INTERNATIONAL AWARD WINNING
HARRIS REFERENCE CATALOG

POSTAGE STAMP PRICES

Confederate States, U.S. Possessions,
U.S. Trust Territories, and
Comprehensive U.S. Stamp Identifier

2025 US/BNA POSTAGE STAMP CATALOG

Starting at just 14 years old, Henry Ellis Harris placed a free ad in the Washington Post in June 1916 offering a risk-free deal - a packet of 10 postage stamps for 50 cents - and steadily grew his customer base. By 1931, Harris had become the biggest name in stamp collecting, with ads in popular magazines like Boys Life, Popular Mechanics, and King Comics, even making it onto matchbook covers. In 1935, Harris published the first 64-page Harris US/BNA Catalog covering the United States and British North America stamps. This catalog has since won seven international awards and continues to be published today as America's best-selling stamp price guide. Now, over 100 years after that first free ad, H.E. Harris remains dedicated to providing high-quality postage stamps, beautifully crafted stamp albums, and the renowned Harris Catalog to collectors.

ISBN: 0794850367

4001 Helton Drive • Building A • Florence, Alabama 35630
Designed in U.S.A. / Printed in China

ABOUT OUR CATALOG PRICES

The prices quoted in this catalog are the prices for which H.E. Harris offers stamps for retail sale at the time of publication. (*Harris no longer offers first day covers for sale.*)

These prices are based on current market values as researched by our staff, but, more importantly, on our day-to-day buying and selling activities in the stamp market.

Although you may certainly use this catalog as a guide to current market prices, you must keep in mind the fact that prices can change in response to varying levels of collector demand, or dealer promotions, and/or special purchases. We are not responsible for typographical errors.

You should also remember that condition is always the key factor in determining the value and price of a given stamp or set of stamps. Unlike some other stamp catalogs, we price U.S. stamps issued up to 1935 in three different condition grades for unused and used examples. For these earlier issues, we have also shown the percentage premium that would apply to Never Hinged Mint examples.

Our illustrated definitions of condition grades are presented on pages XII-XIII.

We have not found it possible to keep every stamp in stock that is listed in this catalog, and we cannot guarantee that we can supply all of the stamps in all conditions that are listed.

However, we will search for any stamp in any condition that a customer may want if that stamp is not in our stock at the time the customer places an order for it.

INDEX

UNITED STATES STAMPS

Air Mail ... 212-218
Air Mail Special Delivery ... 219
Certified Mail ... 219
Envelope Cut Squares & Entires ... 223-233
General Issues ... 1-209
Hunting Permit ... 256-259
Hunting Permit, State ... 260-267
Imperforates ... 210-211
Imperforates, Semi-Postal ... 211
Offices in China ... 220
Officials ... 221-222
Parcel Post ... 222
Parcel Post Due ... 222
Postage Due ... 220
Postal Cards ... 237-249
Postal Cards, Air Mail ... 248-249
Postal Cards, Official ... 250
Postal Cards, Reply ... 249-250
Postal Notes ... 222
Postal Stationery ... 223-233
Postal Stationery, Air Mail ... 234-235
Postal Stationery, Official ... 236
Registration ... 219
Revenues ... 251-255
Semi-Postal ... 209
Special Delivery ... 219
Special Handling ... 222

UNITED STATES RELATED AREAS

Canal Zone ... 268-272
Confederate States ... 272
Cuba ... 273
Guam ... 273
Hawaii ... 273-274
Marshall Islands ... 275-284
Micronesia ... 285-293
Palau ... 294-306
Philippines ... 307
Puerto Rico ... 307
Ryukyu Islands ... 308-313

UNITED NATIONS

Geneva Issues ... 330-336
Geneva Air Letter Sheets & Postal Cards ... 336
New York Air Post ... 327
New York Issues ... 314-327
New York Postal Stationery ... 328-329
Vienna Issues ... 337-343
Vienna Air Letter Sheets & Postal Cards ... 343

CANADA AND PROVINCES

British Columbia & Vancouver Island ... 404
Canada Air Post ... 401-402
Canada Air Post Special Delivery ... 402
Canada General Issues ... 344-400
Canada Officials ... 403-404
Canada Phosphor Tagged Issues ... 401
Canada Postage Due ... 403
Canada Registration ... 403
Canada Semi-Postal ... 401
Canada Special Delivery ... 402
Canada War Tax ... 402
New Brunswick ... 415
Newfoundland ... 405-413
Newfoundland Air Post ... 413-414
Newfoundland Postage Due ... 414
Nova Scotia ... 415
Prince Edward Island ... 416

OTHER FEATURES

Catalog Pricing Policy ... III
Guide for Collectors ... V-XIX
Pictorial Guide to Centering ... XII
Quality and Condition Definitions ... XIII
Stamp Identifier Section ... XIV-XIX
How to Write Your Order ... 417
Discount Coupons ... 418

A GUIDE FOR COLLECTORS

In this section we will attempt to define and explain some of the terms commonly used by stamp collectors. Instead of listing the terms in an alphabetical dictionary or glossary format, we have integrated them. In this way, you can see how an individual term fits within the total picture.

PRODUCTION

The manufacture of stamps involves a number of procedures. We will discuss the major steps here, with emphasis on their implications for stamp collectors. Although we present them separately, modern printing presses may combine one or more operations so that the steps tend to blend together. There also are steps in the process that we do not cover here. While they may be important to the production process, their direct implications for most collectors are minimal.

PLATE MAKING

Before anything can be printed, a printing plate must be made. Using the intaglio printing process (which is explained under **printing**) as an example, the steps involved in plate production are as follows:

- A **master die** is made. The design is recess engraved in a reverse mirror-image. Most master dies consist of only one impression of the design.
- The next step is to prepare a **transfer roll**. The soft steel of the transfer roll is rocked back and forth under pressure against the hardened master die and a series of multiple impressions, called **reliefs**, are created in the transfer roll. Note that the impression on the transfer roll will be raised above the surface, since the roll was pressed into the recesses of the master die.
- Once the transfer roll has been made and hardened, it is used to impress designs in to the soft steel of a **printing plate** that can fit up to 400 impressions of small, definitive-sized stamps or 200 impressions of large, commemorative-sized stamps. This time, the raised design on the transfer roll impresses a recessed design into the plate.

The process is much more complex than this, but these are the basics. Once the printing plate is hardened, it is almost ready to be used to create printed sheets of stamps. Depending on the printing equipment to be used, the printing plate will be shaped to fit around a cylinder for rotary press printing or remain flat for flat-bed press printing. In either form, the plate is then hardened and is ready for use in printing.

DESIGN VARIETIES

The complexity of the platemaking process can result in major or minor flaws. The inspection process will catch most of these flaws, but those that escape detection will result in **plate varieties**.

The early United States Classic issues have been examined in minute detail over the decades. Through **plating** studies, minor differences in individual stamps have been used to identify the position on the printing plate of each design variety. Sometimes called **"flyspeck philately"** because it involves the detection of minute "flyspeck" differences, such plating work has resulted in the identification of some of our greatest rarities. Compare the prices for the one cent blue issues of 1851 and 1857 (#s 5-9 and 18-24) and you will see the tremendous dollar difference that can result from minute design variations. (The Harris Stamp Identifier in this catalog explains the design differences.)

During the plate making or subsequent printing process, plate flaws that are detected will be corrected, sometimes incompletely or incorrectly. Corrections or revisions in an individual die impression or in all plate impressions include the following:

- **Retouching**—minor corrections made in a plate to repair damage or wear.
- **Recutting or re-engraving**—similar to, but more extensive than, retouching. Recutting usually applies to changes made before a plate has been hardened, while re-engraving is performed on a plate that has had to be tempered (softened) after hardening.
- **Redrawing**—the intentional creation of a slightly different design. The insertion of secret marks on the National Bank Notes plates when they were turned over to the Continental Bank Note Company in 1873 can be considered redrawings.
- **Reentry**—the reapplication of a design from a transfer roll to the plate, usually to improve a worn plate. If the reentry is not done completely, or if it is not done precisely on top of the previous design, a double transfer will result. Such double transfers will show on the printed stamp as an extra line at one or more points on the stamp.

Other design varieties may result from undetected plate flaws. A **plate crack** (caused by the hardened plate cracking under wear or pressure) or a **plate scratch** (caused by an object cutting into the plate) will show as an ink line on the printed stamp.

One other group that can be covered here to avoid possible confusion includes **reissues, reprints, special printings and reproductions**. None of these are design varieties that result from plate flaws, corrections or revisions. In fact, reissues, reprints and special printings are made from the same, unchanged plates as the originals. They show no differences in design and usually can be identified only by variations in paper, color or gum. Reproductions (such as U.S. #3 and #4), on the other hand, are made from entirely new plates and, therefore, can be expected to show some variation from the originals.

ERRORS, FREAKS, ODDITIES

"EFOs", as they are called, are printed varieties that result from abnormalities in the production process. They are design varieties, but of a special nature because the result looks different from the norm. When you see them, you know something went wrong. Basically, freaks and oddities can be loosely defined as minor errors. They include the following:

• **Misperforations**, that is, the placement of the perforations within the design rather than at the margins.
• **Foldovers**, caused by a sheet being turned, usually at a corner, before printing and/or perforating. The result is part of a design printed on the reverse of the sheet or placement of perforations at odd angles. Such freaks and oddities may be of relatively minor value, but they do make attractive additions to a collection. Truly major errors, on the other hand, can be of tremendous value. It would not be overstating the case to argue that many collectors are initially drawn to the hobby by the publicity surrounding discoveries of valuable errors and the hope that they might someday do the same. Major errors include the following:
• **Inverts.** These are the most dramatic and most valuable of all major errors and almost always result from printing processes that require more than one pass of a sheet through the presses. If the sheet inadvertently gets "flipped" between passes, the portion printed on the second pass will emerge inverted.
Two definitions we should introduce here are **"frame" and "vignette"**. The vignette is the central design of the stamp; the frame encloses the vignette and, at its outer edges, marks the end of the printed stamp design. Oftentimes, stamps described as inverted centers (vignettes) actually are inverted frames. The center was properly printed in the first pass and the frame was inverted in the second pass.
• **Color errors.** The most noticeable color errors usually involve one or more omitted colors. The sheet may not have made it through the second pass in a two-step printing process. In the past such errors were extremely rare because they were obvious enough to be noticed by inspectors. In modern multi-color printings, the chances of such errors escaping detection have increased. Nonetheless, they still qualify as major errors and carry a significant premium. *Other color errors involve the use of an incorrect color. They may not seem as dramatic as missing colors, but the early issues of many countries include some very rare and valuable examples of these color errors. Although technically not a color error, we can include here one of the most unusual of all errors, the United States 1917 5-cent stamps that are supposed to be blue, but are found in the carmine or rose color of the 2-cent stamps. The error was not caused by a sheet of the 5-centers being printed in the wrong color, as you might expect. Rather, because a few impressions on a 2-cent plate needed reentry, they were removed. But an error was made and the 5-cent design was entered. Thus it is a reentry error, but is described in most catalogs as a color error because that is the apparent result. Whatever the description, the 5-cent denomination surrounded by 2-cent stamps is a real showpiece.
• **Imperfs.** A distinction should be drawn here between imperforate errors and intentionally imperforate stamps. When the latter carry a premium value over their perforated counterparts, it is because they were printed in smaller quantities for specialized usages. They might have been intended, for example, for sale to vending machine manufacturers who would privately perforate the imperforate sheets
On the other hand, errors in which there is absolutely no trace of a perforation between two stamps that were supposed to be perforated carry a premium based on the rarity of the error. Some modern United States coil imperforate errors have been found in such large quantities that they carry little premium value. But imperforate errors found in small quantities represent tremendous rarities.
Be they intentional or errors, imperforate stamps are commonly collected in pairs or larger multiples because it can be extremely difficult—often impossible, to distinguish them from stamps that have had their perforations trimmed away in an attempt to pass them off as more valuable imperfs. Margin singles that show the stamp and a wide, imperforate selvage at one of the edges of the sheet are another collecting option.

PRINTING

There are three basic printing methods:
1. Intaglio, also known as **recess** printing. Line engraved below the surface of the printing plate (that is, in recess) accept the ink and apply it to damp paper that is forced into the recesses of the plate. Intaglio methods include **engraved** and **photogravure (or rotogravure)**. Photogravure is regarded by some as separate from intaglio because the engraving is done by chemical etching and the finished product can be distinguished from hand or machine engraving.
2. Typography. This is similar to intaglio, in that it involves engraving, but the action is in reverse, with the design left at the surface of the plate and the portions to be unprinted cut away. Ink is then applied to the surface design, which is imprinted onto paper. **Typeset** letterpress printing is the most common form of typography.
3. Lithography. This method differs from the previous two in that it involves **surface printing**, rather than engraving. Based on the principle that oil and water do not mix, the design to be printed is applied with a greasy ink onto a plate that is then wet with a watery fluid. Printing ink run across the plate is accepted only at the greased (oiled) points. The ink applies the design to paper that is brought in contact with the plate. **Offset** printing, a modern lithographic method, involves a similar approach, but uses a rubber blanket to transfer the inked design to paper.

PRINTING, CONTINUED

The printing method that was used to produce a given stamp can be determined by close inspection of that stamp.

1. Because the paper is pressed into the grooves of an intaglio plate, when viewed from the surface the design appears to be slightly raised. Running a fingernail lightly across the surface also will reveal this raised effect. When viewed from the back, the design will appear to be recessed (or pressed out toward the surface). Photogravure stamps have a similar appearance and feel, but when viewed under a magnifier, they reveal a series of dots, rather than line engravings.
2. Because the raised design on a plate is pressed into the paper when the typograph process is used, when viewed from the surface, the printing on the stamp does not have the raised effect of an intaglio product. On the other hand, when viewed from the reverse, a raised impression will be evident where the design was imprinted. Overprints often are applied by typography and usually show the raised effect on the back of the stamp.
3. Unlike either of the previous two methods, lithographed stamps look and feel flat. This dull, flat effect can be noticed on any of the United States 1918-20 offset printings, #s 525-536.

"EFOs", as they are called, are printed varieties that result from abnormalities in the production process. They are design varieties, but of a special nature because the result looks different from the norm. When you see them, you know something went wrong. Basically, freaks and oddities can be loosely defined as minor errors. They include the following:

WATERMARKS

This actually is one of the first steps in the stamp production process because it is part of paper manufacturing. A watermark is a slight thinning of the paper pulp, usually in the form of a relevant design. It is applied by devices attached to the rolls on papermaking machines. Without getting involved in the technical aspects, the result is a watermark that can sometimes be seen when held to the light, but more often requires watermark detector fluid.

A word of caution here. Such detector fluids may contain substances that can be harmful when inhaled. This is particularly true of lighter fluids that often are used by collectors in lieu of specially made stamp watermark detector fluids.

Watermarks are used to help detect counterfeits. Although it is possible to reproduce the appearance of a watermark, it is extremely difficult. The authorities have at times been able to identify a counterfeit by the lack of a watermark that should be present or by the presence of an incorrect watermark.

On the other hand, there are occasions when the incorrect or absent watermark did not indicate a counterfeit, but a printing error. The wrong paper may have been used or the paper may have been inserted incorrectly (resulting in an inverted or sideways watermark). The United States 30 cent orange red that is listed among the 1914-17 issues on unwatermarked paper (#467A) is an example of a printing error. It was produced on watermarked paper as part of the 1914-15 series, but a few sheets were discovered without watermarks.

Unfortunately, the difficulty encountered in detecting watermarks on light shades, such as orange or yellow, makes experts very reluctant to identify single copies of #476A. Although not visible, the watermark just might be there.

Because an examination of a full sheet allows the expert to examine the unprinted selvage and all stamps on that sheet at one time, positive identification is possible and most of the stamps that come down to us today as #476A trace back to such full sheets.

GUMMING

Gumming once was almost always applied after printing and before perforating and cutting of sheets into panes. Today, pregummed paper may be used, so the placement of this step in the process cannot be assured—nor is it the sequence of much significance.

The subject of gum will be treated more fully in the **Condition** section of this catalog. At this point, we will only note that certain stamps can be identified by their gum characteristics. Examples include the identification of rotary press stamps by the presence of gum breaker ridges or lines and the detection of the presence of original gum on certain stamps that indicates they can not be a rarer issue that was issued without gum, such as #s 40-47. Others, such as #s 102-111 can be identified in part by their distinctive white, crackly original gum.

PERFORATING

We have already discussed the absence of perforations in the **Errors** section. Here we will concentrate on the perforating process itself.

All perforating machines use devices to punch holes into the printed stamp paper. The holes usually are round and are known as perforations. When two adjacent stamps are separated, the semicircular cutouts are the **perforations**; the remaining paper between the perforations forms **perf tips**, or **"teeth"**.

Most perforations are applied by perforators that contain a full row of punches that are driven through the paper as it is fed through the perforating equipment. **Line Perforators** drive the punches up and down; **rotary perforators** are mounted on cylinders that revolve. There are other techniques, but these are the most common.

To clear up one point of confusion, the **perforation size** (for example, "perf 11") is not the size of the hole or the number of perforations on the side of a given stamp. Rather, it describes the number of perforations that could be fit within two centimeters.

A perf 8 stamp will have visibly fewer perforations than a perf 12 stamp, but it is much harder to distinguish between perf 11 and perf 10-1/2. **Perforation gauges** enable collectors to make these distinctions with relative ease.

TAGGING

Modern, high-speed, mechanical processing of mail has created the need for "tagging" stamps by coating them with a luminescent substance that could be detected under ultraviolet (U.V.) light or by printing them on paper that included such substances. When passed under a machine capable of detecting these substances, an envelope can be positioned and the stamp automatically cancelled, thereby eliminating time-consuming and tedious manual operations. The tagged varieties of certain predominantly untagged stamps, such as #s 1036 and C67, do carry modest premiums. There also are technical differences between phosphorescent and fluorescent types of luminescent substances. But these details are primarily of interest to specialists and will not be discussed in this general work.

PAPER

The fact that we have not devoted more attention to paper should not be an indication of any lack of interest or significance. Books have been written on this one subject alone, and a lack of at least a rudimentary knowledge of the subject can lead to mis-identification of important varieties and result in financial loss.

The three most common categories of paper on which stamps are printed are **wove, laid, and India.** The most frequently used is machine-made **wove paper**, similar to that used for most books. The semiliquid pulp for wove paper is fed onto a fine wire screen and is processed much the same as cloth would be woven. Almost all United States postage stamps are printed on wove paper.

Laid paper is formed in a process that uses parallel wires rather than a uniform screen. As a result, the paper will be thinner where the pulp was in contact with the wires. When held to the light, alternating light and dark lines can be seen. Laid paper varieties have been found on some early United States stamps.

India paper is very thin and tough, without any visible texture. It is, therefore, more suited to obtaining the sharp impressions that are needed for printers' pre-production proofs, rather than to the high-volume printing of stamps.

Other varieties include **bluish** paper, so described because of the tone created by certain substances added to the paper, and silk paper, which contains threads or fibers of silk that usually can be seen on the back of the stamp. Many United States revenue stamps were printed on silk paper.

COLLECTING FORMATS

Whatever the production method, stamps reach the collector in a variety of forms. The most common is in sheet, or more correctly, pane form.

Sheets are the full, uncut units as they come from a press. Before distribution to post offices, these sheets are cut into **panes**. For United States stamps, most regular issues are printed in sheets of 400 and cut into panes of 100; most commemoratives are printed in sheets of 200 and cut into panes of 50. There are numerous exceptions to this general rule, and they are indicated in the mint sheet listings in this catalog. Sheets also are cut in **booklet panes** for only a few stamps—usually four to ten stamps per pane. These panes are assembled in complete booklets that might contain one to five panes, usually stapled together between two covers. An intact booklet is described as **unexploded**; when broken apart it is described as exploded.

Coils are another basic form in which stamps reach post offices. Such stamps are wound into continuous coil rolls, usually containing from 100 to 5,000 stamps, the size depending on the volume needs of the expected customer. Almost all coils are produced with perforations on two opposite sides and straight edges on the remaining two sides. Some serious collectors prefer collecting coils in pairs or strips—two or more adjacent stamps—as further assurance of genuineness. It is much easier to fake a coil single that shows only portions of each perforation hole than a larger unit that shows the complete perf hole.

A variation on this theme is the **coil line pair**—adjacent stamps that show a printed vertical line between. On rotary press stamps the line appears where the two ends of a printing plate meet on a rotary press cylinder. The joint is not complete, so ink falls between the plate ends and is transferred onto the printed coil. On flat plate stamps the guideline is the same as that created for sheet stamps, as described below. **Paste-up** coil pairs are not as popular as line pairs. They were a necessary by-product of flat plate printings in which the coil strips cut from separate sheets had to be pasted together for continuous winding into roll form.

The modern collecting counterpart to coil line pairs is the **plate number strip**—three or five adjacent coil stamps with the plate number displayed on the middle stamp. Transportation coil plate strips have become particularly sought after. On most early coil rolls, the plate numbers were supposed to be trimmed off. Freaks in which the number remains are interesting, but do not carry large premiums since they are regarded as examples of miscut oddities rather than printing errors.

Miniature sheets and souvenir sheets are variations on one theme—small units that may contain only one or at most a much smaller quantity of stamps than would be found on the standard postal panes. Stamps may be issued in miniature sheet format for purposes of expedience, as for example the Bret Harte $5 issue (#2196), which was released in panes of 20 to accommodate the proportionately large demand by collectors for plate blocks rather than single stamps. As the name implies, a souvenir sheet is a miniature sheet that was released as a souvenir to be saved, rather than postally used—although such sheets or the stamps cut out from them can be used as postage. **Note: souvenir cards** are created strictly for promotional and souvenir purposes. They contain stamp reproductions that may vary in size, color or design from the originals and are not valid for postal use.

Often, a common design may be produced in sheet, coil and booklet pane form. The common design is designated by collectors as one **type**, even though it may be assigned many different catalog numbers because of variations in color, size, perforations, printing method, denomination, etc. On the other hand, even minor changes in a basic design represent a new type.

Sheet stamps offer the greatest opportunity for format variation and collecting specialization. Using the following illustration for reference, the varieties that can be derived include the following:

Block (a)—this may be any unit of four stamps or more in at least 2 by 2 format. Unless designated as a different size, blocks are assumed to be blocks of four.

Specialized forms of blocks include:

Arrow block (b)—adjacent stamps at the margin of a sheet, showing the arrow printed in the margin for registration in the printing process, as, for example, in two-color printings. When the arrow designates the point at which a sheet is cut into panes, the result will appear as one leg of the arrow, or V, on each pane. **Guideline block (c)**—similar to arrow block, except that it can be any block that shows the registration line between two rows of two stamps each. **Gutter block**—similar to guideline block, except that an uncolored gutter is used instead of a printed line. The best known United States gutter blocks are those cut from full-sheet "Farley printings". Pairs of stamps from adjacent panes on each side of the gutter form the gutter block. **Imprint, or inscription blocks (d)**—include **copyright, mail early, and ZIP (e) blocks**. On most modern United States sheets, the **selvage (f)**, that is, the margin that borders the outer rows of stamps (f), includes one or more inscriptions in addition to the plate numbers. It may be a copyright protection notice or an inscription that encourages mail users to post their mail early or to use the ZIP code on their mail. Because the inscription appears along the margin, rather than in one of the corners, it is customary to collect copyright blocks and mail early blocks in two rows of three stamps each, with the inscription centered in the margin. The ZIP inscription appears in one of the corners of each pane, so it is collected in corner margin blocks of four. **Plate number block (g)**—this is by far the most popular form of block collecting. On each sheet of stamps, a plate number (or numbers) is printed to identify the printing plate(s) used. Should a damage be discovered, the plate can easily be identified. On flat plate sheets, where the plate number appeared along the margin, the format usually is in plate blocks of six, with the plate number centered in the margin. On rotary press and other sheets where a single plate number appears in one of the four corners of the margin, the customary collecting format is a **corner margin block of four (h)**. This also is true for plate blocks with two plate numbers in two adjacent corner stamps and for modern plates where single digits are used to designate each plate number and the complete series (containing one digit for each printing color) appears in the corner. Before single digits were adopted for modern multi-color printings, the five-digit numbers assigned to each plate might run down a substantial portion of the sheet margin. **Plate strips (i)** are collected in such instances. Their size is two rows times as many stamps as are attached to the margin area that shows all plate numbers. Because a sheet of stamps is cut into separate panes, printing plates include plate numbers that can be seen on each of the cut panes. On modern sheets the plate numbers would be located in each of the four corners of the uncut sheet. Once cut, each of the four panes would show the same plate number in one of its corners. The position of the plate number, which matches the position of the pane on the uncut sheet, is designated as upper left or right and lower left or right. Some specialists seek matched sets. A **matched set** is one of each of the four positions for a given plate number. A **complete matched set** is all positions of all plate numbers for a given issue.

***_**This diagram is for placement purposes only, and is not an exact reproduction of margin markings._**

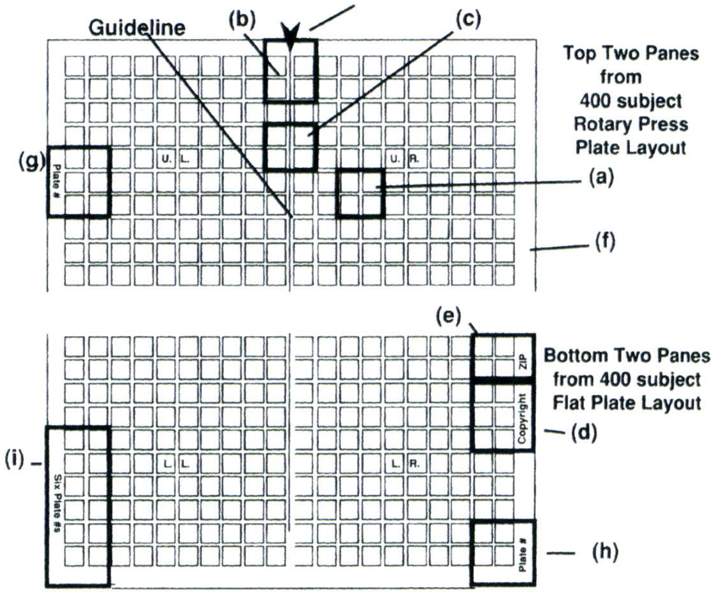

Other definitions that relate in one way or another to the format in which stamps are produced include:

Se-tenant—from the French, meaning joined together. A pair, block, or larger multiple that contains different designs. The 1967 Space Twins issue is an example of a se-tenant pair in which the two different stamps are part of an integral design. The 1968 Historic Flags se-tenant strip contains ten separate designs, each of which can stand alone.

Tete-beche pair—from the French, meaning head-to-tail. Such pairs show adjacent stamps, one of which is upside down in relation to the other.

Proof—any trial impression used in the evaluation of prospective or final designs. Final die proofs—that is, those made from a completed die preparatory to its being used in the production of printing plates—are the standard proof collecting form.

Essay—a partial or complete illustration of a proposed design. In the strict philatelic sense, essays are printed in proof form.

Color trials—a preliminary proof of a stamp design in one or more colors. Trial color proofs are used to select the color in which the stamp will be printed.

Grill—a pattern of embossed cuts that break the stamp paper. See the information at the head of the 1861-67 Issue listings and the section of grills in the Harris Stamp Identifier.

POSTAL MARKINGS

The extensive subject of cancellations and postal markings on stamps and covers is too specialized to present in detail here. Volumes have been written on individual categories of markings—straight line markings, ship cancels, foreign mail cancels, flight covers, etc. In this section we will limit ourselves to the basic definitions related to the stamp and the manner in which it is cancelled, rather than the specialized usage of the envelope to which the stamp is affixed.

- **Manuscript,** or **pen cancels** were the earliest form of "killing" a stamp—that is, marking it to indicate it had been postally used.
- **Handstamps** were created shortly after the first stamps were issued. The early devices might only show a pattern such as a grid and often were carved from cork.
- **Fancy cancels** were an extension of the handstamp. Local postmasters carved cork cancelers that depicted bees, kicking mules, flowers, and hundreds of other figures. Stamps with clear strikes of such fancy cancels usually carry hefty premiums over those with standard cancels.
- **Machine cancels** are applied by mechanical rather than manual means.
- A stamp is **tied** to a cover (or piece) when the cancellation, whatever its form, extends beyond the margins of the stamp onto the cover. Such a tie is one indication of the authenticity of the cover.

Specialized cancellations include the following:

- **Cut cancel**—as the name implies, a cancel that actually cuts the stamp, usually in the form of a thin, straight incision. The most common usage of cut cancels on United States stamps is on Revenue issues.
- **Perfin, or perforated initial**—usually not a cancellation as such, but rather a privately administered punching into the stamp of one or more initials. Most often, the initials were those of a large firm that wished to prevent personal use of their stamps by employees.
- **Precancel**—a cancellation printed on stamps in advance of their sale. The primary purpose of precancels is for sale to large volume mailers, whose mail is delivered to post offices and processed in bulk without necessarily receiving further cancellation.
- **Non-contemporary cancel**—a cancellation applied to a stamp long after the normal period of use for that stamp. A stamp that is worth more used than unused or a damaged unused stamp that would be worth more on cover are examples of candidates for non-contemporary markings.
- **Cancel-to-order, or C.T.O.**—a cancel that is printed on a stamp by an issuing country to give it the appearance of having been used, or to render it invalid for postage in that country. Special fancy cancels or "favor cancels" have been applied at various times in the countries for philatelic reasons.

CATEGORIES

The number of specialized categories into which stamps can be slotted is limited only by the imagination of the individual collector. Some collectors have attempted to collect one of each and every stamp ever issued by every nation that ever existed. Other collectors have concentrated on all the possible varieties and usages of only one stamp. Between these two extremes, stamps can be divided into certain generally accepted categories, whether or not they are used as boundaries for a collection. These categories are as follows:

- **Definitives, or regulars**—stamps that are issued for normal, everyday postage needs. In the United States, they are put on sale for a period limited only by changing rate needs or infrequent issuance of a new definitive series. Post offices can requisition additional stocks of definitives as needed.
- **Commemoratives**—stamps issued to honor a specific event, anniversary, individual or group. They are printed in a predetermined quantity and are intended for sale during a limited period. Although they can be used indefinitely, once stocks are sold out at a local post office, commemoratives usually are not replenished unless the issue has local significance.
- **Pictorials**—stamps that depict a design other than the portrait of an individual or a static design such as a coat of arms or a flag. While some collectors think of these strictly as commemoratives (because most commemoratives are pictorials), some definitives also can be pictorials. Any number of definitives that depict the White House are examples.
- **Airmails, or air posts**—stamps issued specifically for airmail use. Although they do not have to bear a legend, such as "airmail", they usually do. Airmail stamps usually can be used to pay other postage fees.When air flights were a novelty, airmail stamp collecting was an extremely popular specialty. Part of this popularity also can be ascribed to the fact that the first airmail stamps usually were given special attention by issuing postal administrations. Produced using relatively modern technology, they often were among the most attractive of a nation's issues.
- **Zeppelin stamps**—although these do not rate as a major category, they deserve special mention. Zeppelin issues were primarily released for specific use on Zeppelin flights during the 1920s and 1930s. They carried high face values and were issued during the Great Depression period, when most collectors could not afford to purchase them. As a result, most Zeppelin issues are scarce and command substantial premiums. United States "Zepps" are the Graf Zeppelins (C13-C15) and the Century of Progress issue (C18).
- **Back-of-the-book**—specialized stamps that are identified as "back-of-the-book" because of their position in catalogs following the listings of regular and commemorative postal issues. Catalogs identified them with a prefix letter. Some collectors include airmail stamps in this category, in part because they carry a prefix letter (C) and are listed separately. Most collectors treat the airmails as part of a standard collection and begin the back-of-the-book section with semi-postals (B) or, for the United States, special deliveries (E). Other frequently used "b-o-b" categories include postage dues (J), offices in China, or Shanghais (K), officials (O), parcel posts (Q), newspapers (PR), and revenues (R), the latter including "Duck" hunting permit stamps (RW).

CATEGORIES, CONTINUED

Postal stationery and postal cards are the major non-stamp back-of-the-book categories. A complete envelope or card is called an **entire**; the cutout corner from such a piece, showing the embossed or otherwise printed design, is described as a **cut square**.

Some collecting categories do not relate to the intended use of the stamps. Examples include **topicals** (stamps collected by the theme of the design, such as sports, dance, paintings, space, etc.) and **first day covers**. Modern first day covers show a stamp or stamps postmarked in a designated first day city on the official first day of issue. The cancel design will relate to the issue and the cover may bear a privately-printed cachet that further describes and honors the subject of the stamp.

One of the oddities of the hobby is that **stampless covers** are an accepted form of "stamp" collecting. Such covers display a usage without a stamp, usually during the period before stamps were required for the payment of postage. They bear manuscript or handstamps markings such as "due 5," "PAID," etc. to indicate the manner in which postage was paid.

Although they do not constitute a postal marking, we can include **bisects** here for want of a better place. A bisect is a stamp cut in half and used to pay postage in the amount of one-half of the stamp's denomination. The 1847 ten cent stamp (#2) cut in half and used to pay the five cent rate is an example.

Bisects should be collected only on cover and properly tied. They also should reflect an authorized usage, for example, from a post office that was known to lack the proper denomination, and sould pay an amount called for by the usuage shown on the cover.

Not discussed in detail here is the vast subject of **covers**, or postal history. Envelopes, usually but not necessarily showing a postal use, are described by collectors as covers. Early "covers" actually were single letter sheets with a message on one side and folded into the form of an enclosing wrapper when viewed from the outside. The modern aerogramme or air letter is similar in design to these early folded letters.

USED STAMPS

For used stamps, the presence of gum would be the exception, since it would have been removed when the stamp was washed from the envelope, so gum is not a factor on used stamps. The centering definitions, on the other hand, would be the same as for unused issues. In addition, the cancellation would be a factor. We should point out here that we are not referring to the type of cancellation, such as a fancy cancel that might add considerably to the value of a stamp, or a manuscript cancel that reduces its value. Rather, we are referring to the degree to which the cancellation covers the stamp. A **lightly cancelled** used stamp, with all of the main design elements showing and the usage evidenced by an unobtrusive cancel, is the premier condition sought by collectors of used stamps. On the other hand, a stamp whose design has been substantially obliterated by a **heavy cancel** is at best a space filler that should be replaced by a moderate to lightly cancelled example.

PERFORATIONS

The condition of a stamp's perforations can be determined easily by visual examination. While not necessarily perfect, all perforations should have full teeth and clean perforation holes. A **blunt perf** is one that is shorter than it should be, while a **pulled perf** actually shows a portion of the margin or design having been pulled away. **Blind perfs** are the opposite: paper remains where the perforation hole should have been punched out. One irony of the demand for perforation is that **straight edges**, that is, the normal sheet margin straight edge that was produced when flat-plate sheets were cut into panes, are not acceptable to many collectors. In fact, many collectors will prefer a reperforated stamp to a straight edge. (Technically, **"re"perforated** can only apply to a stamp that is being perforated again, as when a damaged or excessive margin has been cut away and new perforations are applied, but we will follow the common practice of including the perforation of normal straight edges in this category). As a result of this preference, many straight edges no longer exist as such. When one considers that they were in the minority to start with (a pane of 100 flat plate stamps would include 19 straight edges) and that even fewer come down to us today, an argument could be made that they may someday be rarities...although it is hard to conceive of anyone paying a premium for straight edges.

FAKES, FAULTS, AND EXPERTISING

Below the first quality level—stamps free of defects—a range of stamps can be found from attractive **"seconds"** that have barely noticeable flaws to **space fillers** that may have a piece missing and which ought to be replaced by a better copy— unless we are talking about great rarities which would otherwise be beyond the budget of most collectors. The more common flaws include **thins, tears, creases, stains, pulled perfs, pinholes** (some dealers and collectors used to display their stamps pinned to boards), **face scuffs** or erasures, and **fading**. Stamps with faults sometimes are **repaired**, either to protect them from further damage or to deceive collectors. While the terms that are applied to stamps that are not genuine often are used interchangeably, they do have specific meaning, as follows:

- **fakes** (in French, faux; in German, falsch)—stamps that appear to be valuable varieties, but which were made from cheaper genuine stamps. Trimming away the perforations to create an imperforate is a common example of a fake.
- **bogus stamps, phantoms, labels**—outright fantasies, usually the product of someone's imagination, produced for amusement rather than deception.

While most stamps are genuine, and the average collector need not be concerned about the possibility of repairs, **expertizing** services do exist for collectors who are willing to pay a fee to obtain an independent opinion on their more valuable stamps.

H.E. Harris Pictorial Guide to Centering

Cat #	Very Fine	Fine	Average
1 to 293 1847 to 1898	Perfs clear of design on all four sides. Margins may not be even.	Perfs well clear of design on at least three sides. But may almost touch design on one side.	Perfs cut into design on at least one side.
294 to 749 1901 to 1934	Perfs clear of design. Margins relatively even on all four sides.	Perfs clear of design. Margins not even on all four sides.	Perfs touch design on at least one side.
750 to Date 1935 to Present	Perfs clear of design. Centered with margins even on all four sides.	Perfs clear of design. Margins may be uneven.	Perfs may touch design on at least one side.

Note: Margins are the area from the edges of stamp to the design. Perfs are the serrations between stamps that aid in separating them.

CENTERING

One major factor in the determination of a stamp's fair value is its **centering**, the relative balance of the stamp design within its margins. Whether the stamp has perforations or is imperforate, its centering can be judged. Because the stamp trade does not have an established system for grading or measuring centering, "eyeballing" has become the standard practice. As a result, one collector's definition may vary from another's. This can create some confusion, but the system seems to work, so it has remained in force. Centering can range from poor to superb, as follows:

- **Poor**—so far off center that a significant portion of the design is lost because of bad centering. On a poorly centered perforated stamp, the perforations cut in so badly that even the perf tips may penetrate the design.
- **Average**—a stamp whose frame or design is cut slightly by the lack of margins on one or two sides. On a perforated stamp, the perf holes might penetrate the stamp, but some margin white space will show on the teeth. Average stamps are accepted by the majority of collectors for 19th century stamps and early 20th century stamps, as well as for the more difficult later issues.
- **Fine**—the perforations are clear of the design, except for those issues that are known to be extremely poorly centered, but the margins on opposite sides will not be balanced, that is, equal to each other. (Note: a stamp whose top and bottom margins are perfectly balanced may still be called fine if the left and right margins differ substantially from each other.)
- **Very fine**—the opposite margins may still appear to differ somewhat, but the stamp is closer to being perfectly centered than it is to being fine centered. Very fine stamps are sought by collectors who are particularly interested in high quality and who are willing to pay the premiums such stamps command.
- **Superb**— perfect centering. They are so scarce that no comprehensive price list could attempt to include a superb category. Superb stamps, when they are available, command very high premiums.
- **"Jumbo"**—an abnormal condition, in which the stamp's margins are oversized compared to those of the average stamp in a given issue. Such jumbos can occur in the plate making process when a design is cut into the printing plate and excessive space is allowed between that design and the adjacent stamps.

Note: Some collectors also define a "fine to very fine" condition, in which the margin balance falls into a mid-range between fine and very fine. In theory it may be an attractive compromise, but in practice the range between fine and very fine is too narrow to warrant a separate intermediate category.

Quality and Condition Definitions

In determining the value of a given stamp, a number of factors have to be taken into consideration. For mint stamps, the condition of the gum, whether or not it has been hinged, and the centering are all major factors that determine their value. For used stamps, the factors to consider are cancellation and centering. The following H.E. Harris guidelines will enable you to determine the quality standards you may choose from in acquiring stamps for your collection.

Mint Stamp Gum

Unused—A stamp that is not cancelled (used), yet has had all the original gum removed. On early U.S. issues this is the condition that the majority of mint stamps exist in, as early collectors often soaked the gum off their stamps to avoid the possibility of the gum drying and splitting.

Original Gum (OG)—A stamp that still retains the adhesive applied when the stamp was made, yet has been hinged or has had some of the gum removed. Mint stamps from #215 to date can be supplied in this condition.

Never Hinged (NH)—A stamp that is in "post office" condition with full gum that has never been hinged. For U.S. #215 to #715 (1935), separate pricing columns or percentages are provided for "Never Hinged" quality. From #772 (1935) to date, all stamps are priced as Never Hinged.

Cancellations

The cancellations on Used stamps range from light to heavy. A lightly cancelled stamp has the main design of the stamp clearly showing through the cancel, while a heavy cancel usually substantially obliterates the design elements of the stamp. In general it should be assumed that Very fine quality stamps will have lighter cancels than Average cancellation stamps.

Heavy Cancel

Light Cancel

GUM

The impact of the condition of the back of an unused stamp (i.e. the **gum**) upon that stamp's value in today's market needs careful consideration. The prices for 19th century stamps vary widely based on this element of condition. Some traditional collectors feel that modern collectors pay too much attention to gum condition. Around the turn of the century, some collectors washed the gum off the stamps to prevent it from cracking and damaging the stamp themselves. But that generation has passed and the practice not only is no longer popular, it is almost unheard of. To some extent the washing of gum is no longer necessary, since modern gums are not as susceptible to cracking. A more important development, however, has been the advent of various mounts that allow the collector to place a stamp in an album without the use of a hinge. With that development, "never hinged" became a premium condition that could be obtained on stamps issued from the 1930s to date. As a result, gum took on added significance, and its absence on 20th century stamps became unacceptable.

The standard definitions that pertain to gum condition are as follows:

- **Original gum, or o.g.**—the gum that was applied when the stamp was produced. There are gradations, from "full" original gum through "partial" original gum, down to "traces". For all intents and purposes, however, a stamp must have most of its original gum to be described as "o.g."
- **Regummed**— the stamp has gum, but it is not that which would have been applied when the stamp was produced. Many collectors will avoid regummed stamps because the gum may hide some repair work. At best, regumming may give the stamp an appearance of completeness, but a premium should not be paid for a stamp that lacks its original gum.
- **Unused**—while many collectors think of this as any stamp that is not used, the narrow philatelic definition indicates a stamp that has no gum or is regummed.
- **Unhinged**—as with "unused", the term has a specific meaning to collectors: a regumming that shows no traces of a hinge mark. Unfortunately, in their confusion some collectors purchase stamps described as "unused" and "unhinged" as if they bore original gum.
- **No gum**—the stamp lacks its gum, either because it was intentionally produced without gum (also described as **ungummed**) or had the gum removed at a later date. It is customary to find 19th century stamps without gum, and the condition is acceptable to all but the most fastidious collectors. On 20th century stamps, original gum is to be expected.
- **Hinged**—the gum shows traces of having been mounted with a hinge. This can range from **lightly hinged** (the gum shows traces, but none of the hinge remains) to **heavily hinged** (a substantial portion of one or more hinge remnants is stuck to the stamp, or a significant portion of the gum has been lost in the removal of a hinge).
- **Thinned**— not only has the gum been removed, but a portion of the stamp paper has been pulled away. A thin usually will show when the stamp is held to a light. One of the faults that may be covered over on regummed stamps is a thin that has been filled in.
- **Never hinged**—as the name implies, the stamp has its original gum in post office condition and has never been hinged. Although some collectors think of **"mint"** stamps as any form of unused, o.g. stamps, the more accepted "mint" definition is never hinged.

UNITED STATES STAMP IDENTIFIER

Shows you how to distinguish between the rare and common U.S. stamps that look alike.

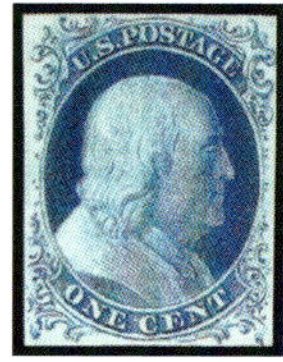

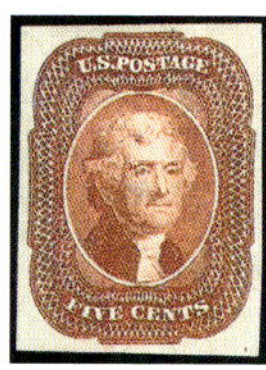

Types of 1¢ Franklin Design of 1851-60

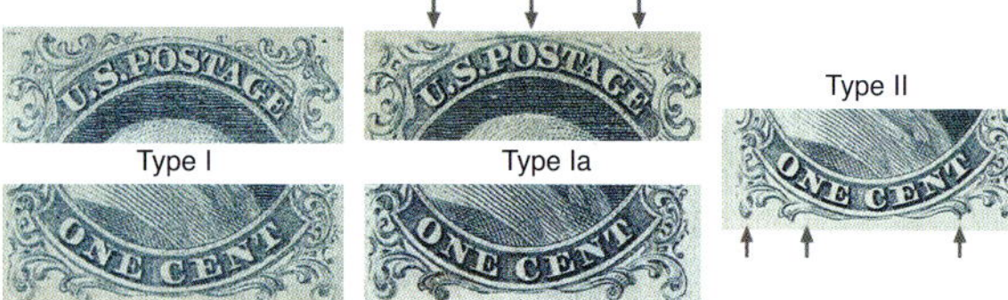

TYPE I has the most complete design of the various types of stamps. At top and bottom there is an unbroken curved line running outside the bands reading "U.S. POSTAGE" and "ONE CENT". The scrolls at bottom are turned under, forming curls. The scrolls and outer line at top are complete.

TYPE Ia is like Type I at bottom but ornaments and curved line at top are partly cut away.

TYPE Ib (not illustrated) is like Type I at top but little curls at bottom are not quite so complete nor clear and scroll work is partly cut away.

TYPE II has the outside bottom line complete, but the little curls of the bottom scrolls and the lower part of the plume ornament are missing. Side ornaments are complete.

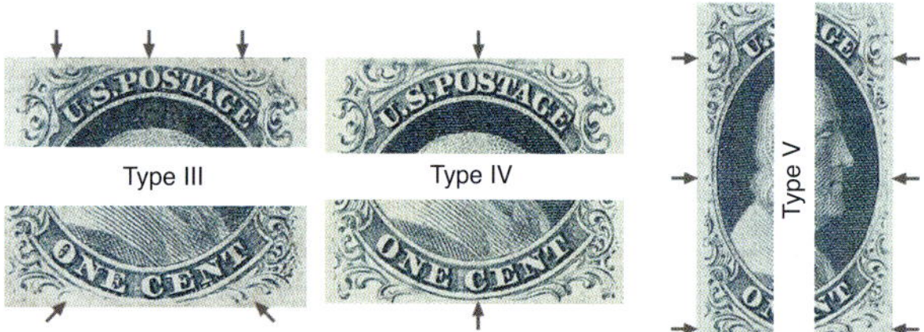

TYPE III has the outside lines at both top and bottom partly cut away in the middle. The side ornaments are complete.

TYPE IIIa (not illustrated) is similar to Type III with the outer line cut away at top or bottom, but not both.

TYPE IV is similar to Type II but the curved lines at top or bottom (or both) have been recut in several different ways, and usually appear thicker than Type IIs.

TYPE V is similar to Type III but has the side ormanents parlty cut away. Type V occurs only on perforated stamps.

Types of 3¢ Washington & 5¢ Jefferson Designs of 1851-60

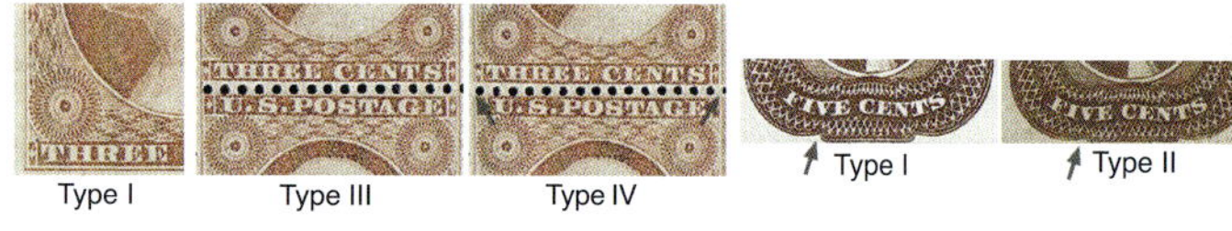

3¢ WASHINGTON

TYPE I has a frame line around the top, bottom and sides.

TYPE III has the frame line removed at top and bottom, while the side frame lines are continuous from the top to bottom of the plate.

TYPE IV is similar to Type III, but the side frame lines were recut individually, and therefore are broken between stamps.

5¢ JEFFERSON

TYPE I is a complete design with projections (arrow) at the top and bottom as well as at the sides.

TYPE II has the projections at the top or bottom partly or completely cut away.

Types of the 10¢ Washington Design of 1851-60

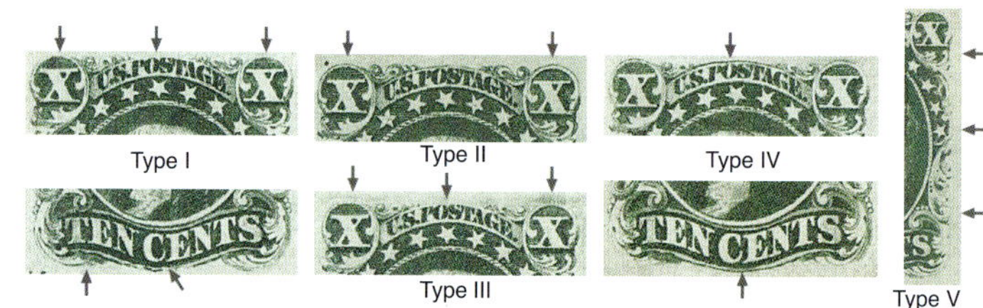

TYPE I has the "shells" at the lower corners practically complete, while the outer line below "TEN CENTS" is very nearly complete. At the top, the outer lines above "U.S. POSTAGE" above the "X" in each corner are broken.

TYPE II has the design complete at the top, but the outer line at the bottom is broken in the middle and the "shells" are partially cut away.

TYPE III has both top and bottom outer lines cut away; similar to Type I at the top and Type II at the bottom.

TYPE IV has the outer lines at the top or bottom of the stamp, or at both place, recut to show more strongly and heavily.

Types I, II, III and IV have complete ornaments at the sides and three small circles or pearls (arrow) at the outer edges of the bottom panel.

TYPE V has the side ornaments, including one or two of the small "pearls" partly cut away. Also, the outside line, over the "X" at the right top, has been partly cut away.

Types of the 12¢ Washington issues of 1851-60

PLATE 1 has stronger, more complete outer frame lines than does Plate 3. Comes imperforate (#17 or perf #36).

PLATE 3 has uneven or broken outer frame lines that are particularly noticeable in the corners. The stamps are perf 15. (#36b)

The 1875 REPRINT plate is similar to plate 1, but the Reprint stamps are greenish black and slightly taller than plate 1 stamps (25mm from top to bottom frame lines versus 24.5 mm) The paper is whiter and the perforations are 12 gauge.

UNITED STATES STAMP IDENTIFIER

Shows you how to distinguish between the rare and common U.S. stamps that look alike.

Types of the 1861 Issue, Grills & Re-Issues

Shortly after the outbreak of the Civil War in 1861, the Post Office demonitized all stamps issued up to that time in order to prevent their use by the Confederacy. Two new sets of designs, consisting of six stamps shown below plus 24¢ and 30¢ demonitized, were prepared by the American Bank Note Company. The first designs, except for the 10¢ and 24¢ values, were not regularly issued and are extremely rare and valuable. The second designs became the regular issue of 1861. The illustrations in the left column show the first (or unissued) designs, which were all printed on thin, semi- transparent paper. The second (or regular) designs are shown at right.

Types of the 1861 Issues

1st

SECOND DESIGN shows a small dash (arrow) under the tip of the ornaments at the right of the figure "1" in the upper left-hand corner of the stamp.

2nd

1st

SECOND DESIGN, 3¢ value, shows a small ball (arrow) at each corner of the design. Also, the ornaments at the corners are larger than in the first design.

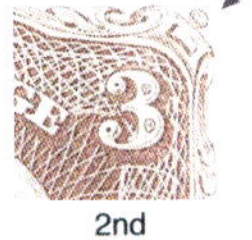
2nd

1st

SECOND DESIGN, 5¢ value has a leaflet (arrow) projecting from the scrolled ornaments at each corner of the stamp.

2nd

1st

FIRST DESIGN has no curved line below the row of stars and there is only one outer line of the ornaments above them.
SECOND DESIGN has a heavy curved line below the row of stars (arrow); ornaments above the stars have double outer line.

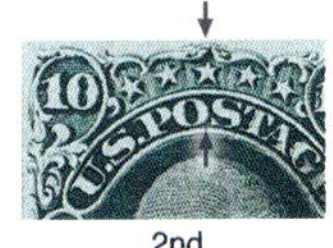
2nd

1st

FIRST DESIGN has rounded corners.
SECOND DESIGN has a oval and a scroll (arrow) in each corner of the design

2nd

Types of the 15¢ "Landing of Columbus" Design of 1869

Type I

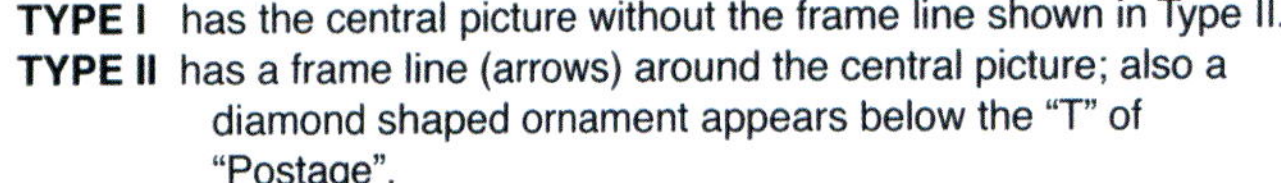
Type II

TYPE I has the central picture without the frame line shown in Type II.
TYPE II has a frame line (arrows) around the central picture; also a diamond shaped ornament appears below the "T" of "Postage".
TYPE III (not illustrated) is like Type I except that the fringe of brown shading lines which appears around the sides and bottom of the picture on Types I and II has been removed.

IDENTIFIER CHART
1861-1867 Bank Notes

Description and Identifying Features				1¢	2¢	3¢	5¢	10¢	12¢	15¢	24¢	30¢	90¢
1861. National. First designs. Thin, semi-transparent paper. No grill.				55		56	57	58[1], 62B	59		60	61	62
1861-62. National. Modified designs[3]. Thicker, opaque paper. No grill.				63		64[2], 65[2], 66[2]	67	68	69		70[2]	71	72
1861-66. National. Thicker, opaque paper. No grill. a. New designs.					73					77			
b. Same designs, new shades.						74[2]	75[2], 76[2]				78[2]		
1867. National. Grills. All on thick, opaque paper.													
Grills	Pts. as seen from stamp face	Area of covered Horiz. x Vert.	# of rows of Pts.										
A	Up	All over	—			79	80					81	
B	Up	18 x 15 mm	22 x 18			82							
C	Up	c. 13 x 16 mm	16-17 x 18-21			83							
D	Down	c. 12 x 14 mm	15 x 17-18		84	85							
Z	Down	c. 11 x 14 mm	13-14 x 17-18	85A	85B	85C		85D	85E	85F			
E	Down	c. 11 x 13 mm	14 x 15-17	86	87	88		89	90	91			
F	Down	c. 9 x 13 mm	11-12 x 15-17	92	93	94	95	96	97	98	99	100	101
1875. National. Re-issues. Hard, white paper. White crackly gum. No grill.				102	103	104	105	106	107	108	109	110	111

FOOTNOTES:
1. #58 does not exist used. Unused, it cannot be distinguished from #62B.
2. Different from corresponding 1861-66 issues only in color.
3. See diagrams for design modification.

UNITED STATES STAMP IDENTIFIER

Shows you how to distinguish between the rare and common U.S. stamps that look alike.

Types of the 1870-71 Through 1887 Bank Notes

The stamps of the 1870-71 issue were printed by the National Bank Note Company. The similar issue of 1873 was printed by the Continental Bank Note Company. When Continental took over the plates previously used by National, they applied the so-called "secret marks" to the designs of the 1¢ through 15¢ denominations by which the two issues can be distinguished as shown below. The illustrations at the left show the original designs of 1870-71; those at the right show secret marks applied to the issue of 1873.

1¢ Secret mark is a small curved mark in the pearl at the left of the figure "1".

7¢ Secret mark is two tiny semicircles drawn around the end of the lines which outline the ball in the lower right-hand corner.

2¢ 1870-71 are red brown. The 1873 issue is brown and in some copies has a small diagonal line under the scroll at the left of the "U.S." (arrow).

10¢ Secret mark is a small semicircle in the scroll at the right-hand side of the central design.

3¢ Secret mark is the heavily shaded ribbon under the letters "RE".

12¢ Secret mark shows the "balls" at the top and bottom on the figure "2" crescent-shaped (right) instead of nearly round as at the left.

6¢ Secret mark shows the first four vertical lines of shading in the lower part of the left ribbon greatly strengthened.

15¢ Secret mark shows as strengthened lines (arrow) in the triangle in the upper left-hand corner, forming a "V".

IDENTIFIER CHART
1870-1887 Bank Notes

Description and Identifying Features	1¢	2¢	3¢	5¢	6¢	7¢	10¢	12¢	15¢	21¢	30¢	90¢
1870-71. National. No secret marks. White wove paper, thin to medium thick. With grills.	134	135	136		137	138	139	140	141	142	143	144
1870-71. National. As above, except without grills.	145	146	147		148	149	150	151	152	153	154[2]	155[2]
1873. Continental. White wove paper, thin to thick. No grills.												
a. With secret marks.	156	157	158		159	160	161	162	163			
b. No secret marks.											165[2]	166[2]
1875. Continental. Special Printing. Same designs as 1873 Continental. Hard, white wove paper. No gum.	167	168	169		170	171	172	173	174	175	176	177
1875. Contineal. New color or denomination. Hard yellowish, wove paper.		178		179								
1875. Continental. Special printing. Same designs as 1875 Continental. Hard, white wove paper. No gum.		180		181								
1879. American. Same designs as 1873-75. Continental. Soft, porous paper.	182	183[3]	184[3]	185	186[3]		188		189[3]		190[3]	191[3]
a. Without secret mark.							187[3]					
1880. American. Special printing. Same as 1879 issue. Soft, porous paper. No gum.	192	193, 203[3]	194[3]	204	195[3]	196	197[3]	198	199[3]	200	201[3]	202[3]
1881-82. American. Designs of 1873. Re-engraved[4]. Soft, porous paper.	206		207[5]		208		209					
1887. American. Same designs as 1881-82. New colors.		214[5]									217	218

FOOTNOTES:

1. See diagrams for secret marks.
2. Corresponding denominations differ from each other only in color.
3. Corresponding denominations differ from each other only in color and gum. The special printings are slightly deeper and richer. The lack of gum is not positive identifier because it can be washed from the 1879 issues.
4. See diagrams for re-engravings.
5. Corresponding denominations differ from each other in color.

UNITED STATES STAMP IDENTIFIER

Shows you how to distinguish between the rare and common U.S. stamps that look alike.

Re-Engraved Designs 1881-82

1¢ has strengthened vertical shading lines in the upper part of the stamp, making the background appear almost solid. Lines of shading have also been added to the curving ornaments in the upper corners.

3¢ has a solid shading line at the sides of the central oval (arrow) that is only about half the previous width. Also a short horizontal line has been cut below the "TS" of "CENTS".

6¢ has only three vertical lines between the edge of the panel and the outside left margin of the stamp. (In the preceding issues, there were four such lines.)

10¢ has only four vertical lines between the left side of the oval and the edge of the shield. (In the preceding issues there were five such lines.) Also, the lines in the background have been made much heavier so that these stamps appear more heavily linked than previous issues.

2¢ Washington Design of 1894-98

TYPE I has horizontal lines of the same thickness within and without the triangle.

TYPE II has horizontal lines which cross the triangle but are thinner within it than without.

TYPE III has thin lines inside the triangle and these do not cross the double frame line of the triangle.

2¢ Columbian "Broken Hat" Variety of 1893

231

As a result of a plate defect, some stamps of the 2¢ Columbian design show a noticeable white notch or gash in the hat worn by the third figure to the left of Columbus. This "broken hat" variety is somewhat less common than the regular 2¢ design.

Broken Hat variety, 231c

4¢ Columbian Blue Error

Collectors often mistake the many shades of the normal 4¢ ultramarine for the rare and valuable blue error. Actually, the "error" is not ultramarine at all, but a deep blue, similar to the deeper blue shades of the 1¢ Columbian.

$1 Perry Design of 1894-95

TYPE I shows circles around the "$1" are broken at point where they meet the curved line below "ONE DOLLAR" (arrows).

TYPE II shows these circles complete.

10¢ Webster design of 1898

TYPE I has an unbroken white curved line below the words "TEN CENTS".

TYPE II shows white line is broken by ornaments at a point just below the "E" in "TEN" and the "T" in "CENTS" (arrows).

2¢ Washington Issue of 1903

Die I
319, 319g, 320

The rounded inner frame line below and to the left "T" in "TWO" has a dark patch of color that narrows, but remains strong across the bottom.

Die II
319f, 320a

2¢ "cap of 2" Variety of 1890

Cap on left "2"

Plate defects in the printing of the 2¢ "Washington" stamp of 1890 accounts for the "Cap of left 2" and "Cap on both 2s" varieties illustrated.

Cap on right "2"

UNITED STATES STAMP IDENTIFIER

Shows you how to distinguish between the rare and common U.S. stamps that look alike.

FRANKLIN AND WASHINGTON ISSUES OF 1908-22

Perforation	Watermark	Other Identifying Features		 ONE CENT	 TWO CENTS	 1 CENT 1	 2 CENTS 2	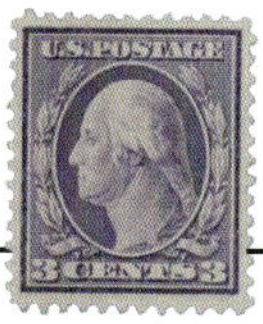 3¢ thru $1 denominations	 8¢ thru $1 denominations
PERF. 12	USPS	White paper		331	332			333-42	422-23
		Bluish gray paper		357	358			359-66	
	USPS	White paper		374	375	405	406	376-82, 407	414-21
COIL 12	USPS	Perf. Horizontal		348	349			350-51	
		Perf. Vertical		352	353			354-56	
	USPS	Perf. Horizontal		385	386				
		Perf. Vertical		387	388			389	
IMPERF.	USPS			343	344			345-47	
	USPS	Flat Plate		383	384	408	409		
		Rotary Press					459		
	Unwmkd.	Flat Plate				481	482-82A	483-85	
		Offset				531	532-34B	535	
COIL 8-1/2	USPS	Perf. Horizontal		390	391	410	411		
		Perf. Vertical		392	393	412	413	394-96	
PERF. 10	USPS								460
	USPS					424	425	426-30	431-40
	Unwmkd.	Flat Plate				462	463	464-69	470-78
		Rotary Press				543			
COIL 10	USPS	Perf. Horizontal	Flat			441	442		
			Rotary			448	449-50		
		Perf. Vertical	Flat			443	444	445-47	
			Rotary			452	453-55	456-58	
	Unwmkd.	Perf. Horizontal				486	487-88	489	
		Perf. Vertical				490	491-92	493-96	497
PERF. 11	USPS				519				
	USPS						461		
	Unwmkd.	Flat Plate				498	499-500	501-07	508-18
		Rotary Press				*544-45	546		
		Offset				525	526-28B	529-30	
Perf. 12-1/2	Unwkmd.	Offset				536			
11 x 10	Unwkmd.	Rotary				538	539-40	541	
10 x 11	Unwkmd.	Rotary				542			

* Design of #544 is 19 mm wide x 22-1/2 mm high. #545 is 19-1/2 to 20 mm wide x 22 mm high.

Size of Flat Plate Design

22mm

18-1/2 to 19mm

Stamps printed by rotary press are always slightly wider or taller on issues prior to 1954. Measurements do not apply to booklet singles.

HOW TO USE THIS IDENTIFICATION CHART

Numbers referred to herein are from Scott's Standard Postage Stamp Catalog. To identify any stamp in this series, first check the type by comparing it with the illustrations at the top of the chart. Then check the perforations, and whether the stamp is single or double line watermarked or unwatermarked. With this information you can quickly find out the Standard Catalog number by checking down and across the chart. For example, a 1¢ Franklin, perf. 12, single line watermark, must be Scott's #374.

UNITED STATES STAMP IDENTIFIER

Shows you how to distinguish between the rare and common U.S. stamps that look alike.

Types of The 2¢ Washington Design of 1912-20

Type I

Type I where the ribbon at left above the figure "2" has one shading line in the first curve, while the ribbon at the right has one shading line in the second curve. Bottom of toga has a faint outline. Top line of toga, from bottom to front of throat, is very faint. Shading lines of the face, terminating in front of the ear, are not joined. Type I occurs on both flat and rotary press printings.

Type Ia is similar to Type I except that all of the lines are stronger. Lines of the Toga button are heavy. Occurs only on flat press printings.

Type Ia

Type II

Type II has ribbons shaded as in Type I. Toga button and shading lines to left of it are heavy. Shading lines in front of ear are joined and end in a strong vertically curved line (arrow). Occurs only on rotary press printings.

Type III where ribbons are shaded with two lines instead of one; otherwise similar to Type II. Occurs on rotary press printings only.

Type III

Type IV

Type IV where top line of toga is broken. Shading lines inside the toga bottom read "Did". The Line of color in the left "2" is very thin and usually broken. Occurs on offset printings only.

Type V in which top line of toga is complete. Toga button has five vertical shaded lines. Line of color in the left "2" is very thin and usually broken. Nose shaded as shown in illustration. Occurs on offset printings only.

Type V

Type Va

Type Va is same as Type V except in shading dots of nose. Third row of dots from bottom has four dots instead of six. Also, the Overall height of Type Va is 1/3 millimeter less than Type V. Occurs on offset printings only.

Type VI is same as Type V except that the line of color in left "2" is very heavy (arrow). Occurs in offset printings only.

Type VI

Type VII

Type VII in which line of color in left "2" is clear and continuous and heavier than Types V or Va, but not as heavy as in Type VI. There are three rows of vertical dots (instead of two) in the shading of the upper lip, and additional dots have been added to hair at top of the head. Occurs on offset printings only.

Types of The 3¢ Washington Design of 1908-20

Type I

TYPE I in which the top line of the toga is weak, as are the top parts of the shading lines that join the toga line. The fifth shading line from the left (arrow) is partly cut away at the top. Also the line between the lips is thin. Occurs on flat and rotary press printings.

Type II

TYPE II where top line of toga is strong and the shading lines that join it are heavy and complete. The line between the lips is heavy. Occurs on flat and rotary press printings.

Type III

TYPE III in which top line of toga is strong, but the fifth shading line from the left (arrow) is missing. The center line of the toga button consists of two short vertical lines with a dot between them. The "P" and "O" of "POSTAGE" are separated by a small line of color. Occurs on offset printings only.

Type IV

TYPE IV in which the shading lines of the toga are complete. The center line of the toga button consists of a single unbroken vertical line running through the dot in the center. The "P" and the "O" of "POSTAGE" are joined. Type IV occurs only in offset printings.

Types of 5¢ Franklin, 10¢ Washington 1847-1947

In the original 5¢ design, the top edge of Franklin's shirt touches the circular frame about at a level with the top of the "F" of "FIVE", while in the 1875 reproduction it is on a level with the top of the figure "5".

In the original 10¢ design, the left edge of Washington's coat points to the "T" of "TEN", and the right edge points between the "T" and "S" of "CENTS". In the reproductions, the left and right outlines of the coat point to the right edge of "X" and to the the center of the "S" of "CENTS" respectively. Also, on the 1875 reprints, the eyes have a sleepy look and the line of the mouth is straighter.

The 1947 "Cipex" Souvenir Sheet, issued on the hundredth anniversary of United States stamps, features reproductions of the two original designs. Stamps cut out of souvenir sheet are, of course, valid postage. However, no difficulty in identification should be encountered since the 1947 reproductions are light blue (5¢) instead of the original red brown, and brownish orange (10¢) instead of the original black.

Commemorative Identifier

The following handy identifier is a list of commemoratives organized alphabetically by key words on the stamp, which are the most prominent after "U.S. Postage," and matches the stamp with its corresponding Scott number.

1948-C 4444f
Abbey, Edwin Austin 3502k
Abbott & Costello 2566
Abstract Expressionists 4444
Abyssinian Cat 2373
Acadia National Park 746, 762, C138, UX601
Acheson, Dean 2755
Achilles 4444j
Acoma Pot 1709, 3873g
Acuff, Roy 3812
Adams
  Ansel 3649p
  Abigail 2146
  John 806, 841, 850, 1687a, 2201, 2216b
  John Quincy 811, 846, 2201, 2216f
Addams, Jane 878
Admiralty Head Lighthouse (WA) 2470, 2474
Adopt a Shelter Pet 4451, 4460
Adopting a Child 3398
Adriatic, S.S. 117,128
Advances in Aviation 3916-25
Adventures of Huckleberry Finn, The 2787
African
  Americans 873, 902, 953, 1085, 1233, 1290, 1361, 1372, 1486, 1490-1491, 1493, 1495, 1554, 1560, 1772, 1790, 1791, 1860, 1865, 2027, 2043, 2051, 2083, 2084, 2097, 2164, 2211, 2223, 2275, 2420, 2496, 2746, 2766, 2816, 2851, 2852, 2854, 2855, 2856, 2857, 2858, 2859, 2860, 2861, 2869g, 2870g, 2956, 2975h, 2982, 2983, 2984, 2985, 2986, 2987, 2988, 2989, 2990, 2991, 2992, 3058, 3096, 3121, 3181, 3182l, 3186c, 3188a, 3190j, 3212, 3214, 3215, 3216, 3217, 3218, 3219, 3273, 3371, 3408a, 3408j, 3408p, 3408r, 3422, 3436, 3501, 3557, 3746, 3834, 3841, 3871, 3896, 3936, 3937, 3996, 4020, 4080, C97, C102, C103, C105
  Elephant Herd 1388
  Violets 2486
Agave Cactus 1943
Aging Together 2011
AIDS Awareness 2806
Ailey, Alvin 3841
Air
  Air Service Emblem C5
  -Cushion Vehicle C123, C126
  Force 1013, 3167, C49
  Force One 4144
  Force, U.S. 3167
  Mail Service, US C74
  Save Our 1413
  Service Emblem C5
Airborne units spearhead attacks 2838d
Aircraft 3142
Aircraft Gun 90mm, Anti 900
Airlift 1341
Airliner, Hypersonic C122, C126
Alabama 1654, 1953, 3561, 3696, 4274
  Statehood 1375
Aladdin & Genie 4195
Alamo, The 776, 778, 1043
Alaska 1681, 1954, 3562, 3697
  (Cook, Captain James) 1732, 1733
  Highway 2635
  Purchase C70
  Statehood 2066, C53, 4374
  Territory 800
  -Yukon Pacific Exposition 370-371
Alaskan
  Malamute 2100
  Brown Bear 2310
Albania 918
Alcoholism, You Can Beat It 1927
Alcott, Louisa May 862
Alexandria C40
Alfred Hitchcock Presents 4414o, UX567
Alger, Horatio 2010
Alice in Wonderland 3913
All Aboard 3333-37
All Heart 4270
All in the Family, TV Series 3189b
Allegiance, Pledge of 2594
Allen,
  Ethan 1071
  Gracie 4414p, UX568
  Steve 4414r, UX584
Alley Oop 3000n
Alliance for Progress 1234
Alliance, French 1753
Allied forces retake New Guinea 2838a
  Nations 537, 907
  Victory 537
Allies
  attack Sicily 2765c
  battle U-Boats 2765a
  Break Codes 2697f
  free Rome, June 4: Paris, August 25 .... 2838f
  in Normandy, D-Day 2838c
  Land in North Africa 2697j
  Liberate Holocaust survivors 2981e
Alligator 1428, 2950, 4033
Allison, Fran 4414k, UX576
Allosaurus 1390, 3136g
Aloha Shirts 4592-4601, 4682-86
Alpha 3142e
Alpha Airplane 3142a
Alpine Skiing 3180
Alpine Tundra 4198
Alta, California, 1st Civil Settlement 1725
Aluminum Group Chair 4333o
Alyssum 4758
Alzheimer's Awareness 4358
Amateur Radio 1260
Amaryllis 4864
Ambulance 2128, 2231
Amber Alert 4031
America
  Beautification of 1318, 1365, 1366
  Smiles 3189m
  Survives the Depression 3185m
America's Libraries 2015
America PUAS 2426, 2512, C121, C127
America/PUASP C131
American 1596, 1597, 1598, 1599, 1603-1606, 1608, 1610-1615
  Architecture 1779-1782, 1838, 1839-1841, 1928-1931, 2019-2022
  Art 3236
  Arts 1484-1487, 1553-1555, 3236
  Automobile Association 1007
  Bald Eagle 1387
  Bankers Association, Jan. 3 987
  Bar Association 1022
  Bicentennial 1432, 1456-1459, 1476-1479, 1480-1483, 1543-1546, 1559-1568, 1629-1631, 1633-1647, 1648-1667, 1668-1674, 1676-1682, 1686-1694, 1704, 1716-1720, 1722, 1726, 1728, 1753, 1789, 1811, 1813, 1816, 1937-1938, 2052
  Cats 2372-2373, 2374-2375
  Chemical Society 1002
  Child 3151e
  Circus 1309
  Copper Rockfish 4423g, UX596
  Credo 1139-1144
  Crocodile 3105d
  Dance 1749-1752
  Dance, Ballet 1749
  Dogs 2098-2101
  Elk 2328
  Flag 1623, 2116
  Folklore 1317, 1330, 1357, 1370, 1470, 1548
  Foxhound 2101
  Goldfinch 1982, 1999, 4890
  Gothic by Grant Wood 3236q
  Horses 2155-2158
  Illustrators 3502
  Indian 565, 695, 1364
  Indian Dances 3072-3076
  Institute of Architects 1089
  Kestrel 2476-2477, 3031-3031A, 3044
  Legion 1369
  Lobster 2304
  Lotus 4046
  Militia 1568
  Music 1252, 1372, 1484, 2110, 2211, 2371, 2550, 2721-2737, 2767-2778, 2849-2861, 2982-2992, 3096-3103. 3154-3165, 3212-19, 3339-3350
  Owls 1760-1763
  Philatelic Society 730-731, 750, 766, 770
  Realism 3184n
  Red Cross 702, 967, 1910
  Revolution 551, 645, 651, 653, 657, 689, 690, 727, 734, 752, 1010, 1729, 1851, 1937-1938
  Revolution Battles 617-619, 629-630, 643-644, 646, 688, 1003, 1361, 1563-1564, 1686, 1722, 1728, 1826
  Samoa 3389
  Shoals Lighthouse (FL) 2473
  Shorthair Cat 2375
  Sign Language 2784
  Society of Civil Engineers 1012
  Sports 1932-1933, 2046, 2097, 2376-2377, 2417
  Streetcar, First 2059
  Trees 1764-1767
  Turners Society 979
  Washington 1675
  Wildlife 2286-2287, 2288-2307, 2308-2316, 2322-2335
  Woman 1152
  Wool Industry 1423
Americana Issue 1581-1582, 1584-1585, 1590-1594, 1616-1619, 1622, 1623, 1625
Americans, African 873, 902, 953, 1085, 1233, 1290, 1361, 1372, 1486, 1490-1491, 1493, 1495, 1554, 1560, 1772, 1790, 1791, 1860, 1865, 2027, 2043, 2051, 2083-2084, 2097, 2164, 2211, 2223, 2275, 2420, 2496, 2746, 2766, C97, C102-C103, C105
AMERIPEX 2145
  '86 .... 2198-2201, 2216-2219
Amethyst 1540
Amish Horse & Buggy C150
Amish Quilt 3524-27
Ammendment, 19th 3184e
Amphipod 3442
Anderson, Marian 3986
  C. Alfred "Chief" 4879
Andrew Wyeth 5212
Anemone 3029
Angelou, Maya 4979
Angels 1268, 1276, 1363, 1471, 3012, 3018, 4477
Angus and Longhorn Cattle 1504
Animal
  Humane, Treatment of 1307
  Muppet 3944g
  Rescue 4451-4461
Annapolis Tercentenary, May 23 984
Antarctic Expedition, Byrd 733, 735, 753, 768
Antarctic Explorers 2386, 2387, 2388, 2389
Antarctic Treaty 1431, C130
Anthem, Flag and 1890, 1891, 1892, 1893
Anthony, Susan B. 784, 1051
Anti-Aircraft Gun, 90mm 900
Antibiotics saves lives 3186b
Antillean Euphonia 3222
Anti-Pollution 1410-1413
Antioch Dunes Evening Primrose 1786
Antique Automobiles 3019-3023a
Apgar, Virginia 2179
Apollo 8 .... 1371, 2633, 2634
Apollo, Soyuz 1569-1570
Appalacians 4045
Appaloosa 2158
Apples 4727-34
Appleseed, Johnny 1317
Appomattox, Civil War Centennial 1182
Apprenticeship 1201
Apte Tarpon Fly 2547
Aquaman 4084h, 4084r
Arbor Day 717
Arc de Triompe 934
Architects, Institute of American 1089
Architecture, American 1779-1782, 1800-1802, 1838-1841, 1928-1931, 2019-2022, 3910
Archives, National 2081
Arctic
  Animals 3288-3292
  Explorations 1128
  Fox 3289
  Hare 3288
  Tundra 3802
Arizona 1680, 1955, 3563, 3698
  National Park (Grand Canyon) 741, 757, 2512
  Statehood 1192, 4627
  USS Memorial 4873
Ark and The Dove, The 736
Arkansas 1657, 1956, 3564, 3699
  River Navigation 1358
  Statehood 782, 2167
Arlen, Harold 3100
Arlington Amphitheater 570, 701
Arlington Green Bridge 4738, U679
Armadillo 2296
Armed
  Forces 926, 929, 934-936, 939, 1026, 1067
  Forces Reserve 1067
Armstrong,
  Edwin 2056
  Louis 2982, 2984
Army
  Medal of Honor 4823, 4823a
  and Navy 900
  Issue 934, 985, 998, 1013, 1067
  Issue, Continental 1565
  Issue, Salvation 1267
Arnaz, Desi 3187l
Arnold, Gen. H.H. "Hap" 2191
Arrival of Lafayette 1010
Arrows E22-E23

Arsenal of Democracy 2559e
Art
  American Indian 3873
  Direction 3772f
  Deco Style (Chrysler Building) 3184j
  Glass 3328
  Hudson River School Paintings 4917-20
Arthur, Chester A. 826, 2218c
Articles of Confederation 1726
Artists . . . 884-888, 1187, 1207, 1241, 1243, 1322, 1335, 1361, 1370, 1386, 1433, 1486, 1553, 1863, 1934, 2182, 4917-20, 4968-72, C71
Arts & Architecture Cover 4333k
Ashe, Arthur 3936
Ashville 4444b
Asia C131
Assassin bug 3351g
Assiniboine Headdress 2501
Aster 2993, 4762
Astronauts 1331, 1434-1435, 1912, 2419, 2632, C76
Atlantic
  Cable 1112
  Cod 2206
Atomic Energy Act 1200
Atoms For Peace 1070
Audubon, John James 874, 1241, 1863, 3236e, 3650, C71
Aurora
  Australis 4123b, 4204
  Borealis 4123a, 4203
Austin, Stephen F. 776, 778
Australia Bicentennial 2370
Australian Shepherd 4458
Austria 919
Authors . . . 859-863, 980, 1250, 1281, 1294, 1327, 1487, 1733, 1832, 1848, 1856-1857, 2010, 2047, 2073, 2094, 2168, 2196-2197, 2350, 2418, 2538, 3134, 3221, 3308, 3433, 3434, 3444, 3557, 3904
Auto Tail Fin 2908-2910
Automobile 296, 1162, 1286A, 1511, 1906, 2381-85, 2437, 2438d, 2905-2906, 4743-47
  Antique 3019-3023a
  Electric 1906
Automobiles 4353-57
Autumn Fern 4850, 4876
Autry, Gene 4449, UX600
Auxiliary Steamship 4549
Avant-garde art, 1913 . . . . . 3183d
Aviation
  advances in 3916-3925
  Commercial 1684
  Naval 1185
  Pioneers of C91-C95, C99-C100, C113-C114, C118-C119, C128-C129
Aviator 2998
Azalea 4622
Azurite 2700
B-10 . . . . . 3142f
B-24 . . . . . 2765d, 3922
B29 3923
Baby
  Boom 3186l
  Buggy 1902
  Coos 3151f
Babyland Rag 3151i
Badger 1922, 2312
Badlands UX602
Bailey Gatzert Riverboat 3095
Bailey, Mildred 2860
Baker, Ella 4384f
Balanchine, George 3843
Balboa, Vasco Nunez de 397, 401
Bald Eagle 1387, 1909, 2309
Baldwin,
  Abraham 1850
  apple 4730, 4731
  James 3871
Ball, Lucille 3523, 4414b, UX575
Ballet 1749, 3237
Balloon Jupiter C54
Ballooning 2530
Balloons, Hot Air 2032-2035
Ballot Box, Early 1584
Baloo 4345
Balsam Fir 4480, 4484
Baltimore
  & Ohio Railroad 1006
  Cathedral 1780
  Checkerspot 4603
  Oriole 1972, 4886
Bankers Association, American 987
Banking and Commerce 1577-1578
Banneker, Benjamin 1804
Banyan 4620
Bar Association, American 1022
Bara, Theda 2827
Barber, Samuel 3162
Barbie Doll 3188i
Barcelona 235
Bardeen, John 4227
Barge fleeting 4710l
Barn Swallow 2286
Barney Google 3000i
Barred Owl 1762
Barrel Cactus 1942
Barry, John 790
Barrymores, The 2012
Bartholdi, Frederic Auguste 2147
Barton, Clara 967, 2975c
Bartram, John & William 3314
Baseball, ... 855, 3402, 4341, 4465, 4466
  Olympic 2619
  Professional 1381, 2016, 2046, 2097, 2417, 3182n, 3184a, ... 3186c, 3187c, 3187j, 3188n, 3191a, 3408, 4080-4083 4694-97, 4697a
  Stadiums 3510-3519
Basie, Count 3096
Basilone, Sgt. John 3963
Basketball 3399, 4950-51
  Centennial 2560
  Naismith— 1189
Bass, Largemouth 2207
Bastogne and Battle of the Bulge 2838j
Bates, Daisy Gatson 4384c
Batman 4084e, 4084o, 4928-35
Bats 3661-3664, 5423
Battle for Leyte Gulf 2838i
Battle of
  Lake Erie 4805
  Bennington 643, 644
  Braddock's Field 688
  Brooklyn 1003
  Bunker Hill 1361, 1564
  Chancellorsville 2975p
  Coral Sea 2697c
  Fallen Timbers 680
  Five Forks 4980
  Fort Stanwix 644
  Gettysburg 2975t, 4788
  Lexington and Concord 1563
  Mobile 1826
  Mobile Bay 4911
  New Orleans 1261, 4952
  Oriskany 644, 1722
  Petersburg 4910
  Saratoga 644
  Shiloh 2975e
  Vicksburg 4787
  White Plains 629, 630
Beach Clean-Up 2954
Beach Umbrella 2443
Beacon on Rocky Mountains C11
Beagle 2098
Beale, Boggs, Lincoln and S. Douglas Debating 1115
Beans 4004, 4011, 4017
Bear
  Black 2299
  Brown 1884
  Polar 1429, 3291
  Smokey, the 2096
Bearberry 2687
Beard, James 4925
Bearden, Romare 4566-69
  Conjunction 4566
  Odyesseus 4567
  Prevalence of Ritual 4568
  Falling Star 4569
Beatles, The "Yellow Submarine" 3188o
Beau Geste 2447
Beaugregory Fish 1827
Beautification of America 1318, 1365-1368, 4716a-e
Beauty and the Beast 4027
Beaver 2316, 4064
Beavertail Cactus 1944
Beckwourth, Jim 2869q, 2870q
Beechcraft 35 Bonanza 3924
Belgium 914
Bell,
  Alexander Graham 893, 1683
  Liberty 627, 1518, 1595, 1618, C57, C62
Bella
  Bella Tribe, Heiltsuk 1834
  Coola Tribe 1837
Bellatrix Lestrange 4844
Benedict, Ruth 2938
Benet, Stephen Vincent 3221
Bengal Tiger, White 2709
Benny, Jack 2564
Bergen
  & McCarthy 2563
  Edgar 2563
Bering
  Glacier 4036
  Land Bridge C131
Berle, Milton 4414a, UX583
Berlin Aircraft 3211
Berlin, Irving 3669
Berlin Wall, Fall of the 3190k
Bernstein, Leonard 3521
Best
  Friend of Charleston 2363
  Wishes 2271, 2396
Bethune, Mary McLeod 2137
Betsy McCall 3151l
Bicycle 1460, 1901, 4687-90
  Tandem 2266
Bierstadt, Albert 3236m, 4346
Big Band
  Leaders 3096-99
  Sounds 3186j
Big Brothers/Big Sisters 2162
Big-White-Tailed Ptarmigan 4198g
Bighorn Sheep 1467, 1880, 1949, 2288, 4198e
Bill of Rights 1312
  Drafting of the 2421
Biloxi Lighthouse 4411, U671, UX564
Biltmore House 1929
Biplane 2436, 2438, 2438c, 2781
Bird of Paradise 3310
Bird Treaty, Migratory 1306
Birds
  & Flowers, State 1953-2002
  of Prey 4608-4612
  songbirds 4882-91
Bishop, Elizabeth 4659
Bison 1883, 2320
Bissell, Emily 1823
Bixby Creek Bridge 4439
Black
  and Tan Coonhound 2101
  Bear 2299
  Heritage 1744, 1771, 1804, 1875, 2016, 2044, 2073, 2137, 2203, 2249, 2371, 2402, 2442, 2567, 2617, 2746, 2816, 2956, 3058, 3121, 3181, 3273, 3371, 3501, 3557, 3746, 3834, 3896, 3996, 4120, 4222, 4403, 4464, 4565, 4624, 4856, 4958, 5056, 5171, 5259, 5349, 5432, 5555, 5663, 5753, 5830
  Hugo L. 2172
  Widow 3351a
Black and Tan Poster 4336
Black-capped Chickadee 1973
Black, White and Tan Cat 4457
Black-footed Ferret 2333, 3105a
Black Pine 4619
Black-tailed
  Jack Rabbit 2305
  Prairie Dog 2325
Blacksmith 1718
Blackwell, Elizabeth 1399
Blair, Montgomery C66
Blake, Eubie 2988
Bliss, Fort 976
Blondie 3000l
Blood Donor 1425
Blue Flag 2663
Blue Hen Chicken 1960
Blue Jay 1757, 1757d, 2318, 2483
Blue Paloverde 3194
Blue-spotted Salamander 3815
Blue Spruce 4481, 4485
Blueberries 3294, 3298, 3302, 3404, 5652, 5653
Bluebird, Eastern 2478, 3033
Bluefin, Tuna 2208
Bluets 2656
Bly, Nellie 3665
BMX Biking 3322, 4690
Boatmen on the Missouri by George Caleb Bingham 3236f
Bobcat 2482, 2332
Bob Parr 4678
"Bobtail" Horsecar 2061
Bobwhite 2301
Boeing 247 3916
Boeing B-29 Superfortress 3923
Bogart, Humphrey 3152, 4671
Bohlen, Charles E. 4076e
Bolivar, Simon 1110-1111
Bombardier beetle 3351m
Bon Homme Richard 983
Bonds and Stamps help 2765g
Bonsai Trees 4618-4622
Boo 4681
Books, Bookmark and Eyeglasses 1585
Boone, Daniel 1357
Borglum, Gutzon, Sculptured Head by 1114
Boston
  Harbor Lighthouse 4793
  State House 1781
  Tea Party 1480-1483
  Terrier 2099
Botanical
  Congress 1376-1379
  Prints 3126-3129
Boulder Dam 774

Bow, Clara 2820
Boxing 2499, 2640, 2766, 3182h, 3183m, 3187k, 4020
Box Turtle 2326
Bowling 2963
Boy Scouts 995, 1145, 2161, 3183j, 4472
Boyd, William. . . . 4414g, UX573
Boys' Clubs of America 1163
Boys in a Pasture 4473
Brachiosaurus 3136d
Bradley, Omar N. 3394
Brain Coral, Beaugregory Fish 1827
Bread Wagon. 2136
Breakfast in Bed by Mary Cassatt. 3236o
Breckenridge, Mary 2942
Breads 4912
Breast Cancer Awareness 3081
Brenda Starr 3000t
Brice, Fanny 2565
Bridge 293, 961, 1012, 1109, 1258, 1721
at Niagara Falls. 297
Bixby Creek 4439
Brooklyn 1012, 2041
Mackinac. 1109, 4438, U674
New River Gorge Bridge. U675, 4511
Sunshine Skyway 4649
Bridger, Jim 2869c, 2870c
Bright Eyes 3230-3234
Bringing Up Father 3000d
Bristlecone Pines. 4049
Broad-billed Hummingbird. 2643
Broad-tailed Hummingbird. 2289
Broadbill Decoy 2138
Broadway Songwriters. 3345-50
Brodsky, Joseph 4654
Brontosaurus 1390, 2425
Brooding Sea Anemones. 4423j, UX595
Brooklyn Bridge 1012, 2041
Brooklyn, Battle of 1003
Brooks, Gwendolyn 4655
Brother Jonathan. 2365
Brown
Bear 1884
Horse with Green Bridle 2979
Pelican 1466, 3105h, 4423a, UX594, 1970
Capped Rosy-Finch 4198j
Thrasher 1962
Brussels Universal and International Exhibition 1104
Bryan, William Jennings 2195
Bryant, Bear. 3143, 3148
Bryce Canyon National Park C139, UX603
Buchanan, James 820, 2217f
James (Wheatland). 1081
Buchanan's No. 999 2847
Buck, Pearl 1848
Buckboard 2124
Buckbreak the Hippogriff 4832
Buffalo . . 287, 569, 700, 1392, 1883, 2320, 3209c, 3467, 3468, 3475, 3484, 3484A, 4041
Bill Cody 2178, 2869
Soldiers. 2818
Buggy 1360, 1370, 1505, 1902
Baby 1418, 1902
Bugs Bunny 3137, 3138, 5494-5503
Bugs Life, A 4677
Building a Nation 4801
Bullfinch, Charles. 1781
Bullfrog 4055
Bull, John. 2364
Bull Run 4523
Bullseye 4680
Bumble 4949
Bunchberry 2675
Bunche, Ralph 1860
Bunker Hill 1034, 1056, 1564
Flag. 1351
Burbank, Luther 876
Bureau of Engraving and Printing 2875
Burgos, Julia de. 4476
Burgoyne Campaign 644, 1728, 2590
Burke, Admiral Arleigh A. 4441
Burma Road 2559a
Burmese 2374
Burns and Allen 4414p, UX568
Burns, George 4414p, UX568
Burr, Raymond. 4414n, UX580
Burroughs, Edgar Rice 4702
Butte 2902, 2902B
in fog 4710d
Butterflies. 1712-1715, 3105f, 4000-4002, 4198f, 4198h, 4198i, 4462, 4603, 4736, 4859
Buzz Lightyear. 4555, 5709-12
By 1945, World War II has uprooted millions. 2981g
Byrd Antarctic Expedition II 733, 735, 753, 768
Richard E. 2388
Cab, Hansom. 1904
Cabbage Patch Kids 3190i
Cable
Car 1442
San Francisco. 1442, 2263
TV 3190f
Caboose, RR. 1905
Cabrillo, Juan Rodriguez 2704
Cactus 1942-1945
Cactus Wren 1955
Cadillac Eldorado 4353
Cadillac, Landing of. 1000
Cagney, James 3329
Calder, Alexander 3198-3202
Caledonia Poster. 4339
Calendula 4755
Calico Cat 4453
Calico Scallop 2120
California 1663, 1957, 3438, 3565, 3700
Condor 1430, 3105i
Gold 954
Gold Rush. 3316
Gull 1996
Pacific International Exposition. 773, 778
Poppy 2651
Sea Lion. 2329
Settlement. 1373
Statehood 997, 3483
Quail 1957
(Yosemite National Park) 740, 751, 756, 769
Calliope Hummingbird. 2646, 4154, 4154a
Calvin, Melvin 4541
Camarasaurus. 3136c
Camel 2392
Camellia. 1877, 1935
Cameras, Motion Picture 1555
Camp Fire Girls 1167, 2163
Camp, Walter. 3810
Campanella, Roy. 4080
Camptosaurus. 3136b
Canada 1324
Goose 1757, 1757c, 2334
US Friendship. 961
Canal 298, 681, 856
Boat 2257
Erie 1325
Cancer
Cancer, Crusade Against 1263
Detection, Early 1754
Candle 1205, 2395
Holder, Rush Lamp and 1610
Cannon 629-630, 1178, 1181
Canoe 1356, 2163, 2353A, 2453, 2454
Canvasback Decoy 2140
Cape Hatteras 1448-1451, 2471
Cape Lookout, North Carolina. 3788
CAPEX '78. . . . . 1757-1757h
Capitol 572, 989, 992, 1202, 1365, 1503, 1590-1591, 1616, 1623, 2114, 2115, 2116, 2532, 2561, 3472, 3648, C64-C65
Capra, Frank 4669
National Sesquicentennial. 989-992
Statue of Freedom on Dome 989
Cardinal 1465, 1757, 1757a, 1965-1966, 1969, 1985, 1987, 1998, 2000, 2480, 2489,4939, 4943
in Snow. 2874
Honeyeater. 3225
CARE. 1439
Carl Fredricksen 4556
Carlson, Chester 2180
Carlyle House, John C40
Carmel, Man and Children of. 1485
Carmel Mission 4650
Carmichael, Hoagy 3103
Carnegie, Andrew 1171
Carney, Art. 4414t, UX572
Carnivorous Plants 3528-3531
Carolina Charter 1230
Carolina-Charleston. 683
Carolina Wren 1992
Carousel
Animals. 2390-2393
Horses 2976-2979a
Carpenters' Hall. 1543
Carreta. 2255
Carriage, Steam 2451
Carrier, Letter. 1238, 1490, 1497, 2420
Cars, Classic 2381-2385
Carson
Kit 2869n, 2870n
Rachel. 1857
Rachel Valley, NV 999
Carter Family, The. 2773, 2776
Carteret, Philip, Landing of 1247
Caruso, Enrico. 2250
Carver, George Washington 953, 3183c
Case Study House. 4333d
Cashman, Nellie 2869k, 2870k
Cash, Johnny. 4789
Cassatt, Mary 1322, 2181, 3236o, 3804-07
Catfish 2209
Cather, Willa 1487
Catlin, George 3236k
Cats 3232, 4452, 4453, 4456, 4457, 4460
American. 2372-2375
Musical 3190b
Catt, Carrie C. 959
Cattle
Angus and Longhorn 1504
Western, in Storm. 292, 3209h, 3210
Celebrate 4196, 4335
Celebrate the Century
1900's. 3182
1910's. 3183
1920's. 3184
1930's. 3185
1940's. 3186
1950's. 3187
1960's. 3188
1970's. 3189
1980's. 3190
1990's. 3191
Celebrity Chefs 4922-26
Cellular Phones. 3191o
Centennial Olympic Games. 3068, 3068a-68t
Center-pivot irrigation 4710h
Century
Of Progress Exposition. 728-731
Flight. C18
20th, Limited 3335
Ceratosaurus. 3136a
Certified Public Accountants 2361
Cha Cha Cha. 3941
Chalic Coral. 1829
Challenger Space Shuttle 2544
Chamberlain, Wilt 4950-51
Champions of Liberty. . 1096, 1110-1111, 1117-1118, 1136-1137
Guiseppe Garibaldi. 1168-1169
Gustaf Mannerheim 1165-1166
Ignacy Jan Paderewski. 1159-1160
Mahatma Gandhi 1174-1175
Masaryk 1147-1148
San Martin 1125-1126
Champlain, Samuel de 4073-4074
Chancellorsville 2975p
Chaney, Lon 2822, 3168
Chaney, Lon, Jr.. 3172
Chanute, Octave C93-C94
Chaplin, Charlie 2821, 3183a
Chapman, Dave. 4546h
Charleston Carolina. 683
Charles,Ray. 4807
Charleston, Best Friend of. 2363
Charlie Parker 2987
Charlotte Amalie Harbor, St. Thomas, Virgin Islands 802
Charter. 2559
Oak 772
Chaplin, Charlie as the Little Tramp 3183a
Chavez, Cesar E. 3781
Chavez, Dennis. 2186
Checkerspot 1713
Chefs. 4922-26
Chemical Society, American 1002
Chemistry 1685
Chen, Joyce. 4924
Chennault, Claire Lee 2187
Cherokee
Seal. 972
Strip 1360
Strip Land Run 2754
Cherry Blossoms 4982-83
Centennial. 4651-4652
Cherry Orchard 4710i
Cherub. 2948, 2949, 2958, 2959, 2960
Chesapeake Bay Retriever 2099
Chestnut, Mary 2975o
Chestnutt, Charles. 4222
Chevrolet Chevelle 4746
Chevrolet Corvette. 3933
Cheyenne Headdress 2502
Chicago, Century of Progress,
Exposition 728-731, 766
Flight. C18
Chicksaw Seal. 972
Chickadee 1971, 1973
Child, Julia. 4926
Children's Stamp 1085
Chief Joseph 1364, 2869f
Chief Shadoo. 683
Child labor reform 3183o
Child on Hobby Horse 1769
Children . . 230, 235, 651, 717, 796, 855, 963, 995, 1005 1007, 1015, 1024, 1073, 1082, 1085, 1087, 1093, 1135, 1149, 1152, 1163, 1167, 1199, 1238, 1273, 1321-1322, 1336, 1342-1343, 1385, 1414, 1426, 1444, 1453, 1455, 1468, 1470, 1483, 1485, 1507, 1549, 1559, 1701, 1703, 1768-1769, 1772, 1788-1799, 1824, 1842, 1910, 1939, 2010-2011, 2026-2027, 2028-2029, 2030, 2063, 2104, 2106-2108, 2153, 2160-2165, 2199, 2244, 2251, 2275, 2367, 2399, 2427
Children's Friendship. 1085
Chili Peppers 4003, 4012, 4013

Chilkat Tlingit Tribe ... 1835
China, Republic of ... 1188
China Clipper ... C115
  Over the Pacific ... C20-C22, C115
Chinese
  Hibiscus ... 3313
  New Year ... 2720, 2817, 2876, 3060, 3120, 3179, 3272, 3370, 3500, 3559, 3747, 3832, 3895, 3997, 4221, 4375, 4435, 4623, 4726,4846, 4957
  Resistance ... 906
Chipmunk ... 1757f
Chisholm
  Shirley ... 4856
Choctaw Seal ... 972
Choreographers ... 4698-4701
Chris-Craft Speedboat ... 4161
Christmas ... 3003-3018, 4424
  4¢ '62 ... 1205
  5¢ '63 ... 1240
  5¢ '64 ... 1254-1257
  5¢ '65 ... 1276
  5¢ '66 ... 1321
  5¢ '67 ... 1336
  6¢ '68 ... 1363
  6¢ '69 ... 1384
  6¢ '70 ... 1414-1418
  8¢ '71 ... 1444-1445
  8¢ '72 ... 1471-1472
  8¢ '73 ... 1507-1508
  10¢ '74 ... 1550-1552
  10¢ '75 ... 1579-1580
  13¢ '76 ... 1701-1703
  13¢ '77 ... 1729-1730
  13¢ '82 ... 2025
  15¢ '78 ... 1768-1769
  15¢ '79 ... 1799-1800
  15¢ '80 ... 1842-1843
  20¢ '81 ... 1939-1940
  20¢ '82 ... 2026-2030
  20¢ '83 ... 2063-2064
  20¢ '84 ... 2107-2108
  22¢ '85 ... 2165-2166
  22¢ '86 ... 2244-2245
  22¢ '87 ... 2367-2368
  25¢ '88 ... 2399-2400
  25¢ '89 ... 2427-2429
  25¢ '90 ... 2514-2516
  29¢ '91 ... 2578-2585
  29¢ '92 ... 2710-2719
  29¢ '93 ... 2789-2803
  29¢ '94 ... 2871-2874
  32¢ '95 ... 3003-3018
  32¢ '96 ... 3107-3117
  32¢ '97 ... 3176-3177
  32¢ '98 ... 3244-3252
  33¢ '99 ... 3355-67
  34¢ '01 ... 3536-3544
  37¢ '02 ... 3675-3691
  37¢ '03 ... 3820-3828
  37¢ '04 ... 3879, 3883-3894
  37¢ '05 ... 3949-3960
  39¢ '06 ... 4100-4116
  41¢ '07 ... 4206-4218
  42¢ '08 ... 4359-4371
  44¢ '09 ... 4424-4432
  44¢ '10 ... 4477-4481
  44¢ '11 ... 4570-4582
  45¢ '12 ... 4711-15
  46¢ '13 ... 4813,4815,4816,4817-20,4821
  49¢ '14 ... 4945, 4946-49
  $1.10 '13 ... 4814
  $1.15 '14 ... 4936
Christmas Cactus ... 4865
Chrysanthemum ... 2994, 4174, 4176
Chrysler 300C ... 4357
Chrysler Building ... 3910b
Church
  Edwin ... 4919
  Frederick ... 3236n
Churchill, Winston ... 1264, 2559, 2559d
Cigar-Store Figure ... 2243
Cinco de Mayo ... 3203, 3309
Cinderella and Prince Charming ... 4026
Cinematography ... 3772g
Circuit Board, Printed ... 1501
Circus ... 2750-2753, 4898-4905
Circus
  American ... 1309
  Posters ... 4898-4905, 4905b, 4905d
  Wagon ... 2452-2452d, 4905d
Cities, Save Our ... 1411
Citizen Kane ... 3186o
City
  Mail Delivery ... 1238
  of Refuge National Park ... C84
Civil
  Aeronautics Conference, International ... 649, 650
  Defense ... 2559g
  Rights Act of 1964 ... 3937g
  Rights Pioneers ... 4384
  Service ... 2053
  War ... 2975, 4910-4911, 4980-81
  War Centennial, Appomattox ... 1182
  War Centennial, Fort Sumter ... 1178
  War Centennial, Gettysburg ... 1180
  War Centennial, Shiloh ... 1179
  War Centennial, The Wilderness ... 1181
  War, Grand Army of the Republic ... 985
  War, Sesquicentennial ... 4522-4523, 4664-4665
  War, Sesquicentennial, Antietam ... 4665
  War, Sesquicentennial, Battle of New Orleans ... 4664
  War, Sesquicentennial, Bull Run ... 4523
  War, Sesquicentennial, Fort Sumpter ... 4522
  War, Sesquicentennial, Gettysburg ... 4788
  War, Sesquicentennial, Vicksburg ... 4787
  War, United Confederate Veterans ... 998
Civilian Conservation Corps ... 2037
Claret Cup Cactus ... 2660
Clark
  Expedition, Lewis and ... 1063, 3854
  George Rogers ... 651
  Grenville ... 1867
  William ... 3856
Classic
  American Aircraft ... 3142
  American Dolls ... 3151
  Books ... 2785-2786, 2788
  Cars ... 2381-2385
  Films ... 2445-2448, 2722
  Mail Transportation ... 2434-2438
Clay, Henry . 140, 151, 162, 173, 198, 227, 259, 274, 284, 309, 1846
Clemens,
  Samuel L. ... 863
  Samuel L. (Mark Twain) ... 1470
Clemente, Roberto ... 2097, 3408j
Clermont ... 370-373, 1270
Cleveland, Grover ... 564, 693, 827, 2218d
Cliff Palace ... 743, 759, 4039
Clifford, J.R. ... 4384b
Cliffs of Green River by Thomas Moran ... 3236l
Cline, Patsy ... 2772, 2777
Clipper, 314 ... 3142r
Clipper Ship ... 4548
Clock Tower, Tokyo and Dogwood Blossoms ... 4985
Cloudscapes ... 3878
Clown ... 1390, 2750, 4905d
Coal Car ... 2259
Coast
  and Geodetic Survey ... 1088
  Guard ... 936
  Redwoods ... 4063
Cobb, Col. David ... 1686, 1686d
Cobb, Ty ... 3408d
Cobra Lily ... 3530
Coburn, Alvin Langdon ... 3649f
Cochran, Jacqueline ... 3066
Cochrane, Mickey ... 3408g
Cocker, Spaniel ... 2099
Cod, Atlantic ... 2206
Cody, Buffalo Bill ... 2177, 2869b, 2870b
Clayton Moore ... 4414m, UX578
Coffeepot
  Curved Spout ... 1778
  Straight-Spout ... 1775
Cog Railway Car ... 2463
Cohan, George M. ... 1756
Colbert, Claudette ... 4669
Cole
  Nat "King" ... 2852
  Thomas ... 4920
Coleman, Bessie ... 2956
Collective Bargaining ... 1558
College Football ... 1382, 2089
Collie ... 2100
Collins, Eddie ... 3408b
Colonial
  American Craftsmen ... 1456-1459
  Post Rider ... 2779
Colorado ... 1670, 1958, 3566, 3701
  (Mesa Verde National Park) ... 743, 759
  Statehood ... 1001, 1711
Coltrane, John ... 2991
Columbia
  District of ... 2561
  University ... 1029
Columbian
  Doll ... 3151b
  Exposition ... 230-245, 2624-2629
  Exposition, World Stamp Expo '92 ... 2616
  World Stamp Expo '92 ... 2624, 2626-2629
Columbus ... 240, 2616, 2620-2623
  Christopher ... 118-119, 230-245, 2616, 2620-2629, 2805
  First Voyage of ... 2620-2623
  Landing ... 118-119
  Landing in Puerto Rico ... 2805
  Monument ... 1076
Comanche Headdress ... 2503
Comedians ... 2562-2566
Comic Strip Classic ... 3000
Comiskey Park, Chicago ... 3517
Commerce, Banking and ... 1578
Commercial Aviation ... 1684
Commodity Rationing ... 2697b
Common
  Buckeye Butterfly ... 4000-4002
  Dolphin ... 2511
  Loon ... 1975
  Merganser ... 4352e
  Sunflower ... 2666
Communications
  for Peace, Echo I— ... 1173
  in Colonial Times ... 1476-1479
Compact Discs ... 3190h
Composers ... 879-883, 962, 1372, 1484, 1755-1756, 1845, 2044, 2110, 2177, 2211, 2371, 2550, 3100-3103
Computer
  Technology ... 3106
  Art and Graphics ... 3191f
Comstock, Henry ... 1130
Concord / German Immigration ... 2040
Concord, Lexington and ... 617-619, 1563
Condor, California ... 1430, 3105i
Coneflower ... 4170, 4184
Conestoga, Wagon ... 2252
Congratulations! ... 2267
Congress
  Liberty of ... 2004
Congressional ... 3334
Conifer, Sprig of ... 1257
Connecticut ... 1637, 1959, 3567, 3702
  Settlement ... 772, 778
  Statehood ... 2340
Conservation
  Corps, Civilian ... 2037
  Energy ... 1547, 1723
  Forest ... 1122
  Range ... 1176
  Soil ... 1133
  Soil and Water ... 2074
  Water ... 1150
  Waterfowl ... 1362
  Wildlife .. 1077-1079, 1098, 1392, 1427-1430, 1464-1467, 1760-1763
Consolidated
  B-24 Liberator ... 3922
  PBY Catalina ... 3917
Constellation ... 3945-3948
  Airplane ... 3142m
Constitution
  Bicentennial ... 2336-2348, 2355-2360, 2412-2415, 2421
  Drafting of the ... 2355-2359
  Nineteenth Amendment ... 1051
  Nineteenth Amendment (Suffrage) ... 784
  Ratification ... 835, 2336-2348
  Signing of the ... 798, 2360
  Thirteenth Amendment ... 902
  US Frigate ... 951
Construction toys ... 3183n
Consumer Education ... 2005
Container Ship ... 4551
Contemplation of Justice ... 1592, 1617
Continental
  Army ... 1565
  Colors, 1776 ... 3403d
  Congress, First ... 1543-1546
  Marines ... 1567
  Navy ... 1566
Contra Costa Wallflower ... 1785
Contributors to the Cause ... 1559-1562
Convergence ... 4444d
Cook, Captain James ... 1732-1733
Coolidge, Calvin ... 834, 2219b
Coon Cat, Maine ... 2374
Coonhound, Black and Tan ... 2101
Cooper
  Gary ... 2447, 4421
  James Fenimore ... 860
  Anna Julia ... 4408
Cooperative for American Relief Everywhere (CARE) ... 1439
Copernicus, Nicolaus ... 1488
Copley
  Elizabeth ... 1273
  John Singleton ... 1273
Copper ... 2701
Coral
  Pink Rose ... 3052
  Reefs ... 1827-1830
  Sea, Battle of ... 2697c
Cord ... 2383
Cori, Gerti ... 4224
Corn ... 4007, 4008, 4014
Cornish-Windsor Covered Bridge ... 4070

Cornwallis
  at Yorktown, Surrender of ... 703
  Surrender of ... 1686
Cornwell, Dean ... 3502j
Coronado Expedition ... 898
Corregidor (Philippines) ... 925, 2697d
Corsair Airplane ... 3142g
Corythosaurus ... 3136m
Cosby Show, The Hit Comedy ... 3190j
Cosmos ... 4761
Costa's Hummingbird ... 2644
Costello, Lou ... 2566
Costume Design ... 3772c
Cottontail ... 2290
Country & Western Music ... 2723, 2771-2778
Covered Wagons ... 290, 950
Cowboys of the Silver Screen ... 4446-49, UX597-600
Cranberry Harvest ... 4710j
Crane
  Black-Necked ... 2867
  Ichabod ... 1548
  Whooping ... 1097, 2868
Crater Lake National Park ... 745, 761, 4040
Crayola Crayons, introduced, 1903 ... 3182d
Crazy Horse ... 1855
Creatures of the Sea ... 2508-2511
Credit Union Act ... 2075
Crested Honeycreeper ... 3224
Crime Prevention ... 2102
Crippled, Hope for the ... 1385
Crockett, Davy ... 1330
Crocodile ... 3105d
Crocus ... 3025
Crosby, Bing ... 2850
Crosley Field, Cincinnati ... 3512
Cross-Country Skiing ... 2810
Crosspatch Fabric Design ... 4333b
Crossword Puzzle, First ... 3183l
Crusade Against Cancer ... 1263
Cub Airplane ... 3142c
Cummings, E.E. ... 4662
Cunningham, Imogen ... 3649q
Curious George ... 3992
Curtiss
  Glenn ... C100
  Jenny ... C1-C3, C74, 3142s
Curved-Spout Coffeepot ... 1778
Cushing, Harvey, M.D. ... 2188
Cutler, Manasseh ... 795
Cycling ... 3119
Cyclamen ... 4862
Czechoslovakia ... 910
Daffodil ... 2761
Daffy Duck ... 3306-3307
Dahlia ... 1878, 2995, 4167, 4179
Daisy
  Orange Gerbera ... 4175, 4177
  Red Gerbera ... 4169, 4181
Daly, Sgt. Major Daniel J. ... 3964
Dam
  Boulder ... 774
  Grand Coulee ... 1009
  Norris ... 1184
Dances, American Indian ... 3072-3076
Dante ... 1268
Dare, Virginia ... 796
Dartmouth College Case ... 1380
Dashiell Parr ... 4678
Daspletosaurus ... 3136k
Davis
  Alexander J. ... 1841
  Dr. Allison ... 2816
  Miles ... 4693
  Sr., Benjamin O. ... 3121
  Jefferson ... 1408, 2975f
Daye Press, Stephen ... 857
Daylight ... 3333
DC Comics Superheroes ... 4084
DC-3 Airplane ... 3142q
DC-4 Skymaster ... C32-C33, C37, C39, C41
D-Day ... 2838c
de Grasse, Count ... 703
de Mille, Agnes ... 3842
De Haviland Biplane ... C6
Dean,
  Dizzy ... 3408s
  James ... 3082
Death Valley ... 4070
Decatur House ... 1440
Decatur, Stephen ... 791
Declaration of Independence ... 120, 1545, 1687
  by John Trumbull ... 1691-1694
  of War ... 2559j
Deep Sea Creatures ... 3439-3443
Deer ... 2390, 4971
  Fawn ... 2479
  Mouse ... 2324
  White-Tailed ... 1888
DeForest Audions ... C86
Delaware ... 1633, 1960, 3568, 3703
  Statehood ... 2336
Delivery of Letter ... E20-E21
Delta Wing Plane Silhouette ... C77
Dempsey, Jack wins title, 1919 ... 3183m
Denmark ... 920
Dental Health ... 1135
Department
  of Agriculture ... O1-O9, O94-O95
  of Justice ... O25-O34, O106-O107
  of State ... O57-O71
  of the Air Force 1947-1997 ... 3167
  of the Interior ... O15-O24, O96-O103
Depression ... 3185m
Desegregation public schools ... 3187f
Desert
  Five Spot ... 2690
  Plants ... 1942-1945
  Shield/Desert Storm ... 2551, 2552
Destroyer "Reuben James' ... 2559f
Detroit ... 1000
Development Energy ... 1724
Devils Tower National Monument ... 1084
Dewey
  George ... 793
  John ... 1291
Diabetes ... 3503
Diamond Head
  Hawaii ... C46
  Lighthouse ... 4146
Dick Tracy ... 3000m
Dickinson
  Emily ... 1436
  John ... 1687e, 1694
Dickson, William ... 3064
Digitalis ... 4756
DiMaggio, Joe ... 4697
Dinah Shore Show ... 4414i, UX569
Dinosaurs (Prehistoric Animals) ... 2422-2425
Diplomats, Distinguised American ... 4076
Directing ... 3772b
Dirksen, Everett ... 1874
Disabled
  American Veterans and Servicemen ... 1421-1422
  International Year of ... 1925
Disco Music ... 3189d
Discovery ... 1733
Diskey, Donald ... 4546d
Disney
  Characters ... 3865-3868, 3912-3915, 4025-4028, 4192-95, 4342-45, 5213-22
  Walt ... 1355
Distant View of Niagara Falls ... 4920
Distinguished Sailors ... 4440-43
District of Columbia ... 2561, 3813
Diver
  Coral ... 2866
  Motorboat ... 2863
  Ship ... 2864
  Ship's Wheel ... 2865
Dix, Dorothea ... 1844
Dizzy Dean ... 3408s
Doby, Larry ... 4695
Dobby the House Elf ... 4831
Doctors ... 949, 1138, 1251, 1399, 1754, 1865, 2013, 2038, 2170, 2188
Dodge Charger Daytona ... 4743
Dog Sled ... 1128, 2135
Dogbane beetle ... 3351e
Dogface ... 1714
Dogs ... 239, 619, 1128, 1307, 1468, 2202, 3230, 4451, 4454, 4455, 4458, 4459, 4547
  American ... 2098-2101
  At Work ... 4604-07
  Military ... 4606
  Rescue ... 4607
  Seeing Eye ... 1787, 4604
  Therapy ... 4605
Dogwood ... 2347
  Blossoms Lace Design ... 2354
Dolls ... 3151
Dolls by
  Martha Chase, "Alabama Baby" ... 3151a
  Izannah Walker ... 3151h
  Ludwig Greiner ... 3151k
  Martha Chase ... 3151d
  Albert Schoenhut ... 3151o
Dolphin ... 4388
Dolphin, Common ... 2511
Dorchester, SS ... 956
Dorsey, Tommy and Jimmy ... 3097
Dot ... 4677
Douglas Debates, Lincoln- ... 1115
Douglas Fir ... 1376
Douglass, Frederick ... 1290, 2975h
Dove ... 2877-2878
Dr. Bunsen, Honeydew, and Beaker ... 3944h
Dr. Seuss "The Cat in the Hat" ... 3187h
Draco Malfoy ... 4841
Dracula ... 3169
Drafting of the
  Bill of Rights ... 2421
  Constitution ... 2355-2359
Dragnet ... 4414e, UX570
Dragon ... 3370
Drew M.D., Charles R. ... 1865
Dreyfuss, Henry ... 4546f
Drive-in movies ... 3187i
Drug Abuse, Prevent ... 1438
Drum ... 1615, 1629-1630
Drummer ... 1479, 1629, 1630
Drummer Nutcracker ... 4360, 4364, 4368
Du Sable, Jean Baptiste Pointe ... 2249
DuBois, W.E.B. ... 2617
Duck Decoys ... 2138-2141
Duck Stamps
  American Eider ... RW24
  American Merganser ... RW23
  Baldpates ... RW9
  Barrow's Goldeneye ... RW65, RW65A
  Black Mallards ... RW7
  Black-Bellied Whistling Duck ... RW57
  Black Scoters ... RW69, RW69A
  Blue Geese ... RW22
  Blue-winged Teal ... RW20
  Buffleheads ... RW15
  Canada Geese ... RW3, RW25, RW43, RW64
  Canvasback Decoy ... RW42
  Canvasback Drake ... RW32
  Canvasbacks ... RW2, RW42, RW49, RW60
  Cinnamon Teal ... RW38, RW52
  Duckling ... RW28
  Emperor Geese ... RW39
  Fulvous Whistling Duck ... RW18, RW53
  Goldeneye Ducks ... RW16
  Greater Scalup ... RW66, RW66A
  Green-winged Teal ... RW6, RW46
  Harlequin Ducks ... RW19
  Hawaiian Nene Geese ... RW31
  Hooded Merganser Drake ... RW45
  Hooded Mergansers ... RW35, RW72, RW72A
  King Eider ... RW58
  Labrador Retriever ... RW26
  Lesser Scaup ... RW56
  Mallard Drake ... RW26
  Mallard Hen ... RW28
  Mallards ... RW47, RW62
  Mallards Alighting ... RW1
  Mottled Duck ... RW67, RW67A
  Northern Pintail ... RW68, RW68A
  Old Squaw Ducks ... RW34
  Pair of Brant ... RW30
  Pintail Drake and Hen Alighting ... RW5
  Pintail Drakes ... RW29
  Pintails ... RW50
  Red-breasted Merganser ... RW61
  Redhead Ducks ... RW13, RW27
  Redheads ... RW54, RW71, RW71A
  Ring-necked Ducks ... RW27
  Ross's Geese ... RW37, RW44, RW73, RW73A
  Ruddy Ducks ... RW8, RW48
  Scaup Ducks ... RW4
  Shoveller ... RW12
  Snow Geese ... RW14, RW55, RW70, RW70A
  Spectacled Eider ... RW59
  Steller's Eiders ... RW40
  Surf Scoters ... RW63
  Trumpeter Swans ... RW17
  Whistling Swans ... RW33
  White-fronted Geese ... RW11
  White-winged Scoters ... RW36
  Widgeons ... RW51
  Wood Ducks ... RW10, RW41, RW79, RW79a
Duck, Wood ... 2484-2485, 2493, 2494
Duesenberg ... 2385
Dulles
  Airport ... 2022
  John Foster Memorial ... 1172
Dug ... 4556
Dumbo ... 4194
Dunbar, Paul Laurence ... 1554
Duncan, Usadora ... 4698
Dung beetle ... 3351n
Dunham, Katherine ... 4700
Dunn, Harvey ... 3502o
Durand, Asher B ... 4918
Dutchman's Breeches ... 2682
Eagan, Eddie ... 2499
Eagle ... 1743, 2598
  and Shield ... 116, 1596, 2431, 2595-2597, 2602-2604, 2907, 3270-3271, 3792-3801, 3844-3853, CE1-CE2

Bald. . .314A, 775, 909-921, 1090, 1131, 1140, 1313, 1344, 1387, 1424, 1831, 1909, 2111-2113, 2122, 2355, 2356-2359, 2394, 2431, 2534-2542, 2605-2606, C67
Golden . . . 4198b, 4610
from Great Seal of the US . . . 1369
in Flight . . . C48, C50
Nebula . . . 3384
Weather Vane . . . 1344
with Shield and Quill Pen . . . 2421
with Shield, Olive Branch and Arrows . . . 2413, C23
Eakins, Thomas . . . 1335
Eames, Charles & Ray . . . 4333, 4333a
Eames Storage Unit . . . 4333n
Earhart, Amelia . . . C68
Early
Ballot Box . . . 1584
Cancer Detection . . . 1754
Football Heroes . . . 3808-3811
Earp, Wyatt . . . 2869j, 2870j
Earth . . 1173, 1193, 1371, 1434, 1569-1570, 1913-1914, 1917, 1919, 2277, 2279, 2282, 2526, 2535, 2570, C122-C123, C125, C126
Clean-Up . . . 2951
Day Issue . . . 2951-2954, 3189a
Earthscapes . . . 4710, 4740
Eastern
Bluebird . . . 2478, 3033, 1977, 1984
Chipmunk . . . 2297
Goldfinch . . . 1967
Hercules beetle . . . 3351l
Hognose Snake . . . 4352d
Easter Red Cedar . . . 4479, 4483
Eastman, George . . . 1062
Ebbets Field, Brooklyn . . . 3510
Ebony jewelwing . . . 3351h
Echo I—Communications for Peace . . . 1173
Ed Sullivan Show . . . 4414j, UX571
Eddy's No. 242 . . . 2845
Edison
Thomas (Electric Light's Golden Jubilee) . . . 654-656
Thomas A. . . . 945
Edmontonia . . . 3136i
Education
Consumer . . . 2005
Higher . . . 1206
Improving . . . 3191e
(Land Grant Colleges) . . . 1065
(Learning Never Ends) . . . 1833
(Nation of Readers) . . . 2106
(Parent-Teachers Association) . . . 1463
Public . . . 2159
Teachers of America . . . 1093
Educators 869-873, 1093, 1291, 1824, 1850, 1852, 1854, 1861, 1920, 2137, 2169, 2171, 2194
Egalite . . . C120
Egg Nebula . . . 3387
EID . . . 3532, 3674, 4117, 4202, 4351, 4416, 4552,4800
Einosaurus . . . 3136j
Einstein, Albert . . . 1285, 1774
Eisenhower, Dwight D. . . 1383, 1393-1395, 1401-1402, 2219g, 2513
El Capitan . . . 740, 751, 756, 769
Elderberry longhorn . . . 3351b
Electric
Automobile . . . 1906
Light's Golden Jubilee . . . 654-656
Streetcar, Early . . . 2060
Theories . . . 2055
Toy Trains
Electronics, Progress in . . . 1500-1502, C86
Elegy to the Spanish Republic . . . 4444g
Elephant
Circus . . . 2753
Herd, African . . . 1388
Elevator . . . 2254
Eliot
Charles W. . . . 871
T.S. . . . 2239
Elk . . . 1886, 4198a
Elkhorn Coral . . . 1828
Elks, Support our Youth . . . 1342
Ellington, Duke . . . 2211
Ellsworth, Lincoln . . . 2389
Elves . . . 3952, 3956, 3960
Ely's No. 10 . . . 2846
Emancipation Proclamation . . . 1233, 4721
Emerson, Ralph Waldo . . . 861
Emigration . . . 290
Emily Post's Etiquette . . . 3184f
Empire State Building . . . 3185b
Empire State Express . . . 295
Employ the Handicapped . . . 1155
Endangered
Flora . . . 1783-1786
Species . . . 3105, 5799
Energy . . . 1723-1724, 2006-2009
Conservation . . . 1547, 1723
Development . . . 1724
Engineering . . . 1012
Engineers, American Society of . . . 1012
English Sundew . . . 3531
Envelopes
sealed . . . 2150
with wax seal . . . 4741
Environment, Preserve the . . . 1527
Eohippus . . . 3077
Ercoupe 415 . . . 3920
Ericsson Memorial, John . . . 628
Erie Canal . . . 1325
Erikson, Leif . . . 1359
E.T. the Extra-Terrestrial . . . 3190m
Evans, Walker . . . 3649m
Everglades National Park . . . 952
Evers, Medgar . . . 4384e
Evening grosbeak . . . 4887
Ewry, Ray . . . 2497
Executive
Branch . . . 2414
Department . . . O10-O14
Mansion . . . 990
Exotic Shorthair Cat . . . 2372
Experiment . . . 2405
Explorer II . . . 2035
Explorers . . . 285, 288
Antarctic . . . 2386-2389
Armstrong . . . C76
Balboa . . . 397
Byrd . . . 733, 735, 768, 2388
Cabrillo . . . 2704
Cook . . . 1732-1733
Coronado . . . 898
de Leon . . . 2024
Ellsworth . . . 2389
Erikson . . . 1359
Greely . . . 2221
Henson . . . 2223
Kane . . . 2220
Lewis and Clark . . . 1063
Marquette . . . 1356
Nicolet . . . 739, 755
Palmer . . . 2386
Peary . . . 1128, 2223
Polar . . . 2220-2223
Powell . . . 1374
Stefansson . . . 2222
Verrazano . . . 1258
Wilkes . . . 2387
Expo '74 . . . 1527
Expositions . . . 230-245, 285-293, 323-330, 370-371, 397-400, 401, 404, 630, 728-731, 735, 750-751, 766, 773, 778, 852-853, 948, 1075-1076, 1104, 1196, 1244, 1310-1311, 1340, 1342-1344, 1527, 1632, 1757, 2006-2009, 2086, 2410, 2616, 2624-2629
Express
International . . . 2542
Mail . . . 1909, 2122, 2394, 2541, 2544A,2842, 3262, 3473, 3648, 4019, 4145, 4269, 4379, 4439, 4650
Extreme Sports . . . 3191d, 3321-3324
Eyeglasses, Books, Bookmark . . . 1585
F6F Hellcat . . . 3918
Fairbanks, Douglas . . . 2088
Fall of Corregidor . . . 2697d
Fallingwater . . . 2019
Family
Planning . . . 1455
Unity . . . 2104
Famous Americans 860-868, 870-893, 945, 953, 960, 965, 975, 980, 986, 988, 1062, 1072, 1121, 1138, 1170-1172, 1177
Fanfin Anglerfish . . . 3439
Fangtooth . . . 3441
Fantasy, Space . . . 2741-2745
Far West Riverboat . . . 3093
Farley, Cal . . . 2934
Farmer's Market . . . 4912-15
Farmers of America, Future . . . 1024
Farming . . . 286
Farnsworth, Philo T. . . . 2058
Farragut, David G. . . . 311, 792, 2975g
Fashion, 1970's . . . 3189k
Faulkner, William . . . 2350
Fawcett, Robert . . . 3502d
Fawkes the Phoenix . . . 4829
Fawn . . . 2479
FDR's New Deal . . . 3185e
Federal
Deposit Insurance Corporation . . . 2071
Hall . . . 1086
Reserve system created, 1913 . . . 3183b
Federated States of Micronesia . . . 2506
Fenway Park, Boston . . . 3516
Fermi, Enrico . . . 3533
Ferns . . . 4848-52, 4874-78, 4973-77, 4973a-77a
Ferrer, Jose . . . 4666
Ferryboat . . . 2466
Feynman, Richard . . . 3909
Fiedler, Arthur . . . 3159
Fields,
Dorothy . . . 3102
W.C. . . . 1803
Fierce fighting frees Manila . . . 2981b
Fife Player . . . 1631
Fifth World Forestry Congress . . . 1156
Fiftieth Anniversary of Statehood (Montana, North Dakota, South Dakota, Washington) . . . 858
Fifty State Flags . . . 1633-1647, 1648-1667, 1668-1682
Fifty-Star and 13-Star Flags . . . 1509
Fifty-Star Runway . . . C72-C73
Figure Skating . . . 3190e, 3555
Fillmore, Millard . . . 818, 2217d
Film Editing . . . 3772h
Films, Classic . . . 2445-2448, 2722
Finding Nemo . . . 4679
Fine Arts . . . 1259
Finger Coral . . . 1830
Finland Independence . . . 1334
Finnish Settlement, Swedish- . . . 836
Finnish Settlement, Swedish (Stamp Collecting) . . . 2200
Fir, Douglas . . . 1376
Balsam . . . 4480, 4484
Fire
Engine Truck . . . 971, 2264
Pumper . . . 1908
Truck . . . 971
Firemen, Volunteer . . . 971
Fireweed . . . 2679
Fireworks . . . 2276
First
Automated Post Office . . . 1164
Baseball World Series, 1903 . . . 3182n
Civil Settlement—Alta, California . . . 1725
Continental Congress . . . 1543-1546
Crossword puzzle, pub., 1913 . . . 3183l
Flight Wright Brothers 1903 . . . 3783
Kentucky Settlement . . . 1542
Moon Landing . . . 2841
Navy Jack . . . 1354, 1566
Stars and Stripes . . . 1350
Supersonic Flight 1947 . . . 3173
Television Camera . . . 2058
Transcontinental telephone line, 1914 . . . 3183e
Voyage of Christopher Columbus . . . 2620-2623
Fischer's Lovebirds . . . 2537
Fish . . . 2205-2209, 2863-2866, 3231
(Anti-Pollution) . . . 1412
Fanfin Anglerfish . . . 3439
Fangtooth . . . 3441
(Louisiana World Exposition) . . . 2086
Medusa . . . 3443
Pumpkinseed Sunfish . . . 2491
Sea Cucumber . . . 3440
(Wildlife Conservation) . . . 1427
Fishing
Boat . . . 2529, 2529C
Flies . . . 2545-2549
Fitzgerald,
Ella . . . 4120
F. Scott . . . 3104
Five Finger Lighthouse . . . 4147
Flag . . . 2880, 2882-2892
and Anthem Issue . . . 1890
and Chalkboard . . . 3283
and Statue of Liberty . . . 3965-3975, 3978, 3979, 3980
29-Star, 1847 . . . 3403t
38-Star . . . 3403q
49-Star, 1912 . . . 1132
50-Star . . . 1153, 3403t
Bennington, c. 1820 . . . 3408h
Brandywine, 1777 . . . 3403f
Centennial, 1876 . . . 3403p
Easton, 1814 . . . 3403j
Forster, 1775 . . . 3403c
Fort Sumter, 1861 . . . 3403o
Francis Hopkins, 1777 . . . 3403e
Great Star, 1837 . . . 3403m
Indian Peace, 1803 . . . 3403i
John Paul Jones, 1779 . . . 3403g
New England, 1775 . . . 3403b
Over Capitol . . . 2115, 2116
Over Farm . . . 3448, 3449, 3450, 3469, 3470, 3495
Over Field . . . 2919
Over Porch . . . 2897, 2913-2916, 2920-2921
Over Yosemite . . . 2280
Peace,1891 . . . 3403r
Pierre L'Enfant, 1783 . . . 3403h
Plane and Globes . . . C90
Sons of Liberty, 1775 . . . 3403a
With Clouds . . . 2278, 2285A
With Fireworks . . . 2276
Flagg, James Montgomery . . . 3502a
Flags . . . 231-233, 329, 372-373, 537, 614, 629-630, 690, 775, 778, 909-921, 923, 938, 942, 1000, 1010, 1034, 1069, 1088, 1123, 1239, 1271, 1275, 1407, 1625, 1645-1647,1648-1667, 1668-1682, 2097, 2204, 2616, 4303, 4487, 4489, 4491

and Anthem. 1892-1893
on Parade 2531
Over Capitol 1623, 2114
Over Mt. Rushmore 2523, 2523A
Over Supreme Court. 1894-1895, 1896
Over White House 1208, 1338-1338G, 2609
US. 288, 372-373, 537, 629, 630, 690, 727, 752, 775, 778, 929, 938, 944, 962, 990-991, 1004, 1010, 1094, 1115, 1132, 1153, 1208, 1249, 1261, 1320, 1338-1338G, 1345-1354, 1383, 1406, 1447, 1509, 1519, 1597-1598, 1618C, 1622, 1630, 1631, 1686, 1686d, 1688, 1890-1891, 1893-1896, 1952, 2103, 2114-2216, 2276, 2278, 2280, 2409, 2419, 2421, 2475, 2522, 2523, 2523A, 2528, 2531, 2593, 2594, 2605-2609, 2879-2893, 2966, 3508, 3549, 3549B, 3550, 3550A, 3620-3625, 3629F, 3630, 3631, 3632, 3632A, 3632C, 3633, 3633A, 3635, 3636, 3636D, 3637, 3777, 3778, 3779, 3780, 3965-3975, 3978, 3979, 3980, 4129-4135, C34, C54, C76, C115, C122-C125, C126, 4228-4247, 4273, 4302, 4519, 4629-4648, 4673-76, 4894-97
with Olympic Rings 2528
Flags, State 1633-1682
Alabama 1654, 4274
Alaska. 1681, 4275
American Samoa 4276
Arizona 1680, 4277
Arkansas. 1657, 4278
California. 1663, 4279
Colorado 1670, 4280
Connecticut. 1637, 4281
Delaware. 1633, 4282
District of Columbia. 4283
Florida. 1659, 4284
Georgia. 1636, 4285
Guam 4286
Hawaii. 1682, 4287
Idaho. 1675, 4288
Illinois 1653, 4289
Indiana 1651, 4290
Iowa 1661, 4291
Kansas 1666, 4292
Kentucky. 1647, 4293
Louisiana 1650, 4294
Maine 1655, 4295
Maryland. 1639, 4296
Massachusetts 1638, 4297
Michigan 1658, 4298
Minnesota. 1664, 4299
Mississippi 1652, 4300
Missouri 1656, 4301
Montana 1673, 4304
Nebraska 1669, 4305
Nevada. 1668, 4306
New Hampshire 1641, 4307
New Jersey. 1635, 4308
New Mexico 1679, 4309
New York. 1643, 4310
North Carolina. 1644, 4311
North Dakota. 1671, 4312
Northern Marianas 4313
Ohio 1649, 4314
Oklahoma 1678, 4315
Oregon 1665, 4316
Pennsylvania 1634, 4317
Puerto Rico. 4318
Rhode Island. 1645, 4319
South Carolina 1640, 4320
South Dakota 1672, 4321
Tennessee 1648, 4322
Texas 1660, 4323
US. 4332
Utah 1677, 4324
Vermont 1646, 4325
Virginia 1642, 4327
Virgin Islands 4326
Washington. 1674,4328
West Virginia. 1667, 4329
Wisconsin 1662, 4330
Wyoming. 1676, 4331
Flamingo 2707
Flanagan, Father. 2171
Flappers do the Charleston. 3184h
Flash, The 4084f, 4084p
Flash Gordon. 3000p
Flathead Headdress 2504
Flies, Fishing 2545-2549
Flight
of the Wright Brothers. 3873
Powered C47
Flik 4677
Flora and Fauna 2476-2483, 2486-2492
Flora, Endangered. 1783-1786
Floral Piece, Lace 2352
Florida. 1659, 1961, 3569, 3704
Settlement. 1271
Hillsboro Inlet 3791
Huguenot-Walloon Monument 616
Statehood 927, 2950
manatee 3105o
panther 3105m
Flower fly. 3351f
Flowers 1158, 1183, 1192, 1256, 1318, 1337, 1365, 1366, 1367, 1375, 1377-1379, 1711, 1737, 1783, 1784-1786, 1807, 1876-1879, 1942, 1944, 1951, 2014, 2074, 2076-2079, 2166, 2268, 2273, 2285, 2347, 2378-2379, 2395, 2416, 2517-2520, 2524-2527, 2647-2696, 2760-2764, 2829-2833, 2993-2997, 3025-3029, 3310-3313, 3454-3465, 3478-3481, 3487-3490, 3836-3837, 4166-75, 4176-85, 4653, 4754-63, 4764, 4765, 4862-65, 4914
Fall Garden. 2993-2997
Garden 2760-2764
State Birds and 1978-2002
Summer Garden 2829-2833
Wildflowers 2647-2696
Winter Garden 3025-3029
Flushing Remonstrance, the 1099
Flying Fortress Airplane. 3142k
Fog Warning, The by Winslow Homer. 3236j
Folk
Art, American. . 1706-1709, 1745-1748, 1775-1778, 1834-1837, 2138-2141, 2238, 2240-2243, 2351-2354, 2390-2393, 2501-2505
Dance 1751
Heroes 3083-3086
Folklore, American. . 1317, 1330, 1357, 1370, 1470, 1548, 1578
Fonda, Henry. 3911
Fontanne, Lynn and Alfred Lunt 3287
Food for Peace—Freedom from Hunger. 1231
Football
Coaches 3143-3150
College 1382, 2089, 2376
Early Heroes. 3808-3811
Professional 3188d, 3188l, 3189e, 3189l, 3190c
Youth. 3400
Forbes, Brig. Gen. John 1123
Forbes Field, Pittsburgh 3515
Ford, Gerald 4199
Ford, Henry 1286A
Ford, John H 4668
Ford
Mustang 3188h, 4745
Thunderbird 3935
Foreign Countries 398, 856, 906, 909-921, 925, 961, 1021, 1104, 1131, 1157-1158, 1188, 1313, 1324, 1334, 1431, 1569, 1570, 1721, 1753, 1757, 2003, 2036, 2040, 2091, 2349, 2370, 2532, C120
Forest
Congress, Fifth World. 1156
Conservation. 1122
Fire Prevention 2096
"...for purple mountain majesties". 1893
Fort
Bliss 976
Dearborn (Chicago) 728, 730, 766
Duquesne (Pitt). 1123
Harrod. 1542
Jefferson Lighthouse 4413, U673, UX566
Kearney 970
McHenry 962, 4921
McHenry, Flag. 1346, 1597, 1598, 1618C
Moultrie Flag. 962, 1345
Nisqually. 1604
Orange, Landing at. 615
Sackville, Surrender of 651
Snelling. 1409
Stanwix. 644
Sumter, Civil War Centennial 1178
Sumter, Civil War Sesquecentennial 4522
Ticonderoga 1071
Fortune's Holly Fern 4848, 4874
Fosse, Bob 4701
Fossil Fuels 2009
Foster,
John 3236a
Stephen Collins. 879
Four
Chaplains 956
Freedoms 908, 2840
Horsemen of Norte Dame. 3184l
4-H Club 1005
49-Star Flag 1132
Fox in Socks 3989
Foxhound, American 2101
Foxx, Jimmie 3408n
Fozzie Bear 3944b
Fragrant Water Lily 2648
France 915, 934
Francis of Assisi. 2023
Francisco, Peter 1562
Frankenstein 3170
Franklin, Benjamin 1, 3, 5, 18-24, 38, 40, 46, 63, 71, 81, 85A, 86, 92, 100, 102, 110, 112, 134, 145, 156, 167, 182, 192, 206, 212, 219, 246-247, 264, 279, 300, 314, 316, 318, 331, 357, 374, 383, 385, 390, 392, 414-423, 431-440, 460, 470-478, 497, 508-518, 523-524, 547, 552, 575, 578, 594, 596-597, 604, 632, 658, 669, 803, 947-948, 1030, 1073, 1393D, 1474, 1687b, 1690, 1693, 1753, 2036, 2052, 2145, 2779, 3139, 4021-4024
Franklinia. 1379
Fraternity. C120
Frederick 3994
Fred &George Weasley. 4839
Free-Blown Glass 3325
Freedom
from Hunger, Food for Peace 1231
of the Press. 1119, 1476-1477, 1593
Riders 3937f
Wheels of 1162
Freedoms, Four. 908, 933
Frémont, John C. 288, 2869j, 2870j
French
Alliance. 1753
Daniel Chester 887
Revolution. C120
Frequency Modulation 2056
Friendship
Apollo 7. 1193
with Morocco. 2349
Frilled Dogwinkle 2117
Fringed Gentian. 2672
From Me To You 4978
Frost
A.B. 3502g
Robert 1526
Fruits and Vegetables 4913
Fulbright Scholarships. 3065
Fulton
Celebration, Hudson- 372-373
Ferry House 1003
Robert. 1270
Fur Seals. 1464
Furness, Frank 1840
Future
Farmers of America 1024
Mail Transportation C122-C126
Spacecraft. 2543
Gable, Clark. 2446, 4669
Gadsby's Tavern C40
Gadsden Purchase 1028
Galaxy NGC1316 3388
Galliard Cut 856
Gallatin, Albert 1279
Gallaudet, Thomas H. 1861
Galvez, Gerneral Bernardo de. 1826
Games, World University. 2748
Gandhi, Mahatma 1174-1175
Gar Wood Speedboat 4163
Garbo, Greta 3943
Garden Flowers. 2760-2764, 2829-2833
Aster 2993
Chrysanthemum 2994
Dahlia 2995
Hydrangea 2996
Rudbeckia. 2997-2997a
Garden, International Peace 2014
Gardening—Horticulture 1100
Garfield, James A. . . . 205, 205C, 216, 224, 256, 271, 282, 305, 558, 587, 638, 664, 675, 723, 825, 2218b
Garibaldi, Guiseppe. 1168-1169
Garland, Judy 2445, 4077
Garner, Erroll 2992
Gasoline Alley 3000h
Gateway Arch 4044
Gato Class. 3377
Gatsby style, The. 3184b
Geddes, Norman Bel 4546g
GeeBee Airplane 3142i
Gee's Bend, Quilts of. 4089-4098
Gehrig, Lou 2417, 3408t
Geisel, Theodor Suess 3835
Gellhorn, Martha 4248
Gemini 4 . . . . . 1332, 2634
General Federation of Women's Clubs 1316
Geodetic, Coast and, Survey. 1088
Geophysical Year, International. 1107
George, Sen. Walter F., Memorial 1170
Georgia 726, 1636, 1962, 3570, 3705
Statehood 2339
Tybee Island 3790
Geothermal Spring 4710c
German Immigration, Concord 2040
Germany surrenders at Reims 2981f
Geronimo. 2869m, 2870m
Gershwin
George 1484
Ira & George. 3345
Get Well! 2268
Gettysburg
Address. 978
Battle of 1180, 2975t, 4788
GI Bill, 1944. . . . . 3186i
Giannini, Amadeo P. 1400
Giant Panda. 2706
Giant Sequoia 1764
Gibbs, Josiah Willard. 3907

Gibson
Althea . . . 4803
Girl . . . 3182m
Josh . . . 3408r
Gifts of Friendship . . . 4982-85
Gila trout . . . 3105j
Gilbert, John . . . 2823
Gilbreth, Lillian M. . . . 1868
Ginny Weasley . . . 4840
Gingerbread Man. . . . 4427, 4431
Gingerbread houses . . . 4817-20
Giraffe . . . 2705
Girl in Red Dress with Cat and Dog by Ammi Phillips . . . 3236c
Girl Scouts . . . 974, 1199, 2251, 3182k
Giving and Sharing . . . 3243
Glacier and Icebergs . . . 4710a
Glacier National Park . . . 748, 764, C149, UX635
Glade Creek Grist Mill . . . 4927, U689
Gladiola . . . 2831
Glass, American . . . 3325-3328
Glass House . . . 3910h
Glassblower . . . 1456
Gleason, Jackie . . . 4414t, UX572
Globes . . . 650, 702, 1016, 1066, 1070, 1112, 1128-1129, 1151, 1156, 1162, 1410-1413, 1439, 1576, 2535-2536, C12, C16-C17, C19, C24, C42-C44, C89-C90, 4740, 4893
Gloriosa Lily . . . 3312
Goddard, Robert H. . . . C69
Goethals, Gen. George W. . . . 856
Go Green . . . 4524
Gold Stars . . . 2765i
Gold Star Mothers . . . 969
Golden Delicious Apple . . . 4728,4733
Golden Gate . . . 399, 567, 698
Bridge . . . 3185l
International Exposition . . . 852
Goldie's Wood Fern . . . 4851, 4877
Golf . . . 1932-1933, 2377, 2965, 3185n
Gompers, Samuel . . . 988
Gone with the Wind . . . 2446, 3185i
Goniopholis . . . 3136e
Goode, Alexander D. . . . 956
Goodman, Benny . . . 3099
Goodnight, Charles . . . 2869l, 2870l
Gottschalk, Louis Moreau . . . 3165
Gowan & Marx . . . 2366
Graces, The Three . . . 895
Graf Zeppelin . . . C13-C15, C18
Graham, Martha . . . 3840
Grand
Army of the Republic, Aug. 29 . . . 985
Canyon . 741, 757, 2512, 3183h, 4054, 4917, C135, UX604
Central Terminal . . . 4739
Coulee Dam . . . 1009
Teton National Park . . . C147, UX636
Union Flag . . . 1352
Grange,
National . . . 1323
Red . . . 3811
Granny Smith Apple . . . 4729,4734
Grant, Cary . . . 3692
Grant, Ulysses S. . . . 223, 255, 270, 281, 303, 314A, 560, 589, 640, 666, 677, 787, 823, 2217i, 2975d
Grassland Habitats . . . 1922
Gray, Asa . . . 4542
Gray
Birch . . . 1767
Owl . . . 1760
Squirrel . . . 2295
White and Tan Cat . . . 4456
Wolf . . . 2322, 3292
Gray's Harbour Lighthouse . . . 4148
Great
Americans Issue . . . 1844-1869, 2167-2173, 2176-2182, 2183-2184, 2184A, 2185-2186, 2188, 2190-2194, 2194A, 2195-2197, 2933, 2938, 2940, 2943
Basin . . . 4051
Film Directors . . . 4668-71
Gonzo and Camilla the Chicken . . . 3944j
Gray Owl . . . 1760
Smoky Mountains National Park . . . 749, 765, 797, C140, UX605
White Throne . . . 747, 763
Blue Heron . . . 1921
Head . . . 746, 7625
Horned Owl . . . 1763
Lakes . . . 1069
Lakes Dunes . . . 4352
Lakes Lighthouses . . . 2969-2973
Plains Prairie . . . 3506
River Road . . . 1319
Salt Lake, Valley of . . . 950
Seal of the United States . . . 1194
Spangled Fritillary . . . 4859
Train Robbery, The 1903 . . . 3182c
Greatest Show on Earth, Circus . . . 2750-2753
Greece . . . 916
Greeley
Adolphus W. . . . 2221
Horace . . . 1177
Green
Arrow . . . 4084d, 4084n
Bay, (WI) . . . 739, 755
Bay Packers . . . 3188d
Lantern . . . 4084b, 4084l
Mountain Boys . . . 643
Nathanael . . . 785
Throated Carib . . . 3223
Greenberg, Hank . . . 4081
Greetings . . . 3245-52
From America . . . 3561-3610, 3696-3745
Griffith, D.W. . . . 1555
Grizzly Bear . . . 1923
Grofé, Ferde . . . 3163
Gropius
House . . . 2021
Walter . . . 2021
Grosbeak, Owl . . . 2284
Grosvenor, Lt. Thomas . . . 1361
Grove, Lefty . . . 3408k
Grumman F6F Hellcat . . . 3918
Guadalcanal, Battle of . . . 2697i
Guava . . . 4257, 4259
Guggenheim Museum . . . 1280
Guitar . . . 1613
Gulf War . . . 3191b
Gunston Hall (Home of George Mason) . . . 1108
Gutenberg Bible . . . 1014
Guthrie, Woody . . . 3213
Habib, Philip C. . . . 4076d
Hacker-Craft Speedboat . . . 4162
Hagatna Bay . . . C143, UX637
Haida Ceremonial Canoe, Tlingit, Chief in . . . 1389
Halas, George . . . 3146, 3150
Hale, Nathan . . . 551, 653
Haley, Bill . . . 2725, 2732
Half Moon . . . 372-373
Hallelujah Poster . . . 4340
Hamer, Fannie Lou . . . 4384e
Hamilton
Alexander . 143, 154, 165, 176, 190, 201, 217, 1053, 1086, 1686e
Alice . . . 2940
Hamilton's Battery, Alexander . . . 629, 630
Hammarskjold, Dag . . . 1203-1204
Hammerstein, Oscar (and Rogers) . . . 3348
Hamster . . . 3234
Hancock
Center . . . 3910l
John . . . 1687d, 1694
Winfield . . . 2975n
Handcar 1880s . . . 1898
Handicapped, Employ the . . . 1155
Handy, W.C. . . . 1372
Hang-it-all . . . 4333g
Hansom Cab . . . 1904
Hanson, John . . . 1941
Hanukkah . . . 3118, 3352, 3547, 3672, 3880, 4118, 4219, 4372, 4433, 4583,4824
Happy
Birthday . . . 2272, 2395, 3558, 3695, 4079, 5635
New Year . . . 2720, 2817, 2876, 3060, 3120, 3179, 3120, 3179, 3272, 3370, 3500, 3559, 3747, 3832, 3895
Harbor
NY, New Amsterdam . . . 1027
Seal . . . 1882, 4423c, UX593
Harbug, Edgar "Yip" . . . 3905
Harding, Warren G. . . . 553, 576, 582, 598, 605, 610-613, 631, 633, 659, 670, 684, 686, 833, 2219a
Hardy, Stan Laurel & Oliver . . . 2562
Harebell . . . 2689
Harlequin Lupine . . . 2664
Harness Racing . . . 2758
Harnett, William M. . . . 1386
Harris
Joel Chandler . . . 980
Patricia Roberts . . . 3371
Harrison
Benjamin . . . 308, 622, 694, 828, 1045, 2218e
William Henry . . . 814, 966, 2201, 2216i
Harrod, Fort . . . 1542
Hart,
Lorenz . . . 3347
Moss . . . 3882
William S. . . . 4448, UX599
Harte, Bret . . . 2196
Hartford, USS . . . 792
Hartlley, David . . . 2052
Harvard, John . . . 2190
Harry Potter . . . 4825-44
Hatter . . . 1459
Hatteras, Cape . . . 1448-1451, 2471
Hawaii . . . 1682, 1963, 3571, 3706
City of Refuge National Park . . . C84
(Cook, Captain James) . . . 1733
Diamond Head . . . C46
Discovery of . . . 647
Goose . . . 1963
Statehood . . . 2080, C55, 4415
Territory . . . 799
Hawaiian
Goose . . . 1963
Wild Broadbean . . . 1784
Missionary Stamp . . . 3694a-94d
Monk seal . . . 3105c
Hawaiian Rain Forest . . . 4474
Ohi'a lehua . . . 4474a, UX611
Hawai'i 'Amakihi . . . 4474a, UX611
Hawai'I 'Elepaio . . . 4474a, UX611
Oma'o . . . 4474d, UX614
Kanawao . . . 4474d, UX614
Ohelo kau-la-au . . . 4474d,UX614
Koele Mountain Damselfly . . . 4474g, UX617
Akala . . . 4474g, UX617
Oha . . . 4474e, UX615
'Akepa . . . 4474b, UX612
'Ope'ape'a . . . 4474b, UX612
Pulelehua . . . 4474f, UX616
Kolea lau nui . . . 4474f, UX616
'Ilihia . . . 4474f, UX616
Jewel Orchid . . . 4474i, UX619
Palapalai . . . 4474i, UX619
'I'iwi . . . 4474c, UX613
Haha . . . 4474c, UX613
'Ala'ala wai nui . . . 4474j, UX620
Happyface Spider . . . 4474j, UX620
Apapane . . . 4474h, UX620
Hawaiian Mint . . . 4474h, UX618
Hawes, Josiah J and Southworth, A.S. . . . 3649a
Hawkins, Coleman . . . 2983
Hawthorne, Nathaniel . . . 2047
Hayden, Robert . . . 4657
Hayes, Helen . . . 4525
Hayes, Rutherford B. . . . 563, 692, 824, 2218a
Head of Freedom, Capitol Dome . . . 573, 4075c
Headdresses . . . 230, 237, 783, C117
Indian . . . 2501-2505
Headmaster Albus Dumbledore . . . 4833
Heade, Martin Johnson . . . 3872
Headless Horseman . . . 1548
Health Research . . . 2087
Healy, George, Portrait by . . . 1113
Heart Health . . . 4625
Hedwig the Owl . . . 4830
Heitsuk, Bella Bella Tribe . . . 1834
Held, John Jr. . . . 3502t
Help End Hunger . . . 2164
Helping Children Learn . . . 3125
Hemingway, Ernest . . . 2418
HemisFair '68 . . . 1340
Hermit Thrush . . . 1997
Hendrix
Jimi . . . 4880
Henry, O. . . . 4705
Henry, Patrick . . . 1052, 1144
Henson,
Jim . . . 3944k
Matthew . . . 2223
Hepburn,
Audrey . . . 3786
Katherine . . . 4461
Herb Robert . . . 2657
Herbert, Victor . . . 881
Herkimer
at Oriskany, by Frederick Yohn . . . 1722
Brig. Gen. Nicholas . . . 644, 1722
Hermitage, The . . . 786, 1037, 1059
Hermit Thrush . . . 1997
Hermoine Granger . . . 4827,4837
Herrmann, Bernard . . . 3341
Hermey . . . 4947
Hersey, John . . . 4249
Hershey, Milton S. . . . 2933
Hershey's Kiss . . . 4122
Heston, Charlton . . . 4892
Hiawatha . . . 3336
Hickok, Wild Bill . . . 2869o, 2870o
Higgins, Marguerite . . . 3668
High Museum of Art . . . 3910j
Higher Education . . . 1206
Highlander Figure . . . 2240
Highway interchange . . . 4710o
Hillsboro Inlet, Florida . . . 3791
Himalayan Cat . . . 2373
Hine, Lewis W. . . . 3649e
Hines, John L. . . . 3393
Hip-hop Culture . . . 3190o
Hispanic Americans . . . 2103
Hispanics . . . 801, 895, 898, 983, 1043, 1110-1111, 1125-1126, 1157, 1234, 1271, 1437, 1826, 2024, 2097, 2103, 2173, 2185, 2247, 2255, 2704, 3166, 3781, C56, C104, C116
Historic
Flags . . . 1345-1354
Preservation . . . 1440-1443

Hitchcock, Alfred . . . 3226, 4414o, UX567
Ho-Chunk Bag . . . 3873d
Hoban, James . . . 1935-1936
Holiday, Billie . . . 2856
Holly . . . 1254
Buddy . . . 2729, 2736
Hollywood Composers . . . 3339-44
Holmes, Oliver Wendell . . . 1288, 1288B, 1305E
Home on the Range . . . 2869a, 2870a
Homemakers . . . 1253
Hometowns honor their returning veterans . . . 2981j
Homer, Winslow . . . 1207, 3236j, 4473
Homestead Act . . . 1198
Honeybee . . . 2281
Honorable Discharge Emblem . . . 940
Honoring Those Who Served . . . 3331
Hoover, Herbert . . . 1269, 2219c
Hopalong Cassidy . . . 4414g, UX573
Hope, Bob . . . 4406
Hope for the Crippled . . . 1385
Hopi Pot . . . 1708
Hopkins
Johns . . . 2194
Mark . . . 870
Hopper, Edward . . . 3236d, 4558
Hornsby, Rogers . . . 3408f
Horse
and Rider . . . 2715, 4968
Racing . . . 1528
Horses
American . . . 2155-2158
Carousel . . . 2391
Racing . . . 1528
Sports . . . 2756-2759
Horticulture—Gardening . . . 1100
Hospice Care . . . 3276
Hospitals, Public . . . 2210
Hostages Come Home . . . 3190d
Hot Air Ballooning . . . 2033, 2034
Hot Rods . . . 4908-4909
Houdini . . . 3651
Household conveniences . . . 3185g
House of Cards . . . 4333l
House of Representatives, US . . . 2412
Houston, Charles Hamilton . . . 4384d
Houston, Sam . . . 776, 778, 1242
Hovercraft . . . C123, C126b
Howdy Doody . . . 4414d, UX574
Howe
Elias . . . 892
Julia Ward . . . 2176
Hubble, Edwin . . . 4226
Huckleberry Finn, the Adventures of . . . 2787
Hudson
-Fulton Celebration . . . 372-373
General . . . 2843
River . . . 372-373, 752
River School Paintings . . . 4917-20
Hughes,
Charles Evans . . . 1195
Langston . . . 3557
Huguenot-Walloon Tercentenary . . . 614-616
Hull, Cordell . . . 1235
Humane Treatment of Animals . . . 1307
Hummingbird . . . 2642-2646, 4857, 4858
Trumpet . . . 4154, 4154a
Humphrey, Hubert H . . . 2189
Hunger
Freedom From—Food for Peace . . . 1231
Help End . . . 2164
Hunt, Richard Morris . . . 1929
Huntington, Samuel . . . 1687
Hurley, Ruby . . . 4384f
Hurston, Zora Neale . . . 3748
Huston, John . . . 4671
Hutchinson Speedboat . . . 4160
Hyacinth . . . 2760, 3900
Hyde Park . . . 930
Hydrangea . . . 2996
Hypersonic Airliner . . . C122, C126
I Love Lucy . . . 3187l, 4414b, UX575
Ice
Dancing . . . 2809
Hockey . . . 2811, 3554
Skating . . . 1698, 2029, 3117, 4937, 4941
Iceboat . . . 2134
Idaho . . . 1675, 1964, 3572, 3707
Statehood . . . 896, 2439
Iiwi . . . 2311
Illinois . . . 1653, 1965, 3573, 3708
Institute of Technology . . . 2020
Statehood . . . 1339
(Windmill) . . . 1741
Immigrants arrive . . . 3182i
Improving Education . . . 3191e
Incredibles, The . . . 4678
Independence
Declaration of . . . 1687
Finland . . . 1334
Hall . . . 1044, 1546, 1622, 1625, 2779
Mexican . . . 1157
Sesquicentennial Exposition . . . 627
Skilled Hands for . . . 1717-1720
Indiana . . . 1651, 1966, 3574, 3709
Statehood . . . 1308
Territory . . . 996
Indian
Paintbrush . . . 2647
Pond Lily . . . 2680
Indians . . 230-231, 237-238, 240, 285, 287, 328, 565, 680, 682-683, 695, 739, 755, 783, 972, 1063, 1187, 1360, 1389, 1426, C117
American . . . 1364
American Art, Navajo Blanket . . . 2238
Centennial . . . 972
Chief Joseph . . . 1364
Crazy Horse . . . 1855
Head Penny . . . 1734
Headdresses . . . 2501-2505
Masks, Pacific Northwest . . . 1834-1837
Red Cloud . . . 2176
Sequoyah . . . 1859
Sitting Bull . . . 2184
Thorpe, Jim . . . 2089
Induction Motor . . . 2057
Industry
Agriculture for Defense . . . 899
Petroleum . . . 1134
Poultry . . . 968
Science & . . . 2031
Wool . . . 1423
Inkwell and Quill . . . 1535, 1581, 1811
Inland Marsh . . . 4710e
Inline Skating . . . 3324
Insects & Spiders . . . 3351
Integrated Circuit, The . . . 3188j
International
Civil Aeronautics Conference . . . 649-650
Cooperation Year . . . 1266
Geophysical Year . . . 1107
Naval Review—Jamestown Festival . . . 1091
Philatelic Exhibition . . . 630
Philatelic Exhibitions . . . 778, 1075-1076, 1310-1311, 1632, 1757, 2145, 2216-2219
Polar Year . . . 4123
Red Cross . . . 1016, 1239
Style of Architecture . . . 3186k
Telecommunication Union . . . 1274
Women's Year . . . 1571
Year of the Child . . . 1772
Year of the Disabled . . . 1925
Youth Year . . . 2160-2163
Interphil 76 . . . 1632
Intrepid . . . 2032
Inventors . 889-893, 945, 1062, 1270, 1286A, 2055, 2567, C45, C69, C91-C94, C113-C114, C118-C119
Inventors, American . . . 2056-2058
Inverted Jenny . . . 4806,C3a
Iowa . . . 1661, 1967, 3575, 3710
Statehood . . . 942, 3088, 3089
Territory . . . 838
Iris . . . 2763, 3903, 4166, 4178
Irish Immigration . . . 3286
Irrigation
center pivot . . . 4710h
Irving, Washington . . . 859, 1548
Isabella, Queen . . . 234, 236-238, 241-244, 2620
Islands, Northern Mariana . . . 2804
It Happened One Night . . . 4669
Itlay invaded by Allies . . . 2765f
Ives, Charles . . . 3164
Ives, Frederic E . . . 3063
Iwo Jima (Marines) . . . 929
Jack-in-the-Box . . . 2791, 2798, 2801
Jack-in-the-Pulpit . . . 2650
Jackson,
Andrew . . . 73, 85B, 87, 93, 103, 135, 146, 157, 168, 178, 180, 183, 193, 203, 211, 211D, 215, 221, 253, 302, 786, 812, 941, 1209, 1225, 1286, 2201, 2216g, 2592
(Battle of New Orleans) . . . 1261
Gen. Stonewall . . . 788, 1408, 2975s
(Hermitage) . . . 1037, 1059
Mahalia . . . 3216
Washington and . . . 2592
Jackson Pollack, Abstract Expressionism . . . 3186h
Jacob's Ladder . . . 2684
James P. "Sulley" Sullivan . . . 4681
Jamestown
Exposition . . . 328-330
Festival, International Naval Review . . . 1091
Founding of . . . 329
Japan
Invades Aleutians . . . 2697e
Opening of . . . 1021
Treaty, US- . . . 1158
US Declares War on . . . 2559j
Japanese Bomb Pearl Harbor . . . 2559i
Japanese Diet, Tokyo, and Dogwood Blossoms . . . 4984
Jay, John . . . 1046, 2052
Jazz and Blues Singers . . . 2854-2861
Jazz Flourishes . . . 3184k
Jazz Musicians . . . 2983-2992
Jeffers, Robinson . . . 1485
Jefferson
Memorial . . . 1510, 1520
Thomas . . . 12, 27-30A, 42, 67, 75-76, 80, 105, 139, 150, 161, 172, 187-188, 197, 209, 228, 260, 275, 310, 324, 561, 590, 641, 667, 678, 807, 842, 851, 1011, 1033, 1055, 1141, 1278, 1299, 1299b, 1687b, 1693, 1779, 2185, 2201, 2216c, 2523, C88
Thomas (Monticello) . . . 1047
Jermoine Granger . . . 4828
Jenny Airplane . . . 3142s
Jessie . . . 4680
Jet Liner . . . C51-C52, C60-C61, C78, C82
Over Capitol . . . C64-C65
Jeweled Top Snail . . . 4423h, UX592
Jitterbug sweeps nation . . . 3186g
Jock Scott . . . 2546
John Bull Locomotive . . . 2364
John Henry . . . 3085
Johnson, Andrew . . . 822, 2217
Johnson,
James P . . . 2985
James Weldon . . . 2371
John H . . . 4624
Joshua . . . 3236h
Lady Bird . . . 4716, 4716a
Lyndon B . . . 1503, 2219i
Robert . . . 2857
Walter . . . 3408i
William H . . . 4653
Johnston, Joseph E . . . 2975m
Joliet, Louis . . . 1356
Jolson, Al . . . 2849
Jones
Bobby . . . 1933, 3185n
Casey . . . 993
John Paul . . . 790, 1789, 1789B
Joplin
Janis . . . 4916
Scott . . . 2044
Jordan,Barbara . . . 4565
Joseph
E. Johnston . . . 2975m
Pulitzer . . . 946
Journalism—Freedom of the Press . . . 1119, 1476-1477, 1593
Journalists . . . 4248-52
Juke Box . . . 2911-2912A, 3132
Julian, Percy Lavon . . . 2746
Jumbo Jets . . . 3189n
Jumping spider . . . 3351t
Jupiter . . . 2573
Jurassic Park . . . 3191k
Balloon . . . C54
Pioneer 10 . . . 1556
Jury Duty . . . 4200
Just, Ernest E . . . 3058
Justice . . . 313
Contemplation of . . . 1592
(Scales of) . . . 1139, 1186
Kahanamoku, Duke . . . 3660
Kahlo, Frida . . . 3509
Kaiser Darren . . . 3932
Kaleidoscope Flowers . . . 4722-25
Kamehameha, King . . . 799
Kane, Elisha Kent . . . 2220
Kansas . . . 1666, 1968, 3576, 3711
City, MO . . . 994
Statehood . . . 1183
Territory . . . 1061
Karloff, Boris . . . 3170, 3171
Karman, Theodore von . . . 2699
Kasebier, Gertrude . . . 3649d
Katzenjammer Kids . . . 3000b
Kearney
Expedition, Gen. Stephen Watts, Oct. 16 . . . 944
Fort . . . 970
Keaton, Buster . . . 2828
Keep in Touch . . . 2274
Keller, Helen/Anne Sullivan . . . 1824
Kelly, Grace . . . 2749
Kelp Forest . . . 4423, UX587-96
Kennedy
John F . . . 1287, 2219h
Memorial . . . 1246
Robert F . . . 1770
Kent, Rockwell . . . 3502q
Kentucky . . . 1647, 1969, 3577, 3712
Settlement, First . . . 1542
Statehood . . . 2636
Kermit the Frog . . . 3944a-3944j

Kern, Jerome 2110
Kertesz, Andre 3649r
Kerosene Table Lamp 1611
Kestrel, American 2476-2477, 3031, 3044
Key, Francis Scott 962
Keystone Cops 2826
Kids Care 2951-2954
Kii Statue C84
Kilauea Volcano 4067
Killer Whale 2508, 2511
Kiwi 4255, 4262
Kindred Spirits by Asher B. Durand 3236g
King
John's Crown 1265
Martin Luther, Jr. 1771, 3188a
Penguins 2708
Salmon 1079
King of Hearts 4404
King Nutcracker 4362, 4366, 4370
Kitten and Puppy 2025
Kline, Franz 3236s
Klondike Gold Rush 3235
Knox, Henry 1851
Knoxville World's Fair 2006-2009
Koala 2370
Korea 921
Korean Veterans 2152
Korean War 3187e
Veterans Memorial 3803
Korngold, Enrich Wolfgang 3344
Kosciuszko, General Thaddeus 734
Kossuth, Lajos 1117-1118
Krazy Kat 3000e
Kukla, Fran & Ollie 4414k, UX576
Kwanza 3175, 3368, 3548, 3673, 3881, 4119, 4220, 4373, 4434, 4584,4845
,La Chaise 4333h
La Fortaleza, PR 801
La Grande Vallee O 4444h
Labor Day 1082
(A. Phllip Randolph) 2402
(Collective Bargaining) 1558
(Gompers, Samuel) 998
Organized 1831
(Perkins, Francis) 1821
Lacemaking 2351-2354
Lady and the Tramp 4028
Lady beetle 3351c
Ladybug 2315
Lady's Slipper 1377, 2077
Lafayette 1010, 1097
Indiana C54
Marquis de 1686d, 1716
Lagoon Nebula 3386
LaGuardia, Fiorello 1397
Lake
Erie,Battle of 4805
Erie 1069
Huron 1069
Michigan 1069
Ontario 1069
Placid, NY, Olympic—Winter Games '32 716
Placid, NY, Olympic—Winter Games '80 1795-1798
Shore Drive, Chicago 3910f
Superior 1069, 4047
Lamps 1206, 1386
Kerosene Table 1611
Rush 1610
Whale Oil 1608
Lancaster County, PA C150, UX638
Land-Grant Colleges 1065
Landing
Craft 1434
of Cadillac 1000
of Carteret 1247
of Columbus 231, 2616, 2622, 2623, 2624, 2625
of the Pilgrims 549, 1420
Landsat 2570
Lange, Dorothea 3649l
Langley, Samuel P. C118
Lanier, Sidney 1446
Lantern, Railroad 1612
LaRabida 239
Large-Flowered Trillium 2652
Lark Bunting 1958
Lasers 3188k
Lasker, Mary 3435B
Lassie 4414f, UX577
Last of the Buffalo, The by Alfred Bierstadt 3236m
Latin Jazz 4349
Latrobe, Benjamin 1780
Laubach, Dr. Frank 1864
Laurel & Hardy 2562
Laurens, John 1686e
Law and Order 1343
Law, World Peace through 1576
Leadbelly 3212
Leaf-nosed Bat 3662
Leatherworker 1720
Lee
General Robert E. 788, 982, 1049, 1408
Jason 964
Robert E. 2975b
Lena Horne 5259
Lefty Grove 3408k
Lefty's Deceiver 2548
Legend of Sleepy Hollow, The 1548
Legends
of Baseball 3408
of Hollywood . . 2967, 3082, 3152, 3226, 3329, 3446, 3523, 3692, 3786, 3876, 3911, 4077, 4421, 4892
of the West 2869, 2870
Leigh, Vivien 2446
Lejeune, Lt. Gen. John A. 3961
Lend Lease 2559c
Leon, Ponce de 2024
Lerner & Loewe 3346
Lesser Long Nosed-bat and Cactus 4155, 4155a
Letter Writing Issue 1806-1810
Letter 1310, 1511, 1805, 2150, 2618
Carriers 1490, 1497, 2420
Lift Spirits 1807
Preserve Memories 1805
Shape Opinions 1809
Letters Mingle Souls 1530, 1532, 1534, 1536
Levendecker, J.C. 3502c
Levertov, Denise 4661
Lewis
and Clark Expedition 1063, 3854
Edna 4922
Francis 1687c
Meriwether 1063, 3854, 3855
Sinclair 1856
Lexington and Concord 617-619, 790, 1563
Leyte Gulf, battle of 2838i
Liberation of Rome and Paris 2838f
Liberte C120
Liberty . . 1034-1042A, 1043-1044A, 1045-1054A, 1055-1059A, C120
Bell 627, 1518, 1595, 1618, 4125, 4126, 4127, 4128, C57, C62
Birth of 618
Head of 1599, 1619
Ship 2559h, 4550
Statue of . . 566, 696, 899, 908, 946, 995, 1035, 1041-1042, 1044-1044A, 1057, 1075, 1320, 1594, 1599, 1619, 1816, 2147, 2224, C35, C58, C63, C80, C87
Torch 1008, 1594, 1816, 2531A
Bell 4437, U667b, U667c
Libraries, America's 2015
Library
Low Memorial 1029
of Congress 2004, 3390
Life Magazine, 1st Issue of 3185c
Lighthouse, Sandy Hook 1605
Lighthouses 1391, 1449, 1605, 1891, 2470-2474, 2969-2973, 3783-3791, 4146-4150, 4409-13, U669-73, UX562-66,4791-95
Lightning Airplane 3142n
Lightning McQueen 4553
Lightning Whelk 2121
Li'l Abner 3000q
Lilac 2764
Lily 1879, 2829, 3530, 4172, 4182
Limner, the Freak 3236b
Limon, Jose 4699
Lincoln
Abraham 77, 85F, 91, 98, 108, 122, 132, 137, 148, 159, 170,186, 195, 208, 222, 254, 269, 280, 304, 315, 317, 367-369, 555, 584, 600, 635, 661, 672, 821, 902, 906, 978, 1036, 1058, 1113-1116, 1143, 1233, 1282, 1303, 2081, 2106, 2217g, 2410, 2433, 2523, 2523A, 2975j, C59, C88, 4380-83, 4860, 4861
-Douglas Debates 1115
Gen. Benjamin 1686b
Memorial 571, 4982
Tad 2106
Lincoln Premiere 4356
Lindbergh, Charles 1710, 2781, C10
Lindbergh flies the Atlantic 3184m
Linquini 4554
Linum 4757
Lions International (Search for Peace) 1326
Lion's Mane Nudibranch 4423d, UX588
Lippman, Walter 1849
Literary Arts . . 1773, 1832, 2047, 2094, 2239, 2350,2418, 2449, 2538, 2698, 2862, 3002, 3104, 3134, 3221, 3308, 3444, 3659, 3748, 3871, 3904, 4030, 4124, 4223, 4386, 4476, 4545
Little
American (Antarctic) 733, 735, 753, 768
House on the Prairie 2786
Mermaid 3914
Nemo in Slumberland 3000c
Orphan Annie 3000j
Rock Nine 3937d
Women 2788
Livingston, Robert R. 323, 1020, 1687a, 1693
Lloyd, Harold 2825
Lockheed
Constellation C35
P-80 Shooting Star 3921
Locks at Sault Ste. Marie 298
Lockwood, Belva Ann 2178
Locomobile 2381
Locomotives . 114, 125, 922, 947, 961, 993, 1006, 1415, 1506, 1511, 1573, 1755, 1897A, 2226, 2362-2366, 2402, 2843-2847
Loesser, Frank 3350
Loewy, Raymond 4546c
Log rafts 4710g
Lombardi, Vince 3145, 3147
London, Jack 2182, 2197
Long, Dr. Crawford W. 875
Long-billed Curlew, Numenius Longrostis by John James Audubon 3236e
Longleaf Pine Forest 3611
Longfellow, Henry W. 864, 4124
Longhorn Cattle, Angus and 1504
Lord Voldermort 4843
Los Angeles, CA. Olympic Issue '32 . . . . 718, 719
Los Angeles Class 3372, 3374
Louis
Armstrong 2982, 2984
Joe 2766
XVI, King 1753
Louisiana 1650, 1970, 3578, 3713
Purchase 3782
Purchase Exposition 323-327, 1020
Statehood 1197, 4667
World Exposition 2086
Lounge Chair & Ottoman 4333f
Lounge Chair Metal 4333p
Love 1475, 1951, 2072, 2143, 2202, 2248, 2378-2379, 2440-2441, 2535-2537, 2618, 2813, 2814, 2814C, 2815, 2948-2949, 3030, 3123, 3124, 3274-75, 3496-3499, 3551, 3657, 3658, 3833, 3898, 3976, 4029, 4122, 4450, 4626,4787, 4955-56, 4959-60, 5155, 5255, 5339, 5431, 5543, 5660-61, 5745-46, 5826
Birds 2813, 2815
(Cherubs) 2957-2960
Love You 2398
Dad! 2270
Mother! 2273
Lovebirds, Fischer's 2537
Low
Juliette Gordon 974
Memorial Library 1029
Lowell, James Russell 866
Luce, Henry 2935
Ludington, Sybil 1559
Luge 2808
Lugosi, Bela 3169
Luna Lovegood 4838
Luna Moth 2293
Lunar
Orbiter 1435, 2571
Rover 1435
Lunch Counter Sit-ins 3937c
Lunch Wagon 2464
Lunt, Alfred & Lynn Fontaine 3287
Luiseno, Basket 3873j
Luther, Martin 2065
Luxembourg 912
Lyndhurst 1841
Lyon, Mary 2169
Lyra Constellation 3947
Maass, Clara 1699
Mackinac Bridge 4438, U674
MacArthur, Gen. Douglas 1424
Macdonough, Thomas 791
MacDowell, Edward A. 882
Mackinac Bridge 1109
Madison
Dolley 1822
Helene 2500
James 262, 277, 312, 479, 808, 843, 2201, 2216d, 2875a, 3545
Madonna and Child 2789, 2790, 2871, 3003, 4206, 4424
Madonna and Child, della Robbia 1768
Maggie Mix-up 3151n
Magi 4945
Magna Carta 1265
Magnolia 3193, 4168, 4180
Magsaysay, Ramon 1096
Mahoning by Franz Kline 3236s
Mail
Car 2265
Car (Postal People) 1489
Car (USPS) 1396
Delivery, City 1238
Express 1909, 2122, 2394, 2541
International Express 2542
Order Business 1468
Overland 1120
Planes and US Map, Two C7, C8, C9
(Pony Express) 894, 1154
Priority 2419, 2540

  Railroad ... 2265
  Transportation, Future ... C122-C123, C125, C126
  Truck ... 2781
  Wagon ... 1903
Mailbox, Rural ... 1703, 1730
Maine ... 1655, 1971, 3579, 3714
  (Christmas) ... 1384
  Coon Cat ... 2374
  (Great Head National Park) ... 746, 762
  Statehood ... 1391
Maisy ... 3990
Make-up ... 3772e
Makeup Rate ... 2521
Malamute, Alaskan ... 2100
Malaria Eradication ... 1194
Malcolm X ... 3273
Mallard ... 1757b
  Decoy ... 2139
Maltese Cat ... 4452
Maltese Falcon, the ... 4671
Mambo ... 3942
Mammoth
  Cave ... 4068
  Woolly ... 3078
Man Ray ... 3649i
Man
  Riding Donkey ... 4969
  Walks on the Moon ... 3188c
Manatee ... 3105o
Mancini, Henry ... 3839
Mann, Horace ... 869
Mannerheim, Gustaf ... 1165-1166
Mantel, Mickey ... 4083
Maps .. 327, 733, 735, 753, 768, 783, 795, 858, 906, 927, 933, 942, 952, 955, 957, 984, 1018, 1067, 1069, 1071, 1092, 1112, 1120, 1131, 1154, 1206, 1232, 1247-1248, 1258, 1274, 1306, 1308, 1319, 1340, 1431, 1690, 1937, 1938, 2220-2223, 2386-2389, 2559, 2620, 2697, 2747, 2765, 2838, 2981, C7-C9, C14, C53, C55, C116-C117, 4893
Marathon ... 3067
March on Washington ... 3937h,4804
Marblehead (Lake Erie) ... 2972
Marbois, Marquis Francois de Barbe ... 1020
Marciano, Rocky ... 3187k
Marconi's Spark Coil and Spark Gap ... 1500
Mariana Islands ... 2804
Marigold ... 2832
Marin, Luis Munoz ... 2173
Marine
  Corps ... 1013
  Corps Reserve ... 1315
  One ... 4144
Mariner
  2 ... 2569
  10 ... 2568
  10/Venus, Mercury ... 1557
Marines ... 929
  assault Tarawa ... 2765j
  Continental ... 1567
  Distinguised ... 3961-3964
  on Guadalcanal ... 2697i
  raise flag on Iwo Jima ... 2981a
Maris, Roger, 61 in '61 ... 3188n
Marquette, Jacques ... 285, 1356
Mars ... 2572, 2631-2632
  Pathfinder and Sojourner ... 3178
  Viking Missions to ... 1759
Marsh Marigold ... 2658
Marshall
  George C ... 1289
  Islands, Republic of the Federated States of Micronesia ... 2506-2507
  James W ... 954
  John ... 263, 278, 313, 480, 1050, 2415
  Plan ... 3141
  Plan, Acheson, Dean ... 2755
  Thurgood ... 3746
Martin, Roberta ... 3217
Marx, Gowan & ... 2366
Marx, Groucho ... 4414h, UX586
Mary Chestnut ... 2975o
Maryland ... 1639, 1972, 3580, 3715
  Settlement ... 736
  Statehood ... 2342
Masaryk, Thomas G ... 1147, 1148
Masks, Pacific Northwest Indian ... 1834, 1835, 1836, 1837
Mason
  George ... 1858
  George (Gunston Hall) ... 1108
Massachusetts ... 1638, 1973, 3581, 3716
  Bay Colony ... 682
  Flag ... 1034, 1056
  Statehood ... 2341
  Windmill ... 1740
Masters, Edgar Lee ... 1405
Masters of American Photography ... 3649
Masterson, Bat ... 2869h, 2870h
Mastodon ... 3079
Matagorda Island Lighthouse ... 4409, U669, UX562
Mater ... 4553
Mathewson, Christy ... 3408c
Matzeliger, Jan ... 2567
Mauldin, Bill ... 4445
Maybeck, Bernard ... 1930
Mayer, Maria Goeppert ... 4543
Mayflower ... 548
  Compact, Signing of ... 550
  (Landing of the Pilgrims) ... 549, 1420
Mayo, Doctors William J. and Charles H. ... 1251
Mazzei, Philip ... C98
McCarthy
  & Bergen ... 2563
  Charlie ... 2563
McClintock, Barbara ... 3906
McCloy, Lt. Commander John ... 4442
McCormack, John ... 2090
McCormick, Cyrus Hall ... 891
McDaniel, Hattie ... 3996
McDowell, Dr. Ephraim ... 1138
McGruff the Crime Dog ... 2102
McHenry Flag, Fort ... 1346
MdKinley, Wiliam G. . 326, 559, 588, 639, 665, 676, 829, 2218f
McLoughlin, John ... 964
McMahon, Sen. Brien ... 1200
McMein, Neysa ... 3502m
McPhatter, Clyde ... 2726, 2733
McQueen's Jupiter ... 2844
Mead, Margaret, anthropologist ... 3184g
Meadow Beauty ... 2649
Meany, George ... 2848
Medal of Honor ... 2013, 2045, 2103,4822-23, 4822a-4823a
Medical Imaging ... 3189o
Medics treat wounded ... 2765b
Medussa ... 3443
Mellon, Andrew W ... 1072
Melville, Herman ... 2094
Memorial ... 1318
  Poppy ... 977
Mendez Vs. Westminster ... 4201
Mendoza, Lydia ... 4786
Mentoring A Child ... 3556
Mercer, Johnny ... 3101
Merchant Marine ... 939, 4548-51
Mercury ... 1557, 2568, 2634
  Helmet and Olive Branch ... E7
  Project ... 1193
Merengue ... 3939
Merganthaler, Ottmar ... 3062
Mermaid ... 1112
Merman, Ethel ... 2853
Mesa Verde National Park ... 743, 759
Messenger
  on Bicycle ... E6, E8-E11
  Running ... E1-E4, E5
Messenger Mission ... 4528
Metropolitan Opera ... 2054
Mexican
  Hat ... 2688
  Independence ... 1157
Mexico, Statehood ... 4591
Michael, Moina ... 977
Micheaux, Oscar ... 4464
Michener, James ... 3427A
Michigan ... 1658, 1974, 3582, 3717
  Landing of Cadillac ... 1000
  State College ... 1065
  Statehood ... 775, 2246
Mickey Mouse ... 3912, 4025, 4192
Micronesia, Federated States of ... 2506-2507
Microphone ... 1502
Microscope ... 1080, 1263, 1754, 1925
Midway, battle of ... 2697g
Mighty Casey ... 3083
Migratory
  Bird Hunting & Conservation Stamp Act ... 2092
  Bird Treaty ... 1306
Mike Wazowskie ... 4681
Miquel Locks, Pedro ... 398
Military
  Academy ... 3560
  Uniforms ... 1565-1568
Militia, American ... 1568
Milk
  Harvey ... 4906
  Wagon ... 2253
Millay, Edna St. Vincent ... 1926
Miller, Petty Officer 3rd Class Doris ... 4443
Millikan, Robert ... 1866
Mineral Heritage ... 1538-1541
Minerals ... 2700-2703
Mingus, Charles ... 2989
Mining Prospector ... 291
Minnesota ... 1664, 1975, 3583, 3718
  (Hubert Humphrey) ... 2190
  Statehood ... 1106, 4266
  Territory ... 981
Minnie Mouse ... 4025
Minute Man, The ... 619
Mirror Lake ... 742, 750, 758, 770
Miss Piggie ... 3944d
Missiing in Action ... 2966
Mission Belfry, CA ... 1373
Missions ... 1373, 1443, C116
Mississippi ... 1652, 1976, 3584, 3719
  (Great River Road) ... 1319
  Missouri River System ... 4065
  River ... 285, 1356
  River Bridge ... 293
  River Delta ... 4058
  Statehood ... 1337
  Territory ... 955
Mississippian Effigy ... 3873f
Missouri ... 1656, 1977, 3585, 3720
  Kansas City ... 994
  River ... 1063
  Statehood ... 1426
Mistletoe ... 1255
Mitchell
  Billy ... 3330
  Margaret ... 2168
  Pass, NE ... 1060
Mix, Tom ... 4447, UX598
Mobile, Battle of ... 1826
Mobile Bay, Battle of ... 4911
Mockingbird ... 2330, 1956, 1961, 1976, 1994, 1995
Model B Airplane ... 3142b
Model T Ford ... 3182a
Modern Dance ... 1752
Mold-Blown Glass ... 3326
Molded Plastic Sculpture ... 4333m
Moloka'I ... 4034
Monarch Butterfly ... 2287, 3351k, 4462
Monarch caterpillar ... 3351j
Monday Night Football ... 3189l
Monitor and Virginia ... 2975a
Monk, Thelonius ... 2990
Monmouth, Battle of (Molly Pitcher) ... 646
Monongahela River ... 681
Monorail ... 1196
Monroe
  James. 325, 562, 591, 603, 642, 668, 679, 810, 845, 1020, 1038, 1105, 2201, 2216e
  Marilyn ... 2967
Monopoly Game, The ... 3185o
Montana ... 1673, 1978, 3586, 3721
  (Glacier National Park) ... 748, 764
  Statehood ... 858, 2401
Monterey Truban Snail ... 4423j, UX595°
Montgomery, Alabama Bus Boycott ... 3937e
Monticello ... 1047
Monument, George Washington ... 2149
Moon . . 126, 1021, 1192, 1345, 1371, 1434-1435, 1548, 1909, 2122, 2246, 2394, 2404, 2419, 2571, 2631, 2634, C124
  First Landing ... 2841, 5399-4000
  Landing ... 2419, 2842, 3188c, 3413, C76
  Rover ... 1435, C124, C126
Moore
  John Bassett ... 1295
  Marianne ... 2449
Moorish Idol ... 1829
Moose ... 1757e, 1887, 2298
Moran, Thomas ... 3236l, 4917
Morgan
  Charles W ... 1441, 2340
  Horse ... 2156
  Silver Dollar ... 1557
Morning Light, S.S ... 1239
Morocco, Friendship with ... 2349
Morill, Justin ... 2941
Morris, Robert ... 1004
Morris Island, South Carolina ... 3789
Morris Township School ... 1606
Morrison's Bumblebee ... 4153, 4153a
Morro Castle, San Juan, Puerto Rico ... 1437
Morse, Samuel F.B ... 890, 924
Morton
  Jelly Roll ... 2986
  Julius Sterling, (Arbor Day) ... 717
Moses
  Grandma ... 1370
  Horace A ... 2095
Moss Campion ... 2686
Mothers
  Gold Star ... 969
  of America ... 737-738, 754
Mother Teresa ... 4475
Motion
  Pictures ... 926, 1555, 1727
  Picture Camera ... 1555
Motorcycle ... 1899, 4085-4088
Mott, Lucretia ... 959
Moultrie Flag, Fort ... 1345
Mount
  Davidson ... 1130
  Hood ... 1124

McKinley National Park . . . 800, 1454, C137
Ranier . . . 2404
Ranier National Park. . . . 742, 750, 758, 770
Rockwell (Mt. Sinopah). . . . 748, 764
Rushmore . . . 2523-2523A, C88
Rushmore Memorial . . . 1011
Surabachi . . . 929
Vernon . . . 785, 1032
Wai'ale'ale. . . . 4066
Washington. . . . 4053
Mountain
Bluebird. . . . 2439, 1964, 1980, 4883
Goat . . . 2323
Habitats. . . . 1923
Lion . . . 2292
McKinley National Park. . . . UX606
Nonprofit . . . 2903-2904A
Ranier National Park. . . . UX607
Movies go 3-D . . . 3187o
Mowgli . . . 4345
Mrs Elizabeth Freake and Baby Mary
by the Freake Limner . . . 3236b
Muddler Minnow . . . 2549
Muir, John . . . 1245, 3182j
Mule Deer . . . 2294
Muller-Munk, Peter . . . 4546a
Mummy, The . . . 3171
Munor Marin, Luis . . . 2173
Muppets. . . . 3944a-3944j
Murphy,
Audie L.. . . . 3396
Robert D. . . . 4076a
Murrow, Edward R. . . . 2812
Muscle cars . . . 4743-47
Muscogee Seal . . . 972
Museum
National Postal . . . 2779
Smithsonian Institution . . . 3059
Music . . . 3772d
American. . . . 1252
and Literature by William Harnett . . . 3236i
Big Band . . . 3096-3099
Films . . . 3772d
Musicals. . . . 2767-2770
Musicians. . . . 1372, 1755, 2110, 2211,2371, 2411
. . . 2721, 2723, 2724-2737, 2771-74, 2775-78
. . . 2849-53,2854-61, 2983-92, 3096-99, 3154-57,
. . . 3212-15, 3216-19, 4880
Muskellunge . . . 2205
Mustang Airplane. . . . 3142a
Muybridge, Eadweard . . . 3061
My
Fair Lady. . . . 2770
Old Kentucky Home State Park . . . 2636
Myron's Discobolus . . . 719
Nagurski, Bronko. . . . 3808
Naismith—Basketball . . . 1189
Nancy . . . 3000o
Narrows Bridge, Verrazano- . . . 1258
Nash
Healey. . . . 3934
Ogden. . . . 3659
Nassau Hall (Princeton University) . . . 1083, 1704
Nation of Readers, A . . . 2106
National
Academy of Science. . . . 1237
Apprenticeship Program . . . 1201
Archives . . . 227, 2081
Capitol. . . . 990-992
Defense . . . 899-901
Education Association. . . . 1093
Farmer's Bank . . . 1931
Gallery of Art. . . . 3910g
Grange . . . 1323
Guard . . . 1017
Letter Writing Week . . . 1805-1810
Park Service . . . 1314
Parks. . . . 740-751, 756-765, 769-770, 952, 1448-1454,
2018, C84, C135, C138, C139, C140, C141
Postal Museum. . . . 2779-2782
Recovery Act. . . . 732
Stamp Exhibition. . . . 735, 768
Native American Culture . . . 2869e, 2870e
Nativity, by John Singleton Copley . . . 1701
NATO. . . . 1008, 1127, 3354
Natural History. . . . 1387-1390
Nature of America . 3293, 3378, 3506, 3611, 3802, 3831, 3899,
4099, 4198, 4352, 4423, 4474
Nautical Figure . . . 2242
Nautilus . . . 1128
Navajo
Blanket . . . 2235-2238
Necklace. . . . 3749-3749B
Weaving . . . 3873h
Naval
Academy, US . . . 794
Aviation. . . . 1185
Review, International . . . 1091
Navigation, Lake . . . 294
Navigation, Ocean. . . . 299
Navy . . . 790-794
Medal of honor . . . 4822, 4822a
Continental . . . 1566
Department. . . . O35-O45
US. . . . 935, 1013, 1067
Nebraska. . . . 1669, 1979, 3587, 3722
Statehood . . . 1328
Territory. . . . 1060
Negro Leagues . . . 3408p,3408r, 4465, 4466
Foster, Rube . . . 4466
Nelson,
Harriet. . . . 4414q, UX579
Ozzie. . . . 4414q, UX579
Thomas, Jr. . . . 1686d, 1687c
Nemo. . . . 4679
Neptune. . . . 1112, 2576
New England . . . 2119
Nessen, Gretta von . . . 4546i
Netherlands. . . . 913, 2003
Neumann, John von . . . 3908
Neuter/Spay. . . . 3670-71
Nevada . . . 1668, 1980, 3588, 3723
Settlement. . . . 999
Statehood . . . 1248, 4907
Nevelson, Louise. . . . 3379-83
Nevers, Ernie. . . . 3809
Nevin, Ethelbert. . . . 883
New
London Harbor Lighthouse . . . 4795
Amsterdam Harbor, NY. . . . 1027
Baseball Records . . . 3191a
England Neptune . . . 2119
Hampshire . . . 1068, 1641, 1981, 3589, 3724
Hampshire Statehood. . . . 2344
Jersey. . . . 1635, 1982, 3590, 3725
Jersey, Settlement . . . 1247
Jersey, Statehood. . . . 2338
Mexico . . . 1679, 1983, 3591, 3726
Mexico (Chavez, Dennis) . . . 2185
Mexico, Statehood . . . 1191, 4591
Orleans. . . . 2407
River Gorge Bridge. . . . 4511, U675
Sweden. . . . C117
Year, Chinese . . . 2817
Year, Happy . . . 2720, 3370, 3500
York. . . . 1643, 1984, C38, 3592, 3727
York City . . . 1027
York City Coliseum . . . 1076
York, Newburgh . . . 727, 731, 767
York, Skyline. . . . C35
York Statehood. . . . 2346
York Stock Exchange . . . 2630
York World's Fair '39. . . . 853
York World's Fair '64. . . . 1244
Newburgh, New York. . . . 752
News of victory hits home . . . 2981i
Newspaper Boys . . . 1015
Newman, Alfred. . . . 3343
Niagara by Frederic Edwin Church . . . 3236n
Niagara Falls . . . 568, 699, C133, UX639
Railway Suspension Bridge . . . 961
Nicolet, Jean . . . 739
Nieu Nederland . . . 614
Nighthawks by Edward Hopper. . . . 3236p
Nimitz, Chester W.. . . . 1869
Nine-Mile Prairie . . . C136, UX640
Nineteenth Amendment. . . . 1406, 2980, 3184e
(Suffrage) . . . 784, 1051, 1406
Nisqually, Fort . . . 1604
Nixon, Richard. . . . 2955
No. 12 by Mark Rothko . . . 3236t
Nobel Prize, The . . . 3504
Noguchi, Isamu . . . 3857-3861
Nonprofit . . . 2902
Norris
Dam . . . 1184
Sen. George W. . . . 1184
Norse-American. . . . 620, 621
North
African Invasion . . . 2697j
Carolina . . . 1644, 1985, 3593, 3728
Carolina, Cape Lookout . . . 3788
Carolina (Great Smoky Mountains
National Park). . . . 749, 765
Carolina Statehood. . . . 2347
Dakota . . . 1671, 1986, 3594, 3729
Dakota Statehood. . . . 858, 2403
Pole. . . . 1128
Northeast Deciduous Forest . . . 3899
Northern
Goshawk. . . . 4608
Harrier. . . . 4612
Kelp Crab . . . 4423i, UX589
Mariana Islands . . . 2804
Sea Lion . . . 2509
Spy Apple . . . 4727, 4732
Northrop YB-49 Flying Wing . . . 3925
Northwest Territory
Ordinance. . . . 795
Sesquicentennial . . . 837
Norway . . . 911
Noyes, Eliot . . . 4546j
Numismatics . . . 2558
Nurse. . . . 702, 1699, 1910
Nursing . . . 1190
Nutcrackers . . . 4360-71
NYU Library . . . 1928
Oakland Bay Bridge, Plane Over. . . . C36
Oakley, Annie. . . . 2869d, 2870d
Ocelot . . . 3105e
Ochoa, Severo. . . . 4544
Ochs, Adolph S. . . . 1700
Ocotillo. . . . 1378
Off the Flordia Keys, Longest Reef . . . 4042
Official
Postal Savings Mail . . . O121-O143
Stamps . . . O1-O161
Oglethorpe, General . . . 726
O Henry . . . 4705
Ohi'a Lehua . . . 2669
Ohio. . . . 1649, 1987, 3595, 3730, 3773
Class. . . . 3375
River Canalization. . . . 681
Statehood . . . 1018, 3773
Oil
Derrick . . . 1134
Wagon. . . . 2130
O'Keeffe, Georgia . . . 3069
Okinawa, the last big battle . . . 2981c
Oklahoma . . . 1678, 1988, 3596, 3731
(Cherokee Strip) . . . 1360
Statehood . . . 1092, 4121
Oklahoma!. . . . 2722, 2769
Okefenokee Swamp . . . C142, US641
Old
Cape Henry, Virginia. . . . 3787
Faithful . . . 744, 760, 1453, 4379
Man of the Mountain. . . . 1068, 2344
North Church . . . 1603
Olivia . . . 3993
Olmstead, Fredrick Law, Landscape Artist . . . 3338
Olympians . . . 2496-2500
Olympic . . . 3068, 3087
Games '32 . . . 716, 718-719
Games '60 . . . 1146
Games '72 . . . 1460-1462, C85
Games '76 . . . 1695-1698
Games '80 . . . 1790-1798, C97
Games '84 . . . 2048-2051, 2067, 2070, 2082-2085,
C101-C112
Games '88 . . . 2369, 2380
Games '92 . . . 2553-2557, 2611-2615, 2637-2641
Games '96 . . . 3068
Games, Athens, Greece . . . 3863
Games, Hockey Player. . . . 1798, 2070, 2611, 2811, 3554
Games, Runner . . . 1697, 1791, 2083, 2555, 2557, 3068c,
3068m, 3068p, 3863, C102
Games, Skater .1698, 1795, 2067, 2612, 2613, 2809, 3555
Games, Skiier. 1696, 1796, 1797, 2068, 2069, 2614, 2807,
2810, 3552, C85
Games, Summer. . . . 1790, 1791-1794, 2082-2085,
2553-2557, 2637-2641, 3068, C97, C101-C104,
Games, Summer (cont.) . . . C105-C108, C109-C112, 4334
Games, Swimmer. . . . 1695, 1792, 2082, 2641, C107
Games, Winter . . . 1795-1798, 2067-2070, 2807-2811,
3552-3555, 3995, C85, 4436
Rings. . . . 2539-2542
Rings and Snowflake . . . 1146
Rings, Flag with . . . 2528
Special . . . 1788
Special, Winter . . . 2142
Omithominus. . . . 3136n
Omnibus . . . 1897, 2225
O'Neil, Capt. William O. "Bucky" . . . 973
O'Neill, Eugene . . . 1294, 1305C
O'Neill, Rose . . . 3502i
One-Room Schoolhouse . . . 1606
Opening of Japan . . . 1021
Opera, Metropolitan. . . . 2054
Opisthias . . . 3136h
Orange and Yellow . . . 4444c
Orange, Landing at Fort . . . 615
Orange Tabby Cat . . . 4460
Orange-Tip . . . 1715
Orbiter
Lunar. . . . 2571
Viking . . . 2572
Orchids . . . 2076-2079, 4474i
Order, Law and . . . 1343
Ordinance, Northwest Territory . . . 795
Oregon. . . . 1665, 1989, 3597, 3732
(Crater Lake National Park) . . . 745, 761
SS. . . . 997

Statehood . . . 1124, 4376
Territory . . . 783, 964
Trail . . . 964, 2747
Organ & Tissue Donation . . . 3227
Organized Labor . . . 1831
Orian Constellation . . . 3946
Oriskany . . . 644
Herkimer at . . . 1722
Mail Transportation . . . C124
Ormandy, Eugene . . . 3161
Ornate
Box Turtle . . . 3818
Chorus Frog . . . 3817
Ornithoimmus . . . 3136n
Oroville Dam . . . 4056
Orson Welles, “Citizen Kane” . . . 3186o
Osprey . . . 2291, 4611
Osteopathic Medicine . . . 1469
O'Sullivan, Timothy H. . . . 3649b
Ott, Mel . . . 4082
Otter, Sea . . . 2510
Ouimet, Francis . . . 2377
Overland Mail . . . 1120, 2869t, 2870t
Overrun Countries . . . 129, 909-921
Oveta Culp . . . 4510
Ovington, Mary White . . . 4384a
Owens, Jesse . . . 2496, 3185j
Owl/Grosbeak . . . 2284-2285
Owl,
American . . . 1760-1763
Snowy . . . 3290
Owney . . . 4547
Oxen . 950, 958, 964, 970, 981, 997, 1019, 1061, 1426, 1487, 1542
Ozzie and Harriet . . . 4414q, UX579
P-47 Thunderbolt . . . 3919
P-51's escort B-17's on boming raids . . . 2838b
P-80 Shooting Star . . . 3921
P.S. Write Soon . . . 1806, 1808, 1810
Pacific
Calypso . . . 2079
Coast Rain Forest . . . 3378
Coral Reef . . . 3831
Crest Trail . . . 4043
Dogwood . . . 3197
Exposition, Alaska-Yukon- . . . 370-371
Exposition, California . . . 773, 778
Northwest Indian Masks . . . 1834-1837
Rock Crab . . . 4423h, UX592
Trust Territories, Northern Mariana Islands . . . 2408
'97 . . . 3130-3131
Packard . . . 2384
Paddlewheel Steamer . . . 1187, 2435, 2438
Paderewski, Ignacy Jan . . . 1159-1160
Paige, Satchel . . . 3408p
Paine, Thomas . . . 1292
Painted Bunting . . . 4885
Painted Fern . . . 4852, 4878
Painting, American . . . 1187, 1207, 1241, 1243, 1273, 1322, 1335, 1361, 1386, 1433, 1553, 1563, 1564, 1629-1631, 1686-1689, 1691-1694, 1704, 1722, 1728, C71
Palace
of the Arts . . . 1930
of the Governors, Santa Fe, NM . . . 1031A, 1054A
Palaeosaniwa . . . 3136l
Palau . . . 2999
Pallid Bat . . . 3663
Palmer, Capt. Nathaniel B. . . . 2386
Palomar Mountain Observatory . . . 966
Pamphleteers . . . 1476
Pan American
Exposition . . . 294-299
Games . . . 2247, C56
Inverts, The . . . 3505
Union . . . 895
Union Building . . . C34
Panama
Canal . . . 398, 856, 3183f
Pacific Expedition . . . 401
Pacific Exposition . . . 397-400A
Panda, Giant . . . 2706
Pansy . . . 3027, 4450
Papanicolaou, Dr. George . . . 1754
Papaya . . . 4256, 4258
Paperwhite . . . 4863
Parakeet . . . 3233
Parasaurolophus . . . 3136o
Parcel Post Postage Due Stamps . . . JQ1-JQ5
Parent Teacher Association . . . 1463
Paris, Treaty of . . . 2052
Parker
Al . . . 3502f
Charlie . . . 2987
Dorothy . . . 2698
Parkman, Francis . . . 1281, 1297
Parks, Rosa . . . 4742
Parrish, Maxfield . . . 3502b
Parrot, Thick-billed . . . 3105b
Partridge, Alden . . . 1854
Pasqueflower . . . 2676
Pass, NE, Mitchell . . . 1060
Passionflower . . . 2674
Patrol Wagon, Police . . . 2258
Patton, Jr., General George S. . . . 1026
Paul, Alice . . . 2943
Paul Bunyan . . . 3084
Pauling, Linus . . . 4225
Payne, Ethel L. . . . 3667
PBY Catalina . . . 3916
Peace
Atoms for . . . 1070
Bridge . . . 1721
Corps . . . 1447, 3188f
Garden, International . . . 2014
of 1783 . . . 727, 731, 752, 767
Symbol . . . 3188m
Through Law, World . . . 1576
Through World Trade, World . . . 1129
Peacetime Draft . . . 2559b
Peach . . . 2487, 2493, 2495
Peale,
Charles Wilson . . . 1789
Rembrandt . . . 3236d
Peanuts . . . 3507
Pear . . . 2488, 2494, 2495A
Pearle Harbor . . . 2559i
Peary, Admiral Robert . . . 1128, 2223
Peashooter Airplane . . . 3142o
Peck, Gregory . . . 4526
Pecos Bill . . . 3086
Pegasus Constellation . . . 3948
Pelican
Brown . . . 1466
Island National Wildlife Refuge . . . 3774
Pember, Phoebe . . . 2975r
Penguins, King . . . 2708
Penn
Academy . . . 1840
William . . . 724
Pennsylvania . . . 1634, 1990, 3598, 3733
Academy of Fine Arts . . . 1064, 1840
Avenue . . . 2561
State University . . . 1065
Statehood . . . 2337
Toleware . . . 1775-1778
Pepper, Claude . . . 3426
Peppers, Chili . . . 4003, 4012, 4013
Percy Crosby's “Skippy” . . . 3151m
Peregrine Falcon . . . 4057, 4609
Performing Arts . . . 1755-1756, 1801, 1803, 2012, 2088, 2090, 2110, 2211, 2250, 2411, 2550
Periodical cicada . . . 3351r
Perisphere . . . 853
Perkins, Frances . . . 1821
Perry
Commodore . . 144, 155, 166, 177, 191, 202, 218, 229, 261
Commodore Oliver Hazard . . . 276-276A
Matthew C. . . . 1021
Perry Mason . . . 4414n, UX580
Pershing, Gen. John J. . . . 1214
Persian Cat . . . 2375
Persistent Trillium . . . 1783
Personal Computers . . . 3190n
Peter Pan . . . 4193
Petersburg, Battle of . . . 4910
Petrified Wood . . . 1538
Petroleum Industry . . . 1134
Phantom of the Opera, The . . . 3168
Pharmacy . . . 1473
Pheasant . . . 2283, 3050-3051, 3055. 1993
Phil Silvers Show . . . 4414l, UX581
Philadelphia
Exchange . . . 1782
Light Horse Flag . . . 1353
Philatelic
Americans, Society of . . . 797
Exhibition, International Centenary . . . 948
Exhibition, Third International . . . 778
Exhibitions 948, 1632, 1757, 2145, 2216-2217, 2218-2219
Exhibitions, Centenary International . . . 948
Exhibitions, Fifth National . . . 1075-1076
Exhibitions, Trans-Mississippi . . . 751
Society, American . . . 730-731, 750, 766, 770
Phillips,
Ammi . . . 3236c
Coles . . . 3502e
Philippines (Corregidor) . . . 925
Phlox . . . 4754
Phoenix . . . 2406
Photography . . . 1758, 3649
George Eastman . . . 1062
Physical Fitness . . . 2043
Sokols . . . 1262
Piaf, Edith . . . 4692
Piano . . . 1615C
Pickett, Bill (Ben Pictured) . . . 2869g
Pickett, Bill . . . 2870g
Pierce
Arrow . . . 2382
Franklin . . . 819, 2217e
Pika . . . 2319
Pilgrim Tercentenary . . . 548-550
Pilgrims . . . 548-550
Landing of the . . . 1420
Pine Cone . . . 2491, 4478, 4479, 4480, 4481, 4482, 4483, 4484, 4485
Pink Rose . . . 2492
Pinks . . . 4760
Pioneer
10 . . . 3189i
10 Jupiter . . . 1556
11 . . . 2573
Pioneers of Aviation . . . C91-C96, C99-C100, C113-C114, C118-C119, C128-C129
Pioneers of Industrial Design . . . 4546
Piper
Cub . . . C129
William T. . . . C129, C132
Piping Plover . . . 3105n, 4352c
Piping Plover Nestlings . . . 4352i
Pitcher, Molly (Battle of Monmouth) . . . 646
Pitts, Zasu . . . 2824
Pittsburgh Steelers . . . 3189e
Pixar Films . . . 4553-57, 4677-81, UX622-26, UX628-32
Plains
Indian . . . 3151g
Prickly Pear . . . 2685
Plan for Better Cities . . . 1333
Plane . . . C77
and Globes . . . C89
Globes and Flag . . . C90
Plants . . . 4915
Plastic Man . . . 4084g, 4084q
Plath, Sylvia . . . 4658
Pledge of Allegiance . . . 2593-2594
Ploesti Refineries, bombing of . . . 2765d
Pluto . . . 2577
Plymouth Hemi Barracuda . . . 4747
Pocahontas . . . 330
Poe, Edgar Allan . . . 986, 4377
Poets . . . 864-868, 986, 1405, 1436, 1446, 1485, 1526, 1554, 1926, 2239, 2449, 4654-4662
Poinsettia . . . 1256, 4816b
Piont Judith Lighthouse . . . 4794
Poland . . . 909
(von Steuben, General) . . . 689
Poland's Millennium . . . 1313
Polar
Bear . . . 1429, 1885, 3291
Explorers . . . 1128, 1431, 2220-2223
Police, Patrol Wagon . . . 2258
Poling, Clark V. . . . 956
Polio . . . 1087, 3187a
Polk, George . . . 4250
Polk, James K. . . . 816, 2217b, 2587
Pollock, Jackson . . . 3186h
Polo . . . 2759
Polo Grounds, New York City . . . 3514
Pomegranate . . . 4253, 4260
Ponderosa Pine . . . 4478, 4482
Pongo and Pup . . . 4342
Pons, Lily . . . 3154
Ponselle, Rosa . . . 3157
Pontiac GTO . . . 4744
Pontiac Safari . . . 4355
Pony Express . . . 894, 1154
Rider . . . 2780
Poor, Salem . . . 1560
Popcorn Wagon . . . 2261
Popeye . . . 3000k
Poppy . . . 4173, 4183
Popular Singers . . . 2849-2853
Porgy & Bess . . . 1484, 2768
Porkfish . . . 1828
Porky Pig . . . 3534-3535
Porter
Cole . . . 2550
David D. . . . 792
Katherine Anne . . . 4030
Portland Head Lighthouse . . . 4791
Portrait of Richard Mather by John Foster . . . 3236a
Portsmouth Harbor Lighthouse . . . 4792
Post
Emily . . . 3182f
Office Department . . . O47-O56, O108
Office Department Building . . . C42
Office, First Automated . . . 1164
Office, Truck . . . E14, E19
Rider . . . 113, 1478
Wiley . . . C95-C96
Stamp Centenary . . . 947, 948
Postwar Baby Boom . . . 3186l
Postal
Conference, International . . . C66
Service 1164, 1238, 1396, 1489-1498, 1572-1575, 2420, 2539

Portsmouth Harbor Ligthouse ... 4792
Posting a Broadside ... 1477
Postman and Motorcycle ... E12-E13, E15-E18
Potomac River ... 1366
Poultry Industry ... 968
Powell, John Wesley ... 1374
Powered Flight ... 3783
POWs-MIAs ... 1422, 2966
Powatan, USS ... 792
Powered Flight ... C47
Prairie Crab Apple ... 3196
Prairie Ironweed ... 4156, 4156a
Preamble to the Constitution ... 2355-2359
Prehistoric Animals ... 2422-2425, 3077-3080, 3136
Preservation of Wildlife Habitats ... 1921-1924
Preserve
the Environment (Expo '74) ... 1527
Wetlands ... 2092
Presidential Issue '38 . 803-804, 806-824, 826-831, 832-834, 839-851
Presidential Libraries ... 3930
Presidents Miniature Sheets '86 ... 2216-2219
Presidents Miniature Sheets '86 (Stamp Collecting) ... 2201
Presley, Elvis ... 2721, 2724, 2731
Pressed Glass ... 3327
Prevent Drug Abuse ... 1438
Priestley, Joseph ... 2038
Primrose ... 4763
Prince Valiant ... 3000s
Princeton
George Washington at ... 1704
University (Nassau Hall) ... 1083
Prinsesse Tam-Tam Poster ... 4338
Printed Circuit Board ... 1501
Printing ... 857
Press ... 857, 1014, 1119, 1476, 1593, 2779
Priority Mail . 2419, 2540, 2543, 2544, 3261, 3472, 3647, 4018, 4144, 4268, 4378, 4438, 4511, 4649
Prisoners of War ... 2966
Proclamation
Emancipation ... 1233
of Peace, American Revolution ... 727, 752
Professor Minerva McGonagall ... 4836
Professor Severus Snape ... 4834
Professional
Baseball ... 1381
Management ... 1920
Progress
Alliance for ... 1232, 1234
in Electronics ... 1500-1502, C86
of Women ... 959
Prohibition enforced ... 3184c
Project Mercury ... 1193
Prominent Americans ... 1278-1283, 1283B, 1284-1286A, 1287-1288, 1288B, 1289-1294, 1299, 1303-1304, 1304C, 1305, 1305C, 1393-1395, 1397-1402
Pronghorn Antelope ... 1078, 1889, 2313, 4048
Propeller, Wooden, and Airplane Radiator ... C4
Prostate Cancer Awareness ... 3315
Providence, RI ... 1164
P.S. Write Soon ... 1806, 1808, 1810
Pteranadon ... 2423
PUAS, America ... 2426, 2512, C121, C127
PUASP, America/ ... C131
Public
Education ... 2159
Hospitals ... 2210
Pueblo Pottery ... 1706-1709
Puerto Rico
(Clemente, Roberto) ... 2097
Columbus Landing in ... 2805
(De Leon, Ponce) ... 2024
Election ... 983
(Marin, Luis Munoz) ... 2173
San Juan ... 1437
Territory ... 801
Pulaski, General ... 690
Pulitzer, Joseph ... 946
Puller, Lt. Gen. Lewis B. ... 3962
Puma ... 1881
Pumper, Fire ... 1908
Pumpkinseed Sunfish ... 2481
Puppy ... 3671
Puppy and Kitten ... 2025
Pure Food and Drug Act ... 1080, 3182f
Purple Finch ... 1981
Purple Heart ... 3784-3784A, 4032, 4263, 4264, 4164, 4390, 4529, 4704, 4704a
Purple Nightshade ... 4153, 4153a
Pushcart ... 2133
Putnam, Rufus ... 795
Pyle
Ernie ... 1398
Howard ... 3502h
Quaking Aspen ... 4072
Quarter
Horse ... 2155
Seated ... 1578
Queen of Hearts ... 4405
Quill
Inkwell and ... 1535, 1581, 1811
Pen ... 1099, 1119, 1230, 1250, 2360, 2421
Quilts
American ... 1745-1748, 3524-3527, 4089-4098
Basket Design ... 1745
Quimby, Harriet ... C128
Rabbit ... 3272
Raccoon ... 1757h, 2331
Racing
Car ... 2262
Horse ... 1528
Radiator, Airplane, and Wooden Propeller ... C4
Radio
Amateur ... 1260
entertains America ... 3184i
Waves ... 1260, 1274, 1329
Raggedy Ann, by Johnny Gruelle ... 3151c
Railroad
Baltimore & Ohio ... 1006
Engineers ... 993
Lantern ... 1612
Mail Car ... 2265
Roundhouse ... 4710m
Transcontinental ... 922
Railway
Car, Cog ... 2463
Mail Car ... 2781
Rainbow Bridge ... 4060
Rainey, "Ma" ... 2859
Ramirez, Martin ... 4968-72
Rand, Ayn ... 3308
Randolph, A. Philip ... 2402
Range Conservation ... 1176
Raphael Semmes ... 2975i
Raspberries ... 3295, 3300, 3303, 3407
Ratification of the Constitution ... 835, 2336-2348
Ration Coupons ... 2697b
Rawlings, Marjorie Kinnan ... 4223
Ray, Man ... 3649i
Rayburn, Sam ... 1202
Read, George ... 1687e, 1694
Readers, A Nation of ... 2106
Reagan, Ronald ... 3897, 4078, 4494
Rebecca Everingham Riverboat ... 3094
Rebecca of Sunnybrook Farm ... 2785
Recognizing Deafness ... 2783
Recovering Species ... 3191g
Recreational Sports ... 2961-2965
Red Ball Express speeds vital supplies, 1944 ... 2838h
Redding, Otis ... 2728, 2735
Red
Admiral Butterfly ... 4352j
Bat ... 3661
Cloud ... 2175
Cross, American ... 702, 967, 1910
Cross, International ... 1016, 1239
Fox ... 1757g, 2335, 3036, 4352b
Grange ... 3811
headed Woodpecker ... 3045
Maids ... 2692
Nosed Reindeer ... 2792, 2797, 2802
Sea Urchin ... 4423b, UX587
Squirrel ... 2489
winged Blackbird ... 2303
Red Skelton Show ... 4414c, UX582
Redding, Otis ... 2728, 2735
Redhead Decoy ... 2141
Red-headed Woodpecker ... 3032
Redwood Forrest ... 4378
Reed, Dr. Walter ... 877
Refuge National Park, City of ... C84
Register and Vote ... 1249, 1344
Reindeer ... 3356, 3357, 3358, 3359, 3360,3361, 3362, 3363, 3364, 3365, 3366, 3367, 4207, 4211, 4215, 4425, 4429 4712, 4714
Religious Freedom in America ... 1099
"Remember the Maine" ... 3192
Remington, Frederic ... 888, 1187, 1934, 3502p
Remy the Rat ... 4554
Renwick, James ... 1838
Representatives, House of ... 2412
Reptiles, Age of ... 1390
Reptiles and Amphibians ... 3814-3818
Republic P-47 Thunderbolt ... 3919
Republic of
China ... 1188
Palau ... 2999
Texas ... 776, 778, 2204
the Marshall Islands ... 2507
Research, Health ... 2087
Residential subdivision ... 4710k
Resolution ... 1733
Restaurantionen ... 620
Retarded Children ... 1549
Reticulate Collared Lizard ... 3816
Reticulated Helmet ... 2118
Retriever,
Chesapeake Bay ... 2099
Golden ... 4455
Yellow Labrador ... 4454
Return to Space ... 3191h
Reuter, Ernst ... 1136-1137
Revel, Bernard ... 2193
Revere, Paul ... 1048, 1059A
Rhead, Frederick Hurten ... 4546b
Rhode Island ... 1645, 1991, 3599, 3734
Flag ... 1349
Red ... 1991
Settlement ... 777
Statehood ... 2348
Windmill ... 1739
Rhodochrosite ... 1541
Rhythm & Blues/Rock & Roll ... 2724-2737
Ribault Monument, Jan ... 616
Richard Nixon ... 2955
Richardson, Henry Hobson ... 1839
Rickenbacker, Eddie ... 2998, 2998a
Riley, James Whitcomb ... 868
Ring Nebula ... 3385
Ring-necked Pheasant ... 1993
Ringmaster ... 2751
Ringtail ... 2302
Rio Grande ... C134, UX642
Rio Grande Blankets ... 3926-3929
Rise of the Spirit of Independence ... 1476-1479
Riverboats ... 3091-3095
River Otter ... 2314
Road Racer ... 4689
Roadrunner ... 1983
Road Runner and Wile E. Coyote ... 3391-3392
Roanoke Island Settlement, Virginia Dare ... 796
Roanoke Voyages ... 2093
Robert E. Lee Riverboat ... 3091
Robeson, Paul ... 3834
Robie House, Chicago ... 3182o
Robin ... 1959, 1974, 2001
Robinson
Edward G. ... 3446
Jackie ... 2016, 3186c, 3408a
Sugar Ray ... 4020
Rochambeau, Count de ... 703
Rock 'n Roll ... 3187m
Rock & Roll/Rhythm & Blues Musicians ... 2721-2737
Rockne, Knute ... 2376
Rockwell, Norman ... 2839, 2840, 3502s
Rocky Marciano, undefeated ... 3187k
Rocky Mountains ... 288, 4062
Beacon on ... C11
Roethke, Theodore ... 4663
Rodgers, Jimmie ... 1755
Rodgers & Hammerstein ... 3348
Rogers,
Roy ... 4446, UX597
Will ... 975, 1801
Rohde, Gilbert ... 4546l
Rojas-Lombardi, Felipe ... 4923
Romanesque Facade ... 4444i
Ron Weasley ... 4826,4827
Roosevelt
Eleanor ... 1236, 2105, 3185d
Franklin D. ... 930-933, 1284, 1298, 1305, 1950, 2219d, 2559d, 3185a
(Rough Riders) ... 973
(Sagamore Hill) ... 1023
Theodore ... 557, 586, 602, 637, 648, 663, 674, 830, 856, 1011, 1039, 2218g, 2523, 3182b, C88,
Roses ... 1737, 1876, 2378-2379, 2490, 2492, 2833, 3049, 3054, 4959
Rose-breasted Grosbeak ... 1959
Roseate Spoonbill ... 2308
Rosebud Orchid ... 2670
Rosetta, Sister ... 3219
Ross
Betsy ... 1004
George ... 1004
Rotary International ... 1066
Rothko, Mark ... 3236t
Rough Riders ... 973
Round-lobed Hepatica ... 2677
Rover
Lunar ... 1435
Surface ... C124, C126C
Rowlf the Dog ... 3944i
Royal
Poinciana ... 3311
Wulff ... 2545
RR Caboose ... 1905
Rube Goldgerg's Inventions ... 3000f
Rubens Peale with Geranium by Rembrandt Peale ... 3236d
Rubeus Hagrid ... 4835
Ruby-throated Hummingbird ... 2642
Rudbeckia ... 2997

Rudolph
the Red-Nosed Reindeer 4946-49
Wilma 3422, 3436
Rue Anemone 2694
Ruffled Grouse 1924, 1990
Rufous Hummingbird 2645
Rural
America 1504-1506
Electrification Administration 2144
Free Delivery 3090
Mailbox 1730
Rush Lamp and Candle Holder 1610
Rushing, Jimmy 2858
Rushmore, Mount 1011, 2523-2523A, C88
Russell,
Charles M. 1243
Richard 1853
Ruth, Babe 2046, 3184a, 3408h
Rutledge, Edward 1687e, 1694
S Class 3373
S.S. Adriatic 117
Saarinen, Eeno 2022
Sabertooth Blenny 1830
Saber-tooth Cat 3080
Sabin, Dr. Albert 3435
Sabine Pass Lighthouse 4410, U670, UX563
Sacagawea 1063, 2869s, 2870s
Sackville, Surrender of Fort 651
Saddlebred Horse 2157
Safety 1007
Traffic 1272
Sagamore Hill (Home of Theodore Roosevelt) 1023
Saguaro Cactus 1192, 1945, 1955, 4035, 4155, 4155a
Sailboat UX633
Saint
Augustine 927
Charles Streetcar 2062
Gaudens, Augustus 886
Lawrence Seaway 1131, 2091
Saipan, Battle of 2838g
Salazar, Ruben 4251
Salem, Peter 1361
Salk, Dr. Jonas 3428
Salomon, Haym 1561
Salsa 3940
Salt evaporation pond 4710f
Salute to Youth 963
Salvation Army 1267
Sam the Eagle and Flag 3944c
Sampson, William T. 793
San Diego, CA 773, 778
San Francisco 567, 698
49ers 3190c
Bay 400-400A
Cable Car 1442, 2263
Discovery of 400A, 404
Garter snake 3105k
(Golden Gate) 567, 698
Oakland Bay Bridge, Plane over C36
San
Gabriel Mission, CA C116
Idlefonso Pot 1707
Juan, Puerto Rico 1437
Martin, Jose de 1125-1126
Xavier del Bac Mission 1443
Sand Island Lighthouse 4412, U672, UX565
Sandburg, Carl 1731
Sandy Hook Lighthouse 1605, 2474
Santa
Claus . . . 1472, 1508, 1800, 2064, 2108, 2579, 2580-2585, 2873, 3004, 3110, 3115, 3537-3544, 3822, 3823, 3826, 3827, 3883-3894, 3949, 3953, 3957, 4713, 4948
Fe, NM 944, 1031A, 1054A
Maria 232
Santa Claus Nutcracker 4361, 4365, 4369
Saratoga
Battle of 1728
US 791
Victory at 2590
Sargent, Gov. Winthrop 955
Saroyan, William 2538
Satellite 1575, 3187d
Saturn 2574
Sault Ste. Marie 1069
Savannah 923
Save Our
Air 1413
Cities 1411
Soil 1410
Water 1412
Save Vanishing Species B4
Savings
and Loans 1911
Bonds, US 2534
Bonds—Servicemen 1320
Saw-Whet Owl 1761, 2284
Sawtooth Mountain, ID 2439
Sawyer, Tom 1470
Saxhorns 1614
Scarlet
Kingsnake 3814
Tanager 2306, 4888
Scenic American Landscapes C133-C150, UX634-43
Schaus swallowtail butterfly 3105f
Schley, Winfield S. 793
School
Bus 2123
Teachers 1093
Schoolhouse, One-Room 1606
Schurz, Carl 1847
Science & Industry 2031
Sciences, The 1237
Scientists 874-878, 953, 1074, 1080, 1285, 1488, 1774, 2699, 2746, 3533, 3906-3909, 4022, 4224-27, 4541-44
Scissor-tailed Flycatcher 1988
Scootles 3151j
Scorpionfly 3351s
Scott
Blanche Stuart C99
General Winfield 24, 142, 153, 164, 175, 200, 786
Jock 2546
Scotts Bluff, NE 1060
Scuba Diving 2863-2866
Screenwriting 3772a
Sea 4893
Creatures of the 2508-2511
Cucumber 3440
Lion, Northern 2509
Otter 2510
Seal 683, 775, 778, 794, 897, 927, 940, 955, 972, 974, 979, 995, 1001-1002, 1005, 1015, 1018, 1066, 1091, 1095-1096, 1127, 1131, 1151, 1156,1167, 1194, 1234, 1266, 1308, 1314, 1419, 1421,1432, 1525, 1559, 1560, 1561, 1565-1570, 1825, 2142, 2336, C40
Surface temperatures 4893
Fur 1464
Harbor 1882
Hawaiian Monk 3105c
Sealed Envelopes 2150
Seamstress 1717
Seaplane 2468
Searchers, the 4668
Search for Peace (Lions International) 1326
Seashells 2117-2121
Seated Liberty Quarter 1578
SEATO 1151
Seattle World's Fair 1196
Secretariat Wins Triple Crown 3189g
Seeing Eye Dogs 1787
Sego Lily 2667
Seinfeld Sitcom Sensation 3191c
Selma, Alabama March 3937i
Seminole
Doll 3873e
Seal 972
Semmes, Raphael 2975i
Senate, US 2413
Seneca Carving 3873i
Sequoyah 1859
Serling, Rod 4414s, UX585
Serra, Father Junipero C116
Service Women 1013
Servicemen
Disabled American Veterans and 1421-1422
Savings Bonds 1320
Sesame Street 3189c, 5394
Sessile Belwort 2662
Sevareid, Eric 4252
Sevier, Gov. John 941
Seward, William H. 370, 371
Shadoo, Chief 683
Shakespeare, Wiliam 1250
Sheeler, Charles 3236r
Shepard, Alan 4527
Sheridan, Gen. Philip 787
Sherman
General William T. 225, 257, 272, 787, 2975q
Roger 1687a, 1693
Shibe Park, Philadelphia 3518
Shield, Eagle and Flags 121
Shiloh, Civil War Centennial 1179, 2975e
Ship
Figurehead 2241
Liberty 2559h
Shipbuilding 1095
Shiprock, NM 1191
Shooting Star 2654
Shore, Dinah 4414i, UX569
Shorthair Cat
American 2375
Exotic 2372
Shoshone Headdress 2505
Shot Heard Round the World, The 3187c
Show Boat 2767
Showy Evening Primrose 2671
Shuttle 1913-1914, 1917, 1919, C125, C126a, C126d
Siamese Cat 2372
Sicily, Invasion of 2765c
Sickle Cell Disease Awareness 3877
Sierra Juniper 4618
Sign Language, American 2783-2784
Signing of the
Constitution 798, 2360
Mayflower Compact 550
Sikorsky, Igor C119
Simpsons 4399-4403, UX557-61
Homer 4399, UX557
Marge 4400, UX558
Bart 4401, UX559
Lisa 4402, UX560
Maggie 4403, UX561
Silver
Centennial 1130
Coffeepot 3759
Silver Bells Wreath 4936
Silver (horse) 4414m, UX578
Silvers, Phil 4414l, UX581
Silversmith 1457
Sims, Admiral William S. 4440
Sinatra, Frank 4265
SIPEX 1310-1311
Sisler, George 3408e
Sitting Bull 2183
Skateboarding 3321
Skaters 3117, 4937, 4941
Skating, inline 3324
Skelton, Red 4414c, UX582
Ski Jumping 3552
Skiing, Alpine 3180
Skilled Hands for Independence 1717-1720
Skylab 1915
Skylab I 1529
Skyscraper apts 4710n
Sled, Dog 1128, 2135
Sleeping Beauty 4344
Sleepy Hollow, Legend of 1548
Sleigh 1384, 1551, 1900, 2400, 2428
Slinky, 1945 . . . . . 3186m
Sloan, John 1433
Slolam 2807
Smiley Face 3189m
Smith
Alfred E. 937
Bessie 2854
Captain John 328
Jessie Willcox 3502l
Kate 4463
W. Eugene 3649n
Smithsonian Institution 943, 1838, 3059
Smokey the Bear 2096
Smooth Solomon's Seal 2691
Snelling, Fort 1409
Snowangel 4940, 4944
Snowboarding 3323, 3553, 4436
Snow-covered buildings 4715
Snowdrop 3028
Snowflakes 4101-4116,4808-12
Snowman . . . 2793, 2796, 2799, 2803, 3950, 3954, 3958, 4209, 4213, 4217,3676, 3677, 3678, 3679, 3680, 3681, 3682, 3683, 3684, 3686, 3687, 3688, 3689, 3690, 3691, 4209, 4213, 4217, 4426, 4430, 4938, 4942
Snow White and the Seven Dwarfs 3185h, 3915
Snowy
Egret 2321
Owl 3290
Soccer, Youth 3401
Social Security Act 2153
Society of Philatelic Americans 797
Softball 2962
Soft Shield Fern 4849, 4875
Soil
Conservation 1133
Conservation, Water and 2074
Save our 1410
Sokols, Physical Fitness— 1262
Solar Energy 2006, 2952
Soldier Nutcracker 4363, 4367, 4371
Solo Transatlantic Flight, Lindbergh's 1710, C10
Songwriters 3100-3103
Sonoran Desert 3293
Soo Locks 1069
Sound 3772j
Recording 1705
Sousa, John Philip 880
South Carolina 1640, 1992, 3600, 3735
Morris Island 3789
Settlement 1407
Statehood 2343
South Dakota 1672, 1993, 3601, 3736
Statehood 858, 2416
South-East Asia Treaty Organization (SEATO) 1151
Southern
Dogface Butterfly 4156, 4156a
Florida Wetland 4099

Magnolia . . . 3193
Sea Otters . . . 4423b, UX587
Southwest Carved Wood Figure . . . 2426, C121
Southworth, Hawes . . . 3649a
Soyuz, Apollo . . . 1569-1570
Space
Accomplishment in (Apollo 8) . . . 1371
Accomplishments in . . . 1331-1332
Achievement Decade . . . 1434-1435
Achievements . . . 1912-1919
Achievement and Exploration . . . 3412
Adventure . . . 2631-2634
(Apollo Soyuz) . . . 1569-1570
Discovery . . . 3238-42
(Echo I—Communications for Peace) . . . 1173
Escaping the Gravity of Earth . . . 3411
Exploration . . . 2568-2577
Exploring the Solar System . . . 3410
Fantasy . . . 2741-2745
Firsts . . . 4527-28
(Fort Bliss) . . . 976
(Future Mail Transportation) . . . C122-C125, C126
(Goddard, Robert H.) . . . C69
(Mariner 10/Venus, Mercury) . . . 1557
(Moon Landing) . . . 2419, C76, 3413
Needle . . . 1196
(Palomar Mountain Observatory) . . . 966
(Pioneer 10/Jupiter) . . . 1556
Probing the Vastness of Space . . . 3409
(Project Mercury) . . . 1193
Shuttle . . . 2544-2544A, 2631, 3261-3262, 3411a, C125, C126a, C126d
Shuttle Program . . . 3190a
(Skylab I) . . . 1529
Vehicle . . . 2543
(Viking Missions) . . . 1759
(von Karman, Theodore) . . . 2699
Spacecraft . . . C122, C125, C126
Spaniel, Cocker . . . 2099
Spanish
American War . . . 3192
Settlement of the Southwest 1598 . . . 3220
Speaker . . . 1502
Speaker, Tris . . . 3408l
Speaker's Stand . . . 1582
Special
Effects . . . 3772i
Occasions . . . 2267-2274, 2395-2398
Olympics . . . 1788, 3191i, 3771
Olympics, Winter . . . 2142
Spectacle Reef (Lake Huron) . . . 2971
Sperry, Lawrence and Elmer . . . C114
Spicebush Swallowtail Butterfly . . . 4736
Spinybacked spider . . . 3351q
Spirit of '76 . . . 1629-1631
"Spirit of St. Louis", Lindbergh's . . . 1710, C10
Split Rock (Lake Superior) . . . 2969
Sport of the Gods Poster . . . 4337
Sport Utility Vechicles . . . 3191m
Sportin' Life . . . 1484
Sports
American . . . 2376-2377
Extreme . . . 3321-3324, 3191d
Recreational . 716-719, 855, 1146, 1189, 1262, 1381-1382, 1460-1462, 1528, 1695-1698, 1702-1703, 1788, 1790-1798, 1932-1933, 2016, 2027, 2029, 2033-2034, 2043, 2046, 2048-2051, 2067-2070, 2082-2085, 2089, 2097, 2142, 2247, 2369, 2376-2377, 2380, 2417, 2496-2500, 2560, 2756-2759, 2766, 2807-2811, 2962, 2965, C56, C85, C97, C101-C112
Sports Balls . . . 5203-5210
Summer . . . 3397
Spotted
Bat . . . 3664
Sandpiper . . . 4352f
Water Beetle . . . 3351o
Spreading Pogonia . . . 2078
Springarn, Joel Elias . . . 4384b
Squashblossoms Lace, Design . . . 2351
Squashes . . . 4006, 4009, 4015
Squirrel . . . 2489
Squirt . . . 4679
St. John, Virgin Islands . . . C145, UX608
St. Joseph (Lake Michigan) . . . 2970
St. Louis World's Fair, 1904 . . . 3182e
Stacking Chairs . . . 4333c
Stagecoach . . . 1120, 1572, 1898A, 2228, 2434, 2438a, 2448
Staggerwing Airplane . . . 3142j
Stamp
Collecting . . . 1474, 2198-2201, 2410, 2433
Expo '89 . . . 2410, 2433, 2433a-2433d
Expo '92, World Columbian . . . 2616
Stampin' the Future . . . 3414-3417
Stand Watie . . . 2975l
Standing Cypress . . . 2695
Stanley Steamer . . . 2132
Stanton
Edwin M. . . . 138, 149, 160, 171, 196
Elizabeth . . . 959
Star Fruit . . . 4254, 4261
Stargell, Willie . . . 4696
Star Route Truck . . . 2125
Star-Spangled Banner, 1814 . . . 3403k
Star Trek . . . 3188e
Stars
and Stripes . . . 2531, 3403
of the Silent Screen . . . 2819-2828
"Stars and Stripes Forever" . . . 3153
Starr, Brenda . . . 3000t
State
Birds & Flowers . . . 1953-2002
Capitols . . . 782, 838, 896, 903-904, 927, 941, 957, 996, 1001, 1232, 1308, 1407, 2337, 2342
Statehood Anniversary . . . 858
Statehood
Alabama . . . 1375
Alaska . . . 2066, C53
Arkansas . . . 2167
California . . . 997
Colorado . . . 1001, 1711
Connecticut . . . 2340
Florida . . . 927, 2950
Georgia . . . 2339
Hawaii . . . 2080, C55
Idaho . . . 896, 2439
Illinois . . . 1339
Indiana . . . 1308
Iowa . . . 942
Kansas . . . 1183
Kentucky . . . 2636
Louisiana . . . 1197
Maine . . . 1391
Maryland . . . 2342
Massachusetts . . . 2341
Michigan . . . 775, 778, 2246
Minnesota . . . 1106
Mississippi . . . 1337
Missouri . . . 1426
Montana . . . 858, 2401
Nebraska . . . 1328
Nevada . . . 1248
New Hampshire . . . 2344
New Jersey . . . 2338
New Mexico . . . 1191
New York . . . 2346
North Carolina . . . 2347
North Dakota . . . 858, 2403
Ohio . . . 1018
Oklahoma . . . 1092
Oregon . . . 1124
Rhode Island . . . 2348
South Carolina . . . 2343
South Dakota . . . 858, 2416
Tennessee . . . 941
Texas . . . 938
Vermont . . . 903, 2533
Virginia . . . 2345
Washington . . . 858, 2404
West Virginia . . . 1232
Wisconsin . . . 957
Wyoming . . . 897, 2444
Statesman, Acheson, Dean . . . 2755
Statler and Waldorf . . . 3944e
Statue of Liberty . . . 566, 696, 899, 908, 946, 995, 1035, 1041-1042, 1044, 1044A, 1057, 1075, 1320, 1594, 1599, 1619, 1816, 2147, 2224, 2599, 3122, 3122E, 3451-3453, 3466, 3476-3477, 3485, 3965-3970, 3972-3975, 3978-3983, 3985, 4486, 4488, 4490, C35, C58, C63, C80, C87
Steam Carriage . . . 2451
Steamboat Willie . . . 4343
Steamboats . . . 2405-2409, 2435, 2438b
Steamship (Savannah) . . . 923
Stearman Airplane . . . 3142l
Steel Industry . . . 1090
Steelers Win Four Super Bowls . . . 3189e
Steeplechase . . . 2756
Stefansson, Vihjalmur . . . 2222
Stegosaurus . . . 1390, 2424, 3136f
Steichen, Edward . . . 3649g
Steinbeck, John . . . 1773
Steiner, Max . . . 3339
Steinmetz, Charles . . . 2055
Stevens, Wallace . . . 4660
Stevenson, Adlai E. . . . 1275
Stewart, James . . . 4197
Stewart, Walter . . . 1686e
Stieglitz, Alfred . . . 3649h
Stillwell, Gen. Joseph . . . 3420
Stock car racing . . . 3187n
Stock Exchange, New York . . . 2630
Stock Market crash, 1929 . . . 3184o
Stocking . . . 2872
Stone
Harlan F. . . . 965
Lucy . . . 1293
Mountain Memorial . . . 1408
Stonewall Jackson . . . 2975s
Stourbridge Lion . . . 2362
Stokowski, Leopold . . . 3158
Straight-Spout Coffeepot . . . 1775
Strand, Paul . . . 3649o
Stratford Hall . . . 788
Stratojet Airplane . . . 3142h
Stravinsky, Igor . . . 1845
Strawberries . . . 3296, 3299, 3305, 3405
Stream Violet . . . 2655
Streamline design . . . 3185k
Streetcars . . . 2059-2062
Streetcar Named Desire, A 1947 . . . 3186n
Strickland, William . . . 1782
Stuart, Gilbert Charles . . . 884
Studebaker Goldenhawk . . . 4354
Studebaker Starliner . . . 3931
Stutz Bearcat . . . 2131
Stuyvesant, Peter . . . 971
Submarines shorten war in Pacific . . . 2838e
Suffrage, Woman . . . 1406
(Belva Ann Lockwood) . . . 2179
(Lucy Stone) . . . 1293
(Susan B. Anthony) . . . 784, 1051
Sugar Bowl . . . 1777
Sullivan
Anne & Helen Keller . . . 1824
Ed . . . 4414j, UX571
Expedition, Maj. Gen. John . . . 657
Louis . . . 1931
Summer Afternoon . . . 4918
Sunday Funnies . . . 4467
Beetle Bailey . . . 4468
Calvin and Hobbes . . . 4468
Archie . . . 4469
Garfield (the cat) . . . 4470
Dennis the Menace . . . 4471
Sun . . 616, 906, 950, 968, 1016, 1188, 1434, 1710, 1723-1724, 1915, 2340, 3410
Tower of the . . . 852
Yat-Sen . . . 906, 1188
Sunflower . . . 4347
Sunflower and Seeds . . . 4005, 4010, 4016
Sunset . . . 4919
Sunshine Skyway Bridge . . . 4649
Super Bowl I . . . 3188l
Super Chief . . . 3337
Supergirl . . . 4084i, 4084s
Superman . . . 3185f, 4084a, 4084k
Supersonic Flight . . . 3173
Support Our Youth—Elks . . . 1342
Supreme Court . . . 991, 1895, 1896, 2415
Black, Hugo . . . 2172
Brandeis, Louis D. . . . 4422c
Brennan, William J., Jr. . . . 4422b
Flag Over . . . 1894
Frankfurter, Felix . . . 4422a
Frieze (American Bar Association) . . . 1022
Holmes, Oliver Wendell . . . 1288, 1288B, 1305E
Jay, John . . . 1046
Justices . . . 4422
Marshall, John . . . 312, 1050
Moore, John Bassett . . . 1295
Story, Joseph . . . 4422d
Warren, Earl . . . 2184A
Surface Rover . . . C124, C126c
Surrender
at Appomattox Court House . . . 4981
at Saratoga . . . 644, 1728
of Cornwallis at Yorktown . . . 703, 1686
Surrey . . . 1907
Sutter's Mill . . . 954
Swallowtail . . . 1712, 4736
Sweden/USA . . . 2036
Swedish
Chef and Fruit . . . 3944f
Finnish Landing . . . 836
Pioneer . . . 958
(Stamp Collecting) . . . 2200
Sweet White Violet . . . 2659
Switzerland . . . 2532
Sylvan Dell Riverboat . . . 3092
Sylvester . . . 3204-3205
Synthetic Fuels . . . 2007
Szell, George . . . 3160
Taft
Sen. Robert A. Memorial . . . 1161
William H. . . . 685, 687, 831, 2218h
Tail fins, chrome . . . 3187g
Take Me Out To The Ballgame . . . 4341
Talking Pictures . . . 1727
Talman, William . . . 4414n, UX580
Tandem Bicycle . . . 2266
Tanner, Henry O. . . . 1486
Tarawa, Invasion of . . . 2765j
Tarbell, Ida M. . . . 3666
Taylor
Zachary . . . 179, 181, 185, 204, 817, 2217c

Robert Robinson....4958
Tea Caddy....1776
Teachers of America....1093
Teague, Walter Dorwin....4546e
Teddy Bear Created....3182k
Teddy Bears....3653-56
Teen fashions....3187b
Telecommunication Union, International....1274
Telegraph....890, 924
Telephone....893, 1683
Telescope....1919, 3409
Television....3186f
Camera, First....2058
Tennessee....1648, 1994, 3602, 3738
Statehood....941, 3070-3071
Valley Authority....2042
Williams....3002
Tennis....2964
Terrell, Mary Church....4384a
Terrier,
Boston....2098, 4459
Wire-Haired Jack Russell....4451
Territorial Issues....799-802
Territories, Pacific Trust, Northern Mariana Islands....2408
Terry, Sonny....3214
Terry and the Pirates....3000r
Tesla, Nikola....2057
Texaco Star Theatre....4414a, UX583
Texas....1660, 1995, 3603, 3739, 4323
(HemisFair '68)....1340
Republic of....776, 778, 2204
Statehood....938, 2968
Windmill....1742
Thank You!....2269, 5519-22
Thanksgiving....3546, 4417, 4418, 4419, 4420
That's All Folks....3534a, 3535a
Thayer, Sylvanus....1852
The Golden Wall....4444a
The Honeymooners....4414t, UX572
The Liver is the Cock's Comb....4444e
The Lone Ranger....4414m, UX578
The Tonight Show....4414r, UX584
The Twilight Zone....4414s, UX585
Theater Dance....1750
Thelonius Monk....2990
Thick-billed parrot....3105b
Thinking of You....2397
Thirteen Mile Woods....C144, USX634
Thirteenth Amendment....902
Thirty Mile Point (Lake Ontario)....2973
Thomas A. Edison....945
Thomas, Danny....4628
Thomson, Charles....1687, 1694
Thoreau, Henry David....1327
Thorpe, Jim....2089, 3183g
Three Graces....895
314 Clipper Airplane....3142r
Thurber, James....2862
Tibbett, Lawrence....3156
Tickseed....2653
Ticonderoga, Fort....1071
Tidal Basin....1318
Tiffany Lamp....3757
Tiger, Amur....B4
Tiger Beetle....4352g
Tiger Stadium, Detroit....3511
Tiger Swallowtail....2300
Tiger, White Bengal....2709
Tilghman, Bill....2869r, 2870r
Timothy Mouse....4194
Tinkerbell....4193
Tiomkin, Dimitri....3340
Titanic Blockbuster Film....3191l
Tlingit
Chief in Haida Ceremonial Canoe....1389
Sculptures....3873c
Tribe....1836
Tokyo Bay....1021
Tokyo Raid....2697a
Toleware, Pennsylvania....1775-1778
Toonerville Folks....3000g
Tops....4333i
Torch....978-979, 1015, 1066, 1096, 1110-1111, 1117-1118, 1125-1126, 1136-1137, 1144, 1147-1148, 1159-1160, 1165-1166, 1168-1169, 1174-1175, 1234, 1308, 2336
Liberty....1594, 1816, 2531A
of Enlightment....901
Toscanini, Arturo....2411
Tourmaline....1539
Touro Synagogue....2017
Tow Truck....2129
Tower of the Sun....852
Toy
Antique....3626-3629, 3638-3645
Ship....2714
Soldier....2794-2795, 2800, 4428, 4432
Steamer....2713, 2717
Train....2712, 2716, 2719
Toy Story 2....4680
Track Racing....2757
Tractor....1162, 2127
Trailer....2547-2548
Traditional Mail Delivery....2434-2438
Traffic Safety....1272
Trail, Oregon....2747
Trains on Inclined Tracks....4970
Trans-Mississippi
Exposition....285-293
Philatelic Exposition....751, 769
Reissue....3209-3210
Transatlantic
Airmail....C24
Flight, Solo....1710, C10
Transcontinental
Railroad....922
Telephone Line....3183e
Transistors....1501
Transpacific Airmail....C20-C22, C115
Transport Plane, Twin-Motor....C25-C31
Transportation....1897-1897A, 1898-1908, 2252-2256, 2258-2266, 2451, 2453, 2457, 2463-2464, 2466, 2468, 2905
Air-Cushion Vehicle....C123, C125, C126b
Airplane....649, 650, 934, 947, 1185, 1511, 1574, 1684, 1710, 2433, 2436, 2438c, 2468, C1, C2-C9, C10-C11, C20-C22, C25-C33, C35-C41, C44-C47, C68, C74, C91-C96, C99, C100, C113-C115, C118-C119, C128-C129
Ambulance....2128, 2231
Automobile....1162, 1286A, 1511, 1906, 2131-2132, 2262, 2381-2385, 2437, 2438d
Balloons....2032-2035, 2530, C54
Bicycle....1460, 1901, 2266, C110
Buggy....1360, 1370, 1505, 1902, 2124
Bus....1897, 2123, 2225
Cable Car....1442, 2263
Caboose, RR....1905
Canoe....2453
Carriage, Steam....2451
Cart....981, 2133
Classic (Mail)....2434-2438
Coal Car....2259
Cog Railway Car....2463
Elevator....2254
Ferryboat....2466
Fire Engine....971, 1908, 2264
Handcar....1898
Horses....235, 240, 287, 289, 400, 400A, 404, 618, 645, 783, 835, 894, 898, 944, 947, 950, 973, 1001, 1003, 1006, 1012, 1028, 1061, 1120, 1123, 1130, 1154, 1176, 1243, 1261, 1360, 1384, 1408, 1416, 1478-1479, 1505, 1528, 1548, 1551, 1559, 1686, 1689, 1794, 1934, 2059, 2341, 2345-2346, 2391, 2400, 2401, 2448
Jeep....2559c
Jet....1017, 1574, 2022, C47, C49, C51-C52, C57-C65, C75, C77-C78, C81-C82, C87, C89-C90, C98, C122, C126a
Locomotive....922, 947, 961, 993, 1006, 1506, 1573, 1755, 1897A, 1905, 2226, 2362-2366, 2402, 3333-3337
Lunar Rover....1435
Lunch Wagon....2464
Mail Car....2265
Monorail....1196
Motorcycle....1899
Railway Car, Cog....2463
Series....1898A, 2123-2132, 2134-2136
Ships and Boats....230-233, 235, 293, 329, 372-373, 398-399, 402-403, 548-549, 567, 614-615, 620-621, 683, 698, 736, 739, 746, 755, 762, 790, 792-793, 802, 836, 856, 923, 936, 939, 947, 951, 956, 984, 994, 997, 1000, 1003, 1010, 1017, 1021, 1027, 1063, 1069, 1088, 1091, 1095, 1109, 1128, 1197, 1207, 1239, 1258, 1270, 1271, 1322, 1325, 1335, 1356, 1358, 1374, 1389, 1409, 1420, 1433, 1441-1442, 1448, 1480-1483, 1567-1568, 1688, 1733, 1793, 1937, 1938, 2040, 2080, 2085, 2091, 2093, 2134, 2163, 2200, 2220, 2260, 2336, 2340, 2342, 2386-2387, 2404-2409, 2435, 2506-2507, 2529, 2529C, 2559, 2621, 2623, C130
Shuttle....C125, C126d
Sled....1128, 1461, 1702-1703, 2027, 2135
Sleigh....1384, 1551, 1900, 1940, 2400
Stagecoach....1120, 1572, 1898A, 2228, 2434, 2438, 2448
Steam Carriage....2451
Streetcar....2059-2062
Surface Rover....C124, C126
Tank....1026, 2559e
Topper (horse)....4414g, UX573
Tractor....1162, 2127
Tractor-Trailer....2457
Tricycle....2126
Truck....1025, 1162, 1572, 2125, 2129, 2457, 2559a, 2635
Wagon....240, 286, 289-290, 323, 783, 950, 958, 964, 970, 981, 997, 1018-1019, 1028, 1061, 1120, 1124, 1360, 1426, 1487, 1542, 1744, 1897, 1903, 1907, 2124, 2128, 2130, 2136, 2253, 2255, 2258, 2261, 2341, 2345-2346, 2403, 2448, 2452, 2452D, 2464
Wheelchair....1155, 1385, 2153, 2256
Zeppelin....C13-C15, C18
Trapeze, Circus....2752
Traynor, Pie....3408o
Treasury Department....O72-O82, O114-O120
Treaty
Antarctic....1431, C130
of Paris....2052
US-Japan....1158
Tree Planting....2953
Treefish....4423j, UX595
Trees....1240, 1245, 1376
American....1764-1767, 3193-3197
Trego, William T....1689
Tricycle....2126
Trident Maple....4621
Tri-Motor Airplane....3142p
Trinity Church....1839
Troops Guarding Train....289
Trout....1427, 3105j
Truck
Star Route....2125
Tow....2129
Trucking Industry....1025
Trudeau, Edward....3432a
True katydid....3351p
Truman, Harry S....1499, 1862, 2219f, 2981h, 3186d
Trumball, John....1361, 1686, 1686d
Trumpet Honeysuckle....2683
Truth, Sojourner....2203
Trylon....853
Tube, TV....1502
Tuberculosis....1823
Tubman, Harriet....1744, 2975k
Tucker, Richard....3155
Tufted Puffins....4737
Tugboat....2260
Tulip....2425-2427, 2517-2520, 2524-2527, 2762, ...3902, 4171, 4185, 4960
Tuna, Bluefin....2208
Tunnel with Cars and Busses....4972
Turk's Cap Lily....2681
Turners Society, American....979
TV Camera, Tube....1502
TV entertains America....3186f
TWA Terminal, New York....3910d
(Twain, Mark), Samuel L. Clemens....863, 1470, 4545
Tweety Bird....3204-3205
Twentieth (20th) Century Limited....3335
Twentieth Century Poets....4654-4662
Twinflower....2665
Twin-Motored Transport Plane....C25-C31
Two Against the White by Charles Sheeler....3236r
Two Medicine Lake....748, 764
Tybee Island, Georgia....3790
Tyler, John....815, 847, 2217a
Tyrannosaurus....2422, 5410-13
U-Boat Battles....2765a
Ulysses S. Grant....2975d
Umbrella Beach....2443
Underground Railroad....2975k
United
Confederate Veteran....998
(Dag Hammarskjold)....1203-1204
Headquarters....1203-1204
International Cooperation Year....1266
Nations....907, 1419, 2974
Nations Conference....928
Nations Memorial,....
Nations Secretariat....3186k
States enters WWI....3183i
(Stevenson, Adlai E.)....1275
Way....2275
Universal
(Classic Mail Transportation)....2434-2437
(Future Mail Transportation)....C126
Postal Union....1530-1537, 3332, C42-C44
Postal Union (Future Mail Transportation)....C122-C125
Uranus....2575
Urban Planning....1333
US
Air Force Academy....3838
Air Mail Service....C74
Canada Friendship....961
Capitol....649-650, 989, 992, 1013, 1152, 1202, 1365, 1368, 1503, 2114-2116, 2532, 2561, 3472, 3648, 4075b, 4983, C64, C65
Celebrates 200th Birthday....3189f
Congress....2559j
Frigate Constitution, Oct. 21....951
House of Representatives....2412
Japan Treaty....1158
Launches satellites....3187d
Map and Two Mail Planes....C7
Military Academy....789, 3560
(Morocco, Friendship With)....2349
Naval Academy....794, 3001
Netherlands....2003
Postage Stamp Centenary....947
Savings Bonds....2534
Senate....2413
Servicemen....1421-1422

& Soviets link up at Elbe River 2981d
Sweden Treaty 2036
Troops clear saipen bunkers 2838g
USA 2193, 2608A, 2608B
and Jet C75, C81
Netherlands 2003
USS
Arizona Memorial 4873
Constellation 3869
Holland 3376
Yorktown Lost 2697g
Utah 950, 1677, 1996, 3604, 3740, 4324
Settlement 950
Statehood 3024
(Zion National Park) 747, 763
Valens, Ritchie 2727, 2734
Valentino, Rudolph 2819
Valley
Carson, NV 999
Forge 645, 1689, 1729
of the Great Salt Lake 950
Van
Buren, Martin 813, 2201, 2216h
der Rohe, Mies 2020
Vanna venturi House 3910c
Vance, Vivian 4414b, UX575
VanDerZee, James 3649k
Varela, Padre Felix 3166
Variscite 2702
VCR's Transform Entertainment .3189h
Vega Airplane 3142d
Vehicle, Space 2543
Velvet ant 3351i
Venus Flytrap 3528
Venus Mercury, Mariner 10/ 1557
Vermillion Rockfish 4423f, UX590
Vermont .1646, 1997, 3605, 3741, 4325
Battle of Bennington and Independence 643
Statehood 903, 2533
Verrazano-Narrows Bridge 1258, 4052, 4872
Verville, Alfred C113
Vesper Sparrow 4352a
Veterans
Administration 1825
Administration of Foreign Wars 1525
Civil War 985, 998
Disabled American 1421
Honoring 3508
Korean 2152
of Foreign Wars 1525
of World War II 940
Vietnam 1802, 2109
World War I 2154
Vicksburg 4787
Victory, Allied 537
Video Games 3190l
Vietnam
Veterans 1802
Memorial 2109, 3190g
War 3188g
Viking
Mission to Mars 1759
Orbiter 2572
Ship 621
Villard, Oswald Garrison 4384c
Vincennes 651
Vintage
Black Cinema 4336-40
Mahogany Speed Boats 4160-63
See Packets 4754-63
Violet, African 2495
Violins, Weaver 1813
Virgin Island 802, 4326, C145, UX608
Virginia 1642, 1998, 3606, 3742, 4327
Bluebells 2668
Capes, Battle of the 1938
of Sagadahock 1095
Old Cape Henry 3787
Rotunda 1779
Windmill 1738
Virtual Reality 3191j
Voice of America 1329
Volcanic Crater 4710b
Volleyball 2961
Voluntarism 2039
Volunteer Firemen 971
Von
Karman, Dr. Theodore 2699
Steuben, Gen. Frederich 689, 1686, 1686d
Nessen,Gretta 4546i
Vote, Register and 1249
Voting Rights Act, 1965 . . . . .3937b
Voyager 2 2574-2576
Voyageurs National Park C148, UX643
V-mail 2765e
Wagner, Honus 3408q
Wagon
Bread 2136
Circus 2452, 2452D
Lunch 2464
Mail 1903
Oil 2130
Walk in the Water 2409
Walker, Dr. Mary 2013
Walker, Madam C.J. 3181
Wallace, Lila and DeWitt 2936
Wallenberg, Raoul 3135
Walloon, Huguenot 614-616
WALL-E 4557
Walt Disney Concert Hall 3910e
Walter Johnson 3408i
Wapiti 1886
War
Department O83-O93, O114-O120
of 1812 4703
Win the 905
Ward, Clara 3218
War Savings Bonds and Stamps .2765g
Warhol, Andy 3652
Warner, Pop 3144, 3149
Warren,
Earl 2184
Robert Penn 3904
Washington
and Jackson 2592
and Lee University 982
at Cambridge 617
at Princeton 1704
at Valley Forge 645, 1729, 1689
Bicentennial Issue 704-715
Booker T. 873, 1074
Bridge 1012
Crossing the Delaware 1688
D.C. 943, 989-992, 2561
Dinah 2730, 2737
(Executive Branch) 2414
George . . . 2, 4, 10-11, 13-17, 25-26, 31-37, 39, 41, 43-45, 47, 62B, 64-66, 68-70, 72, 74, 78-79, 82-83, 85, 85C-85E, 88-90, 94, 96-97, 99, 101, 104, 106-107, 109, 111, 115, 136, 147, 158, 169, 184, 194, 207, 210, 211B, 213-214, 219D, 220, 248-252, 279B, 301, 319-322, 332-342, 353-356, 358-366, 375-382, 384, 386, 388-389, 391, 393-396, 405-413, 424-430, 441-450, 452-459, 461-469, 481-496, 498-507, 519, 525-536, 538-546, 554, 577, 579, 583, 595, 599-599A, 606, 634-634A, 645-647, 660, 671, 688, 703-715, 720-722, 785, 804, 839, 848, 947-948, 982, 1003-1004, 1011, 1031, 1054, 1123, 1139, 1213, 1229, 1283, 1283B, 1304, 1304C, 1686, 1686c, 1688b, 1689, 1689b, 1729, 1952, 2081, 2201, 2216a, 2523, 2592, 3140, 3468A, 3475A, 3482, 3483, 3616-3619, 3819, C88
Headquarters 727, 730, 752, 766
Inauguration 854, 2414
John P. 956
Martha. . .306, 556, 585, 601, 636, 662, 673, 805, 840, 849
Monument. 649-650, 1158, 1366, 2149, 3473
(Mount Ranier National Park) 742, 750, 758, 770
State 1674, 1999, 3607, 3743, 4328
Statehood 858, 2404
(Steamboat) 2408
Territory 1019
(Touro Synagogue) 2017
Water
Conservation 1150
Conservation, Soil and 2074
Lillies 4964-67
Save Our 1412
Waterfowl
Conservation 1362
Preservation Act 2092
Waters
Ethel 2851
Muddy 2855
Watie, Stand 2975l
Watkins, Carleton E. 3649c
Waves of color 4717-20, 4953, 4954
Waxman, Franz 3342
Wayne
Gen. Anthony 680
John 2448, 3876, 4668
We Give Thanks 3546
Weather Vanes 4613-4617
Weaver Violins 1813
W.E.B. DuBois, social activist 3182l
Webb, Jack 4414e, UX570
Webster, Daniel. . 141, 152, 163, 174, 189, 199, 226, 258, 273, 282C, 283, 307, 725, 1380
Webster, Noah 1121
Wedding
Cake 4521, 4602, 4735
Doves 3998-3999
Flowers 4764, 4765, 4764a
Hearts 4271, 4272
Roses 4520
Yes I Do .4765, 4881, 4765, 4881
Wells, Ida B. 2442
West
Benjamin 1553
Gen. Joseph 683
Gull 4423b,UX587
Point, US Military Academy 789
Quoddy Head (ME) 2472
Virginia 1667, 2000, 3608, 3744, 4329,4790
Wildlife 2869p,2870p
Virginia Statehood 1232
Western Gull 4423b, UX587
Western Meadowlark. . . . 1968, 1978, 1979, 1986, 1989, 2002, 4882
Western Tanager 4884
Western Wildlife 2869p, 2870p
Weston, Eward 3649j
Westport Landing, MO. 994
Westwood Children, The by Joshua Johnson 3236h
Wetland Habitats 1921
Whale
Killer 2508
Oil Lamp 1608
Wharton
Edith 1832
Joseph 1920
Wheat Fields 1506
Wheatland (Home of James Buchanan) 1081
Wheel Chair 1155, 1385, 2153, 2256
Wheels of Freedom 1162
Wheelwright 1719
Whistler, James A. McNeill 737-738, 754, 885
Whistler's Mother 737-738, 754
Whitcomb, Jon 3502n
White
Bengal Tiger 2709
Cloud, Head Chief of the Iowas, The by George Catlin 3236k
Footed-Mouse 4352h
House 809, 844, 932, 990, 1208, 1240, 1338, 1338A, 1338D, 1338F, 1338G, 1935-1936, 2219, 2219e, 2609, 3445
House, Little 931
Josh 3215
Minor 3649t
Mountain Avens 2661
Oak 1766
Paul Dudley, Dr. 2170
Pine 1765
Plains, Battle of 629-630
Sanford 1928
Spotted Anemone 4423e, UX591
Sturgeon 4061
Walter 4384d
William Allen 960
White-Tailed Deer 1888, 2317
White-throated sparrow 4891
Whitman, Walt 867
Whitney, Eli 889
Whittier, John Greenleaf 865
Whooping Cranes 1098, 2868
Wightman, Hazel 2498
Wigmaker 1458
Wild
Animals 2705-2709
Columbine 2678
Flax 2696
Pink 2076
Thing 3991
Turkey 1077
Wildcat Airplane 3142t
Wilder, Billy 4670
Wilder, Thornton 3134
Wilderness, Civil War Centennial .1181
Wildflowers 2647-2696
Wildlife 1757, 1880-1889, 2478, 3033
American 2286-2335
Conservation 1077-1079, 1098, 1392, 1427-1430, 1464-1467, 1760-1763
Habitats, Preservation of 1921-1924a
Wile E. Coyote and Road Runner 3391-3392
Wiley, Harvey W. 1080
Wilkes, Lt. Charles 2387
Wilkins, Roy 3501
Willard, Frances E. 872
William T. Sherman 2975q
Williams
Hank 2723, 2771, 2775
Roger 777
Ted 4694
Tennessee 3002
William Carlos 4656
Willie and Joe 2765h
Willis, Frances E.. . . . . .4076b
Willos Ptarmigan 1954
Willkie, Wendell 2192
Wills, Bob. 2774, 2778
Willson, Meredith 3349

Wilson, Woodrow 623, 697, 832, 1040, 2218i, 3183k
Win the War 905
Windmills 1738-1742
Winfield Hancock 2975n
Winged
Airmail Envelope C79, C83
Globe C12, C16-C17, C19, C24
Winogrand, Garry 3649s
Winter
Aconite 3026
Fun 4937-44
Olympic Games '84 2067
Olympic Games '94 2807-2811
Pastime, by Nathaniel Currier 1702
Special Olympics 2142
Wire Base Tables 4333e
Wire Mesh Chair 4333j
Wisconsin 1662, 2001, 3206, 3609, 3745, 4330
Statehood 957, 3206
Tercentenary 739, 755
(Workman's Compensation Law) 1186
Wisdom Statue 3766
Witherspoon, John 1687c
Wizard of Oz, The 2445
Wolf
Howlin' 2861
Man, The 3172
Trap Farm National Park 1452, 2018
Wolfe, Thomas 3444
Wolverine 2327
Woman
American 1152
Clubs, General Federation of 1316
Women
In Military Service 3174
Join War Effort 2697h
Progress of 959
Suffrage 1406, 2980, 3184e
Support war effort 3186e
Voting Rights 2980, 5523
Women, Armed Services 1013
Women's Rights Movement 3189j
Wonder Woman 4084c, 4084m
Wonders
of America 4033-4072
of the Sea 2863-2866
Wood Carved Figurines 2240-2243
Woodchuck 2307
Wood Duck 2484-2485
Wooden Propeller, Airplane Radiator and C4
Woodland Caribou 3105l
Woodland Habitats 1924
Woodpecker, Red-headed 3032
Woodson, Carter G 2073
Woodstock 3188b, 5409
Woody 4680
Wool Industry, American 1423
Wooly Mammoth 3078
Workmen's Compensation 1186
World
Columbian Stamp Expo '92 . . . . 2616, 2624-2629
Cup Soccer Championships 1994, 2834-2837
Exposition, Louisiana 2086
Forestry Congress, Fifth 1156
Health Organization 1194
Peace Through Law 1576
Peace Through World Trade 1129
Of Dinosaurs 3136
Refugee Year 1149
Series 3187j, 3182n
STAMP EXPO '89 . . . . 2410, 2433
STAMP EXPO '92, Columbian 2616, 2624-2629
University Games 2748
War I 537, 2154, 2981d-2981j, 3183i
War II 899-901, 905, 907-908, 909-915, 917-921, 925-926, 929, 934-936, 939-940, 956, 969, 1026, 1289, 1424, 1869, 2186, 2192, 2559, 2697, 2765, 2838, 2981, 3186a
Wide Web 3191n
World's Fair '64 1244
Expo '74 1527
Expo Seattle '62 1196
Knoxville '82 2006-2009
New York 853
Wreath and Toys 1843
Christmas 3245-52, 4814
Silver Bells Wreath 4936
Wright
Airplane 649, C45, C47, C91
Brothers 3182g, C45, C47, C91-C92
Frank Lloyd 1280, 2019
Richard 4386
Russell 4546l
Wrigley Field, Chicago 3519
Wulfenite 2703
Wyeth, N.C 3502r
Wyoming 1676, 2002, 3610, 3746, 4331
Statehood 2444
Toad 3105g
(Yellowstone National Park) 744, 760, 1453
X-Planes 4018-4019
Yale Art and Architecture Building 3910i
Yankee Stadium, New York City 3513
Yat-Sen Sun 906, 1188
Year
International Women's 1571
of the Child, International 1772
of the Disabled, International 1925
2000 3369
Yellow Kid, The 3000a
Yellow . . . .
Bellied Marmot 4198c
Garden spider 3351d
Lady's -Slipper 2077, 2673
Popular 3195
Skunk Cabbage 2693
Submarine, Beatles 3188o
Trumpet 3529
Yellowstone National Park 744, 760, 1453
Yellow-tail Rockfish 4423e, UX591
YMCA Youth Camping 2160
Yoda 4143n, 4205
York, Alvin C 3395
Yorktown
Battle of 703, 1937
Sinking of the 2687g
Surrender of Cornwallis at 703, 1686
-Virginia Capes, Battle of 703, 1937-1938
Yosemite
Falls 4090
Flag over 2280
National Park 740, 751, 756, 769, UX609
You Bet Your Life 4414h, UX586
Young, CY 3408m
Young, Whitney Moore 1875
Youth
Camping, YMCA 2160
Salute to 963
Support our 1342
Year, International 2160-2163
Yugoslavia, Oct. 26 917
Yukon-Pacific Expostion, Alaska- 370-371
Zaharias, Babe 1932
Zeppelin
Between Continents C14
Century of Progress C18
over Atlantic C13
Passing Globe C15
Zia Pot 1706
Zinnia 2830, 4759
Zion National Park 747, 763, C146, UX610
ZIP Code 1511

GENERAL ISSUES

1847 – THE FIRST ISSUE
Imperforate

"For every single letter in manuscript or paper of any kind by or upon which information shall be asked or communicated in writing or by marks or signs conveyed in the mail, for any distance under three hundred miles, five cents; and for any distance over three hundred miles, ten cents . . . and every letter or parcel not exceeding half an ounce in weight shall be deemed a single letter, and every additional weight of half ounce, shall be charged with an additional single postage."

With these words, the Act of March 3, 1845, authorized, but not required, the prepayment of postage effective July 1, 1847, and created a need for the first United States postage stamps. Benjamin Franklin, as the first Postmaster General of the United States and the man generally regarded as the "father" of the postal system, was selected for the 5 cent stamp. As the first President of the United States, George Washington was designated for the 10 cent issue.

The 1847 stamps were released July 1, 1847, but were available only in the New York City post office on that date. The earliest known usages are July 7 for the 5 cent and July 2 for the 10 cent.

The best estimates are that 4,400,000 of the 5 cent and 1,050,000 of the 10 cent stamps reached the public. The remaining stocks were destroyed when the stamps were demonetized and could no longer be used for postage as of July 1, 1851.

Like most 19th century United States stamps, the first Issue is much more difficult to find unused than used. Stamps canceled by "handstamp" marking devices—usually carved from cork—are scarcer than those with manuscript, or "pen", cancels.

Issued without gum, the Reproductions of the 1847 issue were printed from entirely new dies for display at the 1876 Centennial Exposition and were not valid for postal use. The issue also was reproduced on a souvenir sheet issued in 1947 to celebrate the centenary of the First Issue. Differences between the 1847 issue, 1875 Reproductions and 1948 stamps are described in the Stamp Identifier at the front of this catalog. (Page XIX)

1, 3
Franklin

2, 4
Washington

SCOTT NO.	DESCRIPTION	UNUSED VF	UNUSED F	UNUSED AVG	USED VF	USED F	USED AVG
	1847 Imperforate (OG + 100%)						
1	5¢ red brown	3500.00	2000.00	1200.00	600.00	475.00	300.00
1	— Pen cancel	....	....	....	475.00	300.00	200.00
2	10¢ black . . .	20000.00	13000.00	7000.00	1200.00	900.00	700.00
2	— Pen cancel	....	....	....	800.00	700.00	600.00
	1875 Reprints of 1847 Issues, without gum						
3	5¢ red brown	1400.00	950.00	750.00	....	....	....
4	10¢ black	1700.00	1200.00	900.00	....	....	....

1851-61 – THE CLASSIC ISSUES

An act of Congress approved March 3, 1851, enacted new, reduced postage rates, introduced additional rates and made the prepayment of additional postage compulsory. Although the use of postage stamps was not required, the 1851 Act stimulated their use and paved the way for their required usage from July 1, 1855 on.

Under the Act of 1851, the basic prepaid single letter rate (defined as one-half ounce or less) was set at 3 cents. As this would be the most commonly used value, it was decided that a likeness of George Washington should grace the 3 cent stamp. Benjamin Franklin was assigned to the 1 cent stamp, which, among other usages, met the newspaper and circular rates.

Washington also appears on the 10, 12, 24 and 90 cent stamps and Franklin on the 30 cent value. Thomas Jefferson was selected for the new 5 cent stamp that was issued in 1856.

By 1857, improved production techniques and the increasing usage of stamps led to the introduction of perforated stamps that could be more easily separated. The result was the 1857-61 series whose designs are virtually identical to the 1851 set. The 1857-61 perforated stamps were set in the printing plates with very little space between each stamp. As a result, insufficient space was allowed to accommodate the perforations, which often cut into the design on these stamps. In fact, stamps with complete designs and wide margins on all four sides are the exception and command very substantial premiums.

The most fascinating—and most challenging—feature of the 1851-61 stamps is the identification of many major and minor types. An extremely slight design variation can mean a difference of thousands of dollars and collectors even today can apply their knowledge to discover rare, mis-identified types.

The various "Types", identified below by Roman numerals in parentheses, resulted from minor changes in the printing plates caused by wear or plate retouching. The 1851-57 one-cent blue stamp may be the most studied of all the United States issues and is found in seven major catalog-listed Types (14, if we count imperforate and perforated stamps separately), plus countless minor listed and unlisted varieties. A thorough explanation of the differences in the major types for all denominations of the 1857-61 series is contained in the Harris Stamp Identifier in this catalog.

Shortly after the outbreak of the Civil War, the 1851-61 stamps were demonetized to prevent Southern post offices from selling the stamps in the North to raise cash for the Confederate States. After the war, large supplies of unused 1857-61 stamps were located in Southern post offices and purchased by stamp dealers and collectors. This explains the relatively large supply of unused 1857-61 issues that still exist today. The short life and limited use of 90 cent high value, which was issued in 1860, and the 5 cent orange brown, released May 8, 1861, explains why those stamps sell for more used than unused.

5-9, 18-24, 40
Franklin

10, 11, 25, 26, 41
Washington

12, 27-30A, 42
Jefferson

13-16, 31-35, 43
Washington

17, 36, 44
Washington

SCOTT NO.	DESCRIPTION	UNUSED VF	UNUSED F	UNUSED AVG	USED VF	USED F	USED AVG
	1851-57 Imperforate (OG + 100%)						
5	1¢ blue (I).	....	....	....	....	69000.00	....
5A	1¢ blue (Ib).	13000.00	10750.00	8900.00	9500.00	6425.00	4475.00
6	1¢ dark blue (Ia).	22000.00	16700.00	12250.00	11000.00	8000.00	5275.00
7	1¢ blue (II)	500.00	375.00	250.00	250.00	175.00	100.00
8	1¢ blue (III).	9500.00	6000.00	4200.00	2500.00	1500.00	1000.00
8A	1¢ blue (IIIa).	5000.00	3400.00	2100.00	1725.00	1100.00	800.00
9	1¢ blue (IV).	350.00	270.00	175.00	200.00	125.00	85.00
10	3¢ orange brown (I) . .	2000.00	1200.00	800.00	225.00	180.00	140.00
11	3¢ deep claret (I)	200.00	185.00	75.00	30.00	17.25	15.00
12	5¢ red brown (I)	13650.00	10250.00	6750.00	1100.00	600.00	450.00
13	10¢ green (I).	11050.00	8500.00	6000.00	1175.00	650.00	475.00
14	10¢ green (II)	2300.00	1750.00	1350.00	300.00	200.00	180.00
15	10¢ green (III).	2500.00	1800.00	1300.00	300.00	200.00	180.00
16	10¢ green (IV)	18900.00	12500.00	10000.00	2000.00	1500.00	1150.00
17	12¢ black	3250.00	2500.00	1750.00	300.00	200.00	150.00

***NOTE:** For further details on the various types of similar appearing stamps please refer to our U.S. Stamp Identifier.*

37, 45
Washington

38, 46
Franklin

39, 47
Washington

SCOTT NO.	DESCRIPTION	UNUSED VF	UNUSED F	UNUSED AVG	USED VF	USED F	USED AVG
	1857-61 Same design as preceding Issue, Perf. 15-1/2 (†) (OG + 75%)						
18	1¢ blue (I)	1500.00	950.00	700.00	1000.00	550.00	300.00
19	1¢ blue (Ia)	22000.00	12500.00	9125.00	9000.00	5900.00	3790.00
20	1¢ blue (II)	750.00	525.00	400.00	400.00	290.00	160.00
21	1¢ blue (III)	8150.00	5500.00	4200.00	3000.00	1700.00	1200.00
22	1¢ blue (IIIa)	1350.00	950.00	650.00	795.00	425.00	300.00
23	1¢ blue (IV)	4900.00	3400.00	2400.00	1500.00	925.00	600.00
24	1¢ blue (V)	95.00	60.00	35.00	70.00	40.00	30.00
25	3¢ rose (I)	1750.00	1300.00	1000.00	230.00	153.50	97.25
26	3¢ dull red (III)	45.00	25.00	15.00	20.00	7.50	5.00
26a	3¢ dull red (IV)	350.00	265.00	185.00	170.00	120.00	85.00
27	5¢ brick red (I)	22000.00	15750.00	10750.00	2250.00	1685.00	900.00
28	5¢ red brown (I)	20000.00	13000.00	8500.00	2000.00	1350.00	825.00
28A	5¢ Indian red (I)	40000.00	20000.00	13000.00	3600.00	2800.00	2000.00
29	5¢ brown (I)	1800.00	975.00	725.00	590.00	325.00	200.00
30	5¢ orange brown (II)	925.00	650.00	500.00	2100.00	1400.00	800.00
30A	5¢ brown (II)	1250.00	975.00	650.00	475.00	275.00	180.00
31	10¢ green (I)	12000.00	9500.00	6000.00	1500.00	1100.00	650.00
32	10¢ green (II)	3200.00	2200.00	1650.00	450.00	220.00	150.00
33	10¢ green (III)	3200.00	2200.00	1650.00	375.00	295.00	190.00
34	10¢ green (IV)	22500.00	15750.00	12500.00	2600.00	2100.00	1650.00
35	10¢ green (V)	180.00	75.00	50.00	120.00	65.00	45.00
36	12¢ black, Plate I	1100.00	800.00	600.00	550.00	375.00	200.00
36b	12¢ black, Plate III	550.00	380.00	250.00	400.00	275.00	185.00
37	24¢ gray lilac	800.00	500.00	300.00	500.00	400.00	200.00
38	30¢ orange	1250.00	700.00	500.00	700.00	400.00	275.00
39	90¢ blue	1700.00	1100.00	600.00	10000.00	7750.00	5750.00
	1875 Reprints of 1857-61 Issue. Perf. 12 Without Gum						
40	1¢ bright blue	700.00	550.00	300.00	....	....	....
41	3¢ scarlet	5000.00	3200.00	2800.00	....	....	....
42	5¢ orange brown	3000.00	1700.00	1200.00	....	....	....
43	10¢ blue green	4300.00	3200.00	2200.00	....	....	....
44	12¢ greenish black	4500.00	3500.00	2000.00	....	....	....
45	24¢ blackish violet	5600.00	3800.00	2200.00	....	....	....
46	30¢ yellow orange	5400.00	3800.00	2200.00	....	....	....
47	90¢ deep blue	4500.00	3500.00	2000.00	....	....	....

THE 1861-67 ISSUE

The 1861-66 Issue and its 1867 Grilled varieties are among the most interesting and controversial of all stamps. Born out of the need to demonetize previously-issued stamps in the possession of Southern post offices, they were rushed into service shortly after the outbreak of the Civil War.

The controversy begins with the "August Issues", catalog #s 55-62B. It is now generally accepted that all but the 10 and 24 cent values never were issued for use as postage. The set is more aptly described as "First Designs", because they were printed by the National Bank Note Company and submitted to the Post Office Department as fully gummed and perforated sample designs.

63, 85A, 86, 92, 102
Franklin

64-65, 79, 82, 83, 85, 85C, 88, 94, 104
Washington

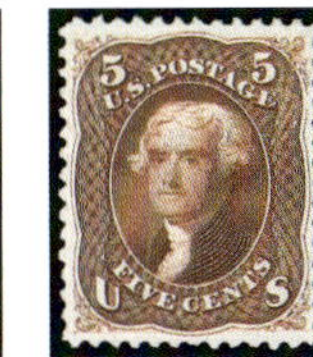
67, 75, 76, 80, 95, 105
Jefferson

62B, 68, 85D, 89, 96, 106
Washington

69, 85E, 90, 97, 107
Washington

70, 78, 99, 109
Washington

71, 81, 100, 110
Franklin

72, 101, 111
Washington

(†) means Issue is actually very poorly centered. Perforations may touch the design on "Fine" quality.

73, 84, 85B, 87, 93, 103
Jackson

77, 85F, 91, 98, 108
Lincoln

SCOTT NO.	DESCRIPTION	UNUSED VF	UNUSED F	UNUSED AVG	USED VF	USED F	USED AVG
	1861 First Design (†) Perf. 12 (OG + 75%)						
62B	10¢ dark green	3600.00	2200.00	1325.00	1900.00	1325.00	875.00
	1861-62 Second Design (†) Perf. 12 (OG + 75%)						
63	1¢ blue	160.00	85.00	60.00	55.00	40.00	25.00
64	3¢ pink	5500.00	3900.00	2800.00	750.00	575.00	400.00
64b	3¢ rose pink	325.00	250.00	190.00	165.00	115.00	90.00
65	3¢ rose	60.00	40.00	28.00	4.50	3.00	2.00
66	3¢ lake	2850.00	2100.00	1500.00	....	....	....
67	5¢ buff	11550.00	7250.00	5500.00	975.00	700.00	550.00
68	10¢ yellow green	500.00	300.00	220.00	85.00	50.00	38.00
69	12¢ black	825.00	600.00	380.00	125.00	80.00	50.00
70	24¢ red lilac	1400.00	800.00	500.00	400.00	200.00	135.00
71	30¢ orange	1280.00	775.00	500.00	250.00	180.00	100.00
72	90¢ blue	1600.00	900.00	600.00	650.00	480.00	325.00
	1861-66 (†) (OG + 75%)						
73	2¢ black	200.00	120.00	75.00	115.00	75.00	45.00
75	5¢ red brown	2800.00	2200.00	1450.00	600.00	475.00	300.00
76	5¢ brown	700.00	450.00	275.00	170.00	120.00	70.00
77	15¢ black	2000.00	1325.00	850.00	220.00	185.00	115.00
78	24¢ lilac	1200.00	725.00	450.00	350.00	175.00	120.00

From 1867 to 1870, grills were embossed into the stamp paper to break the fiber and prevent the eradication of cancellations. The first "A" grilled issues were grilled all over. When postal clerks found that the stamps were as likely to separate along the grill as on the perforations, the Post Office abandoned the "A" grill and tried other configurations, none of which proved to be effective. The Grilled Issues include some of our greatest rarities. The most notable is the 1 cent "Z", only two of which are known to exist. One realized $4,400,000 in a 2024 auction, making it the most valuable United States stamp. The grills are fully explained and identified in the Harris Stamp Identifiers.

SCOTT NO.	DESCRIPTION	UNUSED VF	UNUSED F	UNUSED AVG	USED VF	USED F	USED AVG
	1867 Grill with Points Up A. Grill Covering Entire Stamp (†) (OG + 75%)						
79	3¢ rose	....	5000.00	3500.00	....	1400.00	975.00
80	5¢ brown	....	....	....	....	400000.00	....
81	30¢ orange	....	....	....	....	....	250000.00
	B. Grill about 18 x 15 mm. (OG + 75%)						
82	3¢ rose	....	....	....	....	1000000.00	....
	C. Grill About 13 x 16 mm. (†) (OG + 75%)						
83	3¢ rose	2500.00	1400.00	1000.00	1200.00	800.00	500.00
	1867 Grill with Points Down D. Grill About 12 x 14 mm. (†) (OG + 75%)						
84	2¢ black	10000.00	8000.00	6000.00	8000.00	5000.00	3000.00
85	3¢ rose	3200.00	1800.00	1200.00	1200.00	800.00	500.00
	Z. Grill About 11 x 14 mm. (†) (OG + 75%)						
85A	1¢ blue	....	....	....	....	....	....
85B	2¢ black	7000.00	5000.00	3000.00	1350.00	1050.00	700.00
85C	3¢ rose	9500.00	6750.00	4800.00	3500.00	3050.00	2075.00
85D	10¢ green	....	....	....	750000.00	675000.00	....
85E	12¢ black	8400.00	6250.00	4700.00	2500.00	1900.00	1500.00
85F	15¢ black	....	....	....	2000000.00	....	....
	E. Grill About 11 x 13 mm. (†) (OG + 75%)						
86	1¢ blue	1600.00	1100.00	650.00	775.00	400.00	200.00
87	2¢ black	800.00	615.00	450.00	325.00	190.00	130.00
88	3¢ rose	495.00	375.00	250.00	45.00	30.75	20.50
89	10¢ green	2400.00	1500.00	900.00	375.00	220.00	150.00
90	12¢ black	2200.00	1200.00	850.00	500.00	250.00	160.00
91	15¢ black	5200.00	3000.00	2000.00	750.00	550.00	325.00

Showgard® MOUNTS

All showgard mounts are only available with **black backgrounds.**

Cut Style

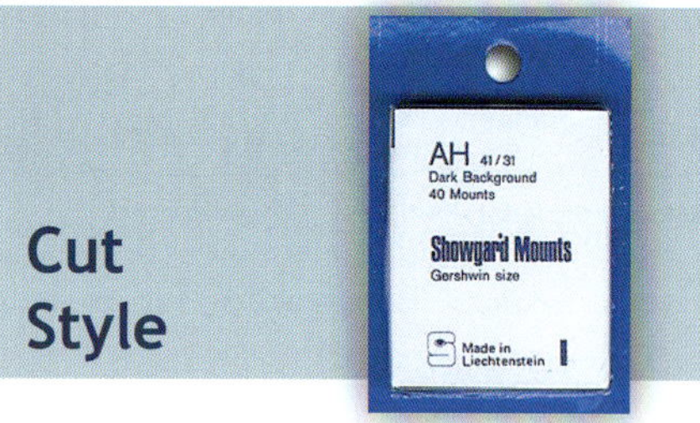

Stock# Showgard	Stock# Harris	Pieces/ Pack	Description	Retail
AH41/31	9SGD10	40	U.S. Semi Jumbo Gershwin, etc.	$4.95
AV31/41	9SGD3184	40	Legends of the West	$4.95
C50/31	9SGD1	40	U.S. Jumbo Singles - Horiz.	$4.95
CV31/50	9SGD2	40	U.S. Jumbo Singles - Vert	$4.95
DH52/36	9SGD3081	30	U.S. Duck Stamps	$4.95
E22/25	9SGD5	40	U.S. Regular Issues	$4.95
EH25/22	9SGD6	40	U.S. Regular Issues - Horiz.	$4.95
J40/25	9SGD3	40	U.S. Comm. - Horiz	$4.95
JV25/40	9SGD4	40	U.S. Comm. - Vert	$4.95
N40/27	9SGD9	40	United Nations	$4.95
S31/31	9SGD3329	40	Celebrate the Century	$4.95
T25/27	9SGD7	40	U.S. Famous Americans	$4.95
U33/27	9SGD8	40	U.N. and Germany	$4.95

Sets

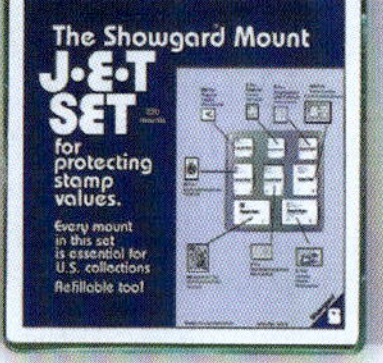

Stock# Showgard	Stock# Harris	Pieces/ Pack	Description	Retail
US2	9SGD11	320	Cut style for U.S. w/tray - 8 sizes	$32.95
US3	9SGD12	75	Strip style w/tray #22-52	$49.95
US01	9SGD63	50	U.S. strip sizes #22-52	$24.50

Plate Block & Covers

Stock# Showgard	Stock# Harris	Pieces/ Pack	Description	Retail
57/55	9SGD13	25	Regular issue U.S. Plate Blocks	$9.95
67/25	9SGD2341	40	U.S. Coil Strips of three	$9.95
105/57	9SGD15	20	U.S. Giori Press. Mdrn. Plate Blk	$9.95
106/55	9SGD14	20	U.S. 3¢, 4¢ Comm. Plate Block	$9.95
127/70	9SGD16	10	U.S. Jumbo Issues Plate Block	$9.95
140/89	9SGD2342	10	Postcards	$9.95
165/94	9SGD17	10	First Day Covers	$9.95

Strips 215mm Long

Stock# Showgard	Stock# Harris	Pieces/ Pack	Description	Retail
20	9SGD18	22	Mini Stamps U.S., etc.	$11.95
22	9SGD19	22	Narrow U.S. Airs	$11.95
24	9SGD20	22	GD and Canada Early U.S.	$11.95
25	9SGD21	22	U.S. Comm. and Regular Issue	$11.95
27	9SGD22	22	U.S. Famous Americans and U.N.	$11.95
28	9SGD23	22	Switzerland, Liechtenstein	$11.95
30	9SGD24	22	U.S. Jamestown, Foreign	$11.95
31	9SGD25	22	U.S. Squares and Semi-Jumbo	$11.95
33	9SGD26	22	GB Issues, Misc. Foreign	$11.95
36	9SGD27	15	Duck Stamps, Misc. Foreign	$11.95
39	9SGD28	15	U.S. Magsaysay, Misc. Foreign	$11.95
41	9SGD29	15	U.S. Vertical Comm. Israel Tabs	$11.95
44	9SGD30	15	U.S. Hatteras Block of four	$11.95
48	9SGD31	15	Can. Reg. Issue and Comm. Blks	$11.95
50	9SGD32	15	U.S. Plain Blocks of four	$11.95
52	9SGD33	15	France Paintings	$11.95
57	9SGD34	15	U.S. Comm. Plate Blocks (4)	$11.95
61	9SGD35	15	Souvenir Sheets, Tab Singles	$11.95

Strips 240mm Long

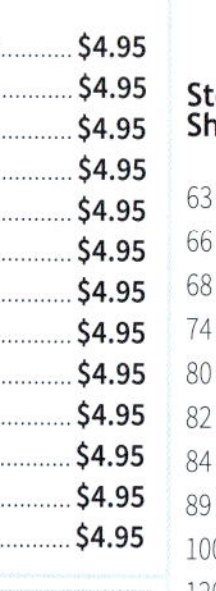

Stock# Showgard	Stock# Harris	Pieces/ Pack	Description	Retail
63	9SGD36	10	U.S. Squares, Plain Blocks (4)	$16.50
66	9SGD37	10	Israel Plate Blocks, etc.	$16.50
68	9SGD38	10	Can. Plate Blocks, $1 Fundy, etc.	$16.50
74	9SGD39	10	U.N. Inscription Blocks (4)	$16.50
80	9SGD40	10	U.S. Comm. Plain Blocks (4)	$16.50
82	9SGD41	10	U.N. Chagall SS, Can. Plate Blks	$16.50
84	9SGD42	10	Israel, Tab Blocks, etc.	$16.50
89	9SGD43	10	U.N. Inscription Blocks (6)	$16.50
100	9SGD44	7	U.S. Squares - Plate Blocks	$16.50
120	9SGD45	7	Miniature Sheets	$16.50

Strips 264mm Long

Stock# Showgard	Stock# Harris	Pieces/ Pack	Description	Retail
70	9SGD46	10	U.S. Jumbo Plate Blocks	$18.95
91	9SGD47	10	GB Souvenir Sheets	$18.95
105	9SGD48	10	GB Blocks, Covers, Cards	$18.95
107	9SGD49	20	U.S. Plate No. Strip (20)	$18.95
111	9SGD54	5	U.S. Floating No. Plate Strips (20)	$18.95
127	9SGD55	5	U.S. UPU and LBJ Plte Blks (15)	$18.95
137	9SGD56	5	GB Coronations, U.N., SS	$18.95
158	9SGD57	5	Souvenir Sheets, Apollo Soyuz, Plate Block	$18.95
175	9SGD2471	5	U.S. Sheets - Love, Christmas	$18.95
188	9SGD2892	5	Marilyn Monroe Miniature Sheets	$18.95
198	9SGD2893	5	Legends of the West Miniature Sheets	$18.95

Miscellaneous

Stock# Showgard	Stock# Harris	Pieces/ Pack	Description	Retail
265/231	9SGD53	5	Full Sheets and Souvenir Cards	$23.50
Group 94	9SGD2650	4	1994 Souvenir Sheets (Clear)	$10.25
MPK	9SGD50	12	Assortment #22-41	$8.95
MPK II	9SGD51	15	Assortment #76-171	$37.95

Blocks

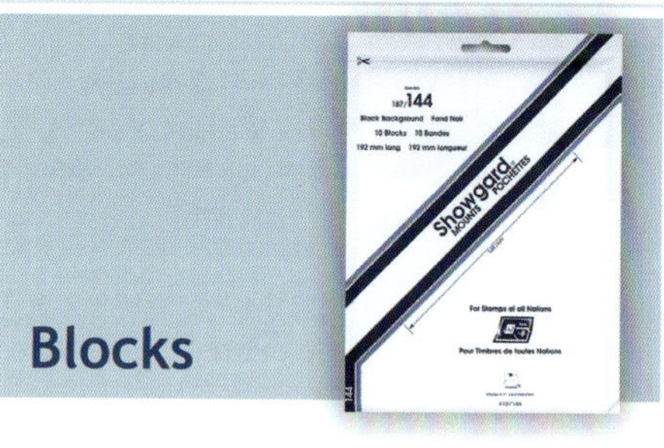

Stock# Showgard	Stock# Harris	Pieces/ Pack	Description	Retail
111/91	9SGD2756	6	Columbian Souvenir Sheets	$9.25
120/207	9SGD2113	4	Ameripex Presidential Sheetless	$10.95
187/144	9SGD61	10	U.N. Flags Sheetlets	$25.95
191/229	9SGD3330	5	Celebrate the Century Sheets (5)	$15.95
192/201	9SGD3071	5	Legends of the West Sheet	$15.75
204/153	9SGD62	5	U.S. Bicentennial and W. Plains SS.	$15.95
229/131	9SGD2713	5	WWII Souvenir Sheets	$17.25
260/25	9SGD2382	25	U.S. Coil Strips (up to 11 stamps)	$14.25
260/40	9SGD58	10	U.S. Postal People Full Strip	$11.25
260/46	9SGD3277	10	U.S. Vending Booklets	$12.50
260/55	9SGD59	10	U.S. 13¢ Eagle Full Strip	$12.50
260/59	9SGD60	10	U.S. Dbl Press Reg. Iss. Strip (20)	$14.50
Group Pac 97	9SGD3274	7	Pacific 97 Issues	$5.75
Trans-Miss	9SGD3341	11	Trans-Miss. Reissues	$5.75
Space	9SGD4122	5	Space Exploration	$7.25

Accommodation Range Mount

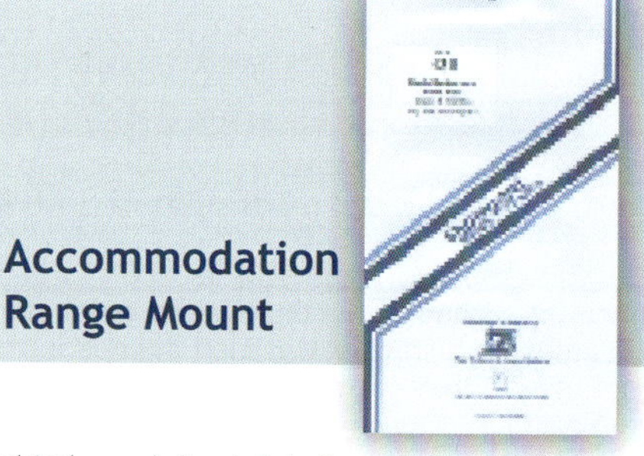

Black Backgrounds, Now includes 5 mounts per pack!

Stock# Showgard	Stock# Harris	Description	Retail
76	9SGD4119	Bright Eyes (Top), Challenger Shuttle Plate Blocks	$13.25
96	9SGD3010	Flowering Trees, Christmas Plate Blocks	$13.25
109	9SGD3122	109 Strip	$13.25
115	9SGD3012	115 Strip	$19.00
117	9SGD4111	117 Strip	$19.00
121	9SGD4112	121 Strip	$19.00
131	9SGD2746	131 Strip	$19.00
135	9SGD4113	135 Strip	$19.00
139	9SGD4114	139 Strip	$19.00
143	9SGD4115	143 Strip	$19.00
147	9SGD3123	Cinco De Mayo, Miniature Sheet	$19.00
151	9SGD4116	Automobiles, Hanukkah, Miniature Sheets	$19.00
163	9SGD3011	Kwanzaa Miniature Sheet	$19.00
167	9SGD4117	IA, TN, Bright Eyes, Miniature Sheets	$19.00
181	9SGD4120	All Aboard	$19.00
201	9SGD3230	World of Dinosaurs, Miniature Sheet	$19.00
215	9SGD4121	Arctic Animals	$19.00
171	9SGD4118	Helping Children	$19.00

To Order Call 800-546-2995

H.E. Harris

SCOTT NO.	DESCRIPTION	UNUSED VF	UNUSED F	UNUSED AVG	USED VF	USED F	USED AVG
	F. Grill About 9 x 13 mm. (†) (OG + 75%)						
92	1¢ blue	1250.00	775.00	500.00	600.00	375.00	200.00
93	2¢ black	375.00	180.00	140.00	100.00	60.00	40.00
94	3¢ red.	220.00	150.00	90.00	15.00	10.00	6.00
95	5¢ brown	1800.00	1400.00	950.00	1125.00	775.00	475.00
96	10¢ yellow green .	1300.00	700.00	400.00	350.00	240.00	135.00
97	12¢ black	1600.00	1000.00	580.00	320.00	275.00	160.00
98	15¢ black	2100.00	1300.00	800.00	400.00	300.00	190.00
99	24¢ gray lilac	4300.00	2500.00	1900.00	2000.00	1200.00	750.00
100	30¢ orange.	4500.00	2600.00	2000.00	1000.00	800.00	500.00
101	90¢ blue	7000.00	4000.00	3000.00	3000.00	2000.00	1200.00

The Re-Issues of the 1861-66 Issue were issued with gum and, while scarce, are found used. They can be distinguished by their bright colors, sharp printing impressions, hard paper and white, crackly original gum.

SCOTT NO.	DESCRIPTION	UNUSED VF	UNUSED F	UNUSED AVG	USED VF	USED F	USED AVG
	1875. Re-Issue of 1861-66 Issue. Hard White Paper (OG + 75%)						
102	1¢ blue	450.00	325.00	225.00	1600.00	1225.00	850.00
103	2¢ black	2000.00	1200.00	875.00	13000.00	9500.00	7000.00
104	3¢ brown red	2200.00	1500.00	1000.00	17000.00	14785.00	10000.00
105	5¢ brown	1400.00	900.00	650.00	7200.00	5000.00	3000.00
106	10¢ green.	1800.00	1400.00	950.00	125000.00	95000.00	77250.00
107	12¢ black	2200.00	1500.00	1100.00	15000.00	12000.00	9250.00
108	15¢ black	2300.00	1800.00	1175.00	35000.00	28000.00	22000.00
109	24¢ deep violet. . .	3200.00	2200.00	1400.00	20000.00	16000.00	13000.00
110	30¢ brownish orange	3400.00	2600.00	1500.00	25000.00	20000.00	16875.00
111	90¢ blue	4200.00	2400.00	1700.00	225000.00	....	130000.00

THE 1869 PICTORIALS

As the first United States series to include pictorial designs, the 1869 issue is one of the most popular today. They were so unpopular that they were removed from sale less than a year after issue. Most protests were directed toward their odd size and the tradition-breaking pictorial designs.

The 1869 issue broke important new ground in the use of two color designs. Not only does this add to their attractiveness; it also is the source for the first United States "Inverted Centers". These inverted errors appear on the bi-colored 15, 24 and 30 cent values. The printing technology of the time required a separate printing pass for each color. On the first pass, the central designs, or vignettes, were printed. The second pass applied the frames.

In a very few instances, the sheets with their central designs already printed were passed upside down through the printing press. As a result, the frames were printed upside down. So the description "inverted center" for the 15 and 24 cent errors is technically incorrect, but the form in which these errors are photographed and displayed is with the center, rather than the frame, inverted.

Used copies of the 1869 Pictorials are not as scarce as might be expected. Any of the stamps above the 3 cent denomination were used on mail to Europe and were saved by collectors overseas. When stamp collecting became popular in the United States and Americans were able to purchase stamps abroad at relatively low prices, many of these used 1869 Pictorials found their way back to this country. On the other hand, because of the short life of the issue in post offices and their sudden withdrawal, unused stamps—particularly the high values—are quite rare.

All values of the 1869 Pictorials are found with the "G" grill. Ungrilled varieties are known on all values except the 6, 10, 12 and type II 15 cent stamps. (The Harris Stamp Identifier describes the difference in the three 15 cent types.)

The 1869 Pictorials were re-issued in 1875 in anticipation of the 1876 Centennial Exposition. Most collectors who had missed the original 1869 issue were delighted to have a second chance to purchase the stamps, which explains why the high value re-issues carry lower prices today than do the original 1869 pictorials. At the time, most collectors did not realize they were buying entirely different stamps. The same designs were used, but the re-issues were issued on a distinctive hard, white paper without grills.

The 1 cent stamp was re-issued a second time, in 1880. This re-issue can be distinguished by the lack of a grill and by the soft, porous paper used by the American Bank Note Company.

112, 123, 133,133a
Franklin

113, 124
Pony Express Rider

114, 125
Locomotive

115, 126
Washington

116, 127
Shield & Eagle

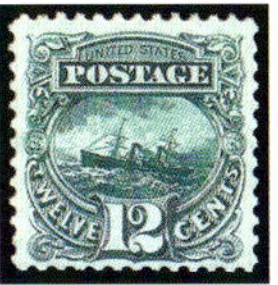

117, 128
S.S. Adriatic

118, 119, 129
Landing of Columbus

120, 130
Signing of Declaration

121, 131
Shield, Eagle & Flags

122, 132
Lincoln

SCOTT NO.	DESCRIPTION	UNUSED VF	UNUSED F	UNUSED AVG	USED VF	USED F	USED AVG
	1869 G. Grill measuring 9-1/2 x 9-1/2 mm. (†) (OG + 75%)						
112	1¢ buff	375.00	190.00	120.00	200.00	150.00	90.00
113	2¢ brown	320.00	195.00	115.00	115.00	90.00	60.00
114	3¢ ultramarine . . .	150.00	80.00	50.00	25.00	18.00	12.00
115	6¢ ultramarine . . .	1300.00	900.00	500.00	220.00	175.00	100.00
116	10¢ yellow	1200.00	750.00	400.00	150.00	120.00	80.00
117	12¢ green.	1200.00	750.00	400.00	150.00	120.00	80.00
118	15¢ brown & blue (I)	4600.00	3000.00	2500.00	950.00	650.00	400.00
119	15¢ brown & blue (II)	1700.00	1000.00	650.00	275.00	190.00	120.00
120	24¢ green & violet	4000.00	2200.00	1500.00	700.00	490.00	320.00
121	30¢ blue & carmine	2000.00	1400.00	1000.00	550.00	350.00	250.00
122	90¢ carmine & black	4500.00	3500.00	2000.00	2400.00	1800.00	1200.00
	1875 Re-Issue of 1869 Issue. Hard White Paper. Without Grill (OG + 75%)						
123	1¢ buff	390.00	275.00	175.00	450.00	325.00	230.00
124	2¢ brown	390.00	275.00	175.00	900.00	650.00	450.00
125	3¢ blue	3000.00	1800.00	1200.00	....	25000.00	....
126	6¢ blue	900.00	550.00	450.00	3500.00	2200.00	1200.00
127	10¢ yellow	950.00	650.00	450.00	2400.00	2000.00	1300.00
128	12¢ green.	1600.00	850.00	550.00	3500.00	2400.00	1350.00
129	15¢ brown & blue (III)	950.00	600.00	400.00	1300.00	900.00	600.00
130	24¢ green & violet	1300.00	850.00	600.00	1900.00	1200.00	900.00
131	30¢ blue & carmine	1400.00	900.00	675.00	3200.00	2300.00	1500.00
132	90¢ carmine & black	2000.00	1550.00	1250.00	6500.00	4800.00	3600.00
	1880 Re-Issue. Soft Porous Paper, Issued Without Grill (†) (#133 OG +50%)						
133	1¢ buff	200.00	150.00	95.00	550.00	450.00	300.00
133a	1¢ brown orange . (issued w/o gum)	425.00	350.00	225.00	650.00	500.00	320.00

(†) means Issue is actually very poorly centered. Perforations may touch the design on "Fine" quality.

THE 1870-88 BANK NOTE ISSUES

The "Bank Notes" are stamps that were issued between 1870 and 1888 by the National, Continental and American Bank Note Companies.

The myriad of varieties, secret marks, papers, grills, re-engravings and special printings produced by the three companies resulted in no less than 87 major catalog listings for what basically amounts to 16 different designs. For collectors, what seems to be the very difficult task of properly identifying all these varieties can be eased by following these guidelines:

1. The chronological order in which the three Bank Note companies produced stamps is their reverse alphabetical order: National, Continental, American.

2. "3, 6, 9" identifies the number of years each of the companies printed stamps within the 18-year Bank Note period. Starting in 1870, National continued its work for 3 more years, until 1873, when the Continental Company began printing stamps. That company served for the next 6 years, until 1879, when American took over the Continental company. Although American printed some later issues, the "Bank Note" period ended 9 years later, in 1888.

3. The first Bank Note issue, the Nationals of 1870-71, continued the practice of grilling stamps. Although some specialists contend there are grilled Continental stamps, for all intents and purposes, if a Bank Note stamp bears a genuine grill, it must be from the 1870-71 National issue.

4. The secret marks on values through the 12 cent, and possibly the 15 cent value, were added when the Continental Company took over. They enabled the government to distinguish between National's work and that of its successor. If a Bank Note stamp did not show a secret mark, the Post Office could identify it as the work of the National Bank Note Company. You can do the same.

5. The paper used by the National and Continental companies is similar, but that of the American Bank Note company is noticably different from the first two. When held to the light, the thick, soft American paper shows its coarse, uneven texture, while that of its two predecessors is more even and translucent. The American Bank Note paper also reveals a yellowish hue when held to the light, whereas the National and Continental papers are whiter.

6. Experienced collectors also apply a "snap test" to identify American Bank Note paper by gently flexing a Bank Note stamp at one of its corners. The American Bank Note paper will not "snap" back into place. The National and Continental stamps, on the other hand, often give off a noticeable sound when the flex is released.

7. By purchasing one Bank Note design put into use after 1882 (which can only be an American) and one early Bank Note stamp without the secret mark, (which can only be a National), the collector has a reference point against which to compare any other Bank Note stamp. If it is a soft paper, it is an American Bank Note issue; if a harder paper, it is either a National or a Continental—and these two can be classified by the absence (National) or presence (Continental) of the secret marks or other distinguishing features or colors. The Harris Stamp Identifier in this catalog provides illustrations of the secret marks and further information on the distinguishing features of the various Bank Notes. With two reference stamps, some practice and the use of the information in this catalog, collectors can turn the "job" of understanding the Bank Notes into a pleasant adventure.

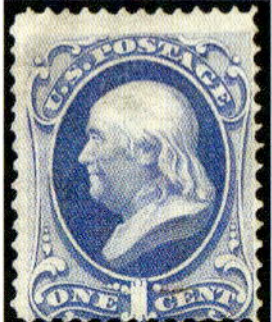

134, 145, 156, 167, 182, 192, 206
Franklin

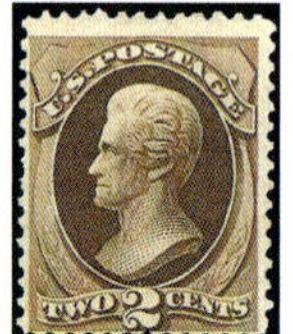

135, 146, 157, 168, 178, 180, 183, 193, 203
Jackson

136, 147, 158, 169, 184, 194, 207, 214
Washington

NOTE: For further details on the various types of similar appearing stamps please refer to our U.S. Stamp Identifier.

(†) means Issue is actually very poorly centered. Perforations may touch the design on "Fine" quality.

137, 148, 159, 170, 186, 195, 208
Lincoln

138, 149, 160, 171, 196
Stanton

139, 150, 161, 172, 187, 188, 197, 209
Jefferson

140, 151, 162, 173, 198
Clay

141, 152, 163, 174, 189, 199
Webster

142, 153, 164, 175, 200
Scott

143, 154, 165, 176, 190, 201, 217
Hamilton

144, 155, 166, 177, 191, 202, 218
Perry

1870 National Bank Note Co., without Secret Marks. With H Grill about (10 x 12 mm. or 8-1/2 x 10 mm.) Perf 12. (†) (OG +75%)

SCOTT NO.	DESCRIPTION	UNUSED VF	UNUSED F	UNUSED AVG	USED VF	USED F	USED AVG
134	1¢ ultramarine . . .	850.00	650.00	500.00	300.00	200.00	110.00
135	2¢ red brown	450.00	360.00	275.00	110.00	85.00	50.00
136	3¢ green.	300.00	200.00	150.00	45.00	30.00	15.00
137	6¢ carmine	2000.00	1700.00	1000.00	600.00	450.00	250.00
138	7¢ vermillion.	1800.00	1250.00	900.00	650.00	450.00	300.00
139	10¢ brown	3000.00	2500.00	1750.00	1300.00	800.00	525.00
140	12¢ dull violet	16800.00	11500.00	6500.00	3800.00	2800.00	1800.00
141	15¢ orange	4750.00	2700.00	1850.00	1500.00	1100.00	650.00
142	24¢ purple	....	....	....	7500.00	6000.00	4300.00
143	30¢ black	10000.00	6750.00	4800.00	4000.00	2800.00	1800.00
144	90¢ carmine	12100.00	7250.00	4500.00	2600.00	1800.00	1200.00

1870-71. National Bank Note Co., without Secret Marks. Without Grill. Perf 12. (†) (OG +75%)

SCOTT NO.	DESCRIPTION	UNUSED VF	UNUSED F	UNUSED AVG	USED VF	USED F	USED AVG
145	1¢ ultramarine . . .	400.00	275.00	150.00	30.00	20.00	15.00
146	2¢ red brown	250.00	155.00	100.00	25.00	16.00	10.50
147	3¢ green.	275.00	170.00	112.00	4.00	2.75	1.60
148	6¢ carmine	675.00	400.00	225.00	50.00	31.00	19.00
149	7¢ vermillion.	700.00	450.00	250.00	165.00	92.00	56.00
150	10¢ brown	850.00	600.00	395.00	63.00	43.00	27.00
151	12¢ dull violet	1500.00	1000.00	600.00	325.00	215.00	135.00
152	15¢ bright orange .	1500.00	1000.00	600.00	350.00	235.00	150.00
153	24¢ purple	1250.00	800.00	550.00	300.00	180.00	120.00
154	30¢ black	4000.00	2800.00	1600.00	450.00	300.00	175.00
155	90¢ carmine	3000.00	2000.00	1150.00	500.00	350.00	200.00

1873. Continental Bank Note Co. Same designs as 1870-71, with Secret Marks, on thin hard grayish white paper. Perf 12 (†) (OG + 75%)

SCOTT NO.	DESCRIPTION	UNUSED VF	UNUSED F	UNUSED AVG	USED VF	USED F	USED AVG
156	1¢ ultramarine . . .	110.00	90.00	65.00	5.00	3.75	2.25
157	2¢ brown	150.00	125.00	75.00	30.00	21.00	12.00
158	3¢ green.	75.00	40.00	25.00	1.25	.75	.50
159	6¢ dull pink	150.00	125.00	85.00	35.00	20.00	14.00
160	7¢ orange vermillion	400.00	325.00	250.00	150.00	105.00	68.00
161	10¢ brown	500.00	250.00	195.00	40.00	28.00	17.00
162	12¢ black violet . .	800.00	600.00	400.00	200.00	130.00	86.00
163	15¢ yellow orange	800.00	600.00	400.00	225.00	150.00	90.00
165	30¢ gray black . . .	1450.00	1250.00	700.00	200.00	130.00	83.00
166	90¢ rose carmine .	1000.00	850.00	500.00	475.00	300.00	175.00

1875 Special Printing–On Hard White Wove Paper–Without Gum Perf. 12

SCOTT NO.	DESCRIPTION	UNUSED VF	UNUSED F	UNUSED AVG	USED VF	USED F	USED AVG
167	1¢ ultramarine . . .	20000.00	13250.00	7500.00	....	....	....
168	2¢ dark brown . . .	10000.00	6500.00	4400.00	....	....	....
169	3¢ blue green	25000.00	16750.00	11250.00	....	....	....
170	6¢ dull rose.	25000.00	16750.00	11250.00	....	....	....
171	7¢ reddish vermillion	6500.00	4300.00	3000.00	....	....	....
172	10¢ pale brown. . .	23500.00	15750.00	10500.00	....	....	....
173	12¢ dark violet . . .	8000.00	5250.00	3800.00	....	....	....
174	15¢ bright orange .	23000.00	15500.00	10250.00	....	....	....
175	24¢ dull purple . . .	5750.00	3800.00	2600.00	....	....	....
176	30¢ greenish black	20000.00	13500.00	9250.00	....	....	....
177	90¢ violet carmine	32500.00	21500.00	15000.00	....	....	....

179, 181, 185, 204
Taylor

205, 205C, 216
Garfield

1875 Continental Bank Note Co.
Hard yellowish paper, Perf 12. (†)
(OG + 50%)

SCOTT NO.	DESCRIPTION	UNUSED VF	UNUSED F	UNUSED AVG	USED VF	USED F	USED AVG
178	2¢ vermillion	145.00	100.00	75.00	20.00	14.00	9.50
179	5¢ blue	350.00	225.00	150.00	45.00	28.00	15.00

1875 Continental Bank Note Co., Special Printings.
Same as 1875, on hard white paper, without gum. Perf 12.

SCOTT NO.	DESCRIPTION	UNUSED VF	UNUSED F	UNUSED AVG	USED VF	USED F	USED AVG
180	2¢ carmine vermillion	80000.00	60000.00	36500.00	....	....	....
181	5¢ bright blue	500000.00	375000.00	235000.00	....	....	....

1879 American Bank Note Co.
Same designs as 1870-71 Issue (with Secret Marks) and 1875 Issue on soft, porous, coarse, yellowish paper. Perf 12. (†)
(OG + 60%)

SCOTT NO.	DESCRIPTION	UNUSED VF	UNUSED F	UNUSED AVG	USED VF	USED F	USED AVG
182	1¢ dark ultramarine	150.00	100.00	80.00	8.00	5.00	3.00
183	2¢ vermilion	60.00	40.00	25.00	5.50	4.00	3.00
184	3¢ green	45.00	35.00	27.00	1.00	.70	.50
185	5¢ blue	185.00	130.00	100.00	26.00	18.00	12.00
186	6¢ pink	350.00	275.00	195.00	45.00	32.50	19.50
187	10¢ brown (no secret mark) . .	1500.00	1000.00	600.00	70.00	50.00	30.00
188	10¢ brown (secret mark)	900.00	600.00	450.00	50.00	36.50	21.95
189	15¢ red orange . . .	100.00	85.00	50.00	40.00	30.00	17.25
190	30¢ full black	400.00	350.00	200.00	150.00	100.00	67.00
191	90¢ carmine	900.00	700.00	525.00	500.00	320.00	230.00

1880 American Bank Note Co., Special Printings.
Same as 1879 Issue, on soft, porous paper, without gum. Perf 12.

SCOTT NO.	DESCRIPTION	UNUSED VF	UNUSED F	UNUSED AVG	USED VF	USED F	USED AVG
192	1¢ dark ultramarine	75000.00	47000.00	28000.00	....	....	....
193	2¢ black brown . . .	28000.00	19750.00	12750.00	....	....	....
194	3¢ blue green	120000.00	75000.00	48000.00	....	....	....
195	6¢ dull rose.	90000.00	55000.00	34000.00	....	....	....
196	7¢ scarlet vermillion	9000.00	6250.00	4200.00	....	....	....
197	10¢ deep brown . .	55000.00	35500.00	21000.00	....	....	....
198	12¢ black purple . .	15000.00	10500.00	7000.00	....	....	....
199	15¢ orange	35000.00	25000.00	18000.00	....	....	....
200	24¢ dark violet . . .	15000.00	10500.00	7000.00	....	....	....
201	30¢ greenish black	25000.00	18000.00	12000.00	....	....	....
202	90¢ dull carmine . .	35000.00	26000.00	18000.00	....	....	....
203	2¢ scarlet vermillion	120000.00	90000.00	60000.00	....	....	....
204	5¢ deep blue	260000.00	200000.00	145000.00	....	....	....

1882 American Bank Note Company Perf 12.
(OG + 60%)

SCOTT NO.	DESCRIPTION	UNUSED VF	UNUSED F	UNUSED AVG	USED VF	USED F	USED AVG
205	5¢ yellow brown . .	110.00	85.00	65.00	15.00	11.00	7.00

1882 American Bank Note Co., Special Printing.
Same as in 1882 Issue, on soft, porous Paper. Perf 12.

SCOTT NO.	DESCRIPTION	UNUSED VF	UNUSED F	UNUSED AVG	USED VF	USED F	USED AVG
205C	5¢ gray brown . . .	....	50000.00	....	....	....	....

210, 211B, 213
Washington

211, 211D, 215
Jackson

212
Franklin

1881-83 American Bank Note Co.
Same designs as 1873, Re-Engraved. On soft, porous paper. Perf 12. (†)
(OG + 100%)

SCOTT NO.	DESCRIPTION	UNUSED VF	UNUSED F	UNUSED AVG	USED VF	USED F	USED AVG
206	1¢ gray blue	45.00	30.00	25.00	1.50	.95	.70
207	3¢ blue green	35.00	25.00	18.00	1.25	.75	.55
208	6¢ rose	250.00	170.00	100.00	130.00	100.00	70.00
208a	6¢ brown red	175.00	150.00	120.00	175.00	130.00	87.50
209	10¢ brown	75.00	65.00	50.00	10.00	7.50	4.50
209b	10¢ black brown . .	1100.00	950.00	600.00	350.00	250.00	150.00
210	2¢ red brown	25.00	17.00	12.00	.75	.45	.35
211	4¢ blue green	100.00	80.00	60.00	32.50	23.00	17.00

1883 American Bank Note Co. Special Printing.
Same design as 1883 Issue, on soft porous paper. Perf 12.

SCOTT NO.	DESCRIPTION	UNUSED VF	UNUSED F	UNUSED AVG	USED VF	USED F	USED AVG
211B	2¢ pale red brown	175.00	100.00	80.00	....	....	....
211D	4¢ deep blue green	50000.00	....	....	....	....	....

1887 American Bank Note Co.
New designs or colors. Perf 12.
(OG + 60%)

SCOTT NO.	DESCRIPTION	UNUSED VF	UNUSED F	UNUSED AVG	USED VF	USED F	USED AVG
212	1¢ ultramarine . . .	50.00	40.00	30.00	3.00	2.15	1.25
213	2¢ green	30.00	18.00	10.00	.60	.40	.30
214	3¢ vermillion	60.00	40.00	25.00	100.00	64.00	40.00

1888 American Bank Note Company.
New Colors Perf 12.
(NH + 100%)

SCOTT NO.	DESCRIPTION	UNUSED O.G. VF	UNUSED O.G. F	UNUSED O.G. AVG	USED VF	USED F	USED AVG
215	4¢ carmine	290.00	187.50	125.00	35.00	25.00	15.00
216	5¢ indigo.	300.00	195.00	130.00	22.50	16.00	3.75
217	30¢ orange brown	400.00	200.00	150.00	125.00	100.00	55.00
218	90¢ purple	1000.00	500.00	300.00	345.00	250.00	150.00

THE 1890-93 SMALL BANK NOTE ISSUES

Unlike the complex Large Bank Notes, the 1890-93 series is the simplest of the 19th century definitive issues. They were printed by the American Bank Note Company and what few printing varieties there are can easily be determined by using the Harris Stamp Identifier.

The two major printing varieties are the 2 cent carmine with a "cap" on the left 2 (#219a) or both 2s (#219c).

The "cap" appears to be just that—a small flat hat just to the right of center on top of the denomination numeral 2. It was caused by a breakdown in the metal of the transfer roll that went undetected while it was being used to enter the designs into a few printing plates.

219
Franklin

219D, 220
Washington

221
Jackson

222
Lincoln

223
Grant

224
Garfield

225
Sherman

226
Webster

227
Clay

228
Jefferson

229
Perry

(NH +100%)

SCOTT NO.	DESCRIPTION	UNUSED O.G. VF	UNUSED O.G. F	UNUSED O.G. AVG	USED VF	USED F	USED AVG
219	1¢ dull blue.	45.00	25.00	20.50	.60	.45	.35
219D	2¢ lake	250.00	180.00	110.00	5.00	3.50	1.85
220	2¢ carmine	35.00	19.00	14.00	.55	.40	.30
220a	Cap on left "2" . . .	250.00	140.00	90.00	....	....	....
220c	Cap on both "2"s .	750.00	400.00	275.00	40.00	25.00	18.50
221	3¢ purple	95.00	60.00	45.00	13.50	8.00	6.00
222	4¢ dark brown . . .	135.00	80.00	60.00	6.50	4.95	3.50
223	5¢ chocolate.	120.00	78.00	54.00	6.50	4.90	3.25
224	6¢ brown red	110.00	70.00	50.00	34.00	23.00	16.00
225	8¢ lilac	95.00	65.00	47.50	20.00	13.00	9.00
226	10¢ green	250.00	160.00	110.00	5.75	3.75	2.25
227	15¢ indigo.	350.00	210.00	150.00	42.00	30.00	19.00
228	30¢ black	550.00	350.00	245.00	58.00	38.00	23.00
229	90¢ orange	700.00	425.00	300.00	175.00	100.00	70.00

230 *In Sight of Land*

231 *Landing of Columbus*

232 *Flagship*

233 *Fleet of Columbus*

234 *Soliciting Aid*

235 *At Barcelona*

236 *Restored To Favor*

237 *Presenting Natives*

238 *Discovery*

239 *At La Rábida*

240 *Recall of Columbus*

241 *Pledging Jewels*

242 *Columbus in Chains*

243 *Describing Third Voyage*

244 *Isabella & Columbus*

245 *Portrait of Columbus*

THE COLUMBIANS

Perhaps the most glamorous of all United States issues is the 1893 Columbians set. Consisting of 16 denominations, the set was issued to celebrate the 1893 World's Columbian Exposition.

Even then, the Post Office Department was aware that stamps could be useful for more than just the prepayment of postage. We quote from an internal Post Office Department report of November 20, 1892:

"During the past summer the determination was reached by the Department to issue, during the progress of the Columbian Exposition at Chicago, a special series of adhesive postage stamps of such a character as would help to signalize the four hundredth anniversary of the discovery of America by Columbus. This course was in accordance with the practice of other great postal administrations on occasions of national rejoicing.

The collecting of stamps is deserving of encouragement, for it tends to the cultivation of artistic tastes and the study of history and geography, especially on the part of the young. The new stamps will be purchased in large quantities simply for the use of collections, without ever being presented in payment of postage; and the stamps sold in this way will, of course, prove a clear gain to the department."

As it turned out, the Columbians issue did sell well, being purchased in large quantities not only by collectors, but by speculators hoping to capitalize on the expected demand for the stamps and the fact that they were supposed to be on sale for only one year, from January 2 to December 31, 1893. (The 8 cent stamp was issued March 3,1893 to meet the new, reduced Registration fee.)

Although sales of the stamps were brisk at the Exposition site in Chicago, speculation proved less than rewarding. The hordes that showed up on the first day of sale in Chicago (January 3rd) and purchased large quantities of the issue ended up taking losses on most of the stamps.

The set was the most expensive postal issue produced to date by the Post Office. The lower denominations matched those of the previous, "Small" Bank Note issue and the 50 cent Columbian replaced the 90 cent Bank Note denomination. But the $1 through $5 denominations were unheard of at that time. The reason for their release was explained in the November 20, 1892 report: "...such high denominations having heretofore been called for by some of the principal post offices".

The Columbians were an instant success. Businesses did not like the wide size, but they usually could obtain the smaller Bank Note issue. Collectors enjoyed the new stamps, although at least one complained that some of the high values purchased by him had straight edges—and was quickly authorized to exchange "the imperfect stamps" for perfect ones.

The one major variety in this set is the 4 cent blue error of color. It is similar to, but richer in color than, the 1 cent Columbian and commands a larger premium over the normal 4 cent ultramarine color.

The imperforates that are known to exist for all values are proofs which were distributed as gifts and are not listed as postage stamps. The only exception, the 2 cent imperforate, is believed to be printers' waste that was saved from destruction.

SCOTT NO.	DESCRIPTION	UNUSED O.G. VF	F	AVG	USED VF	F	AVG
	1893 COLUMBIAN ISSUE (NH + 100%)						
230	1¢ deep blue	25.00	15.00	12.75	.70	.50	.30
231	2¢ brown violet. . .	25.00	18.00	12.75	.30	.25	.20
231C	2¢ "broken hat". . .	70.00	50.00	40.00	3.50	2.50	1.50
232	3¢ green.	70.00	50.00	40.00	25.00	15.00	10.00
233	4¢ ultramarine . . .	90.00	60.00	35.00	11.00	7.50	4.50
234	5¢ chocolate.	90.00	60.00	35.00	11.00	7.50	4.75
235	6¢ purple	90.00	60.00	35.00	45.00	25.00	12.00
236	8¢ magenta	80.00	50.00	40.00	25.00	14.00	10.00
237	10¢ black brown . .	160.00	100.00	80.00	13.00	8.50	5.50
238	15¢ dark green. . .	350.00	250.00	150.00	115.00	70.00	50.00
239	30¢ orange brown	350.00	250.00	150.00	115.00	70.00	50.00
240	50¢ slate blue. . . .	700.00	450.00	350.00	220.00	180.00	140.00
241	$1 salmon.	1450.00	925.00	725.00	700.00	500.00	400.00
242	$2 brown red	1475.00	975.00	775.00	700.00	500.00	400.00
243	$3 yellow green . .	2200.00	1350.00	900.00	900.00	700.00	500.00
244	$4 crimson lake . .	3000.00	1800.00	1500.00	1375.00	1000.00	725.00
245	$5 black	3400.00	2200.00	1700.00	1400.00	1100.00	750.00

(†) means Issue is actually very poorly centered. Perforations may touch the design on "Fine" quality.

246, 247, 264, 279 *Franklin* — 248-252, 265-267, 279B *Washington* — 253, 268 *Jackson* — 254, 269, 280 *Lincoln* — 255, 270, 281 *Grant*

256, 271, 282 *Garfield* — 257, 272 *Sherman* — 258, 273, 282C, 283 *Webster* — 259, 274, 284 *Clay* — 260, 275 *Jefferson*

261, 261A, 276, 276A *Perry* — 262, 277 *Madison* — 263, 278 *Marshall*

1894-98 THE FIRST BUREAU ISSUES

In 1894, the United States Bureau of Engraving and Printing replaced the American Bank Note Company as the contractor for all United States postage stamps. The "First" Bureau issues, as they are commonly known, actually consist of three series, as follows:

The 1894 Series. In order to expedite the transfer of production to the Bureau, the plates then being used by the American Bank Note Company for the 1890-93 Small Bank Notes were modified, small triangles being added in the upper corners. The 1 cent through 15 cent stamps are otherwise essentially the same as the 1890-93 issue although minor variations have been noted on some values. The 30 cent and 90 cent 1890-93 denominations were changed to 50 cents and $1, respectively, and new $2 and $5 denominations were added.

The 1895 Series. To protect against counterfeiting of United Sates stamps, the Bureau adopted the use of watermarked paper. (A scheme for counterfeiting 2 cent stamps had been uncovered around the same time the watermarked paper was being adopted. Some of these counterfeits are known postally used.) This series is almost exactly the same as the 1984 series except for the presence of watermarks. The watermarks can be difficult t detect on this series, particularly on the light-colored stamps, such as the 50 cent, and on used stamps. Since the 1894 unwatermarked stamps (with the exception of the 2 cent carmine type I) are worth more than the 1895 watermarked stamps, collectors will want to examine their 1894 stamps carefully. (Some collectors feel they can recognize the 1894 stamps by their ragged perforations, caused by difficulties the Bureau encountered when it first took over the produciton of postage stamps. This is not a reliable method.)

The 1898 "Color Changes." With the adoption of a Universal Postal Union code that recommended standard colors for international mail, the United States changed the colors for the lower values in the 1895 Series. The stamps were printed on the same watermarked paper as that used for the 1895 Series. Except for the 2 cent,which was changed from carmine to red, the colors of the 1898 Series are easily differentiated from the 1895 set. The 2 cent value is the most complicated of the First Bureau Issues. In addition to the color changes that took place, three different triangle types are known. The differences are attributed to the possibility that the work of engraving the triangles into the American Bank Note plates was performed by several Bureau engravers.

The 10 cent and $1 types I and II can be distinguished by the circles surrounding the numeral denominations. The Type IIs are identical to the circles of the 1890-93 Small Bank Notes.

All stamps in these series are perf. 12. The Harris Stamp Identifier at the front of this catalog provides additional information on the major types and watermarks of all three series.

SCOTT NO.	DESCRIPTION	UNUSED O.G. VF	F	AVG	USED VF	F	AVG
	1894 Unwatermarked (†) (NH + 100%)						
246	1¢ ultramarine . . .	50.00	32.75	23.75	10.50	6.75	4.25
247	1¢ blue	90.00	53.00	37.00	4.00	2.50	1.75
248	2¢ pink (I)	35.00	22.00	16.00	12.50	8.00	5.00
249	2¢ carmine lake (I)	275.00	160.00	110.00	10.00	6.75	4.00
250	2¢ carmine (I)	50.00	32.75	23.00	2.00	1.00	.75
251	2¢ carmine (II) . . .	400.00	250.00	150.00	18.00	12.75	8.00
252	2¢ carmine (III) . . .	165.00	90.00	60.00	20.00	14.50	9.00
253	3¢ purple	145.00	85.00	60.00	17.50	9.75	6.50
254	4¢ dark brown . . .	195.00	110.00	80.00	16.00	9.75	6.25
255	5¢ chocolate	160.00	90.00	70.00	14.00	8.50	5.50
256	6¢ dull brown	210.00	125.00	85.00	39.00	28.00	19.00
257	8¢ violet brown . . .	200.00	130.00	94.00	35.00	21.25	16.95
258	10¢ dark green . . .	375.00	240.00	160.00	20.00	10.00	7.00
259	15¢ dark blue	385.00	240.00	180.00	96.00	58.00	38.00
260	50¢ orange	725.00	425.00	315.00	185.00	115.00	70.00
261	$1 black (I)	1300.00	800.00	550.00	625.00	375.00	260.00
261A	$1 black (II)	2700.00	1750.00	1200.00	1000.00	675.00	450.00
262	$2 bright blue	3600.00	2300.00	1850.00	1500.00	1100.00	725.00
263	$5 dark green	5050.00	3700.00	2900.00	3000.00	2100.00	1500.00
	1895 Double Line Watermark "USPS" (†) (NH + 75%)						
264	1¢ blue	8.50	5.50	3.75	.50	.35	.25
265	2¢ carmine (I)	55.00	35.00	25.00	4.00	2.65	1.75
266	2¢ carmine (II) . . .	60.00	38.50	25.00	6.00	4.20	2.75
267	2¢ carmine (III) . . .	6.50	4.00	3.00	.35	.30	.25
268	3¢ purple	50.00	31.25	22.25	3.00	1.90	1.25
269	4¢ dark brown . . .	65.00	38.00	26.00	4.25	2.85	1.50
270	5¢ chocolate	52.50	36.00	22.00	4.25	2.75	1.75
271	6¢ dull brown	165.00	90.00	65.00	9.00	6.00	4.50
272	8¢ violet brown . . .	85.00	50.00	35.00	3.50	2.00	1.25
273	10¢ dark green . . .	125.00	70.00	50.00	2.75	1.75	1.00
274	15¢ dark blue	300.00	170.00	110.00	27.50	18.00	12.25
275	50¢ orange	375.00	225.00	160.00	75.00	52.50	32.00
276	$1 black (I)	775.00	450.00	310.00	155.00	100.00	64.00
276A	$1 black (II)	1500.00	1000.00	700.00	275.00	195.00	135.00
277	$2 bright blue	1100.00	825.00	625.00	625.00	450.00	305.00
278	$5 dark green	2500.00	1800.00	1050.00	925.00	600.00	425.00
	1898 New Colors (NH + 75%)						
279	1¢ deep green . . .	15.00	9.00	6.50	.50	.35	.25
279B	2¢ red (IV)	13.00	7.50	5.00	.50	.30	.25
279Bc	2¢ rose carmine (IV)	325.00	195.00	120.00	200.00	125.00	95.00
279Bd	2¢ orange red (IV)	17.50	10.00	7.00	2.00	1.50	1.00
280	4¢ rose brown . . .	55.00	37.25	24.75	4.00	2.65	1.75
281	5¢ dark blue	48.00	29.00	18.00	2.75	1.85	1.00
282	6¢ lake	80.00	52.50	40.00	8.00	5.50	3.25
282C	10¢ brown (I)	265.00	180.00	125.00	7.00	4.65	3.00
283	10¢ orange brown (II)	210.00	125.00	78.00	9.00	5.75	3.50
284	15¢ olive green . . .	190.00	115.00	80.00	20.00	12.50	8.75

1898 THE TRANS-MISSISSIPPI ISSUE

Issued for the Trans-Mississippi Exposition in Omaha, Nebraska, the "Omahas", as they also are known, did not receive the same welcome from collectors as that accorded the first commemorative set, the 1893 Columbians. Although the uproar was ascribed to the fact that collectors felt put upon by another set with $1 and $2 values, had the $1 to $5 values in the Columbian series appreciated in value, no doubt the protests would have been muted.

On the other hand, the public at large enjoyed the new issue. The Trans-Mississippi issues depict various works of art and are among the most beautiful stamps ever issued by the United States. The 8 and 10 cent values reproduce works by Frederic Remington and the $1 "Western Cattle in Storm", based on a work by J.A. MacWhirter, is regarded as one of our finest examples of the engraver's art.

As appealing as these stamps are in single colors, the set might have been even more beautiful. The original intent was to print each stamp with the vignette, or central design, in black and the frame in a distinctive second color that would be different for each denomination. That plan had to be dropped when the Bureau was called upon to produce large quantities of revenue stamps at the outbreak of the Spanish-American War.

285
Marquette on the Mississippi

286
Farming in the West

287
Indian Hunting Buffalo

288
Fremont on the Rocky Mountains

289
Troops Guarding Train

290
Hardships of Emigration

291
Western Mining Prospector

292
Western Cattle in Storm

293
Eads Bridge over Mississippi River

SCOTT NO.	DESCRIPTION	UNUSED O.G. VF	F	AVG	USED VF	F	AVG
	1898 Trans-Mississippi Exposition Issue (†) (NH + 100%)						
285	1¢ dark yellow green	55.00	36.75	25.75	10.00	6.50	4.00
286	2¢ copper red............	35.00	23.00	17.50	3.00	2.00	1.25
287	4¢ orange..................	225.00	135.00	95.00	59.00	35.00	22.00
288	5¢ dull blue................	240.00	135.00	92.00	32.00	20.00	11.00
289	8¢ violet brown..........	310.00	200.00	125.00	85.00	55.00	32.00
290	10¢ gray violet...........	260.00	165.00	100.00	56.00	33.00	19.00
291	50¢ sage green.........	950.00	575.00	475.00	250.00	180.00	140.00
292	$1 black.....................	2000.00	1150.00	850.00	990.00	775.00	600.00
293	$2 orange brown.......	2500.00	1600.00	1000.00	1200.00	950.00	700.00

1901 THE PAN-AMERICAN ISSUE

Issued to commemorate the Pan-American Exposition in Buffalo, N.Y., this set depicts important engineering and manufacturing achievements. The beautiful engraving is showcased by the bicolored printing.

294, 294a
Fast Lake Navigation

295, 295a
Fast Express

296, 296a
Automobile

297
Bridge at Niagara Falls

298
Canal at Sault Ste. Marie

299
Fast Ocean Navigation

SCOTT NO.	DESCRIPTION	UNUSED O.G. VF	F	AVG	USED VF	F	AVG
	1901 Pan-American Issue (NH + 75%)						
294-99	1¢-10¢ (6 varieties, complete)	530.00	370.00	300.00	190.00	125.00	80.00
294	1¢ green & black.........	25.00	16.00	12.00	3.00	2.20	1.50
294a	same, center inverted	...	12500.00	...	...	16000.00	...
295	2¢ carmine & black.....	22.00	14.00	11.00	1.30	.90	.40
295a	same, center inverted	...	45000.00	...	...	60000.00	...
296	4¢ deep red brown & black...	90.00	70.00	60.00	24.00	14.00	11.00
296a	same, center inverted	...	40000.00	...	...	...	...
296aS	same, center inverted (Specimen)......	...	7500.00	...	...	...	...
297	5¢ ultramarine & black	90.00	70.00	60.00	24.00	14.00	11.00
298	8¢ brown violet & black	150.00	90.00	70.00	95.00	60.00	40.00
299	10¢ yellow brown & black.	175.00	130.00	90.00	45.00	35.00	20.00

	UNUSED PLATE BLOCKS OF 6 NH F	NH AVG	OG F	OG AVG	UNUSED ARROW BLOCKS NH F	NH AVG	OG F	OG AVG
294	475.00	340.00	285.00	215.00	165.00	105.00	72.50	57.50
295	475.00	340.00	280.00	215.00	160.00	100.00	65.00	50.00
296	3750.00	2750.00	2100.00	1650.00	825.00	575.00	375.00	315.00
297	4200.00	3250.00	2600.00	2000.00	825.00	550.00	400.00	325.00
298	7500.00	5500.00	4000.00	3200.00	1050.00	700.00	500.00	375.00
299	10500.00	8000.00	6000.00	4800.00	1500.00	900.00	695.00	500.00

(†) means Issue is actually very poorly centered.
Perforations may touch the design on "Fine" quality.

THE 1902-03 SERIES

The Series of 1902-03 was the first regular issue designed and produced by the United States Bureau of Engraving and Printing, most of the work on the 1894-98 series having been performed by the American Bank Note Company. (When the Bureau was awarded the contract to produce the 1894 series, they added triangles in the upper corners of the American Bank Note designs.)

The new series filled a number of gaps and was the first United States issue to feature a woman—in this case Martha Washington, on the 8 cent value.

Modern collectors consider the 1902-03 issue one of the finest regular series ever produced by the Bureau.

The intricate frame designs take us back to a period when such work still was affordable. In its time, however, the 1902-03 set was looked upon with disdain. The 2 cent Washington, with its ornate frame design and unflattering likeness of George Washington, came in for particular scorn. Yielding to the clamor, in 1903, less than one year after its release, the Post Office recalled the much criticized 2 cent stamp and replaced it with an attractive, less ornate design that cleaned up Washington's appearance, particularly in the area of the nose, and used a shield design that was less ornate.

The issue marked the first time United States stamps were issued in booklet form, the 1 and 2 cent values being printed in panes of six stamps each. Also for the first time since perforating was adopted in 1857, United States stamps were once again deliberately issued in imperforate form for postal use. The intent was to have such stamps available in sheet and coil form for use in vending machines. The manufacturers of such machines could purchase the imperforate stamps and perforate them to fit their equipment. One of these imperforate issues, the 4 cent brown of 1908 (#314A), ranks as one of the great rarities of 20th century philately. It is found only with the private perforations of the Schermack Mailing Machine Company.

Coil stamps intended for use in stamp affixing and vending machines also made their inaugural appearance with this issue. Their availability was not widely publicized and few collectors obtained copies of these coils. All genuine coils from this series are very rare and extremely valuable. We emphasize the word "genuine" because most coils that are seen actually have been faked by trimming the perforated stamps or fraudulently perforating the imperfs.

The only major design types are found on the 1903 2 cent, catalog #s 319 and 320. Identified as Die I and Die II, the differences are described in the Harris Stamp Identifier.

300, 314, 316, 318
Franklin

301
Washington

302
Jackson

303, 314A
Grant

304, 315, 317
Lincoln

305
Garfield

306
Martha Washington

307
Webster

308
Harrison

309
Clay

310
Jefferson

311
Farragut

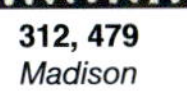

312, 479
Madison

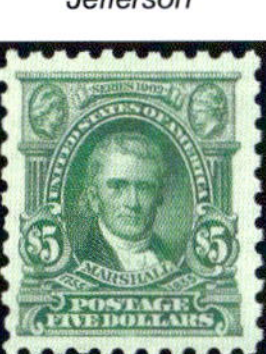

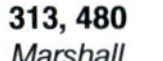

313, 480
Marshall

319-22
Washington

SCOTT NO.	DESCRIPTION	UNUSED O.G. VF	UNUSED O.G. F	UNUSED O.G. AVG	USED VF	USED F	USED AVG
	1902-03 Perf. 12 (†) (NH + 75%)						
300	1¢ blue green	16.00	9.00	6.00	.35	.25	.20
300b	1¢ booklet pane of 6	....	550.00	375.00	....	....	....
301	2¢ carmine	19.50	13.00	8.00	.35	.25	.20
301c	2¢ booklet pane of 6	....	475.00	335.00	....	....	....
302	3¢ brown violet. . .	75.00	43.00	30.00	6.00	3.95	2.25
303	4¢ brown	75.00	43.00	30.00	2.50	1.50	1.00
304	5¢ blue	82.50	50.00	35.00	3.50	1.75	.90
305	6¢ claret	90.00	50.00	35.00	9.00	5.00	3.00
306	8¢ violet black . . .	65.00	35.00	27.00	5.00	2.75	1.75
307	10¢ pale red brown	85.00	50.00	36.00	4.00	2.25	1.50
308	13¢ purple black. .	60.00	35.00	25.00	17.00	11.00	6.50
309	15¢ olive green. . .	225.00	140.00	98.00	17.00	11.00	7.00
310	50¢ orange.	625.00	375.00	260.00	52.00	33.00	23.00
311	$1 black	800.00	525.00	360.00	120.00	73.00	46.00
312	$2 dark blue	1000.00	900.00	550.00	325.00	250.00	180.00
313	$5 dark green. . . .	2500.00	2000.00	1500.00	1000.00	750.00	525.00
	1906-08 Imperforate (NH + 75%)						
	This and all subsequent imperforate issues can usually be priced as unused pairs at double the single price.						
314	1¢ blue green	20.00	15.00	10.00	35.00	20.00	15.00
314A	4¢ brown	....	100000.00	....	....	50000.00	....
315	5¢ blue	600.00	400.00	300.00	1500.00	900.00	650.00
	1908 Coil Stamps. Perf 12 Horizontally						
316	1¢ blue green, pair	....	....	....	....	....	....
317	5¢ blue, pair	....	5800.00	....	....	....	....
	1908 Coil Stamps. Perf 12 Vertically						
318	1¢ blue green, pair	....	5500.00	....	....	....	....
	1903. Perf. 12 (†) (NH + 60%)						
319	2¢ carmine, Die I .	10.00	6.00	4.75	.50	.30	.20
319f	2¢ lake, Die II	17.50	11.00	7.50	1.00	.70	.50
319g	2¢ carmine, Die I, booklet pane of 6 .	....	160.00	......	......	....	....
	1906 Imperforate (NH + 75%)						
320	2¢ carmine, Die I .	55.00	40.00	28.00	79.00	45.00	31.00
320a	2¢ lake, Die I	80.00	65.00	45.00	58.00	40.00	28.00
	1908 Coil Stamps. Perf 12 Horizontally						
321	2¢ carmine, pair . .	....	....	....	....	....	....
	1908 Coil Stamps. Perf 12 Vertically						
322	2¢ carmine, pair . .	....	7500.00	....	....	....	....

SCOTT NO.	UNUSED NH F	UNUSED NH AVG	UNUSED OG F	UNUSED OG AVG	SCOTT NO.	UNUSED NH F	UNUSED NH AVG	UNUSED OG F	UNUSED OG AVG
	PLATE BLOCKS OF 6					**CENTER LINE BLOCKS**			
300	350.00	200.00	215.00	137.50	314	300.00	200.00	180.00	145.00
301	425.00	220.00	235.00	155.00	320	335.00	235.00	200.00	175.00
314	425.00	315.00	290.00	215.00		**ARROW BLOCKS**			
319	295.00	200.00	160.00	115.00	314	235.00	185.00	140.00	110.00
320	415.00	290.00	225.00	175.00	320	250.00	200.00	135.00	100.00

1904 THE LOUISIANA PURCHASE ISSUE

Issued to commemorate the Louisiana Purchase Exposition held in St. Louis in 1904, these stamps were not well received. Collectors at the time did not purchase large quantities of the stamps, and the series was on sale for only seven months. As a result, well centered unused stamps are extremely difficult to locate.

323
Robert R. Livingston

324
Jefferson

325
Monroe

326
McKinley

327
Map of Louisiana Purchase

SCOTT NO.	DESCRIPTION	UNUSED O.G. VF	F	AVG	USED VF	F	AVG
	1904 Louisiana Purchase Issue (NH + 75%)						
323-27	**1¢-10¢ (5 varieties, complete) ......**	**460.00**	**325.00**	**185.00**	**120.00**	**70.00**	**52.00**
323	1¢ green........	45.00	25.00	20.00	8.00	6.00	3.00
324	2¢ carmine......	30.00	22.00	16.00	2.75	2.25	1.25
325	3¢ violet........	120.00	80.00	50.00	40.00	20.00	15.00
326	5¢ dark blue.....	120.00	80.00	50.00	30.00	20.00	15.00
327	10¢ red brown ...	150.00	120.00	100.00	40.00	25.00	20.00

1907 THE JAMESTOWN EXPOSITION ISSUE

This set may be the most difficult United States 20th century issue to find well centered. Issued in April, 1907 for the Jamestown Exposition at Hampton Roads, Virginia, the set was removed from sale when the Exposition closed on November 30th of that year. Very fine copies carry hefty premiums.

328
Capt. John Smith

329
Founding of Jamestown

330
Pocahontas

SCOTT NO.	DESCRIPTION	UNUSED O.G. VF	F	AVG	USED VF	F	AVG
	1907 Jamestown Exposition Issue (NH + 75%)						
328-30	**1¢-5¢ (3 varieties, complete) ......**	**220.00**	**155.00**	**100.00**	**50.00**	**35.00**	**22.00**
328	1¢ green........	35.00	20.00	15.00	6.00	4.00	3.00
329	2¢ carmine......	40.00	20.00	14.00	6.00	4.00	2.00
330	5¢ blue.........	150.00	120.00	80.00	40.00	30.00	20.00

SCOTT NO.	UNUSED PLATE BLOCKS OF 6 NH F	NH AVG	OG F	OG AVG	UNUSED ARROW BLOCKS NH F	NH AVG	OG F	OG AVG
323	550.00	415.00	275.00	220.00	200.00	120.00	130.00	85.00
324	550.00	412.50	290.00	220.00	160.00	100.00	95.00	65.00
325	1750.00	1325.00	1120.00	840.00	550.00	355.00	400.00	265.00
326	1750.00	1150.00	965.00	845.00	675.00	380.00	375.00	250.00
327	3000.00	1950.00	1500.00	1150.00	1100.00	715.00	650.00	530.00
328	700.00	490.00	400.00	300.00	150.00	95.00	100.00	75.00
329	700.00	475.00	415.00	285.00	195.00	110.00	120.00	95.00
330	5000.00	3000.00	2750.00	1950.00	800.00	475.00	400.00	300.00

THE WASHINGTON-FRANKLIN HEADS

The Washington-Franklin Heads—so called because all stamps in the regular series featured the busts of George Washington and Benjamin Franklin—dominated the postal scene for almost two decades. Using a variety of papers, denominations, perforation sizes and formats, watermarks, design modifications and printing processes, almost 200 different major catalog listings were created from two basic designs.

The series started modestly, with the issuance of 12 stamps (#331-342) between November 1908 and January 1909. The modest designs on the new set replaced the ornate 1902-03 series. Their relative simplicity might have relegated the set to a secondary position in 20th century United States philately had it not been for the complexity of the varieties and the years of study the Washington-Franklin Heads now present to collectors.

The first varieties came almost immediately, in the form of imperforate stamps (#343-347) and coils, the latter being offered with horizontal (#348-351) or vertical (#352-356) perforations. The imperfs were intended for the fading vending machine technology that required private perforations while the coils were useful in standardized dispensers that were just coming into their own.

Then, in 1909, the Post Office began its experimentation. In this instance, it was the paper. As noted in our introduction to the 1909 Bluish Papers which follows, the Post Office Department and the Bureau of Engraving and Printing hoped that the new paper would reduce losses due to uneven shrinkage of the white wove paper used at the time. The experimental Washington-Franklin Bluish Papers (#357-66) are now among the most valuable in the series and the 8 cent Bluish Paper (#363) is the highest priced of the major listed items.

Attention was next directed to the double line watermark as the cause of the uneven shrinkage, as well as for weakness and thinning in the paper. As a result, a narrower, single line watermark was adopted for sheet stamps (#374-82), imperforates (#383-84), and coils with horizontal perfs (#385-86) and vertical perfs (#387-89).

Even as these experiments were being conducted, the perforation size was being examined to determine if a change was in order. Up until now, the perf 12 gauge had been used on all Washington-Franklin Heads.

The first perforation change was necessitated by the development of new coil manufacturing equipment. Under the increased pressure of the new equipment, the coil strips with the closely-spaced perf 12 gauge were splitting while being rolled into coils. To add paper between the holes, a perf 8-1/2 gauge was adopted for coil stamps and two new major varieties were created: with horizontal perfs (#390-91) and vertical perfs (#392-396).

Necessity was the driving force behind still more changes in 1912, when stamps with numeral denominations were issued to replace the "ONE CENT" and "TWO CENTS" stamps. This responded to the need for numeral denominations on foreign mail and created new sheets (#410-11) and vertically perforated (#412-13) coils. At the same time, a 7 cent value (#407) was issued to meet changing rate requirements.

In conjunction with the introduction of numerals on the 1 and 2 cent stamps, the design of the 1 cent was changed, with the bust of Washington replacing that of Franklin. Meanwhile, the bust of Franklin, which had been used only on the 1 cent stamp, was placed on all values from 8 cents to the $1 (#414-21) and a ribbon was added across their top to make the high value stamp even more noticeable to postal clerks.

As if to add just a little more variety while all the other changes were being made—but in actuality to use up a supply of old double-line watermark paper—50 cent and $1 issues with double-line watermarks (#422-23) were introduced.

The work with perforation changes on coil stamps carried over to sheet stamps in 1914 with the release of a perf 10 series (#424-40). The perf 10 size was then adapted to coils perforated horizontally (#441-42) and vertically (#443-47).

The transition to Rotary Press printing created new coils perforated 10 horizontally (#448-50) and vertically (#452-58). An imperforate Rotary coil (#459) for vending machine manufacturers also was produced.

A perf 10 double-line watermark $1 (#460) and a perf 11 two-cent sheet stamp (#461) added only slightly to the variety, but were followed by completely new runs on unwatermarked paper: perf 10 sheet stamps (#462-478) and imperforates (#481-84) were produced on the flat plate presses, while the Rotary press was used for coils perforated horizontally (#486-489) and vertically (#490-97).

While all this was taking place, the amazing 5 cent carmine error of color (#485) appeared on certain imperf 2 cent sheets. That same error (in rose, #505) was found when perf 11 sheet stamps (#498-518) were issued. The stamps turned out to be too hard to separate. Another strange issue, a 2 cent stamp on double-line watermark paper but perforated 11 (#519), came about when a small supply of old imperfs (#344) were discovered and put into the postal stream.

New $2 and $5 Franklins (#523-24), the former using an erroneous color, were released. To compensate for plate damage being caused by poor quality offset printings, perf 11 (#525-530) and imperforate (#531-535) were tried—and quickly resulted in a whole new series of "types" that had collectors spending more time with their magnifying glasses than with their families.

Odd perf sizes and printings (#538/546) came about as the Bureau cleaned out old paper stock. Then, in one final change, the Bureau corrected the color of the $2 from orange red and black to carmine and black. Almost 200 different stamps, all from two basic designs!

1909 THE BLUISH PAPERS

The Bluish Paper varieties are found on the 1 through 15 cent Washington-Franklin series of 1908-09 and on the 1909 Commemoratives. According to Post Office notices of the period, the experimental paper was a 30% rag stock that was intended to reduce paper waste. After being wet, a preliminary operation in the printing process, the standard white wove paper often would shrink so much that the perforators would cut into the designs. The rag paper did not solve the problem, the experiment was quickly abandoned and the 1909 Bluish Papers became major rarities.

The Harris Stamp Identifier provides further information on identifying the Washington-Franklin Heads.

331, 343, 348, 352, 357, 374, 383, 385, 387, 390, 392
Franklin

332, 344, 349, 353, 358, 375, 384, 386, 388, 391, 393
Washington

333, 345, 359, 376, 389, 394
Washington

334, 346, 350, 354, 360, 377, 395
Washington

335, 347, 351, 355, 361, 378, 396
Washington

336, 362, 379
Washington

337, 363, 380
Washington

338, 356, 364, 381
Washington

339, 365
Washington

340, 366, 382
Washington

341
Washington

342
Washington

***NOTE:** For further details on the various types of similar appearing stamps please refer to our U.S. Stamp Identifier.*

1908-09 Double Line Watermark "USPS" Perf. 12
(NH + 75%)

SCOTT NO.	DESCRIPTION	UNUSED O.G. VF	UNUSED O.G. F	UNUSED O.G. AVG	USED VF	USED F	USED AVG
331-42	**1¢-$1 (12 varieties, complete) ......**	**1600.00**	**960.00**	**620.00**	**300.00**	**200.00**	**115.00**
331	1¢ green........	11.25	6.50	4.00	1.00	.70	.60
331a	1¢ booklet pane of 6	200.00	145.00	95.00	......	......	......
332	2¢ carmine......	11.25	7.00	4.25	.75	.50	.40
332a	2¢ booklet pane of 6	185.00	120.00	85.00	......	......	......
333	3¢ deep violet (I) .	52.50	29.00	18.00	6.50	4.25	2.50
334	4¢ orange brown .	55.00	34.00	22.00	2.00	1.25	.80
335	5¢ blue.........	72.00	40.00	24.00	3.75	2.60	1.75
336	6¢ red orange....	80.00	50.00	30.00	8.50	5.00	3.25
337	8¢ olive green....	60.00	38.00	24.00	5.50	3.25	2.25
338	10¢ yellow	85.00	58.00	43.00	4.75	2.50	1.50
339	13¢ blue green...	60.00	34.00	23.00	80.00	50.00	29.00
340	15¢ pale ultramarine	82.00	50.00	35.00	12.00	8.00	5.00
341	50¢ violet	400.00	235.00	145.00	45.00	30.00	18.00
342	$1 violet brown...	675.00	400.00	260.00	145.00	100.00	63.00

1908-09 Imperforate
(NH + 75%)

SCOTT NO.	DESCRIPTION	UNUSED O.G. VF	UNUSED O.G. F	UNUSED O.G. AVG	USED VF	USED F	USED AVG
343-47	**1¢-5¢ (5 varieties, complete) ......**	**90.00**	**65.00**	**50.00**	**100.00**	**75.00**	**50.00**
343	1¢ green........	6.00	4.00	3.00	5.75	4.50	2.75
344	2¢ carmine......	6.50	4.50	4.00	5.00	4.00	2.75
345	3¢ deep violet (I) .	16.00	14.00	12.00	28.00	19.00	11.00
346	4¢ orange brown .	18.00	15.00	10.00	28.00	20.00	18.00
347	5¢ blue.........	45.00	30.00	24.00	42.00	30.00	20.00

1908-10 Coil Stamps Perf. 12 Horizontally
(NH + 75%)

SCOTT NO.	DESCRIPTION	UNUSED O.G. VF	UNUSED O.G. F	UNUSED O.G. AVG	USED VF	USED F	USED AVG
348	1¢ green........	48.00	30.00	28.00	55.00	35.00	25.00
349	2¢ carmine......	115.00	80.00	55.00	150.00	80.00	65.00
350	4¢ orange brown .	150.00	100.00	85.00	240.00	160.00	140.00
351	5¢ blue.........	150.00	100.00	85.00	350.00	220.00	160.00

NOTE: **Counterfeits are common on #348-56 and #385-89**

1909 Coil Stamps Perf. 12 Vertically
(NH + 75%)

SCOTT NO.	DESCRIPTION	UNUSED O.G. VF	UNUSED O.G. F	UNUSED O.G. AVG	USED VF	USED F	USED AVG
352	1¢ green........	140.00	80.00	70.00	250.00	175.00	90.00
353	2¢ carmine......	175.00	125.00	82.50	240.00	150.00	70.00
354	4¢ orange brown .	275.00	170.00	110.00	290.00	175.00	110.00
355	5¢ blue.........	300.00	180.00	120.00	350.00	250.00	175.00
356	10¢ yellow	3500.00	2500.00	2000.00	6000.00	4000.00	3000.00

PLATE BLOCKS OF 6

SCOTT NO.	UNUSED NH F	UNUSED NH AVG	UNUSED OG F	UNUSED OG AVG
331	140.00	110.00	100.00	70.00
332	140.00	110.00	100.00	70.00
333	450.00	325.00	290.00	210.00
334	635.00	415.00	400.00	280.00
335	950.00	700.00	600.00	475.00
336	1250.00	900.00	700.00	495.00
337	700.00	495.00	375.00	275.00
338	1000.00	790.00	735.00	475.00
339	750.00	615.00	430.00	320.00
343	125.00	115.00	80.00	60.00
344	175.00	140.00	152.50	110.00
345	330.00	250.00	320.00	240.00
346	600.00	450.00	465.00	390.00
347	650.00	525.00	555.00	400.00

CENTER LINE BLOCKS

SCOTT NO.	UNUSED NH F	UNUSED NH AVG	UNUSED OG F	UNUSED OG AVG
343	80.00	60.00	60.00	45.00
344	105.00	90.00	87.50	55.00
345	250.00	185.00	190.00	155.00
346	325.00	285.00	275.00	200.00
347	450.00	315.00	325.00	230.00

ARROW BLOCKS

SCOTT NO.	UNUSED NH F	UNUSED NH AVG	UNUSED OG F	UNUSED OG AVG
343	57.50	52.00	52.00	37.50
344	100.00	87.50	85.00	55.00
345	240.00	180.00	185.00	150.00
346	295.00	260.00	250.00	175.00
347	390.00	300.00	320.00	210.00

(NH + 75%)

SCOTT NO.	COIL LINE PAIRS UNUSED OG VF	COIL LINE PAIRS UNUSED OG F	COIL LINE PAIRS UNUSED OG AVG	COIL PAIRS UNUSED OG VF	COIL PAIRS UNUSED OG F	COIL PAIRS UNUSED OG AVG
348	365.00	235.00	160.00	180.00	125.00	80.00
349	675.00	450.00	310.00	300.00	215.00	130.00
350	1300.00	1000.00	725.00	650.00	420.00	310.00
351	2250.00	1675.00	1225.00	600.00	400.00	270.00
352	1050.00	765.00	540.00	350.00	250.00	175.00
353	700.00	500.00	350.00	330.00	230.00	165.00
354	1650.00	1100.00	775.00	800.00	570.00	395.00
355	1650.00	1100.00	775.00	800.00	625.00	445.00
356	17500.00	12000.00	9000.00	10000.00	6800.00	4500.00

1909 Bluish Gray paper Perf. 12 (NH + 75%)

SCOTT NO.	DESCRIPTION	UNUSED O.G. VF	UNUSED O.G. F	UNUSED O.G. AVG	USED VF	USED F	USED AVG
357	1¢ green........	105.00	80.00	55.00	175.00	140.00	100.00
358	2¢ carmine......	100.00	75.00	50.00	175.00	140.00	100.00
359	3¢ deep violet (I) .	2400.00	1800.00	1300.00	9800.00	7000.00	6000.00
360	4¢ orange brown .	......	27000.00	18000.00	......	......	......
361	5¢ blue.........	7000.00	3900.00	2800.00	20000.00	15000.00	11500.00
362	6¢ red orange....	2000.00	1200.00	800.00	22500.00	15500.00	11350.00
363	8¢ olive green....	......	30000.00	20000.00	......	......	......
364	10¢ yellow	2500.00	1500.00	1100.00	12000.00	9000.00	8000.00
365	13¢ blue green...	3500.00	2200.00	1500.00	4000.00	2700.00	1850.00
366	15¢ pale ultramarine	1900.00	1400.00	1100.00	13000.00	10000.00	7000.00

THE 1909 COMMEMORATIVES

After the 16-value Columbian commemorative set, the Post Office Department began gradually reducing the number of stamps in subsequent series. The 1909 commemoratives were the first to use the single-stamp commemorative approach that is now the common practice.

The Lincoln Memorial issue was released on the 100th anniversary of the birth of America's 16th President. The Alaska-Yukon was issued for the Alaska-Yukon Exposition held in Seattle to publicize the development of the Alaska territory. The Hudson-Fulton stamp commemorated Henry Hudson's 1609 discovery of the river that bears his name, the 1809 voyage of Robert Fulton's "Clermont" steamboat and the 1909 celebration of those two events.

As noted earlier, the 1909 Commemoratives were issued on experimental "bluish" paper in addition to the white wove standard. The stamps on white wove paper also were issued in imperforate form for private perforation by vending and stamp-affixing machine manufacturers.

367-369
Lincoln

370, 371
William H. Seward

372, 373
S.S. Clermont

SCOTT NO.	DESCRIPTION	UNUSED O.G. VF	UNUSED O.G. F	UNUSED O.G. AVG	USED VF	USED F	USED AVG
	1909 LINCOLN MEMORIAL ISSUE (NH + 50%)						
367	2¢ carmine, perf. .	8.00	5.50	3.50	2.00	1.50	1.00
368	2¢ carmine, imperf.	25.00	15.00	12.00	28.00	18.00	15.00
369	2¢ carmine (bluish paper)	200.00	165.00	115.00	270.00	180.00	140.00
	1909 ALASKA-YUKON ISSUE						
370	2¢ carmine, perf. .	11.00	8.00	5.50	3.00	2.20	1.40
371	2¢ carmine, imperf.	20.00	12.00	10.00	25.00	16.00	10.00
	1909 HUDSON-FULTON ISSUE						
372	2¢ carmine, perf. .	12.50	8.00	6.00	5.00	3.20	2.00
373	2¢ carmine, imperf	22.00	15.00	11.00	30.00	18.00	13.00
	1910-11 Single Line Watermark "USPS" Perf. 12 (NH + 50%)						
374-82	**1¢-15¢ (9 varieties, complete) . . . . . .**	**700.00**	**495.00**	**398.00**	**60.00**	**40.00**	**28.00**
374	1¢ green.	15.00	9.50	6.00	.30	.30	.20
374a	1¢ booklet pane of 6	225.00	145.00	100.00	......	......	......
375	2¢ carmine	14.50	9.00	6.00	.30	.30	.20
375a	2¢ booklet pane of 6	150.00	105.00	66.00	......	......	......
376	3¢ deep violet (I) .	32.50	18.00	12.00	4.25	2.50	1.50
377	4¢ brown	47.50	28.50	21.50	1.25	.85	.55
378	5¢ blue	40.00	24.00	18.00	1.50	1.10	.75
379	6¢ red orange. . . .	60.00	36.00	23.00	2.25	1.25	.85
380	8¢ olive green. . . .	115.00	90.00	70.00	22.00	15.00	11.00
381	10¢ yellow	125.00	95.00	75.00	7.00	5.50	3.75
382	15¢ pale ultramarine	255.00	190.00	170.00	25.00	16.00	11.00
	1911 Imperforate						
383	1¢ green.	3.25	2.70	1.50	2.75	1.75	1.10
384	2¢ carmine	4.20	3.25	2.10	3.00	2.20	1.80

SCOTT NO.	UNUSED NH F	UNUSED NH AVG	UNUSED OG F	UNUSED OG AVG
	PLATE BLOCKS OF 6			
367	225.00	155.00	160.00	110.00
368	385.00	270.00	300.00	220.00
370	320.00	220.00	220.00	150.00
371	475.00	330.00	345.00	235.00
372	400.00	250.00	290.00	200.00
373	475.00	330.00	345.00	235.00
374	150.00	90.00	85.00	60.00
375	150.00	85.00	95.00	70.00
376	350.00	230.00	245.00	220.00
377	390.00	250.00	285.00	185.00
378	325.00	245.00	245.00	185.00
383	100.00	68.75	62.50	45.00
384	210.00	150.00	140.00	95.00

SCOTT NO.	UNUSED NH F	UNUSED NH AVG	UNUSED OG F	UNUSED OG AVG
	CENTER LINE BLOCKS			
368	225.00	165.00	165.00	125.00
371	300.00	200.00	200.00	150.00
373	365.00	265.00	265.00	200.00
383	45.00	30.00	30.00	25.00
384	90.00	55.00	65.00	40.00
	ARROW BLOCKS			
368	180.00	130.00	120.00	110.00
371	235.00	190.00	180.00	135.00
373	265.00	200.00	200.00	160.00
383	42.00	30.00	30.00	20.00
384	50.00	45.00	45.00	36.00

Very Fine Plate Blocks from this period command premiums.

SCOTT NO.	DESCRIPTION	UNUSED O.G. VF	UNUSED O.G. F	UNUSED O.G. AVG	USED VF	USED F	USED AVG
	COIL STAMPS 1910 Perf. 12 Horizontally (NH + 75%)						
385	1¢ green.	60.00	45.00	30.00	48.00	30.00	20.00
386	2¢ carmine	165.00	100.00	70.00	100.00	70.00	55.00
	1910-11 Perf. 12 Vertically (†)						
387	1¢ green.	240.00	180.00	130.00	145.00	110.00	70.00
388	2¢ carmine	1650.00	1200.00	875.00	2100.00	800.00	600.00
389	3¢ deep violet (I) .	......	110000.00	......	......	12500.00	......
	1910 Perf. 8-1/2 Horizontally						
390	1¢ green.	7.00	4.00	3.00	15.00	11.00	8.00
391	2¢ carmine	65.00	38.00	22.00	60.00	42.00	28.00
	1910-13 Perf. 8-1/2 Vertically						
392	1¢ green.	35.00	24.00	15.00	60.00	39.00	25.00
393	2¢ carmine	55.00	38.00	22.00	50.00	30.00	20.00
394	3¢ deep violet (I) .	75.00	55.00	45.00	70.00	45.00	30.00
395	4¢ brown	75.00	55.00	45.00	80.00	75.00	52.00
396	5¢ blue	70.00	50.00	40.00	98.00	68.00	45.00

(NH + 75%)

SCOTT NO.	COIL LINE PAIRS UNUSED OG VF	COIL LINE PAIRS UNUSED OG F	COIL LINE PAIRS UNUSED OG AVG	COIL PAIRS UNUSED OG VF	COIL PAIRS UNUSED OG F	COIL PAIRS UNUSED OG AVG
385	450.00	300.00	195.00	200.00	125.00	87.50
386	1300.00	800.00	550.00	330.00	225.00	130.00
387	1200.00	825.00	585.00	700.00	460.00	310.00
390	50.00	35.00	22.50	25.00	16.50	9.00
391	330.00	235.00	140.00	150.00	100.00	60.00
392	225.00	140.00	95.00	120.00	82.00	48.00
393	325.00	210.00	150.00	155.00	100.00	60.00
394	600.00	395.00	265.00	200.00	135.00	85.00
395	475.00	315.00	225.00	220.00	150.00	95.00
396	450.00	295.00	200.00	210.00	136.00	90.00

THE PANAMA-PACIFIC ISSUE

The Panama-Pacific stamps were issued to commemorate the discovery of the Pacific Ocean in 1513 and the opening of the 1915 Panama-Pacific Exposition that celebrated the completion of the Panama Canal. Released in perf 12 form in 1913, the set of four denominations was changed to perf 10 in 1914. Before the perf change, the 10 cent orange yellow shade was determined to be too light. It was changed to the deeper orange color that is found both perf 12 and perf 10.

Because many collectors ignored the perf 10 stamps when they were issued, these stamps are scarcer than their perf 12 predecessors. In fact, #404 is the rarest 20th century commemorative issue.

397, 401
Balboa

398, 402
Panama Canal

399, 403
Golden Gate

400, 400A, 404
Discovery of San Francisco Bay

SCOTT NO.	DESCRIPTION	UNUSED O.G. VF	UNUSED O.G. F	UNUSED O.G. AVG	USED VF	USED F	USED AVG
	1913 Perf. 12 (NH + 75%)						
397-400A	**1¢-10¢ (5 varieties, complete) . . . .**	**510.00**	**380.00**	**260.00**	**70.00**	**48.50**	**34.00**
397	1¢ green.	25.00	14.00	10.00	2.50	1.70	1.00
398	2¢ carmine	28.00	16.00	12.00	1.75	.90	.75
399	5¢ blue	85.00	65.00	45.00	12.00	8.00	6.00
400	10¢ orange yellow	140.00	114.00	80.00	30.00	22.00	16.00
400A	10¢ orange. . . .	240.00	180.00	118.00	25.00	18.00	12.00
	1914-15 Perf. 10 (NH + 75%)						
401-04	**1¢-10¢ (4 varieties, complete) . . . .**	**1240.00**	**995.00**	**745.00**	**115.00**	**72.00**	**55.00**
401	1¢ green.	35.00	25.00	18.00	9.00	7.00	5.00
402	2¢ carmine	90.00	65.00	52.00	4.50	2.75	1.75
403	5¢ blue	220.00	170.00	120.00	24.00	15.00	10.00
404	10¢ orange. . . .	900.00	740.00	560.00	80.00	50.00	40.00

405/545
Washington

406/546
Washington

426/541
Washington

427, 446, 457, 465, 495, 503
Washington

428, 447, 458, 466, 467, 496, 504, 505
Washington

429, 468, 506
Washington

407, 430, 469, 507
Washington

414, 431, 470, 508
Franklin

415, 432, 471, 509
Franklin

416, 433, 472, 497, 510
Franklin

434, 473, 511
Franklin

417, 435, 474 512
Franklin

513
Franklin

418, 437, 475, 514
Franklin

419, 438, 476, 515
Franklin

420, 439, 476A, 516
Franklin

421, 422, 440, 477, 517
Franklin

423, 478, 518, 460
Franklin

SCOTT NO.	DESCRIPTION	UNUSED O.G. VF	F	AVG	USED VF	F	AVG
	1912-14 Single Line Watermark Perf. 12 (NH + 60%)						
405	1¢ green......	16.50	9.50	5.50	1.00	.80	.65
405b	1¢ booklet pane of 6	95.00	65.00	45.00	......	......	......
406	2¢ carmine (I). .	11.00	7.00	4.25	.75	.65	.50
406a	2¢ booklet pane of 6	95.00	65.00	45.00	......	......	......
407	7¢ black	125.00	75.00	50.00	25.00	16.00	10.50
	1912 Imperforate						
408	1¢ green......	2.75	2.00	1.50	1.50	.95	.65
409	2¢ carmine (I). .	3.95	3.00	2.00	1.50	1.15	.85

SCOTT NO.	UNUSED NH F	AVG	UNUSED OG F	AVG
	PLATE BLOCKS OF 6			
397	350.00	237.50	260.00	167.50
398	450.00	350.00	290.00	200.00
401	425.00	250.00	275.00	195.00
405	160.00	120.00	100.00	70.00
406	160.00	120.00	100.00	70.00
408	32.00	24.00	19.00	14.00
409	56.00	40.00	35.00	25.00

SCOTT NO.	UNUSED NH F	AVG	UNUSED OG F	AVG
	CENTER LINE BLOCKS			
408	15.50	11.00	11.00	8.50
409	17.00	11.95	14.50	9.50
	ARROW BLOCKS			
408	10.00	9.00	7.50	6.00
409	12.00	10.00	10.00	8.00

SCOTT NO.	DESCRIPTION	UNUSED O.G. VF	F	AVG	USED VF	F	AVG
	COIL STAMPS 1912 Perf. 8-1/2 Horizontally (NH + 60%)						
410	1¢ green......	8.95	5.50	3.75	17.50	10.00	5.75
411	2¢ carmine (I). .	14.00	8.50	5.50	14.00	9.00	5.50
	1912 Perf. 8-1/2 Vertically						
412	1¢ green......	32.00	22.00	15.00	40.00	30.00	24.00
413	2¢ carmine (I). .	75.00	43.00	28.00	50.00	40.00	30.00

(NH + 60%)

SCOTT NO.	COIL LINE PAIRS UNUSED OG VF	F	AVG	COIL PAIRS UNUSED OG VF	F	AVG
410	48.00	29.00	18.00	19.00	12.50	8.00
411	70.00	45.00	30.00	30.00	20.00	12.50
412	150.00	100.00	65.00	80.00	60.00	40.00
413	375.00	250.00	170.00	150.00	100.00	65.00

SCOTT NO.	DESCRIPTION	UNUSED O.G. VF	F	AVG	USED VF	F	AVG
	1912-14 Perf. 12 Single Line Watermark (NH + 60%)						
414	8¢ pale olive green	70.00	45.75	30.00	3.50	2.00	1.50
415	9¢ salmon red .	80.00	51.00	30.00	20.00	15.00	10.00
416	10¢ orange yellow	70.00	38.00	24.00	.75	.50	.35
417	12¢ claret brown	70.00	46.00	30.00	7.50	5.00	3.25
418	15¢ gray......	140.00	77.00	50.00	7.00	4.25	3.00
419	20¢ ultramarine	275.00	185.00	115.00	20.00	15.00	10.00
420	30¢ orange red.	160.00	105.00	65.00	20.00	15.00	10.00
421	50¢ violet	575.00	340.00	225.00	30.00	20.00	10.00
	1912 Double Line Watermark "USPS" Perf 12						
422	50¢ violet	350.00	225.00	150.00	30.00	25.00	15.00
423	$1 violet black .	675.00	425.00	250.00	100.00	85.00	60.00
	1914-15 Single Line Watermark, "USPS" Perf. 10 (NH + 60%)						
424-40	**1¢-50¢ (16 varieties, complete) ....**	**2220.00**	**1375.00**	**925.00**	**125.00**	**80.00**	**60.00**
424	1¢ green......	6.50	4.00	2.50	.25	.20	.15
424d	1¢ booklet pane of 6	8.00	4.00	3.00	....	....	....
425	2¢ rose red.....	5.00	2.50	1.75	.25	.20	.15
425e	2¢ booklet pane of 6	30.00	23.00	16.00	....	....	....
426	3¢ deep violet (I)	32.50	20.00	13.00	2.00	1.50	1.00
427	4¢ brown	55.00	34.00	24.00	1.25	.75	.50
428	5¢ blue.......	55.00	39.00	28.00	1.25	.75	.50
429	6¢ red orange. .	70.00	45.00	30.00	3.25	1.75	1.00
430	7¢ black	135.00	79.00	59.00	5.00	3.50	2.25
431	8¢ pale olive green	75.00	48.75	30.00	4.50	3.25	2.25
432	9¢ salmon red .	77.50	42.00	27.00	12.00	7.00	5.00
433	10¢ orange yellow	72.50	43.00	29.00	1.75	1.25	1.00
434	11¢ dark green.	42.50	28.00	20.00	12.00	7.00	5.00
435	12¢ claret brown	40.00	26.00	18.00	8.00	6.00	4.00
437	15¢ gray......	170.00	105.00	80.00	12.00	7.00	5.00
438	20¢ ultramarine	275.00	165.00	115.00	10.00	6.25	4.25
439	30¢ orange red.	400.00	220.00	170.00	28.00	18.00	15.00
440	50¢ violet	800.00	500.00	325.00	28.00	18.00	15.00

UNUSED PLATE BLOCKS OF 6

SCOTT NO.	NH F	AVG	OG F	AVG
414	600.00	400.00	450.00	285.00
415	875.00	612.50	600.00	437.50
416	700.00	450.00	430.00	300.00
417	875.00	595.00	562.50	375.00
418	900.00	650.00	600.00	450.00
424 (6)	75.00	55.00	40.00	27.25
424 (10)	225.00	140.00	155.00	95.00
425 (6)	75.00	40.00	37.50	30.00
425 (10)	225.00	150.00	145.00	100.00
426	350.00	275.00	250.00	150.00
427	600.00	415.00	445.00	315.00
428	500.00	315.00	350.00	210.00
429	525.00	315.00	340.00	200.00
430	1350.00	950.00	900.00	615.00
431	650.00	500.00	500.00	360.00
432	875.00	630.00	650.00	465.00
433	800.00	575.00	600.00	425.00
434	400.00	260.00	290.00	165.00
435	400.00	225.00	270.00	170.00
437	1200.00	850.00	850.00	625.00
438	3850.00	2950.00	2500.00	1950.00
439	6000.00	4275.00	3700.00	2850.00
440	20000.00	13500.00	14500.00	10500.00

SCOTT NO.	DESCRIPTION	UNUSED O.G. VF	F	AVG	USED VF	F	AVG
	COIL STAMPS 1914 Perf. 10 Horizontally (NH + 60%)						
441	1¢ green......	2.75	1.50	1.00	2.50	1.90	1.25
442	2¢ carmine (I). .	17.50	11.00	7.00	50.00	40.00	25.00
	1914 Perf.10 Vertically (NH + 60%)						
443	1¢ green......	50.00	33.00	21.00	40.00	24.00	14.00
444	2¢ carmine (I). .	75.00	44.00	27.00	30.00	21.75	13.50
445	3¢ violet (I)	400.00	255.00	180.00	315.00	200.00	125.00
446	4¢ brown	300.00	200.00	150.00	150.00	90.00	65.00
447	5¢ blue.......	72.50	47.00	33.00	120.00	80.00	50.00

SCOTT NO.	DESCRIPTION	UNUSED O.G. VF	F	AVG	USED VF	F	AVG
	ROTARY PRESS COIL STAMPS 1915-16 Perf. 10 Horizontally (NH + 60%)						
448	1¢ green.	9.50	7.00	4.00	20.00	13.50	8.50
449	2¢ red (I)	3500.00	2100.00	1450.00	725.00	550.00	335.00
450	2¢ carmine (III).	27.50	20.00	14.00	25.00	16.50	8.25
	1914-16 Perf. 10 Vertically (NH + 60%)						
452	1¢ green.	22.50	16.00	12.00	25.00	17.75	12.50
453	2¢ carmine rose (I)	200.00	137.50	93.75	45.00	35.00	25.00
454	2¢ red (II)	145.00	100.00	65.00	25.00	14.25	10.00
455	2¢ carmine (III).	14.00	10.00	6.50	4.50	3.35	1.70
456	3¢ violet (I)	450.00	300.00	190.00	185.00	160.00	140.00
457	4¢ brown	60.00	31.00	22.00	56.00	35.00	21.00
458	5¢ blue.	45.00	30.00	20.00	40.00	38.00	23.00
	1914 Imperforate Coil (NH + 60%)						
459	2¢ carmine (I). .	475.00	375.00	250.00	1400.00	1000.00	....
	1915 Flat Plate Printing Double Line Watermark Perf. 10 (NH + 60%)						
460	$1 violet black .	950.00	550.00	425.00	150.00	125.00	100.00
	1915 Single Line Watermark "USPS" Perf. 11 (NH + 60%)						
461	2¢ pale carmine red (I)	250.00	130.00	73.00	350.00	250.00	170.00
	1916-17 Unwatermarked Perf. 10 (NH + 60%)						
462	1¢ green.	17.50	12.00	8.00	.50	.30	.20
462a	1¢ booklet pane of 6	25.00	16.00	9.50	....	....	....
463	2¢ carmine (I). .	7.95	5.50	3.50	.50	.30	.20
463a	2¢ booklet pane of 6	110.00	80.00	55.00	....	....	....
464	3¢ violet (I)	130.00	70.00	52.00	20.00	15.00	10.00
465	4¢ orange brown	80.00	50.00	30.00	3.25	2.25	1.25
466	5¢ blue.	120.00	65.00	40.00	5.00	3.50	2.00
467	5¢ carmine (error)	1200.00	700.00	550.00	3000.00	2000.00	1500.00
468	6¢ red orange. .	155.00	83.00	50.00	12.00	9.00	7.50
469	7¢ black	210.00	115.00	80.00	15.00	10.00	8.00
470	8¢ olive green .	135.00	75.00	50.00	10.00	8.50	6.00
471	9¢ salmon red .	150.00	83.00	53.00	22.00	15.00	10.00
472	10¢ orange yellow	180.00	94.00	69.00	5.50	3.00	2.00
473	11¢ dark green.	85.00	54.00	31.50	25.00	18.00	15.00
474	12¢ claret brown	140.00	90.00	65.00	10.00	8.00	5.00
475	15¢ gray.	325.00	225.00	130.00	20.00	15.00	10.00
476	20¢ light ultramarine	400.00	220.00	160.00	22.00	15.00	10.00
476A	30¢ orange red.	....	4800.00	....	....	....	....
477	50¢ light violet .	1600.00	950.00	625.00	100.00	80.00	62.00
478	$1 violet black. .	1200.00	690.00	510.00	38.00	23.00	19.00
	Design of 1902-03						
479	$2 dark blue . . .	485.00	335.00	245.00	50.00	40.00	35.00
480	$5 light green . .	425.00	270.00	160.00	55.00	45.00	35.00
	1916-17 Imperforate (NH + 60%)						
481	1¢ green.	2.50	1.75	.75	1.50	1.00	.50
482	2¢ carmine (I). .	2.50	2.00	1.00	1.75	1.25	1.00
483	3¢ violet (I)	35.00	25.00	17.00	18.00	13.00	10.00
484	3¢ violet (II) . . .	22.50	19.00	13.00	14.00	10.00	8.00

(NH + 60%)

SCOTT NO.	COIL LINE PAIRS UNUSED OG VF	F	AVG	COIL PAIRS UNUSED OG VF	F	AVG
441	12.50	8.75	5.00	5.75	3.75	2.50
442	90.00	48.00	30.00	40.00	25.00	16.00
443	180.00	120.00	75.00	100.00	66.00	42.00
444	425.00	300.00	185.00	150.00	88.00	54.00
445	1600.00	900.00	600.00	750.00	495.00	350.00
446	900.00	500.00	350.00	550.00	370.00	275.00
447	325.00	185.00	125.00	175.00	110.00	75.00
448	62.00	39.00	25.00	32.00	18.00	12.00
450	90.00	65.00	40.00	58.00	40.00	28.00
452	115.00	65.00	40.00	47.50	35.00	24.00
453	850.00	500.00	350.00	400.00	250.00	174.00
454	750.00	425.00	325.00	350.00	200.00	140.00
455	90.00	50.00	35.00	32.00	20.00	13.00
456	1350.00	900.00	550.00	900.00	625.00	380.00
457	240.00	130.00	90.00	120.00	80.00	52.00
458	250.00	145.00	95.00	115.00	85.00	50.00
459	1800.00	1250.00	900.00	1350.00	1150.00	900.00

NOTE: For further details on the various types of similar appearing stamps please refer to our U.S. Stamp Identifier.

UNUSED PLATE BLOCKS OF 6

SCOTT NO.	NH F	NH AVG	OG F	OG AVG	SCOTT NO.	NH F	NH AVG	OG F	OG AVG
462	195.00	125.00	125.00	80.00	472	2000.00	1500.00	1500.00	1000.00
463	175.00	110.00	110.00	67.50	473	550.00	400.00	375.00	275.00
464	1500.00	1100.00	1150.00	825.00	474	950.00	600.00	600.00	400.00
465	800.00	500.00	600.00	425.00	481	35.00	25.00	25.00	16.50
466	1100.00	850.00	950.00	565.00	482	35.00	22.00	22.50	17.00
470	750.00	550.00	600.00	350.00	483	200.00	160.00	160.00	110.00
471	850.00	675.00	595.00	400.00	484	150.00	95.00	125.00	85.00
	CENTER LINE BLOCKS					**ARROW BLOCKS**			
481	10.00	6.00	5.00	4.00	481	8.00	5.00	4.00	3.00
482	13.50	8.00	8.50	5.50	482	11.00	7.00	7.75	4.75
483	130.00	95.00	97.50	72.50	483	125.00	90.00	95.00	70.00
484	80.00	55.00	70.00	55.00	484	75.00	50.00	65.00	50.00

SCOTT NO.	DESCRIPTION	UNUSED O.G. VF	F	AVG	USED VF	F	AVG
	ROTARY PRESS COIL STAMPS 1916-19 Perf. 10 Horizontally (NH + 60%)						
486	1¢ green.	1.75	1.00	.50	1.00	.75	.50
487	2¢ carmine (II) .	32.50	19.00	12.00	20.00	12.00	10.00
488	2¢ carmine (III).	5.95	3.75	2.50	5.00	3.50	2.00
489	3¢ violet (I)	7.00	4.50	3.00	2.75	1.95	1.00
	1916-22 Perf. 10 Vertically (NH + 60%)						
490	1¢ green.	1.00	.50	.50	1.00	.50	.50
491	2¢ carmine (II) .	2750.00	1750.00	1100.00	800.00	550.00	375.00
492	2¢ carmine (III).	16.00	9.00	6.00	1.00	.50	.50
493	3¢ violet (I)	37.50	21.00	16.00	7.00	4.25	2.75
494	3¢ violet (II) . . .	22.50	13.00	8.50	2.50	1.50	1.00
495	4¢ orange brown	27.50	15.75	11.00	10.50	6.00	4.00
496	5¢ blue.	7.00	4.00	3.00	2.60	1.75	1.00
497	10¢ orange yellow	35.00	20.00	15.00	25.00	16.50	9.25

(NH + 60%)

SCOTT NO.	COIL LINE PAIRS UNUSED OG VF	F	AVG	COIL PAIRS UNUSED OG VF	F	AVG
486	6.50	4.50	3.50	3.50	2.00	1.25
487	160.00	105.00	75.00	67.50	42.00	25.00
488	28.00	18.00	12.00	12.50	9.00	5.75
489	40.00	30.00	24.00	16.00	10.00	7.00
490	6.00	3.75	1.90	2.50	1.50	1.00
491	......	10000.00	6000.00	6450.00	4500.00	3000.00
492	70.00	50.00	35.00	36.00	20.00	14.00
493	160.00	100.00	70.00	78.75	60.00	35.00
494	90.00	60.00	48.00	47.00	35.00	19.50
495	100.00	75.00	55.00	55.00	35.00	22.00
496	40.00	28.00	19.50	15.00	9.00	7.00
497	160.00	115.00	75.00	75.00	45.00	35.00

1917-19 Flat Plate Printing Perf. 11 (NH + 60%)

SCOTT NO.	DESCRIPTION	UNUSED O.G. VF	F	AVG	USED VF	F	AVG
498/518	**(498-99, 501-04, 506-18) 19 varieties**	**680.00**	**410.00**	**270.00**	**45.00**	**25.00**	**19.00**
498	1¢ green.	.90	.50	.50	.35	.25	.20
498e	1¢ booklet pane of 6	7.50	4.50	3.25	....	....	....
498f	1¢ booklet pane of 30.	1300.00	800.00	550.00	....	....	....
499	2¢ rose (I).	.90	.50	.25	.35	.25	.20
499e	2¢ booklet pane of 6	7.00	4.50	3.50	....	....	....
500	2¢ deep rose (Ia)	400.00	225.00	165.00	300.00	200.00	125.00
501	3¢ light violet (I)	25.00	15.00	10.00	1.00	.70	.50
501b	3¢ booklet pane of 6	95.00	65.00	45.00	....	....	....
502	3¢ dark violet (II)	26.00	15.00	10.00	2.25	1.50	.95
502b	3¢ booklet pane of 6	100.00	56.00	38.00	....	....	....
503	4¢ brown	17.00	10.00	6.00	1.25	.85	.50
504	5¢ blue.	15.00	8.50	5.50	1.00	.75	.45
505	5¢ rose (error) .	895.00	525.00	360.00	700.00	475.00	300.00
506	6¢ red orange. .	22.00	13.00	8.00	.75	.50	.35
507	7¢ black	42.00	25.00	17.00	2.75	2.00	1.10
508	8¢ olive bistre. .	25.00	15.00	9.00	1.50	1.20	.80
509	9¢ salmon red .	24.00	14.00	9.00	4.75	2.95	2.00
510	10¢ orange yellow	30.00	17.00	10.50	.30	.25	.20
511	11¢ light green .	22.50	13.00	8.00	7.50	4.75	3.25
512	12¢ claret brown	22.50	13.00	8.00	1.25	.75	.60
513	13¢ apple green	25.00	14.00	10.00	17.00	10.00	9.00
514	15¢ gray.	64.00	38.00	26.00	2.50	1.50	1.25
515	20¢ light ultramarine	85.00	46.00	34.00	.75	.50	.35
516	30¢ orange red.	70.00	40.00	30.00	2.50	1.50	1.25
517	50¢ red violet . .	100.00	75.00	50.00	1.50	.80	.75
518	$1 violet black .	110.00	75.00	50.00	4.25	2.75	1.75
	1917 Design of 1908-09 Double Line Watermark Perf. 11						
519	2¢ carmine	715.00	385.00	255.00	1800.00	1400.00	800.00

SCOTT NO.	NH F	NH AVG	OG F	OG AVG	SCOTT NO.	NH F	NH AVG	OG F	OG AVG
		UNUSED PLATE BLOCKS OF 6							
498	25.00	18.75	17.95	15.50	511	225.00	125.00	165.00	100.00
499	25.00	18.75	17.95	15.50	512	220.00	125.00	155.00	100.00
501	200.00	150.00	165.00	115.00	513	220.00	150.00	145.00	90.00
502	225.00	200.00	195.00	150.00	514	835.00	465.00	595.00	385.00
503	215.00	165.00	150.00	130.00	515	975.00	565.00	675.00	425.00
504	165.00	100.00	135.00	80.00	516	800.00	475.00	640.00	375.00
506	275.00	200.00	195.00	135.00	517	2000.00	1350.00	1300.00	900.00
507	375.00	285.00	265.00	225.00	518	1750.00	1080.00	1225.00	800.00
508	375.00	255.00	300.00	200.00	519	5000.00	2785.00	3575.00	2150.00
509	220.00	150.00	175.00	120.00			ARROW BLOCK		
510	325.00	270.00	200.00	155.00	518	450.00	280.00	300.00	225.00

523, 547
Franklin

524
Franklin

SCOTT NO.	DESCRIPTION	UNUSED O.G. VF	UNUSED O.G. F	UNUSED O.G. AVG	USED VF	USED F	USED AVG
	1918 Unwatermarked (NH + 60%)						
523	$2 orange red & black	775.00	650.00	400.00	350.00	200.00	125.00
524	$5 deep green & black	300.00	200.00	150.00	60.00	40.00	20.00
	1918-20 Offset Printing Perf. 11 (NH + 60%)						
525	1¢ gray green. .	6.00	4.00	2.50	1.25	.85	.50
526	2¢ carmine (IV)	42.50	30.00	16.00	7.00	5.00	3.25
527	2¢ carmine (V) .	35.00	23.00	14.00	2.25	1.50	.85
528	2¢ carmine (Va)	17.00	11.00	8.00	1.00	.75	.55
528A	2¢ carmine (VI)	72.50	55.00	36.00	2.00	1.50	1.00
528B	2¢ carmine (VII)	38.50	25.00	18.00	.60	.50	.35
529	3¢ violet (III) . . .	7.50	5.50	4.50	.50	.35	.25
530	3¢ purple (IV) . .	2.50	1.75	1.25	.50	.30	.20
	1918-20 Offset Printing Imperforate						
531	1¢ gray green. .	22.50	14.00	10.50	18.00	12.00	10.00
532	2¢ carmine rose (IV)	100.00	71.00	54.00	60.00	50.00	40.00
533	2¢ carmine (V) .	225.00	120.00	135.00	210.00	150.00	110.00
534	2¢ carmine (Va)	42.50	33.00	19.00	27.00	20.00	15.00
534A	2¢ carmine (VI)	130.00	73.00	53.00	44.00	29.00	22.00
534B	2¢ carmine (VII)	2500.00	1800.00	1350.00	1550.00	1275.00	770.00
535	3¢ violet (IV). . .	18.50	13.00	9.00	12.00	10.00	8.50
	1919 Offset Printing Perf. 12-1/2						
536	1¢ gray green. .	40.00	28.00	18.00	45.00	30.00	20.00

537
"Victory" and Flags

SCOTT NO.	DESCRIPTION	UNUSED O.G. VF	UNUSED O.G. F	UNUSED O.G. AVG	USED VF	USED F	USED AVG
	1919 VICTORY ISSUE (NH + 50%)						
537	3¢ violet	18.50	10.50	6.50	5.00	3.50	2.50
	1919-21 Rotary Press Printings—Perf. 11 x 10 (†) (NH + 50%)						
538	1¢ green.	25.00	14.00	9.50	12.00	10.00	8.00
538a	Same, imperf. horizontally. . . .	80.00	50.00	36.00	....	....	....
539	2¢ carmine rose (II)	3300.00	2700.00	1800.00	....	22000.00	....
540	2¢ carmine rose (III)	17.50	10.00	6.00	15.00	12.00	10.50
540a	Same, imperf. horizontally. . . .	85.00	48.00	38.00	....	....	....
541	3¢ violet (II) . . .	80.00	48.00	37.00	45.00	40.00	30.00
	Perf. 10 x 11						
542	1¢ green.	17.00	11.00	7.00	2.25	1.35	1.00
	Perf. 10						
543	1¢ green.	1.35	.75	.50	.75	.40	.20

SCOTT NO.	DESCRIPTION	UNUSED O.G. VF	UNUSED O.G. F	UNUSED O.G. AVG	USED VF	USED F	USED AVG
	Perf. 11						
544	1¢ green (19 x 22-1/2mm)	....	18000.00	14200.00	....	3700.00	....
545	1¢ green (19-1/2 x 22mm)	300.00	200.00	130.00	300.00	185.00	125.00
546	2¢ carmine rose (III)	165.00	110.00	68.25	300.00	185.00	125.00
	1920 Flat Plate Printing Perf. 11						
547	$2 carmine & black	335.00	225.00	130.00	59.00	40.00	30.00

SCOTT NO.	NH F	NH AVG	OG F	OG AVG	SCOTT NO.	NH F	NH AVG	OG F	OG AVG
		UNUSED PLATE BLOCKS OF 6					UNUSED PLATE BLOCKS OF (—)		
525 (6)	45.00	30.00	25.00	20.00	535 (6)	105.00	85.00	85.00	65.00
526 (6)	400.00	275.00	250.00	200.00	536 (6)	250.00	175.00	175.00	135.00
527 (6)	300.00	200.00	180.00	150.00	537 (6)	250.00	175.00	165.00	125.00
528 (6)	150.00	100.00	95.00	60.00	538 (4)	135.00	97.50	90.00	60.00
528A (6)	700.00	450.00	490.00	315.00	540 (4)	130.00	80.00	80.00	50.00
528B (6)	300.00	200.00	195.00	145.00	541 (4)	500.00	350.00	330.00	225.00
529 (6)	100.00	67.50	65.00	45.00	542 (6)	195.00	135.00	135.00	90.00
530 (6)	40.00	26.50	25.00	17.00	543 (4)	35.00	20.00	15.00	10.00
531 (6)	150.00	112.50	110.00	85.00	543 (6)	55.00	32.00	30.00	20.00
532 (6)	650.00	500.00	485.00	375.00	545 (4)	1200.00	800.00	950.00	675.00
533 (6)	2100.00	1800.00	1575.00	1175.00	546 (4)	1000.00	700.00	700.00	475.00
534 (6)	275.00	200.00	435.00	150.00	547 (8)	6000.00	4575.00	4350.00	3150.00
534A (6)	800.00	550.00	525.00	415.00	548 (6)	100.00	65.00	67.50	50.00
					549 (6)	110.00	70.00	75.00	55.00
					550 (6)	725.00	525.00	475.00	330.00
		CENTER LINE					ARROW BLOCKS		
531	80.00	50.00	55.00	35.00	531	60.00	45.00	50.00	40.00
532	325.00	200.00	225.00	145.00	532	275.00	170.00	195.00	120.00
533	2000.00	1250.00	1000.00	650.00	533	1000.00	700.00	700.00	500.00
534	95.00	55.00	70.00	50.00	534	90.00	55.00	60.00	45.00
534A	275.00	200.00	185.00	125.00	534A	220.00	160.00	160.00	120.00
535	90.00	65.00	55.00	40.00	535	85.00	60.00	52.50	37.50
547	1400.00	975.00	1175.00	835.00	547	1275.00	900.00	1100.00	825.00

548
The "Mayflower"

549
Landing of the Pilgrims

550
Signing of the Compact

SCOTT NO.	DESCRIPTION	UNUSED O.G. VF	UNUSED O.G. F	UNUSED O.G. AVG	USED VF	USED F	USED AVG
	1920 PILGRIM TERCENTENARY ISSUE (NH + 50%)						
548-50	**1¢-5¢ (3 varieties, complete) . . . .**	**75.00**	**48.00**	**37.00**	**42.00**	**21.00**	**18.50**
548	1¢ green.	9.50	6.50	4.75	7.00	3.75	2.50
549	2¢ carmine rose	12.00	7.50	4.25	4.50	2.50	2.00
550	5¢ deep blue . .	70.00	40.00	32.00	37.00	20.00	18.00

551, 653
Nathan Hale

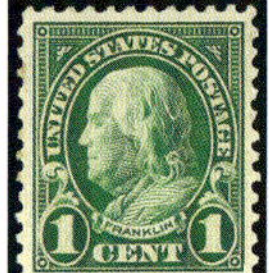
552, 575, 578, 581, 594, 596, 597, 604, 632
Franklin

553, 576, 582, 598, 605, 631, 633
Harding

554, 577, 579, 583, 595, 599-99A, 606, 634-34A
Washington

555, 584, 600, 635
Lincoln

556, 585, 601, 636
Martha Washington

557, 586, 602, 637
Roosevelt

558, 587, 638, 723
Garfield

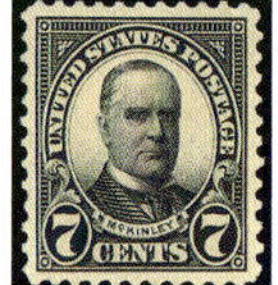
559, 588, 639
McKinley

560, 589, 640
Grant

561, 590, 641
Jefferson

562, 591, 603, 642
Monroe

563, 692
Hayes

564, 693
Cleveland

565, 695
American Indian

566, 696
Statue of Liberty

567, 698
Golden Gate

568, 699
Niagara Falls

569,700
Bison

570, 701
Arlington Amphitheatre

571
Lincoln Memorial

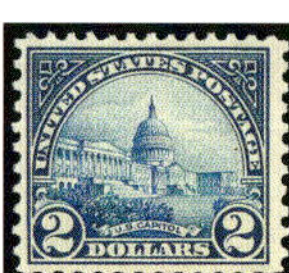
572
U.S. Capitol

573
"America"

SCOTT NO.	DESCRIPTION	UNUSED O.G. VF	F	AVG	USED VF	F	AVG
	THE 1922-25 ISSUE Flat Plate Printings Perf. 11 (NH + 60%)						
551-73	**1/2¢-$5 (23 varieties, complete) . . . .**	**1145.00**	**760.00**	**555.00**	**74.00**	**40.00**	**28.00**
551	1/2¢ olive brown (1925)	.60	.50	.25	.25	.20	.15
552	1¢ deep green (1923)	4.25	3.00	2.25	1.00	.80	.60
552a	1¢ booklet pane of 6	17.50	13.00	9.00	....	....	....
553	1-1/2¢ yellow brown (1925).	5.25	3.25	2.50	2.00	1.35	.95
554	2¢ carmine (1923)	4.50	3.00	2.00	1.00	.80	.60
554c	2¢ booklet pane of 6	12.00	9.00	5.50	....	....	....
555	3¢ violet (1923)	32.50	23.00	15.00	2.00	1.50	1.00
556	4¢ yellow brown (1923).	33.50	24.00	15.00	1.00	.65	.50
557	5¢ dark blue . . .	33.50	24.00	15.00	1.00	.65	.50
558	6¢ red orange. .	60.00	38.00	28.00	2.75	1.75	1.25
559	7¢ black (1923)	17.50	12.00	9.00	2.25	1.25	.90
560	8¢ olive green (1923)	65.00	44.00	31.00	2.00	1.25	.95
561	9¢ rose (1923) .	30.00	18.00	12.00	4.00	2.25	1.50
562	10¢ orange (1923)	35.00	23.00	15.00	.30	.20	.15
563	11¢ light blue . .	4.25	3.00	2.00	.75	.50	.30
564	12¢ brown violet (1923).	15.00	8.00	5.00	.75	.50	.40
565	14¢ blue (1923)	9.00	5.00	3.00	2.50	2.00	1.25
566	15¢ gray.	40.00	23.00	18.00	.25	.20	.15
567	20¢ carmine rose (1923).	40.00	25.00	20.00	.25	.20	.15
568	25¢ yellow green	33.50	21.00	15.00	2.25	1.50	1.25
569	30¢ olive brown (1923).	60.00	39.00	28.00	1.00	.60	.40
570	50¢ lilac	95.00	56.00	45.00	.50	.25	.20
571	$1 violet black (1923)	72.50	48.00	37.00	2.00	1.25	.75
572	$2 deep blue (1923)	165.00	105.00	88.00	18.00	11.00	6.50
573	$5 carmine & blue (1923).	300.00	220.00	160.00	29.00	18.00	12.00
	1923-25 Imperforate						
575	1¢ green.	16.50	12.00	9.00	14.00	8.00	5.50
576	1-1/2¢ yellow brown (1925).	3.25	2.00	1.25	4.75	2.50	2.00
577	2¢ carmine	3.25	2.25	1.25	4.25	2.50	1.75
	Rotary Press Printings 1923 Perf. 11 x 10 (†) (NH + 60%)						
578	1¢ green	100.00	85.00	60.00	250.00	180.00	130.00
579	2¢ carmine . . .	150.00	87.00	62.50	225.00	140.00	100.00
	1923-26 Perf. 10 (†)						
581-91	**1¢-10¢ (11 varieties, complete) . . . .**	**285.00**	**175.00**	**125.00**	**49.00**	**29.00**	**18.00**
581	1¢ green.	18.25	12.00	7.50	1.25	.85	.60
582	1-1/2¢ brown (1925)	6.00	4.00	3.00	1.25	.90	.65
583	2¢ carmine (1924)	4.00	2.00	1.25	.25	.20	.15
583a	2¢ booklet pane of 6 (1924).	110.00	70.00	50.00	....	....	....
584	3¢ violet (1925)	40.00	24.00	17.00	5.00	3.50	2.00
585	4¢ yellow brown (1925).	24.00	16.00	11.00	1.50	1.15	.75
586	5¢ blue (1925) .	24.00	16.00	11.00	1.00	0.50	0.30
587	6¢ red orange (1925)	18.50	10.00	6.50	1.50	.90	.60
588	7¢ black (1926)	25.00	16.00	10.50	18.00	12.00	8.00
589	8¢ olive green (1926)	40.00	24.00	15.00	13.00	8.50	5.00
590	9¢ rose (1926) .	8.00	4.00	3.00	10.00	5.00	3.25
591	10¢ orange (1925)	90.00	55.00	42.00	.55	.45	.35
	Perf. 11 (†)						
594	1¢ green.	....	65000.00	....	....	11000.00	8800.00
595	2¢ carmine	275.00	225.00	170.00	550.00	350.00	225.00
	Perf. 11						
596	1¢ green.	....	....	....	....	200000.00	....

SCOTT NO.		PLATE BLOCKS (6) UNUSED NH VF	F	AVG.	UNUSED OG VF	F	AVG.
551	1/2¢ olive brown (1923)......	25.00	20.00	15.00	15.00	12.00	9.00
552	1¢ deep green (1923).........	52.00	30.00	25.00	32.50	20.00	14.00
553	1-1/2¢ yellow brown (1923)	95.00	80.00	65.00	65.00	55.00	35.00
554	2¢ carmine (1923).............	50.00	30.00	22.50	32.50	21.50	15.00
555	3¢ violet (1923)..................	350.00	225.00	180.00	195.00	150.00	110.00
556	4¢ yellow brown (1923)......	365.00	235.00	185.00	205.00	150.00	110.00
557	5¢ dark blue	375.00	240.00	200.00	210.00	160.00	125.00
558	6¢ red orange......................	750.00	450.00	400.00	500.00	350.00	250.00
559	7¢ black (1923)...................	150.00	100.00	70.00	100.00	65.00	45.00
560	8¢ olive green (1923)	1100.00	740.00	650.00	750.00	500.00	375.00
561	9¢ rose (1923).....................	340.00	225.00	160.00	195.00	160.00	130.00
562	10¢ orange (1923)...............	400.00	290.00	200.00	300.00	200.00	160.00
563	11¢ light blue	55.00	38.00	32.00	45.00	28.00	18.50
564	12¢ brown violet (1923)......	250.00	145.00	100.00	175.00	100.00	80.00
565	14¢ blue (1923)...................	120.00	80.00	57.50	85.00	52.50	42.50
566	15¢ grey	500.00	350.00	240.00	350.00	225.00	175.00
567	20¢ carmine rose (1923)	475.00	320.00	240.00	400.00	220.00	190.00
568	25¢ yellow green	420.00	260.00	200.00	325.00	190.00	125.00
569	30¢ olive brown (1923).......	550.00	375.00	295.00	325.00	225.00	160.00
570	50¢ lilac	1350.00	1000.00	750.00	850.00	600.00	450.00
571	$1 violet black (1923)	800.00	520.00	400.00	550.00	400.00	300.00
572	$2 deep blue (1923)...........	1750.00	1300.00	1000.00	1100.00	850.00	650.00
573(8)	$5 carmine + blue (1923)...	5000.00	3750.00	2800.00	3500.00	2250.00	1750.00

SCOTT NO.		CENTER LINE BLOCKS F/NH	F/OG	AVG/OG	ARROW BLOCKS F/NH	F/OG	AVG/OG
571	$1 violet black	....	....	....	310.00	210.00	140.00
572	$2 deep blue	....	....	....	650.00	450.00	360.00
573	$5 carmine & blue	1100.00	925.00	775.00	1050.00	900.00	750.00
575	1¢ imperforate	58.00	50.00	40.00	55.00	47.50	38.00
576	1-1/2¢ imperforate..............	19.50	15.00	10.50	11.00	8.00	5.00
577	2¢ imperforate.....................	22.50	17.50	12.00	12.00	9.00	7.00

SCOTT NO.		PLATE BLOCKS UNUSED NH VF	F	AVG.	UNUSED OG VF	F	AVG.
575 (6)	1¢ green	160.00	110.00	75.00	110.00	70.00	50.00
576 (6)	1-1/2¢ yellow brown (1925)	50.00	33.00	25.00	35.00	22.00	16.00
577 (6)	2¢ carmine	50.00	34.00	25.00	42.00	25.00	18.00
578	1¢ green	2100.00	1200.00	950.00	1300.00	900.00	675.00
579	2¢ carmine	1100.00	700.00	525.00	695.00	450.00	350.00
581	1¢ green	225.00	140.00	100.00	160.00	100.00	70.00
582	1-1/2¢ brown (1925)...........	85.00	55.00	35.00	60.00	38.00	25.00
583	2¢ carmine (1923)	75.00	45.00	28.50	55.00	33.00	20.00
584	3¢ violet (1925)	400.00	260.00	190.00	260.00	190.00	150.00
585	4¢ yellow green (1925).......	300.00	200.00	157.50	220.00	160.00	115.00
586	5¢ blue (1925)	375.00	240.00	170.00	275.00	170.00	120.00
587	6¢ red orange (1925)	225.00	145.00	95.00	150.00	95.00	65.00
588	7¢ black (1926)	250.00	155.00	100.00	175.00	110.00	70.00
589	8¢ olive green (1926)	400.00	260.00	190.00	275.00	190.00	125.00
590	9¢ rose (1926).....................	115.00	70.00	45.00	80.00	50.00	30.00
591	10¢ orange (1925)..............	1050.00	700.00	500.00	650.00	475.00	380.00

SCOTT NO.	DESCRIPTION	UNUSED VF	F	AVG	USED VF	F	AVG
	1923-29 Rotary Press Coil Stamps (NH + 50%)						
597/606	**597-99, 600-06 (10 varieties). .**	**34.25**	**23.50**	**15.50**	**3.50**	**2.45**	**1.65**
	Perf. 10 Vertically						
597	1¢ green.	.60	.25	.25	1.00	.80	.60
598	1-1/2¢ deep brown (1925).	1.35	1.00	.75	1.00	.65	.50
599	2¢ carmine (I) (1923)	.60	.50	.25	1.00	.80	.60
599A	2¢ carmine (II) (1929).	210.00	115.00	73.50	25.00	15.25	9.75
600	3¢ violet (1924)	13.75	9.00	5.50	1.00	.70	.45
601	4¢ yellow brown	8.25	5.50	4.25	1.50	.75	.45
602	5¢ dark blue (1924)	2.95	1.75	1.25	1.00	.75	.50
603	10¢ orange (1924)	7.25	5.00	3.50	1.00	.75	.50
	Perf. 10 Horizontally						
604	1¢ yellow green (1924)	.60	.50	.25	1.00	.75	.50
605	1-1/2¢ yellow brown (1925).	.75	.50	.25	1.00	.75	.50
606	2¢ carmine	.65	.50	.25	1.00	.75	.50

NOTE: For further details on the various types of similar appearing stamps please refer to our U. S. Stamp Identifier.

SCOTT NO.		UNUSED OG (NH + 40%) COIL LINE PAIRS VF	F	AVG.	COIL PAIRS VF	F	AVG.
597	1¢ green.............................	2.55	1.95	1.40	1.20	.65	.50
598	1-1/2¢ brown (1925)...........	6.75	5.25	4.00	2.70	2.00	1.50
599	2¢ carmine (I).....................	2.15	1.65	1.20	1.25	1.00	.55
599A	2¢ carmine (II) (1929).........	825.00	557.50	375.00	450.00	247.50	157.50
600	3¢ deep violet (1924)	40.00	30.00	23.75	28.00	18.00	11.50
601	4¢ yellow brown	35.75	27.50	22.00	16.50	12.00	8.50
602	5¢ dark blue (1924)............	11.75	9.00	6.00	6.25	4.25	2.75
603	10¢ orange (1924)..............	35.00	27.00	20.00	15.00	10.00	7.00
604	1¢ green (1924)..................	3.40	2.60	1.65	1.25	1.00	.50
605	1-1/2¢ yellow brown (1925)	4.25	3.00	2.00	1.50	1.00	.75
606	2¢ carmine	2.75	2.00	1.35	1.30	1.00	.50

610-613
Harding

SCOTT NO.	DESCRIPTION	UNUSED VF	F	AVG	USED VF	F	AVG
	1923 HARDING MEMORIAL ISSUE (NH + 50%)						
610	2¢ black, perf 11 flat	1.50	1.00	.75	1.00	.75	.50
611	2¢ black, imperf	17.50	10.50	8.00	15.00	10.00	8.00
612	2¢ black, perf 10 rotary . .	27.00	14.00	12.00	6.00	3.50	2.50
613	2¢ black perf 11 rotary	......	......	......	......	45000.00	36500.00

614
Ship "New Netherlands"

615
Landing at Fort Orange

616
Monument at Mayport, Fla.

SCOTT NO.	DESCRIPTION	UNUSED VF	F	AVG	USED VF	F	AVG
	1924 HUGUENOT-WALLOON ISSUE (NH + 40%)						
614-16	**1¢-5¢ (3 varieties, complete) . . . .**	**69.00**	**51.00**	**39.00**	**45.00**	**32.00**	**20.00**
614	1¢ dark green. .	6.50	4.75	3.50	6.50	3.75	3.00
615	2¢ carmine rose	10.00	6.00	4.00	5.50	3.75	2.75
616	5¢ dark blue . . .	60.00	47.00	37.00	37.00	29.00	20.00

617
Washington at Cambridge

618
Birth of Liberty

619
The Minute Man

SCOTT NO.	DESCRIPTION	UNUSED VF	F	AVG	USED VF	F	AVG
	1925 LEXINGTON-CONCORD SESQUICENTENNIAL (NH + 40%)						
617-19	**1¢-5¢ (3 varieties, complete) . . . .**	**76.00**	**56.00**	**42.25**	**41.00**	**30.00**	**20.00**
617	1¢ deep green .	8.75	5.50	4.75	9.50	6.00	4.25
618	2¢ carmine rose	13.50	9.00	6.00	10.50	8.00	6.00
619	5¢ dark blue . . .	60.00	46.00	34.00	29.00	22.00	14.00

SCOTT NO.	DESCRIPTION	UNUSED O.G. VF	F	AVG	USED VF	F	AVG

620
Sloop "Restaurationen"

621
Viking Ship

1925 NORSE-AMERICAN ISSUE (NH + 40%)

SCOTT NO.	DESCRIPTION	UNUSED O.G. VF	F	AVG	USED VF	F	AVG
620-21	**2¢-5¢ (2 varieties, complete) . . . .**	**45.00**	**28.50**	**19.25**	**40.00**	**27.00**	**19.00**
620	2¢ carmine & black	10.25	7.00	5.50	8.00	6.00	4.50
621	5¢ dark blue & black	39.50	24.00	16.00	36.00	24.00	17.00

622, 694
Harrison

623, 697
Wilson

1925-26 Flat Plate Printings, Perf. 11

SCOTT NO.	DESCRIPTION	UNUSED O.G. VF	F	AVG	USED VF	F	AVG
622	13¢ green (1926)	25.00	16.00	11.00	1.25	.75	.60
623	17¢ black	31.50	19.00	15.00	.75	.50	.40

SCOTT NO.	PLATE BLOCKS	UNUSED NH VF	F	AVG.	UNUSED OG VF	F	AVG.
610 (6)	2¢ black perf 11 flat	45.00	30.00	22.00	33.00	23.00	18.00
611 (6)	2¢ black imperf.	210.00	140.00	90.00	160.00	105.00	80.00
611 (4)	2¢ black center line block	110.00	85.00	60.00	77.50	60.00	45.00
611 (4)	2¢ black arrow block	58.00	45.00	32.50	45.00	35.00	25.00
612 (4)	2¢ black perf 10 rotary	500.00	370.00	300.00	390.00	275.00	210.00
614 (6)	1¢ dark green	80.00	54.00	40.00	60.00	39.00	25.00
615 (6)	2¢ carmine rose	150.00	90.00	65.00	110.00	75.00	55.00
616 (6)	5¢ dark blue	620.00	450.00	350.00	510.00	325.00	250.00
617 (6)	1¢ deep green	90.00	50.00	40.00	65.00	40.00	30.00
618 (6)	2¢ carmine rose	160.00	95.00	75.00	115.00	72.00	55.00
619 (6)	5¢ dark blue	510.00	395.00	300.00	410.00	315.00	220.00
620 (8)	2¢ carmine black	325.00	250.00	175.00	235.00	180.00	125.00
621 (8)	5¢ dark blue+black	1050.00	800.00	550.00	815.00	625.00	435.00
622 (6)	13¢ green (1926)	280.00	215.00	150.00	190.00	145.00	105.00
623 (6)	17¢ black	325.00	250.00	175.00	255.00	195.00	136.50

627
Liberty Bell

628
John Ericsson Statue

629, 630
Hamilton's Battery

1926-27 COMMEMORATIVES (NH + 40%)

SCOTT NO.	DESCRIPTION	UNUSED O.G. VF	F	AVG	USED VF	F	AVG
627/644	**627-29, 643-44 (5 varieties, complete) . . . . . .**	**32.00**	**25.00**	**17.00**	**17.00**	**12.00**	**7.50**
	1926 COMMEMORATIVES						
627	2¢ Sesquicentennial	5.75	4.25	3.25	1.00	.80	.55
628	5¢ Ericsson Memorial	16.25	13.00	9.00	7.00	5.00	3.50
629	2¢ White Plains	3.75	2.75	2.00	3.25	2.50	1.50
630	White Plains Sheet of 25.	425.00	300.00	250.00	550.00	425.00	300.00
630V	2¢ Dot over "S" variety.	450.00	350.00	300.00	600.00	475.00	350.00
	Rotary Press Printings Designs of 1922-25 1926 Imperforate						
631	1-1/2¢ yellow brown	4.95	3.75	2.75	6.00	4.25	3.00
631	1-1/2¢ center line block	26.00	20.00	13.50	....	....	....
631	1-1/2¢ arrow block	12.25	9.50	6.50	....	....	....

1926-28 Perf. 11 x 10 1/2

SCOTT NO.	DESCRIPTION	UNUSED O.G. VF	F	AVG	USED VF	F	AVG
632/42	**1¢-10¢ (632-34, 635-42 11 varieties) . . .**	**41.00**	**33.00**	**25.00**	**2.60**	**2.10**	**1.55**
632	1¢ green (1927)	.50	.25	.25	.25	.20	.15
632a	1¢ booklet pane of 6	7.00	5.00	3.50	....	....	....
633	1-1/2¢ yellow brown (1927).	3.75	2.75	2.00	.25	.20	.15
634	2¢ carmine (I). .	.40	.25	.25	.25	.20	.15
634	Electric Eye Plate	5.50	4.25	2.75	....	....	....
634d	2¢ booklet pane of 6	2.15	1.75	1.25	....	....	....
634A	2¢ carmine (II) (1928).	550.00	395.00	255.00	25.00	17.00	11.00
635	3¢ violet (1927)	1.00	.75	.50	.25	.20	.15
636	4¢ yellow brown (1927)	4.25	3.25	2.75	.50	.30	.25
637	5¢ dark blue (1927)	3.95	3.00	2.25	25	.20	.15
638	6¢ red orange (1927)	6.25	4.75	3.50	25	.20	.15
639	7¢ black (1927)	6.00	4.50	3.25	25	.20	.15
640	8¢ olive green (1927)	6.00	4.50	3.25	25	.20	.15
641	9¢ orange red (1931)	4.50	3.50	2.50	25	.20	.15
642	10¢ orange (1927)	6.75	5.50	4.00	.25	.20	.15

643

644

1927 COMMEMORATIVES

SCOTT NO.	DESCRIPTION	UNUSED O.G. VF	F	AVG	USED VF	F	AVG
643	2¢ Vermont. . . .	3.25	2.50	1.75	2.75	2.15	1.50
644	2¢ Burgoyne. . .	6.95	5.50	3.75	5.00	3.95	2.50

645

646

647

648

649

650

1928 COMMEMORATIVES (NH + 40%)

SCOTT NO.	DESCRIPTION	UNUSED O.G. VF	F	AVG	USED VF	F	AVG
645-50	**6 varieties, complete**	**61.00**	**42.00**	**30.00**	**52.00**	**34.00**	**25.00**
645	2¢ Valley Forge	2.50	2.00	1.50	1.50	1.10	.80
646	2¢ Molly Pitcher	2.35	2.00	1.50	2.75	2.25	1.50
647	2¢ Hawaii	7.75	5.00	3.25	7.50	6.00	3.50
648	5¢ Hawaii	32.50	23.00	16.75	33.00	25.00	17.00
649	2¢ Aeronautics .	4.00	2.50	2.00	4.00	2.25	1.50
650	5¢ Aeronautics .	13.50	9.00	7.00	9.00	5.00	3.75

651

654-656

657

1929 COMMEMORATIVES (NH + 40%)

SCOTT NO.	DESCRIPTION	UNUSED O.G. VF	F	AVG	USED VF	F	AVG
651/81	**651, 654-55, 657, 680-81 (6 varieties). . .**	**10.25**	**8.25**	**5.25**	**5.00**	**3.70**	**2.75**
651	2¢ George R. Clark	2.25	1.25	1.25	1.75	1.10	.90
	Same, arrow block of 4	4.50	3.35	2.35	....	....	....
	1929 Design of 1922-25 Rotary Press Printing Perf. 11x10-1/2						
653	1/2¢ olive brown	.60	.50	.50	.25	.20	.15

SCOTT NO.	DESCRIPTION	UNUSED O.G. VF	F	AVG	USED VF	F	AVG
	1929 COMMEMORATIVES						
654	2¢ Edison, Flat, Perf 11	2.15	1.75	1.25	1.75	1.40	1.00
655	2¢ Edison, Rotary, 11x10-1/2	1.50	1.25	1.00	.50	.45	.35
656	2¢ Edison, Rotary Press Coil, Perf. 10 Vertically	28.50	22.00	15.00	3.00	2.35	1.50
657	2¢ Sullivan Expedition	1.60	1.25	1.00	1.75	1.40	1.10
	1929. 632-42 Overprinted Kansas (NH + 50%)						
658-68	**1¢-10¢ (11 varieties, complete) . . . .**	**250.00**	**200.00**	**165.00**	**200.00**	**160.00**	**110.00**
658	1¢ green.	3.00	1.75	1.25	2.10	1.60	1.20
659	1-1/2¢ brown . .	4.25	3.25	2.25	3.25	2.00	1.40
660	2¢ carmine	4.25	3.00	2.00	1.75	1.25	.75
661	3¢ violet	20.00	16.00	14.00	20.00	15.00	12.00
662	4¢ yellow brown	22.00	17.00	12.00	15.00	10.00	7.00
663	5¢ deep blue . .	15.00	12.00	9.00	12.00	9.00	6.00
664	6¢ red orange. .	30.00	25.00	20.00	22.00	18.00	12.00
665	7¢ black	30.00	25.00	20.00	28.00	22.00	18.00
666	8¢ olive green .	80.00	70.00	60.00	70.00	62.00	40.00
667	9¢ light rose . . .	18.00	12.50	10.00	13.00	11.00	7.00
668	10¢ orange yellow	28.00	22.00	18.00	14.00	12.00	10.00
	1929. 632-42 Overprinted Nebraska (NH + 50%)						
669-79	**1¢-10¢, 11 varieties, complete . . . . .**	**330.00**	**240.00**	**185.00**	**210.00**	**164.00**	**120.00**
669	1¢ green.	3.75	3.00	2.20	3.10	2.20	1.60
670	1-1/2¢ brown . .	4.00	2.50	2.00	3.20	2.50	1.80
671	2¢ carmine	4.00	2.50	2.00	2.00	1.50	1.00
672	3¢ violet	12.00	10.50	8.00	17.50	12.00	8.00
673	4¢ yellow brown	22.00	15.00	12.00	18.00	15.50	11.00
674	5¢ deep blue . .	20.00	14.00	11.00	18.00	15.50	11.00
675	6¢ red orange. .	38.00	26.00	22.00	30.00	22.00	16.00
676	7¢ black	28.00	21.00	16.00	22.00	18.00	14.00
677	8¢ olive green .	35.00	26.00	18.00	35.00	24.00	18.00
678	9¢ light rose . . .	40.00	35.00	25.00	38.00	30.00	25.00
679	10¢ orange yellow	125.00	88.00	77.00	32.00	22.00	15.00

SCOTT NO.		PLATE BLOCKS UNUSED NH VF	F	AVG.	UNUSED OG VF	F	AVG.
627 (6)	Sesquicentennial................	65.00	50.00	35.00	49.50	38.00	26.00
628 (6)	5¢ Ericsson Memorial.........	145.00	110.00	77.50	110.00	85.00	60.00
629 (6)	2¢ White Plains	67.50	52.00	35.00	52.00	40.00	30.00
631	1-1/2¢ yellow brown	93.00	71.50	50.00	70.00	55.00	40.00
632	1¢ green.............................	3.25	2.50	1.75	2.60	2.00	1.40
633	1-1/2¢ yellow brown (1927)	120.00	92.50	65.00	90.00	70.00	48.00
634	2¢ carmine (1)....................	2.60	1.95	1.40	2.10	1.70	1.25
635	3¢ violet.............................	15.00	12.50	9.00	10.50	7.50	4.50
636	4¢ yellow brown (1927)......	130.00	95.00	70.00	105.00	80.00	55.00
637	5¢ dark blue (1927)............	29.50	22.50	15.75	22.75	17.50	12.75
638	6¢ red orange (1927)	29.50	22.50	15.75	22.75	17.50	12.75
639	7¢ black (1927)	29.50	22.50	15.75	22.75	17.50	12.75
640	8¢ olive green (1927)	29.50	22.50	15.75	22.75	17.50	12.75
641	9¢ orange red (1931)	30.00	23.00	16.00	23.00	18.00	13.00
642	10¢ orange (1927)..............	43.50	33.50	23.00	34.00	26.00	18.25
643 (6)	2¢ Vermont........................	65.00	50.00	35.00	58.00	42.00	28.00
644 (6)	2¢ Burgoyne.......................	80.00	57.00	42.00	60.00	45.00	30.00
645 (6)	2¢ Valley Forge	58.00	40.00	28.00	41.00	30.00	19.50
646	2¢ Molly Pitcher..................	60.00	42.50	32.00	42.00	33.00	25.00
647	2¢ Hawaii	205.00	140.00	110.00	145.00	110.00	77.00
648	5¢ Hawaii	425.00	315.00	225.00	335.00	260.00	185.00
649 (6)	2¢ Aeronautics	24.00	18.00	12.00	19.50	14.00	10.00
650 (6)	5¢ Aeronautics	115.00	90.00	65.00	85.00	65.00	47.50
651 (6)	2¢ George R. Clark	19.50	15.00	10.00	14.50	11.00	7.50
653	1/2¢ olive brown.................	2.75	2.00	1.25	1.95	1.50	.95
654 (6)	2¢ Edison	51.00	39.50	28.00	40.00	31.50	22.50
655	2¢ Edison	70.00	55.00	40.00	58.00	45.00	30.50
657 (6)	2¢ Sullivan Expedition........	45.00	35.00	26.50	39.50	30.00	22.50
	LINE PAIR						
656	2¢ Edison, coil....................	125.00	95.00	65.00	80.00	62.50	45.00

SCOTT NO.		PLATE BLOCKS UNUSED NH VF	F	AVG.	UNUSED OG VF	F	AVG.
658	1¢ green............................	65.00	40.00	30.00	45.00	30.00	20.00
659	1-1/2¢ brown	80.00	50.00	35.00	60.00	38.00	25.00
660	2¢ carmine	80.00	50.00	35.00	60.00	38.00	25.00
661	3¢ violet.............................	425.00	265.00	200.00	275.00	200.00	225.00
662	4¢ yellow brown	375.00	225.00	150.00	250.00	165.00	115.00
663	5¢ deep blue	275.00	165.00	125.00	185.00	120.00	90.00
664	6¢ red orange.....................	850.00	550.00	400.00	525.00	325.00	225.00
665	7¢ black..............................	850.00	550.00	400.00	525.00	325.00	225.00
666	8¢ olive green.....................	1500.00	900.00	750.00	1000.00	625.00	475.00
667	9¢ light rose........................	450.00	300.00	200.00	295.00	200.00	125.00
668	10¢ orange yellow.............	650.00	425.00	295.00	425.00	285.00	195.00
669	1¢ green............................	85.00	50.00	40.00	55.00	35.00	25.00
670	1-1/2¢ brown	100.00	60.00	40.00	60.00	35.00	25.00
671	2¢ carmine	80.00	50.00	35.00	55.00	35.00	25.00
672	3¢ violet.............................	350.00	200.00	140.00	225.00	135.00	95.00
673	4¢ yellow brown	475.00	300.00	200.00	325.00	200.00	140.00
674	5¢ deep blue	500.00	300.00	200.00	350.00	210.00	150.00
675	6¢ red orange.....................	1000.00	550.00	450.00	650.00	375.00	265.00
676	7¢ black..............................	550.00	325.00	225.00	335.00	215.00	155.00
677	8¢ olive green.....................	750.00	450.00	315.00	475.00	350.00	250.00
678	9¢ light rose........................	1000.00	550.00	400.00	600.00	375.00	265.00
679	10¢ orange yellow.............	2000.00	1200.00	850.00	1200.00	750.00	550.00

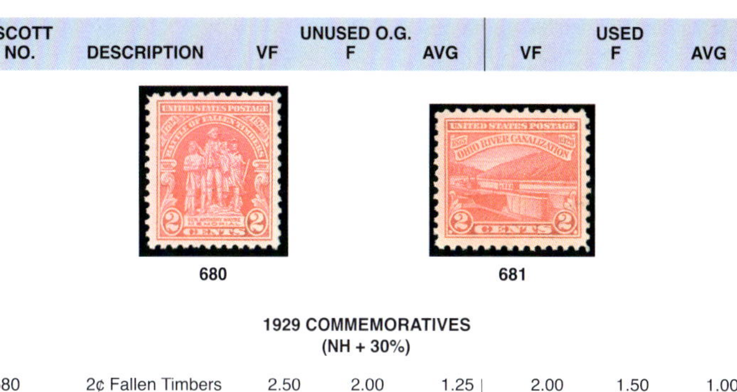

680 681

SCOTT NO.	DESCRIPTION	UNUSED O.G. VF	F	AVG	USED VF	F	AVG
	1929 COMMEMORATIVES (NH + 30%)						
680	2¢ Fallen Timbers	2.50	2.00	1.25	2.00	1.50	1.00
681	2¢ Ohio River Canal	1.50	1.25	1.00	1.25	1.00	.75

682

683

684, 686

685, 687

1930-31 COMMEMORATIVES

SCOTT NO.	DESCRIPTION	UNUSED O.G. VF	F	AVG	USED VF	F	AVG
682/703	**(682-83, 688-90, 702-03) 7 varieties, complete**	**5.50**	**4.10**	**3.10**	**5.35**	**4.15**	**2.85**
	1930 COMMEMORATIVES						
682	2¢ Massachusetts Bay	1.50	1.25	1.00	1.25	1.00	.65
683	2¢ Carolina-Charleston	2.50	2.00	1.50	3.25	2.50	1.75
	1930 Rotary Press Printing Perf. 11 x 10-1/2 (NH + 30%)						
684	1-1/2¢ Harding .	.75	.50	.50	.25	.20	.15
685	4¢ Taft	1.50	1.25	.75	.25	.20	.15
	1930 Rotary Press Coil Stamps Perf. 10 Vertically						
686	1-1/2¢ Harding .	2.95	2.25	1.50	.25	.20	.15
687	4¢ Taft	4.75	3.75	2.50	1.00	.75	.50

688

689

690

SCOTT NO.	DESCRIPTION	UNUSED O.G. VF	F	AVG	USED VF	F	AVG
	1930 COMMEMORATIVES						
688	2¢ Braddock's Field	1.95	1.50	1.00	2.50	1.80	1.25
689	2¢ Von Steuben	1.10	1.00	.75	1.25	.90	.65
	1931 COMMEMORATIVES						
690	2¢ Pulaski	.75	.50	.50	.50	.40	.30

SCOTT NO.		PLATE BLOCKS UNUSED NH VF	F	AVG.	UNUSED OG VF	F	AVG.
680 (6)	2¢ Fallen Timbers...............	48.00	35.00	22.50	36.00	27.50	21.00
681 (6)	2¢ Ohio River Canal...........	33.75	25.00	15.75	26.00	20.00	12.00
682 (6)	2¢ Massachusetts Bay.......	58.50	40.00	27.00	39.00	30.00	18.00
683 (6)	2¢ Carolina-Charleston......	85.00	60.00	40.00	64.50	49.50	36.00
684	1-1/2¢ Harding..................	3.65	2.50	1.70	2.90	2.25	1.65
685	4¢ Taft................................	17.00	12.00	9.00	13.00	10.00	6.00
686	....	15.00	10.75	7.50	10.00	8.00	6.00
687	....	30.00	22.50	15.00	20.00	15.00	10.00
688 (6)	3¢ Braddock's Field...........	71.50	47.50	33.00	52.00	40.00	24.00
689 (6)	2¢ Von Steuben.................	40.00	31.50	18.00	32.50	25.00	15.00
690 (6)	2¢ Pulaski..........................	23.50	17.00	10.75	18.25	14.00	8.50

SCOTT NO.	DESCRIPTION	UNUSED VF	F	AVG	USED VF	F	AVG
	1931 Designs of 1922-26. Rotary Press Printing. (NH + 35%)						
692-701	11¢ to 50¢ (10 varieties, complete)	184.00	140.00	105.00	3.25	2.75	2.25
	Perf. 11 x 10-1/2						
692	11¢ light blue . .	5.50	4.25	3.50	.25	.20	.15
693	12¢ brown violet	10.50	8.00	5.50	.25	.25	.20
694	13¢ yellow green	4.00	3.00	2.25	1.00	.75	.50
695	14¢ dark blue . .	10.50	8.00	5.50	3.00	2.50	1.90
696	15¢ gray......	16.00	12.00	9.00	.25	.20	.15
	Perf. 10-1/2 x 11						
697	17¢ black.....	12.50	9.50	6.50	.50	.40	.30
698	20¢ carmine rose	16.50	13.00	9.00	.25	.20	.15
699	25¢ blue green.	16.00	12.00	9.00	.25	.20	.15
700	30¢ brown	36.50	28.00	21.00	.25	.20	.15
701	50¢ lilac	65.00	50.00	41.00	.25	.20	.15

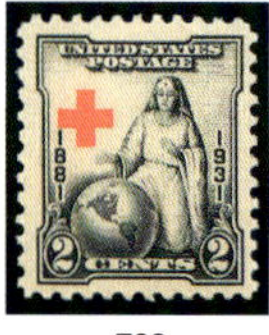
702

703

1931 COMMEMORATIVES (NH + 30%)

SCOTT NO.	DESCRIPTION	UNUSED VF	F	AVG	USED VF	F	AVG
702	2¢ Red Cross. .	.50	.25	.25	.25	.25	.20
702	2¢ arrow block .	1.50	1.00	.65	....	....	....
703	2¢ Yorktown . . .	.60	.50	.50	.75	.50	.40
703	2¢ center line block	3.00	2.15	1.75	....	....	....
703	2¢ arrow block .	2.75	1.95	1.45	....	....	....

1932 WASHINGTON BICENTENNIAL ISSUE

Planning for this set, which celebrated the 200th anniversary of the birth of George Washington, began more than eight years before its release. Despite many suggestions that a pictorial series be created, the final set depicted 12 portraits of Washington at various stages of his life. For reasons of economy, the stamps were produced in single colors and in the same size as regular issues. Nevertheless, the set was an instant success and it was reported that more than a million covers were mailed from Washington, D.C. on January 1, 1932, the first day of issue.

704 705 706 707
708 709 710 711

712

713

714

715

SCOTT NO.	DESCRIPTION	UNUSED VF	F	AVG	USED VF	F	AVG
	(NH + 40%)						
704-15	1/2¢ to 10¢ (12 varieties, complete)	32.00	21.00	16.00	4.50	3.40	2.50
704	1/2¢ olive brown	.35	.25	.25	.25	.20	.15
705	1¢ green......	.40	.25	.25	.25	.20	.15
706	1-1/2¢ brown . .	.75	.50	.25	.25	.25	.20
707	2¢ carmine rose	.40	.25	.25	.25	.20	.15
708	3¢ deep violet. .	.90	.70	.40	.25	.20	.15
709	4¢ light brown. .	.75	.50	.50	.25	.25	.20
710	5¢ blue.......	2.20	1.70	1.20	.50	.25	.20
711	6¢ red orange. .	5.00	3.00	2.00	.25	.20	.15
712	7¢ black......	.95	.75	.50	.50	.30	.20
713	8¢ olive bistre. .	5.00	2.50	2.00	1.50	1.00	.75
714	9¢ pale red....	3.00	2.00	1.20	.30	.25	.20
715	10¢ orange yellow	15.00	10.00	8.00	.25	.20	.15

716

717

718

719

1932 COMMEMORATIVES (NH + 30%)

SCOTT NO.	DESCRIPTION	UNUSED VF	F	AVG	USED VF	F	AVG
716/25	(716-19, 724-25) 6 varieties....	12.75	9.50	7.50	2.10	1.55	1.25
716	2¢ Winter Olympics	.95	.75	.50	.50	.40	.35
717	2¢ Arbor Day . .	.40	.25	.25	.25	.20	.15
718	3¢ Summer Olympics	4.00	3.00	2.50	.25	.20	.15
719	5¢ Summer Olympics	6.00	4.50	3.50	.75	.50	.40

720-722

723

724

725

726

SCOTT NO.	DESCRIPTION	UNUSED VF	F	AVG	USED VF	F	AVG
	1932 Rotary Press						
720	3¢ deep violet. .	.50	.25	.25	.25	.20	.15
720b	3¢ booklet pane of 6	60.00	40.00	28.00	....	....	....
721	3¢ deep violet coil perf 10 vertically	3.95	3.00	2.00	.25	.20	.15
722	3¢ deep violet coil perf 10 horizontally	2.95	2.25	1.50	1.00	.80	.65
723	6¢ Garfield, coil perf 10 vertically	17.50	13.00	9.00	.75	.75	.65
	1932 COMMEMORATIVES						
724	3¢ Penn	1.10	.75	.50	.50	.30	.25
725	3¢ Webster....	1.30	.75	.50	.55	.40	.30

SCOTT NO.		UNUSED OG (NH + 30%) COIL LINE PAIRS VF	F	AVG.	COIL PAIRS VF	F	AVG.
686	1-1/2¢ Harding..................	10.00	8.00	5.50	5.90	4.50	3.00
687	4¢ Taft................................	20.00	15.00	10.00	9.50	7.50	5.00
721	3¢ deep violet perf 10 vertically................	10.75	8.25	5.50	7.90	6.00	4.00
722	3¢ deep violet perf 10 horizontally............	7.75	6.00	4.15	5.90	4.50	3.00
723	6¢ Garfield perf 10 vertically................	71.50	55.00	33.00	35.00	26.00	18.00

SCOTT NO.	DESCRIPTION	UNUSED VF	UNUSED F	UNUSED AVG	USED VF	USED F	USED AVG

727, 752 — 728, 730, 766 — 729, 731, 767

1933 COMMEMORATIVES (NH + 30%)

SCOTT NO.	DESCRIPTION	UNUSED VF	UNUSED F	UNUSED AVG	USED VF	USED F	USED AVG
726/34	**(726-29, 732-34) 7 varieties . . . .**	**3.40**	**2.65**	**2.00**	**2.40**	**1.90**	**1.40**
726	3¢ Oglethorpe .	1.30	.75	.75	.30	.30	.20
727	3¢ Washington's Headquarters . .	.50	.50	.25	.25	.20	.15
728	1¢ Fort Dearborn	.60	.50	.25	.25	.20	.15
729	3¢ Federal Building	.80	.75	.50	.25	.20	.15

Special Printing for A.P.S. Convention
Imperforate: Without Gum

SCOTT NO.	DESCRIPTION	UNUSED VF	UNUSED F	UNUSED AVG	USED VF	USED F	USED AVG
730	1¢ yellow green, sheet of 25	....	42.50	....	....	43.00	....
730a	1¢ yellow green single	1.25	1.00	.75	.75	1.00	.65
731	3¢ violet, sheet of 25	....	33.50	....	....	34.00	....
731a	3¢ violet, single	1.25	1.25	.75	.60	1.25	.90

732

733, 735, 753, 768

734

736

SCOTT NO.	DESCRIPTION	UNUSED VF	UNUSED F	UNUSED AVG	USED VF	USED F	USED AVG
732	3¢ N.R.A.	.40	.25	.25	.25	.20	.15
733	3¢ Byrd.	1.50	1.25	1.00	1.75	1.25	.95
734	5¢ Kosciuszko .	1.50	1.25	1.00	1.50	1.25	.90

1934 NATIONAL PHILATELIC EXHIBITION
Imperforate Without Gum

SCOTT NO.	DESCRIPTION	UNUSED VF	UNUSED F	UNUSED AVG	USED VF	USED F	USED AVG
735	3¢ dark blue, sheet of 6	....	21.50	....	....	17.00	....
735a	3¢ dark blue, single	4.50	4.25	....	2.75	2.50	....

737, 738, 754

739, 755

1934 COMMEMORATIVES (NH + 30%)

SCOTT NO.	DESCRIPTION	UNUSED VF	UNUSED F	UNUSED AVG	USED VF	USED F	USED AVG
736-39	**4 varieties . . . .**	**1.95**	**1.45**	**.85**	**1.15**	**.90**	**.75**
736	3¢ Maryland . . .	.55	.50	.25	.30	.30	.25
737	3¢ Mother's Day, rotary, perf 11 x 10-1/2	.50	.25	.25	.30	.25	.20
738	3¢ Mother's Day, flat, perf 11	.60	.50	.25	.50	.35	.30
739	3¢ Wisconsin . .	.60	.50	.25	.30	.25	.20

For Your Convenience in Ordering, Complete Sets are Listed Before Single Stamp Listings!

740, 751, 756, 769

741, 757

742, 750, 758, 770

743, 759

744, 760

745, 761

746, 762

747, 763

748, 764

749, 765

1934 NATIONAL PARKS ISSUE (NH + 30%)

SCOTT NO.	DESCRIPTION	UNUSED VF	UNUSED F	UNUSED AVG	USED VF	USED F	USED AVG
740-49	**1¢-10¢ (10 varieties, complete) . . . .**	**22.25**	**16.00**	**12.75**	**9.25**	**7.95**	**5.35**
740	1¢ Yosemite . . .	.30	.25	.25	.25	.20	.15
741	2¢ Grand Canyon	.30	.25	.25	.25	.20	.15
742	3¢ Mt. Rainier. .	.50	.25	.25	.25	.20	.15
743	4¢ Mesa Verde.	1.60	1.25	1.00	.75	.65	.45
744	5¢ Yellowstone.	2.00	1.50	1.25	1.75	1.35	.95
745	6¢ Crater Lake.	3.35	2.25	1.75	2.50	1.95	1.25
746	7¢ Acadia	1.75	1.25	1.00	2.00	1.65	1.10
747	8¢ Zion.	4.50	3.50	2.50	4.75	3.65	2.50
748	9¢ Glacier.	4.25	3.00	2.50	1.75	1.30	.90
749	10¢ Great Smoky Mountains	6.50	5.00	4.00	2.50	2.00	1.25

Special Printing for the A.P.S. Convention & Exhibition of Atlantic City
Imperforate Souvenir Sheet
(NH + 30%)

SCOTT NO.	DESCRIPTION	UNUSED VF	UNUSED F	UNUSED AVG	USED VF	USED F	USED AVG
750	3¢ deep violet, sheet of 6	....	45.00	....	....	43.00	....
750a	3¢ deep violet, single	7.25	6.50	....	6.00	5.00	....

Special Printing for Trans-Mississippi Philatelic Exposition and Convention at Omaha
Imperforate Souvenir Sheet
(NH + 30%)

SCOTT NO.	DESCRIPTION	UNUSED VF	UNUSED F	UNUSED AVG	USED VF	USED F	USED AVG
751	1¢ green, sheet of 6	....	16.50	....	....	17.00	....
751a	1¢ green, single	3.25	2.75	....	2.75	2.25	....

SCOTT NO.		PLATE BLOCKS UNUSED NH VF	F	AVG.	UNUSED OG VF	F	AVG.
692	11¢ light blue	22.50	16.50	10.00	16.50	12.75	9.50
693	12¢ brown violet	47.50	32.50	20.00	33.00	25.00	19.75
694	13¢ yellow green	21.50	16.50	10.00	16.50	12.75	9.50
695	14¢ dark blue	50.00	33.50	26.50	37.50	25.00	23.50
696	15¢ grey	65.00	50.00	35.00	49.75	36.00	27.00
697	17¢ black	65.00	47.50	30.00	40.00	30.00	20.00
698	20¢ carmine rose	75.00	55.00	40.00	55.00	43.00	30.00
699	25¢ blue green	75.00	60.00	40.00	55.00	45.00	30.00
700	30¢ brown	145.00	100.00	75.00	105.00	75.00	55.00
701	50¢ lilac	350.00	275.00	155.00	250.00	195.00	115.00
702	2¢ Red Cross	4.00	3.00	2.00	3.00	2.50	1.75
703	2¢ Yorktown (4)	5.75	4.00	2.70	4.25	3.35	2.65
704-15	Washington Bicentennial	590.00	435.00	290.00	445.00	335.00	248.50
704	1/2¢ olive brown	7.50	5.00	3.50	5.50	4.00	3.00
705	1¢ green	7.50	5.00	3.50	5.75	4.50	3.25
706	1-1/2¢ brown	34.50	23.50	17.00	25.00	18.00	13.25
707	2¢ carmine rose	3.00	2.00	1.25	2.25	1.60	1.10
708	3¢ deep violet	25.00	18.50	12.50	21.00	15.00	10.50
709	4¢ light brown	11.50	8.00	6.00	8.50	6.00	4.50
710	5¢ blue	30.00	20.00	16.00	23.50	18.00	14.00
711	6¢ red orange	105.00	80.00	49.50	78.00	60.00	46.50
712	7¢ black	12.00	8.50	6.00	9.00	7.00	5.50
713	8¢ olive bistre	105.00	80.00	49.50	78.00	60.00	40.00
714	9¢ pale red	80.00	55.00	40.00	57.50	42.50	30.00
715	10¢ orange yellow	200.00	150.00	100.00	155.00	115.00	90.00
716 (6)	2¢ Winter Olympics	22.00	16.00	11.00	16.95	13.00	9.50
717	2¢ Arbor Day	14.00	10.50	6.50	10.75	8.25	6.00
718	3¢ Summer Olympics	30.00	22.50	15.00	21.00	15.00	11.00
719	5¢ Summer Olympics	45.00	35.00	25.00	35.00	28.00	20.00
720	3¢ deep violet	2.95	2.00	1.40	2.15	1.65	1.10
724 (6)	3¢ Penn	20.00	14.00	9.50	14.00	11.00	9.00
725 (6)	3¢ Daniel Webster	35.75	26.00	14.00	28.00	22.00	16.00
726 (6)	3¢ Oglethorpe	23.50	16.50	11.00	18.00	14.00	10.00
727	3¢ Washington Hdqrs	10.00	7.00	4.50	7.95	6.00	4.50
728	1¢ Fort Dearborn	3.55	2.75	1.65	2.95	2.25	1.65
729	3¢ Federal Building	6.00	4.00	2.75	4.25	3.35	2.25
732	3¢ N.R.A.	2.95	2.00	1.40	2.55	1.95	1.40
733 (6)	3¢ Byrd	27.50	20.00	13.00	21.00	16.00	13.00
734 (6)	5¢ Kosciuszko	60.00	45.00	28.00	42.95	33.00	25.00
736 (6)	3¢ Maryland	17.50	12.50	8.25	13.00	10.00	8.25
737	3¢ Mother's Day, rotary perf. 11 x 10-1/2	2.95	2.00	1.30	2.40	1.75	1.40
738 (6)	3¢ Mother's Day, flat, perf. 11	8.50	6.50	3.95	6.50	5.00	3.85
739 (6)	3¢ Wisconsin	9.50	7.50	5.00	7.00	5.50	4.00
740-49	10 varieties complete	210.00	160.00	96.50	160.00	125.00	94.00
740 (6)	1¢ Yosemite	3.75	2.65	1.70	2.85	2.00	1.60
741 (6)	2¢ Grand Canyon	4.50	3.25	2.00	3.35	2.50	1.90
742 (6)	3¢ Mt. Rainier	3.50	2.75	1.65	3.00	2.30	1.55
743 (6)	4¢ Mesa Verde	15.50	12.00	7.25	13.00	10.00	7.00
744 (6)	5¢ Yellowstone	19.50	15.00	9.00	14.00	11.00	8.25
745 (6)	6¢ Crater Lake	33.50	26.00	15.50	26.50	20.50	15.50
746 (6)	7¢ Acadia	21.50	16.50	10.00	17.25	13.25	10.00
747 (6)	8¢ Zion	33.50	26.00	15.50	26.50	20.50	15.50
748 (6)	9¢ Glacier	33.50	26.00	15.50	26.50	20.50	15.50
749 (6)	10¢ Great Smoky Mountains	53.50	41.25	24.75	39.00	30.00	23.50

SELECTED U.S. COMMEMORATIVE MINT SHEETS

SCOTT NO.	F/NH SHEET	SCOTT NO.	F/NH SHEET
610 (100)	175.00	709 (100)	72.50
614 (50)	350.00	710 (100)	400.00
615 (50)	500.00	711 (100)	800.00
617 (50)	400.00	712 (100)	90.00
618 (50)	650.00	713 (100)	925.00
620 (100)	1175.00	714 (100)	675.00
627 (50)	275.00	715 (100)	2450.00
628 (50)	775.00	716 (100)	90.00
629 (100)	350.00	717 (100)	45.00
643 (100)	335.00	718 (100)	365.00
644 (50)	325.00	719 (100)	600.00
645 (100)	275.00	724 (100)	100.00
646 (100)	265.00	725 (100)	125.00
647 (100)	895.00	726 (100)	115.00
648 (100)	3895.00	727 (100)	50.00
649 (50)	175.00	728 (100)	55.00
650 (50)	650.00	729 (100)	72.50
651 (50)	95.00	732 (100)	35.00
654 (100)	225.00	733 (50)	135.00
655 (100)	200.00	734 (100)	155.00
657 (100)	175.00	736 (100)	55.00
680 (100)	250.00	737 (50)	22.50
681 (100)	130.00	738 (50)	26.50
682 (100)	145.00	739 (50)	30.00
683 (100)	275.00	740-49 set	925.00
688 (100)	225.00	740 (50)	12.00
689 (100)	110.00	741 (50)	12.00
690 (100)	70.00	742 (50)	20.00
702 (100)	42.50	743 (50)	65.00
703 (50)	28.00	744 (50)	80.00
704-15 set	4975.00	745 (50)	140.00
704 (100)	35.00	746 (50)	75.00
705 (100)	30.00	747 (50)	175.00
706 (100)	95.00	748 (50)	170.00
707 (100)	37.50	749 (50)	300.00
708 (100)	125.00		

THE FARLEY PERIOD

The 1933-35 period was one of great excitement for the hobby. With a stamp collector in the White House, in the person of President Franklin Delano Roosevelt, it was a period during which special Souvenir Sheets were issued for the A.P.S. Convention in 1933 (catalog #730) and the National Philatelic Exhibition in 1934 (#735). Collectors gloried in the limelight.

But there was a darker side, in the form of rare imperforate sheets that were being released to then Postmaster General James A. Farley, President Roosevelt himself, and a few other prominent personages. The protests against the practice grew to unmanageable proportions when word got around that one of the imperforate sheets of the 1934 Mother's Day issue had been offered to a stamp dealer for $20,000. Adding insult to injury, it was learned shortly thereafter that not only were there individual sheets floating around, but full, uncut sheets also had been presented as gifts to a fortunate few.

The outcry that followed could not be stifled. Congress had become involved in the affair and the demands were mounting that the gift sheets be recalled and destroyed. This being deemed impractical or undesirable, another solution was found—one that comes down to us today in the form of "The Farleys".

The solution was to let everyone "share the wealth", so to speak. Instead of recalling the few sheets in existence, additional quantities of the imperforates were issued in the same full sheet form as the gift sheets. Naturally, this step substantially reduced the value of the original, very limited edition, but it satisfied most collectors and left as its legacy "The Farley Issues".

The Farleys were issued March 15, 1935, and consisted of reprints of 20 issues. They remained on sale for three months, a relatively short time by most standards, but more than enough time for collectors who really cared. Although purists felt then—and some still do now—that President Roosevelt would have saved collectors a considerable sum by having the first few sheets destroyed, the issue has provided us with a wondrous selection of Gutters and Lines, arrow blocks, single sheets and full panes.

The collector on a limited budget can fill the spaces in an album with single imperforates. But the Farleys are such an interesting study that owning and displaying at least one of each variety of any one issue is a must. We illustrate here one of the full sheets of the 1 cent Century of Progress Farley Issue. The full sheets consisted of nine panes of 25 stamps each. The individual panes were separated by wide horizontal **(A)** or vertical **(B)** gutters and the gutters of four adjacent sheets formed a cross gutter **(C)**.

NOTE: For #s 753-765 and 771, lines separated the individual panes. The lines ended in arrows at the top, bottom and side margins.

1935 "FARLEY SPECIAL PRINTINGS"
Designs of 1933-34 Imperforate (#752, 753 Perf.) Without Gum

SCOTT NO.		PLATE BLOCK	CENTER LINE BLOCK	ARROW BLOCK T OR B	ARROW BLOCK L OR R	PAIR WITH V. LINE	PAIR WITH H. LINE	FINE UNUSED	FINE USED
752-71	**20 varieties, complete ..**	**.......**	**470.00**	**.......**	**.......**	**135.00**	**91.50**	**35.00**	**29.75**
752	3¢ Newburgh	27.00	50.00	16.50	9.50	8.50	5.00	.45	.40
753	3¢ Byrd....	(6)19.00	95.00	90.00	4.00	42.50	1.80	.75	.75
754	3¢ Mother's Day.......	(6)19.00	9.50	4.00	4.25	1.80	2.00	.75	.65
755	3¢ Wisconsin	(6)19.00	9.50	4.00	4.25	2.00	2.25	.75	.65
756-65	**1¢-10¢ Parks (10 varieties, complete)..**	**295.00**	**150.00**	**140.00**	**140.00**	**42.25**	**43.50**	**19.50**	**17.00**
756	1¢ Yosemite	(6) 5.00	4.00	1.40	1.10	.60	.50	.30	.25
757	2¢ Grand Canyon....	(6) 6.50	5.50	1.55	1.45	.65	.85	.40	.30
758	3¢ Mt. Rainier	(6)16.50	6.50	3.60	4.00	1.55	1.75	.75	.65
759	4¢ Mesa Verde	(6)22.00	11.00	6.00	7.00	2.50	3.10	1.50	1.35
760	5¢ Yellowstone	(6)27.50	16.50	12.00	10.50	5.25	4.75	2.50	2.00
761	6¢ Crater Lake	(6)45.00	22.00	15.00	16.50	6.50	7.50	3.00	2.75
762	7¢ Acadia ..	(6)36.00	18.00	10.50	12.25	4.50	5.50	2.25	2.00
763	8¢ Zion	(6)45.00	20.00	14.50	12.00	7.00	5.50	2.75	2.25
764	9¢ Glacier ..	(6)50.00	22.00	13.00	5.75	5.75	6.50	3.00	2.50
765	10¢ Great Smoky Mountains..	(6)57.50	33.00	25.00	22.00	11.00	10.00	5.00	4.25
766a-70a	**5 varieties, complete ..**	**.......**	**95.00**	**.......**	**.......**	**40.00**	**35.50**	**9.45**	**7.75**
766a	1¢ Fort Dearborn	....	20.00	....	....	9.00	6.50	.85	.65
767a	3¢ Federal Building....	....	21.50	....	....	9.00	6.50	.75	.65
768a	3¢ Byrd....	....	19.00	....	....	8.25	7.25	3.00	2.75
769a	1¢ Yosemite	....	12.00	....	....	7.75	5.50	1.85	1.60
770a	3¢ Mt. Rainier	....	28.00	....	....	11.50	13.00	3.60	3.05
771	16¢ Air Post Special Delivery....	(6)80.00	82.50	15.00	16.50	6.75	8.25	3.50	3.20

U.S. FARLEY ISSUE COMPLETE MINT SHEETS

SCOTT NO.	F/NH SHEET	SCOTT NO.	F/NH SHEET
752-71 set	7500.00	761 (200)	650.00
752 (400)	440.00	762 (200)	500.00
753 (200)	635.00	763 (200)	550.00
754 (200)	190.00	764 (200)	600.00
755 (200)	190.00	765 (200)	950.00
756-65 set	4100.00	766 (225)	400.00
756 (200)	75.00	767 (225)	400.00
757 (200)	90.00	768 (150)	550.00
758 (200)	160.00	769 (120)	275.00
759 (200)	280.00	770 (120)	600.00
760 (200)	450.00	771 (200)	600.00

772, 778a

773, 778b

774

775, 778c

1935-36 COMMEMORATIVES

SCOTT NO.	DESCRIPTION	FIRST DAY COVERS SING	FIRST DAY COVERS PL. BLK.	MINT SHEET	PLATE BLOCK F/NH	UNUSED F/NH	USED F
772/84	**(772-77, 782-84) 9 varieties.......**		**.......**	**.......**	**.......**	**3.60**	**1.75**
772	3¢ Connecticut.........	12.00	19.50	18.50 (50)	2.25	.40	.25
773	3¢ San Diego..........	12.00	19.50	18.50 (50)	1.85	.40	.25
774	3¢ Boulder Dam.........	12.00	19.50	25.00 (50)	(6)3.50	.50	.25
775	3¢ Michigan............	12.00	19.50	22.00 (50)	3.00	.50	.25

776, 778d

777

1936 COMMEMORATIVE

SCOTT NO.	DESCRIPTION	FIRST DAY COVERS SING	FIRST DAY COVERS PL. BLK.	MINT SHEET	PLATE BLOCK F/NH	UNUSED F/NH	USED F
776	3¢ Texas	15.00	25.00	22.00 (50)	2.55	.50	.25
777	3¢ Rhode Island	12.00	19.50	24.00 (50)	3.00	.50	.25

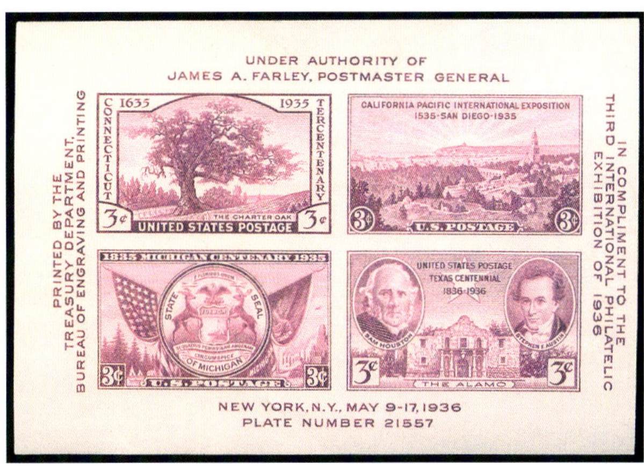

778

782

783

784

1936 THIRD INTERNATIONAL PHILATELIC EXHIBITION "TIPEX" Imperforate Souvenir Sheet Designs of 772, 773, 775, 776

SCOTT NO.	DESCRIPTION	FIRST DAY COVERS SING	FIRST DAY COVERS PL. BLK.	MINT SHEET	PLATE BLOCK F/NH	UNUSED F/NH	USED F
778	red violet, sheet of 4	16.50	....	....	....	3.50	3.00
778a	3¢ Connecticut.........	....	....	....	....	1.00	.75
778b	3¢ San Diego..........	....	....	....	....	1.00	.75
778c	3¢ Michigan...........	....	....	....	....	1.00	.75
778d	3¢ Texas	....	....	....	....	1.00	.75
782	3¢ Arkansas Statehood ..	12.00	19.50	24.00 (50)	3.00	.55	.25
783	3¢ Oregon Territory	12.00	19.50	22.00 (50)	1.85	.45	.25
784	3¢ Suffrage for Women ..	12.00	19.50	31.00 (100)	1.75	.40	.25

FIRST DAY COVERS:

First Day Covers are envelopes cancelled on the "First Day of Issue" of the stamp used on an envelope. Usually they also contain a picture (cachet) on the left side designed to go with the theme of the stamp. From 1935 to 1949, prices listed are for cacheted, addressed covers. From 1950 to date, prices are for cacheted, unaddressed covers. **While we list values for these, H.E. Harris no longer sells them.*

785 786

787

788

789

1936-37 ARMY AND NAVY ISSUE

SCOTT NO.	DESCRIPTION	FIRST DAY COVERS SING	FIRST DAY COVERS PL. BLK.	MINT SHEET	PLATE BLOCK F/NH	UNUSED F/NH	USED F
785-94	10 varieties, complete	57.50	......	......	59.00	5.50	2.30

ARMY COMMEMORATIVES

SCOTT NO.	DESCRIPTION	FIRST DAY COVERS SING	FIRST DAY COVERS PL. BLK.	MINT SHEET	PLATE BLOCK F/NH	UNUSED F/NH	USED F
785	1¢ green	6.00	12.00	15.00 (50)	1.60	.40	.25
786	2¢ carmine	6.00	12.00	17.00 (50)	1.75	.40	.25
787	3¢ purple	6.00	12.00	24.00 (50)	3.00	.60	.25
788	4¢ gray	6.00	14.50	40.00 (50)	12.00	.60	.30
789	5¢ ultramarine	7.00	14.50	43.00 (50)	13.50	.75	.35

790

791

792

793

794

NAVY COMMEMORATIVES

SCOTT NO.	DESCRIPTION	FIRST DAY COVERS SING	FIRST DAY COVERS PL. BLK.	MINT SHEET	PLATE BLOCK F/NH	UNUSED F/NH	USED F
790	1¢ green	6.00	12.00	14.00 (50)	1.75	.30	.25
791	2¢ carmine	6.00	12.00	14.00 (50)	1.85	.35	.25
792	3¢ purple	6.00	12.00	22.00 (50)	2.50	.50	.25
793	4¢ gray	6.00	14.50	42.00 (50)	12.25	.75	.30
794	5¢ ultramarine	7.00	14.50	50.00 (50)	13.25	1.25	.35

795

796

1937 COMMEMORATIVES

SCOTT NO.	DESCRIPTION	FIRST DAY COVERS SING	FIRST DAY COVERS PL. BLK.	MINT SHEET	PLATE BLOCK F/NH	UNUSED F/NH	USED F
795/802	(795-96, 798-802) 7 varieties	....	....	....	....	3.25	2.10
795	3¢ Northwest Ordinance	8.50	16.00	19.00 (50)	2.00	.45	.25
796	5¢ Virginia Dare	8.50	16.00	25.00 (48)	8.50(6)	.45	.30

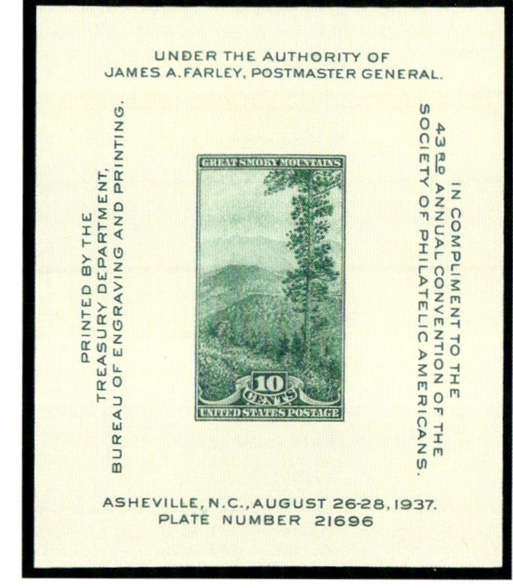

797

1937 S.P.A. CONVENTION ISSUE
Design of 749 Imperforate Souvenir Sheet

SCOTT NO.	DESCRIPTION	FIRST DAY COVERS SING	FIRST DAY COVERS PL. BLK.	MINT SHEET	PLATE BLOCK F/NH	UNUSED F/NH	USED F
797	10¢ blue green	8.50	....	....	....	1.00	.80

798

799

800

801

802

SCOTT NO.	DESCRIPTION	FIRST DAY COVERS SING	FIRST DAY COVERS PL. BLK.	MINT SHEET	PLATE BLOCK F/NH	UNUSED F/NH	USED F
798	3¢ Constitution	10.00	16.00	34.00 (50)	4.00	.75	.25
799	3¢ Hawaii	10.00	16.00	26.00 (50)	2.75	.50	.25
800	3¢ Alaska	10.00	16.00	23.00 (50)	2.75	.50	.25
801	3¢ Puerto Rico	10.00	16.00	29.00 (50)	3.00	.55	.25
802	3¢ Virgin Islands	10.00	16.00	29.00 (50)	3.00	.55	.25

1938 PRESIDENTIAL SERIES

In 1938 a new set of definitive stamps was issued honoring the first 29 presidents, Ben Franklin, Martha Washington, and the White House. These were regular issues that effectively replaced the previous definitive issues of the 1922-25 series.

The "Presidential Series" contained 32 denominations ranging from 1/2¢-$5.00. It is an interesting series because various printing methods were employed. The 1/2¢-50¢ values were printed in single colors on rotary presses using both normal and "electric eye" plates. The $1.00 to $5.00 values were printed in two colors on flat plate presses.

The $1.00 value was reprinted twice, once in 1951 on revenue paper watermarked "USIR" (#832b) and again in 1954. The 1954 issue was "dry printed" on thick white paper, with an experimental colorless gum (832c).

This series in regular and coil form was used for 16 years until it was replaced by the new definitive issues of 1954.

803 | 804, 839, 848 | 805, 840, 849 | 806, 841, 850
807, 842, 851 | 808, 843 | 809, 844 | 810, 845
811, 846 | 812 | 813 | 814
815, 847 | 816 | 817 | 818
819 | 820 | 821 | 822

823 | 824 | 825 | 826
827 | 828 | 829
830 | 831
832 | 833 | 834

SCOTT NO.	DESCRIPTION	FIRST DAY COVERS SING	PL. BLK.	MINT SHEET	PLATE BLOCK F/NH	UNUSED F/NH	USED F
	1938 PRESIDENTIAL SERIES						
803-34	**1/2¢-$5, 32 varieties, complete. . . . .**	**520.00**	**.......**	**.......**	**900.00**	**200.00**	**17.50**
803-31	**1/2¢-50¢, 29 varieties**	**110.00**	**.......**	**.......**	**225.00**	**50.00**	**6.50**
803	1/2¢ Franklin	2.50	5.50	17.00(100)	1.00	.25	.25
804	1¢ G. Washington . . .	2.50	5.50	22.00(100)	1.15	.25	.25
804b	1¢ booklet pane of 6 .	14.00	....	....	....	2.25	....
805	1-1/2¢ M. Washington	2.50	5.50	23.00(100)	1.15	.25	.25
806	2¢ J. Adams.	2.50	5.50	32.00(100)	1.50	.30	.25
806	E.E. Plate Block of 10	....	....	....	7.00	....	....
806b	2¢ booklet pane of 6 .	14.00	....	....	....	6.25	....
807	3¢ Jefferson.	2.50	5.50	30.00(100)	1.50	.30	.25
807	E.E. Plate Block of 10	....	....	....	125.00	....	....
807a	3¢ booklet pane of 6 .	14.00	....	....	....	9.25	....
808	4¢ Madison	2.50	5.50	90.00(100)	5.25	1.00	.25
809	4-1/2¢ White House. .	2.50	5.50	43.00(100)	2.00	.50	.25
810	5¢ J. Monroe	2.50	5.50	52.00(100)	2.50	.50	.25
811	6¢ J.Q. Adams.	2.50	5.50	75.00(100)	3.50	.75	.25
812	7¢ A. Jackson	2.50	5.50	56.00(100)	3.00	.60	.25
813	8¢ Van Buren.	2.50	5.50	75.00(100)	3.75	.80	.25
814	9¢ Harrison	2.50	5.50	66.00(100)	4.00	.75	.25
815	10¢ Tyler	2.50	5.50	58.00(100)	3.00	.60	.25
816	11¢ Polk.	3.75	6.75	94.00(100)	5.00	1.00	.25
817	12¢ Taylor	3.75	6.75	130.00(100)	7.00	1.75	.25
818	13¢ Fillmore.	3.75	6.75	158.00(100)	8.50	1.75	.25
819	14¢ Pierce	3.75	6.75	143.00(100)	7.00	1.75	.25
820	15¢ Buchanan	3.75	6.75	124.00(100)	5.00	1.35	.25
821	16¢ Lincoln	4.50	8.25	194.00(100)	8.75	2.00	.55
822	17¢ Johnson	4.50	8.25	158.00(100)	7.75	2.00	.25
823	18¢ Grant.	4.50	8.25	325.00(100)	17.00	4.00	.25
824	19¢ Hayes	4.50	8.25	214.00(100)	9.00	2.00	.75
825	20¢ Garfield.	4.75	11.25	228.00(100)	9.75	2.25	.25
826	21¢ Arthur	5.25	11.25	215.00(100)	12.00	2.75	.25
827	22¢ Cleveland	5.25	11.25	196.00(100)	12.00	2.00	.75
828	24¢ B. Harrison	6.25	11.25	440.00(100)	20.00	4.00	.30
829	25¢ McKinley.	6.25	13.75	173.00(100)	9.50	1.75	.25
830	30¢ T. Roosevelt	8.50	13.75	670.00(100)	26.00	6.50	.25
831	50¢ Taft	15.00	30.00	895.00(100)	36.00	8.00	.25
	Flat Plate Printing Perf. 11						
832	$1 Wilson.	70.00	150.00	1225.00(100)	55.00	12.00	.25
832	$1 center line block . .	....	....	....	55.00	....	....
832	$1 arrow block	....	....	....	50.00	....	....
832b	$1 Watermarked "USIR"	....	....	....	....	300.00	70.00
832c	$1 dry print thick paper (1954)	35.00	75.00	1100.00(100)	40.00	8.50	.25
833	$2 Harding.	135.00	275.00	....	140.00	25.00	5.50
833	$2 center line block . .	....	....	....	130.00	....	....
833	$2 arrow block	....	....	....	130.00	....	....
834	$5 Coolidge	225.00	400.00	....	600.00	125.00	5.25
834	$5 center line block . .	....	....	....	600.00	....	....
834	$5 arrow block	....	....	....	625.00	....	....

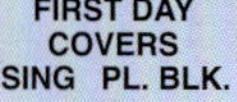

835

836

837

838

1938-39 COMMEMORATIVES

SCOTT NO.	DESCRIPTION	FIRST DAY COVERS SING	FIRST DAY COVERS PL. BLK.	MINT SHEET	PLATE BLOCK F/NH	UNUSED F/NH	USED F
835/58	(835-38, 852-58) 11 varieties, complete	....	....	....	....	7.00	2.15
835	3¢ Ratification	10.00	14.00	35.00(50)	6.00	.70	.25
836	3¢ Swedes-Finns	10.00	14.00	20.00(48)	(6)4.00	.40	.25
837	3¢ Northwest Territory	10.00	14.00	40.00(100)	9.00	.40	.25
838	3¢ Iowa Territory	10.00	14.00	40.00(50)	8.50	.70	.25

1939 PRESIDENTIALS ROTARY PRESS COIL

SCOTT NO.	DESCRIPTION	FIRST DAY COVERS SING	LINE PAIR	MINT SHEET	LINE PAIR	UNUSED F/NH	USED F
839-51	13 varieties, complete	67.50	120.00	....	148.50	36.75	5.30
	Perforated 10 Vertically						
839	1¢ G. Washington	5.00	8.50	....	1.75	.40	.25
840	1-1/2¢ M. Washington	5.00	8.50	....	1.75	.40	.25
841	2¢ J. Adams	5.00	8.50	....	1.85	.45	.25
842	3¢ T. Jefferson	5.00	8.50	....	2.00	.70	.25
843	4¢ J. Madison	5.75	10.50	....	35.00	8.00	.70
844	4-1/2¢ White House	5.75	10.50	....	6.25	.75	.50
845	5¢ J. Monroe	5.75	11.00	....	32.00	5.75	.50
846	6¢ J.Q. Adams	5.75	11.00	....	8.25	1.50	.40
847	10¢ J. Tyler	8.50	16.00	....	56.00	12.00	1.00
	Perforated 10 Horizontally						
848	1¢ G. Washington	5.00	8.50	....	3.25	1.10	.30
849	1-1/2¢ M. Washington	5.00	8.50	....	5.00	1.50	.70
850	2¢ J. Adams	5.00	8.50	....	9.00	3.00	.80
851	3¢ T. Jefferson	5.00	8.50	....	8.75	3.00	.80

852

853

854

855

856

1939 COMMEMORATIVES

SCOTT NO.	DESCRIPTION	FIRST DAY COVERS SING	FIRST DAY COVERS PL. BLK.	MINT SHEET	PLATE BLOCK F/NH	UNUSED F/NH	USED F
852	3¢ Golden Gate	12.00	19.50	20.00(50)	2.00	.40	.25
853	3¢ World's Fair	12.00	19.50	20.00(50)	2.50	.40	.25
854	3¢ Inauguration	12.00	19.50	40.00(50)	(6)7.00	.75	.25
855	3¢ Baseball	37.50	60.00	110.00(50)	12.00	2.00	.30
856	3¢ Panama Canal	17.50	25.00	25.00(50)	(6)5.00	.60	.25

857

858

1939 COMMEMORATIVES

SCOTT NO.	DESCRIPTION	FIRST DAY COVERS SING	FIRST DAY COVERS PL. BLK.	MINT SHEET	PLATE BLOCK F/NH	UNUSED F/NH	USED F
857	3¢ Printing	12.00	19.50	20.00(50)	2.35	.40	.25
858	3¢ Four States	10.00	14.50	30.00(50)	3.75	.75	.25

859

860

861

862

863

1940 FAMOUS AMERICANS ISSUES

SCOTT NO.	DESCRIPTION	FIRST DAY COVERS SING	FIRST DAY COVERS PL. BLK.	MINT SHEET	PLATE BLOCK F/NH	UNUSED F/NH	USED F
859-93	35 varieties, complete	130.00	....	....	475.00	43.00	19.95
	American Authors						
859	1¢ Washington Irving	3.00	4.00	20.00(70)	1.75	.35	.25
860	2¢ James F. Cooper	3.00	4.00	25.00(70)	2.00	.35	.25
861	3¢ Ralph W. Emerson	3.00	4.00	24.00(70)	2.00	.35	.25
862	5¢ Louisa May Alcott	4.00	6.00	45.00(70)	13.00	.60	.35
863	10¢ Samuel L. Clemens	7.50	13.50	180.00(70)	49.50	2.25	1.75

864

865

866

867

868

American Poets

SCOTT NO.	DESCRIPTION	FIRST DAY COVERS SING	FIRST DAY COVERS PL. BLK.	MINT SHEET	PLATE BLOCK F/NH	UNUSED F/NH	USED F
864	1¢ Henry W. Longfellow	3.00	4.00	26.00(70)	3.50	.35	.25
865	2¢ John Whittier	3.00	4.00	24.00(70)	3.50	.35	.25
866	3¢ James Lowell	3.00	4.00	29.00(70)	4.25	.35	.25
867	5¢ Walt Whitman	4.00	6.00	60.00(70)	15.00	.80	.35
868	10¢ James Riley	7.50	11.50	195.00(70)	42.00	2.75	1.75

869

870

871

872

873

American Educators

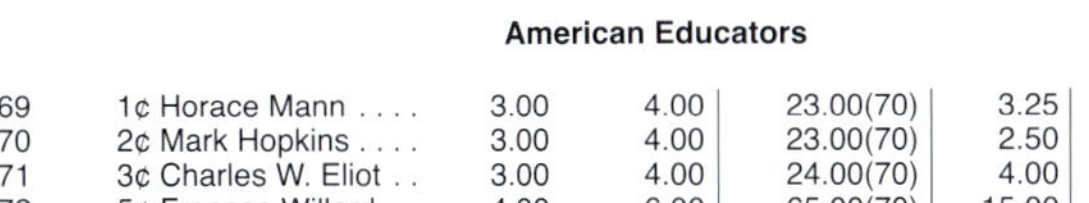

SCOTT NO.	DESCRIPTION	FIRST DAY COVERS SING	FIRST DAY COVERS PL. BLK.	MINT SHEET	PLATE BLOCK F/NH	UNUSED F/NH	USED F
869	1¢ Horace Mann	3.00	4.00	23.00(70)	3.25	.35	.25
870	2¢ Mark Hopkins	3.00	4.00	23.00(70)	2.50	.35	.25
871	3¢ Charles W. Eliot . .	3.00	4.00	24.00(70)	4.00	.40	.25
872	5¢ Frances Willard. . .	4.00	6.00	65.00(70)	15.00	.80	.35
873	10¢ Booker T. Washington	9.50	13.50	295.00(70)	44.00	3.50	1.75

874

875

876

877

878

American Scientists

SCOTT NO.	DESCRIPTION	FIRST DAY COVERS SING	FIRST DAY COVERS PL. BLK.	MINT SHEET	PLATE BLOCK F/NH	UNUSED F/NH	USED F
874	1¢ John J. Audubon. .	3.00	4.00	22.00(70)	1.75	.35	.25
875	2¢ Dr. Crawford Long	3.00	4.00	22.00(70)	1.75	.35	.25
876	3¢ Luther Burbank. . .	3.00	4.00	29.00(70)	1.85	.40	.25
877	5¢ Dr. Walter Reed . .	4.00	6.00	49.00(70)	11.00	.55	.35
878	10¢ Jane Addams . . .	6.00	11.50	145.00(70)	28.00	2.25	1.60

879

880

881

882

883

American Composers

SCOTT NO.	DESCRIPTION	FIRST DAY COVERS SING	FIRST DAY COVERS PL. BLK.	MINT SHEET	PLATE BLOCK F/NH	UNUSED F/NH	USED F
879	1¢ Stephen Foster. . .	3.00	4.00	22.00(70)	1.75	.35	.25
880	2¢ John Philip Sousa.	3.00	4.00	22.00(70)	1.75	.35	.25
881	3¢ Victor Herbert	3.00	4.00	26.00(70)	1.85	.40	.25
882	5¢ Edward A. MacDowell	4.00	6.00	70.00(70)	14.00	.75	.35
883	10¢ Ethelbert Nevin. .	6.00	11.50	360.00(70)	50.00	5.50	2.00

884

885

886

887

888

American Artists

SCOTT NO.	DESCRIPTION	FIRST DAY COVERS SING	FIRST DAY COVERS PL. BLK.	MINT SHEET	PLATE BLOCK F/NH	UNUSED F/NH	USED F
884	1¢ Gilbert Stuart	3.00	4.00	25.00(70)	1.75	.40	.25
885	2¢ James Whistler. . .	3.00	4.00	21.00(70)	1.75	.35	.25
886	3¢ A. Saint-Gaudens .	3.00	4.00	30.00(70)	2.45	.40	.25
887	5¢ Daniel C. French. .	4.00	6.00	55.00(70)	12.50	.85	.35
888	10¢ Frederic Remington	6.00	11.50	185.00(70)	36.00	2.75	1.75

889

890

891

892

893

American Inventors

SCOTT NO.	DESCRIPTION	FIRST DAY COVERS SING	FIRST DAY COVERS PL. BLK.	MINT SHEET	PLATE BLOCK F/NH	UNUSED F/NH	USED F
889	1¢ Eli Whitney	3.00	4.00	30.00(70)	3.25	.40	.25
890	2¢ Samuel Morse . . .	3.00	4.00	42.00(70)	3.35	.70	.25
891	3¢ Cyrus McCormick .	3.00	4.00	32.50(70)	2.75	.55	.25
892	5¢ Elias Howe	4.00	6.00	100.00(70)	18.00	1.50	.45
893	10¢ Alexander G. Bell	8.00	20.00	850.00(70)	85.00	14.00	3.50

894

895

1940 COMMEMORATIVES

SCOTT NO.	DESCRIPTION	FIRST DAY COVERS SING	FIRST DAY COVERS PL. BLK.	MINT SHEET	PLATE BLOCK F/NH	UNUSED F/NH	USED F
894-902	**9 varieties, complete**	....	....	....	....	**3.80**	**1.80**
894	3¢ Pony Express	7.00	11.00	30.00(50)	4.75	.70	.25
895	3¢ Pan Am Union. . . .	5.00	11.00	22.00(50)	4.50	.45	.25

MINT SHEETS: From 1935 to date, we list prices for standard size Mint Sheets in Fine, Never Hinged condition. The number of stamps in each sheet is noted in ( ).

FAMOUS AMERICANS: Later additions to the Famous American series include #945 Edison, #953 Carver, #960 White, #965 Stone, #975 Rogers, #980 Harris, #986 Poe, and #988 Gompers.

896

897

898

1940 COMMEMORATIVES

SCOTT NO.	DESCRIPTION	FIRST DAY COVERS SING	FIRST DAY COVERS PL. BLK.	MINT SHEET	PLATE BLOCK F/NH	UNUSED F/NH	USED F
896	3¢ Idaho Statehood . .	6.00	11.00	29.00(50)	3.50	.60	.25
897	3¢ Wyoming Statehood	6.00	11.00	28.00(50)	3.25	.60	.25
898	3¢ Coronado Expedition	6.00	11.00	32.00(52)	3.75	.75	.25

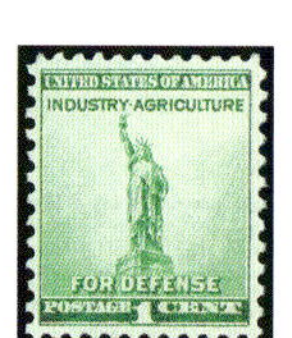

899

900

901

902

NATIONAL DEFENSE ISSUE

SCOTT NO.	DESCRIPTION	FIRST DAY COVERS SING	FIRST DAY COVERS PL. BLK.	MINT SHEET	PLATE BLOCK F/NH	UNUSED F/NH	USED F
899	1¢ Liberty.	4.00	7.00	20.00(100)	1.25	.30	.25
900	2¢ Gun.	4.00	7.00	20.00(100)	1.25	.30	.25
901	3¢ Torch.	4.00	7.00	24.00(100)	1.50	.30	.25
902	3¢ Emancipation	9.00	11.00	27.50(50)	4.75	.60	.35

903

1941-43 COMMEMORATIVES

SCOTT NO.	DESCRIPTION	FIRST DAY COVERS SING	FIRST DAY COVERS PL. BLK.	MINT SHEET	PLATE BLOCK F/NH	UNUSED F/NH	USED F
903-08	**3¢-5¢ 6 varieties. . . .**	....	....	....	....	**4.75**	**1.00**
	1941 COMMEMORATIVES						
903	3¢ Vermont	7.00	10.75	30.00(50)	3.00	.55	.25

904

905

906

1942 COMMEMORATIVES

SCOTT NO.	DESCRIPTION	FIRST DAY COVERS SING	FIRST DAY COVERS PL. BLK.	MINT SHEET	PLATE BLOCK F/NH	UNUSED F/NH	USED F
904	3¢ Kentucky.	5.00	10.75	22.00(50)	2.50	.50	.25
905	3¢ Win The War.	4.50	7.50	52.00(100)	2.25	.55	.25
906	5¢ China Resistance .	12.00	20.00	400.00(50)	36.00	3.50	.45

907

908

1943 COMMEMORATIVES

SCOTT NO.	DESCRIPTION	FIRST DAY COVERS SING	FIRST DAY COVERS PL. BLK.	MINT SHEET	PLATE BLOCK F/NH	UNUSED F/NH	USED F
907	2¢ Allied Nations	6.00	7.50	16.00(100)	1.25	.30	.25
908	1¢ Four Freedoms. . .	6.00	10.50	15.00(100)	1.25	.30	.25

909

910

911

912

913

914

915

916

917

918

919

920

921

1943-44 OVERRUN COUNTRIES SERIES

SCOTT NO.	DESCRIPTION	FIRST DAY COVERS SING	FIRST DAY COVERS PL. BLK.	MINT SHEET	PLATE BLOCK F/NH	UNUSED F/NH	USED F
909-21	**13 varieties, complete**	**50.00**	....	....	**75.00**	**6.50**	**3.50**
909	5¢ Poland	5.00	10.00	24.00(50)	9.00	.40	.25
910	5¢ Czechoslovakia . .	5.00	10.00	20.00(50)	4.00	.40	.25
911	5¢ Norway	5.00	10.00	19.00(50)	2.75	.40	.25
912	5¢ Luxembourg	5.00	10.00	18.00(50)	2.00	.40	.25
913	5¢ Netherlands	5.00	10.00	18.00(50)	2.00	.40	.25
914	5¢ Belgium.	5.00	10.00	18.00(50)	2.00	.40	.25
915	5¢ France	5.00	10.00	20.00(50)	2.00	.75	.25
916	5¢ Greece	5.00	10.00	47.00(50)	16.00	.75	.40
917	5¢ Yugoslavia	5.00	10.00	27.50(50)	8.00	.60	.30
918	5¢ Albania	5.00	10.00	25.00(50)	8.00	.60	.30
919	5¢ Austria.	5.00	10.00	24.00(50)	6.00	.60	.30
920	5¢ Denmark.	5.00	10.00	34.00(50)	8.00	.75	.30
921	5¢ Korea (1944).	5.00	10.00	30.00(50)	8.55	.60	.30

922

923

924

925

926

927

1944 COMMEMORATIVES

SCOTT NO.	DESCRIPTION	FIRST DAY COVERS SING	FIRST DAY COVERS PL. BLK.	MINT SHEET	PLATE BLOCK F/NH	UNUSED F/NH	USED F
922-26	**5 varieties**	....	....	....	....	**1.90**	**1.00**
922	3¢ Railroad	9.00	12.00	32.00(50)	3.50	.55	.25
923	3¢ Steamship	9.00	12.00	20.00(50)	2.50	.40	.25
924	3¢ Telegraph	9.00	12.00	18.00(50)	2.25	.40	.25
925	3¢ Corregidor	9.00	12.00	17.50(50)	2.50	.40	.25
926	3¢ Motion Picture	9.00	12.00	15.00(50)	2.00	.40	.25

928

929

1945-46 COMMEMORATIVES

SCOTT NO.	DESCRIPTION	FIRST DAY COVERS SING	FIRST DAY COVERS PL. BLK.	MINT SHEET	PLATE BLOCK F/NH	UNUSED F/NH	USED F
927-38	**1¢-5¢ (12 varieties, complete)**	....	....	....	....	**4.00**	**2.50**
927	3¢ Florida	10.00	15.00	17.00(50)	2.00	.40	.25
928	5¢ Peace Conference	10.00	15.00	16.00(50)	1.75	.35	.25
929	3¢ Iwo Jima	17.00	20.00	29.00(50)	3.50	.60	.25

930

931

932

933

SCOTT NO.	DESCRIPTION	FIRST DAY COVERS SING	FIRST DAY COVERS PL. BLK.	MINT SHEET	PLATE BLOCK F/NH	UNUSED F/NH	USED F
930	1¢ FDR & Hyde Park	4.00	6.00	7.50(50)	1.10	.30	.25
931	2¢ FDR & "Little White House"	4.00	6.00	8.50(50)	1.10	.30	.25
932	3¢ FDR & White House	4.00	6.00	13.00(50)	1.50	.30	.25
933	5¢ FDR & Globe (1946)	4.00	6.00	17.00(50)	1.75	.35	.25

934

935

936

937

938

SCOTT NO.	DESCRIPTION	FIRST DAY COVERS SING	FIRST DAY COVERS PL. BLK.	MINT SHEET	PLATE BLOCK F/NH	UNUSED F/NH	USED F
934	3¢ Army	10.00	14.00	18.50(50)	2.00	.35	.25
935	3¢ Navy	10.00	14.00	18.50(50)	2.00	.35	.25
936	3¢ Coast Guard	10.00	14.00	14.00(50)	1.75	.35	.25
937	3¢ Al Smith	10.00	14.00	27.00(100)	1.75	.35	.25
938	3¢ Texas Statehood	10.00	14.00	18.00(50)	2.25	.50	.25

939

940

941

942

943

944

1946-47 COMMEMORATIVES

SCOTT NO.	DESCRIPTION	FIRST DAY COVERS SING	FIRST DAY COVERS PL. BLK.	MINT SHEET	PLATE BLOCK F/NH	UNUSED F/NH	USED F
939/52	**(939-47, 949-52) 13 varieties**	....	....	....	....	**4.50**	**2.50**
939	3¢ Merchant Marine	10.00	12.00	15.00(50)	1.50	.35	.25
940	3¢ Honorable Discharge	10.00	12.00	26.00(100)	1.50	.35	.25
941	3¢ Tennessee Statehood	3.00	5.00	15.00(50)	1.50	.35	.25
942	3¢ Iowa Statehood	3.00	5.00	15.00(50)	1.50	.40	.25
943	3¢ Smithsonian Institute	3.00	5.00	15.00(50)	1.50	.40	.25
944	3¢ Kearny Expedition	3.00	5.00	15.00(50)	1.50	.40	.25

945

946

947

1947 COMMEMORATIVES

SCOTT NO.	DESCRIPTION	FIRST DAY COVERS SING	FIRST DAY COVERS PL. BLK.	MINT SHEET	PLATE BLOCK F/NH	UNUSED F/NH	USED F
945	3¢ Thomas A. Edison	3.00	5.00	19.00(70)	1.40	.30	.25
946	3¢ Joseph Pulitzer	3.00	5.00	14.00(50)	1.40	.30	.25
947	3¢ Stamp Centenary	3.00	5.00	15.00(50)	1.50	.30	.25

NEVER HINGED: From 1888 to 1935, Unused OG or Unused prices are for stamps with original gum that have been hinged. If you desire Never Hinged stamps, refer to the NH listings.

SCOTT NO.	DESCRIPTION	FIRST DAY COVERS SING	FIRST DAY COVERS PL. BLK.	MINT SHEET	PLATE BLOCK F/NH	UNUSED F/NH	USED F

"CIPEX" SOUVENIR SHEET

SCOTT NO.	DESCRIPTION	SING	PL. BLK.	MINT SHEET	PLATE BLOCK F/NH	UNUSED F/NH	USED F
948	5¢ & 10¢ Sheet of 2. .	4.00	....	....	....	1.25	1.00
948a	5¢ blue, single stamp	....	....	....	....	.65	.50
948b	10¢ brown orange, single stamp	....	....	....	....	.65	.50

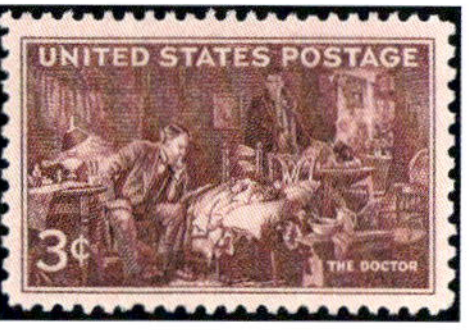

949

950

951

952

953

SCOTT NO.	DESCRIPTION	SING	PL. BLK.	MINT SHEET	PLATE BLOCK F/NH	UNUSED F/NH	USED F
949	3¢ Doctors	8.00	12.00	15.50(50)	1.50	.35	.25
950	3¢ Utah Centennial . .	3.00	5.00	18.00(50)	1.85	.50	.25
951	3¢ "Constitution"	8.00	12.00	13.50(50)	1.50	.40	.25
952	3¢ Everglades National Park.	4.00	6.00	15.50(50)	1.85	.45	.25

954

955

956

957

1948 COMMEMORATIVES

SCOTT NO.	DESCRIPTION	SING	PL. BLK.	MINT SHEET	PLATE BLOCK F/NH	UNUSED F/NH	USED F
953-80	**3¢-5¢ (28 varieties, complete)**	....	....	....	....	**9.25**	**5.50**
953	3¢ George Washington Carver	6.00	10.00	19.00(70)	1.60	.35	.25
954	3¢ Gold Rush.	2.40	5.00	16.00(50)	1.60	.35	.25
955	3¢ Mississippi Territory	2.40	5.00	16.00(50)	1.60	.35	.25
956	3¢ Chaplains	3.00	5.00	16.00(50)	1.60	.35	.25
957	3¢ Wisconsin Statehood	2.40	5.00	16.00(50)	1.75	.45	.25

958

959

960

961

962

963

SCOTT NO.	DESCRIPTION	SING	PL. BLK.	MINT SHEET	PLATE BLOCK F/NH	UNUSED F/NH	USED F
958	5¢ Swedish Pioneer. .	2.40	5.00	16.00(50)	1.80	.35	.25
959	3¢ Women's Progress	2.40	5.00	15.00(50)	1.25	.40	.25
960	3¢ William White	2.40	5.00	18.00(70)	1.50	.35	.25
961	3¢ U.S.-Canada Friendship	2.40	5.00	13.00(50)	1.50	.35	.25
962	3¢ Francis S. Key . . .	2.40	5.00	13.00(50)	1.50	.35	.25
963	3¢ Salute to Youth . . .	2.40	5.00	13.00(50)	1.50	.35	.25

964

965

966

967

968

969

970

SCOTT NO.	DESCRIPTION	SING	PL. BLK.	MINT SHEET	PLATE BLOCK F/NH	UNUSED F/NH	USED F
964	3¢ Oregon Territory . .	2.40	5.00	18.00(50)	2.00	.50	.25
965	3¢ Harlan Stone.	2.40	5.00	18.00(70)	1.50	.35	.25
966	3¢ Mt. Palomar	3.00	5.00	19.00(70)	1.75	.35	.25
967	3¢ Clara Barton	3.00	5.00	13.00(50)	1.60	.35	.25
968	3¢ Poultry	2.40	5.00	16.00(50)	1.75	.35	.25
969	3¢ Gold Star Mothers	2.40	5.00	12.50(50)	1.60	.35	.25
970	3¢ Fort Kearny.	2.40	5.00	17.00(50)	2.00	.45	.25

PLATE BLOCKS: are portions of a sheet of stamps adjacent to the number(s) indicating the printing plate number used to produce that sheet. Flat plate issues are usually collected in plate blocks of six (number opposite middle stamp) while rotary issues are normally corner blocks of four.

971

972

973

974

SCOTT NO.	DESCRIPTION	FIRST DAY COVERS SING	PL. BLK.	MINT SHEET	PLATE BLOCK F/NH	UNUSED F/NH	USED F
971	3¢ Volunteer Firemen	5.00	7.00	14.00(50)	1.50	.35	.25
972	3¢ Indian Centennial .	2.40	5.00	14.00(50)	1.50	.35	.25
973	3¢ Rough Riders	2.40	5.00	16.00(50)	1.50	.35	.25
974	3¢ Juliette Low.	7.00	10.00	14.00(50)	1.70	.35	.25

975

976

977

978

979

980

SCOTT NO.	DESCRIPTION	FIRST DAY COVERS SING	PL. BLK.	MINT SHEET	PLATE BLOCK F/NH	UNUSED F/NH	USED F
975	3¢ Will Rogers	2.40	5.00	20.00(50)	1.70	.40	.25
976	3¢ Fort Bliss.	2.40	5.00	22.00(50)	1.70	.40	.25
977	3¢ Moina Michael . . .	2.40	5.00	13.00(50)	1.50	.35	.25
978	3¢ Gettysburg Address	3.00	5.00	16.00(50)	1.75	.35	.25
979	3¢ American Turners .	2.40	5.00	13.00(50)	1.40	.35	.25
980	3¢ Joel C. Harris	2.40	5.00	19.00(70)	1.40	.35	.25

981

982

983

984

1949-50 COMMEMORATIVES

SCOTT NO.	DESCRIPTION	FIRST DAY COVERS SING	PL. BLK.	MINT SHEET	PLATE BLOCK F/NH	UNUSED F/NH	USED F
981-97	**17 varieties, complete**	....	....	....	....	**5.70**	**3.40**
981	3¢ Minnesota Territory	2.40	4.25	17.00(50)	1.60	.40	.25
982	3¢ Washington & Lee University.	2.40	4.25	12.50(50)	1.35	.35	.25
983	3¢ Puerto Rico.	3.00	4.25	18.00(50)	2.00	.45	.25
984	3¢ Annapolis	3.00	4.25	12.50(50)	1.40	.35	.25

985

986

SCOTT NO.	DESCRIPTION	FIRST DAY COVERS SING	PL. BLK.	MINT SHEET	PLATE BLOCK F/NH	UNUSED F/NH	USED F
985	3¢ G.A.R.	3.00	4.25	18.00(50)	1.65	.35	.25
986	3¢ Edgar A. Poe	3.00	4.25	20.00(70)	1.85	.45	.25

987

988

989

1950 COMMEMORATIVES

SCOTT NO.	DESCRIPTION	FIRST DAY COVERS SING	PL. BLK.	MINT SHEET	PLATE BLOCK F/NH	UNUSED F/NH	USED F
987	3¢ Bankers Association	2.40	4.25	14.00(50)	1.50	.35	.25
988	3¢ Samuel Gompers .	2.40	4.25	18.00(70)	1.50	.35	.25
989	3¢ Statue of Freedom	2.40	4.25	15.00(50)	1.50	.35	.25

990

991

992

993

994

995

996

997

SCOTT NO.	DESCRIPTION	FIRST DAY COVERS SING	PL. BLK.	MINT SHEET	PLATE BLOCK F/NH	UNUSED F/NH	USED F
990	3¢ Executive Mansion	2.40	4.25	18.00(50)	1.75	.50	.25
991	3¢ Supreme Court . . .	2.40	4.25	16.00(50)	1.75	.35	.25
992	3¢ United States Capitol	2.40	4.25	16.00(50)	1.75	.35	.25
993	3¢ Railroad	4.00	5.25	16.00(50)	1.75	.35	.25
994	3¢ Kansas City	2.40	4.25	16.00(50)	1.60	.35	.25
995	3¢ Boy Scouts	7.00	10.00	16.00(50)	1.60	.35	.25
996	3¢ Indiana Territory . .	2.40	4.25	18.00(50)	2.00	.50	.25
997	3¢ California Statehood	2.40	4.25	18.00(50)	2.00	.50	.25

BUY COMPLETE SETS AND SAVE!

998

999

1000

1001

1002

1003

1951-52 COMMEMORATIVES

SCOTT NO.	DESCRIPTION	FIRST DAY COVERS SING	FIRST DAY COVERS PL. BLK.	MINT SHEET	PLATE BLOCK F/NH	UNUSED F/NH	USED F
998-1016	19 varieties, complete	....	....	....	....	6.40	3.95
998	3¢ Confederate Veterans	3.00	4.25	21.00(50)	2.25	.40	.25
999	3¢ Nevada Settlement	2.00	4.25	15.00(50)	1.75	.35	.25
1000	3¢ Landing of Cadillac	2.00	4.25	15.00(50)	1.50	.35	.25
1001	3¢ Colorado Statehood	2.00	4.25	17.00(50)	1.50	.35	.25
1002	3¢ Chemical Society .	2.00	4.25	16.00(50)	1.50	.35	.25
1003	3¢ Battle of Brooklyn .	2.00	4.25	12.50(50)	1.50	.35	.25

1004

1005

1006

1007

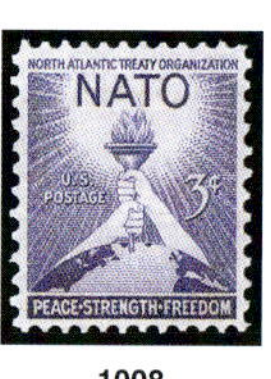
1008

1009

1010

1952 COMMEMORATIVES

SCOTT NO.	DESCRIPTION	FIRST DAY COVERS SING	FIRST DAY COVERS PL. BLK.	MINT SHEET	PLATE BLOCK F/NH	UNUSED F/NH	USED F
1004	3¢ Betsy Ross	2.50	5.50	13.50(50)	1.40	.40	.25
1005	3¢ 4-H Club	6.00	10.00	14.00(50)	1.40	.40	.25
1006	3¢ B. & O. Railroad . .	4.00	6.50	17.50(50)	2.25	.40	.25
1007	3¢ AAA.	2.00	4.25	14.00(50)	1.60	.40	.25
1008	3¢ NATO	2.00	4.25	24.00(100)	1.60	.40	.25
1009	3¢ Grand Coulee Dam	2.00	4.25	18.00(50)	1.75	.40	.25
1010	3¢ Lafayette.	2.00	4.25	13.50(50)	1.40	.40	.25

1011

1012

1013

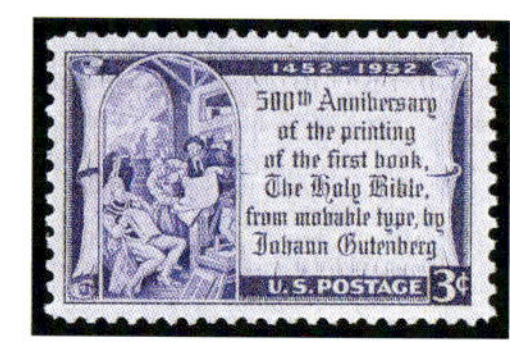
1014

1015

1016

SCOTT NO.	DESCRIPTION	FIRST DAY COVERS SING	FIRST DAY COVERS PL. BLK.	MINT SHEET	PLATE BLOCK F/NH	UNUSED F/NH	USED F
1011	3¢ Mt. Rushmore	2.00	4.25	19.00(50)	2.25	.50	.25
1012	3¢ Civil Engineers . . .	2.00	4.25	12.50(50)	1.40	.35	.25
1013	3¢ Service Women . .	2.25	4.25	13.50(50)	1.40	.35	.25
1014	3¢ Gutenburg Press .	2.00	4.25	13.50(50)	1.40	.35	.25
1015	3¢ Newspaper Boys .	2.00	4.25	12.50(50)	1.40	.35	.25
1016	3¢ Red Cross	3.00	6.25	12.50(50)	1.40	.35	.25

1017

1018

1019

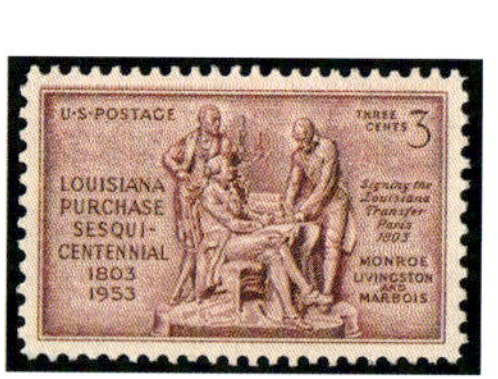
1020

1021

1022

1953-54 COMMEMORATIVES

SCOTT NO.	DESCRIPTION	FIRST DAY COVERS SING	FIRST DAY COVERS PL. BLK.	MINT SHEET	PLATE BLOCK F/NH	UNUSED F/NH	USED F
1017/63	(1017-29, 1060-63) 17 varieties, complete	....	....	....	....	5.55	3.55
1017	3¢ National Guard . . .	2.00	4.25	12.50(50)	1.40	.35	.25
1018	3¢ Ohio Statehood. . .	2.00	4.25	17.50(70)	1.40	.35	.25
1019	3¢ Washington Territory	2.00	4.25	18.00(50)	2.25	.50	.25
1020	3¢ Louisiana Purchase	4.00	6.00	13.50(50)	1.85	.40	.25
1021	5¢ Opening of Japan .	3.00	4.25	14.00(50)	1.50	.40	.25
1022	3¢ American Bar Association	5.00	6.25	14.00(50)	1.50	.40	.25

1023

1024

1025

1026

1027

1028

SCOTT NO.	DESCRIPTION	FIRST DAY COVERS SING	FIRST DAY COVERS PL. BLK.	MINT SHEET	PLATE BLOCK F/NH	UNUSED F/NH	USED F
1023	3¢ Sagamore Hill. . . .	2.00	4.25	12.50(50)	1.40	.35	.25
1024	3¢ Future Farmers. . .	2.00	4.25	12.50(50)	1.40	.35	.25
1025	3¢ Trucking Industry .	2.50	4.50	12.50(50)	1.40	.35	.25
1026	3¢ Gen. George S. Patton	3.00	4.75	12.50(50)	1.40	.35	.25
1027	3¢ New York City. . . .	2.00	4.25	12.50(50)	1.40	.35	.25
1028	3¢ Gadsden Purchase	2.00	4.25	15.00(50)	1.60	.35	.25

1029

1954 COMMEMORATIVES

SCOTT NO.	DESCRIPTION	FIRST DAY COVERS SING	FIRST DAY COVERS PL. BLK.	MINT SHEET	PLATE BLOCK F/NH	UNUSED F/NH	USED F
1029	3¢ Columbia University	2.00	4.25	12.50(50)	1.40	.35	.20

1030

1031, 1054

1031A, 1054A

1032

1033, 1055

1034, 1056

1035, 1057, 1075a

1036, 1058

1037, 1059

1038

1039

1040

1041, 1075b, 1041b

1042

1043

1044

1044A

1045

1046

1047

1048, 1059A

1049

1050

1051

1052

1053

1954-68 LIBERTY SERIES

SCOTT NO.	DESCRIPTION	FIRST DAY COVERS SING	FIRST DAY COVERS PL. BLK.	MINT SHEET	PLATE BLOCK F/NH	UNUSED F/NH	USED F
1030-53	**1/2¢-$5, 27 varieties, complete. . . . .**	**110.00**	**235.00**	....	**385.00**	**100.00**	**12.50**
1030-51	**1/2¢-50¢, 25 varieties**	**55.00**	**115.00**	....	**85.00**	**19.00**	**5.50**
1030	1/2¢ Benjamin Franklin (1955)	2.00	4.25	13.00(100)	1.00	.25	.25
1031	1¢ George Washington	2.00	4.25	20.00(100)	1.25	.25	.25
1031A	1-1/4¢ Palace of Governors (1960) . . .	2.00	4.25	16.00(100)	1.25	.25	.25
1032	1-1/2¢ Mount Vernon.	2.00	4.25	20.00(100)	2.50	.25	.25
1033	2¢ Thomas Jefferson.	2.00	4.25	19.00(100)	1.25	.25	.25
1034	2-1/2¢ Bunker Hill (1959)	2.00	4.25	18.00(100)	1.25	.25	.25
1035	3¢ Statue of Liberty . .	2.00	4.25	23.00(100)	1.25	.35	.25
1035a	3¢ booklet pane of 6 .	3.50	....	....	....	6.00	....
1036	4¢ Abraham Lincoln. .	2.00	4.25	25.00(100)	1.50	.25	.25
1036a	4¢ booklet pane of 6 .	3.00	....	....	....	3.75	....
1037	4-1/2¢ Hermitage (1959)	2.00	4.25	30.00(100)	2.00	.40	.25
1038	5¢ James Monroe . . .	2.00	4.25	30.00(100)	2.00	.40	.25
1039	6¢ T. Roosevelt (1955)	2.00	4.25	40.00(100)	2.25	.60	.25
1040	7¢ Woodrow Wilson (1956)	2.00	4.25	48.00(100)	2.75	.55	.25
1041	8¢ Statue of Liberty (flat plate).	2.00	4.25	30.00(100)	2.50	.40	.25
1041B	8¢ Statue of Liberty . .	2.00	4.25	120.00(100)	6.00	.70	.25
1042	8¢ Liberty re-engraved (1958)	2.00	4.25	35.00(100)	2.00	.45	.25
1043	9¢ Alamo (1956)	2.25	5.00	52.00(100)	3.00	.65	.25
1044	10¢ Independence Hall (1956)	2.25	5.00	52.00(100)	3.00	.60	.25
1044A	11¢ Statue of Liberty (1961)	2.25	5.00	52.00(100)	3.50	.75	.25
1045	12¢ Benjamin Harrison (1959)	2.25	5.00	88.00(100)	4.00	.85	.25
1046	15¢ John Jay (1958) .	2.50	5.25	90.00(100)	5.50	1.25	.25
1047	20¢ Monticello (1956)	2.50	5.25	125.00(100)	6.50	1.30	.25
1048	25¢ Paul Revere (1958)	2.50	5.25	200.00(100)	10.00	2.50	.25
1049	30¢ Robert E. Lee (1955)	3.75	6.00	243.00(100)	17.00	3.00	.25
1050	40¢ John Marshall (1955)	3.75	7.00	280.00(100)	16.00	3.50	.25
1051	50¢ Susan B. Anthony (1955)	5.50	8.50	280.00(100)	15.00	3.00	.25
1052	$1 Patrick Henry (1955)	9.25	17.50	615.00(100)	35.50	7.00	.25
1053	$5 Alexander Hamilton (1956)	50.00	110.00	....	350.00	85.00	10.00

1954-65 COIL STAMPS
Perf. 10 Vertically or Horizontally

SCOTT NO.	DESCRIPTION	FIRST DAY COVERS SING	FIRST DAY COVERS LINE PAIR	MINT SHEET	LINE PAIR	UNUSED F/NH	USED F
1054-59A	**1¢-25¢ (8 varieties, complete). . . . .**	**16.00**	**29.75**	....	**32.00**	**4.65**	**2.75**
1054	1¢ George Washington	2.00	3.75	....	1.25	.30	.25
1054A	1-1/4¢ Palace of Governors(1960)	2.00	3.75	....	3.00	.30	.25
1055	2¢ Thomas Jefferson(1957)	2.00	3.75	....	2.75	.50	.25
1056	2-1/2¢ Bunker Hill Mon. (1959)	2.00	3.75	....	5.00	.45	.30
1057	3¢ Statue of Liberty(1956)	2.00	3.75	....	.85	.25	.25
1058	4¢ Abraham Lincoln (1958)	2.00	3.75	....	1.00	.35	.25
1059	4-1/2¢ Hermitage (1959)	2.00	3.75	....	19.00	2.00	2.00
1059A	25¢ Paul Revere (1965)	2.50	5.00	....	3.50	1.25	.25

NOTE: **Pairs of the above can be priced at two times the single price.**

1060

1061

1062

1063

1954 COMMEMORATIVES

SCOTT NO.	DESCRIPTION	FIRST DAY COVERS SING	FIRST DAY COVERS PL. BLK.	MINT SHEET	PLATE BLOCK F/NH	UNUSED F/NH	USED F
1060	3¢ Nebraska Territory	2.00	4.25	13.00(50)	1.50	.35	.25
1061	3¢ Kansas Territory . .	2.00	4.25	14.00(50)	1.50	.50	.25
1062	3¢ George Eastman .	2.00	4.25	17.00(70)	1.50	.35	.25
1063	3¢ Lewis & Clark	4.00	6.00	16.00(50)	2.25	.65	.25

1064

1065

1066

1067

1069

1068

1955 COMMEMORATIVES

SCOTT NO.	DESCRIPTION	FIRST DAY COVERS SING	FIRST DAY COVERS PL. BLK.	MINT SHEET	PLATE BLOCK F/NH	UNUSED F/NH	USED F
1064-72	**3¢-8¢ (9 varieties, complete)**	....	....	....	....	**2.95**	**1.95**
1064	3¢ Pennsylvania Academy	2.00	4.25	16.00(50)	1.50	.40	.25
1065	3¢ Land Grant Colleges	2.50	4.50	17.00(50)	1.85	.50	.25
1066	8¢ Rotary International	5.00	7.00	20.00(50)	2.00	.55	.25
1067	3¢ Armed Forces Reserve	2.00	4.25	13.00(50)	1.55	.35	.25
1068	3¢ Great Stone Face .	2.00	4.25	19.00(50)	1.75	.45	.25
1069	3¢ Soo Locks.	2.00	4.25	13.00(50)	1.35	.50	.25

1070

1071

1072

SCOTT NO.	DESCRIPTION	FIRST DAY COVERS SING	FIRST DAY COVERS PL. BLK.	MINT SHEET	PLATE BLOCK F/NH	UNUSED F/NH	USED F
1070	3¢ Atoms for Peace . .	2.00	4.25	12.50(50)	1.35	.35	.25
1071	3¢ Fort Ticonderoga .	2.00	4.25	14.00(50)	1.50	.40	.25
1072	3¢ Andrew Mellon . . .	2.00	4.25	19.00(70)	1.75	.40	.25

1073

1074

1075

1956 COMMEMORATIVES

SCOTT NO.	DESCRIPTION	FIRST DAY COVERS SING	FIRST DAY COVERS PL. BLK.	MINT SHEET	PLATE BLOCK F/NH	UNUSED F/NH	USED F
1073/85	**(1073-74, 1076-85) 12 varieties. . . . . . .**	....	....	....	....	**4.00**	**2.00**
1073	3¢ Benjamin Franklin.	2.00	4.25	14.00(50)	1.40	.35	.25
1074	3¢ Booker T. Washington	3.50	5.50	14.00(50)	1.40	.35	.25
1075	3¢ & 8¢ FIPEX Sheet of 2	6.00	....	....	....	3.25	3.25
1075a	3¢ deep violet, single.	....	....	....	....	1.25	1.05
1075b	8¢ violet blue & carmine, single.	....	....	....	....	1.75	1.25

1076

1077

1078

1079

SCOTT NO.	DESCRIPTION	FIRST DAY COVERS SING	FIRST DAY COVERS PL. BLK.	MINT SHEET	PLATE BLOCK F/NH	UNUSED F/NH	USED F
1076	3¢ FIPEX.	2.00	4.25	12.50(50)	1.30	.35	.25
1077	3¢ Wild Turkey.	2.75	4.50	14.00(50)	1.55	.35	.25
1078	3¢ Antelope	2.75	4.50	14.00(50)	1.55	.35	.25
1079	3¢ Salmon	2.75	4.50	14.00(50)	1.55	.35	.25

PLATE BLOCKS: are portions of a sheet of stamps adjacent to the number(s) indicating the printing plate number used to produce that sheet. Flat plate issues are usually collected in plate blocks of six (number opposite middle stamp) while rotary issues are normally corner blocks of four.

1080

1081

1082

SCOTT NO.	DESCRIPTION	FIRST DAY COVERS SING	FIRST DAY COVERS PL. BLK.	MINT SHEET	PLATE BLOCK F/NH	UNUSED F/NH	USED F
1080	3¢ Pure Food & Drug Act	2.00	4.25	13.50(50)	1.35	.35	.25
1081	3¢ "Wheatland"	2.00	4.25	13.50(50)	1.35	.35	.25
1082	3¢ Labor Day.	2.00	4.25	13.50(50)	1.35	.35	.25

1083

1084

1085

SCOTT NO.	DESCRIPTION	FIRST DAY COVERS SING	FIRST DAY COVERS PL. BLK.	MINT SHEET	PLATE BLOCK F/NH	UNUSED F/NH	USED F
1083	3¢ Nassau Hall	2.00	4.25	13.50(50)	1.35	.35	.25
1084	3¢ Devil's Tower	2.00	4.25	16.00(50)	1.75	.50	.25
1085	3¢ Children of the World	2.00	4.25	13.00(50)	1.50	.35	.25

1086

1087

1088

1089

1090

1091

1957 COMMEMORATIVES

SCOTT NO.	DESCRIPTION	FIRST DAY COVERS SING	FIRST DAY COVERS PL. BLK.	MINT SHEET	PLATE BLOCK F/NH	UNUSED F/NH	USED F
1086-99	**14 varieties, complete**	....	....	....	....	**4.35**	**3.00**
1086	3¢ Alexander Hamilton	2.00	4.25	17.00(50)	1.85	.45	.25
1087	3¢ Polio	2.25	4.50	13.00(50)	1.35	.35	.25
1088	3¢ Coast & Geodetic Survey	2.00	4.25	13.00(50)	1.35	.35	.25
1089	3¢ Architects	2.00	4.25	13.00(50)	1.35	.35	.25
1090	3¢ Steel Industry	2.00	4.25	13.00(50)	1.35	.35	.25
1091	3¢ International Naval Review.	2.00	4.25	13.00(50)	1.35	.35	.25

1092

1093

1094

1095

1096

1097

SCOTT NO.	DESCRIPTION	FIRST DAY COVERS SING	FIRST DAY COVERS PL. BLK.	MINT SHEET	PLATE BLOCK F/NH	UNUSED F/NH	USED F
1092	3¢ Oklahoma Statehood	2.00	4.25	15.00(50)	2.00	.50	.25
1093	3¢ School Teachers. .	2.25	4.50	12.50(50)	1.35	.45	.25
1094	4¢ 48-Star Flag	2.00	4.25	12.50(50)	1.35	.35	.25
1095	3¢ Shipbuilding Anniversary	2.00	4.25	17.00(70)	1.50	.35	.25
1096	8¢ Ramon Magsaysay	2.50	4.25	17.00(48)	1.75	.40	.25
1097	3¢ Birth of Lafayette .	2.00	4.25	12.50(50)	1.35	.35	.25

1098

1099

1100

SCOTT NO.	DESCRIPTION	FIRST DAY COVERS SING	FIRST DAY COVERS PL. BLK.	MINT SHEET	PLATE BLOCK F/NH	UNUSED F/NH	USED F
1098	3¢ Whooping Cranes.	2.25	4.50	12.50(50)	1.35	.35	.25
1099	3¢ Religious Freedom	2.00	4.25	12.50(50)	1.35	.35	.25

1104

1105

1106

1107

1958 COMMEMORATIVES

SCOTT NO.	DESCRIPTION	FIRST DAY COVERS SING	FIRST DAY COVERS PL. BLK.	MINT SHEET	PLATE BLOCK F/NH	UNUSED F/NH	USED F
1100-23	**21 varieties, complete**	....	....	....	....	**7.00**	**4.40**
1100	3¢ Gardening & Horticulture.	2.00	4.25	12.50(50)	1.35	.35	.25
1104	3¢ Brussels Exhibition	2.00	4.25	12.50(50)	1.35	.35	.25
1105	3¢ James Monroe . . .	2.00	4.25	25.00(70)	2.00	.35	.25
1106	3¢ Minnesota Statehood	2.00	4.25	14.00(50)	1.75	.40	.25
1107	3¢ Int'l. Geophysical Year	2.00	4.25	12.50(50)	1.35	.35	.25

1108

1109

1110, 1111

1112

SCOTT NO.	DESCRIPTION	FIRST DAY COVERS SING	FIRST DAY COVERS PL. BLK.	MINT SHEET	PLATE BLOCK F/NH	UNUSED F/NH	USED F
1108	3¢ Gunston Hall.	2.00	4.25	12.50(50)	1.30	.35	.25
1109	3¢ Mackinac Bridge. .	2.00	4.25	13.00(50)	1.30	.40	.25
1110	4¢ Simon Bolivar	2.00	4.25	17.00(70)	1.30	.35	.25
1111	8¢ Simon Bolivar	2.00	4.50	28.00(72)	2.50	.40	.25
1112	4¢ Atlantic Cable Centenary	2.00	4.25	14.00(50)	1.30	.35	.25

1113

1114

1115

1116

SCOTT NO.	DESCRIPTION	FIRST DAY COVERS SING	FIRST DAY COVERS PL. BLK.	MINT SHEET	PLATE BLOCK F/NH	UNUSED F/NH	USED F
1113	1¢ Abraham Lincoln (1959)	2.00	4.25	8.00(50)	1.00	.30	.25
1114	3¢ Bust of Lincoln (1959)	2.00	4.25	13.50(50)	1.75	.40	.25
1115	4¢ Lincoln-Douglas Debates.	2.00	4.25	15.00(50)	1.75	.40	.25
1116	4¢ Statue of Lincoln (1959)	2.00	4.25	19.00(50)	2.15	.45	.25

1117, 1118

1119

1120

SCOTT NO.	DESCRIPTION	FIRST DAY COVERS SING	FIRST DAY COVERS PL. BLK.	MINT SHEET	PLATE BLOCK F/NH	UNUSED F/NH	USED F
1117	4¢ Lajos Kossuth. . . .	2.00	4.25	18.00(70)	1.35	.35	.25
1118	8¢ Lajos Kossuth. . . .	2.00	4.50	20.00(72)	1.75	.35	.25
1119	4¢ Freedom of Press.	2.00	4.25	12.50(50)	1.35	.35	.25
1120	4¢ Overland Mail	2.00	4.25	12.50(50)	1.35	.35	.25

Plate blocks will be blocks of 4 stamps unless otherwise noted.

1121

1122

1123

SCOTT NO.	DESCRIPTION	FIRST DAY COVERS SING	FIRST DAY COVERS PL. BLK.	MINT SHEET	PLATE BLOCK F/NH	UNUSED F/NH	USED F
1121	4¢ Noah Webster. . . .	2.00	4.25	17.00(70)	1.25	.35	.25
1122	4¢ Forest Conservation	2.00	4.25	14.00(50)	1.50	.35	.25
1123	4¢ Fort Duquesne . . .	2.00	4.25	12.50(50)	1.25	.35	.25

1124

1125, 1126

1127

1128

1129

1959 COMMEMORATIVES

SCOTT NO.	DESCRIPTION	FIRST DAY COVERS SING	FIRST DAY COVERS PL. BLK.	MINT SHEET	PLATE BLOCK F/NH	UNUSED F/NH	USED F
1124-38	**4¢-8¢, 15 varieties . .**	......	....	....	....	**4.95**	**3.25**
1124	4¢ Oregon Statehood	2.00	4.25	17.00(50)	1.70	.35	.25
1125	4¢ José de San Martin	2.00	4.25	17.00(70)	1.40	.35	.25
1126	8¢ José de San Martin	2.00	4.25	19.50(72)	1.75	.35	.25
1127	4¢ NATO	2.00	4.25	17.00(70)	1.40	.35	.25
1128	4¢ Arctic Exploration .	2.00	4.25	12.50(50)	1.40	.35	.25
1129	8¢ World Peace & Trade	2.00	4.25	19.00(50)	1.95	.40	.25

1130

1131

1132

1133

1134

1135

1136, 1137

1138

SCOTT NO.	DESCRIPTION	FIRST DAY COVERS SING	FIRST DAY COVERS PL. BLK.	MINT SHEET	PLATE BLOCK F/NH	UNUSED F/NH	USED F
1130	4¢ Silver Centennial .	2.00	4.25	19.00(50)	1.95	.50	.25
1131	4¢ St. Lawrence Seaway	2.00	4.25	12.50(50)	1.35	.35	.25
1132	4¢ 49-Star Flag	2.00	4.25	12.50(50)	1.35	.35	.25
1133	4¢ Soil Conservation .	2.00	4.25	13.00(50)	1.40	.35	.25
1134	4¢ Petroleum	2.00	4.25	15.00(50)	1.40	.40	.25
1135	4¢ Dental Health	5.00	7.00	15.00(50)	1.40	.40	.25
1136	4¢ Ernst Reuter	2.00	4.25	17.00(70)	1.40	.35	.25
1137	8¢ Ernst Reuter	2.00	4.25	20.00(72)	1.75	.35	.25
1138	4¢ Dr. Ephraim McDowell	2.00	4.25	18.00(70)	1.50	.35	.25

1139

1140

1141

1142

1143

1144

1960-61 CREDO OF AMERICA SERIES

SCOTT NO.	DESCRIPTION	FIRST DAY COVERS SING	FIRST DAY COVERS PL. BLK.	MINT SHEET	PLATE BLOCK F/NH	UNUSED F/NH	USED F
1139-44	6 varieties, complete	....	....	....	....	1.85	1.15
1139	4¢ Credo—Washington	2.00	4.25	14.00(50)	1.35	.50	.25
1140	4¢ Credo—Franklin . .	2.00	4.25	12.50(50)	1.35	.35	.25
1141	4¢ Credo—Jefferson .	2.00	4.25	14.00(50)	1.35	.50	.25
1142	4¢ Credo—Key	2.00	4.25	12.50(50)	1.35	.35	.25
1143	4¢ Credo—Lincoln. . .	2.00	4.25	12.50(50)	1.35	.35	.25
1144	4¢ Credo—Henry (1961)	2.00	4.25	15.00(50)	1.50	.35	.25

1145

1146

1147, 1148

1149

1150

1151

1152

1153

1960 COMMEMORATIVES

SCOTT NO.	DESCRIPTION	FIRST DAY COVERS SING	FIRST DAY COVERS PL. BLK.	MINT SHEET	PLATE BLOCK F/NH	UNUSED F/NH	USED F
1145-73	4¢-8¢, 29 varieties . .	....	....	....	....	8.85	5.25
1145	4¢ Boy Scouts	8.50	10.50	14.00(50)	1.75	.40	.25
1146	4¢ Winter Olympics . .	2.00	4.25	12.50(50)	1.35	.35	.25
1147	4¢ Thomas Masaryk .	2.00	4.25	17.00(70)	1.35	.35	.25
1148	8¢ Thomas Masaryk .	2.00	4.25	21.00(72)	1.75	.40	.25
1149	4¢ World Refugee Year	2.00	4.25	12.50(50)	1.35	.35	.25
1150	4¢ Water Conservation	2.00	4.25	12.50(50)	1.35	.35	.25
1151	4¢ SEATO	2.00	4.25	17.00(70)	1.50	.35	.25
1152	4¢ American Women .	2.00	4.25	12.50(50)	1.35	.35	.25
1153	4¢ 50-Star Flag	2.00	4.25	15.00(50)	1.50	.35	.25

1154

1155

1156

1157

1158

1159, 1160

1161

1162

1163

SCOTT NO.	DESCRIPTION	FIRST DAY COVERS SING	FIRST DAY COVERS PL. BLK.	MINT SHEET	PLATE BLOCK F/NH	UNUSED F/NH	USED F
1154	4¢ Pony Express	2.00	4.25	15.00(50)	1.70	.45	.25
1155	4¢ Employ the Handicapped	2.00	4.25	12.00(50)	1.35	.35	.25
1156	4¢ World Forestry Congress	2.00	4.25	15.00(50)	1.50	.40	.25
1157	4¢ Mexican Independence	2.00	4.25	12.00(50)	1.35	.35	.25
1158	4¢ U.S.-Japan Treaty	2.00	4.25	17.00(50)	1.70	.35	.25
1159	4¢ Ignacy Paderewski	2.00	4.25	17.00(70)	1.75	.35	.25
1160	8¢ Ignacy Paderewski	2.00	4.25	20.00(72)	1.75	.35	.25
1161	4¢ Robert A. Taft	2.00	4.25	19.00(70)	1.75	.35	.25
1162	4¢ Wheels of Freedom	2.00	4.25	15.00(50)	1.50	.35	.25
1163	4¢ Boys' Club of America	2.25	4.25	12.00(50)	1.40	.35	.25

1164

1165, 1166

1167

1168, 1169

1170

1171

1172

1173

SCOTT NO.	DESCRIPTION	FIRST DAY COVERS SING	PL. BLK.	MINT SHEET	PLATE BLOCK F/NH	UNUSED F/NH	USED F
1164	4¢ Automated Post Office	2.00	4.25	16.00(50)	1.50	.45	.25
1165	4¢ Gustaf Mannerheim	2.00	4.25	17.00(70)	1.40	.30	.25
1166	8¢ Gustaf Mannerheim	2.00	4.25	19.50(72)	1.60	.35	.25
1167	4¢ Camp Fire Girls	5.00	7.25	17.00(50)	1.40	.60	.25
1168	4¢ Giuseppe Garibaldi	2.00	4.25	17.00(70)	1.40	.30	.25
1169	8¢ Giuseppe Garibaldi	2.00	4.25	19.50(72)	1.50	.35	.25
1170	4¢ Walter George	2.00	4.25	20.00(70)	1.50	.50	.25
1171	4¢ Andrew Carnegie	2.00	4.25	17.50(70)	1.25	.35	.25
1172	4¢ John Foster Dulles	2.00	4.25	17.50(70)	1.25	.35	.25
1173	4¢ "ECHO I" Satellite	3.00	6.50	17.00(50)	1.40	.70	.25

1174, 1175

1176

1177

1961 COMMEMORATIVES

SCOTT NO.	DESCRIPTION	FIRST DAY COVERS SING	PL. BLK.	MINT SHEET	PLATE BLOCK F/NH	UNUSED F/NH	USED F
1174/90	**(1174-77, 1183-90) 12 varieties........**	**.......**	**.......**	**.......**	**.......**	**5.75**	**2.55**
1174	4¢ Mahatma Gandhi .	2.00	4.25	20.00(70)	1.35	.50	.25
1175	8¢ Mahatma Gandhi .	2.00	4.25	20.00(72)	1.75	.50	.25
1176	4¢ Range Conservation	2.00	4.25	17.00(50)	1.75	.50	.25
1177	4¢ Horace Greeley . .	2.00	4.25	20.00(70)	1.75	.50	.25

1178

1179

1180

1181

1182

1183

1961-65 CIVIL WAR CENTENNIAL SERIES

SCOTT NO.	DESCRIPTION	FIRST DAY COVERS SING	PL. BLK.	MINT SHEET	PLATE BLOCK F/NH	UNUSED F/NH	USED F
1178-82	**4¢-5¢, 5 varieties, complete ....**	**.......**	**.......**	**.......**	**.......**	**2.75**	**1.05**
1178	4¢ Fort Sumter.	7.50	10.00	20.00(50)	2.00	.60	.25
1179	4¢ Shiloh (1962)	7.50	10.00	22.00(50)	1.75	.40	.25
1180	5¢ Gettysburg (1963).	7.50	10.00	22.00(50)	2.25	.60	.25
1181	5¢ Wilderness (1964)	7.50	10.00	22.00(50)	1.75	.55	.25
1181	Zip Code Block	....	....	....	1.40	....	....
1182	5¢ Appomattox (1965)	7.50	10.00	25.00(50)	3.00	.75	.25
1182	Zip Code Block	....	....	....	3.50	....	....

1184

1185

1186

1187

1188

1189

1190

1961 COMMEMORATIVES

SCOTT NO.	DESCRIPTION	FIRST DAY COVERS SING	PL. BLK.	MINT SHEET	PLATE BLOCK F/NH	UNUSED F/NH	USED F
1183	4¢ Kansas Statehood	2.00	4.25	17.00(50)	1.50	.60	.25
1184	4¢ George W. Norris .	2.00	4.25	12.00(50)	1.30	.35	.25
1185	4¢ Naval Aviation. . . .	2.00	4.25	14.00(50)	1.30	.35	.25
1186	4¢ Workmen's Compensation	2.00	4.25	13.00(50)	1.30	.35	.25
1187	4¢ Frederic Remington	2.00	4.25	15.00(50)	1.30	.35	.25
1188	4¢ Sun Yat-sen	6.00	10.00	34.00(50)	3.75	.85	.25
1189	4¢ Basketball.	9.00	12.00	17.00(50)	1.30	.65	.25
1190	4¢ Nursing	13.50	20.00	17.00(50)	1.30	.65	.25

NOTE: **To determine the VF price on stamps issued from 1941 to date, add 20% to the F/NH or F (used) price (minimum .03 per item). All VF unused stamps from 1941 date priced as NH.**

1191

1192

1193

1194

1962 COMMEMORATIVES

SCOTT NO.	DESCRIPTION	FIRST DAY COVERS SING	PL. BLK.	MINT SHEET	PLATE BLOCK F/NH	UNUSED F/NH	USED F
1191-1207	17 varieties	....	....	....	....	5.40	3.40
1191	4¢ New Mexico Statehood	1.75	4.00	15.00(50)	1.50	.40	.25
1192	4¢ Arizona Statehood	1.75	4.00	15.00(50)	1.50	.35	.25
1193	4¢ Project Mercury	5.00	7.50	14.00(50)	1.40	.35	.25
1194	4¢ Malaria Eradication	1.75	4.00	14.00(50)	1.40	.35	.25

1195

1196

1197

SCOTT NO.	DESCRIPTION	FIRST DAY COVERS SING	PL. BLK.	MINT SHEET	PLATE BLOCK F/NH	UNUSED F/NH	USED F
1195	4¢ Charles Evans Hughes	2.00	4.00	13.00(50)	1.40	.35	.25
1196	4¢ Seattle World's Fair	2.00	4.00	15.00(50)	2.00	.35	.25
1197	4¢ Louisiana Statehood	2.00	4.00	15.00(50)	1.50	.40	.25

1198

1199

1200

1201

1202

1203

1205

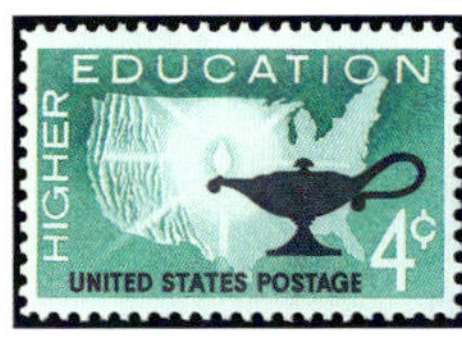

1206

1207

SCOTT NO.	DESCRIPTION	FIRST DAY COVERS SING	PL. BLK.	MINT SHEET	PLATE BLOCK F/NH	UNUSED F/NH	USED F
1198	4¢ Homestead Act.	2.00	4.00	14.00(50)	1.40	.35	.25
1199	4¢ Girl Scouts	7.00	10.00	14.00(50)	1.40	.35	.25
1200	4¢ Brien McMahon	2.00	4.00	14.00(50)	1.50	.35	.25
1201	4¢ Apprenticeship .	2.00	4.00	14.00(50)	1.40	.35	.25
1202	4¢ Sam Rayburn . .	2.00	4.00	17.00(50)	1.50	.35	.25
1203	4¢ Dag Hammarskjold	2.00	4.00	12.00(50)	1.40	.35	.25
1204	same, yellow inverted	5.00	10.25	12.00(50)	1.50	.35	.25
1205	4¢ Christmas 1962	2.00	4.00	23.00(50)	2.00	.35	.25
1206	4¢ Higher Education	2.00	4.00	12.00(50)	1.40	.35	.25
1207	4¢ Winslow Homer	2.00	4.00	12.50(50)	1.40	.35	.25

1208

1209, 1225

1213, 1229

1214

1962-66 REGULAR ISSUE

SCOTT NO.	DESCRIPTION	FIRST DAY COVERS SING	PL. BLK.	MINT SHEET	PLATE BLOCK F/NH	UNUSED F/NH	USED F
1208	5¢ Flag & White House (1963)	2.00	4.25	22.00(100)	1.35	.30	.25
1209	1¢ Andrew Jackson (1963)	2.00	4.00	20.00(100)	2.00	.30	.25
1213	5¢ Washington ...	2.00	4.00	27.50(100)	1.50	.30	.25
1213a	5¢ b. pane of 5—Slog. I	2.50	....	....	....	6.50	....
1213a	5¢ b. pane of 5—Slog. II (1963)	....	....	....	....	20.00	....
1213a	5¢ b. pane of 5—Slog. III (1964)	....	....	....	....	3.50	....
1213c	5¢ Tagged pane of 5 Slogan II (1963). . .	....	....	....	....	105.00	....
1213c	5¢ b. p. of 5—Slog. III (1963)	....	....	....	....	2.50	....
1214	8¢ John J. Pershing (1961)	2.25	5.00	40.00(100)	2.95	.65	.25

Slogan I—Your Mailman Deserves Your Help · Keep Harmful Objects Out of...
Slogan II—Add Zip to Your Mail · Use Zone Numbers for Zip Code.
Slogan III—Add Zip to Your Mail · Always Use Zip Code.

1962-66 COIL STAMPS Perf. 10 Vertically

SCOTT NO.	DESCRIPTION	FIRST DAY COVERS SING	LINE PAIRS	MINT SHEET	LINE PAIRS	UNUSED F/NH	USED F
1225	1¢ Andrew Jackson (1963)	2.00	3.00	....	3.00	.50	.25
1229	5¢ Washington (1963)	2.00	3.00	....	4.00	1.25	.25

1230

1231

1232

1233

1963 COMMEMORATIVES

SCOTT NO.	DESCRIPTION	FIRST DAY COVERS SING	PL. BLK.	MINT SHEET	PLATE BLOCK F/NH	UNUSED F/NH	USED F
1230-41	12 varieties......	....	....	....	....	3.85	2.00
1230	5¢ Carolina Charter	2.00	4.00	14.00(50)	1.50	.40	.25
1231	5¢ Food for Peace	2.00	4.00	12.00(50)	1.40	.35	.25
1232	5¢ West Virginia Statehood	2.00	4.00	15.00(50)	1.70	.50	.25
1233	5¢ Emancipation Proclamation.....	4.00	6.00	12.50(50)	1.70	.35	.25

1234

1235

1236

1237

1238

1239

1240

1241

1242

1243

1963 COMMEMORATIVES

SCOTT NO.	DESCRIPTION	FIRST DAY COVERS SING	FIRST DAY COVERS PL. BLK.	MINT SHEET	PLATE BLOCK F/NH	UNUSED F/NH	USED F
1234	5¢ Alliance for Progress	2.00	4.00	12.00(50)	1.30	.30	.25
1235	5¢ Cordell Hull. . . .	2.00	4.00	12.00(50)	1.75	.40	.25
1236	5¢ Eleanor Roosevelt	2.00	4.00	12.50(50)	1.30	.35	.25
1237	5¢ The Sciences . .	2.00	4.00	12.00(50)	1.30	.30	.25
1238	5¢ City Mail Delivery	2.00	4.00	12.00(50)	1.30	.30	.25
1239	5¢ International Red Cross.	2.00	4.00	12.00(50)	1.30	.30	.25
1240	5¢ Christmas 1963	2.00	4.00	25.00(100)	1.50	.35	.25
1241	5¢ John J. Audubon	2.00	4.00	12.00(50)	1.30	.30	.25

1244

1245

1964 COMMEMORATIVES

SCOTT NO.	DESCRIPTION	FIRST DAY COVERS SING	FIRST DAY COVERS PL. BLK.	MINT SHEET	PLATE BLOCK	UNUSED F/NH	USED
1242-60	**19 varieties. . . . .**	....	....	....	....	**6.95**	**3.90**
1242	5¢ Sam Houston	4.00	6.00	17.50(50)	1.75	.70	.25
1243	5¢ Charles M. Russell	2.00	4.00	15.00(50)	1.75	.35	.25
1244	5¢ New York World's Fair	2.00	4.00	12.50(50)	1.30	.35	.25
1245	5¢ John Muir	2.00	4.00	18.00(50)	2.00	.50	.25

1246

1247

SCOTT NO.	DESCRIPTION	FIRST DAY COVERS SING	FIRST DAY COVERS PL. BLK.	MINT SHEET	PLATE BLOCK F/NH	UNUSED F/NH	USED F
1246	5¢ John F. Kennedy. .	2.50	5.00	17.00(50)	1.75	.50	.25
1247	5¢ New Jersey Tercentenary	1.75	4.00	12.00(50)	1.35	.35	.25

1248

1249

1250

1251

1252

SCOTT NO.	DESCRIPTION	FIRST DAY COVERS SING	FIRST DAY COVERS PL. BLK.	MINT SHEET	PLATE BLOCK F/NH	UNUSED F/NH	USED F
1248	5¢ Nevada Statehood	2.00	4.00	16.00(50)	1.50	.35	.25
1249	5¢ Register and Vote.	2.00	4.00	14.00(50)	1.50	.30	.25
1250	5¢ Shakespeare	2.00	4.00	12.00(50)	1.35	.30	.25
1251	5¢ Mayo Brothers . . .	5.00	7.00	14.00(50)	1.50	.60	.25
1252	5¢ American Music . .	2.00	4.00	12.00(50)	1.35	.30	.25

1253

1254

1255

1256

1257

SCOTT NO.	DESCRIPTION	FIRST DAY COVERS SING	FIRST DAY COVERS PL. BLK.	MINT SHEET	PLATE BLOCK F/NH	UNUSED F/NH	USED F
1253	5¢ Homemakers	2.00	4.00	15.00(50)	1.50	.30	.25
1254-57	5¢ Christmas, 4 varieties, attached .	5.25	7.50	42.00(100)	2.50	2.00	1.50
1254	5¢ Holly	2.75	....	....	....	.40	.25
1255	5¢ Mistletoe	2.75	....	....	....	.40	.25
1256	5¢ Poinsettia	2.75	....	....	....	.40	.25
1257	5¢ Pine Cone.	2.75	....	....	....	.40	.25

COMMEMORATIVES: Commemorative stamps are special issues released to honor or recognize persons, organizations, historical events or landmarks. They are usually issued in the current first class denomination to supplement regular issues.

1258

1259

1260

SCOTT NO.	DESCRIPTION	FIRST DAY COVERS SING	FIRST DAY COVERS PL. BLK.	MINT SHEET	PLATE BLOCK F/NH	UNUSED F/NH	USED
1258	5¢ Verrazano-Narrows. Bridge	2.00	4.00	12.50(50)	1.30	.35	.25
1259	5¢ Modern Art	2.00	4.00	12.00(50)	1.30	.35	.25
1260	5¢ Radio Amateurs . . .	8.00	10.00	23.50(50)	2.50	.60	.25

1261

1262

1263

1264

1265

1965 COMMEMORATIVES

SCOTT NO.	DESCRIPTION	FIRST DAY COVERS SING	FIRST DAY COVERS PL. BLK.	MINT SHEET	PLATE BLOCK F/NH	UNUSED F/NH	USED
1261-76	**5¢-11¢, 16 varieties . .**	....	....	....	....	**5.15**	**3.30**
1261	5¢ Battle of New Orleans	2.00	4.00	14.00(50)	1.75	.40	.25
1262	5¢ Physical Fitness . . .	2.00	4.00	14.00(50)	1.35	.30	.25
1263	5¢ Crusade Against Cancer.	4.00	6.00	12.00(50)	1.35	.30	.25
1264	5¢ Winston Churchill . .	2.00	4.00	12.00(50)	1.35	.40	.25
1265	5¢ Magna Carta.	2.00	4.00	12.00(50)	1.35	.30	.25

1266

1267

1268

1269

1270

1271

1272

1273

SCOTT NO.	DESCRIPTION	FIRST DAY COVERS SING	FIRST DAY COVERS PL. BLK.	MINT SHEET	PLATE BLOCK F/NH	UNUSED F/NH	USED
1266	5¢ International Cooperation Year.	2.00	4.00	12.50(50)	1.25	.30	.25
1267	5¢ Salvation Army	3.00	4.00	12.50(50)	1.25	.30	.25
1268	5¢ Dante Alighieri	2.00	4.00	12.50(50)	1.25	.30	.25
1269	5¢ Herbert Hoover. . . .	2.00	4.00	14.00(50)	1.75	.50	.25
1270	5¢ Robert Fulton	2.00	4.00	14.00(50)	1.20	.45	.25
1271	5¢ Florida Settlement .	2.00	4.00	14.00(50)	1.75	.40	.25
1272	5¢ Traffic Safety.	2.00	4.00	14.00(50)	1.75	.40	.25
1273	5¢ John S. Copley	2.00	4.00	12.00(50)	1.20	.30	.25

1274

1275

1276

SCOTT NO.	DESCRIPTION	FIRST DAY COVERS SING	FIRST DAY COVERS PL. BLK.	MINT SHEET	PLATE BLOCK F/NH	UNUSED F/NH	USED
1274	11¢ Telecom-munication	2.00	4.00	30.00(50)	5.00	.75	.40
1275	5¢ Adlai Stevenson . . .	2.00	4.00	12.00(50)	1.20	.30	.25
1276	5¢ Christmas 1965 . . .	2.00	4.00	28.00(100)	2.00	.30	.25

STAMP HISTORY

THATCHER FERRY BRIDGE

In 1962, during the regular course of business H.E. Harris purchases, at their 4 cent face value, a pane of 50 stamps honoring the Canal Zone's Thatcher Ferry Bridge. Due to a printing error, the silver bridge has been omitted. Harris discovers that his is the only pane from the sheet of 200 printed that has reached the public. Because a recent error in a Dag Hammerskjold stamp prompted the U.S. Postal Service to reprint thousands in order to make the error worthless, Harris questions how the Canal Zone will handle the bridge error. Flooding the market, he insists, would blunt the fun and excitement of stamp collecting. When the Canal Zone says it will reprint the error, Harris sues. March 25, 1965, The Federal District Court in Washington rules in Harris' favor, stopping the Canal Zone authorities from reprinting the stamp error. Viewed as a precendent-setting event in philately, the effort won Harris the respect and awards of his fellow collectors.

1278, 1299

1279

1280

1281, 1297

1282, 1303

1283, 1304

1283B, 1304C

1284, 1298

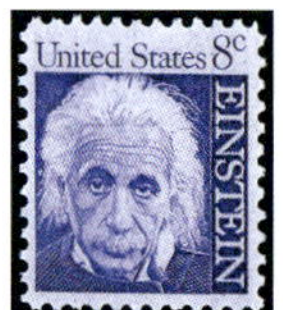

1285

1286

1286A

1287

1288, 1288B, 1288d, 1305E, 1305Ei

1289

1290

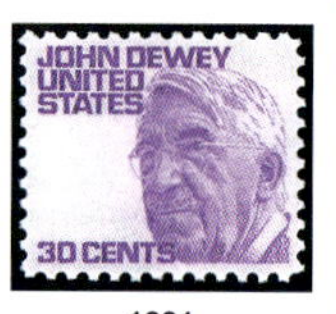

1291

1292

1293

1294, 1305C

1295

1305

1965-78 PROMINENT AMERICAN SERIES

SCOTT NO.	DESCRIPTION	FIRST DAY COVERS SING	FIRST DAY COVERS PL. BLK.	MINT SHEET	PLATE BLOCK F/NH	UNUSED F/NH	USED
1278-95	1¢-$5, 20 varieties, complete (No #1288B or 1288d)	91.50	....	....	150.00	32.50	7.75
1278	1¢ T. Jefferson (1968)	1.75	4.00	12.00(100)	1.00	.25	.25
1278a	1¢ bklt.pane of 8	2.50	....	....	....	1.55	....
1278ae	1¢ test gum	90.00	....	....	....	2.00	....
1278b	1¢ bklt pane of 4 (1971)	18.00	....	....	....	1.00	....
1279	1¼¢ A. Gallatin (1967)	1.75	4.00	18.00(100)	12.00	.25	.25
1280	2¢ F.L. Wright (1966)	1.75	4.00	15.00(100)	.90	.25	.25
1280a	2¢ bklt pane of 5 (1968)	2.50	....	....	....	1.00	....
1280c	2¢ bklt pane of 6 (1971)	18.00	....	....	....	1.00	....
1280ce	2¢ test gum	125.00	....	....	....	1.00	....
1281	3¢ F. Parkman (1967)	1.75	4.00	14.00(100)	1.15	.25	.25
1282	4¢ A. Lincoln	1.75	4.00	22.00(100)	1.15	.25	.25
1283	5¢ G. Washington (1966)	1.75	4.00	23.00(100)	1.15	.25	.25
1283B	5¢ Washington, redrawn (1967)	1.75	4.00	21.00(100)	1.25	.30	.25
1284	6¢ F. D. Roosevelt(1966)	1.75	4.00	24.00(100)	1.35	.35	.25
1284b	6¢ bklt pane of 8 (1967)	3.00	....	....	....	1.75	....
1284c	6¢ bklt pane of 5 (1968)	150.00	....	....	....	1.60	....
1285	8¢ A. Einstein (1966)	4.00	6.00	40.00(100)	2.25	.50	.25
1286	10¢ A. Jackson (1967)	2.00	4.25	48.00(100)	2.25	.50	.25
1286A	12¢ H. Ford (1968)	2.00	4.25	46.00(100)	2.25	.50	.25
1287	13¢ J.F. Kennedy (1967)	2.50	4.50	52.00(100)	3.50	.70	.25
1288	15¢ O.W. Holmes, die I (1968)	2.25	4.50	48.00(100)	2.25	.60	.25
1288d	15¢ Holmes, die II (1979)	....	....	90.00(100)	14.00	1.10	.45
1288B	same, from bklt pane (1978)	2.25	....	....	....	.60	.25
1288Bc	15¢ bklt pane of 8	3.75	....	....	....	4.75	....
1289	20¢ G.C. Marshall (1967)	2.25	4.50	65.00(100)	5.00	.70	.25
1290	25¢ F. Douglass (1967)	5.00	6.00	96.00(100)	5.50	1.20	.25
1291	30¢ J. Dewey (1968)	2.50	5.00	130.00(100)	7.00	1.25	.25
1292	40¢ T. Paine (1968)	2.50	5.00	155.00(100)	6.50	1.50	.25
1293	50¢ L. Stone (1968)	3.75	7.25	210.00(100)	8.00	2.00	.25
1294	$1 E. O'Neil (1967)	6.00	12.50	395.00(100)	18.00	5.00	.25
1295	$5 J. B. Moore (1966)	50.00	115.00	....	70.00	16.00	3.50

BOOKLET PANE SLOGANS

Slogan IV : Mail Early in the Day.
Slogan V: Use Zip Code.

#1278b–Slogans IV and V
#1280a, 1284c–Slogans IV or V

1966-81 COIL STAMPS

SCOTT NO.	DESCRIPTION	FIRST DAY COVERS SING	LINE PAIR	MINT SHEET	LINE PAIR	UNUSED F/NH	USED
1297/1305C	1¢-$1, 9 varieties, (No #1305Ei)	....	....	....	15.00	6.80	2.75
	Perf. 10 Horizontally						
1297	3¢ F. Parkman (1975)	1.75	2.75	....	.70	.25	.25
1298	6¢ F.D. Roosevelt (1967)	1.75	2.75	....	1.70	.40	.25
	Perf. 10 Vertically						
1299	1¢ T. Jefferson (1968)	1.75	2.75	....	.65	.35	.25
1303	4¢ A. Lincoln	1.75	2.75	....	1.00	.35	.25
1304	5¢ G. Washington	1.75	2.75	....	1.00	1.00	.25
1304C	5¢ Washington, redrawn (1981)	1.75	2.75	....	2.75	.30	.25
1305	6¢ F.D. Roosevelt (1968)	1.75	2.75	....	.85	.50	.25
1305E	15¢ O.W. Holmes, die I (1978)	2.00	3.25	....	1.40	.50	.25
1305Ei	15¢ O.W. Holmes, die II (1979)	....	....	....	4.50	1.25	.30
1305C	$1 E. O'Neil (1973)	5.00	9.50	....	10.00	3.95	1.50

1306

1307

1308

1309

1310

1312

1313

1314

1966 COMMEMORATIVES

SCOTT NO.	DESCRIPTION	FIRST DAY COVERS SING	FIRST DAY COVERS PL. BLK.	MINT SHEET	PLATE BLOCK F/NH	UNUSED F/NH	USED
1306/22	(1306-10, 1312-22) 16 varieties	....	....	....	....	5.10	3.35
1306	5¢ Migratory Bird Treaty	2.00	4.25	17.00(50)	1.50	.35	.25
1307	5¢ A.S.P.C.A.	2.00	4.00	14.00(50)	1.50	.35	.25
1308	5¢ Indiana Statehood	2.00	4.00	14.00(50)	1.95	.35	.25
1309	5¢ American Circus	3.00	4.25	14.00(50)	1.60	.35	.25
1310	5¢ SIPEX (single)	2.00	4.00	12.50(50)	1.25	.35	.25
1311	5¢ SIPEX, Imperf Souvenir Sheet	2.00	....	....	....	.35	.25
1312	5¢ Bill of Rights	2.25	4.00	15.00(50)	1.60	.35	.25
1313	5¢ Polish Millennium	2.00	4.00	12.50(50)	1.25	.35	.25
1314	5¢ National Park Service	2.00	4.00	22.00(50)	2.40	.55	.25

1315

1316

1317

1318

1319

1320

SCOTT NO.	DESCRIPTION	FIRST DAY COVERS SING	FIRST DAY COVERS PL. BLK.	MINT SHEET	PLATE BLOCK F/NH	UNUSED F/NH	USED
1315	5¢ Marine Corps Reserve	2.00	4.00	18.00(50)	2.00	.30	.25
1316	5¢ Women's Clubs. . .	2.00	4.00	12.50(50)	1.25	.30	.25
1317	5¢ Johnny Appleseed	2.00	4.00	22.00(50)	1.50	.40	.25
1318	5¢ Beautification	2.00	4.00	15.00(50)	1.50	.55	.25
1319	5¢ Great River Road .	2.00	4.00	15.00(50)	1.50	.40	.25
1320	5¢ Servicemen–Bonds.	2.00	4.00	12.50(50)	1.20	.30	.25

1321

1322

1323

SCOTT NO.	DESCRIPTION	FIRST DAY COVERS SING	FIRST DAY COVERS PL. BLK.	MINT SHEET	PLATE BLOCK F/NH	UNUSED F/NH	USED
1321	5¢ Christmas 1966 . .	1.75	4.00	24.00(100)	1.50	.35	.25
1322	5¢ Mary Cassatt	1.75	4.00	12.00(50)	1.20	.30	.25

1324

1325

1326

1327

1967 COMMEMORATIVES

SCOTT NO.	DESCRIPTION	FIRST DAY COVERS SING	FIRST DAY COVERS PL. BLK.	MINT SHEET	PLATE BLOCK F/NH	UNUSED F/NH	USED
1323-37	**15 varieties, complete. . . . .**	....	....	....	....	**7.50**	**3.25**
1323	5¢ National Grange . . .	2.00	4.00	12.00(50)	1.25	.35	.25
1324	5¢ Canada Centennial.	2.00	4.00	12.00(50)	1.25	.30	.25
1325	5¢ Erie Canal.	2.00	4.00	14.00(50)	1.50	.40	.25
1326	5¢ Search for Peace . .	2.00	4.00	12.00(50)	1.25	.30	.25
1327	5¢ Henry D. Thoreau. .	2.00	4.00	14.00(50)	1.75	.40	.25

1328

1329

1330

SCOTT NO.	DESCRIPTION	FIRST DAY COVERS SING	FIRST DAY COVERS PL. BLK.	MINT SHEET	PLATE BLOCK F/NH	UNUSED F/NH	USED
1328	5¢ Nebraska Statehood	2.00	4.00	20.00(50)	2.00	.30	.25
1329	5¢ Voice of America. . .	4.00	6.00	12.00(50)	1.25	.30	.25
1330	5¢ Davy Crockett.	2.50	4.25	12.00(50)	1.25	.30	.25

1331 1332

SCOTT NO.	DESCRIPTION	FIRST DAY COVERS SING	FIRST DAY COVERS PL. BLK.	MINT SHEET	PLATE BLOCK F/NH	UNUSED F/NH	USED
1331-32	5¢ Space, attached, 2 varieties	12.50	25.00	30.00(50)	3.50	1.75	1.20
1331	5¢ Astronaut	4.00	....	....	....	1.50	.40
1332	5¢ Gemini 4 Capsule. .	4.00	....	....	....	1.50	.40

1333

1334

SCOTT NO.	DESCRIPTION	FIRST DAY COVERS SING	FIRST DAY COVERS PL. BLK.	MINT SHEET	PLATE BLOCK F/NH	UNUSED F/NH	USED
1333	5¢ Urban Planning. . . .	2.00	4.00	12.00(50)	1.20	.30	.25
1334	5¢ Finland Independence	2.00	4.00	12.00(50)	1.20	.30	.25

1335

1336

1337

SCOTT NO.	DESCRIPTION	FIRST DAY COVERS SING	FIRST DAY COVERS PL. BLK.	MINT SHEET	PLATE BLOCK F/NH	UNUSED F/NH	USED
1335	5¢ Thomas Eakins . . .	2.00	4.00	12.00(50)	1.20	.30	.25
1336	5¢ Christmas 1967 . . .	2.00	4.00	12.00(50)	1.20	.30	.25
1337	5¢ Mississippi Statehood	2.00	4.00	17.00(50)	1.75	.45	.25

1338, 1338A, 1338D　　1338F, 1338G

SCOTT NO.	DESCRIPTION	FIRST DAY COVERS SING	FIRST DAY COVERS PL. BLK.	MINT SHEET	PLATE BLOCK	UNUSED F/NH	USED
	GIORI PRESS 1868 Design size: 18½ x 22 mm Perf.11						
1338	6¢ Flag & White House	1.75	4.00	24.00(100)	1.20	.30	.25
	HUCK PRESS Design size: 18 x 21 mm 1969 Coil Stamp Perf. 10 Vertically						
1338A	6¢ Flag & White House	1.75	....		....	5.75	.30	.25
	1970 Perf. 11 x 10½						
1338D	6¢ Flag & White House	2.00	4.25	23.00(100)	5.25(20)	.30	.25
	1971 Perf. 11 x 10½						
1338F	8¢ Flag & White House	2.00	4.25	33.00(100)	8.00(20)	.45	.25
	Coil Stamp Perf. 10 Vertically						
1338G	8¢ Flag & White House	2.00	....	....	....	.45	.25

1339

1340

1968 COMMEMORATIVES

SCOTT NO.	DESCRIPTION	FIRST DAY COVERS SING	FIRST DAY COVERS PL. BLK.	MINT SHEET	PLATE BLOCK	UNUSED F/NH	USED
1339/64	**(1339-40, 1342-64) 25 varieties.........**	....	....	....	....	**11.75**	**5.95**
1339	6¢ Illinois Statehood . .	2.00	4.00	15.00(50)	1.50	.50	.25
1340	6¢ Hemisfair '68.	2.00	4.00	12.00(50)	1.25	.30	.25

1341

SCOTT NO.	DESCRIPTION	FIRST DAY COVERS SING	FIRST DAY COVERS PL. BLK.	MINT SHEET	PLATE BLOCK	UNUSED F/NH	USED
1341	$1 Airlift to Servicemen	8.50	17.50	165.00(50)	15.00	3.95	2.75

1342

1343

1344

SCOTT NO.	DESCRIPTION	FIRST DAY COVERS SING	FIRST DAY COVERS PL. BLK.	MINT SHEET	PLATE BLOCK	UNUSED F/NH	USED
1342	6¢ Support our Youth. .	2.00	4.00	12.00(50)	1.25	.30	.25
1343	6¢ Law and Order	4.00	6.00	19.00(50)	1.95	.45	.25
1344	6¢ Register and Vote . .	2.00	4.00	12.00(50)	1.25	.30	.25

1345

1346

1347

1348

1349

1350

1351

1352

1353

1354

1968 HISTORIC AMERICAN FLAGS

SCOTT NO.	DESCRIPTION	FIRST DAY COVERS SING	FIRST DAY COVERS PL. BLK.	MINT SHEET	PLATE BLOCK	UNUSED F/NH	USED
1345-54	**10 varieties, complete, attached . . . .**	**10.00**	....	**20.00(50)**	**10.00**	**5.25**	....
1345-54	**Same, set of singles .**	**57.50**	....	....	....	**4.25**	**3.25**
1345	6¢ Fort Moultrie Flag . .	6.00	....	....	....	.55	.45
1346	6¢ Fort McHenry Flag .	6.00	....	....	....	.55	.45
1347	6¢ Washington's Cruisers	6.00	....	....	....	.55	.45
1348	6¢ Bennington Flag . . .	6.00	....	....	....	.55	.45
1349	6¢ Rhode Island Flag .	6.00	....	....	....	.55	.45
1350	6¢ First Stars & Stripes	6.00	....	....	....	.55	.45
1351	6¢ Bunker Hill Flag . . .	6.00	....	....	....	.55	.45
1352	6¢ Grand Union Flag . .	6.00	....	....	....	.55	.45
1353	6¢ Philadelphia Light Horse	6.00	....	....	....	.55	.45
1354	6¢ First Navy Jack. . . .	6.00	....	....	....	.55	.45

NOTE: All ten varieties of 1345-54 were printed on the same sheet; therefore, plate and regular blocks are not available for each variety separately. Plate blocks of four will contain two each of #1346, with number adjacent to #1345 only; Zip blocks will contain two each of #1353 and #1354, with inscription adjacent to #1354 only; Mail Early blocks will contain two each of #1347-49 with inscription adjacent to #1348 only. A plate strip of 20 stamps, with two of each variety will be required to have all stamps in plate block form and will contain all marginal inscription.

1355

1356

1357

1358

1359

1360

1361

1968 COMMEMORATIVES

SCOTT NO.	DESCRIPTION	FIRST DAY COVERS SING	FIRST DAY COVERS PL. BLK.	MINT SHEET	PLATE BLOCK	UNUSED F/NH	USED
1355	6¢ Walt Disney.	40.00	50.00	40.00(50)	4.75	1.25	.30
1356	6¢ Father Marquette .	2.00	4.00	15.00(50)	2.25	.50	.25
1357	6¢ Daniel Boone	2.00	4.00	15.00(50)	1.50	.50	.25
1358	6¢ Arkansas River . . .	2.00	4.00	15.00(50)	1.75	.50	.25
1359	6¢ Leif Erikson.	2.00	4.00	12.00(50)	1.25	.50	.25
1360	6¢ Cherokee Strip . . .	2.00	4.00	25.00(50)	2.50	.70	.25
1361	6¢ Trumbull Art	4.00	6.00	14.00(50)	1.30	.40	.25

1362

1363

1364

SCOTT NO.	DESCRIPTION	FIRST DAY COVERS SING	FIRST DAY COVERS PL. BLK.	MINT SHEET	PLATE BLOCK	UNUSED F/NH	USED
1362	6¢ Waterfowl Conservation	2.00	4.00	15.00(50)	1.70	.40	.25
1363	6¢ Christmas 1968 . . .	2.00	....	12.00(50)	3.25(10)	.30	.25
1364	6¢ Chief Joseph.	2.00	4.00	17.00(50)	1.70	.40	.25

1365 1366

1367 1368

1969 COMMEMORATIVES

SCOTT NO.	DESCRIPTION	FIRST DAY COVERS SING	FIRST DAY COVERS PL. BLK.	MINT SHEET	PLATE BLOCK	UNUSED F/NH	USED
1365-86	**22 varieties, complete**	....	....	....	....	**10.25**	**5.00**
1365-68	Beautification, 4 varieties, attached.	6.00	8.50	20.00(50)	3.00	2.50	2.00
1365	6¢ Azaleas & Tulips . .	3.00	....	....	....	1.00	.25
1366	6¢ Daffodils	3.00	....	....	....	1.00	.25
1367	6¢ Poppies.	3.00	....	....	....	1.00	.25
1368	6¢ Crabapple Trees. .	3.00	....	....	....	1.00	.25

1369 1370 1371

SCOTT NO.	DESCRIPTION	FIRST DAY COVERS SING	FIRST DAY COVERS PL. BLK.	MINT SHEET	PLATE BLOCK	UNUSED F/NH	USED
1369	6¢ American Legion. . .	2.00	4.00	12.00(50)	1.40	.30	.25
1370	6¢ Grandma Moses. . .	2.00	4.00	12.00(50)	1.40	.30	.25
1371	6¢ Apollo 8 Moon Orbit	2.50	5.00	22.00(50)	2.40	.50	.25

1372

1373

1374

1375

SCOTT NO.	DESCRIPTION	FIRST DAY COVERS SING	FIRST DAY COVERS PL. BLK.	MINT SHEET	PLATE BLOCK	UNUSED F/NH	USED
1372	6¢ W.C. Handy–Musician	3.50	5.00	13.00(50)	1.50	.40	.25
1373	6¢ California Settlement	2.00	4.00	13.00(50)	1.50	.40	.25
1374	6¢ Major J.W. Powell. .	2.00	4.00	13.00(50)	1.50	.40	.25
1375	6¢ Alabama Statehood	2.00	4.00	13.00(50)	1.50	.40	.25

1376 1377

1378 1379

SCOTT NO.	DESCRIPTION	FIRST DAY COVERS SING	FIRST DAY COVERS PL. BLK.	MINT SHEET	PLATE BLOCK	UNUSED F/NH	USED
1376-79	Bontanical Congress, 4 varieties, attached . .	7.00	9.50	24.00(50)	3.75	2.50	2.25
1376	6¢ Douglas Fir	3.00	....	....	....	1.00	.25
1377	6¢ Lady's-slipper	3.00	....	....	....	1.00	.25
1378	6¢ Ocotillo	3.00	....	....	....	1.00	.25
1379	6¢ Franklinia	3.00	....	....	....	1.00	.25

AVERAGE QUALITY: From 1935 to date, deduct 20% from the Fine price to determine the price for an Average quality stamp.

MINT SHEETS: From 1935 to date, we list prices for standard size Mint Sheets in Fine, Never Hinged condition. The number of stamps in each sheet is noted in ( ).

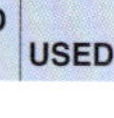

1380

1381

1382

1383

SCOTT NO.	DESCRIPTION	FIRST DAY COVERS SING	FIRST DAY COVERS PL. BLK.	MINT SHEET	PLATE BLOCK	UNUSED F/NH	USED
1380	6¢ Dartmouth College .	2.00	4.00	12.00(50)	1.50	.40	.25
1381	6¢ Professional Baseball	16.00	25.00	30.00(50)	3.00	.60	.30
1382	6¢ College Football . . .	7.00	13.50	20.00(50)	2.00	.40	.25
1383	6¢ Eisenhower.	2.00	4.00	12.00(32)	1.75	.40	.25

1384

1385

1386

SCOTT NO.	DESCRIPTION	FIRST DAY COVERS SING	FIRST DAY COVERS PL. BLK.	MINT SHEET	PLATE BLOCK	UNUSED F/NH	USED
1384	6¢ Christmas 1969 . . .	2.00	....	14.00(50)	3.50(10)	.30	.25
1384a	6¢ precancelled set of 4 cities	....	....	280.00(50)	150.00(10)	4.50	....
1385	6¢ Rehabilitation	2.00	4.00	12.00(50)	1.20	.30	.25
1386	6¢ William M. Harnett .	2.00	4.00	8.00(32)	1.20	.30	.25

1387

1388

1389

1390

1391

1392

1970 COMMEMORATIVES

SCOTT NO.	DESCRIPTION	FIRST DAY COVERS SING	FIRST DAY COVERS PL. BLK.	MINT SHEET	PLATE BLOCK	UNUSED F/NH	USED
1387/1422	**(1387-92, 1405-22) 24 varieties, (No precancels). . . .**	....	....	....	....	**11.85**	**5.75**
1387-90	Natural History, 4 varieties, attached . .	5.00	7.00	12.00(32)	2.25	1.95	1.50
1387	6¢ Bald Eagle	2.50	....	....	....	.50	.25
1388	6¢ Elephant Herd.	2.50	....	....	....	.50	.25
1389	6¢ Haida Canoe.	2.50	....	....	....	.50	.25
1390	6¢ Reptiles.	2.50	....	....	....	.50	.25
1391	6¢ Maine Statehood . .	2.00	4.00	14.00(50)	1.75	.40	.25
1392	6¢ Wildlife–Buffalo. . . .	2.00	4.00	17.00(50)	2.00	.40	.25

1393, 1401

1393D

1394

1395, 1402

1396

1397

1398

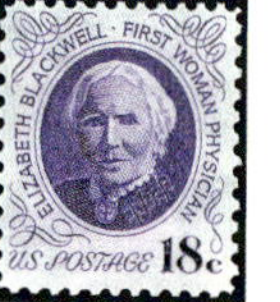

1399

1400

1970-74 REGULAR ISSUE

SCOTT NO.	DESCRIPTION	FIRST DAY COVERS SING	FIRST DAY COVERS PL. BLK.	MINT SHEET	PLATE BLOCK	UNUSED F/NH	USED
1393/1400	**6¢-21¢, 8 varieties, complete (No #1395)**	....	....	....	....	**3.85**	**1.30**
1393	6¢ D. Eisenhower	1.75	4.00	23.00(100)	1.50	.30	.25
1393a	6¢ bklt pane of 8	2.75	....	....	....	1.95	....
1393ae	6¢ test gum	90.00	....	....	....	1.90	....
1393b	6¢ bklt pane of 5– Slogan IV or V	3.75	....	....	....	1.75	....
1393D	7¢ B. Franklin (1972). .	1.75	4.00	28.00(100)	1.75	.35	.25
1394	8¢ Ike–black, blue, red (1971)	1.75	4.00	32.00(100)	1.60	.30	.25
1395	same, deep claret bklt single (1971)	2.50	....	....	....	.45	.25
1395a	8¢ bklt pane of 8	2.50	....	....	....	2.40	....
1395b	8¢ bklt pane of 6	2.25	....	....	....	1.90	....
1395c	8¢ bklt pane of 4, VI & VII (1972).	2.00	....	....	....	1.95	....
1395d	8¢ bklt pane of 7 II or V (1972)	2.50	....	....	....	3.75	....
1396	8¢ Postal Service Emblem (1971)	1.75	4.00	24.00(100)	3.75(12)	.35	.25
1397	14¢ F. LaGuardia (1972)	1.75	4.00	50.00(100)	3.50	.75	.25
1398	16¢ E. Pyle (1971). . . .	2.50	4.50	60.00(100)	3.75	.85	.25
1399	18¢ E. Blackwell (1974)	2.00	4.25	60.00(100)	3.50	.75	.25
1400	21¢ A.P. Giannini (1973)	2.50	4.50	70.00(100)	3.75	.75	.30

1970-71 COIL STAMPS–Perf. 10 Vertically

SCOTT NO.	DESCRIPTION	FIRST DAY COVERS SING	LINE PAIR	MINT SHEET	LINE PAIR	UNUSED F/NH	USED
1401	6¢ D. Eisenhower	1.75	2.75	....	.90	.30	.25
1402	8¢ Eisenhower, claret (1971)	1.75	2.75	....	1.00	.35	.25

1405

1406

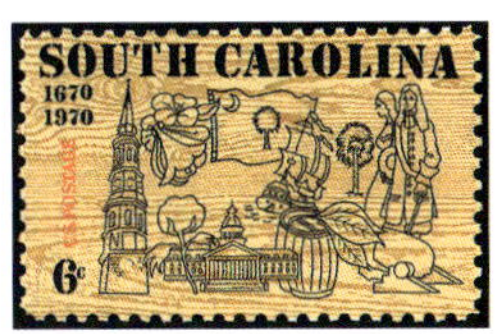

1407

1408

1409

1970 COMMEMORATIVES

SCOTT NO.	DESCRIPTION	FIRST DAY COVERS SING	FIRST DAY COVERS PL. BLK.	MINT SHEET	PLATE BLOCK	UNUSED F/NH	USED
1405	6¢ E.L. Master–Poet . .	2.00	4.00	13.00(50)	1.50	.40	.25
1406	6¢ Woman Suffrage. . .	2.00	4.00	14.00(50)	1.75	.70	.25
1407	6¢ South Carolina Tercentenary	2.00	4.00	12.50(50)	1.50	.50	.25
1408	6¢ Stone Mountain Memorial	2.00	4.00	14.00(50)	1.75	.50	.25
1409	6¢ Fort Snelling	2.00	4.00	19.50(50)	2.00	.50	.25

1412 1413

1410 1411

SCOTT NO.	DESCRIPTION	FIRST DAY COVERS SING	FIRST DAY COVERS PL. BLK.	MINT SHEET	PLATE BLOCK	UNUSED F/NH	USED
1410-13	Anti-Pollution, 4 varieties, attached . .	5.00	7.00	15.00(50)	4.00(10)	2.00	1.75
1410	6¢ Globe & Wheat	2.50	....	....	....	.40	.25
1411	6¢ Globe & City	2.50	....	....	....	.40	.25
1412	6¢ Globe & Bluegill . . .	2.50	....	....	....	.40	.25
1413	6¢ Globe & Seagull . . .	2.50	....	....	....	.40	.25

1414

SCOTT NO.	DESCRIPTION	FIRST DAY COVERS SING	FIRST DAY COVERS PL. BLK.	MINT SHEET	PLATE BLOCK	UNUSED F/NH	USED
1414	6¢ Nativity	1.75	....	12.00(50)	2.75(8)	.30	.25

FIRST DAY COVERS: First Day Covers are envelopes cancelled on the "First Day of Issue" of the stamp used on the envelope. Usually they also contain a picture (cachet) on the left side designed to go with the theme of the stamp. From 1935 to 1949, prices listed are for cacheted, addressed covers. From 1950 to date, prices are for cacheted, unaddressed covers.

1415 1416

1417 1418

SCOTT NO.	DESCRIPTION	FIRST DAY COVERS SING	FIRST DAY COVERS PL. BLK.	MINT SHEET	PLATE BLOCK	UNUSED F/NH	USED
1415-18	Christmas Toys, 4 varieties, attached . .	5.50	....	20.00(50)	5.50(8)	3.75	2.25
1415	6¢ Locomotive	3.00	....	....	....	1.00	.30
1416	6¢ Horse	3.00	....	....	....	1.00	.30
1417	6¢ Tricycle	3.00	....	....	....	1.00	.30
1418	6¢ Doll Carriage.	3.00	....	....	....	1.00	.30

Precancelled

SCOTT NO.	DESCRIPTION	FIRST DAY COVERS SING	FIRST DAY COVERS PL. BLK.	MINT SHEET	PLATE BLOCK	UNUSED F/NH	USED
1414a	6¢ Nativity (precancelled)	4.00	....	14.00(50)	2.75(8)	.30	.25
1415a-18a	Christmas Toys, precancelled, 4 varieties attached .	45.00	....	40.00(50)	8.50(8)	4.25	3.75
1415a	6¢ Locomotive	7.00	....	....	....	1.50	.25
1416a	6¢ Horse	7.00	....	....	....	1.50	.25
1417a	6¢ Tricycle	7.00	....	....	....	1.50	.25
1418a	6¢ Doll Carriage.	7.00	....	....	....	1.50	.25

NOTE: Unused precancels are with original gum, while used are without gum.

1419

1420

SCOTT NO.	DESCRIPTION	FIRST DAY COVERS SING	FIRST DAY COVERS PL. BLK.	MINT SHEET	PLATE BLOCK	UNUSED F/NH	USED
1419	6¢ U.N. 25th Anniversary	2.00	4.00	18.00(50)	1.95	.45	.25
1420	6¢ Pilgrim Landing. . . .	2.00	4.00	12.00(50)	1.35	.35	.25

1421 1422

SCOTT NO.	DESCRIPTION	FIRST DAY COVERS SING	FIRST DAY COVERS PL. BLK.	MINT SHEET	PLATE BLOCK	UNUSED F/NH	USED
1421-22	D.A.V. Servicemen, 2 varieties, attached . .	3.00	5.00	15.00(50)	2.25	.75	.60
1421	6¢ Disabled Veterans .	2.00	....	....	....	.35	.30
1422	6¢ Prisoners of War. . .	2.00	....	....	....	.35	.30

SE-TENANTS: Beginning with the 1964 Christmas issue (#1254-57), the United States has issued numerous Se-Tenant stamps covering a wide variety of subjects. Se-Tenants are issues where two or more different stamp designs are produced on the same sheet in pair, strip or block form. Mint stamps are usually collected in attached blocks, etc.; used are generally saved as single stamps.

1423

1424

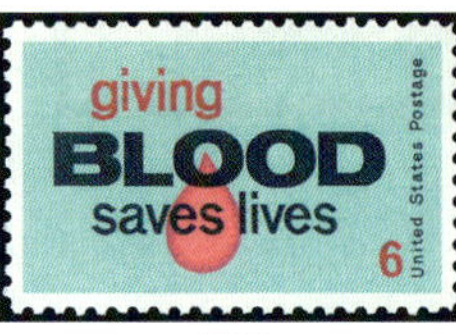

1425

1426

1971 COMMEMORATIVES

SCOTT NO.	DESCRIPTION	FIRST DAY COVERS SING	FIRST DAY COVERS PL. BLK.	MINT SHEET	PLATE BLOCK	UNUSED F/NH	USED
1423-45	**6¢-8¢, 23 varieties complete**	....	....	....	....	9.75	4.95
1423	6¢ Sheep	1.75	4.00	14.00(50)	1.60	.50	.25
1424	6¢ General D. MacArthur	1.75	4.00	14.00(50)	1.60	.50	.25
1425	6¢ Blood Donors	1.75	4.00	12.00(50)	1.35	.30	.25
1426	8¢ Missouri Statehood	1.75	4.00	17.00(50)	5.50(12)	.50	.25

1427 1428

1429 1430

SCOTT NO.	DESCRIPTION	FIRST DAY COVERS SING	FIRST DAY COVERS PL. BLK.	MINT SHEET	PLATE BLOCK	UNUSED F/NH	USED
1427-30	Wildlife Conservation, 4 varieties, attached	5.00	9.00	12.50(32)	2.50	2.00	1.50
1427	8¢ Trout	2.50	....	....	....	.40	.25
1428	8¢ Alligator	2.50	....	....	....	.40	.25
1429	8¢ Polar Bear	2.50	....	....	....	.40	.25
1430	8¢ Condor	2.50	....	....	....	.40	.25

1431

1432

1433

SCOTT NO.	DESCRIPTION	FIRST DAY COVERS SING	FIRST DAY COVERS PL. BLK.	MINT SHEET	PLATE BLOCK	UNUSED F/NH	USED
1431	8¢ Antarctic Treaty	2.00	4.00	14.00(50)	1.75	.40	.25
1432	8¢ American Revolution	2.00	4.00	12.00(50)	1.50	.40	.25
1433	8¢ John Sloan–Artist	2.00	4.00	12.00(50)	1.50	.35	.25

1434 1435

SCOTT NO.	DESCRIPTION	FIRST DAY COVERS SING	FIRST DAY COVERS PL. BLK.	MINT SHEET	PLATE BLOCK	UNUSED F/NH	USED
1434-35	Space Achievements, 2 varieties, attached	3.50	4.50	13.50(50)	1.75	.75	.55
1434	8¢ Moon, Earth, Sun & Landing Craft	2.00	....	....	....	.45	.30
1435	8¢ Lunar Rover	2.00	....	....	....	.45	.30

1436

1437

1438

1439

SCOTT NO.	DESCRIPTION	FIRST DAY COVERS SING	FIRST DAY COVERS PL. BLK.	MINT SHEET	PLATE BLOCK	UNUSED F/NH	USED
1436	8¢ Emily Dickinson	2.00	4.00	14.00(50)	1.70	.40	.25
1437	8¢ San Juan	2.00	4.00	28.00(50)	2.50	.65	.25
1438	8¢ Drug Addiction	2.00	4.00	13.00(50)	2.25(6)	.35	.25
1439	8¢ CARE	2.00	4.00	14.00(50)	2.70(8)	.45	.25

1440 1441

1442 1443

SCOTT NO.	DESCRIPTION	FIRST DAY COVERS SING	FIRST DAY COVERS PL. BLK.	MINT SHEET	PLATE BLOCK	UNUSED F/NH	USED
1440-43	Historic Preservation 4 varieties, attached	5.00	6.00	12.50(32)	2.00	1.75	1.00
1440	8¢ Decatur House	2.50	....	....	....	.40	.25
1441	8¢ Whaling Ship	2.50	....	....	....	.40	.25
1442	8¢ Cable Car	2.50	....	....	....	.40	.25
1443	8¢ Mission	2.50	....	....	....	.40	.25

1444 1445

SCOTT NO.	DESCRIPTION	FIRST DAY COVERS SING	FIRST DAY COVERS PL. BLK.	MINT SHEET	PLATE BLOCK	UNUSED F/NH	USED
1444	8¢ Christmas Nativity. .	2.00	4.00	12.00(50)	4.25(12)	.35	.25
1445	8¢ Christmas Patridge.	2.00	4.00	12.00(50)	4.25(12)	.35	.25

1446

1447

1972 COMMEMORATIVES

SCOTT NO.	DESCRIPTION	FIRST DAY COVERS SING	FIRST DAY COVERS PL. BLK.	MINT SHEET	PLATE BLOCK	UNUSED F/NH	USED
1446/74	**29 varieties, complete. . . . .**	....	....	....	....	**10.15**	**6.00**
1446	8¢ Sidney Lanier–Poet	2.00	4.00	14.00(50)	1.75	.50	.25
1447	8¢ Peace Corps.	2.00	4.00	12.50(50)	2.25(6)	.40	.25

1448 1449

1450 1451

1452

1454

1453

1972 NATIONAL PARKS CENTENNIAL

SCOTT NO.	DESCRIPTION	FIRST DAY COVERS SING	FIRST DAY COVERS PL. BLK.	MINT SHEET	PLATE BLOCK	UNUSED F/NH	USED
1448-54	**2¢-15¢, 7 varieties, complete . . . .**	....	....	....	....	**2.50**	**1.50**
1448-51	Cape Hatteras, 4 varieties, attached.	6.00	7.00	13.00(100)	1.15	1.00	.65
1448	2¢ Ship's Hull.	....	....	....	....	.25	.25
1449	2¢ Lighthouse	....	....	....	....	.25	.25
1450	2¢ Three Seagulls	....	....	....	....	.25	.25
1451	2¢ Two Seagulls	....	....	....	....	.25	.25
1452	6¢ Wolf Trap Farm Park	2.00	4.00	13.00(50)	1.75	.50	.25
1453	8¢ Yellowstone Park . .	2.00	4.00	16.00(32)	2.75	.50	.25
1454	15¢ Mount McKinley . .	2.00	4.00	24.00(50)	2.75	.60	.35

1455

1972 COMMEMORATIVES

SCOTT NO.	DESCRIPTION	FIRST DAY COVERS SING	FIRST DAY COVERS PL. BLK.	MINT SHEET	PLATE BLOCK	UNUSED F/NH	USED
1455	8¢ Family Planning . . .	2.00	4.00	14.00(50)	1.50	.35	.25

1456 1457

1458 1459

SCOTT NO.	DESCRIPTION	FIRST DAY COVERS SING	FIRST DAY COVERS PL. BLK.	MINT SHEET	PLATE BLOCK	UNUSED F/NH	USED
1456-59	Colonial Craftsmen, 4 varieties, attached . .	3.75	4.75	15.00(50)	1.75	1.50	1.20
1456	8¢ Glassmaker	2.25	....	....	....	.45	.25
1457	8¢ Silversmith	2.25	....	....	....	.45	.25
1458	8¢ Wigmaker	2.25	....	....	....	.45	.25
1459	8¢ Hatter	2.25	....	....	....	.45	.25

1460

1461

1462

SCOTT NO.	DESCRIPTION	FIRST DAY COVERS SING	FIRST DAY COVERS PL. BLK.	MINT SHEET	PLATE BLOCK	UNUSED F/NH	USED
1460	6¢ Olympics–Cycling . .	2.10	4.25	12.00(50)	3.25(10)	.30	.25
1461	8¢ Olympics–Bob Sled Racing.	2.10	4.25	12.25(50)	3.25(10)	.35	.25
1462	15¢ Olympics–Foot Racing	2.10	4.25	22.00(50)	6.00(10)	.50	.45

1463

SCOTT NO.	DESCRIPTION	FIRST DAY COVERS SING	FIRST DAY COVERS PL. BLK.	MINT SHEET	PLATE BLOCK	UNUSED F/NH	USED
1463	8¢ Parent Teacher Association	2.00	4.00	14.00(50)	1.50	.40	.25
1463a	Same, Reversed Plate Number	2.00	4.00	15.00(50)	1.75	....	....

1464 1465

1466 1467

SCOTT NO.	DESCRIPTION	FIRST DAY COVERS SING	FIRST DAY COVERS PL. BLK.	MINT SHEET	PLATE BLOCK	UNUSED F/NH	USED
1464-67	Wildlife Conservation, 4 varieties, attached . .	4.00	6.00	17.00(32)	3.25	2.00	1.50
1464	8¢ Fur Seal	2.00	....	....	....	.50	.25
1465	8¢ Cardinal	2.00	....	....	....	.50	.25
1466	8¢ Brown Pelican.	2.00	....	....	....	.50	.25
1467	8¢ Bighorn Sheep	2.00	....	....	....	.50	.25

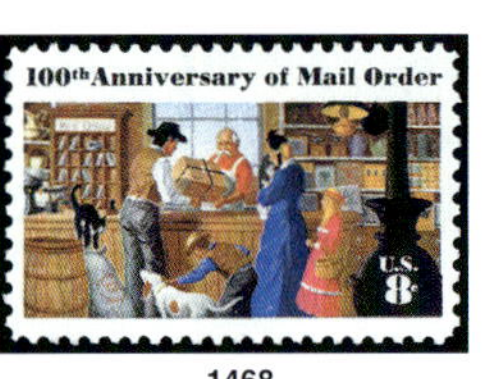

1468

1469

1470

SCOTT NO.	DESCRIPTION	FIRST DAY COVERS SING	FIRST DAY COVERS PL. BLK.	MINT SHEET	PLATE BLOCK	UNUSED F/NH	USED
1468	8¢ Mail Order Business	2.00	4.00	13.00(50)	4.25(12)	.35	.25
1469	8¢ Osteopathic Medicine	2.00	4.25	15.00(50)	2.75(6)	.45	.25
1470	Tom Sawyer–Folklore .	2.00	4.00	14.00(50)	2.25	.35	.25

1471

1472

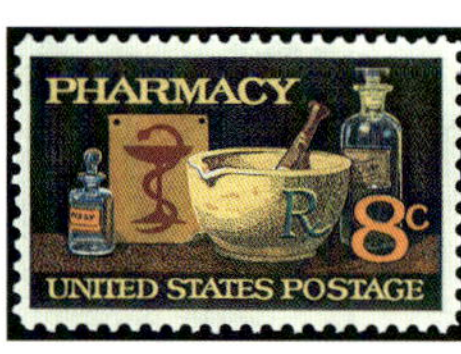

1473

SCOTT NO.	DESCRIPTION	FIRST DAY COVERS SING	FIRST DAY COVERS PL. BLK.	MINT SHEET	PLATE BLOCK	UNUSED F/NH	USED
1471	8¢ Christmas–Virgin Mother	1.75	4.00	13.00(50)	4.50(12)	.35	.25
1472	8¢ Christmas–Santa . . Claus	1.75	4.00	13.00(50)	4.50(12)	.35	.25
1473	8¢ Pharmacy	8.00	10.00	13.00(50)	1.75(4)	.35	.25

1474

1475

SCOTT NO.	DESCRIPTION	FIRST DAY COVERS SING	FIRST DAY COVERS PL. BLK.	MINT SHEET	PLATE BLOCK	UNUSED F/NH	USED
1474	8¢ Stamp Collecting . .	2.00	4.25	10.00(40)	1.50(4)	.35	.25

1476

1477

1478

1479

1973 COMMEMORATIVES

SCOTT NO.	DESCRIPTION	FIRST DAY COVERS SING	FIRST DAY COVERS PL. BLK.	MINT SHEET	PLATE BLOCK	UNUSED F/NH	USED
1475-1508	34 varieties, complete	....	....	....	....	12.00	7.60
1475	8¢ "Love"	2.25	5.00	12.50(50)	2.25(6)	.35	.25

COLONIAL COMMUNICATIONS

SCOTT NO.	DESCRIPTION	FIRST DAY COVERS SING	FIRST DAY COVERS PL. BLK.	MINT SHEET	PLATE BLOCK	UNUSED F/NH	USED
1476	8¢ Pamphlet Printing . .	2.00	4.00	12.50(50)	1.50	.35	.25
1477	8¢ Posting Broadside .	2.00	4.00	12.50(50)	1.50	.35	.25
1478	8¢ Colonial Post Rider.	2.00	4.00	12.50(50)	1.50	.35	.25
1479	8¢ Drummer & Soldiers	2.00	4.00	12.50(50)	1.50	.35	.25

1480 1481

1482 1483

SCOTT NO.	DESCRIPTION	FIRST DAY COVERS SING	FIRST DAY COVERS PL. BLK.	MINT SHEET	PLATE BLOCK	UNUSED F/NH	USED
1480-83	Boston Tea Party, 4 varieties, attached . .	4.50	6.50	16.00(50)	1.85	1.60	1.25
1480	8¢ Throwing Tea	2.25	....	....	....	.45	.25
1481	8¢ Ship	2.25	....	....	....	.45	.25
1482	8¢ Rowboats	2.25	....	....	....	.45	.25
1483	8¢ Rowboat & Dock. . .	2.25	....	....	....	.45	.25

1484

1488

1485

1486

1487

SCOTT NO.	DESCRIPTION	FIRST DAY COVERS SING	FIRST DAY COVERS PL. BLK.	MINT SHEET	PLATE BLOCK	UNUSED F/NH	USED
	AMERICAN ARTS						
1484	8¢ George Gershwin–Composer	2.00	4.00	10.25(40)	4.00(12)	.35	.25
1485	8¢ Robinson Jeffers–Poet	2.00	4.00	10.25(40)	4.25(12)	.35	.25
1486	8¢ Henry O. Tanner–Artist	5.00	6.00	10.25(40)	4.00(12)	.35	.25
1487	8¢ Willa Cather–Novelist	2.00	4.00	14.00(40)	7.00(12)	.60	.25
1488	8¢ Nicolaus Copernicus	2.00	4.00	12.25(40)	1.50	.35	.25

1489

1490

1491

1492

1493

1494

1495

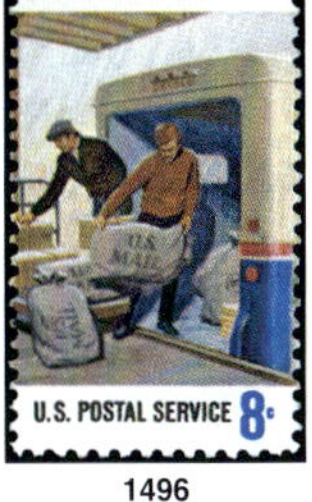

1496

1497

1498

SCOTT NO.	DESCRIPTION	FIRST DAY COVERS SING	FIRST DAY COVERS PL. BLK.	MINT SHEET	PLATE BLOCK	UNUSED F/NH	USED
	1973 POSTAL SERVICE EMPLOYEES						
1489-98	**10 varieties, complete, attached . .**	**6.50**	**........**	**18.00(50)**	**9.00(20)**	**4.50**	**3.60**
1489-98	**Set of singles, complete**	**22.00**	**........**	**........**	**........**	**4.25**	**3.25**
1489	8¢ Window Clerk	2.25	....	....	....	.45	.35
1490	8¢ Mail Pickup	2.25	....	....	....	.45	.35
1491	8¢ Conveyor Belt	2.25	....	....	....	.45	.35
1492	8¢ Sacking Parcels . . .	2.25	....	....	....	.45	.35
1493	8¢ Mail Cancelling	2.25	....	....	....	.45	.35
1494	8¢ Manual Sorting	2.25	....	....	....	.45	.35
1495	8¢ Machine Sorting . . .	2.25	....	....	....	.45	.35
1496	8¢ Loading Truck	2.25	....	....	....	.45	.35
1497	8¢ Letter Carrier	2.25	....	....	....	.45	.35
1498	8¢ Rural Delivery	2.25	....	....	....	.45	.35

1499

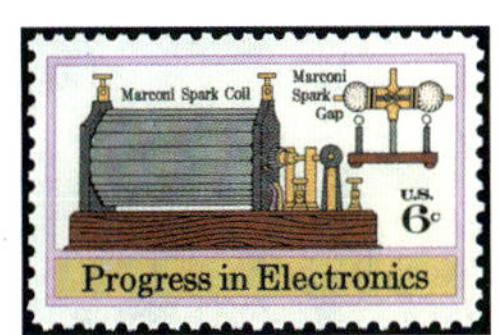

1500

1501

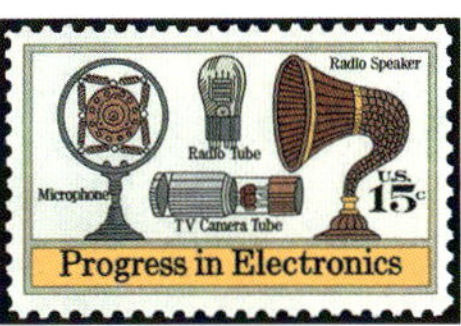

1502

1503

SCOTT NO.	DESCRIPTION	FIRST DAY COVERS SING	FIRST DAY COVERS PL. BLK.	MINT SHEET	PLATE BLOCK	UNUSED F/NH	USED
	1973 COMMEMORATIVES						
1499	8¢ Harry S. Truman . . .	2.00	4.00	12.00(32)	2.25	.50	.25
1500	6¢ Electronics	2.00	4.00	12.00(50)	1.50	.35	.25
1501	8¢ Electronics	2.00	4.00	14.00(50)	1.75	.35	.25
1502	15¢ Electronics	2.00	4.00	25.00(50)	2.50	.60	.40
1503	8¢ Lyndon B. Johnson.	2.00	4.00	12.00(32)	5.50(12)	.50	.25

1504

1505

1506

SCOTT NO.	DESCRIPTION	FIRST DAY COVERS SING	FIRST DAY COVERS PL. BLK.	MINT SHEET	PLATE BLOCK	UNUSED F/NH	USED
	1973-74 RURAL AMERICA						
1504	8¢ Angus Cattle	2.00	4.00	16.50(50)	1.85	.45	.25
1505	10¢ Chautauqua (1974)	2.00	4.00	16.50(50)	1.85	.45	.25
1506	10¢ Winter Wheat (1974)	2.00	4.00	14.00(50)	1.85	.45	.25

1507

1508

SCOTT NO.	DESCRIPTION	FIRST DAY COVERS SING	FIRST DAY COVERS PL. BLK.	MINT SHEET	PLATE BLOCK	UNUSED F/NH	USED
	1973 CHRISTMAS						
1507	8¢ Madonna.	2.25	3.25	13.00(50)	4.25(12)	.40	.25
1508	8¢ Christmas Tree	2.25	3.25	13.00(50)	4.25(12)	.40	.25

1509, 1519

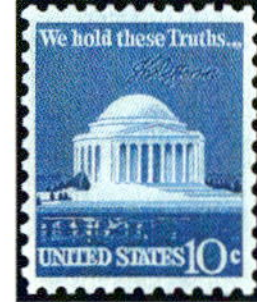

1510, 1520

1511

1518

1973-74 REGULAR ISSUES

SCOTT NO.	DESCRIPTION	FIRST DAY COVERS SING	FIRST DAY COVERS PL. BLK.	MINT SHEET	PLATE BLOCK	UNUSED F/NH	USED
1509	10¢ Crossed Flags . . .	2.25	4.00	32.00(100)	7.75(20)	.40	.25
1510	10¢ Jefferson.Memorial	2.25	4.00	34.00(100)	2.50	.50	.25
1510b	10¢ bklt pane of 5– Slogan VIII.	2.25	....	....	....	1.85	....
1510c	10¢ bklt pane of 8	2.25	....	....	....	3.00	....
1510d	10¢ bklt pane of 6 (1974)	2.25	....	....	....	6.50	....
1511	10¢ Zip Code Theme (1974)	2.25	4.00	29.50(100)	2.75(8)	.35	.25

BOOKLET PANE SLOGANS

VI–Stamps in This Book.... VII– This Book Contains 25.... VIII–Paying Bills....

COIL STAMPS Perf.10 Vertically

SCOTT NO.	DESCRIPTION	FIRST DAY COVERS SING	LINE PAIR	MINT SHEET	LINE PAIR	UNUSED F/NH	USED
1518	6.3¢ Liberty Bell.	2.25	2.75	....	.90	.40	.25
1519	10¢ Crossed Flags . . .	2.25	....	....	....	.50	.25
1520	10¢ Jefferson Memorial	2.25	2.75	....	1.25	.40	.25

1525

1526

1527

1528

1529

1974 COMMEMORATIVES

SCOTT NO.	DESCRIPTION	FIRST DAY COVERS SING	FIRST DAY COVERS PL. BLK.	MINT SHEET	PLATE BLOCK	UNUSED F/NH	USED
1525-52	**28 varieties, complete. . . . .**	....	....	....	....	**11.00**	**6.00**
1525	10¢ Veterans of Foreign Wars	2.25	4.00	14.00(50)	1.50	.40	.25
1526	10¢ Robert Frost	2.25	4.00	16.50(50)	1.85	.40	.25
1527	10¢ Environment– EXPO '74.	2.25	4.00	16.00(40)	6.00(12)	.40	.25
1528	10¢ Horse Racing	2.25	4.00	19.50(50)	6.00(12)	.40	.25
1529	10¢ Skylab Project. . . .	2.25	4.00	14.25(50)	1.75	.40	.25

1530

1531

1532

1533

1534

1535

1536

1537

1974 UNIVERSAL POSTAL UNION

SCOTT NO.	DESCRIPTION	FIRST DAY COVERS SING	FIRST DAY COVERS PL. BLK.	MINT SHEET	PLATE BLOCK	UNUSED F/NH	USED
1530-37	**8 varieties, attached .**	**6.00**	....	**13.00(32)**	**7.50(16)**	**3.50(8)**	**2.95**
1530-37	**Set of singles, complete**	**17.50**	....	....	....	**3.25**	**2.25**
1530	10¢ Raphael	2.75	....	....	....	.50	.35
1531	10¢ Hokusai.	2.75	....	....	....	.50	.35
1532	10¢ J.F. Peto	2.75	....	....	....	.50	.35
1533	10¢ J.E. Liotard	2.75	....	....	....	.50	.35
1534	10¢ G. Terborch.	2.75	....	....	....	.50	.35
1535	10¢ J.B.S. Chardin . . .	2.75	....	....	....	.50	.35
1536	10¢ T. Gainsborough . .	2.75	....	....	....	.50	.35
1537	10¢ F. de Goya	2.75	....	....	....	.50	.35

1538

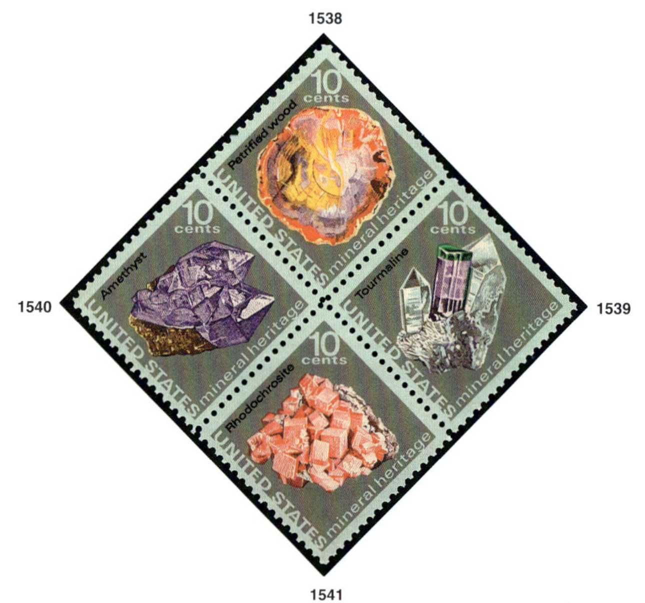

1540 1539

1541

1974 COMMEMORATIVES

SCOTT NO.	DESCRIPTION	FIRST DAY COVERS SING	FIRST DAY COVERS PL. BLK.	MINT SHEET	PLATE BLOCK	UNUSED F/NH	USED
1538-41	Mineral Heritage, 4 varieties, attached . .	3.50	5.00	18.00(48)	2.25	1.75	1.25
1538	10¢ Petrified Wood . . .	2.25	....	....	....	.50	.25
1539	10¢ Tourmaline	2.25	....	....	....	.50	.25
1540	10¢ Amethyst.	2.25	....	....	....	.50	.25
1541	10¢ Rhodochrosite . . .	2.25	....	....	....	.50	.25

1542

SCOTT NO.	DESCRIPTION	FIRST DAY COVERS SING	FIRST DAY COVERS PL. BLK.	MINT SHEET	PLATE BLOCK	UNUSED F/NH	USED
1542	10¢ Fort Harrod Bicentennial.........	2.25	4.00	15.00(50)	1.75	.40	.25

1543 1544

1545 1546

SCOTT NO.	DESCRIPTION	FIRST DAY COVERS SING	FIRST DAY COVERS PL. BLK.	MINT SHEET	PLATE BLOCK	UNUSED F/NH	USED
1543-46	Continental Congress, 4 varieties, attached ..	4.50	6.00	17.00(50)	2.25	1.75	1.25
1543	10¢ Carpenter's Hall ..	2.25	....	....	....	.40	.25
1544	10¢ Quote–First Congress	2.25	....	....	....	.40	.25
1545	10¢ Quote–Declaration–of Independence	2.25	....	....	....	.40	.25
1546	10¢ Independence Hall	2.25	....	....	....	.40	.25

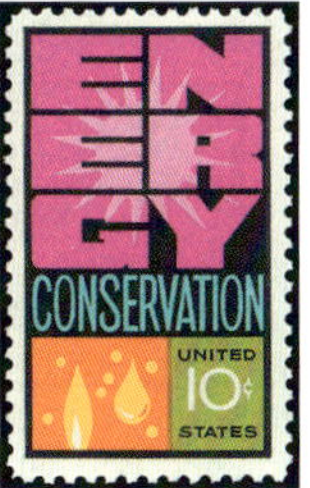

1547 1548 1549

SCOTT NO.	DESCRIPTION	FIRST DAY COVERS SING	FIRST DAY COVERS PL. BLK.	MINT SHEET	PLATE BLOCK	UNUSED F/NH	USED
1547	10¢ Energy Conservation	2.25	4.00	17.00(50)	1.90	.45	.25
1548	10¢ Sleepy Hollow...	2.25	4.00	15.00(50)	1.75	.40	.25
1549	10¢ Retarded Children	2.25	4.00	19.00(50)	1.90	.40	.25

1550 1551 1552

SCOTT NO.	DESCRIPTION	FIRST DAY COVERS SING	FIRST DAY COVERS PL. BLK.	MINT SHEET	PLATE BLOCK	UNUSED F/NH	USED
1550	10¢ Christmas–Angel .	2.25	4.00	14.00(50)	4.50(10)	.35	.25
1551	10¢ Christmas–Currier & Ives..............	2.25	4.00	14.00(50)	5.00(12)	.35	.25
1552	10¢ Christams–Dove of Peace.......	2.25	4.00	18.00(50)	9.50(20)	.40	.25
1552	same	....	....	....	5.50(12)	....	....

1553 1554 1555

1975 COMMEMORATIVES

SCOTT NO.	DESCRIPTION	FIRST DAY COVERS SING	FIRST DAY COVERS PL. BLK.	MINT SHEET	PLATE BLOCK	UNUSED F/NH	USED
1553-80	**8¢-10¢, 28 varieties, complete...........**	....	....	....	....	**12.00**	**6.25**
1553	10¢ Benjamin West–Arts	2.25	4.00	16.00(50)	5.00(10)	.45	.25
1554	10¢ Paul Dunbar–Arts .	2.25	4.00	18.00(50)	5.00(10)	.45	.25
1555	10¢ D.W. Griffith–Arts .	2.25	4.00	17.00(50)	2.00	.45	.25

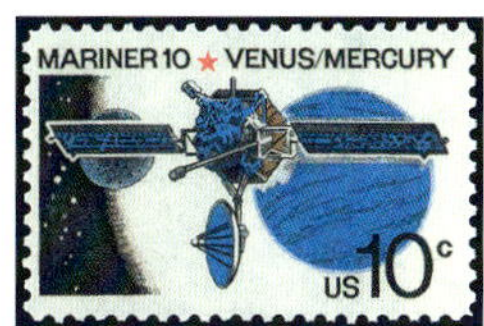

1556 1557

1558

SCOTT NO.	DESCRIPTION	FIRST DAY COVERS SING	FIRST DAY COVERS PL. BLK.	MINT SHEET	PLATE BLOCK	UNUSED F/NH	USED
1556	10¢ Pioneer 10	2.25	4.00	16.00(50)	2.00	.45	.25
1557	10¢ Mariner 10	2.25	4.00	16.00(50)	2.00	.45	.25
1558	10¢ Collective Bargaining	2.25	4.00	16.00(50)	3.25(8)	.40	.25

1559 1560

1561 1562

SCOTT NO.	DESCRIPTION	FIRST DAY COVERS SING	FIRST DAY COVERS PL. BLK.	MINT SHEET	PLATE BLOCK	UNUSED F/NH	USED
1559	8¢ Sybil Ludington....	2.25	4.00	14.00(50)	4.00(10)	.35	.25
1560	10¢ Salem Poor......	2.25	4.00	16.00(50)	5.00(10)	.45	.25
1561	10¢ Haym Salomon...	2.25	4.00	16.00(50)	5.00(10)	.45	.25
1562	18¢ Peter Francisco ..	2.25	4.00	27.50(50)	8.00(10)	.70	.40

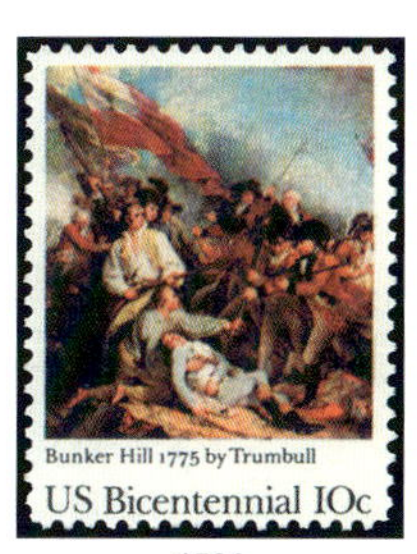

1563 1564

SCOTT NO.	DESCRIPTION	FIRST DAY COVERS SING	FIRST DAY COVERS PL. BLK.	MINT SHEET	PLATE BLOCK	UNUSED F/NH	USED
1563	10¢ Lexington-Concord	2.25	4.00	15.00(40)	5.75(12)	.45	.25
1564	10¢ Battle of Bunker Hill	2.25	4.00	16.00(40)	5.50(12)	.45	.25

1565

1566

1567

1568

SCOTT NO.	DESCRIPTION	FIRST DAY COVERS SING	PL. BLK.	MINT SHEET	PLATE BLOCK	UNUSED F/NH	USED
1565-68	Military Uniforms, 4 varieties, attached . .	4.00	6.00	17.00(50)	5.75(12)	1.75	1.30
1565	10¢ Continental Army .	2.25	....	....	....	.50	.25
1566	10¢ Continental Navy .	2.25	....	....	....	.50	.25
1567	10¢ Continental Marines	2.25	....	....	....	.50	.25
1568	10¢ American Militia . .	2.25	....	....	....	.50	.25

1569
1570

SCOTT NO.	DESCRIPTION	FIRST DAY COVERS SING	PL. BLK.	MINT SHEET	PLATE BLOCK	UNUSED F/NH	USED
1569-70	Apollo-Soyuz Mission, . 2 varieties, attached . .	3.00	4.50	11.00(24)	5.75(12)	.95	.65
1569	10¢ Docked	2.25	....	....	....	.50	.30
1570	10¢ Docking.	2.25	....	....	....	.50	.30

1571

SCOTT NO.	DESCRIPTION	FIRST DAY COVERS SING	PL. BLK.	MINT SHEET	PLATE BLOCK	UNUSED F/NH	USED
1571	10¢ International Women's Year	2.25	4.00	14.00(50)	2.40(6)	.35	.25

1572 1573

1574 1575

SCOTT NO.	DESCRIPTION	FIRST DAY COVERS SING	PL. BLK.	MINT SHEET	PLATE BLOCK	UNUSED F/NH	USED
1572-75	Postal Service Bicentennial, 4 varieties, attached . .	4.00	5.00	19.00(50)	5.50(12)	1.85	1.50
1572	10¢ Stagecoach & Trailer	2.25	....	....	....	.50	.25
1573	10¢ Locomotives	2.25	....	....	....	.50	.25
1574	10¢ Airplanes.	2.25	....	....	....	.50	.25
1575	10¢ Satellite.	2.25	....	....	....	.50	.25

World Peace through LAW USA 10c

1576

1577 1578

SCOTT NO.	DESCRIPTION	FIRST DAY COVERS SING	PL. BLK.	MINT SHEET	PLATE BLOCK	UNUSED F/NH	USED
1576	10¢ World Peace through Law	2.25	4.00	15.00(50)	2.00	.45	.25
1577-78	Banking & Commerce, 2 varieties, attached . .	2.50	3.75	15.00(40)	2.25	1.00	.70
1577	10¢ Banking.	2.25	....	....	....	.60	.25
1578	10¢ Commerce	2.25	....	....	....	.60	.25

1579

1580

SCOTT NO.	DESCRIPTION	FIRST DAY COVERS SING	PL. BLK.	MINT SHEET	PLATE BLOCK	UNUSED F/NH	USED
1579	(10¢) Madonna	2.25	4.00	15.00(50)	5.00(12)	.45	.25
1580	(10¢) Christmas Card .	2.25	4.00	15.00(50)	5.00(12)	.45	.25
1580b	(10¢) Christmas Card, perf. 10 1/2 x 11	....	....	66.00(50)	19.00(12)	1.40	.80

1581, 1811

1582

1584

1585

1590, 1591, 1616

1592, 1617

1593

1594, 1816

1595, 1618

1596

1597, 1598, 1618C

1599, 1619

1603

1604

1605

1606

1608

1610

1611

1612

1975-81 AMERICANA ISSUE

SCOTT NO.	DESCRIPTION	FIRST DAY COVERS SING	FIRST DAY COVERS PL. BLK.	MINT SHEET	PLATE BLOCK	UNUSED F/NH	USED
1581/1612	1¢-$5, (No #1590, 1590a, 1595, or 1598) 19 varieties, complete	51.50	....	....	155.00	33.50	6.95
1581	1¢ Inkwell & Quill (1977)	2.25	4.00	10.00(100)	1.25	.35	.25
1582	2¢ Speaker's Stand (1977)	2.25	4.00	10.00(100)	2.00	.25	.25
1584	3¢ Ballot Box (1977) . .	2.25	4.00	17.00(100)	2.00	.30	.25
1585	4¢ Books & Eyeglasses (1977)	2.25	4.00	18.00(100)	2.00	.30	.25
1590	9¢ Capitol, from bklt pane (1977)	15.00	....	....	....	1.25	1.00
1590a	same, perf 10 (1977) . .	....	....	....	....	33.00	....
1590,1623	Attached pair, from bklt pane	....	....	....	....	1.75	....
1590a, 1623b	Attached pair, perf. 10 .	....	....	....	....	35.00	....
1591	9¢ Capitol, grey paper .	2.25	4.00	30.00(100)	1.75	.40	.25
1592	10¢ Justice (1977)	2.25	4.00	32.00(100)	1.75	.40	.25
1593	11¢ Printing Press	2.25	4.00	36.00(100)	2.25	.50	.25
1594	12¢ Torch (1981)	2.25	4.00	38.50(100)	2.50	.50	.25
1595	13¢ Liberty Bell from bklt pane	2.25	....	....	....	.50	.25
1595a	13¢ bklt pane of 6	2.25	....	....	....	3.25	....
1595b	13¢ bklt pane of 7– Slogan VIII	2.50	....	....	....	3.50	....
1595c	13¢ bklt pane of 8	2.50	....	....	....	3.75	....
1595d	13¢ bklt pane of 5– Slogan IX (1976)	2.25	....	....	....	3.50	....
	VIII–Paying Bills... IX–Collect Stamps...						
1596	13¢ Eagle & Shield . . .	2.25	4.00	40.00(100)	7.00(12)	.50	.25
1597	15¢ Fort McHenry Flag (1978)	2.25	4.00	43.00(100)	12.00(20)	.50	.25
1598	same, from bklt pane . . (1978)	2.25	....	....	....	.90	.25
1598a	15¢ bklt pane of 8	3.00	....	....	....	8.50	....
1599	16¢ Statue of Liberty (1978)	2.25	4.00	52.00(100)	3.00	.60	.30
1603	24¢ Old North Church .	2.25	4.00	72.00(100)	4.50	.95	.25
1604	28¢ Fort Nisqually (1978)	2.25	4.00	92.00(100)	5.75	1.10	.35
1605	29¢ Lighthouse (1978)	2.25	4.00	100.00(100)	5.75	1.20	.50
1606	30¢ School House (1979)	2.25	4.00	100.00(100)	6.00	1.20	.30
1608	50¢ "Betty" Lamp (1979)	2.50	5.25	150.00(100)	9.00	2.00	.30
1610	$1 Rush Lamp (1979) .	3.50	17.50	305.00(100)	16.00	3.50	.30
1610c	Same, candle flame inverted.......		....	....	....	14500.00	....
1611	$2 Kerosene Lamp (1978)	7.00	14.50	600.00(100)	32.50	7.25	.85
1612	$5 Conductor's Lantern (1979)	15.00	31.50	1375.00(100)	74.00	16.00	3.00

1613

1614

1615

1615C

1975-79 COIL STAMPS Perforated Vertically

SCOTT NO.	DESCRIPTION	FIRST DAY COVERS SING	FIRST DAY COVERS PL. BLK.	MINT SHEET	LINE PR.	UNUSED F/NH	USED
1613-19	3.1¢-16¢, 9 varieties, . complete	....	....	....	12.50	3.75	1.80
1613	3.1¢ Guitar (1979)	2.25	2.75	....	1.20	.45	.25
1614	7.7¢ Saxhorns (1976) .	2.25	2.75	....	1.50	.60	.40
1615	7.9¢ Drum (1976)	2.25	2.75	....	1.40	.60	.40
1615C	8.4¢ Piano (1978)	2.25	2.75	....	5.00	.60	.40
1616	9¢ Capitol (1976)	2.25	2.75	....	1.30	.60	.40
1617	10¢ Justice (1977)	2.25	2.75	....	1.25	.50	.25
1618	13¢ Liberty Bell	2.25	2.75	....	1.50	.60	.30
1618C	15¢ Fort McHenry Flag (1978)	2.25	....	....	....	.85	.25
1619	16¢ Statue of Liberty (1978)	2.25	2.75	....	2.50	.75	.60

COIL LINE PAIRS: are two connected coil stamps with a line the same color as the stamps printed between the two stamps. This line usually appears every 20 to 30 stamps on a roll depending on the issue.

1622, 1625

1623, 1623b

1975-77 REGULAR ISSUES

SCOTT NO.	DESCRIPTION	FIRST DAY COVERS SING	FIRST DAY COVERS PL. BLK.	MINT SHEET	PLATE BLOCK	UNUSED F/NH	USED
1622	13¢ Flag & Independence Hall, 11 x 10½	2.25	4.00	40.00(100)	12.00(20)	.55	.25
1622c	same, perf. 11 (1981) .	....	....	150.00(100)	90.00(20)	1.20	....
1623	13¢ Flag & Capitol from bklt pane, perf 11 x 10½ (1977)	3.00	....	....	....	.50	.50
1623a	bklt pane of 8 (one–1590, seven–1623)	30.00	....	....	....	4.00	3.75
1623b	13¢ Flag & Capitol from bklt pane, perf. 10	2.25	....	....	....	.90	.75
1623c	bklt pane of 8 (one–1590a, seven–1623b)	17.00	....	....	....	30.00	....

1975 COIL STAMP

SCOTT NO.	DESCRIPTION	FIRST DAY COVERS SING	FIRST DAY COVERS PL. BLK.	MINT SHEET	PLATE BLOCK	UNUSED F/NH	USED
1625	13¢ Flag & Independence Hall	2.25	....	....	3.75	.55	.25

1629 1630 1631

1632

1976 COMMEMORATIVES

SCOTT NO.	DESCRIPTION	FIRST DAY COVERS SING	FIRST DAY COVERS PL. BLK.	MINT SHEET	PLATE BLOCK	UNUSED F/NH	USED
1629/1703	(1629-32, 1683-85, 1690-1703) 21 varieties	....	....	....	....	12.80	3.50
1629-31	Spirit of '76 , 3 varieties, attached	3.00	6.00	22.00(50)	7.25(12)	1.75	1.25
1629	13¢ Boy Drummer	2.00	....	....	....	.60	.25
1630	13¢ Older Drummer . . .	2.00	....	....	....	.60	.25
1631	13¢ Fifer	2.00	....	....	....	.60	.25
1632	13¢ Interphil	2.25	4.00	19.00(50)	2.25	.50	.25

1633

1682

1976 BICENTENNIAL STATE FLAGS
Complete Set Printed in One Sheet of 50 Stamps

1633 *Delaware*
1634 *Pennsylvania*
1635 *New Jersey*
1636 *Georgia*
1637 *Connecticut*
1638 *Massachusetts*
1639 *Maryland*
1640 *South Carolina*
1641 *New Hampshire*
1642 *Virginia*
1643 *New York*
1644 *North Carolina*
1645 *Rhode Island*
1646 *Vermont*
1647 *Kentucky*
1648 *Tennessee*
1649 *Ohio*
1650 *Louisiana*
1651 *Indiana*
1652 *Mississippi*
1653 *Illinois*
1654 *Alabama*
1655 *Maine*
1656 *Missouri*
1657 *Arkansas*
1658 *Michigan*
1659 *Florida*
1660 *Texas*
1661 *Iowa*
1662 *Wisconsin*
1663 *California*
1664 *Minnesota*
1665 *Oregon*
1666 *Kansas*
1667 *West Virginia*
1668 *Nevada*
1669 *Nebraska*
1670 *Colorado*
1671 *North Dakota*
1672 *South Dakota*
1673 *Montana*
1674 *Washington*
1675 *Idaho*
1676 *Wyoming*
1677 *Utah*
1678 *Oklahoma*
1679 *New Mexico*
1680 *Arizona*
1681 *Alaska*
1682 *Hawaii*

SCOTT NO.	DESCRIPTION	FIRST DAY COVERS SING	FIRST DAY COVERS PL. BLK.	MINT SHEET	PLATE BLOCK	UNUSED F/NH	USED

1976 BICENTENNIAL STATE FLAGS
Complete Set Printed in One Sheet of 50 Stamps
Continued

SCOTT NO.	DESCRIPTION	SING	PL. BLK.	MINT SHEET	PLATE BLOCK	UNUSED F/NH	USED
1633-82	13¢ State Flags, 50 varieties, attached.	....	....	29.00(50)	....	29.00	....
	Set of 50 singles	95.00	....	....	....	....	18.75
	Singles of above	2.50	....	....	....	1.00	.50

1683

1684

1685

SCOTT NO.	DESCRIPTION	SING	PL. BLK.	MINT SHEET	PLATE BLOCK	UNUSED F/NH	USED
1683	13¢ Telephone	2.25	4.00	28.00(50)	2.75	.60	.25
1684	13¢ Aviation	2.25	4.00	20.00(50)	8.50(10)	.75	.25
1685	13¢ Chemistry	2.25	4.00	25.00(50)	7.50(12)	.60	.25

1686

1687

1976 BICENNTENNIAL SOUVENIR SHEETS

SCOTT NO.	DESCRIPTION	SING	PL. BLK.	MINT SHEET	PLATE BLOCK	UNUSED F/NH	USED
1686-89	4 varieties, complete . .	32.50	....	....	....	30.00	27.00
1686	13¢ Cornwallis Surrender	6.00	....	....	....	5.00	4.75
1686a-e	13¢ singles, each.	3.50	....	....	....	1.20	1.10
1687	18¢ Independence. . . .	7.50	....	....	....	7.00	6.50
1687a-e	18¢ singles, each.	3.75	....	....	....	1.60	1.50
1688	24¢ Washington Crossing Delaware	9.50	....	....	....	9.00	8.25
1688a-e	24¢ singles, each.	4.25	....	....	....	1.90	1.80
1689	31¢ Washington at Valley Forge	11.50	....	....	....	12.00	10.50
1689a-e	31¢ singles, each.	5.25	....	....	....	2.40	2.30

1690

1691 1692 1693 1694

SCOTT NO.	DESCRIPTION	SING	PL. BLK.	MINT SHEET	PLATE BLOCK	UNUSED F/NH	USED
1690	13¢ Benjamin Franklin.	2.25	4.00	21.00(50)	2.25	.50	.25
1691-94	Declaration of Independence, 4 varieties, attached . .	5.00	10.00	26.00(50)	12.00(16)	3.50	3.00
1691	13¢ Delegation members	2.25	....	....	....	1.10	.25
1692	13¢ Adams, etc.	2.25	....	....	....	1.10	.25
1693	13¢ Jefferson, Franklin, etc.	2.25	....	....	....	1.10	.25
1694	13¢ Hancock, Thomson, etc.	2.25	....	....	....	1.10	.25

1695

1696

1697

1698

SCOTT NO.	DESCRIPTION	SING	PL. BLK.	MINT SHEET	PLATE BLOCK	UNUSED F/NH	USED
1695-98	Olympic Games, 4 varieties, attached . .	4.00	6.00	24.00(50)	7.50(12)	2.40	1.95
1695	13¢ Diving	2.25	....	....	....	.75	.25
1696	13¢ Skiing	2.25	....	....	....	.75	.25
1697	13¢ Running	2.25	....	....	....	.75	.25
1698	13¢ Skating	2.25	....	....	....	.75	.25

1699

1700

SCOTT NO.	DESCRIPTION	SING	PL. BLK.	MINT SHEET	PLATE BLOCK	UNUSED F/NH	USED
1699	13¢ Clara Maass	2.25	4.00	17.00(40)	7.00(12)	.60	.25
1700	13¢ Adolph S. Ochs. . .	2.25	4.00	16.00(32)	2.50	.60	.25

1701

1702, 1703

SCOTT NO.	DESCRIPTION	SING	PL. BLK.	MINT SHEET	PLATE BLOCK	UNUSED F/NH	USED
1701	13¢ Nativity	2.25	....	20.00(50)	6.50(12)	.55	.25
1702	13¢ "Winter Pastime" (Andreati).	2.25	....	20.00(50)	5.50(10)	.55	.25
1703	13¢ "Winter Pastime" (Gravure Int.)	2.25	....	22.00(50)	13.00(20)	.55	.25

1704

1705

1977 COMMEMORATIVES

SCOTT NO.	DESCRIPTION	FIRST DAY COVERS SING	FIRST DAY COVERS PL. BLK.	MINT SHEET	PLATE BLOCK	UNUSED F/NH	USED
1704-30	**27 varieties, complete**	....	....	....	....	**13.00**	**5.00**
1704	13¢ Princeton	2.25	4.00	16.00(40)	5.50(10)	.60	.25
1705	13¢ Sound Recording .	2.25	4.00	20.00(50)	2.25	.60	.25

1708 1709

1706 1707

SCOTT NO.	DESCRIPTION	FIRST DAY COVERS SING	FIRST DAY COVERS PL. BLK.	MINT SHEET	PLATE BLOCK	UNUSED F/NH	USED
1706-09	Pueblo Art, 4 varieties, attached . .	4.00	....	19.00(40)	6.50(10)	3.00	2.50
1706	13¢ Zia.	2.25	....	....	....	.75	.25
1707	13¢ San Ildefonso	2.25	....	....	....	.75	.25
1708	13¢ Hopi	2.25	....	....	....	.75	.25
1709	13¢ Acoma.	2.25	....	....	....	.75	.25

1710

1711

SCOTT NO.	DESCRIPTION	FIRST DAY COVERS SING	FIRST DAY COVERS PL. BLK.	MINT SHEET	PLATE BLOCK	UNUSED F/NH	USED
1710	13¢ Transatlantic Flight	3.00	5.00	22.00(50)	7.50(12)	.50	.25
1711	13¢ Colorado Statehood	2.25	4.00	22.00(50)	7.50(12)	.50	.25

1712

1713

Mint Sheets: From 1935 to date, we list prices for standard size Mint Sheets Fine, Never Hinged condition. The number of stamps in each sheet is noted in ( ).

1714

1715

1716

SCOTT NO.	DESCRIPTION	FIRST DAY COVERS SING	FIRST DAY COVERS PL. BLK.	MINT SHEET	PLATE BLOCK	UNUSED F/NH	USED
1712-15	Butterflies, 4 varieties, attached . .	4.00	6.00	22.00(50)	7.50(12)	3.00	2.50
1712	13¢ Swallowtail	2.25	....	....	....	.60	.25
1713	13¢ Checkerspot	2.25	....	....	....	.60	.25
1714	13¢ Dogface	2.25	....	....	....	.60	.25
1715	13¢ Orange-Tip	2.25	....	....	....	.60	.25
1716	13¢ Lafayette.	2.25	6.00	17.00(40)	2.25	.50	.25

1717 1718

1719 1720

SCOTT NO.	DESCRIPTION	FIRST DAY COVERS SING	FIRST DAY COVERS PL. BLK.	MINT SHEET	PLATE BLOCK	UNUSED F/NH	USED
1717-20	Skilled Hands, 4 varieties, attached . .	4.00	....	22.00(50)	7.25(12)	2.50	2.00
1717	13¢ Seamstress.	2.25	....	....	....	.60	.25
1718	13¢ Blacksmith	2.25	....	....	....	.60	.25
1719	13¢ Wheelwright	2.25	....	....	....	.60	.25
1720	13¢ Leatherworker. . . .	2.25	....	....	....	.60	.25

1721

1722

1723

1724

SCOTT NO.	DESCRIPTION	FIRST DAY COVERS SING	FIRST DAY COVERS PL. BLK.	MINT SHEET	PLATE BLOCK	UNUSED F/NH	USED
1721	13¢ Peace Bridge	2.25	4.00	21.00(50)	3.00	.50	.25
1722	13¢ Herkimer at Oriskany	2.25	4.00	17.50(40)	5.25(10)	.50	.25
1723-24	Energy, 2 varieties, attached . .	2.50	....	18.00(40)	7.25(12)	1.10	.85
1723	13¢ Conservation	2.25	....	....	....	.60	.25
1724	13¢ Development	2.25	....	....	....	.60	.25

1725

1726

1727

1728

1729

1730

SCOTT NO.	DESCRIPTION	FIRST DAY COVERS SING	FIRST DAY COVERS PL. BLK.	MINT SHEET	PLATE BLOCK	UNUSED F/NH	USED
1725	13¢ Alta California	2.25	4.00	20.00(50)	2.25	.45	.25
1726	13¢ Articles of Confederation	2.25	4.00	20.00(50)	2.25	.45	.25
1727	13¢ Talking Pictures . .	2.25	4.00	20.00(50)	2.25	.45	.25
1728	13¢ Surrender at Saratoga	2.25	....	17.50(40)	5.25(10)	.45	.25
1729	13¢ Washington, Christmas	2.50	....	48.00(100)	13.00(20)	.60	.25
1730	13¢ Rural Mailbox, Christmas	2.50	....	39.00(100)	5.25(10)	.50	.25

1731

1732

1733

1978 COMMEMORATIVES

SCOTT NO.	DESCRIPTION	FIRST DAY COVERS SING	FIRST DAY COVERS PL. BLK.	MINT SHEET	PLATE BLOCK	UNUSED F/NH	USED
1731/69	**(1731-33, 1744-56, 1758-69) 28 varieties .**	....	....	....	....	**19.50**	**7.00**
1731	13¢ Carl Sandburg . . .	2.25	4.00	22.00(50)	2.50	.50	.25
1732-33	Captain Cook, 2 varieties, attached . .	2.00	....	24.00(50)	12.00(20)	1.50	1.20
1732	13¢ Captain Cook (Alaska)	2.25	4.00	....	2.50	.55	.25
1733	13¢ "Resolution" (Hawaii)	2.25	4.00	....	2.50	.55	.25

NOTE: The Plate Block set includes #1732 & 1733 Plate Blocks of four.

1734

1735, 1736, 1743

1737

1978-80 DEFINITIVES

SCOTT NO.	DESCRIPTION	FIRST DAY COVERS SING	FIRST DAY COVERS PL. BLK.	MINT SHEET	PLATE BLOCK	UNUSED F/NH	USED
1734	13¢ Indian Head Penny	2.25	4.00	58.00(150)	2.50	.60	.25
1735	(15¢) "A" Defintive (Gravure)	2.25	4.00	45.00(100)	2.50	.60	.25
1736	same (Intaglio), from bklt pane	2.25	....	....	....	.60	.25
1736a	15¢ "A" bklt pane of 8 .	3.50	....	....	....	4.50	....
1737	15¢ Roses	2.25	....	....	....	.60	.25
1737a	same, bklt pane of 8 . .	4.00	....	....	....	4.50	....

1738 1739 1740 1741 1742

SCOTT NO.	DESCRIPTION	FIRST DAY COVERS SING	FIRST DAY COVERS PL. BLK.	MINT SHEET	PLATE BLOCK	UNUSED F/NH	USED
1738-42	Windmills, strip of 5, attached (1980)	5.00	....	....	....	3.00	2.25
1738	15¢ Virginia Windmill . .	2.25	....	....	....	.70	.25
1739	15¢ Rhode Island Windmill	2.25	....	....	....	.70	.25
1740	15¢ Massachusetts Windmill	2.25	....	....	....	.70	.25
1741	15¢ Illinois Windmill . . .	2.25	....	....	....	.70	.25
1742	15¢ Texas Windmill . . .	2.25	....	....	....	.70	.25
1742a	Same, bklt pane of 10 .	6.00	....	....	....	6.00	....

1978 COIL STAMP

SCOTT NO.	DESCRIPTION	FIRST DAY COVERS SING	LINE PR.	MINT SHEET	LINE PR.	UNUSED F/NH	USED
1743	(15¢) "A" Definitive	2.25	2.75	....	1.65	.55	.20

1745

1744

1746

1747

1748

SCOTT NO.	DESCRIPTION	FIRST DAY COVERS SING	FIRST DAY COVERS PL. BLK.	MINT SHEET	PLATE BLOCK	UNUSED F/NH	USED
1744	13¢ Harriet Tubman. . .	5.00	7.00	29.00(50)	9.50(12)	.65	.25
1745-48	Quilts, 4 varieties, attached	3.50	....	30.00(48)	12.00(12)	3.00	2.00
1745	13¢ Flowers	2.25	....	....	....	.75	.25
1746	13¢ Stars	2.25	....	....	....	.75	.25
1747	13¢ Stripes	2.25	....	....	....	.75	.25
1748	13¢ Plaid	2.25	....	....	....	.75	.25

1750

1749 1752

1751

SCOTT NO.	DESCRIPTION	FIRST DAY COVERS SING	FIRST DAY COVERS PL. BLK.	MINT SHEET	PLATE BLOCK	UNUSED F/NH	USED
1749-52	American Dance, 4 varieties, attached . .	5.00	....	22.00(48)	7.75(12)	3.00	2.00
1749	13¢ Ballet.	2.25	....	....	....	.75	.25
1750	13¢ Theater	2.25	....	....	....	.75	.25
1751	13¢ Folk.	2.25	....	....	....	.75	.25
1752	13¢ Modern	2.25	....	....	....	.75	.25

1753 1754 1755 1756

SCOTT NO.	DESCRIPTION	FIRST DAY COVERS SING	FIRST DAY COVERS PL. BLK.	MINT SHEET	PLATE BLOCK	UNUSED F/NH	USED
1753	13¢ French Alliance . . .	2.25	4.00	16.00(40)	2.25	.50	.25
1754	13¢ Dr. Papanicolaou .	2.25	4.00	20.00(50)	2.25	.60	.25
1755	13¢ Jimmie Rodgers . .	2.25	4.00	23.00(50)	8.00(12)	.75	.25
1756	15¢ George M. Cohan.	2.25	4.00	23.00(50)	8.00(12)	.75	.25

1757

1978 CAPEX SOUVENIR SHEET

SCOTT NO.	DESCRIPTION	FIRST DAY COVERS SING	FIRST DAY COVERS PL. BLK.	MINT SHEET	PLATE BLOCK	UNUSED F/NH	USED
1757	$1.04 CAPEX	4.25	....	19.00(6)	4.00	3.50	3.00
1757a	13¢ Cardinal	2.25	....	....	....	.45	.40
1757b	13¢ Mallard	2.25	....	....	....	.45	.40
1757c	13¢ Canada Goose . . .	2.25	....	....	....	.45	.40
1757d	13¢ Blue Jay	2.25	....	....	....	.45	.40
1757e	13¢ Moose.	2.25	....	....	....	.45	.40
1757f	13¢ Chipmunk	2.25	....	....	....	.45	.40
1757g	13¢ Red Fox	2.25	....	....	....	.45	.40
1757h	13¢ Raccoon	2.25	....	....	....	.45	.40

1758

1759

SCOTT NO.	DESCRIPTION	FIRST DAY COVERS SING	FIRST DAY COVERS PL. BLK.	MINT SHEET	PLATE BLOCK	UNUSED F/NH	USED
1758	15¢ Photography	2.25	4.00	17.00(40)	7.25(12)	.60	.25
1759	15¢ Viking Mission. . . .	2.25	4.00	23.00(50)	3.00	.60	.25

1760

1761

1762

1763

SCOTT NO.	DESCRIPTION	FIRST DAY COVERS SING	FIRST DAY COVERS PL. BLK.	MINT SHEET	PLATE BLOCK	UNUSED F/NH	USED
1760-63	American Owls, 4 varieties, attached.	5.00	6.00	30.00(50)	3.50	3.00	2.00
1760	15¢ Great Gray	2.25	....	....	....	.70	.25
1761	15¢ Saw-Whet.	2.25	....	....	....	.70	.25
1762	15¢ Barred Owl	2.25	....	....	....	.70	.25
1763	15¢ Great Horned	2.25	....	....	....	.70	.25

1764 1765

1766 1767

SCOTT NO.	DESCRIPTION	FIRST DAY COVERS SING	FIRST DAY COVERS PL. BLK.	MINT SHEET	PLATE BLOCK	UNUSED F/NH	USED
1764-67	Trees, 4 varieties, attached.	5.00	....	28.00(40)	12.00(12)	3.25	2.00
1764	15¢ Giant Sequoia. . . .	2.25	....	....	....	.70	.25
1765	15¢ Pine	2.25	....	....	....	.70	.25
1766	15¢ Oak.	2.25	....	....	....	.70	.25
1767	15¢ Birch	2.25	....	....	....	.70	.25

1768

1769

SCOTT NO.	DESCRIPTION	FIRST DAY COVERS SING	FIRST DAY COVERS PL. BLK.	MINT SHEET	PLATE BLOCK	UNUSED F/NH	USED
1768	15¢ Madonna, Christmas	2.25	4.00	44.00(100)	7.25(12)	.60	.25
1769	15¢ Hobby Horse, Christmas	2.25	4.00	44.00(100)	8.25(12)	.60	.25

1770

1771

1979 COMMEMORATIVES

SCOTT NO.	DESCRIPTION	FIRST DAY COVERS SING	FIRST DAY COVERS PL. BLK.	MINT SHEET	PLATE BLOCK	UNUSED F/NH	USED
1770/1802	**(1770-94, 1799-1802) 29 varieties, complete**	....	....	....	....	**17.50**	**6.00**
1770	15¢ Robert F. Kennedy	2.25	4.00	25.00(48)	2.75	.65	.25
1771	15¢ Martin L. King, Jr. .	3.00	5.00	25.00(50)	8.50(12)	.75	.25

1772

1773

1774

SCOTT NO.	DESCRIPTION	FIRST DAY COVERS SING	FIRST DAY COVERS PL. BLK.	MINT SHEET	PLATE BLOCK	UNUSED F/NH	USED
1772	15¢ International Year of the Child	2.25	4.00	23.50(50)	2.75	.65	.25
1773	15¢ John Steinbeck . . .	2.25	4.00	25.00(50)	2.75	.65	.25
1774	15¢ Albert Einstein. . . .	3.00	5.00	25.00(50)	3.25	.75	.25

U.S. BICENTENNIAL: The U.S.P.S. issued stamps commemorating the 200th anniversary of the struggle for independence from 1775 through 1783. These include numbers: 1432, 1476-83, 1543-46, 1559-68, 1629-31, 1633-82, 1686-89, 1691-94, 1704, 1716-20, 1722, 1726, 1728-29, 1753, 1789, 1826, 1937-38, 1941, 2052 and C98.

SCOTT NO.	DESCRIPTION	FIRST DAY COVERS SING	FIRST DAY COVERS PL. BLK.	MINT SHEET	PLATE BLOCK	UNUSED F/NH	USED

1775 1776

1777 1778

1779 1780

1781 1782

SCOTT NO.	DESCRIPTION	SING	PL. BLK.	MINT SHEET	PLATE BLOCK	UNUSED F/NH	USED
1775-78	Pennsylvania Toleware, 4 varieties, attached . .	5.00	....	20.00(40)	6.75(10)	2.50	2.00
1775	15¢ Coffee Pot.	2.25	....	....	....	.75	.25
1776	15¢ Tea Caddy	2.25	....	....	....	.75	.25
1777	15¢ Sugar Bowl	2.25	....	....	....	.75	.25
1778	15¢ Coffee Pot.	2.25	....	....	....	.75	.25
1779-82	Architecture, 4 varieties, attached.	5.00	6.00	27.00(48)	4.00	3.50	2.75
1779	15¢ Virginia Rotunda . .	2.25	....	....	....	1.00	.25
1780	15¢ Baltimore Cathedral	2.25	....	....	....	1.00	.25
1781	15¢ Boston State House	2.25	....	....	....	1.00	.25
1782	15¢ Philadelphia Exchange	2.25	....	....	....	1.00	.25

1783

1784

1785

1786

SCOTT NO.	DESCRIPTION	SING	PL. BLK.	MINT SHEET	PLATE BLOCK	UNUSED F/NH	USED
1783-86	Endangered Flora, 4 varieties, attached . .	5.00	....	25.00(50)	8.25(12)	2.75	2.25
1783	15¢ Trillium	2.25	....	....	....	.75	.25
1784	15¢ Broadbean	2.25	....	....	....	.75	.25
1785	15¢ Wallflower.	2.25	....	....	....	.75	.25
1786	15¢ Primrose	2.25	....	....	....	.75	.25

1787

1788

1789, 1789a

1790

SCOTT NO.	DESCRIPTION	SING	PL. BLK.	MINT SHEET	PLATE BLOCK	UNUSED F/NH	USED
1787	15¢ Guide Dog	2.25	....	24.00(50)	12.00(20)	.70	.25
1788	15¢ Special Olympics .	2.25	....	24.00(50)	6.00(10)	.65	.25
1789	15¢ John Paul Jones perf. 11 x 12.	2.25	....	24.00(50)	6.00(10)	.65	.25
1789a	same, perf. 11	2.25	....	35.00(50)	9.00(10)	1.00	.30

NOTE: #1789a may be included in year date sets and special offers and not 1789.

SCOTT NO.	DESCRIPTION	SING	PL. BLK.	MINT SHEET	PLATE BLOCK	UNUSED F/NH	USED
1790	10¢ Summer Olympics, Javelin Thrower	2.25	4.00	15.00(50)	5.25(12)	.40	.25

1791 1792

1793 1794

SCOTT NO.	DESCRIPTION	SING	PL. BLK.	MINT SHEET	PLATE BLOCK	UNUSED F/NH	USED
1791-94	Summer Olympics, 4 varieties, attached . .	5.00	....	24.00(50)	8.25(12)	2.50	2.00
1791	15¢ Runners	2.25	....	....	....	.70	.25
1792	15¢ Swimmers.	2.25	....	....	....	.70	.25
1793	15¢ Rowers	2.25	....	....	....	.70	.25
1794	15¢ Equestrian	2.25	....	....	....	.70	.25

1795 1796

1797 1798

1980

SCOTT NO.	DESCRIPTION	SING	PL. BLK.	MINT SHEET	PLATE BLOCK	UNUSED F/NH	USED
1795-98	Winter Olympics, 4 varieties, attached . .	5.00	....	25.00(50)	8.25(12)	2.75	2.00
1795	15¢ Skater.	2.25	....	....	....	.70	.25
1796	15¢ Downhill Skier. . . .	2.25	....	....	....	.70	.25
1797	15¢ Ski Jumper	2.25	....	....	....	.70	.25
1798	15¢ Hockey	2.25	....	....	....	.70	.25
1795a-98a	same, perf. 11, attached	....	....	45.00(50)	15.00(12)	4.50	3.50
1795a	15¢ Skater.	....	....	....	....	1.20	.75
1796a	15¢ Downhill Skier. . . .	....	....	....	....	1.20	.75
1797a	15¢ Ski Jumper	....	....	....	....	1.20	.75
1798a	15¢ Hockey	....	....	....	....	1.20	.75

SCOTT NO.	DESCRIPTION	FIRST DAY COVERS SING	PL. BLK.	MINT SHEET	PLATE BLOCK	UNUSED F/NH	USED

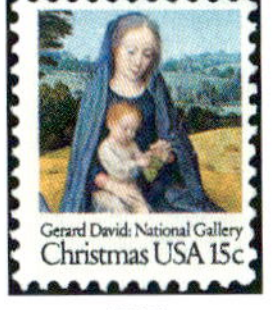

1799

1800

1979 COMMEMORATIVES

1799	15¢ Christmas–Madonna	2.25	....	44.00(100)	7.25(12)	.60	.25
1800	15¢ Christmas–Santa Claus	2.25	....	49.00(100)	8.00(12)	.70	.25

1801

1802

1801	15¢ Will Rogers	3.00	....	25.00(50)	8.00(12)	.70	.25
1802	15¢ Vietnam Veterans .	3.00	5.25	27.00(50)	8.00(10)	.70	.25

1803

1804

1980 COMMEMORATIVES

1795/1843	(1795-98, 1803-10, 1821-43) 35 varieties, complete	....	....	....	....	23.00	7.50
1803	15¢ W.C. Fields	2.25	4.00	24.00(50)	7.25(12)	.60	.25
1804	15¢ Benjamin Banneker	2.25	4.00	27.00(50)	8.75(12)	.70	.25

1805

1806, 1808, 1810

1807

1809

1805-10	6 varieties, attached . .	4.50	....	32.00(60)	24.00(36)	4.25	2.75
1805-06	2 varieties, attached . .	2.50	....	....	....	....	....
1807-08	2 varieties, attached . .	2.50	....	....	....	....	....
1809-10	2 varieties, attached . .	2.50	....	....	....	....	....
1805	15¢ "Letters Preserve Memories"	2.25	....	....	....	.75	.35
1806	15¢ claret & multicolor .	2.25	....	....	....	.75	.35
1807	15¢ "Letters Lift Spirits"	2.25	....	....	....	.75	.35
1808	15¢ green & multicolor.	2.25	....	....	....	.75	.35
1809	15¢ "Letters Shape Opinions"	2.25	....	....	....	.75	.35
1810	15¢ red, white & blue . .	2.25	....	....	....	.75	.35

1813

1818, 1819, 1820

SCOTT NO.	DESCRIPTION	FIRST DAY COVERS SING	PL. BLK.	MINT SHEET	PLATE BLOCK	UNUSED F/NH	USED

1980-81 Coil Stamps, Perf. 10 Vertically

			LINE PR.		LINE PR.		
1811	1¢ Inkwell & Quill	2.25	2.75	....	.60	.20	.25
1813	3.5¢ Two Violins	2.25	2.75	....	1.40	.30	.25
1816	12¢ Torch (1981)	2.25	2.75	....	2.25	.50	.40
1818	(18¢) "B" definitive	2.50	3.50	55.00(100)	3.25	.70	.25
1819	(18¢) "B" definitive, from bklt pane	2.25	....	....	....	.70	.25
1819a	(18¢) "B" bklt pane of 8	4.00	....	....	....	5.25	....

1981 Coil Stamp Perf. Vertically

1820	(18¢) "B" definitive	2.25	2.75	....	2.00	.75	.25

1821

1822

1823

1825

1826

1824

1821	15¢ Frances Perkins . .	2.25	4.00	23.00(50)	2.50	.55	.25
1822	15¢ Dolley Madison . . .	2.25	4.00	72.00(150)	2.75	.60	.25
1823	15¢ Emily Bissell	2.25	4.00	23.00(50)	2.50	.60	.25
1824	15¢ Helen Keller & Anne Sullivan.	2.25	4.00	27.00(50)	3.00	.60	.25
1825	15¢ Veterans Administration	2.25	4.00	25.00(50)	2.50	.60	.25
1826	15¢ General Bernardo . deGalvez	2.25	4.00	25.00(50)	3.50	.60	.25

1827

1828

1829

1830

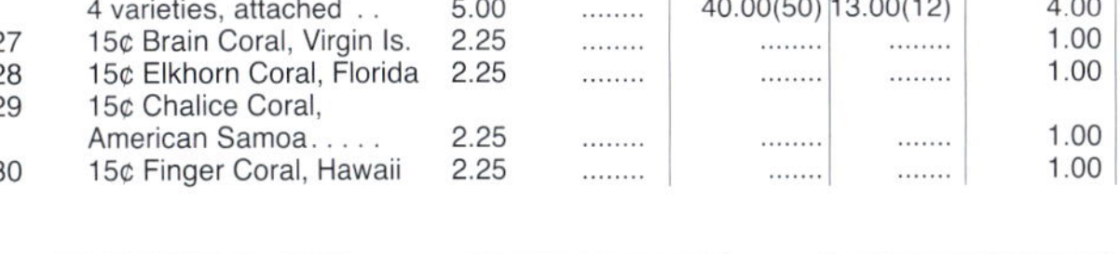

1827-30	Coral Reefs, 4 varieties, attached . .	5.00	....	40.00(50)	13.00(12)	4.00	2.75
1827	15¢ Brain Coral, Virgin Is.	2.25	....	....	....	1.00	.30
1828	15¢ Elkhorn Coral, Florida	2.25	....	....	....	1.00	.30
1829	15¢ Chalice Coral, American Samoa	2.25	....	....	....	1.00	.30
1830	15¢ Finger Coral, Hawaii	2.25	....	....	....	1.00	.30

1831

1832

1833

1831	15¢ Organized Labor . .	2.25	4.00	29.00(50)	10.00(12)	.65	.25
1832	15¢ Edith Wharton	2.25	4.00	25.00(50)	2.75	.65	.25
1833	15¢ Education	2.25	4.00	25.00(50)	3.75(6)	.65	.25

SCOTT NO.	DESCRIPTION	FIRST DAY COVERS SING	PL. BLK.	MINT SHEET	PLATE BLOCK	UNUSED F/NH	USED

1834 1835

1836 1837

SCOTT NO.	DESCRIPTION	FIRST DAY COVERS SING	PL. BLK.	MINT SHEET	PLATE BLOCK	UNUSED F/NH	USED
1834-37	American Folk Art, 4 varieties, attached . .	5.00	....	24.00(40)	9.00(10)	3.25	2.00
1834	15¢ Bella Bella Tribe . .	2.25	....	....	....	1.00	.25
1835	15¢ Chilkat Tlingit Tribe	2.25	....	....	....	1.00	.25
1836	15¢ Tlingit Tribe.	2.25	....	....	....	1.00	.25
1837	15¢ Bella Coola Tribe .	2.25	....	....	....	1.00	.25

1838 1839

1840 1841

SCOTT NO.	DESCRIPTION	FIRST DAY COVERS SING	PL. BLK.	MINT SHEET	PLATE BLOCK	UNUSED F/NH	USED
1838-41	American Architecture, 4 varieties, attached . .	4.00	5.00	25.00(40)	3.50	3.00	2.00
1838	15¢ Smithsonian Inst. .	2.25	....	....	....	1.00	.25
1839	15¢ Trinity Church	2.25	....	....	....	1.00	.25
1840	15¢ Penn Academy . . .	2.25	....	....	....	1.00	.25
1841	15¢ Lyndhurst	2.25	....	....	....	1.00	.25

1842

1843

SCOTT NO.	DESCRIPTION	FIRST DAY COVERS SING	PL. BLK.	MINT SHEET	PLATE BLOCK	UNUSED F/NH	USED
1842	15¢ Madonna.	2.25	4.00	22.50(50)	7.00(12)	.55	.25
1843	15¢ Christmas Wreath & Toy.	2.25	4.00	23.50(50)	12.00(20)	.55	.25

SE-TENANTS: Beginning with the 1964 Christmas issue (#1254-57), the United States has issued numerous Se-Tenant stamps covering a wide variety of subjects. Se-Tenants are issues where two or more different stamp designs are produced on the same sheet in pair, strip or block form. Mint stamps are usually collected in attached blocks, etc.; used are generally saved as single stamps.

SCOTT NO.	DESCRIPTION	FIRST DAY COVERS SING	PL. BLK.	MINT SHEET	PLATE BLOCK	UNUSED F/NH	USED

1844 1845 1846 1847 1848 1849 1850 1851 1852 1853 1854 1855 1856 1857 1858 1859 1860 1861 1862 1863 1864 1865 1866 1867 1868 1869

1980-85 GREAT AMERICANS

SCOTT NO.	DESCRIPTION	FIRST DAY COVERS SING	PL. BLK.	MINT SHEET	PLATE BLOCK	UNUSED F/NH	USED
1844-69	**1¢-50¢, 26 varieties, complete. . . . .**	....	....	....	....	**17.50**	**6.40**
1844	1¢ Dorothea Dix, 11.2, (1983)	2.25	4.00	13.00(100)	5.00(20)	.25	.25
1844c	1¢ Dorothea Dix, 10.9, small block tagging . . .	....	....	16.00(100)	5.00(20)	.25	.25
1844d	1¢ Dorothea Dix, 10.95 large block tagging . . .	....	....	17.00(100)	7.00(20)	.85	.45
1845	2¢ Igor Stravinsky (1982)	2.25	4.00	13.00(100)	1.25	.25	.25
1846	3¢ Henry Clay (1983) .	2.25	4.00	21.00(100)	2.25	.25	.25
1847	4¢ Carl Schurz (1983) .	2.25	4.00	22.00(100)	1.35	.25	.25
1848	5¢ Pearl Buck (1983). .	2.25	4.00	38.00(100)	3.00	.70	.25
1849	6¢ Walter Lippmann (1985)	2.25	4.00	23.00(100)	6.25(20)	.40	.25
1850	7¢ Abraham Baldwin (1985)	2.25	4.00	33.00(100)	7.75(20)	.60	.25
1851	8¢ Henry Knox (1985) .	2.25	4.00	29.00(100)	1.75	.30	.25
1852	9¢ Sylvanus Thayer (1985)	2.25	4.00	33.00(100)	8.00(20)	.40	.25
1853	10¢ Richard Russell (1984)	2.25	4.00	53.00(100)	15.00(20)	.60	.25
1854	11¢ Partridge (1985) . .	2.25	4.00	64.00(100)	4.00	.65	.25
1855	13¢ Crazy Horse (1982)	2.25	4.00	49.00(100)	3.00	.50	.40
1856	14¢ Sinclair Lewis (1985)	2.25	4.00	66.00(100)	17.00(20)	.80	.25
1857	17¢ Rachel Carson (1981)	2.25	4.00	53.00(100)	3.25	.60	.25
1858	18¢ George Mason (1981)	2.25	4.00	58.00(100)	3.75	.60	.25
1859	19¢ Sequoyah	2.25	4.00	65.00(100)	3.75	.75	.40
1860	20¢ Ralph Bunche (1982)	2.25	4.00	79.00(100)	4.00	.80	.25
1861	20¢ T. H. Gallaudet (1983)	2.25	4.00	80.00(100)	4.75	1.00	.25

SCOTT NO.	DESCRIPTION	FIRST DAY COVERS SING	FIRST DAY COVERS PL. BLK.	MINT SHEET	PLATE BLOCK	UNUSED F/NH	USED
1862	20¢ Harry Truman (1984)	2.25	4.00	65.00(100)	17.50(20)	.80	.25
1862a	same, Bullseye perf. .	....	....	....	6.50	.95	....
1863	22¢ J. Audubon (1985)	2.25	4.00	75.00(100)	18.00(20)	.80	.25
1863a	same, Bullseye perf. .	....	....	....	28.00	1.00	....
1864	30¢ F.C. Laubach (1984)	2.25	4.00	98.00(100)	24.00(20)	1.00	.25
1864a	same, Bullseye perf. .	....	....	....	7.00	1.25	....
1865	35¢ Charles Drew (1981)	2.25	4.50	140.00(100)	8.00	1.50	.40
1866	37¢ Robert Millikan (1982)	2.25	4.50	125.00(100)	7.00	1.20	.25
1867	39¢ Grenville Clark(1985)	2.25	4.50	125.00(100)	33.00(20)	1.50	.25
1867c	Large Block Tagging Perf 10.9	....	....	365.00(100)	85.00	4.25	0.70
1867d	Large Block Tagging Perf 11.2	....	....	200.00(100)	11.00	2.25	0.35
1868	40¢ Lillian Gilbreth (1984)	2.25	4.50	125.00(100)	31.00(20)	1.50	.25
1868a	same, Bullseye perf. .	....	....	170.00(100)	8.50	1.60	....
1869	50¢ Chester Nimitz (1985)	2.25	4.50	155.00(100)	13.00	1.80	.25
1869a	same, Bullseye perf. .	....	....	205.00(100)	13.00	2.25	0.35

1874

1875

1981 COMMEMORATIVES

SCOTT NO.	DESCRIPTION	FIRST DAY COVERS SING	FIRST DAY COVERS PL. BLK.	MINT SHEET	PLATE BLOCK	UNUSED F/NH	USED
1874/1945	**(1874-79, 1910-45) 42 varieties, complete**	....	....	....	....	**32.00**	**10.50**
1874	15¢ Everett Dirksen. . .	2.25	4.00	22.00(50)	2.50	.60	.25
1875	15¢ Whitney Moore Young	2.25	4.00	26.00(50)	3.00	.70	.25

1876 1877

1878 1879

SCOTT NO.	DESCRIPTION	FIRST DAY COVERS SING	FIRST DAY COVERS PL. BLK.	MINT SHEET	PLATE BLOCK	UNUSED F/NH	USED
1876-79	Flowers, 4 varieties, attached . .	5.00	6.00	30.00(48)	3.50	3.25	2.60
1876	18¢ Rose.	2.25	....	....	....	.80	.25
1877	18¢ Camellia	2.25	....	....	....	.80	.25
1878	18¢ Dahlia	2.25	....	....	....	.80	.25
1879	18¢ Lily	2.25	....	....	....	.80	.25

1880 1881 1882 1883 1884

1885 1886 1887 1888 1889

1981 WILDLIFE DEFINITIVES

SCOTT NO.	DESCRIPTION	FIRST DAY COVERS SING	FIRST DAY COVERS PL. BLK.	MINT SHEET	PLATE BLOCK	UNUSED F/NH	USED
1880-89	Wildlife, set of singles .	17.00	....	....	....	11.00	2.75
1880	18¢ Bighorned Sheep .	2.25	....	....	....	1.25	.30
1881	18¢ Puma	2.25	....	....	....	1.25	.30
1882	18¢ Seal	2.25	....	....	....	1.25	.30
1883	18¢ Bison.	2.25	....	....	....	1.25	.30
1884	18¢ Brown Bear.	2.25	....	....	....	1.25	.30
1885	18¢ Polar Bear.	2.25	....	....	....	1.25	.30
1886	18¢ Elk.	2.25	....	....	....	1.25	.30
1887	18¢ Moose.	2.25	....	....	....	1.25	.30
1888	18¢ White-tailed Deer .	2.25	....	....	....	1.25	.30
1889	18¢ Pronghorned Antelope	2.25	....	....	....	1.25	.30
1889a	Wildlife, bklt pane of 10	6.50	....	....	....	12.00	....

1890 1891 1892

1893 1894, 1895, 1896

1981 FLAG AND ANTHEM ISSUE

SCOTT NO.	DESCRIPTION	FIRST DAY COVERS SING	FIRST DAY COVERS PL. BLK.	MINT SHEET	PLATE BLOCK	UNUSED F/NH	USED
1890	18¢ "Waves of Grain" .	2.25	4.00	58.00(100)	15.00(20)	.75	.25
	1981 Coil Stamp Perf. 10 Vertically						
			PLATE# STRIP 3		**PLATE# STRIP 3**		
1891	18¢ "Shining Sea"	2.25	....	....	6.00	.80	.25
	same, plate strip of 5 . .	....	....	....	....	7.50	....
	1981						
1892	6¢ Stars, from bklt pane	2.25	....	....	....	1.20	1.00
1893	18¢ "Purple Mountains" from bklt pane	2.25	....	....	....	.75	.25
1892-93	6¢ & 18¢ as above, attached pair	....	....	....	....	2.75	2.00
1893a	2-1892, 6-1893 bklt pane of 8.	5.25	....	....	....	5.00	5.00
			PLATE BLOCK		**PLATE BLOCK**		
1894	20¢ Flag & Supreme Court	2.25	4.00	85.00(100)	22.50(20)	1.10	.25
			PLATE# STRIP 3		**PLATE# STRIP 3**		
1895	20¢ Flag & Supreme Court	2.25	5.00	....	5.25	.75	.25
	same, plate strip of 5 . .	....	....	....	....	6.00	....
1896	20¢ Flag & Supreme Court, from bklt pane	2.25	....	....	....	.80	.25
1896a	20¢ bklt pane of 6	3.50	....	....	....	4.25	....
1896b	20¢ bklt pane of 10 . . .	5.50	....	....	....	8.00	....

1897

1897A

1898

1898A

1899

Sleigh 1880s USA 5.2c Auth Nonprofit Org
1900

1901

1902

1903

1904

1905

1906

1907

1908

NOTE: #1898A—"Stagecoach 1890s" is 19-1/2 mm long.

1981-84 Perf. 10 Vertically TRANSPORTATION COILS

SCOTT NO.	DESCRIPTION	FIRST DAY COVERS SING	PLATE# STRIP 3	MINT SHEET	PLATE# STRIP 3	UNUSED F/NH	USED
1897-1908	1¢-20¢, 14 varieties, complete	29.50	....	....	....	4.50	3.10
1897	1¢ Omnibus (1983) . . .	2.25	17.50	....	.70	.25	.25
1897A	2¢ Locomotive (1982) .	2.25	25.00	....	.75	.25	.25
1898	3¢ Handcar (1983). . . .	2.25	25.00	....	1.05	.25	.25
1898A	4¢ Stagecoach (1982) .	2.25	22.50	....	1.80	.25	.25
1899	5¢ Motorcycle (1983). .	2.25	25.00	....	1.25	.25	.25
1900	5.2¢ Sleigh (1983)	2.25	37.50	....	5.00	.35	.25
1901	5.9¢ Bicycle (1982) . . .	2.25	37.50	....	5.00	.50	.40
1902	7.4¢ Baby Buggy (1984)	2.25	25.00	....	5.00	.50	.40
1903	9.3¢ Mail Wagon	2.25	42.50	....	4.00	.50	.25
1904	10.9¢ Hansom Cab (1982)	2.25	40.00	....	8.00	.50	.40
1905	11¢ Caboose (1984) . .	2.25	40.00	....	4.00	.50	.25
1906	17¢ Electric Car.	2.25	37.50	....	3.75	.70	.25
1907	18¢ Surrey.	2.25	55.00	....	4.00	.75	.25
1908	20¢ Fire Pumper	2.25	55.00	....	3.75	.75	.25

PRECANCELLED COILS

The following are for precancelled, unused, never hinged stamps. Stamps without gum sell for less.

SCOTT NO.		PL# STRIP 3	UNUSED
1895b	20¢ Supreme Court	45.00	1.00
1898Ab	4¢ Stagecoach.	5.00	.35
1900a	5.2¢ Sleigh.	6.00	.30
1901a	5.9¢ Bicycle	18.00	.45
1902a	7.4¢ Baby Buggy	6.00	.40
1903a	9.3¢ Mail Wagon	4.50	.40
1904a	10.9¢ Hansom Cab	18.00	.50
1905a	11¢ Caboose	4.50	.45
1906a	17¢ Electric Car	5.00	.55

PLATE NUMBER STRIPS OF 5

SCOTT NO.	UNUSED F/NH	SCOTT NO.	UNUSED F/NH	SCOTT NO.	UNUSED F/NH
1897	.95	1903	9.00	1901A	25.00
1897A	.85	1904	10.00	1902A	8.00
1898	1.20	1905	5.50	1903A	5.25
1898A	2.00	1906	4.00	1904A	30.00
1899	1.60	1907	5.25	1905A	5.25
1900	9.00	1908	5.00	1906A	7.00
1901	9.00	1898Ab	8.00		
1902	8.00	1900A	8.00		

1909

1983 EXPRESS MAIL BOOKLET SINGLE

SCOTT NO.	DESCRIPTION	SING	PL. BLK.	MINT SHEET	PLATE BLOCK	UNUSED F/NH	USED
1909	$9.35 Eagle & Moon . .	75.00	....	....	....	35.00	22.50
1909a	$9.35 bklt pane of 3 . . .	200.00	....	....	....	105.00	....

1910

1911

1981 COMMEMORATIVES (Continued)

SCOTT NO.	DESCRIPTION	SING	PL. BLK.	MINT SHEET	PLATE BLOCK	UNUSED F/NH	USED
1910	18¢ American Red Cross	2.25	4.00	27.75(50)	3.25	.60	.25
1911	18¢ Savings & Loans Assoc.	2.25	4.00	25.75(50)	3.00	.60	.25

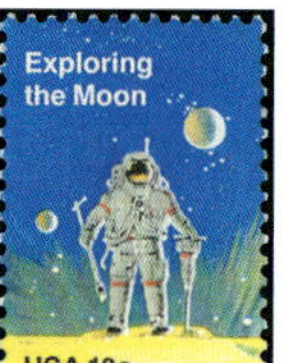

1912

1913

1914

1915

1916

1917

1918

1919

SCOTT NO.	DESCRIPTION	FIRST DAY COVERS SING	PL. BLK.	MINT SHEET	PLATE BLOCK	UNUSED F/NH	USED
1912-19	Space Achievement, 8 varieties, attached . .	6.00	9.00	32.00(48)	7.25(8)	5.75	5.50
1912-19	same, set of singles. . .	15.50	....	....	....	....	2.50
1912	18¢ Exploring the Moon	2.00	....	....	....	1.00	.35
1913	18¢ Releasing Boosters	2.00	....	....	....	.80	.35
1914	18¢ Cooling Electric Systems.	2.00	....	....	....	.80	.35
1915	18¢ Understanding the Sun	2.00	....	....	....	.80	.35
1916	18¢ Probing the Planets	2.00	....	....	....	.80	.35
1917	18¢ Shuttle and Rockets	2.00	....	....	....	.80	.35
1918	18¢ Landing.	2.00	....	....	....	.80	.35
1919	18¢ Comprehending the Universe	2.00	....	....	....	.80	.35

1920

SCOTT NO.	DESCRIPTION	SING	PL. BLK.	MINT SHEET	PLATE BLOCK	UNUSED F/NH	USED
1920	18¢ Professional Management	2.25	4.00	26.50(50)	3.25	.65	.25

1921

1922

1923

1924

SCOTT NO.	DESCRIPTION	SING	PL. BLK.	MINT SHEET	PLATE BLOCK	UNUSED F/NH	USED
1921-24	Wildlife Habitats, 4 varieties, attached . .	5.00	6.00	38.00(50)	5.00	4.00	3.00
1921	18¢ Blue Heron	2.25	....	....	....	.90	.25
1922	18¢ Badger	2.25	....	....	....	.90	.25
1923	18¢ Grizzly Bear	2.25	....	....	....	.90	.25
1924	18¢ Ruffled Grouse . . .	2.25	....	....	....	.90	.25

1925

1926

1927

SCOTT NO.	DESCRIPTION	FIRST DAY COVERS SING	FIRST DAY COVERS PL. BLK.	MINT SHEET	PLATE BLOCK	UNUSED F/NH	USED
1925	18¢ Disabled Persons .	2.25	4.00	26.00(50)	3.25	.75	.25
1926	18¢ Edna St. Vincent Millay	2.25	4.00	26.00(50)	3.25	.75	.25
1927	18¢ Alcoholism	4.50	7.00	60.00(50)	47.50(20)	.75	.25

1928 1929

1930 1931

SCOTT NO.	DESCRIPTION	FIRST DAY COVERS SING	FIRST DAY COVERS PL. BLK.	MINT SHEET	PLATE BLOCK	UNUSED F/NH	USED
1928-31	American Architecture, 4 varieties, attached . .	5.00	6.00	26.00(40)	4.25	3.75	3.00
1928	18¢ New York Univ. Library	2.25	....	....	....	1.00	.25
1929	18¢ Biltmore House. . .	2.25	....	....	....	1.00	.25
1930	18¢ Palace of the Arts .	2.25	....	....	....	1.00	.25
1931	18¢ National Farmers Bank	2.25	....	....	....	1.00	.25

1932

1933

SCOTT NO.	DESCRIPTION	FIRST DAY COVERS SING	FIRST DAY COVERS PL. BLK.	MINT SHEET	PLATE BLOCK	UNUSED F/NH	USED
1932	18¢ Babe Zaharias . . .	12.00	15.00	30.00(50)	4.50	.90	.30
1933	18¢ Bobby Jones.	15.00	18.00	39.00(50)	6.00	1.20	.30

1934

1935

1936

1937 1938

SCOTT NO.	DESCRIPTION	FIRST DAY COVERS SING	FIRST DAY COVERS PL. BLK.	MINT SHEET	PLATE BLOCK	UNUSED F/NH	USED
1934	18¢ Coming Through the Rye	2.25	4.50	32.00(50)	3.75	.80	.25
1935	18¢ James Hoban	2.25	4.00	29.00(50)	3.25	.70	.25
1936	20¢ James Hoban	2.25	4.00	33.00(50)	3.25	.70	.30
1937-38	Yorktown/Virginia Capes, 2 varieties, attached . .	2.00	4.00	34.00(50)	3.50	1.75	1.25
1937	18¢ Yorktown.	2.25	....	....	....	1.00	.30
1938	18¢ Virginia Capes . . .	2.25	....	....	....	1.00	.30

1939

1940

1941

SCOTT NO.	DESCRIPTION	FIRST DAY COVERS SING	FIRST DAY COVERS PL. BLK.	MINT SHEET	PLATE BLOCK	UNUSED F/NH	USED
1939	(20¢) Madonna & Child	2.25	4.00	54.00(100)	3.25	.75	.25
1940	(20¢) Christmas Toy . .	2.25	4.00	28.00(50)	3.25	.75	.25
1941	20¢ John Hanson	2.25	4.00	29.50(50)	3.25	.75	.25

1943

1942 1944 1945

SCOTT NO.	DESCRIPTION	FIRST DAY COVERS SING	FIRST DAY COVERS PL. BLK.	MINT SHEET	PLATE BLOCK	UNUSED F/NH	USED
1942-45	Desert Plants, 4 varieties, attached . .	5.00	6.00	29.00(40)	4.00	3.75	3.00
1942	20¢ Barrel Cactus	2.25	....	....	....	1.00	.25
1943	20¢ Agave	2.25	....	....	....	1.00	.25
1944	20¢ Beavertail Cactus .	2.25	....	....	....	1.00	.25
1945	20¢ Saguaro	2.25	....	....	....	1.00	.25

1946, 1947, 1948

1949

1981-1982 Regular Issues

SCOTT NO.	DESCRIPTION	FIRST DAY COVERS SING	FIRST DAY COVERS PL. BLK.	MINT SHEET	PLATE BLOCK	UNUSED F/NH	USED
1946	(20¢) "C" Eagle, 11x10½	2.25	4.00	65.00(100)	3.75	.75	.25
			LINE PAIR		LINE PAIR		
1947	(20¢) "C" Eagle, coil. . .	2.25	2.75	....	2.75	.95	.25
1948	(20¢) "C" Eagle, from pane	2.25	....	....	....	.95	.25
1948a	same, bklt pane of 10 .	6.00	....	....	....	8.00	....
1949	20¢ Bighorned Sheep, blue, from bklt pane (1982) .	2.25	....	....	....	.95	.25
1949a	same, bklt pane of 10 .	6.00	....	....	....	8.50	....
1949c	Type II, from bklt pane.	....	....	....	....	2.25	.40
1949d	same, bklt pane of 10 .	....	....	....	....	20.00	....

1950 1951

1952

1982 COMMEMORATIVES

SCOTT NO.	DESCRIPTION	FIRST DAY COVERS SING	FIRST DAY COVERS PL. BLK.	MINT SHEET	PLATE BLOCK	UNUSED F/NH	USED
1950/2030	(1950-52, 2003-04, 2006-30) 30 varieties	....	....	....	....	26.00	7.00
1950	20¢ Franklin D. Roosevelt	2.25	4.00	31.00(48)	3.25	.80	.25
1951	20¢ LOVE, perf. 11 . . .	1.85	4.25	31.00(50)	3.25	.65	.25
1951a	same, perf. 11x 10½ . .	....	....	48.00(50)	5.50	1.10	.75

NOTE: **Perforations will be mixed on Used #1951.**

SCOTT NO.	DESCRIPTION	FIRST DAY COVERS SING	FIRST DAY COVERS PL. BLK.	MINT SHEET	PLATE BLOCK	UNUSED F/NH	USED
1952	20¢ George Washington	2.25	4.00	30.00(50)	3.75	.80	.25

1982 STATE BIRDS AND FLOWERS

1953

1973

1953	*Alabama*	**1978**	*Montana*
1954	*Alaska*	**1979**	*Nebraska*
1955	*Arizona*	**1980**	*Nevada*
1956	*Arkansas*	**1981**	*New Hampshire*
1957	*California*	**1982**	*New Jersey*
1958	*Colorado*	**1983**	*New Mexico*
1959	*Connecticut*	**1984**	*New York*
1960	*Delaware*	**1985**	*North Carolina*
1961	*Florida*	**1986**	*North Dakota*
1962	*Georgia*	**1987**	*Ohio*
1963	*Hawaii*	**1988**	*Oklahoma*
1964	*Idaho*	**1989**	*Oregon*
1965	*Illinois*	**1990**	*Pennsylvania*
1966	*Indiana*	**1991**	*Rhode Island*
1967	*Iowa*	**1992**	*South Carolina*
1968	*Kansas*	**1993**	*South Dakota*
1969	*Kentucky*	**1994**	*Tennessee*
1970	*Louisiana*	**1995**	*Texas*
1971	*Maine*	**1996**	*Utah*
1972	*Maryland*	**1997**	*Vermont*
1973	*Massachusetts*	**1998**	*Virginia*
1974	*Michigan*	**1999**	*Washington*
1975	*Minnesota*	**2000**	*West Virginia*
1976	*Mississippi*	**2001**	*Wisconsin*
1977	*Missouri*	**2002**	*Wyoming*

1966

2002

Perf. 10½ x 11

SCOTT NO.	DESCRIPTION	FIRST DAY COVERS SING	FIRST DAY COVERS PL. BLK.	MINT SHEET	PLATE BLOCK	UNUSED F/NH	USED
1953-2002	20¢, 50 varieties, attached		....	38.00(50)	....	38.00	....
	set of singles.	86.00	....	....	....	40.00	25.00
	singles of above	2.00	....	....	....	1.25	.65
1953a-2002a	same, perf. 11.	....	....	48.00(50)	....	48.00	....
	singles of above	....	....	....	....	50.00	

NOTE: **Used singles will not be sorted by perf. sizes.**

2003

2004

2005

SCOTT NO.	DESCRIPTION	FIRST DAY COVERS SING	FIRST DAY COVERS PL. BLK.	MINT SHEET	PLATE BLOCK	UNUSED F/NH	USED
2003	20¢ USA/Netherlands .	2.25	4.00	32.00(50)	17.00(20)	.70	.25
2004	20¢ Library of Congress	2.25	4.00	49.00(50)	5.00	1.25	.25
			PLATE# STRIP 3		**PLATE# STRIP 3**		
2005	20¢ Consumer Education, Coil	2.25	60.00	....	18.00	1.20	.25
	same, plate strips of 5 .	....	....	....	....	50.00	....

2006 2007

2008 2009

SCOTT NO.	DESCRIPTION	FIRST DAY COVERS SING	FIRST DAY COVERS PL. BLK.	MINT SHEET	PLATE BLOCK	UNUSED F/NH	USED
2006-09	World's Fair, 4 varieties, attached . .	5.00	6.00	36.00(50)	4.50	4.00	2.00
2006	20¢ Solar Energy.	2.25	....	....	....	1.00	.25
2007	20¢ Synthetic Fuels . .	2.25	....	....	....	1.00	.25
2008	20¢ Breeder Reactor . .	2.25	....	....	....	1.00	.25
2009	20¢ Fossil Fuels	2.25	....	....	....	1.00	.25

2010

2011

2012

SCOTT NO.	DESCRIPTION	FIRST DAY COVERS SING	FIRST DAY COVERS PL. BLK.	MINT SHEET	PLATE BLOCK	UNUSED F/NH	USED
2010	20¢ Horatio Alger.	2.25	4.00	29.00(50)	3.25	.70	.25
2011	20¢ Aging Together . . .	2.25	4.00	29.00(50)	3.25	.70	.25
2012	20¢ Barrymores.	2.25	4.00	30.00(50)	3.25	.70	.25

2013

2014

2015

SCOTT NO.	DESCRIPTION	FIRST DAY COVERS SING	FIRST DAY COVERS PL. BLK.	MINT SHEET	PLATE BLOCK	UNUSED F/NH	USED
2013	20¢ Dr. Mary Walker . .	2.25	4.00	29.50(50)	3.25	.70	.25
2014	20¢ Peace Garden . . .	2.25	4.00	48.00(50)	6.00	1.20	.25
2015	20¢ America's Libraries	2.25	4.00	29.00(50)	3.25	.60	.25

2016

2017

2018

SCOTT NO.	DESCRIPTION	FIRST DAY COVERS SING	FIRST DAY COVERS PL. BLK.	MINT SHEET	PLATE BLOCK	UNUSED F/NH	USED
2016	20¢ Jackie Robinson . .	7.00	13.50	90.00(50)	11.00	2.50	.25
2017	20¢ Touro Synagogue .	3.00	4.00	40.00(50)	18.00(20)	.85	.25
2018	20¢ Wolf Trap Farm. . .	2.25	4.00	29.00(50)	3.25	.75	.25

PLATE BLOCKS: are portions of a sheet of stamps adjacent to the number(s) indicating the printing plate number used to produce that sheet. Flat plate issues are usually collected in plate blocks of six (number opposite middle stamp) while rotary issues are normally corner blocks of four.

2019 2020

2021 2022

SCOTT NO.	DESCRIPTION	FIRST DAY COVERS SING	FIRST DAY COVERS PL. BLK.	MINT SHEET	PLATE BLOCK	UNUSED F/NH	USED
2019-22	American Architecture, 4 varieties, attached . .	5.00	6.00	32.00(40)	4.50	4.00	3.25
2019	20¢ Fallingwater Mill Run	2.25	....	....	....	1.25	.25
2020	20¢ Illinois Inst. Tech . .	2.25	....	....	....	1.25	.25
2021	20¢ Gropius House . . .	2.25	....	....	....	1.25	.25
2022	20¢ Dulles Airport	2.25	....	....	....	1.25	.25

2023

2024

2025

2026

SCOTT NO.	DESCRIPTION	FIRST DAY COVERS SING	FIRST DAY COVERS PL. BLK.	MINT SHEET	PLATE BLOCK	UNUSED F/NH	USED
2023	20¢ St. Francis of Assisi	2.25	4.00	30.00(50)	3.25	.75	.25
2024	20¢ Ponce de Leon . . .	2.25	4.00	39.00(50)	20.00(20)	1.00	.25
2025	13¢ Kitten & Puppy, Christmas	2.25	4.00	25.00(50)	2.50	.60	.25
2026	20¢ Madonna & Child, Christmas	2.25	4.00	30.00(50)	17.00(20)	.75	.25

2027 2028

2029 2030

SCOTT NO.	DESCRIPTION	FIRST DAY COVERS SING	FIRST DAY COVERS PL. BLK.	MINT SHEET	PLATE BLOCK	UNUSED F/NH	USED
2027-30	Winter Scenes, Christmas, 4 varieties, attached . .	4.00	5.00	38.00(50)	5.00	4.25	3.50
2027	20¢ Sledding	2.25	....	....	....	1.25	.25
2028	20¢ Snowman	2.25	....	....	....	1.25	.25
2029	20¢ Skating	2.25	....	....	....	1.25	.25
2030	20¢ Decorating	2.25	....	....	....	1.25	.25

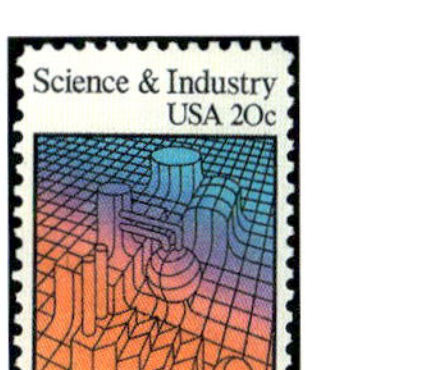

2031

1983 COMMEMORATIVES

SCOTT NO.	DESCRIPTION	FIRST DAY COVERS SING	FIRST DAY COVERS PL. BLK.	MINT SHEET	PLATE BLOCK	UNUSED F/NH	USED
2031-65	**13¢-20¢, 35 varieties, complete. . . . .**	....	....	....	....	**28.40**	**7.70**
2031	20¢ Science & Industry	2.25	4.00	29.00(50)	3.25	.75	.25

2033

2032 2034 2035

SCOTT NO.	DESCRIPTION	FIRST DAY COVERS SING	FIRST DAY COVERS PL. BLK.	MINT SHEET	PLATE BLOCK	UNUSED F/NH	USED
2032-35	20¢ Ballooning, 4 varieties, attached . .	5.00	6.00	33.00(40)	4.00	3.55	2.50
2032	20¢ Intrepid	2.25	....	....	....	1.10	.25
2033	20¢ Red, white, & blue balloon.	2.25	....	....	....	1.10	.25
2034	20¢ Yellow, gold & green balloon.	2.25	....	....	....	1.10	.25
2035	20¢ Explorer II	2.25	....	....	....	1.10	.25

2036

2037

2038

SCOTT NO.	DESCRIPTION	FIRST DAY COVERS SING	FIRST DAY COVERS PL. BLK.	MINT SHEET	PLATE BLOCK	UNUSED F/NH	USED
2036	20¢ USA/Sweden	2.25	4.00	29.00(50)	3.25	.70	.25
2037	20¢ Civilian Conservation Corps.	2.25	4.00	29.00(50)	3.25	.70	.25
2038	20¢ Joseph Priestley . .	2.25	4.00	29.00(50)	3.25	.70	.25

2039

2040

2041

SCOTT NO.	DESCRIPTION	FIRST DAY COVERS SING	FIRST DAY COVERS PL. BLK.	MINT SHEET	PLATE BLOCK	UNUSED F/NH	USED
2039	20¢ Volunteerism.	2.25	4.00	34.50(50)	18.00(20)	.70	.25
2040	20¢ German Immigrants	2.25	4.00	29.00(50)	3.00	.70	.25
2041	20¢ Brooklyn Bridge . .	3.00	5.00	30.00(50)	3.00	.70	.25

SCOTT NO.	DESCRIPTION	FIRST DAY COVERS SING	FIRST DAY COVERS PL. BLK.	MINT SHEET	PLATE BLOCK	UNUSED F/NH	USED

2042

2043

2044

SCOTT NO.	DESCRIPTION	FIRST DAY COVERS SING	FIRST DAY COVERS PL. BLK.	MINT SHEET	PLATE BLOCK	UNUSED F/NH	USED
2042	20¢ Tennessee Valley Authority	2.25	4.00	30.00(50)	16.00(20)	.70	.25
2043	20¢ Physical Fitness . .	2.25	4.00	30.00(50)	16.00(20)	.70	.25
2044	20¢ Scott Joplin.	2.25	4.00	35.00(50)	4.00	.75	.25

2045

2046

2047

SCOTT NO.	DESCRIPTION	FIRST DAY COVERS SING	FIRST DAY COVERS PL. BLK.	MINT SHEET	PLATE BLOCK	UNUSED F/NH	USED
2045	20¢ Medal of Honor. . .	6.00	8.00	35.00(40)	4.50	1.00	.25
2046	20¢ Babe Ruth.	8.00	16.00	75.00(50)	10.00	2.00	.25
2047	20¢ Nathaniel Hawthorne	2.25	4.00	32.50(50)	4.00	.75	.25

2048 2049

2050 2051

SCOTT NO.	DESCRIPTION	FIRST DAY COVERS SING	FIRST DAY COVERS PL. BLK.	MINT SHEET	PLATE BLOCK	UNUSED F/NH	USED
2048-51	Olympics, 4 varieties, attached . .	5.00	6.00	29.00(50)	3.50	3.00	2.75
2048	13¢ Discus.	2.25	....	....	....	1.00	.30
2049	13¢ High Jump	2.25	....	....	....	1.00	.30
2050	13¢ Archery	2.25	....	....	....	1.00	.30
2051	13¢ Boxing.	2.25	....	....	....	1.00	.30

2052

2053

2054

SCOTT NO.	DESCRIPTION	FIRST DAY COVERS SING	FIRST DAY COVERS PL. BLK.	MINT SHEET	PLATE BLOCK	UNUSED F/NH	USED
2052	20¢ Treaty of Paris . . .	2.25	4.00	24.00(40)	3.25	.75	.25
2053	20¢ Civil Service	2.25	4.00	32.00(50)	18.00(20)	.75	.25
2054	20¢ Metropolitan Opera	2.25	4.00	30.00(50)	3.25	.75	.25

MINT SHEETS: From 1935 to date, we list prices for standard size Mint Sheets in Fine, Never Hinged condition. The number of stamps in each sheet is noted in ( ).

SCOTT NO.	DESCRIPTION	FIRST DAY COVERS SING	FIRST DAY COVERS PL. BLK.	MINT SHEET	PLATE BLOCK	UNUSED F/NH	USED

2055 2056

2057 2058

SCOTT NO.	DESCRIPTION	FIRST DAY COVERS SING	FIRST DAY COVERS PL. BLK.	MINT SHEET	PLATE BLOCK	UNUSED F/NH	USED
2055-58	Inventors, 4 varieties, attached . .	5.00	6.00	38.00(50)	4.50	4.00	3.00
2055	20¢ Charles Steinmetz	2.25	....	....	....	1.35	.25
2056	20¢ Edwin Armstrong .	2.25	....	....	....	1.35	.25
2057	20¢ Nikola Tesla	2.25	....	....	....	1.35	.25
2058	20¢ Philo T. Farnsworth	2.25	....	....	....	1.35	.25

2059 2060

2061 2062

SCOTT NO.	DESCRIPTION	FIRST DAY COVERS SING	FIRST DAY COVERS PL. BLK.	MINT SHEET	PLATE BLOCK	UNUSED F/NH	USED
2059-62	Streetcars, 4 varieties, attached . .	5.00	6.00	40.00(50)	4.50	4.00	3.00
2059	20¢ First Streetcar. . . .	2.25	....	....	....	1.25	.25
2060	20¢ Electric Trolley . . .	2.25	....	....	....	1.25	.25
2061	20¢ "Bobtail"	2.25	....	....	....	1.25	.25
2062	20¢ St. Charles Streetcar	2.25	....	....	....	1.25	.25

2063

2064

SCOTT NO.	DESCRIPTION	FIRST DAY COVERS SING	FIRST DAY COVERS PL. BLK.	MINT SHEET	PLATE BLOCK	UNUSED F/NH	USED
2063	20¢ Madonna.	2.25	4.00	32.00(50)	3.75	.75	.25
2064	20¢ Santa Claus	2.25	4.00	32.00(50)	16.00(20)	.85	.25

2065

SCOTT NO.	DESCRIPTION	FIRST DAY COVERS SING	FIRST DAY COVERS PL. BLK.	MINT SHEET	PLATE BLOCK	UNUSED F/NH	USED
2065	20¢ Martin Luther	2.25	4.00	33.00(50)	3.75	.85	.25

2066

1984 COMMEMORATIVES

SCOTT NO.	DESCRIPTION	FIRST DAY COVERS SING	PL. BLK.	MINT SHEET	PLATE BLOCK	UNUSED F/NH	USED
2066-2109	44 varieties, complete	....	....	....	....	37.50	9.30
2066	20¢ Alaska Statehood .	2.25	4.00	32.00(50)	3.25	.70	.25

2067

2068

2069

2070

SCOTT NO.	DESCRIPTION	FIRST DAY COVERS SING	PL. BLK.	MINT SHEET	PLATE BLOCK	UNUSED F/NH	USED
2067-70	Winter Olympics, 4 varieties, attached . .	5.00	6.00	36.00(50)	4.50	3.50	3.00
2067	20¢ Ice Dancing.	2.25	....	....	....	1.10	.30
2068	20¢ Downhill Skiing . . .	2.25	....	....	....	1.10	.30
2069	20¢ Cross Country Skiing	2.25	....	....	....	1.10	.30
2070	20¢ Hockey	2.25	....	....	....	1.10	.30

2071

2072

2073

2074

SCOTT NO.	DESCRIPTION	FIRST DAY COVERS SING	PL. BLK.	MINT SHEET	PLATE BLOCK	UNUSED F/NH	USED
2071	20¢ Federal Deposit Insurance Corporation	2.25	4.00	29.00(50)	3.25	.75	.25
2072	20¢ Love	1.95	4.00	29.00(50)	16.50(20)	.75	.25
2073	20¢ Carter G. Woodson	3.00	4.00	32.00(50)	3.50	.75	.25
2074	20¢ Conservatiion	2.25	4.00	29.00(50)	3.25	.75	.25

2076

2077

2075

2078

2079

SCOTT NO.	DESCRIPTION	FIRST DAY COVERS SING	PL. BLK.	MINT SHEET	PLATE BLOCK	UNUSED F/NH	USED
2075	20¢ Credit Union	1.95	4.50	29.00(50)	3.25	.70	.25
2076-79	Orchids, 4 varieties, attd.	4.00	5.00	34.00(48)	3.75	3.25	2.75
2076	20¢ Wildpink	2.25	....	....	....	.95	.25
2077	20¢ Lady's-slipper	2.25	....	....	....	.95	.25
2078	20¢ Spreading Pogonia	2.25	....	....	....	.95	.25
2079	20¢ Pacific Calypso . . .	2.25	....	....	....	.95	.25

2080

2081

SCOTT NO.	DESCRIPTION	FIRST DAY COVERS SING	PL. BLK.	MINT SHEET	PLATE BLOCK	UNUSED F/NH	USED
2080	20¢ Hawaii Statehood .	2.25	4.00	32.00(50)	3.50	.75	.25
2081	20¢ National Archives .	2.25	4.00	34.00(50)	3.75	.85	.25

2082

2083

2084

2085

SCOTT NO.	DESCRIPTION	FIRST DAY COVERS SING	PL. BLK.	MINT SHEET	PLATE BLOCK	UNUSED F/NH	USED
2082-85	Olympics, 4 varieties, attached.	5.00	6.00	37.00(50)	5.00	4.50	4.00
2082	20¢ Men's Diving.	2.25	....	....	....	1.20	.25
2083	20¢ Long Jump	2.25	....	....	....	1.20	.25
2084	20¢ Wrestling.	2.25	....	....	....	1.20	.25
2085	20¢ Women's Kayak . .	2.25	....	....	....	1.20	.25

2086

2087

2088

SCOTT NO.	DESCRIPTION	FIRST DAY COVERS SING	PL. BLK.	MINT SHEET	PLATE BLOCK	UNUSED F/NH	USED
2086	20¢ Louisiana Exposition	2.25	4.00	36.00(40)	4.50	.95	.25
2087	20¢ Health Research. .	2.25	4.00	32.00(50)	3.50	.70	.25
2088	20¢ Douglas Fairbanks	2.25	4.00	49.00(50)	26.00(20)	1.30	.30

2089

2090

2091

SCOTT NO.	DESCRIPTION	FIRST DAY COVERS SING	PL. BLK.	MINT SHEET	PLATE BLOCK	UNUSED F/NH	USED
2089	20¢ Jim Thorpe	4.50	8.00	66.00(50)	8.50	2.00	.30
2090	20¢ John McCormack .	3.00	4.00	30.00(50)	3.25	.65	.25
2091	20¢ St. Lawrence Seaway	3.00	4.00	30.00(50)	3.25	.65	.25

SE-TENANTS: Beginning with the 1964 Christmas issue (#1254-57), the United States has issued numerous Se-Tenant stamps covering a wide variety of subjects. Se-Tenants are issues where two or more different stamp designs are produced on the same sheet in pair, strip or block form. Mint stamps are usually collected in attached blocks, etc.—Used are generally saved as single stamps. Our Se-Tenant prices follow in this collecting pattern.

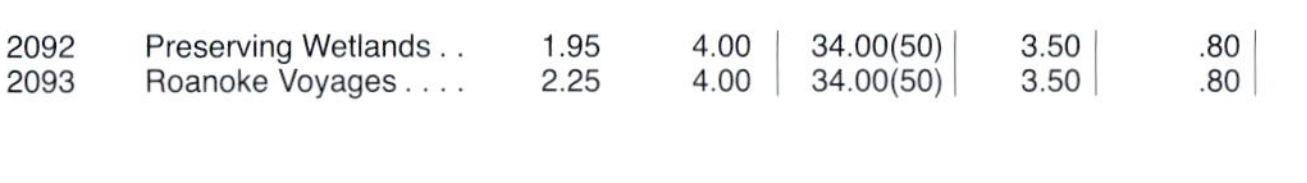

2092 2093

SCOTT NO.	DESCRIPTION	FIRST DAY COVERS SING	FIRST DAY COVERS PL. BLK.	MINT SHEET	PLATE BLOCK	UNUSED F/NH	USED
2092	Preserving Wetlands . .	1.95	4.00	34.00(50)	3.50	.80	.25
2093	Roanoke Voyages	2.25	4.00	34.00(50)	3.50	.80	.25

2094 2095 2096 2097

SCOTT NO.	DESCRIPTION	FIRST DAY COVERS SING	FIRST DAY COVERS PL. BLK.	MINT SHEET	PLATE BLOCK	UNUSED F/NH	USED
2094	20¢ Herman Melville .	2.25	4.00	29.00(50)	3.25	.70	.25
2095	20¢ Horace Moses . .	2.25	4.00	31.00(50)	19.00(20)	.90	.25
2096	20¢ Smokey Bear . . .	2.25	4.00	34.00(50)	3.50	.90	.25
2097	20¢ Roberto Clemente	12.00	20.00	95.00(50)	10.00	2.00	.50

2098 2099

2100 2101

SCOTT NO.	DESCRIPTION	FIRST DAY COVERS SING	FIRST DAY COVERS PL. BLK.	MINT SHEET	PLATE BLOCK	UNUSED F/NH	USED
2098-2101	American Dogs, 4 varieties, attached .	5.00	6.00	32.50(40)	4.75	4.25	3.75
2098	20¢ Beagle, Boston Terrier	2.25	....	....	....	1.25	.25
2099	20¢ Chesapeake Bay Retriever, Cocker Spaniel	2.25	....	....	....	1.25	.25
2100	20¢ Alaskan Malamute, Collie	2.25	....	....	....	1.25	.25
2101	20¢ Black & Tan Coonhound, American Foxhound . .	2.25	....	....	....	1.25	.25

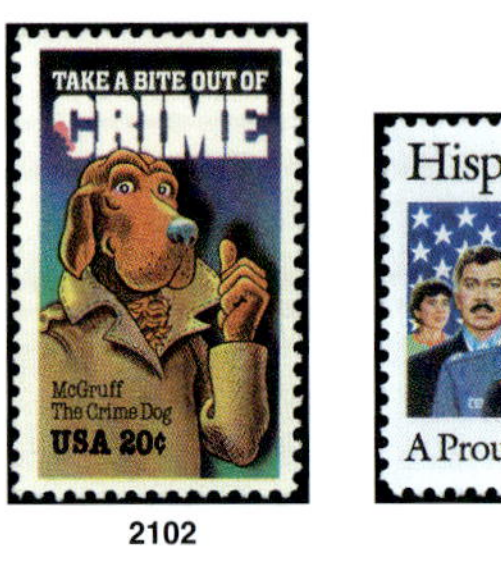

2102 2103 2104

SCOTT NO.	DESCRIPTION	FIRST DAY COVERS SING	FIRST DAY COVERS PL. BLK.	MINT SHEET	PLATE BLOCK	UNUSED F/NH	USED
2102	20¢ Crime Prevention .	2.25	4.00	29.00(50)	3.25	.60	.25
2103	20¢ Hispanic Americans	3.00	4.00	28.00(40)	4.00	.60	.25
2104	20¢ Family Unity	2.25	4.00	36.00(50)	20.00(20)	1.00	.25

2105 2106 2107

SCOTT NO.	DESCRIPTION	FIRST DAY COVERS SING	FIRST DAY COVERS PL. BLK.	MINT SHEET	PLATE BLOCK	UNUSED F/NH	USED
2105	20¢ Eleanor Roosevelt	2.25	4.00	28.00(40)	3.25	.70	.25
2106	20¢ Nation of Readers	2.25	4.00	33.00(50)	4.00	1.10	.30
2107	20¢ Madonna & Child .	2.25	4.00	29.00(50)	3.25	.60	.25

2108 2109

SCOTT NO.	DESCRIPTION	FIRST DAY COVERS SING	FIRST DAY COVERS PL. BLK.	MINT SHEET	PLATE BLOCK	UNUSED F/NH	USED
2108	20¢ Santa Claus	1.35	4.00	30.00(50)	3.25	.60	.30
2109	20¢ Vietnam Veterans .	5.00	4.00	32.00(40)	4.65	1.00	.30

2110

1985 COMMEMORATIVES

SCOTT NO.	DESCRIPTION	FIRST DAY COVERS SING	FIRST DAY COVERS PL. BLK.	MINT SHEET	PLATE BLOCK	UNUSED F/NH	USED
2110/2166	**(2110, 2137-47, 2152-66) 27 varieties . . . .**	....	....	....	....	**33.50**	**7.50**
2110	22¢ Jerome Kern	2.25	4.00	32.00(50)	3.25	.70	.25

2111-2113 2114, 2115 2116

1985 REGULAR ISSUES

SCOTT NO.	DESCRIPTION	FIRST DAY COVERS SING	FIRST DAY COVERS PL. BLK.	MINT SHEET	PLATE BLOCK	UNUSED F/NH	USED
2111	(22¢) "D" Eagle	2.25	4.00	72.00(100)	25.00(20)	.90	.25
			PLATE# STRIP 3		PLATE# STRIP 3		
2112	(22¢) "D" Eagle, coil. . .	2.25	21.00	....	6.75	.75	.25
	same, plate strip of 5 . . .	....	....	....	....	10.00	....
2113	(22¢) "D" Eagle from bklt pane	2.25	....	....	....	1.25	.25
2113a	same, bklt pane of 10 .	7.50	....	....	....	10.00	....
			PLATE BLOCK		PLATE BLOCK		
2114	22¢ Flag over Capitol	2.25	4.00	75.00(100)	4.00	.80	.25
			PLATE# STRIP 3		PLATE# STRIP 3		
2115	22¢ Flag over Capitol, coil	2.25	27.50	....	3.75	.85	.25
	same, plate strip of 5 . . .	....	....	....	....	5.50	....
2115a	same, narrow block tagging	....	....	....	4.50	.85	.25
	same, plate strip of 5 . . .	....	....	....	....	5.50	....
2115b	same, wide & tall block tagging	....	....	....	65.00	2.00	....
	same, plate strip of 5 . . .	....	....	....	....	85.00	....
2115c	22¢ Flag over Capitol "T" Coil (1985-87)	2.90	....	....	4.50	.90	.75
	same, plate strip of 5 . . .	....	....	....	....	6.00	....
2116	22¢ Flag over Capitol from booklet pane	2.25	....	....	....	1.00	.25
2116a	same, bklt pane of 5 . . .	2.90	....	....	....	5.00	....

SCOTT NO.	DESCRIPTION	FIRST DAY COVERS SING	PL. BLK.	MINT SHEET	PLATE BLOCK	UNUSED F/NH	USED

2117

2118

2119

2120

2121

1985 SEASHELLS FROM BOOKLET PANE

SCOTT NO.	DESCRIPTION	FIRST DAY COVERS SING	PL. BLK.	MINT SHEET	PLATE BLOCK	UNUSED F/NH	USED
2117-21	Shells, strip of 5, attached	3.00	....	....	....	4.25	4.00
2117	22¢ Frilled Dogwinkle .	2.25	....	....	....	.90	.25
2118	22¢ Reticulated Helmet	2.25	....	....	....	.90	.25
2119	22¢ New England Neptune	2.25	....	....	....	.90	.25
2120	22¢ Calico Scallop. . . .	2.25	....	....	....	.90	.25
2121	22¢ Lightning Whelk . .	2.25	....	....	....	.90	.25
2121a	22¢ Seashells, bklt pane of 10.	7.50	....	....	....	8.00	6.50

2122

1985 EXPRESS MAIL STAMP FROM BOOKLET PANE

SCOTT NO.	DESCRIPTION	FIRST DAY COVERS SING	PL. BLK.	MINT SHEET	PLATE BLOCK	UNUSED F/NH	USED
2122	$10.75 Eagle & Moon .	65.00	....	....	....	40.00	15.00
2122a	same, bklt pane of 3 . .	160.00	....	....	....	115.00	....
2122b	Type II, from bklt pane .	....	....	....	....	45.00	20.00
2122c	same, bklt pane of 3 . .	....	....	....	....	135.00	....

2123

2124

2125

2126

2127

2128

2129

2130

2131

2132

2133

2134

2135

2136

TRANSPORTATION COILS 1985-87 PERF. 10

SCOTT NO.	DESCRIPTION	FIRST DAY COVERS SING	PLATE# STRIP 3	MINT SHEET	PLATE# STRIP 3	UNUSED F/NH	USED
2123	3.4¢ School Bus	2.00	11.50	....	1.50	.35	.30
2124	4.9¢ Buckboard	2.00	14.00	....	1.25	.35	.30
2125	5.5¢ Star Route Truck (1986)	2.00	15.00	....	2.50	.35	.30
2126	6¢ Tricycle	2.00	14.00	....	3.25	.35	.30
2127	7.1¢ Tractor (1987) . .	2.00	15.00	....	3.15	.35	.30
2128	8.3¢ Ambulance.	2.00	14.00	....	1.95	.35	.30
2129	8.5¢ Tow Truck (1987)	2.00	12.50	....	4.00	.35	.30
2130	10.1¢ Oil Wagon	2.00	12.50	....	8.00	1.00	.30
2131	11¢ Stutz Bearcat . . .	2.00	18.00	....	2.75	.40	.30
2132	12¢ Stanley Steamer.	2.00	15.00	....	3.00	.60	.30
2133	12.5¢ Pushcart	2.00	15.00	....	4.75	.40	.30
2134	14¢ Iceboat	2.00	15.00	....	2.50	.40	.30
2135	17¢ Dog Sled (1986) .	2.00	12.50	....	5.75	.70	.30
2136	25¢ Bread Wagon (1986)	2.00	15.00	....	4.00	.80	.25

PRECANCELLED COILS

The following are for precancelled, unused, never hinged stamps. Stamps without gum sell for less.

SCOTT NO.		PL# STRIP 3	UNUSED
2123a	3.4¢ School Bus.	7.50	.35
2124a	4.9¢ Buckboard	2.35	.35
2125a	5.5¢ Star Route Truck	2.50	.35
2126a	6¢ Tricycle	2.75	.35
2127a	7.1¢ Tractor	4.00	.35
2127b	7.1¢ Tractor, precancel (1989).	3.25	.35
2128a	8.3¢ Ambulance.	2.50	.35
2129a	8.5¢ Tow Truck.	4.25	.35
2130a	10.1¢ Oil Wagon	3.75	.35
2130b	10.1¢ Oil Wagon, red precancel (1988)	4.00	.35
2132a	12¢ Stanley Steamer	4.00	.60
2132b	12¢ Stanley Steamer "B" Press	18.00	1.85
2133a	12.5¢ Pushcart.	4.00	.40

PLATE NUMBER STRIPS OF 5

SCOTT NO.	UNUSED F/NH	SCOTT NO.	UNUSED F/NH	SCOTT NO.	UNUSED F/NH
2123	2.00	2132	4.50	2127A	4.50
2124	1.80	2133	4.75	2127Av	3.25
2125	2.75	2134	3.50	2128A	3.00
2126	2.40	2135	6.00	2129A	4.50
2127	3.50	2136	6.50	2130A	3.50
2128	2.75	2123A	7.00	2130Av	3.25
2129	5.00	2124A	2.50	2132A	4.50
2130	8.50	2125A	3.50	2132B	25.00
2131	3.00	2126A	3.00	2133A	4.50

2137

1985 COMMEMORATIVES (continued)

SCOTT NO.	DESCRIPTION	FIRST DAY COVERS SING	PL. BLK.	MINT SHEET	PLATE BLOCK	UNUSED F/NH	USED
2137	22¢ Mary Bethune	2.25	4.00	40.00(50)	5.00	1.00	.25

2138 2139

2140 2141

SCOTT NO.	DESCRIPTION	FIRST DAY COVERS SING	PL. BLK.	MINT SHEET	PLATE BLOCK	UNUSED F/NH	USED
2138-41	Duck Decoys, 4 varieties, attached . .	5.00	6.00	65.00(50)	7.00	6.00	5.00
2138	22¢ Broadbill	2.25	....	....	....	1.75	.40
2139	22¢ Mallard	2.25	....	....	....	1.75	.40
2140	22¢ Canvasback	2.25	....	....	....	1.75	.40
2141	22¢ Redhead.	2.25	....	....	....	1.75	.40

2142

2143

2144

2145

SCOTT NO.	DESCRIPTION	FIRST DAY COVERS SING	FIRST DAY COVERS PL. BLK.	MINT SHEET	PLATE BLOCK	UNUSED F/NH	USED
2142	22¢ Winter Special Olympics	2.25	4.00	49.00(40)	7.00	1.70	.25
2143	22¢ "LOVE"	1.95	4.00	34.00(50)	3.50	.70	.25
2144	22¢ Rural Electricity. . .	2.25	....	46.00(50)	28.00(20)	1.50	.25
2145	22¢ Ameripex '86.	2.25	4.00	34.00(48)	3.75	1.00	.25

2146

2147

SCOTT NO.	DESCRIPTION	FIRST DAY COVERS SING	FIRST DAY COVERS PL. BLK.	MINT SHEET	PLATE BLOCK	UNUSED F/NH	USED
2146	22¢ Abigail Adams. . . .	2.25	4.00	33.00(50)	3.75	.85	.25
2147	22¢ Frederic Bartholdi .	2.25	4.00	34.00(50)	4.00	1.00	.25

2149

2150

1985 REGULAR ISSUE COILS

SCOTT NO.	DESCRIPTION	SING	PLATE# STRIP 3		PLATE# STRIP 3	UNUSED F/NH	USED
2149	18¢ George Washington	2.25	50.00	....	3.50	.85	.30
	same, plate strip of 5 . .	....	....	....	....	4.50	....
2149a	18¢ George Washington, precancel.	....	....	....	3.25	.70	.40
	same, plate strip of 5 . .	....	....	....	....	4.00	....
2150	21.1¢ Envelope	2.25	32.50	....	3.75	.90	.60
	same, plate strip of 5 . .	....	....	....	....	5.50	....
2150a	21.1¢ Envelope, precancel	....	....	....	3.85	.75	.50
	same, plate strip of 5 . .	....	....	....	....	5.25	....

2152

2153

2154

SCOTT NO.	DESCRIPTION	FIRST DAY COVERS SING	FIRST DAY COVERS PL. BLK.	MINT SHEET	PLATE BLOCK	UNUSED F/NH	USED
2152	22¢ Korean War Veterans	3.00	4.00	41.50(50)	5.00	1.00	.25
2153	22¢ Social Security . . .	2.25	4.00	32.00(50)	3.50	1.00	.25
2154	22¢ World War I Veterans	3.00	4.00	58.00(50)	5.00	1.00	.25

2155 2156

2157 2158

SCOTT NO.	DESCRIPTION	FIRST DAY COVERS SING	FIRST DAY COVERS PL. BLK.	MINT SHEET	PLATE BLOCK	UNUSED F/NH	USED
2155-58	American Horses, 4 varieties, attached . .	5.00	6.00	68.00(40)	10.00	8.00	5.00
2155	22¢ Quarter Horse. . . .	2.25	....	....	....	2.25	.50
2156	22¢ Morgan	2.25	....	....	....	2.25	.50
2157	22¢ Saddlebred	2.25	....	....	....	2.25	.50
2158	22¢ Appaloosa.	2.25	....	....	....	2.25	.50

2160

2159

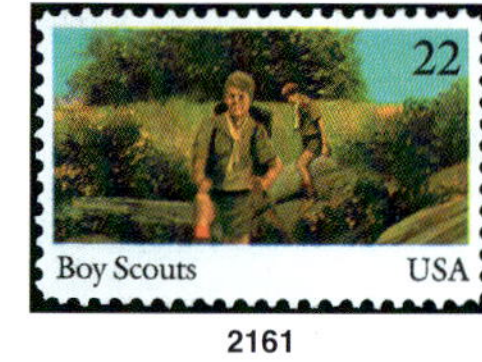

2161

2162

2163

SCOTT NO.	DESCRIPTION	FIRST DAY COVERS SING	FIRST DAY COVERS PL. BLK.	MINT SHEET	PLATE BLOCK	UNUSED F/NH	USED
2159	22¢ Public Education. .	2.25	4.00	50.00(50)	5.00	1.20	.25
2160-63	Youth Year, 4 varieties, attached . .	5.00	6.00	61.00(50)	8.00	6.00	4.50
2160	22¢ YMCA	2.25	....	....	....	1.75	.40
2161	22¢ Boy Scouts	2.25	....	....	....	1.75	.40
2162	22¢ Big Brothers & Big Sisters	2.25	....	....	....	1.75	.40
2163	22¢ Camp Fire.	2.25	....	....	....	1.75	.40

2164

2165

2166

2167

SCOTT NO.	DESCRIPTION	FIRST DAY COVERS SING	FIRST DAY COVERS PL. BLK.	MINT SHEET	PLATE BLOCK	UNUSED F/NH	USED
2164	22¢ Help End Hunger .	2.25	4.00	32.75(50)	3.25	.70	.25
2165	22¢ Madonna & Child .	2.25	4.00	32.00(50)	3.25	.60	.25
2166	22¢ Poinsettia	2.25	4.00	38.00(50)	3.25	.60	.25
2167	22¢ Arkansas Statehood	2.25	4.00	39.00(50)	5.00	1.00	.25

2168 2169 2170 2171

2172 2173 2175 2176

2177 2178 2179 2180

2181 2182, 2197 2183 2184

2185 2186 2187 2188

2189 2190 2191 2192

2193 2194 2195 2196

1986-93 GREAT AMERICANS

SCOTT NO.	DESCRIPTION	FIRST DAY COVERS SING	PL. BLK.	MINT SHEET	PLATE BLOCK	UNUSED F/NH	USED
2168-96	(28 varieties)		....	....	225.00	45.00	12.50
2168	1¢ Margaret Mitchell . .	5.00	6.00	11.00(100)	1.15	.30	.25
2169	2¢ Mary Lyon (1987) . .	2.25	4.00	11.00(100)	1.15	.30	.25
2170	3¢ Dr. Paul D. White . .	2.25	4.00	14.00(100)	1.00	.30	.25
2171	4¢ Father Flanagan . . .	2.25	4.00	20.00(100)	1.00	.30	.25
2172	5¢ Hugo L. Black	2.25	4.00	35.00(100)	2.00	.50	.25
2173	5¢ Luis Muñoz Marin (1990)	2.25	4.00	38.00(100)	2.25	.30	.25
2175	10¢ Red Cloud (1987) .	2.25	4.00	45.00(100)	2.50	.40	.25
2176	14¢ Julia Ward Howe (1987)	2.25	4.00	60.00(100)	2.75	1.00	.25
2177	15¢ Buffalo Bill Cody (1988)	2.25	4.00	90.00(100)	12.00	1.00	.25
2178	17¢ Belva Ann Lockwood	2.25	4.00	60.00(100)	3.25	1.00	.25
2179	20¢ Virginia Apgar (1994)	2.25	4.00	62.00(100)	3.75	1.00	.25
2180	21¢ Chester Carlson (1988)	2.25	4.00	68.00(100)	3.75	1.00	.50
2181	23¢ Mary Cassatt (1988)	2.25	4.00	73.00(100)	4.00	1.00	.25
2182	25¢ Jack London (1988)	2.25	4.00	73.00(100)	4.25	1.00	.25
2182a	as above bklt pane of 10	8.00	....	....	....	7.75	....
2183	28¢ Sitting Bull (1989) .	2.25	....	125.00(100)	7.00	1.30	.50
2184	29¢ Earl Warren (1992)	2.25	4.00	110.00(100)	6.00	1.00	.25
2185	29¢ Thomas Jefferson (1993)	2.25	4.75	110.00(100)	6.00(4)	1.00	.25
2185b	same, Plate Block of 8 .	....	....	....	8.75(8)	....	....
2186	35¢ Dennis Chavez (1991)	2.25	4.00	107.00(100)	6.00	1.20	.50
2187	40¢ Claire Lee Chennault (1990)	3.00	5.00	120.00(100)	7.00	1.35	.25
2188	45¢ Dr. Harvey Cushing (1988)	1.85	4.25	142.00(100)	9.00	1.50	.25

SCOTT NO.	DESCRIPTION	FIRST DAY COVERS SING	PL. BLK.	MINT SHEET	PLATE BLOCK	UNUSED F/NH	USED
2189	52¢ Hubert Humphrey (1991)	2.00	4.50	160.00(100)	9.00	1.75	.25
2190	56¢ John Harvard	3.00	4.50	167.00(100)	10.00	1.75	.25
2191	65¢ H.H. Arnold (1988)	3.00	4.25	195.00(100)	11.00	2.25	.25
2192	75¢ Wendell Willkie (1992)	2.75	5.50	238.00(100)	13.00	2.75	.25
2193	$1 Dr. Bernard Revel . .	5.00	10.00	375.00(100)	20.00	4.00	.50
2194	$1 John Hopkins (1989)	5.00	10.00	60.00(20)	15.00	3.75	.50
2195	$2 William Jennings Bryan	8.00	10.00	595.00(100)	29.00	6.75	1.00
2196	$5 Bret Harte (1987) . .	17.50	28.50	290.00(20)	73.00	17.00	3.50
2197	25¢ Jack London, bklt single (1988)	2.25	....	....	....	.90	.25
2197a	as above bklt pane (6), perf.10	5.00	....	....	....	5.25	....

2198

2199

2200

2201

1986 COMMEMORATIVES

SCOTT NO.	DESCRIPTION	FIRST DAY COVERS SING	PL. BLK.	MINT SHEET	PLATE BLOCK	UNUSED F/NH	USED
2167/2245	(2167, 2202-04, 2210-11, 2220-24, 2235-45) 22 varieties		....	....	....	24.00	5.95
2198	22¢ Cover & Handstamp	2.25	....	....	....	.90	.55
2199	22¢ Collector with Album	2.25	....	....	....	.90	.55
2200	22¢ No. 836 under magnifier	2.25	....	....	....	.90	.55
2201	22¢ President sheet. . .	2.25	....	....	....	.90	.55
2201a	Stamp Collecting bklt pane, 4 varieties, attached . .	6.00	....	....	....	3.50	2.60

2202

2203

2204

SCOTT NO.	DESCRIPTION	FIRST DAY COVERS SING	PL. BLK.	MINT SHEET	PLATE BLOCK	UNUSED F/NH	USED
2202	22¢ LOVE	1.95	4.25	39.00(50)	4.00	1.00	.25
2203	22¢ Sojourner Truth. . .	3.00	4.00	41.00(50)	4.50	1.00	.25
2204	22¢ Texas Republic . . .	3.00	4.00	44.00(50)	6.00	1.25	.25

BOOKLET PANE SINGLES: Traditionally, booklet panes have been collected only as intact panes since, other than the straight edged sides, they were identical to sheet stamps. However, starting with the 1971 8¢ Eisenhower stamp, many issues differ from the comparative sheet stamp or may even be totally different issues (e.g. #1738-42 Windmills). These newer issues are now collected as booklet singles or panes—both methods being acceptable.

2205

2206

2207

2208

2209

SCOTT NO.	DESCRIPTION	FIRST DAY COVERS SING	FIRST DAY COVERS PL. BLK.	MINT SHEET	PLATE BLOCK	UNUSED F/NH	USED
2205	22¢ Muskellunge	2.25	....	....	....	1.85	.35
2206	22¢ Altantic Cod	2.25	....	....	....	1.85	.35
2207	22¢ Largemouth Bass .	2.25	....	....	....	1.85	.35
2208	22¢ Bluefin Tuna	2.25	....	....	....	1.85	.35
2209	22¢ Catfish	2.25	....	....	....	1.85	.35
2209a	Fish, bklt pane, 5 varieties, attached.	6.50	....	....	....	8.50	6.00

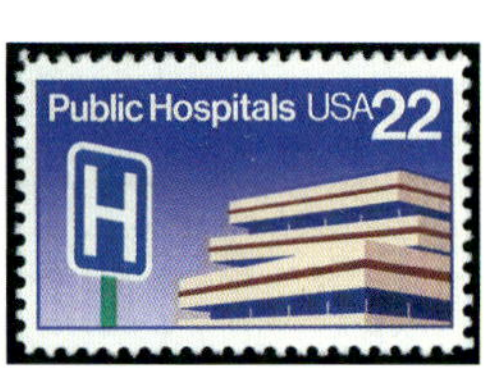

2210

2211

SCOTT NO.	DESCRIPTION	FIRST DAY COVERS SING	FIRST DAY COVERS PL. BLK.	MINT SHEET	PLATE BLOCK	UNUSED F/NH	USED
2210	22¢ Public Hospitals . .	2.25	4.00	34.00(50)	3.75	.75	.25
2211	22¢ Duke Ellington . . .	4.00	6.00	38.00(50)	4.50	1.00	.25

1986 PRESIDENTS MINIATURE SETS
Complete set printed on 4 miniature sheets of 9 stamps each.

2216a *Washington*
2216b *Adams*
2216c *Jefferson*
2216d *Madison*
2216e *Monroe*
2216f *J.Q. Adams*
2216g *Jackson*
2216h *Van Buren*
2216i *W.H. Harrison*
2217a *Tyler*
2217b *Polk*
2217c *Taylor*
2217d *Fillmore*
2217e *Pierce*
2217f *Buchanan*
2217g *Lincoln*
2217h *A. Johnson*
2217i *Grant*
2218a *Hayes*
2218b *Garfield*
2218c *Arthur*
2218d *Cleveland*
2218e *B. Harrison*
2218f *McKinley*
2218g *T. Roosevelt*
2218h *Taft*
2218i *Wilson*
2219a *Harding*
2219b *Coolidge*
2219c *Hoover*
2219d *F.D. Roosevelt*
2219e *White House*
2219f *Truman*
2219g *Eisenhower*
2219h *Kennedy*
2219i *L.B. Johnson*

2216

1986 AMERIPEX '86 MINIATURE SHEETS

SCOTT NO.	DESCRIPTION	FIRST DAY COVERS SING	FIRST DAY COVERS PL. BLK.	MINT SHEET	PLATE BLOCK	UNUSED F/NH	USED
2216-19	22¢ 36 varieties complete in 4 minature sheets	29.95	....	....	....	35.00	30.00
2216a-19i	set of 36 singles.	70.00	....	....	....	40.00	22.50

2220 2221

2222 2223

1986 COMMEMORATIVES

SCOTT NO.	DESCRIPTION	FIRST DAY COVERS SING	FIRST DAY COVERS PL. BLK.	MINT SHEET	PLATE BLOCK	UNUSED F/NH	USED
2220-23	Explorers, 4 varieties, attached . .	6.00	7.00	50.00(50)	6.00	5.00	4.50
2220	22¢ Elisha Kent Kane .	2.50	....	....	....	1.40	.40
2221	22¢ Adolphus W. Greely	2.50	....	....	....	1.40	.40
2222	22¢ Vilhjalmur Stefansson	2.50	....	....	....	1.40	.40
2223	22¢ R.E. Peary, M. Henson	2.50	....	....	....	1.40	.40

2224

SCOTT NO.	DESCRIPTION	FIRST DAY COVERS SING	FIRST DAY COVERS PL. BLK.	MINT SHEET	PLATE BLOCK	UNUSED F/NH	USED
2224	22¢ Statue of Liberty . .	4.00	6.00	38.00(50)	4.00	.80	.25

2225

2226

2228

1986-91 TRANSPORTATION COILS–"B" Press
Perf. 10 Vertically

SCOTT NO.	DESCRIPTION	FIRST DAY COVERS SING	PLATE# STRIP 3	MINT SHEET	PLATE# STRIP 3	UNUSED F/NH	USED
2225	1¢ Omnibus	2.25	6.50	....	.85	.25	.25
	same, plate strip of 5 . .	....	....	....	....	1.20	....
2225a	1¢ Omnibus, untagged (1991)	....	....	....	1.50	.25	.25
	same, plate strip of 5 . .	....	....	....	....	2.00	....
2226	2¢ Locomotive (1987) .	2.25	6.50	....	1.00	.25	.20
	same, plate strip of 5 . .	....	....	....	....	1.20	....
2226a	plate strip of 5	....	....	....	....	2.50	....
2226b	2¢ Locomative, untagged (1994)	....	....	....	1.25	.25	.25
2228	4¢ Stagecoach.	....	....	....	2.50	.30	.25
	same, plate strip of 5 . .	....	....	....	....	2.00	....
2228a	same, overall tagging (1990)	....	....	....	7.00	.60	.30
	same, plate strip of 5 . .	....	....	....	....	10.00	....
2231	8.3¢ Ambulance precancelled (1986). . .	....	....	....	7.00	2.00	.60
	same, plate strip of 5 . .	....	....	....	....	8.00	....

#2225—"¢" sign eliminated. #1897 has "1¢".
#2226—inscribed "2 USA". #1897A inscribed "USA 2¢".
#2228—"Stagecoach 1890s" is 17 mm long.

SCOTT NO.	DESCRIPTION	FIRST DAY COVERS SING	FIRST DAY COVERS PL. BLK.	MINT SHEET	PLATE BLOCK	UNUSED F/NH	USED

2235 2236 2237 2238

1986 COMMEMORATIVES (continued)

SCOTT NO.	DESCRIPTION	FDC SING	FDC PL. BLK.	MINT SHEET	PLATE BLOCK	UNUSED F/NH	USED
2235-38	Navajo Art, 4 varieties, attached . .	4.00	5.00	51.00(50)	6.50	6.00	3.50
2235	22¢ Navajo Art.	2.25	....	....	....	1.75	.25
2236	22¢ Navajo Art.	2.25	....	....	....	1.75	.25
2237	22¢ Navajo Art.	2.25	....	....	....	1.75	.25
2238	22¢ Navajo Art.	2.25	....	....	....	1.75	.25

2239

SCOTT NO.	DESCRIPTION	FDC SING	FDC PL. BLK.	MINT SHEET	PLATE BLOCK	UNUSED F/NH	USED
2239	22¢ T.S. Eliot	2.25	4.00	38.00(50)	4.00	1.00	.25

2240 2241 2242 2243

SCOTT NO.	DESCRIPTION	FDC SING	FDC PL. BLK.	MINT SHEET	PLATE BLOCK	UNUSED F/NH	USED
2240-43	Woodcarved Figurines, 4 varieties, attached . .	4.00	5.00	39.00(50)	4.50	4.25	3.00
2240	22¢ Highlander Figure.	2.25	....	....	....	1.10	.30
2241	22¢ Ship Figurehead . .	2.25	....	....	....	1.10	.30
2242	22¢ Nautical Figure . . .	2.25	....	....	....	1.10	.30
2243	22¢ Cigar Store Figure	2.25	....	....	....	1.10	.30

2244

2245

SCOTT NO.	DESCRIPTION	FDC SING	FDC PL. BLK.	MINT SHEET	PLATE BLOCK	UNUSED F/NH	USED
2244	22¢ Madonna.	2.25	4.00	66.00(100)	4.00	.75	.25
2245	22¢ Village Scene	2.25	4.00	66.00(100)	4.00	.75	.25

2246

2247

2248

2249 2250 2251

1987 COMMEMORATIVES

SCOTT NO.	DESCRIPTION	FDC SING	FDC PL. BLK.	MINT SHEET	PLATE BLOCK	UNUSED F/NH	USED
2246/2368	(2246-51, 2275, 2336-38, 2349-54, 2360-61, 2367-68) 20 varieties	....	....	....	....	18.50	5.25
2246	22¢ Michigan Statehood	2.25	4.00	39.00(50)	4.50	1.00	.25
2247	22¢ Pan American Games	2.25	4.00	38.00(50)	4.00	.95	.25
2248	22¢ LOVE	3.00	4.50	68.00(100)	4.00	.95	.25
2249	22¢ Jean Baptiste Pointe du Sable	2.25	4.00	36.00(50)	4.00	.95	.25
2250	22¢ Enrico Caruso. . . .	2.25	4.00	36.00(50)	4.00	.95	.25
2251	22¢ Girls Scouts	2.25	4.00	36.00(50)	4.00	.95	.25

2252 2253 2254 2255

2256

2257

2258

2259

2260

2261

2262

2263

2264

2265

2266

1987-93 TRANSPORTATION COILS

SCOTT NO.	DESCRIPTION	FDC SING	PLATE# STRIP 3	MINT SHEET	PLATE# STRIP 3	UNUSED F/NH	USED
2252	3¢ Conestoga Wagon (1988)	2.25	9.00	....	1.25	.25	.25
2252a	same, untagged (1992)	....	9.00	....	2.50	.25	.25
2253	5¢ Milk Wagon.	2.25	9.00	....	1.90	.25	.25
2254	5.3¢ Elevator,precancel ('88)	2.25	9.00	....	1.90	.40	.25
2255	7.6¢ Carreta, precancel ('88)	2.25	9.00	....	3.25	.40	.25
2256	8.4¢ Wheel Chair, precancel (1988)	2.25	9.00	....	3.50	.40	.25
2257	10¢ Canal Boat	2.25	9.00	....	3.50	.40	.25
2257a	same, overall tagging (1993).......		9.00	....	12.00	3.00	.25
2258	13¢ Police Wagon, precancel (1988)	2.25	9.00	....	6.00	.90	.25
2259	13.2¢ Railroad Coal Car, precancel (1988)	2.25	9.00	....	3.50	.40	.25
2260	15¢ Tugboat (1988) . . .	2.25	9.00	....	4.00	.50	.25
2260a	same, overall tagging (1990).......		9.00	....	6.00	.75	.25
2261	16.7¢ Popcorn Wagon, precancel (1988)	2.25	9.00	....	4.00	.60	.25
2262	17.5¢ Racing Car.	2.25	9.00	....	5.25	1.25	.35
2262a	17.5¢ Racing Car, precancel (1988)	2.25	9.00	....	5.25	.90	.55
2263	20¢ Cable Car (1988) .	2.25	9.00	....	4.50	.70	.25
2263b	same, overall tagging (1990).......		9.00	....	11.00	1.85	.40
2264	20.5¢ Fire Engine, precancel (1988)	2.25	9.00	....	8.00	1.50	.55
2265	21¢ Railroad Mail Car, precancel (1988)	2.25	9.00	....	4.00	.80	.45
2266	24.1¢ Tandem Bicycle, precancel (1988)	2.25	9.00	....	6.00	1.20	.90

SCOTT NO.	DESCRIPTION	FIRST DAY COVERS SING	PL. BLK.	MINT SHEET	PLATE BLOCK	UNUSED F/NH	USED

PLATE NUMBER STRIPS OF 5

SCOTT NO.	UNUSED F/NH	SCOTT NO.	UNUSED F/NH	SCOTT NO.	UNUSED F/NH
2252	1.40	2257a	18.00	2262a	8.00
2252a	3.50	2258	7.50	2263	7.00
2253	2.50	2259	5.00	2263b	14.00
2254	2.50	2260	6.25	2264	10.00
2255	3.50	2260a	8.00	2265	6.00
2256	3.50	2261	4.75	2266	7.00
2257	4.50	2262	7.00		

2267

2268

2269

2270

2271

2272

2273

2274

1987 SPECIAL OCCASIONS BOOKLET PANE

SCOTT NO.	DESCRIPTION	FDC SING	FDC PL. BLK.	MINT SHEET	PLATE BLOCK	UNUSED F/NH	USED
2267	22¢ Congratulations! . .	2.25	....	....	....	2.00	.55
2268	22¢ Get Well!	2.25	....	....	....	2.00	.55
2269	22¢ Thank You!	2.25	....	....	....	2.00	.55
2270	22¢ Love You, Dad! . . .	2.25	....	....	....	2.00	.55
2271	22¢ Best Wishes!	2.25	....	....	....	2.00	.55
2272	22¢ Happy Birthday! . .	2.25	....	....	....	2.00	.55
2273	22¢ Love You, Mother!	2.25	....	....	....	2.00	.55
2274	22¢ Keep in Touch! . . .	2.25	....	....	....	2.00	.55
2274a	Special Occasions bklt pane of 10, attached . .	17.00	....	....	....	15.00	....

NOTE: **#2274a contains 1 each of #2268-71, 2273-74 and 2 each of #2267 and 2272.**

2275

1987 COMMEMORATIVES (continued)

SCOTT NO.	DESCRIPTION	FDC SING	FDC PL. BLK.	MINT SHEET	PLATE BLOCK	UNUSED F/NH	USED
2275	22¢ United Way	2.25	4.00	34.00(50)	3.50	1.00	.25

2276

2277, 2279, 2282, 2282a

2278, 2285A, 2285Ac

1987-88 REGULAR ISSUE

SCOTT NO.	DESCRIPTION	FDC SING	FDC PL. BLK.	MINT SHEET	PLATE BLOCK	UNUSED F/NH	USED
2276	22¢ Flag & Fireworks. .	2.25	4.00	68.00(100)	4.00	1.00	.25
2276a	bklt pane of 20	12.50	....	....	....	13.50	....
2277	(25¢) "E" Earth (1988) .	2.25	4.00	72.00(100)	4.50	.95	.25
2278	25¢ Flag with Clouds (1988)	2.25	4.00	72.00(100)	5.00	1.00	.25

2280

2281

2283, 2283a

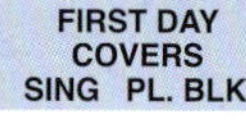

2284

2285, 2285b

SCOTT NO.	DESCRIPTION	FDC SING	PLATE # STRIP 3	MINT SHEET	PLATE# STRIP 3	UNUSED F/NH	USED
2279	(25¢) "E" Earth coil (1988)	2.25	7.50	....	4.50	.80	.25
	same, plate strip of 5 . .	....	....	....	....	5.00	....
2280	25¢ Flag over Yosemite, coil (1988)	2.25	7.50	....	4.50	.90	.25
	same, plate strip of 5 . .	....	....	....	....	6.00	....
2280a	25¢ Flag over Yosemite, phosphor (1989)	2.25	....	....	5.00	.95	.25
	same, plate strip of 5 . .	....	....	....	....	6.50	....
2281	25¢ Honey Bee, coil (1988)	2.25	7.50	....	5.00	.85	.25
	same, plate strip of 5 . .	....	....	....	....	6.50	....
2282	(25¢) "E" Earth, bklt single (1988)	2.25	....	....	....	.85	.25
2282a	(25¢) "E" Earth, bklt pane of 10.	7.25	....	....	....	9.75	....
2283	25¢ Pheasant bklt single (1988)	2.25	....	....	....	1.50	.25
2283a	25¢ Pheasant, bklt pane of 10.	7.25	....	....	....	10.00	....
2283b	25¢ Pheasant, (red omitted) bklt single.	....	....	....	....	11.00	....
2283c	25¢ Pheasant, (red omitted) bklt pane of 10	....	....	....	....	105.00	....
2284	25¢ Grosbeak, bklt single (1988)	2.25	....	....	....	1.00	.25
2285	25¢ Owl bklt single . . .	2.25	....	....	....	1.00	.25
2285b	25¢ Owl/Grosbeck, bklt pane of 10	7.25	....	....	....	8.75	....
2285A	25¢ Flag with Clouds, bklt single.	2.25	....	....	....	.95	.25
2285Ac	as above, bklt pane of 6 (1988)	4.00	....	....	....	5.75	....

2286

2310

2335

1987 AMERICAN WILDLIFE

2286 *Barn Swallow*
2287 *Monarch Butterfly*
2288 *Bighorn Sheep*
2289 *Broad-tailed Humming-bird*
2290 *Cottontail*
2291 *Osprey*
2292 *Mountain Lion*
2293 *Luna Moth*
2294 *Mule Deer*
2295 *Gray Squirrel*
2296 *Armadillo*
2297 *Eastern Chipmunk*
2298 *Moose*
2299 *Black Bear*
2300 *Tiger Swallowtail*
2301 *Bobwhite*
2302 *Ringtail*
2303 *Red-winged Blackbird*
2304 *American Lobster*
2305 *Black-tailed Jack Rabbit*
2306 *Scarlet Tanager*
2307 *Woodchuck*
2308 *Roseate Spoonbill*
2309 *Bald Eagle*
2310 *Alaskan Brown Bear*
2311 *Iiwi*
2312 *Badger*
2313 *Pronghorn*
2314 *River Otter*
2315 *Ladybug*
2316 *Beaver*
2317 *White-tailed Deer*
2318 *Blue Jay*
2319 *Pika*
2320 *Bison*
2321 *Snowy Egret*
2322 *Gray Wolf*
2323 *Mountain Goat*
2324 *Deer Mouse*
2325 *Black-tailed Prairie Dog*
2326 *Box Turtle*
2327 *Wolverine*
2328 *American Elk*
2329 *California Sea Lion*
2330 *Mockingbird*
2331 *Raccoon*
2332 *Bobcat*
2333 *Black-footed Ferret*
2334 *Canada Goose*
2335 *Red Fox*

SCOTT NO.	DESCRIPTION	FDC SING	FDC PL. BLK.	MINT SHEET	PLATE BLOCK	UNUSED F/NH	USED
2286-2335	22¢, 50 varieties, attached.	70.00	....	45.00(50)	....	45.00	....
	set of singles	86.00	....	....	....	50.00	30.00
	singles of above, each	2.00	....	....	....	1.50	.75

2336

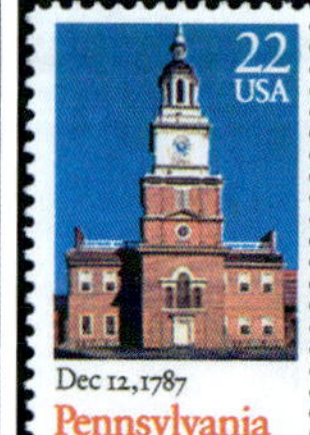

2337

2338

2339

2340

2341

2342

2343

2344

2345

2346

2347

2348

1987-90 COMMEMORATIVES

SCOTT NO.	DESCRIPTION	FIRST DAY COVERS SING	FIRST DAY COVERS PL. BLK.	MINT SHEET	PLATE BLOCK	UNUSED F/NH	USED
2336	22¢ Delaware Statehood	2.25	4.00	40.00(50)	4.00	1.00	.25
2337	22¢ Pennsylvania Statehood	2.25	4.00	40.00(50)	4.00	1.00	.25
2338	22¢ New Jersey Statehood	2.25	4.00	40.00(50)	4.00	1.00	.25
2339	22¢ Georgia Statehood (1988)	2.25	4.00	40.00(50)	4.00	1.00	.35
2340	22¢ Connecticut Statehood (1988)	2.25	4.00	40.00(50)	4.00	1.00	.25
2341	22¢ Massachusetts Statehood (1988)	2.25	4.00	40.00(50)	4.00	1.00	.40
2342	22¢ Maryland Statehood (1988)	2.25	4.00	40.00(50)	4.00	1.00	.40
2343	25¢ South Carolina Statehood (1988)	2.25	4.00	40.00(50)	4.00	1.00	.25
2344	25¢ New Hampshire Statehood (1988)	2.25	4.00	40.00(50)	4.00	1.00	.25
2345	25¢ Virginia Statehood (1988)	2.25	4.00	40.00(50)	4.00	1.00	.25
2346	25¢ New York Statehood (1988)	2.25	4.00	40.00(50)	4.00	1.00	.25
2347	25¢ North Carolina Statehood (1989)	2.25	4.00	45.00(50)	5.50	1.50	.25
2348	25¢ Rhode Island Statehood (1990)	2.25	9.00	45.00(50)	5.50	1.50	.25

2349

2350

SCOTT NO.	DESCRIPTION	FIRST DAY COVERS SING	FIRST DAY COVERS PL. BLK.	MINT SHEET	PLATE BLOCK	UNUSED F/NH	USED
2349	22¢ Morocco	2.25	4.00	35.00(50)	3.75	.80	.25
2350	22¢ William Faulkner	2.25	4.00	37.00(50)	4.75	1.25	.25

2351 2352

2353 2354

SCOTT NO.	DESCRIPTION	FIRST DAY COVERS SING	FIRST DAY COVERS PL. BLK.	MINT SHEET	PLATE BLOCK	UNUSED F/NH	USED
2351-54	Lacemaking, 4 varieties, attached	4.00	5.00	38.00(40)	5.00	4.50	3.50
2351	22¢ Lace, Ruth Maxwell	2.25	....	....	....	1.25	.30
2352	22¢ Lace, Mary McPeek	2.25	....	....	....	1.25	.30
2353	22¢ Lace, Leslie K. Saari	2.25	....	....	....	1.25	.30
2354	22¢ Lace, Trenna Ruffner	2.25	....	....	....	1.25	.30

2355

2356

2357

2358

2359

SCOTT NO.	DESCRIPTION	FIRST DAY COVERS SING	FIRST DAY COVERS PL. BLK.	MINT SHEET	PLATE BLOCK	UNUSED F/NH	USED
2355	22¢ "The Bicentennial"	2.25	....	....	....	1.50	.30
2356	22¢ "We the people"	2.25	....	....	....	1.50	.30
2357	22¢ "Establish justice"	2.25	....	....	....	1.50	.30
2358	22¢ "And secure"	2.25	....	....	....	1.50	.30
2359	22¢ "Do ordain"	2.25	....	....	....	1.50	.30
2359a	Drafting of Constitution bklt pane, 5 varieties, attached	4.60	....	....	....	6.75	6.50

2360

2361

SCOTT NO.	DESCRIPTION	FIRST DAY COVERS SING	FIRST DAY COVERS PL. BLK.	MINT SHEET	PLATE BLOCK	UNUSED F/NH	USED
2360	22¢ Signing of U.S. Constitution	2.25	4.00	45.00(50)	4.50	1.00	.25
2361	22¢ Certified Public Accountants	12.00	15.00	75.00(50)	7.50	1.75	.25

2362

2363

2364

2365

2366

LOCOMOTIVES ISSUE

SCOTT NO.	DESCRIPTION	FIRST DAY COVERS SING	FIRST DAY COVERS PL. BLK.	MINT SHEET	PLATE BLOCK	UNUSED F/NH	USED
2362	22¢ "Stourbridge Lion, 1829"	2.25	....	....	....	1.25	.25
2363	22¢ "Best Friend of Charleston, 1830"	2.25	....	....	....	1.25	.25
2364	22¢ "John Bull, 1831"	2.25	....	....	....	1.25	.25
2365	22¢ "Brother Jonathan, 1832"	2.25	....	....	....	1.25	.25
2366	22¢ "Gowan + Marx, 1839"	2.25	....	....	....	1.25	.25
2366a	Locomotives, bklt pane, 5 varieties, attached	4.60	....	....	....	5.00	4.75

2367

2368

SCOTT NO.	DESCRIPTION	FIRST DAY COVERS SING	FIRST DAY COVERS PL. BLK.	MINT SHEET	PLATE BLOCK	UNUSED F/NH	USED
2367	22¢ Madonna	2.25	4.00	68.00(100)	4.00	.90	.25
2368	22¢ Ornament	2.25	4.00	68.00(100)	4.00	.90	.25

2369

2370

2371

2372 2373

Siamese Cat, Exotic Shorthair Cat — Abyssinian Cat, Himalayan Cat

Maine Coon Cat, Burmese Cat — American Shorthair Cat, Persian Cat

2374 2375

2376

2377

2378

1988 COMMEMORATIVES

SCOTT NO.	DESCRIPTION	FIRST DAY COVERS SING	FIRST DAY COVERS PL. BLK.	MINT SHEET	PLATE BLOCK	UNUSED F/NH	USED
2339/2400	(2339-46, 2369-80, 2386-93, 2399-2400) 30 varieties	....	....	....	....	29.00	9.00
2369	22¢ Winter Olympics	2.25	4.00	47.00(50)	7.00	1.50	.25
2370	22¢ Australia Bicentennial	2.25	4.00	28.00(50)	3.50	.75	.25
2371	22¢ James Weldon Johnson	2.25	4.00	44.00(50)	5.00	1.00	.30
2372-75	Cats, 4 varieties, attached	8.00	12.00	40.00(40)	6.50	5.00	4.00
2372	22¢ Siamese, Exotic Shorthair	2.25	....	....	....	1.50	.75
2373	22¢ Abyssinian, Himalayan	2.25	....	....	....	1.50	.75
2374	22¢ Maine Coon, Burmese	2.25	....	....	....	1.50	.75
2375	22¢ American Shorthair, Persian	2.25	....	....	....	1.50	.75
2376	22¢ Knute Rockne	4.00	6.00	45.00(50)	4.75	1.20	.50
2377	25¢ Francis Ouimet	8.00	10.00	48.00(50)	7.00	1.25	.30
2378	25¢ LOVE	2.25	4.00	72.00(100)	4.00	.85	.25

2379

2380

SCOTT NO.	DESCRIPTION	FIRST DAY COVERS SING	FIRST DAY COVERS PL. BLK.	MINT SHEET	PLATE BLOCK	UNUSED F/NH	USED
2379	45¢ LOVE	2.25	4.00	67.50(50)	7.00	1.50	.25
2380	25¢ Summer Olympics	2.25	4.00	46.00(50)	4.75	1.00	.25

2381

2382

2383

1932 Packard

2384

2385

SCOTT NO.	DESCRIPTION	FIRST DAY COVERS SING	FIRST DAY COVERS PL. BLK.	MINT SHEET	PLATE BLOCK	UNUSED F/NH	USED
2381	25¢ Locomobile	2.25	....	....	....	2.00	.40
2382	25¢ Pierce-Arrow	2.25	....	....	....	2.00	.40
2383	25¢ Cord	2.25	....	....	....	2.00	.40
2384	25¢ Packard	2.25	....	....	....	2.00	.40
2385	25¢ Duesenberg	2.25	....	....	....	2.00	.40
2385a	Classic Automobiles bklt pane , 5 varieties, attached	4.60	....	....	....	9.00	7.00

BOOKLET PANE SINGLES: Traditionally, booklet panes have been collected only as intact panes since, other than the straight edged sides, they were identical to sheet stamps. However, starting with the 1971 8¢ Eisenhower stamp, many issues differ from the comparative sheet stamp or may even be totally different issues (e.g. #1738-42 Windmills). These newer issues are now collected as booklet singles or panes—both methods being acceptable.

SCOTT NO.	DESCRIPTION	FIRST DAY COVERS SING	FIRST DAY COVERS PL. BLK.	MINT SHEET	PLATE BLOCK	UNUSED F/NH	USED

2386 2387

2388 2389

SCOTT NO.	DESCRIPTION	FIRST DAY COVERS SING	FIRST DAY COVERS PL. BLK.	MINT SHEET	PLATE BLOCK	UNUSED F/NH	USED
2386-89	Antarctic Explorers, 4 varieties, attached . .	4.00	5.00	48.00(50)	6.00	5.75	4.00
2386	25¢ Nathaniel Palmer .	2.25	....	....	....	1.50	.45
2387	25¢ Lt. Charles Wilkes.	2.25	....	....	....	1.50	.45
2388	25¢ Richard E. Byrd . .	2.25	....	....	....	1.50	.45
2389	25¢ Lincoln Ellsworth. .	2.25	....	....	....	1.50	.45

2390

2391

2392

2393

SCOTT NO.	DESCRIPTION	FIRST DAY COVERS SING	FIRST DAY COVERS PL. BLK.	MINT SHEET	PLATE BLOCK	UNUSED F/NH	USED
2390-93	Carousel Animals, 4 varieties, attached . .	4.00	5.00	52.50(50)	6.75	6.00	4.00
2390	25¢ Deer	2.25	....	....	....	1.60	.30
2391	25¢ Horse	2.25	....	....	....	1.60	.30
2392	25¢ Camel	2.25	....	....	....	1.60	.30
2393	25¢ Goat	2.25	....	....	....	1.60	.30

2394

SCOTT NO.	DESCRIPTION	FIRST DAY COVERS SING	FIRST DAY COVERS PL. BLK.	MINT SHEET	PLATE BLOCK	UNUSED F/NH	USED
2394	$8.75 Express Mail . . .	32.00	70.00	535.00(20)	125.00	30.00	10.00

2395

2396

2397

2398

SCOTT NO.	DESCRIPTION	FIRST DAY COVERS SING	FIRST DAY COVERS PL. BLK.	MINT SHEET	PLATE BLOCK	UNUSED F/NH	USED
2395-2398	Special Occasions, bklt singles.	7.00	....	....	....	4.50	1.85
2396a	Bklt pane (6) with gutter 3–#2395 + 3–#2396 . .	4.60	....	....	....	6.00	5.00
2398a	Bklt pane (6) with gutter 3–#2397 + 3–#2398 . .	4.60	....	....	....	6.00	5.00

2399

2400

SCOTT NO.	DESCRIPTION	FIRST DAY COVERS SING	FIRST DAY COVERS PL. BLK.	MINT SHEET	PLATE BLOCK	UNUSED F/NH	USED
2399	25¢ Madonna and Child	2.25	4.00	36.00(50)	3.75	1.00	.25
2400	25¢ One Horse Sleigh .	2.25	4.00	36.00(50)	3.75	1.00	.25

2401

2402

1989 COMMEMORATIVES

SCOTT NO.	DESCRIPTION	FIRST DAY COVERS SING	FIRST DAY COVERS PL. BLK.	MINT SHEET	PLATE BLOCK	UNUSED F/NH	USED
2347/2437	**(2347, 2401-04, 2410-14, 2416-18, 2420-28, 2434-37) 26 varieties . . . .**	**........**	**........**	**........**	**........**	**27.75**	**6.25**
2401	25¢ Montana Statehood	2.25	4.00	60.00(50)	7.00	1.50	.25
2402	25¢ A.P. Randolph	3.00	4.00	55.00(50)	5.00	1.20	.25

2403

2404

SCOTT NO.	DESCRIPTION	FIRST DAY COVERS SING	FIRST DAY COVERS PL. BLK.	MINT SHEET	PLATE BLOCK	UNUSED F/NH	USED
2403	25¢ North Dakota Statehood	2.25	4.00	65.00(50)	7.00	1.50	.25
2404	25¢ Washington Statehood	2.25	4.00	60.00(50)	7.00	1.50	.25

2405

2406

2407

2408

2409

SCOTT NO.	DESCRIPTION	FIRST DAY COVERS SING	FIRST DAY COVERS PL. BLK.	MINT SHEET	PLATE BLOCK	UNUSED F/NH	USED
2405	25¢ "Experiment,1788-90"	2.25	....	....	....	1.40	.35
2406	25¢ "Phoenix, 1809" . .	2.25	....	....	....	1.40	.35
2407	25¢ "New Orleans, 1812"	2.25	....	....	....	1.40	.35
2408	25¢ "Washington, 1816"	2.25	....	....	....	1.40	.35
2409	25¢ "Walk in the Water,1818"	2.25	....	....	....	1.40	.35
2409a	Steamboat, bklt pane, 5 varieties, attached . .	6.00	....	....	....	6.50	4.00
2409av	same, bklt pane, unfolded	....	....	....	....	12.00	....

2410

2411

SCOTT NO.	DESCRIPTION	FIRST DAY COVERS SING	FIRST DAY COVERS PL. BLK.	MINT SHEET	PLATE BLOCK	UNUSED F/NH	USED
2410	25¢ World Stamp Expo '89	2.25	4.00	36.00(50)	3.75	1.00	.25
2411	25¢ Arturo Toscanini . .	2.25	4.00	38.00(50)	3.75	1.00	.25

2412  2413  2414  2415

SCOTT NO.	DESCRIPTION	FIRST DAY COVERS SING	FIRST DAY COVERS PL. BLK.	MINT SHEET	PLATE BLOCK	UNUSED F/NH	USED
2412	25¢ U.S. House of Representatives.	2.25	4.00	45.00(50)	4.50	1.00	.25
2413	25¢ U.S. Senate	2.25	4.00	58.00(50)	5.25	1.15	.25
2414	25¢ Executive Branch .	2.25	4.00	40.00(50)	4.00	1.00	.25
2415	25¢ U.S. Supreme Court (1990)	2.25	4.00	40.00(50)	4.00	1.00	.25

2416

SCOTT NO.	DESCRIPTION	FIRST DAY COVERS SING	FIRST DAY COVERS PL. BLK.	MINT SHEET	PLATE BLOCK	UNUSED F/NH	USED
2416	25¢ South Dakota Statehood	2.25	4.00	55.00(50)	6.00	1.50	.25

2417

2418

SCOTT NO.	DESCRIPTION	FIRST DAY COVERS SING	FIRST DAY COVERS PL. BLK.	MINT SHEET	PLATE BLOCK	UNUSED F/NH	USED
2417	25¢ Lou Gehrig	5.00	8.00	55.00(50)	6.00	1.20	.30
2418	25¢ Ernest Hemingway	2.25	4.00	42.50(50)	4.50	1.00	.25

2419

SCOTT NO.	DESCRIPTION	FIRST DAY COVERS SING	FIRST DAY COVERS PL. BLK.	MINT SHEET	PLATE BLOCK	UNUSED F/NH	USED
2419	$2.40 Moon Landing . .	7.50	15.75	165.00(20)	40.00	10.00	5.00

2420

2421

SCOTT NO.	DESCRIPTION	FIRST DAY COVERS SING	FIRST DAY COVERS PL. BLK.	MINT SHEET	PLATE BLOCK	UNUSED F/NH	USED
2420	25¢ Letter Carriers. . . .	2.25	4.00	29.00(50)	4.00	1.00	.25
2421	25¢ Bill of Rights	2.25	4.00	43.00(50)	5.00	1.25	.25

2422 2423

2424 2425

SCOTT NO.	DESCRIPTION	FIRST DAY COVERS SING	FIRST DAY COVERS PL. BLK.	MINT SHEET	PLATE BLOCK	UNUSED F/NH	USED
2422-25	Prehistoric Animals, 4 attached	5.00	7.00	38.00(40)	5.50	5.00	3.75
2422	25¢ Tyrannosaurus Rex	2.50	....	....	....	1.40	.25
2423	25¢ Pteranodon.	2.50	....	....	....	1.40	.25
2424	25¢ Stegosaurus	2.50	....	....	....	1.40	.25
2425	25¢ Brontosaurus	2.50	....	....	....	1.40	.25

2426

SCOTT NO.	DESCRIPTION	FIRST DAY COVERS SING	FIRST DAY COVERS PL. BLK.	MINT SHEET	PLATE BLOCK	UNUSED F/NH	USED
2426	25¢ Kachina Doll	2.25	4.00	38.00(50)	4.00	1.00	.25

2427  2428, 2429  2431

SCOTT NO.	DESCRIPTION	FIRST DAY COVERS SING	FIRST DAY COVERS PL. BLK.	MINT SHEET	PLATE BLOCK	UNUSED F/NH	USED
2427	25¢ Madonna & Child .	1.75	4.00	40.00(50)	4.00	1.00	.25
2427a	same, bklt pane of 10 .	7.25	....	....	....	9.00	....
2427av	same, bklt pane, unfolded	....	....	....	....	15.00	....
2428	25¢ Sleigh full of Presents	2.25	4.00	40.00(50)	4.00	.85	.25
2429	25¢ Sleigh full of Presents, bklt single.	2.25	....	....	....	.90	.25
2429a	same, bklt pane of 10 .	7.25	....	....	....	9.00	....
2429av	same, bklt pane, unfolded	....	....	....	....	19.00	....
2431	25¢ Eagle & Shield, self-adhesive	1.95	....	....	....	1.25	.75
2431a	same, bklt pane of 18 .	32.00	....	....	....	18.00	....
2431	same, coil	....	....	....	3.00(3)	1.25	....

2433

SCOTT NO.	DESCRIPTION	FIRST DAY COVERS SING	FIRST DAY COVERS PL. BLK.	MINT SHEET	PLATE BLOCK	UNUSED F/NH	USED
2433	$3.60 World Stamp Expo, Imperf. Souvenir Sheet	15.00	....	....	....	22.00	18.00

2434 2435 2436 2437

SCOTT NO.	DESCRIPTION	FIRST DAY COVERS SING	FIRST DAY COVERS PL. BLK.	MINT SHEET	PLATE BLOCK	UNUSED F/NH	USED
2434-37	Classic Mail Delivery, 4 attached	5.00	7.00	40.00(40)	5.75	5.00	4.00
2434	25¢ Stagecoach.	2.25	....	....	....	1.50	.40
2435	25¢ Paddlewheel Steamer	2.25	....	....	....	1.50	.40
2436	25¢ Biplane	2.25	....	....	....	1.50	.40
2437	25¢ Automobile	2.25	....	....	....	1.50	.40
2438	$1.00 Classic Mail Delivery Imperf. Souvenir Sheet	4.50	....	....	....	8.00	6.50

2439

2440, 2441

2442

1990 COMMEMORATIVES

SCOTT NO.	DESCRIPTION	FIRST DAY COVERS SING	FIRST DAY COVERS PL. BLK.	MINT SHEET	PLATE BLOCK	UNUSED F/NH	USED
2348/2515	**(2348, 2415, 2439-40, 2442, 2444-49, 2496-2500, 2506-15, 26 varieties . . . .**	....	....	....	....	**32.00**	**6.25**
2439	25¢ Idaho Statehood . .	2.25	4.00	60.00(50)	5.00	1.50	.25
2440	25¢ LOVE	2.25	4.00	44.00(50)	4.00	1.50	.25
2441	25¢ LOVE, bklt single .	2.25	....	....	....	1.25	.25
2441a	25¢ LOVE bklt pane of 10	8.65	....	....	....	10.00	....
2441av	same, bklt pane, unfolded	....	....	....	....	50.00	....
2442	25¢ Ida B. Wells	3.00	4.00	60.00(50)	5.00	1.50	.25

2443

2444

2445

2446

2449

2447

2448

SCOTT NO.	DESCRIPTION	FIRST DAY COVERS SING	FIRST DAY COVERS PL. BLK.	MINT SHEET	PLATE BLOCK	UNUSED F/NH	USED
2443	15¢ Umbrella, bklt single	2.25	....	....	....	.60	.25
2443a	15¢ Umbrella, bklt pane of 10.	5.75	....	....	....	5.00	3.40
2443av	same, bklt pane, unfolded	....	....	....	....	10.00	....
2444	25¢ Wyoming Statehood	8.00	10.00	60.00(50)	6.00	1.75	.25
2445-48	Classic Films, 4 varieties, attached . .	8.00	7.00	65.00(40)	8.00	7.50	5.00
2445	25¢ Wizard of OZ	4.00	....	....	....	2.25	.35
2446	25¢ Gone with the Wind	4.00	....	....	....	2.25	.35
2447	25¢ Beau Geste.	4.00	....	....	....	2.25	.35
2448	25¢ Stagecoach.	4.00	....	....	....	2.25	.35
2449	25¢ Marianne Craig Moore	2.25	4.00	48.00(50)	5.00	1.50	.20

2451

2452, 2452B, 2452D

2453, 2454

2457, 2458

2463

2464

2466

2468

1990-95 TRANSPORTATION COILS

SCOTT NO.	DESCRIPTION	FIRST DAY COVERS SING	PLATE# STRIP 3	MINT SHEET	PLATE# STRIP 3	UNUSED F/NH	USED
2451	4¢ Steam Carriage (1991)	2.25	6.50	....	1.50	.25	.25
	same, plate strip of 5	....	....	....	....	1.60	....
2451b	4¢ Steam Carriage, untagged	......	....	....	1.50	.25	.25
	same, plate strip of 5		....	....	....	1.60	....
2452	5¢ Circus Wagon	2.25	6.50	....	1.50	.25	.25
	same, plate strip of 5	....	....	....	....	2.00	....
2452a	5¢ Circus Wagon, untagged	....	....	....	3.50	.25	.25
	same, plate strip of 5	....	....	....	....	4.00	....
2452B	5¢ Circus Wagon, Gravure (1992)	2.25	6.50	....	1.50	.35	.25
	same, plate strip of 5 . .	....	....	....	....	2.50	....
2452D	5¢ Circus Wagon, coil (Reissue, 1995 added)	3.00	10.00	....	2.00	.35	.25
	same, plate strip of 5 . .	....	....	....	....	3.00	....
2453	5¢ Canoe, precancel, brown (1991)	2.25	6.50	....	2.00	.35	.25
	same, plate strip of 5 . .	....	....	....	....	2.75	....
2454	5¢ Canoe, precancel, red (1991)	2.25	6.50	....	2.50	.35	.25
	same, plate strip of 5 . .	....	....	....	....	3.00	....
2457	10¢ Tractor Trailer (1991)	2.25	6.50	....	3.00	.45	.25
	same, plate strip of 5 . .	....	....	....	....	4.25	....
2458	10¢ Tractor Trailer, Gravure (1994)	2.25	6.50	....	6.00	.70	.50
	same, plate strip of 5 . .	....	....	....	....	8.00	....
2463	20¢ Cog Railway Car, coil	1.95	10.00	....	4.00	.70	.25
	same, plate strip of 5 . .	....	....	....	....	6.00	....
2464	23¢ Lunch Wagon (1991)	2.25	6.50	....	5.00	.85	.25
	same, plate strip of 5 . .	....	....	....	....	7.00	....
2466	32¢ Ferryboat, coil. . . .	1.95	10.00	....	6.75	1.25	.25
	same, plate strip of 5 . .	....	....	....	....	8.75.	....
2468	$1 Seaplane, coil	3.00	10.00	....	15.00	4.00	1.00
	same, plate strip of 5 . .	....	....	....	....	21.50	....

2470 2471 2472 2473 2474

SCOTT NO.	DESCRIPTION	FIRST DAY COVERS SING	FIRST DAY COVERS PL. BLK.	MINT SHEET	PLATE BLOCK	UNUSED F/NH	USED
2470	25¢ Admiralty Head Lighthouse	2.25	....	....	....	2.25	.25
2471	25¢ Cape Hatteras Lighthouse	2.25	....	....	....	2.25	.25
2472	25¢ West Quoddy Head Lighthouse	2.25	....	....	....	2.25	.25
2473	25¢ American Shoals Lighthouse	2.25	....	....	....	2.25	.25
2474	25¢ Sandy Hook Lighthouse	2.25	....	....	....	2.25	.25
2474a	Lighthouse, bklt pane, 5 varieties	4.60	....	....	....	12.00	6.50
2474av	Same, bklt pane, unfolded	....	....	....	....	18.00	....

2475

SCOTT NO.	DESCRIPTION	FIRST DAY COVERS SING	FIRST DAY COVERS PL. BLK.	MINT SHEET	PLATE BLOCK	UNUSED F/NH	USED
2475	25¢ ATM Plastic Stamp, single	2.25	....	....	....	1.75	1.25
2475a	Same, pane of 12	20.00	....	....	....	13.00	....

2476 2477 2478 2479

2480 2481 2482 2483

1990-95 REGULAR ISSUE

SCOTT NO.	DESCRIPTION	FIRST DAY COVERS SING	FIRST DAY COVERS PL. BLK.	MINT SHEET	PLATE BLOCK	UNUSED F/NH	USED
2476	1¢ Kestrel (1991)	2.25	4.00	10.00(100)	.90	.25	.25
2477	1¢ Kestrel (redesign 1¢, 1995)	2.25	4.00	10.00(100)	.90	.25	.25
2478	3¢ Bluebird (1993)	2.25	4.00	15.00(100)	1.50	.25	.25
2479	19¢ Fawn (1993)	2.25	4.00	58.00(100)	5.00	.75	.25
2480	30¢ Cardinal (1993)	2.25	4.00	85.00(100)	5.25	1.10	.80
2481	45¢ Pumpkinseed Sunfish (1992)	2.00	4.50	135.00(100)	7.75	1.50	.75
2482	$2 Bobcat	6.00	14.00	110.00(20)	28.00	6.50	1.15
2483	20¢ Blue Jay, bklt single (1995)	1.95	....	....	....	.85	.30
2483a	same, bklt pane of 10	9.00	....	....	....	9.00	....
2483av	same, bklt pane, unfolded	....	....	....	....	11.00	....

2484, 2485 2486 2487, 2493, 2495 2488, 2494, 2495A

2489 2490 2491 2492

SCOTT NO.	DESCRIPTION	FIRST DAY COVERS SING	FIRST DAY COVERS PL. BLK.	MINT SHEET	PLATE BLOCK	UNUSED F/NH	USED
2484	29¢ Wood Duck, bklt single (BEP) (1991)	2.25	....	....	....	.95	.25
2484a	same, bklt pane of 10 (BEP)	9.00	....	....	....	9.50	....
2484av	same, bklt pane, unfolded	....	....	....	....	13.00	....
2485	29¢ Wood Duck, bklt single (KCS) (1991)	2.25	....	....	....	1.20	.25
2485a	same, bklt pane of 10 (KCS)	9.00	....	....	....	10.50	....
2485av	same, bklt pane, unfolded	....	....	....	....	14.00	....
2486	29¢ African Violet, bklt single	2.25	....	....	....	1.10	.25
2486a	same, bklt pane of 10	9.00	....	....	....	12.00	....
2486av	same, bklt pane, unfolded	....	....	....	....	14.00	....
2487	32¢ Peach, bklt single	1.95	....	....	....	1.25	.25
2488	32¢ Pear, bklt single	1.95	....	....	....	1.25	.25
2488a	32¢ Peach & Pear, bklt pane of 10	7.25	....	....	....	12.00	....
2488av	same, bklt pane, unfolded	....	....	....	....	15.00	....
2489	29¢ Red Squirrel, self-adhesive (1993)	2.25	....	....	....	1.10	.45
2489a	same, bklt pane of 18	13.50	....	....	....	20.00	....
2489v	same, coil	....	....	....	3.00(3)	1.10	....
2490	29¢ Rose, self-adhesive (1993)	2.25	....	....	....	1.10	.40
2490a	same, bklt pane of 18	13.50	....	....	....	20.00	....
2491	29¢ Pine Cone, self-adhesive	2.25	....	....	....	1.10	.40
2491a	same, bklt pane of 18	13.50	....	....	....	19.00	....
2492	32¢ Pink Rose, self-adhesive	1.95	....	....	....	1.10	.30
2492a	same, bklt pane of 20	14.50	....	....	....	20.00	....
2492b	same, bklt pane of 15	11.50	....	....	....	18.00	....
2493	32¢ Peach, self-adhesive	1.95	....	....	....	1.10	.30
2494	32¢ Pear, self-adhesive	1.95	....	....	....	1.10	.30
2494a	32¢ Peach & Pear, self-adhesive, bklt pane of 20	14.50	....	....	....	22.00	....
2495	32¢ Peach, self-adhesive coil (1993)	1.95	....	....	15.00(3)	3.50	....
2495A	32¢ Pear, self-adhesive coil	1.95	....	....	....	3.50	....
2495Ab	plate strip of 5	....	....	....	....	20.00	....

2496

2497

2498

2499

2500

SCOTT NO.	DESCRIPTION	FIRST DAY COVERS SING	FIRST DAY COVERS PL. BLK.	MINT SHEET	PLATE BLOCK	UNUSED F/NH	USED
2496-2500	Olympians, strip of 5, attached	7.50	10.00	35.00(35)	12.00(10)	7.00	5.00
2496	25¢ Jesse Owens	2.40	....	....	....	1.75	.50
2497	25¢ Ray Ewry	2.40	....	....	....	1.75	.50
2498	25¢ Hazel Wightman	2.40	....	....	....	1.75	.50
2499	25¢ Eddie Eagan	2.40	....	....	....	1.75	.50
2500	25¢ Helene Madison	2.40	....	....	....	1.75	.50

2501

2502

2503

2504

2505

SCOTT NO.	DESCRIPTION	FIRST DAY COVERS SING	FIRST DAY COVERS PL. BLK.	MINT SHEET	PLATE BLOCK	UNUSED F/NH	USED
2501-05	25¢ Headdresses strip of 5					9.00	
2501	25¢ Assiniboine	2.40	....	....	....	2.00	.40
2502	25¢ Cheyenne	2.40	....	....	....	2.00	.40
2503	25¢ Comanche	2.40	....	....	....	2.00	.40
2504	25¢ Flathead	2.40	....	....	....	2.00	.40
2505	25¢ Shoshone	2.40	....	....	....	2.00	.40
2505a	25¢ bklt pane of 10 . . .	7.85	....	....	....	18.00	....
2505av	same, bklt pane, unfolded	....	....	....	....	25.00	....

2506 2507

SCOTT NO.	DESCRIPTION	FIRST DAY COVERS SING	FIRST DAY COVERS PL. BLK.	MINT SHEET	PLATE BLOCK	UNUSED F/NH	USED
2506-07	Micronesia + Marshall Islands 2 varieties, attached . .	5.00	6.00	48.00(50)	5.00	2.00	1.30
2506	25¢ Micronesia	2.50	....	....	....	1.00	.25
2507	25¢ Marshall Islands . .	2.50	....	....	....	1.00	.25

2508 2509

2510 2511

1990 REGULAR ISSUES

SCOTT NO.	DESCRIPTION	FIRST DAY COVERS SING	FIRST DAY COVERS PL. BLK.	MINT SHEET	PLATE BLOCK	UNUSED F/NH	USED
2508-11	Sea Creatures, ... 4 varieties, attached . .	5.00	6.00	37.00(40)	6.00	5.50	3.50
2508	25¢ Killer Whales.	2.50	....	....	....	1.40	.40
2509	25¢ Northern Sea Lions	2.50	....	....	....	1.40	.40
2510	25¢ Sea Otter	2.50	....	....	....	1.40	.40
2511	25¢ Common Dolphin .	2.50	....	....	....	1.40	.40

2512

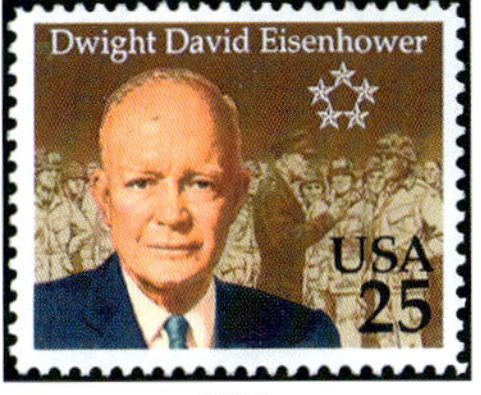

2513

2514

2515, 2516

SCOTT NO.	DESCRIPTION	FIRST DAY COVERS SING	FIRST DAY COVERS PL. BLK.	MINT SHEET	PLATE BLOCK	UNUSED F/NH	USED
2512	25¢ Americas Issue (Grand Canyon).	2.25	4.00	42.00(50)	5.00	1.25	.25
2513	25¢ Dwight D. Eisenhower	2.25	4.00	38.00(40)	5.00	1.25	.25
2514	25¢ Madonna & Child– Antonello	2.25	4.00	38.00(50)	3.50	.95	.25
2514a	same, bklt pane of 10 .	6.50	....	....	....	10.00	....
2514av	same, bklt pane, unfolded	....	....	....	....	15.00	....
2515	25¢ Christmas Tree . . .	2.25	4.00	38.00(50)	4.00	.75	.25
2516	25¢ Christmas Tree bklt single.	2.25	....	....	....	1.50	.25
2516a	same, bklt pane of 10 .	6.00	....	....	....	12.00	....
2516av	same, bklt pane, unfolded	....	....	....	....	19.50	....

2517- 2519, 2520

1991 REGULAR ISSUES

SCOTT NO.	DESCRIPTION	FIRST DAY COVERS SING	FIRST DAY COVERS PL. BLK.	MINT SHEET	PLATE BLOCK	UNUSED F/NH	USED
2517	(29¢) 'F' Flower	2.25	4.25	90.00(100)	4.25	.95	.25
			PLATE # STRIP 3		PLATE# STRIP 3		
2518	(29¢) "F" Flower, coil . .	2.25	10.00	....	4.00	.95	.25
	same, plate strip of 5 . .	....	....	....	....	6.00	....
2519	(29¢) "F" Flower, bklt single (BEP).	2.25	....	....	....	1.00	.25
2519a	same, bklt pane of 10 (BEP)	6.50	....	....	....	11.00	....
2520	(29¢) "F" Flower, bklt single (KCS).	3.00	....	....	....	3.50	.70
2520a	same, bklt pane of 10 (KCS)	6.50	....	....	....	30.00	....

2521

2522

SCOTT NO.	DESCRIPTION	FIRST DAY COVERS SING	FIRST DAY COVERS PL. BLK.	MINT SHEET	PLATE BLOCK	UNUSED F/NH	USED
2521	(4¢) "F" Make-up Rate.	2.25	4.25	17.00(100)	1.00	.20	.25
2522	(29¢) "F" ATM Plastic Stamp, single.	2.25	....	....	....	1.00	.50
2522a	same, pane of 12.	9.00	....	....	....	16.00	....

2523, 2523A

SCOTT NO.	DESCRIPTION	FIRST DAY COVERS SING	PLATE# STRIP 3	MINT SHEET	PLATE# STRIP 3	UNUSED F/NH	USED
2523	29¢ Flag over Mt. Rushmore, coil	2.25	10.00	....	5.00	1.50	.25
	same, plate strip of 5 .		....	....	....	7.00	....
2523A	29¢ Falg over Mt. Rushmore, photogravure coil	2.25	10.00	....	5.00	1.50	1.00
	same, plate strip of 5 .	....	....	....	....	7.50	....

2524-27

SCOTT NO.	DESCRIPTION	FIRST DAY COVERS SING	FIRST DAY COVERS PL. BLK.	MINT SHEET	PLATE BLOCK	UNUSED F/NH	USED
2524	29¢ Flower..........	2.25	4.25	90.00(100)	5.00	1.00	.25
2524A	29¢ Flower, perf. 13...	....	....	155.00(100)	55.00	1.40	.50
			PLATE# STRIP 3		PLATE# STRIP 3		
2525	29¢ Flower, coil rouletted	2.25	10.00	....	5.00	1.20	.25
	same, plate strip of 5..	....	....	....	....	7.00	....
2526	29¢ Flower, coil, perf (1992)	2.25	10.00	....	5.50	1.30	.25
	same, plate strip of 5..	....	....	....	....	8.00	....
2527	29¢ Flower, bklt single	2.25	....	....	....	1.20	.25
2527a	same, bklt pane of 10 .	6.50	....	....	....	9.50	....
2527av	same, bklt pane, unfolded	....	....	....	....	12.00	....

2528

2529, 2529C

2530

2531

2531A

SCOTT NO.	DESCRIPTION	FIRST DAY COVERS SING	PLATE# STRIP 3	MINT SHEET	PLATE# STRIP3	UNUSED F/NH	USED
2528	29¢ Flag with Olympic Rings, bklt single..........	2.25	....	....	....	1.10	.25
2528a	same, bklt pane of 10 .	6.50	....	....	....	10.00	....
2528av	same, bklt pane, unfolded	....	....	....	....	12.00	....
2529	19¢ Fishing Boat Type I	2.25	10.00	....	4.00	.75	.25
	same, plate strip of 5..	....	....	....	....	5.00	....
2529a	same, Type II (1993) ..	....	....	....	4.50	.75	.40
	same, plate strip of 5..	....	....	....	....	5.50	....
2529C	19¢ Fishing Boat (reengraved)	2.25	10.00	....	9.00	1.25	.60
	same, plate strip of 5..	....	....	....	....	11.50	....
2530	19¢ Hot-Air Balloon bklt single..........	2.25	....	....	....	.70	.25
2530a	same, bklt pane of 10 .	10.00	....	....	....	6.75	.25
2530av	same, bklt pane, unfolded	....	....	....	....	8.00	....
2531	29¢ Flags on Parade ..	2.25	4.25	95.00(100)	5.00	1.25	.25
2531A	29¢ Liberty Torch ATM Stamp	2.25	....	....	....	1.25	.30
2531Ab	same, pane of 18.....	15.00	....	....	....	18.00	....

2532

1991 COMMEMORATIVES

SCOTT NO.	DESCRIPTION	FIRST DAY COVERS SING	FIRST DAY COVERS PL. BLK.	MINT SHEET	PLATE BLOCK	UNUSED F/NH	USED
2532/2579	(2532-35, 2537-38, 2550-51, 2553-61, 2567, 2578-79) 29 varieties	....	....	....	....	32.00	11.50
2532	50¢ Switzerland......	2.25	5.00	58.00(40)	7.00	1.75	.40

2533

2534

2535, 2536

2537

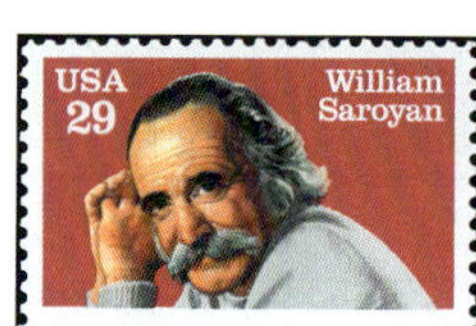
2538

2539

SCOTT NO.	DESCRIPTION	FIRST DAY COVERS SING	FIRST DAY COVERS PL. BLK.	MINT SHEET	PLATE BLOCK	UNUSED F/NH	USED
2533	29¢ Vermont Statehood	2.25	4.25	56.00(50)	6.00	1.50	.25
2534	29¢ Savings Bonds ...	2.25	4.25	45.00(50)	4.75	1.00	.25
2535	29¢ Love	2.25	4.25	43.00(50)	4.75	1.00	.25
2535a	29¢ Love, perf 11.....	2.25	4.25	65.00(50)	8.50	1.50	.25
2536	29¢ Love, bklt single..	2.25	....	....	....	1.00	.25
2536a	same, bklt pane of 10 .	6.50	....	....	....	10.00	....
2536av	same, bklt pane, unfolded	....	....	....	....	13.00	....
2537	52¢ Love	2.25	5.00	80.00(50)	8.50	1.75	.35
2538	29¢ William Saroyan ..	2.25	4.25	45.00(50)	5.00	1.00	.25
2539	$1 USPS/Olympic Rings	3.00	6.50	58.00(20)	15.00	3.50	1.50

2540

SCOTT NO.	DESCRIPTION	FIRST DAY COVERS SING	FIRST DAY COVERS PL. BLK.	MINT SHEET	PLATE BLOCK	UNUSED F/NH	USED
2540	$2.90 Eagle and Olympic Rings.......	10.00	16.50	210.00(20)	55.00	13.00	5.50

2541

2542

SCOTT NO.	DESCRIPTION	FIRST DAY COVERS SING	FIRST DAY COVERS PL. BLK.	MINT SHEET	PLATE BLOCK	UNUSED F/NH	USED
2541	$9.95 Express Mail ...	27.00	50.00	600.00(20)	150.00	33.00	11.00
2542	$14.00 Express Mail ..	35.00	67.50	825.00(20)	200.00	45.00	23.00

2543

2544

2544A

SCOTT NO.	DESCRIPTION	FIRST DAY COVERS SING	FIRST DAY COVERS PL. BLK.	MINT SHEET	PLATE BLOCK	UNUSED F/NH	USED
2543	$2.90 Space Vehicle, priority mail	8.00	17.50	375.00(40)	45.00	10.00	2.75
2544	$3 Challenger Shuttle, priority mail (1995)....	8.00	17.50	170.00(20)	42.00	9.00	3.00
2544A	$10.75 Endeavour Shuttle, express mail (1995)...	27.50	57.50	625.00(20)	155.00	30.00	10.00
2544b	Challenger Shuttle, Priority Mail (1996).....	....	....	180.00(20)	42.00	10.00	3.50

2545 2546

2547 2548

2549

SCOTT NO.	DESCRIPTION	FIRST DAY COVERS SING	FIRST DAY COVERS PL. BLK.	MINT SHEET	PLATE BLOCK	UNUSED F/NH	USED
2545	29¢ "Royal Wulff".	2.25	....	....	....	2.00	.25
2546	29¢ "Jock Scott".	2.25	....	....	....	2.00	.25
2547	29¢ "Apte Tarpon"	2.25	....	....	....	2.00	.25
2548	29¢ "Lefty's Deceiver" .	2.25	....	....	....	2.00	.25
2549	29¢ "Muddler Minnow".	2.25	....	....	....	2.00	.25
2549a	Fishing Flies, bklt pane, 5 varieties, attached . .	4.50	....	....	....	12.00	9.00
2549av	same, bklt pane, unfolded	....	....	....	....	18.00	....

2550 2551, 2552

SCOTT NO.	DESCRIPTION	FIRST DAY COVERS SING	FIRST DAY COVERS PL. BLK.	MINT SHEET	PLATE BLOCK	UNUSED F/NH	USED
2550	29¢ Cole Porter	2.25	4.25	50.00(50)	5.00	1.10	.25
2551	29¢ Desert Storm	2.25	4.25	50.00(50)	4.75	1.10	.25
2552	29¢ Desert Storm, bklt single.	2.25	....	....	....	2.50	.25
2552a	same, bklt pane of 5 . .	4.75	....	....	....	5.50	....
2552av	same, bklt pane, unfolded	....	....	....	....	7.50	....

2553

2554 2555

2556 2557

2558

SCOTT NO.	DESCRIPTION	FIRST DAY COVERS SING	FIRST DAY COVERS PL. BLK.	MINT SHEET	PLATE BLOCK	UNUSED F/NH	USED
2553-57	Summer Olympics, 5 varieties, attached . .	4.50	....	38.00(40)	12.00(10)	5.25	4.50
2553	29¢ Pole Vault	2.25	....	....	....	1.10	.60
2554	29¢ Discus.	2.25	....	....	....	1.10	.60
2555	29¢ Sprinters	2.25	....	....	....	1.10	.60
2556	29¢ Javelin	2.25	....	....	....	1.10	.60
2557	29¢ Hurdles	2.25	....	....	....	1.10	.60
2558	29¢ Numismatics.	2.25	4.25	60.00(50)	6.00	1.30	.60

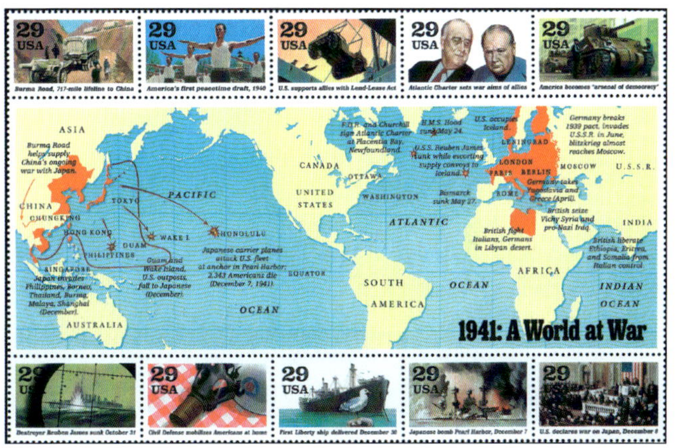

2559

SCOTT NO.	DESCRIPTION	FIRST DAY COVERS SING	FIRST DAY COVERS PL. BLK.	MINT SHEET	PLATE BLOCK	UNUSED F/NH	USED
2559	$2.90 World War II, 1941, souvenir sheet of 10 . .	14.00	....	22.00(20)	....	14.00	11.00
2559a	29¢ Burma Road	3.00	....	....	....	1.35	.75
2559b	29¢ Peacetime Draft . .	3.00	....	....	....	1.35	.75
2559c	29¢ Lend-Lease Act. . .	3.00	....	....	....	1.35	.75
2559d	29¢ Atlantic Charter. . .	3.00	....	....	....	1.35	.75
2559e	29¢ "Arsenal of Democracy"	3.00	....	....	....	1.35	.75
2559f	29¢ Destroyer "Reuben James".	3.00	....	....	....	1.35	.75
2559g	29¢ Civil Defense	3.00	....	....	....	1.35	.75
2559h	29¢ Liberty Ship.	3.00	....	....	....	1.35	.75
2559i	29¢ Pearl Harbor	3.00	....	....	....	1.35	.75
2559j	29¢ Declaration of War on Japan	3.00	....	....	....	1.35	.75

2560

SCOTT NO.	DESCRIPTION	FIRST DAY COVERS SING	FIRST DAY COVERS PL. BLK.	MINT SHEET	PLATE BLOCK	UNUSED F/NH	USED
2560	29¢ Basketball.	3.00	4.50	65.00(50)	6.50	1.50	.25

2561

SCOTT NO.	DESCRIPTION	FIRST DAY COVERS SING	FIRST DAY COVERS PL. BLK.	MINT SHEET	PLATE BLOCK	UNUSED F/NH	USED
2561	29¢ District of Columbia	2.25	4.25	45.00(50)	4.50	1.30	.25

2562

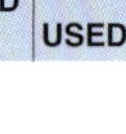
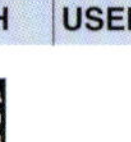
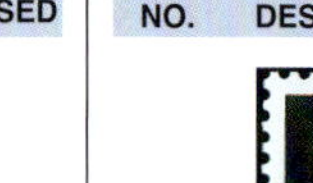

2563

2564

2565

2566

SCOTT NO.	DESCRIPTION	FIRST DAY COVERS SING	FIRST DAY COVERS PL. BLK.	MINT SHEET	PLATE BLOCK	UNUSED F/NH	USED
2562	29¢ Laurel and Hardy .	2.25	....	....	....	1.50	.35
2563	29¢ Bergen and McCarthy	2.25	....	....	....	1.50	.35
2564	29¢ Jack Benny	2.25	....	....	....	1.50	.35
2565	29¢ Fanny Brice	2.25	....	....	....	1.50	.35
2566	29¢ Abbott and Costello	2.25	....	....	....	1.50	.35
2566a	Comedians, bklt pane of 10.	8.00	....	....	....	13.00	9.50
2566av	same, bklt pane, unfolded	....	....	....	....	17.00	....

2567

SCOTT NO.	DESCRIPTION	FIRST DAY COVERS SING	FIRST DAY COVERS PL. BLK.	MINT SHEET	PLATE BLOCK	UNUSED F/NH	USED
2567	29¢ Jan Matzeliger . . .	2.25	4.25	45.00(50)	4.75	1.20	.25

2568

2569

2570

2571

2572

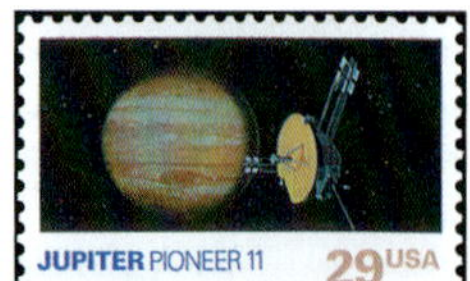

2573

2574

2575

NEPTUNE VOYAGER 2 29USA

2576

2577

SCOTT NO.	DESCRIPTION	FIRST DAY COVERS SING	FIRST DAY COVERS PL. BLK.	MINT SHEET	PLATE BLOCK	UNUSED F/NH	USED
2568	29¢ Mercury and Mariner 10	2.25	....	....	....	1.50	.40
2569	29¢ Venus and Mariner 2	2.25	....	....	....	1.50	.40
2570	29¢ Earth and Landsat	2.25	....	....	....	1.50	.40
2571	29¢ Moon and Lunar Orbiter	2.25	....	....	....	1.50	.40
2572	29¢ Mars and Viking Orbiter	2.25	....	....	....	1.50	.40
2573	29¢ Jupiter and Pioneer 11	2.25	....	....	....	1.50	.40
2574	29¢ Saturn and Voyager 2	2.25	....	....	....	1.50	.40
2575	29¢ Uranus and Voyager 2	2.25	....	....	....	1.50	.40
2576	29¢ Neptune and Voyager 2	2.25	....	....	....	1.50	.40
2577	29¢ Pluto, "Not Yet Explored"	2.25	....	....	....	1.50	.40
2577a	Space Explorations, bklt pane of 10.	9.00	....	....	....	14.00	12.00
2577av	same, bklt pane, unfolded	....	....	....	....	20.00	....

2578

2579-81

2582

2583

2584

2585

SCOTT NO.	DESCRIPTION	FIRST DAY COVERS SING	FIRST DAY COVERS PL. BLK.	MINT SHEET	PLATE BLOCK	UNUSED F/NH	USED
2578	(29¢) Christmas– Traditional	2.25	4.25	45.00(50)	4.75	1.00	.25
2578a	same, bklt pane of 10 .	7.00	....	....	....	10.00	....
2578av	same, bklt pane, unfolded	....	....	....	....	15.00	....
2579	(29¢) Christmas– Contemporary	2.25	4.25	45.00(50)	4.75	.95	.25
2580-85	(29¢) Santa & Chimney set of 6 singles.	12.00	....	....	....	13.50	3.50
2581b-85a	same, bklt pane of 4 .	....	....	....	....	28.00	....
2581-85av	same, bklt pane of 4, unfolded.	20.00	....	....	....	32.50	....

NOTE: **The far left brick from the top row of the chimney is missing from Type II, No. 2581**

2587

2590

1992-95 Regular Issues

SCOTT NO.	DESCRIPTION	FIRST DAY COVERS SING	FIRST DAY COVERS PL. BLK.	MINT SHEET	PLATE BLOCK	UNUSED F/NH	USED
2587	32¢ James K. Polk (1995)	1.95	4.75	120.00(100)	7.00	1.75	.25
2590	$1 "Surrender at Saratoga" (1994)	4.00	6.50	60.00(20)	15.00	3.50	1.00

2592

SCOTT NO.	DESCRIPTION	FIRST DAY COVERS SING	FIRST DAY COVERS PL. BLK.	MINT SHEET	PLATE BLOCK	UNUSED F/NH	USED
2592	$5 Washington & Jackson (1994)	22.00	30.00	300.00(20)	68.00	16.50	3.00

2593, 2594

SCOTT NO.	DESCRIPTION	FIRST DAY COVERS SING	FIRST DAY COVERS PL. BLK.	MINT SHEET	PLATE BLOCK	UNUSED F/NH	USED
2593	29¢ Pledge of Allegiance (black) bklt single.	2.25	....	....	....	1.00	.25
2593a	same, bklt pane of 10 .	7.00	....	....	....	10.00	....
2593av	same, bklt pane, unfolded	....	....	....	....	14.00	....
2594	29¢ Pledge of Allegiance (red) bklt single (1993).	2.25	....	....	....	1.50	.25
2594a	same, bklt pane of 10 .	7.00	....	....	....	11.00	....
2594av	same, bklt pane, unfolded	....	....	....	....	14.00	....

2595-97

2598

2599

1992-94 Self-Adhesive Stamps

SCOTT NO.	DESCRIPTION	FIRST DAY COVERS SING	FIRST DAY COVERS PL. BLK.	MINT SHEET	PLATE BLOCK	UNUSED F/NH	USED
2595	29¢ Eagle & Shield (brown) bklt single	2.25	....	....	....	1.20	.30
2595a	same, bklt pane of 17 .	12.00	....	....	....	18.00	....
2595v	same, coil	2.50	....	....	....	1.20	.30
2596	29¢ Eagle & Shield (green) bklt single	1.75	....	....	....	1.20	.30
2596a	same, bklt pane of 17 .	12.00	....	....	....	18.00	....
2596v	same, coil	2.50	....	....	....	1.20	.30
2597	29¢ Eagle & Shield (red) bklt single	2.25	....	....	....	1.20	.30
2597a	same, bklt pane of 17 .	12.00	....	....	....	18.00	....
2597v	same, coil	2.50	....	....	....	1.20	.30
2598	29¢ Eagle (1994).	2.25	....	....	....	1.20	.30
2598a	same, bklt pane of 18 .	13.50	....	....	....	18.00	....
2598v	29¢ Eagle, coil.	2.50	....	....	10.00(3)	1.20	....
2598b	same, plate strip of 5 . .	....	....	....	....	12.00	....
2599	29¢ Statue of Liberty (1994)	2.25	....	....	....	1.20	.30
2599a	same, bklt pane of 18 .	13.50	....	....	....	18.00	....
2599v	29¢ Statue of Liberty, coil	2.50	....	....	10.00(3)	1.20	....
2599b	same, plate strip of 5 . .	....	....	....	....	12.00	....

2602

2603, 2604

2605

2606-08

2609

1991-93 Regular Issue

SCOTT NO.	DESCRIPTION	FIRST DAY COVERS SING	PLATE# STRIP 3	MINT SHEET	PLATE# STRIP 3	UNUSED F/NH	USED
2602	(10¢) Eagle, Bulk-Rate coil.	2.25	10.00	....	3.00	.40	.25
	same, plate strip of 5 . .	....	....	....	....	4.00	....
2603	(10¢) Eagle, Bulk-Rate coil (orange-yellow) (BEP)	2.25	10.00	....	3.00	.40	.25
	same, plate strip of 5 . .	....	....	....	....	4.00	....
2604	(10¢) Eagle, Bulk-Rate coil (Stamp Ventures) (gold) (1993)	2.25	10.00	....	3.00	.40	.25
2605	23¢ Flag, Presort First-Class	2.25	10.00	....	4.00	.75	.30
	same, plate strip of 5 . .	....	....	....	....	5.50	....
2606	23¢ USA, Presort First-Class (ABN) (1992)	2.25	10.00	....	4.50	.75	.30
	same, plate strip of 5 . .	....	....	....	....	7.00	....
2607	23¢ USA, Presort First-Class (BEP) (1992)	2.25	10.00	....	4.50	.75	.30
	same, plate strip of 5 . .	....	....	....	....	7.00	....
2608	23¢ USA, Presort First-Class (Stamp Ventures) (1993)	2.25	10.00	....	7.00	1.40	.30
	same, plate strip of 5 . .	....	....	....	....	10.00	....
2609	29¢ Flag over White House, coil (1992)	2.25	10.00	....	5.00	1.20	.25
	same, plate strip of 5 . .	....	....	....	....	7.00	....

2611

2612

2613

2614

2615

1992 COMMEMORATIVES

SCOTT NO.	DESCRIPTION	FIRST DAY COVERS SING	FIRST DAY COVERS PL. BLK.	MINT SHEET	PLATE BLOCK	UNUSED F/NH	USED
2611/2720	**(2611-23, 2630-41, 2697-2704, 2710-14, 2720) 48 varieties . . . .**	....	....	....	....	**50.00**	**16.50**
2611-15	Winter Olympics, 5 varieties, attached . .	6.00	....	40.00(35)	12.00(10)	5.75	4.50
2611	29¢ Hockey	2.25	....	....	....	1.30	.25
2612	29¢ Figure Skating . . .	2.25	....	....	....	1.30	.25
2613	29¢ Speed Skating . . .	2.25	....	....	....	1.30	.25
2614	29¢ Skiing	2.25	....	....	....	1.30	.25
2615	29¢ Bobsledding	2.25	....	....	....	1.30	.25

2616

2617

SCOTT NO.	DESCRIPTION	FIRST DAY COVERS SING	FIRST DAY COVERS PL. BLK.	MINT SHEET	PLATE BLOCK	UNUSED F/NH	USED
2616	29¢ World Columbian Expo	2.25	4.25	45.00(50)	4.75	1.50	.25
2617	29¢ W.E.B. Du Bois. . .	3.00	4.25	52.00(50)	5.50	1.50	.25

2618

2619

SCOTT NO.	DESCRIPTION	FIRST DAY COVERS SING	FIRST DAY COVERS PL. BLK.	MINT SHEET	PLATE BLOCK	UNUSED F/NH	USED
2618	29¢ Love	2.25	4.25	45.00(50)	4.50	.95	.25
2619	29¢ Olympic Baseball .	3.75	5.50	52.00(50)	6.50	1.25	.25

2620 2621 2622 2623

SCOTT NO.	DESCRIPTION	FIRST DAY COVERS SING	FIRST DAY COVERS PL. BLK.	MINT SHEET	PLATE BLOCK	UNUSED F/NH	USED
2620-23	First Voyage of Columbus	4.00	5.00	40.00(40)	5.50	4.25	4.00
2620	29¢ Seeking Isabella's Support	2.25	....	....	....	1.25	.35
2621	29¢ Crossing the Atlantic	2.25	....	....	....	1.25	.35
2622	29¢ Approaching Land	2.25	....	....	....	1.25	.35
2623	29¢ Coming Ashore . . .	2.25	....	....	....	1.25	.35

2624

2625

2626

2627

2628

2629

SCOTT NO.	DESCRIPTION	FIRST DAY COVERS SING	FIRST DAY COVERS PL. BLK.	MINT SHEET	PLATE BLOCK	UNUSED F/NH	USED
2624-29	1¢-$5 Columbian Souvenir Sheets (6). . .	55.00	....	....	....	50.00	40.00
2624a-29a	same, set of 16 singles	105.00	....	....	....	54.00	39.00

2630

SCOTT NO.	DESCRIPTION	FIRST DAY COVERS SING	FIRST DAY COVERS PL. BLK.	MINT SHEET	PLATE BLOCK	UNUSED F/NH	USED
2630	29¢ NY Stock Exchange	4.00	6.00	35.00(40)	4.75	1.00	.25

2631 2632

2633

2634

SCOTT NO.	DESCRIPTION	FIRST DAY COVERS SING	FIRST DAY COVERS PL. BLK.	MINT SHEET	PLATE BLOCK	UNUSED F/NH	USED
2631-34	Space, US/Russian Joint Issue	4.00	5.00	48.00(50)	5.50	5.00	3.50
2631	29¢ Cosmonaut & Space Shuttle	2.50	....	....	....	1.30	.40
2632	29¢ Astronaut & Mir Space Station	2.50	....	....	....	1.30	.40
2633	29¢ Apollo Lunar Module & Sputnik	2.50	....	....	....	1.30	.40
2634	29¢ Soyuz, Mercury & Gemini Space Craft . . .	2.50	....	....	....	1.30	.40

2635

2636

SCOTT NO.	DESCRIPTION	FIRST DAY COVERS SING	FIRST DAY COVERS PL. BLK.	MINT SHEET	PLATE BLOCK	UNUSED F/NH	USED
2635	29¢ Alaska Highway . .	2.25	4.75	45.00(50)	4.75	1.20	.25
2636	29¢ Kentucky Statehood	2.25	4.75	45.00(50)	4.75	1.20	.25

2637

2638

2639

2640

2641

SCOTT NO.	DESCRIPTION	FIRST DAY COVERS SING	FIRST DAY COVERS PL. BLK.	MINT SHEET	PLATE BLOCK	UNUSED F/NH	USED
2637-41	Summer Olympics, 5 varieties, attached . .	5.50	....	39.00(35)	14.00(10)	6.00	5.00
2637	29¢ Soccer	2.25	....	....	....	1.30	.75
2638	29¢ Women's Gymnastics	2.25	....	....	....	1.30	.75
2639	29¢ Volleyball	2.25	....	....	....	1.30	.75
2640	29¢ Boxing.	2.25	....	....	....	1.30	.75
2641	29¢ Swimming	2.25	....	....	....	1.30	.75

2642

2643

2644

2645

2646

SCOTT NO.	DESCRIPTION	FIRST DAY COVERS SING	FIRST DAY COVERS PL. BLK.	MINT SHEET	PLATE BLOCK	UNUSED F/NH	USED
2642	29¢ Ruby-throated Hummingbird	2.25	....	....	....	1.30	.60
2643	29¢ Broad-billed Hummingbird	2.25	....	....	....	1.30	.60
2644	29¢ Costa's Hummingbird	2.25	....	....	....	1.30	.60
2645	29¢ Rufous Hummingbird	2.25	....	....	....	1.30	.60
2646	29¢ Calliope Hummingbird	2.25	....	....	....	1.30	.60
2646a	29¢ Hummingbirds, bklt pane, 5 vareities, attached . .	5.00	....	....	....	5.75	....
2646av	same, bklt pane, unfolded	....	....	....	....	6.50	....

2647

2648

2649

1992 WILDFLOWERS

2647 *Indian Paintbrush*
2648 *Fragrant Water Lily*
2649 *Meadow Beauty*
2650 *Jack-in-the-Pulpit*
2651 *California Poppy*
2652 *Large-Flowered Trillium*
2653 *Tickseed*
2654 *Shooting Star*
2655 *Stream Violet*
2656 *Bluets*
2657 *Herb Robert*
2658 *Marsh Marigold*
2659 *Sweet White Violet*
2660 *Claret Cup Cactus*
2661 *White Mountain Avens*
2662 *Sessile Bellwort*
2663 *Blue Flag*
2664 *Harlequin Lupine*
2665 *Twinflower*
2666 *Common Sunflower*
2667 *Sego Lily*
2668 *Virginia Bluebells*
2669 *Ohi'a Lehua*
2670 *Rosebud Orchid*
2671 *Showy Evening Primrose*
2672 *Fringed Gentian*
2673 *Yellow Lady's Slipper*
2674 *Passionflower*
2675 *Bunchberry*
2676 *Pasqueflower*
2677 *Round-lobed Hepatica*
2678 *Wild Columbine*
2679 *Fireweed*
2680 *Indian Pond Lily*
2681 *Turk's Cap Lily*
2682 *Dutchman's Breeches*
2683 *Trumpet Honeysuckle*
2684 *Jacob's Ladder*
2685 *Plains Prickly Pear*
2686 *Moss Campion*
2687 *Bearberry*
2688 *Mexican Hat*
2689 *Harebell*
2690 *Desert Five Spot*
2691 *Smooth Solomon's Seal*
2692 *Red Maids*
2693 *Yellow Skunk Cabbage*
2694 *Rue Anemone*
2695 *Standing Cypress*
2696 *Wild Flax*

SCOTT NO.	DESCRIPTION	FIRST DAY COVERS SING	FIRST DAY COVERS PL. BLK.	MINT SHEET	PLATE BLOCK	UNUSED F/NH	USED
2647-96	29¢ Wildflowers, 50 varieties, attached .	70.00	....	55.00(50)	....	55.00	....
	set of singles	86.00	....	....	....	....	29.00
	singles of above, each.	1.75	....	....	....	1.50	.85

2697

SCOTT NO.	DESCRIPTION	FIRST DAY COVERS SING	FIRST DAY COVERS PL. BLK.	MINT SHEET	PLATE BLOCK	UNUSED F/NH	USED
2697	$2.90 World War II (1942) Souvenir Sheet of 10. .	12.00	....	22.50(20)	....	14.00	11.00
2697a	29¢ Tokyo Raid	2.50	....	....	....	1.35	.75
2697b	29¢ Commodity Rationing	2.50	....	....	....	1.35	.75
2697c	29¢ Battle of Coral Sea	2.50	....	....	....	1.35	.75
2697d	29¢ Fall of Corregidor .	2.50	....	....	....	1.35	.75
2697e	29¢ Japan Invades Aleutians	2.50	....	....	....	1.35	.75
2697f	29¢ Allies Break Codes	2.50	....	....	....	1.35	.75
2697g	29¢ USS Yorktown Lost	2.50........	....	....	....	1.35	.75
2697h	29¢ Women Join War Effort	2.50	....	....	....	1.35	.75
2697i	29¢ Marines on Guadalcanal	2.50	....	....	....	1.35	.75
2697j	29¢ Allies Land in North Africa	2.50	....	....	....	1.35	.75

2698

2699

SCOTT NO.	DESCRIPTION	FIRST DAY COVERS SING	FIRST DAY COVERS PL. BLK.	MINT SHEET	PLATE BLOCK	UNUSED F/NH	USED
2698	29¢ Dorothy Parker . . .	2.25	4.75	45.00(50)	5.00	1.50	.25
2699	29¢ Dr. T. von Karman.	2.25	4.75	45.00(50)	4.75	1.50	.25

2700

2701

2704

2702

2703

SCOTT NO.	DESCRIPTION	FIRST DAY COVERS SING	FIRST DAY COVERS PL. BLK.	MINT SHEET	PLATE BLOCK	UNUSED F/NH	USED
2700-03	Minerals, 4 varieties, attached . .	5.00	4.00	55.00(40)	7.00	6.50	4.00
2700	29¢ Azurite.	2.25	....	....	....	1.50	.75
2701	29¢ Copper	2.25	....	....	....	1.50	.75
2702	29¢ Variscite	2.25	....	....	....	1.50	.75
2703	29¢ Wulfenite.	2.25	....	....	....	1.50	.75
2704	29¢ Juan Rodriguez Cabrillo	2.25	4.75	49.00(50)	4.75	1.00	.25

2705

2706

2707

2708

2709

SCOTT NO.	DESCRIPTION	FIRST DAY COVERS SING	FIRST DAY COVERS PL. BLK.	MINT SHEET	PLATE BLOCK	UNUSED F/NH	USED
2705	29¢ Giraffe.	2.25	....	....	....	1.25	.40
2706	29¢ Giant Panda	2.25	....	....	....	1.25	.40
2707	29¢ Flamingo.	2.25	....	....	....	1.25	.40
2708	29¢ King Penguins . . .	2.25	....	....	....	1.25	.40
2709	29¢ White Bengal Tiger	2.25	....	....	....	1.25	.40
2709a	29¢ Wild Animals, bklt pane of 5.	5.00	....	....	....	6.00	4.50
2709av	same, bklt pane , unfolded	....	....	....	....	7.75	....

2710

SCOTT NO.	DESCRIPTION	FIRST DAY COVERS SING	FIRST DAY COVERS PL. BLK.	MINT SHEET	PLATE BLOCK	UNUSED F/NH	USED
2710	29¢ Christmas–Traditional	2.25	4.75	45.00(50)	5.00	1.00	.25
2710a	same, bklt pane of 10 .	9.00	....	....	....	9.00	....
2710av	same, bklt pane, unfolded	....	....	....	....	12.00	....

2711, 2715 2712, 2716, 2719

2713, 2717 2714, 2718

SCOTT NO.	DESCRIPTION	FIRST DAY COVERS SING	FIRST DAY COVERS PL. BLK.	MINT SHEET	PLATE BLOCK	UNUSED F/NH	USED
2711-14	Christmas Toys, 4 varieties, attached . .	4.00	5.00	52.00(50)	6.00	5.50	4.50
2711	29¢ Hobby Horse.	2.25	....	....	....	1.50	.30
2712	29¢ Locomotive	2.25	....	....	....	1.50	.30
2713	29¢ Fire Engine	2.25	....	....	....	1.50	.30
2714	29¢ Steamboat	2.25	....	....	....	1.50	.30
2715	29¢ Hobby Horse (gravure) bklt single.	2.25	....	....	....	1.50	.30
2716	29¢ Locomotive (gravure) bklt single.	2.25	....	....	....	1.50	.30
2717	29¢ Fire Engine (gravure) bklt single.	2.25	....	....	....	1.50	.30
2718	29¢ Steamboat (gravure) bklt single.	2.25	....	....	....	1.50	.30
2718a	29¢ Christmas Toys (gravure) bklt pane of 4.	9.00	....	....	....	7.00	5.50
2718av	same, bklt pane, unfolded	....	....	....	....	9.00	....
2719	29¢ Locomotive ATM, self-adhesive	2.25	....	....	....	1.20	.75
2719a	same, bklt pane of 18 .	13.50	....	....	....	18.00	....

2720

SCOTT NO.	DESCRIPTION	FIRST DAY COVERS SING	FIRST DAY COVERS PL. BLK.	MINT SHEET	PLATE BLOCK	UNUSED F/NH	USED
2720	29¢ Happy New Year. .	3.00	4.75	27.00(20)	6.50	1.20	.25

2721

2722

2723

1993 COMMEMORATIVES

SCOTT NO.	DESCRIPTION	FIRST DAY COVERS SING	FIRST DAY COVERS PL. BLK.	MINT SHEET	PLATE BLOCK	UNUSED F/NH	USED
2721/2806	**(2721-30, 2746-59, 2765-66, 2771-74, 2779-89, 2791-94, 2804-06) 57 varieties**	....	....	....	....	**74.00**	**25.00**
2721	29¢ Elvis Presley.	2.00	5.00	35.00(40)	4.50	1.00	.25
2722	29¢ "Oklahoma!"	2.25	4.75	35.00(40)	4.00	1.00	.25
2723	29¢ Hank Williams. . . .	2.25	4.75	75.00(40)	9.00	2.00	.25
2723a	29¢ Hank Williams, perf. 11.2 x 11.4.	....	....	400.00(40)	100.00	15.00	10.00

2724, 2731

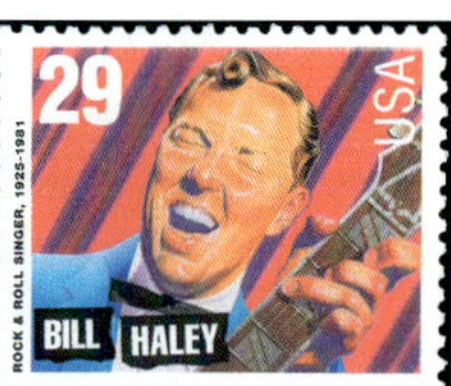

2725, 2732

2726, 2733

2727, 2734

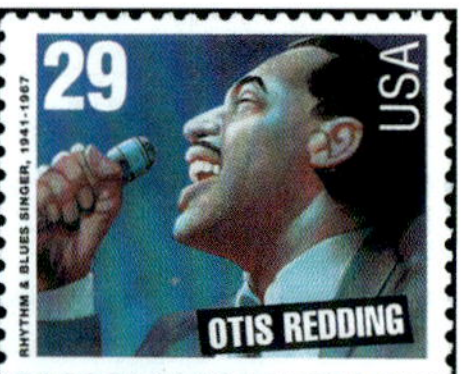

2728, 2735

2729, 2736

2730, 2737

SCOTT NO.	DESCRIPTION	FIRST DAY COVERS SING	FIRST DAY COVERS PL. BLK.	MINT SHEET	PLATE BLOCK	UNUSED F/NH	USED
2724-30	Rock & Roll/Rhythm & Blues, 7 varieties, attached . .	12.00	....	50.00(35)	14.00(8)	11.00	9.00
2724-30	same, Top Plate Block of 10	....	....	....	18.00(10)	....	....
2724	29¢ Elvis Presley	3.00	....	....	....	1.50	1.25
2725	29¢ Bill Haley.	3.00	....	....	....	1.50	1.25
2726	29¢ Clyde McPhatter . .	3.00	....	....	....	1.50	1.25
2727	29¢ Ritchie Valens. . . .	3.00	....	....	....	1.50	1.25
2728	29¢ Otis Redding.	3.00	....	....	....	1.50	1.25
2729	29¢ Buddy Holly	3.00	....	....	....	1.50	1.25
2730	29¢ Dinah Washington	3.00	....	....	....	1.50	1.25
2731	29¢ Elvis Presley, bklt single.	3.00	....	....	....	1.25	.50
2732	29¢ Bill Haley, bklt single	3.00	....	....	....	1.25	.50
2733	29¢ Clyde McPhatter, bklt single.	3.00	....	....	....	1.25	.50
2734	29¢ Ritchie Valens, bklt single.	3.00	....	....	....	1.25	.50
2735	29¢ Otis Redding, bklt single.	3.00	....	....	....	1.25	.50
2736	29¢ Buddy Holly, bklt single.	3.00	....	....	....	1.25	.50
2737	29¢ Dinah Washington, bklt single.	3.00	....	....	....	1.25	.50
2737a	same, bklt pane of 8 . .	10.00	....	....	....	12.00	....
2737av	same, bklt pane, unfolded	....	....	....	....	14.00	....
2737b	same, bklt pane of 4 . .	5.00	....	....	....	6.50	....
2737bv	same, bklt pane, unfolded	....	....	....	....	7.50	....

2741

2742

2743

2744

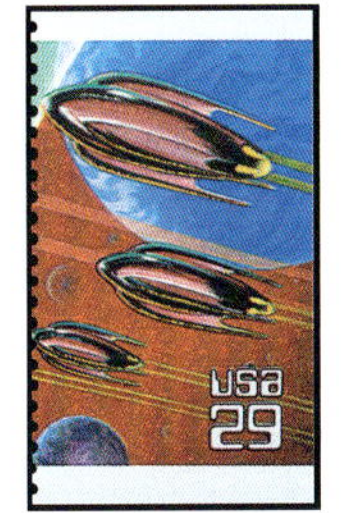

2745

SCOTT NO.	DESCRIPTION	FIRST DAY COVERS SING	FIRST DAY COVERS PL. BLK.	MINT SHEET	PLATE BLOCK	UNUSED F/NH	USED
2741	29¢ Saturn & 3 Rockets	2.25	....	....	....	1.00	.35
2742	29¢ 2 Flying Saucers. .	2.25	....	....	....	1.00	.35
2743	29¢ 3 Rocketeers	2.25	....	....	....	1.00	.35
2744	29¢ Winged Spaceship	2.25	....	....	....	1.00	.35
2745	29¢ 3 Space Ships . . .	2.25	....	....	....	1.00	.35
2745a	29¢ Space Fantasy, bklt pane of 5.	4.50	....	....	....	5.25	4.00
2745av	same, bklt pane, unfolded	....	....	....	....	6.75	....

2746

2747

2748

2749

2750 2751

2752 2753

SCOTT NO.	DESCRIPTION	FIRST DAY COVERS SING	FIRST DAY COVERS PL. BLK.	MINT SHEET	PLATE BLOCK	UNUSED F/NH	USED
2746	29¢ Percy Lavon Julian	3.00	4.75	48.00(50)	5.00	1.20	.25
2747	29¢ Oregon Trail	2.25	4.75	48.00(50)	5.00	1.70	.25
2748	29¢ World University Games	2.25	4.75	45.00(50)	4.75	.95	.25
2749	29¢ Grace Kelly.	3.00	4.75	49.00(50)	5.00	.95	.25
2750-53	Circus, 4 varieties, attached	5.00	6.00	45.00(40)	9.00(6)	5.00	4.00
2750	29¢ Clown	2.25	....	....	....	1.35	.30
2751	29¢ Ringmaster	2.25	....	....	....	1.35	.30
2752	29¢ Trapeze Artist	2.25	....	....	....	1.35	.30
2753	29¢ Elephant	2.25	....	....	....	1.35	.30

2754

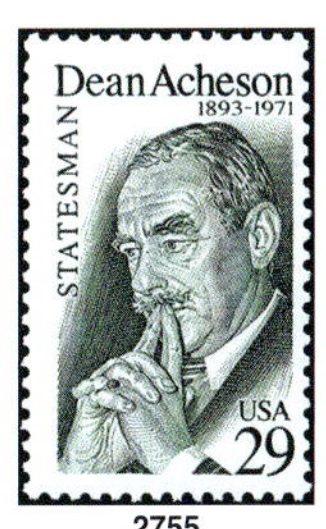

2755

SCOTT NO.	DESCRIPTION	FIRST DAY COVERS SING	FIRST DAY COVERS PL. BLK.	MINT SHEET	PLATE BLOCK	UNUSED F/NH	USED
2754	29¢ Cherokee Strip . . .	2.25	4.75	30.00(20)	7.00	1.50	.25
2755	29¢ Dean Acheson . . .	2.25	4.75	45.00(50)	5.00	1.10	.25

2756 2757

2758 2759

SCOTT NO.	DESCRIPTION	FIRST DAY COVERS SING	FIRST DAY COVERS PL. BLK.	MINT SHEET	PLATE BLOCK	UNUSED F/NH	USED
2756-59	Sporting Horses, 4 varieties, attached . .	7.50	9.75	45.00(40)	6.00	5.75	4.50
2756	29¢ Steeplechase	3.00	....	....	....	1.25	.75
2757	29¢ Thoroughbred	3.00	....	....	....	1.25	.75
2758	29¢ Harness	3.00	....	....	....	1.25	.75
2759	29¢ Polo	3.00	....	....	....	1.25	.75

2760

2761

2762

2763 2764

SCOTT NO.	DESCRIPTION	FIRST DAY COVERS SING	FIRST DAY COVERS PL. BLK.	MINT SHEET	PLATE BLOCK	UNUSED F/NH	USED
2760	29¢ Hyacinth	2.25	....	....	....	1.15	.30
2761	29¢ Daffodil	2.25	....	....	....	1.15	.30
2762	29¢ Tulip	2.25	....	....	....	1.15	.30
2763	29¢ Iris	2.25	....	....	....	1.15	.30
2764	29¢ Lilac	2.25	....	....	....	1.15	.30
2764a	Garden Flowers, bklt pane of 5	4.50	....	....	....	6.50	4.00
2764av	same, bklt pane, unfolded	....	....	....	....	8.50	....

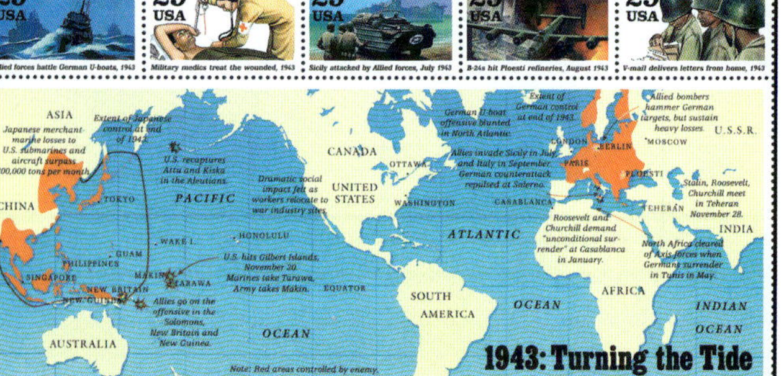

2765

SCOTT NO.	DESCRIPTION	FIRST DAY COVERS SING	FIRST DAY COVERS PL. BLK.	MINT SHEET	PLATE BLOCK	UNUSED F/NH	USED
2765	$2.90 World War II, 1943, Souvenir Sheet of 10	12.00	....	22.50(20)	....	14.00	11.00
2765a	29¢ Allies battle U-boats	2.50	....	....	....	1.35	.75
2765b	29¢ Medics treat wounded	2.50	....	....	....	1.35	.75
2765c	29¢ Allies attack Sicily	2.50	....	....	....	1.35	.75
2765d	29¢ B-24's hit Ploesti refineries	2.50	....	....	....	1.35	.75
2765e	29¢ V-Mail	2.50	....	....	....	1.35	.75
2765f	29¢ Italy invaded by Allies	2.50	....	....	....	1.35	.75
2765g	29¢ Bonds and Stamps help	2.50	....	....	....	1.35	.75
2765h	29¢ "Willie and Joe"	2.50	....	....	....	1.35	.75
2765i	29¢ Gold Stars	2.50	....	....	....	1.35	.75
2765j	29¢ Marines assault Tarawa	2.50	....	....	....	1.35	.75

2766

SCOTT NO.	DESCRIPTION	FIRST DAY COVERS SING	FIRST DAY COVERS PL. BLK.	MINT SHEET	PLATE BLOCK	UNUSED F/NH	USED
2766	29¢ Joe Louis	5.00	6.00	48.00(50)	5.00	1.50	.25

2767

2768

2769

2770

SCOTT NO.	DESCRIPTION	FIRST DAY COVERS SING	FIRST DAY COVERS PL. BLK.	MINT SHEET	PLATE BLOCK	UNUSED F/NH	USED
2767	29¢ "Show Boat"	2.50	....	....	....	1.75	.30
2768	29¢ "Porgy & Bess"	2.50	....	....	....	1.75	.30
2769	29¢ "Oklahoma!"	2.50	....	....	....	1.75	.30
2770	29¢ "My Fair Lady"	2.50	....	....	....	1.75	.30
2770a	Broadway Musicals, bklt pane of 4	6.00	....	....	....	6.00	....
2770av	same, bklt pane, unfolded	....	....	....	....	8.50	....

2771, 2775

2772, 2777

2773, 2776

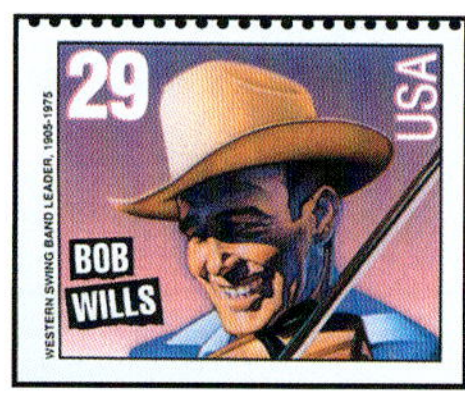

2774, 2778

SCOTT NO.	DESCRIPTION	FIRST DAY COVERS SING	FIRST DAY COVERS PL. BLK.	MINT SHEET	PLATE BLOCK	UNUSED F/NH	USED
2771-74	Country Music, 4 varieties, attached	6.00	7.00	28.00(20)	7.50	6.50	6.00
2771	29¢ Hank Williams	2.50	....	....	....	1.50	.65
2772	29¢ Patsy Cline	2.50	....	....	....	1.50	.65
2773	29¢ The Carter Family	2.50	....	....	....	1.50	.65
2774	29¢ Bob Wills	2.50	....	....	....	1.50	.65
2775	29¢ Hank Williams, bklt single	2.50	....	....	....	1.20	.30
2776	29¢ The Carter Family, bklt single	2.50	....	....	....	1.20	.30
2777	29¢ Patsy Cline, bklt single	2.50	....	....	....	1.20	.30
2778	29¢ Bob Wills, bklt single	2.50	....	....	....	1.20	.30
2778a	Country Music, bklt pane of 4	5.00	....	....	....	4.75	....
2778av	same, bklt pane, unfolded	....	....	....	....	6.50	....

2779 2780

2781 2782

2783

2784

SCOTT NO.	DESCRIPTION	FIRST DAY COVERS SING	FIRST DAY COVERS PL. BLK.	MINT SHEET	PLATE BLOCK	UNUSED F/NH	USED
2779-82	National Postal Museum, 4 varieties, attached . .	4.00	5.00	27.00(20)	7.75	6.50	5.00
2779	29¢ Ben Franklin	2.25	....	....	....	1.75	1.00
2780	29¢ Soldier & Drum . . .	2.25	....	....	....	1.75	1.00
2781	29¢ Lindbergh	2.25	....	....	....	1.75	1.00
2782	29¢ Stamps & Bar Code	2.25	....	....	....	1.75	1.00
2783-84	American Sign Language/ Deaf Communication, 2 varieties, attached . .	2.50	4.75	22.00(20)	5.50	2.00	1.25
2783	29¢ Mother/Child	2.25	....	....	....	1.10	.35
2784	29¢ Hand Sign.	2.25	....	....	....	1.10	.35

2785 2786

2787 2788

SCOTT NO.	DESCRIPTION	FIRST DAY COVERS SING	FIRST DAY COVERS PL. BLK.	MINT SHEET	PLATE BLOCK	UNUSED F/NH	USED
2785-88	Youth Classics, 4 varieties, attached . .	5.00	6.00	47.00(40)	7.00	6.00	4.50
2785	29¢ Rebecca of Sunnybrook Farm	2.25	....	....	....	1.60	.45
2786	29¢ Little House on the Prairie	2.25	....	....	....	1.60	.45
2787	29¢ Adventures of Huckleberry Finn	2.25	....	....	....	1.60	.45
2788	29¢ Little Women.	2.25	....	....	....	1.60	.45

2789, 2790

2791, 2798, 2801

2792, 2797, 2802

2793, 2796, 2799, 2803

2794, 2795, 2800

SCOTT NO.	DESCRIPTION	FIRST DAY COVERS SING	FIRST DAY COVERS PL. BLK.	MINT SHEET	PLATE BLOCK	UNUSED F/NH	USED
2789	29¢ Christmas–Traditional	2.25	4.75	45.00(50)	5.25	1.00	.25
2790	29¢ Christmas–Traditional, bklt single.	2.25	....	....	....	1.00	.25
2790a	same, bklt pane of 4 . .	3.00	....	....	....	4.00	....
2790av	same, bklt pane, unfolded	....	....	....	....	6.00	....
2791-94	Christmas–Contemporary, 4 varieties, attached . .	3.00	4.75	55.00(50)	6.50	5.50	4.00

SCOTT NO.	DESCRIPTION	FIRST DAY COVERS SING	FIRST DAY COVERS PL. BLK.	MINT SHEET	PLATE BLOCK	UNUSED F/NH	USED
2791	29¢ Jack-in-the-Box. . .	2.25	....	....	....	1.25	.25
2792	29¢ Red-Nosed Reindeer	2.25	....	....	....	1.25	.25
2793	29¢ Snowman	2.25	....	....	....	1.25	.25
2794	29¢ Toy Soldier Blowing Horn.	2.25	....	....	....	1.25	.25
2795	29¢ Toy Soldier Blowing Horn, bklt single.	2.25	....	....	....	1.40	.25
2796	29¢ Snowman, bklt single	2.25	....	....	....	1.40	.25
2797	29¢ Red-Nosed Reindeer, bklt single.	2.25	....	....	....	1.40	.25
2798	29¢ Jack-in-the-Box, bklt single.	2.25	....	....	....	1.40	.25
2798a	same, bklt pane of 10 .	7.00	....	....	....	12.00	....
2798av	same, bklt pane, unfolded	....	....	....	....	16.00	....
2799-2802v	29¢ Christmas–Contemporary, coil.	....	....	....	18.00(8)	7.50(4)	....
2802b	same, plate strip of 5 . .	....	....	....	....	14.00	....
2799	29¢ Snowman, self-adhesive (3 buttons)	2.25	....	....	....	1.25	.80
2800	29¢ Toy Soldier Blowing Horn, self-adhesive . . .	2.25	....	....	....	1.25	.80
2801	29¢ Jack-in-the-Box, self-adhesive	2.25	....	....	....	1.25	.80
2802	29¢ Red-Nosed Reindeer, self-adhesive	2.25	....	....	....	1.25	.80
2802a	same, bklt pane of 12 .	9.00	....	....	....	17.00	....
2803	29¢ Snowman, self-adhesive (2 buttons)	2.25	....	....	....	1.25	.80
2803a	same, bklt pane of 18 .	13.50	....	....	....	18.00	....

2804

2805

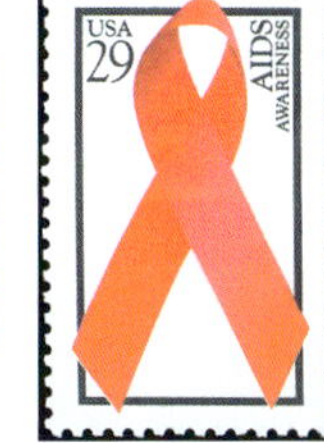

2806

SCOTT NO.	DESCRIPTION	FIRST DAY COVERS SING	FIRST DAY COVERS PL. BLK.	MINT SHEET	PLATE BLOCK	UNUSED F/NH	USED
2804	29¢ Commonwealth of North Mariana Islands .	2.25	4.75	25.00(20)	6.00	1.75	.25
2805	29¢ Columbus Landing in Puerto Rico	2.25	4.75	48.00(50)	4.75	1.20	.25
2806	29¢ AIDS Awareness. .	2.25	4.75	45.00(50)	4.50	1.20	.25
2806a	29¢ AIDS Awareness, bklt single.	2.25	....	....	....	1.10	.25
2806b	same, bklt pane of 5 . .	9.00	....	....	....	4.00	....
2806bv	same, bklt pane, unfolded	....	....	....	....	6.50	....

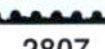

2807

2808

2809

2810

2811

1994 COMMEMORATIVES

SCOTT NO.	DESCRIPTION	FIRST DAY COVERS SING	FIRST DAY COVERS PL. BLK.	MINT SHEET	PLATE BLOCK	UNUSED F/NH	USED
2807/76	**(2807-12, 2814C-28, 2834-36, 2838-39, 2848-68, ... 2871-72, 2876) 59 varieties**	....	....	....	....	**80.00**	**35.50**
2807-11	Winter Olympics, 5 varieties, attached . .	5.00	....	22.00(20)	12.00(10)	7.00	6.00
2807	29¢ Alpine Skiing.	2.25	....	....	....	1.50	.50
2808	29¢ Luge	2.25	....	....	....	1.50	.50
2809	29¢ Ice Dancing.	2.25	....	....	....	1.50	.50
2810	29¢ Cross Country Skiing	2.25	....	....	....	1.50	.50
2811	29¢ Ice Hockey	2.25	....	....	....	1.50	.50

2812

2813

2815

2814

1994 COMMEMORATIVES (continued)

SCOTT NO.	DESCRIPTION	FIRST DAY COVERS SING	FIRST DAY COVERS PL. BLK.	MINT SHEET	PLATE BLOCK	UNUSED F/NH	USED
2812	29¢ Edward R. Murrow	2.25	4.75	65.00(50)	8.00	1.75	.25
2813	29¢ Love (sunrise), self-adhesive	2.25	....	....	....	1.25	.30
2813a	same, bklt pane of 18	13.50	....	....	....	18.00	....
2813v	29¢ Love (sunrise), self-adhesive coil	2.50	....	....	7.00(3)	1.40	....
2813b	same, plate strip of 5	....	....	....	....	10.00	....
2814	29¢ Love (dove), bklt single	2.25	....	....	....	1.10	.30
2814a	same, bklt pane of 10	7.00	....	....	....	11.00	....
2814av	same, bklt pane, unfolded	....	....	....	....	12.00	....
2814C	29¢ Love (dove)	2.25	4.75	48.00(50)	5.00	1.20	.25
2815	52¢ Love (dove)	2.00	4.50	75.00(50)	9.00(4)	1.75	.40
....	same, plate block of 10	....	....	....	16.00(10)	....	....

2816

2817

2818

SCOTT NO.	DESCRIPTION	FIRST DAY COVERS SING	FIRST DAY COVERS PL. BLK.	MINT SHEET	PLATE BLOCK	UNUSED F/NH	USED
2816	29¢ Allison Davis	2.25	4.75	30.00(20)	8.00	1.50	.25
2817	29¢ Chinese New Year of the Dog	2.25	4.75	29.00(20)	8.00	1.75	.25
2818	29¢ Buffalo Soldiers	4.00	5.00	20.00(20)	4.75	1.50	.25

2819

2820

2821

2822

2823

2824

2825

2826

2827

2828

SCOTT NO.	DESCRIPTION	FIRST DAY COVERS SING	FIRST DAY COVERS PL. BLK.	MINT SHEET	PLATE BLOCK	UNUSED F/NH	USED
2819	29¢ Rudolph Valentino	2.25	....	....	....	2.00	.95
2920	29¢ Clara Bow	2.25	....	....	....	2.00	.95
2821	29¢ Charlie Chaplin	2.25	....	....	....	2.00	.95
2822	29¢ Lon Chaney	2.25	....	....	....	2.00	.95
2823	29¢ John Gilbert	2.25	....	....	....	2.00	.95
2824	29¢ Zasu Pitts	2.25	....	....	....	2.00	.95
2825	29¢ Harold Lloyd	2.25	....	....	....	2.00	.95
2826	29¢ Keystone Cops	2.25	....	....	....	2.00	.95
2827	29¢ Theda Bara	2.25	....	....	....	2.00	.95
2828	29¢ Buster Keaton	2.25	....	....	....	2.00	.95
2819-28	Silent Screen Stars, 10 varieties, attached	7.00	....	59.00(40)	22.50(10)	18.00	15.00

2829

2830

2831

2832

2833

SCOTT NO.	DESCRIPTION	FIRST DAY COVERS SING	FIRST DAY COVERS PL. BLK.	MINT SHEET	PLATE BLOCK	UNUSED F/NH	USED
2829	29¢ Lily	2.25	....	....	....	1.25	.30
2830	29¢ Zinnia	2.25	....	....	....	1.25	.30
2831	29¢ Gladiola	2.25	....	....	....	1.25	.30
2832	29¢ Marigold	2.25	....	....	....	1.25	.30
2833	29¢ Rose	2.25	....	....	....	1.25	.30
2833a	Summer Garden Flowers, bklt pane of 5	4.50	....	....	....	6.00	5.00
2833av	same, bklt pane, unfolded	....	....	....	....	7.50	....

2834

2835

2836

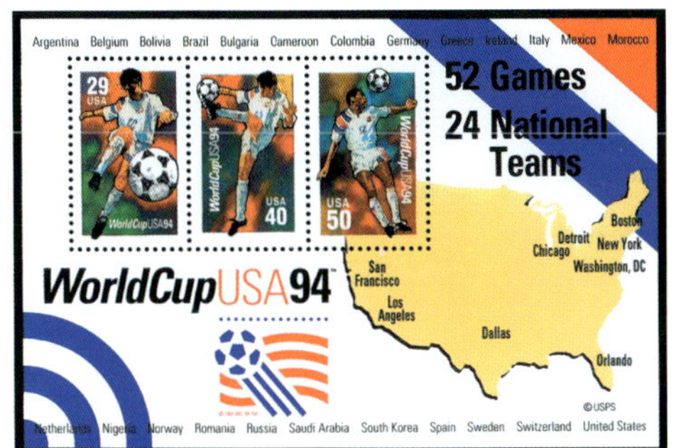

2837

SCOTT NO.	DESCRIPTION	FIRST DAY COVERS SING	PL. BLK.	MINT SHEET	PLATE BLOCK	UNUSED F/NH	USED
2834	29¢ World Cup Soccer	2.25	4.75	20.00(20)	4.50	1.00	.50
2835	40¢ World Cup Soccer	2.25	4.75	25.00(20)	5.50	1.50	1.00
2836	50¢ World Cup Soccer	2.25	5.50	28.00(20)	6.50	1.75	1.25
2837	29¢-50¢ World Cup Soccer Souvenir Sheet	3.50	....	....	....	7.00	4.00

2838

SCOTT NO.	DESCRIPTION	FIRST DAY COVERS SING	PL. BLK.	MINT SHEET	PLATE BLOCK	UNUSED F/NH	USED
2838	$2.90 World War II, 1944, Souvenir Sheet of 10. .	12.00	....	49.50(20)	....	30.00	20.00
2838a	29¢ Allied forces retake New Guinea.	2.50	....	....	....	2.75	1.00
2838b	29¢ P-51s escort B-17s on bombing raids	2.50	....	....	....	2.75	1.00
2838c	29¢ Allies in Normandy, D-Day, June 6	2.50	....	....	....	2.75	1.00
2838d	29¢ Airborne units spearhead attacks. . . .	2.50	....	....	....	2.75	1.00
2838e	29¢ Submarines shorten war in Pacific	2.50	....	....	....	2.75	1.00
2838f	29¢ Allies free Rome, June 4; Paris , August 25	2.50	....	....	....	2.75	1.00
2838g	29¢ U.S. troops clear Saipan bunkers	2.50	....	....	....	2.75	1.00
2838h	29¢ Red Ball Express speeds vital supplies . .	2.50	....	....	....	2.75	1.00
2838i	29¢ Battle for Leyte Gulf, October, 23-26.	2.50	....	....	....	2.75	1.00
2838j	29¢ Bastogne and Battle of the Bulge, December. .	2.50	....	....	....	2.75	1.00

2839

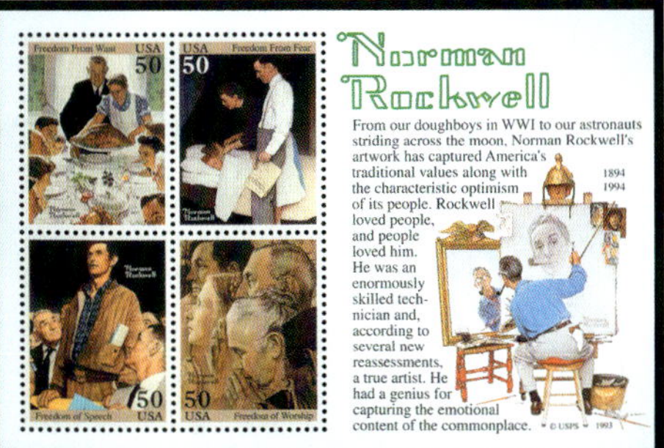

2840

SCOTT NO.	DESCRIPTION	FIRST DAY COVERS SING	PL. BLK.	MINT SHEET	PLATE BLOCK	UNUSED F/NH	USED
2839	29¢ Norman Rockwell .	1.75	4.75	48.00(50)	4.50	1.75	.75
2840	50¢ "Four Freedoms" Souvenir Sheets	5.00	....	....	....	9.00	7.00

2841

SCOTT NO.	DESCRIPTION	FIRST DAY COVERS SING	PL. BLK.	MINT SHEET	PLATE BLOCK	UNUSED F/NH	USED
2841	29¢ Moon Landing 25th Anniversary, Sheet of 12	12.00	....	....	....	16.00	....
2841a	29¢ Moon Landing 25th Anniversary, single stamp	1.75	....	....	....	1.50	.50

2842

SCOTT NO.	DESCRIPTION	FIRST DAY COVERS SING	PL. BLK.	MINT SHEET	PLATE BLOCK	UNUSED F/NH	USED
2842	$9.95 Moon Landing Express Mail Stamp.	27.00	50.00	675.00(20)	150.00	30.00	25.00

2843

2844

2845

2846

2847

SCOTT NO.	DESCRIPTION	FIRST DAY COVERS SING	PL. BLK.	MINT SHEET	PLATE BLOCK	UNUSED F/NH	USED
2843	29¢ Hudson's General.	2.25	....	....	....	1.50	.35
2844	29¢ McQueen's Jupiter	2.25	....	....	....	1.50	.35
2845	29¢ Eddy's No. 242 . . .	2.25	....	....	....	1.50	.35
2846	29¢ Ely's No. 10	2.25	....	....	....	1.50	.35
2847	29¢ Buchanan's No. 999	2.25	....	....	....	1.50	.35
2847a	Locomotives, bklt pane of 5.	4.50	....	....	....	6.00	4.25
2847av	same, bklt pane, unfolded	....	....	....	....	8.00	....

2848

SCOTT NO.	DESCRIPTION	FIRST DAY COVERS SING	PL. BLK.	MINT SHEET	PLATE BLOCK	UNUSED F/NH	USED
2848	29¢ George Meany . . .	1.75	4.75	45.00(50)	4.50	1.00	.25

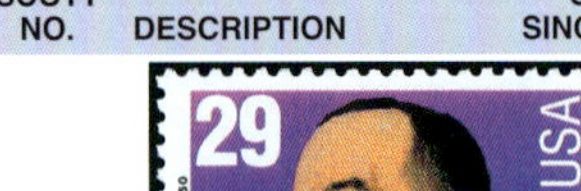

2849

2850

2851

2852

2853

SCOTT NO.	DESCRIPTION	FIRST DAY COVERS SING	FIRST DAY COVERS PL. BLK.	MINT SHEET	PLATE BLOCK	UNUSED F/NH	USED
2849-53	Popular Singers, 5 varieties, attached . .	8.00	....	30.00(20)	15.00(6)	9.50	6.00
2849	29¢ Al Jolson	3.00	....	....	....	1.75	1.00
2850	29¢ Bing Crosby	3.00	....	....	....	1.75	1.00
2851	29¢ Ethel Waters	3.00	....	....	....	1.75	1.00
2852	29¢ Nat "King" Cole . . .	3.00	....	....	....	1.75	1.00
2853	29¢ Ethel Merman	3.00	....	....	....	1.75	1.00
....	same, Plate Block of 12	....	....	....	22.50(12)	....	....

2854

2855

2856

2857

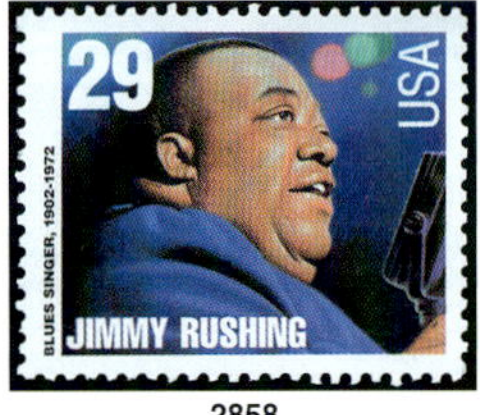

2858

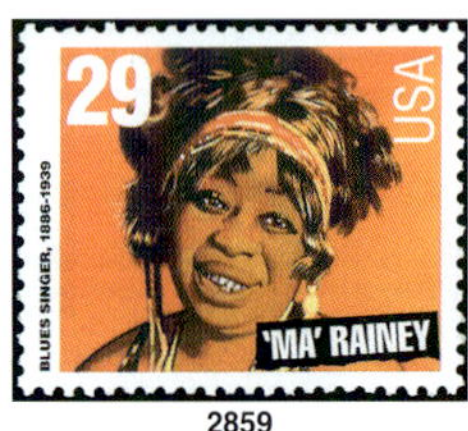

2859

2860

2861

SCOTT NO.	DESCRIPTION	FIRST DAY COVERS SING	FIRST DAY COVERS PL. BLK.	MINT SHEET	PLATE BLOCK	UNUSED F/NH	USED
2854-61	Blues & Jazz Singers, 8 varieties, attached .	12.00	....	58.00(35)	22.00(10)	23.00	12.00
....	same, Horizontal Plate Block of 10 w/Top Label	....	....	....	26.00(10)	....	....
2854	29¢ Bessie Smith. . . .	3.00	....	....	....	2.00	1.25
2855	29¢ Muddy Waters . .	3.00	....	....	....	2.00	1.25
2856	29¢ Billie Holiday	3.00	....	....	....	2.00	1.25
2857	29¢ Robert Johnson .	3.00	....	....	....	2.00	1.25
2858	29¢ Jimmy Rushing . .	3.00	....	....	....	2.00	1.25
2859	29¢ "Ma" Rainey	3.00	....	....	....	2.00	1.25
2860	29¢ Mildred Bailey . . .	3.00	....	....	....	2.00	1.25
2861	29¢ Howlin' Wolf	3.00	....	....	....	2.00	1.25

2862

SCOTT NO.	DESCRIPTION	FIRST DAY COVERS SING	FIRST DAY COVERS PL. BLK.	MINT SHEET	PLATE BLOCK	UNUSED F/NH	USED
2862	29¢ James Thurber . . .	1.75	4.75	45.00(50)	4.75	1.00	.25

2863 2864

2865 2866

SCOTT NO.	DESCRIPTION	FIRST DAY COVERS SING	FIRST DAY COVERS PL. BLK.	MINT SHEET	PLATE BLOCK	UNUSED F/NH	USED
2863-66	Wonders of the Sea, 4 varieties, attached . .	5.00	6.00	35.00(24)	7.00	6.50	5.00
2863	29¢ Diver & Motorboat.	2.25	....	....	....	1.75	.55
2864	29¢ Diver & Ship	2.25	....	....	....	1.75	.55
2865	29¢ Diver & Ship's Wheel	2.25	....	....	....	1.75	.55
2866	29¢ Diver & Coral	2.25	....	....	....	1.75	.55

2867 2868

SCOTT NO.	DESCRIPTION	FIRST DAY COVERS SING	FIRST DAY COVERS PL. BLK.	MINT SHEET	PLATE BLOCK	UNUSED F/NH	USED
2867-68	Cranes.	4.00	5.00	19.50(20)	5.00	2.25	1.50
2867	29¢ Black-Necked Crane	3.00	....	....	....	1.15	.30
2868	29¢ Whooping Crane. .	3.00	....	....	....	1.15	.30

2869

Legends of the West

2869a	*Home on the Range*	**2869k**	*Nellie Cashman*
2869b	*Buffalo Bill Cody*	**2869l**	*Charles Goodnight*
2869c	*Jim Bridger*	**2869m**	*Geronimo*
2869d	*Annie Oakley*	**2869n**	*Kit Carson*
2869e	*Native American Culture*	**2869o**	*Wild Bill Hickok*
2869f	*Chief Joseph*	**2869p**	*Western Wildlife*
2869g	*Bill Pickett*	**2869q**	*Jim Beckwourth*
2869h	*Bat Masterson*	**2869r**	*Bill Tilghman*
2869i	*John Fremont*	**2869s**	*Sacagawea*
2869j	*Wyatt Earp*	**2869t**	*Overland Mail*

2869g

2870g

SCOTT NO.	DESCRIPTION	FIRST DAY COVERS SING	FIRST DAY COVERS PL. BLK.	MINT SHEET	PLATE BLOCK	UNUSED F/NH	USED
2869	Legends of the West, 20 varieties, attached .	....	....	30.00(20)	....	30.00	25.00
....	set of singles	31.50	....	....	....	....	17.00
....	singles of above, each.	....	....	....	....	....	1.00
2869v	same as above, uncut sheet of 120 (6 panes)	....	....	100.00(120)	....	100.00	....
....	block of 40 with vertical or horizontal, gutter between (2 panes)	....	....	27.50(40)	....	27.50	....
....	block of 24 with vertical gutter	....	....	20.75(24)	....	20.75	....
....	block of 25 with horizontal gutter	....	....	21.50(25)	....	21.50	....
....	cross gutter block of 20	....	....	....	....	31.00	....
....	cross gutter block of 4 .	....	....	....	....	17.00	....
....	vertical pair with horizontal gutter	....	....	....	....	2.75	....
....	horizontal pair with vertical gutter	....	....	....	....	2.75	....
2870	Legends of the West, (Recallled), 20 varieties, attached.	....	....	200.00(20)	....	200.00	....

2871

2872

2873

2874

SCOTT NO.	DESCRIPTION	FIRST DAY COVERS SING	FIRST DAY COVERS PL. BLK.	MINT SHEET	PLATE BLOCK	UNUSED F/NH	USED
2871	29¢ Christmas–Traditional	2.25	4.75	45.00(50)	5.00	1.25	.25
2871a	29¢ Christmas–Traditional bklt single.	2.25	....	....	....	1.10	.30
2871b	same, bklt pane of 10 .	9.00	....	....	....	10.00	....
2871bv	same, bklt pane, unfolded	....	....	....	....	12.00	....
2872	29¢ Christmas Stocking	2.25	4.75	45.00(50)	5.00	1.25	.25
2872v	29¢ Christmas Stocking, bklt single.	2.25	....	....	....	1.25	.25
2872a	same, bklt pane of 20 .	....	....	....	....	20.00	....
2872av	same, bklt pane, unfolded	....	....	....	....	26.00	....
2873	29¢ Santa Claus, self-adhesive	2.25	....	....	....	1.20	.25
2873a	same, bklt pane of 12 .	9.00	....	....	....	14.00	....
2874	29¢ Cardinal in Snow, self-adhesive	2.25	....	....	....	1.50	1.20
2874a	same, bklt pane of 18 .	13.50	....	....	....	18.00	....

2875

SCOTT NO.	DESCRIPTION	FIRST DAY COVERS SING	FIRST DAY COVERS PL. BLK.	MINT SHEET	PLATE BLOCK	UNUSED F/NH	USED
2875	$2 B.E.P. Souvenir Sheet of 4 (Madison)	25.00	....	....	....	25.00	20.00
2875a	single from above ($2 Madison)	6.00	....	....	....	5.00	3.00

2876

2877, 2878

SCOTT NO.	DESCRIPTION	FIRST DAY COVERS SING	FIRST DAY COVERS PL. BLK.	MINT SHEET	PLATE BLOCK	UNUSED F/NH	USED
2876	29¢ Year of the Boar . .	3.00	4.75	24.00(20)	5.75	1.25	.45
2877	(3¢) "G" Make-up Rate (ABN, bright blue)	2.25	4.75	17.00(100)	1.00	.25	.25
2878	(3¢) "G" Make-up Rate (SVS, dark blue)	2.25	4.75	20.00(100)	1.25	.25	.25

2879, 2880 — 2881-85, 2889-92 — 2886, 2887 — 2888

SCOTT NO.	DESCRIPTION	FIRST DAY COVERS SING	FIRST DAY COVERS PL. BLK.	MINT SHEET	PLATE BLOCK	UNUSED F/NH	USED
2879	(20¢) "G" Old Glory Postcard Rate (BEP, black "G") .	2.25	4.75	80.00(100)	9.50	.75	.25
2880	(20¢) "G" Old Glory Postcard Rate (SVS, red "G") . . .	2.25	4.75	110.00(100)	25.00	1.00	.25
2881	(32¢) "G" Old Glory (BEP, black "G").	2.25	4.75	350.00(100)	80.00	3.00	.50
2882	(32¢) "G" Old Glory (SVS, red "G")	2.25	4.75	96.00(100)	9.00	1.10	.25
2883	(32¢) "G" Old Glory, bklt single (BEP, black "G")	2.25	....	....	....	1.10	.25
2883a	same, bklt pane of 10 .	7.25	....	....	....	10.00	....
2884	(32¢) "G" Old Glory, bklt single (ABN, blue "G") .	2.25	....	....	....	1.25	.25
2884a	same, bklt pane of 10 .	7.25	....	....	....	10.00	....
2885	(32¢) "G" Old Glory, bklt single (KCS, red "G"). .	2.25	....	....	....	1.50	.25
2885a	same, bklt pane of 10 .	7.25	....	....	....	14.00	....
2886	(32¢) "G", self-adhesive	2.25	....	....	....	1.10	.30
2886a	same, bklt pane of 18 .	13.50	....	....	....	16.00	....
2887	(32¢) "G" Old Glory, self-adhesive (blue shading)	2.25	....	....	....	1.25	.85
2887a	same, bklt pane of 18 .	13.50	....	....	....	20.00	....

SCOTT NO.	DESCRIPTION	SING	PLATE# STRIP 3	MINT SHEET	PLATE# STRIP 3	UNUSED F/NH	USED
2886b	(32¢) "G" Old Glory, coil	....	....	....	14.00	2.50	....
2888	(25¢) Old Glory First-Class Presort, coil	2.25	10.00	....	6.75	1.50	.65
2889	(32¢) "G" Old Glory, coil (BEP, black "G").	2.25	10.00	....	12.50	3.00	.85
2890	(32¢) "G" Old Glory, coil (ABN, blue "G") . . .	2.25	10.00	....	6.25	1.10	.25
2891	(32¢) "G" Old Glory, coil (SVS, red "G")	2.25	10.00	....	9.00	1.50	.40
2892	(32¢) "G" Old Glory, coil (SVS, red "G") rouletted	2.25	10.00	....	8.00	1.50	.20

2893 — 2897, 2913-16, 2920, 2921 — 2902, 2902B — 2903, 2904, 2904A, 2904B

2905, 2906 — 2907 — 2908-10 — 2911, 2912, 2912A, 2912B

1995-97 Regular Issues

SCOTT NO.	DESCRIPTION	SING	PL. BLK.	MINT SHEET	PLATE BLOCK	UNUSED F/NH	USED
2893	(5¢) "G" Old Glory, Nonprofit, coil.	1.95	10.00	....	4.50	1.00	.40
2897	32¢ Flag over Porch . .	1.95	4.75	100.00(100)	7.50	1.50	.25

1995-97 Regular Issue Coils

SCOTT NO.	DESCRIPTION	SING	PLATE# STRIP 3	MINT SHEET	PLATE# STRIP 3	UNUSED F/NH	USED
2902	(5¢) Butte, Nonprofit, coil	1.95	10.00	....	2.00	.30	.25
2902B	(5¢) Butte, self-adhesive coil	1.95	....	....	2.75	.45	.25
2903	(5¢) Mountain, (BEP, violet 1996)	2.25	10.00	....	2.00	.25	.25
2904	(5¢) Mountain (SVS, blue 1996)	2.25	10.00	....	4.00	.45	.25
2904A	(5¢) Mountain, self-adhesive coil.	2.25	....	....	4.00	.45	.25
2904B	(5¢) Mountain, self-adhesive coil (1997)	2.25	....	....	4.00	.45	.25
2905	(10¢) Automobile, Bulk Rate, coil	2.25	10.00	....	3.75	.45	.35
2905a	(10¢) Automobile, Large, "1995" date (1996). . . .	....	....	....	6.50	.45	.25
2906	(10¢) Automobile, self-adhesive coil.	2.25	....	....	6.00	.65	.25
2907	(10¢) Eagle, bulk-rate, coil (1996)	2.25	....	....	7.50	.80	.35
2908	(15¢) Auto Tail Fin, Presorted First-Class Card, coil (BEP).	2.25	10.00	....	3.50	.50	.45
2909	(15¢) Auto Tail Fin, Presorted First-Class Card, coil (SVS).	2.25	10.00	....	3.50	.50	.45
2910	(15¢) Auto Tail Fin, self-adhesive coil. . . .	2.25	....	....	3.75	.55	.45
2911	(25¢) Juke Box, Presorted First-Class, coil (BEP)	2.25	10.00	....	5.75	.80	.45
2912	(25¢) Juke Box, Presorted First-Class, coil (SVS)	2.25	10.00	....	5.75	.85	.45
2912A	(25¢) Juke Box, self-adhesive coil. . . .	2.25	....	....	6.00	1.10	.45
2912B	(25¢) Juke Box, self-adhesive coil (1997)	2.25	....	....	6.00	1.25	.45
2913	32¢ Flag over Porch, coil (BEP, red date) . .	2.25	10.00	....	6.00	1.10	.25
2914	32¢ Flag over Porch, coil (SVS, blue date)	2.25	10.00	....	7.00	1.10	.70
2915	32¢ Flag over Porch, self-adhesive coil (Die Cut 8.7)	2.25	....	....	14.00	1.60	.80
2915A	32¢ Flag over Porch, self-adhesive coil (1996, Die Cut 9.8)	2.25	....	....	8.00	1.40	.30
2915B	32¢ Flag over Porch, self-adhesive coil (1996, Die Cut 11.5)	2.25	....	....	9.00	1.50	1.00
2915C	32¢ Flag over Porch, self-adhesive coil (1996, Die Cut 10.9)	10.00	....	....	29.00	3.00	2.00
2915D	32¢ Flag over Porch, self adhesive coil (1997)	2.25	....	....	14.00	2.40	1.50

PLATE NUMBER STRIPS OF 5

SCOTT NO.	UNUSED F/NH	SCOTT NO.	UNUSED F/NH	SCOTT NO.	UNUSED F/NH
2886b	20.00	2904	2.95	2912	7.50
2888	10.00	2904A	6.00	2912A	8.75
2889	20.00	2904B	7.50	2912B	9.00
2890	9.50	2905	4.00	2913	8.00
2891	10.00	2906	8.00	2914	10.00
2892	14.00	2907	9.00	2915	15.00
2893	7.00	2908	4.00	2915A	10.00
2902	3.00	2909	4.00	2915B	12.00
2902B	4.00	2910	5.00	2915C	35.00
2903	2.50	2911	7.50	2915D	23.00

2919

1995-97 Booklet Panes

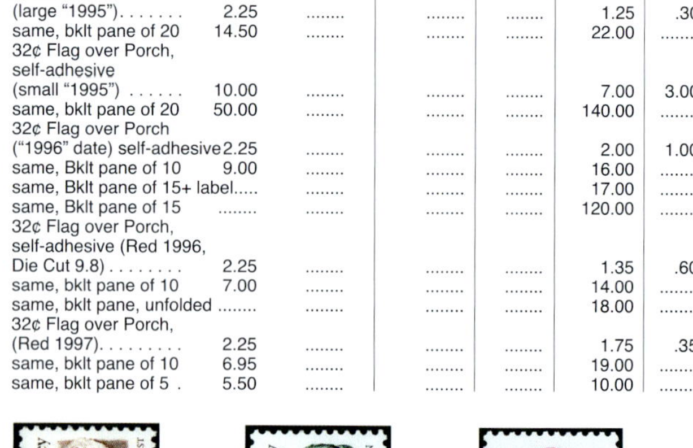

SCOTT NO.	DESCRIPTION	SING	PL. BLK.	MINT SHEET	PLATE BLOCK	UNUSED F/NH	USED
2916	32¢ Flag over Porch, bklt single.	2.25	....	....	....	1.10	.25
2916a	same, bklt pane of 10	7.25	....	....	....	10.00	....
2916av	same, bklt pane, unfolded	....	....	....	....	12.00	....
2919	32¢ Flag over Field self-adhesive	2.25	....	....	....	1.25	.65
2919a	same, bklt pane of 18	13.50	....	....	....	20.00	....
2920	32¢ Flag over Porch, self-adhesive (large "1995").	2.25	....	....	....	1.25	.30
2920a	same, bklt pane of 20	14.50	....	....	....	22.00	....
2920b	32¢ Flag over Porch, self-adhesive (small "1995")	10.00	....	....	....	7.00	3.00
2920c	same, bklt pane of 20	50.00	....	....	....	140.00	....
2920D	32¢ Flag over Porch ("1996" date) self-adhesive	2.25	....	....	....	2.00	1.00
2920De	same, Bklt pane of 10	9.00	....	....	....	16.00	....
2920f	same, Bklt pane of 15+ label	....	....	....	....	17.00	....
2920h	same, Bklt pane of 15	....	....	....	....	120.00	....
2921	32¢ Flag over Porch, self-adhesive (Red 1996, Die Cut 9.8)	2.25	....	....	....	1.35	.60
2921a	same, bklt pane of 10	7.00	....	....	....	14.00	....
2921av	same, bklt pane, unfolded	....	....	....	....	18.00	....
2921b	32¢ Flag over Porch, (Red 1997).	2.25	....	....	....	1.75	.35
2921c	same, bklt pane of 10	6.95	....	....	....	19.00	....
2921d	same, bklt pane of 5 .	5.50	....	....	....	10.00	....

2933

2934

2935

2936

2938

2940

2941

2942

2943

1995-99 GREAT AMERICANS

SCOTT NO.	DESCRIPTION	FIRST DAY COVERS SING	FIRST DAY COVERS PL. BLK.	MINT SHEET	PLATE BLOCK	UNUSED F/NH	USED
2933	32¢ Milton S. Hershey .	2.25	4.75	120.00(100)	7.50	1.40	.55
2934	32¢ Carl Farley (1996).	2.25	4.75	110.00(100)	7.00	1.30	.50
2935	32¢ Henry R. Luce (1998)	2.25	4.75	20.00(20)	5.50	1.15	.80
2936	32¢ Lila & DeWitt Wallace (1998)	2.25	4.75	20.00(20)	5.50	1.10	.90
2938	46¢ Ruth Benedict . . .	2.25	5.00	150.00(100)	8.50	1.75	1.05
2940	55¢ Alice Hamilton. . . .	2.25	5.00	155.00(100)	9.00	1.85	.35
2941	55¢ Justin Morrill (1999)	2.25	5.00	30.00(20)	8.50	1.85	.35
2942	77¢ Mary Breckenridge (1998)	2.25	5.50	48.00(20)	12.00	2.75	1.55
2943	78¢ Alice Paul	2.25	5.50	245.00(100)	14.00	2.75	.50

2948

2949

2950

1995 COMMEMORATIVES

SCOTT NO.	DESCRIPTION	FIRST DAY COVERS SING	FIRST DAY COVERS PL. BLK.	MINT SHEET	PLATE BLOCK	UNUSED F/NH	USED
2948/3023	**(2948, 2950-58, 2961-68, 2974, 2976-92, 2998-99, 3001-07, 3019-23) 50 varieties . . . .**	....	....	....	....	**90.00**	**32.00**
2948	(32¢) Love (Cherub) . .	2.25	4.75	46.00(50)	5.00	1.10	.25
2949	(32¢) Love (Cherub), self-adhesive	2.25	....	....	....	1.25	.25
2949a	same, bklt pane of 20 .	14.50	....	....	....	20.00	....
2950	32¢ Florida Statehood .	2.25	4.75	25.00(20)	7.00	1.60	.25

2951 2952

2953 2954

SCOTT NO.	DESCRIPTION	FIRST DAY COVERS SING	FIRST DAY COVERS PL. BLK.	MINT SHEET	PLATE BLOCK	UNUSED F/NH	USED
2951-54	Kids Care About Environment, 4 varieties, attached.	4.00	4.75	18.00(16)	5.50	4.95	3.50
2951	32¢ Earth in a Bathtub.	2.25	....	....	....	1.20	.35
2952	32¢ Solar Energy.	2.25	....	....	....	1.20	.35
2953	32¢ Tree Planting	2.25	....	....	....	1.20	.35
2954	32¢ Beach Clean-Up . .	2.25	....	....	....	1.20	.35

2955

2956

2957, 2959

2958

2960

SCOTT NO.	DESCRIPTION	FIRST DAY COVERS SING	FIRST DAY COVERS PL. BLK.	MINT SHEET	PLATE BLOCK	UNUSED F/NH	USED
2955	32¢ Richard M. Nixon .	2.25	4.75	65.00(50)	6.00	1.35	.30
2956	32¢ Bessie Coleman . .	2.25	4.75	60.00(50)	7.00	1.50	.30
2957	32¢ Love (Cherub). . . .	2.25	4.75	55.00(50)	6.00	1.25	.25
2958	55¢ Love (Cherub). . . .	2.50	5.00	83.00(50)	8.00	1.85	.60
2959	32¢ Love (Cherub), bklt single.	2.25	....	....	....	1.30	.30
2959a	same, bklt pane of 10 .	7.25	....	....	....	10.00	....
2959av	same, bklt pane, unfolded	....	....	....	....	12.00	....
2960	55¢ Love (Cherub), self-adhesive	2.50	....	....	....	1.85	.70
2960a	same, bklt pane of 20 .	23.50	....	....	....	30.00	9.95

2961

2962

2963

2964

2965

SCOTT NO.	DESCRIPTION	FIRST DAY COVERS SING	FIRST DAY COVERS PL. BLK.	MINT SHEET	PLATE BLOCK	UNUSED F/NH	USED
2961-65	Recreational Sports, 5 varieties, attached . .	7.00	....	22.00(20)	13.00(10)	6.00	4.50
2961	32¢ Volleyball	3.00	....	....	....	1.20	1.00
2962	32¢ Softball	3.00	....	....	....	1.20	1.00
2963	32¢ Bowling.	3.00	....	....	....	1.20	1.00
2964	32¢ Tennis	3.00	....	....	....	1.20	1.00
2965	32¢ Golf.	3.00	....	....	....	1.20	1.00

2966

2967

2968

SCOTT NO.	DESCRIPTION	FIRST DAY COVERS SING	FIRST DAY COVERS PL. BLK.	MINT SHEET	PLATE BLOCK	UNUSED F/NH	USED
2966	32¢ POW & MIA	3.00	4.00	20.00(20)	5.00	1.20	.30
2967	32¢ Marilyn Monroe. . .	4.00	5.00	30.00(20)	6.00	1.75	.35
2967v	same as above, uncut sheet of 120 (6 panes)	....	....	180.00(120)	....	....	....
....	block of 8 with vertical gutter	....	....	....	....	50.00	....
....	cross gutter block of 8 .	....	....	....	....	65.00	....
....	vertical pair with horizontal gutter	....	....	....	....	5.50	....
....	horizontal pair with vertical gutter	....	....	....	....	9.50	....
2968	32¢ Texas Statehood. .	3.00	4.75	28.00(20)	5.50	1.35	.35

2969 2970 2971

2972 2973 2974

SCOTT NO.	DESCRIPTION	FIRST DAY COVERS SING	FIRST DAY COVERS PL. BLK.	MINT SHEET	PLATE BLOCK	UNUSED F/NH	USED
2969	32¢ Split Rock Lighthouse	2.25	....	....	....	2.00	.40
2970	32¢ St. Joseph Lighthouse	2.25	....	....	....	2.00	.40
2971	32¢ Spectacle Reef Lighthouse	2.25	....	....	....	2.00	.40
2972	32¢ Marblehead Lighthouse	2.25	....	....	....	2.00	.40
2973	32¢ Thirty Mile Point Lighthouse	2.25	....	....	....	2.00	.40
2973a	Great Lakes Lighthouses, bklt pane of 5	5.50	....	....	....	10.00	6.50
2973av	same, bklt pane, unfolded	....		....	....	12.00	....
2974	32¢ United Nations . . .	1.75	4.75	19.00(20)	4.75	1.00	.25

2975

CIVIL WAR

2975a	*Monitor-Virginia*	**2975k**	*Harriet Tubman*
2975b	*Robert E. Lee*	**2975l**	*Stand Watie*
2975c	*Clara Barton*	**2975m**	*Joseph E. Johnston*
2975d	*Ulysses S. Grant*	**2975n**	*Winfield Hancock*
2975e	*Shiloh*	**2975o**	*Mary Chestnut*
2975f	*Jefferson Davis*	**2975p**	*Chancellorsville*
2975g	*David Farragut*	**2975q**	*William T. Sherman*
2975h	*Frederick Douglass*	**2975r**	*Phoebe Pember*
2975i	*Raphael Semmes*	**2975s**	*"Stonewall" Jackson*
2975j	*Abraham Lincoln*	**2975t**	*Gettysburg*

SCOTT NO.	DESCRIPTION	FIRST DAY COVERS SING	FIRST DAY COVERS PL. BLK.	MINT SHEET	PLATE BLOCK	UNUSED F/NH	USED
2975	32¢ Civil War, 20 varieties, attached .	....	....	35.00(20)	....	35.00	30.00
....	set of singles	35.00	....	....	....	....	25.00
....	singles of above, each.	....	....	....	....	....	1.25
2975v	32¢ Civil War, uncut sheet of 120 (6 panes)	....	....	150.00(120)	....	150.00	....
....	cross gutter block of 20	....	....	....	....	55.00	....
....	cross gutter block of 4	....	....	....	....	27.50	....
....	vertical pair with horizontal gutter	....	....	....	....	6.00	....
....	horizontal pair with vertical gutter	....	....	....	....	6.00	....

2976 2977 2978 2979

SCOTT NO.	DESCRIPTION	FIRST DAY COVERS SING	FIRST DAY COVERS PL. BLK.	MINT SHEET	PLATE BLOCK	UNUSED F/NH	USED
2976-79	Carousel Horses, 4 varieties, attached . .	4.00	4.75	23.00(20)	5.75	5.00	3.75
2976	32¢ Palamino.	2.25	....	....	....	1.25	.45
2977	32¢ Pinto Pony	2.25	....	....	....	1.25	.45
2978	32¢ Armored Jumper. .	2.25	....	....	....	1.25	.45
2979	32¢ Brown Jumper . . .	2.25	....	....	....	1.25	.45

2980

SCOTT NO.	DESCRIPTION	FIRST DAY COVERS SING	FIRST DAY COVERS PL. BLK.	MINT SHEET	PLATE BLOCK	UNUSED F/NH	USED
2980	32¢ Women's Suffrage	1.95	4.75	44.00(40)	5.00	1.10	.30

2981

SCOTT NO.	DESCRIPTION	FIRST DAY COVERS SING	FIRST DAY COVERS PL. BLK.	MINT SHEET	PLATE BLOCK	UNUSED F/NH	USED
2981	$3.20 World War II (1945) Souvenir Sheet of 10. .	8.25	....	40.00(20)	....	22.00	15.00
2981a	32¢ Marines raise flag on Iwo Jima	2.25	....	....	....	2.50	1.00
2981b	32¢ Fierce fighting frees Manila	2.25	....	....	....	2.50	1.00
2981c	32¢ Okinawa, the last big battle	2.25	....	....	....	2.50	1.00
2981d	32¢ U.S. & Soviets link up at Elbe River	2.25	....	....	....	2.50	1.00
2981e	32¢ Allies liberate Holocaust survivors	2.25	....	....	....	2.50	1.00
2981f	32¢ Germany surrenders at Reims	2.25	....	....	....	2.50	1.00
2981g	32¢ By 1945, World War II has uprooted millions. .	2.25	....	....	....	2.50	1.00
2981h	32¢ Truman announces Japan's surrender	2.25	....	....	....	2.50	1.00
2981i	32¢ News of victory hits home	2.25	....	....	....	2.50	1.00
2981j	32¢ Hometowns honor their returning veterans	2.25	....	....	....	2.50	1.00

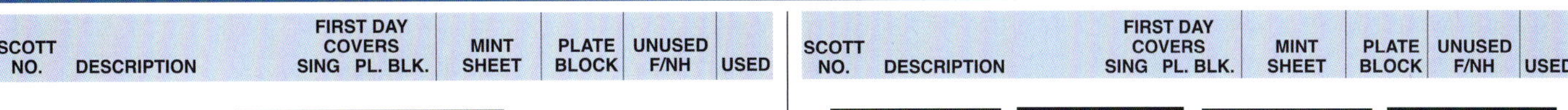

2982

SCOTT NO.	DESCRIPTION	FIRST DAY COVERS SING	FIRST DAY COVERS PL. BLK.	MINT SHEET	PLATE BLOCK	UNUSED F/NH	USED
2982	32¢ Louis Armstrong . .	1.95	4.75	25.00(20)	5.50	1.50	.50

2983 2984

2985 2986 2987 2988 2989 2990 2991 2992

SCOTT NO.	DESCRIPTION	FIRST DAY COVERS SING	FIRST DAY COVERS PL. BLK.	MINT SHEET	PLATE BLOCK	UNUSED F/NH	USED
2983-92	Jazz Musicians, 10 varieties attached	8.25	....	65.00(20)	35.00(10)	32.00	24.00
2983	32¢ Coleman Hawkins.	2.25	....	....	....	3.00	2.50
2984	32¢ Louis Armstrong . .	2.25	....	....	....	3.00	2.50
2985	32¢ James P. Johnson	2.25	....	....	....	3.00	2.50
2986	32¢ "Jelly Roll" Morton.	2.25	....	....	....	3.00	2.50
2987	32¢ Charlie Parker. . . .	2.25	....	....	....	3.00	2.50
2988	32¢ Eubie Blake	2.25	....	....	....	3.00	2.50
2989	32¢ Charles Mingus. . .	2.25	....	....	....	3.00	2.50
2990	32¢ Thelonius Monk . .	2.25	....	....	....	3.00	2.50
2991	32¢ John Coltrane	2.25	....	....	....	3.00	2.50
2992	32¢ Erroll Garner.	2.25	....	....	....	3.00	2.50

2993 2994 2995 2996

2997

2998

2999

SCOTT NO.	DESCRIPTION	FIRST DAY COVERS SING	FIRST DAY COVERS PL. BLK.	MINT SHEET	PLATE BLOCK	UNUSED F/NH	USED
2993	32¢ Aster	2.25	....	....	....	1.25	.40
2994	32¢ Chrysanthemum . .	2.25	....	....	....	1.25	.40
2995	32¢ Dahlia	2.25	....	....	....	1.25	.40
2996	32¢ Hydrangea	2.25	....	....	....	1.25	.40
2997	32¢ Rudbeckia.	2.25	....	....	....	1.25	.40
2997a	Fall Garden Flowers, bklt pane of 5.	5.50	....	....	....	6.00	4.00
2997av	same, bklt pane, unfolded	....	....	....	....	9.00	....
2998	60¢ Eddie Rickenbacker	2.25	5.00	100.00(50)	10.00	3.25	.50
2998a	Large, 1995 date (1999)	2.25	5.00	128.00(50)	16.00	2.75	1.00
2999	32¢ Republic of Palau .	2.25	4.75	46.00(50)	5.00	1.20	.25

3000
COMIC STRIPS

3000a *The Yellow Kid*
3000b *Katzenjammer Kids*
3000c *Little Nemo*
3000d *Bringing Up Father*
3000e *Krazy Kat*
3000f *Rube Goldberg*
3000g *Toonerville Folks*
3000h *Gasoline Alley*
3000i *Barney Google*
3000j *Little Orphan Annie*
3000k *Popeye*
3000l *Blondie*
3000m *Dick Tracy*
3000n *Alley Oop*
3000o *Nancy*
3000p *Flash Gordon*
3000q *Li'l Abner*
3000r *Terry and the Pirates*
3000s *Prince Valiant*
3000t *Brenda Starr*

SCOTT NO.	DESCRIPTION	FIRST DAY COVERS SING	FIRST DAY COVERS PL. BLK.	MINT SHEET	PLATE BLOCK	UNUSED F/NH	USED
3000	32¢ Comic Strips, 20 varieties, attached .	....	....	25.00(20)	....	25.00	20.00
....	set of singles	50.00	....	....	....	12.75	
....	single of above, each. .	....	....	....	....	....	1.00

SCOTT NO.	DESCRIPTION	FIRST DAY COVERS SING	FIRST DAY COVERS PL. BLK.	MINT SHEET	PLATE BLOCK	UNUSED F/NH	USED
	COMIC STRIPS (continued)						
3000v	32¢ Comic Strips, uncut sheet of 120 (6 panes)	....	....	120.00(120)	....	120.00	....
....	cross gutter block of 20	....	....	....	....	40.00	....
....	cross gutter block of 4	....	....	....	....	18.50	....
....	vertical pair with horizontal gutter	....	....	....	....	4.50	....
....	horizontal pair with vertical gutter	....	....	....	....	4.50	....

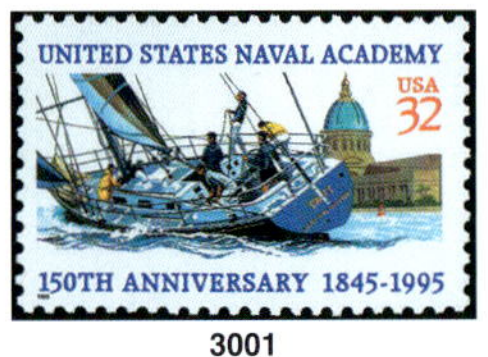

3001

3002

SCOTT NO.	DESCRIPTION	FIRST DAY COVERS SING	FIRST DAY COVERS PL. BLK.	MINT SHEET	PLATE BLOCK	UNUSED F/NH	USED
3001	32¢ Naval Academy. . .	2.25	4.75	35.00(20)	8.00	1.50	.35
3002	32¢ Tennessee Williams	2.25	4.75	25.00(20)	6.00	1.50	.40

3003

3004, 3010, 3016

3005, 3009, 3015

3006, 3011, 3017

3007, 3008, 3014

3012, 3018

SCOTT NO.	DESCRIPTION	FIRST DAY COVERS SING	FIRST DAY COVERS PL. BLK.	MINT SHEET	PLATE BLOCK	UNUSED F/NH	USED
3003	32¢ Madonna & Child .	2.25	4.75	47.00(50)	5.00	1.00	.25
3003a	32¢ Madonna & Child, bklt single.	2.25	....	....	....	1.10	.25
3003b	same, bklt pane of 10 .	7.25	....	....	....	10.00	....
3003bv	same, bklt pane, unfolded	....	....	....	....	11.50	....
3004-07	Santa & Children with Toys, 4 varieties, attached . .	4.00	4.75	50.00(50)	6.50	5.00	4.00
3004	32¢ Santa at Chimney.	2.25	....	....	....	1.65	.40
....	same, bklt single	2.25	....	....	....	1.65	.40
3005	32¢ Girl holding Jumping Jack	2.25	....	....	....	1.65	.40
....	same, bklt single	2.25	....	....	....	1.65	.40
3006	32¢ Boy holding Toy Horse	2.25	....	....	....	1.65	.40
....	same, bklt single	2.25	....	....	....	1.65	.40
3007	32¢ Santa working on Sled	2.25	....	....	....	1.65	.40
....	same, bklt single	2.25	....	....	....	1.65	.40
3007b	32¢ Santa & Children with Toys, bklt pane of 10 (3 each of 3004-05) . . .	7.25	....	....	....	12.50	....
....	same, bklt pane unfolded	....	....	....	....	14.00	....
3007c	32¢ Santa & Children with Toys, bklt pane of 10 (3 each of 3006-07) . . .	7.25	....	....	....	12.50	....
....	same, bklt pane, unfolded	....	....	....	....	14.00	....
3008	32¢ Santa working on Sled, self-adhesive	2.25	....	....	....	1.75	.50
3009	32¢ Girl holding Jumping Jack, self-adhesive . . .	2.25	....	....	....	1.75	.50
3010	32¢ Santa at Chimney, self-adhesive	2.25	....	....	....	1.75	.50
3011	32¢ Boy holding Toy Horse, self-adhesive	2.25	....	....	....	1.75	.50
3011a	32¢ Santa & Children with Toys, self-adhesive, pane of 20	14.50	....	....	....	30.00	....
3012	32¢ Midnight Angel, self-adhesive	2.25	....	....	....	1.25	.45
3012a	same, bklt pane of 20 .	14.50	....	....	....	22.50	....

3013

SCOTT NO.	DESCRIPTION	FIRST DAY COVERS SING	FIRST DAY COVERS PL. BLK.	MINT SHEET	PLATE BLOCK	UNUSED F/NH	USED
3013	32¢ Children Sledding, self-adhesive	2.25	....	....	....	1.25	.80
3013a	same, bklt pane of 18 .	13.00	....	....	....	20.00	....
3014-17	Santa & Children with Toys, self-adhesive, coil strip of 4	....	....	....	45.00(8)	20.00	....
3017a	same, plate strip of 5 . .	....	....	....	....	35.00	....
3014	32¢ Santa working on Sled, self-adhesive coil	2.25	....	....	....	5.50	1.35
3015	32¢ Girl holding Jumping Jack, self-adhesive coil	2.25	....	....	....	5.50	1.35
3016	32¢ Santa at Chimney, self-adhesive coil	2.25	....	....	....	5.50	1.35
3017	32¢ Boy holding Toy Horse, self-adhesive coil	2.25	....	....	....	5.50	1.35
3018	32¢ Midnight Angel, self-adhesive coil	3.00	....	....	17.75(3)	1.75	1.00

3019

3020

3021

3022

3023

SCOTT NO.	DESCRIPTION	FIRST DAY COVERS SING	FIRST DAY COVERS PL. BLK.	MINT SHEET	PLATE BLOCK	UNUSED F/NH	USED
3019-23	Antique Automobiles, 5 varieties, attached . .	5.50	....	30.00(25)	12.50(10)	7.50	6.50
3019	32¢ 1893 Duryea.	2.25	....	....	....	1.50	.90
3020	32¢ 1894 Haynes	2.25	....	....	....	1.50	.90
3021	32¢ 1898 Columbia . . .	2.25	....	....	....	1.50	.90
3022	32¢ 1899 Winton	2.25	....	....	....	1.50	.90
3023	32¢ 1901 White	2.25	....	....	....	1.50	.90

3024

3025

3026

3027

3028

3029

1996 COMMEMORATIVES

SCOTT NO.	DESCRIPTION	FIRST DAY COVERS SING	FIRST DAY COVERS PL. BLK.	MINT SHEET	PLATE BLOCK	UNUSED F/NH	USED
3024/3118	(3024, 3030, 3058-67, 3069-70, 3072-88, 3090-3104, 3106-11, 3118) 53 varieties	....	....	....	....	68.00	25.50
3024	32¢ Utah Statehood. . .	2.25	4.75	65.00(50)	7.00	1.85	.40
3025	32¢ Crocus	2.25	....	....	....	1.85	.40
3026	32¢ Winter Aconite . . .	2.25	....	....	....	1.85	.40
3027	32¢ Pansy	2.25	....	....	....	1.85	.40
3028	32¢ Snowdrop	2.25	....	....	....	1.85	.40
3029	32¢ Anemone	2.25	....	....	....	1.85	.40
3029a	Winter Garden Flowers, bklt pane of 5.	5.50	....	....	....	6.50	5.00
3029av	same, bklt pane, unfolded	....	....	....	....	7.75	....

3030

3031, 3031A, 3044

3032, 3045

3033

3036, 3036a

3048, 3053

3049, 3054

3050, 3051, 3055

3052, 3052E

SCOTT NO.	DESCRIPTION	FIRST DAY COVERS SING	FIRST DAY COVERS PL. BLK.	MINT SHEET	PLATE BLOCK	UNUSED F/NH	USED
3030	32¢ Love (Cherub), self-adhesive	2.25	....	....	....	1.25	.25
3030a	same, bklt pane of 20 .	14.50	....	....	....	22.00	9.95
3030b	same, bklt pane of 15 .	11.50	....	....	....	15.00	....
3031	1¢ Kestrel, self-adhesive	2.25	....	10.00(50)	1.15	.25	.25
3031A	1¢ Kestrel, self-adhesive (2000)	1.95	....	12.00(50)	1.15	.25	.25
3032	2¢ Red-headed Woodpecker	2.25	4.75	15.00(100)	1.25	.25	.25
3033	3¢ Eastern Bluebird (redesign 3¢)	2.25	4.75	16.00(100)	1.35	.25	.25
3036	$1 Red Fox, self-adhesive	5.00	10.00	125.00(20)	25.00	8.00	.75
3036a	$1 Red Fox, 11.75 X 11(2002)	....	....	130.00(20)	30.00	9.00	.85
3044	1¢ Kestrel, coil.	2.25	5.00	....	1.00	.25	.25
	same, plate strip of 5 . .	....	....	....	....	1.50	....
3044a	1¢ Kestrel, large date, coil(1999)	2.25	5.00	....	1.00	.25	.25
3045	2¢ Red-headed Wood-pecker, coil.	2.25	....	....	1.00	.25	.25
	same, plate strip of 5 . .	....	....	....	....	1.50	....
3048	20¢ Blue Jay, self-adhesive (1996)	2.25	....	....	....	.75	.30
3048a	same, bklt pane of 10 .	8.00	....	....	....	7.25	....
3049	32¢ Yellow Rose, self-adhesive	2.25	....	....	....	1.10	.25
3049a	same, bklt pane of 20 .	14.50	....	....	....	20.00	....
3049b	same, bklt pane of 4 . .	....	....	....	....	5.50	....
3049c	same, bklt pane of 5 and label		....	....	....	6.75	....
3049d	same, bklt pane of 6 . .	....	....	....	....	6.75	....
3050	20¢ Ring-necked Pheasant, self-adhesive	2.25	....	....	....	.90	.25
3050a	same, bklt pane of 10 .	9.00	....	....	....	9.25	....

SCOTT NO.	DESCRIPTION	FIRST DAY COVERS SING	FIRST DAY COVERS PL. BLK.	MINT SHEET	PLATE BLOCK	UNUSED F/NH	USED
3050b	20¢ Pheasant, die cut 11	2.25	....	....	....	5.25	.85
3050c	same, bklt pane of 10 .	5.50	....	....	....	45.00	....
3051	20¢ Ring-necked Pheasant, die cut 10 1/2 x 11, self-adhesive	2.25	....	....	....	1.60	1.00
	die cut 10 1/2.	2.25	....	....	....	13.00	6.00
3051b	same, bklt pane of 5, (4 #3051, 1 #3051a) . .	3.50	....	....	....	17.50	....
3052	33¢ Coral Pink Rose, self-adhesive (1999) . .	2.25	....	....	....	1.35	.30
3052a	same, bklt pane of 4 . .	3.00	....	....	....	5.25	....
3052b	same, bklt pane of 5 . .	3.75	....	....	....	6.50	....
3052c	same, bklt pane of 6 . .	4.50	....	....	....	7.50	....
3052d	same, bklt pane of 20 .	14.50	....	....	....	20.00	....
3052E	33¢ Coral Pink Rose, die-cut 10.75 x 10.5, self-adhesive (2000) . .	2.25	....	....	....	1.40	.30
3052Ef	same, bklt pane of 20 .	14.50	....	....	....	18.00	....
3053	20¢ Blue Jay, self-adhesive, coil (1996)	2.25	....	....	6.50	1.00	.25
3054	32¢ Yellow Rose, self-adhesive coil (1997)	2.25	....	....	7.00	1.00	.25
	same, plate strip of 5 . .	....	....	....	....	8.00	....
3055	20¢ Ring-necked Pheasant, self-adhesive coil (1998)	2.25	....	....	4.00	.80	.25
	same, plate strip of 5 . .	....	....	....	....	6.00	....

3058

3059

3060

SCOTT NO.	DESCRIPTION	FIRST DAY COVERS SING	FIRST DAY COVERS PL. BLK.	MINT SHEET	PLATE BLOCK	UNUSED F/NH	USED
3058	32¢ Ernest Just	3.00	4.75	22.50(20)	5.00	1.50	.25
3059	32¢ Smithsonian Institution	2.25	4.75	19.50(20)	5.00	1.20	.25
3060	32¢ Year of the Rat . . .	2.25	4.75	25.00(20)	5.50	1.40	.25

3061

3062

3063

3064

SCOTT NO.	DESCRIPTION	FIRST DAY COVERS SING	FIRST DAY COVERS PL. BLK.	MINT SHEET	PLATE BLOCK	UNUSED F/NH	USED
3061-64	Pioneers of Communication, 4 varieties, attached . .	4.00	4.75	22.00(20)	5.50	5.00	3.25
3061	32¢ Eadweard Muybridge	2.25	....	....	....	1.55	.65
3062	32¢ Ottmar Mergenthaler	2.25	....	....	....	1.55	.65
3063	32¢ Frederic E. Ives . .	2.25	....	....	....	1.55	.65
3064	32¢ William Dickson . .	2.25	....	....	....	1.55	.65

3066

3065

3067

SCOTT NO.	DESCRIPTION	FIRST DAY COVERS SING	FIRST DAY COVERS PL. BLK.	MINT SHEET	PLATE BLOCK	UNUSED F/NH	USED
3065	32¢ Fulbright Scholarships	2.25	4.75	70.00(50)	8.00	1.85	.25
3066	50¢ Jacqueline Cochran	2.25	5.00	83.00(50)	8.50	2.00	.60
3067	32¢ Marathon	3.00	4.75	20.00(20)	5.00	1.00	.25

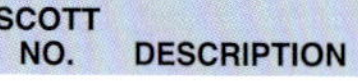

3068

1996 SUMMER OLYMPIC GAMES

3068a	*Decathlon*	**3068k**	*Beach volleyball*
3068b	*Men's canoeing*	**3068l**	*Men's rowing*
3068c	*Women's running*	**3068m**	*Men's sprints*
3068d	*Women's diving*	**3068n**	*Women's swimming*
3068e	*Men's cycling*	**3068o**	*Women's softball*
3068f	*Freestyle wrestling*	**3068p**	*Men's hurdles*
3068g	*Women's gymnastics*	**3068q**	*Men's swimming*
3068h	*Women's sailboarding*	**3068r**	*Men's gymnastics*
3068i	*Men's shot put*	**3068s**	*Equestrian*
3068j	*Women's soccer*	**3068t**	*Men's basketball*

SCOTT NO.	DESCRIPTION	FIRST DAY COVERS SING	FIRST DAY COVERS PL. BLK.	MINT SHEET	PLATE BLOCK	UNUSED F/NH	USED
3068	32¢ Centennial Olympic Games, 20 varieties, attached	....	....	25.00(20)	....	25.00	20.00
....	set of singles	35.00	....	....	....	....	17.00
....	single of above, each.	....	....	....	....	....	1.00
3068v	same as above, uncut sheet of 120 (6 panes)	....	....	135.00(120)	....	135.00	....
....	cross gutter block of 20	....	....	....	....	35.00	....
....	cross gutter block of 4	....	....	....	....	19.50	....
....	vertical pair with horizontal gutter	....	....	....	....	4.50	....
....	horizontal pair with vertical gutter	....	....	....	....	4.50	....

3069

3070, 3071

SCOTT NO.	DESCRIPTION	FIRST DAY COVERS SING	FIRST DAY COVERS PL. BLK.	MINT SHEET	PLATE BLOCK	UNUSED F/NH	USED
3069	32¢ Georgia O'Keeffe	2.25	....	23.00(15)	7.50	1.75	.25
3070	32¢ Tennessee Statehood	2.25	4.75	60.00(50)	6.00	1.25	.25
3071	32¢ Tennessee Statehood, self-adhesive	2.25	....	....	....	1.40	.40
3071a	same, bklt pane of 20	14.50	....	....	....	30.00	....

3072

3073

3074

3075

3076

SCOTT NO.	DESCRIPTION	FIRST DAY COVERS SING	FIRST DAY COVERS PL. BLK.	MINT SHEET	PLATE BLOCK	UNUSED F/NH	USED
3072-76	American Indian Dances, 5 varieties, attached	5.50	....	28.00(20)	16.00(10)	8.00	7.00
3072	32¢ Fancy Dance	2.25	....	....	....	1.50	.85
3073	32¢ Butterfly Dance	2.25	....	....	....	1.50	.85
3074	32¢ Traditional Dance	2.25	....	....	....	1.50	.85
3075	32¢ Raven Dance	2.25	....	....	....	1.50	.85
3076	32¢ Hoop Dance	2.25	....	....	....	1.50	.85

3077 3078

3079 3080

SCOTT NO.	DESCRIPTION	FIRST DAY COVERS SING	FIRST DAY COVERS PL. BLK.	MINT SHEET	PLATE BLOCK	UNUSED F/NH	USED
3077-80	Prehistoric Animals, 4 varieties, attached	4.00	4.75	22.00(20)	5.50	5.00	3.50
3077	32¢ Eohippus	2.25	....	....	....	1.25	.40
3078	32¢ Woolly Mammoth	2.25	....	....	....	1.25	.40
3079	32¢ Mastodon	2.25	....	....	....	1.25	.40
3080	32¢ Saber-tooth Cat	2.25	....	....	....	1.25	.40

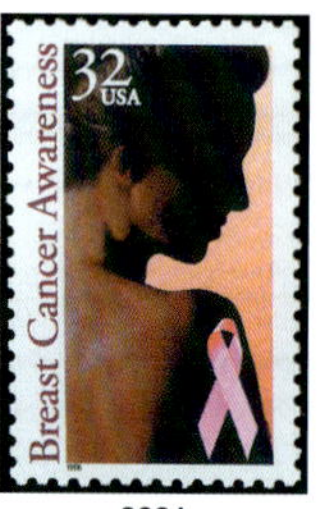

3081

3082

SCOTT NO.	DESCRIPTION	FIRST DAY COVERS SING	FIRST DAY COVERS PL. BLK.	MINT SHEET	PLATE BLOCK	UNUSED F/NH	USED
3081	32¢ Breast Cancer Awareness	2.25	4.75	20.00(20)	5.00	1.10	.25
3082	32¢ James Dean	3.00	4.75	25.00(20)	6.00	1.50	.25
....	vertical pair with horizontal gutter	....	....	....	....	4.50	....
....	horizontal pair with vertical gutter	....	....	....	....	7.00	....

3083 3084 3085 3086

SCOTT NO.	DESCRIPTION	FIRST DAY COVERS SING	FIRST DAY COVERS PL. BLK.	MINT SHEET	PLATE BLOCK	UNUSED F/NH	USED
3083-86	Folk Heroes, 4 varieties, attached . .	4.00	4.75	25.00(20)	7.00	6.00	4.75
3083	32¢ Mighty Casey	2.25	....	....	....	1.60	1.05
3084	32¢ Paul Bunyan	2.25	....	....	....	1.60	1.05
3085	32¢ John Henry	2.25	....	....	....	1.60	1.05
3086	32¢ Pecos Bill	2.25	....	....	....	1.60	1.05

3087

3088, 3089

SCOTT NO.	DESCRIPTION	FIRST DAY COVERS SING	FIRST DAY COVERS PL. BLK.	MINT SHEET	PLATE BLOCK	UNUSED F/NH	USED
3087	32¢ Olympic Discus Thrower	2.25	4.75	27.50(20)	6.00	1.50	.30
3088	32¢ Iowa Statehood. . .	2.25	4.75	65.00(50)	7.00	1.75	.30
3089	32¢ Iowa Statehood, self-adhesive	2.25	....	....	....	1.25	.35
3089a	same, bklt pane of 20 .	14.50	....	....	....	22.00	....

3090

SCOTT NO.	DESCRIPTION	FIRST DAY COVERS SING	FIRST DAY COVERS PL. BLK.	MINT SHEET	PLATE BLOCK	UNUSED F/NH	USED
3090	32¢ Rural Free Delivery	2.25	4.75	30.00(20)	7.00	1.50	.30

3091

3092

3093

3094

3095

SCOTT NO.	DESCRIPTION	FIRST DAY COVERS SING	FIRST DAY COVERS PL. BLK.	MINT SHEET	PLATE BLOCK	UNUSED F/NH	USED
3091-95	Riverboats, 5 varieties, attached . .	6.50	....	25.00(20)	14.00(10)	7.00	5.00
3091	32¢ Robt. E. Lee	2.25	....	....	....	1.50	.40
3092	32¢ Sylvan Dell	2.25	....	....	....	1.50	.40
3093	32¢ Far West	2.25	....	....	....	1.50	.40
3094	32¢ Rebecca Everingham	2.25	....	....	....	1.50	.40
3095	32¢ Bailey Gatzert. . . .	2.25	....	....	....	1.50	.40
3091-95b	32¢ Riverboats, special die cutting, 5 attached	....	....		210.00(10)	97.00	....
3095b	same, as above, pane of 20	....	....	325.00(20)	....	325.00	....

3098 3099

3096 3097

SCOTT NO.	DESCRIPTION	FIRST DAY COVERS SING	FIRST DAY COVERS PL. BLK.	MINT SHEET	PLATE BLOCK	UNUSED F/NH	USED
3096-99	Big Band Leaders, 4 varieties, attached . .	6.00	7.00	25.00(20)	6.50	6.00	4.50
3096	32¢ Count Basie	2.25	....	....	....	1.60	.85
3097	32¢ Tommy & Jimmy Dorsey	2.25	....	....	....	1.60	.85
3098	32¢ Glenn Miller	2.25	....	....	....	1.60	.85
3099	32¢ Benny Goodman. .	2.25	....	....	....	1.60	.85

3102 3103

3100 3101

SCOTT NO.	DESCRIPTION	FIRST DAY COVERS SING	FIRST DAY COVERS PL. BLK.	MINT SHEET	PLATE BLOCK	UNUSED F/NH	USED
3100-03	Songwriters, 4 varieties, attached . .	6.00	7.00	25.00(20)	6.00	5.50	4.50
3100	32¢ Harold Arlen	2.25	....	....	....	1.50	.75
3101	32¢ Johnny Mercer . . .	2.25	....	....	....	1.50	.75
3102	32¢ Dorothy Fields . . .	2.25	....	....	....	1.50	.75
3103	32¢ Hoagy Carmichael	2.25	....	....	....	1.50	.75

3104

SCOTT NO.	DESCRIPTION	FIRST DAY COVERS SING	FIRST DAY COVERS PL. BLK.	MINT SHEET	PLATE BLOCK	UNUSED F/NH	USED
3104	23¢ F. Scott Fitzgerald.	2.25	4.75	45.00(50)	5.00	1.20	.25

SE-TENANTS: Beginning with the 1964 Christmas issue (#1254-57), the United States has issued numerous Se-Tenant stamps covering a wide variety of subjects. Se-Tenants are issues where two or more different stamp designs are produced on the same sheet in pair, strip or block form. Mint stamps are usually collected in attached blocks, etc.—Used are generally saved as single stamps. Our Se-Tenant prices follow in this collecting pattern.

3105

ENDANGERED SPECIES

3105a	*Black-footed ferret*	**3105i**	*California condor*
3105b	*Thick-billed parrot*	**3105j**	*Gila trout*
3105c	*Hawaiian monk seal*	**3105k**	*San Francisco garter snake*
3105d	*American crocodile*	**3105l**	*Woodland caribou*
3105e	*Ocelot*	**3105m**	*Florida panther*
3105f	*Schaus swallowtail butterfly*	**3105n**	*Piping plover*
3105g	*Wyoming toad*	**3105o**	*Florida manatee*
3105h	*Brown pelican*		

SCOTT NO.	DESCRIPTION	FIRST DAY COVERS SING	FIRST DAY COVERS PL. BLK.	MINT SHEET	PLATE BLOCK	UNUSED F/NH	USED
3105	32¢ Endangered Species, 15 varieties, attached .	15.00	....	22.00(15)	....	22.00	17.00
....	set of singles	27.50	....	....	....	....	12.00
....	singles of above, each.	....	....	....	....	....	1.25

3106

3107, 3112

SCOTT NO.	DESCRIPTION	FIRST DAY COVERS SING	FIRST DAY COVERS PL. BLK.	MINT SHEET	PLATE BLOCK	UNUSED F/NH	USED
3106	32¢ Computer Technology	2.25	4.75	40.00(40)	5.00	1.00	.25
3107	32¢ Madonna & Child	2.25	4.75	47.00(50)	5.00	1.00	.25

3108, 3113 — 3109, 3114 — 3110, 3115 — 3111, 3116

SCOTT NO.	DESCRIPTION	FIRST DAY COVERS SING	FIRST DAY COVERS PL. BLK.	MINT SHEET	PLATE BLOCK	UNUSED F/NH	USED
3108-11	Christmas Family Scenes, 4 varieties, attached .	4.00	4.75	55.00(50)	6.00	5.50	4.00
3108	32¢ Family at Fireplace	2.25	....	....	....	1.25	.35
3109	32¢ Decorating Tree .	2.25	....	....	....	1.25	.35
3110	32¢ Dreaming of SantaClaus	2.25	....	....	....	1.25	.35
3111	32¢ Holiday Shopping	2.25	....	....	....	1.25	.35
3112	32¢ Madonna & Child, self-adhesive	2.25	....	....	....	1.25	.30
3112a	same, bklt pane of 20	14.50	....	....	....	21.00	....
3113	32¢ Family at Fireplace, self-adhesive	2.25	....	....	....	1.25	.35
3114	32¢ Decorating Tree, self-adhesive	2.25	....	....	....	1.25	.35
3115	32¢ Dreaming of Santa Claus, self-adhesive	2.25	....	....	....	1.25	.35
3116	32¢ Holiday Shopping, self-adhesive	2.25	....	....	....	1.25	.35
3116a	Christmas Family Scenes, self-adhesive, bklt pane of 20	14.50	....	....	....	20.00	....

3117 — 3118

SCOTT NO.	DESCRIPTION	FIRST DAY COVERS SING	FIRST DAY COVERS PL. BLK.	MINT SHEET	PLATE BLOCK	UNUSED F/NH	USED
3117	32¢ Skaters, self-adhesive	2.25	....	....	....	1.70	1.00
3117a	same, bklt pane of 18	13.00	....	....	....	19.00	....
3118	32¢ Hanukkah, self-adhesive	2.25	....	22.00(20)	4.50	1.00	.25

3119

SCOTT NO.	DESCRIPTION	FIRST DAY COVERS SING	FIRST DAY COVERS PL. BLK.	MINT SHEET	PLATE BLOCK	UNUSED F/NH	USED
3119	50¢ Cycling, sheet of 2	4.00	....	....	....	4.50	4.00
3119a-b	same, set of 2 singles	5.00	....	....	....	5.00	3.00

3120

3121

1997 COMMEMORATIVES

SCOTT NO.	DESCRIPTION	FIRST DAY COVERS SING	FIRST DAY COVERS PL. BLK.	MINT SHEET	PLATE BLOCK	UNUSED F/NH	USED
3120/75	**(3120-21, 3125, 3130-31, 3134-35, 3141, 3143-50, 3152-75) 40 varieties .**	....	....	....	....	**50.00**	**26.00**
3120	32¢ Year of the Ox. . . .	3.00	....	24.00(20)	5.50	1.25	.25
3121	32¢ Benjamin O. Davis, Sr.	3.00	4.75	30.00(20)	5.50	1.50	.50

3122

SCOTT NO.	DESCRIPTION	FIRST DAY COVERS SING	FIRST DAY COVERS PL. BLK.	MINT SHEET	PLATE BLOCK	UNUSED F/NH	USED
3122	32¢ Statue of Liberty, self-adhesive (1997) .	2.25	....	....	....	1.45	.25
3122a	same, bklt pane of 20	14.50	....	....	....	22.00	....
3122b	same, bklt pane of 4 .	4.75	....	....	....	5.00	....
3122c	same, bklt pane of 5 .	5.00	....	....	....	6.00	....
3122d	same, bklt pane of 6 .	5.75	....	....	....	12.00	....
3122E	32¢ Statue of Liberty, die cut 11.5 x 11.8 . . .	....	....	....	....	2.75	1.00
3122Ef	same, bklt pane of 20	....	....	....	....	40.00	....
3122Eg	same, bklt pane of 6 .	....	....	....	....	15.00	....

3123

3124

SCOTT NO.	DESCRIPTION	FIRST DAY COVERS SING	FIRST DAY COVERS PL. BLK.	MINT SHEET	PLATE BLOCK	UNUSED F/NH	USED
3123	32¢ Swans, self-adhesive	2.25	....	....	....	1.25	.35
3123a	same, bklt pane of 20	14.50	....	....	....	20.00	....
3124	55¢ Swans, self-adhesive	2.50	....	....	....	2.00	.60
3124a	same, bklt pane of 20	19.75	....	....	....	30.00	....

3125

SCOTT NO.	DESCRIPTION	FIRST DAY COVERS SING	FIRST DAY COVERS PL. BLK.	MINT SHEET	PLATE BLOCK	UNUSED F/NH	USED
3125	32¢ Helping Children Learn	2.25	4.75	19.50(20)	5.00	1.10	.30

3126, 3128

3127, 3129

SCOTT NO.	DESCRIPTION	FIRST DAY COVERS SING	FIRST DAY COVERS PL. BLK.	MINT SHEET	PLATE BLOCK	UNUSED F/NH	USED
3126	32¢ Citron, Moth, Larvae, Pupa, Beetle, self-adhesive (Die Cut 10.9 x 10.2) . .	2.25	....	....	....	1.15	.35
3127	32¢ Flowering Pineapple, Cockroaches, self-adhesive (Die Cut 10.9 x 10.2) . .	2.25	....	....	....	1.15	.35
3127a	same, bklt pane of 20 (10–#3126, 10–#3127)	14.50	....	....	....	20.00	....
3128	32¢ Citron, Moth, Larvae, Pupa, Beetle, self-adhesive (Die Cut 11.2 x 10.8) . .	2.25	....	....	....	1.95	1.30
3128a	same, stamp sideways	2.25	....	....	....	6.00	3.50
3128b	same, bklt pane of 5 (2–#3128 & #3129, 1–#3128a)	5.50	....	....	....	13.00	....
3129	32¢ Flowering Pineapple, Cockroaches, self-adhesive (Die Cut 11.2 x 10.8) . .	2.25	....	....	....	1.95	1.30
3129a	same, stamp sideways	2.25	....	....	....	12.00	4.00
3129b	same, bklt pane of 5 (2–#3128 & #3129, 1–#3129a)	5.50	....	....	....	19.00	....

3130

3131

SCOTT NO.	DESCRIPTION	FIRST DAY COVERS SING	FIRST DAY COVERS PL. BLK.	MINT SHEET	PLATE BLOCK	UNUSED F/NH	USED
3130-31	32¢ Stagecoach & Ship, (Pacific '97) 2 varieties, attached.	3.00	4.75	19.00(16)	6.00	2.75	2.00
3130	32¢ Ship	2.25	....	....	....	1.40	.35
3131	32¢ Stagecoach.	2.25	....	....	....	1.40	.35
3130-31v	same, as above, uncut sheet of 96 (6 panes)	....	....	110.00(96)	....	110.00	....
....	block of 32 with vertical or horizontal gutter between (2 panes)	....	....	37.50(32)	....	37.50	....
....	cross gutter block of 16	....	....	....	....	30.00	....
....	vertical pairs with horizontal gutter	....	....	....	....	10.00	....
....	horizontal pairs with vertical gutter	....	....	....	....	8.00	....

3132

SCOTT NO.	DESCRIPTION	FIRST DAY COVERS SING	FIRST DAY COVERS PL. BLK.	MINT SHEET	PLATE BLOCK	UNUSED F/NH	USED
3132	(25¢) Juke Box, self-adhesive linerless coil.	2.25	....	....	10.00(3)	2.35	1.25
	same, plate strip of 5 . .	....	....	....	....	15.00	....
3133	32¢ Flag Over Porch, self-adhesive, linerless coil	2.25	....	....	11.00(3)	2.00	1.10
	same, plate strip of 5 . .	....	....	....	....	15.00	....

3134

3135

SCOTT NO.	DESCRIPTION	FIRST DAY COVERS SING	FIRST DAY COVERS PL. BLK.	MINT SHEET	PLATE BLOCK	UNUSED F/NH	USED
3134	32¢ Thornton Wilder . .	2.25	4.75	20.00(20)	5.25	1.10	.30
3135	32¢ Raoul Wallenberg .	3.00	4.75	20.00(20)	5.25	1.10	.30

3136

DINOSAURS

3136a	*Ceratosaurus*	**3136f**	*Stegosaurus*	**3136k**	*Daspletosaurus*
3136b	*Camptosaurus*	**3136g**	*Allosaurus*	**3136l**	*Palaeosaniwa*
3136c	*Camarasaurus*	**3136h**	*Opisthias*	**3136m**	*Corythosaurus*
3136d	*Brachiosaurus*	**3136i**	*Edmontonia*	**3136n**	*Ornithominus*
3136e	*Goniopholis*	**3136j**	*Einiosaurus*	**3136o**	*Parasaurolophus*

SCOTT NO.	DESCRIPTION	FIRST DAY COVERS SING	FIRST DAY COVERS PL. BLK.	MINT SHEET	PLATE BLOCK	UNUSED F/NH	USED
3136	32¢ Dinosaurs, 15 varieties, attached	11.50	....	....	....	20.00	18.00
....	set of singles	26.50	....	....	....	....	12.00
....	singles of above, each	....	....	....	....	....	1.00

3137, 3138

SCOTT NO.	DESCRIPTION	FIRST DAY COVERS SING	FIRST DAY COVERS PL. BLK.	MINT SHEET	PLATE BLOCK	UNUSED F/NH	USED
3137	32¢ Bugs Bunny, self-adhesive, pane of 10	9.50	....	....	....	13.00	....
3137a	same, single from pane	2.50	....	....	....	1.25	.35
3137b	same, pane of 9 (#3137a)	....	....	....	....	10.00	....
3137c	same, pane of 1 (#3137a)	....	....	....	....	2.50	....
3137v	same, top press sheet (6 panes) ...		....	350.00	....	350.00	....
3137v	same, bottom press w/ plate# (6 panes)		....	800.00	....	800.00	....
....	pane of 10 from press sheet	....	....	95.00	....	95.00	....
....	pane of 10 from press sheet w/ plate#		....	500.00	....	500.00	....

SCOTT NO.	DESCRIPTION	FIRST DAY COVERS SING	PL. BLK.	MINT SHEET	PLATE BLOCK	UNUSED F/NH	USED
	1997 COMMEMORATIVES (continued)						
3138	32¢ Bugs Bunny, self-adhesive, Die Cut, pane of 10 . . .	....	....	....	....	130.00	....
3138a	same, single from pane	....	....	....	....	....	....
3138b	same, pane of 9 (#3138a)	....	....	....	....	....	....
3138c	same, pane of 1 (#3138a)	....	....	....	....	....	....

3139

3140

SCOTT NO.	DESCRIPTION	FIRST DAY COVERS SING	PL. BLK.	MINT SHEET	PLATE BLOCK	UNUSED F/NH	USED
3139	50¢ Benjamin Franklin, Souvenir Sheet of 12 (Pacific '97)	25.00	....	....	....	22.00	20.00
3139a	same, single from sheet	5.00	....	....	....	1.90	1.50
3140	60¢ George Washington, Souvenir Sheet of 12 (Pacific '97)	25.00	....	....	....	25.00	24.00
3140a	same, single from sheet	5.00	....	....	....	2.00	1.50

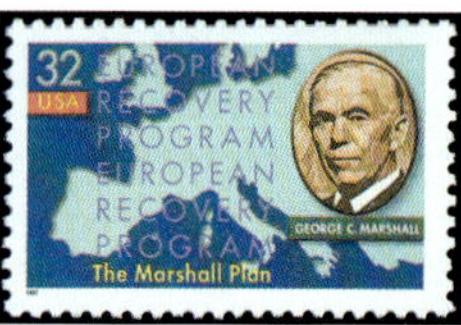

3141

SCOTT NO.	DESCRIPTION	FIRST DAY COVERS SING	PL. BLK.	MINT SHEET	PLATE BLOCK	UNUSED F/NH	USED
3141	32¢ Marshall Plan	1.95	4.75	20.00(20)	5.00	1.00	.30

3142

CLASSIC AMERICAN AIRCRAFT

3142a	*Mustang*	**3142k**	*Flying Fortress*
3142b	*Model B*	**3142l**	*Stearman*
3142c	*Cub*	**3142m**	*Constellation*
3142d	*Vega*	**3142n**	*Lightning*
3142e	*Alpha*	**3142o**	*Peashooter*
3142f	*B-10*	**3142p**	*Tri-Motor*
3142g	*Corsair*	**3142q**	*DC-3*
3142h	*Stratojet*	**3142r**	*314 Clipper*
3142i	*GeeBee*	**3142s**	*Jenny*
3142j	*Staggerwing*	**3142t**	*Wildcat*

SCOTT NO.	DESCRIPTION	FIRST DAY COVERS SING	PL. BLK.	MINT SHEET	PLATE BLOCK	UNUSED F/NH	USED
3142	32¢ Classic American Aircraft, 20 varieties, attached .	....	....	25.00(20)	....	25.00	20.00
....	set of singles	35.00	....	....	....	....	14.00
....	singles of above, each.	....	....	....	....	....	1.00
3142v	same as above, uncut sheet of 120 (6 panes)	....	....	125.00(120)	....	125.00	....
....	cross gutter block of 20	....	....	....	....	28.00	....
....	cross gutter block of 4 .	....	....	....	....	18.50	....
....	vertical pair with horizontal gutter	....	....	....	....	3.50	....
....	horizontal pair with vertical gutter	....	....	....	....	3.50	....

3143, 3148 3144, 3149

3145, 3147 3146, 3150

SCOTT NO.	DESCRIPTION	FIRST DAY COVERS SING	PL. BLK.	MINT SHEET	PLATE BLOCK	UNUSED F/NH	USED
3143-46	Legendary Football Coaches, 4 varieties, attached . .	4.00	4.75	25.00(20)	5.50	5.25	4.00
3143	32¢ Paul "Bear" Bryant	2.25	....	....	....	1.30	1.30
3144	32¢ Glenn "Pop" Warner	2.25	....	....	....	1.30	1.30
3145	32¢ Vince Lombardi. . .	2.25	....	....	....	1.30	1.30
3146	32¢ George Halas	2.25	....	....	....	1.30	1.30
3147	32¢ Vince Lombardi. . .	2.25	4.75	24.00(20)	5.50	1.30	1.30
3148	32¢ Paul "Bear" Bryant	2.25	4.75	24.00(20)	5.50	1.30	1.30
3149	32¢ Glenn "Pop" Warner	2.25	4.75	24.00(20)	5.50	1.30	1.30
3150	32¢ George Halas	2.25	4.75	24.00(20)	5.50	1.30	1.30

3151

CLASSIC AMERICAN DOLLS

3151a	*"Alabama Baby," and doll by Martha Chase*	**3151i**	*"Babyland Rag"*
3151b	*"Columbian Doll"*	**3151j**	*"Scootles"*
3151c	*Johnny Gruelle's "Raggedy Ann"*	**3151k**	*Doll by Ludwig Greiner*
3151d	*Doll by Martha Chase*	**3151l**	*"Betsy McCall"*
3151e	*"American Child"*	**3151m**	*Percy Crosby's "Skippy"*
3151f	*"Baby Coos"*	**3151n**	*"Maggie Mix-up"*
3151g	*Plains Indian*	**3151o**	*Dolls by Albert Schoenhut*
3151h	*Doll by Izannah Walker*		

SCOTT NO.	DESCRIPTION	FIRST DAY COVERS SING	FIRST DAY COVERS PL. BLK.	MINT SHEET	PLATE BLOCK	UNUSED F/NH	USED
3151	32¢ Classic American Dolls, 15 varieties, attached .	....	....	22.50(15)	....	22.50	18.00
....	set of singles	30.00	....	....	....	....	14.00
....	singles of above. each.	....	....	....	....	....	1.00

3152

SCOTT NO.	DESCRIPTION	FIRST DAY COVERS SING	FIRST DAY COVERS PL. BLK.	MINT SHEET	PLATE BLOCK	UNUSED F/NH	USED
3152	32¢ Humphrey Bogart .	3.00	....	27.00(20)	6.00	1.50	.35
3152v	same, as above, uncut sheet of 120 (6 panes)	....	....	125.00(120)	....	125.00	....
....	block of 8 with vertical gutter........		....	....	....	18.00	....
....	cross gutter block of 8 .	....	....	....	....	21.00	....
....	vertical pair with horizontal gutter	....	....	....	....	3.50	....
....	horizontal pair with vertical gutter	....	....	....	....	5.00	....

3153

SCOTT NO.	DESCRIPTION	FIRST DAY COVERS SING	FIRST DAY COVERS PL. BLK.	MINT SHEET	PLATE BLOCK	UNUSED F/NH	USED
3153	32¢ "The Stars & Stripes Forever".	2.25	4.75	47.00(50)	5.00	1.00	.30

3154

3155

3156

3157

SCOTT NO.	DESCRIPTION	FIRST DAY COVERS SING	FIRST DAY COVERS PL. BLK.	MINT SHEET	PLATE BLOCK	UNUSED F/NH	USED
3154-57	Opera Singers, 4 varieties, attached . .	4.00	4.75	22.00(20)	5.50	4.75	4.00
3154	32¢ Lily Pons.	2.25	....	....	....	1.25	1.00
3155	32¢ Richard Tucker . . .	2.25	....	....	....	1.25	1.00
3156	32¢ Lawrence Tibbett .	2.25	....	....	....	1.25	1.00
3157	32¢ Rosa Ponselle . . .	2.25	....	....	....	1.25	1.00

3158

3159

3160

3161

3162

3163

3164

3165

SCOTT NO.	DESCRIPTION	FIRST DAY COVERS SING	FIRST DAY COVERS PL. BLK.	MINT SHEET	PLATE BLOCK	UNUSED F/NH	USED
3158-65	Composers and Conductors, 8 varieties, attached . .	7.00	....	39.00(20)	20.00(8)	17.00	10.00
3158	32¢ Leopold Stokowski	2.25	....	....	....	2.00	1.00
3159	32¢ Arthur Fiedler	2.25	....	....	....	2.00	1.00
3160	32¢ George Szell.	2.25	....	....	....	2.00	1.00
3161	32¢ Eugene Ormandy .	2.25	....	....	....	2.00	1.00
3162	32¢ Samuel Barber . . .	2.25	....	....	....	2.00	1.00
3163	32¢ Ferde Grofé	2.25	....	....	....	2.00	1.00
3164	32¢ Charles Ives	2.25	....	....	....	2.00	1.00
3165	32¢ Louis Moreau Gottschalk	2.25	....	....	....	2.00	1.00

3166

3167

SCOTT NO.	DESCRIPTION	FIRST DAY COVERS SING	FIRST DAY COVERS PL. BLK.	MINT SHEET	PLATE BLOCK	UNUSED F/NH	USED
3166	32¢ Padre Félix Varela	2.25	4.75	19.00(20)	4.75	1.00	.50
3167	32¢ U.S. Air Force 50th Anniverary	4.00	6.00	19.00(20)	4.75	1.25	.30

3168

3169

3170

3171

3172

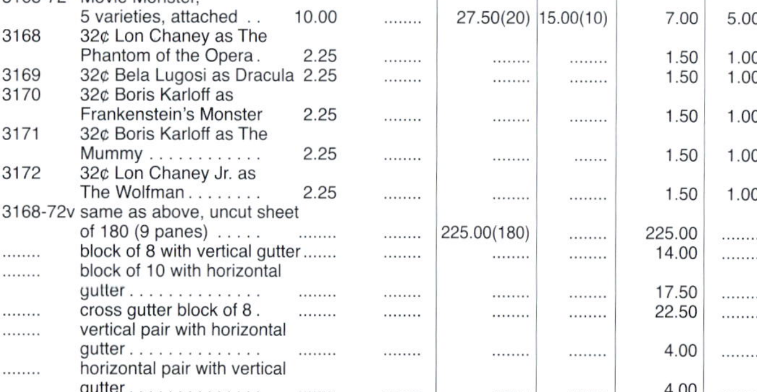

SCOTT NO.	DESCRIPTION	FIRST DAY COVERS SING	FIRST DAY COVERS PL. BLK.	MINT SHEET	PLATE BLOCK	UNUSED F/NH	USED
3168-72	Movie Monster, 5 varieties, attached . .	10.00	....	27.50(20)	15.00(10)	7.00	5.00
3168	32¢ Lon Chaney as The Phantom of the Opera .	2.25	....	....	....	1.50	1.00
3169	32¢ Bela Lugosi as Dracula	2.25	....	....	....	1.50	1.00
3170	32¢ Boris Karloff as Frankenstein's Monster	2.25	....	....	....	1.50	1.00
3171	32¢ Boris Karloff as The Mummy	2.25	....	....	....	1.50	1.00
3172	32¢ Lon Chaney Jr. as The Wolfman	2.25	....	....	....	1.50	1.00
3168-72v	same as above, uncut sheet of 180 (9 panes)	....	....	225.00(180)	....	225.00	....
....	block of 8 with vertical gutter	....	....	....	....	14.00	....
....	block of 10 with horizontal gutter	....	....	....	....	17.50	....
....	cross gutter block of 8 .	....	....	....	....	22.50	....
....	vertical pair with horizontal gutter	....	....	....	....	4.00	....
....	horizontal pair with vertical gutter	....	....	....	....	4.00	....

3173

SCOTT NO.	DESCRIPTION	FIRST DAY COVERS SING	FIRST DAY COVERS PL. BLK.	MINT SHEET	PLATE BLOCK	UNUSED F/NH	USED
3173	32¢ First Supersonic Flight, 50th Anniversary	3.00	4.75	20.00(20)	5.00	1.00	.30

3174

SCOTT NO.	DESCRIPTION	FIRST DAY COVERS SING	FIRST DAY COVERS PL. BLK.	MINT SHEET	PLATE BLOCK	UNUSED F/NH	USED
3174	32¢ Women in Military Service.	3.00	4.75	24.00(20)	6.25	1.35	.35

3175

SCOTT NO.	DESCRIPTION	FIRST DAY COVERS SING	FIRST DAY COVERS PL. BLK.	MINT SHEET	PLATE BLOCK	UNUSED F/NH	USED
3175	32¢ Kwanzaa.	3.00	4.75	47.00(50)	5.00	1.00	.30
....	same, as above, uncut sheet of 250 (5 panes)	....	....	725.00(250)	....	....	....

3176

3177

SCOTT NO.	DESCRIPTION	FIRST DAY COVERS SING	FIRST DAY COVERS PL. BLK.	MINT SHEET	PLATE BLOCK	UNUSED F/NH	USED
3176	32¢ Madonna & Child, self-adhesive	2.25	....	....	....	1.00	.25
3176a	same, bklt pane of 20 .	14.50	....	....	....	19.00	....
3177	32¢ American Holly, self-adhesive	2.25	....	....	....	1.00	.25
3177a	same, bklt pane of 20 .	14.50	....	....	....	19.00	....
3177b	same, bklt pane of 4 . .	3.00	....	....	....	5.50	....
3177c	same, bklt pane of 5 . .	3.75	....	....	....	6.75	....
3177d	same, bklt pane of 6 . .	4.50	....	....	....	7.25	....

3178

SCOTT NO.	DESCRIPTION	FIRST DAY COVERS SING	FIRST DAY COVERS PL. BLK.	MINT SHEET	PLATE BLOCK	UNUSED F/NH	USED
3178	$3 Mars Rover Sojourner, Souvenir Sheet	14.00	....	....	....	9.50	5.00
....	same, as above, uncut sheet of 18 souvenir sheets .	....	....	175.00(18)	....	175.00	....
3178v	single souvenir sheet from uncut sheet of 18.		....	....	....	10.50	....

3179

1998 COMMEMORATIVES

SCOTT NO.	DESCRIPTION	FIRST DAY COVERS SING	FIRST DAY COVERS PL. BLK.	MINT SHEET	PLATE BLOCK	UNUSED F/NH	USED
3179/3252	**(3179-81, 3192-3203, 3206, 3211-27, 3230-35, 3237-43, 3249-52) 50 varieties**	....	....	....	....	**72.00**	**27.00**
3179	32¢ Year of the Tiger . .	3.00	4.75	22.50(20)	5.50	1.20	.30

3180 3181

SCOTT NO.	DESCRIPTION	FIRST DAY COVERS SING	FIRST DAY COVERS PL. BLK.	MINT SHEET	PLATE BLOCK	UNUSED F/NH	USED
3180	32¢ Alpine Skiing.	2.25	4.75	25.00(20)	6.00	1.75	.30
3181	32¢ Madam C.J. Walker	3.00	4.75	22.50(20)	5.50	1.50	.35

3182

CELEBRATE THE CENTURY 1900s

3182a *Model T Ford*
3182b *Theodore Roosevelt*
3182c *"The Great Train Robbery" 1903*
3182d *Crayola Crayons, introduced, 1903*
3182e *St. Louis World's Fair, 1904*
3182f *Pure Food & Drug Act, 1906*
3182g *Wright Brothers first flight, 1903*
3182h *Boxing match in painting*
3182i *Immigrants arrive.*
3182j *John Muir, preservationist*
3182k *"Teddy" bear created*
3182l *W.E.B. DuBois, social activist*
3182m *Gibson Girl*
3182n *First baseball World Series, 1903*
3182o *Robie House, Chicago*

SCOTT NO.	DESCRIPTION	FIRST DAY COVERS SING	FIRST DAY COVERS PL. BLK.	MINT SHEET	PLATE BLOCK	UNUSED F/NH	USED
3182	32¢ Celebrate the Century 1900's, 15 varieties, attached.	17.50	....	18.00(15)	....	18.00	14.00
....	set of singles	32.00	....	....	....	....	12.00
....	singles of above, each.	....	....	....	....	....	1.00
3182v	same as above, uncut sheet of 60 (4 panes)	....	....	70.00(4)	....	70.00	....

3183

CELEBRATE THE CENTURY 1910s

3183a *Charlie Chaplin as the Little Tramp*
3183b *Federal Reserve system created, 1913*
3183c *George Washington Carver*
3183d *Avant-garde art, 1913*
3183e *First-Transcontinental telephone line, 1914*
3183f *Panama Canal opens, 1914*
3183g *Jim Thorpe wins decathlon, 1912*
3183h *Grand Canyon National Park, 1913*
3183i *United States enters WWI*
3183j *Boy Scouts, 1910*
3183k *Woodrow Wilson*
3183l *First crossword puzzle, pub., 1913*
3183m *Jack Dempsey wins title, 1919*
3183n *Construction toys*
3183o *Child labor reform*

SCOTT NO.	DESCRIPTION	FIRST DAY COVERS SING	FIRST DAY COVERS PL. BLK.	MINT SHEET	PLATE BLOCK	UNUSED F/NH	USED
3183	32¢ Celebrate the Century 1910's, 15 varieties, attached.	17.50	....	18.00(15)	....	18.00	14.00
....	set of singles	32.00	....	....	....	....	12.00
....	singles of above, each.	....	....	....	....	....	1.00
3183v	same as above, uncut sheet of 60 (4 panes)	....	....	70.00(4)	....	70.00	....

3184

CELEBRATE THE CENTURY 1920s

3184a *Babe Ruth*
3184b *The Gatsby style*
3184c *Prohibition enforced*
3184d *Electric toy trains*
3184e *19th Ammendment*
3184f *Emily Post's Etiquette*
3184g *Margaret Mead, anthropologist*
3184h *Flappers do the Charleston*
3184i *Radio entertains America*
3184j *Art Deco style (Chrysler Building)*
3184k *Jazz flourishes*
3184l *Four Horsemen of Notre Dame*
3184m *Lindbergh flies the Atlantic*
3184n *American realism*
3184o *Stock Market crash, 1929*

SCOTT NO.	DESCRIPTION	FIRST DAY COVERS SING	FIRST DAY COVERS PL. BLK.	MINT SHEET	PLATE BLOCK	UNUSED F/NH	USED
3184	32¢ Celebrate the Century 1920's, 15 varieties, attached.	17.50	....	18.00(15)	....	18.00	14.00
....	set of singles	32.00	....	....	....	....	12.00
....	singles of above, each.	....	....	....	....	....	1.00
3184v	same, as above, uncut sheet of 60 (4 panes)	....	....	70.00(4)	....	70.00	....

3185

CELEBRATE THE CENTURY 1930s

3185a *Franklin D. Roosevelt*
3185b *Empire State Building*
3185c *1st Issue of Life Magazine*
3185d *Eleanor Roosevelt*
3185e *FDR's New Deal*
3185f *Superman arrives*
3185g *Household conveniences*
3185h *"Snow White and the Seven Dwarfs"*
3185i *"Gone with the Wind"*
3185j *Jesse Owens*
3185k *Streamline design*
3185l *Golden Gate Bridge*
3185m *America survives the Depression*
3185n *Bobby Jones wins Grand Slam*
3185o *The Monopoly Game*

SCOTT NO.	DESCRIPTION	FIRST DAY COVERS SING	FIRST DAY COVERS PL. BLK.	MINT SHEET	PLATE BLOCK	UNUSED F/NH	USED
3185	32¢ Celebrate the Century 1930's, 15 varieties, attached.	17.50	....	18.00(15)	....	18.00	14.00
....	set of singles	32.00	....	....	....	....	12.00
....	singles of above, each.	....	....	....	....	....	1.00
3185v	same as above, uncut sheet of 60 (4 panes)	....	....	70.00(4)	....	70.00	....

3186

CELEBRATE THE CENTURY 1940s

3186a *World War II*
3186b *Antibiotics save lives*
3186c *Jackie Robinson*
3186d *Harry S. Truman*
3186e *Women support war effort*
3186f *TV entertains America*
3186g *Jitterbug sweeps nation*
3186h *Jackson Pollock, Abstract Expressionism*
3186i *GI Bill, 1944*
3186j *Big Band Sounds*
3186k *Intl. Style of Architecture*
3186l *Postwar Baby Boom*
3186m *Slinky, 1945*
3186n *"A Streetcar Named Desire" 1947*
3186o *Orson Welles' "Citizen Kane"*

SCOTT NO.	DESCRIPTION	FIRST DAY COVERS SING	FIRST DAY COVERS PL. BLK.	MINT SHEET	PLATE BLOCK	UNUSED F/NH	USED
3186	33¢ Celebrate the Century 1940's, 15 varieties, attached...........	17.50	....	22.00(15)	....	22.00	15.00
....	set of singles........	32.00	....	....	....	....	14.00
....	singles of above, each.	....	....	....	....	....	.85
3186v	same as above, uncut sheet of 60 (4 panes)......	....	....	70.00(4)	....	70.00	1.00

3187

CELEBRATE THE CENTURY 1950s

3187a *Polio vaccine developed*
3187b *teen fashions*
3187c *The "Shot Heard Round the World"*
3187d *US launches satellites*
3187e *Korean War*
3187f *Desegregation public schools*
3187g *Tail fins, chrome*
3187h *Dr. Seuss "The Cat in the Hat"*
3187i *Drive-in movies*
3187j *World series rivals*
3187k *Rocky Marciano, undefeated*
3187l *"I Love Lucy"*
3187m *Rock 'n Roll*
3187n *Stock car racing*
3187o *Movies go 3-D*

SCOTT NO.	DESCRIPTION	FIRST DAY COVERS SING	FIRST DAY COVERS PL. BLK.	MINT SHEET	PLATE BLOCK	UNUSED F/NH	USED
3187	33¢ Celebrate the Century 1950's, 15 varieties, attached...........	17.50	....	22.00(15)	....	22.00	15.00
....	set of singles........	32.00	....	....	....	....	14.00
....	singles of above, each.	....	....	....	....	....	1.00
3187v	same as above, uncut sheet of 60 (4 panes)......	....	....	70.00(4)	....	70.00	....

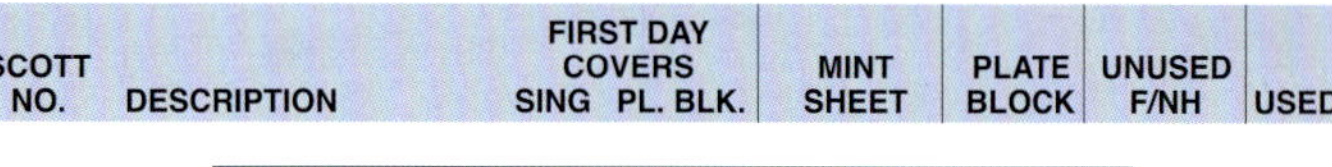

3188

CELEBRATE THE CENTURY 1960s

3188a *"I Have a Dream" Martin Luther King*
3188b *Woodstock*
3188c *Man Walks on the Moon*
3188d *Green Bay Packers*
3188e *Star Trek*
3188f *The Peace Corps*
3188g *The Vietnam War*
3188h *Ford Mustang*
3188i *Barbie Doll*
3188j *The Integrated Circuit*
3188k *Lasers*
3188l *Super Bowl I*
3188m *Peace Symbol*
3188n *Roger Maris, 61 in '61*
3188o *The Beatles "Yellow Submarine"*

SCOTT NO.	DESCRIPTION	FIRST DAY COVERS SING	FIRST DAY COVERS PL. BLK.	MINT SHEET	PLATE BLOCK	UNUSED F/NH	USED
3188	33¢ Celebrate the Century 1960's, 15 varieties, attached...........	17.50	....	22.00(15)	....	22.00	15.00
....	set of singles........	32.00	....	....	....	....	14.00
....	singles of above, each.	....	....	....	....	....	1.00
3188v	same as above, uncut sheet of 60 (4 panes)......	....	....	70.00(4)	....	70.00	....

3189

CELEBRATE THE CENTURY 1970s

3189a *Earth Day Celebrated*
3189b *"All in the Family", TV Series*
3189c *Sesame Street*
3189d *Disco Music*
3189e *Steelers Win Four Super Bowls*
3189f *U.S. Celebrates 200th Birthday*
3189g *Secretariat Wins Triple Crown*
3189h *VCR's Transform Entertainment*
3189i *Pioneer 10*
3189j *Women's Rights Movement*
3189k *1970's Fashion*
3189l *Monday Night Football*
3189m *America Smiles*
3189n *Jumbo Jets*
3189o *Medical Imaging*

SCOTT NO.	DESCRIPTION	FIRST DAY COVERS SING	FIRST DAY COVERS PL. BLK.	MINT SHEET	PLATE BLOCK	UNUSED F/NH	USED
3189	33¢ Celebrate the Century 1970's, 15 varieties, attached...........	17.50	....	22.00(15)	....	22.00	15.00
....	set of singles........	32.00	....	....	....	....	14.00
....	singles of above, each.	....	....	....	....	....	1.00
3189v	same as above, uncut sheet of 60 (4 panes)......	....	....	70.00(4)	....	70.00	....

SCOTT NO.	DESCRIPTION	FIRST DAY COVERS SING	FIRST DAY COVERS PL. BLK.	MINT SHEET	PLATE BLOCK	UNUSED F/NH	USED

3190

CELEBRATE THE CENTURY 1980s

3190a *Space Shuttle program*
3190b *Cats, Musucal Smash*
3190c *San Francisco 49ers*
3190d *Hostages Come Home*
3190e *Figure Skating*
3190f *Cable TV*
3190g *Vietnam Veterans Memorial*
3190h *Compact Discs*
3190i *Cabbage Patch Kids*
3190j *"The Cosby Show", Hit Comedy*
3190k *Fall of the Berlin Wall*
3190l *Video Games*
3190m *"E.T. The Extra-Terrestrial"*
3190n *Personal Computers*
3190o *Hip-hop Culture*

SCOTT NO.	DESCRIPTION	FIRST DAY COVERS SING	FIRST DAY COVERS PL. BLK.	MINT SHEET	PLATE BLOCK	UNUSED F/NH	USED
3190	33¢ Celebrate the Century 1980's, 15 varieties, attached.	17.50	....	22.00(15)	....	22.00	15.00
....	set of singles	32.00	....	....	....	....	14.00
....	singles of above, each.	....	....	....	....	....	1.00
3190v	same as above, uncut sheet of 60 (4 panes)	....	....	70.00(4)	....	70.00	....

3191

CELEBRATE THE CENTURY 1990s

3191a *New Baseball Records*
3191b *Gulf War*
3191c *"Seinfield" Sitcom Sensation*
3191d *Extreme Sports*
3191e *Improving Education*
3191f *Computer Art and Graphics*
3191g *Recovering Species*
3191h *Return to Space*
3191i *Special Olympics*
3191j *Virtual Reality*
3191k *"Jurassic Park"*
3191l *"Titanic" Blockbuster Film*
3191m *Sport Utility Vehicles*
3191n *World Wide Web*
3191o *Cellular Phones*

SCOTT NO.	DESCRIPTION	FIRST DAY COVERS SING	FIRST DAY COVERS PL. BLK.	MINT SHEET	PLATE BLOCK	UNUSED F/NH	USED
3191	33¢ Celebrate the Century 1990's, 15 varieties, attached.	17.50	....	22.00(15)	....	22.00	15.00
....	set of singles	32.00	....	....	....	....	14.00
....	singles of above, each.	....	....	....	....	....	1.00
3191v	same as above, uncut sheet of 60 (4 panes)	....	....	70.00(4)	....	70.00	....

3192

SCOTT NO.	DESCRIPTION	FIRST DAY COVERS SING	FIRST DAY COVERS PL. BLK.	MINT SHEET	PLATE BLOCK	UNUSED F/NH	USED
3192	32¢ "Remember the Maine"	3.00	4.75	27.00(20)	6.75	1.50	.30

3193 3194 3195

3196 3197

SCOTT NO.	DESCRIPTION	FIRST DAY COVERS SING	FIRST DAY COVERS PL. BLK.	MINT SHEET	PLATE BLOCK	UNUSED F/NH	USED
3193-97	Flowering Trees, self-adhesive, 5 varieties, attached.	5.75	....	26.00(20)	15.00(10)	7.00	5.00
3193	32¢ Southern Magnolia	2.25	....	....	....	1.10	.40
3194	32¢ Blue Paloverde . .	2.25	....	....	....	1.10	.40
3195	32¢ Yellow Poplar . . .	2.25	....	....	....	1.10	.40
3196	32¢ Prairie Crab Apple	2.25	....	....	....	1.10	.40
3197	32¢ Pacific Dogwood.	2.25	....	....	....	1.10	.40

3198

3199

3200

3201

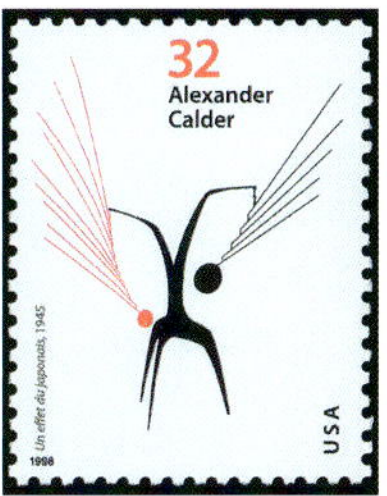

3202

SCOTT NO.	DESCRIPTION	FIRST DAY COVERS SING	FIRST DAY COVERS PL. BLK.	MINT SHEET	PLATE BLOCK	UNUSED F/NH	USED
3198-3202	Alexander Calder, 5 varieties, attached.	5.75	....	27.00(20)	16.00(10)	7.50	5.50
3198	32¢ Black Cascade, 13 Verticals, 1959 . . .	1.95	....	....	....	1.50	1.00
3199	32¢ Untitled, 1965 . . .	1.95	....	....	....	1.50	1.00
3200	32¢ Rearing Stallion, 1928	1.95	....	....	....	1.50	1.00
3201	32¢ Potrait of a Young Man, c. 1945.	1.95	....	....	....	1.50	1.00
3202	32¢ Un Effet du Japonais, 1945.	1.95	....	....	....	1.50	1.00
3198-3202v	same, as above, uncut sheet of 120 (6 panes)	....	....	140.00(120)	....	....	....

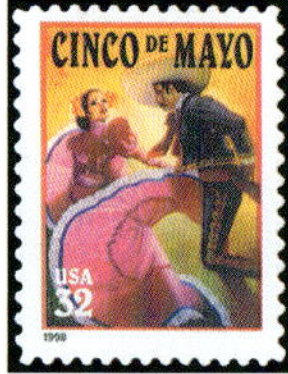

3203

SCOTT NO.	DESCRIPTION	FIRST DAY COVERS SING	FIRST DAY COVERS PL. BLK.	MINT SHEET	PLATE BLOCK	UNUSED F/NH	USED
3203	32¢ Cinco De Mayo, self-adhesive	2.25	4.75	22.00(20)	5.75	1.10	.30
3203v	same as above, uncut sheet of 180 (9 panes)	....	....	180.00(180)	....	180.00	....
....	cross gutter block of 4 .	....	....	....	....	16.00	....
....	vertical pair with horizontal gutter	....	....	....	....	3.00	....
....	horizontal pair with vertical gutter	....	....	....	....	3.00	....

3204, 3205

SCOTT NO.	DESCRIPTION	FIRST DAY COVERS SING	FIRST DAY COVERS PL. BLK.	MINT SHEET	PLATE BLOCK	UNUSED F/NH	USED
3204	32¢ Sylvester & Tweety, self-adhesive, pane of 10	12.00	....	....	....	12.00	....
3204a	same, single from pane	2.25	....	....	....	1.35	.35
3204b	same, pane of 9 (#3204a)	....	....	....	....	9.75	....
3204c	same, pane of 1 (#3204a)	7.00	....	....	....	2.75	....
....	same, top press sheet of 60 (6 panes)	....	....	100.00(60)	....	100.00	....
....	same, bottom press sheet of 60 (6 panes)	....	....	175.00(60)	....	175.00	....
....	same, pane of 10 from press sheet	....	....	....	....	17.50	....
....	same, pane of 10 from press sheet w/ plate # .	....	....	....	....	80.00	....
....	vert. pair with horiz. gutter	....	....	....	....	10.00	....
....	horiz pair with vert. gutter	....	....	....	....	20.00	....
3205	32¢ Sylvester & Tweety, self-adhesive, Die-Cut, pane of 10	20.00	....	....	....	22.00	....
3205a	same, single from pane	....	....	....	....	1.75	....
3205b	same, pane of 9 (#3205a)	....	....	....	....	14.00	....
3205c	same, pane of 1, imperf.	12.00	....	....	....	6.00	....

3206

SCOTT NO.	DESCRIPTION	FIRST DAY COVERS SING	FIRST DAY COVERS PL. BLK.	MINT SHEET	PLATE BLOCK	UNUSED F/NH	USED
3206	32¢ Wisconsin, self-adhesive	1.95	4.75	20.00(20)	5.00	1.20	.30

3207, 3207a

3208, 3208a

SCOTT NO.	DESCRIPTION	FIRST DAY COVERS SING	PLATE# STRIP 3	MINT SHEET	PLATE# STRIP 3	UNUSED F/NH	USED
3207	(5¢) Wetlands, Nonprofit, coil	2.25	10.00	....	1.85	.25	.25
	same, plate strip of 5 . .	....	....	....	....	2.00	....
3207A	same, self-adhesive coil	2.25	....	....	1.85	.25	.25
	same, plate strip of 5 . .	....	....	....	....	2.00	....
3207Ab	same, self-adhesive coil, large date.	....	....	....	3.75	.40	.25
....	same, plate strip of 5 . .	....	....	....	....	4.50	....
3208	(25¢) Diner, Presorted First-Class, coil	1.95	10.00	....	5.00	1.00	.50
3208a	same, self-adhesive coil, die cut 9.7	1.95	....	....	6.00	1.00	.50
....	same, plate strip of 5 . .	....	....	....	....	7.00	....

3209

SCOTT NO.	DESCRIPTION	FIRST DAY COVERS SING	FIRST DAY COVERS PL. BLK.	MINT SHEET	PLATE BLOCK	UNUSED F/NH	USED
3209	1¢-$2 Trans-Mississippi, Souvenir Sheet of 9 . . .	12.00	....	....	....	18.00	13.00
....	same, set of 9 singles .	18.00	....	....	....	16.00	12.00
3209v	block of 9 with horiz. gutter	....	....	....	....	60.00	....
3209v	vert. pair with horiz. gutter	....	....	....	....	12.50	....

3210

SCOTT NO.	DESCRIPTION	FIRST DAY COVERS SING	FIRST DAY COVERS PL. BLK.	MINT SHEET	PLATE BLOCK	UNUSED F/NH	USED
3210	$1 Cattle in Storm, Souvenir Sheet of 9 . . .	17.50	....	....	....	32.00	22.00
....	same, single stamp . . .	....	....	....	....	3.75	2.50
3209-10	same, press sheet of 54 (6 panes, 3–#3209 & 3–#3210)	....	....	175.00(54)	....	175.00	....
3210v	cross gutter block of 12	....	....	....	....	85.00	....
3210v	vert. pair with horiz. gutter	....	....	....	....	12.50	....
3210v	horiz. pair with vert. gutter	....	....	....	....	12.50	....

3211

SCOTT NO.	DESCRIPTION	FIRST DAY COVERS SING	FIRST DAY COVERS PL. BLK.	MINT SHEET	PLATE BLOCK	UNUSED F/NH	USED
3211	32¢ Berlin Airlift, 50th Anniversary	1.95	4.75	25.00(20)	6.00	1.35	.30

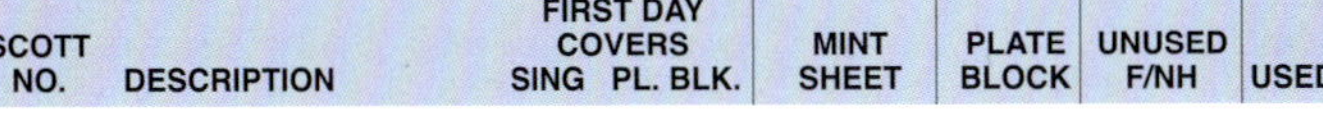

3212 3213

3215 3214

SCOTT NO.	DESCRIPTION	FIRST DAY COVERS SING	FIRST DAY COVERS PL. BLK.	MINT SHEET	PLATE BLOCK	UNUSED F/NH	USED
3212-15	Folk Musicains, 4 varieties, attached . .	12.00	14.00	32.00(20)	8.00	7.00	5.00
	Same, Top plate block of 8		....	....	15.00(8)	....	....
3212	32¢ Huddie "Leadbelly" Ledbetter	3.00	....	....	....	1.75	1.00
3213	32¢ Woody Guthrie . . .	3.00	....	....	....	1.75	1.00
3214	32¢ Sonny Terry	3.00	....	....	....	1.75	1.00
3215	32¢ Josh White	3.00	....	....	....	1.75	1.00

3216 3217

3218 3219

SCOTT NO.	DESCRIPTION	FIRST DAY COVERS SING	FIRST DAY COVERS PL. BLK.	MINT SHEET	PLATE BLOCK	UNUSED F/NH	USED
3216-19	Gospel Singers, 4 varieties, attached . .	12.00	14.00	36.00(20)	8.00	7.00	4.00
	Same, Top plate block of 8		....	....	16.00(8)	....	....
3216	32¢ Mahalia Jackson. .	3.00	....	....	....	1.75	1.00
3217	32¢ Roberta Martin . . .	3.00	....	....	....	1.75	1.00
3218	32¢ Clara Ward	3.00	....	....	....	1.75	1.00
3219	32¢ Sister Rosetta Tharpe	3.00	....	....	....	1.75	1.00

3220

3221

SCOTT NO.	DESCRIPTION	FIRST DAY COVERS SING	FIRST DAY COVERS PL. BLK.	MINT SHEET	PLATE BLOCK	UNUSED F/NH	USED
3220	32¢ Spanish Settlement of the Southwest	2.25	4.75	19.50(20)	4.75	1.20	.25
3221	32¢ Stephen Vincent Benet	2.25	4.75	19.50(20)	4.75	1.20	.35

3222 3223

3224 3225

SCOTT NO.	DESCRIPTION	FIRST DAY COVERS SING	FIRST DAY COVERS PL. BLK.	MINT SHEET	PLATE BLOCK	UNUSED F/NH	USED
3222-25	Tropical Birds, 4 varieties, attached . .	5.00	6.00	22.00(20)	6.50	6.00	4.00
3222	32¢ Antillean Euphonia	2.25	....	....	....	1.25	.75
3223	32¢ Green-throated Carib	2.25	....	....	....	1.25	.75
3224	32¢ Crested Honeycreeper	2.25	....	....	....	1.25	.75
3225	32¢ Cardinal Honeyeater	2.25	....	....	....	1.25	.75

3226

SCOTT NO.	DESCRIPTION	FIRST DAY COVERS SING	FIRST DAY COVERS PL. BLK.	MINT SHEET	PLATE BLOCK	UNUSED F/NH	USED
3226	32¢ Alfred Hitchcock .	2.25	....	26.00(20)	6.00	1.50	.35
3226v	same as above, uncut sheet of 120 (6 panes)	....	....	120.00(120)	....	120.00	....
....	block of 8 with vertical gutter.....		....	....	....	18.00	....
....	cross gutter block of 8	....	....	....	....	25.00	....
....	vertical pair with horizontal gutter	....	....	....	....	4.50	....
....	horizontal pair with vertical gutter	....	....	....	....	6.00	....

3227

3230

3231

PRESORTED STD

3228, 3229

SCOTT NO.	DESCRIPTION	FIRST DAY COVERS SING	FIRST DAY COVERS PL. BLK.	MINT SHEET	PLATE BLOCK	UNUSED F/NH	USED
3227	32¢ Organ & Tissue Donation, self-adhesive	2.25	....	22.00(20)	5.50	1.20	.25
3228	(10¢) Modern Bicycle, self-adhesive coil, die cut 9.8	2.25	....	....	3.00(3)	.40	.25
	same, plate strip of 5 .	....	....	....	....	4.00	....
3228a	large "1998" date	....	....	....	3.50(3)	.75	.50
....	same, plate strip of 5 .	....	....	....	....	4.50	....
3229	(10¢) Modern Bicycle, coil	2.25	10.00	....	3.00(3)	.40	.25
	same, plate strip of 5 .	....	....	....	....	3.75	....

3232

3233

1998 COMMEMORATIVES (continued)

3234

SCOTT NO.	DESCRIPTION	FIRST DAY COVERS SING	FIRST DAY COVERS PL. BLK.	MINT SHEET	PLATE BLOCK	UNUSED F/NH	USED
3230-34	Bright Eyes, self-adhesive, 5 varieties, attached .	12.00	....	28.00(20)	15.00(10)	7.00	6.00
3230	32¢ Bright Eyes Dog .	3.00	....	....	....	1.50	.45
3231	32¢ Bright Eyes Fish .	3.00	....	....	....	1.50	.45
3232	32¢ Bright Eyes Cat. .	3.00	....	....	....	1.50	.45
3233	32¢ Bright Eyes Parakeet	3.00	....	....	....	1.50	.45
3234	32¢ Bright Eyes Hamster	3.00	....	....	....	1.50	.45

3235

SCOTT NO.	DESCRIPTION	FIRST DAY COVERS SING	FIRST DAY COVERS PL. BLK.	MINT SHEET	PLATE BLOCK	UNUSED F/NH	USED
3235	32¢ Klondike Gold Rush	2.25	....	22.00(20)	6.00	1.20	.25

3236

AMERICAN ART

3236a *"Portrait of Richard Mather," by John Foster*
3236b *"Mrs. Elizabeth Freake and Baby Mary," by The Freake Limner*
3236c *"Girl in Red Dress with Cat and Dog," by Ammi Phillips*
3236d *"Rubens Peale with Geranium," by Rembrandt Peale*
3236e *"Long-billed Curlew, Numenius Longrostris," by John James Audubon*
3236f *"Boatmen on the Missouri," by George Caleb Bingham*
3236g *"Kindred Spirits," by Asher B. Durand*
3236h *"The Westwood Children," by Joshua Johnson*
3236i *"Music and Literature," by William Harnett*
3236j *"The Fog Warning," by Winslow Homer*
3236k *"The White Cloud, Head Chief of the Iowas," by George Catlin*
3236l *"Cliffs of Green River," by Thomas Moran*
3236m *"The Last of the Buffalo," by Alfred Bierstadt*
3236n *"Niagara," by Frederic Edwin Church*
3236o *"Breakfast in Bed," by Mary Cassatt*
3236p *"Nighthawks," by Edward Hopper*
3236q *"American Gothic," by Grany Wood*
3236r *"Two Against the White," by Charles Sheeler*
3236s *"Mahoning," by Franz Kline*
3236t *"No. 12," by Mark Rothko*

SCOTT NO.	DESCRIPTION	FIRST DAY COVERS SING	FIRST DAY COVERS PL. BLK.	MINT SHEET	PLATE BLOCK	UNUSED F/NH	USED
3236	32¢ American Art, 20 varieties, attached	....	....	30.00(20)	....	30.00	25.00
....	set of singles	35.00	....	....	....	....	19.00
....	same as above, uncut sheet of 120 (6 panes)	....	....	175.00(120)	....	175.00	....
....	block of 24 with vert. gutter	....	....	....	....	27.50	....
....	block of 25 with horiz. gutter	....	....	....	....	32.50	....
....	cross gutter block of 20	....	....	....	....	40.00	....
....	vert. pair with horiz. gutter	....	....	....	....	7.00	....

AMERICAN ART (continued)

SCOTT NO.	DESCRIPTION	FIRST DAY COVERS SING	FIRST DAY COVERS PL. BLK.	MINT SHEET	PLATE BLOCK	UNUSED F/NH	USED
....	horiz. pair with vert. gutter	....	....	....	....	9.00	....
....	horiz. blk of 8 with vert. gutter		....	....	....	....	....
....	vert. blk of 10 with horiz. gutter		....	....	....	....	....

3237

3243

SCOTT NO.	DESCRIPTION	FIRST DAY COVERS SING	FIRST DAY COVERS PL. BLK.	MINT SHEET	PLATE BLOCK	UNUSED F/NH	USED
3237	32¢ Ballet.	1.95	....	23.00(20)	6.00	1.50	.35
....	same,uncut sheet of 120 (6 panes)	....	....	115.00(120)	....	115.00	....
....	cross gutter blk of 4 . .	....	....	....	....	13.00	....
....	vert. pair with horiz. gutter	....	....	....	....	3.00	....
....	horiz. pair with vert. gutter	....	....	....	....	3.00	....

3238

3239

3240

3241

3244

3242

SCOTT NO.	DESCRIPTION	FIRST DAY COVERS SING	FIRST DAY COVERS PL. BLK.	MINT SHEET	PLATE BLOCK	UNUSED F/NH	USED
3238-42	Space Discovery, 5 varieties, attached .	5.75	11.00	24.00(20)	15.00(10)	7.50	6.50
3238	32¢ Space City	2.25	....	....	....	1.50	1.00
3239	32¢ Space ship landing	2.25	....	....	....	1.50	1.00
3240	32¢ Person in space suit	2.25	....	....	....	1.50	1.00
3241	32¢ Space Ship taking off	2.25	....	....	....	1.50	1.00
3242	32¢ Large domed structure	2.25	....	....	....	1.50	1.00
3238-42v	same, uncut sheet of 180 (9 panes)	....	....	185.00(180)	....	185.00	....
....	cross gutter blk of 10 .	....	....	....	....	27.50	....
....	vert. blk of 10 with horiz. gutter	....	....	....	....	20.00	....
....	horiz. pair with vert. gutter	....	....	....	....	3.50	....
....	vert. pair with horiz. gutter	....	....	....	....	3.50	....

3245, 3249

3246, 3250

3247, 3251

3248, 3252

SCOTT NO.	DESCRIPTION	FIRST DAY COVERS SING	FIRST DAY COVERS PL. BLK.	MINT SHEET	PLATE BLOCK	UNUSED F/NH	USED
3243	32¢ Giving and Sharing, self-adhesive	2.25	4.75	22.00(20)	5.50	1.20	.30
3244	32¢ Madonna & Child, self-adhesive	2.25	....	....	....	1.50	.25
3244a	same, booklet pane of 20	14.50	....	....	....	20.00	....
3245	32¢ Evergreen Wreath, self-adhesive	2.25	....	....	....	4.00	1.00
3246	32¢ Victorian Wreath, self-adhesive	2.25	....	....	....	4.00	1.00
3247	32¢ Chili Pepper Wreath, self-adhesive	2.25	....	....	....	4.00	1.00
3248	32¢ Tropical Wreath self-adhesive	2.25	....	....	....	4.00	1.00

SCOTT NO.	DESCRIPTION	FIRST DAY COVERS SING	FIRST DAY COVERS PL. BLK.	MINT SHEET	PLATE BLOCK	UNUSED F/NH	USED
3248a	32¢ Christmas Wreaths, self-adhesive, bklt pane of 4	4.00	....	....	....	20.00	....
3248b	same, bklt pane of 5 .	5.00	....	....	....	25.00	....
3248c	same, bklt pane of 6 .	5.50	....	....	....	30.00	....
3249-52	32¢ Christmas Wreaths, self-adhesive, 4 varieties, attached.	4.00	4.75	60.00(20)	15.00	13.00	....
3249-52a	die cut 11.7x11.6	....	....	....	....	19.00	....
3249	32¢ Evergreen Wreath, self-adhesive	2.25	....	....	....	2.50	.75
3249a	32¢ Evergreen Wreath, self-adhesive, die-cut 11.7x11.6	2.25	....	....	....	2.75	1.00
3250	32¢ Victorian Wreath, self-adhesive	2.25	....	....	....	2.50	.75
3250a	32¢ Victorian Wreath, self-adhesive, die-cut 11.7x11.6	2.25	....	....	....	2.75	1.00
3251	32¢ Chili Pepper Wreath, self-adhesive	2.25	....	....	....	2.50	.75
3251a	32¢ Chili Pepper Wreath, self-adhesive, die-cut 11.7x11.6	2.25	....	....	....	2.75	1.00
3252	32¢ Tropical Wreath, self-adhesive	2.25	....	....	....	2.50	.75
3252a	32¢ Tropical Wreath, self-adhesive, die-cut 11.7x11.6	2.25	....	....	....	2.75	1.00
3252c	same, bklt pane of 20	14.50	....	....	....	55.00	....
3252e	bklt pane of 20, 5 each of 3249a-52a + label . . .	14.50	....	....	....	60.00	....

3257, 3258

3259, 3263

3260, 3264, 3265, 3266, 3267, 3268, 3269

SCOTT NO.	DESCRIPTION	FIRST DAY COVERS SING	FIRST DAY COVERS PL. BLK.	MINT SHEET	PLATE BLOCK	UNUSED F/NH	USED
3257	(1¢) Weather Vane (white USA)	2.25	3.50	11.00(50)	1.10	.25	.25
3258	(1¢) Weather Vane (pale blue USA)	2.25	3.50	11.00(50)	1.10	.25	.25
3259	22¢ Uncle Sam, self-adhesive	2.25	4.75	14.00(20)	3.75	.75	.35
3259a	22¢ Uncle Sam, die cut 10.8	....	....	30.00(20)	12.00	3.50	1.35
3260	(33¢) Uncle Sam's Hat	2.25	4.75	50.00(50)	7.00	1.25	.35

3261

3262

SCOTT NO.	DESCRIPTION	FIRST DAY COVERS SING	FIRST DAY COVERS PL. BLK.	MINT SHEET	PLATE BLOCK	UNUSED F/NH	USED
3261	$3.20 Space Shuttle Landing, self-adhesive	7.50	26.50	200.00(20)	46.00	11.00	5.00
3262	$11.75 Piggyback Space Shuttle, self-adhesive	28.50	95.00	695.00(20)	150.00	38.00	22.00
3263	22¢ Uncle Sam, self adhesive coil	2.25	....	....	5.75	.85	.35
....	same, plate strip of 5 .	....	....	....	....	6.50	....
3264	(33¢) Uncle Sam's Hat, coil	2.25	10.00	....	8.00	1.20	.65
....	same, plate strip of 5 .	....	....	....	....	9.50	....
3265	(33¢) Uncle Sam's Hat, self-adhesive coil, die cut 9.9	2.25	....	....	11.00	1.25	.30
....	same, plate strip of 5 .	....	....	....	....	12.00	....
3266	(33¢) Uncle Sam's Hat, self-adhesive coil, die cut 9.7	2.25	....	....	20.00(3)	3.00	1.65
....	same, plate strip of 5 .	....	....	....	....	24.00	....
3267	(33¢) Uncle Sam's Hat, self-adhesive, die cut 9.9	2.25	....	....	....	1.25	.30
3267a	same, bklt pane of 10	7.25	....	....	....	10.00	....
3268	(33¢) Uncle Sam's Hat, self-adhesive, die cut 11.2 x 11.1	2.25	....	....	....	1.25	.30
3268a	same, bklt pane of 10	7.25	....	....	....	10.00	....
3268b	(33¢) Uncle Sam's Hat, d/c 11	....	....	....	....	1.25	.50
3268c	same, bklt pane of 20	14.50	....	....	....	23.00	....
3269	(33¢) Uncle Sam's Hat, self-adhesive, die cut 8	2.25	....	....	....	1.30	.75
3269a	same, bklt pane of 18	13.50	....	....	....	20.00	....

SCOTT NO.	DESCRIPTION	FIRST DAY COVERS SING	FIRST DAY COVERS PL. BLK.	MINT SHEET	PLATE BLOCK	UNUSED F/NH	USED
3270	(10¢) Eagle, Presorted Std. coil, d/c 9.8, small date	2.25	....	....	3.00(3)	.40	.25
3270a	same, large date	....	....	....	10.00(3)	.85	.50
	plate strip of 5	....	....	....	....	12.00	....
3271	(10¢) Eagle, Presorted Std., self-adhesive coil d/c 9.9	2.25	....	....	4.00	.40	.25
....	same, plate strip of 5 .	....	....	....	4.50	....	....
3271a	same, large date	....	....	....	12.00(5)	1.25	.30

3270, 3271

3272

3273

1999 COMMEMORATIVES

SCOTT NO.	DESCRIPTION	FIRST DAY COVERS SING	FIRST DAY COVERS PL. BLK.	MINT SHEET	PLATE BLOCK	UNUSED F/NH	USED
3272/3369	**(3272-73, 3276, 3286-92, 3308-09, 3314-3350, 3352, 3354, 3356-59, 3368-69) 56 varieties . . . .**	....	....	....	....	**84.00**	**28.00**
3272	33¢ Year of the Rabbit.	2.25	4.75	22.00(20)	5.00	1.25	.25
3273	33¢ Malcolm X, Civil Rights, self-adhesive	2.25	4.75	24.00(20)	6.00	1.50	.25

3274

3275

SCOTT NO.	DESCRIPTION	FIRST DAY COVERS SING	FIRST DAY COVERS PL. BLK.	MINT SHEET	PLATE BLOCK	UNUSED F/NH	USED
3274	33¢ Love, self-adhesive	2.25	....	....	....	1.25	.25
3274a	same, bklt pane of 20	14.50	....	....	....	20.00	....
3275	55¢ Love, self-adhesive	2.50	....	30.00(20)	7.50	1.70	.50

3276

3277, 3278, 3279, 3280, 3281, 3282

3283

SCOTT NO.	DESCRIPTION	FIRST DAY COVERS SING	FIRST DAY COVERS PL. BLK.	MINT SHEET	PLATE BLOCK	UNUSED F/NH	USED
3276	33¢ Hospice Care, self-adhesive	2.25	4.75	20.00(20)	5.00	1.00	.25
3277	33¢ Flag and City . . .	2.25	4.75	250.00(100)	48.00	2.50	.75
3278	33¢ Flag and City, self-adhesive, die cut 11.1	1.95	4.75	25.00(20)	6.00	1.10	.25
3278a	same, bklt pane of 4 .	4.00	....	....	....	5.25	....
3278b	same, bklt pane of 5 .	5.00	....	....	....	6.75	....
3278c	same, bklt pane of 6 .	5.50	....	....	....	8.00	....
3278d	same, bklt pane of 10	7.25	....	....	....	18.00	....
3278e	same, bklt pane of 20	14.50	....	....	....	21.00	....
3278F	33¢ Flag and City, self-adhesive, die cut 11.5x11.75	2.25	....	....	....	1.95	.50
3278Fg	same, bklt pane of 20	14.50	....	....	....	36.00	....
3278i	Flag and City, die cut 11.25	2.25	....	....	....	5.00	2.50
3278j	same, bklt pane of 10	7.25	....	....	....	45.00	....
3279	33¢ Flag and City, self-adhesive, die cut 9.8	2.25	....	....	....	1.25	.30
3279a	same, bklt pane of 10	7.25	....	....	....	13.00	....
3280	33¢ Flag and City, coil d/c 9.9	2.25	....	....	6.00	1.15	.25
....	same, plate strip of 5 .	....	....	....	....	7.75	....
3280a	33¢ Flag and City coil, large date.	....	....	....	....	2.50	1.15
....	same, plate strip of 5 .	....	....	....	....	14.00	....
3281	33¢ Flag and City, self-adhesive coil (square corners) large date	2.25	....	....	7.00	1.25	.25
....	same, plate strip of 5 .	....	....	....	....	8.50	....
3281c	same, small date, type II	2.25	....	....	10.00(3)	2.00	.25
....	same, plate strip of 5 .	....	....	....	....	12.00	....
3281d	same, small date, type I	....	....	....	....	7.00	....
....	plate and strip of 5. . .	....	....	....	....	50.00	....

SCOTT NO.	DESCRIPTION	FIRST DAY COVERS SING	FIRST DAY COVERS PL. BLK.	MINT SHEET	PLATE BLOCK	UNUSED F/NH	USED
3282	33¢ Flag and City, self-adhesive coil (round corners)	2.25	....	....	6.00(3)	1.50	.60
....	same, plate strip of 5 .	....	....	....	....	10.00	....
3283	33¢ Flag and Chalkboard, self-adhesive	2.25	....	....	....	1.25	.50
3283a	same, bklt pane of 18	13.50	....	....	....	20.00	....

3286

3287

SCOTT NO.	DESCRIPTION	FIRST DAY COVERS SING	FIRST DAY COVERS PL. BLK.	MINT SHEET	PLATE BLOCK	UNUSED F/NH	USED
3286	33¢ Irish Immigration .	2.25	4.75	22.00(20)	5.50	1.20	.25
3287	33¢ Alfred Lunt & Lynn Fontanne, Actors	2.25	4.75	20.00(20)	4.75	1.20	.25

3288 3289 3290

3291 3292

SCOTT NO.	DESCRIPTION	FIRST DAY COVERS SING	FIRST DAY COVERS PL. BLK.	MINT SHEET	PLATE BLOCK	UNUSED F/NH	USED
3288-92	Arctic Animals, 5 varieties, attached .	12.00	....	20.00(15)	15.00(10)	7.50	5.00
3288	33¢ Arctic Hare	2.25	....	....	....	1.50	.75
3289	33¢ Arctic Fox	2.25	....	....	....	1.50	.75
3290	33¢ Snowy Owl	2.25	....	....	....	1.50	.75
3291	33¢ Polar Bear.	2.25	....	....	....	1.50	.75
3292	33¢ Gray Wolf	2.25	....	....	....	1.50	.75

3293
SONORAN DESERT

3293a *Cactus wren, brittlebush, teddy bear cholla*
3293b *Desert tortoise*
3293c *White-winged dove, prickly pear*
3293d *Gambel quail*
3293e *Saquaro cactus*
3293f *Desert mule deer*
3293g *Desert cottontail, hedgehog cactus*
3293h *Gila monster*
3293i *Western diamondback rattlesnake, cactus mouse*
3293j *Gila woodpecker*

SCOTT NO.	DESCRIPTION	FIRST DAY COVERS SING	FIRST DAY COVERS PL. BLK.	MINT SHEET	PLATE BLOCK	UNUSED F/NH	USED
3293	33¢ Sonoran Desert, 10 varieties, attached, self-adhesive	....	....	16.00(10)	....	16.00	....
....	set of singles	18.50	....	....	....	....	9.00
3293v	same, uncut sheet of 60 (6 panes)	....	....	80.00(60)	....	80.00	....

3294, 3298, 3302 3295, 3299, 3303 3296, 3300, 3304 3297, 3301, 3305

SCOTT NO.	DESCRIPTION	FIRST DAY COVERS SING	FIRST DAY COVERS PL. BLK.	MINT SHEET	PLATE BLOCK	UNUSED F/NH	USED
3294	33¢ Blueberries, self-adhesive, die cut 11.2 x 11.7	2.25	....	....	....	1.30	.30
3294a	same, dated "2000" . .	2.25	....	....	....	1.75	.30
3295	33¢ Raspberries, self-adhesive, die cut 11.2 x 11.7	2.25	....	....	....	1.50	.30
3295a	same, dated "2000" . .	2.25	....	....	....	1.75	.30
3296	33¢ Strawberries, self-adhesive, die cut 11.2x 11.7	2.25	....	....	....	1.50	.30
3296a	same, dated "2000" . .	2.25	....	....	....	1.75	.30
3297	33¢ Blackberries, self-adhesive, die cut 11.2 x 11.7	2.25	....	....	....	1.50	.30
3297b	same, bklt pane of 20 (3294-97 x 5 of each)	14.50	....	....	....	27.00	....
3297a	same, dated "2000" . .	2.25	....	....	....	1.75	.30
3297d	same, bklt pane of 20	14.50	....	....	....	34.00	....
3297e	same, block of 4, (#3294a-96a, 3297c) .	4.00	....	....	....	8.50	....
3298	33¢ Blueberries, self-adhesive, die cut 9.5 x 10	2.25	....	....	....	1.75	.55
3299	33¢ Strawberries, self-adhesive, die cut 9.5 x 10	2.25	....	....	....	1.75	.55
3300	33¢ Raspberries, self-adhesive, die cut 9.5 x 10	2.25	....	....	....	1.75	.55
3301	33¢ Blackberries, self-adhesive, die cut 9.5 x 10	2.25	....	....	....	1.75	.55
3301a	same, bklt pane of 4 (3298-3301 x 1)	4.00	....	....	....	8.00	....
3301b	same, bklt pane of 5, (3298, 3299, 3301, 3300 x 2)	5.00	....	....	....	10.00	....
3301c	same, bklt pane of 6, (3300, 3301, 3298 x 2, 3299)	6.00	....	....	....	12.00	....
3302-05	33¢ Berries, self-adhesive coil, strip of 4, attached	4.00	....	....	....	10.00	....
3302	33¢ Blueberries, self-adhesive coil	2.25	....	....	....	2.00	.50
3303	33¢ Raspberries, self-adhesive coil	2.25	....	....	....	2.00	.50
3304	33¢ Blackberries, self-adhesive coil	2.25	....	....	....	2.00	.50
3305	33¢ Strawberries, self-adhesive coil	2.25	....	....	....	2.00	.50
3302-05	33¢ Berries, self-adhesive coil, pl# strip of 5 (3302 x 2, 3303-05 x 1)	10.00	....	....	....	16.00(5)	....

3306, 3307 3308

SCOTT NO.	DESCRIPTION	FIRST DAY COVERS SING	FIRST DAY COVERS PL. BLK.	MINT SHEET	PLATE BLOCK	UNUSED F/NH	USED
3306	33¢ Daffy Duck, self-adhesive, pane of 10	12.00	....	....	....	12.50	....
3306a	same, single from pane	2.25	....	....	....	1.25	.45
3306b	same, pane of 9 (3306a)	....	....	....	....	9.50	....
3306c	same, pane of 1 (3306a)	7.00	....	....	....	2.50	....
3306v	same, top press sheet of 60 (6 panes)	....	....	80.00(60)	....	80.00	....
....	same, bottom press sheet of 60 w/ plate # (6 panes)	....	....	110.00(60)	....	110.00	....
....	same, pane of 10 from press sheet	....	....	....	....	15.00	....
....	same, pane of 10 from press sheet with plate #	....	....	....	....	85.00	....
....	vert. pair with horiz. gutter	....	....	....	....	5.00	....
....	horiz. pair with vert. gutter	....	....	....	....	10.00	....
3307	33¢ Daffy Duck, self-adhesive, die cut, pane of 10	15.00	....	....	....	23.00	....
3307a	same, single from pane	....	....	....	....	2.00	....
3307b	same, pane of 9 (3307a)	....	....	....	....	16.00	....
3307c	same, pane of 1, imperf.	12.00	....	....	....	6.00	....
3308	33¢ Ayn Rand	2.25	4.75	20.00(20)	5.00	1.10	.35

3309

SCOTT NO.	DESCRIPTION	FIRST DAY COVERS SING	FIRST DAY COVERS PL. BLK.	MINT SHEET	PLATE BLOCK	UNUSED F/NH	USED
3309	33¢ Cinco De Mayo, self-adhesive	2.25	4.75	20.00(20)	5.00	1.10	.30

3310

3311

3312

3313

SCOTT NO.	DESCRIPTION	FIRST DAY COVERS SING	FIRST DAY COVERS PL. BLK.	MINT SHEET	PLATE BLOCK	UNUSED F/NH	USED
3310-13	33¢ Tropical Flowers, self-adhesive, 4 varieties, attached.	8.00	....	....	....	5.00	5.00
3310	33¢ Bird of Paradise, self-adhesive	2.25	....	....	....	1.25	.35
3311	33¢ Royal Poinciana, self-adhesive	2.25	....	....	....	1.25	.35
3312	33¢ Gloriosa Lily, self-adhesive	2.25	....	....	....	1.25	.35
3313	33¢ Chinese Hibiscus, self-adhesive	2.25	....	....	....	1.25	.35
3313a	same, bklt pane of 20 (3310-13 x 5)	....	....	....	....	22.00	....

3314

3315

3316

SCOTT NO.	DESCRIPTION	FIRST DAY COVERS SING	FIRST DAY COVERS PL. BLK.	MINT SHEET	PLATE BLOCK	UNUSED F/NH	USED
3314	33¢ John & William Bartram, Botanists	2.25	4.75	20.00(20)	5.00	1.10	.30
3315	33¢ Prostate Cancer Awareness.	2.25	4.75	20.00(20)	5.00	1.10	.30
3316	33¢ California Gold Rush	2.25	4.75	20.00(20)	5.00	1.10	.30

3317

3318

3319

3320

SCOTT NO.	DESCRIPTION	FIRST DAY COVERS SING	FIRST DAY COVERS PL. BLK.	MINT SHEET	PLATE BLOCK	UNUSED F/NH	USED
3317-20	Aquarium Fish, self-adhesive, 4 varieties, attached.	8.00	....	25.00(20)	11.00(8)	6.50	6.00
3317	33¢ Yellow fish, red fish, cleaner shrimp	2.25	....	....	....	1.40	.35
3318	33¢ Fish, thermometer	2.25	....	....	....	1.40	.35
3319	33¢ Red fish, blue fish	2.25	....	....	....	1.40	.35
3320	33¢ Fish, heater.	2.25	....	....	....	1.40	.35

3321

3322

3323

3324

SCOTT NO.	DESCRIPTION	FIRST DAY COVERS SING	FIRST DAY COVERS PL. BLK.	MINT SHEET	PLATE BLOCK	UNUSED F/NH	USED
3321-24	Xtreme Sports, self-adhesive, 4 varieties, attached.	8.00	....	22.00(20)	5.00	4.50	4.00
3321	33¢ Skateboarding . .	2.25	....	....	....	1.25	.45
3322	33¢ BMX biking	2.25	....	....	....	1.25	.45
3323	33¢ Snowboarding. . .	2.25	....	....	....	1.25	.45
3324	33¢ Inline skating. . . .	2.25	....	....	....	1.25	.45

3325

3326

3327

3328

SCOTT NO.	DESCRIPTION	FIRST DAY COVERS SING	FIRST DAY COVERS PL. BLK.	MINT SHEET	PLATE BLOCK	UNUSED F/NH	USED
3325-28	American Glass, 4 varieties, attached .	10.00	....	30.00(15)	....	10.00	5.00
3325	33¢ Freeblown glass .	3.00	....	....	....	2.25	.45
3326	33¢ Mold-blown glass	3.00	....	....	....	2.25	.45
3327	33¢ Pressed glass. . .	3.00	....	....	....	2.25	.45
3328	33¢ Art glass	3.00	....	....	....	2.25	.45

3329

SCOTT NO.	DESCRIPTION	FIRST DAY COVERS SING	FIRST DAY COVERS PL. BLK.	MINT SHEET	PLATE BLOCK	UNUSED F/NH	USED
3329	33¢ James Cagney . .	1.95	4.75	28.00(20)	7.00	1.50	.35

3330

3331

3332

SCOTT NO.	DESCRIPTION	FIRST DAY COVERS SING	FIRST DAY COVERS PL. BLK.	MINT SHEET	PLATE BLOCK	UNUSED F/NH	USED
3330	55¢ General William "Billy" Mitchell, self-adhesive	2.50	....	32.00(20)	7.75	1.75	.75
3331	33¢ Honoring Those Who Served, self-adhesive	2.25	....	25.00(20)	5.50	1.50	.30
3332	45¢ Universal Postal Union	2.25	5.00	27.00(20)	6.50	1.60	1.00

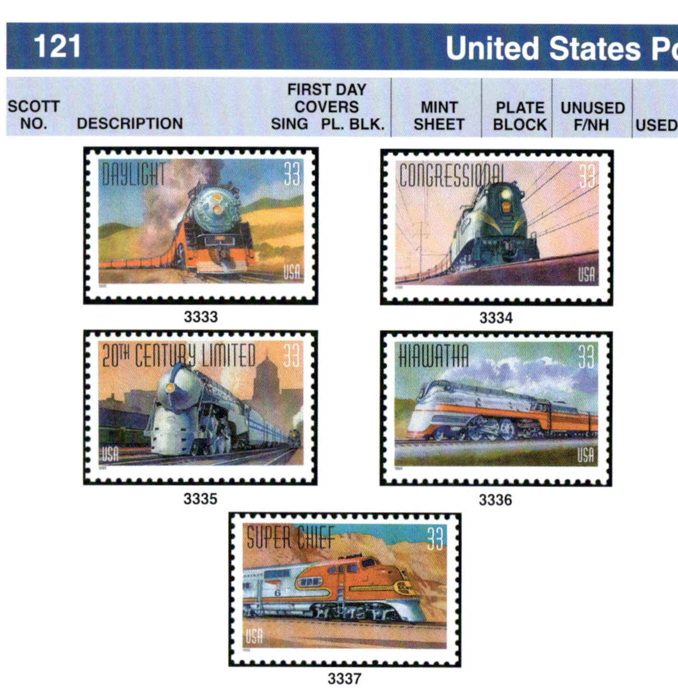

3333 3334 3335 3336 3337

SCOTT NO.	DESCRIPTION	FIRST DAY COVERS SING	FIRST DAY COVERS PL. BLK.	MINT SHEET	PLATE BLOCK	UNUSED F/NH	USED
3333-37	33¢ Famous Trains, 5 varieties, attached .	10.00	15.00	25.00(20)	14.00(8)	7.00	7.00
3333	33¢ Daylight.	3.00	....	....	....	1.40	.45
3334	33¢ Congressional. . .	3.00	....	....	....	1.40	.45
3335	33¢ 20th Century Limited	3.00	....	....	....	1.40	.45
3336	33¢ Hiawatha.	3.00	....	....	....	1.40	.45
3337	33¢ Super Chief.	3.00	....	....	....	1.40	.45
3333-37v	same, uncut sheet of 120 (6 panes)	....	....	175.00(120)	....	175.00	....
....	block of 8 with horiz. gutter	....	....	....	....	22.50	....
....	block of 10 with vert. gutter	....	....	....	....	23.50	....
....	cross gutter block of 8	....	....	....	....	25.00	....
....	horiz. pair with vert. gutter	....	....	....	....	4.00	....
....	vert. pair with horiz. gutter	....	....	....	....	4.00	....

3338

SCOTT NO.	DESCRIPTION	FIRST DAY COVERS SING	FIRST DAY COVERS PL. BLK.	MINT SHEET	PLATE BLOCK	UNUSED F/NH	USED
3338	33¢ Frederick Law Olmstead, Landscape Architect .	1.95	4.75	19.50(20)	5.00	1.10	.30

3339 3340

3341 3342 3343 3344

SCOTT NO.	DESCRIPTION	FIRST DAY COVERS SING	FIRST DAY COVERS PL. BLK.	MINT SHEET	PLATE BLOCK	UNUSED F/NH	USED
3339-44	33¢ Hollywood Composers, 6 varieties, attached .	12.00	17.00	30.00(20)	14.00(6)	12.00	8.00
....	same, plate block of 8	....	....	....	18.00	....	....
3339	33¢ Max Steiner	3.00	....	....	....	1.75	.95
3340	33¢ Dimitri Tiomkin . .	3.00	....	....	....	1.75	.95
3341	33¢ Bernard Herrmann	3.00	....	....	....	1.75	.95
3342	33¢ Franz Waxman . .	3.00	....	....	....	1.75	.95
3343	33¢ Alfred Newman . .	3.00	....	....	....	1.75	.95
3344	33¢ Erich Wolfgang Korngold	3.00	....	....	....	1.75	.95

3345 3346

3347 3348 3349 3350

SCOTT NO.	DESCRIPTION	FIRST DAY COVERS SING	FIRST DAY COVERS PL. BLK.	MINT SHEET	PLATE BLOCK	UNUSED F/NH	USED
3345-50	33¢ Broadway Songwriters, 6 varieties, attached .	12.00	17.00	30.00(20)	14.00(6)	12.00	7.75
....	same, plate block of 8	....	....	18.00	....	....	
3345	33¢ Ira & George Gershwin	3.00	....	....	....	1.75	1.00
3346	33¢ Lerner & Loewe .	3.00	....	....	....	1.75	1.00
3347	33¢ Lorenz Hart.	3.00	....	....	....	1.75	1.00
3348	33¢ Rodgers & Hammerstein	3.00	....	....	....	1.75	1.00
3349	33¢ Meredith Willson.	3.00	....	....	....	1.75	1.00
3350	33¢ Frank Loesser. . .	3.00	....	....	....	1.75	1.00

3351

INSECTS & SPIDERS

3351a *Black Widow*
3351b *Elderberry longhorn*
3351c *Lady beetle*
3351d *Yellow garden spider*
3351e *Dogbane beetle*
3351f *Flower fly*
3351g *Assassin bug*
3351h *Ebony jewelwing*
3351i *Velvet ant*
3351j *Monarch caterpillar*
3351k *Monarch butterfly*
3351l *Eastern hercules beetle*
3351m *Bombardier beetle*
3351n *Dung beetle*
3351o *Spotted water beetle*
3351p *True Katydid*
3351q *Spinybacked spider*
3351r *Periodical cicada*
3351s *Scorpionfly*
3351t *Jumping spider*

INSECTS & SPIDERS (continued)

SCOTT NO.	DESCRIPTION	FIRST DAY COVERS SING	FIRST DAY COVERS PL. BLK.	MINT SHEET	PLATE BLOCK	UNUSED F/NH	USED
3351	33¢ Insects & Spiders, 20 varieties, attached .	....	....	25.00(20)	....	25.00	18.00
....	set of singles	37.50	....	....	....	....	14.00
....	same, uncut sheet of 80 (4 panes)	....	....	100.00(80)	....	100.00	....
....	same, block of 10 with vert. gutter	....	....	....	....	25.00	....
....	same, block of 8 with horiz. gutter	....	....	....	....	25.00	....
....	same, cross gutter block of 20.	....	....	....	....	35.00	....
....	same, vert. pair with horiz. gutter	....	....	....	....	3.00	....
....	same, horiz. pair with vert. gutter	....	....	....	....	3.00	....

3352

SCOTT NO.	DESCRIPTION	FIRST DAY COVERS SING	FIRST DAY COVERS PL. BLK.	MINT SHEET	PLATE BLOCK	UNUSED F/NH	USED
3352	33¢ Hanukkah, self-adhesive	2.25	4.75	20.00(20)	5.00	1.10	.30

3353

SCOTT NO.	DESCRIPTION	FIRST DAY COVERS SING	FIRST DAY COVERS PL. BLK.	MINT SHEET	PLATE BLOCK	UNUSED F/NH	USED
3353	22¢ Uncle Sam, coil. .	1.95	....	....	5.00	.75	.50
....	same, plate strip of 5 .	....	....	....	....	6.00	....

3354

3355

SCOTT NO.	DESCRIPTION	FIRST DAY COVERS SING	FIRST DAY COVERS PL. BLK.	MINT SHEET	PLATE BLOCK	UNUSED F/NH	USED
3354	33¢ NATO, 50th Anniv.	2.25	4.75	20.00(20)	5.00	1.10	.35
3355	33¢ Madonna & Child, self-adhesive	2.25	....	....	....	1.20	.25
3355a	same, bklt pane of 20	14.50	....	....	....	22.00	....

3356, 3360, 3364

3357, 3361, 3365

3358, 3362, 3366

3359, 3363, 3367

SCOTT NO.	DESCRIPTION	FIRST DAY COVERS SING	FIRST DAY COVERS PL. BLK.	MINT SHEET	PLATE BLOCK	UNUSED F/NH	USED
3356-59	33¢ Christmas Deer, self-adhesive	4.00	....	49.00(20)	12.50	11.00	....
3356	33¢ Christmas Deer, gold & red, self-adhesive	2.25	....	....	....	2.75	.85
3357	33¢ Christmas Deer, gold & blue, self-adhesive	2.25	....	....	....	2.75	.85
3358	33¢ Christmas Deer, gold & purple, self-adhesive	2.25	....	....	....	2.75	.85
3359	33¢ Christmas Deer, gold & green, self-adhesive	2.25	....	....	....	2.75	.85
3360	33¢ Christmas Deer, gold & red, bklt single, self-adhesive	2.25	....	....	....	1.75	.45
3361	33¢ Christmas Deer, gold & blue, bklt single, self-adhesive	2.25	....	....	....	1.75	.45
3362	33¢ Christmas Deer, gold & purple, bklt single, self-adhesive	2.25	....	....	....	1.75	.45
3363	33¢ Christmas Deer, gold & green, bklt single, self-adhesive	2.25	....	....	....	1.75	.45
3363a	same, bklt pane of 20	14.50	....	....	....	38.00	....
3364	33¢ Christmas Deer, gold & red, bklt single, (21x19mm), self-adhesive	2.25	....	....	....	2.25	.65
3365	33¢ Christmas Deer, gold & blue, bklt single, (21x19mm), self-adhesive	2.25	....	....	....	2.25	.65
3366	33¢ Christmas Deer, gold & purple, bklt single, (21x19mm), self-adhesive	2.25	....	....	....	2.25	.65
3367	33¢ Christmas Deer, gold & green, bklt single, (21x19mm), self-adhesive	2.25	....	....	....	2.25	.65
3367a	same, bklt pane of 4 (3364-67 x 1)	4.00	....	....	....	10.00	....
3367b	same, bklt pane of 5 (3364, 3366, 3367, 3365 x 2)	5.00	....	....	....	12.00	....
3367c	same, bklt pane of 6 (3365, 3367, 3364 x 2, 3366)	6.00	....	....	....	15.00	....

3368

3369

SCOTT NO.	DESCRIPTION	FIRST DAY COVERS SING	FIRST DAY COVERS PL. BLK.	MINT SHEET	PLATE BLOCK	UNUSED F/NH	USED
3368	33¢ Kwanzaa, self-adhesive	2.25	....	20.00(20)	5.00	1.10	.35
3369	33¢ Baby New Year, self-adhesive	2.25	....	20.00(20)	5.00	1.10	.35

3370

3371

3372

2000 COMMEMORATIVES

SCOTT NO.	DESCRIPTION	FIRST DAY COVERS SING	FIRST DAY COVERS PL. BLK.	MINT SHEET	PLATE BLOCK	UNUSED F/NH	USED
3370/3446	**(3370-72, 3379-90, 3393-3402 3414-17, 3438-46) 38 varieties. . . . . . .**	....	....	....	....	**46.00**	**20.00**
3370	33¢ Year of the Dragon	2.25	4.75	23.00(20)	5.50	1.20	.35
3371	33¢ Patricia Roberts Harris, self-adhesive	2.25	....	24.00(20)	6.00	1.50	.35
3372	33¢ Los Angeles Class Submarine (microprint USPS)	2.25	4.75	23.00(20)	5.50	1.20	.35

3373

3374

3375

3376

3377

SCOTT NO.	DESCRIPTION	FIRST DAY COVERS SING	FIRST DAY COVERS PL. BLK.	MINT SHEET	PLATE BLOCK	UNUSED F/NH	USED
3373	22¢ S Class Submarine	2.25	....	....	....	1.50	2.00
3374	33¢ Los Angeles Class Submarine (no microprint)	2.25	....	....	....	2.00	2.50
3375	55¢ Ohio Class Submarine	2.50	....	....	....	2.50	3.75
3376	60¢ USS Holland Submarine	2.50	....	....	....	3.00	3.50
3377	$3.20 Gato Class Submarine	7.50	....	....	....	12.00	9.00
3377a	same, bklt pane of 5, (#3373-77).	12.00	....	....	....	18.00	....
....	same, complete booklet of 2 panes	....	....	....	....	32.00	....

3378

PACIFIC COAST RAIN FOREST

3378a	*Harlequin duck*	3378f	*Winter wren*
3378b	*Dwarf oregongrape, snail-eating ground beetle*	3378g	*Pacific giant salamander, Rough-skinned newt*
3378c	*American dipper*	3378h	*Western tiger swallowtail*
3378d	*Cutthroat trout*	3378i	*Douglas squirrel, foliose lichen*
3378e	*Roosevelt elk*	3378j	*Foliose lichen, banana slug*

SCOTT NO.	DESCRIPTION	FIRST DAY COVERS SING	FIRST DAY COVERS PL. BLK.	MINT SHEET	PLATE BLOCK	UNUSED F/NH	USED
3378	33¢ Pacific Coast Rain Forest, 10 varieties, attached, self-adhesive	....	....	14.00(10)	....	14.00	....
....	set of singles	25.00	....	....	....	....	6.00
3378v	same, uncut sheet of 60 (6 panes)	....	....	60.00(60)	....	60.00	....

3379

3380

3381

3382

3383

SCOTT NO.	DESCRIPTION	FIRST DAY COVERS SING	FIRST DAY COVERS PL. BLK.	MINT SHEET	PLATE BLOCK	UNUSED F/NH	USED
3379-83	33¢ Louise Nevelson, (1899-1988), Sculptor, 5 varieties, attached .	10.00	15.00	20.00(20)	12.00(10)	6.00	4.50
3379	33¢ Silent Music I . . .	2.25	....	....	....	1.40	.90
3380	33¢ Royal Tide I. . . .	2.25	....	....	....	1.40	.90
3381	33¢ Black Chord	2.25	....	....	....	1.40	.90
3382	33¢ Nightsphere-Light	2.25	....	....	....	1.40	.90
3383	33¢ Dawn's Wedding Chapel I.	2.25	....	....	....	1.40	.75

3384

3385

3386

3387 3388

SCOTT NO.	DESCRIPTION	FIRST DAY COVERS SING	FIRST DAY COVERS PL. BLK.	MINT SHEET	PLATE BLOCK	UNUSED F/NH	USED
3384-88	33¢ Hubble Space Telescope Images, 5 varieties, attached.	10.00	15.00	23.00(20)	12.00(10)	6.00	4.55
3384	33¢ Eagle Nebula . . .	3.00	....	....	....	1.40	.55
3385	33¢ Ring Nebula	3.00	....	....	....	1.40	.55
3386	33¢ Lagoon Nebula . .	3.00	....	....	....	1.40	.55
3387	33¢ Egg Nebula.	3.00	....	....	....	1.40	.55
3388	33¢ Galaxy NGC1316	3.00	....	....	....	1.40	.55

3389

3390

SCOTT NO.	DESCRIPTION	FIRST DAY COVERS SING	FIRST DAY COVERS PL. BLK.	MINT SHEET	PLATE BLOCK	UNUSED F/NH	USED
3389	33¢ American Samoa	2.25	4.75	30.00(20)	8.00	1.85	1.00
3390	33¢ Library of Congress	2.25	4.75	20.00(20)	5.00	1.10	.35

3391, 3392

SCOTT NO.	DESCRIPTION	FIRST DAY COVERS SING	FIRST DAY COVERS PL. BLK.	MINT SHEET	PLATE BLOCK	UNUSED F/NH	USED
3391	33¢ Road Runner & Wile E. Coyote, self-adhesive, pane of 10	12.00	....	....	....	14.00	....
3391a	same, single from pane	2.25	....	....	....	1.50	.35
3391b	same, pane of 9 (3391a)	....	....	....	....	11.00	....
3391c	same, pane of 1 (3391a)	7.00	....	....	....	3.50	....
....	same, top press sheet of 60 (6 panes) w/ plate #	....	....	80.00(60)	....	80.00	....
....	same, bottom press sheet of 60 (6 panes) w/ plate #	....	....	95.00(60)	....	95.00	....
....	same, pane of 10 from press sheet	....	....	....	....	15.00	....
....	same, pane of 10 with plate # on front . .	....	....	....	....	65.00	....
....	vert. pair with horiz. gutter	....	....	....	....	4.00	....
....	horiz. pair with vert. gutter	....	....	....	....	8.00	....
3392	33¢ Road Runner & Wile E. Coyote, die cut, pane of 10. . .	15.00	....	....	....	50.00	....
3392a	same, single from pane	....	....	....	....	4.00	....
3392b	same, pane of 9 (3392a)	....	....	....	....	42.00	....
3392c	same, pane of 1, imperf.	12.00	....	....	....	11.00	....

3393 3394

3395 3396

SCOTT NO.	DESCRIPTION	FIRST DAY COVERS SING	FIRST DAY COVERS PL. BLK.	MINT SHEET	PLATE BLOCK	UNUSED F/NH	USED
3393-96	33¢ Distinguished Soldiers, 4 varieties, attached .	8.00	12.00	29.00(20)	7.00	5.75	5.00
3393	33¢ Major General John L. Hines (1868-1968). . .	2.25	....	....	....	1.50	.45
3394	33¢ General Omar N. Bradley (1893-1981) .	2.25	....	....	....	1.50	.45
3395	33¢ Sergeant Alvin C. York (1887-1964). . . .	2.25	....	....	....	1.50	.45
3396	33¢ Second Lieutenant Audie L. Murphy (1924-71)	2.25	....	....	....	1.50	.45

3397

3398

SCOTT NO.	DESCRIPTION	FIRST DAY COVERS SING	FIRST DAY COVERS PL. BLK.	MINT SHEET	PLATE BLOCK	UNUSED F/NH	USED
3397	33¢ Summer Sports. .	2.25	4.75	20.00(20)	4.75	1.10	.30
3398	33¢ Adoption, self-adhesive	2.25	....	20.00(20)	4.75	1.10	.30

3399 3400

3401 3402

SCOTT NO.	DESCRIPTION	FIRST DAY COVERS SING	FIRST DAY COVERS PL. BLK.	MINT SHEET	PLATE BLOCK	UNUSED F/NH	USED
3399-3402	33¢ Youth Team Sports, 4 varieites, attached .	8.00	12.00	20.00(20)	5.00	4.75	4.00
3399	33¢ Basketball.	3.00	....	....	....	1.40	.85
3400	33¢ Football.	3.00	....	....	....	1.40	.85
3401	33¢ Soccer	3.00	....	....	....	1.40	.85
3402	33¢ Baseball	3.00	....	....	....	1.40	.85

3403

THE STARS AND STRIPES

3403a	*Sons of Liberty Flag, 1775*	**3403k**	*Star-Spangled Banner, 1814*
3403b	*New England, 1775*	**3403l**	*Bennington Flag, c.1820*
3403c	*Forster Flag, 1775*	**3403m**	*Great Star Flag, 1837*
3403d	*Continental Colors, 1776*	**3403n**	*29-Star Flag, 1847*
3403e	*Francis Hopkinson Flag, 1777*	**3403o**	*Fort Sumter Flag, 1861*
3403f	*Brandywine Flag, 1777*	**3403p**	*Centennial Flag, 1876*
3403g	*John Paul Jones Flag, 1779*	**3403q**	*38-Star Flag*
3403h	*Pierre L'Enfant Flag, 1783*	**3403r**	*Peace Flag, 1891*
3403i	*Indian Peace Flag, 1803*	**3403s**	*48-Star Flag, 1912*
3403j	*Easton Flag, 1814*	**3403t**	*50-Star Flag, 1960*

SCOTT NO.	DESCRIPTION	FIRST DAY COVERS SING	FIRST DAY COVERS PL. BLK.	MINT SHEET	PLATE BLOCK	UNUSED F/NH	USED
3403	33¢ The Stars & Stripes, 20 varieties, attached, self-adhesive	....	....	25.00(20)	....	25.00	....
....	set of singles	37.50	....	....	....	....	15.00
3403v	same, uncut sheet of 120 (6 panes)	....	....	150.00(120)	....	150.00	....
....	same, block of 8 with horiz. gutter	....	....	....	....	18.00	....
....	same, block of 10 with vert. gutter	....	....	....	....	20.00	....
....	same, cross gutter block of 20	....	....	....	....	40.00	....
....	vert. pair with horiz. gutter	....	....	....	....	4.50	....
....	horiz. pair with vert. gutter	....	....	....	....	4.50	....

3404

3405

3406

3407

SCOTT NO.	DESCRIPTION	FIRST DAY COVERS SING	FIRST DAY COVERS PL. BLK.	MINT SHEET	PLATE BLOCK	UNUSED F/NH	USED
3404	33¢ Blueberries, self-adhesive linerless coil	2.25	....	....	....	3.50	1.50
3405	33¢ Strawberries, self-adhesive linerless coil	2.25	....	....	....	3.50	1.50
3406	33¢ Blackberries, self-adhesive linerless coil	2.25	....	....	....	3.50	1.50
3407	33¢ Raspberries, self-adhesive linerless coil	2.25	....	....	....	3.50	1.50
3404-07	33¢ Berries, self-adhesive linerless coil, strip of 4	5.00	....	....	....	15.00	....
....	same, pl# strip of 5 . .	....	....	....	....	22.00	....

3408

LEGENDS OF BASEBALL

3408a	*Jackie Robinson*	**3408k**	*Lefty Grove*
3408b	*Eddie Collins*	**3408l**	*Tris Speaker*
3408c	*Christy Mathewson*	**3408m**	*Cy Young*
3408d	*Ty Cobb*	**3408n**	*Jimmie Foxx*
3408e	*George Sisler*	**3408o**	*Pie Traynor*
3408f	*Rogers Hornsby*	**3408p**	*Satchel Paige*
3408g	*Mickey Cochrane*	**3408q**	*Honus Wagner*
3408h	*Babe Ruth*	**3408r**	*Josh Gibson*
3408i	*Walter Johnson*	**3408s**	*Dizzy Dean*
3408j	*Roberto Clemente*	**3408t**	*Lou Gehrig*

SCOTT NO.	DESCRIPTION	FIRST DAY COVERS SING	FIRST DAY COVERS PL. BLK.	MINT SHEET	PLATE BLOCK	UNUSED F/NH	USED
3408	33¢ Legends of Baseball, 20 varieties, attached, self-adhesive	....	....	25.00(20)	....	25.00	....
....	set of singles	37.50	....	....	....	....	15.00
3408v	same, uncut sheet of 120 (6 panes)	....	....	135.00(120)	....	135.00	....
....	cross gutter block of 20	....	....	....	....	40.00	....
....	block of 8 with vert. gutter	....	....	....	....	22.50	....
....	block of 10 with horiz. gutter	....	....	....	....	22.50	....
....	vert. pair with horiz. gutter	....	....	....	....	3.50	....
....	horiz. pair with vert. gutter	....	....	....	....	4.50	....

3409

SCOTT NO.	DESCRIPTION	FIRST DAY COVERS SING	FIRST DAY COVERS PL. BLK.	MINT SHEET	PLATE BLOCK	UNUSED F/NH	USED
3409	60¢ Probing the Vastness of Space, souvenir sheet of 6..........	15.00	....	....	....	23.00	....
3409a	60¢ Hubble Space Telescope	3.00	....	....	....	4.00	3.00
3409b	60¢ National Radio Astronomy Observatory	3.00	....	....	....	4.00	3.00
3409c	60¢ Keck Observatory	3.00	....	....	....	4.00	3.00
3409d	60¢ Cerro Tololo Inter-American Observatory	3.00	....	....	....	4.00	3.00
3409e	60¢ Mt. Wilson Observatory	3.00	....	....	....	4.00	3.00
3409f	60¢ Arecibo Observatory	3.00	....	....	....	4.00	

3410

3411

SCOTT NO.	DESCRIPTION	FIRST DAY COVERS SING	FIRST DAY COVERS PL. BLK.	MINT SHEET	PLATE BLOCK	UNUSED F/NH	USED
3410	$1 Exploring the Solar System, souvenir sheet of 5...............	13.50	....	....	....	28.00	....
3410a	$1 Solar eclipse.....	3.50	....	....	....	5.50	3.00
3410b	$1 Cross-section of sun	3.50	....	....	....	5.50	3.00
3410c	$1 Sun and Earth....	3.50	....	....	....	5.50	3.00
3410d	$1 Sun & solar flare..	3.50	....	....	....	5.50	3.00
3410e	$1 Sun with clouds ..	3.50	....	....	....	5.50	3.00
3411	$3.20 Escaping the Gravity of Earth hologram, souvenir sheet of 2 ..	16.50	....	....	....	35.00	....
3411a	$3.20 International Space Station hologram, from souvenir sheet..	7.50	....	....	....	18.00	13.00
3411b	$3.20 Astronauts Working hologram, from souvenir sheet	7.50	....	....	....	18.00	13.00

3412

SCOTT NO.	DESCRIPTION	FIRST DAY COVERS SING	FIRST DAY COVERS PL. BLK.	MINT SHEET	PLATE BLOCK	UNUSED F/NH	USED
3412	$11.75 Space Achievement and Exploration hologram, souvenir sheet of 1 ..	27.50	....	....	....	47.50	....

3413

SCOTT NO.	DESCRIPTION	FIRST DAY COVERS SING	FIRST DAY COVERS PL. BLK.	MINT SHEET	PLATE BLOCK	UNUSED F/NH	USED
3413	$11.75 Landing on the Moon hologram, souvenir sheet of 1..........	27.50	....	....	....	47.50	....

3414

3415

3416

3417

SCOTT NO.	DESCRIPTION	FIRST DAY COVERS SING	FIRST DAY COVERS PL. BLK.	MINT SHEET	PLATE BLOCK	UNUSED F/NH	USED
3414-17	33¢ Stampin' the Future, 4 varieties, attached .	8.00	10.00	20.00(20)	10.00(8)	5.50	4.00
3414	33¢ Designed by Zachary Canter	2.25	....	....	....	1.40	.50
3415	33¢ Designed by Sarah Lipsey	2.25	....	....	....	1.40	.50
3416	33¢ Designed by Morgan Hill	2.25	....	....	....	1.40	.50
3417	33¢ Designed by Ashley Young	2.25	....	....	....	1.40	.50

3420

3422, 3436

3426

3427

3427A

3428

3430

3431, 3432

3432A

3432B

3433, 3434

3435

2000-2009 DISTINGUISHED AMERICANS

SCOTT NO.	DESCRIPTION	FIRST DAY COVERS SING	FIRST DAY COVERS PL. BLK.	MINT SHEET	PLATE BLOCK	UNUSED F/NH	USED
3420	10¢ Joseph W. Stilwell	2.25	4.00	7.00(20)	1.75	.40	.25
3422	23¢ Wilma Rudolph, self-adhesive, die cut 11.25 x 10.75 .	2.25	4.75	15.00(20)	3.50	.85	.40
3426	33¢ Claude Pepper . .	2.25	4.75	20.00(20)	5.00	1.10	.55
3427	58¢ Margaret Chase Smith, self-adhesive (2007) .	2.25	5.50	32.00(20)	8.50	1.75	.65
3427a	59¢ James A. Michener	2.25	5.50	32.00(20)	8.50	1.75	.70
3428	63¢ Dr. Jonas Salk (2006)	2.25	6.00	34.00(20)	9.25	1.85	.70
3430	75¢ Harriett Beecher Stowe, self-adhesive (2007) .	2.95	6.00	38.00(20)	10.50	2.25	.95
3431	76¢ Hattie W. Caraway, die cut 11	2.95	5.50	54.00(20)	16.00	3.00	.60
3432	76¢ Hattie W. Caraway, die cut 11.5 x 11.	....	....	135.00(20)	36.00	8.00	4.00
3432a	76¢ Edward Trudeau .	2.95	5.75	37.00(20)	9.50	2.50	.95
3432b	78¢ Mary Lasker (2009)	3.75	....	34.00(20)	9.50	2.25	.75
3433	83¢ Edna Ferber, die cut 11 x 11.5.	2.95	5.50	52.00(20)	14.00	3.00	.95
3434	83¢ Edna Ferber, die cut 11.25 (2003). .	2.95	5.50	48.00(20)	13.00	2.75	.90
3435	87¢ Dr. Albert Sabin (2006)	2.95	5.50	46.00(20)	12.00	2.75	.95
3436	23¢ Wilma Rudolph, self-adhesive, die cut 11.25 x 10.75 .	2.25	....	....	....	.85	.50
3436a	same, bklt pane of 4 .	3.00	....	....	....	3.25	....
3436b	same, bklt pane of 6 .	4.00	....	....	....	4.75	....
3436c	same, bklt pane of 10	6.75	....	....	....	7.50	....

3438

SCOTT NO.	DESCRIPTION	FIRST DAY COVERS SING	FIRST DAY COVERS PL. BLK.	MINT SHEET	PLATE BLOCK	UNUSED F/NH	USED
3438	33¢ California Statehood, self-adhesive	2.25	....	22.00(20)	6.00	1.50	.40

3439

3440

3441

3442

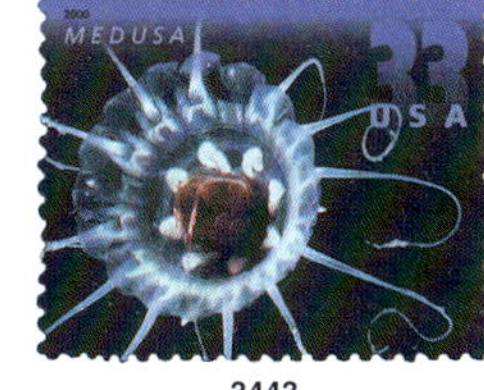

3443

SCOTT NO.	DESCRIPTION	FIRST DAY COVERS SING	FIRST DAY COVERS PL. BLK.	MINT SHEET	PLATE BLOCK	UNUSED F/NH	USED
3439-43	33¢ Deep Sea Creatures, 5 varieities attached. .	5.75	11.00	20.00(15)	....	7.00	4.75
3439	33¢ Fanfin Anglerfish.	2.25	....	....	....	1.40	.85
3440	33¢ Sea Cucumber . .	2.25	....	....	....	1.40	.85
3441	33¢ Fangtooth	2.25	....	....	....	1.40	.85
3442	33¢ Amphipod	2.25	....	....	....	1.40	.85
3443	33¢ Medusa.	2.25	....	....	....	1.40	.85

3444

3445

3446

SCOTT NO.	DESCRIPTION	FIRST DAY COVERS SING	FIRST DAY COVERS PL. BLK.	MINT SHEET	PLATE BLOCK	UNUSED F/NH	USED
3444	33¢ Thomas Wolfe . .	2.25	4.75	20.00(20)	4.75	1.10	.30
3445	33¢ White House	2.25	4.75	35.00(20)	9.00	2.00	.35
3446	33¢ Edward G. Robinson	2.25	4.75	49.00(20)	12.00	3.00	2.00
....	same, uncut sheet of 120 (6 panes)	....	....	175.00(120)	....	240.00	....
....	cross gutter block of 8	....	....	....	....	35.00	....
....	block of 8 with vert. gutter	....	....	....	....	24.00	....
....	horiz. pair with vert. gutter	....	....	....	....	6.00	....
....	vert. pair with horiz. gutter	....	....	....	....	4.50	....

3447

3448, 3449, 3450,

3451, 3452, 3453

SCOTT NO.	DESCRIPTION	FIRST DAY COVERS SING	FIRST DAY COVERS PL. BLK.	MINT SHEET	PLATE BLOCK	UNUSED F/NH	USED
3447	10¢ New York Public Library Lion, coil	2.25	....	....	4.00	.50	.25
....	same, pl# strip of 5 . .	....	....	....	....	5.00	....
3447a	10¢ New York Public Library, self-adhesive, coil, die cut 11.5	2.25	....	....	....	.75	.60
....	same, pl# strip of 5 . .	....	....	....	....	5.00	....
3448	(34¢) Flag over Farm.	2.25	4.75	45.00(20)	12.00	1.50	.75
3449	(34¢) Flag over Farm self-adhesive	2.25	4.75	30.00(20)	6.00	1.30	.30
3450	(34¢) Flag over Farm, self-adhesive	2.25	....	....	....	1.60	.75
3450a	same, bklt pane of 18	14.00	....	....	....	29.00	....
3451	(34¢) Statue of Liberty, self-adhesive	2.25	....	....	....	1.20	.35
3451a	same, bklt pane of 20	14.50	....	....	....	24.00	....
3451b	same, bklt pane of 4 .	4.00	....	....	....	7.00	....
3451c	same, bklt pane of 6 .	5.50	....	....	....	10.50	....
3452	(34¢) Statue of Liberty, coil	2.25	....	....	7.00	1.25	.25
....	same, pl# strip of 5 . .	....	....	....	....	9.00	....
3453	(34¢) Statue of Liberty, self-adhesive coil. . . .	1.95	....	....	10.00	1.25	.25
....	same, pl# strip of 5 . .	....	....	....	....	12.00	....
3453b	same, large date	....	....	....	15.00(3)	1.80	.30

3454, 3458, 3465

3455, 3459, 3464

3456, 3460, 3463

3457, 3461, 3462

SCOTT NO.	DESCRIPTION	FIRST DAY COVERS SING	FIRST DAY COVERS PL. BLK.	MINT SHEET	PLATE BLOCK	UNUSED F/NH	USED
3454-57	(34¢) Flowers, self-adhesive, 4 varieties attached . .	4.25	....	....	....	7.50	....
3454	(34¢) Fressia, self-adhesive, die cut 10.25 x 10.75 .	2.25	....	....	....	2.50	.40
3455	(34¢) Symbidium Orchid, self-adhesive, die cut 10.25 x 10.75.	2.25	....	....	....	2.50	.40
3456	(34¢) Longiflorum Lily, self-adhesive, die cut 10.25 x 10.75.	2.25	....	....	....	2.50	.40
3457	(34¢) Asian Hydrid, self-adhesive, die cut 10.25 x 10.75.	2.25	....	....	....	2.50	.40
3457b	same, bklt pane of 4 (3454-57).	4.00	....	....	....	8.50	....
3457c	same, bklt pane of 6 (3456, 3457, 3454 x 2 3455 x 2)	5.50	....	....	....	14.00	....
3457d	same, bklt pane of 6 (3454, 3455, 3456 x 2 3457 x 2)	5.50	....	....	....	14.00	....
3457e	(34¢) Flowers, bklt pane of 20, self-adhesive (5 each 3457a + label)	14.50	....	....	....	36.00	....
3458-61	(34¢) Flowers, self-adhesive, 4 varieties attached . .	4.25	....	....	....	18.00	....
3458	(34¢) Fressia, bklt single, self-adhesive, die cut 11.5 x 11.75	2.25	....	....	....	5.50	1.00
3459	(34¢) Symbidium Orchid, bklt single, self-adhesive, die cut 11.5 x 11.75 . .	2.25	....	....	....	5.50	1.00
3460	(34¢) Longiflorum Lily, bklt single, self-adhesive, die cut 11.5 x 11.75 . .	2.25	....	....	....	5.50	1.00
3461	(34¢) Asian Hybrid Lily, bklt single, self-adhesive, die cut 11.5 x 11.75 . .	2.25	....	....	....	5.50	1.00
3461b	same, bklt pane of 20, self-adhesive (2 each 3461a, 3 each 3457a)	14.50	....	....	....	70.00	....
3461c	same, bklt pane of 20, self-adhesive (2 each 3457a, 3 each 3461a)	14.50	....	....	....	90.00	....
3462	(34¢) Longiflorum Lily, self-adhesive coil. . . .	2.25	....	....	....	5.00	.60
3463	(34¢) Asian Hybrid Lily, self-adhesive coil. . . .	2.25	....	....	....	5.00	60
3464	(34¢) Symbidium Orchid, self-adhesive coil. . . .	2.25	....	....	....	5.00	.60
	self-adhesive coil. . . .	2.25	....	....	....	5.00	.60
3462-65	(34¢) Flowers, self- adhesive coil, strip of 4	4.25	....	....	....	20.00	....
....	same, pl# strip of 5 . .	....	....	....	....	28.00	....

3466, 3476, 3477, 3485

3467, 3468, 3475, 3484, 3484A

3468A, 3475A

3469, 3470

3471

3471A

2001 REGULAR ISSUES

SCOTT NO.	DESCRIPTION	FIRST DAY COVERS SING	FIRST DAY COVERS PL. BLK.	MINT SHEET	PLATE BLOCK	UNUSED F/NH	USED
3466	34¢ Statue of Liberty, self-adhesive coil, die cut 9.75 (round corners)	2.25	....	....	8.50	1.30	.50
....	same, pl# strip of 5 . .	....	....	....	11.00	....	....
3467	21¢ Buffalo	2.25	4.75	100.00(100)	30.00	1.50	.75
3468	21¢ Buffalo. self-adhesive	2.25	4.75	16.00(20)	4.50	.90	.75
3468A	23¢ George Washington, self-adhesive	2.25	4.75	15.00(20)	4.00	.90	.75
3469	34¢ Flag over Farm . .	2.25	4.75	170.00(100)	38.00	1.50	.90
3470	34¢ Flag over Farm, self-adhesive	2.25	4.75	28.00(20)	8.00	2.00	.50
3471	55¢ Eagle, self-adhesive	2.50	5.00	45.00(20)	11.00	2.25	.80
3471A	57¢ Eagle, self-adhesive	2.50	5.00	41.00(20)	11.00	2.50	80

3472

3473

SCOTT NO.	DESCRIPTION	FIRST DAY COVERS SING	FIRST DAY COVERS PL. BLK.	MINT SHEET	PLATE BLOCK	UNUSED F/NH	USED
3472	$3.50 Capitol Dome, self-adhesive	8.00	30.00	210.00(20)	48.00	12.00	5.00
3473	$12.25 Washington Monument, self-adhesive	30.00	98.50	700.00(20)	155.00	40.00	12.00
3475	21¢ Buffalo, self-adhesive coil. . . .	2.25	....	....	5.00	.75	.35
....	same, pl# strip of 5 . .	....	....	....	....	6.00	....
3475A	23¢ George Washington, self-adhesive coil. . . .	2.25	....	....	....	1.20	.30
....	same, pl# strip of 5 . .	....	....	....	....	9.00	....
3476	34¢ Statue of Liberty, coil.	2.25	....	....	7.00	1.50	.40
....	same, pl# strip of 5 . .	....	....	....	....	9.00	....
3477	34¢ Statue of Liberty, self-adhesive coil die cut 9.75 (square corners)	2.25	....	....	7.75	1.50	.25
....	same, pl# strip of 5 . .	....	....	....	....	10.00	....

3478, 3489

3479, 3490

3480, 3488

3481, 3487

SCOTT NO.	DESCRIPTION	FIRST DAY COVERS SING	FIRST DAY COVERS PL. BLK.	MINT SHEET	PLATE BLOCK	UNUSED F/NH	USED
3478	34¢ Longiflorum, self-adhesive coil. . . .	2.25	....	....	....	2.50	.50
3479	34¢ Asain Hybrid Lily, self-adhesive coil. . . .	2.25	....	....	....	2.50	50
3480	34¢ Symbidium Orchid, self-adhesive coil. . . .	2.25	....	....	....	2.50	.50
3481	34¢ Fressia, self-adhesive coil. . . .	2.25	....	....	....	2.50	.50
3478-81	34¢ Flowers, self-adhesive, coil, strip of 4	4.25	....	....	....	9.00	....
....	same, pl# strip of 5 . .	....	....	....	....	14.00	....

3482, 3483 | 3491, 3493 | 3492, 3494 | 3495

SCOTT NO.	DESCRIPTION	FIRST DAY COVERS SING	FIRST DAY COVERS PL. BLK.	MINT SHEET	PLATE BLOCK	UNUSED F/NH	USED
3482	20¢ George Washington, self-adhesive, die cut 11.25	2.25	....	....	....	1.00	.50
3482a	same, bklt pane of 10	5.50	....	....	....	9.50	....
3482b	same, bklt pane of 4, die cut 11.25 x 11. . . .	3.00	....	....	....	6.50	....
3482c	same, bklt pane of 6, die cut 11.25 x 11. . . .	4.00	....	....	....	5.00	....
3483	20¢ George Washington, self-adhesive, die cut 10.5 x 11.25.	2.25	....	....	....	7.00	1.80
3483a	same, bklt pane of 4 (2 each 3482-3483) . .	3.00	....	....	....	22.00	....
3483b	same, bklt pane of 6 (3 each 3482-3483) . .	4.00	....	....	....	33.00	....
3483c	same, bklt pane of 10, die cut 10.5 x 11 (3482 x 5 at L, 3483 x 5 at R) . .	5.50	....	....	....	38.00	....
3483d	same, bklt pane of 4 (2 each 3482-3483), die cut 11.25 x 11. . . .	....	....	....	....	20.00	....
3483e	same, bklt pane of 6 (2 each 3482-3483), die cut 11.25 x 11. . . .	....	....	....	....	34.00	....
3483f	same, bklt pane of 10 (5 each 3482-3483), die cut 11.25 x 11. . . .	....	....	....	....	38.00	....
3483g	pair, 3482 at left, 3483 at right.	....	....	....	....	8.50	....
3483h	pair 3483 at left, 3482 at right.	....	....	....	....	8.50	....
3484	21¢ Buffalo, self-adhesive, die cut 11.25	2.25	....	....	....	1.00	.50
3484b	same, bklt pane of 4 .	3.00	....	....	....	4.00	....
3484c	same, bklt pane of 6 .	4.00	....	....	....	5.00	....
3484d	same, bklt pane of 10	5.50	....	....	....	9.50	....
3484A	21¢ Buffalo, self-adhesive, die cut 10.5 X 11.25. .	2.25	....	....	....	7.00	2.50
3484Ae	same, bklt pane of 4 (3484 x 2 at L, 3484A x 2 at R)	....	....	....	....	22.00	....
3484Af	same, bklt pane of 6 (3484 x 3 at L, 3484A x 3 at R)	....	....	....	....	34.00	....
3484Ag	same, bklt pane of 10 (3484 x 5 at L, 3484A x 5 at R)	....	....	....	....	38.00	....
3484Ah	same, bklt pane of 4 (3484A x 2 at L, 3484 x 2 at R)	....	....	....	....	23.00	....
3484Ai	same, bklt pane of 6 (3484A x 3 at L, 3484 x 3 at R)	....	....	....	....	34.00	....
3484Aj	same, bklt pane of 10 (3484A x 5 at L, 3484 x 5 at R)	....	....	....	....	38.00	....
3484Ak	same, pair (3484 at L, 3484A at R)	....	....	....	....	7.50	....
3484Al	same, pair (3484A at L, 3484 at R)	....	....	....	....	8.00	....
3485	34¢ Statue of Liberty, self-adhesive	2.25	....	....	....	1.45	.25
3485a	same, bklt pane of 10	7.25	....	....	....	14.00	....
3485b	same, bklt pane of 20	14.50	....	....	....	28.00	....
3485c	same, bklt pane of 4 .	4.00	....	....	....	7.00	....
3485d	same, bklt pane of 6 .	5.50	....	....	....	9.50	....
3487-90	34¢ Flowers, self-adhesive 4 varieties attached . .	4.25	....	....	....	6.00	3.50
3487	34¢ Fressia, self-adhesive, die cut 10.25 x 10.75 .	2.25	....	....	....	1.75	.35
3488	34¢ Symbidium Orchid, self-adhesive, die cut 10.25 x 10.75.	2.25	....	....	....	1.75	.35
3489	34¢ Longiflorum Lily, self-adhesive, die cut 10.25 x 10.75.	2.25	....	....	....	1.75	.35
3490	34¢ Asian Hybrid Lily, self-adhesive, die cut 10.25 x 10.75.	2.25	....	....	....	1.75	.35
3490b	same, bklt pane of 4 (3487-90 x 1)	4.00	....	....	....	6.50	....
3490c	same, bklt pane of 6 (3489-3490, 3487 x 2, 3488 x 2)	5.50	....	....	....	8.50	....
3490d	same, bklt pane of 6 (3487-3488, 3498 x 2 3490 x 2)	5.50	....	....	....	8.50	....
3490e	same, bklt pane of 20 (3487-90 x 5 + label) .	14.50	....	....	....	28.00	....
3491	34¢ Apple, self-adhesive	2.25	....	....	....	1.75	.25
3492	34¢ Orange, self-adhesive	2.25	....	....	....	1.75	.25
3491-92	34¢ Apple & Orange, Pair	2.50	....	....	....	3.50	....
3492b	34¢ Apple & Orange, bklt pane of 20, self-adhesive	14.50	....	....	....	26.00	....
3493	34¢ Apple, self-adhesive, die cut 11.5 x 10.75 . .	2.25	....	....	....	2.50	.65
3494	34¢ Orange, self-adhesive, die cut 11.5 x 10.75 . .	2.25	....	....	....	2.50	.65
3493-94	34¢ Apple & Orange, Pair	2.50	....	....	....	5.00	....
3494b	same, bklt pane of 4 (3493 x 2, 3494 x 2). .	4.00	....	....	....	10.00	....

SCOTT NO.	DESCRIPTION	FIRST DAY COVERS SING	FIRST DAY COVERS PL. BLK.	MINT SHEET	PLATE BLOCK	UNUSED F/NH	USED
3494c	same, bklt pane of 6 (3493 x 3, 3494 x 3) (3493 at UL).	5.50	....	....	....	15.00	....
3494d	same, bklt pane of 6 (3493 x 3, 3494 x 3) (3494 at UL).	5.50	....	....	....	15.00	....
3495	34¢ Flag over Farm, self-adhesive	1.95	....	....	....	2.00	.50
3495a	same, ATM bklt pane of 18	14.00	....	....	....	37.00	....

3496 | 3497, 3498 | 3499

SCOTT NO.	DESCRIPTION	FIRST DAY COVERS SING	FIRST DAY COVERS PL. BLK.	MINT SHEET	PLATE BLOCK	UNUSED F/NH	USED
3496	34¢ LOVE, self-adhesive, die cut 11.75	2.25	....	....	....	1.50	.30
3496a	same, bklt pane of 20	14.50	....	....	....	30.00	....
3497	34¢ LOVE, self-adhesive, die cut 11.25	2.25	....	....	....	1.50	.30
3497a	same, bklt pane of 20	14.50	....	....	....	30.00	....
3498	34¢ LOVE, self-adhesive, die cut 11.5 x 10.75 . .	2.25	....	....	....	2.50	.30
3498a	same, bklt pane of 4 .	4.00	....	....	....	9.00	....
3498b	same, bklt pane of 6 .	5.50	....	....	....	12.00	....
3499	55¢ LOVE, self-adhesive	2.50	5.00	35.00(20)	8.50	1.85	.65

3500 | 3501

2001 COMMEMORATIVES

SCOTT NO.	DESCRIPTION	FIRST DAY COVERS SING	FIRST DAY COVERS PL. BLK.	MINT SHEET	PLATE BLOCK	UNUSED F/NH	USED
3500/3548	**(3500-01, 3503-04, 3507-19, 3521, 3523-33, 3536-40, 3545-48) 38 varieties. . . . . . .**	....	....	....	....	**49.00**	**13.50**
3500	34¢ Year of the Snake	2.25	4.75	25.00(20)	6.00	1.50	.35
3501	34¢ Roy Wilkins, self-adhesive	2.25	4.75	27.00(20)	6.50	1.50	.30

3502

AMERICAN ILLUSTRATORS

3502a *Marine Corps poster*
3502b *"Interlude (The Lute Players)"*
3502c *Advertisement for Arrow Collars and Shirts*
3502d *Advertisement for Carrier Corp. Refrigeration*
3502e *Advertisement for Luxite Hosiery*
3502f *Illustration for correspondence school lesson*
3502g *"Br'er Rabbit"*
3502h *"An Attack on a Galleon"*
3502i *Kewpie and Kewpie Doodle Dog*
3502j *Illustration for cover of True Magazine*
3502k *"Galahad's Departure"*
3502l *"The First Lesson"*
3502m *Illustration for cover of McCall's*
3502n *"Back Home for Keeps"*
3502o *"Something for Supper"*
3502p *"A Dash for the Timber"*
3502q *Illustration for "Moby Dick"*
3502r *"Captain Bill Bones"*
3502s *Illustration for The Saturday Evening Post*
3502t *"The Girl He Left Behind"*

SCOTT NO.	DESCRIPTION	FIRST DAY COVERS SING	FIRST DAY COVERS PL. BLK.	MINT SHEET	PLATE BLOCK	UNUSED F/NH	USED

AMERICAN ILLUSTRATORS (Continued)

SCOTT NO.	DESCRIPTION	FIRST DAY COVERS SING	FIRST DAY COVERS PL. BLK.	MINT SHEET	PLATE BLOCK	UNUSED F/NH	USED
3502	34¢ American Illustrators, 20 varieties, attached, self-adhesive	....	....	25.00(20)	....	25.00	....
....	set of singles	37.50	....	....	....	....	15.00
3502v	same, uncut sheet of 80 (4 panes)	....	....	120.00(80)	....	120.00	....
....	cross gutter block of 20	....	....	....	....	60.00	....
....	block of 8 with horiz. gutter	....	....	....	....	40.00	....
....	block of 10 with vert. gutter	....	....	....	....	40.00	....
....	vert. pair with horiz. gutter	....	....	....	....	7.00	....
....	horiz. pair with vert. gutter	....	....	....	....	7.00	....

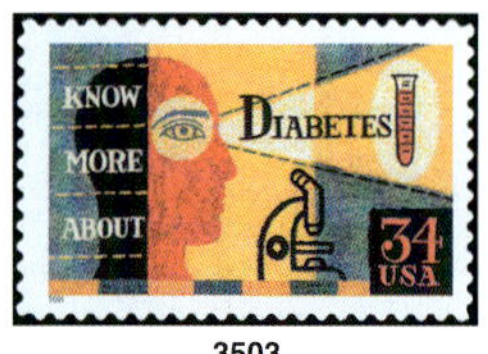

3503

3504

SCOTT NO.	DESCRIPTION	FIRST DAY COVERS SING	FIRST DAY COVERS PL. BLK.	MINT SHEET	PLATE BLOCK	UNUSED F/NH	USED
3503	34¢ Diabetes Awareness	2.25	4.75	22.00(20)	5.75	1.25	.30
3504	34¢ Nobel Prize Centenary	2.25	4.75	22.00(20)	5.75	1.25	.30

3505

SCOTT NO.	DESCRIPTION	FIRST DAY COVERS SING	FIRST DAY COVERS PL. BLK.	MINT SHEET	PLATE BLOCK	UNUSED F/NH	USED
3505	1¢-80¢ Pan-American Expo. Invert Souvenir Sheet of 7	10.00	....	....	....	12.00	8.00
....	same, uncut sheet of 28 (4 panes)	....	....	....	....	60.00	....

3506

GREAT PLAINS PRAIRIE

3506a *Pronghorns, Canada geese*
3506b *Burrowing owls, American buffalos*
3506c *American buffalo, Black-tailed prairie dogs, wild alfalfa*
3506d *Black-tailed prairie dogs, American Buffalo*
3506e *Painted lady butterfly, American buffalo, prairie coneflowers, prairie wild roses*
3506f *Western Meadowlark, camel cricket, prairie coneflowers, prairie wild flowers*
3506g *Badger, Harvester ants*
3506h *Eastern short-horned lizard, plains gopher*
3506i *Plains spadefoot, dung beetle, prairie roses*
3506j *Two-striped grasshopper, Ord's kangaroo rat*

SCOTT NO.	DESCRIPTION	FIRST DAY COVERS SING	FIRST DAY COVERS PL. BLK.	MINT SHEET	PLATE BLOCK	UNUSED F/NH	USED
3506	34¢ Great Plains Prairie, 10 varieties, attached, self-adhesive	....	....	15.00(10)	....	15.00	....
....	set of singles	19.50	....	....	....	....	7.00
3506v	same, uncut sheet of 60 (6 panes)	....	....	60.00(60)	....	60.00	....

SCOTT NO.	DESCRIPTION	FIRST DAY COVERS SING	FIRST DAY COVERS PL. BLK.	MINT SHEET	PLATE BLOCK	UNUSED F/NH	USED

3509

3507

3508

SCOTT NO.	DESCRIPTION	FIRST DAY COVERS SING	FIRST DAY COVERS PL. BLK.	MINT SHEET	PLATE BLOCK	UNUSED F/NH	USED
3507	34¢ Peanuts, self-adhesive	2.25	4.75	25.00(20)	6.50	1.50	.35
3508	34¢ US Veterans, self-adhesive	2.25	4.75	34.00(20)	7.00	1.85	.35
3509	34¢ Frida Kahlo	2.25	4.75	22.00(20)	5.50	1.25	.30

3510 3511

3512 3513

3514 3515

3516 3517

3518 3519

BASEBALL'S LEGENDARY PLAYING FIELDS

3510 *Ebbets Field*
3511 *Tiger Stadium*
3512 *Crosley Field*
3513 *Yankee Stadium*
3514 *Polo Grounds*
3515 *Forbes Field*
3516 *Fenway Park*
3517 *Comiskey Park*
3518 *Shibe Park*
3519 *Wrigley Field*

SCOTT NO.	DESCRIPTION	FIRST DAY COVERS SING	FIRST DAY COVERS PL. BLK.	MINT SHEET	PLATE BLOCK	UNUSED F/NH	USED
3510-19	34¢ Baseball's Legendary Playing Fields, 10 varieties, self-adhesive	7.25	....	25.00(20)	15.00(10)	14.00	12.00
....	set of singles	25.00	....	....	....	....	6.00
3510-19v	same, uncut sheet of 160 (8 panes)	....	....	160.00(160)	....	160.00	....
....	cross gutter block of 12	....	....	....	....	25.00	....
....	block of 10 with vert. gutter	....	....	....	....	15.00	....
....	block of 4 with horiz. gutter	....	....	....	....	7.50	....
....	vert. pair with horiz. gutter	....	....	....	....	3.50	....
....	horiz. pair with vert. gutter	....	....	....	....	3.50	....

3520 3521

3522

SCOTT NO.	DESCRIPTION	FIRST DAY COVERS SING	FIRST DAY COVERS PL. BLK.	MINT SHEET	PLATE BLOCK	UNUSED F/NH	USED
3520	10¢ Atlas Statue, coil self-adhesive, die cut 8.5	2.25	....	4.00	.35	.25	
....	same, pl# strip of 5 . .	....	....	....	....	4.50	....
3521	34¢ Leonard Bernstein	2.25	4.75	20.00(20)	5.00	1.10	.40
3522	15¢ Woody Wagon, self-adhesive coil	2.25	....	....	4.00	.50	.40
....	same, pl# strip of 5 . .	....	....	....	....	5.00	....

3523

SCOTT NO.	DESCRIPTION	FIRST DAY COVERS SING	FIRST DAY COVERS PL. BLK.	MINT SHEET	PLATE BLOCK	UNUSED F/NH	USED
3523	34¢ Lucille Ball, self-adhesive	2.25	4.75	28.00(20)	6.50	1.50	.35
3523v	same, uncut sheet of 180 (9 panes)	....	....	185.00(180)	....	185.00	....
....	cross gutter block of 8	....	....	....	....	30.00	....
....	block of 8 with vert. gutter	....	....	....	....	22.50	....
....	vert. pair with horiz. gutter	....	....	....	....	3.00	....
....	horiz. pair with vert. gutter	....	....	....	....	4.00	....

3524 3525

3526 3527

SCOTT NO.	DESCRIPTION	FIRST DAY COVERS SING	FIRST DAY COVERS PL. BLK.	MINT SHEET	PLATE BLOCK	UNUSED F/NH	USED
3524-27	34¢ Amish Quilts, 4 varieties attached . .	4.25	5.25	22.00(20)	5.50	5.00	4.00
3524	34¢ Diamond in the Square	2.25	....	....	....	1.30	.50
3525	34¢ Lone Star	2.25	....	....	....	1.30	.50
3526	34¢ Sunshine and Shadow	2.25	....	....	....	1.30	.50
3527	34¢ Double Ninepatch Variation	2.25	....	....	....	1.30	.50

3528 3529 3530 3531

SCOTT NO.	DESCRIPTION	FIRST DAY COVERS SING	FIRST DAY COVERS PL. BLK.	MINT SHEET	PLATE BLOCK	UNUSED F/NH	USED
3528-31	34¢ Carnivorous Plants, 4 varieties attached . .	4.25	5.25	23.00(20)	5.25	5.00	4.00
3528	34¢ Venus Flytrap . . .	2.25	....	....	....	1.30	.40
3529	34¢ Yellow Trumpet . .	2.25	....	....	....	1.30	.40
3530	34¢ Cobra	2.25	....	....	....	1.30	.40
3531	34¢ English Sundew .	2.25	....	....	....	1.30	.40

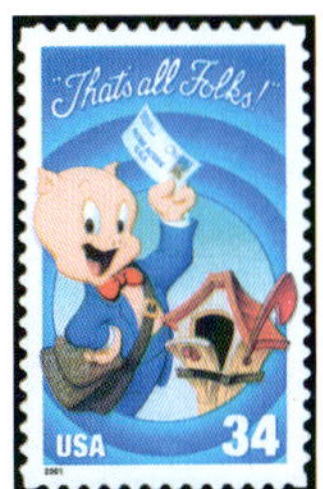
3532 3533 3534, 3535

SCOTT NO.	DESCRIPTION	FIRST DAY COVERS SING	FIRST DAY COVERS PL. BLK.	MINT SHEET	PLATE BLOCK	UNUSED F/NH	USED
3532	34¢ "Eid Mubarak", self-adhesive	2.25	4.75	21.00(20)	5.50	1.25	.30
3533	34¢ Enrico Fermi, self-adhesive	2.25	4.75	22.00(20)	5.50	1.25	.30
3534	34¢ That's All Folks, self-adhesive, pane of 10	12.50	....	....	....	18.00	....
3534a	same, single from pane	2.50	....	....	....	1.50	.30
3534b	same, pane of 9 (3534a)	....	....	....	....	12.00	....
3534c	same, pane of 1 (3534a)	7.25	....	....	....	3.25	....
....	same, top press sheet of 60 (6 panes) w/ pl# . .	....	....	80.00(60)	....	80.00	....
....	same, bottom press sheet of 60 (6 panes) w/ pl#	....	....	95.00(60)	....	95.00	....
....	same, pane of 10 from press sheet	....	....	....	....	15.00	....
....	same, pane of 10 w/ pl# on front.	....	....	....	....	70.00	....
....	vert. pair with horiz. gutter	....	....	....	....	4.00	....
....	horiz. pair with vert. gutter	....	....	....	....	7.50	....
3535	34¢ That's All Folks, die cut, self-adhesive, pane of 10	15.00	....	....	....	85.00	....
3535a	same, single form pane	....	....	....	....	8.00	....
3535b	same, pane of 9 (3435a)	....	....	....	....	65.00	....
3535c	same, pane of 1, imperf.	12.50	....	....	....	25.00	....

3536

SCOTT NO.	DESCRIPTION	FIRST DAY COVERS SING	FIRST DAY COVERS PL. BLK.	MINT SHEET	PLATE BLOCK	UNUSED F/NH	USED
3536	34¢ Madonna and Child, self-adhesive	2.25	....	....	....	1.30	.25
3536a	same, bklt pane of 20	14.50	....			25.00	....

3537, 3537a, 3541 3538, 3538a, 3542 3539, 3539a, 3543 3540, 3540a, 3544

SCOTT NO.	DESCRIPTION	FIRST DAY COVERS SING	FIRST DAY COVERS PL. BLK.	MINT SHEET	PLATE BLOCK	UNUSED F/NH	USED
3537-40	34¢ Santas, self-adhesive, 4 varieties attach, large date	4.25	5.25	30.00(20)	6.50	5.75	....
3537	34¢ Santa w/ horse, large date	2.25	....	....	....	1.40	.50
3538	34¢ Santa w/ horn, large date	2.25	....	....	....	1.40	.50
3539	34¢ Santa w/ drum, large date	2.25	....	....	....	1.40	.50
3540	34¢ Santa w/ dog, large date	2.25	....	....	....	1.40	.50

SCOTT NO.	DESCRIPTION	FIRST DAY COVERS SING	FIRST DAY COVERS PL. BLK.	MINT SHEET	PLATE BLOCK	UNUSED F/NH	USED
3537a-40a	34¢ Santas, self-adhesive, 4 varieties attach, small date	4.25	5.25	....	....	5.75	4.50
3537a	34¢ Santa w/ horse, small date	2.25	....	....	....	1.30	.60
3538a	34¢ Santa w/ horn, small date	2.25	....	....	....	1.30	.60
3539a	34¢ Santa w/ drum, small date	2.25	....	....	....	1.30	.60
3540a	34¢ Santa w/ dog, small date	2.25	....	....	....	1.30	.60
3540d	same, bklt pane of 20, 3537a-40a x 5 + label	14.50	....	....	....	28.00	....
3537b-40e	34¢ Santas, self-adhesive, 4 varieties attach, large date	4.25	5.25	....	....	15.00	11.00
3537b	34¢ Santa w/ horse, large date	2.25	....	....	....	4.00	.75
3538b	34¢ Santa w/ horn, large date	2.25	....	....	....	4.00	.75
3539b	34¢ Santa w/ drum, large date	2.25	....	....	....	4.00	.75
3540e	34¢ Santa w/ dog, large date	2.25	....	....	....	4.00	.75
3540g	same, bklt pane of 20, 3537b-40e x 5 + label	14.50	....	....	....	65.00	....
3541-44	34¢ Santas, self-adhesive, 4 varieties attach, green denom.	4.25	....	....	....	7.50	....
3541	34¢ Santa w/ horse, green denom	2.25	....	....	....	1.85	.50
3542	34¢ Santa w/ horn, green denom	2.25	....	....	....	1.85	.50
3543	34¢ Santa w/ drum, green denom.	2.25	....	....	....	1.85	.50
3544	34¢ Santa w/ dog, green denom	2.25	....	....	....	1.85	.50
3544b	same, bklt pane of 4 (3541-3544).	4.00	....	....	....	8.00	....
3544c	same, bklt pane of 6 (3543-44, 3541-42 x 2)	5.50	....	....	....	12.00	....
3544d	same, bklt pane of 6 (3541-42, 3543-44 x 2)	5.50	....	....	....	12.00	....

3545

SCOTT NO.	DESCRIPTION	FIRST DAY COVERS SING	FIRST DAY COVERS PL. BLK.	MINT SHEET	PLATE BLOCK	UNUSED F/NH	USED
3545	34¢ James Madison .	2.25	4.75	25.00(20)	6.00	1.25	.30
3545v	same, uncut sheet of 120 (6 panes)	....	....	150.00(120)	....	150.00	....
....	cross gutter block of 4	....	....	....	....	11.00	....
....	horiz. pair with vert. gutter	....	....	....	....	4.50	....
....	vert. pair with horiz. gutter	....	....	....	....	3.50	....

3546

3547

3548

SCOTT NO.	DESCRIPTION	FIRST DAY COVERS SING	FIRST DAY COVERS PL. BLK.	MINT SHEET	PLATE BLOCK	UNUSED F/NH	USED
3546	34¢ We Give Thanks, self-adhesive	2.25	4.75	20.00(20)	5.00	1.10	.35
3547	34¢ Hanukkah, self-adhesive	2.25	4.75	22.00(20)	5.50	1.25	.30
3548	34¢ Kwanzaa, self-adhesive	2.25	4.75	22.00(20)	5.50	1.25	.30

3549, 3549B, 3550, 3550A

3551

SCOTT NO.	DESCRIPTION	FIRST DAY COVERS SING	FIRST DAY COVERS PL. BLK.	MINT SHEET	PLATE BLOCK	UNUSED F/NH	USED
3549	34¢ United We Stand, self-adhesive	2.25	....	....	....	1.75	.30
3549a	same, bklt pane of 20	14.50	....	....	....	36.00	....
3549B	34¢ United We Stand, die cut 10.5 x 10.75 on 2 or 3 sides	2.25	....	....	....	1.90	.30
3549Bc	same, bklt pane of 4 .	4.00	....	....	....	7.50	....
3549Bd	same, bklt pane of 6 .	5.50	....	....	....	11.00	....
3549Be	same, bklt pane of 20 (double-sided)	....	....	....	....	38.00	....
3550	34¢ United We Stand, self-adhesive coil (square corners)	2.25	....	....	....	1.40	.30
....	same, pl# strip of 5 . .	....	....	....	....	12.00	....
3550A	34¢ United We Stand, self-adhesive coil, (round corners)	2.25	....	....	....	1.40	.40
....	same, pl# strip of 5 . .	....	....	....	....	12.00	....
3551	57¢ Love, self-adhesive	2.50	5.00	32.00(20)	8.00	1.75	.50

3554 3555

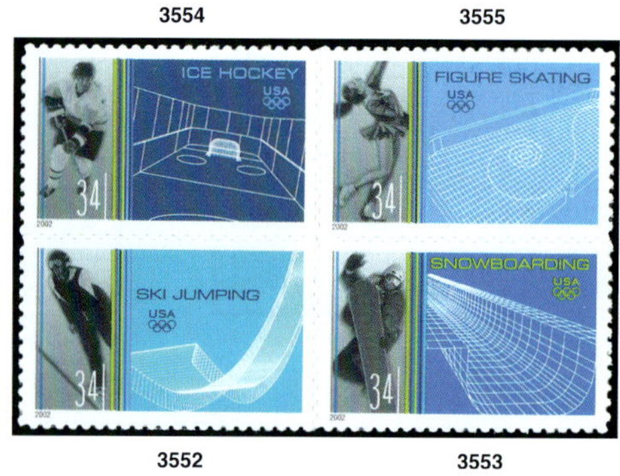

3552 3553

2002 COMMEMORATIVES

SCOTT NO.	DESCRIPTION	FIRST DAY COVERS SING	FIRST DAY COVERS PL. BLK.	MINT SHEET	PLATE BLOCK	UNUSED F/NH	USED
3552/3695	**(3552-60, 3650-56, 3659-74, 3676-79, 3692, 3695) 38 varieties**	....	....	....	....	**55.00**	**12.50**
3552-55	34¢ Winter Olympics, self-adhesive, 4 varieties attached.	4.25	5.25	28.00(20)	7.00	6.00	4.00
3552	34¢ Ski Jumping	2.25	....	....	....	1.60	.40
3553	34¢ Snowboarding. . .	2.25	....	....	....	1.60	.40
3554	34¢ Ice Hockey	2.25	....	....	....	1.60	.40
3555	34¢ Figure Skating . .	2.25	....	....	....	1.60	.40
3552-55v	same, uncut sheet of 180 (9 panes)	....	....	185.00(180)	....	185.00	....
....	cross gutter block of 8	....	....	....	....	25.00	....
....	block of 4 with vert. gutter	....	....	....	....	8.00	....
....	block of 8 with horiz. gutter	....	....	....	....	11.50	....
....	vert. pair with horiz. gutter	....	....	....	....	3.00	....
....	horiz. pair with vert. gutter	....	....	....	....	2.00	....

3556

3557

SCOTT NO.	DESCRIPTION	FIRST DAY COVERS SING	FIRST DAY COVERS PL. BLK.	MINT SHEET	PLATE BLOCK	UNUSED F/NH	USED
3556	34¢ Mentoring a Child, self-adhesive	2.25	4.75	22.00(20)	5.50	1.20	.30
3557	34¢ Langston Hughes, self-adhesive	2.25	4.75	25.00(20)	6.50	1.50	.30

3558

SCOTT NO.	DESCRIPTION	FIRST DAY COVERS SING	FIRST DAY COVERS PL. BLK.	MINT SHEET	PLATE BLOCK	UNUSED F/NH	USED
3558	34¢ Happy Birthday, self-adhesive	2.25	4.75	20.00(20)	5.00	1.20	.30

3559

3560

SCOTT NO.	DESCRIPTION	FIRST DAY COVERS SING	FIRST DAY COVERS PL. BLK.	MINT SHEET	PLATE BLOCK	UNUSED F/NH	USED
3559	34¢ Year of the Horse, self-adhesive	2.25	4.75	27.00(20)	7.00	1.50	.30
3560	34¢ Military Academy Bicentennial, self-adhesive	2.25	4.75	20.00(20)	5.00	1.00	.30

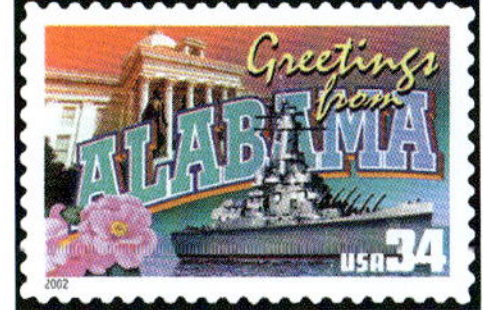
3561

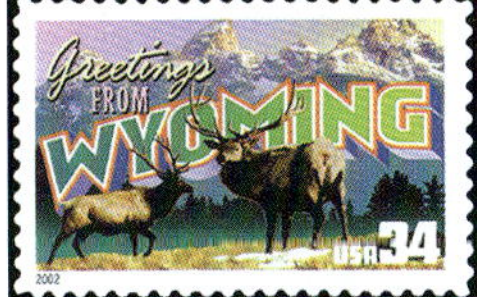
3610

GREETINGS FROM AMERICA

3561	*Alabama*	**3578**	*Louisiana*	**3595**	*Ohio*
3562	*Alaska*	**3579**	*Maine*	**3596**	*Oklahoma*
3563	*Arizona*	**3580**	*Maryland*	**3597**	*Oregon*
3564	*Arkansas*	**3581**	*Massachusetts*	**3598**	*Pennsylvania*
3565	*California*	**3582**	*Michigan*	**3599**	*Rhode Island*
3566	*Colorado*	**3583**	*Minnesota*	**3600**	*South Carolina*
3567	*Connecticut*	**3584**	*Mississippi*	**3601**	*South Dakota*
3568	*Delaware*	**3585**	*Missouri*	**3602**	*Tennessee*
3569	*Florida*	**3586**	*Montana*	**3603**	*Texas*
3570	*Georgia*	**3587**	*Nebraska*	**3604**	*Utah*
3571	*Hawaii*	**3588**	*Nevada*	**3605**	*Vermont*
3572	*Idaho*	**3589**	*New Hampshire*	**3606**	*Virginia*
3573	*Illinois*	**3590**	*New Jersey*	**3607**	*Washington*
3574	*Indiana*	**3591**	*New Mexico*	**3608**	*West Virginia*
3575	*Iowa*	**3592**	*New York*	**3609**	*Wisconsin*
3576	*Kansas*	**3593**	*North Carolina*	**3610**	*Wyoming*
3577	*Kentucky*	**3594**	*North Dakota*		

SCOTT NO.	DESCRIPTION	FIRST DAY COVERS SING	FIRST DAY COVERS PL. BLK.	MINT SHEET	PLATE BLOCK	UNUSED F/NH	USED
3561-3610	34¢ Greetings from America, self-adhesive, 50 varieties attached. .	....	....	50.00(50)	....	50.00	....
....	set of singles.	120.00	....	....	....	....	40.00
	singles each			....	....	....	1.00

3611

LONGLEAF PINE FOREST

3611a *Bachman's sparrow*
3611b *Northern bobwhite, yellow pitcher plants*
3611c *Fox squirrel, red-bellied woodpecker*
3611d *Brown-headed nuthatch*
3611e *Broadhead skink, yellow pitcher plants, pipeworts*
3611f *Eastern towhee, yellow pitcher plants, meadow beauties, toothache grass*
3611g *Gray Fox, gopher tortoise*
3611h *Blind click beetle, sweetbay, pine woods freefrog*
3611i *Rosebuds orchid, pipeworts, southern toad, yellow pitcher plants*
3611j *Grass-pink orchid, yellow-sided skimmer, pipeworts*

SCOTT NO.	DESCRIPTION	FIRST DAY COVERS SING	FIRST DAY COVERS PL. BLK.	MINT SHEET	PLATE BLOCK	UNUSED F/NH	USED
3611	34¢ Longleaf Pine Forest, 10 varieties, attached, self-adhesive	....	....	25.00(10)	....	25.00	....
....	set of singles	25.00	....	....	....	....	10.00
3611v	same, uncut sheet of 90 (9 panes)	....	....	100.00(90)	....	100.00	....

3612

3613, 3614, 3615

3616, 3617, 3618, 3619

3620, 3621, 3622, 3623, 3624, 3625

SCOTT NO.	DESCRIPTION	FIRST DAY COVERS SING	FIRST DAY COVERS PL. BLK.	MINT SHEET	PLATE BLOCK	UNUSED F/NH	USED
3612	5¢ Toleware coffee pot, coil	2.25	....	....	....	.25	.25
....	same, pl# strip of 5 . .	....	....	....	....	2.50	....
3613	3¢ Lithographed Star (year at LL)	2.25	4.75	6.00(50)	1.20	.25	.25
3614	3¢ Photogravure Star (year at LR)	2.25	4.75	6.00(50)	1.20	.25	.25
3615	3¢ Star, coil	2.25	....	....	....	.25	.25
....	same, pl# strip of 5 . .	....	....	....	....	2.00	....
3616	23¢ George Washington	2.25	4.75	150.00(100)	38.00	1.10	.45
3617	23¢ George Washington, self-adhesive coil. . . .	2.25	....	....	....	.75	.40
....	same pl# strip of 5. . .	....	....	....	....	5.50	....
3618	23¢ George Washington, self-adhesive die cut 11.25	2.25	....	....	....	.95	.45
3618a	same, bklt pane of 4 .	3.00	....	....	....	4.00	....
3618b	same, bklt pane of 6 .	4.00	....	....	....	6.00	....
3618c	same, bklt pane of 10	6.75	....	....	....	8.00	....
3619	23¢ George Washington, self-adhesive, die cut 10.5 x 11.25	1.95	....	....	....	6.00	2.75
3619a	same, bklt pane of 4 (3619 x 2 at L, 3618 x 2 at R)........		....	....	....	13.00	....
3619b	same, bklt pane of 6 (3619 x 3 at L, 3618 x 3 at R)........		....	....	....	21.00	....
3619c	same, bklt pane of 4 (3618 x 2 at L, 3619 x 2 at R)........		....	....	....	14.00	....
3619d	same, bklt pane of 6 (3618 x 3 at L, 3619 x 3 at R)		....	....	....	21.00	....
3619e	same, bklt pane of 10 (3619 x 5 at L, 3618 x 5 at R)........		....	....	....	30.00	....
3619f	same, bklt pane of 10 (3618 x 5 at L, 3619 at R)	....	....	....	....	30.00	....
3619g	same, pair (3619 at L, 3618 at R)	....	....	....	....	6.50	....
3619h	same, pair (3618 at L, 3619 at R)	....	....	....	....	6.50	....
3620	(37¢) Flag	2.25	4.75	155.00(100)	23.00	1.40	1.00
3621	(37¢) Flag, self-adhesive	2.25	4.75	30.00(20)	8.00	1.55	.35
3622	(37¢) Flag, self-adhesive coil	2.25	....	....	....	1.50	.25
....	same, pl# strip of 5 . .	....	....	....	....	11.00	....
3623	(37¢) Flag, self-adhesive, die cut 11.25	2.25	....	....	....	1.25	.25
3623a	same, bklt pane of 20	....	....	....	....	24.00	....
3624	(37¢) Flag, self-adhesive, die cut 10.5 x 10.75. .	2.25	....	....	....	1.75	.65
3624a	same, bklt pane of 4 .	4.00	....	....	....	5.75	....
3624b	same, bklt pane of 6 .	5.50	....	....	....	8.50	....
3624c	same, bklt pane of 20	15.00	....	....	....	33.00	....
3625	(37¢) Flag, self-adhesive, die cut 8.	2.25	....	....	....	1.60	.45
3625a	same, ATM bklt pane of 18	15.00	....	....	....	32.00	....

3626, 3639, 3642

3627,3638, 3643

3628, 3641, 3644

3629, 3640, 3645

SCOTT NO.	DESCRIPTION	FIRST DAY COVERS SING	FIRST DAY COVERS PL. BLK.	MINT SHEET	PLATE BLOCK	UNUSED F/NH	USED
3626	(37¢) Toy mail wagon, self-adhesive	2.25	....	....	....	1.40	.40
3627	(37¢) Toy locomotive, self-adhesive	2.25	....	....	....	1.40	.40
3628	(37¢) Toy taxicab, self-adhesive	2.25	....	....	....	1.40	.40
3629	(37¢) Toy fire pumper, self-adhesive	2.25	....	....	....	1.40	.40
3626-29	(37¢) Antique Toys, self-adhesive, 4 varieties attached . .	4.25	....	....	....	6.00	4.50
3629b	same, bklt pane of 4 (3626-29 x 1)	4.25	....	....	....	6.00	....
3629c	same, bklt pane of 6 (3627, 3629, 3626 x 2, 3628 x 2)	5.50	....	....	....	9.50	....
3629d	same, bklt pane of 6 . (3626, 3628, 3627 x 2, 3629 x 2)	5.50	....	....	....	9.50	....
3629e	same, bklt pane of 20	15.00	....	....	....	25.00	....
3629F	37¢ Flag.	2.25	4.75	135.00(100)	26.00	1.50	1.00

3629F, 3630, 3631, 3632, 3632A, 3632C, 3633, 3633A, 3633B, 3635, 3636, 3636D, 3637

SCOTT NO.	DESCRIPTION	FIRST DAY COVERS SING	FIRST DAY COVERS PL. BLK.	MINT SHEET	PLATE BLOCK	UNUSED F/NH	USED
3630	37¢ Flag, self-adhesive	2.25	4.75	24.00(20)	8.00	1.20	.30
3631	37¢ Flag, coil	2.25	....	....	....	1.50	.30
....	same, pl# strip of 5 . .	....	....	....	....	12.00	....
3632	37¢ Flag, self-adhesive coil, die cut 10 vert.	2.25	....	....	....	1.25	.30
....	same, pl# strip of 5 . .	....	....	....	....	10.00	....
3632A	37¢ Flag coil, die cut 10, flag lacking star point.	2.25	....	....	....	1.25	.55
....	same, pl# strip of 5 . .	....	....	....	....	10.00	....
3632C	37¢ Flag, self-adhesive coil, die cut 11.75 (2004). .	2.25	....	....	....	1.25	.80
....	same, pl# strip of 5 . .	....	....	....	....	10.00	....
3633	37¢ Flag, self-adhesive coil, die cut 8.5 vert.	2.25	....	....	....	1.25	.60
....	same, pl# strip of 5 . .	....	....	....	....	10.00	....

SCOTT NO.	DESCRIPTION	FIRST DAY COVERS SING	FIRST DAY COVERS PL. BLK.	MINT SHEET	PLATE BLOCK	UNUSED F/NH	USED
3633A	37¢ Flag coil, die cut 8.5, right angel corners. . .	1.95	....	....	....	3.00	1.00
....	same, pl# strip of 5 . .	....	....	....	....	20.00	....
3633B	37¢ Flag coil, die cut 9.5 (dated 2005)	2.25	....	....	....	10.00	.75
....	same, plt. strip of 5 . .	....	....	....	....	53.00	....
3634	37¢ Flag, self-adhesive, die cut 11	2.25	....	....	....	1.50	1.20
3634a	same, bklt pane of 10	....	....	....	....	16.00	....
3634b	same, self-adhesive, bklt single, dated 2003 . . .	2.25	....	....	....	1.60	1.20
3634c	same, bklt pane of 4 (3634b)	4.25	....	....	....	6.00	....
3634d	same, bklt pane of 6 (3634b)	5.50	....	....	....	9.00	....
3634e	same, die cut 11.3 . . .	....	....	....	....	1.35	.35
3634f	same, bklt pane of 10 of 3634e.	....	....	....	....	9.00	....
3635	37¢ Flag, self-adhesive, die cut 11.25	2.25	....	....	....	1.25	.50
3635a	same, bklt pane of 20	....	....	....	....	25.00	....
3636	37¢ Flag, self-adhesive, die cut 10.5 x 10.75 . .	2.25	....	....	....	3.00	.60
3636a	same, bklt pane of 4 .	....	....	....	....	4.00	....
3636b	same, bklt pan of 6 . .	....	....	....	....	5.00	....
3636c	same, bklt pane of 20	....	....	....	....	28.00	....
3636D	37¢ Flag, die cut 11.25 x 11, self-adhesive	2.25	....	....	....	1.85	.85
3636De	same, bklt pane of 20	....	....	....	....	37.00	....
3637	37¢ Flag, self-adhesive, die cut 8	2.25	....	....	....	1.50	.85
3637a	same, ATM bklt pane of 18	15.00	....	....	....	28.00	....
3638	37¢ Toy locomotive, self-adhesive coil, die cut 8.5 horiz.	2.25	....		....	1.75	.50
3639	37¢ Toy mail wagon, self-adhesive coil, die cut 8.5 horiz.	2.25	....		....	1.75	.50
3640	37¢ Toy fire pumper, self-adhesive coil, die cut 8.5 horiz.	2.25	....		....	1.75	.50
3641	37¢ Toy taxicab, self-adhesive coil, die cut 8.5 horiz.	2.25	....		....	1.75	.50
3638-41	37¢ Antique Toys, self-adhesive coil, strip of 4.	4.25	....	....	....	6.50	5.00
....	same, pl# strip of 5 . .	....	....	....	....	15.50	....
3642	37¢ Toy mail wagon, self-adhesive, die cut 11	2.25	....	....	....	1.50	.50
3642a	same, die cut 11x11.25, 2003	2.25	....	....	....	1.50	.50
3643	37¢ Toy locomotive, self-adhesive, die cut 11	2.25	....	....	....	1.50	.50
3643a	same, die cut 11x11.25, 2003	2.25	....	....	....	1.50	.50
3644	37¢ Toy taxicab, self-adhesive, die cut 11	2.25	....	....	....	1.50	.50
3644a	same, die cut 11x11.25, 2003	2.25	....	....	....	1.50	.50
3645	37¢ Toy fire pumper, self-adhesive, die cut 11	2.25	....	....	....	1.50	.50
3645f	same, die cut 11x11.25, 2003	2.25	....	....	....	1.50	.50
3642-45	37¢ Antique Toys, self-adhesive, 4 varieties attach.	4.25	....	....	....	6.00	4.00
3645b	same, bklt pane of 4 (3642-45 x 1)	4.25	....	....	....	9.00	....
3645c	same, bklt pane of 6 (3643, 3645, 3642 x 2, 3644 x 2)	5.50	....	....	....	8.00	....
3645d	same, bklt pane of 6 (3642, 3644, 3642 x 2, 3645 x 2)	5.50	....	....	....	8.00	....
3645e	same, bklt pane of 20	15.00	....	....	....	26.00	....
3645g	37¢ Antique Toys, self-adhesive, blk of 4 (3642a, 3643a, 3644a, 3645f)	4.25	....	....	....	6.00	....
3645h	same, bklt pane of 20	15.00	....	....	....	32.00	....

3646

SCOTT NO.	DESCRIPTION	FIRST DAY COVERS SING	FIRST DAY COVERS PL. BLK.	MINT SHEET	PLATE BLOCK	UNUSED F/NH	USED
3646	60¢ Coverlet Eagle, self-adhesive	2.75	5.50	35.00(20)	8.00	2.00	.50

3648

3647

SCOTT NO.	DESCRIPTION	FIRST DAY COVERS SING	FIRST DAY COVERS PL. BLK.	MINT SHEET	PLATE BLOCK	UNUSED F/NH	USED
3647	$3.85 Jefferson Memorial, self-adhesive	8.75	35.00	230.00(20)	52.00	13.00	7.75
3647A	same, die cut 11x10.75, dated 2003.	8.75	35.00	235.00(20)	54.00	14.00	8.75
3648	$13.65 Capitol Dome, self-adhesive	35.00	105.00	775.00(20)	175.00	44.00	12.00

3649

MASTERS OF AMERICAN PHOTOGRAPHY

3649a *Albert Sands Southworth & Josiah Johnson Hawes*
3649b *Timothy H. O'Sullivan*
3649c *Carleton E. Watkins*
3649d *Getrude Kasebier*
3649e *Lewis W. Hine*
3649f *Alvin Langdon Coburn*
3649g *Edward Steichen*
3649h *Alfred Steiglitz*
3649i *Man Ray*
3649j *Edward Weston*
3649k *James VanDerZee*
3649l *Dorothea Lange*
3649m *Walker Evans*
3649n *Eugene Smith*
3649o *Paul Strand*
3649p *Ansel Adams*
3649q *Imogen Cunningham*
3649r *Andre Kertesz*
3649s *Garry Winogrand*
3649t *Minor White*

SCOTT NO.	DESCRIPTION	FIRST DAY COVERS SING	FIRST DAY COVERS PL. BLK.	MINT SHEET	PLATE BLOCK	UNUSED F/NH	USED
3649	37¢ Masters of American Photography, self-adhesive, 20 varieties attached .	....	....	30.00(20)	....	30.00	....
....	same, set of singles. .	50.00	....	....	....	....	17.00

3650

3652

3651

SCOTT NO.	DESCRIPTION	FIRST DAY COVERS SING	FIRST DAY COVERS PL. BLK.	MINT SHEET	PLATE BLOCK	UNUSED F/NH	USED
3650	37¢ John James Audubon, self-adhesive	2.25	4.75	28.00(20)	6.50	1.75	.30
3651	37¢ Harry Houdini, self-adhesive	2.25	4.75	26.00(20)	6.00	1.50	.30
3652	37¢ Andy Warhol, self-adhesive	2.25	4.75	29.00(20)	7.00	1.50	.30

3653 3654

3655 3656

SCOTT NO.	DESCRIPTION	FIRST DAY COVERS SING	FIRST DAY COVERS PL. BLK.	MINT SHEET	PLATE BLOCK	UNUSED F/NH	USED
3653-56	37¢ Teddy Bears, self-adhesive, 4 varieties attached.	5.00	6.00	30.00(20)	6.75	6.00	5.00
3653	37¢ Bruin Teddy Bear	2.25	....	....	....	1.75	.50
3654	37¢ Stick Teddy Bear.	2.25	....	....	....	1.75	.50
3655	37¢ Gund Teddy Bear	2.25	....	....	....	1.75	.50
3656	37¢ Ideal Teddy Bear.	2.25	....	....	....	1.75	.50

3657

3658

3659

SCOTT NO.	DESCRIPTION	FIRST DAY COVERS SING	FIRST DAY COVERS PL. BLK.	MINT SHEET	PLATE BLOCK	UNUSED F/NH	USED
3657	37¢ Love, self-adhesive	2.25	....	....	....	1.25	.35
....	same, bklt pane of 20	15.00	....	....	....	22.00	....
3658	60¢ Love, self-adhesive	2.75	5.50	35.00(20)	9.00	2.20	.75
3659	37¢ Ogden Nash, self-adhesive	2.25	4.75	22.50(20)	5.50	1.40	.35

3661

3660

3662

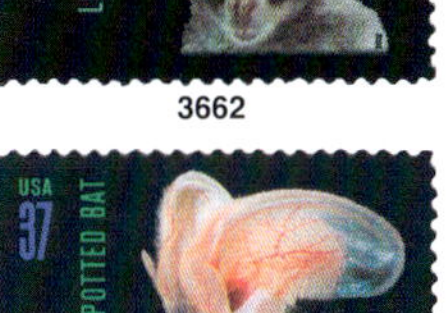
3663

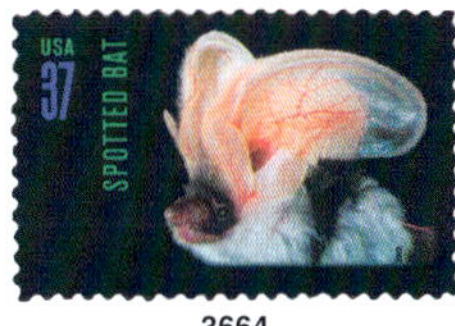
3664

SCOTT NO.	DESCRIPTION	FIRST DAY COVERS SING	FIRST DAY COVERS PL. BLK.	MINT SHEET	PLATE BLOCK	UNUSED F/NH	USED
3660	37¢ Duke Kahanamoku, self-adhesive	2.25	4.75	22.00(20)	5.50	1.25	.35
3661-64	37¢ American Bats, self-adhesive, 4 varieties attached.	4.25	4.75	28.50(20)	7.25	7.00	4.00
3661	37¢ Red Bat.	2.25	....	....	....	1.75	.45
3662	37¢ Leaf-nosed Bat . .	2.25	....	....	....	1.75	.45
3663	37¢ Pallid Bat	2.25	....	....	....	1.75	.45
3664	37¢ Spotted Bat.	2.25	....	....	....	1.75	.45

3665 3666

3667 3668

3669

SCOTT NO.	DESCRIPTION	FIRST DAY COVERS SING	FIRST DAY COVERS PL. BLK.	MINT SHEET	PLATE BLOCK	UNUSED F/NH	USED
3665-68	37¢ Women In Journalism, self-adhesive, 4 varieties attached.	6.00	7.00	37.00(20)	9.00	8.00	5.00
3665	37¢ Nellie Bly.	2.25	....	....	....	2.00	.50
3666	37¢ Ida M. Tarbell. . . .	2.25	....	....	....	2.00	.50
3667	37¢ Ethel L. Payne . .	2.25	....	....	....	2.00	.50
3668	37¢ Marguerite Higgins	2.25	....	....	....	2.00	.50
3669	37¢ Irving Berlin, self-adhesive	2.25	4.75	25.00(20)	6.00	1.25	.30

3670 3671

SCOTT NO.	DESCRIPTION	FIRST DAY COVERS SING	FIRST DAY COVERS PL. BLK.	MINT SHEET	PLATE BLOCK	UNUSED F/NH	USED
3670-71	37¢ Neuter and Spay, self-adhesive, 2 varieites attached.	4.00	4.75	25.00(20)	6.00	3.50	2.00
3670	37¢ Kitten	2.25	....	....	....	2.00	.40
3671	37¢ Puppy	2.25	....	....	....	2.00	.40

3672

3673

3674

SCOTT NO.	DESCRIPTION	FIRST DAY COVERS SING	FIRST DAY COVERS PL. BLK.	MINT SHEET	PLATE BLOCK	UNUSED F/NH	USED
3672	37¢ Hanukkah, self-adhesive	2.25	4.75	25.00(20)	6.00	1.30	.40
3673	37¢ Kwanzaa, self-adhesive	2.25	4.75	21.00(20)	5.50	1.20	.40
3674	37¢ EID, self-adhesive	2.25	4.75	21.00(20)	5.50	1.20	.40

3675

SCOTT NO.	DESCRIPTION	FIRST DAY COVERS SING	FIRST DAY COVERS PL. BLK.	MINT SHEET	PLATE BLOCK	UNUSED F/NH	USED
3675	37¢ Madonna & Child, self-adhesive	2.25	4.75	....	....	1.50	.30
....	same, bklt pane of 20	15.00	....	....	....	27.00	....

3676, 3683, 3684, 3688

3677, 3680, 3685, 3689

3678, 3681, 3686, 3690

3679, 3682, 3687, 3691

SCOTT NO.	DESCRIPTION	FIRST DAY COVERS SING	FIRST DAY COVERS PL. BLK.	MINT SHEET	PLATE BLOCK	UNUSED F/NH	USED
3676-79	37¢ Snowmen, self-adhesive, 4 varieties attached . .	6.00	7.00	32.00(20)	8.50	8.00	4.75
3676	37¢ Snowman with red and green scarf	2.25	....	....	....	2.00	1.25
3677	37¢ Snowman with blue scarf.	2.25	....	....	....	2.00	1.25
3578	37¢ Snowman with pipe	2.25	....	....	....	2.00	1.25
3679	37¢ Snowman with top hat	2.25	....	....	....	2.00	1.25
3680	37¢ Snowman with blue scarf, self-adhesive coil	2.25	....	....	....	2.50	.75
3681	37¢ Snowman with pipe, self-adhesive coil. . . .	2.25	....	....	....	2.50	.75
3682	37¢ Snowman with top hat, self-adhesive coil. . . .	2.25	....	....	....	2.50	.75
3683	37¢ Snowman with red and green scarf, self-adhesive coil	2.25	....	....	....	2.50	.75
3680-83	37¢ Snowmen, self-adhesive coil, strip of 4	4.25	....	....	....	12.00	....
....	same, pl# strip of 5 . .	....	....	....	....	21.00	....
3684	37¢ Snowman with red and green scarf, large design	2.25	....	....	....	1.75	.50
3685	37¢ Snowman with blue scarf, large design . . .	2.25	....	....	....	1.75	.50
3686	37¢ Snowman with pipe, large design	2.25	....	....	....	1.75	.50
3687	37¢ Snowman with top hat, large design.	2.25	....	....	....	1.75	.50
3684-87	37¢ Snowman, self-adhesive, 4 varieties attached . .	4.25	....	....	....	7.00	4.75
3687b	same, bklt pane of 20 (3684-87 x 5 + label) .	15.00	....	....	....	36.00	....
3688	37¢ Snowman with red and green scarf, small design	2.25	....	....	....	2.25	.75
3689	37¢ Snowman with blue scarf, small design. . .	2.25	....	....	....	2.25	.75
3690	37¢ Snowman with pipe, small design.	2.25	....	....	....	2.25	.75
3691	37¢ Snowman with top hat, small design.	2.25	....	....	....	2.25	.75
3688-91	37¢ Snowmen , self-adhesive, 4 varieties attached . .	4.25	....	....	....	10.00	6.25
3691b	same, bklt pane of 4, (3688-91).	4.25	....	....	....	10.00	....
3691c	same, bklt pane of 6 (3690-91, 3688-89 x 2)	5.50	....	....	....	15.00	....
3691d	same, bklt pane of 6 (3688-89, 3690-91 x 2)	5.50	....	....	....	15.00	....

3693, 3775, 3785

3692

3695

SCOTT NO.	DESCRIPTION	FIRST DAY COVERS SING	FIRST DAY COVERS PL. BLK.	MINT SHEET	PLATE BLOCK	UNUSED F/NH	USED
3692	37¢ Cary Grant, self-adhesive	2.25	4.75	30.00(20)	7.00	1.50	.40
3693	(5¢) Sea Coast coil, self-adhesive	2.25	....	....	....	.25	.20
....	same, pl# strip of 5 . .	....	....	....	....	2.50	....

The "Hawaiian Missionary" Stamps of 1851-1853

The first official Hawaiian post office was established in December 1850. Postmaster Henry M. Whitney had stamps printed locally in three denominations. Philatelists call these rare stamps "Hawaiian Missionaries" because virtually all were used by Christian missionaries on outbound mail. Only 28 covers with Missionary stamps are known to exist; only the Dawson cover (right) bears the 2¢ stamp. The two 13¢ stamps were unusual as they prepaid postage in two countries–Hawaii and the U.S.

3694

SCOTT NO.	DESCRIPTION	FIRST DAY COVERS SING	FIRST DAY COVERS PL. BLK.	MINT SHEET	PLATE BLOCK	UNUSED F/NH	USED
3694	37¢ Hawaiian Missionary, souvenir sheet of 4 . .	5.00	....	....	....	8.00	6.00
3694a	37¢ Hawaii 2¢ of 1851	2.25	....	....	....	2.00	1.00
3694b	37¢ Hawaii 5¢ of 1851	2.25	....	....	....	2.00	1.00
3694c	37¢ Hawaii 13¢ of 1851	2.25	....	....	....	2.00	1.00
3694d	37¢ Hawaii 13¢ of 1852	2.25	....	....	....	2.00	1.00
3695	37¢ Happy Birthday, self-adhesive	2.25	4.75	25.00(20)	6.00	1.20	.30

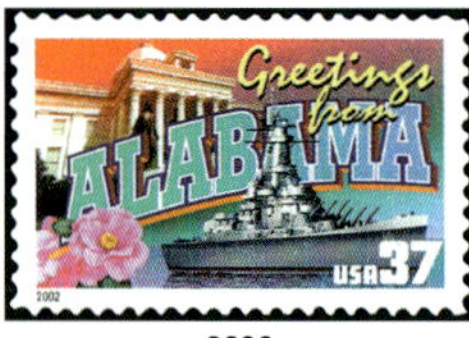

3696

3745

GREETINGS FROM AMERICA

3696	*Alabama*	**3713**	*Louisiana*	**3730**	*Ohio*
3697	*Alaska*	**3714**	*Maine*	**3731**	*Oklahoma*
3698	*Arizona*	**3715**	*Maryland*	**3732**	*Oregon*
3699	*Arkansas*	**3716**	*Massachusetts*	**3733**	*Pennsylvania*
3700	*California*	**3717**	*Michigan*	**3734**	*Rhode Island*
3701	*Colorado*	**3718**	*Minnesota*	**3735**	*South Carolina*
3702	*Connecticut*	**3719**	*Mississippi*	**3736**	*South Dakota*
3703	*Delaware*	**3720**	*Missouri*	**3737**	*Tennessee*
3704	*Florida*	**3721**	*Montana*	**3738**	*Texas*
3705	*Georgia*	**3722**	*Nebraska*	**3739**	*Utah*
3706	*Hawaii*	**3723**	*Nevada*	**3740**	*Vermont*
3707	*Idaho*	**3724**	*New Hampshire*	**3741**	*Virginia*
3708	*Illinois*	**3725**	*New Jersey*	**3742**	*Washington*
3709	*Indiana*	**3726**	*New Mexico*	**3743**	*West Virginia*
3710	*Iowa*	**3727**	*New York*	**3744**	*Wisconsin*
3711	*Kansas*	**3728**	*North Carolina*	**3745**	*Wyoming*
3712	*Kentucky*	**3729**	*North Dakota*		

SCOTT NO.	DESCRIPTION	FIRST DAY COVERS SING	FIRST DAY COVERS PL. BLK.	MINT SHEET	PLATE BLOCK	UNUSED F/NH	USED
3696-3745	37¢ Greetings from America, self-adhesive, 50 varieties attached. .	....	....	50.00(50)	....	50.00	....
....	set of singles.	120.00	....	....	....	....	35.00
	singles each	....		....	....	....	.85

3746

3747

ZORA NEALE HURSTON 37 USA
3748

2003 COMMEMORATIVES

SCOTT NO.	DESCRIPTION	FIRST DAY COVERS SING	FIRST DAY COVERS PL. BLK.	MINT SHEET	PLATE BLOCK	UNUSED F/NH	USED
3746/3824	**(3746-48, 3771, 3773-74, 3781-82, 3786-91, 3803, 3808-18, 3821-24) 30 varieties. . . . . . .**	....	....	....	....	**45.00**	**10.50**
3746	37¢ Thurgood Marshall, self-adhesive	2.25	4.75	28.00(20)	7.00	1.50	.30
3747	37¢ Year of the Ram, self-adhesive	2.25	4.75	25.00(20)	6.00	1.50	.30
3748	37¢ Zora Neale Hurston, self-adhesive	2.25	4.75	30.00(20)	7.50	2.00	.30

3749, 3749a, 3758, 3758a

3750, 3751, 3752, 3753, 3758b

3754, 3759

3755, 3761

3756

3757, 3762

AMERICAN DESIGN SERIES

SCOTT NO.	DESCRIPTION	FIRST DAY COVERS SING	FIRST DAY COVERS PL. BLK.	MINT SHEET	PLATE BLOCK	UNUSED F/NH	USED
3749	1¢ Tiffany Lamp, self-adhesive (2007).	2.25	4.75	3.00(20)	.95	.25	.25
3749a	1¢ Tiffany Lamp.	2.95	5.75	4.25(20)	1.00	.25	.25
3750	2¢ Navajo Necklace, self-adhesive	2.25	4.75	5.00(20)	.90	.25	.25
3751	same, self-adhesvie, die cut 11.25 X 11.5 . .	2.25	4.75	8.00(20)	1.75	.40	.25
3752	same, w/ USPS micro-printing, self-adhesive, die cut 11.25 X 11 . . .	2.25	4.75	7.00(20)	1.75	.30	.25
3753	same, die cut 11.5 X 11, (2007 date)	2.25	4.75	6.00(20)	1.25	.30	.25
3754	3¢ Silver Coffeepot, self-adhesive (2007).	2.25	4.75	4.50(20)	1.25	.25	.25
3755	4¢ Chippendale Chair, self-adhesive (2004) .	2.25	4.75	5.50(20)	1.20	.25	.25
3756	5¢ Toleware, self-adhesive	2.25	4.75	6.00(20)	1.40	.35	.25
3756a	5¢ Toleware, 11.25x10.75 (dated 2007)	2.25	4.75	6.00(20)	1.40	.35	.35
3757	10¢ American Clock, self-adhesive	2.25	4.75	7.00(20)	1.50	.35	.25
3758	1¢ Tiffany Lamp, coil (2003)	2.25	....	....	....	.25	.25
....	same, pl# strip of 5 . .	....	....	....	....	2.25	....
3758a	1¢ Tiffany Lamp, coil (2008) perf 10	2.25	....	....	....	.25	.25
....	same, pl# strip of 5 . .	....	....	....	....	2.25	....
3758b	2¢ Navajo Necklace Perf 9.75 vert. (2011)	....	3.75	....	....	.25	....
....	same, plate number strip of 5		....	....	....	2.25	....
3759	3¢ Silver Coffeepot, coil	2.25	....	....	....	.25	.25
....	same, pl# strip of 5 . .	....	....	....	....	8.00	....
3761	4¢ Chippendale Chair, coil (2007)	2.25	....	....	....	.25	.25
....	same, pl# strip of 5 . .	....	....	....	....	3.00	.25
3761A	4¢ Chippendale Chair, Chair Coil (ap) (2013 Date)	2.75	....	....	....	.30	.25
....	Same, Plate # strip of 5	....	....	....	....	1.50	....
3762	10¢ American Clock, coil	2.25	....	....	....	.30	.25
....	same, pl# strip of 5 . .	....	....	....	....	3.00	....
3763	10¢ American Clock (2008)	....	....	....	....	.30	.25
....	same, plate strip of 5.	....	....	....	....	4.00	....
3763A	10¢ American Clock Coil (untagged) (2008 Date)	....	....	....	....	.30	.25
....	Same, Plate # strip of 5	....	....	....	....	4.00	....

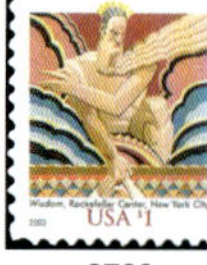

3766

3769

3770

3771

SCOTT NO.	DESCRIPTION	FIRST DAY COVERS SING	FIRST DAY COVERS PL. BLK.	MINT SHEET	PLATE BLOCK	UNUSED F/NH	USED
3766	$1 Wisdom, self-adhesive	3.50	7.50	61.00(20)	14.50	3.25	.70
3766a	$1 Wisdom, (2008) die cut 11.25x11	3.50	7.50	60.00(20)	13.50	3.00	.70
3769	(10¢) New York Library Lion, perf. 10 vert. . . .	2.25	....	....	4.00(3)	.30	.20
....	same, pl# strip of 5 . .	....	....	....	....	6.00	....
3770	(10¢) Atlas Statue, self-adhesive coil, die cut 11 dated 2003.	2.25	....	....	....	.30	.25
....	same, pl# strip of 5 . .	....	....	....	....	6.00	....
3771	80¢ Special Olympics, self-adhesive	3.00	7.00	45.00(20)	12.00	2.50	1.00

3772

AMERICAN FILM MAKING

3772a	*Screenwriting*	3772d	*Music*	3772g	*Cinematography*
3772b	*Directing*	3772e	*Make-up*	3772h	*Film editing*
3772c	*Costume design*	3772f	*Art Direction*	3772i	*Special effects*
				3772j	*Sound*

SCOTT NO.	DESCRIPTION	FIRST DAY COVERS SING	FIRST DAY COVERS PL. BLK.	MINT SHEET	PLATE BLOCK	UNUSED F/NH	USED
3772	37¢ American Film Making, self-adhesive, 10 varieties attached.	....	....	15.00(10)	....	15.00	13.50
....	set of singles	25.00	....	....	....	....	7.00

3773 3774 3781 3782

SCOTT NO.	DESCRIPTION	FIRST DAY COVERS SING	FIRST DAY COVERS PL. BLK.	MINT SHEET	PLATE BLOCK	UNUSED F/NH	USED
3773	37¢ Ohio Statehood, self-adhesive	2.25	4.75	22.00(20)	5.50	1.20	.30
3774	37¢ Pelican Island National Wildlife Refuge, self-adhesive	2.25	4.75	22.00(20)	6.00	1.35	.30
3775	(5¢) Sea Coast coil, perf. 9.75 vert.	2.25	....	....	....	.30	.25
....	same, pl# strip of 5 . .	....	....	....	....	2.75	....

3776 3777 3778 3779

3780 3783 3784, 3784A 3786

SCOTT NO.	DESCRIPTION	FIRST DAY COVERS SING	FIRST DAY COVERS PL. BLK.	MINT SHEET	PLATE BLOCK	UNUSED F/NH	USED
3776	37¢ Uncle Sam on Bicycle	2.25	....	....	....	1.50	1.00
3777	37¢ 1888 Pres. Campaign badge.	2.25	....	....	....	1.50	1.00
3778	37¢ 1893 Silk bookmark	2.25	....	....	....	1.50	1.00
3779	37¢ Modern hand fan	2.25	....	....	....	1.50	1.00
3780	37¢ Carving of woman with flag & sword	2.25	....	....	....	1.50	1.00
3776-80	37¢ Old Glory, self-adhesive, 5 varieties attached . .	5.00	....	....	....	7.00	....
3780b	same, complete booklet of 2 panes	....	....	....	....	25.00	....
3781	37¢ Cesar E. Chavez, self-adhesive	2.25	4.75	22.00(20)	5.50	1.20	.30
3782	37¢ Louisiana Purchase, self-adhesive	2.25	4.75	34.00(20)	8.00	1.50	.35

SCOTT NO.	DESCRIPTION	FIRST DAY COVERS SING	FIRST DAY COVERS PL. BLK.	MINT SHEET	PLATE BLOCK	UNUSED F/NH	USED
3783	37¢ First Flight of the Wright Brothers, self-adhesive	2.25	....	15.00(10)	....	1.85	.45
3783a	same, bklt pane of 9 .	....	....	....	....	13.00	....
3783b	same, bklt pane of 1 .	7.00	....	....	....	4.50	....
3784	37¢ Purple Heart, self-adhesive	2.25	4.75	22.00(20)	5.50	1.20	.45
3784A	37¢ Purple Heart, self-adhesive, die cut 10.75 x 10.25.	2.25	4.75	22.00(20)	5.50	1.20	.50
3785	(5¢) Sea Coast coil, four-side die cuts.	2.25	....	....	....	.35	.25
....	same, pl# strip of 5 . .	....	....	....	....	2.50	....
3785A	(5¢) Sea Coast coil, die cut 9.25 x 10	2.25	....	....	....	.35	.25
....	same, pl# strip of 5 . .	....	....	....	....	2.50	....
3786	37¢ Audrey Hepburn, self-adhesive	2.25	4.75	40.00(20)	10.00	2.00	.30

3787 3788 3789

3790 3792–3801, 3792a–3801a 3791

SCOTT NO.	DESCRIPTION	FIRST DAY COVERS SING	FIRST DAY COVERS PL. BLK.	MINT SHEET	PLATE BLOCK	UNUSED F/NH	USED
3787-91	37¢ Southern Lighthouses, self-adhesive, 5 varieties attached.	5.00	....	47.00(20)	28.00(10)	12.00	10.00
3787	37¢ Old Cape Henry, Virginia.	2.25	....	....	....	2.00	.65
3788	37¢ Cape Lookout, North Carolina	2.25	....	....	....	2.00	.65
3788a	same, dropped denomination......	....	....	....	....	....	....
3789	37¢ Morris Island, South Carolina.	2.25	....	....	....	2.00	.65
3790	37¢ Tybee Island, Georgia	2.25	....	....	....	2.00	.65
3791	37¢ Hillsboro Inlet, Florida	2.25	....	....	....	2.00	.65
3791b	same, strip of 5 (3787, 3788a, 3789-91)	....	....	....	....	....	....
3792	(25¢) Eagle, gray with gold eagle, coil.	2.25	....	....	....	1.00	.60
3792a	same, serpentine die cut 11.5(2005)	2.25	....	....	....	1.00	.60
3793	(25¢) Eagle, gold with red eagle, coil	2.25	....	....	....	1.00	.60
3793a	same, serpentine die cut 11.5(2005)	2.25	....	....	....	1.00	.60
3794	(25¢) Eagle, dull blue with gold eagle, coil .	2.25	....	....	....	1.00	.60
3794a	same, serpentine die cut 11.5(2005)	2.25	....	....	....	1.00	.60
3795	(25¢) Eagle, gold with Prussian blue eagle, coil	2.25	....	....	....	1.00	.60
3795a	same, serpentine die cut 11.5(2005)	2.25	....	....	....	1.00	.60
3796	(25¢) Eagle, green with gold eagle, coil.	2.25	....	....	....	1.00	.60
3796a	same, die cut 11.5(2005)	2.25	....	....	....	1.00	.60
3797	(25¢) Eagle, gold with gray eagle, coil	2.25	....	....	....	1.00	.60
3797a	same, die cut 11.5(2005)	2.25	....	....	....	1.00	.60
3798	(25¢) Eagle, Prussian blue with gold eagle, coil	2.25	....	....	....	1.00	.60
3798a	same, die cut 11.5(2005)	2.25	....	....	....	1.00	.60
3799	(25¢) Eagle, gold with dull blue eagle, coil . .	2.25	....	....	....	1.00	.60
3799a	same, die cut 11.5(2005)	2.25	....	....	....	1.00	.60
3800	(25¢) Eagle, red with gold eagle, coil.	2.25	....	....	....	1.00	.60
3800a	same, die cut 11.5(2005)	2.25	....	....	....	1.00	.60
3801	(25¢) Eagle, gold with green eagle, coil	2.25	....	....	....	1.00	.60
3801a	same, die cut 11.5(2005)	2.25	....	....	....	1.00	.60
3792-3801	(25¢) Eagle, self-adhesive coil, strip of 10	6.00	....	....	....	12.00	....
....	same, pl# strip of 11 .	....	....	....	....	14.00	....
3792a-3801a	same, self-adhesive, coil strip of 10, serpentine die cut 11.5(dated 2005) .	6.00	....	....	....	12.00	....
....	same, plt. strip of 11 .	....	....	....	....	14.00	....

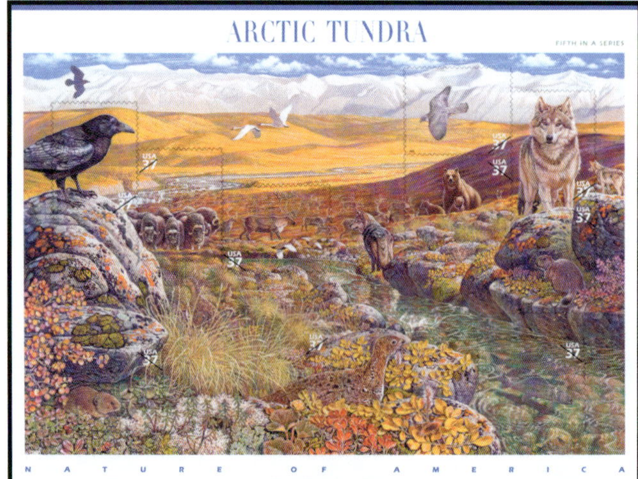

3802

ARCTIC TUNDRA

3802a	*Gyrfalcon*	**3802f**	*Caribou & willow ptarmigans*
3802b	*Gray wolf*	**3802g**	*Arctic ground squirrel*
3802c	*Common raven*	**3802h**	*Willow ptarmigan & bearberry*
3802d	*Musk oxen & caribou*	**3802i**	*Arctic grayling*
3802e	*Grizzly bears & caribou*	**3802j**	*Singing vole, thin-legged spider, lingonberry, Labrador tea*

SCOTT NO.	DESCRIPTION	FIRST DAY COVERS SING	FIRST DAY COVERS PL. BLK.	MINT SHEET	PLATE BLOCK	UNUSED F/NH	USED
3802	37¢ Arctic Tundra, 10 varieties, attached, self-adhesive	....	....	15.00(10)	....	15.00	....
	set of singles	25.00	....	....	....	....	7.00

3803

SCOTT NO.	DESCRIPTION	FIRST DAY COVERS SING	FIRST DAY COVERS PL. BLK.	MINT SHEET	PLATE BLOCK	UNUSED F/NH	USED
3803	37¢ Korean War Veterans, Memorial, self-adhesive	2.25	4.75	21.00(20)	5.50	1.20	.30

3804 3805 3806 3807

SCOTT NO.	DESCRIPTION	FIRST DAY COVERS SING	FIRST DAY COVERS PL. BLK.	MINT SHEET	PLATE BLOCK	UNUSED F/NH	USED
3804	37¢ Young Mother . . .	2.25	....	....	....	1.50	.40
3805	37¢ Children Playing .	2.25	....	....	....	1.50	.40
3806	37¢ On a Balcony . . .	2.25	....	....	....	1.50	.40
3807	37¢ Child in Straw Hat	2.25	....	....	....	1.50	.40
3804-07	37¢ Mary Cassatt Paintings, self-adhesive, 4 varieties attached.	4.25	....	....	....	6.00	4.00
3807b	same, bklt pane of 20 (3804-07 x 5)	15.00	....	....	....	30.00	....

3808

3809

3810 3811

SCOTT NO.	DESCRIPTION	FIRST DAY COVERS SING	FIRST DAY COVERS PL. BLK.	MINT SHEET	PLATE BLOCK	UNUSED F/NH	USED
3808-11	37¢ Early Football Heroes, self-adhesive, 4 varieties attached.	4.25	4.75	25.00(20)	6.50	6.00	5.00
3808	37¢ Bronko Nagurski.	2.25	....	....	....	1.50	.40
3809	37¢ Ernie Nevers. . . .	2.25	....	....	....	1.50	.40
3810	37¢ Walter Camp. . . .	2.25	....	....	....	1.50	.40
3811	37¢ Red Grange	2.25	....	....	....	1.50	.40

3812

3813

SCOTT NO.	DESCRIPTION	FIRST DAY COVERS SING	FIRST DAY COVERS PL. BLK.	MINT SHEET	PLATE BLOCK	UNUSED F/NH	USED
3812	37¢ Roy Acuff, self-adhesive	2.25	4.75	24.00(20)	6.00	1.25	.30
3813	37¢ District of Columbia, self-adhesive	2.25	4.75	22.00(16)	6.00	1.50	.40

3814

3815

3816

3817

3818

3819

3820

SCOTT NO.	DESCRIPTION	FIRST DAY COVERS SING	FIRST DAY COVERS PL. BLK.	MINT SHEET	PLATE BLOCK	UNUSED F/NH	USED
3814-18	37¢ Reptiles & Amphibians, self-adhesive, 5 varieties attached.	5.00	10.50	28.00(20)	15.00	7.50	5.00
3814	37¢ Scarlet Kingsnake	2.25	....	....	....	1.50	.50
3815	37¢ Blue-Spotted Salamander	2.25	....	....	....	1.50	.50
3816	37¢ Reticulate Lizard.	2.25	....	....	....	1.50	.50
3817	37¢ Ornate Chorus Frog	2.25	....	....	....	1.50	.50
3818	37¢ Ornate Box Turtle	2.25	....	....	....	1.50	.50
3819	23¢ George Washington, self-adhesive, die cut 11	2.25	4.75	30.00(20)	12.00	2.00	.75
3820	37¢ Madonna & Child, self-adhesive (2003) .	2.25	....	....	....	1.30	.40
3820a	same, bklt pane of 20	....	....	....	....	24.00	....

3821, 3825 3822, 3826 3823, 3827 3824, 3828

SCOTT NO.	DESCRIPTION	FIRST DAY COVERS SING	FIRST DAY COVERS PL. BLK.	MINT SHEET	PLATE BLOCK	UNUSED F/NH	USED
3821-24	37¢ Christmas Music Makers, self-adhesive, 4 varieties attached.	4.25	4.75	34.00(20)	7.50	7.00	4.00
3821	37¢ Reindeer with Pipes	2.25	....	....	....	2.00	.75
3822	37¢ Santa Claus with Drum	2.25	....	....	....	2.00	.75
3823	37¢ Santa Claus with Trumpet	2.25	....	....	....	2.00	.75
3824	37¢ Reindeer with Horn	2.25	....	....	....	2.00	.75
3824b	same, bklt pane of 20, (3821-24 x 5 + label) .	15.00	....	....	....	34.00	....
3825	37¢ Reindeer with Pipes, die cut 10.5 x 10.75 . .	2.25	....	....	....	2.00	1.00
3826	37¢ Santa Claus with Drum, die cut 10.5 x 10.75 . .	2.25	....	....	....	2.00	1.00
3827	37¢ Santa Claus with Trumpet die cut 10.5 x 10.75 . .	2.25	....	....	....	2.00	1.00
	die cut 10.5 x 10.75 . .	2.25	....	....	....	2.00	1.00
3825-28	37¢ Christmas Music Makers, self-adhesive, 4 varieties attached, die cut 10.5 x 10.75	4.25	....	....	....	7.00	4.00
3828b	same, bklt pane of 4 (3825-28)	4.25	....	....	....	7.00	....
3828c	same, bklt pane of 6 (3827-28, 3825-26 x 2)	5.50	....	....	....	11.00	....
3828d	same, bklt pane of 6 (3825-26, 3827-28 x 2)	5.50	....	....	....	11.00	....

3829, 3829A, 3830, 3830D

SCOTT NO.	DESCRIPTION	FIRST DAY COVERS SING	FIRST DAY COVERS PL. BLK.	MINT SHEET	PLATE BLOCK	UNUSED F/NH	USED
3829	37¢ Snowy Egret, self-adhesive coil, die cut 8.5	1.95	....	....	....	1.25	.40
....	same, pl# strip of 5 . .	....	....	....	....	10.00	....
3829A	37¢ Snowy Egret, self-adhesive coil, die cut 9.5	1.95	....	....	....	1.25	.35
....	same, pl# strip of 5 . .	....	....	....	....	11.00	....
3830	37¢ Snowy Egret, self adhesive	2.25	....	....	....	1.25	.35
3830a	same, bklt pane of 20	....	....	....	....	26.00	....
3830D	37¢ Snowy Egret, w/ USPS microprinting . .	2.25	....	....	....	10.00	1.50
3830Dc	Booklet Pane of 20 . .	....	....	....	....	170.00	....

3831

PACIFIC CORAL REEF

3831a *Emperor angelfish, blue & mound coral*
3831b *Humphead wrasse, Moorish idol*
3831c *Bumphead parrotfish*
3831d *Black-spotted puffer, threadfin butterflyfish*
3831e *Hawksbill turtle, palette surgeonfish*
3831f *Pink anemonefish, sea anemone*
3831g *Snowflake moray eel, Spanish dancer*
3831h *Lionfish*
3831i *Triton's trumpet*
3831j *Oriental sweetlips, bluestreak cleaner wrasse, mushroom coral*

SCOTT NO.	DESCRIPTION	FIRST DAY COVERS SING	FIRST DAY COVERS PL. BLK.	MINT SHEET	PLATE BLOCK	UNUSED F/NH	USED
3831	37¢ Pacific Coral Reef, 10 varieties, attached, self-adhesive	....	....	15.00(10)	....	15.00	....
....	set of singles	25.00	....	....	....	....	7.00

2004 COMMEMORATIVES

SCOTT NO.	DESCRIPTION	FIRST DAY COVERS SING	FIRST DAY COVERS PL. BLK.	MINT SHEET	PLATE BLOCK	UNUSED F/NH	USED
3832/3886	(3832, 3834-35, 3837-43 3854, 3857-63, 3865-71, 3876-77, 3880-86) 34 varieties		....	....	....	45.00	18.00

3832

3834

3835

SCOTT NO.	DESCRIPTION	FIRST DAY COVERS SING	FIRST DAY COVERS PL. BLK.	MINT SHEET	PLATE BLOCK	UNUSED F/NH	USED
3832	37¢ Year of the Monkey, self-adhesive	2.25	4.75	22.00(20)	5.50	1.20	.40
3833	37¢ Candy Hearts, self-adhesive	2.25	....	....	....	1.20	.30
3833a	same, bklt pane of 20	....	....	....	....	23.00	....
3834	37¢ Paul Robeson, self-adhesive	2.25	4.75	25.00(20)	6.00	1.50	.35
3835	37¢ Theodore Seuss Geisel (Dr. Seuss) self-adhesive	2.25	4.75	22.00(20)	5.00	1.50	.35

3836

3833

3837

SCOTT NO.	DESCRIPTION	FIRST DAY COVERS SING	FIRST DAY COVERS PL. BLK.	MINT SHEET	PLATE BLOCK	UNUSED F/NH	USED
3836	37¢ White Lilacs and Pink Roses, self-adhesive	2.25	....	....	....	1.20	.30
3836a	same, bklt pane of 20	....	....	....	....	23.00	....
3837	60¢ Five varieties of Pink Roses, self-adhesive .	2.75	5.50	42.00(20)	9.50	2.35	1.00

3838

3839

SCOTT NO.	DESCRIPTION	FIRST DAY COVERS SING	FIRST DAY COVERS PL. BLK.	MINT SHEET	PLATE BLOCK	UNUSED F/NH	USED
3838	37¢ United States Air Force Academy, self-adhesive	2.25	4.75	22.00(20)	5.50	1.20	.35
3839	37¢ Henry Mancini, self-adhesive	2.25	4.75	22.00(20)	5.50	1.20	.35

3840

3841

3842

3843

SCOTT NO.	DESCRIPTION	FIRST DAY COVERS SING	FIRST DAY COVERS PL. BLK.	MINT SHEET	PLATE BLOCK	UNUSED F/NH	USED
3840-43	37¢ American Choreographers, self-adhesive, 4 varieties attached.	4.25	4.75	25.00(20)	12.00	6.00	5.00
3840	37¢ Martha Graham .	2.25	....	....	....	1.50	.70
3841	37¢ Alvin Ailey	2.25	....	....	....	1.50	.70
3842	37¢ Agnes de Mille . .	2.25	....	....	....	1.50	.70
3843	37¢ George Balanchine	2.25	....	....	....	1.50	.70

3844, 3845, 3846, 3847, 3848, 3849, 3850, 3851, 3852, 3853

SCOTT NO.	DESCRIPTION	FIRST DAY COVERS SING	FIRST DAY COVERS PL. BLK.	MINT SHEET	PLATE BLOCK	UNUSED F/NH	USED
3844-3853	(25¢) Eagle, water activated coil, strip of 10, perf. 9.75	6.00	....	....	....	20.00	....
....	same, pl# strip of 11 .	....	....	....	....	26.00	....
3844	(25¢) Eagle, gray with gold eagle, coil, perf. 9.75	2.25	....	....	....	2.00	.75
3845	(25¢) Eagle, gold with green eagle, coil, perf. 9.75.	2.25	....	....	....	2.00	.75
3846	(25¢) Eagle, red with gold eagle, coil, perf. 9.75.	2.25	....	....	....	2.00	.75
3847	(25¢) Eagle, gold with dull blue eagle, coil, perf. 9.75	2.25	....	....	....	2.00	.75
3848	(25¢) Eagle, Prussian blue with gold eagle, coil, perf. 9.75	2.25	....	....	....	2.00	.75
3849	(25¢) Eagle, gold with gray eagle, coil, perf. 9.75	2.25	....	....	....	2.00	.75
3850	(25¢) Eagle, Prussian green with gold eagle, coil, perf. 9.75	2.25	....	....	....	2.00	.75
3851	(25¢) Eagle, gold with Prussian blue eagle, coil, perf. 9.75	2.25	....	....	....	2.00	.75
3852	(25¢) Eagle, dull blue with gold eagle, coil, perf. 9.75	2.25	....	....	....	2.00	.75
3853	(25¢) Eagle, gold with red eagle, coil, perf. 9.75	2.25	....	....	....	2.00	.75

3855

3854

3856

SCOTT NO.	DESCRIPTION	FIRST DAY COVERS SING	FIRST DAY COVERS PL. BLK.	MINT SHEET	PLATE BLOCK	UNUSED F/NH	USED
3854	37¢ Lewis & Clark Bicentennial, self-adhesive	2.25	4.75	35.00(20)	9.00	2.00	.40
3855	37¢ Lewis & Clark Bicentennial, Lewis booklet single .	2.25	....	....	....	1.75	1.00
3856	37¢ Lewis & Clark Bicentennial, Clark booklet single . .	2.25	....	....	....	1.75	1.00
3855-56	37¢ Lewis & Clark, pair	5.00	....	....	....	3.75	....
3856b	37¢ Lewis & Clark: The Corps of Discovery, 1804-06, self-adhesive, bklt pane of 10	....	....	....	....	20.00	....
	complete booklet	....	....	....	....	38.00	....

3857

3858

3859

3860

3861

SCOTT NO.	DESCRIPTION	FIRST DAY COVERS SING	FIRST DAY COVERS PL. BLK.	MINT SHEET	PLATE BLOCK	UNUSED F/NH	USED
3857-61	37¢ Isamu Noguchi, self-adhesive, 5 varieties attached.	5.00	9.50	25.00(20)	14.00(10)	7.00	7.00
3857	37¢ Akari 25N	2.25	....	....	....	1.50	1.00
3858	37¢ Margaret La Farge Osborn	2.25	....	....	....	1.50	1.00
3859	37¢ Black Sun	2.25	....	....	....	1.50	1.00
3860	37¢ Mother and Child	2.25	....	....	....	1.50	1.00
3861	37¢ Figure (detail) . . .	2.25	....	....	....	1.50	1.00

3862

3864, 3874, 3874a, 3875

3863

SCOTT NO.	DESCRIPTION	FIRST DAY COVERS SING	FIRST DAY COVERS PL. BLK.	MINT SHEET	PLATE BLOCK	UNUSED F/NH	USED
3862	37¢ National WWII Memorial, self-adhesive	2.25	4.75	25.00(20)	6.00	1.50	.40
3863	37¢ 2004 Olympic Games, Athens, Greece, self-adhesive	2.25	4.75	22.00(20)	5.50	1.25	.30
3864	(5¢) Sea Coast, coil, perf. 9.75 vert.	2.25	....	....	....	.35	.25
....	same, pl # strip of 5 . .	....	....	....	....	2.50	....

3865 3866

3867 3868

SCOTT NO.	DESCRIPTION	FIRST DAY COVERS SING	FIRST DAY COVERS PL. BLK.	MINT SHEET	PLATE BLOCK	UNUSED F/NH	USED
3865-68	37¢ Art of Disney: Friendship, self-adhesive, 4 varieties attached.	4.25	4.75	30.00(20)	7.00	6.50	4.00
3865	37¢ Goofy, Mickey Mouse, Donald Duck .	2.25	....	....	....	1.75	.85
3866	37¢ Bambi, Thumper .	2.25	....	....	....	1.75	.85
3867	37¢ Mufasa, Simba . .	2.25	....	....	....	1.75	.85
3868	37¢ Jiminy Cricket, Pinocchio.	2.25	....	....	....	1.75	.85

3869

3870

SCOTT NO.	DESCRIPTION	FIRST DAY COVERS SING	FIRST DAY COVERS PL. BLK.	MINT SHEET	PLATE BLOCK	UNUSED F/NH	USED
3869	37¢ U.S.S. Constellation, self-adhesive	2.25	4.75	24.00(20)	6.00	1.50	.35
3870	37¢ R. Buckminster Fuller, self-adhesive	2.25	4.75	24.00(20)	5.50	1.40	.35

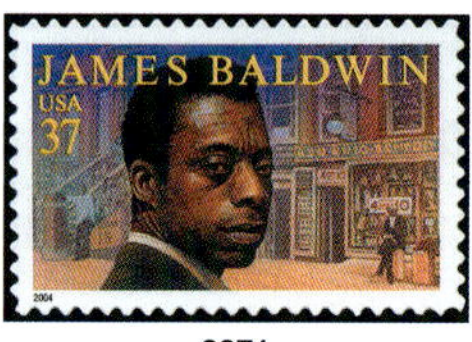

3871

3872

SCOTT NO.	DESCRIPTION	FIRST DAY COVERS SING	FIRST DAY COVERS PL. BLK.	MINT SHEET	PLATE BLOCK	UNUSED F/NH	USED
3871	37¢ James Baldwin, self-adhesive	2.25	4.75	22.00(20)	5.50	1.20	.35
3872	37¢ Giant Magnolias, self-adhesive	2.25	....	....	....	1.20	.40
3872a	same, bklt pane of 20	....	....	....	....	26.00	....

3873

ART OF THE AMERICAN INDIAN

3873a	*Mimbres bowl*	**3873f**	*Mississippian dffigy*
3873b	*Kutenai parfleche*	**3873g**	*Acoma pot*
3873c	*Tlingit sculptures*	**3873h**	*Navajo weaving*
3873d	*Ho-Chunk bag*	**3873i**	*Seneca carving*
3873e	*Seminole doll*	**3873j**	*Luiseno basket*

SCOTT NO.	DESCRIPTION	FIRST DAY COVERS SING	FIRST DAY COVERS PL. BLK.	MINT SHEET	PLATE BLOCK	UNUSED F/NH	USED
3873	37¢ Art of the American Indian, 10 varieties attached.	....	....	28.00(10)	....	28.00	....
....	set of singles	25.00	....	....	....	....	8.00
3874	(5¢) Sea Coast, coil, perf. 10 vert., self-adhesive	2.25	....	....	....	.55	.30
....	same, pl# strip of 5 . .	....	....	....	....	4.75	....
3874a	(5¢) Sea Coast with small date, coil, die cut 10 vert., self-adhesive	2.25	....	....	....	.45	.30
....	same, pl# strip of 5 . .	....	....	....	....	3.50	....
3875	(5¢) Sea Coast, coil, perf. 11.5 vert., self-adhesive	2.25	....	....	....	.45	.30
....	same, pl# strip of 5 . .	....	....	....	....	3.50	....

3876

3877

SCOTT NO.	DESCRIPTION	FIRST DAY COVERS SING	FIRST DAY COVERS PL. BLK.	MINT SHEET	PLATE BLOCK	UNUSED F/NH	USED
3876	37¢ John Wayne	2.25	4.75	28.00(20)	6.50	1.50	.40
....	same, uncut sheet of 120	....	....	120.00(20)	....	120.00	....
....	cross gutter block of 8	....	....	....	....	21.00	....
....	block of 8 with vert. gutter	....	....	....	....	13.50	....
....	horizontal pair with vertical gutter.	....	....	....	....	4.00	....
....	vertical pair with horizontal gutter.	....	....	....	....	3.00	....
3877	37¢ Sickle Cell Disease Awareness.	2.25	4.75	22.00(20)	5.50	1.20	.40

3878

CLOUDSCAPES

3878a	*Cirrus radiatus*	**3878i**	*Altocumulus castellanus*
3878b	*Cirrostratus fibratus*	**3878j**	*Alotcumulus lenticularis*
3878c	*Cirrocumulus undulatus*	**3878k**	*Stratocumulus undulatus*
3878d	*Cumulonimbus mammatus*	**3878l**	*Stratus opacus*
3878e	*Cumulonimbus incus*	**3878m**	*Cumulus humilis*
3878f	*Alocumulus stratiformis*	**3878n**	*Cumulus congestus*
3878g	*Altostratus translucidus*	**3878o**	*Cumulonimbus with tornado*
3878h	*Altocumulus undulatus*		

SCOTT NO.	DESCRIPTION	FIRST DAY COVERS SING	FIRST DAY COVERS PL. BLK.	MINT SHEET	PLATE BLOCK	UNUSED F/NH	USED
3878	37¢ Cloudscapes, 15 varieties attached .	35.00	....	24.00(15)	....	24.00	....
....	set of singles	35.00	....	....	....	....	14.00

3879

3880

SCOTT NO.	DESCRIPTION	FIRST DAY COVERS SING	FIRST DAY COVERS PL. BLK.	MINT SHEET	PLATE BLOCK	UNUSED F/NH	USED
3879	37¢ Madonna & Child, self-adhesive, die cut 10.75 x 11	2.25	....	....	....	1.25	.30
3879a	same, bklt pane of 20	....	....	....	....	26.00	....
3880	37¢ Hanukkah-Dreidel, self-adhesive	2.25	4.75	21.00(20)	5.50	1.25	.30

3881

3882

SCOTT NO.	DESCRIPTION	FIRST DAY COVERS SING	FIRST DAY COVERS PL. BLK.	MINT SHEET	PLATE BLOCK	UNUSED F/NH	USED
3881	37¢ Kwanzaa-People in Robes, self-adhesive	2.25	4.75	21.00(20)	5.50	1.25	.35
3882	37¢ Moss Hart, self-adhesive	2.25	4.75	21.00(20)	5.50	1.25	.40

3883, 3887, 3892

3884, 3888, 3891

3885, 3889, 3894

3886, 3890, 3893

SCOTT NO.	DESCRIPTION	FIRST DAY COVERS SING	FIRST DAY COVERS PL. BLK.	MINT SHEET	PLATE BLOCK	UNUSED F/NH	USED
3883-86	37¢ Santa Christmas Ornaments, self-adhesive, 4 attached	4.25	4.75	27.00(20)	7.00	6.00	4.25
3883	37¢ Purple Santa Ornament	2.25	....	....	....	1.85	.55
3884	37¢ Green Santa Ornament	2.25	....	....	....	1.85	.55
3885	37¢ Blue Santa Ornament	2.25	....	....	....	1.85	.55
3886	37¢ Red Santa Ornament	2.25	....	....	....	1.85	.55
3886b	same, bklt pane of 20	....	....	....	....	32.00	....
3887	37¢ Purple Santa Ornament, die cut 10.25 x 10.75 .	2.25	....	....	....	1.85	.55
3888	37¢ Green Santa Ornament, die cut 10.25 x 10.75 .	2.25	....	....	....	1.85	.55
3889	37¢ Blue Santa Ornament, die cut 10.25 x 10.75 .	2.25	....	....	....	1.85	.55
3890	37¢ Red Santa Ornament, die cut 10.25 x 10.75 .	2.25	....	....	....	1.85	.55
3887-90	37¢ Santa Christmas Ornaments, self-adhesive, 4 attached die cut 10.25 x 10.75.	4.25	....	....	....	7.75	3.50
3890b	same, bklt pane of 4 .	4.25	....	....	....	7.75	....
3890c	same, bklt pane of 6 (3889-90, 3887-88 x 2)	5.50	....	....	....	12.00	....
3890d	same, bklt pane of 6 (3887-88, 3889-90 x 2)	5.50	....	....	....	12.00	....
3891	37¢ Green Santa Ornament, die cut 8 . .	2.25	....	....	....	3.00	1.00
3892	37¢ Purple Santa Ornament, die cut 8 . .	2.25	....	....	....	3.00	1.00
3893	37¢ Red Santa Ornament, die cut 8 . .	2.25	....	....	....	3.00	1.00
3894	37¢ Blue Santa Ornament, die cut 8 . .	2.25	....	....	....	3.00	1.00
3891-94	37¢ Christmas Ornaments, self-adhesive, 4 attached, die cut 8.	4.25	....	....	....	14.00	4.00
3894b	same, bklt pane of 18	15.00	....	....	....	52.00	....

3895

CHINESE NEW YEAR TYPES OF 1992-2004

3895a	*Rat*	**3895g**	*Horse*
3895b	*Ox*	**3895h**	*Ram*
3895c	*Tiger*	**3895i**	*Monkey*
3895d	*Rabbit*	**3895j**	*Rooster*
3895e	*Dragon*	**3895k**	*Dog*
3895f	*Snake*	**3895l**	*Boar*

SCOTT NO.	DESCRIPTION	FIRST DAY COVERS SING	FIRST DAY COVERS PL. BLK.	MINT SHEET	PLATE BLOCK	UNUSED F/NH	USED
3895	37¢ Chinese New Year, self-adhesive, 24 varieties attached .	....	....	30.00(24)	....	30.00	....
....	set of singles	23.50	....	....	....	....	13.00

2005 COMMEMORATIVES

SCOTT NO.	DESCRIPTION	FIRST DAY COVERS SING	FIRST DAY COVERS PL. BLK.	MINT SHEET	PLATE BLOCK	UNUSED F/NH	USED
3896/3964	**(3896-97, 3904-3909, 3911-25, 3930, 3936 3938-43, 3945-52 3961-64) 43 varieties**		....	....	....	**56.00**	**27.00**

3896

3897

3898

SCOTT NO.	DESCRIPTION	FIRST DAY COVERS SING	FIRST DAY COVERS PL. BLK.	MINT SHEET	PLATE BLOCK	UNUSED F/NH	USED
3896	37¢ Marian Anderson, self-adhesive	3.00	4.75	27.00(20)	6.25	1.20	.40
3897	37¢ Ronald Reagan, self-adhesive	3.00	4.75	22.00(20)	5.50	1.35	.40
....	same, uncut sheet of 120	....	....	120.00(120)	....	120.00	....
....	cross gutter block of 4	....	....	....	....	9.50	....
....	horiz. pair with vert. gutter	....	....	....	....	4.00	....
....	vert. pair with horiz. gutter	....	....	....	....	3.00	....
3898	37¢ Love-Hand and Flower Bouquet, self-adhesive	3.00	....	....	....	1.20	.30
3898a	same, bklt pane of 20	....	....	....	....	22.00	....

NORTHEAST DECIDUOUS FOREST

NATURE OF AMERICA

3899

NORTHEAST DECIDUOUS FOREST

3899a	*Eastern buckmouth*	**3899f**	*Long-tailed weasel*
3899b	*Red-shouldered hawk*	**3899g**	*Wild turkey*
3899c	*Eastern red bat*	**3899h**	*Ovenbird*
3899d	*White-tailed deer*	**3899i**	*Red eft*
3899e	*Black bear*	**3899j**	*Eastern chipmunk*

SCOTT NO.	DESCRIPTION	FIRST DAY COVERS SING	FIRST DAY COVERS PL. BLK.	MINT SHEET	PLATE BLOCK	UNUSED F/NH	USED
3899	37¢ Northeast Deciduous Forest, self-adhesive, 10 varieties attached .	....	....	15.00(10)	....	15.00	....
....	set of singles	25.00	....	....	....	....	7.75

3900 3901 3902 3903

SCOTT NO.	DESCRIPTION	FIRST DAY COVERS SING	FIRST DAY COVERS PL. BLK.	MINT SHEET	PLATE BLOCK	UNUSED F/NH	USED
3900	37¢ Hyacinth	3.00	....	....	....	1.75	.45
3901	37¢ Daffodil	3.00	....	....	....	1.75	.45
3902	37¢ Tulip	3.00	....	....	....	1.75	.45
3903	37¢ Iris.	3.00	....	....	....	1.75	.45
3900-03	37¢ Spring Flowers, self-adhesive, 4 varieties attached . .	4.25	....	....	....	7.00	....
3903b	same, bklt pane of 20	....	....	....	....	32.00	....

3904

3905

SCOTT NO.	DESCRIPTION	FIRST DAY COVERS SING	FIRST DAY COVERS PL. BLK.	MINT SHEET	PLATE BLOCK	UNUSED F/NH	USED
3904	37¢ Robert Penn Warren, self-adhesive	3.00	4.75	22.00(20)	5.50	1.50	.35
3905	37¢ Yip Harburg, self-adhesive	3.00	4.75	22.00(20)	5.50	1.50	.35

3906 3907

3908 3909

SCOTT NO.	DESCRIPTION	FIRST DAY COVERS SING	FIRST DAY COVERS PL. BLK.	MINT SHEET	PLATE BLOCK	UNUSED F/NH	USED
3906-09	37¢ American Scientists, self-adhesive, 4 attached	4.25	4.75	27.00(20)	7.00	6.00	3.50
3906	37¢ Barbara McClintock	3.00	....	....	....	1.50	.60
3907	37¢ Josiah Willard Gibbs	3.00	....	....	....	1.50	.60
3908	37¢ John von Neuman	3.00	....	....	....	1.50	.60
3909	37¢ Richard Feynman	3.00	....	....	....	1.50	.60
....	same, plate blk of 8 with Top Label.	....	....	....	10.00(8)	....	....

3910

MODERN AMERICAN ARCHITECTURE

3910a	*Guggenheim Museum*	**3910g**	*National Gallery of Art*
3910b	*Chrysler Building*	**3910h**	*Glass House*
3910c	*Vanna Venturi House*	**3910i**	*Yale Art and Architecture Bldg.*
3910d	*TWA Terminal*	**3910j**	*High Museum of Atlanta*
3910e	*Walt Disney Concert Hall*	**3910k**	*Exeter Academy Library*
3910f	*860-880 Lake Shore Drive*	**3910l**	*Hancock Center*

SCOTT NO.	DESCRIPTION	FIRST DAY COVERS SING	FIRST DAY COVERS PL. BLK.	MINT SHEET	PLATE BLOCK	UNUSED F/NH	USED
3910	37¢ Modern American Architecture, self-adhesive, 12 varieties attached. .	....	....	15.00(12)	....	15.00	....
....	set of singles	....	....	....	....	....	9.00

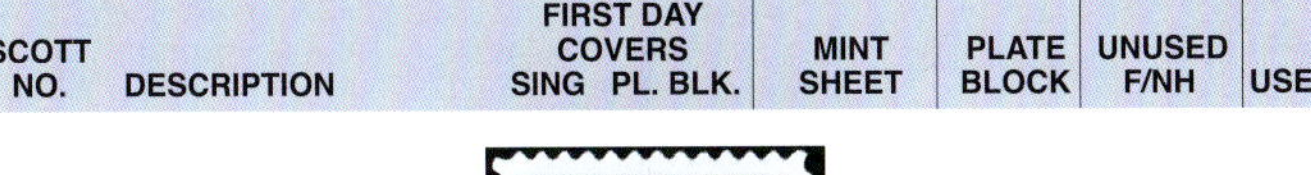

3911

SCOTT NO.	DESCRIPTION	FIRST DAY COVERS SING	FIRST DAY COVERS PL. BLK.	MINT SHEET	PLATE BLOCK	UNUSED F/NH	USED
3911	37¢ Henry Fonda, self-adhesive	3.00	4.75	30.00(20)	8.00	1.50	.50
....	same, uncut sheet of 180	....	....	270.00(180)	....	270.00	....

3912 3913

3914 3915

SCOTT NO.	DESCRIPTION	FIRST DAY COVERS SING	FIRST DAY COVERS PL. BLK.	MINT SHEET	PLATE BLOCK	UNUSED F/NH	USED
3912-15	37¢ Disney Characters, self-adhesive, 4 attached	4.25	4.75	24.00(20)	6.50	6.00	3.50
3912	37¢ Pluto, Mickey Mouse	3.00	....	....	....	1.50	.50
3913	37¢ Mad Hatter, Alice	3.00	....	....	....	1.50	.50
3914	37¢ Flounder, Ariel. . .	3.00	....	....	....	1.50	.50
3915	37¢ Snow White, Dopey	3.00	....	....	....	1.50	.50

3916

3917

3918

3919

3920

3921

3922

3923

3924

3925

ADVANCES IN AVIATION

3916	Boeing 247	**3921**	Lockheed P80 Shooting Star
3917	Consolidated PBY Catalina	**3922**	Consolidated B24 Liberator
3918	Grumman F6F	**3923**	Boeing B29 Superfortress
3919	Republic P47 Thunderbolt	**3924**	Beechcraft 35 Bonanza
3920	E & R Corp. Ercoupe 415	**3925**	Northrop YB-49 Flying Wing

SCOTT NO.	DESCRIPTION	FIRST DAY COVERS SING	FIRST DAY COVERS PL. BLK.	MINT SHEET	PLATE BLOCK	UNUSED F/NH	USED
3916-25	37¢ Advances in Aviation, self-adhesive, 10 attached	25.00	....	25.00(20)	16.00(10)	15.00	11.00
....	set of singles	....	....		....	15.00	9.00

3926

3927

3928

3929

SCOTT NO.	DESCRIPTION	FIRST DAY COVERS SING	FIRST DAY COVERS PL. BLK.	MINT SHEET	PLATE BLOCK	UNUSED F/NH	USED
3926	37¢ Blanket w/ yellow, orange, and red stripes	3.00	....	....	....	1.50	.85
3927	37¢ Blanket w/ black, orange red, and yellow	3.00	....	....	....	1.50	.85
3928	37¢ Blanket w/ yellow and black diamonds. .	3.00	....	....	....	1.50	.85
3929	37¢ Blanket w/ zigzag diamonds.	3.00	....	....	....	1.50	.85
3926-29	37¢ Rio Grande Blankets, self-adhesive, 4 attached	4.25	....	....	....	6.50	4.00
3929b	same, bklt pane of 20	15.00	....	....	....	29.00	....

3930

3931

3936

3932

3933

3934

3935

SCOTT NO.	DESCRIPTION	FIRST DAY COVERS SING	FIRST DAY COVERS PL. BLK.	MINT SHEET	PLATE BLOCK	UNUSED F/NH	USED
3930	37¢ Presidential Libraries Act, 50th Anniv., self-adhesive	3.00	4.75	22.00(20)	5.50	1.25	.35
3931	37¢ 1953 Studebaker Starliner	3.00	....	....	....	1.50	.50
3932	37¢ 1954 Kaiser Darren	3.00	....	....	....	1.50	.50
3933	37¢ 1953 Chevrolet Corvette	3.00	....	....	....	1.50	.50
3934	37¢ 1952 Nash Healey	3.00	....	....	....	1.50	.50
3935	37¢ 1955 Ford Thunderbird	3.00	....	....	....	1.50	.50
3935b	same, bklt pane of 20	15.00	....	....	....	30.00	....
3936	37¢ Arthur Ashe, self-adhesive	3.00	4.75	22.00(20)	5.50	1.20	.40

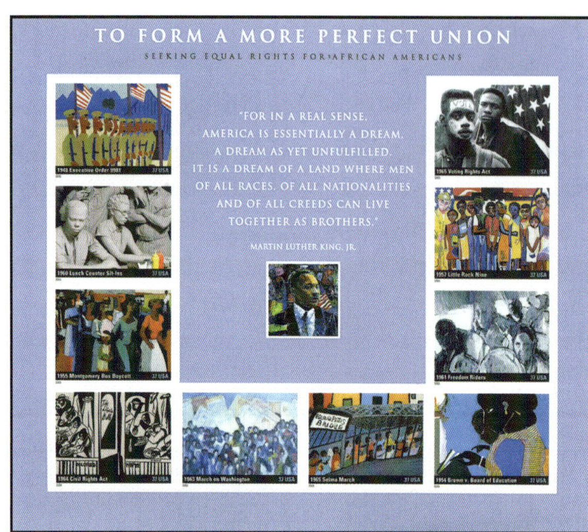

3937

TO FORM A MORE PERFECT UNION

3937a 1948 Executive Order 9981
3937b 1965 Voting Rights Act
3937c 1960 Lunch Counter Sit-Ins
3937d 1957 Litte Rock Nine
3937e 1955 Montgomery Bus Boycott
3937f 1961 Freedom Riders
3937g 1964 Civil Rights Act
3937h 1963 March on Washington
3937i 1965 Selma March
3937j 1954 Brown vs. Board of Education

SCOTT NO.	DESCRIPTION	FIRST DAY COVERS SING	FIRST DAY COVERS PL. BLK.	MINT SHEET	PLATE BLOCK	UNUSED F/NH	USED
3937	37¢ To Form A More Perfect Union, self-adhesive, 10 attached. .	15.00	....	18.00(10)	....	18.00	10.00
....	set of singles	....	....	....	....	18.00	8.75

3938

3939

3943

3940

3941

3942

SCOTT NO.	DESCRIPTION	FIRST DAY COVERS SING	FIRST DAY COVERS PL. BLK.	MINT SHEET	PLATE BLOCK	UNUSED F/NH	USED
3938	37¢ Child Health, self-adhesive	3.00	4.75	24.00(20)	6.00	1.35	.35
3939-42	37¢ Let's Dance, self-adhesive, 4 attached .	4.25	4.75	30.00(20)	14.00	7.50	5.75
3939	37¢ Merengue	3.00	....	....	....	1.75	1.25
3940	37¢ Salsa.	3.00	....	....	....	1.75	1.25
3941	37¢ Cha Cha Cha . . .	3.00	....	....	....	1.75	1.25
3942	37¢ Mambo	3.00	....	....	....	1.75	1.25
3943	37¢ Greta Garbo, self-adhesive	3.00	4.75	22.00(20)	5.50	1.20	1.25

3944

JIM HENSON AND THE MUPPETS

3944a Kermit the Frog
3944b Fozzie Bear
3944c Sam the Eagle and flag
3944d Miss Piggy
3944e Statler and Waldorf
3944f The Swedish Chef and fruit
3944g Animal
3944h Dr. Brunsen Honeydew and Beaker
3944i Rowlf the Dog
3944j The Great Gonzo and Camilia
3944k Jim Henson

SCOTT NO.	DESCRIPTION	FIRST DAY COVERS SING	FIRST DAY COVERS PL. BLK.	MINT SHEET	PLATE BLOCK	UNUSED F/NH	USED
3944	37¢ Jim Henson and the Muppets, self-adhesive, 11 varieties attached. .	12.00	....	15.00(11)	....	15.00	....
....	set of singles	30.00	....	....	....	15.00	9.00

3945

3946

3947

3948

SCOTT NO.	DESCRIPTION	FIRST DAY COVERS SING	FIRST DAY COVERS PL. BLK.	MINT SHEET	PLATE BLOCK	UNUSED F/NH	USED
3945-48	37¢ Constellations, self-adhesive, 4 attached	4.25	4.75	28.00(20)	6.50	6.00	4.00
3945	37¢ Leo	3.00	....	....	....	1.75	.90
3946	37¢ Orion.	3.00	....	....	....	1.75	.90
3947	37¢ Lyra.	3.00	....	....	....	1.75	.90
3948	37¢ Pegasus	3.00	....	....	....	1.75	.90

3949, 3953, 3957

3950, 3954, 3958

3951, 3955, 3959

3952, 3956, 3960

SCOTT NO.	DESCRIPTION	FIRST DAY COVERS SING	FIRST DAY COVERS PL. BLK.	MINT SHEET	PLATE BLOCK	UNUSED F/NH	USED
3949-52	37¢ Christmas Cookies, self-adhesive, 4 attached	4.25	4.75	28.00(20)	6.75	6.00	4.00
3949	37¢ Santa Claus cookie	3.00	....	....	....	1.50	.55
3950	37¢ Snowmen cookie	3.00	....	....	....	1.50	.55
3951	37¢ Angel cookie	3.00	....	....	....	1.50	.55
3952	37¢ Elves cookie	3.00	....	....	....	1.50	.55
3953	37¢ Santa Claus cookie, die cut 10.75 X 11 . . .	3.00	....	....	....	1.75	.60
3954	37¢ Snowmen cookie, die cut 10.75 X 11 . . .	3.00	....	....	....	1.75	.60
3955	37¢ Angel cookie, die cut 10.75 X 11 . . .	3.00	....	....	....	1.75	.60
3956	37¢ Elves cookie, die cut 10.75 X 11 . . .	3.00	....	....	....	1.75	.60
3953-56	37¢ Christmas cookies, self-adhesive, 4 attached, die cut 10.75 X 11 . . .	4.25	....	....	....	7.50	4.00
3956b	same, bklt pane of 20	....	....	....	....	38.00	....

SCOTT NO.	DESCRIPTION	FIRST DAY COVERS SING	FIRST DAY COVERS PL. BLK.	MINT SHEET	PLATE BLOCK	UNUSED F/NH	USED
3957	37¢ Santa Claus cookie, die cut 10.5 X 10.75. .	3.00	....	....	....	2.00	1.00
3958	37¢ Snowmen cookie, die cut 10.5 X 10.75. .	3.00	....	....	....	2.00	1.00
3959	37¢ Angel cookie, die cut 10.5 X 10.75. .	3.00	....	....	....	2.00	1.00
3960	37¢ Elves cookie, die cut 10.5 X 10.75. .	3.00	....	....	....	2.00	1.00
3957-60	37¢ Christmas Cookies, self-adhesvie, 4 attached die cut 10.5 X 10.75. .	4.25	....	....	....	8.50	5.50
3960b	same, booklet pane of 4	4.25	....	....	....	8.50	....
3960c	same, bklt pane of 6 (3959-60, 3957-58 X 2)	5.50	....	....	....	14.00	....
3960d	same, bklt pane of 6 (3957-58, 3959-60 X 2)	5.50	....	....	....	14.00	....

3961 3962

3963 3964

SCOTT NO.	DESCRIPTION	FIRST DAY COVERS SING	FIRST DAY COVERS PL. BLK.	MINT SHEET	PLATE BLOCK	UNUSED F/NH	USED
3961-64	37¢ Distinguished Marines, self-adhesive, 4 attached	4.25	4.75	28.00(20)	6.50	6.00	5.00
....	same, plate block of 8	....	....	....	12.00(8)	....	....
3961	37¢ Lt. General John A. Lejeune.	3.00	....	....	....	1.50	1.05
3962	37¢ Lt. General Lewis B. Puller.	3.00	....	....	....	1.50	1.05
3963	37¢ Sgt. John Basilone	3.00	....	....	....	1.50	1.05
3964	37¢ Sgt. Major Daniel J. Daly	3.00	....	....	....	1.50	1.05

3965-3975

3976

3978-3983, 3985

SCOTT NO.	DESCRIPTION	FIRST DAY COVERS SING	FIRST DAY COVERS PL. BLK.	MINT SHEET	PLATE BLOCK	UNUSED F/NH	USED
3965	(39¢) Flag and Statue of Liberty	3.00	4.75	120.00(100)	18.00	1.50	1.00
3966	(39¢) Flag and Statue of Liberty, self-adhesive	3.00	4.75	24.00(20)	7.00	1.50	.40
3966a	same, bklt pane of 20	16.00	....	....	....	30.00	....
3967	(39¢) Flag and Statue of Liberty, coil, die cut 9.75.	3.00	....	....	....	1.50	.70
....	same, pl# strip of 5 . .	....	....	....	....	12.00	....
3968	(39¢) Flag and Statue of Liberty, self-adhesive coil, die cut 8.5.	3.00	....	....	....	1.50	.35
....	same, pl# strip of 5 . .	....	....	....	....	13.00	....
3969	(39¢) Flag and Statue of Liberty, coil, die cut 10.25	3.00	....	....	....	2.00	.35
....	same, pl# strip of 5 . .	....	....	....	....	14.00	....
3970	(39¢) Flag and Statue of Liberty, self-adhesive coil, die cut 9.5.	3.00	....	....	....	3.00	.35
....	same, pl# strip of 5 . .	....	....	....	....	18.00	....
3972	(39¢) Flag and Statue of Liberty, self-adhesive die cut 11.25 X 10.75.	3.00	....	....	....	1.50	.35
3972a	same, bklt pane of 20	16.00	....	....	....	26.00	....
3973	(39¢) Flag and Statue of Liberty, self-adhesive die cut 10.25 X 10.75	3.00	....	....	....	1.50	.25
3973a	same, bklt pane of 20	16.00	....	....	....	26.00	....
3974	(39¢) Flag and Statue of Liberty, self-adhesive die cut 11.25 X 10.75.	3.00	....	....	....	1.80	.70
3974a	same, bklt pane of 4. .	4.50	....	....	....	8.00	....
3974b	same, bklt pane of 6 .	6.00	....	....	....	12.00	....

SCOTT NO.	DESCRIPTION	FIRST DAY COVERS SING	FIRST DAY COVERS PL. BLK.	MINT SHEET	PLATE BLOCK	UNUSED F/NH	USED
3975	(39¢) Flag and Statue of Liberty, self-adhesive die cut 8.	3.00	....	....	....	1.55	.35
....	same, bklt pane of 18	16.00	....	....	....	32.00	....
3976	(39¢) Birds	3.00	....	....	....	1.60	.35
3976a	same, bklt pane of 20	30.00	....	....	....	31.00	....
3978	39¢ Flag and Statue of Liberty, self-adhesive die cut 11.25 X 10.75.	3.00	4.75	26.00(20)	6.50	1.50	.35
3978a	same, bklt pane of 10	....	....	....	....	15.00	....
3978b	same, bklt pane of 20	....	....	....	....	32.00	....
3979	39¢ Flag and Statue of Liberty, coil, perf 10	3.00	....	....	....	1.50	.40
....	same, pl# strip of 5 . .	....	....	....	....	9.00	....
3980	same, self-adhesive coil, die cut 11	3.00	....	....	....	1.50	.90
....	same, pl# strip of 5 . .	....	....	....	....	9.50	....
3981	same self-adhesive coil w/ USPS micro die cut 9.5	3.00	....	....	....	2.00	.45
....	same, pl# strip of 5 . .	....	....	....	....	12.00	....
3982	same, self-adhesive coil, die cut 10.25 vertical .	3.00	....	....	....	1.50	.40
....	same, pl# strip of 5 . .	....	....	....	....	10.00	....
3983	same, self-adhesive coil, die cut 8.5	3.00	....	....	....	1.50	.45
....	same, pl# strip of 5 . .	....	....	....	....	10.00	....
3985	39¢ Flag and Statue of Liberty, self-adhesive, die cut 11.25 X 10.75 on 2 or 3 sides.	3.00	....	....	....	1.50	.50
3985a	same, bklt pane of 20	....	....	....	....	26.00	....
3985b	same, die cut 11.1 on 2 or 3	3.00	....	....	....	1.50	.75
3985c	same, bklt pane of 4 .	....	....	....	....	6.00	....
3985d	same, bklt pane of 6 .	....	....	....	....	8.50	....

2006 COMMEMORATIVES

SCOTT NO.	DESCRIPTION	FIRST DAY COVERS SING	FIRST DAY COVERS PL. BLK.	MINT SHEET	PLATE BLOCK	UNUSED F/NH	USED
3987/4119	**(3987-96, 4020, 4021-28, 4030-32, 4073, 4077-83 4085-88, 4101-04 4117-19) 41 varieties**		**........**	**........**	**........**	**60.00**	**20.00**

3987 3988 3989 3990

3991 3992 3993 3994

FAVORITE CHILDREN'S BOOK ANIMALS

3987	The Very Hungry Caterpillar	**3991**	Wild Thing
3988	Wilbur	**3992**	Curious George
3989	Fox in Socks	**3993**	Olivia
3990	Maisy	**3994**	Frederick

SCOTT NO.	DESCRIPTION	FIRST DAY COVERS SING	FIRST DAY COVERS PL. BLK.	MINT SHEET	PLATE BLOCK	UNUSED F/NH	USED
3987-94	39¢ Children's Book Animals, self-adhesive 8 attached	10.00	....	25.00(16)	14.00(8)	12.50	10.00
....	set of singles	....	....	....	....	....	5.50
....	same, uncut sheet of 96	....	....	90.00(96)	....	90.00	....
....	cross gutter block of 8	....	....	....	....	17.50	....
....	blk of 8 w/ horiz. gutter	....	....	....	....	10.00	....
....	blk of 8 w/ vert. gutter	....	....	....	....	9.00	....
....	horz. pair w/ vert. gutter	....	....	....	....	2.50	....
....	vert. pair w/ horz. gutter	....	....	....	....	2.50	....

3995

3996

SCOTT NO.	DESCRIPTION	FIRST DAY COVERS SING	FIRST DAY COVERS PL. BLK.	MINT SHEET	PLATE BLOCK	UNUSED F/NH	USED
3995	39¢ 2006 Winter Olympic games, Turin, Italy, self-adhesive	3.00	4.75	24.00(20)	6.00	1.35	.40
3996	39¢ Hattie McDaniel, self-adhesive	3.00	4.75	25.00(20)	6.50	1.60	.40

SCOTT NO.	DESCRIPTION	FIRST DAY COVERS SING	FIRST DAY COVERS PL. BLK.	MINT SHEET	PLATE BLOCK	UNUSED F/NH	USED

CHINESE NEW YEAR TYPES OF 1992-2004

3997a	Rat	**3997g**	Horse
3997b	Ox	**3997h**	Ram
3997c	Tiger	**3997i**	Monkey
3997d	Rabbit	**3997j**	Rooster
3997e	Dragon	**3997k**	Dog
3997f	Snake	**3997l**	Boar

SCOTT NO.	DESCRIPTION	FIRST DAY COVERS SING	FIRST DAY COVERS PL. BLK.	MINT SHEET	PLATE BLOCK	UNUSED F/NH	USED
3997	39¢ Chinese New Year self-adhesive, 12 varieties attached . . .	....	....	20.00(12)	....	20.00	....
	set of singles	32.00	....	....	....	20.00	10.00

3998

4000, 4001, 4002

3999

SCOTT NO.	DESCRIPTION	FIRST DAY COVERS SING	FIRST DAY COVERS PL. BLK.	MINT SHEET	PLATE BLOCK	UNUSED F/NH	USED
3998	39¢ Wedding Doves, Dove Facing Left, self-adhesive	3.00	....	....	....	1.50	.35
3998a	same, bklt pane of 20	16.00	....	....	....	26.00	....
3999	63¢ Wedding Doves, Dove Facing Right, self-adhesive	3.00	....	....	....	3.00	1.80
3999a	same, bklt pane of 40	....	....	....	....	65.00	....
4000	24¢ Common Buckeye butterfly	3.00	4.75	77.00(100)	14.00	.90	.65
4001	24¢ Common Buckeye butterfly self-adhesive, die cut 11	3.00	4.75	15.00(20)	5.00	.90	.35
4001a	same, single from bklt. pane, die cut 10.75 X11.25	3.00	....	....	....	.85	.35
4001b	same, bklt pane of 10 (4001a)	....	....	....	....	8.50	....
4001c	same, bklt pane of 4 (4001a)	....	....	....	....	3.50	....
4001d	same, bklt pane of 6 (4001a)	....	....	....	....	5.00	....
4002	24¢ Common Buckeye butterfly, self-adhesive, coil, die cut 8.5.	3.00	....	....	....	.85	.30
....	same, pl# strip of 5 . .	....	....	....	....	6.00	....

4003, 4008, 4013

4004, 4009, 4014

4005, 4010, 4015

4006, 4011, 4016

4007, 4012, 4017

SCOTT NO.	DESCRIPTION	FIRST DAY COVERS SING	FIRST DAY COVERS PL. BLK.	MINT SHEET	PLATE BLOCK	UNUSED F/NH	USED
4003	39¢ Chili Peppers, self-adhesive, coil . . .	3.00	....	....	....	2.50	.60
4004	39¢ Beans, self-adhesive, coil	3.00	....	....	....	2.50	.60
4005	39¢ Sunflower and Seeds self-adhesive, coil . . .	3.00	....	....	....	2.50	.60
4006	39¢ Squashes, self-adhesive, coil	3.00	....	....	....	2.50	.60
4007	39¢ Corn, self-adhesive, coil	3.00	....	....	....	2.50	.60
4003-07	39¢ Crops of the Americas, coil, strip of 5	5.00	....	....	....	14.00	3.50
....	same, pl# strip of 5 . .	....	....	....	....	16.00	....
....	same, pl# strip of 11 .	....	....	....	....	30.00	....
4008	39¢ Chili Peppers, self-adhesive, bklt single, die cut 10.75 X 10.5. .	3.00	....	....	....	2.25	.40
4009	39¢ Beans, self-adhesive bklt single, die cut 10.75 X 10.5	3.00	....	....	....	2.25	.40
4010	39¢ Sunflower and Seeds self-adhesive, bklt single, die cut 10.75 X 10.5. .	3.00	....	....	....	2.25	.40
4011	39¢ Squashes, self-adhesive, bklt single die cut 10.75 X 10.5. .	3.00	....	....	....	2.25	.40
4012	39¢ Corn, self-adhesive bklt single, die cut 10.75 X 10.5	3.00	....	....	....	2.25	.40
4012b	same, bklt pane of 20	....	....	....	....	34.00	....
4013	39¢ Chili Peppers, self-adhesive, bklt single, die cut 10.75 X 11.25.	3.00	....	....	....	1.65	.75

SCOTT NO.	DESCRIPTION	FIRST DAY COVERS SING	FIRST DAY COVERS PL. BLK.	MINT SHEET	PLATE BLOCK	UNUSED F/NH	USED
4014	39¢ Beans, self-adhesive bklt single, die cut 10.75 X11.25	3.00	....	....	....	1.65	.75
4015	39¢ Sunflower and Seeds self-adhesive, bklt single, die cut 10.75 X11.25 .	3.00	....	....	....	1.65	.75
4016	39¢ Squashes, self-adhesive, bklt single die cut 10.75 X 11.25.	3.00	....	....	....	1.65	.75
4016a	same, bklt pane of 4 .	....	....	....	....	6.00	....
4017	39¢ Corn, self-adhesive bklt single, die cut 10.75 X 11.25	3.00	....	....	....	1.65	.75
4017b	same, bklt pane of 4 .	....	....	....	....	6.00	....
4017c	same, bklt pane of 6 (4013-16, 4017 X 2). .	....	....	....	....	13.00	....
4017d	same, bklt pane of 6 (4013-15, 4017, 4016 X2)	....	....	....	....	13.00	....

4018

4020

4019

SCOTT NO.	DESCRIPTION	FIRST DAY COVERS SING	FIRST DAY COVERS PL. BLK.	MINT SHEET	PLATE BLOCK	UNUSED F/NH	USED
4018	$4.05 X-Plane, self-adhesive	9.00	25.00	205.00(20)	50.00	12.00	8.00
4019	$14.40 X-Plane, self-adhesive	30.00	75.00	690.00(20)	180.00	41.00	30.00
4020	39¢ Sugar Ray Robinson, self-adhesive	3.00	4.75	23.00(20)	5.50	1.25	.50

4021 4022

4023 4024

SCOTT NO.	DESCRIPTION	FIRST DAY COVERS SING	FIRST DAY COVERS PL. BLK.	MINT SHEET	PLATE BLOCK	UNUSED F/NH	USED
4021-24	39¢ Benjamin Franklin (1706-90), self-adhesive 4 attached	4.25	4.75	38.00(20)	10.00	8.50	....
4021	39¢ Benjamin Franklin Statesman	3.00	....	....	....	2.00	1.10
4022	39¢ Benjamin Franklin Scientist.	3.00	....	....	....	2.00	1.10
4023	39¢ Benjamin Franklin Printer	3.00	....	....	....	2.00	1.10
4024	39¢ Benjamin Franklin Postmaster	3.00	....	....	....	2.00	1.10

4025 4026

4027 4028

SCOTT NO.	DESCRIPTION	FIRST DAY COVERS SING	FIRST DAY COVERS PL. BLK.	MINT SHEET	PLATE BLOCK	UNUSED F/NH	USED
4025-28	39¢ Disney Characters, self-adhesive, 4 attached	4.25	4.75	25.00(20)	6.50	6.00	....

SCOTT NO.	DESCRIPTION	FIRST DAY COVERS SING	PL. BLK.	MINT SHEET	PLATE BLOCK	UNUSED F/NH	USED
4025	39¢ Mickey and Minnie Mouse	3.00	....	....	....	1.30	.50
4026	39¢ Cinderella and Prince Charming	3.00	....	....	....	1.30	.50
4027	39¢ Beauty and the Beast	3.00	....	....	....	1.30	.50
4028	39¢ Lady and the Tramp	3.00	....	....	....	1.30	.50

4029

4030

SCOTT NO.	DESCRIPTION	FIRST DAY COVERS SING	PL. BLK.	MINT SHEET	PLATE BLOCK	UNUSED F/NH	USED
4029	39¢ Lovebirds, self-adhesive	3.00	....	....	....	1.50	.35
4029a	same, bklt pane of 20	....	....	....	....	32.00	....
4030	39¢ Katherine Anne Porter self-adhesive	3.00	4.75	24.00(20)	5.75	1.50	.35

4031

4032

SCOTT NO.	DESCRIPTION	FIRST DAY COVERS SING	PL. BLK.	MINT SHEET	PLATE BLOCK	UNUSED F/NH	USED
4031	39¢ Amber Alert, self-adhesive	3.00	4.75	24.00(20)	5.75	1.50	.40
4032	39¢ Purple Heart, self-adhesive	3.00	4.75	24.00(20)	5.75	1.50	.35

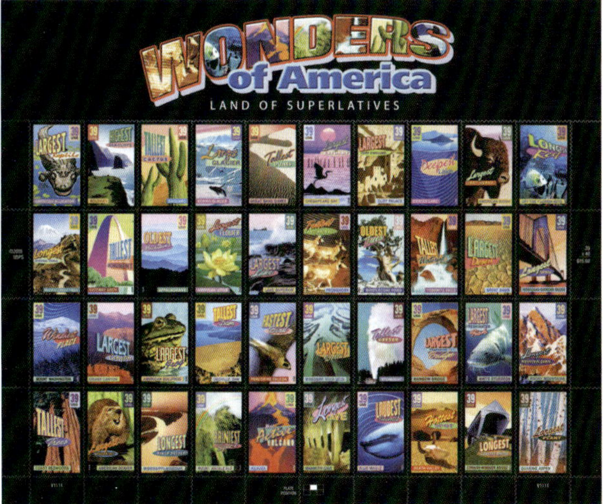

4033-4072

WONDERS OF AMERICA

4033 American Alligator
4034 Moloka'i
4035 Saguaro
4036 Bering Glacier
4037 Great Sand Dunes
4038 Chesapeake Bay
4039 Cliff Palace
4040 Crater Lake
4041 American Bison
4042 Off the Florida Keys
4043 Pacific Crest Trail
4044 Gateway Arch
4045 Appalachians
4046 American Lotus
4047 Lake Superior
4048 Pronghorn
4049 Bristlecone Pines
4050 Yosemite Falls
4051 Great Basin
4052 Verrazano-Narrows Bridge
4053 Mount Washington
4054 Grand Canyon
4055 American Bullfrog
4056 Oroville Dam
4057 Peregrine Falcon
4058 Mississippi River Delta
4059 Steamboat Geyser
4060 Rainbow Bridge
4061 White Sturgeon
4062 Rocky Mountains
4063 Coast Redwoods
4064 American Beaver
4065 Mississippi-Missouri
4066 Mount Wai'ale'ale
4067 Kilauea
4068 Mammoth Cave
4069 Blue Whale
4070 Death Valley
4071 Cornish-Windsor Bridge
4072 Quaking Aspen

SCOTT NO.	DESCRIPTION	FIRST DAY COVERS SING	PL. BLK.	MINT SHEET	PLATE BLOCK	UNUSED F/NH	USED
4033-72	39¢ Wonders of America, self-adhesive, 40 attached	....	....	40.00(40)	....	40.00	....
....	same, set of singles. .	....	....	....	....	40.00	34.00

4073, 4074a

SCOTT NO.	DESCRIPTION	FIRST DAY COVERS SING	PL. BLK.	MINT SHEET	PLATE BLOCK	UNUSED F/NH	USED
4073	39¢ Samuel de Champlain, self-adhesive	3.00	4.75	24.00(20)	6.00	1.40	.50
4074	39¢ Samuel de Champlain, souvenir sheet of 4 (joint issue,4074a x 2 and Canada 2156a x 2)	....	....	....	....	12.00	....
4074a	same, single from s/s .	....	....	....	....	2.50	1.60

4075

SCOTT NO.	DESCRIPTION	FIRST DAY COVERS SING	PL. BLK.	MINT SHEET	PLATE BLOCK	UNUSED F/NH	USED
4075	$1-$5 Washington 2006 World Exhibition, souvenir sheet of 3 . .	....	....	....	....	27.00	....
4075a	$1 Lincoln Memorial .	4.50	....	....	....	4.00	2.00
4075b	$2 U.S. Capitol	7.50	....	....	....	7.00	4.00
4075c	$5 "America"	15.00	....	....	....	17.00	10.00

4076

SCOTT NO.	DESCRIPTION	FIRST DAY COVERS SING	PL. BLK.	MINT SHEET	PLATE BLOCK	UNUSED F/NH	USED
4076	39¢ Distinguished American Diplomats, self-adhesive, souvenir sheet of 6 . .	15.00	....	....	....	12.00	....
4076a	39¢ Robert D. Murphy	3.00	....	....	....	2.00	1.25
4076b	39¢ Frances E. Willis.	3.00	....	....	....	2.00	1.25
4076c	39¢ Hiram Bingham IV	3.00	....	....	....	2.00	1.25
4076d	39¢ Philip C. Habib . .	3.00	....	....	....	2.00	1.25
4076e	39¢ Charles E. Bohlen	3.00	....	....	....	2.00	1.25
4076f	39¢ Clifton R. Wharton Sr.	3.00	....	....	....	2.00	1.25

4077

4078

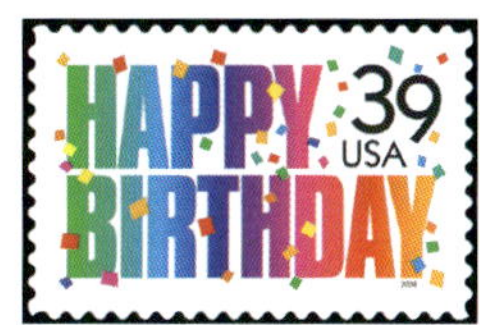

4079

SCOTT NO.	DESCRIPTION	FIRST DAY COVERS SING	PL. BLK.	MINT SHEET	PLATE BLOCK	UNUSED F/NH	USED
4077	39¢ Judy Garland, self-adhesive	3.00	4.75	32.00(20)	7.50	1.75	.50
....	same, uncut sheet of 120	....	....	120.00(120)	....	120.00	....
....	block of 8 with vert. gutter	....	....	....	....	10.50	....
....	cross gutter block of 8	....	....	....	....	18.00	....
....	horiz. pair with vert. gutter	....	....	....	....	4.00	....
....	vert. pair with horiz. gutter	....	....	....	....	3.00	....
4078	39¢ Ronald Reagan, self-adhesive	3.00	4.75	30.00(20)	7.00	1.75	.45
4079	39¢ Happy Birthday, Self-adhesive.	3.00	4.75	24.00(20)	6.00	1.50	.50

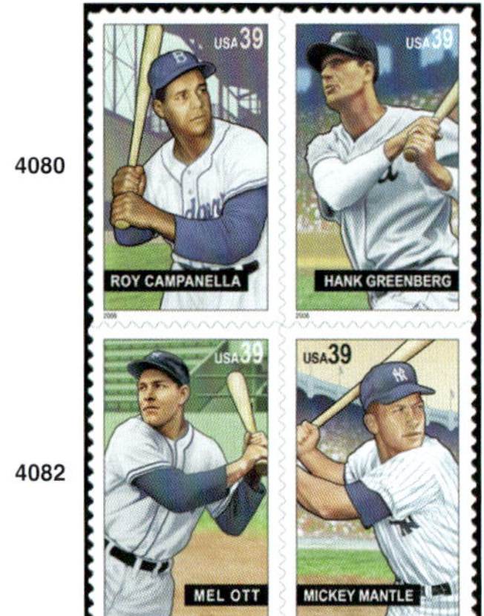

4080 4081

4082 4083

SCOTT NO.	DESCRIPTION	FIRST DAY COVERS SING	FIRST DAY COVERS PL. BLK.	MINT SHEET	PLATE BLOCK	UNUSED F/NH	USED
4080-83	39¢ Baseball Sluggers, self-adhesive, 4 attached	4.25	4.75	24.00(20)	6.50	6.00	....
4080	39¢ Roy Campanella.	3.00	....	....	....	1.60	.55
4081	39¢ Hank Greenberg.	3.00	....	....	....	1.60	.55
4082	39¢ Mel Ott	3.00	....	....	....	1.60	.55
4083	39¢ Mickey Mantle. . .	3.00	....	....	....	1.60	.55
....	same, uncut sheet of 120	....	....	120.00(120)	....	120.00	....
....	cross gutter blk of 8 . .	....	....	....	....	18.00	....
....	blk of 8 with vert. gutter	....	....	....	....	10.50	....
....	horz. pair with vert. gutter	....	....	....	....	4.00	....
....	vert. pair with horz. gutter	....	....	....	....	4.00	....

4084

D.C. COMICS SUPER HEROES

4084a Superman
4084b Green Lantern
4084c Wonder Woman
4084d Green Arrow
4084e Batman
4084f The Flash
4084g Plastic Man
4084h Aquaman
4084i Supergirl
4084j Hawkman
4084k Superman Cover
4084l Green Lantern Cover
4084m Wonder Woman Cover
4084n Green Arrow Cover
4084o Batman Cover
4084p The Flash Cover
4084q Plastic Man Cover
4084r Aquaman Cover
4084s Supergirl Cover
4084t Hawkman Cover

SCOTT NO.	DESCRIPTION	FIRST DAY COVERS SING	FIRST DAY COVERS PL. BLK.	MINT SHEET	PLATE BLOCK	UNUSED F/NH	USED
4084	39¢ D.C. Comics Super Heroes, self-adhesive, 20 varieties attached .	....	....	28.00(20)	....	28.00	....
....	same, uncut sheet of 80	....	....	75.00(80)	....	75.00	....
....	cross gutter block of 20	....	....	....	....	25.00	....
....	horz. pair w/ vert. gutter	....	....	....	....	4.00	....
....	vert. pair w/ horz. gutter	....	....	....	....	4.00	....
....	set of singles	....	....	....	....	....	16.00

4085 4086

4087 4088

SCOTT NO.	DESCRIPTION	FIRST DAY COVERS SING	FIRST DAY COVERS PL. BLK.	MINT SHEET	PLATE BLOCK	UNUSED F/NH	USED
4085-88	39¢ Motorcycles, self-adhesive, 4 attached .	4.25	4.75	30.00(20)	7.75	6.50	....
4085	39¢ 1940 Indian Four	3.00	....	....	....	1.75	.60
4086	39¢ 1918 Cleveland. .	3.00	....	....	....	1.75	.60
4087	39¢ 1970 Chopper. . .	3.00	....	....	....	1.75	.60
4088	39¢ 1965 Harley Davidson Electa-Glide.	3.00	....	....	....	1.75	.60

4089 4090 4091 4092

4093 4094 4095 4096

4097 4098

SCOTT NO.	DESCRIPTION	FIRST DAY COVERS SING	FIRST DAY COVERS PL. BLK.	MINT SHEET	PLATE BLOCK	UNUSED F/NH	USED
4089-98	39¢ Quilts of Gee's Bend, Alabama, self-adhesive, 10 attached	....	....	....	....	17.00	....
4089	39¢ House Variation by Mary Lee Bendolph . .	3.00	....	....	....	1.75	.85
4090	39¢ Pig in a Pen Medallion by Minnie Sue Coleman	3.00	....	....	....	1.75	.85
4091	39¢ Nine Patch by Ruth P. Mosely.	3.00	....	....	....	1.75	.85
4092	39¢ Housetop Four Block Half Log Cabin by Lottie Mooney	3.00	....	....	....	1.75	.85
4093	39¢ Roman Stripes Variation by Loretta Pettway. . .	3.00	....	....	....	1.75	.85
4094	39¢ Chinese Coins Variation by Arlonzia Pettway . .	3.00	....	....	....	1.75	.85
4095	39¢ Blocks and Strips by Annie Mae Young . . .	3.00	....	....	....	1.75	.85
4096	39¢ Medallion by Loretta Pettway	3.00	....	....	....	1.75	.85
4097	39¢ Bars and String-pierced Columns by Jessie T. Pettway	3.00	....	....	....	1.75	.85
4098	39¢ Medallion with Checkerboard Center by Patty Ann Williams	3.00	....	....	....	1.75	.85
4098b	same, bklt pane of 20 (4089-4098 x 2)	....	....	....	....	30.00	....

4099

SOUTHERN FLORIDA WETLANDS

4099a Snail Kite
4099b Wood Storks
4099c Florida Panther
4099d Bald Eagle
4099e American Crocodile
4099f Roseate Spoonbills
4099g Everglades Mink
4099h Cape Sable Seaside Sparrow
4099i American Alligator
4099j White Ibis

SCOTT NO.	DESCRIPTION	FIRST DAY COVERS SING	FIRST DAY COVERS PL. BLK.	MINT SHEET	PLATE BLOCK	UNUSED F/NH	USED
4099	39¢ Southern Florida Wetlands, self-adhesive, 10 attached	....	....	15.00(10)	....	15.00	....
....	set of singles	20.00	....	....	....	15.00	8.50

4100

SCOTT NO.	DESCRIPTION	FIRST DAY COVERS SING	FIRST DAY COVERS PL. BLK.	MINT SHEET	PLATE BLOCK	UNUSED F/NH	USED
4100	39¢ Madonna and Child, self-adhesive	3.00	....	....	....	1.50	.40
4100a	same, bklt pane of 20	....	....	....	....	28.00	....

4103, 4107, 4111, 4114

4102, 4106, 4110, 4115

4101, 4105, 4109, 4113

4104, 4108, 4112, 4116

SCOTT NO.	DESCRIPTION	FIRST DAY COVERS SING	FIRST DAY COVERS PL. BLK.	MINT SHEET	PLATE BLOCK	UNUSED F/NH	USED
4101-04	39¢ Snowflakes, self-adhesive, die cut 11.25 x 11, 4 attached	4.25	4.75	30.00(20)	7.50	6.00	....
4101	39¢ Spindly Arms and Branches	3.00	....	....	....	1.50	.50
4102	39¢ Leafy Arms	3.00	....	....	....	1.50	.50
4103	39¢ Large Center. . . .	3.00	....	....	....	1.50	.50
4104	39¢ Arms w/ Wide Centers	3.00	....	....	....	1.50	.50
4105-08	39¢ Snowflakes, self-adhesive, die cut 11.25 x 11.5, 4 attached	4.25	....	....	....	8.50	....
4105	39¢ Spindly Arms and Branches	3.00	....	....	....	1.75	.50
4106	39¢ Leafy Arms	3.00	....	....	....	1.75	.50
4107	39¢ Large Center. . . .	3.00	....	....	....	1.75	.50
4108	39¢ Arms w/ Wide Centers	3.00	....	....	....	1.75	.50
4108b	same, bklt pane of 20 (4105-08 x 5)	....	....	....	....	32.00	....
4109-12	39¢ Snowflakes, self-adhesive, die cut 11.25 x 11, 4 attached	4.25	....	....	....	7.50	....
4109	39¢ Spindly Arms and Branches	3.00	....	....	....	1.75	1.25
4110	39¢ Leafy Arms	3.00	....	....	....	1.75	1.25
4111	39¢ Large Center. . . .	3.00	....	....	....	1.75	1.25
4112	39¢ Arms w/ Wide Centers	3.00	....	....	....	1.75	1.25
4112b	same, bklt pane of 4 (4109-12)	....	....	....	....	8.00	....
4112c	same, bklt pane of 6 (4111-4112, 4109-4110 x 2).	....	....	....	....	12.00	....
4112d	same, bklt pane of 6 (4109-4110, 4111-4112 x 2). .	....	....	....	....	12.00	....
4113-16	39¢ Snowflakes, die cut 8, self-adhesive, 4 attached	4.25	....	....	....	9.00	....
4113	39¢ Spindly Arms and Branches.	3.00	....	....	....	2.00	1.75
4114	39¢ Large Center	3.00	....	....	....	2.00	1.75
4115	39¢ Leafy Arms.	3.00	....	....	....	2.00	1.75
4116	39¢ Arms w/ Wide Centers	3.00	....	....	....	2.00	1.75
4116b	same, bklt pane of 18 (4113 x 5, 4114 x 4, 4115 x 5, 4116 x 4)	....	....	....	....	30.00	....

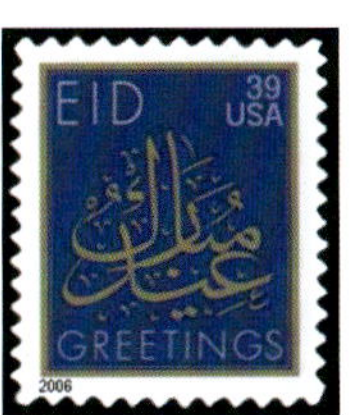
4117

4119

4118

SCOTT NO.	DESCRIPTION	FIRST DAY COVERS SING	FIRST DAY COVERS PL. BLK.	MINT SHEET	PLATE BLOCK	UNUSED F/NH	USED
4117	39¢ EID, self-adhesive	3.00	4.75	22.00(20)	5.50	1.50	.85
4118	39¢ Hanukkah-Dreidal, self-adhesive	3.00	4.75	22.00(20)	5.50	1.50	.40
4119	39¢ Kwanzaa-People self-adhesive	3.00	4.75	22.00(20)	5.50	1.50	.40

2007 COMMEMORATIVES

SCOTT NO.	DESCRIPTION	FIRST DAY COVERS SING	FIRST DAY COVERS PL. BLK.	MINT SHEET	PLATE BLOCK	UNUSED F/NH	USED
4120/4220	(4120, 4121, 4124, 4136, 4146-4150, 4160-4163, 4192-4197, 4199-4205, 4207-4210, 4219, 4220) 32 varieties	....		....	....	44.00	15.00

4120

4121

4122

SCOTT NO.	DESCRIPTION	FIRST DAY COVERS SING	FIRST DAY COVERS PL. BLK.	MINT SHEET	PLATE BLOCK	UNUSED F/NH	USED
4120	39¢ Ella Fitzgerald, self-adhesive	3.00	4.75	22.00(20)	5.50	1.50	.40
4121	39¢ Oklahoma Statehood self-adhesive	3.00	4.75	22.00(20)	5.50	1.50	.40
4122	39¢ Hershey's Kiss, self-adhesive	3.00	4.75	28.00(20)	....	1.50	.40
4122a	same, bklt pane of 20	....	....	....	....	28.00	....

4123

SCOTT NO.	DESCRIPTION	FIRST DAY COVERS SING	FIRST DAY COVERS PL. BLK.	MINT SHEET	PLATE BLOCK	UNUSED F/NH	USED
4123	84¢ International Polar Year, self-adhesive, souvenir sheet of 2 . .	....	....	....	....	8.00	....
4123a	84¢ Aurora Borealis . .	4.00	....	....	....	5.00	2.50
4123b	84¢ Aurora Australis .	4.00	....	....	....	5.00	2.50

4124

4125, 4126, 4127, 4128, 4437

4129, 4130, 4132, 4133, 4134, 4135

SCOTT NO.	DESCRIPTION	FIRST DAY COVERS SING	FIRST DAY COVERS PL. BLK.	MINT SHEET	PLATE BLOCK	UNUSED F/NH	USED
4124	39¢ Henry Wadsworth Longfellow, self-adhesive	3.00	4.75	21.00(20)	5.50	1.50	.40
4125	(41¢) Forever Liberty Bell, self-adhesive, large micro print	3.50	....	....	....	1.50	.35
4125a	same, bklt pane of 20	....	....	....	....	27.00	....
4125b	(42¢) Forever, Liberty Bell, large micro print, bell 16mm wide dated 2008	3.50	....	....	....	1.50	.35
4125c	same, bklt pane of 20	....	....	....	....	27.00	....
4125f	(44¢) Forever, dated 2009, large micro, bell 16mm wide	....	....	....	....	1.50	.45
4125g	same, booklet pane of 20	....	....	....	....	27.00	....
4126	(41¢) Forever, Liberty Bell, self-adhesive, small micro print	3.50	....	....	....	1.50	.35
4126a	same, bklt pane of 20	....	....	....	....	27.00	....
4126b	(42¢) Forever, Liberty Bell, small micro print, bell 16mm wide dated 2008	3.50	....	....	....	1.50	.45
4126c	same, bklt pane of 20	....	....	....	....	27.00	....
4126d	(44¢) Forever, dated 2009, small micro, bell 16mm wide	....	....	....	....	1.50	.45
4126e	same, booklet pane of 20	....	....	....	....	27.00	....
4127	(41¢) Forever Liberty Bell, self-adhesive, medium micro print	3.50	....	....	....	2.00	.35
4127a	same, bklt pane of 20	....	....	....	....	38.00	....
....	solid tagging	....	....	....	....	160.00	....
4127b	same, bklt pane of 4 .	....	....	....	....	5.25	....
4127c	same, bklt pane of 6 .	....	....	....	....	7.75	....
4127d	(42¢) Forever Liberty Bell, med. micro print, bell 15 wide, mottled tagging dated 2008	3.50	....	....	....	2.00	.65
4127e	(42¢) Forever Liberty Bell, dbl-sided, bklt pane of 20	....	....	....	....	36.00	....
4127f	(42¢) Forever Liberty Bell, dated 2008, small type, solid tagging	3.50	....	....	....	1.50	....
4127g	(42¢) Forever Liberty Bell, dated 2008, small type, solid tagging, bklt pane of 4		....	....	....	5.25	....

SCOTT NO.	DESCRIPTION	FIRST DAY COVERS SING	FIRST DAY COVERS PL. BLK.	MINT SHEET	PLATE BLOCK	UNUSED F/NH	USED
4127h	(42¢) Forever Liberty Bell, (2008), bklt pane of 6........	....	....	....	....	7.75	....
	same, vending bklt of 20	....	....	....	....	29.00	....
4127i	(44¢) Forever Liberty Bell, dated 2009 in copper....	3.50	....	....	....	1.50	.65
4127j	(44¢) Forever Liberty Bell, double sided pane of 20...	....	....	....	....	27.00	....
4128	(41¢) Forever Liberty Bell, self-adhesive, ATM . .	3.50	....	....	....	1.50	.60
4128a	same, bklt pane of 18	....	....	....	....	28.00	....
4128b	(42¢) Forever, Liberty Bell large micro print, bell 16mm wide dated 2009	3.50	....	....	....	1.50	.65
4128c	same, bklt pane of 18	....	....	....	....	27.00	....
4129	(41¢) American Flag, die cut 11.25	3.50	5.00	127.00(100)	16.00	1.50	1.05
4130	(41¢) American Flag, self-adhesive, 11.25 x 10.75	3.50	5.00	24.00(20)	5.75	1.80	.45
4131	(41¢) American Flag, coil, die cut 9.75.	3.50	....	....	....	1.50	.65
	same, pl# strip of 5 . .	....	....	....	....	10.50	....
4132	(41¢) American Flag, coil, self-adhesive, die cut 9.5	3.50	....	....	....	1.50	.40
	same, pl# strip of 5 . .	....	....	....	....	10.50	....
4133	(41¢) American Flag, coil, self-adhesive, die cut 11	3.50	....	....	....	1.50	.40
	same, pl# strip of 5 . .	....	....	....	....	10.50	....
4134	(41¢) American Flag, coil, self-adhesive, die cut 8.5	3.50	....	....	....	1.50	.40
	same, pl# strip of 5 . .	....	....	....	....	10.00	....
4135	(41¢) American Flag, coil, self-adhesive, rounded corners, die cut 11 . . .	3.50	....	....	....	1.70	1.15
	same, pl# strip of 5 . .	....	....	....	....	12.00	....

4136

4137, 4139, 4141, 4142

4138, 4140

SCOTT NO.	DESCRIPTION	FIRST DAY COVERS SING	FIRST DAY COVERS PL. BLK.	MINT SHEET	PLATE BLOCK	UNUSED F/NH	USED
4136	41¢ Settlement of James-town, self-adhesive . .	3.50	5.00	30.00(20)	....	1.50	.50
4137	26¢ Florida Panther, water-activated, ...	3.00	4.75	78.00(100)	13.50	.85	.35
4138	17¢ Big Horn Sheep, self-adhesive	3.00	4.00	13.00(20)	3.50	.75	.35
4139	26¢ Florida Panther, self-adhesive	3.00	4.75	16.00(20)	4.50	.85	.35
4140	17¢ Big Horn Sheep, self-adhesive, coil . . .	3.00	....	....	....	.75	.35
	same, pl# strip of 5 . .	....	....	....	....	6.75	....
4141	26¢ Florida Panther, self-adhesive, coil . . .	3.00	....	....	....	1.00	.35
	same, pl# strip of 5 . .	....	....	....	....	9.00	....
4142	26¢ Florida Panther, self-adhesive	3.00	....	....	....	1.00	.30
4142a	same, bklt pane of 10	....	....	....	....	10.00	....

STAR WARS

4143a Darth Vader
4143b Millennium Falcon
4143c Emperor Palpatine
4143d Anakin Skywalker and Obi-Wan Kenobi
4143e Luke Skywalker
4143f Princess Leia & R2-D2
4143g C-3PO
4143h Queen Padme Amidala
4143i Obi-Wan Kenobi
4143j Boba Fett
4143k Darth Maul
4143l Chewbacca and Han Solo
4143m X-wing Starfighter
4143n Yoda
4143o Stormtroopers

4143

SCOTT NO.	DESCRIPTION	FIRST DAY COVERS SING	FIRST DAY COVERS PL. BLK.	MINT SHEET	PLATE BLOCK	UNUSED F/NH	USED
4143	41¢ Star Wars, self-adhesive, 15 attached	....	....	22.00(15)	....	22.00	....
....	same, set of singles. .	....	....	....	....	22.00	15.00

4144

4145

SCOTT NO.	DESCRIPTION	FIRST DAY COVERS SING	FIRST DAY COVERS PL. BLK.	MINT SHEET	PLATE BLOCK	UNUSED F/NH	USED
4144	$4.60 Air Force One, self-adhesive	10.00	30.00	230.00(20)	58.00	13.00	10.00
4145	$16.25 Marine One, self-adhesive	35.00	80.00	800.00(20)	200.00	46.00	30.00

4146 4147 4148 4149 4150

SCOTT NO.	DESCRIPTION	FIRST DAY COVERS SING	FIRST DAY COVERS PL. BLK.	MINT SHEET	PLATE BLOCK	UNUSED F/NH	USED
4146-50	41¢ Pacific Lighthouses, self-adhesive, 5 attached	5.50	8.00	30.00(20)	16.00(10)	8.50	....
4146	41¢ Diamond Head . .	3.50	....	....	....	1.75	.50
4147	41¢ Five Finger	3.50	....	....	....	1.75	.50
4148	41¢ Grays Harbor . . .	3.50	....	....	....	1.75	.50
4149	41¢ Umpqua River. . .	3.50	....	....	....	1.75	.50
4150	41¢ St. George Reef .	3.50	....	....	....	1.75	.50

4151

4152

SCOTT NO.	DESCRIPTION	FIRST DAY COVERS SING	FIRST DAY COVERS PL. BLK.	MINT SHEET	PLATE BLOCK	UNUSED F/NH	USED
4151	41¢ Wedding Hearts, self-adhesive	3.50	....	....	....	1.50	.35
4151a	same, bklt pane of 20	....	....	....	....	27.00	....
4152	58¢ Wedding Hearts, self-adhesive	4.00	5.50	33.00(20)	8.00	1.85	.65

4153 4154

4155 4156

SCOTT NO.	DESCRIPTION	FIRST DAY COVERS SING	FIRST DAY COVERS PL. BLK.	MINT SHEET	PLATE BLOCK	UNUSED F/NH	USED
4153-56	41¢ Pollination, self-adhesive, 4 attached .	4.50	....	....	....	7.00	....
4153	41¢ Purple Nightshade and Morrison's Bumblebee, type I, straight edge at left . .	3.50	....	....	....	1.50	.55
4153a	same, type II, straight edge at right.	3.50	....	....	....	1.50	.55
4154	41¢ Hummingbird Trumpet and Calliope Hummingbird, type I, straight edge at right	3.50	....	....	....	1.50	.55
4154a	same, type II, straight edge at left.	3.50	....	....	....	1.50	.55
4155	41¢ Saguaro and Lesser Long-nosed Bat, type I, straight edge at left . .	3.50	....	....	....	1.50	.55
4155a	same, type II, straight edge at right.	3.50	....	....	....	1.50	.55
4156	41¢ Prairie Ironweed and Southern Dogface Butterfly, type I, straight edge at right	3.50	....	....	....	1.50	.55
4156a	same, type II, straight edge at left.	3.50	....	....	....	1.50	.55
4156b	same, blk of 4 (4153-4156)	4.50	....	....	....	6.00	....
4156c	same, blk of 4 (4153a-4156a)	4.50	....	....	....	6.00	....
4156d	same, bklt pane of 20 (4153-4156 x 3, 4153a-4156a x 2)	4.50	....	....	....	28.00	....

SCOTT NO.	DESCRIPTION	FIRST DAY COVERS SING	FIRST DAY COVERS PL. BLK.	MINT SHEET	PLATE BLOCK	UNUSED F/NH	USED
4157	(10¢) Patriotic Banner, self-adhesive, round corners	....	....	....	....	.35	.25
....	same, pl# strip of 5 . .	....	....	....	....	3.50	....
4158	(10¢) Patriotic Banner, self-adhesive, straight corners	....	....	....	....	.35	.25
....	same, pl# strip of 5 . .	....	....	....	....	4.75	....

4159

MARVEL COMICS SUPER HEROES

4159a Spider-Man
4159b The Incredible Hulk
4159c Sub-Mariner
4159d The Thing
4159e Captain America
4159f Silver Surfer
4159g Spider-Woman
4159h Iron Man
4159i Elektra
4159j Wolverine
4159k Spider-Man Cover
4159l Incredible Hulk Cover
4159m Sub-Mariner Cover
4159n Fantastic Four Cover
4159o Captain America Cover
4159p Silver Surfer Cover
4159q Spider-Woman Cover
4159r Iron Man Cover
4159s Elektra Cover
4159t X-Men Cover

SCOTT NO.	DESCRIPTION	FIRST DAY COVERS SING	FIRST DAY COVERS PL. BLK.	MINT SHEET	PLATE BLOCK	UNUSED F/NH	USED
4159	41¢ Marvel Comics Super Heroes, self-adhesive, 20 varieties attached .	....	....	29.00(20)	....	29.00	....
	same, set of singles. .	....	....	....	....	29.00	20.00

4160 4161 4162 4163

SCOTT NO.	DESCRIPTION	FIRST DAY COVERS SING	FIRST DAY COVERS PL. BLK.	MINT SHEET	PLATE BLOCK	UNUSED F/NH	USED
4160-63	41¢ Vintage Mahogany Speedboats, self-adhesive, 4 attached .	4.50	6.50	18.00(12)	14.00(8)	7.00	....
4160	41¢ 1915 Hutchinson	....	....	....	....	1.75	1.00
4161	41¢ 1945 Chris-Craft	....	....	....	....	1.75	1.00
4162	41¢ 1939 Hacker-Craft	....	....	....	....	1.75	1.00
4163	41¢ 1931 Gar Wood .	....	....	....	....	1.75	1.00

4157, 4158

4165, 4165a

4164

SCOTT NO.	DESCRIPTION	FIRST DAY COVERS SING	FIRST DAY COVERS PL. BLK.	MINT SHEET	PLATE BLOCK	UNUSED F/NH	USED
4164	41¢ Purple Heart, self-adhesive	3.50	5.00	24.00(20)	5.50	1.50	.40
4165	41¢ Louis Comfort Tiffany, self-adhesive	3.50	....	....	....	1.50	.40
4165a	same, bklt pane of 20	....	....	....	....	28.00	....
4166-75	41¢ Flowers Strip of 10	....	....	....	....	25.00	....
	same, plate strip of 11	....	....	....	....	35.00	....
4166	41¢ Iris S/A coil	$3.75	....	....	....	2.75	.85
4167	41¢ Dahalia S/A coil .	$3.75	....	....	....	2.75	.85
4168	41¢ Magnolia S/A coil	$3.75	....	....	....	2.75	.85
4169	41¢ Red Gerbera Daisy, S/A coil.	$3.75	....	....	....	2.75	.85
4170	41¢ Coneflower S/A coil	$3.75	....	....	....	2.75	.85
4171	41¢ Tulip S/A coil. . . .	$3.75	....	....	....	2.75	.85
4172	41¢ Water Lily S/A coil	$3.75	....	....	....	2.75	.85
4173	41¢ Poppy S/A coil . .	$3.75	....	....	....	2.75	.85
4174	41¢ Chrysanthemum, S/A coil.	$3.75	....	....	....	2.75	.85
4175	41¢ Orange Gerbera Daisy, S/A coil	$3.75	....	....	....	2.75	.85

4166, 4178

4167, 4179

4168, 4180

4169, 4181

4170, 4184

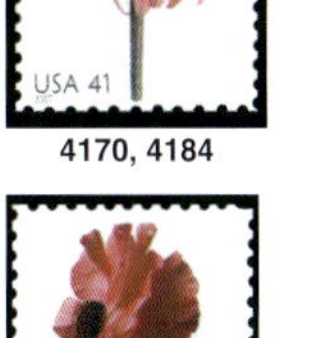

4171, 4185

4172, 4182

4173, 4183

4174, 4176

4175, 4177

SCOTT NO.	DESCRIPTION	FIRST DAY COVERS SING	FIRST DAY COVERS PL. BLK.	MINT SHEET	PLATE BLOCK	UNUSED F/NH	USED
4176	41¢ Chrysanthemum, booklet single	$3.75	....	....	....	1.50	.60
4177	41¢ Orange Gerbera Daisy, booklet single	$3.75	....	....	....	1.50	.60
4178	41¢ Iris, bklt single. . .	$3.75	....	....	....	1.50	.60
4179	41¢ Dahalia, bklt single	$3.75	....	....	....	1.50	.60
4180	41¢ Magnolia, bklt single	$3.75	....	....	....	1.50	.60
4181	41¢ Red Gerbera Daisy, booklet single	$3.75	....	....	....	1.50	.60
4182	41¢ Water Lily, bklt single	$3.75	....	....	....	1.50	.60
4183	41¢ Poppy, bklt single	$3.75	....	....	....	1.50	.60
4184	41¢ Coneflower, booklet single.	$3.75	....	....	....	1.50	.60
4185	41¢ Tulip, bklt single. .	$3.75	....	....	....	1.50	.60
4185a	41¢ Flowers dbl-sided, booklet pane	....	....	....	....	29.00	....
4186	41¢ Flag S/A coil, die cut 9.5, microprint, rt. side of flagpole . . .	3.75	....	....	....	1.50	.35
	same, plate strip of 5 .	....	....	....	....	12.00	....
4187	41¢ Flag S/A coil, die cut 11, microprint, left side of flagpole. . .	3.75	....	....	....	1.50	.35
	same, plate strip of 5 .	....	....	....	....	12.00	....
4188	41¢ Flag S/A coil, 8.5 perpendicular corners,	3.75	....	....	....	1.50	.35
	same, plate strip of 5 .	....	....	....	....	12.00	....
4189	41¢ Flag S/A coil, die cut 11 w/round corners,	3.75	....	....	....	1.50	.35
	same, plate strip of 5 .	....	....	....	....	12.00	....
4190	41¢ Flag bklt single, S/A die-cut 11.25x10.75, microprint rt. side of pole	3.75	....	....	....	1.50	.35
4190a	same bklt pane of 10 .	....	....	....	....	13.00	....
4191	41¢ Flag bklt single, S/A die-cut 11.25x10.75, microprint left side of pole	3.75	....	....	....	1.50	.35
4191a	same bklt pane of 20 .	....	....	....	....	27.00	....

4192 4193 4194 4195

4186-91

4196

SCOTT NO.	DESCRIPTION	FIRST DAY COVERS SING	FIRST DAY COVERS PL. BLK.	MINT SHEET	PLATE BLOCK	UNUSED F/NH	USED
4192-95	41¢ Magic of Disney, 4 attached,.	4.25	4.75	24.00 (20)	6.50	6.00	....
4192	41¢ Mickey Mouse. . .	3.75	....	....	....	1.50	.50
4193	41¢ Peter Pan & Tinkerbell	3.75	....	....	....	1.50	.50
4194	41¢ Dumbo & Timothy Mouse	3.75	....	....	....	1.50	.50
4195	41¢ Aladdin & Genie .	3.75	....	....	....	1.50	.50
4196	41¢ Celebrate	3.75	4.50	22.00 (20)	5.50	1.50	.35

4197

SCOTT NO.	DESCRIPTION	FIRST DAY COVERS SING	FIRST DAY COVERS PL. BLK.	MINT SHEET	PLATE BLOCK	UNUSED F/NH	USED
4197	41¢ James Stewart . .	3.75	4.50	30.00 (20)	7.50	1.75	.50

4198

ALPINE TUNDRA

4198a	*Elk*	**4198f**	*Magdalena Alpine Butterfly*
4198b	*Golden Eagle*	**4198g**	*Big-White-Tailed Ptarmigan*
4198c	*Yellow-bellied marmot*	**4198h**	*Rocky Mountain Parnassian Butterfly*
4198d	*American Pike*	**4198i**	*Melissa Arctic Butterfly*
4198e	*Big Horn Sheep*	**4198j**	*Brown-Capped Rosy-Finch*

SCOTT NO.	DESCRIPTION	FIRST DAY COVERS SING	FIRST DAY COVERS PL. BLK.	MINT SHEET	PLATE BLOCK	UNUSED F/NH	USED
4198	41¢ Alpine Tundra,						
	sheet of 10	....	....	15.00 (10)	....	15.00	....
	set of singles	20.00	....	....	....	15.00	9.00

4199

4200

4201

SCOTT NO.	DESCRIPTION	FIRST DAY COVERS SING	FIRST DAY COVERS PL. BLK.	MINT SHEET	PLATE BLOCK	UNUSED F/NH	USED
4199	41¢ Gerald R. Ford . .	3.75	4.50	24.00 (20)	6.00	1.50	.40
4200	41¢ Jury Duty.	3.75	4.50	24.00 (20)	6.00	1.50	.40
4201	41¢ Mendez v. Westminster	3.75	4.50	24.00 (20)	6.00	1.50	.40

4202

SCOTT NO.	DESCRIPTION	FIRST DAY COVERS SING	FIRST DAY COVERS PL. BLK.	MINT SHEET	PLATE BLOCK	UNUSED F/NH	USED
4202	41¢ EID	3.75	4.50	22.00 (20)	5.50	1.40	.35

4203

4204

SCOTT NO.	DESCRIPTION	FIRST DAY COVERS SING	FIRST DAY COVERS PL. BLK.	MINT SHEET	PLATE BLOCK	UNUSED F/NH	USED
4203-04	41¢ Polar Lights	4.25	4.75	32.00 (20)	9.50	3.50	....
4203	41¢ Aurora Borealis. . .	3.75	....	....	....	1.75	.65
4204	41¢ Aurora Australis . .	3.75	....	....	....	1.75	.65

4205

4206

SCOTT NO.	DESCRIPTION	FIRST DAY COVERS SING	FIRST DAY COVERS PL. BLK.	MINT SHEET	PLATE BLOCK	UNUSED F/NH	USED
4205	41¢ Yoda	3.75	4.50	24.00 (20)	6.00	1.50	.40
4206	41¢ Madonna of the Carnation,						
	by Bernardino Luini . .	3.75	....	....	....	1.30	.35
4206a	same, double-sided,						
	booklet pane of 20. . .	....	....	....	....	24.00	....

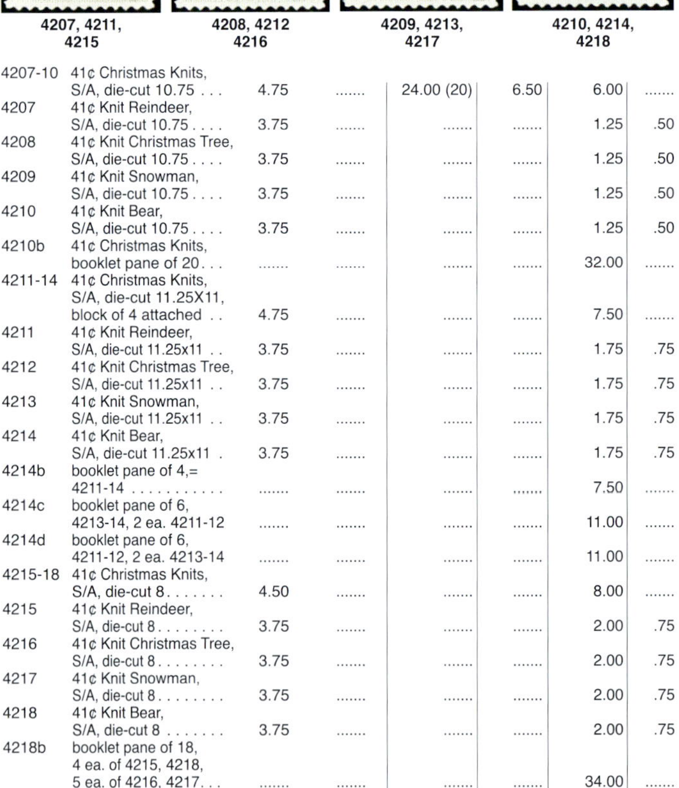

4207, 4211, 4215

4208, 4212 4216

4209, 4213, 4217

4210, 4214, 4218

SCOTT NO.	DESCRIPTION	FIRST DAY COVERS SING	FIRST DAY COVERS PL. BLK.	MINT SHEET	PLATE BLOCK	UNUSED F/NH	USED
4207-10	41¢ Christmas Knits,						
	S/A, die-cut 10.75 . . .	4.75	....	24.00 (20)	6.50	6.00	....
4207	41¢ Knit Reindeer,						
	S/A, die-cut 10.75	3.75	....	....	....	1.25	.50
4208	41¢ Knit Christmas Tree,						
	S/A, die-cut 10.75	3.75	....	....	....	1.25	.50
4209	41¢ Knit Snowman,						
	S/A, die-cut 10.75	3.75	....	....	....	1.25	.50
4210	41¢ Knit Bear,						
	S/A, die-cut 10.75	3.75	....	....	....	1.25	.50
4210b	41¢ Christmas Knits,						
	booklet pane of 20. . .	....	....	....	....	32.00	....
4211-14	41¢ Christmas Knits,						
	S/A, die-cut 11.25X11,						
	block of 4 attached . .	4.75	....	....	....	7.50	....
4211	41¢ Knit Reindeer,						
	S/A, die-cut 11.25x11 . .	3.75	....	....	....	1.75	.75
4212	41¢ Knit Christmas Tree,						
	S/A, die-cut 11.25x11 . .	3.75	....	....	....	1.75	.75
4213	41¢ Knit Snowman,						
	S/A, die-cut 11.25x11 . .	3.75	....	....	....	1.75	.75
4214	41¢ Knit Bear,						
	S/A, die-cut 11.25x11 .	3.75	....	....	....	1.75	.75
4214b	booklet pane of 4,=						
	4211-14	....	....	....	....	7.50	....
4214c	booklet pane of 6,						
	4213-14, 2 ea. 4211-12	....	....	....	....	11.00	....
4214d	booklet pane of 6,						
	4211-12, 2 ea. 4213-14	....	....	....	....	11.00	....
4215-18	41¢ Christmas Knits,						
	S/A, die-cut 8.	4.50	....	....	....	8.00	....
4215	41¢ Knit Reindeer,						
	S/A, die-cut 8.	3.75	....	....	....	2.00	.75
4216	41¢ Knit Christmas Tree,						
	S/A, die-cut 8.	3.75	....	....	....	2.00	.75
4217	41¢ Knit Snowman,						
	S/A, die-cut 8.	3.75	....	....	....	2.00	.75
4218	41¢ Knit Bear,						
	S/A, die-cut 8	3.75	....	....	....	2.00	.75
4218b	booklet pane of 18,						
	4 ea. of 4215, 4218,						
	5 ea. of 4216, 4217. . .	....	....	....	....	34.00	....

4219

4220

SCOTT NO.	DESCRIPTION	FIRST DAY COVERS SING	FIRST DAY COVERS PL. BLK.	MINT SHEET	PLATE BLOCK	UNUSED F/NH	USED
4219	41¢ Hanukkah S/A,						
	die-cut 10.75x11	3.75	4.50	22.00 (20)	5.50	1.40	.45
4220	41¢ Kwanzaa, S/A,						
	die-cut, 11x10.75.	3.75	4.50	22.00 (20)	5.50	1.40	.45

2008 COMMEMORATIVES

SCOTT NO.	DESCRIPTION	FIRST DAY COVERS SING	FIRST DAY COVERS PL. BLK.	MINT SHEET	PLATE BLOCK	UNUSED F/NH	USED
4221/4373	(4221-4227, 4248-4252, 4265, 4266, 4334, 4335, 4336-4345, 4349-4351, 4353-4357, 4358, 4372, 4373) 37 varieties	....		....	....	52.00	24.00

4221 4222 4223

SCOTT NO.	DESCRIPTION	SING	PL. BLK.	MINT SHEET	PLATE BLOCK	UNUSED F/NH	USED
4221	41¢ Year of the Rat, SA. .	3.75	....	17.00 (12)	....	1.50	.45
4222	41¢ Charles W. Chestnutt	3.75	....	24.00 (20)	5.50	1.50	.45
4223	41¢ Marjorie Kinnan Rawlings	3.75	4.50	24.00 (20)	5.50	1.50	.45

4224 4225 4226 4227

SCOTT NO.	DESCRIPTION	SING	PL. BLK.	MINT SHEET	PLATE BLOCK	UNUSED F/NH	USED
4224-27	41¢ American Scientists. .	4.50	7.50	25.00 (20)	12.00(8)	6.00	....
4224	41¢ Gerty Cori.	3.75	....	....	....	1.50	.90
4225	41¢ Linus Pauling. . . .	3.75	....	....	....	1.50	.90
4226	41¢ Edwin Hubble. . .	3.75	....	....	....	1.50	.90
4227	41¢ John Bardeed. . .	3.75	....	....	....	1.50	.90

4229, 4233, 4237, 4241, 4245 — 4230, 4234, 4238, 4242, 4246 — 4231, 4235, 4239, 4243, 4247 — 4228, 4232, 4236, 4240, 4244

SCOTT NO.	DESCRIPTION	SING	PL. BLK.	MINT SHEET	PLATE BLOCK	UNUSED F/NH	USED
4228-31	42¢ Flag 24/7, W/A coil.	6.50	....	....	....	9.00	....
	same, plate # strip of 5	....	....	....	....	20.00	....
	same, plate # strip of 9	....	....	....	....	30.00	....
4228	42¢ Flag at Dusk, W/A coil.	3.50	....	....	....	2.50	.85
4229	42¢ Flag at Night, W/A coil.	3.50	....	....	....	2.50	.85
4230	42¢ Flag at Dawn, W/A coil.	3.50	....	....	....	2.50	.85
4231	42¢ Flag at Midday, W/A coil.	3.50	....	....	....	2.50	.85
4232-35	42¢ Flag 24/7, S/A coil 9.5 (AP).	6.50	....	....	....	7.50	....
	same, plate # strip of 5	....	....	....	....	12.00	....
	same, plate # strip of 9	....	....	....	....	18.00	....
4232	42¢ Flag at Dusk, S/A coil 9.5 (AP).	3.50	....	....	....	2.50	.60
4233	42¢ Flag at Night, S/A coil 9.5 (AP).	3.50	....	....	....	2.50	.60
4234	42¢ Flag at Dawn, S/A coil 9.5 (AP)	3.50	....	....	....	2.50	.60
4235	42¢ Flag at Midday, S/A coil 9.5 (AP).	3.50	....	....	....	2.50	.60
4236-39	42¢ Flag 24/7, S/A coil, 11 perpend. corners (SSP)	6.50	....	....	....	7.50	....
	same, plate # strip of 5	....	....	....	....	13.00	....
	same, plate # strip of 9	....	....	....	....	19.00	....
4236	42¢ Flag at Dusk, S/A coil, 11 perpend. corners (SSP)	3.50	....	....	....	2.50	.60
4237	42¢ Flag at Night, S/A coil, 11 perpend. corners (SSP)	3.50	....	....	....	2.50	.60
4238	42¢ Flag at Dawn, S/A coil, 11 perpend. corners (SSP)	3.50	....	....	....	2.50	.60
4239	42¢ Flag at Midday, S/A coil, 11 perpend. corners (SSP)	3.50	....	....	....	2.50	.60
4240-43	42¢ Flag 24/7, S/A coil, 8.5 perpend. corners (AV)	6.50	....	....	....	7.50	....
	same, plate # strip of 5	....	....	....	....	13.00	....
	same, plate # strip of 9	....	....	....	....	18.00	....
4240	42¢ Flag at Dusk, S/A coil, 8.5 perpend. corners (AV)	3.50	....	....	....	2.50	.60
4241	42¢ Flag at Night, S/A coil, 8.5 perpend. corners (AV)	3.50	....	....	....	2.50	.60
4242	42¢ Flag at Dawn, S/A coil, 8.5 perpend. corners (AV)	3.50	....	....	....	2.50	.60
4243	42¢ Flag at Midday, S/A coil, 8.5 perpend. corners (AV)	3.50	....	....	....	2.50	.60
4244-47	42¢ Flag 24/7, S/A coil, 11 rounded corners (AV)	6.50	....	....	....	7.50	....
	same, plate # strip of 5	....	....	....	....	13.00	....
	same, plate # strip of 9	....	....	....	....	18.00	....
4244	42¢ Flag at Dusk, S/A coil, 11 rounded corners (AV)	3.50	....	....	....	2.50	.60
4245	42¢ Flag at Night, S/A coil, 11 rounded corners (AV)	3.50	....	....	....	2.50	.60
4246	42¢ Flag at Dawn, S/A coil, 11 rounded corners (AV)	3.50	....	....	....	2.50	.60
4247	42¢ Flag at Midday, S/A coil, 11 rounded corners (AV)	3.50	....	....	....	2.50	.60

4248 4249 4250 4251 4252

SCOTT NO.	DESCRIPTION	SING	PL. BLK.	MINT SHEET	PLATE BLOCK	UNUSED F/NH	USED
4248-52	42¢ American Journalists	4.50	7.50	35.00(20)	18.00(10)	9.00	....
	same	....	....	....	12.00(8)	....	....
4248	42¢ Martha Gellhorn. .	3.75	....	....	....	2.00	1.00
4249	42¢ John Hersey. . . .	3.75	....	....	....	2.00	1.00
4250	42¢ George Polk. . . .	3.75	....	....	....	2.00	1.00
4251	42¢ Ruben Salazar. . .	3.75	....	....	....	2.00	1.00
4252	42¢ Eric Sevareid. . . .	3.75	....	....	....	2.00	1.00

4253,4258 4254,4259 4255,4260 4256,4261 4257,4262

SCOTT NO.	DESCRIPTION	SING	PL. BLK.	MINT SHEET	PLATE BLOCK	UNUSED F/NH	USED
4253-57	27¢ Tropical Fruit. . . .	4.75	....	19.00(20)	12.00(10)	6.00	....
4253	27¢ Pomegranate. . . .	2.50	....	....	....	1.25	.50
4254	27¢ Star Fruit.	2.50	....	....	....	1.25	.50
4255	27¢ Kiwi.	2.50	....	....	....	1.25	.50
4256	27¢ Papaya	2.50	....	....	....	1.25	.50
4257	27¢ Guava.	2.50	....	....	....	1.25	.50
4258-62	27¢ Tropical Fruit. . . .	4.75	....	....	....	9.00	....
	same, plate strip of 5 .	....	....	....	....	15.00	....
	same, plate strip of 11	....	....	....	....	22.00	....
4258	27¢ Pomegranate Coil	2.50	....	....	....	2.00	.50
4259	27¢ Star Fruit Coil. . .	2.50	....	....	....	2.00	.50
4260	27¢ Kiwi Coil.	2.50	....	....	....	2.00	.50
4261	27¢ Papaya Coil	2.50	....	....	....	2.00	.50
4262	27¢ Guava Coil.	2.50	....	....	....	2.00	.50

4263, 4264

SCOTT NO.	DESCRIPTION	SING	PL. BLK.	MINT SHEET	PLATE BLOCK	UNUSED F/NH	USED
4263	42¢ Purple Heart	3.50	4.75	148.00 (100)	40.00	1.70	.70
4264	42¢ Purple Heart, S/A	3.50	4.75	24.00 (20)	6.00	1.50	.45

4265 4266

SCOTT NO.	DESCRIPTION	SING	PL. BLK.	MINT SHEET	PLATE BLOCK	UNUSED F/NH	USED
4265	42¢ Frank Sinatra . . .	3.75	4.75	24.00 (20)	6.00	1.50	.40
4266	42¢ Minnesota Statehood	3.75	4.75	22.00 (20)	5.50	1.50	.40

4267 4268 4269

SCOTT NO.	DESCRIPTION	FIRST DAY COVERS SING	FIRST DAY COVERS PL. BLK.	MINT SHEET	PLATE BLOCK	UNUSED F/NH	USED
4267	69¢ Dragonfly	3.75	5.00	55.00 (20)	9.00	3.00	1.25
4268	$4.80 Mount Rushmore	12.00	....	245.00 (20)	65.00	14.00	10.00
4269	$16.50 Hoover Dam . .	35.00	....	800.00 (20)	200.00	45.00	35.00

4270 4271 4272

SCOTT NO.	DESCRIPTION	FIRST DAY COVERS SING	FIRST DAY COVERS PL. BLK.	MINT SHEET	PLATE BLOCK	UNUSED F/NH	USED
4270	42¢ All Heart	3.75	....	....	....	1.40	.40
4270a	42¢ All Heart, pane of 20	....	....	....	....	27.00	....
4271	42¢ Weddings	3.75	....	....	....	1.40	.40
4271a	42¢ Weddings, pane of 20	12.00	....	....	....	27.00	....
4272	59¢ Silver Heart	3.75	....	32.00(20)	9.00	2.00	.75

4273 4332

SCOTT NO.	DESCRIPTION	FIRST DAY COVERS SING	FIRST DAY COVERS PL. BLK.	MINT SHEET	PLATE BLOCK	UNUSED F/NH	USED
4273-82	42¢ Flags of Our Nation, coil strip of 11	....	....	....	....	14.00	....
	same, plate # strip of 10	....	....	....	....	19.00	....
4273	42¢ American Flag. . .	3.75	....	....	....	1.50	.75
4274	42¢ Alabama Flag . . .	3.75	....	....	....	1.50	.75
4275	42¢ Alaska Flag.	3.75	....	....	....	1.50	.75
4276	42¢ American Samoa Flag	3.75	....	....	....	1.50	.75
4277	42¢ Arizona Flag . . .	3.75	....	....	....	1.50	.75
4278	42¢ Arkansas Flag. . .	3.75	....	....	....	1.50	.75
4279	42¢ California Flag . .	3.75	....	....	....	1.50	.75
4280	42¢ ColoradoFlag . . .	3.75	....	....	....	1.50	.75
4281	42¢ Connecticut Flag	3.75	....	....	....	1.50	.75
4282	42¢ Deleware Flag . .	3.75	....	....	....	1.50	.75
4283-92	42¢ Flags of Our Nation	....	....	....	....	14.00	....
	coil strip of 10	....	....	....	....	19.00	....
4283	42¢ District of Columbia Flag	3.75	....	....	....	1.50	.75
4284	42¢ Florida Flag.	3.75	....	....	....	1.50	.75
4285	42¢ Georgia Flag. . . .	3.75	....	....	....	1.50	.75
4286	42¢ Guam Flag	3.75	....	....	....	1.50	.75
4287	42¢ Hawaii Flag.	3.75	....	....	....	1.50	.75
4288	42¢ Idaho Flag.	3.75	....	....	....	1.50	.75
4289	42¢ Illinois Flag	3.75	....	....	....	1.50	.75
4290	42¢ Indiana Flag	3.75	....	....	....	1.50	.75
4291	42¢ Iowa Flag	3.75	....	....	....	1.50	.75
4292	42¢ Kansas Flag	3.75	....	....	....	1.50	.75
4293-4302	44¢ Flags of Our Nation, coil strip of 10	12.00	....	....	....	14.00	....
	same, plate # strip of 11	....	....	....	....	19.00	....
4293	44¢ Kentucky Flag. . .	3.75	....	....	....	1.50	.75
4294	44¢ Louisiana Flag . .	3.75	....	....	....	1.50	.75
4295	44¢ Maine Flag	3.75	....	....	....	1.50	.75
4296	44¢ Maryland Flag. . .	3.75	....	....	....	1.50	.75
4297	44¢ Massachusetts . .	3.75	....	....	....	1.50	.75
4298	44¢ Michigan Flag . . .	3.75	....	....	....	1.50	.75
4299	44¢ Minnesota Flag. .	3.75	....	....	....	1.50	.75
4300	44¢ Mississippi Flag .	3.75	....	....	....	1.50	.75
4301	44¢ Missouri Flag . . .	3.75	....	....	....	1.50	.75
4302	44¢ American Flag & Wheat.	3.75	....	....	....	1.50	.75
4303-12	44¢ Flags of Our Nation. coil strip of 10.	12.00	....	....	....	14.00	....
	same, plate strip of 11	....	....	....	....	19.00	....
4303	44¢ American Flag and Mountains	3.75	....	....	....	1.50	.75
4304	44¢ Montana Flag . . .	3.75	....	....	....	1.50	.50
4305	44¢ Nebraska Flag . .	3.75	....	....	....	1.50	.50
4306	44¢ Nevada Flag	3.75	....	....	....	1.50	.50
4307	44¢ New Hampshire Flag	3.75	....	....	....	1.50	.50
4308	44¢ New Jersey Flag.	3.75	....	....	....	1.50	.50
4309	44¢ New Mexico Flag	3.75	....	....	....	1.50	.50
4310	44¢ New York Flag . .	3.75	....	....	....	1.50	.50
4311	44¢ North Carolina Flag	3.75	....	....	....	1.50	.50
4312	44¢ North Dakota Flag	3.75	....	....	....	1.50	.50
4313-22	(44¢) Flags of Our Nation	....	....	....	....	14.00	....
	same, plate # strip of 11	....	....	....	....	19.00	....
4313	(44¢) N. Marianas Flag	3.75	....	....	....	1.50	.75
4314	(44¢) Ohio Flag	3.75	....	....	....	1.50	.75
4315	(44¢) Oklahoma Flag.	3.75	....	....	....	1.50	.75
4316	(44¢) Oregon Flag . . .	3.75	....	....	....	1.50	.75
4317	(44¢) Pennsylvania Flag	3.75	....	....	....	1.50	.75
4318	(44¢) Puerto Rico Flag	3.75	....	....	....	1.50	.75
4319	(44¢) Rhode Island Flag	3.75	....	....	....	1.50	.75
4320	(44¢) South Carolina Flag	3.75	....	....	....	1.50	.75
4321	(44¢) South Dakota Flag	3.75	....	....	....	1.50	.75
4322	(44¢) Tennessee Flag	3.75	....	....	....	1.50	.75
4323-32	(45¢) Flags of our Nation		....	....	....	40.00	....
	same, plate strip of 11		....	....	....	46.00	....
4323	(45¢) Texas Flag	3.75	....	....	....	4.00	1.75
4324	(45¢) Utah Flag	3.75	....	....	....	4.00	1.75
4325	(45¢) Vermont Flag . .	3.75	....	....	....	4.00	1.75
4326	(45¢) Virgin Islands Flag	3.75	....	....	....	4.00	1.75
4327	(45¢)Virginia Flag . . .	3.75	....	....	....	4.00	1.75
4328	(45¢) Washington Flag	3.75	....	....	....	4.00	1.75
4329	(45¢) West Virginia Flag	3.75	....	....	....	4.00	1.75
4330	(45¢) Wisconsin Flag.	3.75	....	....	....	4.00	1.75
4331	(45¢) Wyoming Flag .	3.75	....	....	....	4.00	1.75
4332	(45¢) American Flag and Fruited Plain	3.75	....	....	....	4.00	1.75

4333

CHARLES (1907-78) AND RAY (1912-88) EAMES, DESIGNERS

- **4333a** *Christmas card depicting Charles and Ray Eames*
- **4333b** *"Crosspatch" fabric design*
- **4333c** *Stacking chairs*
- **4333d** *Case Study House #8, Pacific Palisades, CA*
- **4333e** *Wire-base table*
- **4333f** *Lounge chair and ottoman*
- **4333g** *Hang-it-all*
- **4333h** *La Chaise*
- **4333i** *Scene from film, "Tops"*
- **4333j** *Wire mesh chair*
- **4333k** *Cover of May 1943 edition of California Arts & Architecture Magazine*
- **4333l** *House of Cards*
- **4333m** *Molded plywood sculpture*
- **4333n** *Eames Storage Unit*
- **4333o** *Aluminum group chair*
- **4333p** *Molded plywood chair*

SCOTT NO.	DESCRIPTION	FIRST DAY COVERS SING	FIRST DAY COVERS PL. BLK.	MINT SHEET	PLATE BLOCK	UNUSED F/NH	USED
4333	42¢ Charles & Ray Eames	....	....	25.00 (16)	....	25.00	....
4333a	42¢ Charles & Ray Eames	3.75	....	....	....	1.75	.75
4333b	42¢ Crosspatch Fabric Design	3.75	....	....	....	1.75	.75
4333c	42¢ Stacking Chairs .	3.75	....	....	....	1.75	.75
4333d	42¢ Case Study House No.8	3.75	....	....	....	1.75	.75
4333e	42¢ Wire Base Tables	3.75	....	....	....	1.75	.75
4333f	42¢ Lounge Chair & Ottoman	3.75	....	....	....	1.75	.75
4333g	42¢ Hang-It-All.	3.75	....	....	....	1.75	.75
4333h	42¢ La Chaise	3.75	....	....	....	1.75	.75
4333i	42¢ "Tops".	3.75	....	....	....	1.75	.75
4333j	42¢ Wire Mesh Chair	3.75	....	....	....	1.75	.75
4333k	42¢ "Arts & Architecture" Cover	3.75	....	....	....	1.75	.75
4333l	42¢ House of Cards .	3.75	....	....	....	1.75	.75
4333m	42¢ Molded Plywood Sculpture	3.75	....	....	....	1.75	.75
4333n	42¢ Eames Storage Unit	3.75	....	....	....	1.75	.75
4333o	42¢ Aluminum Group Chair	3.75	....	....	....	1.75	.75
4333p	42¢ Molded Plywood Chair	3.75	....	....	....	1.75	.75

4334 4335

SCOTT NO.	DESCRIPTION	FIRST DAY COVERS SING	FIRST DAY COVERS PL. BLK.	MINT SHEET	PLATE BLOCK	UNUSED F/NH	USED
4334	Summer Olympics . . .	3.75	4.50	25.00 (20)	6.50	1.60	.40
4335	42¢ Celebrate	3.75	4.50	22.00 (20)	6.00	1.50	.40

4336 4337 4338 4339 4340

SCOTT NO.	DESCRIPTION	FIRST DAY COVERS SING	FIRST DAY COVERS PL. BLK.	MINT SHEET	PLATE BLOCK	UNUSED F/NH	USED
4336-40	42¢ Vintage Black Cinema		....	30.00(20)	15.00(10)	8.50	....
4336	42¢ Poster for "Black & Tan"	3.75	....	....	....	1.60	1.50
4337	42¢ Poster for "The Sport of the Gods"	3.75	....	....	....	1.60	1.50
4338	42¢ Poster for "Prinsesse Tam-Tam".....	3.75	....	....	....	1.60	1.50
4339	42¢ Poster for "Caldonia"	3.75	....	....	....	1.60	1.50
4340	42¢ Poster for "Hallelujah"	3.75	....	....	....	1.60	1.50

SCOTT NO.	DESCRIPTION	FIRST DAY COVERS SING	PL. BLK.	MINT SHEET	PLATE BLOCK	UNUSED F/NH	USED
4341	42¢ Take Me Out To Ballgame	3.75	4.50	25.00 (20)	6.50	1.50	.40
4342-45	42¢ Art of Disney. . . .	4.25	4.75	24.00 (20)	7.50	7.00	....
4342	42¢ Lucky & Pongo, from 101 Dalmations . .	3.75	....	....	....	1.60	.75
4343	42¢ Steamboat Willie .	3.75	....	....	....	1.60	.75
4344	42¢ Sleeping Beauty. .	3.75	....	....	....	1.60	.75
4345	42¢ Mowgli & Baloo, from Jungle Book	3.75	....	....	....	1.60	.75
4346	42¢ Albert Bierstadt . .	3.75	4.50	....	....	1.50	.45
4346a	42¢ Albert Bierstadt bklt pane of 20.	....	....	....	....	26.00	....
4347	42¢ Sunflower	3.75	....	....	....	1.50	.35
4347a	same, bklt pane of 20	....	....	....	....	26.00	....
4348	5¢ Sea Coast, coil (2008) water-activated	....	....	....	....	.30	.25
	same, plate strip of 5..	....	....	....	....	3.75	....
4349	42¢ Latin Jazz	3.75	....	24.00(20)	5.50	1.50	.40
4350	42¢ Bette Davis	3.75	....	36.00(20)	8.00	1.85	.50
4351	42¢ EID, die cut 11 . .	3.75	....	24.00(20)	5.50	1.50	.90
4352	42¢ Great Lakes Dunes, sheet of 10.	....	....	17.00	....	17.00	....
	set of singles	20.00	....	....	....	....	9.00
4353-57	42¢ Automobiles of the 1950's	3.75	....	25.00(20)	15.00 (10)	7.50	....
4353	42¢ 1959 Cadillac Eldorado	....	....	....	....	1.50	.85
4354	42¢ 1957 Studebaker Golden Hawk.	....	....	....	....	1.50	.85
4355	42¢ 1957 Pontiac Safari	....	....	....	....	1.50	.85
4356	42¢ 1957 Lincoln Premiere	....	....	....	....	1.50	.85
4357	42¢ 1957 Chrysler 300C	....	....	....	....	1.50	.85
4358	42¢ Alzheimer's Awareness	....	......:	22.00	5.50	1.50	.40
4359	42¢ Virgin and Child, Botticelli.	3.75	....	....	....	1.50	.40
4359a	same, bklt pane of 20	....	....	....	....	26.00	....
4360-63	42¢ Nutcrackers, block of 4, die cut 10.75x11	....	....	....	....	8.50	....
4360	42¢ Drummer Nutcracker, die cut 10.75x11	3.75	....	....	....	1.75	1.00
4361	42¢ Santa Claus Nutcracker, die cut 10.75x11	3.75	....	....	....	1.75	1.00
4362	42¢ King Nutcracker, die cut 10.75x11	3.75	....	....	....	1.75	1.00
4363	42¢ Soldier Nutcracker, die cut 10.75x11	3.75	....	....	....	1.75	1.00
4363b	42¢ Nutcracker, pane of 20	....	....	....	....	34.00	....
4364-67	42¢ Nutcrackers, block of 4 die cut 11.25x11.	....	....	....	....	7.50	....
4364	42¢ Drummer Nutcracker, die cut 11.25x11.	3.75	....	....	....	2.00	1.25
4365	42¢ Santa Claus Nutcracker, die cut 11.25x11.	3.75	....	....	....	2.00	1.25
4366	42¢ King Nutcracker, die cut 11.25x11.	3.75	....	....	....	2.00	1.25
4367	42¢ Soldier Nutcracker, die cut 11.25x11.	3.75	....	....	....	2.00	1.25
4367b	42¢ Nutcracker, bklt pane of 4.	....	....	....	....	7.50	....
4367c	42¢ Nutcracker, (2 each 4366, 4367) bklt pane of 6.	....	....	....	....	11.00	....
4367d	42¢ Nutcracker, (2 each 4364, 4365) bklt pane of 6.	....	....	....	....	11.00	....
4367bk	42¢ Nutcracker, bklt pane of 20, complete	....	....	....	....	34.00	....
4368-71	42¢ Nutcrackers, block of 4, die cut 8 . .	4.75	....	....	....	9.00	....
4368	42¢ Drummer Nutcracker, die cut 8.	3.75	....	....	....	2.00	1.00
4369	42¢ Santa Claus Nutcracker, die cut 8.	3.75	....	....	....	2.00	1.00
4370	42¢ King Nutcracker, die cut 8.	3.75	....	....	....	2.00	1.00
4371	42¢ Soldier Nutcracker, die cut 8.	3.75	....	....	....	2.00	1.00
4371b	42¢ Nutcracker, bklt pane of 18.	....	....	....	....	34.00	....

GREAT LAKES DUNES

4352a	Vesper Sparrow	**4352f**	Spotted Sandpiper
4352b	Red Fox	**4352g**	Tiger Beetle
4352c	Piping Plover	**4352h**	White Footed Mouse
4352d	Eastern Hognose Snake	**4352i**	Piper Plover Nestings
4352e	Common Mergansers	**4352j**	Red Admiral Butterfly

4372

4373

SCOTT NO.	DESCRIPTION	FIRST DAY COVERS SING	FIRST DAY COVERS PL. BLK.	MINT SHEET	PLATE BLOCK	UNUSED F/NH	USED
4372	42¢ Hanukkah	3.75	....	24.00(20)	6.00	1.50	.75
4373	42¢ Kwanzaa.	3.75	....	24.00(20)	6.00	1.50	.75

2009 COMMEMORATIVES

SCOTT NO.	DESCRIPTION	FIRST DAY COVERS SING	FIRST DAY COVERS PL. BLK.	MINT SHEET	PLATE BLOCK	UNUSED F/NH	USED
4374/4434	**(4374-4377, 4380-83, 4386, 4406, 4407, 4408, 4409-4413, 4415, 4416, 4417-4420, 4421, 4433, 4434) 26 varieties**		**......**	**.........**	**.........**	**43.00**	**27.50**

4374

4375

SCOTT NO.	DESCRIPTION	FIRST DAY COVERS SING	FIRST DAY COVERS PL. BLK.	MINT SHEET	PLATE BLOCK	UNUSED F/NH	USED
4374	42¢ Alaska Statehood	3.75	....	22.00(20)	5.50	1.40	.40
4375	42¢ Year of the Ox. . .	3.75	....	14.00(12)	5.50	1.40	.40

4376

4377

SCOTT NO.	DESCRIPTION	FIRST DAY COVERS SING	FIRST DAY COVERS PL. BLK.	MINT SHEET	PLATE BLOCK	UNUSED F/NH	USED
4376	42¢ Oregon Statehood	3.75	....	22.00(20)	5.50	1.50	.40
4377	42¢ Edgar Allen Poe .	3.75	....	22.00(20)	5.50	1.50	.40

4378

4379

SCOTT NO.	DESCRIPTION	FIRST DAY COVERS SING	FIRST DAY COVERS PL. BLK.	MINT SHEET	PLATE BLOCK	UNUSED F/NH	USED
4378	$4.95 Redwood Forest	12.00	....	245.00(20)	60.00	14.00	10.00
4379	$17.50 Old Faithful . .	35.00	....	840.00(20)	195.00	48.00	30.00

4380

4381

4382

4383

SCOTT NO.	DESCRIPTION	FIRST DAY COVERS SING	FIRST DAY COVERS PL. BLK.	MINT SHEET	PLATE BLOCK	UNUSED F/NH	USED
4380-83	42¢ Lincoln, strip of 4	5.75	....	34.00(20)	16.00(8)	8.50	....
4380	42¢ Lincoln as Rail Splitter	4.75	....	....	....	2.00	.75
4381	42¢ Lincoln as Lawyer	4.75	....	....	....	2.00	.75
4382	42¢ Lincoln as Politician	4.75	....	....	....	2.00	.75
4383	42¢ Lincoln as President	4.75	....	....	....	2.00	.75

4384

SCOTT NO.	DESCRIPTION	FIRST DAY COVERS SING	FIRST DAY COVERS PL. BLK.	MINT SHEET	PLATE BLOCK	UNUSED F/NH	USED
4384	42¢ Civil Rights Pioneers	....	....	....	....	14.00	....
4384a	42¢ Mary Church Terrell & Mary White Ovington	....	....	....	....	2.25	1.50
4384b	42¢ J R Clifford & Joel Elias Spingarn..	....	....	....	....	2.25	1.50
4384c	42¢ Oswald Garrison Villard & Daisy Gatson Bates	....	....	....	....	2.25	1.50
4384d	42¢ Charles Hamilton Houston & Walter White.	....	....	....	....	2.25	1.50
4384e	Medgar Evers & Fannie Lou Hamer..	....	....	....	....	2.25	1.50
4384f	Ella Baker & Ruby Hurley	....	....	....	....	2.25	1.50

4385

4386

SCOTT NO.	DESCRIPTION	FIRST DAY COVERS SING	FIRST DAY COVERS PL. BLK.	MINT SHEET	PLATE BLOCK	UNUSED F/NH	USED
4385	10¢ Patriotic Banner. .	3.75	....	....	....	.50	.30
	same, plate strip of 5..		....	....	....	6.00	....
4386	61¢ Richard Wright . .	3.75	....	30.00	8.00	2.00	.85

4387, 4389

4388

4390

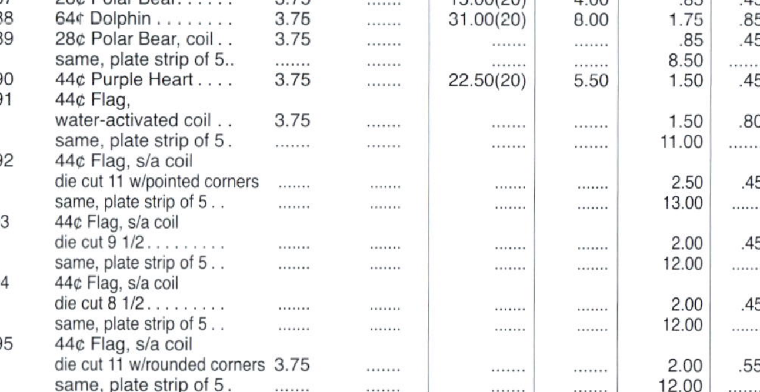

SCOTT NO.	DESCRIPTION	FIRST DAY COVERS SING	FIRST DAY COVERS PL. BLK.	MINT SHEET	PLATE BLOCK	UNUSED F/NH	USED
4387	28¢ Polar Bear.	3.75	....	15.00(20)	4.00	.85	.45
4388	64¢ Dolphin	3.75	....	31.00(20)	8.00	1.75	.85
4389	28¢ Polar Bear, coil . .	3.75	....	....	....	.85	.45
	same, plate strip of 5..		....	....	....	8.50	....
4390	44¢ Purple Heart	3.75	....	22.50(20)	5.50	1.50	.45
4391	44¢ Flag, water-activated coil . .	3.75	....	....	....	1.50	.80
	same, plate strip of 5 .	....	....	....	....	11.00	....
4392	44¢ Flag, s/a coil die cut 11 w/pointed corners	....	....	....	....	2.50	.45
	same, plate strip of 5 . .	....	....	....	....	13.00	....
4393	44¢ Flag, s/a coil die cut 9 1/2.	....	....	....	....	2.00	.45
	same, plate strip of 5 . .	....	....	....	....	12.00	....
4394	44¢ Flag, s/a coil die cut 8 1/2.	....	....	....	....	2.00	.45
	same, plate strip of 5 . .	....	....	....	....	12.00	....
4395	44¢ Flag, s/a coil die cut 11 w/rounded corners	3.75	....	....	....	2.00	.55
	same, plate strip of 5 .	....	....	....	....	12.00	....
4396	44¢ American Flag. . .	3.75	....	....	....	1.50	.45
	same, conv. bklt of 10	....	....	....	....	14.00	....

4391-4396

4397

4398

SCOTT NO.	DESCRIPTION	FIRST DAY COVERS SING	FIRST DAY COVERS PL. BLK.	MINT SHEET	PLATE BLOCK	UNUSED F/NH	USED
4397	44¢ Wedding Rings . .	3.75	....	28.00(20)	7.00	1.50	.40
4398	61¢ Wedding Cake . .	3.75	....	40.00(20)	10.00	2.50	.85

4399

4400

4401

4402

4403

SCOTT NO.	DESCRIPTION	FIRST DAY COVERS SING	PL. BLK.	MINT SHEET	PLATE BLOCK	UNUSED F/NH	USED
4399	44¢ Homer Simpson .	3.75	....	....	....	1.50	.85
4400	44¢ Marge Simpson .	3.75	....	....	....	1.50	.85
4401	44¢ Bart Simpson . . .	3.75	....	....	....	1.50	.85
4402	44¢ Lisa Simpson . . .	3.75	....	....	....	1.50	.85
4403	44¢ Maggie Simpson.	3.75	....	....	....	1.50	.85
4403a	Simpson's, bklt pane of 20.	....	....	....	....	30.00	....

4404

4405

SCOTT NO.	DESCRIPTION	FIRST DAY COVERS SING	PL. BLK.	MINT SHEET	PLATE BLOCK	UNUSED F/NH	USED
4404	44¢ King of Hearts. . .	3.75	....	....	....	1.50	.50
4405	44¢ Queen of Hearts .	3.75	....	....	....	1.50	.50
4405a	King and Queen of Hearts, conv. bklt of 20.	....	....	....	....	30.00	....

4406

SCOTT NO.	DESCRIPTION	FIRST DAY COVERS SING	PL. BLK.	MINT SHEET	PLATE BLOCK	UNUSED F/NH	USED
4406	44¢ Bob Hope	3.75	....	35.00(20)	8.50	1.75	.50

4407

4408

SCOTT NO.	DESCRIPTION	FIRST DAY COVERS SING	PL. BLK.	MINT SHEET	PLATE BLOCK	UNUSED F/NH	USED
4407	44¢ Celebrate	3.75	....	22.00(20)	5.50	1.50	.40
4408	44¢ Anna Julia Cooper	3.75	....	24.00(20)	5.50	1.50	.50

4409 4410 4411 4412 4413

SCOTT NO.	DESCRIPTION	FIRST DAY COVERS SING	PL. BLK.	MINT SHEET	PLATE BLOCK	UNUSED F/NH	USED
4409-13	44¢ Gulf Coast Lighthouses	6.00	....	28.00(20)	16.00	9.00	....
4409	44¢ Matagorda Island Lighthouse	2.50	....	....	....	1.75	.75
4410	44¢ Sabine Pass Lighthouse	2.50	....	....	....	1.75	.75
4411	44¢ Biloxi Lighthouse. .	2.50	....	....	....	1.75	.75
4412	44¢ Sand Island Lighthouse	2.50	....	....	....	1.75	.75
4413	44¢ Fort Jefferson Lighthouse	2.50	....	....	....	1.75	.75

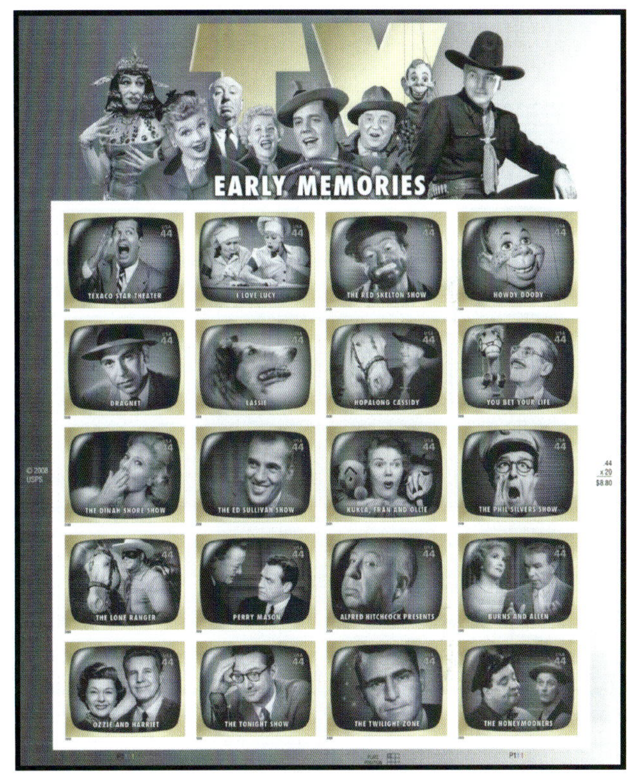

4414

EARLY TV MEMORIES

4414a	*Milton Berle*	**4414k**	*Kukla, Fran & Ollie*
4414b	*I Love Lucy*	**4414l**	*Phil Silvers Show*
4414c	*The Red Skelton Show*	**4414m**	*The Lone Ranger*
4414d	*Howdy Doody*	**4414n**	*Perry Mason*
4414e	*Dragnet*	**4414o**	*Alfred Hitchcock*
4414f	*Lassie*	**4414p**	*Burns & Allen*
4414g	*Hopalong Cassidy*	**4414q**	*Ozzie & Harriet*
4414h	*Groucho Marx*	**4414r**	*The Tonight Show*
4414i	*Dinah Shore Show*	**4414s**	*The Twilight Zone*
4414j	*The Ed Sullivan Show*	**4414t**	*The Honeymooners*

SCOTT NO.	DESCRIPTION	FIRST DAY COVERS SING	PL. BLK.	MINT SHEET	PLATE BLOCK	UNUSED F/NH	USED
4414	44¢ Early TV Memories	20.00	....	30.00 (20)	....	30.00	....
	Set of Singles		....		....		18.00
	Singles		....		....		1.00

4415

4416

SCOTT NO.	DESCRIPTION	FIRST DAY COVERS SING	PL. BLK.	MINT SHEET	PLATE BLOCK	UNUSED F/NH	USED
4415	44¢ Hawaii Statehood .	2.25	7.50	48.00 (20)	10.00	2.50	.50
4416	44¢ EID	2.25	....	22.00 (20)	6.00	1.50	.50

4417 4418 4419 4420

SCOTT NO.	DESCRIPTION	FIRST DAY COVERS SING	FIRST DAY COVERS PL. BLK.	MINT SHEET	PLATE BLOCK	UNUSED F/NH	USED
4417-20	44¢ Thanksgiving Day Parade	5.25	....	23.00 (20)	12.00 (8)	6.50	....
4417	44¢ Crowd, Street Sign, Bear Balloon	2.25	....	....	....	1.50	.55
4418	44¢ Drum Major, Musicians	2.25	....	....	....	1.50	.55
4419	44¢ Musicians, Balloon, Horse	2.25	....	....	....	1.50	.55
4420	44¢ Cowboy, Turkey Balloon	2.25	....	....	....	1.50	.55

4421

SCOTT NO.	DESCRIPTION	FIRST DAY COVERS SING	FIRST DAY COVERS PL. BLK.	MINT SHEET	PLATE BLOCK	UNUSED F/NH	USED
4421	44¢ Gary Cooper.	2.25	....	35.00 (20)	8.50	1.75	.60

4422

SCOTT NO.	DESCRIPTION	FIRST DAY COVERS SING	FIRST DAY COVERS PL. BLK.	MINT SHEET	PLATE BLOCK	UNUSED F/NH	USED
4422	Supreme Court Justices S/S of 4	4.75	....	....	....	7.00	5.00
4422a	44¢ Felix Frankfurter . .	2.25	....	....	....	1.75	1.00
4422b	44¢ William J. Brennan, Jr.	2.25	....	....	....	1.75	1.00
4422c	44¢ Louis D. Brandeis .	2.25	....	....	....	1.75	1.00
4422d	44¢ Joseph Story.	2.25	....	....	....	1.75	1.00

4423

KELP FOREST

4423a *Brown Pelican*
4423b *Western Gull, Southern Sea Otters, Red Sea Urchin*
4423c *Harbor Seal*
4423d *Lion's Mane Nudibranch*
4423e *Yellow-tail Rockfish, White-spotted Rose Anemone*
4423f *Vermillion Rockfish*
4423g *Copper Rockfish*
4423h *Pacific Rock Crab, Jeweled Top Snail*
4423i *Northern Kelp Crab*
4423j *Treefish, Monterey Turban Snail, Brooding Sea Anemone*

SCOTT NO.	DESCRIPTION	FIRST DAY COVERS SING	FIRST DAY COVERS PL. BLK.	MINT SHEET	PLATE BLOCK	UNUSED F/NH	USED
4423	44¢ Kelp Forest	10.00	....	18.00 (10)	....	18.00	....
	Set of Singles	....		....	....	18.00	8.00

4424

SCOTT NO.	DESCRIPTION	FIRST DAY COVERS SING	FIRST DAY COVERS PL. BLK.	MINT SHEET	PLATE BLOCK	UNUSED F/NH	USED
4424	44¢ Madonna & Sleeping Child	2.25	....	....	....	1.50	.45
4424a	same, booklet pane of 20	....	....	....	....	28.00	....

4425, 4429 4426, 4430 4427, 4431 4428, 4432

SCOTT NO.	DESCRIPTION	FIRST DAY COVERS SING	FIRST DAY COVERS PL. BLK.	MINT SHEET	PLATE BLOCK	UNUSED F/NH	USED
4425-28	44¢ Winter Holidays, block of 4	5.00	....	....	....	7.50	....
4425	44¢ Reindeer, die cut 10.75x11	2.25	....	....	....	1.75	.50
4426	44¢ Snowman, die cut 10.75x11	2.25	....	....	....	1.75	.50
4427	44¢ Gingerbread Man, die cut 10.75x11	2.25	....	....	....	1.75	.50
4428	44¢ Toy Soldier, die cut 10.75x11	2.25	....	....	....	1.75	.50
4428b	Booklet pane of 20, 5 each 4425-28	....	....	....	....	34.00	....
4429-32	44¢ Winter Holidays, block of 4	5.00	....	....	....	7.50	....
4429	44¢ Reindeer, die cut 8	2.25	....	....	....	1.75	.60
4430	44¢ Snowman, die cut 8	2.25	....	....	....	1.75	.60
4431	44¢ Gingerbread Man, die cut 8.	2.25	....	....	....	1.75	.60
4432	44¢ Toy Soldier, die cut 8	2.25	....	....	....	1.75	.60
4432b	Booklet pane of 18, 5 each: 4429, 4431 4 each: 4430, 4432	....	....	....	....	30.00	....

4433

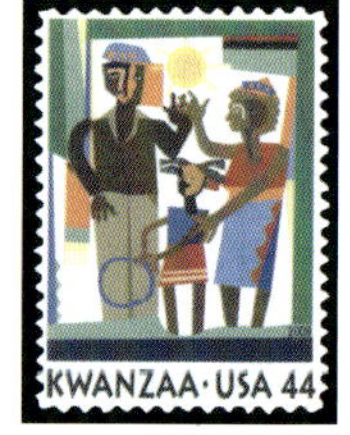

4434

SCOTT NO.	DESCRIPTION	FIRST DAY COVERS SING	FIRST DAY COVERS PL. BLK.	MINT SHEET	PLATE BLOCK	UNUSED F/NH	USED
4433	44¢ Hanukkah	2.25	....	22.00 (20)	5.50	1.50	.50
4434	44¢ Kwanzaa.	2.25	....	22.00 (20)	5.50	1.50	.50

2010 COMMEMORATIVES

SCOTT NO.	DESCRIPTION	FIRST DAY COVERS SING	FIRST DAY COVERS PL. BLK.	MINT SHEET	PLATE BLOCK	UNUSED F/NH	USED
4435/4477	**(4435, 4436, 4440-4443, 4445, 4446-61, 4463-73, 4475, 4476, 4477) 37 varieties**	**........**		**........**	**........**	**55.00**	**18.00**

4435

4436

SCOTT NO.	DESCRIPTION	FIRST DAY COVERS SING	FIRST DAY COVERS PL. BLK.	MINT SHEET	PLATE BLOCK	UNUSED F/NH	USED
4435	44¢ Year of the Tiger . .	2.25	....	15.00 (12)	....	1.75	.55
4436	44¢ 2010 Olympics Snowboarder	2.25	4.75	22.00 (20)	5.50	1.25	.45
4437	44¢ Forever Liberty Bell, dated in copper "2009", medium microprinting, bell 16mm, die-cut 11.25x10.75	2.25	....	....	....	1.50	.55
4437a	same, booklet pane of 18	....	....	....	....	26.00	....

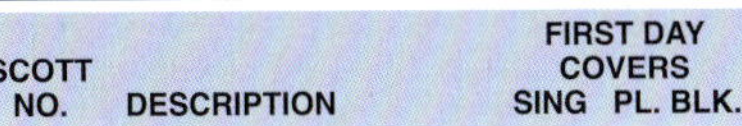

4438

4439

SCOTT NO.	DESCRIPTION	FIRST DAY COVERS SING	FIRST DAY COVERS PL. BLK.	MINT SHEET	PLATE BLOCK	UNUSED F/NH	USED
4438	$4.90 Mackinac Bridge.	12.00	....	235.00 (20)	60.00	15.00	10.00
4439	$18.30 Bixby Creek Bridge	39.00	....	875.00 (20)	215.00	55.00	35.00

4440 4441 4442 4443

SCOTT NO.	DESCRIPTION	FIRST DAY COVERS SING	FIRST DAY COVERS PL. BLK.	MINT SHEET	PLATE BLOCK	UNUSED F/NH	USED
4440-43	44¢ Distinguished Sailors, block of 4	5.25	7.50	24.00 (20)	5.50 (4) 10.00 (8)	6.50	....
4440	Admiral William S. Sims	2.25	....	....	....	1.75	1.00
4441	Admiral Arleigh A. Burke	2.25	....	....	....	1.75	1.00
4442	Lt. Commander John McCloy	2.25	....	....	....	1.75	1.00
4443	Petty Officer 3rd Class Doris Miller	2.25	....	....	....	1.75	1.00

4444

ABSTRACT EXPRESSIONISTS

4444a	*The Golden Wall*	**4444f**	*1948-C*
4444b	*Ashville*	**4444g**	*Elegy to the Spanish Republic*
4444c	*Orange and yellow*	**4444h**	*La Grande Vallee O*
4444d	*Howdy Doody*	**4444i**	*Romanesque Façade*
4444e	*The Liver is the Cock's Comb*	**4444j**	*Achilles*

SCOTT NO.	DESCRIPTION	FIRST DAY COVERS SING	FIRST DAY COVERS PL. BLK.	MINT SHEET	PLATE BLOCK	UNUSED F/NH	USED
4444	Abstract Expressionists	....	20.00	....	....	20.00	....
	set of singles.	....	....	....	....	....	10.00
	singles each	....	....	....	....	....	1.00

4445

SCOTT NO.	DESCRIPTION	FIRST DAY COVERS SING	FIRST DAY COVERS PL. BLK.	MINT SHEET	PLATE BLOCK	UNUSED F/NH	USED
4445	44¢ Bill Mauldin	2.25	....	22.00 (20)	5.75	1.50	.45

4446 4447 4448 4449

SCOTT NO.	DESCRIPTION	FIRST DAY COVERS SING	FIRST DAY COVERS PL. BLK.	MINT SHEET	PLATE BLOCK	UNUSED F/NH	USED
4446-49	44¢ Cowboys of the Silver Screen	5.75	....	32.00 (20)	8.00	7.50	....
4446	44¢ Roy Rogers	2.25	....	....	....	2.00	1.00
4447	44¢ Tom Mix	2.25	....	....	....	2.00	1.00
4448	44¢ William S Hart	2.25	....	....	....	2.00	1.00
4449	44¢ Gene Autry.	2.25	....	....	....	2.00	1.00

4450

SCOTT NO.	DESCRIPTION	FIRST DAY COVERS SING	FIRST DAY COVERS PL. BLK.	MINT SHEET	PLATE BLOCK	UNUSED F/NH	USED
4450	44¢ Love: Pansies in a basket	2.25	....	28.00(20)	6.50	1.50	.40

4451 4452 4453 4454 4455 4456 4457 4458 4459

4460

SCOTT NO.	DESCRIPTION	FIRST DAY COVERS SING	FIRST DAY COVERS PL. BLK.	MINT SHEET	PLATE BLOCK	UNUSED F/NH	USED
4451-60	44¢ Adopt a Shelter Pet	11.50	....	32.00(20)	19.00(10)	17.50	....
4451	44¢ Wire-haired Jack Russell Terrier	2.25	....	....	....	1.50	.65
4452	44¢ Maltese Cat	2.25	....	....	....	1.50	.65
4453	44¢ Calico Cat	2.25	....	....	....	1.50	.65
4454	44¢ Yellow Labrador retriever	2.25	....	....	....	1.50	.65
4455	44¢ Golden retriever. . .	2.25	....	....	....	1.50	.65
4456	44¢ Gray, white and tan cat	2.25	....	....	....	1.50	.65
4457	44¢ Black, white and tan cat	2.25	....	....	....	1.50	.65
4458	44¢ Australian shepherd	2.25	....	....	....	1.50	.65
4459	44¢ Boston terrier.	2.25	....	....	....	1.50	.65
4460	44¢ Orange tabby cat. .	2.25	....	....	....	1.50	.65

4461

4462

SCOTT NO.	DESCRIPTION	FIRST DAY COVERS SING	FIRST DAY COVERS PL. BLK.	MINT SHEET	PLATE BLOCK	UNUSED F/NH	USED
4461	44¢ Katharine Hepburn	2.25	....	24.00(20)	6.00	1.50	.45
4462	64¢ Monarch Butterfly...	2.25	....	31.00(20)	7.50	2.00	1.15

4463

4464

SCOTT NO.	DESCRIPTION	FIRST DAY COVERS SING	FIRST DAY COVERS PL. BLK.	MINT SHEET	PLATE BLOCK	UNUSED F/NH	USED
4463	44¢ Kate Smith.	2.25	....	21.00(20)	5.75	1.50	.45
4464	44¢ Oscar Micheaux. . .	3.75	....	20.00(20)	5.75	1.50	.45

4465 4466

SCOTT NO.	DESCRIPTION	FIRST DAY COVERS SING	FIRST DAY COVERS PL. BLK.	MINT SHEET	PLATE BLOCK	UNUSED F/NH	USED
4465-66	44¢ Negro Leagues Baseball, attached pair.	4.25	7.50	22.00(20)	5.75	3.25	1.25
4465	44¢ Play at Home.	2.50	....	....	....	1.50	.65
4466	44¢ Rube Foster.	2.50	....	....	....	1.50	.65

4467 4468 4469 4470 4471

SCOTT NO.	DESCRIPTION	FIRST DAY COVERS SING	FIRST DAY COVERS PL. BLK.	MINT SHEET	PLATE BLOCK	UNUSED F/NH	USED
4467-71	44¢ Sunday Funnies. . .	4.25	7.50	31.00(20)	18.00(10)	8.00	....
4467	44¢ Beetle Bailey	2.50	....	....	....	1.50	.75
4468	44¢ Calvin and Hobbes	2.50	....	....	....	1.50	.75
4469	44¢ Archie.	2.50	....	....	....	1.50	.75
4470	44¢ Garfield	2.50	....	....	....	1.50	.75
4471	44¢ Dennis the Menace	2.50	....	....	....	1.50	.75

4472

4473

SCOTT NO.	DESCRIPTION	FIRST DAY COVERS SING	FIRST DAY COVERS PL. BLK.	MINT SHEET	PLATE BLOCK	UNUSED F/NH	USED
4472	44¢ Scouting.	2.50	3.75	21.00(20)	5.50	1.50	.45
4473	44¢ Boys in Pasture, Winslow Homer	2.50	3.75	21.00(20)	5.50	1.50	.25

4474

HAWAIIAN RAIN FOREST

4474a *Hawaii 'amakihi, Hawaii 'elepaio*
4474b *'Akepa, 'ope'ape'a*
4474c *'I'iwi, haha*
4474d *'Oma'o, kanawao, 'ohelo kau lau nui*
4474e *'Oha*
4474f *Pulehua, kelea lau nui, 'ilihia*
4474g *Koele Mountain damselfly, 'akala*
4474h *Apapane, Hawaiian Mint*
4474i *Jewel Orchid*
4474j *Happyface spider, 'ala'ala wai nui*

SCOTT NO.	DESCRIPTION	FIRST DAY COVERS SING	FIRST DAY COVERS PL. BLK.	MINT SHEET	PLATE BLOCK	UNUSED F/NH	USED
4474	44¢ Hawaiian Rain Forest sheet	10.00		15.00(10)	....	15.00	....
	set of singles		....	....	....	15.00	10.00

4475

4476

4477

SCOTT NO.	DESCRIPTION	FIRST DAY COVERS SING	FIRST DAY COVERS PL. BLK.	MINT SHEET	PLATE BLOCK	UNUSED F/NH	USED
4475	44¢ Mother Teresa	2.50	3.75	22.00(20)	5.50	1.50	.45
4476	44¢ Julia de Burgos . . .	2.50	3.75	21.00(20)	5.50	1.50	.45
4477	44¢ Angel with Lute . . .	2.50	3.75	21.00(20)	5.50	1.50	.45

4478 4479 4480 4481

SCOTT NO.	DESCRIPTION	FIRST DAY COVERS SING	FIRST DAY COVERS PL. BLK.	MINT SHEET	PLATE BLOCK	UNUSED F/NH	USED
4478-81	(44¢) Forever Pine cones, die cut	11.00	5.50	....	....	16.00	....
4478	(44¢) Forever Ponderosa Pine	2.25	....	....	....	4.00	.50
4479	(44¢) Forever Easter Red Cedar	2.25	....	....	....	4.00	.50
4480	(44¢) Forever Balsam Fir	2.25	....	....	....	4.00	.50
4481	(44¢) Forever Blue Spruce	2.25	....	....	....	4.00	.50
4481b	(44¢) Forever pine cones, die cut 11, bklt pane of 20	....	....	....	....	75.00	....
4482-85	(44¢) Forever pine cones, die cut 11.25x10.75 . . .	5.50	....	....	....	14.00	....
4482	(44¢) Forever Ponderosa Pine	2.25	....	....	....	2.50	.60
4483	(44¢) Forever Eastern Red Cedar	2.25	....	....	....	4.00	.60
4484	(44¢) Forever Balsam Fir	2.25	....	....	....	2.50	.60
4485	(44¢) Forever Blue Spruce	2.25	....	....	....	4.00	.60
4485b	(44¢) Forever pine cones, d/c 11.25x10.75, bklt pane of 18	....	....	....	....	65.00	....

4486, 4488, 4490 4487, 4489, 4491

SCOTT NO.	DESCRIPTION	FIRST DAY COVERS SING	FIRST DAY COVERS PL. BLK.	MINT SHEET	PLATE BLOCK	UNUSED F/NH	USED
4486-87	(44¢) Forever Lady Liberty & Flag (AP) D/C 9.5 (MICRO forever)		....	....	....	5.00	....
	same, plate strip of 5 . .	....	....	....	16.00	....	....
4486	(44¢) Forever Lady Liberty, (AP) D/C 9.5.	2.25	....	....	....	3.00	.45
4487	(44¢) Forever Flag, (AP) D/C 9.5.	2.25	....	....	....	3.00	.45
4488-89	(44¢) Forever Lady Liberty & Flag, (SSP) D/C 11 (MICRO forever)		....	....	....	5.00	....
	same, plate strip of 5 . .	....	....	....	16.00	....	....
4488	(44¢) Forever Lady Liberty, (SSP) D/C 11	2.25	....	....	....	3.00	.45
4489	(44¢) Forever Flag	2.25	....	....	....	3.00	.45
4490-91	(44¢) Forever Lady Liberty & Flag, (AV) D/C 8.5 (MICRO forever)		....	....	......	5.00	....
	same, plate strip of 5 . .	....	....	....	16.00	....	....
4490	(44¢) Forever Lady Liberty, (AV) D/C 8.5	2.25	....	....	....	3.00	.45
4491	(44¢)Forever Flag.	2.25	....	....	....	3.00	.45

2011 COMMEMORATIVES

SCOTT NO.	DESCRIPTION	FIRST DAY COVERS SING	FIRST DAY COVERS PL. BLK.	MINT SHEET	PLATE BLOCK	UNUSED F/NH	USED
4492/4584	**(4492-4494, 4497-4503, 4522-4523, 4525-4528, 4530, 4541-4545, 4547-4558, 4565-4569, 4583-4584) 41 varieties**		**........**	**.........**	**.........**	**74.00**	**25.00**

4492

4493

SCOTT NO.	DESCRIPTION	FIRST DAY COVERS SING	FIRST DAY COVERS PL. BLK.	MINT SHEET	PLATE BLOCK	UNUSED F/NH	USED
4492	(44¢) Year of the Rabbit	2.25	....	25.00(12)	....	2.25	.45
4493	(44¢) Kansas Statehood	2.25	....	28.00(20)	6.50	1.75	.45

4495

4494

4496

SCOTT NO.	DESCRIPTION	FIRST DAY COVERS SING	FIRST DAY COVERS PL. BLK.	MINT SHEET	PLATE BLOCK	UNUSED F/NH	USED
4494	(44¢) Ronald Reagan . .	2.25	....	35.00(20)	9.00	2.00	.50
4495	(5¢) Art Deco Bird, Non-Profit Coil		2.25	....	....	.25	.25
	same, plate number strip of 5		....	....	....	1.70	....
4496	44¢ Quill and Inkwell Coil		2.25	....	....	1.25	.50
	same, plate number strip of 5		....	....	....	12.00	....

4497-4501

SCOTT NO.	DESCRIPTION	FIRST DAY COVERS SING	FIRST DAY COVERS PL. BLK.	MINT SHEET	PLATE BLOCK	UNUSED F/NH	USED
4497-4501	Latin Music Legends	....	....	35.00(20)	18.00(10)	9.00	....
4497	(44¢) Tito Fuente	2.25	....	....	....	2.00	.65
4498	(44¢) Carmen Miranda .	2.25	....	....	....	2.00	.65
4499	(44¢) Selena.	2.25	....	....	....	2.00	.65
4500	(44¢) Carlos Gardel . . .	2.25	....	....	....	2.00	.65
4501	(44¢) Celia Cruz	2.25	....	....	....	2.00	.65

4502

4503

4504

SCOTT NO.	DESCRIPTION	FIRST DAY COVERS SING	FIRST DAY COVERS PL. BLK.	MINT SHEET	PLATE BLOCK	UNUSED F/NH	USED
4502	(44¢) Celebrate.	2.25	....	35.00(20)	7.00	1.80	.45
4503	(44¢) Jazz.	2.25	....	35.00(20)	7.00	1.80	.45
4504	20¢ George Washington	2.25	....	12.00(20)	2.50	.60	.45

4505-09

SCOTT NO.	DESCRIPTION	FIRST DAY COVERS SING	FIRST DAY COVERS PL. BLK.	MINT SHEET	PLATE BLOCK	UNUSED F/NH	USED
4505-09	29¢ Herbs.	....	....	38.00(20)	20.00(10)	10.00	....
4505	29¢ Oregano.	2.25	....	....	....	2.20	.55
4506	29¢ Flax	2.25	....	....	....	2.20	.55
4507	29¢ Foxglove	2.25	....	....	....	2.20	.55
4508	29¢ Lavender	2.25	....	....	....	2.20	.55
4509	29¢ Sage	2.25	....	....	....	2.20	.55

4510

4511

4512

SCOTT NO.	DESCRIPTION	FIRST DAY COVERS SING	FIRST DAY COVERS PL. BLK.	MINT SHEET	PLATE BLOCK	UNUSED F/NH	USED
4510	84¢ Oveta Culp Hobby .	3.75	....	55.00	12.00	3.00	.85
4511	$4.95 New River Gorge Bridge	12.00	....	235.00	55.00	14.00	6.75
4512	20¢ George Washington Coil	2.25	....	....		.50	.35
	same, plate # strip of 5 .	....	....	....	7.00	....	....

4513-17

SCOTT NO.	DESCRIPTION	FIRST DAY COVERS SING	FIRST DAY COVERS PL. BLK.	MINT SHEET	PLATE BLOCK	UNUSED F/NH	USED
4513-17	29¢ Herbs Coil	....	....	....	....	12.00	....
	same, plate # strip of 5 .	....	....	....	16.00	....	....
4513	29¢ Oregano Coil	2.25	....	....	....	2.50	.40
4514	29¢ Flax Coil.	2.25	....	....	....	2.50	.40
4515	29¢ Foxglove Coil.	2.25	....	....	....	2.50	.40
4516	29¢ Lavender Coil	2.25	....	....	....	2.50	.40
4517	29¢ Sage Coil.	2.25	....	....	....	2.50	.40

4518-19

SCOTT NO.	DESCRIPTION	FIRST DAY COVERS SING	FIRST DAY COVERS PL. BLK.	MINT SHEET	PLATE BLOCK	UNUSED F/NH	USED
4518-19	(44¢) Lady Liberty and Flag	3.75	....	....	....	3.50	....
4518	(44¢) Lady Liberty.	2.25	....	....	....	1.75	.70
4519	(44¢) Flag.	2.25	....	....	....	1.75	.70
4519b	Booklet pane of 18, (44¢) Lady Liberty & Flag		....	....	....	30.00	....

4520

4521

SCOTT NO.	DESCRIPTION	FIRST DAY COVERS SING	FIRST DAY COVERS PL. BLK.	MINT SHEET	PLATE BLOCK	UNUSED F/NH	USED
4520	(44¢) Wedding Roses. .	2.25	....	125.00(20)	25.00	5.50	.50
4521	64¢ Wedding Cake. . . .	2.75	....	70.00(20)	18.00	4.00	2.00

4522-4523

SCOTT NO.	DESCRIPTION	FIRST DAY COVERS SING	FIRST DAY COVERS PL. BLK.	MINT SHEET	PLATE BLOCK	UNUSED F/NH	USED
4522-23	(44¢) Civil War Sesquicentennial	3.75	....	24.00(12)	....	4.00	....
4522	(44¢) Battle of Fort Sumter	2.25	....	....	....	2.00	.65
4523	(44¢) First Battle of Bull Run	2.25	....	....	....	2.00	.65

4524

GO GREEN

- 4524a *Buy local produce, reduce bags*
- 4524b *Fix Water Leaks*
- 4524c *Share rides*
- 4524d *Turn off lights when not in use*
- 4524e *Choose to walk*
- 4524f *Go green, step by step*
- 4524g *Compost*
- 4524h *Let nature do the work*
- 4524i *Recycle more*
- 4524j *Ride a bike*
- 4524k *Plant trees*
- 4524l *Insulate the home*
- 4524m *Use public transportation*
- 4524n *Use efficient light bulbs*
- 4524o *Adjust the thermostat*
- 4524p *Maintain tire pressure*

SCOTT NO.	DESCRIPTION	FIRST DAY COVERS SING	FIRST DAY COVERS PL. BLK.	MINT SHEET	PLATE BLOCK	UNUSED F/NH	USED
4524	(44¢) Go Green Pane of 16	....	....	24.00(16)	....	24.00	....
	same, set of singles . . .	....	....	....	....	....	14.00

4525

4526

SCOTT NO.	DESCRIPTION	FIRST DAY COVERS SING	FIRST DAY COVERS PL. BLK.	MINT SHEET	PLATE BLOCK	UNUSED F/NH	USED
4525	(44¢) Helen Hayes	2.25	....	28.00(20)	6.50	1.75	.50
4526	(44¢) Gregory Peck . . .	2.25	....	48.00(20)	11.00	2.50	1.00

4527

4528

SCOTT NO.	DESCRIPTION	FIRST DAY COVERS SING	FIRST DAY COVERS PL. BLK.	MINT SHEET	PLATE BLOCK	UNUSED F/NH	USED
4527-28	(44¢) Space Firsts	3.75	....	28.00(20)	6.50	3.50	1.50
4527	(44¢) Alan B. Shepard, Jr.	2.25	....	....	....	1.75	.65
4528	(44¢) Messenger Mission	2.25	....	....	....	1.75	.65

4529

4530

SCOTT NO.	DESCRIPTION	FIRST DAY COVERS SING	FIRST DAY COVERS PL. BLK.	MINT SHEET	PLATE BLOCK	UNUSED F/NH	USED
4529	(44¢) Purple Heart	2.25	....	28.00(20)	6.50	1.75	.45
4530	(44¢) Indianapolis 500 .	2.25	....	28.00(20)	6.50	1.75	.45

4531-4540

SCOTT NO.	DESCRIPTION	FIRST DAY COVERS SING	FIRST DAY COVERS PL. BLK.	MINT SHEET	PLATE BLOCK	UNUSED F/NH	USED
4531-40	(44¢) Garden of Love . .	12.00	....	75.00(20)	40.00(10)	35.00	....
4531	(44¢) Pink Flower	2.25	....	....	....	3.75	.80
4532	(44¢) Red Flower	2.25	....	....	....	3.75	.80
4533	(44¢) Blue Leaves	2.25	....	....	....	3.75	.80
4534	(44¢) Butterfly.	2.25	....	....	....	3.75	.80
4535	(44¢) Green Vine Leaves	2.25	....	....	....	3.75	.80
4536	(44¢) Blue Flower	2.25	....	....	....	3.75	.80
4537	(44¢) Doves	2.25	....	....	....	3.75	.80
4538	(44¢) Orange Red Flowers	2.25	....	....	....	3.75	.80
4539	(44¢) Strawberry.	2.25	....	....	....	3.75	.80
4540	(44¢) Yellow Orange Flowers	2.25	....	....	....	3.75	.80

4541

4542

4543

4544

SCOTT NO.	DESCRIPTION	FIRST DAY COVERS SING	FIRST DAY COVERS PL. BLK.	MINT SHEET	PLATE BLOCK	UNUSED F/NH	USED
4541-44	(44¢) American Scientists	5.75	....	32.00(20)	15.00(8)	7.00	....
4541	(44¢) Melvin Calvin. . . .	2.75	....	....	....	1.75	.80
4542	(44¢) Asa Gray	2.75	....	....	....	1.75	.80
4543	(44¢) Maria Goeppert Mayer	2.75	....	....	....	1.75	.80
4544	(44¢) Severo Ochoa . . .	2.75	....	....	....	1.75	.80

4545

SCOTT NO.	DESCRIPTION	FIRST DAY COVERS SING	FIRST DAY COVERS PL. BLK.	MINT SHEET	PLATE BLOCK	UNUSED F/NH	USED
4545	(44¢) Mark Twain	2.50	....	30.00(20)	6.50	1.75	.45

4546

PIONEERS OF AMERICAN INDUSTRIAL DESIGN

4546a	*Peter Muller-Munk*	**4546g**	*Norman Bel Geddes*
4546b	*Frederick Hurten Rhead*	**4546h**	*Dave Chapman*
4546c	*Raymond Loewy*	**4546i**	*Greta von Nessen*
4546d	*Donald Deskey*	**4546j**	*Eliot Noyes*
4546e	*Walter Dorwin Teague*	**4546k**	*Russel Wright*
4546f	*Henry Dreyfuss*	**4546l**	*Gilbert Rohde*

SCOTT NO.	DESCRIPTION	FIRST DAY COVERS SING	FIRST DAY COVERS PL. BLK.	MINT SHEET	PLATE BLOCK	UNUSED F/NH	USED
4546	(44¢) Pioneers of American Industrial Design.	15.00	....	22.00(12)	....	22.00	....
	set of singles.	....	....	....	....	22.00	15.00

4547

SCOTT NO.	DESCRIPTION	FIRST DAY COVERS SING	FIRST DAY COVERS PL. BLK.	MINT SHEET	PLATE BLOCK	UNUSED F/NH	USED
4547	(44¢) Owney the Postal Dog	2.75	....	38.00(20)	10.00	2.25	.60

4548

4549

4550

4551

SCOTT NO.	DESCRIPTION	FIRST DAY COVERS SING	FIRST DAY COVERS PL. BLK.	MINT SHEET	PLATE BLOCK	UNUSED F/NH	USED
4548-51	(44¢) U.S. Merchant Marine	4.75	....	28.00(20)	8.00	7.00	....
4548	(44¢) Clipper Ship.	2.75	....	....	....	1.75	.75
4549	(44¢) Auxiliary Steamship	2.75	....	....	....	1.75	.75
4550	(44¢) Liberty Ship	2.75	....	....	....	1.75	.75
4551	(44¢) Container Ship . .	2.75	....	....	....	1.75	.75

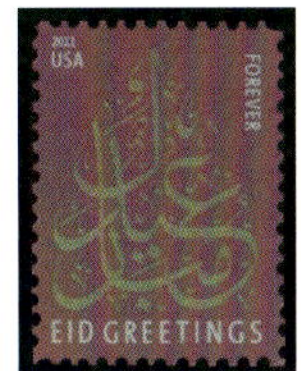

4552

SCOTT NO.	DESCRIPTION	FIRST DAY COVERS SING	FIRST DAY COVERS PL. BLK.	MINT SHEET	PLATE BLOCK	UNUSED F/NH	USED
4552	(44¢) EID	2.75	.....	28.00(20)	6.50	1.75	.50

4553-57

SCOTT NO.	DESCRIPTION	FIRST DAY COVERS SING	FIRST DAY COVERS PL. BLK.	MINT SHEET	PLATE BLOCK	UNUSED F/NH	USED
4553-57	(44¢) Pixar Films: Send a Hello	5.50	....	32.00(20)	16.00(10)	9.00	....
4553	(44¢) Lightening McQueen & Mater	3.25	....	....	....	1.80	.70
4554	(44¢) Remy the Rat & Linquini	3.25	....	....	....	1.80	.70
4555	(44¢) Buzz Lightyear & Two Aliens	3.25	....	....	....	1.80	.70
4556	(44¢) Carl Frederickson & Dug	3.25	....	....	....	1.80	.70
4557	(44¢) Wall-E	3.25	....	....	....	1.80	.70

4559, 4561, 4563

4558

4560, 4562, 4564

SCOTT NO.	DESCRIPTION	FIRST DAY COVERS SING	FIRST DAY COVERS PL. BLK.	MINT SHEET	PLATE BLOCK	UNUSED F/NH	USED
4558	(44¢) Edward Hopper . .	2.75	....	45.00(20)	10.00	2.25	.50
4559	(44¢) Lady Liberty (AP)	2.75	....	....	....	2.25	.65
4560	(44¢) American Flag (AP)	2.75	....	....	....	2.25	.65
4560A	Booklet pane of 20	....	....	....	....	45.00	....
4561	(44¢) Lady Liberty (SSP)	2.75	....	....	....	2.25	.65
4562	(44¢) American Flag (SSP)	2.75	....	....	....	2.25	.65
4562A	Booklet pane of 20	....	....	....	....	45.00	....
4563	(44¢) Lady Liberty (AV).	2.75	....	....	....	2.25	.65
4564	(44¢) American Flag (AV)	2.75	....	....	....	2.25	.65
4564B	Booklet pane of 20	....	....	....	....	45.00	....

4565

4566

4567

4570

4568

4569

SCOTT NO.	DESCRIPTION	FIRST DAY COVERS SING	FIRST DAY COVERS PL. BLK.	MINT SHEET	PLATE BLOCK	UNUSED F/NH	USED
4565	(44¢) Barbara Jordan . .	2.75	....	40.00(20)	9.00	2.00	.50
4566-69	(44¢) Romare Bearden.	5.50	....	30.00(16)	14.00(6)	9.00	....
4566	(44¢) Conjunction	2.75	....	....	....	2.00	1.25
4567	(44¢) Odyesseus	2.75	....	....	....	2.00	1.25
4568	(44¢) Prevalence of Ritual	2.75	....	....	....	2.00	1.25
4569	(44¢) Falling Star	2.75	....	....	....	2.00	1.25
4570	(44¢) Madonna, Raphael	2.75	....	....	....	1.75	.35
4570a	same, booklet pane of 20	....	....	....	....	30.00	....

4571, 4575, 4579

4572, 4576, 4580

4573, 4577, 4581

4574, 4578, 4582

SCOTT NO.	DESCRIPTION	FIRST DAY COVERS SING	FIRST DAY COVERS PL. BLK.	MINT SHEET	PLATE BLOCK	UNUSED F/NH	USED
4571-74	(44¢)Christmas Ornaments, bklt of 4, 10 3/4x11, microprinted on collar	....	....	....	....	11.00	....
4571	(44¢) Red Ornament. . .	2.75	....	....	....	3.00	.70
4572	(44¢) Blue Ornament, green ribbon	2.75	....	....	....	3.00	.70
4573	(44¢) Blue Ornament, red ribbon	2.75	....	....	....	3.00	.70
4574	(44¢) Green Ornament .	2.75	....	....	....	3.00	.70
4574b	Same, booklet pane of 20	....	....	....	....	55.00	....
4575-78	(44¢) Christmas Ornaments, bklt of 4, ... 10 3/4x11, microprinted not on collar	2.75	....	....	....	11.00	....
4575	(44¢) Red Ornament. . .	2.75	....	....	....	3.00	.70
4576	(44¢) Blue Ornament, green ribbon	2.75	....	....	....	3.00	.70
4577	(44¢) Blue Ornament, red ribbon	2.75	....	....	....	3.00	.70
4578	(44¢) Green Ornament .	2.75	....	....	....	3.00	.70
4578b	Same, booklet pane of 20	....	....	....	....	55.00	....
4579-82	(44¢) Christmas Ornament, bklt of 4, 11 1/4x11	....	....	....	....	15.00	....
4579	(44¢) Red Ornament. . .	2.75	....	....	....	3.75	.70
4580	(44¢) Blue Ornament, green ribbon	2.75	....	....	....	3.75	.70
4581	(44¢) Blue Ornament, red ribbon	2.75	....	....	....	3.75	.70
4582	(44¢) Green Ornament .	2.75	....	....	....	3.75	.70
4582bm	Same, booklet pane of 18	....	....	....	....	60.00	....

4583

4584

SCOTT NO.	DESCRIPTION	FIRST DAY COVERS SING	FIRST DAY COVERS PL. BLK.	MINT SHEET	PLATE BLOCK	UNUSED F/NH	USED
4583	(44¢) Hanukkah	2.75	....	35.00(20)	6.50	1.75	.45
4584	(44¢) Kwanzaa	2.75	....	35.00(20)	6.50	1.75	.45

4585-90

SCOTT NO.	DESCRIPTION	FIRST DAY COVERS SING	FIRST DAY COVERS PL. BLK.	MINT SHEET	PLATE BLOCK	UNUSED F/NH	USED
4585-90	(25¢) Eagles presort, strip of 6	4.75	....	....	....	10.00	....
	same, plate strip of 7 . .	....	....	....	....	18.00	....
4585	(25¢) Eagle, green	2.50	....	....	....	1.70	.60
4586	(25¢) Eagle, blue green	2.50	....	....	....	1.70	.60
4587	(25¢) Eagle, blue green	2.50	....	....	....	1.70	.60
4588	(25¢) Eagle, red violet .	2.50	....	....	....	1.70	.60
4589	(25¢) Eagle, brown orange	2.50	....	....	....	1.70	.60
4590	(25¢) Eagle, yellow orange	2.50	....	....	....	1.70	.60

2012 COMMEMORATIVES

SCOTT NO.	DESCRIPTION	FIRST DAY COVERS SING	FIRST DAY COVERS PL. BLK.	MINT SHEET	PLATE BLOCK	UNUSED F/NH	USED
4591/4705	**(4591, 4623-4625, 4627-4628, 4651-4665, 4667-4671, 4677-4681, 4687-4703, 4705) 49 varieties . . . .**	**.......**	**.......**	**.......**	**.......**	**108.00**	**40.00**

4591

SCOTT NO.	DESCRIPTION	FIRST DAY COVERS SING	FIRST DAY COVERS PL. BLK.	MINT SHEET	PLATE BLOCK	UNUSED F/NH	USED
4591	(44¢) New Mexico.	2.75	5.75	30.00(20)	6.50	1.75	.50

4592-96

SCOTT NO.	DESCRIPTION	FIRST DAY COVERS SING	FIRST DAY COVERS PL. BLK.	MINT SHEET	PLATE BLOCK	UNUSED F/NH	USED
4592-96	32¢ Aloha Shirts, strip of 5	5.25	....	44.00(20)	22.00(10)	12.00	....
4592	32¢ Surfers and Palm Trees	2.50	....	....	....	2.25	.55
4593	32¢ Surfers.	2.50	....	....	....	2.25	.55
4594	32¢ Fossil Fish	2.50	....	....	....	2.25	.55
4595	32¢ Shells.	2.50	....	....	....	2.25	.55
4596	32¢ Fish and Starfish . .	2.50	....	....	....	2.25	.55
4597-4601	32¢ Aloha Shirts, coil strip of 5	5.25	....	....	....	10.00	....
4597	32¢ Fish and Starfish . .	2.50	....	....	....	2.00	.55
4598	32¢ Surfers and Palm Trees	2.50	....	....	....	2.00	.55
4599	32¢ Surfers.	2.50	....	....	....	2.00	.55
4600	32¢ Fossil Fish	2.50	....	....	....	2.00	.55
4601	32¢ Shells.	2.50	....	....	....	2.00	.55
	Same, plate # strip of 5	....	....	....	....	16.00	....
	Same, plate # strip of 11	....	....	....	....	30.00	....

4602

4603

4604

4605

4606

4607

SCOTT NO.	DESCRIPTION	FIRST DAY COVERS SING	FIRST DAY COVERS PL. BLK.	MINT SHEET	PLATE BLOCK	UNUSED F/NH	USED
4602	65¢ Wedding Cake	2.75	....	85.00(20)	18.00	4.00	.95
4603	65¢ Baltimore Checkerspot	2.75	....	85.00(20)	22.00	4.50	1.25
4604-07	65¢ Dogs at Work, 4 attached	7.50	....	34.00(20)	10.50	10.00	....
4604	65¢ Seeing Eye Dog. . .	2.75	....	....	....	2.25	1.00
4605	65¢ Therapy Dog	2.75	....	....	....	2.25	1.00
4606	65¢ Military Dog	2.75	....	....	....	2.25	1.00
4607	65¢ Rescue Dog.	2.75	....	....	....	2.25	1.00

4608-4612

SCOTT NO.	DESCRIPTION	FIRST DAY COVERS SING	FIRST DAY COVERS PL. BLK.	MINT SHEET	PLATE BLOCK	UNUSED F/NH	USED
4608-12	85¢ Birds of Prey, strip of 5	10.75	....	75.00(20)	35.00(10)	18.00	....
4608	85¢ Northern Goshawk	3.50	....	....	....	3.75	3.00
4609	85¢ Peregrine Falcon . .	3.50	....	....	....	3.75	3.00
4610	85¢ Golden Eagle.	3.50	....	....	....	3.75	3.00
4611	85¢ Osprey.	3.50	....	....	....	3.75	3.00
4612	85¢ Northern Harrier. . .	3.50	....	....	....	3.75	3.00

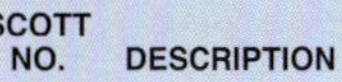

4613-4617

SCOTT NO.	DESCRIPTION	FIRST DAY COVERS SING	FIRST DAY COVERS PL. BLK.	MINT SHEET	PLATE BLOCK	UNUSED F/NH	USED
4613-17	45¢ Weather Vanes, coil strip of 5	6.75	....	....	....	8.00	....
	Same, plate # strip of 5	....	....	....	....	11.00	....
	Same, plate # strip of 11	....	....	....	....	18.00	....
4613	45¢ Rooster With Perch	2.75	....	....	....	1.75	.60
4614	45¢ Cow	2.75	....	....	....	1.75	.60
4615	45¢ Eagle	2.75	....	....	....	1.75	.60
4616	45¢ Rooster	2.75	....	....	....	1.75	.60
4617	45¢ Centaur	2.75	....	....	....	1.75	.60

4618

4619

4620

4621

4622

SCOTT NO.	DESCRIPTION	FIRST DAY COVERS SING	FIRST DAY COVERS PL. BLK.	MINT SHEET	PLATE BLOCK	UNUSED F/NH	USED
4618-22	(45¢) Bonsai, strip of 5 .	6.75	....	....	....	17.00	....
4618	(45¢) Sierra Juniper . . .	2.50	....	....	....	3.50	.70
4619	(45¢) Black Pine	2.50	....	....	....	3.50	.70
4620	(45¢) Banyan	2.50	....	....	....	3.50	.70
4621	(45¢) Trident Maple . . .	2.50	....	....	....	3.50	.70
4622	(45¢) Azalea	2.50	....	....	....	3.50	.70
4622b	Booklet pane of 20	....	....	....	....	65.00	....

4623

4624

4625

4626

4627

4628

SCOTT NO.	DESCRIPTION	FIRST DAY COVERS SING	FIRST DAY COVERS PL. BLK.	MINT SHEET	PLATE BLOCK	UNUSED F/NH	USED
4623	(45¢) Chinese New Year	2.50	....	24.00(12)	....	2.00	.50
4624	(45¢) John H. Johnson .	2.50	....	30.00(20)	6.50	1.75	.50
4625	(45¢) Heart Health	2.50	....	30.00(20)	6.50	1.75	.50
4626	(45¢) Love Ribbons . . .	2.50	....	30.00(20)	6.50	1.75	.50
4627	(45¢) Arizona Statehood Cent..	2.50	....	30.00(20)	6.50	1.75	.50
4628	(45¢) Danny Thomas . .	2.75	....	30.00(20)	6.50	1.75	.50
4629-32	(45¢) Flag Strip of 4, d/c 8.5 vertical	....	....	....	....	9.00	....
4629	(45¢) Flag & Equality coil, d/c 8.5 vertical	2.50	....	....	....	2.25	.80
4630	(45¢) Flag & Justice coil, d/c 8.5 vertical	2.50	....	....	....	2.25	.80

4629, 4633, 4637, 4643, 4647 — 4630, 4634, 4638, 4644, 4648 — 4631, 4635, 4639, 4641, 4645 — 4632, 4636, 4640, 4642, 4646

SCOTT NO.	DESCRIPTION	FIRST DAY COVERS SING	FIRST DAY COVERS PL. BLK.	MINT SHEET	PLATE BLOCK	UNUSED F/NH	USED
4631	(45¢) Flag & Freedom coil, d/c 8.5 vertical	2.50	....	....	....	2.25	.80
4632	(45¢) Flag & Liberty coil, d/c 8.5 vertical	2.50	....	....	....	2.25	.80
	Same, plate # strip of 5	....	....	....	....	11.00	....
	Same, plate # strip of 11	....	....	....	....	15.00	....
4633-36	(45¢) Flag strip of 4, d/c 9.5 vertical	....	....	....	....	9.00	....
4633	(45¢) Flag & Equality coil, d/c 9.5 vertical	2.50	....	....	....	2.25	.80
4634	(45¢) Flag & Justice coil, d/c 9.5 vertical	2.50	....	....	....	2.25	.80
4635	(45¢) Flag & Freedom coil, d/c 9.5 vertical	2.50	....	....	....	2.25	.80
4636	(45¢) Flag & Liberty coil, d/c 9.5 vertical	2.50	....	....	....	2.25	.80
	Same, plate # strip of 5	....	....	....	....	11.00	....
	Same, plate # strip of 11	....	....	....	....	15.00	....
4637-40	(45¢) Flag strip of 4, d/c 11 vertical	....	....	....	....	9.00	....
4637	(45¢) Flag & Equality coil, d/c 11 vertical	2.50	....	....	....	2.25	.80
4638	(45¢) Flag & Justice coil, d/c 11 vertical	2.50	....	....	....	2.25	.80
4639	(45¢) Flag & Freedom coil, d/c 11 vertical	2.50	....	....	....	2.25	.80
4640	(45¢) Flag & Liberty coil, d/c 11 vertical	2.50	....	....	....	2.25	.80
	Same, plate # strip of 5	....	....	....	....	11.00	....
	Same, plate # strip of 11	....	....	....	....	15.00	....
4641-44	(45¢) Flag block of 4 from bklt, colored dots in stars, 18.5 mm from LL to LR corners of flag	5.50	....	....	....	9.00	....
4641	(45¢) Flag & Freedom bklt Single, colored dots in stars . . .	2.50	....	....	....	2.25	.80
4642	(45¢) Flag & Liberty bklt single, colored dots in stars . . .	2.50	....	....	....	2.25	.80
4643	(45¢) Flag & Equality bklt single, colored dots in stars . . .	2.50	....	....	....	2.25	.80
4644	(45¢) Flag & Justice bklt single, colored dots in stars . . .	2.50	....	....	....	2.25	.80
4644b	Same, bklt pane of 20. .	....	....	....	....	45.00	....
4645-48	(45¢) Flag block of 4 from bklt, dark dots in stars, 19mm from LL to LR corners of flag	5.50	....	....	....	9.00	....
4645	(45¢) Flag & Freedom bklt single, dark dots in stars	2.50	....	....	....	2.25	.80
4646	(45¢) Flag & Liberty bklt single, dark dots in stars	2.50	....	....	....	2.25	.80
4647	(45¢) Flag & Equality bklt single, dark dots in stars	2.50	....	....	....	2.25	.80
4648	(45¢) Flag & Justice bklt single, dark dots in stars	2.50	....	....	....	2.25	.80
4648b	Same, bklt pane of 20. .	....	....	....	....	45.00	....

4649

4650

4651-4652

SCOTT NO.	DESCRIPTION	FIRST DAY COVERS SING	FIRST DAY COVERS PL. BLK.	MINT SHEET	PLATE BLOCK	UNUSED F/NH	USED
4649	$5.15 Sunshine Skyway Bridge	12.00	....	235.00(20)	55.00	15.00	12.00
4650	$18.95 Carmel Mission.	39.00	....	425.00(20)	185.00	50.00	40.00
4651-52	(45¢) Cherry Blossom Centennial	3.75	....	40.00(20)	8.00	4.00	....
	Same, plate block of 8 .	....	....	....	9.00(8)	....	....
4651	(45¢) Cherry Blossoms & Washington Monument.	2.50	....	....	....	2.25	.75
4652	(45¢) Cherry Blossoms & Jefferson Memorial	2.50	....	....	....	2.25	.75

4653

SCOTT NO.	DESCRIPTION	FIRST DAY COVERS SING	FIRST DAY COVERS PL. BLK.	MINT SHEET	PLATE BLOCK	UNUSED F/NH	USED
4653	(45¢) Flowers, by William H. Johnson. . . .	2.50	....	38.00(20)	9.00	2.25	.50
	Same	....	....	....	20.00(10)	....	....

4654-63

SCOTT NO.	DESCRIPTION	FIRST DAY COVERS SING	FIRST DAY COVERS PL. BLK.	MINT SHEET	PLATE BLOCK	UNUSED F/NH	USED
4654-63	(45¢) Twentieth Century Poets	10.00	....	80.00(20)	45.00(10)	38.00	....
4654	(45¢) Joseph Brodsky. .	2.50	....	....	....	4.00	2.75
4655	(45¢) Gwendolyn Brooks	2.50	....	....	....	4.00	2.75
4656	(45¢) William Carlos Williams	2.50	....	....	....	4.00	2.75
4657	(45¢) Robert Hayden . .	2.50	....	....	....	4.00	2.75
4658	(45¢) Sylvia Plath	2.50	....	....	....	4.00	2.75
4659	(45¢) Elizabeth Bishop .	2.50	....	....	....	4.00	2.75
4660	(45¢) Wallace Stevens .	2.50	....	....	....	4.00	2.75
4661	(45¢) Denise Levertov .	2.50	....	....	....	4.00	2.75
4662	(45¢) E.E. Cummings . .	2.50	....	....	....	4.00	2.75
4663	(45¢) Theodore Roethke	3.75	....	....	....	4.00	2.75

4664 4665

SCOTT NO.	DESCRIPTION	FIRST DAY COVERS SING	FIRST DAY COVERS PL. BLK.	MINT SHEET	PLATE BLOCK	UNUSED F/NH	USED
4664-65	(45¢) Civil War Sesquicentennial	3.75	....	24.00(12)	....	4.00	....
4664	(45¢) Battle of New Orleans	2.50	....	....	....	2.00	.80
4665	(45¢) Battle of Antietam	2.50	....	....	....	2.00	.80

4666

4667

SCOTT NO.	DESCRIPTION	FIRST DAY COVERS SING	FIRST DAY COVERS PL. BLK.	MINT SHEET	PLATE BLOCK	UNUSED F/NH	USED
4666	(45¢) Jose Ferrer	2.50	....	30.00(20)	6.50	1.75	.65
4667	(45¢) Louisiana Statehood Bicentennial	2.50	....	35.00(20)	8.00	2.00	.45

4668-4671

4672, 4672a

SCOTT NO.	DESCRIPTION	FIRST DAY COVERS SING	FIRST DAY COVERS PL. BLK.	MINT SHEET	PLATE BLOCK	UNUSED F/NH	USED
4668-71	(45¢) Great Film Directors	5.50	....	38.00(20)	10.00	8.00	....
	Same	....	....	....	9.00(8)	....	....
4668	(45¢) John Ford, "The Searchers", John Wayne	2.75	....	....	....	2.25	1.00
4669	(45¢) Frank Capra, "It Happened One Night", Clark Gable and Claudette Colbert	2.75	....	....	....	2.25	1.00
4670	(45¢) Billy Wilder, "Some Like It Hot", Marilyn Monroe.	2.75	....	....	....	2.25	1.00
4671	(45¢) John Huston, "The Maltese Falcon", Humphrey Bogart	2.75	....	....	....	2.25	1.00
4672	1¢ Bobcat	2.25	....	....	....	.25	.25
	Same, plate # strip of 5	....	....	....	.95	....	....
4672a	1¢ Bobcat (dated 2015)	....	....	....	....	.25	.25
	Same, Plate # Strip of 5	....	....	....	1.00	....	....

4673 4674

4675 4676

SCOTT NO.	DESCRIPTION	FIRST DAY COVERS SING	FIRST DAY COVERS PL. BLK.	MINT SHEET	PLATE BLOCK	UNUSED F/NH	USED
4673-76	(45¢) Flags, block or 4 from booklet, colored dots in stars, 19.25 mm from LL to LR corners of flag	5.25	....	....	....	9.00	....
4673	(45¢) Flag & Freedom bklt single, colored dots in stars . . .	2.50	....	....	....	2.25	1.00
4674	(45¢) Flag & Liberty bklt single, colored dots in stars . . .	2.50	....	....	....	2.25	1.00
4675	(45¢) Flag & Equality bklt single, colored dots in stars . . .	2.50	....	....	....	2.25	1.00
4676	(45¢) Flag & Justice bklt single, colored dots in stars . . .	2.50	....	....	....	2.25	1.00
4676b	Same, booklet pane of 10	....	....	....	....	20.00	....

4677-81

SCOTT NO.	DESCRIPTION	FIRST DAY COVERS SING	FIRST DAY COVERS PL. BLK.	MINT SHEET	PLATE BLOCK	UNUSED F/NH	USED
4677-81	(45¢) Pixar Mail a Smile	6.75	....	38.00(20)	20.00(10)	10.00	....
4677	(45¢) Flik & Dot from "A Bug's Life"	2.75	....	....	....	2.00	.65
4678	(45¢) Bob Parr & Dashiell Parr from "The Incredibles"	2.75	....	....	....	2.00	.65
4679	(45¢) Nemo & Squirt from "Finding Nemo".	2.75	....	....	....	2.00	.65
4680	(45¢) Jessie, Woody, & Bullseye from "Toy Story 2".	2.75	....	....	....	2.00	.65
4681	(45¢) Boo, Mike Wazowskie & James P. "Sulley" Sullivan from Monsters, Inc..	2.75	....	....	....	2.00	.65

SCOTT NO.	DESCRIPTION	FIRST DAY COVERS SING	FIRST DAY COVERS PL. BLK.	MINT SHEET	PLATE BLOCK	UNUSED F/NH	USED

4682-4686

SCOTT NO.	DESCRIPTION	SING	PL. BLK.	MINT SHEET	PLATE BLOCK	UNUSED F/NH	USED
4682-86	32¢ Aloha shirts, strip of 5 from booklet	5.00	....	....	....	65.00	....
4682	32¢ Surfers & Palm Trees	2.50	....	....	....	13.00	3.00
4683	32¢ Fossil Fish	2.50	....	....	....	13.00	3.00
4684	32¢ Fish & Starfish	2.50	....	....	....	13.00	3.00
4685	32¢ Surfers	2.50	....	....	....	13.00	3.00
4686	32¢ Shells	2.50	....	....	....	13.00	3.00
4686b	32¢ Aloha shirts, bklt pane of 10	....	....	....	....	120.00	....

4687-4690

SCOTT NO.	DESCRIPTION	SING	PL. BLK.	MINT SHEET	PLATE BLOCK	UNUSED F/NH	USED
4687-90	(45¢) Bicycling	5.75	....	30.00(20)	12.00(8)	7.00	....
4687	(45¢) Child on bicycle with Training Wheels	2.50	....	....	....	1.75	.90
4688	(45¢) Commuter on Bicycle with Panniers	2.50	....	....	....	1.75	.90
4689	(45¢) Road Racer	2.50	....	....	....	1.75	.90
4690	(45¢) BMX Biker	2.50	....	....	....	1.75	.90

4691

4692 4693

SCOTT NO.	DESCRIPTION	SING	PL. BLK.	MINT SHEET	PLATE BLOCK	UNUSED F/NH	USED
4691	(45¢) Scouting	2.50	....	35.00(20)	8.00	2.00	.50
4692-93	(45¢) Musicians	3.75	....	21.00(20)	7.50(5)	4.00	....
	same.	....	....	30.00(20)	18.00(10)	....	....
4692	(45¢) Edith Piaf.	2.50	....	....	....	2.00	1.00
4693	(45¢) Miles Davis	2.50	....	....	....	2.00	1.00

4694 4695

4696 4697

SCOTT NO.	DESCRIPTION	SING	PL. BLK.	MINT SHEET	PLATE BLOCK	UNUSED F/NH	USED
4694	(45¢) Ted Williams	2.50	....	28.00(20)	6.50(4)	1.75	.70
	. . . .	....	....	....	12.00(8)	....	....
4695	(45¢) Larry Doby.	2.50	....	28.00(20)	6.50(4)	1.75	.70
	. . . .	....	....	....	12.00(8)	....	....
4696	(45¢) Willie Stargell . . .	2.50	....	28.00(20)	6.50(4)	1.75	.70
	. . . .	....	....	....	12.00(8)	....	....
4697	(45¢) Joe DiMaggio . . .	2.50	....	28.00(20)	6.50(4)	1.75	.70
	. . . .	....	....	....	12.00(8)	....	....
4697a	(45¢) Major League Baseball All-Stars	6.50	....	30.00(20)	7.00(4)	7.00	....
	. . . .	....	....	....	14.00(8)	....	....

4698

4699

4700

4701

SCOTT NO.	DESCRIPTION	SING	PL. BLK.	MINT SHEET	PLATE BLOCK	UNUSED F/NH	USED
4698-4701	(45¢) Innovative Choreographers	5.50	....	30.00(20)	14.00(8)	7.00	....
4698	(45¢) Isadora Duncan. .	2.50	....	....	....	1.75	1.00
4699	(45¢) Jose Limon	2.50	....	....	....	1.75	1.00
4700	(45¢) Katherine Dunham	2.50	....	....	....	1.75	1.00
4701	(45¢) Bob Fosse.	2.50	....	....	....	1.75	1.00

4702 4703

SCOTT NO.	DESCRIPTION	SING	PL. BLK.	MINT SHEET	PLATE BLOCK	UNUSED F/NH	USED
4702	(45¢) Edgar Rice Burroughs	2.50	....	28.00(20)	6.50(4)	1.75	.50
4703	(45¢) War of 1812 Bicentennial	2.50	....	35.00(20)	....	2.25	.50

4704, 4704b 4705

SCOTT NO.	DESCRIPTION	SING	PL. BLK.	MINT SHEET	PLATE BLOCK	UNUSED F/NH	USED
4704	(45¢) Purple Heart	2.50	....	28.00(20)	6.50(4)	1.75	.40
4704b	(49¢) Purple Heart(dated 2014)	....	....	28.00	6.50(4)	1.75	.40
4705	(45¢) O. Henry	2.50	....	28.00(20)	6.50(4)	1.75	.45

4706 4707 4708 4709

SCOTT NO.	DESCRIPTION	SING	PL. BLK.	MINT SHEET	PLATE BLOCK	UNUSED F/NH	USED
4706-09	(45¢) Flags, 11.25x10.75 colored dots in stars . . .	....	....	....	....	7.00	......
4706	(45¢) Flag and Freedom	2.50	....	....	....	1.75	1.50
4707	(45¢) Flag and Liberty .	2.50	....	....	....	1.75	1.50
4708	(45¢) Flag and Justice .	2.50	....	....	....	1.75	1.50
4709	(45¢) Flag and Equality	2.50	....	....	....	1.75	1.50
4709b	(45¢) Flags ATM booklet pane of 18.	....	....	....	....	30.00	......

4710

EARTHSCAPES

- **4710a** *Glacier & Icebergs*
- **4710b** *Volcanic Crater*
- **4710c** *Geothermal Spring*
- **4710d** *Butte in Fog*
- **4710e** *Inland Marsh*
- **4710f** *Salt Evaporation Pond*
- **4710g** *Log Rafts*
- **4710h** *Center-Pivot Irrigation*
- **4710i** *Cherry Orchard*
- **4710j** *Cranberry Harvest*
- **4710k** *Residential Subdivision*
- **4710l** *Barge Fleeting*
- **4710m** Railroad Roundhouse
- **4710n** *Skyscraper Apartments*
- **4710o** *Highway Interchange*

SCOTT NO.	DESCRIPTION	SING	PL. BLK.	MINT SHEET	PLATE BLOCK	UNUSED F/NH	USED
4710	(45¢) Earthscapes	2.50	....	28.00	....	28.00	......
	Set of Singles						20.00

4711

4712 4713

4714 4715

SCOTT NO.	DESCRIPTION	SING	PL. BLK.	MINT SHEET	PLATE BLOCK	UNUSED F/NH	USED
4711	(45¢) Holy Family & Donkey	2.50	....	....	....	2.00	.45
4711a	same, booklet pane of 20	....	....	....	....	38.00	......
4712-15	(45¢) Christmas Santa & Sleigh	....	....	....	....	9.00	......
4712	(45¢) Reindeer in Flight & Moon	2.50	....	....	....	2.25	.60
4713	(45¢) Santa and Sleigh.	2.50	....	....	....	2.25	.60
4714	(45¢) Reindeer over roof	2.50	....	....	....	2.25	.60
4715	(45¢) Snow-covered buildings	2.50	....	....	....	2.25	.60
4715a	same, booklet pane of 20	....	....	....	....	40.00	......

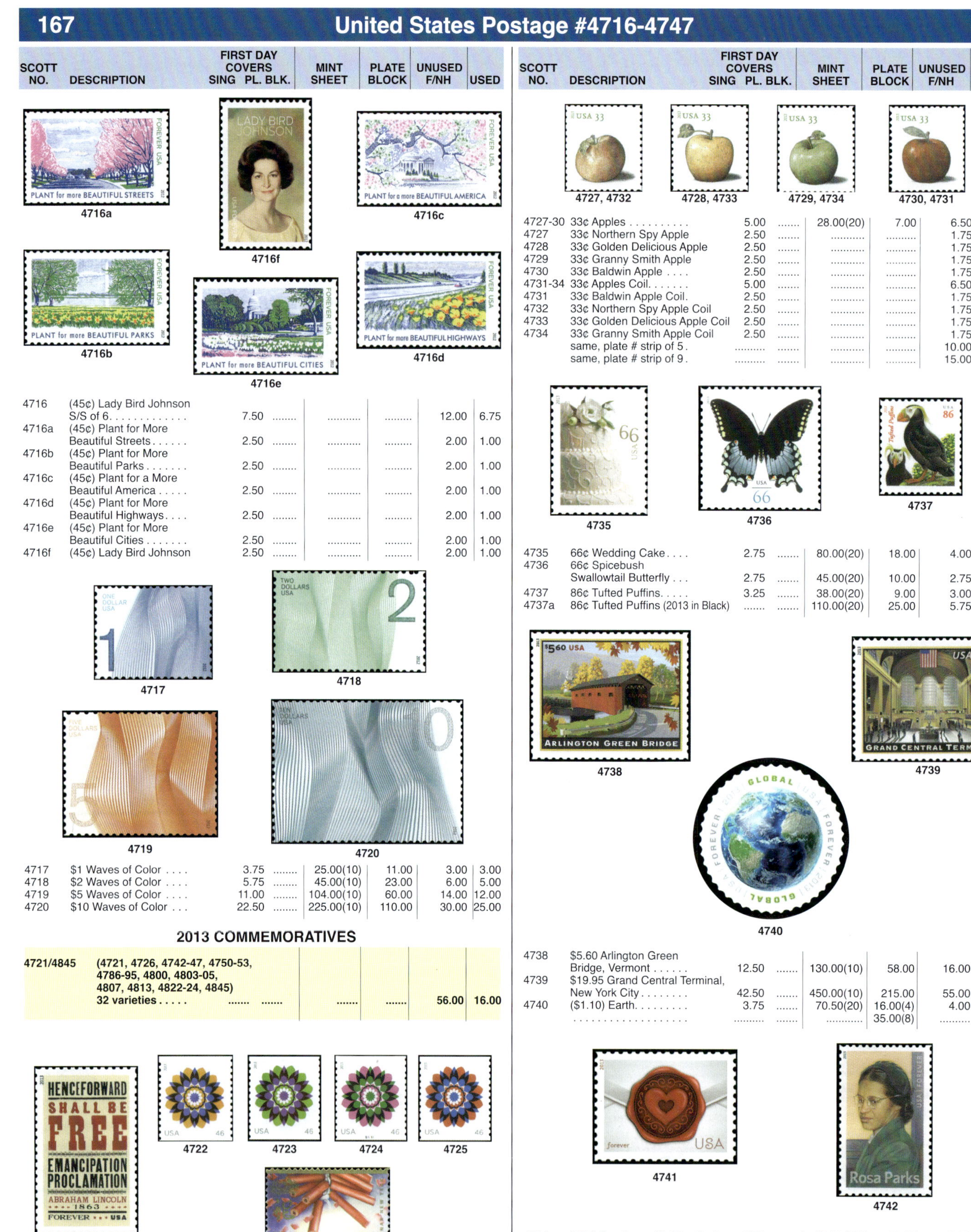

4716a 4716f 4716c 4716b 4716e 4716d

SCOTT NO.	DESCRIPTION	FIRST DAY COVERS SING	FIRST DAY COVERS PL. BLK.	MINT SHEET	PLATE BLOCK	UNUSED F/NH	USED
4716	(45¢) Lady Bird Johnson S/S of 6.	7.50	....	....	....	12.00	6.75
4716a	(45¢) Plant for More Beautiful Streets.	2.50	....	....	....	2.00	1.00
4716b	(45¢) Plant for More Beautiful Parks	2.50	....	....	....	2.00	1.00
4716c	(45¢) Plant for a More Beautiful America	2.50	....	....	....	2.00	1.00
4716d	(45¢) Plant for More Beautiful Highways. . . .	2.50	....	....	....	2.00	1.00
4716e	(45¢) Plant for More Beautiful Cities	2.50	....	....	....	2.00	1.00
4716f	(45¢) Lady Bird Johnson	2.50	....	....	....	2.00	1.00

4717 4718 4719 4720

SCOTT NO.	DESCRIPTION	FIRST DAY COVERS SING	FIRST DAY COVERS PL. BLK.	MINT SHEET	PLATE BLOCK	UNUSED F/NH	USED
4717	$1 Waves of Color	3.75	....	25.00(10)	11.00	3.00	3.00
4718	$2 Waves of Color	5.75	....	45.00(10)	23.00	6.00	5.00
4719	$5 Waves of Color	11.00	....	104.00(10)	60.00	14.00	12.00
4720	$10 Waves of Color . . .	22.50	....	225.00(10)	110.00	30.00	25.00

2013 COMMEMORATIVES

SCOTT NO.	DESCRIPTION	FIRST DAY COVERS SING	FIRST DAY COVERS PL. BLK.	MINT SHEET	PLATE BLOCK	UNUSED F/NH	USED
4721/4845	**(4721, 4726, 4742-47, 4750-53, 4786-95, 4800, 4803-05, 4807, 4813, 4822-24, 4845) 32 varieties . . . . .**	....	....	....	....	**56.00**	**16.00**

4721 4722 4723 4724 4725 4726

SCOTT NO.	DESCRIPTION	FIRST DAY COVERS SING	FIRST DAY COVERS PL. BLK.	MINT SHEET	PLATE BLOCK	UNUSED F/NH	USED
4721	(45¢) Emancipation Proclamation	2.50	....	28.00(20)	6.50	1.75	.60
4722-25	46¢ Kaleidoscope Flowers Coil	5.50	....	....	....	8.00	....
4722	46¢ Yellow Orange	2.50	....	....	....	2.00	.75
4723	46¢ Yellow Green	2.50	....	....	....	2.00	.75
4724	46¢ Red Violet	2.50	....	....	....	2.00	.75
4725	46¢ Red	2.50	....	....	....	2.00	.75
	same, plate # strip of 5 .	....	....	....	12.00	....	....
	same, plate # strip of 9 .	....	....	....	18.00	....	....
4726	(45¢) Chinese New Year	2.50	....	24.00(12)	....	2.00	.55

4727, 4732 4728, 4733 4729, 4734 4730, 4731

SCOTT NO.	DESCRIPTION	FIRST DAY COVERS SING	FIRST DAY COVERS PL. BLK.	MINT SHEET	PLATE BLOCK	UNUSED F/NH	USED
4727-30	33¢ Apples	5.00	....	28.00(20)	7.00	6.50	....
4727	33¢ Northern Spy Apple	2.50	....	....	....	1.75	.60
4728	33¢ Golden Delicious Apple	2.50	....	....	....	1.75	.60
4729	33¢ Granny Smith Apple	2.50	....	....	....	1.75	.60
4730	33¢ Baldwin Apple	2.50	....	....	....	1.75	.60
4731-34	33¢ Apples Coil.	5.00	....	....	....	6.50	....
4731	33¢ Baldwin Apple Coil.	2.50	....	....	....	1.75	.80
4732	33¢ Northern Spy Apple Coil	2.50	....	....	....	1.75	.80
4733	33¢ Golden Delicious Apple Coil	2.50	....	....	....	1.75	.80
4734	33¢ Granny Smith Apple Coil	2.50	....	....	....	1.75	.80
	same, plate # strip of 5 .	....	....	....	....	10.00	....
	same, plate # strip of 9 .	....	....	....	....	15.00	....

4735 4736 4737

SCOTT NO.	DESCRIPTION	FIRST DAY COVERS SING	FIRST DAY COVERS PL. BLK.	MINT SHEET	PLATE BLOCK	UNUSED F/NH	USED
4735	66¢ Wedding Cake	2.75	....	80.00(20)	18.00	4.00	1.00
4736	66¢ Spicebush Swallowtail Butterfly . . .	2.75	....	45.00(20)	10.00	2.75	.85
4737	86¢ Tufted Puffins.	3.25	....	38.00(20)	9.00	3.00	2.00
4737a	86¢ Tufted Puffins (2013 in Black)	....	....	110.00(20)	25.00	5.75	4.00

4738 4739 4740

SCOTT NO.	DESCRIPTION	FIRST DAY COVERS SING	FIRST DAY COVERS PL. BLK.	MINT SHEET	PLATE BLOCK	UNUSED F/NH	USED
4738	$5.60 Arlington Green Bridge, Vermont	12.50	....	130.00(10)	58.00	16.00	10.00
4739	$19.95 Grand Central Terminal, New York City	42.50	....	450.00(10)	215.00	55.00	40.00
4740	($1.10) Earth.	3.75	....	70.50(20)	16.00(4)	4.00	1.75
	. . . .	....	....	....	35.00(8)	....	....

4741 4742

SCOTT NO.	DESCRIPTION	FIRST DAY COVERS SING	FIRST DAY COVERS PL. BLK.	MINT SHEET	PLATE BLOCK	UNUSED F/NH	USED
4741	(46¢) Envelope with Wax Seal	2.50	....	40.00(20)	10.00	2.25	.50
4742	(46¢) Rosa Parks	2.50	....	40.00(20)	10.00	2.25	.50
	. . . .	....	....	....	8.25(8)	....	....
4743-47	(46¢) Muscle Cars	....	....	40.00(20)	20.00(10)	10.00	....
4743	(46¢) 1969 Dodge Charger Daytona	....	....	....	....	2.00	.60
4744	(46¢) 1966 Pontiac GTO	....	....	....	....	2.00	.60
4745	(46¢) 1967 Ford Mustang Shelby GT.	....	....	....	....	2.00	.60
4746	(46¢) 1970 Chevrolet Chevelle SS	....	....	....	....	2.00	.60
4747	(46¢) 1970 Plymouth Hemi Barracuda.	....	....	....	....	2.00	.60

4743

4744

4745

4746

4747

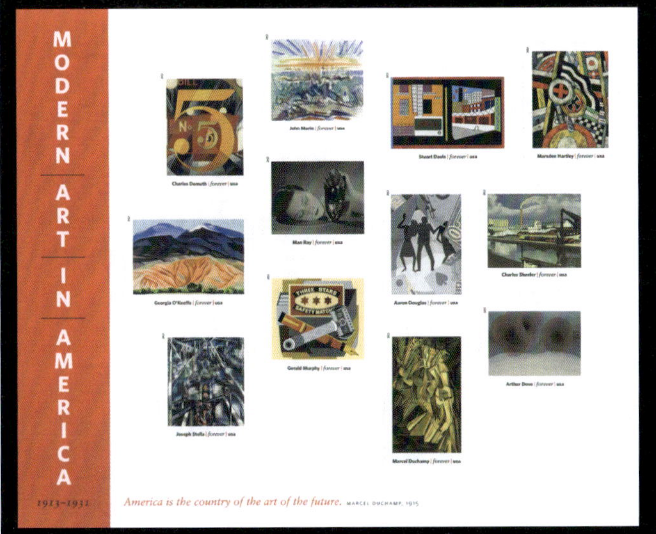

4748

MODERN ART IN AMERICA

4748a *I Saw The Figure 5 (Demuth)*
4748b *Sunset, Main Coast, (Marin)*
4748c *House and Street (Davis)*
4748d *Painting, number 5 (Hartley)*
4748e *Black Mesa Landscape (O'Keefe)*
4748f *Noire et Blanche (Ray)*
4748g *The Prodigal Son (Douglas)*
4748h *American Landscape (Sheeler)*
4748i *Brooklyn Bridge (Stella)*
4748j *Razor (Murphy)*
4748k *Nude Descending a Staircase (Duchamp)*
4748l *Fog Horns (Dove)*

SCOTT NO.	DESCRIPTION	FIRST DAY COVERS SING	PL. BLK.	MINT SHEET	PLATE BLOCK	UNUSED F/NH	USED
4748	(46¢) Modern Art in America	13.00		25.00(12)		25.00	
	Set of Singles						15.00

4749

4750

4751

4752

4753

SCOTT NO.	DESCRIPTION	FIRST DAY COVERS SING	PL. BLK.	MINT SHEET	PLATE BLOCK	UNUSED F/NH	USED
4749	46¢ Patriotic Star Coil. .	2.50				1.75	.40
	same, plate number strip of 5				10.00		
4750-53	(46¢) La Florida	6.25		30.00(16)	9.00	8.00	
4750	(46¢) Red and Pink Hibiscus	2.75				2.00	.75
4751	(46¢) Yellow Cannas. . .	2.75				2.00	.75
4752	(46¢) Red, White and Purple Morning Glories	2.75				2.00	.75
4753	(46¢) White and Purple Passion Flowers.	2.75				2.00	.75

4754

4755

4756

4757

4758

4759

4760

4761

4762

4763

SCOTT NO.	DESCRIPTION	FIRST DAY COVERS SING	PL. BLK.	MINT SHEET	PLATE BLOCK	UNUSED F/NH	USED
4754-63	(46¢) Vintage Seed Packets, block of 10	12.50				38.00	
4754	(46¢) Phlox	2.75				4.00	1.00
4755	(46¢) Calendula	2.75				4.00	1.00
4756	(46¢) Digitalis	2.75				4.00	1.00
4757	(46¢) Linum	2.75				4.00	1.00
4758	(46¢) Alyssum.	2.75				4.00	1.00
4759	(46¢) Zinnias.	2.75				4.00	1.00
4760	(46¢) Pinks	2.75				4.00	1.00
4761	(46¢) Cosmos.	2.75				4.00	1.00
4762	(46¢) Aster	2.75				4.00	1.00
4763	(46¢) Primrose	2.75				4.00	1.00
4763b	same, booklet pane of 20					80.00	

4764, 4764a

4765

SCOTT NO.	DESCRIPTION	FIRST DAY COVERS SING	PL. BLK.	MINT SHEET	PLATE BLOCK	UNUSED F/NH	USED
4764	(46¢) Where Dreams Blossom flowers	2.75		35.00(20)	8.00	2.00	.50
4764a	(49¢) Wedding Flowers Dated 2014.	2.50		45.00(20)	10.00	2.50	.30
4765	66¢ Wedding Flowers and "Yes I Do"	3.75		55.00(20)	12.00	3.00	1.25

4766, 4770, 4777, 4780, 4784, 4798

4767, 4771, 4774, 4781, 4785, 4799

4768, 4772, 4775, 4778, 4782, 4796

4769, 4773, 4776, 4779, 4783, 4797

SCOTT NO.	DESCRIPTION	FIRST DAY COVERS SING	PL. BLK.	MINT SHEET	PLATE BLOCK	UNUSED F/NH	USED
4766-69	(46¢) Flags Forever Coil, D/C 8.5 (AD)	5.75				10.00	
	same, plate # strip of 5 .					16.00	
	same, plate # strip of 9 .					25.00	
4766	(46¢) Flag in Autumn, S/A Coil, 8.5 (AD)	2.75				2.25	.40
4767	(46¢) Flag in Winter, S/A Coil, 8.5 (AD)	2.75				2.25	.40
4768	(46¢) Flag in Spring, S/A Coil, 8.5 (AD)	2.75				2.25	.40
4769	(46¢) Flag in Summer, S/A Coil, 8.5 (AD)	2.75				2.25	.40
4770-73	(46¢) Flags Forever Coil, D/C 9.5 (AP)	5.75				10.00	
	same, plate # strip of 5 .					16.00	
	same, plate # strip of 9 .					25.00	
4770	(46¢) Flag in Autumn, S/A Coil, 9.5 (AP)	2.75				2.25	.40
4771	(46¢) Flag in Winter, S/A Coil, 9.5 (AP)	2.75				2.25	.40
4772	(46¢) Flag in Spring, S/A Coil, 9.5 (AP)	2.75				2.25	.40

SCOTT NO.	DESCRIPTION	FIRST DAY COVERS SING	FIRST DAY COVERS PL. BLK.	MINT SHEET	PLATE BLOCK	UNUSED F/NH	USED
4773	(46¢) Flag in Autumn, S/A Coil, 9.5 (AP)	2.75	......	......	......	3.00	.40
4774-77	(46¢) Flags Forever Coil, D/C 11 (SSP)	5.75	......	......	......	14.00	......
	same, plate # strip of 5	......	......	......	......	20.00	......
	same, plate # strip of 9	......	......	......	......	35.00	......
4774	(46¢) Flag in Winter, S/A Coil, 11 (SSP)	2.75	......	......	......	2.00	.40
4775	(46¢) Flag in Spring, S/A Coil, 11 (SSP)	2.75	......	......	......	2.00	.40
4776	(46¢) Flag in Summer, S/A Coil, 11 (SSP)	2.75	......	......	......	2.00	.40
4777	(46¢) Flag in Autumn, S/A Coil, 11 (SSP)	2.75	......	......	......	2.00	.40
4778-81	Flags Forever, booklet stamps, Microprint at Lower Left Corner of Flag (AP)	5.75	......	......	......	8.50	......
4778	(46¢) Flag in Spring, booklet single, Microprint at Lower Left Corner of Flag (AP)	2.75	......	......	......	2.00	.40
4779	(46¢) Flag in Summer, booklet single, Microprint at Lower Left Corner of Flag (AP)	2.75	......	......	......	2.00	.40
4780	(46¢) Flag in Autumn, booklet single, Microprint at Lower Left Corner of Flag (AP)	2.75	......	......	......	2.00	.40
4781	(46¢) Flag in Winter, booklet single, Microprint at Lower Left Corner of Flag (AP)	2.75	......	......	......	2.00	.40
4781	same, booklet pane of 20	......	......	......	......	38.00	......
4782-85	Flag Forever, booklet stamps, microprinted near top of pole or at lower left near rope (SSP)	5.75	......	......	......	7.50	......
4782a-4785a	Flags Forever, bklt stmps, Microprint near top of pole or lower left near rope (SSP) overall tag	5.75	......	......	......	7.50	......
4782b-4785b	Flags Forever, bklt stmps, Microprint near top of pole or lower left near rope (SSP) overall tag, 2014 date	5.75	......	......	......	7.50	......
4782a	(46¢) Flag in Spring, Booklet Single,(SSP) overall tagging	2.75	......	......	......	1.75	.40
4782b	(46¢) Flag in Spring, Booklet Single, (SSP) overall tagging, 2014 date	2.75	......	......	......	1.75	.40
4783	(46¢) Flag in Summer,Bkl.Sng, (SSP)		2.75	......	......	1.75	.40
4783a	(46¢) Flag in Summer,Booklet single, (SSP) overall tagging	2.75	......	......	......	1.50	.40
4783b	(46¢) Flag in Summer,Booklet single, (SSP) overall tagging, 2014 date	2.75	......	......	......	1.75	.40
4784	(46¢) Flag in Autumn,Bkl.Sng, (SSP)		2.75			1.75	.40
4784a	(46¢) Flag in Autumn,Booklet Single, (SSP) overall tagging	2.75	......	......	......	1.75	.40
4784b	(46¢) Flag in Autumn,Booklet Single, (SSP) overall tagging, 2014 date	2.75	......	......	......	1.75	.40
4785	(46¢) Flag in Winter, Bkl.Sng, (SSP)		2.75			1.75	.40
4785a	(46¢) Flag in Winter, Booklet Single, (SSP) overall tagging	2.75	......	......	......	1.75	.40
4785b	(46¢) Flag in Winter, Booklet Single, (SSP) overall tagging, 2014 date	2.75	......	......	......	1.75	.40
4785d	same, booklet pane of 20 (4782-85)	22	......	......	......	34.00	.40
4785f	same, booklet pane of 10 overall tagging (4782a-85a)	22	......	......	......	20.00	.40
4785h	same, booklet pane of 20 overall tagging, 2014 date(4782b-85b)	22	......	......	......	34.00	.40

4786

SCOTT NO.	DESCRIPTION	SING	PL. BLK.	MINT SHEET	PLATE BLOCK	UNUSED F/NH	USED
4786	(46¢) Lydia Mendoza	2.75	......	25.00(16)	......	1.75	.55

4787

4788

SCOTT NO.	DESCRIPTION	SING	PL. BLK.	MINT SHEET	PLATE BLOCK	UNUSED F/NH	USED
4787-88	(46¢) Civil War Sesquicentennial	3.75	......	24.00 (12)	......	4.00	......
4787	(46¢) Battle of Vicksburg	2.75	......	......	......	2.00	1.00
4788	(46¢) Battle of Gettysburg	2.75	......	......	......	2.00	1.00

4789 4790 4791-95 4800

SCOTT NO.	DESCRIPTION	FIRST DAY COVERS SING	FIRST DAY COVERS PL. BLK.	MINT SHEET	PLATE BLOCK	UNUSED F/NH	USED
4789	(46¢) Johnny Cash	2.75	......	24.00(16)	......	1.75	.30
4790	(46¢) West Virginia Statehood, 150th Anniversary	2.75	......	28.00(20)	6.50	1.75	.30
4791-95	(46¢) New England Coastal Lighthouses	7.50	......	40.00(20)	20.00(10)	10.00	......
4791	(46¢) Portland Head Lighthouse, Maine	2.75	......	......	......	2.00	.80
4792	(46¢) Portsmouth Harbor Lighthouse, New Hampshire	2.75	......	......	......	2.00	.80
4793	(46¢) Boston Harbor Lighthouse, Massachusetts	2.75	......	......	......	2.00	.80
4794	(46¢) Point Judith Lighthouse, Rhode Island	2.75	......	......	......	2.00	.80
4795	(46¢) New London Harbor Lighthouse, Connecticut	2.75	......	......	......	2.00	.80
4796-99	(46¢) Flags Forever, D/C 11 1/4 X 11 1/2	5.75	......	......	......	12.00	......
4796	(46¢) Flag in Spring, Booklet Single, D/C 11 1/4 X 11 1/2	2.75	......	......	......	3.00	......
4797	(46¢) Flag in Summer,Booklet single, D/C 11 1/4 X 11 1/2	2.75	......	......	......	3.00	......
4798	(46¢) Flag in Autumn,Booklet Single, D/C 11 1/4 X 11 1/2	2.75	......	......	......	3.00	......
4799	(46¢) Flag in Winter, Booklet Single, D/C 11.25 X 11.5	2.75	......	......	......	3.00	......
4799b	Double Sided Booklet pane of 20			......	......	55.00	......
4800	(46¢) EID	2.75	......	28.00(20)	6.50	1.75	1.00

4801
MADE IN AMERICA - BUILDING A NATION

4801a *Airplane Mechanic (Lewis Hine)*
4801b *Derrick Man, Empire State Building (Hine)*
4801c *Millinery Apprentice (Hine)*
4801d *Man on Hoisting Ball, Empire State Building (Hine)*
4801e *Lineotype Operator (Hine)*
4801f *Welder On Empire State Building (Hine)*
4801g *Coal Miner (Anonymous)*
4801h *Riverters, Empire State Building (Hine)*
4801i *Powerhouse Mechanic (Hine)*
4801j *Railroad Track Walker (Hine)*
4801k *Textile Worker (Hine)*
4801l *Man Guiding Beam on Empire State Building (Hine)*

SCOTT NO.	DESCRIPTION	SING	PL. BLK.	MINT SHEET	PLATE BLOCK	UNUSED F/NH	USED
4801	(46¢) Building a Nation	13.50	......	24.00(12)	......	24.00	......

4802

4803

4804

4805

SCOTT NO.	DESCRIPTION	SING	PL. BLK.	MINT SHEET	PLATE BLOCK	UNUSED F/NH	USED
4802	1¢ Bobcat coil (SSP) die cut 9.75, (2013)	2.75	......	......	.75	.25	.25
4803	(46¢) Althea Gibson	2.75	......	35.00(20)	8.00	2.00	.50
4804	(46¢) 1963 March on Washington	2.75	......	28.00(20)	6.50	1.75	.50
4805	(46¢) Battle of Lake Erie	2.75	......	28.00(20)	......	1.75	.50

4806a

4807

4808-12

SCOTT NO.	DESCRIPTION	FIRST DAY COVERS SING	FIRST DAY COVERS PL. BLK.	MINT SHEET	PLATE BLOCK	UNUSED F/NH	USED
4806	$2 Inverted Jenny Sheet of 6	27.00				30.00	
4806a	Same., single stamp	6.50				6.00	4.00
4807	(46¢) Ray Charles	2.75		24.00(16)		1.75	.50
4808-12	(10¢) Snowflakes, Presorted	3.75				2.00	
	same, plate number strip of 11					9.00	
	same, plate number strip of 5	4.25				4.50	
4808	(10¢) light blue & multicolored					1.50	.25
4809	(10¢) pale blue & multicolored					1.50	.25
4810	(10¢) light blue & multicolored					1.50	.25
4811	(10¢) pale blue & multicolored					1.50	.25
4812	(10¢) lilac & multicolored					1.50	.25

4813

4814

4815

4816, 4816b, 4816c, 4821

SCOTT NO.	DESCRIPTION	FIRST DAY COVERS SING	FIRST DAY COVERS PL. BLK.	MINT SHEET	PLATE BLOCK	UNUSED F/NH	USED
4813	(46¢) Holy Family & Donkey			45.00(20)	10.00	2.25	.25
4814	($1.10) Christmas Wreath			45.00(10)	20.00	5.00	1.50
4815	(46¢) Virgin & Child by Jan Gossaert	2.75				2.25	.30
4815a	same, booklet pane of 20					38.00	
4816	(46¢) Poinsettia	4.25				2.25	.30
4816a	same, booklet pane of 20					38.00	
4816b	(46¢) Poinsettia, Dated 2014	2.75				2.25	.30
4816c	Same, Booklet Pane of 20 Dated 2014					38.00	

4817-4820

4822, 4822a, 4822b

4823, 4823a 4823b

4824

SCOTT NO.	DESCRIPTION	FIRST DAY COVERS SING	FIRST DAY COVERS PL. BLK.	MINT SHEET	PLATE BLOCK	UNUSED F/NH	USED
4817-20	(46¢) Gingerbread Houses					9.00	
4817	(46¢) Gingerbread House with Red Door	2.75				2.25	.30
4818	(46¢) Gingerbread House with Blue Door	2.75				2.25	.30
4819	(46¢) Gingerbread House with Green Door	2.75				2.25	.30
4820	(46¢) Gingerbread House with Orange Door	2.75				2.25	.30
4820b	same, booklet pane of 20					40.00	
4821	(46¢) Poinsettia	2.75				2.25	.30
4821a	same, booklet pane of 18					38.00	
4822-23	(46¢) Medal of Honor	4.50		35.00(20)	6.50	4.00	
4822-23a	(49¢) Medal of Honor, Dated 2014	3.75		35.00(20)	6.50	4.00	
4822	(46¢) Navy Medal of Honor	2.75				2.00	.55
4822a	(49¢) Navy Medal of Honor Dated 2014	2.50				2.00	.55
4822b	(49¢) Navy Medal of Honor Dated 2015	2.75				2.00	1.50
4823	(46¢) Army Medal of Honor	2.75				2.00	.55
4823a	(49¢) Army Medal of Honor Dated 2014	2.50				2.00	.55
4823b	(49¢) Army Medal of Honor Dated 2015	2.75				2.00	1.50
4824	(46¢) Hanukkah	2.75		28.00(20)	6.50	1.75	.55

4825 4826

4827 4828

4829 4830

4831 4832

4833 4834

4835 4836

4837 4838

4839 4840

4841 4842

4843 4844

SCOTT NO.	DESCRIPTION	FIRST DAY COVERS SING	FIRST DAY COVERS PL. BLK.	MINT SHEET	PLATE BLOCK	UNUSED F/NH	USED
4825-44	(46¢) Harry Potter booklet, 5 panes of 4 stamps each	22.00				40.00	
4825	(46¢) Harry Potter	2.75				2.50	1.25
4826	(46¢) Harry potter and Ron Weasley	2.75				2.50	1.25
4827	(46¢) Harry Potter, Ron Weasley, Hermione Granger	2.75				2.50	1.25
4828	(46¢) Hermione Granger	2.75				2.50	1.25
4828a	same, booklet pane of 4					10.00	
4829	(46¢) Harry Potter and Fawkes the Phoenix	2.75				2.50	1.25
4830	(46¢) Hedwig the Owl	2.75				2.50	1.25
4831	(46¢) Dobby the House Elf	2.75				2.50	1.25
4832	(46¢) Harry Potter and Buckbeak the Hippogriff	2.75				2.50	1.25
4832a	same, booklet pane of 4					10.00	
4833	(46¢) Headmaster Albus Dumbledore	2.75				2.50	1.25
4834	(46¢) Professor Severus Snape	2.75				2.50	1.25
4835	(46¢) Rubeus Hagrid	2.75				2.50	1.25
4836	(46¢) Professor Minerva McGonagall	2.75				2.50	1.25
4836a	same, booklet pane of 4					10.00	
4837	(46¢) Harry Potter, Ron Weasley & Hermione Granger	2.75				2.50	1.25
4838	(46¢) Luna Lovegood	2.75				2.50	1.25
4839	(46¢) Fred and George Weasley	2.75				2.50	1.25
4840	(46¢) Ginny Weasley	2.75				2.50	1.25
4840a	same, booklet pane of 4					10.00	
4841	(46¢) Draco Malfoy	2.75				2.50	1.25
4842	(46¢) Harry Potter	2.75				2.50	1.25
4843	(46¢) Lord Voldermort.	2.75				2.50	1.25
4844	(46¢) Bellatrix Lestrange	2.75				2.50	1.25
4844a	same, booklet pane of 4					10.00	

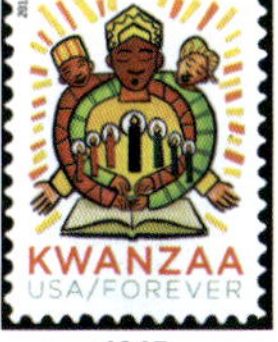

4845

SCOTT NO.	DESCRIPTION	FIRST DAY COVERS SING	FIRST DAY COVERS PL. BLK.	MINT SHEET	PLATE BLOCK	UNUSED F/NH	USED
4845	(46¢) Kwanzaa	2.75		28.00(20)	6.50	1.75	1.00

2014 COMMEMORATIVES

SCOTT NO.	DESCRIPTION	FIRST DAY COVERS SING	FIRST DAY COVERS PL. BLK.	MINT SHEET	PLATE BLOCK	UNUSED F/NH	USED
4846/4951	(4846, 4856, 4866, 4880, 4892, 4898-4907, 4910-16, 4921-26, 4928-35, 4950-51) 38 varieties	....	....	....	....	85.00	....

4846

4847

SCOTT NO.	DESCRIPTION	FIRST DAY COVERS SING	FIRST DAY COVERS PL. BLK.	MINT SHEET	PLATE BLOCK	UNUSED F/NH	USED
4846	(46¢) Chinese New Year Year of the Horse	2.75	....	22.00(12)	....	2.00	.60
4847	(46¢) Love	2.75	....	40.00(20)	6.50	2.25	.50

4848 4849 4850

4851 4852

SCOTT NO.	DESCRIPTION	FIRST DAY COVERS SING	FIRST DAY COVERS PL. BLK.	MINT SHEET	PLATE BLOCK	UNUSED F/NH	USED
4848-52	49¢ Ferns Coil	6.75	....	....	....	10.00	....
	same, plate number strip of 5	2.75	....	....	....	12.00	....
4848	49¢ Fortune's Holly Fern	2.75	....	....	....	2.00	.90
4849	49¢ Soft Shield Fern. . .	2.75	....	....	....	2.00	.90
4850	49¢ Autumn Fern	2.75	....	....	....	2.00	.90
4851	49¢ Goldie's Wood Fern	2.75	....	....	....	2.00	.90
4852	49¢ Painted Fern	2.75	....	....	....	2.00	.90

4855,4853, 4868-71

4856

4857, 4858

SCOTT NO.	DESCRIPTION	FIRST DAY COVERS SING	FIRST DAY COVERS PL. BLK.	MINT SHEET	PLATE BLOCK	UNUSED F/NH	USED
4853	(49¢) Ft. McHenry Flag & Fireworks Coil D/C 8.5 (CCL)	2.75	....	....	....	2.25	....
	same, plate number strip of 5		....	....	....	12.00	....
4854	(49¢) Ft. McHenry Flag & Fireworks Coil D/C 9.5 (AP).	2.75	....	....	....	2.25	....
	same, plate number strip of 5		....	....	....	12.00	....
4855	(49¢) Ft. McHenry Flag & Fireworks D/c 11.25x10.75	2.75	....	....	....	2.25	....
4855a	same, booklet pane of 20	2.75	....	....	....	45.00	....
4856	(49¢) Shirley Chisholm .	2.75	....	38.00(20)	6.50	1.75	.70
4857	34¢ Hummingbird	2.75	....	38.00(20)	6.50	1.75	.30
4858	34¢ Hummingbird coil. .	2.75	....	....	....	1.75	.30
	same, plate number strip of 5		....	....	....	10.00	....

4859

4860

SCOTT NO.	DESCRIPTION	FIRST DAY COVERS SING	FIRST DAY COVERS PL. BLK.	MINT SHEET	PLATE BLOCK	UNUSED F/NH	USED
4859	70¢ Great Spangled Fritillary	3.50	....	50.00(20)	10.00	3.00	1.00
4860	21¢ Lincoln	2.75	....	18.00(20)	4.00	1.00	.30
4861	21¢ Lincoln Coil	2.75	....	....	....	1.00	.30
	Same, plate number strip of 5		....	....	....	6.00	....

4862

4863

4864

4865

SCOTT NO.	DESCRIPTION	FIRST DAY COVERS SING	FIRST DAY COVERS PL. BLK.	MINT SHEET	PLATE BLOCK	UNUSED F/NH	USED
4862-65	(49¢) Winter Flowers . .	5.75	....	....	....	10.00	....
4862	(49¢) Cyclamen	2.75	....	....	....	2.00	.35
4863	(49¢) Paperwhite	2.75	....	....	....	2.00	.35
4864	(49¢) Amaryllis	2.75	....	....	....	2.00	.35
4865	(49¢) Christmas Cactus	2.75	....	....	....	2.00	.35
4865a	(49¢) Winter Flowers, booklet pane of 20		....	....	....	40.00	....

4866

4867

SCOTT NO.	DESCRIPTION	FIRST DAY COVERS SING	FIRST DAY COVERS PL. BLK.	MINT SHEET	PLATE BLOCK	UNUSED F/NH	USED
4866	91¢ Ralph Ellison	3.75	....	58.00(20)	12.00	3.25	1.00
4867	70¢ Wedding Cake	3.50	....	100.00(20)	20.00	5.00	1.50
4868	(49¢) Fort McHenry Flag & Fireworks coil D/C 11 Microprint in Fireworks above flagpole (SSP)	2.75	....	....	....	2.00	.30
	same, plate number strip of 5		....	....	....	12.00	....
4869	(49¢) Fort McHenry Flag & Fireworks D/C 11.25x11.5 with no Microprint	2.75	....	....	....	2.00	.30
	same, booklet pane of 20		....	....	....	40.00	....
4870	(49¢) Fort McHenry Flag & Fireworks D/C 11.25x10.75 with Microprint in fireworks	2.75	....	....	....	2.00	.30
	same, booklet pane of 20			....	....	40.00	....
4871	(49¢) Fort McHenry Flag & Fireworks D/C 11.25x11 thin paper	2.75	....	....	....	1.75	.30
	same, booklet pane of 18		....	....	....	35.00	....

4872

4873

SCOTT NO.	DESCRIPTION	FIRST DAY COVERS SING	FIRST DAY COVERS PL. BLK.	MINT SHEET	PLATE BLOCK	UNUSED F/NH	USED
4872	$5.60 Verrazano-Narrows Bridge	12.50	....	250.00(10)	55.00	15.00	10.00
4873	$19.99 USS Arizona Memorial	45	....	430.00(10)	180.00	50.00	30.00
4874-78	(49¢) Ferns coil.	7.50	....	....	....	18.00	....
	same, plate number strip of 5		....	....	....	22.00	....
	same, Plate Number strip of 11		....	....	....	45.00	....
4874	(49¢) Fortune's Holly Fern	2.75	....	....	....	2.25	1.50
4875	(49¢) Soft Shield Fern .	2.75	....	....	....	2.25	1.50
4876	(49¢) Autumn Fern	2.75	....	....	....	2.25	1.50
4877	(49¢) Goldie's Wood Fern	2.75	....	....	....	2.25	1.50
4878	(49¢) Painted Fern	2.75	....	....	....	2.25	1.50

4879

4880

4881

SCOTT NO.	DESCRIPTION	FIRST DAY COVERS SING	FIRST DAY COVERS PL. BLK.	MINT SHEET	PLATE BLOCK	UNUSED F/NH	USED
4879	70¢ C. Alfred "Chief" Anderson	3.25	....	45.00 (20)	9.00	2.50	1.00
4880	(49¢) Jimi Hendrix	2.75	....	28.00(16)	....	2.00	.70
4881	70¢ Yes I Do	3.25	....	75.00(20)	18.00	5.00	3.00

4882 4883 4884 4885

4886 4887 4888

4889 4890 4891

SCOTT NO.	DESCRIPTION	FIRST DAY COVERS SING	FIRST DAY COVERS PL. BLK.	MINT SHEET	PLATE BLOCK	UNUSED F/NH	USED
4882-91	(49¢) Songbirds	11.00				28.00	
4882	(49¢) Western Meadowlark	2.75				3.00	.70
4883	(49¢) Mountain Bluebird	2.75				3.00	.70
4884	(49¢) Western Tanager.	2.75				3.00	.70
4885	(49¢) Painted Bunting. .	2.75				3.00	.70
4886	(49¢) Baltimore Oriole .	2.75				3.00	.70
4887	(49¢) Evening Grosbeak	2.75				3.00	.70
4888	(49¢) Scarlet Tanager. .	2.75				3.00	.70
4889	(49¢) Rose-breasted Grosbeak	2.75				3.00	.70
4890	(49¢) American Goldfinch	2.75				3.00	.70
4891	(49¢) White-throated Sparrow	2.75				3.00	.70
4891b	Same, booklet pane of 20, 2 each 4882-91.				55.00		

4892

4893

SCOTT NO.	DESCRIPTION	FIRST DAY COVERS SING	FIRST DAY COVERS PL. BLK.	MINT SHEET	PLATE BLOCK	UNUSED F/NH	USED
4892	(49¢) Charlton Heston .	2.75		30.00(20)	6.50	1.75	.55
4893	($1.15) Map of Sea Surface Temperatures	3.75		45.00(10)	18.00	4.50	1.00

4894 4895 4896 4897

SCOTT NO.	DESCRIPTION	FIRST DAY COVERS SING	FIRST DAY COVERS PL. BLK.	MINT SHEET	PLATE BLOCK	UNUSED F/NH	USED
4894-97	(49¢) Flags coil.	6.25				7.00	
	same, plate number strip of 5					12.00	
	same, plate number strip of 9					16.00	
4894	(49¢) Flag with 5 full & 3 partial stars.	2.75				1.75	.30
4895	(49¢) Flag with 3 full stars	2.75				1.75	.30
4896	(49¢) Flag with 4 full & 2 partial stars	2.75				1.75	.30
4897	(49¢) Flag with 2 full and 2 partial stars	2.75				1.75	.30

4898 4899

4902 4903

4900 4901

4904 4905

SCOTT NO.	DESCRIPTION	FIRST DAY COVERS SING	FIRST DAY COVERS PL. BLK.	MINT SHEET	PLATE BLOCK	UNUSED F/NH	USED
4898-4905	(49¢) Circus Posters. . .	10.50		35.00(16)		18.00	
4898	(49¢) Barnum and Bailey Circus Poster with Clown.	2.75				2.25	.90
4899	(49¢) Sells-Floto Circus Poster	2.75				2.25	.90
4900	(49¢) Ringling Bros. Barnum & Bailey Circus Poster with Dainty Miss Leitzel	2.75				2.25	.90
4901	(49¢) Al G. Barnes Wild Animal Circus Poster . .	2.75				2.25	.90
4902	(49¢) Ringling Bros. Shows Poster with Hillary Long	2.75				2.25	.90
4903	(49¢) Barnum and Bailey Circus Poster with Tiger	2.75				2.25	.90
4904	(49¢) Ringling Bros. Barnum and Bailey Circus Poster with Elephant	2.75				2.25	.90
4905	(49¢) Carl Hagenbeck-Wallace Circus Poster	2.75				2.25	.90

4905v

SCOTT NO.	DESCRIPTION	FIRST DAY COVERS SING	FIRST DAY COVERS PL. BLK.	MINT SHEET	PLATE BLOCK	UNUSED F/NH	USED
4905v	Circus Posters Souvenir Sheet, die cut, from year book					130.00	
4905c	Circus Posters Souvenir Sheet, Imperf, from press sheets					20.00	

4906

4907

SCOTT NO.	DESCRIPTION	FIRST DAY COVERS SING	FIRST DAY COVERS PL. BLK.	MINT SHEET	PLATE BLOCK	UNUSED F/NH	USED
4906	(49¢) Harvey Milk	2.50	....	40.00(20)	8.00	2.00	.70
4907	(49¢) Nevada	2.50	....	30.00(20)	6.50	1.75	.70

4908

4909

SCOTT NO.	DESCRIPTION	FIRST DAY COVERS SING	FIRST DAY COVERS PL. BLK.	MINT SHEET	PLATE BLOCK	UNUSED F/NH	USED
4908-09	(49¢) Hot Rods	3.75	....	....	....	4.00	....
4908	(49¢) Rear of 1932 Ford "Deuce" Roadster.	2.50	....	....	....	2.25	.70
4909	(49¢) Front of 1932 Ford "Deuce" Roadster.	2.50	....	....	....	2.25	.70
4909B	Same, Booklet Pane of 20	....	....	....	....	40.00	....

4910

4911

SCOTT NO.	DESCRIPTION	FIRST DAY COVERS SING	FIRST DAY COVERS PL. BLK.	MINT SHEET	PLATE BLOCK	UNUSED F/NH	USED
4910-11	(49¢) Civil War	3.75	....	24.00(12)	....	4.00	....
4910	(49¢) Battle of Petersburg	2.50	....	....	....	2.25	1.50
4911	(49¢) Battle of Mobile Bay	2.50	....	....	....	2.25	1.50

4912-4915

SCOTT NO.	DESCRIPTION	FIRST DAY COVERS SING	FIRST DAY COVERS PL. BLK.	MINT SHEET	PLATE BLOCK	UNUSED F/NH	USED
4912-15	(49¢) Farmer's Market .	5.75	....	38.00(20)	16.00(8)	8.00	....
4912	(49¢) Breads.	2.75	....	....	....	2.25	.70
4913	(49¢) Fruits and Vegetables	2.75	....	....	....	2.25	.70
4914	(49¢) Flowers	2.75	....	....	....	2.25	.70
4915	(49¢) Plants	2.75	....	....	....	2.25	.70

4916

4921

SCOTT NO.	DESCRIPTION	FIRST DAY COVERS SING	FIRST DAY COVERS PL. BLK.	MINT SHEET	PLATE BLOCK	UNUSED F/NH	USED
4916	(49¢) Janis Joplin	2.75	....	30.00(16)	....	2.25	.55
4917-20	(49¢) Hudson River School Paintings Block of 4	5.75	....	....	....	9.00	....
4917	(49¢) Grand Canyon by Thomas Moran	2.50	....	....	....	2.25	.70
4918	(49¢) Summer Afternoon by Asher B Durand	2.50	....	....	....	2.25	.70
4919	(49¢) Sunset by Frederic Edwin Church.	2.50	....	....	....	2.25	.70
4920	(49¢) Distant View of Niagara Falls by Thomas Cole. .	2.50	....	....	....	2.25	.70
4920b	Booklet Pane of 20, Hudson River School Paintings .	....	....	....	....	45.00	....
4921	(49¢) Ft. McHenry, War of 1812	2.50	....	30.00(20)	....	1.75	.70

4917 4918

4919 4920

4922 4923 4924 4925 4926

SCOTT NO.	DESCRIPTION	FIRST DAY COVERS SING	FIRST DAY COVERS PL. BLK.	MINT SHEET	PLATE BLOCK	UNUSED F/NH	USED
4922-26	(49¢) Celebrity Chefs . .	6.75	....	38.00(20)	18.00(10)	10.00	....
4922	(49¢) Edna Lewis	2.50	....	....	....	2.25	1.00
4923	(49¢) Felipe Rojas-Lombardi	2.50	....	....	....	2.25	1.00
4924	(49¢) Joyce Chen	2.50	....	....	....	2.25	1.00
4925	(49¢) James Beard. . . .	2.50	....	....	....	2.25	1.00
4926	(49¢) Julia Child	2.50	....	....	....	2.25	1.00

4927

4936

4928-4935

SCOTT NO.	DESCRIPTION	FIRST DAY COVERS SING	FIRST DAY COVERS PL. BLK.	MINT SHEET	PLATE BLOCK	UNUSED F/NH	USED
4927	$5.75 Glade Creek Grist Mill	12.50	....	130.00(10)	58.00	16.00	10.00
4928-35	(49¢) Batman	9.25	....	45.00(20)	....	24.00	....
4928	(49¢) Bat Signal	2.75	....	....	....	3.50	2.00
4929	(49¢) Bat Signal	2.75	....	....	....	3.50	2.00
4930	(49¢) Bat Signal	2.75	....	....	....	3.50	2.00
4931	(49¢) Bat Signal	2.75	....	....	....	3.50	2.00
4932	(49¢) Batman, Yellow Background	2.75	....	....	....	2.50	1.00
4933	(49¢) Batman and Bat Signal	2.75	....	....	....	2.50	1.00
4934	(49¢) Batman and Rope	2.75	....	....	....	2.50	1.00
4935	(49¢) Batman, Blue Background	2.75	....	....	....	2.50	1.00
4936	($1.15) Silver Bells Wreath	3.75	....	40.00(10)	18.00	5.00	1.00

4937, 4941 · 4938, 4942 · 4939, 4943 · 4940, 4944

SCOTT NO.	DESCRIPTION	FIRST DAY COVERS SING	FIRST DAY COVERS PL. BLK.	MINT SHEET	PLATE BLOCK	UNUSED F/NH	USED
4937-40	(49¢) Winter Fun.					11.00	
4937	(49¢) Skaters					2.75	.35
4938	(49¢) Child Making Snowman					2.75	.35
4939	(49¢) Cardinal.					2.75	.35
4940	(49¢) Child Making Snow Angel					2.75	.35
4940b	Same, Booklet Pane of 20					55.00	
4941-44	(49¢) Winter Fun.					16.00	
4941	(49¢) Skaters					4.00	1.75
4942	(49¢) Child Making Snowman					4.00	1.75
4943	(49¢) Cardinal.					4.00	1.75
4944	(49¢) Child Making Snow Angel					4.00	1.75
4944b	Same, ATM Booklet Pane of 18					75.00	

4946

4945

4949

4947

4948

SCOTT NO.	DESCRIPTION	FIRST DAY COVERS SING	FIRST DAY COVERS PL. BLK.	MINT SHEET	PLATE BLOCK	UNUSED F/NH	USED
4945	(49¢) Magi	2.75				2.25	.30
4945a	Same, Booklet Pane of 20					45.00	
4946-49	(49¢) Rudolph the Red-Nosed Reindeer.	5.75				9.00	
4946	(49¢) Rudolph the Red-Nosed Reindeer.	2.75				2.25	.35
4947	(49¢) Hermey and Rudolph					2.25	.35
4948	(49¢) Santa Claus.					2.25	.35
4949	(49¢) Bumble					2.25	.35
4949b	Same, Booklet Pane of 20					40.00	

4950-4951

SCOTT NO.	DESCRIPTION	FIRST DAY COVERS SING	FIRST DAY COVERS PL. BLK.	MINT SHEET	PLATE BLOCK	UNUSED F/NH	USED
4950-51	(49¢) Wilt Chamberlain.	5.75		35.00(18)	8.00	4.00	
4950	(49¢) Wilt Chamberlain in Philadelphia Warriors Uniform	2.75				2.25	.75
4951	(49¢) Wilt Chamberlain in Los Angelos Lakers Uniform	2.75				2.25	.75

2015 COMMEMORATIVES

SCOTT NO.	DESCRIPTION	FIRST DAY COVERS SING	FIRST DAY COVERS PL. BLK.	MINT SHEET	PLATE BLOCK	UNUSED F/NH	USED
4952/5020	**(4952, 4957-58, 4968-72, 4979-87, 4988a, 5003, 5008-12, 5020) 27 varieties . . . .**					**63.00**	

4952

SCOTT NO.	DESCRIPTION	FIRST DAY COVERS SING	FIRST DAY COVERS PL. BLK.	MINT SHEET	PLATE BLOCK	UNUSED F/NH	USED
4952	(49¢) Battle of New Orleans	2.75		30.00(20)		2.00	.30

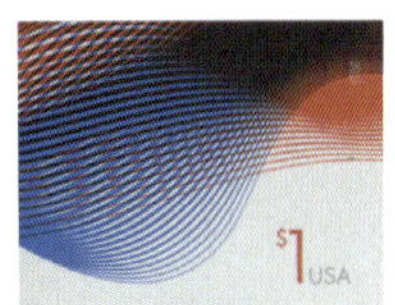
4953

4954

SCOTT NO.	DESCRIPTION	FIRST DAY COVERS SING	FIRST DAY COVERS PL. BLK.	MINT SHEET	PLATE BLOCK	UNUSED F/NH	USED
4953	$1 Patriotic Waves	3.75		22.50(10)	9.00	3.00	1.00
4954	$2 Patriotic Waves	5.75		45.00(10)	18.00	5.00	5.00

4955 · 4956 · 4957

SCOTT NO.	DESCRIPTION	FIRST DAY COVERS SING	FIRST DAY COVERS PL. BLK.	MINT SHEET	PLATE BLOCK	UNUSED F/NH	USED
4955-56	(49¢) Love	3.75		30.00(20)	8.00	4.00	
4955	(49¢) Love, Red	2.75				2.25	1.00
4956	(49¢) Love, Red and Gray	2.75				2.25	1.00
4957	(49¢) Chinese New Year	2.75		24.00(12)		2.25	.90

4959

4958

4960

4961

4962

4963

SCOTT NO.	DESCRIPTION	FIRST DAY COVERS SING	FIRST DAY COVERS PL. BLK.	MINT SHEET	PLATE BLOCK	UNUSED F/NH	USED
4958	(49¢) Robert Robinson Taylor	2.75		30.00(20)	8.00	2.00	.30
4959	(49¢) Red & Black Rose & Heart	2.75		100.00(20)	25.00	5.00	.30
4960	70¢ Black & Red, Tulip & Heart	2.75		125.00(20)	30.00	6.00	3.00
4961-63	(10¢) Stars and Stripes					1.50	
	Same, Plate # Strip of 5					5.00	
4961	(10¢) Stripes at Left, Stars at Right					.50	.25
4962	(10¢) Stars & White Stripe					.50	.25
4963	(10¢) Stars at Left, Stripes at Right					.50	.25

4964 · 4965 · 4966 · 4967

SCOTT NO.	DESCRIPTION	FIRST DAY COVERS SING	FIRST DAY COVERS PL. BLK.	MINT SHEET	PLATE BLOCK	UNUSED F/NH	USED
4964-67	(49¢) Water Lilies	6.50				9.00	
4964	(49¢) Pale Pink Water Lily	2.75				2.25	.30
4965	(49¢) Red Water Lily. . .	2.75				2.25	.30
4966	(49¢) Purple Water Lily .	2.75				2.25	.30
4967	(49¢) White Water Lily .	2.75				2.25	.30
4967b	Same, Booklet Pane of 20					45.00	

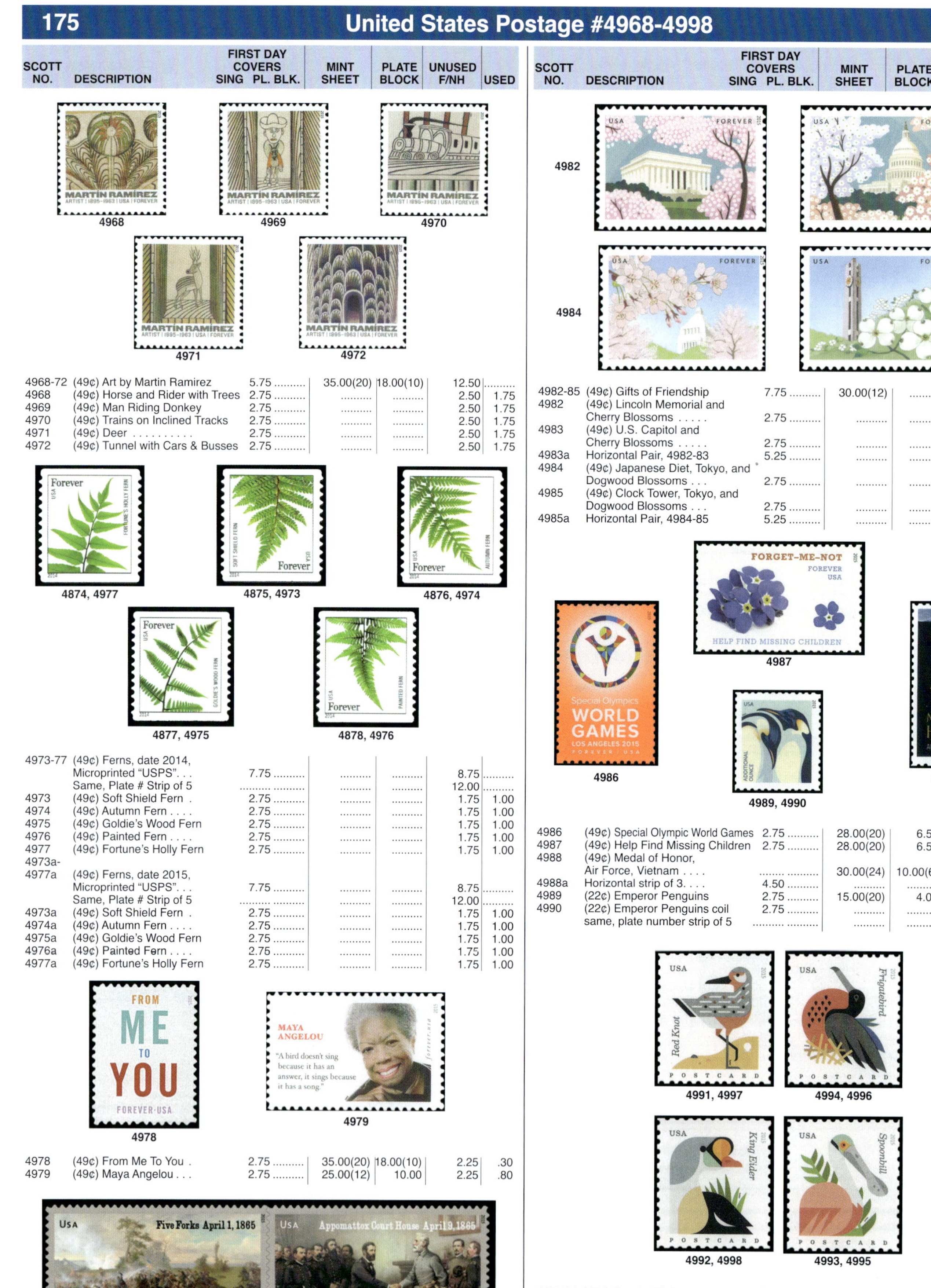

4968 4969 4970 4971 4972

SCOTT NO.	DESCRIPTION	FIRST DAY COVERS SING	FIRST DAY COVERS PL. BLK.	MINT SHEET	PLATE BLOCK	UNUSED F/NH	USED
4968-72	(49¢) Art by Martin Ramirez	5.75		35.00(20)	18.00(10)	12.50	
4968	(49¢) Horse and Rider with Trees	2.75				2.50	1.75
4969	(49¢) Man Riding Donkey	2.75				2.50	1.75
4970	(49¢) Trains on Inclined Tracks	2.75				2.50	1.75
4971	(49¢) Deer	2.75				2.50	1.75
4972	(49¢) Tunnel with Cars & Busses	2.75				2.50	1.75

4874, 4977 4875, 4973 4876, 4974 4877, 4975 4878, 4976

SCOTT NO.	DESCRIPTION	FIRST DAY COVERS SING	FIRST DAY COVERS PL. BLK.	MINT SHEET	PLATE BLOCK	UNUSED F/NH	USED
4973-77	(49¢) Ferns, date 2014, Microprinted "USPS". . .	7.75				8.75	
	Same, Plate # Strip of 5					12.00	
4973	(49¢) Soft Shield Fern	2.75				1.75	1.00
4974	(49¢) Autumn Fern	2.75				1.75	1.00
4975	(49¢) Goldie's Wood Fern	2.75				1.75	1.00
4976	(49¢) Painted Fern	2.75				1.75	1.00
4977	(49¢) Fortune's Holly Fern	2.75				1.75	1.00
4973a-4977a	(49¢) Ferns, date 2015, Microprinted "USPS". . .	7.75				8.75	
	Same, Plate # Strip of 5					12.00	
4973a	(49¢) Soft Shield Fern	2.75				1.75	1.00
4974a	(49¢) Autumn Fern	2.75				1.75	1.00
4975a	(49¢) Goldie's Wood Fern	2.75				1.75	1.00
4976a	(49¢) Painted Fern	2.75				1.75	1.00
4977a	(49¢) Fortune's Holly Fern	2.75				1.75	1.00

4978 4979

SCOTT NO.	DESCRIPTION	FIRST DAY COVERS SING	FIRST DAY COVERS PL. BLK.	MINT SHEET	PLATE BLOCK	UNUSED F/NH	USED
4978	(49¢) From Me To You	2.75		35.00(20)	18.00(10)	2.25	.30
4979	(49¢) Maya Angelou	2.75		25.00(12)	10.00	2.25	.80

4980 4981

SCOTT NO.	DESCRIPTION	FIRST DAY COVERS SING	FIRST DAY COVERS PL. BLK.	MINT SHEET	PLATE BLOCK	UNUSED F/NH	USED
4980-81	(49¢) Civil War Sheet			24.00(12)		4.00	
4980	(49¢) Battle of Five Forks	2.50				2.25	1.75
4981	(49¢) Surrender at Appomattox Court House	2.50				2.25	1.75

4982 4983 4984 4985

SCOTT NO.	DESCRIPTION	FIRST DAY COVERS SING	FIRST DAY COVERS PL. BLK.	MINT SHEET	PLATE BLOCK	UNUSED F/NH	USED
4982-85	(49¢) Gifts of Friendship	7.75		30.00(12)		16.00	
4982	(49¢) Lincoln Memorial and Cherry Blossoms	2.75				4.00	2.00
4983	(49¢) U.S. Capitol and Cherry Blossoms	2.75				4.00	2.00
4983a	Horizontal Pair, 4982-83	5.25				8.00	
4984	(49¢) Japanese Diet, Tokyo, and Dogwood Blossoms	2.75				4.00	2.00
4985	(49¢) Clock Tower, Tokyo, and Dogwood Blossoms	2.75				4.00	2.00
4985a	Horizontal Pair, 4984-85	5.25				8.00	

4987 4986 4988, 4988a 4989, 4990

SCOTT NO.	DESCRIPTION	FIRST DAY COVERS SING	FIRST DAY COVERS PL. BLK.	MINT SHEET	PLATE BLOCK	UNUSED F/NH	USED
4986	(49¢) Special Olympic World Games	2.75		28.00(20)	6.50	1.75	.35
4987	(49¢) Help Find Missing Children	2.75		28.00(20)	6.50	1.75	.35
4988	(49¢) Medal of Honor, Air Force, Vietnam			30.00(24)	10.00(6)		
4988a	Horizontal strip of 3	4.50				5.50	
4989	(22¢) Emperor Penguins	2.75		15.00(20)	4.00	1.25	.30
4990	(22¢) Emperor Penguins coil	2.75				1.00	.30
	same, plate number strip of 5					5.00	

4991, 4997 4994, 4996 4992, 4998 4993, 4995

SCOTT NO.	DESCRIPTION	FIRST DAY COVERS SING	FIRST DAY COVERS PL. BLK.	MINT SHEET	PLATE BLOCK	UNUSED F/NH	USED
4991-94	(35¢) Coastal Birds	4.75		24.00(20)	5.50	5.00	
4991	(35¢) Red Knot	2.75				1.40	1.00
4992	(35¢) King Elder	2.75				1.40	1.00
4993	(35¢) Spoonbill	2.75				1.40	1.00
4994	(35¢) Frigate Bird	2.75				1.40	1.00
4995-98	Coastal Birds coil	4.75				5.00	
	same, plate number strip of 5					8.00	
4995	(35¢) Spoonbill coil	2.75				1.40	.45
4996	(35¢) Frigate Bird coil	2.75				1.40	.45
4997	(35¢) Red Knot coil	2.75				1.40	.45
4998	(35¢) King Elder coil	2.75				1.40	.45

4999

5000

5002

SCOTT NO.	DESCRIPTION	FIRST DAY COVERS SING	FIRST DAY COVERS PL. BLK.	MINT SHEET	PLATE BLOCK	UNUSED F/NH	USED
4999	(71¢) Eastern Tiger Swallowtail Butterfly	3.25		55.00(20)	12.00	3.00	1.00
5000	(71¢) Wedding Cake	3.25		100.00(20)	20.00	5.00	2.00

5001

5003

SCOTT NO.	DESCRIPTION	FIRST DAY COVERS SING	FIRST DAY COVERS PL. BLK.	MINT SHEET	PLATE BLOCK	UNUSED F/NH	USED
5001	(71¢) Flowers and Yes, I Do	3.25		100.00(20)	20.00	5.00	2.00
5002	(71¢) Tulip and Hearts	3.25		100.00(20)	20.00	5.00	2.00

5004, 5007b

5005, 5007b

5006, 5007b

5007, 5007b

SCOTT NO.	DESCRIPTION	FIRST DAY COVERS SING	FIRST DAY COVERS PL. BLK.	MINT SHEET	PLATE BLOCK	UNUSED F/NH	USED
5003	(93¢) Flannery O'Connor	3.75		39.00(20)	8.50	2.50	1.00
5004-07	(49¢) Summer Harvest	6.50				8.00	
5004	(49¢) Watermelons					2.00	.70
5005	(49¢) Sweet Corn					2.00	.70
5006	(49¢) Cantaloupes					2.00	.70
5007	(49¢) Tomatoes					2.00	.70
5007b	same, booklet pane of 20					40.00	

5008

5009

SCOTT NO.	DESCRIPTION	FIRST DAY COVERS SING	FIRST DAY COVERS PL. BLK.	MINT SHEET	PLATE BLOCK	UNUSED F/NH	USED
5008	(49¢) Coast Guard	2.75		30.00(20)	8.00	2.00	.50
5009	(49¢) Elvis Presley	3.50		24.00(20)		2.00	.50

5010

5011

5012

SCOTT NO.	DESCRIPTION	FIRST DAY COVERS SING	FIRST DAY COVERS PL. BLK.	MINT SHEET	PLATE BLOCK	UNUSED F/NH	USED
5010-11	(49¢) World Stamp Show	4.25		38.00(20)	8.00	5.00	
5010	(49¢) World Stamp Show, red	2.75				2.25	2.00
5011	(49¢) World Stamp Show, blue	2.75				2.25	2.00
5012	(49¢) Ingrid Bergman	2.75		40.00(20)	8.00	2.25	.70

5013 5014 5015 5016 5017 5018

SCOTT NO.	DESCRIPTION	FIRST DAY COVERS SING	FIRST DAY COVERS PL. BLK.	MINT SHEET	PLATE BLOCK	UNUSED F/NH	USED
5013-18	(25¢) eagles, strip of 6, D/C 10.25	5.75				15.00	
	same, plate number strip of 7					28.00	
5013	(25¢) Green					2.50	1.25
5014	(25¢) Blue/Green					2.50	1.25
5015	(25¢) Blue					2.50	1.25
5016	(25¢) Red/Violet					2.50	1.25
5017	(25¢) Brown/Orange					2.50	1.25
5018	(25¢) Yellow/Orange					2.50	1.25

5019

5020

SCOTT NO.	DESCRIPTION	FIRST DAY COVERS SING	FIRST DAY COVERS PL. BLK.	MINT SHEET	PLATE BLOCK	UNUSED F/NH	USED
5019	(49¢) Celebrate, 2015 date	2.75		30.00(20)	8.00	2.25	.40
5020	(49¢) Paul Newman	2.75		30.00(20)	8.00	2.25	.70

5021, 5030b

5022, 5030b

5023, 5030b

5024, 5030b

5025, 5030b

5026, 5030b

5027, 5030b

5028, 5030b

5029, 5030b

5030, 5030b

SCOTT NO.	DESCRIPTION	FIRST DAY COVERS SING	FIRST DAY COVERS PL. BLK.	MINT SHEET	PLATE BLOCK	UNUSED F/NH	USED
5021-30	(49¢) Charlie Brown Christmas	12.00				30.00	
5021	(49¢) Charlie Brown carrying Christmas Tree					3.50	1.00
5022	(49¢) Charlie Brown, Pigpen and Dirty Snowman					3.50	1.00
5023	(49¢) Snoopy, Lucy, Violet, Sally and Schroder Skating					3.50	1.00
5024	(49¢) Characters, Dog House and ChristmasTree					3.50	1.00
5025	(49¢) Linus and Christmas Tree					3.50	1.00
5026	(49¢) Charlie Brown looking in Mailbox					3.50	1.00
5027	(49¢) Charlie Brown and Linus behind brick wall					3.50	1.00
5028	(49¢) Charlie Brown, Linus and Christmas Tree					3.50	1.00
5029	(49¢) Charlie Brown screaming, Snoopy decorating dog house					3.50	1.00
5030	(49¢) Charlie Brown hanging ornament on Christmas Tree					3.50	1.00
5030b	same, booklet pane of 20					60.00	

5031, 5034b

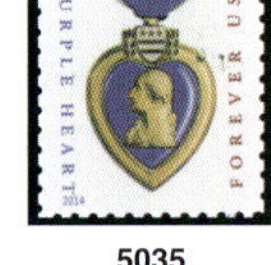

5035

5032, 5034b

5033, 5034b

5034, 5034b

SCOTT NO.	DESCRIPTION	FIRST DAY COVERS SING	FIRST DAY COVERS PL. BLK.	MINT SHEET	PLATE BLOCK	UNUSED F/NH	USED
5031-34	(49¢) Geometric Snowflakes	5.75	....	....	....	12.00	....
5031	(49¢) Purple and Lilac .	2.75	....	....	....	3.00	.90
5032	(49¢) Dark blue and blue	2.75	....	....	....	3.00	.90
5033	(49¢) Dark green and green	2.75	....	....	....	3.00	.90
5034	(49¢) Crimson and pink	2.75	....	....	....	3.00	.90
5034b	same, booklet pane of 20	....	....	....	....	50.00	....
5035	(49¢) Purple Heart, "USPS" microprinted at left	....	....	30.00(20)	6.50	1.75	.30

2016 COMMEMORATIVES

5036/5153	**(5036, 5056-57, 5059-60, 5062-76, 5091-92, 5100, 5105, 5132-35, 5141-42, 5149-53) 35 varieties**	....	....	....	....	**80.00**	....

5036

5037

5038

5039

SCOTT NO.	DESCRIPTION	FIRST DAY COVERS SING	FIRST DAY COVERS PL. BLK.	MINT SHEET	PLATE BLOCK	UNUSED F/NH	USED
5036	(49¢) Quilled Paper Hearts	2.75	....	45.00(20)	10.00	2.50	.50
5037	1¢ Apples coil	2.75	....	....	....	.20	.20
	same, plate strip of 5 . .	....	....	....	....	1.45	....
5038	5¢ Pinot Noir Grapes coil	2.75	....	....	....	.30	.30
	same, plate number strip of 5	....	....	....	....	1.75	....
5039	10¢ Red Pears coil	2.75	....	....	....	.35	.30
	same, plate number strip of 5	....	....	....	....	2.25	....

5040

5041

SCOTT NO.	DESCRIPTION	FIRST DAY COVERS SING	FIRST DAY COVERS PL. BLK.	MINT SHEET	PLATE BLOCK	UNUSED F/NH	USED
5040	$6.45 La Cueva del Indio, Puerto Rico.	14.00	....	150.00(10)	65.00	18.00	12.00
5041	$22.95 Columbia River Gorge	47.00	....	650.00(10)	300.00	75.00	25.00

5042

5043

5044

5045

5046

5047

5048

5049

5050

5052, 5053, 5054, 5055

5051

SCOTT NO.	DESCRIPTION	FIRST DAY COVERS SING	FIRST DAY COVERS PL. BLK.	MINT SHEET	PLATE BLOCK	UNUSED F/NH	USED
5042-51	(49¢) Botanical Art	11.00	....	....	....	25.00	....
5042	(49¢) Corn Lilies	2.75	....	....	....	2.50	1.00
5043	(49¢) Tulips.	2.75	....	....	....	2.50	1.00
5044	(49¢) Tulips.	2.75	....	....	....	2.50	1.00
5045	(49¢) Dahlias	2.75	....	....	....	2.50	1.00
5046	(49¢) Stocks	2.75	....	....	....	2.50	1.00
5047	(49¢) Roses	2.75	....	....	....	2.50	1.00
5048	(49¢) Japanese Irises . .	2.75	....	....	....	2.50	1.00
5049	(49¢) Tulips.	2.75	....	....	....	2.50	1.00
5050	(49¢) Petunias	2.75	....	....	....	2.50	1.00
5051	(49¢) Jonquils.	2.75	....	....	....	2.50	1.00
5051b	same, booklet pane of 10	....	....	....	....	25.00	....
5051c	same, booklet pane of 20	....	....	....	....	60.00	....
5052	(49¢) Flag, d/c 11, SSP coil	2.75	....	....	....	1.50	.30
	microprinted USPS to right of pole under flag	....	....	....	....	....	....
	same, plate number strip of 5	....	....	....	....	10.00	....
5053	(49¢) Flag, d/c 9.5, AP coil	2.75	....	....	....	1.50	.30
	microprinted USPS on second white flag stripe.	....	....	....	....	....	....
	same, plate number strip of 5	....	....	....	....	10.00	....
5054	(49¢) Flag, 11.25x10.75, SSP booklet	2.75	....	....	....	1.50	.30
	microprinted USPS to right of pole under the flag	....	....	....	....	....	....
5054a	same, booklet pane of 10	....	....	....	....	15.00	....
5054b	same, booklet pane of 20	....	....	....	....	30.00	....
5055	(49¢) Flag, 11.25x10.75, AP booklet	2.75	....	....	....	1.50	.30
	microprinted USPS on second white flag stripe.	....	....	....	....	....	....
5055a	same, booklet pane of 20	....	....	....	....	30.00	....

5056

5057

5058

SCOTT NO.	DESCRIPTION	FIRST DAY COVERS SING	FIRST DAY COVERS PL. BLK.	MINT SHEET	PLATE BLOCK	UNUSED F/NH	USED
5056	(49¢) Richard Allen. . . .	2.75	....	30.00(20)	6.50	1.75	.70
5057	(49¢) Chinese New Year Year of the Monkey. . . .	2.75	....	24.00(12)	....	2.25	1.00
5058	($1.20) Moon	4.25	....	55.00(10)	25.00	6.00	1.25

5059

5060

5061

SCOTT NO.	DESCRIPTION	FIRST DAY COVERS SING	FIRST DAY COVERS PL. BLK.	MINT SHEET	PLATE BLOCK	UNUSED F/NH	USED
5059	(49¢) Sarah Vaughan . .	2.75	....	30.00(16)	....	2.25	1.00
5060	(47¢) Shirley Temple. . .	2.75	....	50.00(20)	10.00	3.00	1.00
5061	(5¢) USA Star Nonprofit coil	2.75	....	....	....	.35	.30
	same, plate strip of 5 . .	....	....	....	....	2.00	....

5062 5063

SCOTT NO.	DESCRIPTION	FIRST DAY COVERS SING	FIRST DAY COVERS PL. BLK.	MINT SHEET	PLATE BLOCK	UNUSED F/NH	USED
5062	(47¢) World Stamp Show - NY 2016, red	2.75	....	25.00(12)	....	2.25	1.50
5063	(47¢) World Stamp Show - NY 2016, blue.	2.75	....	25.00(12)	....	2.25	1.50
5062-63	(47¢) World Stamp Folio of 24	....	....	50.00(24)	....	....	....

5064

SCOTT NO.	DESCRIPTION	FIRST DAY COVERS SING	FIRST DAY COVERS PL. BLK.	MINT SHEET	PLATE BLOCK	UNUSED F/NH	USED
5064	(47¢) Repeal of the Stamp Act, Souvenir Sheet of 10 . .	....	....	....	....	20.00	....
	Single from souvenir sheet	....	....	....	....	2.25	1.00

5065 5066

5067 5068

SCOTT NO.	DESCRIPTION	FIRST DAY COVERS SING	FIRST DAY COVERS PL. BLK.	MINT SHEET	PLATE BLOCK	UNUSED F/NH	USED
5065-68	(47¢) Service Cross Medals	6.25	....	24.00(12)	....	8.00	....
5065	(47¢) Distinguished Service Cross	2.75	....	....	....	2.25	1.75
5066	(47¢) Navy Cross	2.75	....	....	....	2.25	1.75
5067	(47¢) Air Force Cross . .	2.75	....	....	....	2.25	1.75
5068	(47¢) Coast Guard Cross	2.75	....	....	....	2.25	1.75

5069 5070 5071

5072

5073

5074

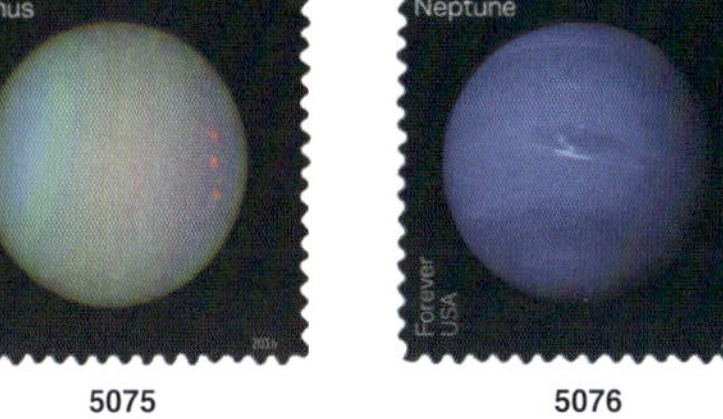

5075 5076

SCOTT NO.	DESCRIPTION	FIRST DAY COVERS SING	FIRST DAY COVERS PL. BLK.	MINT SHEET	PLATE BLOCK	UNUSED F/NH	USED
5069-76	(47¢) Views of Our Planet	....	....	55.00(16)	26.00(8)	24.00	....
5069	(47¢) Mercury	....	....	....	....	3.00	3.00
5070	(47¢) Venus	....	....	....	....	3.00	3.00
5071	(47¢) Earth	....	....	....	....	3.00	3.00
5072	(47¢) Mars	....	....	....	....	3.00	3.00
5073	(47¢) Jupiter	....	....	....	....	3.00	3.00
5074	(47¢) Saturn	....	....	....	....	3.00	3.00
5075	(47¢) Uranus.	....	....	....	....	3.00	3.00
5076	(47¢) Neptune.	....	....	....	....	3.00	3.00

5077 5078

SCOTT NO.	DESCRIPTION	FIRST DAY COVERS SING	FIRST DAY COVERS PL. BLK.	MINT SHEET	PLATE BLOCK	UNUSED F/NH	USED
5077-78	(47¢) Pluto Explored, Souvenir Sheet of 4 . . .	....	....	....	....	6.00	....
5077	(47¢) Pluto Single.	....	....	....	....	3.00	2.00
5078	(47¢) New Horizons Spacecraft Single	....	....	....	....	3.00	2.00

5079a 5079b 5079c

5079d 5079e 5079f

SCOTT NO.	DESCRIPTION	FIRST DAY COVERS SING	FIRST DAY COVERS PL. BLK.	MINT SHEET	PLATE BLOCK	UNUSED F/NH	USED
5079	(47¢) Classics Forever, pane of 6	7.00	....	14.00	....	....	....
	set of singles	16.00	....	....	....	14.00	9.00

5080

NATIONAL PARK SERVICE

5080a	*Iceberg in Glacier Bay*	5080i	*Aerial View of Theadore Roosevelt*
5080b	*Mount Rainer*	5080j	*Water Lily*
5080c	*Scenery in the Grand Tetons*	5080k	*Admin Building at Frijoles Canyon*
5080d	*Bass Harbor Head Lighthouse*	5080l	*Everglades*
5080e	*The Grand Canyon of Arizona*	5080m	*Rainbow at Haleakaia*
5080f	*Horses at Assateague Island*	5080n	*Bison at Yellowstone*
5080g	*Ship Balclutha*	5080o	*Carlsbad Caverns*
5080h	*Stone Arch*	5080p	*Heron at Gulf Islands*

SCOTT NO.	DESCRIPTION	FIRST DAY COVERS SING	PL. BLK.	MINT SHEET	PLATE BLOCK	UNUSED F/NH	USED
5080	(47¢) National Park Service	38.00(16)	....	30.00(16)	....	....	20.00

5081

5082

5083

5084

5085

5086

5087

5088

5089

5090

SCOTT NO.	DESCRIPTION	FIRST DAY COVERS SING	PL. BLK.	MINT SHEET	PLATE BLOCK	UNUSED F/NH	USED
5081-90	(47¢) Colorful Celebrations	22.00(10)	....	....	....	25.00	....
5081	(47¢) Light Blue Bird & Flowers	....	....	....	....	2.50	1.00
5082	(47¢) Orange Birds & Flowers	....	....	....	....	2.50	1.00
5083	(47¢) Violet Flowers . . .	....	....	....	....	2.50	1.00
5084	(47¢) Rose Pink Flowers	....	....	....	....	2.50	1.00
5085	(47¢) Light Blue Flowers	....	....	....	....	2.50	1.00
5086	(47¢) Orange Flowers. .	....	....	....	....	2.50	1.00
5087	(47¢) Violet Birds and Flowers	....	....	....	....	2.50	1.00
5088	(47¢) Rose Pink Bird & Flowers	....	....	....	....	2.50	1.00
5089	(47¢) Rose Pink Flowers	....	....	....	....	2.50	1.00
5090	(47¢) Violet Birds & Flowers	....	....	....	....	2.50	1.00
5090b	same, double sided convertible booklet of 20.	....	....	....	....	50.00	....

5091

5092

SCOTT NO.	DESCRIPTION	FIRST DAY COVERS SING	PL. BLK.	MINT SHEET	PLATE BLOCK	UNUSED F/NH	USED
5091	(47¢) Indiana Statehood	2.75	....	30.00(20)	8.00	2.00	.70
5092	(47¢) EID Greetings . . .	2.75	....	28.00(20)	6.50	1.75	.70

5093

5095

5094

5096

5097

SCOTT NO.	DESCRIPTION	FIRST DAY COVERS SING	PL. BLK.	MINT SHEET	PLATE BLOCK	UNUSED F/NH	USED
5093-97	(47¢) Soda Fountain Favorites	12.00(5)	....	....	....	10.00	....
5093	(47¢) Ice Cream Cone .	....	....	....	....	2.00	.90
5094	(47¢) Egg Cream	....	....	....	....	2.00	.90
5095	(47¢) Banana Split	....	....	....	....	2.00	.90
5096	(47¢) Root Beer Float. .	....	....	....	....	2.00	.90
5097	(47¢) Hot Fudge Sundae	....	....	....	....	2.00	.90
5097c	same, double sided convertible booklet of 20.	....	....	....	....	40.00	....

5098

5099

5100

SCOTT NO.	DESCRIPTION	FIRST DAY COVERS SING	PL. BLK.	MINT SHEET	PLATE BLOCK	UNUSED F/NH	USED
5098-99	(25¢) Star Quilts coil . . .	2.75	....	....	....	1.90	.70
	same, plate number strip of 5	....	....	....	....	4.25	....
5098	(25¢) Red, White & Blue Center Star	....	....	....	....	1.00	.30
5099	(25¢) Blue & Red Center Star	....	....	....	....	1.00	.30
5100	(47¢) James Escalante.	2.75	....	30.00(20)	8.00	2.00	1.00

5101

5102

5103

5104

5105

SCOTT NO.	DESCRIPTION	FIRST DAY COVERS SING	PL. BLK.	MINT SHEET	PLATE BLOCK	UNUSED F/NH	USED
5101-04	(47¢) Pick-up Trucks. . .	4.00	....	....	....	9.00	....
5101	(47¢) 1938 International Harvester	....	....	....	....	2.25	.60
5102	(47¢) 1953 Chevy.	....	....	....	....	2.25	.60
5103	(47¢) 1948 Ford F1. . . .	....	....	....	....	2.25	.60
5104	(47¢) 1965 Ford F100. .	....	....	....	....	2.25	.60
5104b	same, convertible bklt of 20	....	....	....	....	45.00	....
5105	(89¢) Henry James. . . .	3.50	....	48.00(20)	12.00	3.00	2.00

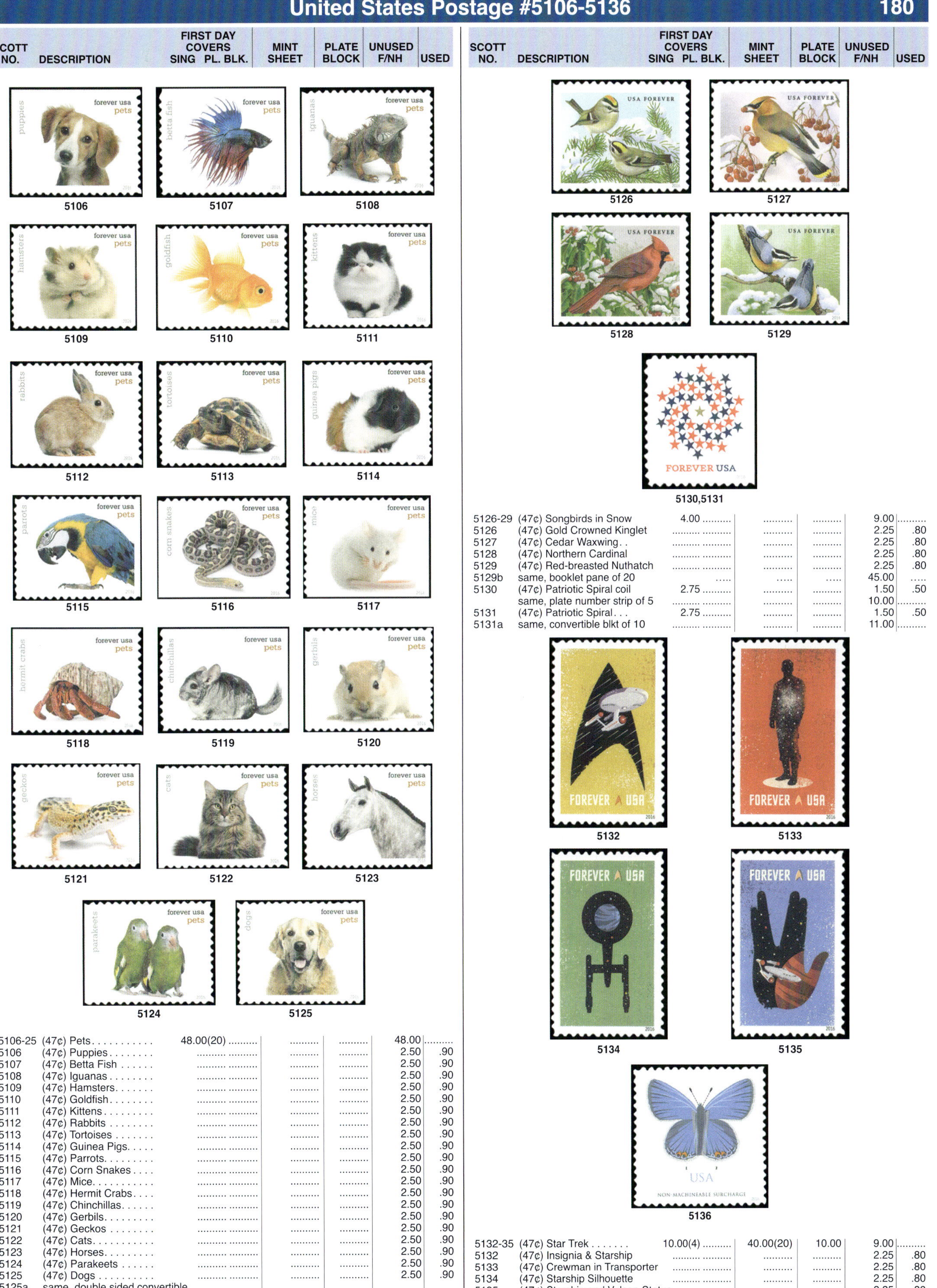

SCOTT NO.	DESCRIPTION	FIRST DAY COVERS SING	PL. BLK.	MINT SHEET	PLATE BLOCK	UNUSED F/NH	USED
5106-25	(47¢) Pets.	48.00(20)	....	....	....	48.00	....
5106	(47¢) Puppies	....	....	....	....	2.50	.90
5107	(47¢) Betta Fish	....	....	....	....	2.50	.90
5108	(47¢) Iguanas	....	....	....	....	2.50	.90
5109	(47¢) Hamsters.	....	....	....	....	2.50	.90
5110	(47¢) Goldfish.	....	....	....	....	2.50	.90
5111	(47¢) Kittens.	....	....	....	....	2.50	.90
5112	(47¢) Rabbits	....	....	....	....	2.50	.90
5113	(47¢) Tortoises	....	....	....	....	2.50	.90
5114	(47¢) Guinea Pigs.	....	....	....	....	2.50	.90
5115	(47¢) Parrots.	....	....	....	....	2.50	.90
5116	(47¢) Corn Snakes	....	....	....	....	2.50	.90
5117	(47¢) Mice.	....	....	....	....	2.50	.90
5118	(47¢) Hermit Crabs. . . .	....	....	....	....	2.50	.90
5119	(47¢) Chinchillas.	....	....	....	....	2.50	.90
5120	(47¢) Gerbils.	....	....	....	....	2.50	.90
5121	(47¢) Geckos	....	....	....	....	2.50	.90
5122	(47¢) Cats.	....	....	....	....	2.50	.90
5123	(47¢) Horses.	....	....	....	....	2.50	.90
5124	(47¢) Parakeets	....	....	....	....	2.50	.90
5125	(47¢) Dogs	....	....	....	....	2.50	.90
5125a	same, double sided convertible booklet of 20.	....	....	....	....	48.00	....

SCOTT NO.	DESCRIPTION	FIRST DAY COVERS SING	PL. BLK.	MINT SHEET	PLATE BLOCK	UNUSED F/NH	USED
5126-29	(47¢) Songbirds in Snow	4.00	....	....	....	9.00	....
5126	(47¢) Gold Crowned Kinglet	....	....	....	....	2.25	.80
5127	(47¢) Cedar Waxwing. .	....	....	....	....	2.25	.80
5128	(47¢) Northern Cardinal	....	....	....	....	2.25	.80
5129	(47¢) Red-breasted Nuthatch	....	....	....	....	2.25	.80
5129b	same, booklet pane of 20		.....	.....	.....	45.00	.....
5130	(47¢) Patriotic Spiral coil	2.75	....	....	....	1.50	.50
	same, plate number strip of 5	....	....	....	....	10.00	....
5131	(47¢) Patriotic Spiral. . .	2.75	....	....	....	1.50	.50
5131a	same, convertible blkt of 10	....	....	....	....	11.00	....
5132-35	(47¢) Star Trek	10.00(4)	....	40.00(20)	10.00	9.00	....
5132	(47¢) Insignia & Starship	....	....	....	....	2.25	.80
5133	(47¢) Crewman in Transporter	....	....	....	....	2.25	.80
5134	(47¢) Starship Silhouette	....	....	....	....	2.25	.80
5135	(47¢) Starship and Vulcan Statue	....	....	....	....	2.25	.80
5136	(68¢) Eastern Tailed-Blue Butterfly	3.25	....	75.00(20)	15.00	3.75	1.00

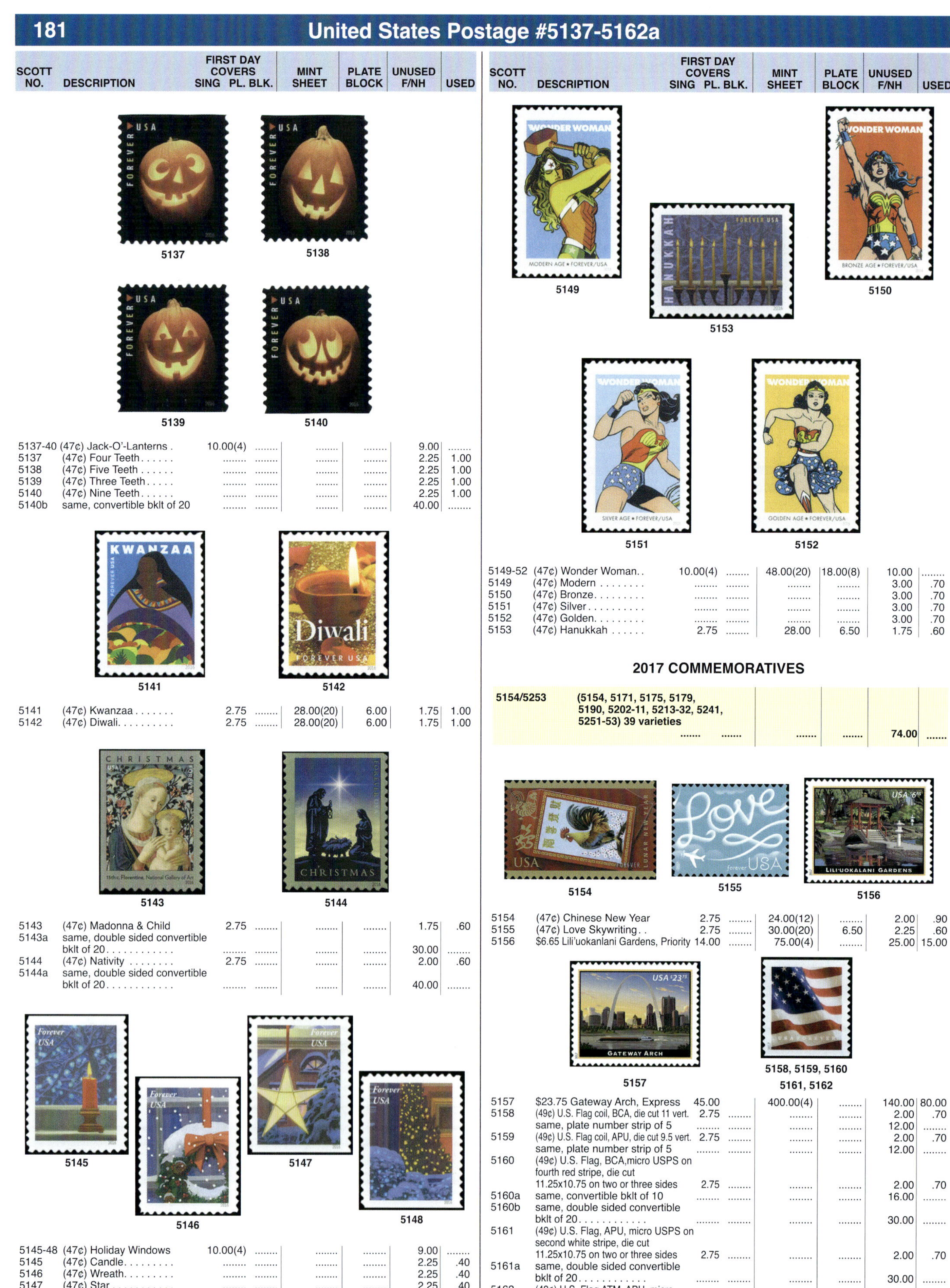

5137 5138 5139 5140

SCOTT NO.	DESCRIPTION	FIRST DAY COVERS SING	FIRST DAY COVERS PL. BLK.	MINT SHEET	PLATE BLOCK	UNUSED F/NH	USED
5137-40	(47¢) Jack-O'-Lanterns .	10.00(4)	....	....	....	9.00	....
5137	(47¢) Four Teeth......	....	....	....	....	2.25	1.00
5138	(47¢) Five Teeth	....	....	....	....	2.25	1.00
5139	(47¢) Three Teeth.....	....	....	....	....	2.25	1.00
5140	(47¢) Nine Teeth......	....	....	....	....	2.25	1.00
5140b	same, convertible bklt of 20	....	....	....	....	40.00	....

5141 5142

SCOTT NO.	DESCRIPTION	FIRST DAY COVERS SING	FIRST DAY COVERS PL. BLK.	MINT SHEET	PLATE BLOCK	UNUSED F/NH	USED
5141	(47¢) Kwanzaa	2.75	....	28.00(20)	6.00	1.75	1.00
5142	(47¢) Diwali..........	2.75	....	28.00(20)	6.00	1.75	1.00

5143 5144

SCOTT NO.	DESCRIPTION	FIRST DAY COVERS SING	FIRST DAY COVERS PL. BLK.	MINT SHEET	PLATE BLOCK	UNUSED F/NH	USED
5143	(47¢) Madonna & Child	2.75	....	....	....	1.75	.60
5143a	same, double sided convertible bklt of 20............	....	....	....	....	30.00	....
5144	(47¢) Nativity	2.75	....	....	....	2.00	.60
5144a	same, double sided convertible bklt of 20............	....	....	....	....	40.00	....

5145 5146 5147 5148

SCOTT NO.	DESCRIPTION	FIRST DAY COVERS SING	FIRST DAY COVERS PL. BLK.	MINT SHEET	PLATE BLOCK	UNUSED F/NH	USED
5145-48	(47¢) Holiday Windows	10.00(4)	....	....	....	9.00	....
5145	(47¢) Candle.........	....	....	....	....	2.25	.40
5146	(47¢) Wreath.........	....	....	....	....	2.25	.40
5147	(47¢) Star	....	....	....	....	2.25	.40
5148	(47¢) Tree...........	....	....	....	....	2.25	.40
5148b	same, double sided convertible bklt of 20............	....	....	....	....	40.00	....

5149 5153 5150 5151 5152

SCOTT NO.	DESCRIPTION	FIRST DAY COVERS SING	FIRST DAY COVERS PL. BLK.	MINT SHEET	PLATE BLOCK	UNUSED F/NH	USED
5149-52	(47¢) Wonder Woman. .	10.00(4)	....	48.00(20)	18.00(8)	10.00	....
5149	(47¢) Modern	....	....	....	....	3.00	.70
5150	(47¢) Bronze.........	....	....	....	....	3.00	.70
5151	(47¢) Silver..........	....	....	....	....	3.00	.70
5152	(47¢) Golden.........	....	....	....	....	3.00	.70
5153	(47¢) Hanukkah	2.75	....	28.00	6.50	1.75	.60

2017 COMMEMORATIVES

SCOTT NO.	DESCRIPTION	FIRST DAY COVERS SING	FIRST DAY COVERS PL. BLK.	MINT SHEET	PLATE BLOCK	UNUSED F/NH	USED
5154/5253	**(5154, 5171, 5175, 5179, 5190, 5202-11, 5213-32, 5241, 5251-53) 39 varieties**	....	....	....	....	**74.00**	....

5154 5155 5156

SCOTT NO.	DESCRIPTION	FIRST DAY COVERS SING	FIRST DAY COVERS PL. BLK.	MINT SHEET	PLATE BLOCK	UNUSED F/NH	USED
5154	(47¢) Chinese New Year	2.75	....	24.00(12)	....	2.00	.90
5155	(47¢) Love Skywriting. .	2.75	....	30.00(20)	6.50	2.25	.60
5156	$6.65 Lili'uokalani Gardens, Priority	14.00	....	75.00(4)	....	25.00	15.00

5157 5158, 5159, 5160 5161, 5162

SCOTT NO.	DESCRIPTION	FIRST DAY COVERS SING	FIRST DAY COVERS PL. BLK.	MINT SHEET	PLATE BLOCK	UNUSED F/NH	USED
5157	$23.75 Gateway Arch, Express	45.00		400.00(4)	....	140.00	80.00
5158	(49¢) U.S. Flag coil, BCA, die cut 11 vert.	2.75	....	....	....	2.00	.70
	same, plate number strip of 5	....	....	....	....	12.00	....
5159	(49¢) U.S. Flag coil, APU, die cut 9.5 vert.	2.75	....	....	....	2.00	.70
	same, plate number strip of 5	....	....	....	....	12.00	....
5160	(49¢) U.S. Flag, BCA,micro USPS on fourth red stripe, die cut 11.25x10.75 on two or three sides	2.75	....	....	....	2.00	.70
5160a	same, convertible bklt of 10	....	....	....	....	16.00	....
5160b	same, double sided convertible bklt of 20............	....	....	....	....	30.00	....
5161	(49¢) U.S. Flag, APU, micro USPS on second white stripe, die cut 11.25x10.75 on two or three sides	2.75	....	....	....	2.00	.70
5161a	same, double sided convertible bklt of 20............	....	....	....	....	30.00	....
5162	(49¢) U.S. Flag ATM, APU, micro USPS on second stripe near blue field, die cut 11.25x10.75 .	2.75	....	....	....	4.00	1.75
5162a	same, booklet pane of 18	.....	.....	.....	....	68.00	.....

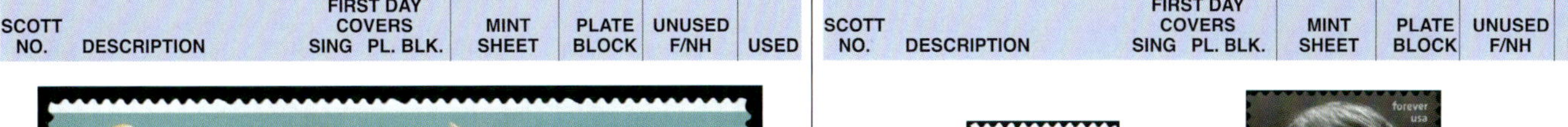

5163, 5169 | 5164, 5170 | 5165, 5167 | 5166, 5168

SCOTT NO.	DESCRIPTION	FIRST DAY COVERS SING	FIRST DAY COVERS PL. BLK.	MINT SHEET	PLATE BLOCK	UNUSED F/NH	USED
5163-66	(34¢) Seashells.	8.00(4)	....	24.00(20)	12.00(8)	5.00	....
5163	(34¢) Queen Conch, die cut 11.25x10.75 . . .	....	....	....	....	1.25	.60
5164	(34¢) Pacific Calico Scallop, die cut 11.25x10.75	....	....	....	....	1.25	.60
5165	(34¢) Alphabet Cone Shell, die cut 11.25x10.75	....	....	....	....	1.25	.60
5166	(34¢) Zebra Nerite Shell, die cut 11.25x10.75	....	....	....	....	1.25	.60
5167-70	(34¢) Seashells coil . . .	8.00(4)	....	....	....	4.00	....
	same, plate number strip of 5	....	....	....	....	8.00	....
5167	(34¢) Alphabet Cone Shell, die cut 9.75 vertical. . . .	....	....	....	....	1.00	.40
5168	(34¢) Zebra Nerite Shell, die cut 9.75 vertical	....	....	....	....	1.00	.40
5169	(34¢) Queen Conch, die cut 9.75 vertical	....	....	....	....	1.00	.40
5170	(34¢) Pacific Calico Scallop, die cut 9.75 vertical	....	....	....	....	1.00	.40

5171

5172

SCOTT NO.	DESCRIPTION	FIRST DAY COVERS SING	FIRST DAY COVERS PL. BLK.	MINT SHEET	PLATE BLOCK	UNUSED F/NH	USED
5171	(49¢) Dorothy Height . .	2.75	....	30.00(20)	8.00	2.00	.70
5172	(5¢) USA Star Coil	2.75	....	....	....	.30	.30
	same, plate number strip of 5	....	....	....	....	1.75	....

5173

OSCAR DE LA RENTA

5173a *Photograph of ODLR*
5173b *Bright pink and gray fabric*
5173c *Green dress*
5173d *Black and white fabric*
5173e *Red dress*
5173f *Floral fabric with dull green*
5173g *Blue dress*
5173h *Floral fabric with white*
5173i *Yellow dress*
5173j *Pink, white and gray floral fabric*
5173k *Pink dress*

SCOTT NO.	DESCRIPTION	FIRST DAY COVERS SING	FIRST DAY COVERS PL. BLK.	MINT SHEET	PLATE BLOCK	UNUSED F/NH	USED
5173	(49¢) Oscar de la Renta	....	....	40.00(11)	....	....	....

5174

5175

SCOTT NO.	DESCRIPTION	FIRST DAY COVERS SING	FIRST DAY COVERS PL. BLK.	MINT SHEET	PLATE BLOCK	UNUSED F/NH	USED
5174	(21¢) Uncle Sam's Hat .	2.75	....	16.00(20)	3.50	.95	.30
5175	(49¢) John F. Kennedy .	2.75	....	24.00(12)	8.00	2.25	.70

5177

5178

5179

SCOTT NO.	DESCRIPTION	FIRST DAY COVERS SING	FIRST DAY COVERS PL. BLK.	MINT SHEET	PLATE BLOCK	UNUSED F/NH	USED
5177	5¢ Pinot Noir Grapes . .	2.75	....	3.80(20)	1.50	.30	.30
5178	10¢ Red Pears, die cut 11.25x11	2.75	....	5.50(20)	1.50	.35	.30
5179	(49¢) Nebraska Statehood	2.75	....	30.00(20)	6.50	2.00	.70

5180

5181

5182

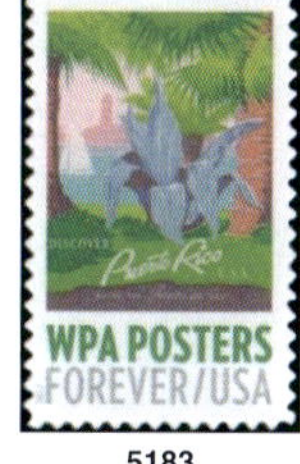

5183

5184

5185

5186

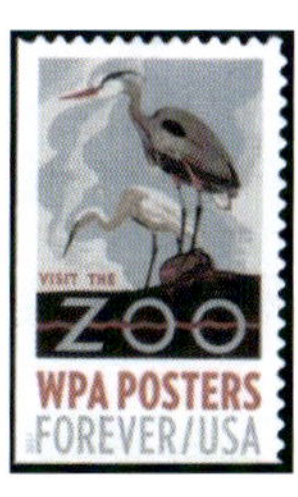

5187

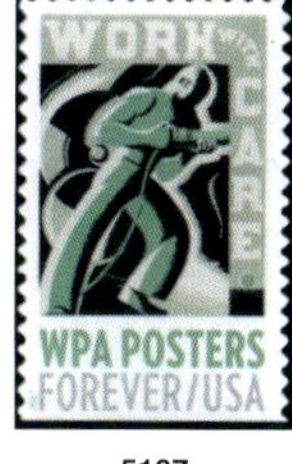

5188

5189

SCOTT NO.	DESCRIPTION	FIRST DAY COVERS SING	FIRST DAY COVERS PL. BLK.	MINT SHEET	PLATE BLOCK	UNUSED F/NH	USED
5180-89	(49¢) WPA Posters. . . .	22.00(10)	....	....	....	22.00	....
5180	(49¢) WPA-See America Welcome to Montana . .	....	....	....	....	2.25	.70
5181	(49¢) WPA-Work Pays America	....	....	....	....	2.25	.70
5182	(49¢) WPA-Field Day . .	....	....	....	....	2.25	.70
5183	(49¢) WPA-Discover Puerto Rico	....	....	....	....	2.25	.70
5184	(49¢) WPA-City of NY Municipal Airports.	....	....	....	....	2.25	.70
5185	(49¢) WPA-Foreign Trade Zone	....	....	....	....	2.25	.70
5186	(49¢) WPA-Visit the Zoo	....	....	....	....	2.25	.70
5187	(49¢) WPA-Work with Care	....	....	....	....	2.25	.70
5188	(49¢) WPA-National Parks Preserve Wild Life	....	....	....	....	2.25	.70
5189	(49¢) WPA-Hiking	....	....	....	....	2.25	.70
5189b	same, double sided convertible bklt of 20.	....	....	....	....	38.00	....

5190

5191

SCOTT NO.	DESCRIPTION	FIRST DAY COVERS SING	FIRST DAY COVERS PL. BLK.	MINT SHEET	PLATE BLOCK	UNUSED F/NH	USED
5190	(49¢) Mississippi Statehood	2.75	....	30.00(20)	6.50	2.00	.70
5191	(70¢) Robert Panara. . .	3.00	....	35.00(20)	8.00	2.25	1.75

5192

5193

5194

5195

5196

5197

SCOTT NO.	DESCRIPTION	FIRST DAY COVERS SING	FIRST DAY COVERS PL. BLK.	MINT SHEET	PLATE BLOCK	UNUSED F/NH	USED
5192-97	(49¢) Delicioso, Latin American Dishes .	12.00(6)	....	....	....	12.00	....
5192	(49¢) Tamales.	....	....	....	....	2.00	.70
5193	(49¢) Flan	....	....	....	....	2.00	.70
5194	(49¢) Sancocho	....	....	....	....	2.00	.70
5195	(49¢) Empanadas.	....	....	....	....	2.00	.70
5196	(49¢) Chili Relleno	....	....	....	....	2.00	.70
5197	(49¢) Ceviche	....	....	....	....	2.00	.70
5197b	same, double sided convertible bklt of 20.	....	....	....	....	35.00	....

5198

5199

5200

SCOTT NO.	DESCRIPTION	FIRST DAY COVERS SING	FIRST DAY COVERS PL. BLK.	MINT SHEET	PLATE BLOCK	UNUSED F/NH	USED
5198	($1.15) Echeveria Plant, Global	4.00	....	35.00(10)	14.00	4.00	.90
5199	(49¢) Boutonniere.	2.75	....	30.00(20)	6.50	2.00	.60
5200	(70¢) Corsage.	2.75	....	35.00(20)	8.00	2.25	.80

5201

5202

SCOTT NO.	DESCRIPTION	FIRST DAY COVERS SING	FIRST DAY COVERS PL. BLK.	MINT SHEET	PLATE BLOCK	UNUSED F/NH	USED
5201	3¢ Strawberries coil, die cut 10 vertical	2.75	....	....	....	.30	.30
	same, plate number strip of 5	....	....	....	....	1.75	....
5202	(49¢) Henry David Thoreau	2.75	....	30.00(20)	6.50	2.00	.95

5203

5204

5205

5206

5207

5208

5209

5210

SCOTT NO.	DESCRIPTION	FIRST DAY COVERS SING	FIRST DAY COVERS PL. BLK.	MINT SHEET	PLATE BLOCK	UNUSED F/NH	USED
5203-10	(49¢) Sports Balls.	20.00(8)	.....	28.00(16)	18.50(8)	15.00	.....
5203	(49¢) Football	.....	.....	.....	.....	2.00	0.70
5204	(49¢) Volleyball.	.....	.....	.....	.....	2.00	0.70
5205	(49¢) Soccer.	.....	.....	.....	.....	2.00	0.70
5206	(49¢) Golf	.....	.....	.....	.....	2.00	0.70
5207	(49¢) Baseball	.....	.....	.....	.....	2.00	0.70
5208	(49¢) Basketball	.....	.....	.....	.....	2.00	0.70
5209	(49¢) Tennis	.....	.....	.....	.....	2.00	0.70
5210	(49¢) Kickball	.....	.....	.....	.....	2.00	0.70

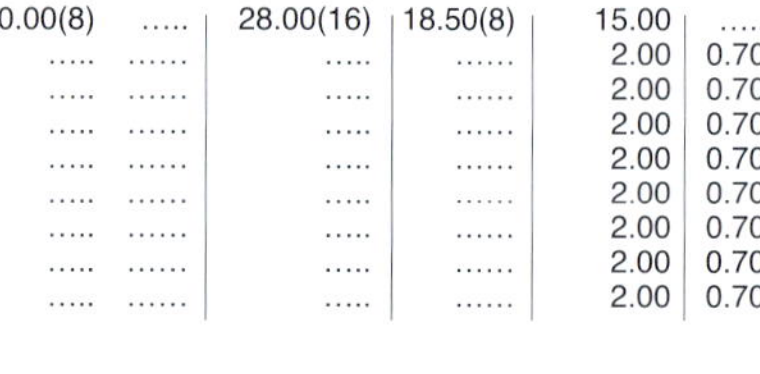

5211

SCOTT NO.	DESCRIPTION	FIRST DAY COVERS SING	FIRST DAY COVERS PL. BLK.	MINT SHEET	PLATE BLOCK	UNUSED F/NH	USED
5211	(49¢) Total Eclipse	2.75	....	30.00(16)	6.50	2.00	.70

5212

ANDREW WYETH

5212a *Wind from the Sea*
5212b *Big Room*
5212c *Christina's World*
5212d *Alvaro & Christin*
5212e *Frostbitten*
5212f *Sailor's Valentine*
5212g *Soaring*
5212h *North Light*
5212i *Spring Fed*
5212j *The Carry*
5212k *Young Bull*
5212l *My Studio*

SCOTT NO.	DESCRIPTION	FIRST DAY COVERS SING	FIRST DAY COVERS PL. BLK.	MINT SHEET	PLATE BLOCK	UNUSED F/NH	USED
5212	(49¢) Andrew Wyeth. . .	25.00(12)	.....	30.00(12)	.....	.....	.....

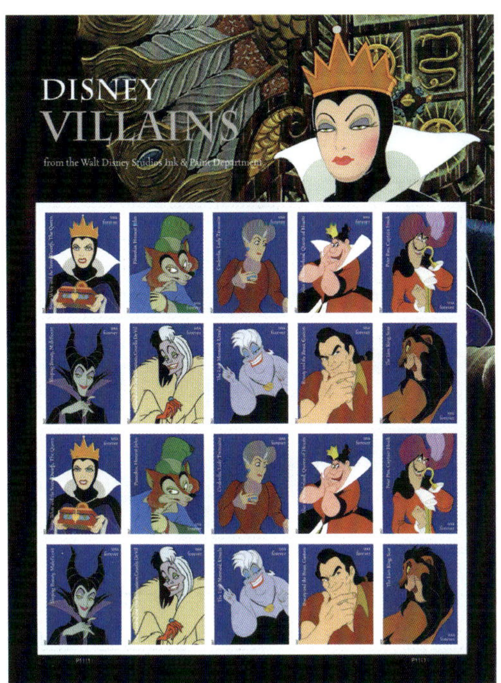

5213-5222

SCOTT NO.	DESCRIPTION	FIRST DAY COVERS SING	PL. BLK.	MINT SHEET	PLATE BLOCK	UNUSED F/NH	USED
5213-22	(49¢) Disney Villians. . .	22.00(10)	.....	35.00(20)	25.00(10)	20.00(10)	.....
5213	(49¢) The Queen, Snow White	.....	......	.....	......	2.25	1.00
5214	(49¢) Honest John, Pinocchio	.....	......	.....	......	2.25	1.00
5215	(49¢) Lady Tremaine, Cinderella	.....	......	.....	......	2.25	1.00
5216	(49¢) Queen of Hearts, Alice in Wonderland	.....		......	....	2.25	1.00
5217	(49¢) Captain Hook, Peter Pan	.....	......	.....	......	2.25	1.00
5218	(49¢) Maleficent, Sleeping Beauty	.....	......	.....	......	2.25	1.00
5219	(49¢) Cruella De Vil, 101 Dalmations.....		......	.....	......	2.25	1.00
5220	(49¢) Ursula, Little Mermaid	.....	......	.....	......	2.25	1.00
5221	(49¢) Gaston, Beauty and the Beast.....		......	.....	......	2.25	1.00
5222	(49¢) Scar, The Lion King	.....	......	.....	......	2.25	1.00

5223

5224

5225

5226

5227

SCOTT NO.	DESCRIPTION	FIRST DAY COVERS SING	PL. BLK.	MINT SHEET	PLATE BLOCK	UNUSED F/NH	USED
5223-27	(49¢) Sharks.	12.00(5)	.....	30.00(20)	18.00(10)	8.50(5)	.....
5223	(49¢) Mako	.....	......	.....	......	2.00	1.00
5224	(49¢) Whale	.....	......	.....	......	2.00	1.00
5225	(49¢) Tresher	.....	......	.....	......	2.00	1.00
5226	(49¢) Hammerhead . . .	.....	......	.....	......	2.00	1.00
5227	(49¢) Great White.	.....	......	.....	......	2.00	1.00

5228

5229

5230

5231

5232

SCOTT NO.	DESCRIPTION	FIRST DAY COVERS SING	PL. BLK.	MINT SHEET	PLATE BLOCK	UNUSED F/NH	USED
5228-32	(49¢) Protect Pollinators	12.00(5)	.....	45.00(20)	24.00(10)	12.00(5)	.....
5228	(49¢) Monarch on Purple Coneflower.....		......	.....	......	2.50	0.95
5229	(49¢) Honeybee on Golden Ragwort.....		......	.....	......	2.50	0.95
5230	(49¢) Monarch on Red Zinnia	.....	......	.....	......	2.50	0.95
5231	(49¢) Honeybee on Purple Aster	.....	......	.....	......	2.50	0.95
5232	(49¢) Monarch on Goldenrod	.....	......	.....	......	2.50	0.95

5233, 5237

5234, 5238

5235, 5239

5236, 5240

SCOTT NO.	DESCRIPTION	FIRST DAY COVERS SING	PL. BLK.	MINT SHEET	PLATE BLOCK	UNUSED F/NH	USED
5233-36	(49¢) Flowers from the Garden	8.00(4)	.....	.....	.....	8.00	.....
	same, plate number strip of 5	.....	.....	.....	.....	14.00	.....
5233	(49¢) Red Camellias in Yellow Pitcher	.....	.....	.....	.....	2.25	0.95
5234	(49¢) Flowers in White Vase	.....	.....	.....	.....	2.25	0.95
5235	(49¢) Peonies in Clear Vase	.....	.....	.....	.....	2.25	0.95
5236	(49¢) Hydrangeas in Blue Pot	.....	.....	.....	.....	2.25	0.95
5237-40	(49¢) Flowers from the Garden	8.00(4)	.....	.....	.....	8.00	.....
5237	(49¢) Red Camellias in Yellow Pitcher	.....	.....	.....	.....	2.25	0.95
5238	(49¢) Flowers in White Vase	.....	.....	.....	.....	2.25	0.95
5239	(49¢) Peonies in Clear Vase	.....	.....	.....	.....	2.25	0.95
5240	(49¢) Hydrangeas in Blue Pot	.....	.....	.....	.....	2.25	0.95
5240b	same, double-sided bklt pane of 20		.....	.....	.....	38.00	.....

5241,5242

5243 5244

5245 5246

SCOTT NO.	DESCRIPTION	FIRST DAY COVERS SING	PL. BLK.	MINT SHEET	PLATE BLOCK	UNUSED F/NH	USED
5241	(49¢) Father Theodore Hesburgh	2.75	.....	30.00(20)	6.50	2.00	0.60
5242	(49¢) Father Theodore Hesburgh, coil	2.75	.....	.....	.....	2.00	0.95
	same, plate number strip of 5	.....	.....	.....	.....	14.00	.....
5243-46	(49¢) The Snowy Day, Ezra Jack Keats	8.00(4)	.....	.....	.....	8.00	.....
5243	(49¢) Making Snowball.	.....	.....	.....	.....	2.00	0.60
5244	(49¢) Sliding	.....	.....	.....	.....	2.00	0.60
5245	(49¢) Making Snow Angel	.....	.....	.....	.....	2.00	0.60
5246	(49¢) Leaving Footprints	.....	.....	.....	.....	2.00	0.60
5246b	same, double-sided bklt pane of 20		.....	.....	.....	30.00	.....

5247 5248 5249 5250

SCOTT NO.	DESCRIPTION	FIRST DAY COVERS SING	FIRST DAY COVERS PL. BLK.	MINT SHEET	PLATE BLOCK	UNUSED F/NH	USED
5247-50	(49¢) Christmas Carols.	8.00(4)	.....	.....	.....	8.00	.....
5247	(49¢) Deck the Halls . . .	.....	.....	.....	.....	2.00	0.60
5248	(49¢) Silent Night	.....	.....	.....	.....	2.00	0.60
5249	(49¢) Jingle Bells	.....	.....	.....	.....	2.00	0.60
5250	(49¢) Jolly Old St. Nicholas	.....	.....	.....	.....	2.00	0.60
5250b	same, double-sided bklt pane of 20	.....	.....	.....	.....	30.00	.....

5251

SCOTT NO.	DESCRIPTION	FIRST DAY COVERS SING	FIRST DAY COVERS PL. BLK.	MINT SHEET	PLATE BLOCK	UNUSED F/NH	USED
5251	(49¢) National Museum of African American History and Culture	2.75	.....	30.00(20)	6.50	2.00	0.95

5252 5253

SCOTT NO.	DESCRIPTION	FIRST DAY COVERS SING	FIRST DAY COVERS PL. BLK.	MINT SHEET	PLATE BLOCK	UNUSED F/NH	USED
5252-53	(49¢) History of Ice Hockey	5.00(2)	.....	30.00(20)	6.50	4.00	.....
5252	(49¢) Player Wearing Gear	.....	.....	.....	.....	2.00	0.70
5253	(49¢) Player Wearing Hat & Scarf	.....	.....	.....	.....	2.00	0.70
5253c	(49¢) History of Ice Hockey, souvenir sheet of 2.	.....	.....	.....	.....	4.50	.....
5252a	(49¢) Player Wearing Gear	.....	.....	.....	.....	2.25	1.00
5253a	(49¢) Player Wearing Hat & Scarf	.....	.....	.....	.....	2.25	1.00

2018 COMMEMORATIVES

SCOTT NO.	DESCRIPTION	FIRST DAY COVERS SING	FIRST DAY COVERS PL. BLK.	MINT SHEET	PLATE BLOCK	UNUSED F/NH	USED
5254/5338	**(5254, 5259, 5264-79, 5281-84, 5299-5305, 5307-10, 5312-16, 5321-30, 5337-38) 50 varieties**	....	....	....	....	**106.00**	....

5254

5255

5256

SCOTT NO.	DESCRIPTION	FIRST DAY COVERS SING	FIRST DAY COVERS PL. BLK.	MINT SHEET	PLATE BLOCK	UNUSED F/NH	USED
5254	(49¢) Year of the Dog	2.75	.....	20.00(12)	.....	2.00	0.60
5255	(49¢) Love Flourishes	2.75	.....	45.00(20)	8.00	2.50	0.60
5256	2¢ Lemon, coil.	.....	.....	.....	.....	0.30	0.30
	same, plate number strip of 5	.....	.....	.....	.....	1.75	.....

5257

5259

5258

5260, 5261 5262, 5263

SCOTT NO.	DESCRIPTION	FIRST DAY COVERS SING	FIRST DAY COVERS PL. BLK.	MINT SHEET	PLATE BLOCK	UNUSED F/NH	USED
5257	$6.70 Byodo-In-Temple, Priority	20.00	.....	80.00(4)	.....	20.00	20.00
5258	$24.70 Sleeping Bear Dunes, Express.	48.00	.....	350.00(4)	.....	95.00	40.00
5259	(50¢) Lena Horne	2.75	.....	30.00(20)	6.50	2.00	0.70
5260	(50¢) U.S. Flag coil, die cut 9.5 vert.	2.75	.....	.....	.....	2.00	0.70
	same, plate number strip of 5	.....	.....	.....	.....	12.00	.....
5261	(50¢) U.S. Flag coil, die cut 11 vert.	2.75	.....	.....	.....	2.00	0.70
	same, plate number strip of 5	.....	.....	.....	.....	12.00	.....
5262	(50¢) U.S. Flag, micro USPS at left of flag	2.75	.....	.....	.....	2.00	0.70
5262a	same, double-sided bklt pane of 20	.....	.....	.....	.....	35.00	.....
5263	(50¢) U.S. Flag, micro USPS at right of flag	2.75	.....	.....	.....	2.00	0.70
5263a	same, double-sided bklt pane of 20	.....	.....	.....	.....	35.00	.....

5264

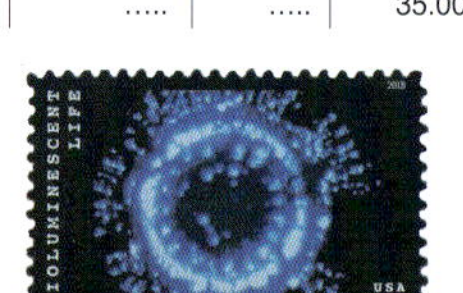

5265

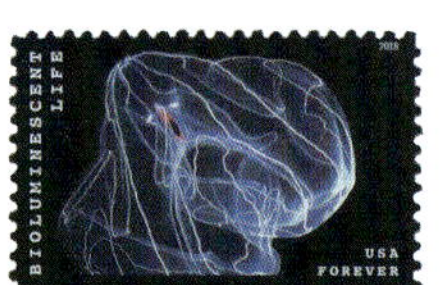

5266

5267

5268

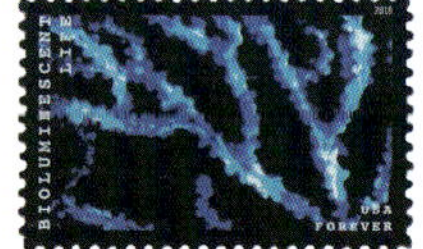

5269

5270

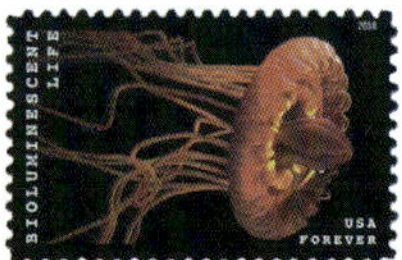

5271

5272

5273

SCOTT NO.	DESCRIPTION	FIRST DAY COVERS SING	FIRST DAY COVERS PL. BLK.	MINT SHEET	PLATE BLOCK	UNUSED F/NH	USED
5264-73	(50¢) Bioluminescent Life .	45.00(20)	.....	48.00(20)	.....	30.00(10)	.....
5264	(50¢) Octopus	.....	.....	.....	.....	3.00	2.25
5265	(50¢) Jellyfish	.....	.....	.....	.....	3.00	2.25
5266	(50¢) Comb Jelly.	.....	.....	.....	.....	3.00	2.25
5267	(50¢) Mushrooms	.....	.....	.....	.....	3.00	2.25
5268	(50¢) Firefly	.....	.....	.....	.....	3.00	2.25
5269	(50¢) Bamboo Coral	.....	.....	.....	.....	3.00	2.25
5270	(50¢) Marine Worm	.....	.....	.....	.....	3.00	2.25
5271	(50¢) Crown Jellyfish.	.....	.....	.....	.....	3.00	2.25
5272	(50¢) Marine Worm	.....	.....	.....	.....	3.00	2.25
5273	(50¢) Sea Pen.	.....	.....	.....	.....	3.00	2.25

5274  5275

SCOTT NO.	DESCRIPTION	FIRST DAY COVERS SING	FIRST DAY COVERS PL. BLK.	MINT SHEET	PLATE BLOCK	UNUSED F/NH	USED
5274	(50¢) Illinois Statehood	2.75	.....	30.00(20)	6.50	2.00	0.70
5275	(50¢) Mister Rogers	2.75	.....	40.00(20)	10.00	3.00	0.70

5276  5277  5278  5279

SCOTT NO.	DESCRIPTION	FIRST DAY COVERS SING	FIRST DAY COVERS PL. BLK.	MINT SHEET	PLATE BLOCK	UNUSED F/NH	USED
5276-79	(50¢) STEM Education . . .	15.00(4)	.....	35.00(20)	16.00(8)	8.00	.....
5276	(50¢) Science	.....	.....	.....	.....	2.00	1.00
5277	(50¢) Technology.	.....	.....	.....	.....	2.00	1.00
5278	(50¢) Engineering	.....	.....	.....	.....	2.00	1.00
5279	(50¢) Math.	.....	.....	.....	.....	2.00	1.00

5281 5282 5283 5284 5280

SCOTT NO.	DESCRIPTION	FIRST DAY COVERS SING	FIRST DAY COVERS PL. BLK.	MINT SHEET	PLATE BLOCK	UNUSED F/NH	USED
5280	(50¢) Peace Rose	2.75	.....	.....	.....	2.00	0.60
5280a	same, double-sided bklt pane of 20	.....	.....	.....	.....	30.00	.....
5281	(50¢) Air Mail Centenary, blue	2.75	.....	30.00(20)	6.50	2.00	0.70
5282	(50¢) Air Mail Centenary, red	2.75	.....	30.00(20)	6.50	2.00	0.70
5283	(50¢) Sally Ride.	2.75	.....	30.00(20)	6.50	2.00	0.70
5284	(50¢) Flag Act of 1818 Bicentennial	2.75	.....	30.00(20)	6.50	2.00	0.70

5285 5286 5287 5288 5289 5290 5291 5292  5293  5294

SCOTT NO.	DESCRIPTION	FIRST DAY COVERS SING	FIRST DAY COVERS PL. BLK.	MINT SHEET	PLATE BLOCK	UNUSED F/NH	USED
5285-94	(50¢) Frozen Treats.	22.00(10)	.....	.....	.....	18.00(10)	.....
5285	(50¢) Green striped pop . .	.....	......	.....	......	2.00	0.70
5286	(50¢) Watermelon, striped pops	.....	......	.....	......	2.00	0.70
5287	(50¢) Twin pop at right. . . .	.....	......	.....	......	2.00	0.70
5288	(50¢) Bitten pop at left. . . .	.....	......	.....	......	2.00	0.70
5289	(50¢) Sprinkle-topped pops	.....	......	.....	......	2.00	0.70
5290	(50¢) Chocolate, vanilla, strawberry pops	.....	......	.....	......	2.00	0.70
5291	(50¢) Bitten pop at right. . .	.....	......	.....	......	2.00	0.70
5292	(50¢) Sprinkle-topped pop at left	.....	......	.....	......	2.00	0.70
5293	(50¢) Chocolate pop at left	.....	......	.....	......	2.00	0.70
5294	(50¢) Sprinkle-topped at right	.....	......	.....	......	2.00	0.70
5294b	same, double-sided bklt pane of 20	.....	......	.....	.....	34.00	.....

5295  5296  5297

SCOTT NO.	DESCRIPTION	FIRST DAY COVERS SING	FIRST DAY COVERS PL. BLK.	MINT SHEET	PLATE BLOCK	UNUSED F/NH	USED
5295	$1 Statue of Freedom	.....	.....	30.00(10)	12.00	3.50	1.25
5296	$2 Statue of Freedom	.....	.....	55.00(10)	24.00	6.50	3.50
5297	$5 Statue of Freedom	.....	.....	55.00(4)	.....	15.00	8.00

5298

O BEAUTIFUL

5298a Death Valley National Park
5298b Three Fingers Mountain
5298c Double Rainbow over Kansas Field
5298d Great Smoky Mountains
5298e Field of Wheat, Wisconsin
5298f Plowed Wheat Field
5298g Grasslands Wildlife Management Area
5298h Field of Wheat, Montana
5298i Yosemite National Park
5298j Crater Lake National Park
5298k Monument Valley Navajo Tribal Park
5298l Maroon Bells
5298m Sunrise Near Orinda, California
5298n Pigeon Point
5298o Edna Valley
5298p Livermore
5298q Napali Coast State Wilderness Park
5298r Lone Ranch Beach
5298s Canaveral National Seashore
5298t Bailey Island

SCOTT NO.	DESCRIPTION	FIRST DAY COVERS SING	FIRST DAY COVERS PL. BLK.	MINT SHEET	PLATE BLOCK	UNUSED F/NH	USED
5298	(50¢) O Beautiful	45.00(20)	.....	60.00(20)	.....	.....	18.00

5299

5300

SCOTT NO.	DESCRIPTION	FIRST DAY COVERS SING	FIRST DAY COVERS PL. BLK.	MINT SHEET	PLATE BLOCK	UNUSED F/NH	USED
5299	(50¢) Scobby-Doo.......	2.75	.....	24.00(12)	6.50	2.00	0.70
5300	(50¢) World War I, Turning the Tide	2.75	.....	30.00(20)	6.50	2.00	0.70

5301, 5306a

5302

5303

5304

5305

SCOTT NO.	DESCRIPTION	FIRST DAY COVERS SING	FIRST DAY COVERS PL. BLK.	MINT SHEET	PLATE BLOCK	UNUSED F/NH	USED
5301-05	(50¢) Art of Magic	12.00(5)	.....	38.00(20)	22.00(10)	10.00(5)	.....
5301	(50¢) Rabbit in Hat	.....	.....	.....	.....	2.25	1.50
5302	(50¢) Fortune Teller......	.....	.....	.....	.....	2.25	1.50
5303	(50¢) Woman Hoop......	.....	.....	.....	.....	2.25	1.50
5304	(50¢) Empty Bird Cage ...	.....	.....	.....	.....	2.25	1.50
5305	(50¢) Bird in Flower......	.....	.....	.....	.....	2.25	1.50
5306	(50¢) Art of Magic, souvenir sheet of 3	.....	.....	.....	.....	6.00	.....

5307 5308 5309 5310

SCOTT NO.	DESCRIPTION	FIRST DAY COVERS SING	FIRST DAY COVERS PL. BLK.	MINT SHEET	PLATE BLOCK	UNUSED F/NH	USED
5307-10	(50¢) Dragons..........	15.00(4)	.....	38.00(20)	10.00(4)	9.00	.....
5307	(50¢) Green Dragon and Castle		.....	.....	.....	2.25	1.50
5308	(50¢) Purple Dragon and Castle		.....	.....	.....	2.25	1.50
5309	(50¢) Dragon and Ship ...	.....	.....	.....	.....	2.25	1.50
5310	(50¢) Dragon and Pagoda.....	.....	.....	.....		2.25	1.50

5311

SCOTT NO.	DESCRIPTION	FIRST DAY COVERS SING	FIRST DAY COVERS PL. BLK.	MINT SHEET	PLATE BLOCK	UNUSED F/NH	USED
5311	($1.15) Poinsettia	4.00	.....	30.00(10)	12.00(4)	3.50	1.00

5312 5313 5314 5315

SCOTT NO.	DESCRIPTION	FIRST DAY COVERS SING	FIRST DAY COVERS PL. BLK.	MINT SHEET	PLATE BLOCK	UNUSED F/NH	USED
5312-15	(50¢) John Lennon	15.00(4)	.....	30.00(16)	.....	9.00	.....
5312	(50¢) Red	.....	.....	.....	.....	2.25	0.80
5313	(50¢) Red Lilac	.....	.....	.....	.....	2.25	0.80
5314	(50¢) Violet	.....	.....	.....	.....	2.25	0.80
5315	(50¢) Blue	.....	.....	.....	.....	2.25	0.80

5316

SCOTT NO.	DESCRIPTION	FIRST DAY COVERS SING	FIRST DAY COVERS PL. BLK.	MINT SHEET	PLATE BLOCK	UNUSED F/NH	USED
5316	(50¢) Honoring First Responders.......	2.75	.....	30.00(20)	6.50(4)	2.00	0.70

5317

5318

5319

5320

SCOTT NO.	DESCRIPTION	FIRST DAY COVERS SING	FIRST DAY COVERS PL. BLK.	MINT SHEET	PLATE BLOCK	UNUSED F/NH	USED
5317-20	(50¢) Birds in Winter	15.00(4)	.....	......	.....	9.00	.....
5317	(50¢) Chickadee	.....	.....	.....	.....	2.25	0.80
5318	(50¢) Cardinal	.....	.....	.....	.....	2.25	0.80
5319	(50¢) Woodpecker.......	.....	.....	.....	.....	2.25	0.80
5320	(50¢) Blue Jay...........	.....	.....	.....	.....	2.25	0.80
5320b	same, double-sided bklt pane of 20	.....	.....	.....	.....	35.00	.....

5321

5322

5323

5324

5325

5326

5327

5328

5329

5330

SCOTT NO.	DESCRIPTION	FIRST DAY COVERS SING	FIRST DAY COVERS PL. BLK.	MINT SHEET	PLATE BLOCK	UNUSED F/NH	USED
5321-30	(50¢) Hot Wheels	35.00(10)	.....	30.00(20)	.....	18.00(10)	.....
5321	(50¢) Purple Passion.	.....	.....	.....	.....	2.00	1.50
5322	(50¢) Rocket-Bye-Baby. . .	.....	.....	.....	.....	2.00	1.50
5323	(50¢) Rigor Motor	.....	.....	.....	.....	2.00	1.50
5324	(50¢) Rodger Dodger	.....	.....	.....	.....	2.00	1.50
5325	(50¢) Mach Speeder	.....	.....	.....	.....	2.00	1.50
5326	(50¢) Twin Mill.	.....	.....	.....	.....	2.00	1.50
5327	(50¢) Bone Shaker	.....	.....	.....	.....	2.00	1.50
5328	(50¢) HW40.	.....	.....	.....	.....	2.00	1.50
5329	(50¢) Deora II	.....	.....	.....	.....	2.00	1.50
5330	(50¢) Sharkruiser	.....	.....	.....	.....	2.00	1.50

5332

5333

5334

5335

5336

5331 5337

5338

SCOTT NO.	DESCRIPTION	FIRST DAY COVERS SING	FIRST DAY COVERS PL. BLK.	MINT SHEET	PLATE BLOCK	UNUSED F/NH	USED
5331	(50¢) Madonna and Child .	2.75	.....	.....	.....	2.00	0.95
5331a	same, double-sided bklt pane of 20	.....	.....	.....	.....	30.00	.....
5332-35	(50¢) Sparkling Holiday Santas	8.00(4)	.....	.....	.....	8.00	.....
5332	(50¢) Santa Head	.....	.....	.....	.....	2.00	0.60
5333	(50¢) Santa and Wreath . .	.....	.....	.....	.....	2.00	0.60
5334	(50¢) Santa and Book	.....	.....	.....	.....	2.00	0.60
5335	(50¢) Santa and Card	.....	.....	.....	.....	2.00	0.60
5335b	same, double-sided bklt pane of 20	.....	.....	.....	.....	30.00	.....
5336	(50¢) Sparkling Holiday Santa, souvenir sheet	.....	.....	.....	.....	2.50	.....
5337	(50¢) Kwanzaa	2.75	.....	30.00(20)	6.50(4)	2.00	0.95
5338	(50¢) Hanukkah.	2.75	.....	30.00(20)	6.50(4)	2.00	0.95

2019 COMMEMORATIVES

SCOTT NO.	DESCRIPTION	FIRST DAY COVERS SING	FIRST DAY COVERS PL. BLK.	MINT SHEET	PLATE BLOCK	UNUSED F/NH	USED
5340/5423M	**(5340, 5349, 5360, 5371-80, 5382-93, 5399-5404, 5409-14, 5420-23) 41 varieties**	**.......**	**.......**	**.......**	**.......**	**74.00**	**.......**

5339

5340

SCOTT NO.	DESCRIPTION	FIRST DAY COVERS SING	FIRST DAY COVERS PL. BLK.	MINT SHEET	PLATE BLOCK	UNUSED F/NH	USED
5339	(50¢) Love Hearts	2.75	.....	30.00(20)	8.00(4)	2.00	0.60
5340	(50¢) Year of the Boar. . . .	2.75	.....	24.00(12)	.....	2.00	0.60

5341

5342, 5343

5344, 5345

5346

SCOTT NO.	DESCRIPTION	FIRST DAY COVERS SING	FIRST DAY COVERS PL. BLK.	MINT SHEET	PLATE BLOCK	UNUSED F/NH	USED
5341	(15¢) Uncle Sam Hat, coil.....	.....	.....	.....	.....	0.30	0.30
	same, plate number strip of 5	.....	.....	.....	.....	3.00	.....
5342	(55¢) U.S. Flag coil, die cut 11	2.75	.....	.....	.....	1.50	0.60
	same, plate number strip of 5	.....	.....	.....	.....	10.50	.....
5343	(55¢) U.S. Flag coil, die cut 9.5	2.75	.....	.....	.....	1.50	0.60
	same, plate number strip of 5	.....	.....	.....	.....	10.50	.....
5344	(55¢) U.S. Flag, micro USPS at upper left	2.75	.....	.....	.....	1.50	0.60
5344a	same, double-sided bklt pane of 20	.....	.....	.....	.....	24.50	.....
5345	(55¢) U.S. Flag, micro USPS at right	2.75	.....	.....	.....	1.50	0.60
5345a	same, double-sided bklt pane of 20	.....	.....	.....	.....	24.50	.....
5346	(70¢) California Dogface Butterfly	3.00	.....	30.00(20)	7.50(4)	2.00	0.70

5347

5348

SCOTT NO.	DESCRIPTION	FIRST DAY COVERS SING	FIRST DAY COVERS PL. BLK.	MINT SHEET	PLATE BLOCK	UNUSED F/NH	USED
5347	($7.35) Joshua Tree, Priority Mail	20.00	.....	140.00(4)	.....	40.00	20.00
5348	($25.50) Bethesda Fountain, Express Mail	50.00	.....	595.00(4)	.....	180.00	50.00

SCOTT NO.	DESCRIPTION	FIRST DAY COVERS SING	FIRST DAY COVERS PL. BLK.	MINT SHEET	PLATE BLOCK	UNUSED F/NH	USED

5349

SCOTT NO.	DESCRIPTION	SING	PL. BLK.	MINT SHEET	PLATE BLOCK	UNUSED F/NH	USED
5349	(55¢) Gregory Hines	2.75	.....	30.00(20)	6.50(4)	2.00	0.70

5350 5351 5352

5353 5354 5355 5356

5357

5358

5359

SCOTT NO.	DESCRIPTION	SING	PL. BLK.	MINT SHEET	PLATE BLOCK	UNUSED F/NH	USED
5350-59	(55¢) Cactus Flowers	30.00(10)	.....	.....	.....	25.00	.....
5350	(55¢) Opuntia Engelmannii	.....	.....	.....	.....	2.50	0.90
5351	(55¢) Rebutia Minuscula.....	.....	.....	.....	.....	2.50	0.90
5352	(55¢) Echinocereus Dasyacanthus	.....	.....	.....	.....	2.50	0.90
5353	(55¢) Echinocereus Poselgeri	.....	.....	.....	.....	2.50	0.90
5354	(55¢) Echinocereus Coccineus	.....	.....	.....	.....	2.50	0.90
5355	(55¢) Pelecyphora Aselliformis	.....	.....	.....	.....	2.50	0.90
5356	(55¢) Parodia Microsperma	.....	.....	.....	.....	2.50	0.90
5357	(55¢) Echinocereus Horizonthalonius	.....	.....	.....	.....	2.50	0.90
5358	(55¢) Thelocactus Heterochromus	.....	.....	.....	.....	2.50	0.90
5359	(55¢) Parodia Scopa	.....	.....	.....	.....	2.50	0.90
5359b	same, double-sided bklt pane of 20	.....	.....	.....	.....	50.00	.....

5360

5361, 5362

SCOTT NO.	DESCRIPTION	SING	PL. BLK.	MINT SHEET	PLATE BLOCK	UNUSED F/NH	USED
5360	(55¢) Alabama Statehood.............	2.75	.....	30.00(20)	6.50(4)	2.00	0.70
5361	(55¢) Star Ribbon	2.75	.....	30.00(20)	6.50(4)	2.00	0.60
5362	(55¢) Star Ribbon coil.............	2.75	.....	.....	.....	2.00	0.60
	same, plate number strip of 5	.....	.....	.....	.....	12.00	.....

5363, 5369 5364, 5370 5365, 5367 5366, 5368

SCOTT NO.	DESCRIPTION	SING	PL. BLK.	MINT SHEET	PLATE BLOCK	UNUSED F/NH	USED
5363-66	(35¢) Coral Reefs	6.00(4)	.....	18.00(20)	8.00(8)	4.00	.....
5363	(35¢) French Angelfish	.....	.....	.....	.....	1.00	0.95
5364	(35¢) Spotted Moray Eel.....	.....	.....	.....	.....	1.00	0.95
5365	(35¢) Grouper and Neon Gobies	.....	.....	.....	.....	1.00	0.95
5366	(35¢) Blue-striped Grunts.....	.....	.....	.....	.....	1.00	0.95
5367-70	(35¢) Coral Reefs coil	6.00(4)	.....	.....	.....	4.00	.....
	same, plate number strip of 5	.....	.....	.....	.....	7.00	.....
5367	(35¢) Grouper and Neon Gobies coil	.....	.....	.....	.....	1.00	0.95
5368	(35¢) Blue-striped Grunts coil	.....	.....	.....	.....	1.00	0.95
5369	(35¢) French Angelfish coil.....	.....	.....	.....	.....	1.00	0.95
5370	(35¢) Spotted Moray Eel coil	.....	.....	.....	.....	1.00	0.95

5371

SCOTT NO.	DESCRIPTION	SING	PL. BLK.	MINT SHEET	PLATE BLOCK	UNUSED F/NH	USED
5371	(55¢) Marvin Gaye.............	2.75	.....	28.00(16)	.....	2.00	0.70

5372

5373 5374

5375 5376

SCOTT NO.	DESCRIPTION	SING	PL. BLK.	MINT SHEET	PLATE BLOCK	UNUSED F/NH	USED
5372-76	(55¢) Post Office Murals..............	15.00(5)	.....	18.00(10)	.....	9.00	.....
5372	(55¢) Piggott, Arkansas...........	.....	.....	.....	.....	2.00	0.80
5373	(55¢) Florence, Colorado...........	.....	.....	.....	.....	2.00	0.80
5374	(55¢) Rockville, Maryland...........	.....	.....	.....	.....	2.00	0.80
5375	(55¢) Anadarko, Oklahoma...........	.....	.....	.....	.....	2.00	0.80
5376	(55¢) Deming, New Mexico...........	.....	.....	.....	.....	2.00	0.80

5377

SCOTT NO.	DESCRIPTION	SING	PL. BLK.	MINT SHEET	PLATE BLOCK	UNUSED F/NH	USED
5377	(55¢) Maureen Connolly Brinker...	2.75	.....	30.00(20)	6.50(4)	2.00	0.70

5378 5379 5380

SCOTT NO.	DESCRIPTION	FIRST DAY COVERS SING	FIRST DAY COVERS PL. BLK.	MINT SHEET	PLATE BLOCK	UNUSED F/NH	USED
5378-80	Transcontinental Railroad...........	10.00(3)	.....	28.00(18)	10.00(6)	6.00	.....
5378	(55¢) Jupiter Locomotive...........	.....	.....	.....	.....	2.00	0.80
5379	(55¢) Golden Spike	.....	.....	.....	.....	2.00	0.80
5380	(55¢) No. 119 Locomotive...........	.....	.....	.....	.....	2.00	0.80

5381
WILD AND SCENIC RIVERS

5381a *Merced River*
5381b *Owyhee River*
5381c *Koyukuk River*
5381d *Niobrara River*
5381e *Snake River*
5381f *Flathead River*
5381g *Missouri River*
5381h *Skagit River*
5381i *Deschutes River*
5381j *Tlikakila River*
5381k *Ontonagon River*
5381l *Clarion River*

SCOTT NO.	DESCRIPTION	FIRST DAY COVERS SING	FIRST DAY COVERS PL. BLK.	MINT SHEET	PLATE BLOCK	UNUSED F/NH	USED
5381	(55¢) Wild and Scenic Rivers...	40.00(12)	.....	22.00	.....	.....	20.00

5382 5383 5384 5385 5386

5387 5388 5389 5390 5391

SCOTT NO.	DESCRIPTION	FIRST DAY COVERS SING	FIRST DAY COVERS PL. BLK.	MINT SHEET	PLATE BLOCK	UNUSED F/NH	USED
5382-91	(55¢) Art of Ellsworth Kelly	35.00(10)	.....	30.00(20)	20.00(10)	18.00	.....
5382	(55¢) Yellow White, 1961 .	.....	.....	.....	.....	2.00	1.50
5383	(55¢) Colors for a Large Wall, 1951	.....	.....	.....	.....	2.00	1.50
5384	(55¢) Blue Red Rocker, 1963	.....	.....	.....	.....	2.00	1.50
5385	(55¢) Spectrum I, 1953 . . .	.....	.....	.....	.....	2.00	1.50
5386	(55¢) South Ferry, 1956 . .	.....	.....	.....	.....	2.00	1.50
5387	(55¢) Blue Green, 1962. . .	.....	.....	.....	.....	2.00	1.50
5388	(55¢) Orange Red Relief, 1990	.....	.....	.....	.....	2.00	1.50
5389	(55¢) Meschers, 1951	.....	.....	.....	.....	2.00	1.50
5390	(55¢) Red Blue, 1964	.....	.....	.....	.....	2.00	1.50
5391	(55¢) Gaza, 1956	.....	.....	.....	.....	2.00	1.50

5392 5393

SCOTT NO.	DESCRIPTION	FIRST DAY COVERS SING	FIRST DAY COVERS PL. BLK.	MINT SHEET	PLATE BLOCK	UNUSED F/NH	USED
5392	(55¢) USS Missouri..............	2.75	.....	30.00(20)	6.50(4)	2.00	0.70
5393	(55¢) Pres. George H.W. Bush	2.75	.....	30.00(20)	6.50(4)	2.00	0.60

5394
SESAME STREET

5394a *Big Bird*
5394b *Ernie*
5394c *Bert*
5394d *Cookie Monster*
5394e *Rosita*
5394f *The Count*
5394g *Oscar*
5394h *Abby Cadabby*
5394i *Herry Monster*
5394j *Julia*
5394k *Guy Smiley*
5394l *Snuffleupagus*
5394m *Elmo*
5394n *Telly*
5394o *Grover*
5394p *Zoe*

SCOTT NO.	DESCRIPTION	FIRST DAY COVERS SING	FIRST DAY COVERS PL. BLK.	MINT SHEET	PLATE BLOCK	UNUSED F/NH	USED
5394	(55¢) Sesame Street.	50.00(16)	.....	30.00 (16)	.....	.....	.....

5395 5396

5397 5398

SCOTT NO.	DESCRIPTION	FIRST DAY COVERS SING	FIRST DAY COVERS PL. BLK.	MINT SHEET	PLATE BLOCK	UNUSED F/NH	USED
5395-98	(55¢) Frogs	15.00(4)	.....	.....	.....	6.50	.....
5395	(55¢) Pacific Tree Frog.............	.....	.....	.....	.....	2.00	0.70
5396	(55¢) Northern Leopard Frog.....	.....	.....	.....	.....	2.00	0.70
5397	(55¢) American Green Tree Frog	.....	.....	.....	.....	2.00	0.70
5398	(55¢) Squirrel Tree Frog.....	.....	.....	.....	.....	2.00	0.70
5398b	same, double-sided bklt pane of 20	.....	.....	.....	.....	30.00	.....

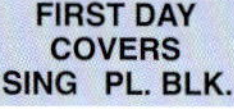

5399

5400

SCOTT NO.	DESCRIPTION	FIRST DAY COVERS SING	PL. BLK.	MINT SHEET	PLATE BLOCK	UNUSED F/NH	USED
5399-5400	(55¢) 50th Anniv. First Moon Landing	6.00(2)	.....	30.00(24)	6.50(4)	4.00	.....
5399	(55¢) Adwin E. Aldrin Jr. on Moon	....	.....	.....	.....	2.00	0.70
5400	(55¢) Moon Landing Site.....	....	.....	.....	.....	2.00	0.70

5401 5402 5403 5404

SCOTT NO.	DESCRIPTION	FIRST DAY COVERS SING	PL. BLK.	MINT SHEET	PLATE BLOCK	UNUSED F/NH	USED
5401-04	(55¢) State and County Fairs	18.00(4)	.....	30.00(20)	12.00(8)	6.50	.....
5401	(55¢) Farmers Unloading Fruits	.....	.....	.....	.....	2.00	1.50
5402	(55¢) Girl and Farm Animals.....	.....	.....	.....	.....	2.00	1.50
5403	(55¢) Parents and Children.....	.....	.....	.....	.....	2.00	1.50
5404	(55¢) Child and Candy Apple.....	.....	.....	.....	.....	2.00	1.50

5405

5406

5407

5408

SCOTT NO.	DESCRIPTION	FIRST DAY COVERS SING	PL. BLK.	MINT SHEET	PLATE BLOCK	UNUSED F/NH	USED
5405-08	(55¢) Military Working Dogs	15.00(4)	.....	.....	.....	6.50	.....
5405	(55¢) German Shepherd.....	.....	.....	.....	.....	2.00	1.00
5406	(55¢) Labrador Retriever.....	.....	.....	.....	.....	2.00	1.00
5407	(55¢) Belgian Malinois..........	.....	.....	.....	.....	2.00	1.00
5408	(55¢) Dutch Shepherd..........	.....	.....	.....	.....	2.00	1.00
5408b	same, double-sided bklt pane of 20	.....	.....	.....	.....	30.00	.....

5409

SCOTT NO.	DESCRIPTION	FIRST DAY COVERS SING	PL. BLK.	MINT SHEET	PLATE BLOCK	UNUSED F/NH	USED
5409	(55¢) 50th Anniv. Woodstock	2.75	.....	30.00(20)	6.50(4)	2.00	0.70

5410

5411

5412

5413

SCOTT NO.	DESCRIPTION	FIRST DAY COVERS SING	PL. BLK.	MINT SHEET	PLATE BLOCK	UNUSED F/NH	USED
5410-13	(55¢) Tyrannosaurus Rex .	15.00(4)	.....	30.00(16)	8.00(4)	7.50	.....
5410	(55¢) Juvenile Tyrannosaurus Rex, Egg, Insect	.....	.....	.....	.....	2.00	1.50
5411	(55¢) Adult Tyrannosaurus Rex	.....	.....	.....	.....	2.00	1.50
5412	(55¢) Young Adult Tyrannosaurus Rex	.....	.....	.....	.....	2.00	1.50
5413	(55¢) Juvenile Tyrannosaurus Rex, Mammal	.....	.....	.....	.....	2.00	1.50

5414

SCOTT NO.	DESCRIPTION	FIRST DAY COVERS SING	PL. BLK.	MINT SHEET	PLATE BLOCK	UNUSED F/NH	USED
5414	(85¢) Walt Whitman.	3.20	.....	40.00(20)	10.00(4)	3.00	1.95

5415 5416

5417

5418

SCOTT NO.	DESCRIPTION	FIRST DAY COVERS SING	PL. BLK.	MINT SHEET	PLATE BLOCK	UNUSED F/NH	USED
5415-18	(55¢) Winter Berries	15.00(4)	.....	.....	.....	9.00	.....
5415	(55¢) Winterberry	.....	.....	.....	.....	2.25	0.70
5416	(55¢) Juniper Berry	.....	.....	.....	.....	2.25	0.70
5417	(55¢) Beautyberry	.....	.....	.....	.....	2.25	0.70
5418	(55¢) Soapberry	.....	.....	.....	.....	2.25	0.70
5418b	same, double-sided bklt pane of 20	.....	.....	.....	.....	35.00	.....

5419

SCOTT NO.	DESCRIPTION	FIRST DAY COVERS SING	PL. BLK.	MINT SHEET	PLATE BLOCK	UNUSED F/NH	USED
5419	Purple Heart	2.75	.....	28.00(20)	6.50(4)	2.00	0.70

5420 5421 5422

5423

SCOTT NO.	DESCRIPTION	FIRST DAY COVERS SING	PL. BLK.	MINT SHEET	PLATE BLOCK	UNUSED F/NH	USED
5420-23	(55¢) Spooky Silhouettes .	15.00(4)	.....	35.00(20)	7.00(4)	6.50	.....
5420	(55¢) Cat and Raven.	.....	.....	.....	.....	2.00	1.50
5421	(55¢) Ghosts	.....	.....	.....	.....	2.00	1.50
5422	(55¢) Spider and Web	.....	.....	.....	.....	2.00	1.50
5423	(55¢) Bats	.....	.....	.....	.....	2.00	1.50

5424

5425

5426

5427

SCOTT NO.	DESCRIPTION	FIRST DAY COVERS SING	FIRST DAY COVERS PL. BLK.	MINT SHEET	PLATE BLOCK	UNUSED F/NH	USED
5424-27	(55¢) Holiday Wreaths. . . .	15.00(4)	.....	.....	.....	6.50	.....
5424	(55¢) Aspidistra Leaf Wreath	.....	.....	.....	.....	2.00	1.50
5425	(55¢) Pine Cone Wreath . .	.....	.....	.....	.....	2.00	1.50
5426	(55¢) Hydrangea, Eucalyptus Wreath	.....	.....	.....	.....	2.00	1.50
5427	(55¢) Woodland Bush Ivy, Red Winterberry Wreath	.....	.....	.....	.....	2.00	1.50
5427b	same, double-sided bklt pane of 20	.....	.....	.....	.....	30.00	.....

2020 COMMEMORATIVES

SCOTT NO.	DESCRIPTION	FIRST DAY COVERS SING	FIRST DAY COVERS PL. BLK.	MINT SHEET	PLATE BLOCK	UNUSED F/NH	USED
5428/5542	**(5428, 5432, 5434, 5455, 5456, 5461-70, 5471-74, 5475-79, 5480-83 5494-5503, 5504-13, 5514-18, 5519-22, 5523, 5524, 5530, 5531, 5542) 62 varieties**	.....	.....	.....	.....	**105.00**	.....

5428

5429

5430

SCOTT NO.	DESCRIPTION	FIRST DAY COVERS SING	FIRST DAY COVERS PL. BLK.	MINT SHEET	PLATE BLOCK	UNUSED F/NH	USED
5428	(55¢) Year of the Rat	2.75	.....	30.00(20)	5.50(4)	2.00	0.70
5429	$7.75 Big Bend National Park, Priority Mail	20.00	.....	70.00(4)	.....	18.00	20.00
5430	$26.35 Grand Island Ice Caves, Express Mail	58.00	.....	250.00(4)	.....	65.00	50.00

5431

5432

5433

SCOTT NO.	DESCRIPTION	FIRST DAY COVERS SING	FIRST DAY COVERS PL. BLK.	MINT SHEET	PLATE BLOCK	UNUSED F/NH	USED
5431	(55¢) Love Hearts	2.75	.....	30.00(20)	6.50(4)	2.00	0.70
5432	(55¢) Gwen Ifill, Journalist.....	2.75	.....	30.00(20)	6.50(4)	2.00	1.00
5433	(10¢) Presorted USA Star, coil	.....	.....	.....	.....	0.30	0.30
	same, plate number strip of 5	.....	.....	.....	.....	2.00	.....

5434

SCOTT NO.	DESCRIPTION	FIRST DAY COVERS SING	FIRST DAY COVERS PL. BLK.	MINT SHEET	PLATE BLOCK	UNUSED F/NH	USED
5434	Let's Celebrate	2.75	.....	30.00(20)	6.50(4)	2.00	.70

5435, 5452

5436, 5453

5437, 5454

5438, 5449

5439, 5445

5440, 5446

5441, 5447

5442, 5448

5443, 5450

5455

5444, 5451

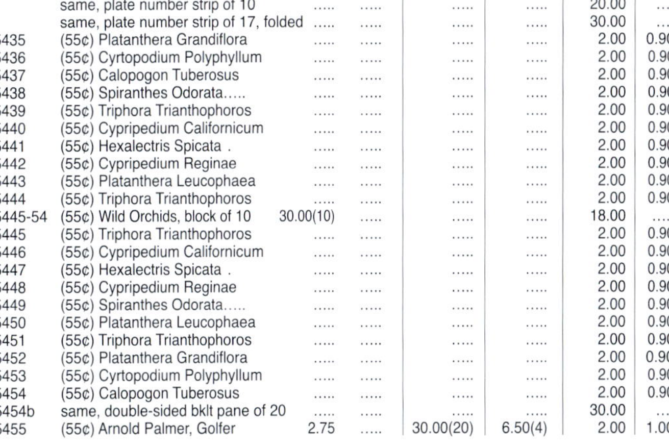

SCOTT NO.	DESCRIPTION	FIRST DAY COVERS SING	FIRST DAY COVERS PL. BLK.	MINT SHEET	PLATE BLOCK	UNUSED F/NH	USED
5435-44	(55¢) Wild Orchids Coil strip of 10	30.00(10)	.....	.....	.....	18.00	.....
	same, plate number strip of 10	.....	.....	.....	.....	20.00	.....
	same, plate number strip of 17, folded	.....	.....	.....	.....	30.00	.....
5435	(55¢) Platanthera Grandiflora	.....	.....	.....	.....	2.00	0.90
5436	(55¢) Cyrtopodium Polyphyllum	.....	.....	.....	.....	2.00	0.90
5437	(55¢) Calopogon Tuberosus	.....	.....	.....	.....	2.00	0.90
5438	(55¢) Spiranthes Odorata.....	.....	.....	.....	.....	2.00	0.90
5439	(55¢) Triphora Trianthophoros	.....	.....	.....	.....	2.00	0.90
5440	(55¢) Cypripedium Californicum	.....	.....	.....	.....	2.00	0.90
5441	(55¢) Hexalectris Spicata .	.....	.....	.....	.....	2.00	0.90
5442	(55¢) Cypripedium Reginae	.....	.....	.....	.....	2.00	0.90
5443	(55¢) Platanthera Leucophaea	.....	.....	.....	.....	2.00	0.90
5444	(55¢) Triphora Trianthophoros	.....	.....	.....	.....	2.00	0.90
5445-54	(55¢) Wild Orchids, block of 10	30.00(10)	.....	.....	.....	18.00	.....
5445	(55¢) Triphora Trianthophoros	.....	.....	.....	.....	2.00	0.90
5446	(55¢) Cypripedium Californicum	.....	.....	.....	.....	2.00	0.90
5447	(55¢) Hexalectris Spicata .	.....	.....	.....	.....	2.00	0.90
5448	(55¢) Cypripedium Reginae	.....	.....	.....	.....	2.00	0.90
5449	(55¢) Spiranthes Odorata.....	.....	.....	.....	.....	2.00	0.90
5450	(55¢) Platanthera Leucophaea	.....	.....	.....	.....	2.00	0.90
5451	(55¢) Triphora Trianthophoros	.....	.....	.....	.....	2.00	0.90
5452	(55¢) Platanthera Grandiflora	.....	.....	.....	.....	2.00	0.90
5453	(55¢) Cyrtopodium Polyphyllum	.....	.....	.....	.....	2.00	0.90
5454	(55¢) Calopogon Tuberosus	.....	.....	.....	.....	2.00	0.90
5454b	same, double-sided bklt pane of 20	.....	.....	.....	.....	30.00	.....
5455	(55¢) Arnold Palmer, Golfer	2.75	.....	30.00(20)	6.50(4)	2.00	1.00

5456

5457

5458

SCOTT NO.	DESCRIPTION	FIRST DAY COVERS SING	FIRST DAY COVERS PL. BLK.	MINT SHEET	PLATE BLOCK	UNUSED F/NH	USED
5456	(55¢) Maine Statehood . . .	2.75	.....	30.00(20)	6.50(4)	2.00	.70
5457	(55¢) Boutoniere	2.75	.....	30.00(20)	6.50(4)	2.00	0.70
5458	(70¢) Corsage	3.75	.....	38.00(20)	8.00(4)	2.50	1.00

5459

5460

SCOTT NO.	DESCRIPTION	FIRST DAY COVERS SING	FIRST DAY COVERS PL. BLK.	MINT SHEET	PLATE BLOCK	UNUSED F/NH	USED
5459	(55¢) Earth Day.	2.75	.....	.....	.....	2.00	0.70
5459a	same, double-sided bklt pane of 20	.....	.....	.....	.....	30.00	.....
5460	($1.20) Global Chrysanthemum	5.00	.....	30.00(10)	12.00(4)	3.00	1.00

5461

5462

5463

5464

5465

5466

5467

5468

5469

5470

SCOTT NO.	DESCRIPTION	FIRST DAY COVERS SING	FIRST DAY COVERS PL. BLK.	MINT SHEET	PLATE BLOCK	UNUSED F/NH	USED
5461-70	(55¢) American Gardens . .	30.00(10)	.....	30.00(20)	20.00(10)	18.00	.....
5461	(55¢) Brooklyn Botanic, New York	.....	.....	.....	.....	.....	1.50
5462	(55¢) Stan Hywet Hall, Ohio	.....	.....	.....	.....	2.00	1.50
5463	(55¢) Dumbarton Oaks, DC	.....	.....	.....	.....	2.00	1.50
5464	(55¢) Coastal Maine Botanical, Maine	.....	.....	.....	.....	.....	1.50
5465	(55¢) Chicago Botanic, Illinois	.....	.....	.....	.....	2.00	1.50
5466	(55¢) Winterthur, Delaware	.....	.....	.....	.....	2.00	1.50
5467	(55¢) Biltmore, North Carolina	.....	.....	.....	.....	2.00	1.50
5468	(55¢) Alfred B Maclay, Florida	.....	.....	.....	.....	2.00	1.50
5469	(55¢) Huntington Botanical, California	.....	.....	.....	.....	2.00	1.50
5470	(55¢) Norfolk Botanical, Virginia	.....	.....	.....	.....	2.00	1.50

5471

5472

5473

5474

SCOTT NO.	DESCRIPTION	FIRST DAY COVERS SING	FIRST DAY COVERS PL. BLK.	MINT SHEET	PLATE BLOCK	UNUSED F/NH	USED
5471-74	(55¢) Voices of the Harlem Renaissance	15.00(4)	.....	30.00(20)	10.00(8)	6.50	.....
5471	(55¢) Nella Larsen.	.....	.....	.....	.....	2.00	1.50
5472	(55¢) Arturo Schomburg . .	.....	.....	.....	.....	2.00	1.50
5473	(55¢) Anne Spencer	.....	.....	.....	.....	2.00	1.50
5474	(55¢) Alain Locke	.....	.....	.....	.....	2.00	1.50

5475

5476

5477

5478 5479

SCOTT NO.	DESCRIPTION	FIRST DAY COVERS SING	FIRST DAY COVERS PL. BLK.	MINT SHEET	PLATE BLOCK	UNUSED F/NH	USED
5475-79	(55¢) Enjoy the Great Outdoors	18.00(5)	.....	35.00(20)	15.00(10)	9.00	.....
5475	(55¢) Child building Sandcastle	.....	.....	.....	.....	2.00	0.95
5476	(55¢) Canoeing	.....	.....	.....	.....	2.00	0.95
5477	(55¢) Hiking.	.....	.....	.....	.....	2.00	0.95
5478	(55¢) Bicycling.	.....	.....	.....	.....	2.00	0.95
5479	(55¢) Cross-country Skiing	.....	.....	.....	.....	2.00	0.95

5480

5481

5482

5483

SCOTT NO.	DESCRIPTION	FIRST DAY COVERS SING	FIRST DAY COVERS PL. BLK.	MINT SHEET	PLATE BLOCK	UNUSED F/NH	USED
5480-83	(55¢) Hip Hop	12.00(4)	.....	30.00(20)	7.00(4)	6.50	.....
5480	(55¢) MC with Microphone	.....	.....	.....	.....	2.00	0.95
5481	(55¢) B-boy Dancing	.....	.....	.....	.....	2.00	0.95
5482	(55¢) Graffiti Art.	.....	.....	.....	.....	2.00	0.95
5483	(55¢) DJ at Turntable	.....	.....	.....	.....	2.00	0.95

5484

5485

5486

5487

5488

5489

5490

5491

5492

5493

SCOTT NO.	DESCRIPTION	FIRST DAY COVERS SING	FIRST DAY COVERS PL. BLK.	MINT SHEET	PLATE BLOCK	UNUSED F/NH	USED
5484-93	(55¢) Fruits and Vegetables, block of 10.	30.00(10)	.....	.....	.....	18.00	.....
5484	(55¢) Plums.	.....	.....	.....	.....	2.00	0.90
5485	(55¢) Tomatoes	.....	.....	.....	.....	2.00	0.90
5486	(55¢) Carrots.	.....	.....	.....	.....	2.00	0.90
5487	(55¢) Lemons	.....	.....	.....	.....	2.00	0.90
5488	(55¢) Blueberries.	.....	.....	.....	.....	2.00	0.90
5489	(55¢) Grapes.	.....	.....	.....	.....	2.00	0.90
5490	(55¢) Lettuce.	.....	.....	.....	.....	2.00	0.90
5491	(55¢) Strawberries.	.....	.....	.....	.....	2.00	0.90
5492	(55¢) Eggplant.	.....	.....	.....	.....	2.00	0.90
5493	(55¢) Figs	.....	.....	.....	.....	2.00	0.90
5493b	same, double-sided bklt pane of 20	.....	.....	.....	.....	30.00	.....

5494 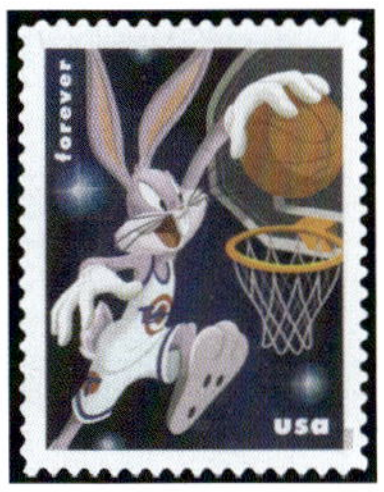 5495  5496

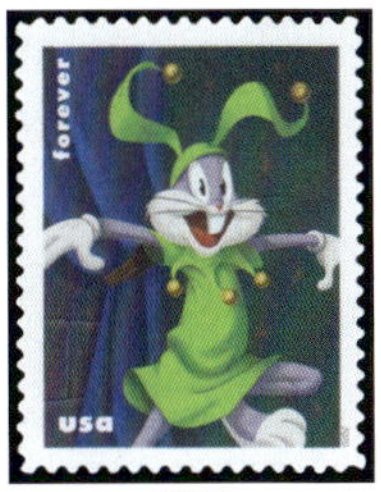

5497  5498

5499  5500  5501

5502  5503

SCOTT NO.	DESCRIPTION	FIRST DAY COVERS SING	FIRST DAY COVERS PL. BLK.	MINT SHEET	PLATE BLOCK	UNUSED F/NH	USED
5494-5503	(55¢) Bugs Bunny, 80th Anniv.	30.00(10)	.....	30.00(20)	18.00(10)	16.00	.....
5494	(55¢) Barber	.....	.....	.....	.....	2.00	1.50
5495	(55¢) Basketball Player . . .	.....	.....	.....	.....	2.00	1.50
5496	(55¢) Celebrity.	.....	.....	.....	.....	2.00	1.50
5497	(55¢) Court Jester	.....	.....	.....	.....	2.00	1.50
5498	(55¢) Brunhilde	.....	.....	.....	.....	2.00	1.50
5499	(55¢) Mermaid.	.....	.....	.....	.....	2.00	1.50
5500	(55¢) Piano Player	.....	.....	.....	.....	2.00	1.50
5501	(55¢) Super-Rabbit	.....	.....	.....	.....	2.00	1.50
5502	(55¢) Baseball Player	.....	.....	.....	.....	2.00	1.50
5503	(55¢) WWII Soldier	.....	.....	.....	.....	2.00	1.50

5504  5505  5506  5507

5508  5509  5510  5511

5512  5513

SCOTT NO.	DESCRIPTION	FIRST DAY COVERS SING	FIRST DAY COVERS PL. BLK.	MINT SHEET	PLATE BLOCK	UNUSED F/NH	USED
5504-13	(55¢) Ruth Asawa	30.00(10)	.....	30.00(20)	18.00(10)	16.00	.....
5504	(55¢) Three Sculptures, 1958-1978	.....	.....	.....	.....	2.00	1.50
5505	(55¢) Sculpture, 1959	.....	.....	.....	.....	2.00	1.50
5506	(55¢) Sculpture, 1958	.....	.....	.....	.....	2.00	1.50
5507	(55¢) Sculpture, 1955	.....	.....	.....	.....	2.00	1.50
5508	(55¢) Sculpture, 1955	.....	.....	.....	.....	2.00	1.50
5509	(55¢) Sculpture, 1980	.....	.....	.....	.....	2.00	1.50
5510	(55¢) Sculpture, 1978	.....	.....	.....	.....	2.00	1.50
5511	(55¢) Sculpture, 1952	.....	.....	.....	.....	2.00	1.50
5512	(55¢) Sculpture, 1954	.....	.....	.....	.....	2.00	1.50
5513	(55¢) Six Sculptures, Various Years	.....	.....	.....	.....	2.00	1.50

5514  5515  5516

5517  5518

SCOTT NO.	DESCRIPTION	FIRST DAY COVERS SING	FIRST DAY COVERS PL. BLK.	MINT SHEET	PLATE BLOCK	UNUSED F/NH	USED
5514-18	(55¢) Innovation	15.00(5)	.....	35.00(20)	15.00(10)	9.00	.....
5514	(55¢) Computing	.....	.....	.....	.....	2.00	1.50
5515	(55¢) Biomedicine	.....	.....	.....	.....	2.00	1.50
5516	(55¢) Genome Sequencing	.....	.....	.....	.....	2.00	1.50
5517	(55¢) Robotics.	.....	.....	.....	.....	2.00	1.50
5518	(55¢) Solar Technology . . .	.....	.....	.....	.....	2.00	1.50

5519  5520  5521  5522

SCOTT NO.	DESCRIPTION	FIRST DAY COVERS SING	FIRST DAY COVERS PL. BLK.	MINT SHEET	PLATE BLOCK	UNUSED F/NH	USED
5519-22	(55¢) Thank You	15.00(4)	.....	30.00(20)	8.00(4)	6.50	.....
5519	(55¢) Rose Brown & Gold .	.....	.....	.....	.....	2.00	1.50
5520	(55¢) Olive & Gold.	.....	.....	.....	.....	2.00	1.50
5521	(55¢) Slate Blue & Gold . .	.....	.....	.....	.....	2.00	1.50
5522	(55¢) Violet & Gold	.....	.....	.....	.....	2.00	1.50

5523

5524, 5524v

5525

SCOTT NO.	DESCRIPTION	FIRST DAY COVERS SING	FIRST DAY COVERS PL. BLK.	MINT SHEET	PLATE BLOCK	UNUSED F/NH	USED
5523	(55¢) Women Suffrage Centenary	2.75	.....	30.00(20)	6.50(4)	2.00	0.70
5524	(55¢) Mayflower, 400th Anniversary	2.75	.....	30.00(20)	6.50(4)	2.00	0.80
5524v	same as above, commemorative book with progressive color proofs, limited 2500	.....	.....	.....	.....	200.00	.....
5525	(55¢) Our Lady of Guapulo	2.75	.....	.....	.....	2.00	0.70
5525a	same, double-sided bklt pane of 20	.....	.....	.....	.....	30.00	.....

5526 5527 5528 5529

SCOTT NO.	DESCRIPTION	FIRST DAY COVERS SING	FIRST DAY COVERS PL. BLK.	MINT SHEET	PLATE BLOCK	UNUSED F/NH	USED
5526-29	(55¢) Holiday Delights. . . .	15.00(4)	.....	.....	.....	6.50	.....
5526	(55¢) Ornament.	.....	.....	.....	.....	2.00	0.70
5527	(55¢) Christmas Tree	.....	.....	.....	.....	2.00	0.70
5528	(55¢) Christmas Stocking .	.....	.....	.....	.....	2.00	0.70
5529	(55¢) Reindeer	.....	.....	.....	.....	2.00	0.70
5529b	same, double-sided bklt pane of 20	.....	.....	.....	.....	30.00	.....

5530 5531

SCOTT NO.	DESCRIPTION	FIRST DAY COVERS SING	FIRST DAY COVERS PL. BLK.	MINT SHEET	PLATE BLOCK	UNUSED F/NH	USED
5530	(55¢) Hanukkah.	2.75	.....	30.00(20)	6.50(4)	2.00	0.70
5531	(55¢) Kwanzaa	2.75	.....	30.00(20)	6.50(4)	2.00	0.70

5532 5533 5534 5535

5536 5537 5538 5539

5540 5541

SCOTT NO.	DESCRIPTION	FIRST DAY COVERS SING	FIRST DAY COVERS PL. BLK.	MINT SHEET	PLATE BLOCK	UNUSED F/NH	USED
5532-41	(55¢) Winter Scenes, block of 10.	30.00(10)	.....	.....	.....	18.00	.....
5532	(55¢) Deer.	.....	.....	.....	.....	2.00	0.90
5533	(55¢) Cardinal	.....	.....	.....	.....	2.00	0.90
5534	(55¢) Snowy Morning	.....	.....	.....	.....	2.00	0.90
5535	(55¢) Red Barn with Wreath	.....	.....	.....	.....	2.00	0.90
5536	(55¢) Barred Owl.	.....	.....	.....	.....	2.00	0.90
5537	(55¢) Blue Jay.	.....	.....	.....	.....	2.00	0.90
5538	(55¢) Mackenzie Barn. . . .	.....	.....	.....	.....	2.00	0.90
5539	(55¢) Rabbit	.....	.....	.....	.....	2.00	0.90
5540	(55¢) After the Snowfall. . .	.....	.....	.....	.....	2.00	0.90
5541	(55¢) Belgian Draft Horses	.....	.....	.....	.....	2.00	0.90
5541b	same, double-sided bklt pane of 20	.....	.....	.....	.....	30.00	.....

5542

SCOTT NO.	DESCRIPTION	FIRST DAY COVERS SING	FIRST DAY COVERS PL. BLK.	MINT SHEET	PLATE BLOCK	UNUSED F/NH	USED
5542	(55¢) Drug Free USA	2.75	.....	30.00(20)	6.50(4)	2.00	0.70

2021 COMMEMORATIVES

SCOTT NO.	DESCRIPTION	FIRST DAY COVERS SING	FIRST DAY COVERS PL. BLK.	MINT SHEET	PLATE BLOCK	UNUSED F/NH	USED
5555/5643	**(5555, 5556, 5557, 5573-82, 5583-92 5593, 5594-97, 5598-5607, 5608, 5609-13, 5614, 5619, 5620, 5621-25 5626, 5627-34, 5636-39, 5640-43) 69 varieties**	.....	.....	.....	.....	**125.00**	.....

5543 5544, 5545

SCOTT NO.	DESCRIPTION	FIRST DAY COVERS SING	FIRST DAY COVERS PL. BLK.	MINT SHEET	PLATE BLOCK	UNUSED F/NH	USED
5543	(55¢) Love.	2.75	.....	30.00(20)	6.50(4)	2.00	0.70
5544	(20¢) Brush Rabbit	2.75	.....	8.00(20)	2.25(4)	0.50	0.30
5545	(20¢) Brush Rabbit, coil. . .	2.75	.....	.....	.....	0.50	0.30
	same, plate number strip of 5	.....	.....	.....	.....	3.00	.....

5546, 5553 5547, 5550

5548, 5552 5549, 5551

SCOTT NO.	DESCRIPTION	FIRST DAY COVERS SING	FIRST DAY COVERS PL. BLK.	MINT SHEET	PLATE BLOCK	UNUSED F/NH	USED
5546-49	(36¢) Barns	15.00(4)	.....	25.00(20)	5.50(4)	5.00	.....
5546	(36¢) Round Barn	.....	.....	.....	.....	1.25	0.60
5547	(36¢) Barn, Windmill	.....	.....	.....	.....	1.25	0.60
5548	(36¢) Forebay Barn.	.....	.....	.....	.....	1.25	0.60
5549	(36¢) Snow-covered Barn .	.....	.....	.....	.....	1.25	0.60
5550-53	(36¢) Barns	15.00(4)	.....	.....	.....	5.00	.....
	same, plate number strip of 5	.....	.....	.....	.....	8.50	.....
5550	(36¢) Barn, Windmill	.....	.....	.....	.....	1.25	0.60
5551	(36¢) Snow-covered Barn .	.....	.....	.....	.....	1.25	0.60
5552	(36¢) Forebay Barn.	.....	.....	.....	.....	1.25	0.60
5553	(36¢) Round Barn	.....	.....	.....	.....	1.25	0.60

5554

5555

SCOTT NO.	DESCRIPTION	FIRST DAY COVERS SING	FIRST DAY COVERS PL. BLK.	MINT SHEET	PLATE BLOCK	UNUSED F/NH	USED
5554	$7.95 Castillo de San Marcos	20.00	.....	75.00(4)	.....	20.00	10.00
5555	(55¢) August Wilson, Playwright	2.75	.....	30.00(20)	6.50(4)	2.00	0.70

5556  5557

SCOTT NO.	DESCRIPTION	FIRST DAY COVERS SING	FIRST DAY COVERS PL. BLK.	MINT SHEET	PLATE BLOCK	UNUSED F/NH	USED
5556	(55¢) Year of the Ox	2.75	.....	30.00(20)	6.50(4)	2.00	0.70
5557	(55¢) Dr. Chien-Shiung Wu, Nuclear Physicist.	2.75	.....	30.00(20)	6.50(4)	2.00	0.70

5558  5559  5560

5561  5562

5563  5564  5565

5566  5567

SCOTT NO.	DESCRIPTION	FIRST DAY COVERS SING	FIRST DAY COVERS PL. BLK.	MINT SHEET	PLATE BLOCK	UNUSED F/NH	USED
5558-67	(55¢) Garden Beauty, block of 10.	30.00(10)	.....	.....	.....	18.00	.....
5558	(55¢) Pink Dogwood	.....	.....	.....	.....	2.00	0.90
5559	(55¢) Orange and Yellow Tulip	.....	.....	.....	.....	2.00	0.90
5560	(55¢) Allium	.....	.....	.....	.....	2.00	0.90
5561	(55¢) Pink Moth Orchid . . .	.....	.....	.....	.....	2.00	0.90
5562	(55¢) Magenta Dahlia	.....	.....	.....	.....	2.00	0.90
5563	(55¢) Yellow Moth Orchid .	.....	.....	.....	.....	2.00	0.90
5564	(55¢) Sacred Lotus	.....	.....	.....	.....	2.00	0.90
5565	(55¢) White Asiatic Lily . . .	.....	.....	.....	.....	2.00	0.90
5566	(55¢) Rose Pink and White Tulip	.....	.....	.....	.....	2.00	0.90
5567	(55¢) Pink American Lotus	.....	.....	.....	.....	2.00	0.90
5567b	same, double-sided bklt pane of 20	.....	.....	.....	.....	35.00	.....

5568

SCOTT NO.	DESCRIPTION	FIRST DAY COVERS SING	FIRST DAY COVERS PL. BLK.	MINT SHEET	PLATE BLOCK	UNUSED F/NH	USED
5568	(75¢) Colorado Hairstreak Butterfly	3.00	.....	50.00(20)	9.00(4)	2.50	1.00

5569  5570  5571  5572

SCOTT NO.	DESCRIPTION	FIRST DAY COVERS SING	FIRST DAY COVERS PL. BLK.	MINT SHEET	PLATE BLOCK	UNUSED F/NH	USED
5569-72	(55¢) Espresso Drinks15.00(4)	.....	.....	.....	.....	6.50	.....
5569	(55¢) Caffe Latte	.....	.....	.....	.....	2.00	0.80
5570	(55¢) Espresso Drinks.	.....	.....	.....	.....	2.00	0.80
5571	(55¢) Caffe Mocha.	.....	.....	.....	.....	2.00	0.80
5572	(55¢) Cappuccino	.....	.....	.....	.....	2.00	0.80
5572b	same, double-sided bklt pane of 20	.....	.....	.....	.....	35.00	.....

5573  5574  5575

5576  5577  5578  5579

5580

5581

5582

SCOTT NO.	DESCRIPTION	FIRST DAY COVERS SING	FIRST DAY COVERS PL. BLK.	MINT SHEET	PLATE BLOCK	UNUSED F/NH	USED
5573-82	(55¢) Star Wars Movie Droids	30.00(10)	.....	35.00(20)	20.00(10)	18.00	.....
5573	(55¢) IG-11	.....	.....	.....	.....	2.00	1.00
5574	(55¢) R2-D2	.....	.....	.....	.....	2.00	1.00
5575	(55¢) K-2SO	.....	.....	.....	.....	2.00	1.00
5576	(55¢) D-O	.....	.....	.....	.....	2.00	1.00
5577	(55¢) L3-37	.....	.....	.....	.....	2.00	1.00
5578	(55¢) BB-8.	.....	.....	.....	.....	2.00	1.00
5579	(55¢) C-3PO	.....	.....	.....	.....	2.00	1.00
5580	(55¢) Gonk Droid.	.....	.....	.....	.....	2.00	1.00
5581	(55¢) 2-1B	.....	.....	.....	.....	2.00	1.00
5582	(55¢) Chopper.	.....	.....	.....	.....	2.00	1.00

5584  5585

5583  5586

5588  5589

5587  5590

5591  5592

SCOTT NO.	DESCRIPTION	FIRST DAY COVERS SING	FIRST DAY COVERS PL. BLK.	MINT SHEET	PLATE BLOCK	UNUSED F/NH	USED
5583-92	(55¢) Heritage Breeds. . . .	30.00(10)	.....	35.00(20)	20.00(10)	18.00	.....
5583	(55¢) Mulefoot Hog	.....	.....	.....	.....	2.00	1.00
5584	(55¢) Wyandotte Chicken .	.....	.....	.....	.....	2.00	1.00
5585	(55¢) Milking Devon Cow .	.....	.....	.....	.....	2.00	1.00
5586	(55¢) Narragansett Turkey	.....	.....	.....	.....	2.00	1.00
5587	(55¢) American Mammoth Donkey	.....	.....	.....	.....	2.00	1.00
5588	(55¢) Cotton Patch Goose	.....	.....	.....	.....	2.00	1.00
5589	(55¢) San Clemente Island Goat	.....	.....	.....	.....	2.00	1.00
5590	(55¢) American Cream Draft Horse	.....	.....	.....	.....	2.00	1.00
5591	(55¢) Cayuga Duck	.....	.....	.....	.....	2.00	1.00
5592	(55¢) Barbados Blackbelly Sheep	.....	.....	.....	.....	2.00	1.00

5594 5595

5593

5596  5597

SCOTT NO.	DESCRIPTION	FIRST DAY COVERS SING	FIRST DAY COVERS PL. BLK.	MINT SHEET	PLATE BLOCK	UNUSED F/NH	USED
5593	(55¢) Go For Broke, WWII	2.75	.....	30.00(20)	6.50(4)	2.00	0.80
5594-97	(55¢) Paintings by Emilio Sanchez	15.00(4)	.....	30.00(20)	14.00(8)	7.50	.....
5594	(55¢) Los Toldos, 1973 . . .	.....	.....	.....	.....	2.00	1.00
5595	(55¢) Ty's Place, 1976. . . .	.....	.....	.....	.....	2.00	1.00
5596	(55¢) En el Souk, 1972 . . .	.....	.....	.....	.....	2.00	1.00
5597	(55¢) Untitled, 1981.	.....	.....	.....	.....	2.00	1.00

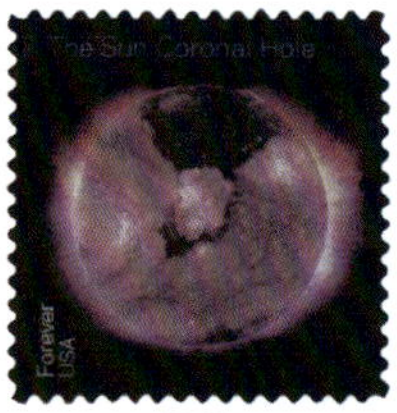

5598  5599  5600

5601  5602

5603  5604  5605

5606  5607

SCOTT NO.	DESCRIPTION	FIRST DAY COVERS SING	FIRST DAY COVERS PL. BLK.	MINT SHEET	PLATE BLOCK	UNUSED F/NH	USED
5598-5607	(55¢) Sun Science.	30.00(10)	.....	35.00(20)	20.00(10)	18.00	.....
5598	(55¢) Coronal Hole, rose. .	.....	.....	.....	.....	2.00	1.00
5599	(55¢) Coronal Loops, orange red	.....	.....	.....	.....	2.00	1.00
5600	(55¢) Solar Flare, blue . . .	.....	.....	.....	.....	2.00	1.00
5601	(55¢) Active Sun	.....	.....	.....	.....	2.00	1.00
5602	(55¢) Plasma Blast	.....	.....	.....	.....	2.00	1.00
5603	(55¢) Coronal Loops	.....	.....	.....	.....	2.00	1.00
5604	(55¢) Sun Sunspots	.....	.....	.....	.....	2.00	1.00
5605	(55¢) Plasma Blast	.....	.....	.....	.....	2.00	1.00
5606	(55¢) Solar Flare, aqua . . .	.....	.....	.....	.....	2.00	1.00
5607	(55¢) Coronal Hole, tan. . .	.....	.....	.....	.....	2.00	1.00

5608

SCOTT NO.	DESCRIPTION	FIRST DAY COVERS SING	FIRST DAY COVERS PL. BLK.	MINT SHEET	PLATE BLOCK	UNUSED F/NH	USED
5608	(55¢) Yogi Berra	2.75	.....	30.00(20)	6.50(4)	2.00	0.80

5609

5610

5611

5612

5613

SCOTT NO.	DESCRIPTION	FIRST DAY COVERS SING	FIRST DAY COVERS PL. BLK.	MINT SHEET	PLATE BLOCK	UNUSED F/NH	USED
5609-13	(55¢) Tap Dance	15.00(5)	.....	35.00(20)	20.00(10)	10.00(5)	.....
5609	(55¢) Max Pollak, buff	.....	.....	.....	.....	2.00	1.00
5610	(55¢) Michela Marino Lerman, rose	.....	.....	.....	.....	2.00	1.00
5611	(55¢) Derick Grant, greenish blue	.....	.....	.....	.....	2.00	1.00
5612	(55¢) Dormeshia Sumbry-Edwards, light blue	.....	.....	.....	.....	2.00	1.00
5613	(55¢) Ayodele Casel, bister	.....	.....	.....	.....	2.00	1.00

5614

SCOTT NO.	DESCRIPTION	FIRST DAY COVERS SING	FIRST DAY COVERS PL. BLK.	MINT SHEET	PLATE BLOCK	UNUSED F/NH	USED
5614	(55¢) Mystery Message. . .	2.75	.....	30.00(20)	6.50(4)	2.00	0.80

5615

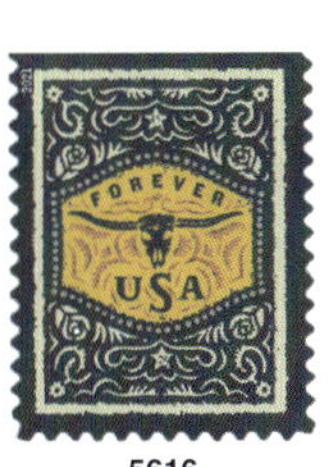
5616

5617

5618

SCOTT NO.	DESCRIPTION	FIRST DAY COVERS SING	FIRST DAY COVERS PL. BLK.	MINT SHEET	PLATE BLOCK	UNUSED F/NH	USED
5615-18	(55¢) Western Wear	15.00(4)	.....	.....	.....	7.50	.....
5615	(55¢) Cowboy Hat, Snakes & Roses	.....	.....	.....	.....	2.00	0.80
5616	(55¢) Belt Buckle, Roses, Star & Spurs	.....	.....	.....	.....	2.00	0.80
5617	(55¢) Cowboy Boot, Roses, Carti & Star	.....	.....	.....	.....	2.00	0.80
5618	(55¢) Western Shirt, Roses, Cacti & Star.	.....	.....	.....	.....	2.00	0.80
5618b	same, double-sided bklt pane of 20	.....	.....	.....	.....	35.00	.....

5619

5620

SCOTT NO.	DESCRIPTION	FIRST DAY COVERS SING	FIRST DAY COVERS PL. BLK.	MINT SHEET	PLATE BLOCK	UNUSED F/NH	USED
5619	(95¢) Ursula K. LeGuin . . .	3.50	.....	50.00(20)	10.50(4)	3.00	1.50
5620	(55¢) Raven Story	2.75	.....	30.00(20)	6.00(4)	2.00	0.80

5621

5622

5623

5624

5625

SCOTT NO.	DESCRIPTION	FIRST DAY COVERS SING	FIRST DAY COVERS PL. BLK.	MINT SHEET	PLATE BLOCK	UNUSED F/NH	USED
5621-25	(55¢) Mid-Atlantic Lighthouse	15.00(5)	.....	35.00(20)	20.00(10)	10.00	.....
5621	(55¢) Montauk Point	.....	.....	.....	.....	2.00	1.00
5622	(55¢) Navesink Twin	.....	.....	.....	.....	2.00	1.00
5623	(55¢) Erie Harbor......	.....	.....	.....	.....	2.00	1.00
5624	(55¢) Harbor of Refuge..........	.....	.....	.....	.....	2.00	1.00
5625	(55¢) Thomas Point Shoal.....	.....	.....	.....	.....	2.00	1.00

5626

SCOTT NO.	DESCRIPTION	FIRST DAY COVERS SING	FIRST DAY COVERS PL. BLK.	MINT SHEET	PLATE BLOCK	UNUSED F/NH	USED
5626	(55¢) Missouri Statehood .	2.75	.....	30.00(20)	6.50(4)	2.00	0.80

5627

5628

5629

5630

5631

5632

5633

5634

SCOTT NO.	DESCRIPTION	FIRST DAY COVERS SING	FIRST DAY COVERS PL. BLK.	MINT SHEET	PLATE BLOCK	UNUSED F/NH	USED
5627-34	(55¢) Backyard Games . . .	24.00(8)	.....	30.00(16)	18.00(8)	16.00(8)	.....
5627	(55¢) Horseshoes	.....	.....	.....	.....	2.00	1.00
5628	(55¢) Bocce.	.....	.....	.....	.....	2.00	1.00
5629	(55¢) Flying Disc.....	.....	.....	.....	.....	2.00	1.00
5630	(55¢) Croquet.....	.....	.....	.....	.....	2.00	1.00
5631	(55¢) Pick-Up Baseball	.....	.....	.....	.....	2.00	1.00
5632	(55¢) Tetherball	.....	.....	.....	.....	2.00	1.00
5633	(55¢) Badminton	.....	.....	.....	.....	2.00	1.00
5634	(55¢) Cornhole	.....	.....	.....	.....	2.00	1.00

5635

SCOTT NO.	DESCRIPTION	FIRST DAY COVERS SING	FIRST DAY COVERS PL. BLK.	MINT SHEET	PLATE BLOCK	UNUSED F/NH	USED
5635	(58¢) Happy Birthday	2.75	.....	30.00(20)	6.50(4)	2.00	0.80

SCOTT NO.	DESCRIPTION	FIRST DAY COVERS SING	PL. BLK.	MINT SHEET	PLATE BLOCK	UNUSED F/NH	USED
5636-39	(58¢) Message Monsters .	15.00(4)	.....	30.00(20)	14.00(8)	7.50	.....
5636	(58¢) Pink & Red Monster.....	.....	.....	.....	.....	2.00	1.00
5637	(58¢) Four-Armed Monster.....	.....	.....	.....	.....	2.00	1.00
5638	(58¢) Tentacled Monster.....	.....	.....	.....	.....	2.00	1.00
5639	(58¢) Red-Headed Monster.....	.....	.....	.....	.....	2.00	1.00
5640-43	(58¢) Day of the Dead. . . .	15.00(4)	.....	30.00(20)	14.00(8)	7.50	.....
5640	(58¢) Girl Skull	.....	.....	.....	.....	2.00	1.00
5641	(58¢) Man Skull.	.....	.....	.....	.....	2.00	1.00
5642	(58¢) Woman Skull	.....	.....	.....	.....	2.00	1.00
5643	(58¢) Boy Skull	.....	.....	.....	.....	2.00	1.00
5644-47	(58¢) Christmas.	15.00(4)	.....	.....	.....	7.50	.....
5644	(58¢) Santa Claus on Roof.....	.....	.....	.....	.....	2.00	0.80
5645	(58¢) Santa Claus on Fireplace	.....	.....	.....	.....	2.00	0.80
5646	(58¢) Head of Santa Claus.....	.....	.....	.....	.....	2.00	0.80
5647	(58¢) Santa Claus, Sleigh & Reindeer	.....	.....	.....	.....	2.00	0.80
5647b	same, double-sided bklt pane of 20	.....	.....	.....	.....	35.00	.....
5648-51	(58¢) Otters in Snow	15.00(4)	.....	.....	.....	7.50	.....
5648	(58¢) Otter in Water.	.....	.....	.....	.....	2.00	0.80
5649	(58¢) Otter, Tail at Right . .	.....	.....	.....	.....	2.00	0.80
5650	(58¢) Otter, Tail at Left.	.....	.....	.....	.....	2.00	0.80
5651	(58¢) Otter in Snow.	.....	.....	.....	.....	2.00	0.80
5651b	same, double-sided bklt pane of 20	.....	.....	.....	.....	35.00	.....

2022 COMMEMORATIVES

SCOTT NO.	DESCRIPTION	FIRST DAY COVERS SING	PL. BLK.	MINT SHEET	PLATE BLOCK	UNUSED F/NH	USED
5662/5739	(5662, 5663, 5668-71, 5683, 5688-92, 5693, 5694-97, 5702, 5703-07, 5708, 5709-12, 5715-19, 5720, 5737, 5738, 5739) 37 varieties	.....	.....	.....	.....	57.00	.....
5652	4¢ Blueberries, die cut 11 1/4x11	3.00	.....	5.00(20)	1.20(4)	0.30	0.30
5653	4¢ Blueberries, coil, die cut 10 3/4	3.00	.....	.....	.....	0.30	0.30
	same, plate number strip of 5	.....	.....	.....	.....	1.75	.....
5654	(58¢) Flags, micro above lower connector at left.	3.00	.....	28.00(20)	6.00(4)	1.60	0.70
5655	(58¢) Flags, coil, die cut 10 3/4	3.00	.....	.....	.....	1.60	0.70
	same, plate number strip of 5	.....	.....	.....	.....	10.50	.....
5656	(58¢) Flags, coil, die cut 11.....	3.00	.....	.....	.....	1.60	0.70
	same, plate number strip of 5	.....	.....	.....	.....	10.50	.....
5657	(58¢) Flags, coil, die cut 9 1/2, micro above lowest flag.....	3.00	.....	.....	.....	1.60	0.70
	same, plate number strip of 5	.....	.....	.....	.....	10.50	.....
5658	(58¢) Flags, micro above lower connector at left.	3.00	.....	.....	.....	1.60	0.70
	same, double-sided bklt pane of 20	.....	.....	.....	.....	30.00	.....
5659	(58¢) Flags, micro above lowest flag	3.00	.....	.....	.....	1.60	0.70
	same, double-sided bklt pane of 20	.....	.....	.....	.....	30.00	.....
5660-61	(58¢) Love.	6.00(2)	.....	28.00(20)	6.00(4)	3.00	.....
5660	(58¢) Blue Gray.	.....	.....	.....	.....	1.60	0.70
5661	(58¢) Pink	.....	.....	.....	.....	1.60	0.70
5662	(58¢) Year of the Tiger. . . .	3.00	.....	28.00(20)	6.00(4)	1.60	0.80
5663	(58¢) Edmonia Lewis, Sculptor	3.00	.....	28.00(20)	6.00(4)	1.60	0.80

5664

5665

SCOTT NO.	DESCRIPTION	FIRST DAY COVERS SING	PL. BLK.	MINT SHEET	PLATE BLOCK	UNUSED F/NH	USED
5664-65	(5¢) Butterfly Garden Flowers, nonprofit	6.00(2)	.....	.....	.....	0.60	.....
5664	(5¢) Cosmos	.....	.....	.....	.....	0.30	0.30
5665	(5¢) Scabiosas	.....	.....	.....	.....	0.30	0.30
	same, plate number strip of 5	.....	.....	.....	.....	2.00	.....

5666

5667

SCOTT NO.	DESCRIPTION	FIRST DAY COVERS SING	FIRST DAY COVERS PL. BLK.	MINT SHEET	PLATE BLOCK	UNUSED F/NH	USED
5666	$8.95 Monument Valley. . .	30.00	.....	75.00(4)	.....	20.00	12.00
5667	$26.95 Palace of Fine Arts	60.00	.....	230.00(4)	.....	60.00	30.00

5668

5669

5670

5671

SCOTT NO.	DESCRIPTION	FIRST DAY COVERS SING	FIRST DAY COVERS PL. BLK.	MINT SHEET	PLATE BLOCK	UNUSED F/NH	USED
5668-71	(58¢) Title IX Civil Rights Law	15.00(4)	.....	28.00(20)	6.00(4)	6.00	.....
5668	(58¢) Runner.	.....	.....	.....	.....	1.60	0.90
5669	(58¢) Swimmer.....	.....	.....	.....	.....	1.60	0.90
5670	(58¢) Gymnast......	.....	.....	.....	.....	1.60	0.90
5671	(58¢) Soccer Player.... . ..	.....	.....	.....	.....	1.60	0.90

5672

5673

5674

5675

SCOTT NO.	DESCRIPTION	FIRST DAY COVERS SING	FIRST DAY COVERS PL. BLK.	MINT SHEET	PLATE BLOCK	UNUSED F/NH	USED
5672-75	(58¢) Mountain Flora.	15.00(4)	.....	.....	.....	6.00	.....
	same, plate number strip of 7	.....	.....	.....	.....	14.00	.....
5672	(58¢) Wood Lily.	.....	.....	.....	.....	1.60	0.80
5673	(58¢) Alpine Buttercup......	.....	.....	.....	.....	1.60	0.80
5674	(58¢) Woods' Rose..... . . .	.....	.....	.....	.....	1.60	0.80
5675	(58¢) Pasqueflower...	.....	.....	.....	.....	1.60	0.80

5676

5677

5678

5679

SCOTT NO.	DESCRIPTION	FIRST DAY COVERS SING	FIRST DAY COVERS PL. BLK.	MINT SHEET	PLATE BLOCK	UNUSED F/NH	USED
5676-79	(58¢) Mountain Flora.	15.00(4)	.....	.....	.....	6.00	.....
5676	(58¢) Wood Lily.	.....	.....	.....	.....	1.60	0.80
5677	(58¢) Alpine Buttercup......	.....	.....	.....	.....	1.60	0.80
5678	(58¢) Woods' Rose..... . . .	.....	.....	.....	.....	1.60	0.80
5679	(58¢) Pasqueflower...	.....	.....	.....	.....	1.60	0.80
5679b	same, double-sided bklt pane of 20	.....	.....	.....	.....	30.00	.....

5680

5681

5682

5683

SCOTT NO.	DESCRIPTION	FIRST DAY COVERS SING	FIRST DAY COVERS PL. BLK.	MINT SHEET	PLATE BLOCK	UNUSED F/NH	USED
5680	($1.30) African Daisy.	6.00	.....	30.00(10)	12.00(4)	3.00	1.30
5681	(58¢) Tulips	3.00	.....	28.00(20)	6.00(4)	1.60	0.80
5682	(78¢) Sunflower Bouquet .	3.25	.....	32.00(20)	7.00(4)	1.80	0.90
5683	(58¢) Shel Silverstein, Writer	3.00	.....	28.00(20)	6.00(4)	1.60	0.90

5684

5685

5686

5687

SCOTT NO.	DESCRIPTION	FIRST DAY COVERS SING	FIRST DAY COVERS PL. BLK.	MINT SHEET	PLATE BLOCK	UNUSED F/NH	USED
5684-87	(15¢) Flags on Barns, presorted standard	12.00(4)	.....	.....	.....	1.50	.....
5684	(10¢) Flag on Red Barn. . .	.....	.....	.....	.....	0.35	0.30
5685	(10¢) Flag on White Barn in Winter	.....	.....	.....	.....	0.35	0.30
5686	(10¢) Flag on White Barn .	.....	.....	.....	.....	0.35	0.30
5687	(10¢) Flag on Barn Near Windmill...	.....	.....	.....	.....	0.35	0.30
	same, plate number strip of 5	.....	.....	.....	.....	4.00	.....

5688

5689

5690

5691

5692

SCOTT NO.	DESCRIPTION	FIRST DAY COVERS SING	FIRST DAY COVERS PL. BLK.	MINT SHEET	PLATE BLOCK	UNUSED F/NH	USED
5688-92	(58¢) Painting by George Morrison.	18.00(5)	.....	28.00(20)	15.00(10)	8.00(5)	.....
5688	(58¢) Sun and River	.....	.....	.....	.....	1.60	1.00
5689	(58¢) Phenomena Against the Crimson.	.....	.....	.....	.....	1.60	1.00
5690	(58¢) Lake Superior Landscape	.....	.....	.....	.....	1.60	1.00
5691	(58¢) Spirit Path, New Day, Red Rock Variation...	.....	.....	.....	.....	1.60	1.00
5692	(58¢) Untitled, 1995...... .	.....	.....	.....	.....	1.60	1.00

5693

SCOTT NO.	DESCRIPTION	FIRST DAY COVERS SING	FIRST DAY COVERS PL. BLK.	MINT SHEET	PLATE BLOCK	UNUSED F/NH	USED
5693	(58¢) Eugenie Clark, Ichthyologist	3.00	.....	28.00(20)	6.00(4)	1.60	0.90

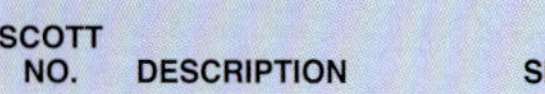

5694

5695

5696

5697

SCOTT NO.	DESCRIPTION	FIRST DAY COVERS SING	FIRST DAY COVERS PL. BLK.	MINT SHEET	PLATE BLOCK	UNUSED F/NH	USED
5694-97	(58¢) Women's Rowing . . .	12.00(4)	.....	28.00(20)	13.00(8)	.....	.....
5694-95	(58¢) Women's Rowing in Red, pair	.....	.....	.....	.....	4.00	.....
5696-97	(58¢) Women's Rowing in Blue, pair	.....	.....	.....	.....	4.00	.....
5694	(58¢) Women in Red, No Oar Splash.	.....	.....	.....	.....	1.60	0.90
5695	(58¢) Women in Red, Oar Splash	.....	.....	.....	.....	1.60	0.90
5696	(58¢) Women in Blue, Oar Splash	.....	.....	.....	.....	1.60	0.90
5697	(58¢) Women in Blue, No Oar Splash.	.....	.....	.....	.....	1.60	0.90

5698

MIGHTY MISSISSIPPI

5698a *Headwater of the Mississppi River*
5698b *Great River Road*
5698c *Steamboat American Queen*
5698d *Sailboat and Limestone Cliff*
5698e *Gateway arch and Skyline*
5698f *Fort Jefferson Hill Park*
5698g *Curved Levee and Farmland*
5698h *Towboat Pushing Barges*
5698i *Crescent City Connections Bridges*
5698j *Cypress Trees in Bayou*

SCOTT NO.	DESCRIPTION	FIRST DAY COVERS SING	FIRST DAY COVERS PL. BLK.	MINT SHEET	PLATE BLOCK	UNUSED F/NH	USED
5698	(58¢) Mighty Mississippi	32.00(10)	.....	14.00(10)	.....	.....	.....

5700

5699

5701

SCOTT NO.	DESCRIPTION	FIRST DAY COVERS SING	FIRST DAY COVERS PL. BLK.	MINT SHEET	PLATE BLOCK	UNUSED F/NH	USED
5699	(78¢) Katherine Graham, Publisher	3.25	.....	32.00(20)	7.00(4)	1.80	1.00
5700	$2 Floral Geometry	.....	.....	35.00(10)	18.00(4)	5.00	3.00
5701	$5 Floral Geometry	.....	.....	40.00(4)	.....	11.00	8.00

5703

5702

5704

5705

5706

5707

SCOTT NO.	DESCRIPTION	FIRST DAY COVERS SING	FIRST DAY COVERS PL. BLK.	MINT SHEET	PLATE BLOCK	UNUSED F/NH	USED
5702	(58¢) Nancy Reagan, First Lady	3.00	.....	28.00(20)	6.00(4)	1.60	0.80
5703-07	(60¢) Mariachi	18.00(5)	.....	28.00(20)	15.00(10)	8.00(5)	.....
5703	(60¢) Guitarist and Moon .	.....	.....	.....	.....	1.60	1.00
5704	(60¢) Guitarist and Sun. . .	.....	.....	.....	.....	1.60	1.00
5705	(60¢) Violinist and Sun . . .	.....	.....	.....	.....	1.60	1.00
5706	(60¢) Bass Guitarist and Sun	.....	.....	.....	.....	1.60	1.00
5707	(60¢) Trumpet Player and Sun	.....	.....	.....	.....	1.60	1.00

5708

SCOTT NO.	DESCRIPTION	FIRST DAY COVERS SING	FIRST DAY COVERS PL. BLK.	MINT SHEET	PLATE BLOCK	UNUSED F/NH	USED
5708	(60¢) Pete Seeger, Music Icons	3.00	.....	25.00(16)	.....	1.60	0.80

5709

5710

5711

5712

SCOTT NO.	DESCRIPTION	FIRST DAY COVERS SING	FIRST DAY COVERS PL. BLK.	MINT SHEET	PLATE BLOCK	UNUSED F/NH	USED
5709-12	(60¢) Go Beyond, Buzz Lightyear	15.00(4)	.....	28.00(20)	13.00(8)	6.00(4)	.....
5709	(60¢) Head in Profile	.....	.....	.....	.....	1.60	1.00
5710	(60¢) Standing Legs Visible	.....	.....	.....	.....	1.60	1.00
5711	(60¢) Running	.....	.....	.....	.....	1.60	1.00
5712	(60¢) Standing Feet Not Visible	.....	.....	.....	.....	1.60	1.00

National Marine Sanctuaries

5713

NATIONAL MARINE SANCTUARIES

5713a *Balloon Fish*
5713b *Red-Footed Boobies*
5713c *Humpback Whale*
5713d *Sea Stacks*
5713e *Mallows Bay*
5713f *Farallon Islands*
5713g *Elkhorn Coral*
5713h *Hawaiian Mon Deal*
5713i *Queen Angelfish*
5713j *Sea Otter*
5713k *Rockfish Exploring Reef*
5713l *Atlantic Sea Nettle*
5713m *Sea Lions*
5713n *Sand Tiger Shark*
5713o *Corals and Fish*
5713p *Ice on Shoreline*

SCOTT NO.	DESCRIPTION	FIRST DAY COVERS SING	FIRST DAY COVERS PL. BLK.	MINT SHEET	PLATE BLOCK	UNUSED F/NH	USED
5713	(60¢) National Marine Sanctuaries	45.00(16)	.....	25.00(16)	.....	.....	20.00

5714

SCOTT NO.	DESCRIPTION	FIRST DAY COVERS SING	FIRST DAY COVERS PL. BLK.	MINT SHEET	PLATE BLOCK	UNUSED F/NH	USED
5714	(60¢) Elephants.	3.00	.....	.....	.....	1.60	0.70
	same, double-sided bklt pane of 20	.....	.....	.....	.....	28.00	.....

5715

5716

5717

5718

5719

SCOTT NO.	DESCRIPTION	FIRST DAY COVERS SING	FIRST DAY COVERS PL. BLK.	MINT SHEET	PLATE BLOCK	UNUSED F/NH	USED
5715-19	(60¢) Pony Cars	18.00(5)	.....	28.00(20)	15.00(10)	8.00(5)	.....
5715	(60¢) 1969 Ford Mustang Boss 302	.....	.....	.....	.....	1.60	1.00
5716	(60¢) 1970 Dodge Challenger R/T	.....	.....	.....	.....	1.60	1.00
5717	(60¢) 1969 Chevrolet Camaro Z/28	.....	.....	.....	.....	1.60	1.00
5718	(60¢) 1967 Mercury Cougar XR-7 GT	.....	.....	.....	.....	1.60	1.00
5719	(60¢) 1969 AMC Javelin SST	.....	.....	.....	.....	1.60	1.00

5720

5721

SCOTT NO.	DESCRIPTION	FIRST DAY COVERS SING	FIRST DAY COVERS PL. BLK.	MINT SHEET	PLATE BLOCK	UNUSED F/NH	USED
5720	(60¢) James Webb Space Telescope	3.00	.....	28.00(20)	.....	1.60	0.80
5721	(60¢) Virgin and Child	3.00	.....	.....	.....	1.60	0.80
	same, double-sided bklt pane of 20	.....	.....	.....	.....	28.00	.....

5722

5723

5724

5725

SCOTT NO.	DESCRIPTION	FIRST DAY COVERS SING	FIRST DAY COVERS PL. BLK.	MINT SHEET	PLATE BLOCK	UNUSED F/NH	USED
5722-25	(60¢) Holiday Elves.	15.00(4)	.....	.....	.....	6.00	.....
5722	(60¢) Elf and Teddy Bear...	..	.....	.....	.....	1.60	0.90
5723	(60¢) Elf Tying Ribbon. . . .	.....	.....	.....	.....	1.60	0.90
5724	(60¢) Elf with Toy Car	.....	.....	.....	.....	1.60	0.90
5725	(60¢) Elf with Rocket.	.....	.....	.....	.....	1.60	0.90
5725b	same, double-sided bklt pane of 20	.....	.....	.....	.....	30.00	.....

5726a

5726b

5726c

5726d

5726e

5726f

5726g

5726h

5726i

5726j

SCOTT NO.	DESCRIPTION	FIRST DAY COVERS SING	FIRST DAY COVERS PL. BLK.	MINT SHEET	PLATE BLOCK	UNUSED F/NH	USED
5726	(60¢) Peanuts, Charles M. Schulz	35.00(10)	.....	30.00(20)	.....	.....	12.00
5726a	(60¢) Charlie Brown	.....	.....	.....	.....	1.60	1.25
5726b	(60¢) Lucy	.....	.....	.....	.....	1.60	1.25
5726c	(60¢) Franklin	.....	.....	.....	.....	1.60	1.25
5726d	(60¢) Sally.	.....	.....	.....	.....	1.60	1.25
5726e	(60¢) Pigpen	.....	.....	.....	.....	1.60	1.25
5726f	(60¢) Linus	.....	.....	.....	.....	1.60	1.25
5726g	(60¢) Snoopy and Woodstock	.....	.....	.....	.....	1.60	1.25
5726h	(60¢) Schroeder	.....	.....	.....	.....	1.60	1.25
5726i	(60¢) Peppermint Patty . . .	.....	.....	.....	.....	1.60	1.25
5726j	(60¢) Marcie	.....	.....	.....	.....	1.60	1.25

5727 5728 5729

5730 5731

5732 5733 5734

5735 5736

SCOTT NO.	DESCRIPTION	FIRST DAY COVERS SING	FIRST DAY COVERS PL. BLK.	MINT SHEET	PLATE BLOCK	UNUSED F/NH	USED
5727-36	(60¢) Snowy Beauty	35.00(10)	.....	.....	.....	15.00	.....
5727	(60¢) Camellia.	.....	.....	.....	.....	1.60	1.00
5728	(60¢) Winter Aconite	.....	.....	.....	.....	1.60	1.00
5729	(60¢) Crocuses	.....	.....	.....	.....	1.60	1.00
5730	(60¢) Hellebore	.....	.....	.....	.....	1.60	1.00
5731	(60¢) Winterberry	.....	.....	.....	.....	1.60	1.00
5732	(60¢) Pansies	.....	.....	.....	.....	1.60	1.00
5733	(60¢) Plum Blossoms	.....	.....	.....	.....	1.60	1.00
5734	(60¢) Grape Hyacinths . . .	.....	.....	.....	.....	1.60	1.00
5735	(60¢) Daffodils.	.....	.....	.....	.....	1.60	1.00
5736	(60¢) Ranunculus	.....	.....	.....	.....	1.60	1.00
5736b	same, double-sided bklt pane of 20		.....	.....	.....	30.00	.....

5737 5738 5739

SCOTT NO.	DESCRIPTION	FIRST DAY COVERS SING	FIRST DAY COVERS PL. BLK.	MINT SHEET	PLATE BLOCK	UNUSED F/NH	USED
5737	(60¢) Kwanzaa	3.00	.....	28.00(20)	6.00(4)	1.60	0.80
5738	(60¢) Women Cryptologists of WWII	3.00	.....	28.00(20)	6.00(4)	1.60	0.90
5739	(60¢) Hanukkah.	3.00	.....	28.00(20)	6.00(4)	1.60	0.80

2023 COMMEMORATIVES

SCOTT NO.	DESCRIPTION	FIRST DAY COVERS SING	FIRST DAY COVERS PL. BLK.	MINT SHEET	PLATE BLOCK	UNUSED F/NH	USED
5744/5821	**(5744, 5753, 5754, 5757, 5758-62, 5763-66, 5792-96, 5797, 5798, 5801, 5803-07, 5820, 5821) 28 varieties**	.....	.....	.....	.....	**45.00**	.....

5740, 5741

5742, 5743

5744

SCOTT NO.	DESCRIPTION	FIRST DAY COVERS SING	FIRST DAY COVERS PL. BLK.	MINT SHEET	PLATE BLOCK	UNUSED F/NH	USED
5740	(24¢) School Bus.	3.00	.....	11.00(20)	2.50(4)	0.60	0.30
5741	(24¢) School Bus, coil	3.00	.....	.....	.....	0.60	0.30
	same, plate number strip of 5	.....	.....	.....	.....	5.00	.....
5742	40¢ Red Fox, die cut 11.25 X 11	3.00	.....	22.00(20)	4.25(4)	1.00	0.70
5743	40¢ Red Fox, coil, die cut 11 vert.	3.00	.....	.....	.....	1.00	0.70
	same, plate number strip of 5	.....	.....	.....	.....	7.50	.....
5744	(60¢) Year of the Rabbit . .	3.00	.....	28.00(20)	6.00(4)	1.60	0.90

5745

5746

SCOTT NO.	DESCRIPTION	FIRST DAY COVERS SING	FIRST DAY COVERS PL. BLK.	MINT SHEET	PLATE BLOCK	UNUSED F/NH	USED
5745-46	(60¢) Love, Kitten and Puppy	6.00(2)	.....	28.00(20)	6.00(4)	3.00	0.90
5745	(60¢) Kitten and Heart. . . .	.....	.....	.....	.....	1.60	0.90
5746	(60¢) Puppy and Heart	.....	.....	.....	.....	1.60	0.90

5747, 5750

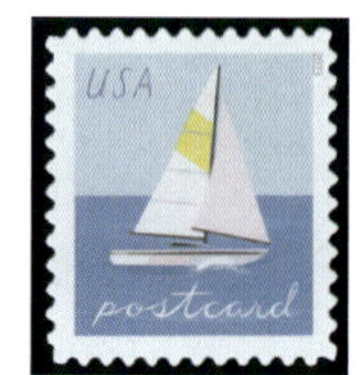
5748, 5749

SCOTT NO.	DESCRIPTION	FIRST DAY COVERS SING	FIRST DAY COVERS PL. BLK.	MINT SHEET	PLATE BLOCK	UNUSED F/NH	USED
5747-48	(48¢) Sailboats	6.00(2)	.....	22.00(20)	5.00(4)	2.30	.....
5747	(48¢) Two Sailboats.	.....	.....	.....	.....	1.20	0.70
5748	(48¢) One Sailboat	.....	.....	.....	.....	1.20	0.70
5749-50	(48¢) Sailboats, coil, die cut 9.5 vert.	6.00(2)	.....	.....	.....	2.30	.....
5749	(48¢) One Sailboat	.....	.....	.....	.....	1.20	0.70
5750	(48¢) Two Sailboats.	.....	.....	.....	.....	1.20	0.70
	same, plate number strip of 5	.....	.....	.....	.....	7.50	.....

5751

5752

SCOTT NO.	DESCRIPTION	FIRST DAY COVERS SING	FIRST DAY COVERS PL. BLK.	MINT SHEET	PLATE BLOCK	UNUSED F/NH	USED
5751	$9.65 Florida Everglades .	30.00	.....	80.00(4)	.....	22.00	12.00
5752	$28.75 Great Smoky Mounatins	60.00	.....	235.00(4)	.....	65.00	35.00

5753

5754

SCOTT NO.	DESCRIPTION	FIRST DAY COVERS SING	FIRST DAY COVERS PL. BLK.	MINT SHEET	PLATE BLOCK	UNUSED F/NH	USED
5753	(63¢) Ernest J. Gaines, Writer	3.00	.....	28.00(20)	6.00(4)	1.60	0.90
5754	(63¢) Women's Soccer . . .	3.00	.....	28.00(20)	6.00(4)	1.60	0.90

5755

5756, 5756A

5757

SCOTT NO.	DESCRIPTION	FIRST DAY COVERS SING	FIRST DAY COVERS PL. BLK.	MINT SHEET	PLATE BLOCK	UNUSED F/NH	USED
5755	$10 Floral Geometry	.....		80.00(4)	.....	22.00	15.00
5756	(5¢) Stars and Bars, coil, die cut 10.75 vert.	3.00	.....	.....	.....	0.30	0.30
	same, plate number strip of 5	.....	.....	.....	.....	2.00	.....
5756A	(5¢) Stars and Bars, coil, large date, DC 10.75 same, plate number strip of 5	3.00	....	....	....	0.35 2.00	0.30 .....
5757	(63¢) Toni Morrison, Writer	3.00	.....	28.00(20)	6.00(4)	1.60	0.90

5758  5759 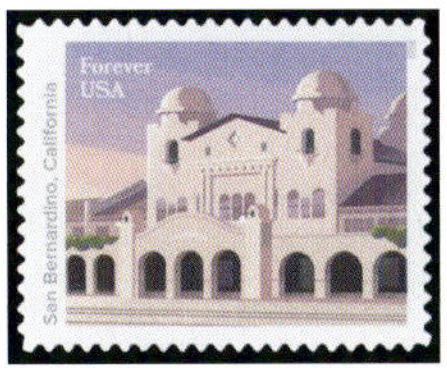 5760

5761  5762

SCOTT NO.	DESCRIPTION	FIRST DAY COVERS SING	FIRST DAY COVERS PL. BLK.	MINT SHEET	PLATE BLOCK	UNUSED F/NH	USED
5758-62	(63¢) Historic Railroad Stations	18.00(5)	.....	28.00(20)	15.00(10)	8.00(5)	.....
5758	(63¢) Point of Rocks Station	.....	.....	.....	.....	1.60	1.00
5759	(63¢) Mail Street Station ...	..	.....	.....	.....	1.60	1.00
5760	(63¢) Santa Fe Station . . .	.....	.....	.....	.....	1.60	1.00
5761	(63¢) Tamaqua Station	..	.....	.....	.....	1.60	1.00
5762	(63¢) Union Terminal.	.....	.....	.....	.....	1.60	1.00

5763  5764

5765  5766

SCOTT NO.	DESCRIPTION	FIRST DAY COVERS SING	FIRST DAY COVERS PL. BLK.	MINT SHEET	PLATE BLOCK	UNUSED F/NH	USED
5763-66	(63¢) Art of the Skateboard	15.00(4)	.....	28.00(20)	13.00(8)	6.00(4)	.....
5763	(63¢) Tlingit Athabascan Salmon Design	.....	.....	.....	.....	1.60	1.00
5764	(63¢) Abstract Design	.....	.....	.....	.....	1.60	1.00
5765	(63¢) Navajo Design	.....	.....	.....	.....	1.60	1.00
5766	(63¢) Jaguar Design	.....	.....	.....	.....	1.60	1.00

5773, 5777  5767, 5778  5774, 5779  5771, 5780

5768, 5781  5770, 5782  5769, 5783  5772, 5784

5776, 5785  5775, 5786

SCOTT NO.	DESCRIPTION	FIRST DAY COVERS SING	FIRST DAY COVERS PL. BLK.	MINT SHEET	PLATE BLOCK	UNUSED F/NH	USED
5767-76	(63¢) Tulip Blossoms, coil, die cut 10.75	35.00(10)	.....	.....	.....	15.00(10)	.....
	same, plate number strip of 10	.....	.....	.....	.....	20.00	.....
5767	(63¢) Pink, Yellowish Base	.....	.....	.....	.....	1.60	1.00
5768	(63¢) Purple, White Base .	.....	.....	.....	.....	1.60	1.00
5769	(63¢) Pink, Orange	.....	.....	.....	.....	1.60	1.00
5770	(63¢) Lilac	.....	.....	.....	.....	1.60	1.00
5771	(63¢) Orange, Red	.....	.....	.....	.....	1.60	1.00
5772	(63¢) Dark Purple	.....	.....	.....	.....	1.60	1.00
5773	(63¢) Brownish, White Base	.....	.....	.....	.....	1.60	1.00
5774	(63¢) Pink, White Base . . .	.....	.....	.....	.....	1.60	1.00
5775	(63¢) Pink, Yellowish Background	.....	.....	.....	.....	1.60	1.00
5776	(63¢) White, Purple Base .	.....	.....	.....	.....	1.60	1.00

SCOTT NO.	DESCRIPTION	FIRST DAY COVERS SING	FIRST DAY COVERS PL. BLK.	MINT SHEET	PLATE BLOCK	UNUSED F/NH	USED
5777-86	(63¢) Tulip Blossoms, die cut 10.75X11	35.00(10)	.....	.....	.....	15.00(10)	.....
5777	(63¢) Brownish, White Base	.....	.....	.....	.....	1.60	1.00
5778	(63¢) Pink, Yellowish Base	.....	.....	.....	.....	1.60	1.00
5779	(63¢) Pink, White Base . . .	.....	.....	.....	.....	1.60	1.00
5780	(63¢) Orange, Red	.....	.....	.....	.....	1.60	1.00
5781	(63¢) Purple, White Base .	.....	.....	.....	.....	1.60	1.00
5782	(63¢) Lilac	.....	.....	.....	.....	1.60	1.00
5783	(63¢) Pink, Orange	.....	.....	.....	.....	1.60	1.00
5784	(63¢) Dark Purple	.....	.....	.....	.....	1.60	1.00
5785	(63¢) White, Purple Base .	.....	.....	.....	.....	1.60	1.00
5786	(63¢) Pink, Yellowish Background	.....	.....	.....	.....	1.60	1.00
5786b	same, double-sided bklt pane of 20	.....	.....	.....	.....	30.00	.....

5787  5788, 5789, 5789A 5790, 5791

SCOTT NO.	DESCRIPTION	FIRST DAY COVERS SING	FIRST DAY COVERS PL. BLK.	MINT SHEET	PLATE BLOCK	UNUSED F/NH	USED
5787	(63¢) Freedom, micro right of lowest stripe	3.00	.....	28.00(20)	6.00(4)	1.60	0.70
5788	(63¢) Freedom, coil, die cut 9.5	3.00	.....	.....	.....	1.60	0.70
	same, plate number strip of 5	.....	.....	.....	.....	10.50	.....
5789	(63¢) Freedom, coil, die cut 10.75	3.00	.....	.....	.....	1.60	0.70
	same, plate number strip of 5	.....	.....	.....	.....	10.50	.....
5789A	(63¢) Freedom, coil, die cut 11	3.00	.....	.....	.....	1.60	0.70
	same, plate number strip of 5	.....	.....	.....	.....	10.50	.....
5790	(63¢) Freedom, micro below left flag field	3.00	.....	.....	.....	1.60	0.70
	same, double-sided bklt pane of 20	.....	.....	.....	.....	30.00	.....
5791	(63¢) Freedom, micro right of lowest stripe	3.00	.....	.....	.....	1.60	0.70
	same, double-sided bklt pane of 20	.....	.....	.....	.....	30.00	.....

5792  5793  5794

5795  5796

SCOTT NO.	DESCRIPTION	FIRST DAY COVERS SING	FIRST DAY COVERS PL. BLK.	MINT SHEET	PLATE BLOCK	UNUSED F/NH	USED
5792-96	(63¢) Roy Liechtenstein . .	18.00(5)	.....	28.00(20)	15.00(10)	8.00(5)	.....
5792	(63¢) Standing Explosion, 1965	.....	.....	.....	.....	1.60	1.00
5793	(63¢) Modern Painting I, 1966	.....	.....	.....	.....	1.60	1.00
5794	(63¢) Still Life Crystal Bowl, 1972	.....	.....	.....	.....	1.60	1.00
5795	(63¢) Still Life Goldfish, 1972	.....	.....	.....	.....	1.60	1.00
5796	(63¢) Woman Portrait, 1979	.....	.....	.....	.....	1.60	1.00

5797

5798

SCOTT NO.	DESCRIPTION	FIRST DAY COVERS SING	FIRST DAY COVERS PL. BLK.	MINT SHEET	PLATE BLOCK	UNUSED F/NH	USED
5797	(63¢) Tomie dePaola, Author	3.00	.....	28.00(20)	6.00(4)	1.60	0.90
5798	(63¢) Chief Standing Bear.	3.00	.....	28.00(20)	6.00(4)	1.60	0.90

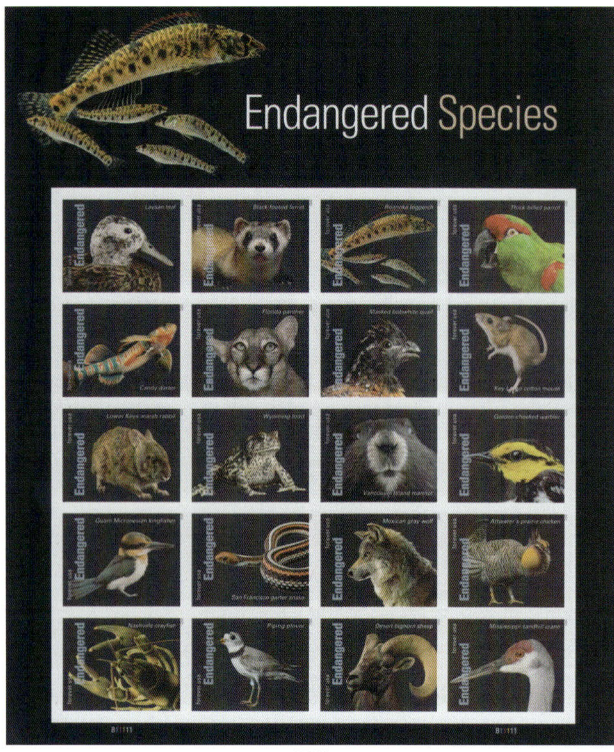

5799

ENDANGERED SPECIES

5799a *Laysan Teal*
5799b *Black-footed Ferret*
5799c *Roanoake Logperch*
5799d *Thick-billed Parrot*
5799e *Candy Darter*
5799f *Florida Panther*
5799g *Masked Bobwhite Quail*
5799h *Key Largo Cotton Mouse*
5799i *Lower Keys Marsh Rabbit*
5799j *Wyoming Toad*
5799k *Vancouver Island Marmot*
5799l *Gold-cheeked Warbler*
5799m *Guam Micronesia Kingfisher*
5799n *San Francisco Garter Snake*
5799o *Mexican Gray Wolf*
5799p *Attwater's Prairie Chicken*
5799q *Nashville Crayfish*
5799r *Piping Plover*
5799s *Desert Bighorn Sheep*
5799t *Mississippi Sandhill Crane*

SCOTT NO.	DESCRIPTION	FIRST DAY COVERS SING	FIRST DAY COVERS PL. BLK.	MINT SHEET	PLATE BLOCK	UNUSED F/NH	USED
5799	(63¢) Endangered Species	55.00(20)	.....	30.00(20)	.....	.....	22.00

5800

WATERFALLS

5800a *Deer Creek Falls, AZ*
5800b *Nevada Fall, CA*
5800c *Harrison Wight Falls, PA*
5800d *Lower Falls, Yellow River, WY*
5800e *Waimoku Falls, HI*
5800f *Stewart Falls, UT*
5800g *Niagara Falls, NY*
5800h *Dark Hollow Falls, VA*
5800i *Grotto Falls, TN*
5800j *Sunbeam Falls, WA*
5800k *LaSalle Canyon Waterfall, IL*
5800l *Upper Falls, NC*

SCOTT NO.	DESCRIPTION	FIRST DAY COVERS SING	FIRST DAY COVERS PL. BLK.	MINT SHEET	PLATE BLOCK	UNUSED F/NH	USED
5800	(63¢) Waterfalls	40.00(12)	.....	22.00(12)	.....	.....	14.00

5801

SCOTT NO.	DESCRIPTION	FIRST DAY COVERS SING	FIRST DAY COVERS PL. BLK.	MINT SHEET	PLATE BLOCK	UNUSED F/NH	USED
5801	(66¢) John Lewis, Writer . .	3.00	.....	28.00(20)	6.00(4)	1.60	0.90

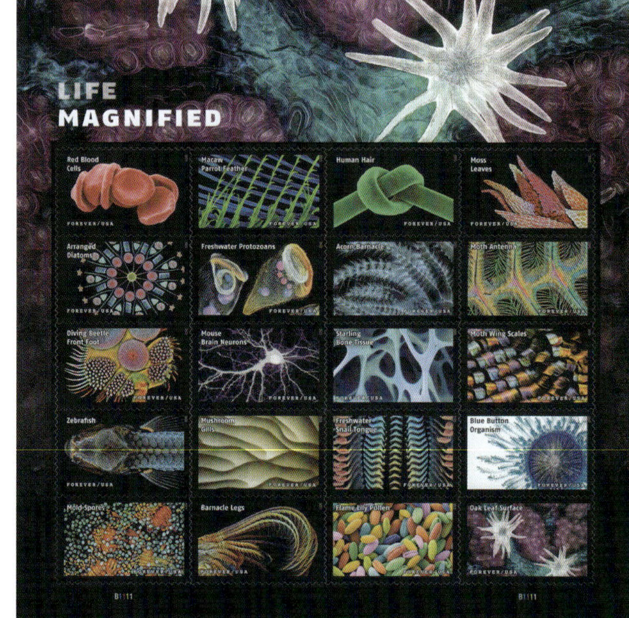

5802

LIFE MAGNIFIED

5802a *Red Blood Cells*
5802b *Macaw Parrot Feather*
5802c *Human Hair*
5802d *Moss Leaves*
5802e *Arranged Diatoms*
5802f *Freshwater Protozoans*
5802g *Acorn Barnacle*
5802h *Moth Antenna*
5802i *Diving Beetle Front Foot*
5802j *Mouse Brain Neurons*
5802k *Starling Bone Tissue*
5802l *Moth Wing Scales*
5802m *Zebrafish*
5802n *Mushroom Gills*
5802o *Freshwater Snail Tongue*
5802p *Blue Button Organism*
5802q *Mold Spores*
5802r *Barnacle Legs*
5802s *Flame Lily Pollen*
5802t *Oak Leaf Surface*

SCOTT NO.	DESCRIPTION	FIRST DAY COVERS SING	FIRST DAY COVERS PL. BLK.	MINT SHEET	PLATE BLOCK	UNUSED F/NH	USED
5802	(66¢) Life Magnified . . .	65.00(20)	.....	30.00(20)	.....	.....	25.00

5803

5804

5805

5806

5807

SCOTT NO.	DESCRIPTION	FIRST DAY COVERS SING	FIRST DAY COVERS PL. BLK.	MINT SHEET	PLATE BLOCK	UNUSED F/NH	USED
5803-07	(66¢) Thinking of You	18.00(5)	.....	28.00(20)	15.00(10)	8.00(5)	.....
5803	(66¢) Butterfly, Flower, Dog, Cake	.....	.....	.....	.....	1.60	1.00
5804	(66¢) Sun, Flower, Horseshoe, Dandelion	.....	.....	.....	.....	1.60	1.00
5805	(66¢) Leaf, Bouquet, Bandage, Party Hat, Ice Cream.		.....	.....	.....	1.60	1.00
5806	(66¢) Rainbow, Ice Cream, Clover, Cat, Cupcake		.....	.....	.....	1.60	1.00
5807	(66¢) Thumbs Up, Balloons, XOOX, Cup		.....	.....	.....	1.60	1.00

5808  5809  5810  5811

SCOTT NO.	DESCRIPTION	FIRST DAY COVERS SING	FIRST DAY COVERS PL. BLK.	MINT SHEET	PLATE BLOCK	UNUSED F/NH	USED
5808-11	(25¢) Bridges-Presort, coil, diecut 10	15.00(4)	.....	.....	.....	2.50(4)	.....
	same, plate number strip of 7	.....	.....	.....	.....	8.00	.....
5808	(25¢) Bob Kerrey Pedestrian Bridge	.....	.....	.....	.....	0.60	0.30
5809	(25¢) Skydance Bridge . . .	.....	.....	.....	.....	0.60	0.30
5810	(25¢) Iowa-Illinois Memorial Bridge.	.....	.....	.....	.....	0.60	0.30
5811	(25¢) Arrigoni Bridge	.....	.....	.....	.....	0.60	0.30

5812  5813  5814  5815

SCOTT NO.	DESCRIPTION	FIRST DAY COVERS SING	FIRST DAY COVERS PL. BLK.	MINT SHEET	PLATE BLOCK	UNUSED F/NH	USED
5812-15	(66¢) Pinatas.	15.00(4)	.....	.....	.....	6.00	.....
5812	(25¢) Donkey Facing Left .	.....	.....	.....	.....	1.60	0.90
5813	(25¢) Star Purple Background	.....	.....	.....	.....	1.60	0.90
5814	(25¢) Star Green Background	.....	.....	.....	.....	1.60	0.90
5815	(25¢) Donkey Facing Right	.....	.....	.....	.....	1.60	0.90
5815b	same, double-sided bklt pane of 20		.....	.....	.....	30.00	.....

5816  5817  5818  5819

SCOTT NO.	DESCRIPTION	FIRST DAY COVERS SING	FIRST DAY COVERS PL. BLK.	MINT SHEET	PLATE BLOCK	UNUSED F/NH	USED
5816-19	(66¢) Christmas Snow Globes	15.00(4)	.....	.....	.....	6.00	.....
5816	(66¢) Snowman.	.....	.....	.....	.....	1.60	0.90
5817	(66¢) Santa Claus	.....	.....	.....	.....	1.60	0.90
5818	(66¢) Reindeer	.....	.....	.....	.....	1.60	0.90
5819	(66¢) Christmas Tree	.....	.....	.....	.....	1.60	0.90
5819b	same, double-sided bklt pane of 20	.....	.....	.....	.....	30.00	.....

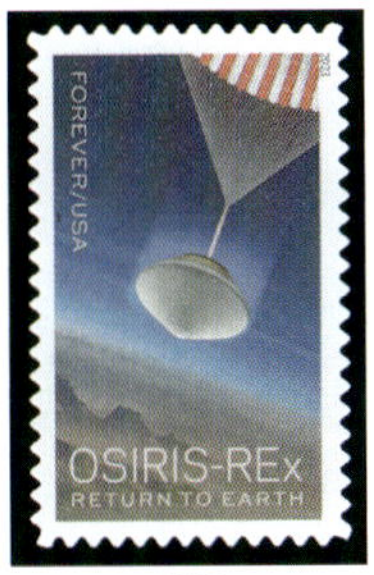

5820 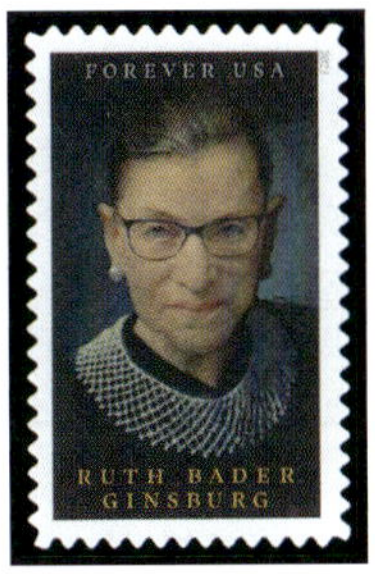 5821

SCOTT NO.	DESCRIPTION	FIRST DAY COVERS SING	FIRST DAY COVERS PL. BLK.	MINT SHEET	PLATE BLOCK	UNUSED F/NH	USED
5820	(66¢) OSIRIS-REx Capsule	3.00	.....	28.00(20)	6.00(4)	1.60	0.90
5821	(66¢) Ruth Bader Ginsburg, Associate Justice	3.00	.....	28.00(20)	6.00(4)	1.60	0.90

5822  5823  5824  5825

SCOTT NO.	DESCRIPTION	FIRST DAY COVERS SING	FIRST DAY COVERS PL. BLK.	MINT SHEET	PLATE BLOCK	UNUSED F/NH	USED
5822-25	(66¢) Winter Woodand Animals	15.00(4)	.....	.....	.....	6.00	.....
5822	(66¢) Deer.	.....	.....	.....	.....	1.60	0.90
5823	(66¢) Rabbit	.....	.....	.....	.....	1.60	0.90
5824	(66¢) Owl.	.....	.....	.....	.....	1.60	0.90
5825	(66¢) Fox.	.....	.....	.....	.....	1.60	0.90
5825b	same, double-sided bklt pane of 20	.....	.....	.....	.....	30.00	.....

2024 COMMEMORATIVES

5826

SCOTT NO.	DESCRIPTION	FIRST DAY COVERS SING	FIRST DAY COVERS PL. BLK.	MINT SHEET	PLATE BLOCK	UNUSED F/NH	USED
5826	(66¢) Love, Dove with Letter	3.00	.....	28.00(20)	6.00(4)	1.60	.....

5827  5828

SCOTT NO.	DESCRIPTION	FIRST DAY COVERS SING	FIRST DAY COVERS PL. BLK.	MINT SHEET	PLATE BLOCK	UNUSED F/NH	USED
5827	$9.85 Pillars of Creation. . .	30.00	.....	80.00(4)	.....	22.00	.....
5828	$30.45 Cosmic Cliffs	60.00	.....	240.00(4)	.....	70.00	.....

5829  5830

SCOTT NO.	DESCRIPTION	FIRST DAY COVERS SING	FIRST DAY COVERS PL. BLK.	MINT SHEET	PLATE BLOCK	UNUSED F/NH	USED
5829	(68¢) Year of the Dragon. .	3.00	.....	28.00(20)	6.00(4)	1.60	.....
5830	(68¢) Constance Baker Motley, Federal Judge	3.00	.....	28.00(20)	6.00(4)	1.60	.....

5831

SCOTT NO.	DESCRIPTION	FIRST DAY COVERS SING	FIRST DAY COVERS PL. BLK.	MINT SHEET	PLATE BLOCK	UNUSED F/NH	USED
5831	($1.16) Saul Bellow, Literary Arts	4.00	.....	50.00(20)	10.00(4)	2.70	.....

5832

SCOTT NO.	DESCRIPTION	FIRST DAY COVERS SING	FIRST DAY COVERS PL. BLK.	MINT SHEET	PLATE BLOCK	UNUSED F/NH	USED
5832	(10¢) Radiant Star-presort coil, perf. 10.75	3.00	.....	.....	.....	0.35	.....
	same, plate number strip of 5	.....	.....	.....	.....	3.00	.....

5833

SCOTT NO.	DESCRIPTION	FIRST DAY COVERS SING	FIRST DAY COVERS PL. BLK.	MINT SHEET	PLATE BLOCK	UNUSED F/NH	USED
5833	(68¢) John Wooden.	3.00	.....	30.00(20)	7.00(4)	1.60	.....

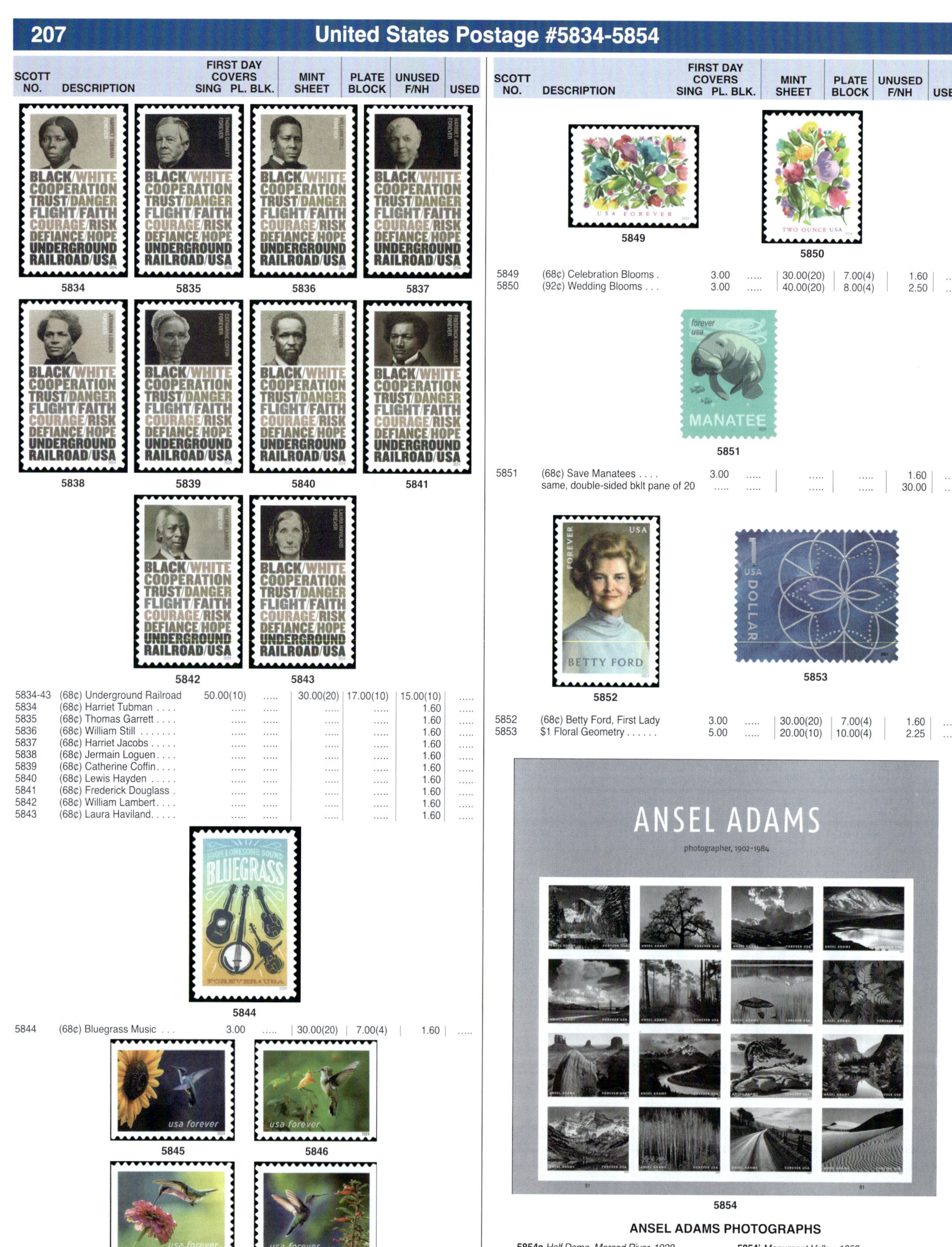

5834 5835 5836 5837 5838 5839 5840 5841 5842 5843

SCOTT NO.	DESCRIPTION	FIRST DAY COVERS SING	FIRST DAY COVERS PL. BLK.	MINT SHEET	PLATE BLOCK	UNUSED F/NH	USED
5834-43	(68¢) Underground Railroad	50.00(10)	.....	30.00(20)	17.00(10)	15.00(10)	.....
5834	(68¢) Harriet Tubman	.....	.....	.....	.....	1.60	.....
5835	(68¢) Thomas Garrett	.....	.....	.....	.....	1.60	.....
5836	(68¢) William Still	.....	.....	.....	.....	1.60	.....
5837	(68¢) Harriet Jacobs	.....	.....	.....	.....	1.60	.....
5838	(68¢) Jermain Loguen	.....	.....	.....	.....	1.60	.....
5839	(68¢) Catherine Coffin. . . .	.....	.....	.....	.....	1.60	.....
5840	(68¢) Lewis Hayden	.....	.....	.....	.....	1.60	.....
5841	(68¢) Frederick Douglass .	.....	.....	.....	.....	1.60	.....
5842	(68¢) William Lambert	.....	.....	.....	.....	1.60	.....
5843	(68¢) Laura Haviland.	.....	.....	.....	.....	1.60	.....

5844

SCOTT NO.	DESCRIPTION	FIRST DAY COVERS SING	FIRST DAY COVERS PL. BLK.	MINT SHEET	PLATE BLOCK	UNUSED F/NH	USED
5844	(68¢) Bluegrass Music . . .	3.00	.....	30.00(20)	7.00(4)	1.60	.....

5845 5846 5847 5848

SCOTT NO.	DESCRIPTION	FIRST DAY COVERS SING	FIRST DAY COVERS PL. BLK.	MINT SHEET	PLATE BLOCK	UNUSED F/NH	USED
5845-48	(68¢) Garden Delights-Hummingbirds	15.00(4)	.....	.....	.....	6.00	.....
5845	(68¢) Hummingbird, Sunflower	.....	.....	.....	.....	1.60	.....
5846	(68¢) Hummingbird, Touch-me-not	.....	.....	.....	.....	1.60	.....
5847	(68¢) Hummingbird, Zinnia	.....	.....	.....	.....	1.60	.....
5848	(68¢) Hummingbird, Sugar Flowers	.....	.....	.....	.....	1.60	.....
5848b	same, double-sided bklt pane of 20	.....	.....	.....	.....	30.00	.....

5849 5850

SCOTT NO.	DESCRIPTION	FIRST DAY COVERS SING	FIRST DAY COVERS PL. BLK.	MINT SHEET	PLATE BLOCK	UNUSED F/NH	USED
5849	(68¢) Celebration Blooms .	3.00	.....	30.00(20)	7.00(4)	1.60	.....
5850	(92¢) Wedding Blooms . . .	3.00	.....	40.00(20)	8.00(4)	2.50	.....

5851

SCOTT NO.	DESCRIPTION	FIRST DAY COVERS SING	FIRST DAY COVERS PL. BLK.	MINT SHEET	PLATE BLOCK	UNUSED F/NH	USED
5851	(68¢) Save Manatees	3.00	.....	.....	.....	1.60	.....
	same, double-sided bklt pane of 20	.....	.....	.....	.....	30.00	.....

5852 5853

SCOTT NO.	DESCRIPTION	FIRST DAY COVERS SING	FIRST DAY COVERS PL. BLK.	MINT SHEET	PLATE BLOCK	UNUSED F/NH	USED
5852	(68¢) Betty Ford, First Lady	3.00	.....	30.00(20)	7.00(4)	1.60	.....
5853	$1 Floral Geometry	5.00	.....	20.00(10)	10.00(4)	2.25	.....

5854

ANSEL ADAMS PHOTOGRAPHS

5854a *Half Dome, Merced River, 1938*
5854b *Oak Tree, Sunset City, 1962*
5854c *Thundercloud, Ellery Lake, 1934*
5854d *Denali & Wonder Lake, 1947*
5854e *Golden Gate Bridge, Baker Beach, 1953*
5854f *Road & Fog, Del Monte Forest, 1964*
5854g *Rock & Grass, Moraine Lake 1936*
5854h *Leaves, Mount Rainier, 1942*
5854i *Monument Valley, 1958*
5854j *Tetons & Snake River, 1942*
5854k *Jeffrey Pine, Sentinel Dome, 1940*
5854l *Mirror Lake, Mount Watkins, 1935*
5854m *Maroon Bells, 1951*
5854n *Aspens, Dawn, Autumn, 1937*
5854o *Road After Rain, 1960*
5854p *Dunes, 1963*

SCOTT NO.	DESCRIPTION	FIRST DAY COVERS SING	FIRST DAY COVERS PL. BLK.	MINT SHEET	PLATE BLOCK	UNUSED F/NH	USED
5854	(68¢) Ansel Adams Photographs	60.00(16)	.....	28.00(16)	.....	.....	.....

5855 5856

5857 5858

5859 5860

5861 5862

5863 5864

SCOTT NO.	DESCRIPTION	FIRST DAY COVERS SING	PL. BLK.	MINT SHEET	PLATE BLOCK	UNUSED F/NH	USED
5855-64	(68¢) Carnival Nights	50.00(10)	.....	30.00(20)	17.00(10)	15.00(10)	.....
5855	(68¢) Wave Swinger Ride .	.....	.....	.....	.....	1.60	.....
5856	(68¢) Midway Gondola Wheel & Ring of Fire	.....	.....	.....	.....	1.60	.....
5857	(68¢) Gondola Wheels . . .	.....	.....	.....	.....	1.60	.....
5858	(68¢) Gondola Wheel, Multi Color	.....	.....	.....	.....	1.60	.....
5859	(68¢) Gondola Wheel, Red Orange	.....	.....	.....	.....	1.60	.....
5860	(68¢) Gondola, Wave Swinger & Midway Food	.....	.....	.....	.....	1.60	.....
5861	(68¢) Gondola Wheel, Fireworks	.....	.....	.....	.....	1.60	.....
5862	(68¢) Round-Up Ride	.....	.....	.....	.....	1.60	.....
5863	(68¢) Carousel Horse	.....	.....	.....	.....	1.60	.....
5864	(68¢) Gondola Wheel & Wave Swinger, Fireworks	.....	.....	.....	.....	1.60	.....

5865 5866

5867 5868

5869 5870

SCOTT NO.	DESCRIPTION	FIRST DAY COVERS SING	PL. BLK.	MINT SHEET	PLATE BLOCK	UNUSED F/NH	USED
5865-70	(68¢) Protect Sea Turtles .	25.00(6)	.....	28.00(18)	20.00(12)	10.00(6)	.....
5865	(68¢) Kemp's Ridley	.....	.....	.....	.....	1.60	.....
5866	(68¢) Green.	.....	.....	.....	.....	1.60	.....
5867	(68¢) Leatherback.	.....	.....	.....	.....	1.60	.....
5868	(68¢) Loggerhead	.....	.....	.....	.....	1.60	.....
5869	(68¢) Hawksbill	.....	.....	.....	.....	1.60	.....
5870	(68¢) Olive Ridley	.....	.....	.....	.....	1.60	.....

5871, 5878, 5879 5872, 5875, 5880 5873, 5776, 5881 5874, 5877, 5882

SCOTT NO.	DESCRIPTION	FIRST DAY COVERS SING	PL. BLK.	MINT SHEET	PLATE BLOCK	UNUSED F/NH	USED
5871-74	(68¢) U.S. Flags, coil, die cut 9.5	15.00(4)	.....	.....	.....	6.00	.....
	same, plate number strip of 5	.....	.....	.....	.....	18.00	.....
5871	(68¢) Flag, Blue Sky Top, Cloud Bottom	.....	.....	.....	.....	1.60	.....
5872	(68¢) Flag, Dark Clouds . .	.....	.....	.....	.....	1.60	.....
5873	(68¢) Flag, Cloud Top & Bottom	.....	.....	.....	.....	1.60	.....
5874	(68¢) Flag, Blue Sky, Clouds Top	.....	.....	.....	.....	1.60	.....
5875-78	(68¢) U.S. Flags, coil, die cut 11.5	15.00(4)	.....	.....	.....	6.00	.....
	same, plate number strip of 5	.....	.....	.....	.....	18.00	.....
5875	(68¢) Flag, Dark Clouds . .	.....	.....	.....	.....	1.60	.....
5876	(68¢) Flag, Cloud Top & Bottom	.....	.....	.....	.....	1.60	.....
5877	(68¢) Flag, Blue Sky, Clouds Top	.....	.....	.....	.....	1.60	.....
5878	(68¢) Flag, Blue Sky Top, Cloud Bottom	.....	.....	.....	.....	1.60	.....
5879-82	(68¢) U.S. Flags, coil, die cut 10	15.00(4)	.....	.....	.....	6.00	.....
	same, plate number strip of 5	.....	.....	.....	.....	18.00	.....
5879	(68¢) Flag, Blue Sky Top, Cloud Bottom	.....	.....	.....	.....	1.60	.....
5880	(68¢) Flag, Dark Clouds . .	.....	.....	.....	.....	1.60	.....
5881	(68¢) Flag, Cloud Top & Bottom	.....	.....	.....	.....	1.60	.....
5882	(68¢) Flag, Blue Sky, Clouds Top	.....	.....	.....	.....	1.60	.....

5883, 5887 5884, 5888 5885, 5889 5886, 5890

SCOTT NO.	DESCRIPTION	FIRST DAY COVERS SING	PL. BLK.	MINT SHEET	PLATE BLOCK	UNUSED F/NH	USED
5883-86	(68¢) U.S. Flags 18.75 mm X 21.5 mm image	15.00(4)	.....	.....	.....	6.00	.....
5883	(68¢) Flag, Cloud Top & Bottom	.....	.....	.....	.....	1.60	.....
5884	(68¢) Flag, Blue Sky, Clouds Top	.....	.....	.....	.....	1.60	.....
5885	(68¢) Flag, Blue Sky Top, Cloud Bottom	.....	.....	.....	.....	1.60	.....
5886	(68¢) Flag, Dark Clouds . .	.....	.....	.....	.....	1.60	.....
5886b	same, double-sided bklt pane of 20	.....	.....	.....	.....	30.00	.....
5887-90	(68¢) U.S. Flags 18.25 mm X 21 mm image	15.00(4)	.....	.....	.....	6.00	.....
5887	(68¢) Flag, Cloud Top & Bottom	.....	.....	.....	.....	1.60	.....
5888	(68¢) Flag, Blue Sky, Clouds Top	.....	.....	.....	.....	1.60	.....
5889	(68¢) Flag, Blue Sky Top, Cloud Bottom	.....	.....	.....	.....	1.60	.....
5890	(68¢) Flag, Dark Clouds . .	.....	.....	.....	.....	1.60	.....
5890b	same, double-sided bklt pane of 20	.....	.....	.....	.....	30.00	.....

5891 5892

5893 5894

5895

SCOTT NO.	DESCRIPTION	FIRST DAY COVERS SING	PL. BLK.	MINT SHEET	PLATE BLOCK	UNUSED F/NH	USED
5891-95	(68¢) Horses	18.00(5)	.....	30.00(20)	17.00(10)	8.00(5)	.....
5891	(68¢) Horse, Brown Spots Facing Left	.....	.....	.....	.....	1.60	.....
5892	(68¢) Horse, White Blaze Facing Forward	.....	.....	.....	.....	1.60	.....
5893	(68¢) Horse, Arabian Facing Right	.....	.....	.....	.....	1.60	.....
5894	(68¢) Horse, Brown with Bridle	.....	.....	.....	.....	1.60	.....
5895	(68¢) Horse, Long White Mane	.....	.....	.....	.....	1.60	.....

SCOTT NO.	DESCRIPTION	FIRST DAY COVERS SING	PL. BLK.	MINT SHEET	PLATE BLOCK	UNUSED F/NH	USED

5896

SHAKER DESIGN

5896a *Meeting Room*
5896b *Tannery*
5896c *Spinning Wheel*
5896d *Staircases*
5896e *Dwelling House Hallway*
5896f *Silk Neckerchiefs*
5896g *Rocking Chair*
5896h *Bentwood Box Detail*
5896i *Heater Stove*
5896j *Cupboard, Oval Boxes*
5896k *Bentwood Boxes, Carriers*
5896l *Cheese Baskets*

SCOTT NO.	DESCRIPTION	FIRST DAY COVERS SING	PL. BLK.	MINT SHEET	PLATE BLOCK	UNUSED F/NH	USED
5896	(68¢) Shaker Design	55.00(12)	.....	22.00(12)	.....	.....	.....

SEMI-POSTAL

B1 (1998 year date)

B2

SCOTT NO.	DESCRIPTION	FIRST DAY COVERS SING	PL. BLK.	MINT SHEET	PLATE BLOCK	UNUSED F/NH	USED
	1998						
B1	(32¢ + 8¢) Breast Cancer	2.25	5.50	30.00(20)	5.50	1.50	.50
	2002						
B2	(34¢ + 11¢) Heroes of 2001	2.50	5.50	30.00(20)	5.50	1.50	.50

B3

B4

SCOTT NO.	DESCRIPTION	FIRST DAY COVERS SING	PL. BLK.	MINT SHEET	PLATE BLOCK	UNUSED F/NH	USED
	2003						
B3	(37¢ + 8¢)Stop Family Violence	2.50	5.50	30.00(20)	5.50	1.50	.50
	2011						
B4	(44¢ + 11¢) Save Vanishing Species	2.70	....	35.00(20)	7.00	2.00	.65

B5 (2014 year date)

B6

SCOTT NO.	DESCRIPTION	FIRST DAY COVERS SING	PL. BLK.	MINT SHEET	PLATE BLOCK	UNUSED F/NH	USED
	2015						
B5	(49¢ + 11¢) Breast Cancer Semi-Postal (2014 date)	2.75	....	35.00(20)	7.00	2.00	.75
	2017						
B6	(49¢ + 11¢) Alzheimers	$2.75	....	35.00(20)	7.00	2.00	.90

B7

SCOTT NO.	DESCRIPTION	FIRST DAY COVERS SING	PL. BLK.	MINT SHEET	PLATE BLOCK	UNUSED F/NH	USED
	2019						
B7	(55¢ + 10¢) Healing PTSD	$2.75	....	35.00(20)	6.50	1.50	.90

In July of 2012, the United States Postal Service released the first self-adhesive imperforate (no die-cuts) press sheets. This section covers the imperforate press sheets, mint sheets or booklet panes, plate blocks or se-tentants, and mint singles from the press sheets.

Due to the popularity of these issues, the current prices are subject to change.

SCOTT NO.	DESCRIPTION	IMPERF PRESS SHEET	IMPERF MINT SHEET OR BOOKLET	IMPERF PLATE BLOCK	IMPERF UNUSED F/NH
	2012				
4694	(45¢) Ted Williams	200.00(120)	45.00(20)	19.50(8)	3.00
4695	(45¢) Larry Doby.	200.00(120)	45.00(20)	19.50(8)	3.00
4696	(45¢) Willie Stargell . . .	200.00(120)	45.00(20)	19.50(8)	3.00
4697	(45¢) Joe DiMaggio . . .	200.00(120)	45.00(20)	19.50(8)	3.00
4694-97a	(45¢) Major League Baseball	350.00(120)	70.00 (20)	35.00(8)	15.00
4703	(45¢) War of 1812 Bicentennial	200.00(100)	55.00(20)	9.00(4)	3.00
4704	(45¢) Purple Heart	100.00(60)	50.00(20)	9.00(4)	3.00
4710	(45¢) Earthscapes	750.00(135)	70.00(15)	....	....
4711c	(45¢) Holy Family & Donkey	375.00(200)	45.00(20)	....	2.25
	same, 3 convertible panes of 20	130.00(60)	45.00(20)	....	....
4712-15	(45¢) Christmas Santa & Sleigh	400.00(200)	45.00(20)	....	8.00
	same, 3 convertible panes of 20	130.00(60)	45.00(20)	....	....
4716	(45¢) Lady Bird Johnson	375.00(96)	30.00(6)	....	....
	2013				
4721	(45¢) Emancipation Proclamation	300.00(200)	40.00(20)	9.00(4)	2.25
4726	(45¢) Chinese New Year	150.00(108)	25.00(12)	....	2.25
4727-30	33¢ Apples	250.00(200)	30.00(20)	7.25(4)	7.00
4735	66¢ Wedding Cake. . . .	900.00(200)	90.00(20)	15.00(4)	4.00
4736	66¢ Spicebush Swallowtail	475.00(200)	60.00(20)	9.00(4)	3.25
4737	86¢ Tufted Puffins.	300.00(120)	75.00(20)	15.00(4)	4.25
4740	($1.10) Earth Global . .	300.00(120)	100.00(20)	20.00(4)	6.00
4741	(46¢) Envelope with wax seal	250.00(120)	45.00(20)	6.75(4)	2.25
4742	(46¢) Rosa Parks	450.00(200)	55.00(20)	6.75(4)	2.25
4743-47	(46¢) Muscle Cars	450.00(200)	55.00(20)	22.00(10)	10.00
4748	(46¢) Modern Art in America	300.00(60)	80.00(12)	....	......
4750-53	(46¢) La Florida	450.00(160)	65.00(16)	11.00(4)	10.00
4764	(46¢) Where Dreams Blossom	300.00(160)	45.00(20)	9.00(4)	2.75
4765	66¢ Wedding Flowers and "Yes I Do"	400.00(180)	50.00(20)	12.00(4)	3.25
4786	(46¢) Lydia Mendoza . .	175.00(200)	30.00(16)	....	2.25
4787-88	(46¢) Civil War	200.00(72)	45.00(12)	....	6.00
4789	(46¢) Johnny Cash	185.00(128)	30.00(16)	....	2.25
4790	(46¢) West Virginia Statehood	250.00(200)	35.00(20)	9.50(4)	2.25
4791-95	(46¢) New England Lighthouses	250.00(120)	55.00(20)	22.50(10)	11.00
4800	(46¢) EID	275.00(160)	45.00(20)	9.50(4)	2.25
4801	(46¢) Made in America .	350.00(60)	85.00(12)	....	....
4803	(46¢) Althea Gibson . . .	400.00(200)	45.00(20)	9.50(4)	2.25
4804	(46¢) 1963 March on Washington	275.00(200)	35.00(20)	9.50(4)	2.25
4805	(46¢) 1812 Battle of Lake Erie	150.00(120)	30.00(20)	....	2.25
4806	$2 Inverted Jenny	500.00(36)	90.00(6)	....	14.00
4807	(46¢) Ray Charles	275.00(144)	40.00(16)	....	2.25
4813	(46¢) Holy Family & Donkey	375.00(200)	45.00(20)	9.50(4)	2.25
4814	($1.10) Christmas Wreath	225.00(60)	45.00(20)	15.00(4)	4.25
4815a	(46¢) Virgin & Child, convertible booklet of 20.	250.00(160)	40.00(20)	....	2.25
4816a	(46¢) Poinsettia, convertible booklet of 20.	325.00(160)	50.00(20)	....	2.25
4817-20	(46¢) Gingerbread Houses, convertible booklet of 20	300.00(160)	50.00(20)	....	9.50
4822-23	(46¢) Medal of Honor . .	100.00(60)	50.00(20)	9.50(4)	9.00
4824	(46¢) Hanukkah	180.00(160)	35.00(20)	9.50(4)	2.25
4825-44	(46¢) Harry Potter.	400.00(120)	....	....	....
4845	(46¢) Kwanzaa	180.00(160)	35.00(20)	9.50(4)	2.25
	2014				
4822a-4823a	(49¢) Medal of Honor, dated 2014	100.00(60)	45.00(20)	9.50(4)	9.00
4846	(46¢) Chinese New Year	195.00(120)	30.00(12)	.....	2.25
4847	(46¢) Love	250.00(120)	50.00(20)	9.50(4)	2.25
4856	(29¢) Shirley Chisholm .	300.00(160)	50.00(20)	9.50(4)	2.25
4859	70¢ Great Spangled Fritillary	480.00(200)	60.00(20)	10.00(4)	3.75
4860	21¢ Abraham Lincoln . .	60.00(60)	30.00(20)	4.50(4)	1.50
4862-65	(49¢) Winter Flowers, convertible booklet of 20	350.00(160)	35.00(20)	.....	8.00
4866	91¢ Ralph Ellison	525.00(200)	70.00(20)	15.00(4)	4.00
4873	$19.95 USS Arizona Memorial	1600.00(30)	600.00(10)	220.00(4)	60.00
4879	70¢ Alfred "Chief" Anderson	350.00(160)	50.00(20)	9.50(4)	3.25
4880	(49¢) Jimi Hendrix	300.00(144)	40.00(16)	.....	2.25
4882-91	(49¢) Songbrids, convertible booklet of 20	400.00(160)	50.00(20)	.....	25.00
4892	(49¢) Charlton Heston .	225.00(180)	35.00(20)	9.50(4)	2.25
4893	($1.15) Map of Sea Surface Temperatures	200.00(50)	50.00(10)	18.00(4)	4.00
4898-4905	(49¢) Circus Posters. . .	250.00(96)	50.00(16)	....	18.00(8)
4906	(49¢) Harvey Milk	525.00(240)	50.00(20)	9.50(4)	2.25
4907	(49¢) Nevada Statehood	280.00(240)	35.00(20)	9.50(4)	2.25
4908-09	(49¢) Hot Rods, convert. bklt of 20	280.00(140)	55.00(20)	.....	5.00
4910-11	(49¢) Civil War	150.00(72)	35.00(12)	.....	8.00
4912-15	(49¢) Farmer's Market .	200.00(100)	50.00(20)	17.50(8)	11.00
4916	(49¢) Janis Joplin	280.00(144)	50.00(16)	.....	2.25
4917-20	(49¢) Hudson River School, convertible booklet of 20	150.00(80)	50.00(20)	.....	9.50
4921	(49¢) Ft. McHenry, War of 1812	125.00(100)	35.00(20)	.....	2.25

SCOTT NO.	DESCRIPTION	IMPERF PRESS SHEET	IMPERF MINT SHEET OR BOOKLET	IMPERF PLATE BLOCK	IMPERF UNUSED F/NH
	2014, continued				
4922-26	(49¢) Celebrity Chefs . .	280.00(180)	35.00(20)	25.00(10)	12.00
4927	$5.75 Glade Creek Grist Mill	950.00(60)	180.00(10)	90.00(4)	22.25
4928-35	(49¢) Batman	380.00(180)	55.00(20)	.....	30.00(8)
4936	($1.15) Silver Bells Wreath	250.00(60)	55.00(10)	18.00(4)	4.50
4937-40	(49¢) Winter Fun, convert. bklt of 20	225.00(120)	55.00(20)	.....	9.50
4945	(49¢) Magi, convert. bklt of 20	350.00(160)	55.00(20)	.....	2.25
4946-49	(49¢) Rudolph, convert. bklt of 20	250.00(120)	55.00(20)	.....	9.50
4950-51	(49¢) Wilt Chamberlain.	190.00(144)	30.00(18)	9.50(4)	4.50
	2015				
4952	(49¢) Battle of New Orleans	125.00(100)	35.00(10)	......	2.25
4953	$1 Patriotic Waves	350.00(140)	35.00(10)	16.00(4)	4.00
4954	$2 Patriotic Waves	480.00(100)	60.00(10)	30.00(4)	8.00
4955-56	(49¢) Hearts Forever . .	130.00(60)	35.00(20)	9.50(4)	5.00
4957	(49¢) Chinese New Year	190.00(144)	25.00(12)	......	2.25
4958	(49¢) Robert Robinson Taylor	150.00(120)	45.00(20)	9.50(4)	2.25
4959	(49¢) Rose & Heart . . .	750.00(240)	85.00(20)	9.50(4)	2.25
4960	70¢ Tulip & Heart	975.00(240)	90.00(20)	10.00(4)	3.75
4964-67	(49¢) Water Lilies, convertible booklet of 20.	480.00(240)	55.00(20)	......	9.50
4968-72	(49¢) Art of Martin Ramirez	400.00(240)	40.00(20)	20.00(10)	12.00
4978	(49¢) From Me To You .	500.00(240)	45.00(20)	20.00(10)	2.25
4979	(49¢) Maya Angelou . . .	180.00(96)	30.00(20)	9.50(4)	2.25
4980-81	(49¢) Civil War	1000.00(72)	235.00(12)	......	35.00
4982-85	(49¢) Gifts of Friendship	180.00(72)	35.00(12)	......	......
4986	(49¢) Special Olympics World Games	100.00(80)	35.00(20)	9.50(4)	2.25
4987	(49¢) Forget-Me-Nots Missing Children.	150.00(120)	35.00(20)	9.50(4)	2.25
4988a	(49¢) Medal of Honor, strip of 3, dated 2015 . .	100.00(72)	50.00(24)	12.00(6)	9.00
4989	(22¢) Emperor Penguins	150.00(200)	15.00(20)	5.00(4)	1.25
4991-94	(35¢) Coastal Birds. . . .	225.00(200)	30.00(20)	5.50(4)	5.00
4999	(71¢) Eastern Tiger Swallowtail	300.00(120)	55.00(20)	12.00(4)	3.00
5003	(93¢) Flannery O'Connor	300.00(120)	60.00(20)	15.00(4)	3.25
5004-07	(49¢) Summer Harvest, convertible bklt of 20. . .	300.00(160)	45.00(20)	......	9.50
5008	(49¢) Coast Guard	225.00(120)	45.00(20)	9.50(4)	2.25
5009	(49¢) Elvis Presley	350.00(144)	35.00(20)	......	2.25
5010-11	(49¢) 2016 World Stamp Show	200.00(120)	50.00(20)	9.50(4)	5.00
5012	(49¢) Ingrid Bergman . .	380.00(180)	45.00(20)	9.50(4)	2.25
5020	(49¢) Paul Newman . . .	160.00(120)	40.00(20)	9.50(4)	2.25
5021-30	(49¢) Charlie Brown, convertible booklet of 20	370.00(160)	50.00(20)	......	25.00
5031-34	(49¢) Geometric Snowflakes, convertible booklet of 20	250.00(120)	50.00(20)	......	9.50
	2016				
5036	(49¢) Quilled Paper Heart	480.00(200)	45.00(20)	9.50(4)	2.25
5040	$6.45 La Cueva del Indio	950.00(60)	190.00(10)	85.00(4)	20.00
5041	$22.95 Columbia River Gorge	5000.00(30)	2000.00(10)	500.00(4)	200.00
5042-51	(49¢) Botanical Art, convertible bklt of 20.	1500.00(160)	225.00(20)	......	110.00
5056	(49¢) Richard Allen. . . .	320.00(120)	65.00(20)	11.00(4)	3.00
5057	(49¢) Chinese New Year	150.00(72)	30.00(12)	......	2.25
	2021				
5543	(55¢) Love	......(160)	60.00(20)	18.00(4)	3.75
5555	(55¢) August Wilson . . .	......(120)	65.00(20)	18.00(4)	3.75
5556	(55¢) Year of the Ox . . .	......(80)	80.00(20)	18.00(4)	3.75
5557	(55¢) Chien-Shiung Wu	......(120)	190.00(20)	45.00(4)	14.00
5573-82	(55¢) Star Wars Droids.	......(160)	175.00(20)	90.00(10)	80.00
5583-92	(55¢) Heritage Breeds .	......(80)	175.00(20)	90.00(10)	80.00
5593	(55¢) Go for Broke	......(120)	60.00(20)	18.00(4)	3.75
5594-97	(55¢) Emilio Sanchez . .	......(180)	60.00(20)	30.00(8)	18.00
5598-5607	(55¢) Sun Science	......(120)	175.00(20)	90.00(10)	80.00
5608	(55¢) Yogi Berra	......(120)	60.00(20)	18.00(4)	3.75
5609-13	(55¢) Tap Dance	......(120)	80.00(20)	35.00(10)	20.00
5614	(55¢) Mystery Message	......(160)	60.00(20)	18.00(4)	3.75
5620	(55¢) Raven Story	......(120)	450.00(20)	100.00(4)	28.00
5621-25	(55¢) Mid-Atlantic Lighthouse	......(120)	60.00(20)	35.00(10)	20.00
5626	(55¢) Missouri Statehood	......(120)	60.00(20)	18.00(4)	3.75
5627-34	(55¢) Backyard Games	......(160)	50.00(16)	30.00(8)	25.00
5636-39	(58¢) Message Monsters	......(60)	55.00(20)	22.00(8)	10.00
5640-43	(58¢) Day of the Dead .	......(160)	55.00(20)	22.00(8)	10.00

SCOTT NO.	DESCRIPTION	IMPERF PRESS SHEET	IMPERF MINT SHEET OR BOOKLET	IMPERF PLATE BLOCK	IMPERF UNUSED F/NH
2022					
5660-61	(58c) Love, blue gray & pink	.....(160)	40.00(20)	9.50(4)	4.75
5662	(58c) Year of the Tiger .	.....(80)	40.00(20)	.....	2.75
5663	(58c) Edmonia Lewis . .	.....(80)	40.00(20)	9.50(4)	2.75
5668-71	(58c) Title IX Civil Rights Law	.....(180)	40.00(20)	9.50(4)	9.50
5683	(58c) The Giving Tree, Shel Silverstein	.....(120)	55.00(20)	9.50(4)	2.75
5688-92	(58c) George Morrison .	.....(180)	55.00(20)	22.00(10)	12.00
5693	(58c) Eugenie Clark . . .	.....(120)	40.00(20)	9.50(4)	2.75
5694-97	(58c) Womens' Rowing	.....(180)	40.00(20)	16.00(8)	9.50
5698	(58c) Mighty Mississippi	.....(60)	25.00(10)	.....	.....
5702	(58c) Nancy Reagan. . .	.....(60)	40.00(20)	9.50(4)	2.75
5703-07	(60c) Mariachi.	.....(120)	40.00(20)	20.00(10)	12.00
5708	(60c) Pete Seeger	.....(144)	30.00(16)	.....	2.75
5709-12	(60c) Go Beyond, Buzz Lightyear	.....(180)	40.00(20)	16.00(8)	9.50
5713	(60c) National Marine Sanctuaries	.....(96)	30.00(16)	.....	.....
5715-19	(60c) Pony Cars	.....(120)	40.00(20)	20.00(10)	12.00
5720	(60c) James Webb Space Telescope	.....(120)	40.00(20)	9.50(4)	2.75
5726	(60c) Peanuts, Charles M. Schulz	.....(120)	55.00(20)	.....	.....
5738	(60c) Women Cryptologists	.....(60)	40.00(20)	9.50(4)	2.75
2023					
5744	(60c) Year of the Rabbit	.....(80)	40.00(20)	.....	2.75
5745-46	(60c) Love, Puppy and Kitten	.....(160)	40.00(20)	9.50(4)	4.75
5753	(63c) Ernest J. Gaines .	.....(180)	40.00(20)	9.50(4)	2.75
5754	(63c) Women's Soccer .	.....(120)	40.00(20)	9.50(4)	2.75
5757	(63c) Toni Morrison. . . .	.....(120)	40.00(20)	9.50(4)	2.75
5758-62	(63c) Historic Railroad Stations	.....(80)	40.00(20)	20.00(10)	12.00
5763-66	(63c) Art of the Skateboard	.....(120)	40.00(20)	16.00(8)	9.50
5792-96	(63c) Roy Liechtenstein	.....(80)	40.00(20)	20.00(10)	12.00
5797	(63c) Tomie dePaola. . .	.....(180)	40.00(20)	9.50(4)	2.75
5798	(63c) Chief Standing Bear	.....(180)	40.00(20)	9.50(4)	2.75
5799	(63c) Endangered Species	.....(80)	60.00(20)	.....	.....
5800	(63c) Waterfalls	....	30.00(12)	.....	.....

**2023 - 2024 Imperf Issues will be listed in the next edition.*

SCOTT NO.	DESCRIPTION	IMPERF PRESS SHEET	IMPERF MINT SHEET OR BOOKLET	IMPERF PLATE BLOCK	IMPERF UNUSED F/NH
Semi-Postals					
B5	(49¢ + 11¢) Breast Cancer	380.00(240)	40.00(20)	9.50(4)	2.25

SCOTT NO.	DESCRIPTION	UNUSED O.G. VF	F	AVG	USED VF	F	AVG

AIR POST

C1-C3
Curtiss Jenny Biplane

C4
Airplane Propeller

C5
Badge of Air Service

C6
Airplane

1918 (C1-6 NH + 75%)

SCOTT NO.	DESCRIPTION	UNUSED O.G. VF	F	AVG	USED VF	F	AVG
C1-3	**6¢-24¢, 3 varieties, complete.........**	**250.00**	**200.00**	**176.00**	**115.00**	**95.00**	**80.00**
C1	6¢ orange	75.00	60.00	55.00	35.00	29.00	23.00
C2	16¢ green	85.00	70.00	60.00	38.00	30.00	27.00
C3	24¢ carmine rose & blue	95.00	75.00	65.00	45.00	40.00	35.00
C3a	same, center inverted	....	800000.00	....	....	....	....

SCOTT NO.		CENTER LINE BLOCKS F/NH	F/OG	A/OG	ARROW BLOCKS F/NH	F/OG	A/OG
C1	6¢ orange	800.00	425.00	280.00	550.00	385.00	255.00
C2	16¢ green	625.00	400.00	325.00	550.00	360.00	285.00
C3	24¢ carmine rose & blue	650.00	425.00	330.00	575.00	370.00	275.00

1923

SCOTT NO.	DESCRIPTION	UNUSED O.G. VF	F	AVG	USED VF	F	AVG
C4-6	**8¢-24¢, 3 varieties, complete.........**	**225.00**	**165.00**	**145.00**	**85.00**	**68.00**	**50.00**
C4	8¢ dark green	25.00	20.00	15.00	15.00	12.00	10.00
C5	16¢ dark blue......	95.00	80.00	70.00	35.00	28.00	20.00
C6	24¢ carmine.......	110.00	70.00	65.00	38.00	30.00	22.00

C7-C9
Map of U.S. and Airplanes

1926-30 (C7-12 NH + 50%)

SCOTT NO.	DESCRIPTION	UNUSED O.G. VF	F	AVG	USED VF	F	AVG
C7-9	**10¢-20¢, 3 varieties, complete.........**	**17.50**	**14.50**	**9.50**	**5.95**	**5.00**	**3.45**
C7	10¢ dark blue......	3.75	3.10	2.40	.65	.50	.35
C8	15¢ olive brown....	4.25	3.60	2.75	3.00	2.50	1.75
C9	20¢ yellow green (1927)	11.50	9.00	7.00	2.75	2.25	1.65

C10
Lindbergh's Airplane "Spirit of St. Louis"

1927 LINDBERGH TRIBUTE ISSUE

SCOTT NO.	DESCRIPTION	UNUSED O.G. VF	F	AVG	USED VF	F	AVG
C10	10¢ dark blue......	10.75	8.25	6.00	2.85	2.20	1.75
C10a	same, bklt pane of 3	125.00	95.00	67.50	....	....	....

C11
Beacon and Rocky Mountains

C12, C16, C17, C19
Winged Globe

1928 BEACON

SCOTT NO.	DESCRIPTION	UNUSED O.G. VF	F	AVG	USED VF	F	AVG
C11	5¢ carmine & blue ..	6.50	4.75	3.25	.90	.70	.50

1930 Flat Plate Printing, Perf.11

SCOTT NO.	DESCRIPTION	UNUSED O.G. VF	F	AVG	USED VF	F	AVG
C12	5¢ violet..........	12.50	9.75	8.50	.85	.65	.50

C13
Graf Zeppelin

C14

C15

1930 GRAF ZEPPELIN ISSUE (NH + 50%)

SCOTT NO.	DESCRIPTION	UNUSED O.G. VF	F	AVG	USED VF	F	AVG
C13-15	**65¢-$2.60, 3 varieties, complete........**	**1620.00**	**1465.00**	**1265.00**	**1500.00**	**1180.00**	**965.00**
C13	65¢ green	300.00	250.00	200.00	275.00	210.00	175.00
C14	$1.30 brown.......	425.00	370.00	320.00	450.00	375.00	295.00
C15	$2.60 blue	900.00	850.00	750.00	800.00	600.00	500.00

1931-32 Rotary Press Printing. Perf. 10½ x 11, Designs as #C12 (C16-C24 NH + 40%)

SCOTT NO.	DESCRIPTION	UNUSED O.G. VF	F	AVG	USED VF	F	AVG
C16	5¢ violet..........	8.00	6.00	5.00	.80	.55	.40
C17	8¢ olive bistre	3.25	2.75	2.15	.55	.40	.35

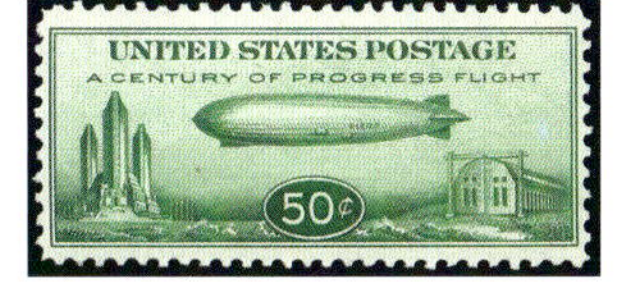

C18
Graf Zeppelin

1933 CENTURY OF PROGRESS ISSUE

SCOTT NO.	DESCRIPTION	UNUSED O.G. VF	F	AVG	USED VF	F	AVG
C18	50¢ green	100.00	90.00	75.00	80.00	70.00	60.00

1934 DESIGN OF 1930

SCOTT NO.	DESCRIPTION	UNUSED O.G. VF	F	AVG	USED VF	F	AVG
C19	6¢ dull orange	3.75	3.00	2.00	.45	.35	.25

C20-22
China Clipper

1935 TRANS-PACIFIC ISSUE

SCOTT NO.	DESCRIPTION	UNUSED O.G. VF	F	AVG	USED VF	F	AVG
C20	25¢ blue..........	1.55	1.25	1.05	1.10	.90	.80

1937. Type of 1935 Issue, Date Omitted

SCOTT NO.	DESCRIPTION	UNUSED O.G. VF	F	AVG	USED VF	F	AVG
C21	20¢ green	12.00	10.00	7.50	2.00	1.65	1.35
C22	50¢ carmine.......	12.00	10.25	7.75	5.40	4.50	3.75

C23
Eagle

1938

SCOTT NO.	DESCRIPTION	UNUSED O.G. VF	F	AVG	USED VF	F	AVG
C23	6¢ dark blue & carmine	.65	.55	.45	.35	.30	.25

C24
Winged Globe

1939 TRANS-ATLANTIC ISSUE

SCOTT NO.	DESCRIPTION	UNUSED O.G. VF	F	AVG	USED VF	F	AVG
C24	30¢ dull blue	12.50	11.00	10.00	1.70	1.50	1.20

AIR POST PLATE BLOCKS #C1-C24

SCOTT NO.		UNUSED NH VF	F	AVG	UNUSED O.G. VF	F	AVG
C1(6)	6¢ orange.	1550.00	1150.00	925.00	1050.00	875.00	600.00
C2(6)	16¢ green.	2100.00	1975.00	1575.00	1400.00	1100.00	900.00
C3(12)	24¢ carmine rose & blue	2800.00	2000.00	1825.00	1800.00	1700.00	1300.00
C4(6)	8¢ dark green.	610.00	450.00	360.00	350.00	300.00	260.00
C5(6)	16¢ dark blue	3400.00	2700.00	2250.00	2200.00	2000.00	1650.00
C6(6)	24¢ carmine	4300.00	3300.00	2825.00	2800.00	2200.00	1900.00
C7(6)	10¢ dark blue	77.00	55.00	49.00	54.00	41.50	30.00
C8(6)	15¢ olive brown . . .	85.00	66.00	52.75	60.00	50.00	44.00
C9(6)	20¢ yellow green . .	185.00	155.00	125.00	110.00	90.00	80.00
C10(6)	10¢ dark blue	200.00	188.00	165.00	135.00	115.00	85.00
C11(6)	5¢ carmine & blue .	85.00	65.00	54.00	60.00	46.50	31.50
C12(6)	5¢ violet	285.00	220.00	175.00	215.00	165.00	120.00
C13(6)	65¢ green.	5200.00	3800.00	3000.00	3300.00	2600.00	2100.00
C14(6)	$1.30 brown	12500.00	1100.00	8000.00	8000.00	7000.00	5500.00
C15(6)	$2.60 blue	19000.00	18000.00	13000.00	12000.00	10000.00	8000.00
C16(4)	5¢ violet	150.00	135.00	105.00	110.00	95.00	65.00
C17(4)	8¢ olive bistre.	58.50	45.00	36.00	40.00	30.00	24.00
C18(4)	50¢ green.	1400.00	1150.00	800.00	950.00	795.00	635.00
C19(4)	6¢ dull orange	39.50	33.00	26.00	30.00	25.00	20.00
C20(6)	25¢ blue	33.00	27.50	22.00	26.50	22.00	17.50
C21(6)	20¢ green.	125.00	105.00	90.00	115.00	100.00	85.00
C22(6)	50¢ carmine	125.00	90.00	75.00	90.00	75.00	65.00
C23(4)	6¢ dark blue & carmine	19.00	15.00	12.00	15.00	12.00	9.00
C24(6)	30¢ dull blue.	185.00	155.00	135.00	155.00	130.00	95.00

C25-C31

1941-44 TRANSPORT ISSUE

SCOTT NO.	DESCRIPTION	FIRST DAY COVERS SING	PL. BLK.	MINT SHEET	PLATE BLOCK	UNUSED F/NH	USED
C25-31	**6¢-50¢, 7 varieties, complete. . . . .**	....	....	....	**127.50**	**23.95**	**5.60**
C25	6¢ Transport Plane . . .	7.00	10.00	15.00(50)	1.25	.30	.25
C25a	same, bklt pane of 3 . .	30.00	....	....	....	4.25	....
C26	8¢ Transport Plane . . .	6.00	11.25	16.00(50)	2.20	.30	.25
C27	10¢ Transport Plane . .	8.00	15.00	82.50(50)	9.00	1.65	.25
C28	15¢ Transport Plane . .	8.00	15.00	150.00(50)	13.95	3.25	.40
C29	20¢ Transport Plane . .	10.00	20.00	125.00(50)	14.00	2.75	.40
C30	30¢ Transport Plane . .	20.00	30.00	140.00(50)	14.00	3.00	.40
C31	50¢ Transport Plane . .	28.50	68.75	575.00(50)	65.00	14.00	4.25

C32

1946

SCOTT NO.	DESCRIPTION	FIRST DAY COVERS SING	PL. BLK.	MINT SHEET	PLATE BLOCK	UNUSED F/NH	USED
C32	5¢ DC-4 Skymaster . . .	2.00	4.25	13.00(50)	1.00	.30	.25

C33, C37, C39, C41

C34

C35

C36

1947

SCOTT NO.	DESCRIPTION	FIRST DAY COVERS SING	PL. BLK.	MINT SHEET	PLATE BLOCK	UNUSED F/NH	USED
C33-36	**5¢-25¢, 4 varieties, complete. . . . .**	....	....	....	....	**2.10**	**.70**
C33	5¢ DC-4 Skymaster . . .	2.00	4.25	25.00(100)	1.20	.30	.25
C34	10¢ Pan American Bldg.	2.00	4.25	19.00(50)	2.00	.45	.25
C35	15¢ New York Skyline .	2.00	4.25	26.00(50)	2.75	.60	.30
C36	25¢ Plane over Bridge .	2.00	5.00	75.00(50)	7.50	1.60	.30

1948
Rotary Press Coil–Perf. 10 Horiz.

SCOTT NO.	DESCRIPTION	FIRST DAY COVERS SING	LINE PR.	MINT SHEET	LINE PR.	UNUSED F/NH	USED
C37	5¢ DC-4 Skymaster. . .	2.00	4.25	....	12.00	1.40	1.00

C38

C40

SCOTT NO.	DESCRIPTION	FIRST DAY COVERS SING	PL. BLK.	MINT SHEET	PLATE BLOCK	UNUSED F/NH	USED
C38	5¢ New York Jubliee . .	2.00	4.25	22.00(100)	5.25	.30	.25

1949

SCOTT NO.	DESCRIPTION	FIRST DAY COVERS SING	PL. BLK.	MINT SHEET	PLATE BLOCK	UNUSED F/NH	USED
C39	6¢ DC-4 Skymaster (as #C33).	2.00	4.25	23.00(100)	1.50	.30	.25
C39a	same, bklt pane of 6 . .	10.00	....	....	....	14.00	....
C40	6¢ Alexandria, Virginia.	2.00	4.25	12.00(50)	1.30	.35	.25

Rotary Press Coil–Perf. 10 Horiz.

SCOTT NO.	DESCRIPTION	FIRST DAY COVERS SING	LINE PR.	MINT SHEET	LINE PR.	UNUSED F/NH	USED
C41	6¢ DC-4 Skymaster (as#C37)	2.00	4.25	....	22.00	4.25	.25

NOTE: Unused Air Mail coil pairs can be supplied at two times the single price.

C42

C43

C44

1949 U.P.U. ISSUES

SCOTT NO.	DESCRIPTION	FIRST DAY COVERS SING	PL. BLK.	MINT SHEET	PLATE BLOCK	UNUSED F/NH	USED
C42-44	**10¢-25¢, 3 varieties, complete. . . . .**	....	....	....	....	**1.90**	**1.35**
C42	10¢ Post Office	2.00	4.25	17.50(50)	1.85	.40	.30
C43	15¢ Globe & Doves . . .	3.00	5.00	25.00(50)	2.25	.60	.45
C44	25¢ Plane & Globe . . .	4.00	6.25	42.00(50)	7.25	1.10	.75

C45

C46

C47

1949-58

SCOTT NO.	DESCRIPTION	FIRST DAY COVERS SING	PL. BLK.	MINT SHEET	PLATE BLOCK	UNUSED F/NH	USED
C45-51	**7 varieties, complete.**	....	....	....	....	**9.00**	**2.30**
C45	6¢ Wright Brothers (1949)	2.00	4.25	25.00(50)	2.00	.50	.25
C46	80¢ Hawaii (1952)	15.00	35.00	350.00(50)	35.00	8.00	2.00
C47	6¢ Powered Flight (1953)	2.00	4.25	12.00(50)	1.30	.30	.25

C48, C50

1949-58 (continued)

SCOTT NO.	DESCRIPTION	FIRST DAY COVERS SING	FIRST DAY COVERS PL. BLK.	MINT SHEET	PLATE BLOCK	UNUSED F/NH	USED
C48	4¢ Eagle (1954)	2.00	4.25	24.00(100)	1.95	.30	.25

C49

C51, C52, C60, C61

SCOTT NO.	DESCRIPTION	FIRST DAY COVERS SING	FIRST DAY COVERS PL. BLK.	MINT SHEET	PLATE BLOCK	UNUSED F/NH	USED
C49	6¢ Air Force (1957) . .	2.00	4.25	17.00(50)	1.85	.40	.25
C50	5¢ Eagle (1958)	2.00	4.25	19.50(100)	1.90	.30	.25
C51	7¢ Silhouette of Jet, blue (1958)	2.00	4.25	24.00(100)	1.40	.35	.25
C51a	same, bklt pane of 6 .	8.00	....	....	....	14.00	....

Rotary Press Coil–Perf. 10 Horiz.

SCOTT NO.	DESCRIPTION	FIRST DAY COVERS SING	LINE PR.	MINT SHEET	LINE PR.	UNUSED F/NH	USED
C52	7¢ Silhouette of Jet, blue	2.00	3.25	....	24.00	2.75	.25

C53

C54

1959

SCOTT NO.	DESCRIPTION	FIRST DAY COVERS SING	FIRST DAY COVERS PL. BLK.	MINT SHEET	PLATE BLOCK	UNUSED F/NH	USED
C53-56	**4 varieties, complete .**	....	....	....	....	**1.50**	**.85**
C53	7¢ Alaska Statehood . .	2.00	4.25	19.00(50)	1.85	.45	.25
C54	7¢ Balloon Jupiter	2.00	4.25	23.00(50)	2.55	.55	.25

C55

C56

SCOTT NO.	DESCRIPTION	FIRST DAY COVERS SING	FIRST DAY COVERS PL. BLK.	MINT SHEET	PLATE BLOCK	UNUSED F/NH	USED
C55	7¢ Hawaii Statehood .	2.00	4.25	19.00(50)	2.00	.45	.25
C56	10¢ Pan-Am Games .	2.00	4.25	20.00(50)	2.25	.55	.35

C57

C58, C63

C59

C62

1959-66 REGULAR ISSUES

SCOTT NO.	DESCRIPTION	FIRST DAY COVERS SING	FIRST DAY COVERS PL. BLK.	MINT SHEET	PLATE BLOCK	UNUSED F/NH	USED
C57/63	**(C57-60, C62-63) 6 varieties........**	....	....	....	....	**3.90**	**1.90**

1959-66

SCOTT NO.	DESCRIPTION	FIRST DAY COVERS SING	FIRST DAY COVERS PL. BLK.	MINT SHEET	PLATE BLOCK	UNUSED F/NH	USED
C57	10¢ Liberty Bell (1960)	2.00	4.25	55.00(50)	7.00	1.55	1.00
C58	15¢ Statue of Liberty . .	2.00	4.25	24.00(50)	2.50	.55	.25
C59	25¢ Abraham Lincoln (1960)	2.00	4.25	43.00(50)	4.25	.90	.25

1960. Design of 1958

SCOTT NO.	DESCRIPTION	FIRST DAY COVERS SING	FIRST DAY COVERS PL. BLK.	MINT SHEET	PLATE BLOCK	UNUSED F/NH	USED
C60	7¢ Jet Plane, carmine .	2.00	4.25	22.50(100)	1.50	.35	.25
C60a	same, bklt pane of 6 . .	9.00	....	....	....	17.00	....

Rotary Press Coil–Perf. 10 Horiz.

SCOTT NO.	DESCRIPTION	FIRST DAY COVERS SING	LINE PR.	MINT SHEET	LINE PR.	UNUSED F/NH	USED
C61	7¢ Jet Plane, carmine	2.00	3.25	....	50.00	5.50	.35

1961-67

SCOTT NO.	DESCRIPTION	FIRST DAY COVERS SING	FIRST DAY COVERS PL. BLK.	MINT SHEET	PLATE BLOCK	UNUSED F/NH	USED
C62	13¢ Liberty Bell	2.00	4.25	25.00(50)	2.70	.60	.25
C63	15¢ Statue re-drawn . .	2.00	4.25	25.00(50)	2.60	.60	.25

C64, C65

1962-64

SCOTT NO.	DESCRIPTION	FIRST DAY COVERS SING	FIRST DAY COVERS PL. BLK.	MINT SHEET	PLATE BLOCK	UNUSED F/NH	USED
C64/69	**(C64, C66-69) 5 varieties**	....	....	....	....	**2.00**	**1.25**

1962

SCOTT NO.	DESCRIPTION	FIRST DAY COVERS SING	FIRST DAY COVERS PL. BLK.	MINT SHEET	PLATE BLOCK	UNUSED F/NH	USED
C64	8¢ Plane & Capitol. . . .	2.00	4.25	25.00(100)	1.40	.30	.25
C64b	same, bklt pane of 5, Slogan I	1.95	....	....	....	9.00	....
C64b	bklt pane of 5, Slogan II, (1963)	....	....	....	....	90.00	....
C64b	bklt pane of 5, Slogan III (1964)	....	....	....	....	15.00	....
C64c	bklt pane of 5 tagged, Slogan III (1964)	....	....	....	....	2.25	....

SLOGAN I–Your Mailman Deserves Your Help... SLOGAN II–Use Zone Numbers..

SLOGAN III–Always Use Zip Code....

Rotary Press Coil–Perf. 10 Horiz.

SCOTT NO.	DESCRIPTION	FIRST DAY COVERS SING	LINE PR.	MINT SHEET	LINE PR.	UNUSED F/NH	USED
C65	8¢ Plane & Capitol. . . .	2.00	3.25	....	8.00	.65	.30

C66

C67

C68

1963

SCOTT NO.	DESCRIPTION	FIRST DAY COVERS SING	FIRST DAY COVERS PL. BLK.	MINT SHEET	PLATE BLOCK	UNUSED F/NH	USED
C66	15¢ Montgomery Blair .	2.00	4.25	29.00(50)	4.00	.75	.60
C67	6¢ Bald Eagle	2.00	4.25	35.00(100)	2.25	.30	.25
C68	8¢ Amelia Earhart	2.00	4.25	20.00(50)	2.00	.40	.25

C69

1964

SCOTT NO.	DESCRIPTION	FIRST DAY COVERS SING	FIRST DAY COVERS PL. BLK.	MINT SHEET	PLATE BLOCK	UNUSED F/NH	USED
C69	8¢ Dr. Robert H. Goddard	2.00	5.00	20.00(50)	2.25	.50	.25

C70

C71

C72, C73

1967-69

SCOTT NO.	DESCRIPTION	FIRST DAY COVERS SING	PL. BLK.	MINT SHEET	PLATE BLOCK	UNUSED F/NH	USED
C70/76	(C70-72, C74-76) 6 varieties........		....	....	....	2.95	1.00

1967-68

SCOTT NO.	DESCRIPTION	FIRST DAY COVERS SING	PL. BLK.	MINT SHEET	PLATE BLOCK	UNUSED F/NH	USED
C70	8¢ Alaska Purchase. . .	2.00	4.25	19.00(50)	2.25	.45	.25
C71	20¢ "Columbia Jays" . .	2.00	4.25	44.00(50)	4.50	1.00	.25
C72	10¢ 50-Stars (1968). . .	2.00	4.25	32.50(100)	1.80	.40	.25
C72b	same, bklt pane of 8 . .	3.00	....	....	....	3.25	....
C72c	same, bklt pane of 5, Slogan IV or V	140.00	....	....	....	5.75	....

SLOGAN IV–Mail Early in the Day... SLOGAN V–Use Zip Code...

1968 Rotary Press Coil–Perf. 10 Vert.

SCOTT NO.	DESCRIPTION	FIRST DAY COVERS SING	LINE PR.	MINT SHEET	LINE PR.	UNUSED F/NH	USED
C73	10¢ 50-Star	2.00	3.25	....	2.75	.50	.35

C74

C75

SCOTT NO.	DESCRIPTION	FIRST DAY COVERS SING	PL. BLK.	MINT SHEET	PLATE BLOCK	UNUSED F/NH	USED
C74	10¢ Air Mail Anniversary	2.00	4.25	15.00(50)	3.10	.40	.25
C75	20¢ "USA" & Plane . . .	2.00	4.25	29.00(50)	3.25	.75	.25

C76

1969

SCOTT NO.	DESCRIPTION	FIRST DAY COVERS SING	PL. BLK.	MINT SHEET	PLATE BLOCK	UNUSED F/NH	USED
C76	10¢ Man on the Moon .	6.00	14.50	15.00(32)	2.25	.50	.35

C77

C78, C82

C79, C83

1971-73

SCOTT NO.	DESCRIPTION	FIRST DAY COVERS SING	PL. BLK.	MINT SHEET	PLATE BLOCK	UNUSED F/NH	USED
C77-81	9¢-21¢, 5 varieties, complete.	....	....	....	....	2.25	1.25
C77	9¢ Delta Winged Plane	2.00	4.25	28.00(100)	1.75	.40	.30
C78	11¢ Silhouette of Plane	2.00	4.25	35.00(100)	2.00	.45	.25
C78b	same, precanceled . . .		....	....	....	....	.50
C78a	11¢ bklt pane of 4	2.25	....	....	....	1.65	....
C79	13¢ Letter (1973).	2.00	4.25	38.00(100)	2.25	.50	.25
C79b	same, precanceled . . .	....	....	....	....	1.50	1.00
C79a	13¢ bklt pane of 5	2.25	....	....	....	2.50	....

C80

SCOTT NO.	DESCRIPTION	FIRST DAY COVERS SING	PL. BLK.	MINT SHEET	PLATE BLOCK	UNUSED F/NH	USED
C80	17¢ Liberty Head	2.00	4.25	27.00(50)	3.00	.65	.25
C81	21¢ "USA" & Plane . . .	2.00	4.25	29.00(50)	3.25	.70	.25

Rotary Press Coils–Perf. 10 Vert.

SCOTT NO.	DESCRIPTION	FIRST DAY COVERS SING	LINE PR.	MINT SHEET	LINE PR.	UNUSED F/NH	USED
C82	11¢ Silhouette of Jet . .	2.00	3.25	....	1.25	.45	.25
C83	13¢ Letter	2.00	3.25	....	1.50	.55	.25

C84

C85

1972-76

SCOTT NO.	DESCRIPTION	FIRST DAY COVERS SING	PL. BLK.	MINT SHEET	PLATE BLOCK	UNUSED F/NH	USED
C84-90	11¢-31¢, 7 varieties, complete.	....	....	....	....	4.70	1.50

1972

SCOTT NO.	DESCRIPTION	FIRST DAY COVERS SING	PL. BLK.	MINT SHEET	PLATE BLOCK	UNUSED F/NH	USED
C84	11¢ City of Refuge	2.00	4.25	22.00(50)	2.40	.50	.25
C85	11¢ Olympics	2.00	4.25	18.50(50)	4.50(10)	.45	.35

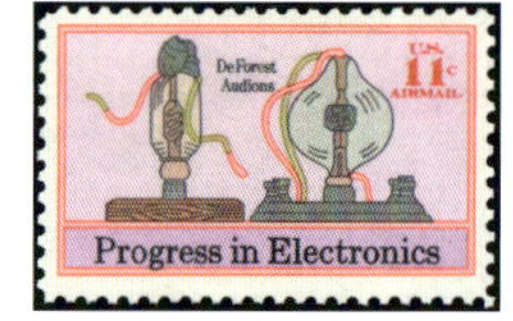

C86

1973

SCOTT NO.	DESCRIPTION	FIRST DAY COVERS SING	PL. BLK.	MINT SHEET	PLATE BLOCK	UNUSED F/NH	USED
C86	11¢ Electronics	2.00	4.25	26.50(50)	2.50	.55	.25

C87

C88

1974

SCOTT NO.	DESCRIPTION	FIRST DAY COVERS SING	PL. BLK.	MINT SHEET	PLATE BLOCK	UNUSED F/NH	USED
C87	18¢ Statue of Liberty . .	2.00	4.25	27.50(50)	2.75	.65	.50
C88	26¢ Mt. Rushmore	2.00	4.25	50.00(50)	5.00	1.25	.25

C89

C90

1976

SCOTT NO.	DESCRIPTION	FIRST DAY COVERS SING	PL. BLK.	MINT SHEET	PLATE BLOCK	UNUSED F/NH	USED
C89	25¢ Plane & Globes. . .	2.00	4.25	37.00 (50)	3.85	.90	.25
C90	31¢ Plane, Flag & Globes	2.00	4.25	47.00 (50)	4.75	1.10	.25

C91 C92

1978-80

SCOTT NO.	DESCRIPTION	FIRST DAY COVERS SING	FIRST DAY COVERS PL. BLK.	MINT SHEET	PLATE BLOCK	UNUSED F/NH	USED
C91-100	**21¢-40¢, 10 varieties, complete. . . . .**	....	....	....	....	**11.50**	**5.35**
C91-92	Wright Brothers, 2 varieties, attached . .	2.40	5.00	95.00(100)	5.75	2.25	1.75
C91	31¢ Wright Brothers & Plane	2.00	....	....	....	1.00	.60
C92	31¢ Wright Brothers & Shed	2.00	....	....	....	1.00	.60

C93 C94

1979

SCOTT NO.	DESCRIPTION	FIRST DAY COVERS SING	FIRST DAY COVERS PL. BLK.	MINT SHEET	PLATE BLOCK	UNUSED F/NH	USED
C93-94	Octave Chanute, 2 varieties, attached . .	2.40	5.00	85.00(100)	5.00	2.10	1.75
C93	21¢ Chanute & Plane .	2.00	....	....	....	1.00	.75
C94	21¢ Chanute & 2 Planes	2.00	....	....	....	1.00	.75

C95 C96

SCOTT NO.	DESCRIPTION	FIRST DAY COVERS SING	FIRST DAY COVERS PL. BLK.	MINT SHEET	PLATE BLOCK	UNUSED F/NH	USED
C95-96	Wiley Post, 2 varieties, attached . .	2.40	5.00	165.00(100)	13.50	3.50	2.75
C95	25¢ Post & Plane.	2.00	....	....	....	1.80	1.10
C96	25¢ Plane & Post.	2.00	....	....	....	1.80	1.10

C97

SCOTT NO.	DESCRIPTION	FIRST DAY COVERS SING	FIRST DAY COVERS PL. BLK.	MINT SHEET	PLATE BLOCK	UNUSED F/NH	USED
C97	31¢ High Jumper	2.00	4.25	48.00(50)	15.00(12)	1.05	.80

C98 C99

1980

SCOTT NO.	DESCRIPTION	FIRST DAY COVERS SING	FIRST DAY COVERS PL. BLK.	MINT SHEET	PLATE BLOCK	UNUSED F/NH	USED
C98	40¢ Philip Mazzei . . .	2.00	4.25	65.00(50)	18.00 (12)	1.40	.35
C98a	40¢ Philip Mazzei, perf. 10-1/2x11-1/4	2.00	4.25 387.00(50)	140.00 (12)	9.00	2.25	
C99	28¢ Blanche S. Scott.	2.00	4.25	42.50(50)	14.00 (12)	1.10	.35

C100

SCOTT NO.	DESCRIPTION	FIRST DAY COVERS SING	FIRST DAY COVERS PL. BLK.	MINT SHEET	PLATE BLOCK	UNUSED F/NH	USED
C100	35¢ Glenn Curtiss . . .	2.00	4.25	48.00(50)	15.00(12)	1.20	.35

C101 C102 C103 C104

1983-85

SCOTT NO.	DESCRIPTION	FIRST DAY COVERS SING	FIRST DAY COVERS PL. BLK.	MINT SHEET	PLATE BLOCK	UNUSED F/NH	USED
C101-16	**28¢-44¢, 16 varieties, complete. . . . .**	....	....	....	....	**21.50**	**11.50**

1983

SCOTT NO.	DESCRIPTION	FIRST DAY COVERS SING	FIRST DAY COVERS PL. BLK.	MINT SHEET	PLATE BLOCK	UNUSED F/NH	USED
C101-04	Summer Olympics, 4 varieties, attached . .	3.50	4.50	55.00(50)	6.50	5.75	4.50
C101	28¢ Women's Gymnastics	2.00	....	....	....	1.50	.95
C102	28¢ Hurdles.	2.00	....	....	....	1.50	.95
C103	28¢ Women's Basketball	2.00	....	....	....	1.50	.95
C104	28¢ Soccer	2.00	....	....	....	1.50	.95

C105 C106 C107 C108

SCOTT NO.	DESCRIPTION	FIRST DAY COVERS SING	FIRST DAY COVERS PL. BLK.	MINT SHEET	PLATE BLOCK	UNUSED F/NH	USED
C105-08	Summer Olympics, 4 varieties, attached .	4.50	5.75	60.00(50)	7.25	6.00	4.75
C105	40¢ Shot Put	2.00	....	....	....	1.55	.95
C106	40¢ Men's Gymnastics	2.00	....	....	....	1.55	.95
C107	40¢ Women's Swimming	2.00	....	....	....	1.55	.95
C108	40¢ Weight Lifting . . .	2.00	....	....	....	1.55	.95

C109 C110 C111 C112

SCOTT NO.	DESCRIPTION	FIRST DAY COVERS SING	FIRST DAY COVERS PL. BLK.	MINT SHEET	PLATE BLOCK	UNUSED F/NH	USED
C109-12	Summer Olympics, 4 varieties, attached .	4.00	5.00	76.00(50)	10.00	6.75	5.00
C109	35¢ Fencing.	2.00	....	....	....	1.75	1.25
C110	35¢ Cycling	2.00	....	....	....	1.75	1.25
C111	35¢ Volleyball	2.00	....	....	....	1.75	1.25
C112	35¢ Pole Vault	2.00	....	....	....	1.75	.1.25

C113 C114

C115 C116

1985

SCOTT NO.	DESCRIPTION	FIRST DAY COVERS SING	FIRST DAY COVERS PL. BLK.	MINT SHEET	PLATE BLOCK	UNUSED F/NH	USED
C113	33¢ Alfred Verville . . .	2.00	4.25	48.00(50)	5.25	1.15	.40
C114	39¢ Lawrence and Elmer Sperry	2.00	4.25	59.00(50)	6.75	1.40	.45
C115	44¢ Transpacific	2.00	4.25	63.00(50)	7.25	1.50	.45
C116	44¢ Junipero Serra . .	2.00	4.25	73.00(50)	10.00	1.75	.65

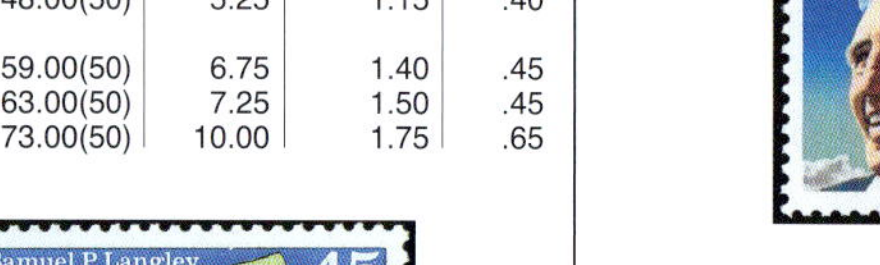

C117

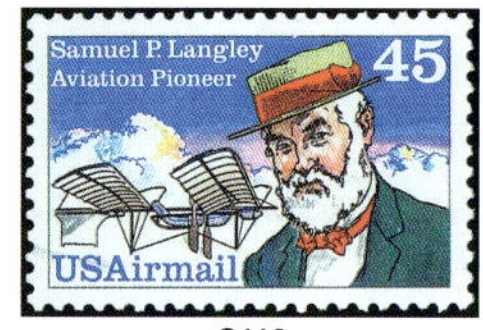

C118

C119

1988

SCOTT NO.	DESCRIPTION	FIRST DAY COVERS SING	FIRST DAY COVERS PL. BLK.	MINT SHEET	PLATE BLOCK	UNUSED F/NH	USED
C117	44¢ New Sweden . . .	2.50	7.50	75.00(50)	10.00	1.65	1.25
C118	45¢ Samuel Langley .	2.00	4.25	67.50(50)	7.00	1.65	.35
C119	36¢ Igor Sikorsky. . . .	2.00	4.25	55.00(50)	6.00	1.40	.60

C120

C121

1989

SCOTT NO.	DESCRIPTION	FIRST DAY COVERS SING	FIRST DAY COVERS PL. BLK.	MINT SHEET	PLATE BLOCK	UNUSED F/NH	USED
C120-25	**6 varieties, complete** .	....	....	....	....	**9.00**	**6.00**
C120	45¢ French Revolution	2.00	4.25	39.00(30)	7.00	1.60	1.10
C121	45¢ Americas Issue (Key Marco Cat)	2.00	4.25	87.50(50)	8.00	1.85	1.00

C122

C123

C124

C125

SCOTT NO.	DESCRIPTION	FIRST DAY COVERS SING	FIRST DAY COVERS PL. BLK.	MINT SHEET	PLATE BLOCK	UNUSED F/NH	USED
C122-25	Futuristic Mail Delivery, 4 varieties, attached .	8.00	10.00	65.00(40)	8.50	6.50	5.25
C122	45¢ Spacecraft	2.00	....	....	....	1.75	1.25
C123	45¢ Air Suspended Hover	2.00	....	....	....	1.75	1.25
C124	45¢ Moon Rover	2.00	....	....	....	1.75	1.25
C125	45¢ Space Shuttle . . .	2.00	....	....	....	1.75	1.25
C126	$1.80 Futuristic Mail Imperf. Souvenir Sheet	6.50	....	....	....	9.00	6.75

C127 C128

1990-93

SCOTT NO.	DESCRIPTION	FIRST DAY COVERS SING	FIRST DAY COVERS PL. BLK.	MINT SHEET	PLATE BLOCK	UNUSED F/NH	USED
C127/C132	**1990-93, 6 varieties complete**	....	....	....	....	**12.00**	**4.50**
C127	45¢ Americas Issue (Island Beach)	2.00	4.25	88.00(50)	10.00	2.00	1.00
C128	50¢ Harriet Quimby . .	2.00	4.25	72.50(50)	8.00	1.80	.55
C128b	50¢ Harriet Quimby, reissue, bullseye perf. (1993) .	....	....	85.00(50)	10.00	2.00	1.35

C129, C132 C130

SCOTT NO.	DESCRIPTION	FIRST DAY COVERS SING	FIRST DAY COVERS PL. BLK.	MINT SHEET	PLATE BLOCK	UNUSED F/NH	USED
C129	40¢ William Piper. . . .	2.00	4.25	65.00(50)	7.50	1.35	.50
C130	50¢ Antarctic Treaty. .	2.00	4.25	73.00(50)	8.00	1.50	.80

C131

SCOTT NO.	DESCRIPTION	FIRST DAY COVERS SING	FIRST DAY COVERS PL. BLK.	MINT SHEET	PLATE BLOCK	UNUSED F/NH	USED
C131	50¢ America (Bering Strait) (1991)	2.00	4.25	85.00(50)	8.00	1.75	.80
C132	40¢ William Piper, reissue, bullseye perf. (1993) .	....	....	330.00(50)	83.00	6.00	1.00

C133

C134 C135

C136

C137

1999-2012

SCOTT NO.	DESCRIPTION	FIRST DAY COVERS SING	FIRST DAY COVERS PL. BLK.	MINT SHEET	PLATE BLOCK	UNUSED F/NH	USED
C133-50	**20 varieties complete**	....	....	**225.00**		**50.00**	**20.00**
C133	48¢ Niagara Falls . . .	2.25	5.50	29.00(20)	8.00	1.75	.55
C134	40¢ Rio Grande	2.10	5.00	24.00(20)	6.00	1.40	.75
C135	60¢ Grand Canyon . .	2.25	5.00	36.00(20)	9.00	2.00	.40
C136	70¢ Nine-Mile Prairie, Nebraska	2.50	6.00	42.00(20)	12.00	2.50	.60
C137	80¢ Mt. McKinley. . . .	2.75	6.50	48.00(20)	13.00	2.75	.70

C138, C138a, C138b

C139

C140

C141

SCOTT NO.	DESCRIPTION	FIRST DAY COVERS SING	PL. BLK.	MINT SHEET	PLATE BLOCK	UNUSED F/NH	USED
C138	60¢ Acadia National Park	2.50	5.00	44.00(20)	10.00	2.50	.50
C138a	60¢ Acadia National Park die cut 11.5 x 11.75 . .	2.75	5.50	50.00(20)	12.00	2.80	.55
C138b	same as above, with "2005" date	2.75	5.50	44.00(20)	11.00	2.40	.50
C139	63¢ Bryce Canyon National Park, self adhesive . .	2.25	6.00	36.00(20)	9.00	2.00	.70
C140	75¢ Great Smoky Mountains National Park, self-adhesive	2.25	6.00	42.00(20)	11.00	2.50	.80
C141	84¢ Yosemite National Park, self-adhesive	2.50	6.50	47.00(20)	12.00	2.75	.80

C142

C143

C144

C145

2007-12

SCOTT NO.	DESCRIPTION	FIRST DAY COVERS SING	PL. BLK.	MINT SHEET	PLATE BLOCK	UNUSED F/NH	USED
C142	69¢ Okefenokee Swamp, self-adhesive	2.50	6.00	37.00(20)	9.00	2.25	.80
C143	90¢ Hagatna Bay, self-adhesive.	2.75	6.50	49.00(20)	12.00	3.00	1.05
C144	72¢ New Hampshire River Scene.	3.75	4.75	34.00(20)	9.00	2.00	1.00
C145	94¢ St. John, US Virgin Islands. . . .	3.75	4.75	47.00(20)	12.00	3.00	1.55

C146

C147

C148

C149

C150

SCOTT NO.	DESCRIPTION	FIRST DAY COVERS SING	PL. BLK.	MINT SHEET	PLATE BLOCK	UNUSED F/NH	USED
C146	79¢ Zion National Park	3.75	....	48.00(20)	12.00	3.00	2.00
C147	98¢ Grand Teton National Park.	3.75	....	48.00(20)	12.00	3.00	1.25
C148	80¢ Voyagers National Park	3.50	....	60.00(20)	16.00	4.00	3.00
C149	85¢ Glaciers National Park, Montana.	3.50	....	100.00(20)	24.00	6.00	3.00
C150	$1.05 Amish Horse & Buggy, Lancaster County, Pennsylvania	4.25	....	60.00(20)	12.00	3.00	1.50

AIR MAIL SPECIAL DELIVERY STAMPS

SCOTT NO.	DESCRIPTION	PLATE BLOCK F/NH	F	AVG	UNUSED F/NH	F	AVG	USED F	AVG

771, CE1, CE2

SCOTT NO.	DESCRIPTION	PLATE BLOCK F/NH	F	AVG	UNUSED F/NH	F	AVG	USED F	AVG
CE1	16¢ dark blue (1934)	25.00	18.00	14.50	1.10	.80	.60	.70	.55
CE2	16¢ red & blue (1936)	14.00	10.00	8.00	.85	.65	.50	.35	.25
CE2	same, center line block	6.00	4.00	2.00	....	....	....	....	....
CE2	same, arrow block of 4	5.00	3.50	2.75	....	....	....	....	....

SPECIAL DELIVERY STAMPS

E1

E2, E3

E4, E5

(E1-E14 for VF Centering–Fine Price + 35%)

SCOTT NO.	DESCRIPTION	UNUSED NH F	AVG	UNUSED OG F	AVG	USED F	AVG
	1885 Inscribed "Secures Immediate Delivery at Special Delivery Office" Perf. 12						
E1	10¢ blue	1000.00	650.00	450.00	300.00	60.00	40.00
	1888 Inscribed "Secures Immediate Delivery at any Post Office"						
E2	10¢ blue	900.00	680.00	450.00	350.00	38.00	22.00
	1893						
E3	10¢ orange	580.00	400.00	250.00	175.00	40.00	25.00
	1894 Same type as preceding issue, but with line under "Ten Cents" Unwatermarked						
E4	10¢ blue	1900.00	1350.00	750.00	450.00	75.00	50.00
	1895 Double Line Watermark						
E5	10¢ blue	400.00	275.00	190.00	120.00	10.00	6.00

E6, E8-11

E7

SCOTT NO.	DESCRIPTION	UNUSED NH F	AVG	UNUSED OG F	AVG	USED F	AVG
	1902						
E6	10¢ ultramarine	675.00	440.00	350.00	225.00	12.00	8.00
	1908						
E7	10¢ green	185.00	120.00	80.00	55.00	50.00	40.00
	1911 Single Line Watermark						
E8	10¢ ultramarine	275.00	175.00	125.00	75.00	12.00	9.00
	1914 Perf. 10						
E9	10¢ ultramarine	500.00	300.00	200.00	130.00	14.00	11.00
	1916 Unwatermarked Perf. 10						
E10	10¢ pale ultra	775.00	500.00	350.00	220.00	50.00	35.00
	1917 Perf. 11						
E11	10¢ ultramarine	60.00	45.00	30.00	20.00	.95	.70
E11	same, plate block of 6	550.00	400.00	325.00	225.00	....	....

SCOTT NO.	DESCRIPTION	PLATE BLOCK F/NH	F	AVG	UNUSED F/NH	F	AVG	USED F	AVG

E12, E15

E14, E19

1922-25 Flat Plate Printing Perf. 11

SCOTT NO.	DESCRIPTION	PLATE BLOCK F/NH	F	AVG	UNUSED F/NH	F	AVG	USED F	AVG
E12	10¢ gray violet	(6) 950.00	700.00	550.00	75.00	50.00	30.00	1.50	1.35
E13	15¢ deep orange (1925)	(6) 800.00	650.00	475.00	85.00	60.00	40.00	2.00	1.25
E14	20¢ black (1925)	(6) 80.00	60.00	40.00	4.75	2.75	1.90	2.50	1.75

SCOTT NO.	DESCRIPTION	FIRST DAY COVERS SING	PL. BLK.	MINT SHEET	PLATE BLOCK	UNUSED F/NH	USED
	1927-51 Rotary Press Printing Perf. 11 x 10½						
E15-19	**10¢-20¢, 5 varieties .**	....	....	....	**50.00**	**9.00**	**3.25**
E15	10¢ gray violet	....	....	80.00(50)	7.00	1.30	.30
E16	15¢ orange (1931)...	....	....	67.00(50)	6.50	1.30	.30
E17	13¢ blue (1944)	9.00	20.00	62.00(50)	5.00	1.20	.30
E18	17¢ orange yellow (1944)	12.00	28.00	245.00(50)	28.00	4.00	2.75
E19	20¢ black (1951)	5.00	12.50	105.00(50)	12.00	1.95	.25

E20

E22

SCOTT NO.	DESCRIPTION	FIRST DAY COVERS SING	PL. BLK.	MINT SHEET	PLATE BLOCK	UNUSED F/NH	USED
	1954-57						
E20	20¢ deep blue	2.50	6.25	32.00(50)	3.50	.70	.20
E21	30¢ lake (1957)	2.50	6.25	43.00(50)	4.50	1.00	.20
	1969-71						
E22	45¢ carmine & violet blue	2.50	6.25	74.00(50)	8.00	1.60	.35
E23	60¢ violet blue & carmine (1971)	2.75	6.75	88.00(50)	9.00	1.85	.20

REGISTRATION STAMP

F1

1911 Registration

SCOTT NO.	DESCRIPTION	UNUSED NH F	AVG	UNUSED OG F	AVG	USED F	AVG
F1	10¢ ultramarine	200.00	135.00	95.00	60.00	12.00	8.00

U.S. CERTIFIED STAMP

FA1

1955 Certified Mail

SCOTT NO.	DESCRIPTION	FIRST DAY COVERS SING	PL. BLK.	MINT SHEET	PLATE BLOCK	UNUSED F/NH	USED
FA1	15¢ red	2.50	6.25	32.00(50)	6.25	.65	.50

J1-J28

J29-J68

1879 Unwatermarked Perf. 12

SCOTT NO.	DESCRIPTION	UNUSED NH F	UNUSED NH AVG	UNUSED OG F	UNUSED OG AVG	USED F	USED AVG
J1	1¢ brown	275.00	165.00	95.00	70.00	17.00	11.00
J2	2¢ brown	1200.00	900.00	450.00	450.00	20.00	14.00
J3	3¢ brown	325.00	270.00	120.00	75.00	7.50	6.00
J4	5¢ brown	1900.00	1300.00	750.00	600.00	80.00	38.00
J5	10¢ brown	2700.00	1800.00	1100.00	800.00	80.00	60.00
J6	30¢ brown	1000.00	700.00	500.00	300.00	70.00	55.00
J7	50¢ brown	1900.00	1400.00	700.00	450.00	80.00	60.00
	1884-89						
J15	1¢ red brown	225.00	165.00	85.00	55.00	8.00	6.50
J16	2¢ red brown	275.00	200.00	100.00	70.00	7.00	5.00
J17	3¢ red brown	2900.00	2300.00	1180.00	875.00	350.00	275.00
J18	5¢ red brown	1600.00	1200.00	750.00	475.00	50.00	36.00
J19	10¢ red brown	1600.00	1450.00	750.00	460.00	40.00	30.00
J20	30¢ red brown	385.00	350.00	275.00	185.00	70.00	60.00
J21	50¢ red brown	4400.00	3000.00	2000.00	1450.00	250.00	185.00
	1891						
J22	1¢ bright claret	100.00	75.00	44.00	30.00	2.25	1.25
J23	2¢ bright claret	110.00	85.00	45.00	34.00	2.25	1.25
J24	3¢ bright claret	225.00	160.00	85.00	65.00	18.00	12.00
J25	5¢ bright claret	350.00	225.00	125.00	80.00	18.00	12.00
J26	10¢ bright claret	600.00	450.00	250.00	180.00	35.00	20.00
J27	30¢ bright claret	2000.00	1600.00	800.00	550.00	300.00	175.00
J28	50¢ bright claret	2100.00	1600.00	800.00	600.00	225.00	150.00
	1894 Unwatermarked Perf. 12 (†)						
J29	1¢ pale vermillion	6500.00	4200.00	2850.00	2250.00	750.00	600.00
J30	2¢ dark vermillion	2250.00	1375.00	900.00	700.00	400.00	255.00
J31	1¢ deep claret	325.00	260.00	90.00	70.00	14.00	12.00
J32	2¢ deep claret	300.00	250.00	75.00	50.00	12.00	9.00
J33	3¢ deep claret	625.00	400.00	225.00	175.00	55.00	40.00
J34	5¢ deep claret	1050.00	825.00	350.00	270.00	60.00	48.00
J35	10¢ deep claret	1200.00	900.00	450.00	300.00	45.00	35.00
J36	30¢ deep claret	1450.00	925.00	650.00	425.00	250.00	150.00
J36b	30¢ pale rose	1300.00	1000.00	600.00	400.00	225.00	125.00
J37	50¢ deep claret	5000.00	3800.00	2250.00	1750.00	850.00	600.00
	1895 Double Line Watermark Perf. 12 (†)						
J38	1¢ deep claret	48.00	40.00	18.00	13.50	1.50	1.00
J39	2¢ deep claret	48.00	40.00	18.00	13.50	1.50	1.00
J40	3¢ deep claret	300.00	250.00	120.00	90.00	4.50	3.00
J41	5¢ deep claret	325.00	275.00	130.00	100.00	4.50	3.00
J42	10¢ deep claret	325.00	275.00	130.00	100.00	7.00	5.50
J43	30¢ deep claret	1900.00	1300.00	800.00	650.00	70.00	60.00
J44	50¢ deep claret	1300.00	900.00	500.00	350.00	55.00	48.00
	1910-12 Single Line Watermark Perf. 12						
J45	1¢ deep claret	135.00	105.00	50.00	40.00	6.00	4.50
J46	2¢ deep claret	125.00	95.00	45.00	35.00	3.00	2.00
J47	3¢ deep claret	1800.00	1500.00	750.00	600.00	60.00	45.00
J48	5¢ deep claret	350.00	250.00	150.00	115.00	15.00	10.00
J49	10¢ deep claret	375.00	225.00	165.00	125.00	25.00	18.00
J50	50¢ deep claret (1912)	3200.00	2300.00	1200.00	900.00	185.00	150.00
	1914 Single Line Watermark Perf. 10						
J52	1¢ carmine lake	275.00	150.00	95.00	65.00	16.00	12.00
J53	2¢ carmine lake	225.00	130.00	75.00	55.00	1.25	.80
J54	3¢ carmine lake	3500.00	2500.00	1200.00	900.00	85.00	60.00
J55	5¢ carmine lake	175.00	135.00	60.00	45.00	7.00	5.00
J56	10¢ carmine lake	250.00	200.00	95.00	75.00	5.00	3.00
J57	30¢ carmine lake	650.00	400.00	300.00	185.00	60.00	40.00
J58	50¢ carmine lake	....	....	18500.00	15500.00	1600.00	1300.00
	1916 Unwatermarked Perf. 10						
J59	1¢ rose	11000.00	7500.00	5000.00	3500.00	750.00	600.00
J60	2¢ rose	800.00	600.00	325.00	250.00	80.00	60.00

SCOTT NO.	DESCRIPTION	PLATE BLOCK (OG) F/NH	PLATE BLOCK (OG) F	PLATE BLOCK (OG) AVG	UNUSED (OG) F/NH	UNUSED (OG) F	UNUSED (OG) AVG	USED F	USED AVG
	1917 Unwatermarked Perf. 11								
J61	1¢ carmine rose . .(6)	85.00	53.00	35.00	11.00	5.00	3.00	.30	.25
J62	2¢ carmine rose . .(6)	85.00	53.00	35.00	11.00	5.00	3.00	.30	.25
J63	3¢ carmine rose . .(6)	170.00	95.00	70.00	45.00	17.00	10.00	.95	.45
J64	5¢ carmine . . . . . .(6)	240.00	150.00	95.00	40.00	16.00	8.00	.95	.45
J65	10¢ carmine rose .(6)	450.00	190.00	145.00	75.00	30.00	18.00	1.25	.85
J66	30¢ carmine rose	....	....	....	300.00	150.00	95.00	2.50	2.00
J67	50¢ carmine rose	....	....	....	425.00	160.00	85.00	1.25	.85
	1925								
J68	1/2¢ dull red . . . . .(6)	20.00	15.00	12.50	2.00	1.25	1.00	.30	.25

J69-J76, J79-J86

J77, J78, J87

J88-J104

1930 Perf. 11

SCOTT NO.	DESCRIPTION	PLATE BLOCK (OG) F/NH	PLATE BLOCK (OG) F	PLATE BLOCK (OG) AVG	UNUSED (OG) F/NH	UNUSED (OG) F	UNUSED (OG) AVG	USED F	USED AVG
J69	1/2¢ carmine . . . .(6)	70.00	55.00	40.00	11.00	6.00	5.00	2.00	1.50
J70	1¢ carmine . . . . . .(6)	80.00	60.00	45.00	7.50	3.50	2.50	.40	.30
J71	2¢ carmine . . . . . .(6)	55.00	60.00	50.00	10.00	6.00	4.00	.40	.25
J72	3¢ carmine . . . . . .(6)	450.00	300.00	250.00	55.00	35.00	25.00	3.00	2.50
J73	5¢ carmine . . . . . .(6)	400.00	300.00	230.00	50.00	22.00	17.00	6.00	4.00
J74	10¢ carmine . . . . .(6)	675.00	300.00	350.00	100.00	75.00	60.00	2.50	1.85
J75	30¢ carmine	....	....	....	350.00	160.00	125.00	4.50	3.75
J76	50¢ carmine	....	....	....	500.00	325.00	250.00	2.50	1.75
J77	$1 scarlet . . . .(6)	325.00	260.00	210.00	75.00	60.00	40.00	.40	.30
J78	$5 scarlet . . . .(6)	350.00	295.00	220.00	95.00	50.00	38.00	.40	.30
	1931 Rotary Press Printing Perf. 11 x 10½								
J79-86	**1/2¢-50¢, 8 varieties, complete**	....	....	....	**30.00**	**24.00**	**15.00**	**1.90**	**1.50**
J79	1/2¢ dull carmine	28.00	20.00	18.00	1.75	1.00	.75	.30	.25
J80	1¢ dull carmine	2.25	1.80	1.25	.35	.30	.25	.30	.25
J81	2¢ dull carmine	2.25	1.80	1.25	.35	.30	.25	.30	.25
J82	3¢ dull carmine	3.10	2.50	1.75	.35	.30	.25	.30	.25
J83	5¢ dull carmine	4.75	3.75	3.00	.40	.35	.25	.30	.25
J84	10¢ dull carmine	9.75	7.50	5.50	1.90	1.25	.40	.30	.25
J85	30¢ dull carmine	60.00	45.00	33.00	12.00	8.00	6.00	.30	.25
J86	50¢ dull carmine	95.00	65.00	50.00	17.00	12.50	10.00	.30	.25
	1956 Rotary Press Printing Perf. 10½ x 11								
J87	$1 scarlet	260.00	210.00	....	50.00	40.00	....	.30	....

SCOTT NO.	DESCRIPTION	MINT SHEET	PLATE BLOCK F/NH	PLATE BLOCK F	UNUSED F/NH	UNUSED F	USED F
	1959						
J88-101	**1/2¢-$5, 14 varieties, complete**	....	....	....	**20.50**	**14.50**	**3.90**
J88	1/2¢ carmine rose & black	400.00(100)	210.00	175.00	1.85	1.50	1.50
J89	1¢ carmine rose & black	9.50(100)	1.25	.75	.30	.25	.25
J90	2¢ carmine rose & black	13.00(100)	1.25	.75	.30	.25	.25
J91	3¢ carmine rose & black	14.00(100)	1.00	.70	.30	.25	.25
J92	4¢ carmine rose & black	20.00(100)	1.25	.85	.30	.25	.25
J93	5¢ carmine rose & black	20.00(100)	1.00	.70	.30	.25	.25
J94	6¢ carmine rose & black	20.00(100)	1.35	.90	.30	.25	.25
J95	7¢ carmine rose & black	32.00(100)	2.25	1.75	.30	.25	.25
J96	8¢ carmine rose & black	32.00(100)	2.25	1.75	.30	.25	.25
J97	10¢ carmine rose & black	32.00(100)	1.80	1.30	.45	.30	.25
J98	30¢ carmine rose & black	97.00(100)	5.25	4.25	1.55	1.00	.25
J99	50¢ carmine rose & black	155.00(100)	7.00	5.75	2.00	1.50	.25
J100	$1 carmine rose & black	310.00(100)	17.00	12.00	3.75	2.75	.25
J101	$5 carmine rose & black	1500.00(100)	72.00	60.00	17.00	13.00	.50
	1978-1985						
J102	11¢ carmine rose & black	37.00(100)	4.00	....	.45	....	.50
J103	13¢ carmine rose & black	42.00(100)	2.95	....	.50	....	.50
J104	17¢ carmine rose & black	116.00(100)	40.00	....	.75	....	.55

OFFICES IN CHINA

SHANGHAI
2¢
CHINA

1919
K1-16: U.S. Postage
498-518 surcharged

SHANGHAI
2 Cts.
CHINA

1922
K17-18: U.S. Postage 498-528B
with local surcharge

SCOTT NO.	DESCRIPTION	UNUSED NH F	UNUSED NH AVG	UNUSED OG F	UNUSED OG AVG	USED F	USED AVG
	1919						
K1	2¢ on 1¢ green	75.00	50.00	35.00	25.00	50.00	40.00
K2	4¢ on 2¢ rose	75.00	50.00	35.00	25.00	50.00	40.00
K3	6¢ on 3¢ violet	160.00	125.00	75.00	50.00	115.00	85.00
K4	8¢ on 4¢ brown	160.00	135.00	75.00	50.00	115.00	85.00
K5	10¢ on 5¢ blue	180.00	145.00	75.00	50.00	115.00	85.00
K6	12¢ on 6¢ red orange	225.00	185.00	100.00	60.00	165.00	111.00
K7	14¢ on 7¢ black	230.00	190.00	90.00	60.00	180.00	120.00
K8	16¢ on 8¢ olive bister	185.00	130.00	75.00	50.00	125.00	90.00
K8a	16¢ on 8¢ olive green	165.00	125.00	75.00	50.00	110.00	95.00
K9	18¢ on 9¢ salmon red	175.00	135.00	70.00	50.00	150.00	100.00
K10	20¢ on 10¢ orange yellow	165.00	125.00	70.00	50.00	125.00	80.00
K11	24¢ on 12¢ brown carmine	225.00	175.00	70.00	50.00	130.00	70.00
K11a	24¢ on 12¢ claret brown	280.00	200.00	115.00	80.00	175.00	110.00
K12	30¢ on 15¢ gray	225.00	160.00	100.00	60.00	200.00	160.00
K13	40¢ on 20¢ deep ultra.	325.00	235.00	150.00	90.00	285.00	200.00
K14	60¢ on 30¢ orange red	300.00	200.00	150.00	90.00	240.00	180.00
K15	$1 on 50¢ light violet	1350.00	950.00	600.00	400.00	850.00	600.00
K16	$2 on $1 violet brown	1200.00	800.00	600.00	400.00	750.00	450.00
	1922 LOCAL ISSUES						
K17	2¢ on 1¢ green	300.00	200.00	140.00	90.00	170.00	125.00
K18	4¢ on 2¢ carmine	300.00	200.00	140.00	90.00	150.00	120.00

OFFICIAL STAMPS

O1-O9, O94, O95

O10-O14

O15-O24, O96-O103

O25-O34, O106, O107

Except for the Post Office Department, portraits for the various denominations are the same as on the regular issues of 1870-73

1873 Printed by the Continental Bank Note Co.
Thin hard paper
(OG + 40%)
(O1-O120 for VF Centering–Fine Price + 50%)

DEPARTMENT OF AGRICULTURE

SCOTT NO.	DESCRIPTION	UNUSED F	UNUSED AVG	USED F	USED AVG
O1	1¢ yellow	225.00	140.00	175.00	130.00
O2	2¢ yellow	200.00	115.00	80.00	50.00
O3	3¢ yellow	180.00	110.00	18.00	13.00
O4	6¢ yellow	220.00	140.00	65.00	45.00
O5	10¢ yellow	440.00	250.00	175.00	130.00
O6	12¢ yellow	375.00	225.00	220.00	145.00
O7	15¢ yellow	345.00	240.00	200.00	160.00
O8	24¢ yellow	345.00	240.00	190.00	125.00
O9	30¢ yellow	475.00	325.00	250.00	190.00

EXECUTIVE DEPARTMENT

SCOTT NO.	DESCRIPTION	UNUSED F	UNUSED AVG	USED F	USED AVG
O10	1¢ carmine	750.00	500.00	410.00	280.00
O11	2¢ carmine	490.00	410.00	225.00	155.00
O12	3¢ carmine	650.00	475.00	225.00	165.00
O13	6¢ carmine	800.00	675.00	450.00	350.00
O14	10¢ carmine	1100.00	800.00	700.00	500.00

DEPARTMENT OF THE INTERIOR

SCOTT NO.	DESCRIPTION	UNUSED F	UNUSED AVG	USED F	USED AVG
O15	1¢ vermillion	65.00	50.00	11.00	8.50
O16	2¢ vermillion	65.00	50.00	13.00	11.00
O17	3¢ vermillion	70.00	55.00	7.00	5.75
O18	6¢ vermillion	65.00	50.00	11.00	9.00
O19	10¢ vermillion	65.00	50.00	22.00	18.00
O20	12¢ vermillion	80.00	60.00	13.00	10.00
O21	15¢ vermillion	180.00	140.00	26.00	22.00
O22	24¢ vermillion	160.00	130.00	21.00	18.00
O23	30¢ vermillion	240.00	200.00	21.00	17.00
O24	90¢ vermillion	290.00	250.00	48.00	38.00

DEPARTMENT OF JUSTICE

SCOTT NO.	DESCRIPTION	UNUSED F	UNUSED AVG	USED F	USED AVG
O25	1¢ purple	230.00	210.00	100.00	85.00
O26	2¢ purple	280.00	240.00	110.00	95.00
O27	3¢ purple	290.00	240.00	38.00	24.00
O28	6¢ purple	280.00	240.00	45.00	36.00
O29	10¢ purple	290.00	240.00	90.00	70.00
O30	12¢ purple	240.00	195.00	70.00	60.00
O31	15¢ purple	420.00	360.00	185.00	165.00
O32	24¢ purple	1150.00	920.00	400.00	355.00
O33	30¢ purple	1200.00	900.00	340.00	250.00
O34	90¢ purple	1800.00	1400.00	800.00	700.00

O35-O45

O47-O56, O108

O57-O67

O68-O71

NAVY DEPARTMENT
(OG + 30%)

SCOTT NO.	DESCRIPTION	UNUSED F	UNUSED AVG	USED F	USED AVG
O35	1¢ ultramarine	150.00	120.00	55.00	46.00
O36	2¢ ultramarine	155.00	125.00	30.00	26.00
O37	3¢ ultramarine	160.00	130.00	14.00	10.00
O38	6¢ ultramarine	175.00	140.00	23.00	14.00
O39	7¢ ultramarine	600.00	500.00	240.00	185.00
O40	10¢ ultramarine	200.00	160.00	38.00	25.00
O41	12¢ ultramarine	215.00	170.00	38.00	25.00
O42	15¢ ultramarine	350.00	310.00	60.00	35.00
O43	24¢ ultramarine	400.00	350.00	64.00	38.00
O44	30¢ ultramarine	300.00	280.00	45.00	26.00
O45	90¢ ultramarine	900.00	800.00	375.00	320.00

OFFICIAL STAMPS: From 1873 to 1879, Congress authorized the use of Official Stamps to prepay postage on government mail. Separate issues were produced for each department so that mailing costs could be assigned to that department's budget. Penalty envelopes replaced Official Stamps on May 1, 1879.

O72-O82, O109-O113

O83-O93, O1140-O120

POST OFFICE DEPARTMENT

SCOTT NO.	DESCRIPTION	UNUSED F	UNUSED AVG	USED F	USED AVG
O47	1¢ black	22.00	17.00	12.00	8.00
O48	2¢ black	25.00	18.00	10.00	7.00
O49	3¢ black	10.00	7.00	2.50	1.00
O50	6¢ black	26.00	20.00	7.00	5.00
O51	10¢ black	120.00	85.00	52.00	40.00
O52	12¢ black	115.00	95.00	12.00	8.00
O53	15¢ black	125.00	90.00	19.00	12.00
O54	24¢ black	175.00	130.00	23.00	15.00
O55	30¢ black	185.00	135.00	24.00	16.00
O56	90¢ black	210.00	130.00	24.00	16.00

DEPARTMENT OF STATE

SCOTT NO.	DESCRIPTION	UNUSED F	UNUSED AVG	USED F	USED AVG
O57	1¢ dark green	240.00	150.00	70.00	55.00
O58	2¢ dark green	280.00	225.00	95.00	75.00
O59	3¢ bright green	195.00	140.00	24.00	18.00
O60	6¢ bright green	195.00	145.00	30.00	20.00
O61	7¢ dark green	300.00	185.00	60.00	45.00
O62	10¢ dark green	210.00	135.00	55.00	40.00
O63	12¢ dark green	270.00	185.00	110.00	75.00
O64	15¢ dark green	285.00	225.00	95.00	78.00
O65	24¢ dark green	485.00	450.00	230.00	175.00
O66	30¢ dark green	450.00	390.00	185.00	145.00
O67	90¢ dark green	900.00	700.00	300.00	250.00
O68	$2 green & black	1450.00	1100.00	2000.00	1400.00
O69	$5 green & black	6400.00	5000.00	10000.00	7000.00
O70	$10 green & black	4450.00	3600.00	6000.00	5500.00
O71	$20 green & black	4800.00	4200.00	4450.00	2900.00

TREASURY DEPARTMENT
(OG + 30%)

SCOTT NO.	DESCRIPTION	UNUSED F	UNUSED AVG	USED F	USED AVG
O72	1¢ brown	120.00	90.00	10.00	8.00
O73	2¢ brown	125.00	95.00	8.50	7.00
O74	3¢ brown	110.00	90.00	2.50	1.25
O75	6¢ brown	120.00	90.00	4.50	3.50
O76	7¢ brown	230.00	190.00	37.00	30.00
O77	10¢ brown	230.00	190.00	12.00	8.00
O78	12¢ brown	260.00	200.00	9.00	7.00
O79	15¢ brown	270.00	220.00	12.00	8.00
O80	24¢ brown	575.00	450.00	90.00	70.00
O81	30¢ brown	375.00	275.00	12.00	8.00
O82	90¢ brown	425.00	330.00	15.00	12.00

WAR DEPARTMENT

SCOTT NO.	DESCRIPTION	UNUSED F	UNUSED AVG	USED F	USED AVG
O83	1¢ rose	230.00	180.00	14.00	10.00
O84	2¢ rose	230.00	180.00	14.00	10.00
O85	3¢ rose	230.00	180.00	5.00	3.50
O86	6¢ rose	600.00	475.00	11.00	9.00
O87	7¢ rose	160.00	135.00	85.00	65.00
O88	10¢ rose	140.00	110.00	24.00	18.00
O89	12¢ rose	250.00	220.00	13.00	10.00
O90	15¢ rose	85.00	70.00	16.00	13.00
O91	24¢ rose	85.00	70.00	13.00	11.00
O92	30¢ rose	125.00	110.00	13.00	11.00
O93	90¢ rose	195.00	165.00	55.00	45.00

1879 Printed by American Bank Note Co.
Soft Porous Paper

DEPARTMENT OF AGRICULTURE

SCOTT NO.	DESCRIPTION	UNUSED F	UNUSED AVG	USED F	USED AVG
O94	1¢ yellow	6000.00	4900.00	....	....
O95	3¢ yellow	525.00	450.00	120.00	75.00

DEPARTMENT OF INTERIOR

SCOTT NO.	DESCRIPTION	UNUSED F	UNUSED AVG	USED F	USED AVG
O96	1¢ vermillion	275.00	230.00	320.00	240.00
O97	2¢ vermillion	10.00	8.00	3.50	2.50
O98	3¢ vermillion	9.00	7.00	3.25	2.25
O99	6¢ vermillion	11.00	8.00	13.00	10.00
O100	10¢ vermillion	95.00	80.00	80.00	70.00
O101	12¢ vermillion	225.00	185.00	120.00	100.00
O102	15¢ vermillion	375.00	210.00	400.00	290.00
O103	24¢ vermillion	4200.00	3500.00	6200.00	....

DEPARTMENT OF JUSTICE

SCOTT NO.	DESCRIPTION	UNUSED F	UNUSED AVG	USED F	USED AVG
O106	3¢ bluish purple	175.00	140.00	110.00	85.00
O107	6¢ bluish purple	450.00	385.00	260.00	195.00

POST OFFICE DEPARTMENT

SCOTT NO.	DESCRIPTION	UNUSED F	UNUSED AVG	USED F	USED AVG
O108	3¢ black	32.00	27.00	9.00	6.00

TREASURY DEPARTMENT

SCOTT NO.	DESCRIPTION	UNUSED F	UNUSED AVG	USED F	USED AVG
O109	3¢ brown	80.00	60.00	11.00	8.75
O110	6¢ brown	180.00	130.00	55.00	48.00
O111	10¢ brown	250.00	215.00	75.00	45.00
O112	30¢ brown	2400.00	2000.00	440.00	350.00
O113	90¢ brown	4600.00	3400.00	600.00	375.00

SCOTT NO.	DESCRIPTION	UNUSED F	UNUSED AVG	USED F	USED AVG
	WAR DEPARTMENT				
O114	1¢ rose red	8.00	5.00	4.50	3.75
O115	2¢ rose red	13.00	10.00	4.50	3.75
O116	3¢ rose red	13.00	10.00	2.25	1.50
O117	6¢ rose red	12.00	9.00	3.25	2.50
O118	10¢ rose red	64.00	44.00	45.00	30.00
O119	12¢ rose red	60.00	40.00	13.00	8.00
O120	30¢ rose red	190.00	120.00	86.00	60.00

1910-11

SCOTT NO.	DESCRIPTION	UNUSED NH F	UNUSED NH AVG	UNUSED OG F	UNUSED OG AVG	USED F	USED AVG
	Double Line Watermark						
O121	2¢ black	40.00	25.00	20.00	11.00	2.50	1.75
O122	50¢ dark green	380.00	250.00	175.00	135.00	65.00	48.00
O123	$1 ultramarine	460.00	350.00	225.00	175.00	17.00	12.00
	Single Line Watermark						
O124	1¢ dark violet	25.00	15.00	10.00	7.00	2.25	1.75
O125	2¢ black	130.00	75.00	60.00	35.00	7.50	5.00
O126	10¢ carmine	50.00	30.00	20.00	15.00	2.25	1.75

O127-O136

O138-O143

SCOTT NO.	DESCRIPTION	FIRST DAY COVERS SING	FIRST DAY COVERS PL. BLK.	MINT SHEET	PLATE BLOCK	UNUSED	USED
	1983-89						
O127	1¢ Great Seal	2.00	4.25	11.00(100)	1.20	.25	.25
O128	4¢ Great Seal	2.00	4.25	14.00(100)	1.20	.25	.25
O129	13¢ Great Seal	2.00	4.25	40.00(100)	2.50	.50	2.25
O129A	14¢ Great Seal (1985)	2.00	....	40.00(100)	....	.50	.55
O130	17¢ Great Seal	2.00	4.25	60.00(100)	3.50	.60	.50
O132	$1 Great Seal	5.75	14.25	300.00(100)	14.00	4.00	2.25
O133	$5 Great Seal	16.50	41.25	1100.00(100)	65.00	15.00	10.00
			PLATE# STRIP 3		PLATE# STRIP 3		
O135	20¢ Great Seal, coil	2.00	30.00	....	19.50	2.00	2.25
O136	22¢ Seal, coil (1985)	2.00	....	....	....	1.60	2.50
	1985 Non-Denominated Issues						
O138	(14¢) Great Seal, postcard D	2.00	30.00	640.00(100)	45.00	5.50	12.00
O138A	15¢ Great Seal, coil (1988)	2.00	....	....	....	.85	1.25
O138B	20¢ Great Seal, coil (1988)	2.00	....	....	....	.90	.75
			PLATE# STRIP 3		PLATE# STRIP 3		
O139	(22¢) Great Seal "D" coil (1985)	2.00	80.00	....	60.00	5.50	11.00
O140	(25¢) Great Seal "E" coil (1988)	2.00	....	....	....	1.30	2.25
O141	25¢ Great Seal, coil (1988)	2.00	....	....	....	1.25	.90
O143	1¢ Great Seal (1989)	2.00	....	10.00(100)	....	.25	.25

O144

O145

O146

O146A

O147

O148

1991-94

SCOTT NO.	DESCRIPTION	FIRST DAY COVERS SING	FIRST DAY COVERS PL. BLK.	MINT SHEET	PLATE BLOCK	UNUSED	USED
O144	(29¢) Great Seal "F" coil	2.00	....	....	....	1.75	1.10
O145	29¢ Great Seal, coil	2.00	....	....	....	1.25	.70
O146	4¢ Great Seal	2.00	....	20.00(100)	....	.40	.45
O146A	10¢ Great Seal	2.00	....	35.00(100)	....	.65	.50
O147	19¢ Great Seal	2.00	....	65.00(100)	....	.70	.95
O148	23¢ Great Seal	2.00	....	80.00(100)	....	1.10	1.10

O151

O152

O153

O154

O155 O156

O157, O158, O159, O160, O162

O161, O163

SCOTT NO.	DESCRIPTION	FIRST DAY COVERS SING	FIRST DAY COVERS PL. BLK.	MINT SHEET	PLATE BLOCK	UNUSED	USED
	1993-95						
O151	$1 Great Seal	6.00	....	600.00(100)	....	6.00	4.00
O152	(32¢) Great Seal "G" coil	2.75	....	....	....	1.00	1.25
O153	32¢ Official Mail	1.95	....	....	....	3.25	2.00
O154	1¢ Official Mail	1.95	....	10.00(100)	....	.25	.35
O155	20¢ Official Mail	1.95	....	70.00(100)	....	.90	1.00
O156	23¢ Official Mail	1.95	....	90.00(100)	....	1.00	1.10
	1999-2009						
O157	33¢ Great Seal, coil	1.95	....	....	....	2.50	1.75
O158	34¢ Great Seal, coil	1.95	....	....	....	2.60	1.50
O159	37¢ Great Seal, coil	1.95	....	....	....	1.40	1.10
....	same, pl# strip of 5	....	....	....	....	13.00	....
O160	39¢ Great Seal, coil	1.95	....	....	....	1.25	1.00
....	same, pl# strip of 5	....	....	....	....	13.00	....
O161	$1 Great Seal	2.75	....	45.00(20)	9.00	2.25	1.25
O162	41¢ Great Seal, water-activated, coil	2.25	....	....	....	1.35	.90
....	same, pl# strip of 5	....	....	....	....	15.00	....
O163	1¢ Official Stamp, s/a die cut 11.5x10.75	3.75	....	7.00(20)	....	.25	.25

PARCEL POST STAMPS

Q1-Q12 Various Designs

SPECIAL HANDLING STAMPS

QE1-QE4

PARCEL POST DUE STAMPS

JQ1-JQ5

(Q1-QE4a for VF Centering–Fine Price + 40%)

SCOTT NO.	DESCRIPTION	UNUSED NH F	UNUSED NH AVG	UNUSED OG F	UNUSED OG AVG	USED F	USED AVG
	1912-13 Parcel Post–All Printed in Carmine Rose						
Q1	1¢ Post Office Clerk	15.00	10.00	7.00	5.00	2.00	1.50
Q2	2¢ City Carrier	20.00	12.00	10.00	7.00	1.50	1.20
Q3	3¢ Railway Clerk	45.00	30.00	20.00	15.00	7.00	5.50
Q4	4¢ Rural Carrier	115.00	85.00	50.00	30.00	4.00	2.85
Q5	5¢ Mail Train	100.00	70.00	50.00	40.00	3.00	2.50
Q6	10¢ Steamship	170.00	120.00	80.00	50.00	4.00	3.00
Q7	15¢ Auto Service	185.00	135.00	80.00	55.00	16.00	13.00
Q8	20¢ Airplane	400.00	200.00	200.00	125.00	32.00	28.00
Q9	25¢ Manufacturing	200.00	120.00	75.00	55.00	9.00	7.00
Q10	50¢ Dairying	800.00	500.00	350.00	220.00	52.00	39.00
Q11	75¢ Harvesting	270.00	160.00	120.00	70.00	42.00	36.00
Q12	$1 Fruit Growing	600.00	550.00	250.00	200.00	48.00	38.00
	1912 Parcel Post Due						
JQ1	1¢ dark green	30.00	20.00	12.00	8.00	5.00	4.00
JQ2	2¢ dark green	250.00	150.00	100.00	65.00	18.00	15.00
JQ3	5¢ dark green	45.00	30.00	20.00	12.00	6.00	5.00
JQ4	10¢ dark green	450.00	300.00	200.00	130.00	50.00	44.00
JQ5	25¢ dark green	300.00	200.00	120.00	80.00	6.00	5.00
	1925-29 Special Handling						
QE1	10¢ yellow green	5.00	3.75	3.00	2.50	1.50	1.20
QE2	15¢ yellow green	5.50	40.00	3.50	2.25	2.00	1.20
QE3	20¢ yellow green	8.50	6.00	5.00	4.00	1.95	1.35
QE4	25¢ deep green	50.00	30.00	21.00	16.00	8.00	5.00
QE4a	25¢ yellow green	50.00	40.00	30.00	19.00	18.00	14.00

POSTAL NOTE STAMPS

PN1-P18

All values printed in black

SCOTT NO.	DESCRIPTION	UNUSED F/NH	UNUSED F/OG	USED F
PN1-18	1¢-90¢, 18 varieties, complete	42.00	35.00	5.00

ENVELOPES

U1-U10
Washington

U19-U24
Franklin

U26, U27
Washington

1853-55

SCOTT NO.	DESCRIPTION	UNUSED ENTIRE	UNUSED CUT SQ.	USED CUT SQ.
U1	3¢ red on white, die 1	1650.00	400.00	38.00
U2	3¢ red on buff, die 1	875.00	95.00	35.00
U3	3¢ red on white, die 2	3800.00	1000.00	52.00
U4	3¢ red on buff, die 2	3275.00	500.00	45.00
U5	3¢ red on white, die 3	26000.00	6000.00	600.00
U6	3¢ red on buff, die 3	......	5200.00	105.00
U7	3¢ red on white, die 4	......	5500.00	160.00
U8	3¢ red on buff, die 4	......	8500.00	485.00
U9	3¢ red on white, die 5	150.00	45.00	45.00
U10	3¢ red on buff, die 5	80.00	25.00	25.00
U11	6¢ red on white	400.00	325.00	100.00
U12	6¢ red on buff	365.00	150.00	100.00
U13	6¢ green on white	600.00	275.00	165.00
U14	6¢ green on buff	400.00	225.00	130.00
U15	10¢ green on white, die 1	750.00	500.00	110.00
U16	10¢ green on buff, die 1	475.00	180.00	100.00
U17	10¢ green on white, die 2	725.00	400.00	150.00
U18	10¢ green on buff, die 2	650.00	375.00	110.00

1860-61

SCOTT NO.	DESCRIPTION	UNUSED ENTIRE	UNUSED CUT SQ.	USED CUT SQ.
U19	1¢ blue on buff, die 1	90.00	35.00	15.50
W20	1¢ blue on buff, die 1	130.00	70.00	55.00
W21	1¢ blue on manila, die 1	135.00	65.00	45.00
W22	1¢ blue on orange, die 1	6500.00	3200.00	......
U23	1¢ blue on orange, die 2	850.00	625.00	350.00
U24	1¢ blue on buff, die 3	725.00	365.00	110.00
U26	3¢ red on white	60.00	30.00	18.00
U27	3¢ red on buff	50.00	25.00	15.00
U28	3¢ & 1¢ red & blue on white	525.00	260.00	240.00
U29	3¢ & 1¢ red & blue on buff	525.00	260.00	260.00
U30	6¢ red on white	3500.00	2200.00	1750.00
U31	6¢ red on buff	5500.00	3700.00	1600.00
U32	10¢ green on white	10000.00	1400.00	460.00
U33	10¢ green on buff	3500.00	1500.00	420.00

U34-U37

U40-U41

Washington

1861

SCOTT NO.	DESCRIPTION	UNUSED ENTIRE	UNUSED CUT SQ.	USED CUT SQ.
U34	3¢ pink on white	65.00	30.00	6.00
U35	3¢ pink on buff	65.00	35.00	6.50
U36	3¢ pink on blue (letter sheet)	250.00	75.00	75.00
U37	3¢ pink on orange	4500.00	3000.00	......
U38	6¢ pink on white	220.00	110.00	85.00
U39	6¢ pink on buff	225.00	65.00	65.00
U40	10¢ yellow green on white	80.00	45.00	35.00
U41	10¢ yellow green on buff	80.00	45.00	35.00
U42	12¢ brown & red on buff	480.00	185.00	185.00
U43	20¢ blue & red on buff	460.00	260.00	225.00
U44	24¢ green & red on buff	640.00	220.00	220.00
U45	40¢ red & black on buff	750.00	325.00	425.00

U46-U49

U50-W57

Jackson

1863-64

SCOTT NO.	DESCRIPTION	UNUSED ENTIRE	UNUSED CUT SQ.	USED CUT SQ.
U46	2¢ black on buff, die 1	85.00	55.00	25.00
W47	2¢ black on dark manila, die 1	125.00	110.00	70.00
U48	2¢ black on buff, die 2	4800.00	2500.00	......
U49	2¢ black on orange, die 2	4200.00	2000.00	......
U50	2¢ black on buff, die 3	45.00	20.00	12.00
W51	2¢ black on buff, die 3	700.00	460.00	280.00
U52	2¢ black on orange, die 3	40.00	23.00	12.00
W53	2¢ black on dark manila, die 3	180.00	50.00	42.00
U54	2¢ black on buff, die 4	40.00	20.00	10.00
W55	2¢ black on buff, die 4	170.00	100.00	70.00
U56	2¢ black on orange, die 4	38.00	25.00	12.00
W57	2¢ black on light manila, die 4	40.00	25.00	15.00

U58-1

U66-U67

Washington

1864-65

SCOTT NO.	DESCRIPTION	UNUSED ENTIRE	UNUSED CUT SQ.	USED CUT SQ.
U58	3¢ pink on white	22.00	12.00	1.80
U59	3¢ pink on buff	22.00	12.00	3.20
U60	3¢ brown on white	140.00	70.00	40.00
U61	3¢ brown on buff	120.00	50.00	30.00
U62	6¢ pink on white	190.00	110.00	30.00
U63	6¢ pink on buff	120.00	48.00	30.00
U64	6¢ purple on white	120.00	58.00	28.00
U65	6¢ purple on buff	75.00	50.00	22.00
U66	9¢ lemon on buff	600.00	400.00	255.00
U67	9¢ orange on buff	220.00	130.00	95.00
U68	12¢ brown on buff	620.00	300.00	280.00
U69	12¢ red brown on buff	185.00	130.00	60.00
U70	18¢ red on buff	185.00	90.00	98.00
U71	24¢ blue on buff	230.00	90.00	98.00
U72	30¢ green on buff	225.00	120.00	85.00
U73	40¢ rose on buff	365.00	110.00	260.00

U74-W77, U108-U121
Franklin

U78-W81, U122-W158
Jackson

U82-U84, U159-U169
Washington

U172-U180
Taylor

U85-U87, U181-U184
Lincoln

U88, U185, U186
Stanton

U89-U92, U187-U194
Jefferson

U93-U95, U195-U197
Clay

U96-U98, U198-U200
Webster

U99-U101, U201-U203
Scott

U102-U104, U204-U210, U336-U341
Hamilton

U105-U107, U211-U217, U342-U347
Perry

NOTE: For details on die or silmilar appearing varieties of envelopes, please refer to the Scott Specialized Catalogue.

SCOTT NO.	DESCRIPTION	UNUSED ENTIRE	UNUSED CUT SQ.	USED CUT SQ.
	1870-71 REAY ISSUE			
U74	1¢ blue on white	97.00	60.00	34.00
U74a	1¢ ultramarine on white	150.00	75.00	38.00
U75	1¢ blue on amber	72.00	46.00	30.00
U75a	1¢ ultramarine on amber	105.00	72.00	31.00
U76	1¢ blue on orange	42.00	23.00	16.00
W77	1¢ blue on manila	95.00	53.00	38.00
U78	2¢ brown on white	77.00	48.00	18.00
U79	2¢ brown on amber	46.00	26.00	12.00
U80	2¢ brown on orange	21.00	14.00	7.00
W81	2¢ brown on manila	66.00	32.00	23.00
U82	3¢ green on white	22.00	10.00	1.25
U83	3¢ green on amber	23.00	9.00	2.25
U84	3¢ green on cream	23.00	12.00	5.00
U85	6¢ dark red on white	77.00	42.00	22.00
U86	6¢ dark red on amber	92.00	48.00	22.00
U87	6¢ dark red on cream	96.00	48.00	26.00
U88	7¢ vermillon on amber	96.00	68.00	200.00
U89	10¢ olive black on white	1400.00	1000.00	925.00
U90	10¢ olive black on amber	1400.00	1000.00	925.00
U91	10¢ brown on white	167.00	105.00	74.00
U92	10¢ brown on amber	178.00	115.00	54.00
U93	12¢ plum on white	280.00	142.00	84.00
U94	12¢ plum on amber	263.00	145.00	120.00
U95	12¢ plum on cream	405.00	280.00	260.00
U96	15¢ red orange on white	215.00	92.00	90.00
U97	15¢ red orange on amber	426.00	230.00	310.00
U98	15¢ red orange on cream	455.00	385.00	380.00
U99	24¢ purple on white	225.00	155.00	155.00
U100	24¢ purple on amber	400.00	240.00	350.00
U101	24¢ purple on cream	525.00	330.00	575.00
U102	30¢ black on white	340.00	115.00	120.00
U103	30¢ black on amber	710.00	285.00	500.00
U104	30¢ black on cream	425.00	260.00	525.00
U105	90¢ carmine on white	275.00	185.00	375.00
U106	90¢ carmine on amber	910.00	355.00	975.00
U107	90¢ carmine on cream	625.00	300.00	2550.00
	1874-86 PLIMPTON ISSUE			
U108	1¢ dark blue on white, die 1	320.00	248.00	72.00
U109	1¢ dark blue on amber, die 1	245.00	215.00	78.00
U110	1¢ dark blue on cream, die 1	......	1800.00	......
U111	1¢ dark blue on orange, die 1	46.00	31.00	18.00
U111a	1¢ light blue on orange, die 1	46.00	31.00	18.00
W112	1¢ dark blue on manila, die 1	155.00	87.00	45.00
U113	1¢ light blue on white, die 2	3.25	2.50	1.25
U113a	1¢ dark blue on white, die 2	30.00	10.00	8.00
U114	1¢ light blue on amber, die 2	9.00	5.00	4.50
U115	1¢ blue on cream, die 2	12.50	6.00	5.00
U116	1¢ light blue on orange, die 2	1.40	.85	.50
U116a	1¢ dark blue on orange, die 2	17.00	10.00	2.75
U117	1¢ light blue on blue, die 2	19.00	10.00	5.50
U118	1¢ light blue on fawn, die 2	18.00	10.00	5.50
U119	1¢ light blue on manila, die 2	22.00	10.00	3.60
W120	1¢ light blue on manila, die 2	3.50	2.25	1.20
W120a	1¢ dark blue on manila, die 2	17.00	9.50	8.00
U121	1¢ blue on amber manila, die 2	33.00	22.00	11.00
U122	2¢ brown on white, die 1	200.00	160.00	63.00
U123	2¢ brown on amber, die 1	152.00	82.00	48.00
U124	2¢ brown on cream, die 1	......	1275.00	......
W126	2¢ brown on manila, die 1	330.00	180.00	88.00
W127	2¢ vermillon on manila, die 1	4900.00	3300.00	260.00
U128	2¢ brown on white, die 2	138.00	72.00	40.00
U129	2¢ brown on amber, die 2	161.00	110.00	48.00
W131	2¢ brown on manila, die 2	38.00	23.00	17.50
U132	2¢ brown on white, die 3	148.00	90.00	30.00
U133	2¢ brown on amber, die 3	655.00	485.00	85.00
U134	2¢ brown on white, die 4	2275.00	1500.00	165.00
U135	2¢ brown on amber, die 4	748.00	550.00	130.00
U136	2¢ brown on orange, die 4	115.00	75.00	30.00
W137	2¢ brown on manila, die 4	148.00	90.00	42.00
U139	2¢ brown on white, die 5	102.00	77.00	38.00
U140	2¢ brown on amber, die 5	172.00	115.00	64.00
W141	2¢ brown on manila, die 5	58.00	50.00	28.00
U142	2¢ vermillon on white, die 5	15.00	11.00	5.75
U143	2¢ vermillon on amber, die 5	16.00	11.00	5.75
U144	2¢ vermillon on cream, die 5	32.00	27.00	8.00
U146	2¢ vermillon on blue, die 5	235.00	155.00	42.00
U147	2¢ vermillon on fawn, die 5	18.00	12.00	5.50
W148	2¢ vermillon on manila, die 5	11.00	5.00	4.50
U149	2¢ vermillon on white, die 6	115.00	77.00	35.00
U150	2¢ vermillon on amber, die 6	85.00	52.00	18.00
U151	2¢ vermillon on blue, die 6	22.00	15.00	11.00
U152	2¢ vermillon on fawn, die 6	22.00	16.00	5.00
U153	2¢ vermillon on white, die 7	128.00	92.00	32.00
U154	2¢ vermillon on amber, die 7	475.00	455.00	95.00
W155	2¢ vermillon on manila, die 7	56.00	25.00	12.00
U156	2¢ vermillon on white, die 8	3800.00	1800.00	180.00
W158	2¢ vermillon on manila,die 8	200.00	120.00	65.00
U159	3¢ green on white, die 1	65.00	45.00	12.00
U160	3¢ green on amber, die 1	82.00	45.00	12.00
U161	3¢ green on cream, die 1	85.00	52.00	16.00
U163	3¢ green on white, die 2	5.50	1.75	.40
U164	3¢ green on amber, die 2	5.50	1.75	.75
U165	3¢ green on cream, die 2	22.00	12.00	7.00
U166	3¢ green on blue,die 2	20.00	12.00	7.00
U167	3¢ green on fawn, die 2	11.00	6.00	4.00
U168	3¢ green on white, die 3	5100.00	1600.00	95.00
U169	3¢ green on amber, die 3	870.00	570.00	130.00
U172	5¢ blue on white, die 1	27.00	18.00	12.00
U173	5¢ blue on amber, die 1	27.00	18.00	13.00
U174	5¢ blue on cream, die 1	220.00	148.00	49.00
U175	5¢ blue on blue, die 1	77.00	46.00	20.00
U176	5¢ blue on fawn, die 1	310.00	177.00	72.00
U177	5¢ blue on white, die 2	27.00	15.00	11.00
U178	5¢ blue on amber, die 2	27.00	15.00	11.00
U179	5¢ blue on blue, die 2	66.00	35.00	14.00
U180	5¢ blue on fawn, die 2	250.00	150.00	60.00
U181	6¢ red on white	26.00	16.00	7.00
U182	6¢ red on amber	29.00	16.00	7.00
U183	6¢ red on cream	95.00	60.00	18.00
U184	6¢ red on fawn	37.50	25.00	14.00
U185	7¢ vermilion on white	......	2000.00	
U186	7¢ vermilion on amber	235.00	185.00	77.00
U187	10¢ brown on white,die 1	74.00	50.00	25.00
U188	10¢ brown on amber, die 1	198.00	100.00	38.00
U189	10¢ chocolate on white, die 2	16.00	9.00	4.50
U190	10¢ chocolate on amber, die 2	18.00	10.00	7.75
U191	10¢ brown on buff, die 2	26.00	21.00	9.00
U192	10¢ brown on blue, die 2	28.00	23.00	9.00
U193	10¢ brown on manila, die 2	31.00	22.00	11.00
U194	10¢ brown/amber manila, die 2	34.00	28.00	10.00
U195	12¢ plum on white	700.00	375.00	110.00
U196	12¢ plum on amber	375.00	300.00	195.00
U197	12¢ plum on cream	950.00	240.00	185.00
U198	15¢ orange on white	115.00	62.00	42.00
U199	15¢ orange on amber	345.00	200.00	120.00
U200	15¢ orange on cream	975.00	675.00	370.00
U201	24¢ purple on white	275.00	215.00	180.00
U202	24¢ purple on amber	275.00	200.00	130.00
U203	24¢ purple on cream	800.00	200.00	130.00
U204	30¢ black on white	95.00	68.00	29.00
U205	30¢ black on amber	165.00	90.00	68.00
U206	30¢ black on cream	825.00	410.00	380.00
U207	30¢ black on oriental buff	200.00	130.00	85.00
U208	30¢ black on blue	200.00	120.00	85.00
U209	30¢ black on manila	200.00	220.00	85.00
U210	30¢ black on amber manila	200.00	205.00	120.00
U211	90¢ carmine on white	185.00	130.00	88.00
U212	90¢ carmine on amber	320.00	230.00	310.00
U213	90¢ carmine on cream	3500.00	1800.00	
U214	90¢ carmine on oriental buff	370.00	220.00	280.00
U215	90¢ carmine on blue	295.00	210.00	260.00
U216	90¢ carmine on manila	280.00	180.00	280.00
U217	90¢ carmine on amber manila	325.00	165.00	220.00

U218-U221, U582
Pony Express Rider and Train

U222-U226
Garfield

Die 1. Single thick line under "POSTAGE" Die 2. Two thin lines under "POSTAGE"

SCOTT NO.	DESCRIPTION	UNUSED ENTIRE	UNUSED CUT SQ.	USED CUT SQ.
	1876 CENTENNIAL ISSUE			
U218	3¢ red on white, die 1	80.00	55.00	30.00
U219	3¢ green on white, die 1	78.00	50.00	19.00
U221	3¢ green on white, die 2	105.00	58.00	27.00
	1882-86			
U222	5¢ brown on white	14.00	6.00	3.20
U223	5¢ brown on amber	14.00	6.00	3.75
U224	5¢ brown on oriental buff	220.00	150.00	75.00
U225	5¢ brown on blue	148.00	100.00	40.00
U226	5¢ brown on fawn	550.00	410.00	......

U227-U230
Washington

SCOTT NO.	DESCRIPTION	UNUSED ENTIRE	UNUSED CUT SQ.	USED CUT SQ.
	1883 OCTOBER			
U227	2¢ red on white	12.00	6.00	2.50
U228	2¢ red on amber	14.00	7.00	3.00
U229	2¢ red on blue	16.00	11.00	5.50
U230	2¢ red on fawn	19.00	11.00	5.50

U231-U249, U260-W292
Washington

U250-U259
Jackson

1883 NOVEMBER
Four Wavy Lines in Oval

SCOTT NO.	DESCRIPTION	UNUSED ENTIRE	UNUSED CUT SQ.	USED CUT SQ.
U231	2¢ red on white	13.00	7.00	2.50
U232	2¢ red on amber	14.00	8.00	4.00
U233	2¢ red on blue	20.00	11.00	8.00
U234	2¢ red on fawn	14.00	9.00	5.00
W235	2¢ red on manila	35.00	24.00	6.50

1884 JUNE

SCOTT NO.	DESCRIPTION	UNUSED ENTIRE	UNUSED CUT SQ.	USED CUT SQ.
U236	2¢ red on white	25.00	15.00	4.50
U237	2¢ red on amber	31.00	18.00	11.00
U238	2¢ red on blue	52.00	31.00	13.00
U239	2¢ red on fawn	38.00	27.00	12.00
U240	2¢ red on white (3-1/2links)	195.00	115.00	50.00
U241	2¢ red on amber (3-1/2links)	2800.00	1000.00	340.00
U243	2¢ red on white (2 links)	215.00	150.00	90.00
U244	2¢ red on amber (2links)	560.00	425.00	105.00
U245	2¢ red on blue (2links)	825.00	500.00	225.00
U246	2¢ red on fawn (2links)	755.00	475.00	210.00
U247	2¢ red on white (round O)	4600.00	3600.00	775.00
U248	2¢ red on amber	....	5400.00	800.00
U249	2¢ red on fawn (round O)	2200.00	1450.00	800.00

1883-86

SCOTT NO.	DESCRIPTION	UNUSED ENTIRE	UNUSED CUT SQ.	USED CUT SQ.
U250	4¢ green on white, die 1	8.50	5.00	3.75
U251	4¢ green on amber,die 1	9.50	6.50	4.00
U252	4¢ green on buff, die 1	22.00	14.00	10.00
U253	4¢ green on blue, die 1	22.00	14.00	7.00
U254	4¢ green on manila, die 1	24.00	16.00	8.00
U255	4¢ green/amber manila,die 1	40.00	31.00	11.00
U256	4¢ green on white, die 2	23.00	13.00	6.00
U257	4¢ green on amber, die 2	31.00	19.00	8.00
U258	4¢ green on manila, die 2	31.00	16.00	8.00
U259	4¢ green/amber manila,die 2	31.00	16.00	8.00

1884 MAY

SCOTT NO.	DESCRIPTION	UNUSED ENTIRE	UNUSED CUT SQ.	USED CUT SQ.
U260	2¢ brown on white	24.00	20.00	6.00
U261	2¢ brown on amber	24.00	20.00	7.00
U262	2¢ brown on blue	36.00	24.00	11.00
U263	2¢ brown on fawn	25.00	19.00	9.50
W264	2¢ brown on manila	31.00	20.00	12.00

1884 JUNE

SCOTT NO.	DESCRIPTION	UNUSED ENTIRE	UNUSED CUT SQ.	USED CUT SQ.
U265	2¢ brown on white	34.00	20.00	7.00
U266	2¢ brown on amber	91.00	81.00	48.00
U267	2¢ brown on blue	35.00	25.00	10.00
U268	2¢ brown on fawn	28.00	19.00	12.00
W269	2¢ brown on manila	43.00	36.00	16.00
U270	2¢ brown on white (2links)	205.00	150.00	55.00
U271	2¢ brown on amber (2links)	655.00	525.00	120.00
U273	2¢ brown on white (round O)	455.00	325.00	120.00
U274	2¢ brown on amber (round O)	455.00	325.00	115.00
U276	2¢ brown on fawn (round O)	1500.00	1000.00	725.00

1884-86
Two Wavy Lines in Oval

SCOTT NO.	DESCRIPTION	UNUSED ENTIRE	UNUSED CUT SQ.	USED CUT SQ.
U277	2¢ brown on white, die 1	.90	.60	.25
U277a	2¢ brown lake on white, die 1	28.00	23.00	22.00
U278	2¢ brown on amber, die 1	1.75	.75	.50
U279	2¢ brown on buff, die 1	10.00	7.00	2.25
U280	2¢ brown on blue, die 1	5.75	3.75	2.25
U281	2¢ brown on fawn, die 1	7.00	4.00	2.50
U282	2¢ brown on manila, die 1	22.00	16.00	4.25
W283	2¢ brown on manila, die 1	12.00	8.75	6.00
U284	2¢ brown/amber manila, die 1	18.00	11.00	6.00
U285	2¢ red on white, die 1	1600.00	775.00	......
U286	2¢ red on blue, die 1	400.00	360.00	......
W287	2¢ red on manila, die 1	235.00	165.00	......
U288	2¢ brown on white, die 2	935.00	400.00	53.00
U289	2¢ brown on amber, die 2	30.00	21.00	14.00
U290	2¢ brown on blue, die 2	2800.00	1950.00	325.00
U291	2¢ brown on fawn, die 2	56.00	38.00	27.00
W292	2¢ brown on manila, die 2	43.00	31.00	20.00

NOTE: For details on die or silmilar appearing varieties of envelopes, please refer to the Scott Specialized Catalogue.

U293
Grant

1886

SCOTT NO.	DESCRIPTION	UNUSED ENTIRE	UNUSED CUT SQ.	USED CUT SQ.
U293	2¢ green on white	....	....	....
	Entire letter sheet	45.00	....	23.00

U294-U304, U352-W357
Franklin

U305-U323, U358-U370
Washington

U324-U329
Jackson

U330-U335, U377-U378
Grant

1887-94

SCOTT NO.	DESCRIPTION	UNUSED ENTIRE	UNUSED CUT SQ.	USED CUT SQ.
U294	1¢ blue on white	1.10	.60	.35
U295	1¢ dark blue on white	11.50	8.50	3.00
U296	1¢ blue on amber	7.25	4.00	1.50
U297	1¢ dark blue on amber	77.00	56.00	27.00
U300	1¢ blue on manila	1.40	.75	.40
W301	1¢ blue on manila	1.75	.90	.35
U302	1¢ dark blue on manila	43.00	33.00	13.00
W303	1¢ dark blue on manila	31.00	18.00	12.00
U304	1¢ blue on amber manila	20.00	14.00	5.50
U305	2¢ green on white, die 1	46.00	22.00	11.00
U306	2¢ green on amber, die 1	66.00	51.00	18.00
U307	2¢ green on buff, die 1	150.00	110.00	36.00
U308	2¢ green on blue, die 1	......	22000.00	1300.00
U309	2¢ green on manila, die 1	......	......	800.00
U311	2¢ green on white, die 2	.90	.40	.30
U312	2¢ green on amber, die 2	.95	.55	.30
U313	2¢ green on buff, die 2	1.40	.70	.35
U314	2¢ green on blue, die 2	1.40	.75	.35
U315	2¢ green on manila, die 2	3.60	2.25	.60
W316	2¢ green on manila, die 2	15.50	6.50	3.00
U317	2¢ green/amber manila, die 2	6.95	3.25	2.00
U318	2¢ green on white, die 3	230.00	160.00	15.00
U319	2¢ green on amber, die 3	300.00	220.00	27.00
U320	2¢ green on buff, die 3	287.00	215.00	50.00
U321	2¢ green on blue, die 3	355.00	225.00	71.50
U322	2¢ green on manila, die 3	410.00	330.00	70.00
U323	2¢ green/amber manila, die 3	875.00	500.00	150.00
U324	4¢ carmine on white	7.25	3.50	2.25
U325	4¢ carmine on amber	9.00	4.25	3.75
U326	4¢ carmine on oriental buff	18.50	8.75	4.00
U327	4¢ carmine on blue	16.50	7.75	4.25
U328	4¢ carmine on manila	16.50	10.00	7.50
U329	4¢ carmine on amber/manila	16.50	8.75	4.00
U330	5¢ blue on white, die 1	10.00	5.00	5.00
U331	5¢ blue on amber, die 1	14.00	6.00	3.00
U332	5¢ blue on oriental buff, die 1	22.00	7.00	5.00
U333	5¢ blue on blue, die 1	22.00	12.00	6.50
U334	5¢ blue on white, die 2	55.00	30.00	13.00
U335	5¢ blue on amber, die 2	28.00	18.00	8.00
U336	30¢ red brown on white	87.00	65.00	50.00
U337	30¢ red brown on amber	87.00	65.00	50.00
U338	30¢ red brown/oriental buff	86.00	65.00	50.00
U339	30¢ red brown on blue	86.00	65.00	50.00
U340	30¢ red brown on manila	86.00	65.00	50.00
U341	30¢ red brown/amber manila	86.00	65.00	50.00
U342	90¢ purple on white	120.00	88.00	93.00
U343	90¢ purple on amber	150.00	110.00	93.00
U344	90¢ purple on oriental buff	165.00	115.00	93.00
U345	90¢ purple on blue	175.00	115.00	95.00
U346	90¢ purple on manila	182.00	110.00	95.00
U347	90¢ purple on amber manila	182.00	120.00	95.00

U348-U351
Columbus and Liberty, with Shield and Eagle

1893 COLUMBIAN ISSUE

SCOTT NO.	DESCRIPTION	UNUSED ENTIRE	UNUSED CUT SQ.	USED CUT SQ.
U348	1¢ deep blue on white	4.00	2.50	1.40
U349	2¢ violet on white	4.50	3.00	.75
U350	5¢ chocolate on white	17.00	10.00	9.00
U351	10¢ slate brown on white	78.00	38.00	34.00

U371-U373

U374-W376

Lincoln

1899

SCOTT NO.	DESCRIPTION	UNUSED ENTIRE	UNUSED CUT SQ.	USED CUT SQ.
U352	1¢ green on white	4.00	1.85	.30
U353	1¢ green on amber	12.00	6.50	1.80
U354	1¢ green on oriental buff	24.00	19.00	3.00
U355	1¢ green on blue	24.00	19.00	8.00
U356	1¢ green on manila	7.50	3.00	1.10
W357	1¢ green on manila	12.00	4.00	1.25
U358	2¢ carmine on white, die 1	8.00	3.25	2.00
U359	2¢ carmine on amber, die 1	42.00	27.00	16.00
U360	2¢ carmine on buff, die 1	42.00	27.00	13.00
U361	2¢ carmine on blue, die 1	92.00	77.00	38.00
U362	2¢ carmine on white,die 2	.85	.40	.25
U363	2¢ carmine on amber. die 2	3.75	2.25	.25
U364	2¢ carmine on buff, die 2	3.75	1.55	.25
U365	2¢ carmine on blue, die 2	4.50	2.00	.60
W366	2¢ carmine on manila, die 2	16.00	9.75	3.50
U367	2¢ carmine on white, die 3	14.00	8.00	3.00
U368	2¢ carmine on amber, die 3	18.00	12.00	7.00
U369	2¢ carmine on buff, die 3	44.00	29.00	14.00
U370	2¢ carmine on blue, die 3	34.00	16.00	11.00
U371	4¢ brown on white, die 1	38.00	23.00	14.00
U372	4¢ brown on amber, die 1	40.00	23.00	14.00
U373	4¢ brown on white, die 2	......	......	1300.00
U374	4¢ brown on white, die 3	35.00	18.00	9.00
U375	4¢ brown on amber, die 3	88.00	70.00	26.00
W376	4¢ brown on manila, die 3	38.00	19.00	11.00
U377	5¢ blue on white, die 3	23.00	14.00	11.00
U378	5¢ blue on amber, die 3	31.00	22.00	11.50

U379-W384
Franklin

U385-W389, U395-W399
Washington

U390-W392
Grant

U393, U394
Lincoln

U400-W405, U416, U417
Franklin

U406-W415, U418, U419
Washington

1903

SCOTT NO.	DESCRIPTION	UNUSED ENTIRE	UNUSED CUT SQ.	USED CUT SQ.
U379	1¢ green on white	1.40	.85	.25
U380	1¢ green on amber	26.00	18.00	2.25
U381	1¢ green on oriental buff	31.00	22.00	3.00
U382	1¢ green on blue	38.00	26.00	5.00
U383	1¢ green on manila	6.25	4.75	1.00
W384	1¢ green on manila	5.25	3.50	.50
U385	2¢ carmine on white	1.50	.60	.30
U386	2¢ carmine on amber	4.25	2.75	.55
U387	2¢ carmine on oriental buff	4.00	2.50	.35
U388	2¢ carmine on blue	3.50	2.25	.60
W389	2¢ carmine on manila	32.00	25.00	11.00
U390	4¢ chocolate on white	36.00	28.00	13.00
U391	4¢ chocolate on amber	35.00	25.00	13.00
W392	4¢ chocolate on manila	58.00	32.00	13.00
U393	5¢ blue on white	36.00	25.00	13.00
U394	5¢ blue on amber	36.00	25.00	13.00

1904 RECUT DIE

SCOTT NO.	DESCRIPTION	UNUSED ENTIRE	UNUSED CUT SQ.	USED CUT SQ.
U395	2¢ carmine on white	2.00	1.00	.35
U396	2¢ carmine on amber	15.00	10.00	1.20
U397	2¢ carmine on oriental buff	9.00	7.00	1.50
U398	2¢ carmine on blue	7.00	5.00	1.10
W399	2¢ carmine on manila	36.00	18.00	11.00

1907-16

SCOTT NO.	DESCRIPTION	UNUSED ENTIRE	UNUSED CUT SQ.	USED CUT SQ.
U400	1¢ green on white	.65	.40	.25
U401	1¢ green on amber	4.00	2.25	.50
U402	1¢ green on oriental buff	16.00	11.00	1.50
U403	1¢ green on blue	16.00	11.00	2.00
U404	1¢ green on manila	6.50	3.75	2.10
W405	1¢ green on manila	2.50	1.25	.30
U406	2¢ brown red on white	3.00	1.25	.25
U407	2¢ brown red on amber	9.00	7.00	3.00
U408	2¢ brown red on oriental buff	14.00	10.00	2.00
U409	2¢ brown red on blue	9.25	6.00	2.10
W410	2¢ brown red on manila	66.00	48.00	36.00
U411	2¢ carmine on white	1.25	.35	.25
U412	2¢ carmine on amber	1.25	.65	.25
U413	2¢ carmine on oriental buff	1.50	.75	.25
U414	2¢ carmine on blue	1.50	.75	.25
W415	2¢ carmine on manila	11.00	7.00	2.50
U416	4¢ black on white	14.00	6.50	3.50
U417	4¢ black on amber	17.00	9.50	3.00
U418	5¢ blue on white	16.00	8.00	2.85
U419	5¢ blue on amber	26.00	18.00	13.00

U420-U428, U440-U442
Franklin

U429-U439, U443-U445, U481-U485, U529-U531
Washington

1916-32

SCOTT NO.	DESCRIPTION	UNUSED ENTIRE	UNUSED CUT SQ.	USED CUT SQ.
U420	1¢ green on white	.40	.35	.25
U421	1¢ green on amber	1.25	.80	.35
U422	1¢ green on oriental buff	3.50	2.50	1.20
U423	1¢ green on blue	1.00	.60	.40
U424	1¢ green on manila	9.50	7.50	4.80
W425	1¢ green on manila	.95	.30	.25
U426	1¢ green on brown (glazed)	66.00	53.00	19.25
W427	1¢ green on brown (glazed)	91.00	78.50	35.00
U428	1¢ green on brown (unglazed)	27.00	18.00	9.00
U429	2¢ carmine on white	.45	.30	.25
U430	2¢ carmine on amber	.50	.30	.25
U431	2¢ carmine on oriental buff	5.75	2.50	.70
U432	2¢ carmine on blue	.65	.40	.25
W433	2¢ carmine on manila	.55	.35	.30
W434	2¢ carmine on brown (glazed)	126.00	100.00	55.00
W435	2¢ carmine/brown (unglazed)	126.00	100.00	55.00
U436	3¢ dark violet on white	.75	.60	.25
U436f	3¢ purple on white (1932)	.75	.55	.25
U436h	3¢ carmine on white (error)	62.00	38.00	33.00
U437	3¢ dark violet on amber	6.00	2.70	1.20
U437a	3¢ purple on amber (1932)	11.00	6.00	1.25
U437g	3¢ carmine on amber (error)	600.00	525.00	360.00
U437h	3¢ black on amber (error)	300.00	200.00	......
U438	3¢ dark violet on buff	38.00	31.00	1.80
U439	3¢ purple on blue (1932)	.80	.35	.25
U439a	3¢ dark violet on blue	18.00	11.00	3.00
U439g	3¢ carmine on blue (error)	500.00	400.00	320.00
U440	4¢ black on white	4.50	2.25	.60
U441	4¢ black on amber	5.50	3.75	.90
U442	4¢ black on blue	6.00	3.75	1.00
U443	5¢ blue on white	7.50	4.00	3.00
U444	5¢ blue on amber	8.00	5.00	2.30
U445	5¢ blue on blue	9.75	4.50	3.50

1920-21 SURCHARGED

2 CENTS

Type 1

Type 2

SCOTT NO.	DESCRIPTION	UNUSED ENTIRE	UNUSED CUT SQ.	USED CUT SQ.
U446	2¢ on 3¢ dark violet on white ....(U436)	26.00	18.00	11.75

Surcharge on Envelopes of 1916-21 Type 2

SCOTT NO.	DESCRIPTION	UNUSED ENTIRE	UNUSED CUT SQ.	USED CUT SQ.
U447	2¢ on 3¢ dark violet on white, rose ....(U436)	18.00	11.00	7.70
U448	2¢ on 3¢ dark violet on white ....(U436)	5.00	3.00	2.10
U449	2¢ on 3¢ dark violet on amber ....(U437)	12.00	8.00	6.50
U450	2¢ on 3¢ dark violet on oriental buff..............(U438)	27.00	21.00	16.00
U451	2¢ on 3¢ dark violet on blue..........................(U439)	26.00	17.00	11.00

Type 3

Surcharge on Envelopes of 1874-1921
Type 3 bars 2mm apart

SCOTT NO.	DESCRIPTION	UNUSED ENTIRE	UNUSED CUT SQ.	USED CUT SQ.
U454	2¢ on 2¢ carmine on white ....(U429)	260.00	175.00	......
U455	2¢ on 2¢ carmine on amber ....(U430)	4300.00	2300.00	......
U456	2¢ on 2¢ carmine on oriental buff ....(U431)	395.00	300.00	......
U457	2¢ on 2¢ carmine on blue ....(U432)	495.00	400.00	......
U458	2¢ on 3¢ dark violet on white ....(U436)	1.15	.65	.40
U459	2¢ on 3¢ dark violet on amber ....(U437)	7.00	4.00	1.20
U460	2¢ on 3¢ dark violet on oriental buff ....(U438)	6.25	4.75	2.25
U461	2¢ on 3¢ dark violet on blue ....(U439)	10.00	7.00	1.20
U462	2¢ on 4¢ chocolate on white ....(U390)	900.00	650.00	275.00
U463	2¢ on 4¢ chocolate on amber ....(U391)	1550.00	1300.00	375.00
U464	2¢ on 5¢ blue on white.................................(U443)	2050.00	1500.00	......

Type 4 like Type 3, but bars 1-1/2 mm apart

SCOTT NO.	DESCRIPTION	UNUSED ENTIRE	UNUSED CUT SQ.	USED CUT SQ.
U465	2¢ on 1¢ green on white ....(U420)	2100.00	1400.00	......
U466A	2¢ on 2¢ carmine on white ....(U429)	1500.00	850.00	......
U467	2¢ on 3¢ green on white ....(U163)	600.00	450.00	......
U468	2¢ on 3¢ dark violet on white ....(U436)	1.20	.85	.50
U469	2¢ on 3¢ dark violet on amber ....(U437)	5.50	4.75	2.50
U470	2¢ on 3¢ dark violet on oriental buff ....(U438)	12.50	7.25	3.00
U471	2¢ on 3¢ dark violet on blue ....(U439)	15.50	8.75	2.00
U472	2¢ on 4¢ chocolate on white ....(U390)	34.00	16.00	13.00
U473	2¢ on 4¢ chocolate on amber ....(U391)	34.00	19.00	11.00
U474	2¢ on 1¢ on 3¢ dark violet on white ....(U436)	420.00	325.00	......
U475	2¢ on 1¢ on 3¢ dark violet on amber ....(U437)	500.00	300.00	......

Type 5 Type 6 Type 7

Surcharge on Envelope of 1916-21 Type 5

SCOTT NO.	DESCRIPTION	UNUSED ENTIRE	UNUSED CUT SQ.	USED CUT SQ.
U476	2¢ on 3¢ dark violet on amber ....(U437)	525.00	300.00	......

Surcharge on Envelope of 1916-21 Type 6

SCOTT NO.	DESCRIPTION	UNUSED ENTIRE	UNUSED CUT SQ.	USED CUT SQ.
U477	2¢ on 3¢ dark violet on white ....(U436)	215.00	150.00	......
U478	2¢ on 3¢ dark violet on amber ....(U437)	500.00	375.00	......

Surcharge on Envelope of 1916-21 Type 7

SCOTT NO.	DESCRIPTION	UNUSED ENTIRE	UNUSED CUT SQ.	USED CUT SQ.
U479	2¢ on 3¢ dark violet on white (black) ....(U436)	595.00	475.00	......

1925

SCOTT NO.	DESCRIPTION	UNUSED ENTIRE	UNUSED CUT SQ.	USED CUT SQ.
U481	1-1/2¢ brown on white...	.65	.30	.30
U481b	1-1/2¢ purple on white (error)	130.00	105.00	......
U482	1-1/2¢ brown on amber...	1.90	1.20	.45
U483	1-1/2¢ brown on blue	2.75	1.80	1.00
U484	1-1/2¢ brown on manila	14.50	8.00	3.75
W485	1-1/2¢ brown on manila	2.00	1.00	.30

Type 8

Surcharge on Envelopes of 1887 Type 8

SCOTT NO.	DESCRIPTION	UNUSED ENTIRE	UNUSED CUT SQ.	USED CUT SQ.
U486	1-1/2¢ on 2¢ green on white ....(U311)	1650.00	925.00	......
U487	1-1/2¢ on 2¢ green on amber ....(U312)	1800.00	1500.00	......

Surcharge on Envelopes of 1899 Type 8

SCOTT NO.	DESCRIPTION	UNUSED ENTIRE	UNUSED CUT SQ.	USED CUT SQ.
U488	1-1/2¢ on 1¢ green on white ....(U352)	1050.00	700.00	......
U489	1-1/2¢ on 1¢ green on amber ....(U353)	225.00	138.00	70.00

Surcharge on Envelopes of 1907-10 Type 8

SCOTT NO.	DESCRIPTION	UNUSED ENTIRE	UNUSED CUT SQ.	USED CUT SQ.
U490	1-1/2¢ on 1¢ green on white ....(U400)	12.00	7.00	4.20
U491	1-1/2¢ on 1¢ green on amber ....(U401)	13.00	12.00	3.00
U492	1-1/2¢ on 1¢ green on oriental buff ....(U402a)	750.00	625.00	155.00
U493	1-1/2¢ on 1¢ green on blue ....(U403c)	180.00	130.00	70.00
U494	1-1/2¢ on 1¢ green on manila ....(U404)	625.00	425.00	110.00

Surcharge on Envelopes of 1916-21 Type 8

SCOTT NO.	DESCRIPTION	UNUSED ENTIRE	UNUSED CUT SQ.	USED CUT SQ.
U495	1-1/2¢ on 1¢ green on white ....(U420)	1.25	.85	.30
U496	1-1/2¢ on 1¢ green on amber ....(U421)	31.00	22.00	14.00
U497	1-1/2¢ on 1¢ green on oriental buff ....(U422)	9.00	5.00	2.50
U498	1-1/2¢ on 1¢ green on blue ....(U423)	2.50	1.65	.90
U499	1-1/2¢ on 1¢ green on manila ....(U424)	22.00	14.00	8.00
U500	1-1/2¢ on 1¢ green on brown (unglazed)......(U428)	115.00	92.00	40.00
U501	1-1/2¢ on 1¢ green on brown (glazed) ....(U426)	115.00	92.00	36.00
U502	1-1/2¢ on 2¢ carmine on white ....(U429)	525.00	300.00	......
U503	1-1/2¢ on 2¢ carmine on oriental buff .... (U431)	540.00	400.00	......
U504	1-1/2¢ on 2¢ carmine on blue ....(U432)	570.00	495.00	......

Surcharge on Envelopes of 1925 Type 8

SCOTT NO.	DESCRIPTION	UNUSED ENTIRE	UNUSED CUT SQ.	USED CUT SQ.
U505	1-1/2¢ on 1-1/2¢ brown on white ....(U481)	695.00	525.00	.....
U506	1-1/2¢ on 1-1/2¢ brown on blue ....(U483)	695.00	525.00	.....

Type 9

Surcharge on Envelopes of 1899 Type 9

SCOTT NO.	DESCRIPTION	UNUSED ENTIRE	UNUSED CUT SQ.	USED CUT SQ.
U508	1-1/2¢ on 1¢ green on amber ....(U353)	105.00	72.00	.....

Surcharge on Envelopes of 1903 Type 9

SCOTT NO.	DESCRIPTION	UNUSED ENTIRE	UNUSED CUT SQ.	USED CUT SQ.
U508A	1-1/2¢ on 1¢ green on white ....(U379)	7000.00	4800.00	.....
U509	1-1/2¢ on 1¢ green on amber ....(U380)	34.00	21.00	14.00
U509B	1-1/2¢ on 1¢ green on oriental buff ....(U381)	85.00	68.00	50.00

Surcharge on Envelopes of 1907-10 Type 9

SCOTT NO.	DESCRIPTION	UNUSED ENTIRE	UNUSED CUT SQ.	USED CUT SQ.
U510	1-1/2¢ on 1¢ green on white ....(U400)	6.00	3.00	1.50
U511	1-1/2¢ on 1¢ green on amber ....(U401)	400.00	275.00	105.00
U512	1-1/2¢ on 1¢ green on oriental buff ....(U402)	17.00	9.00	4.75
U513	1-1/2¢ on 1¢ green on blue ....(U403)	11.00	7.00	5.00
U514	1-1/2¢ on 1¢ green on manila ....(U404)	54.00	42.00	12.00
U515	1-1/2¢ on 1¢ green on white ....(U420)	.80	.45	.25
U516	1-1/2¢ on 1¢ green on amber ....(U421)	76.00	58.00	32.00
U517	1-1/2¢ on 1¢ green on oriental buff ....(U422)	12.00	8.00	1.50
U518	1-1/2¢ on 1¢ green on blue ....(U423)	12.00	7.00	1.50
U519	1-1/2¢ on 1¢ green on manila ....(U424)	52.00	36.00	13.00
U520	1-1/2¢ on 2¢ carmine on white ....(U429)	525.00	375.00	.....
U521	1-1/2¢ on 1¢ green on white, magenta surcharged ....(U420)	7.50	5.00	4.00

U522

U523-U528

U522: Die 1, "E" of "POSTAGE" has center bar shorter than top bar.

U522a: Die 2, "E" of "POSTAGE" has center and top bars same length.

U525: Die 1 "S" of "POSTAGE" even with "T".

U525a: Die 2 "S" of "POSTAGE" higher than "T".

1926 SESQUICENTENNIAL EXPOSITION

SCOTT NO.	DESCRIPTION	UNUSED ENTIRE	UNUSED CUT SQ.	USED CUT SQ.
U522	2¢ carmine on white, die 1	2.50	1.75	.75
U522a	2¢ carmine on white, die 2	12.50	9.00	5.50

1932 WASHINGTON BICENTENNIAL

SCOTT NO.	DESCRIPTION	UNUSED ENTIRE	UNUSED CUT SQ.	USED CUT SQ.
U523	1¢ olive green on white...	2.00	1.25	1.00
U524	1-1/2¢ chocolate on white.......................................	3.25	2.25	2.00
U525	2¢ carmine on white, die 1	.75	.50	.25
U525a	2¢ carmine on white, die 2	100.00	85.00	22.00
U526	3¢ violet on white	3.00	2.50	.50
U527	4¢ black on white	25.00	22.00	21.00
U528	5¢ dark blue on white..	6.00	5.00	21.00

1932 Designs of 1916-32

SCOTT NO.	DESCRIPTION	UNUSED ENTIRE	UNUSED CUT SQ.	USED CUT SQ.
U529	6¢ orange on white	11.00	7.25	5.00
U530	6¢ orange on amber...	18.00	13.00	11.00
U531	6¢ orange on blue..	18.00	13.00	11.00

U532 Franklin · U533 · U535 Washington

1950

SCOTT NO.	DESCRIPTION	FIRST DAY COVER	UNUSED ENTIRE	USED CUT SQ.
U532	1¢ green	2.00	8.75	2.50
U533	2¢ carmine	2.00	1.45	.35
U534	3¢ dark violet	2.00	.75	.30

1952

SCOTT NO.	DESCRIPTION	FIRST DAY COVER	UNUSED ENTIRE	USED CUT SQ.
U535	1-1/2¢ brown	....	7.25	4.00

U537, U538, U552, U556 · U539, U540, U545, U553

Surcharge on Envelopes of 1916-32, 1950, 1965, 1971

1958

SCOTT NO.	DESCRIPTION	FIRST DAY COVER	UNUSED ENTIRE	USED CUT SQ.
U536	4¢ red violet	1.75	1.00	.30
U537	2¢ & 2¢ (4¢) carmine (U429)	......	5.25	2.00
U538	2¢ & 2¢ (4¢) carmine (U533)	......	1.25	1.50
U539	3¢ & 1¢ (4¢) purple, die1 (U436a)	......	18.50	12.00
U539a	3¢ & 1¢ (4¢) purple, die 7 (U436e)	......	15.00	10.00
U539b	3¢ & 1¢ (4¢) purple, die 9 (U436f)	......	36.00	17.00
U540	3¢ & 1¢ (4¢) dark violet (U534)	......	.70	1.25

U541 Franklin · U542 Washington

1960

SCOTT NO.	DESCRIPTION	FIRST DAY COVER	UNUSED ENTIRE	USED CUT SQ.
U541	1-1/4¢ turquoise	1.75	1.00	.60
U542	2-1/2¢ dull blue	1.75	1.15	.60

U543

SCOTT NO.	DESCRIPTION	FIRST DAY COVER	UNUSED ENTIRE	USED CUT SQ.
U543	4¢ Pony Express	2.00	.80	.40

U544 Lincoln · U546

1962

SCOTT NO.	DESCRIPTION	FIRST DAY COVER	UNUSED ENTIRE	USED CUT SQ.
U544	5¢ dark blue	1.75	1.20	.25

Surcharge on Envelope of 1958

SCOTT NO.	DESCRIPTION	FIRST DAY COVER	UNUSED ENTIRE	USED CUT SQ.
U545	4¢+1¢ red violet (U536)	......	1.80	1.35

1964

SCOTT NO.	DESCRIPTION	FIRST DAY COVER	UNUSED ENTIRE	USED CUT SQ.
U546	5¢ New York World's Fair	1.75	.75	.45

U547, U548, U548A, U566  · U549  · U550  · U551

1965-69

SCOTT NO.	DESCRIPTION	FIRST DAY COVER	UNUSED ENTIRE	USED CUT SQ.
U547	1-1/4¢ brown	1.75	.95	.55
U548	1-4/10¢ brown (1968)	1.75	1.25	.55
U548A	1-6/10¢ orange (1969)	1.75	1.15	.55
U549	4¢ bright blue	1.75	1.15	.25
U550	5¢ bright purple	1.75	1.00	.25
U551	6¢ light green (1968)	1.75	1.00	.25

U554

1968

1958 Type Surcharges on Envelopes of 1965

SCOTT NO.	DESCRIPTION	FIRST DAY COVER	UNUSED ENTIRE	USED CUT SQ.
U552	4¢ & 2¢ (6¢) blue (U549)	9.00	4.25	2.25
U553	5¢ & 1¢ (6¢) purple (U550)	9.00	4.00	3.00

1970

SCOTT NO.	DESCRIPTION	FIRST DAY COVER	UNUSED ENTIRE	USED CUT SQ.
U554	6¢ Moby Dick	1.75	.65	.25

U555 · U557

1971

SCOTT NO.	DESCRIPTION	FIRST DAY COVER	UNUSED ENTIRE	USED CUT SQ.
U555	6¢ Conference on Youth	1.75	.90	.25
U556	1-7/10¢ deep lilac	1.75	.40	.25
U557	8¢ ultramarine	1.75	.60	.25

U561 & U562 Surcharge

SCOTT NO.	DESCRIPTION	FIRST DAY COVER	UNUSED ENTIRE	USED CUT SQ.
U561	6¢ & (2¢) (8¢) green (on U551)	4.00	1.25	1.35
U562	6¢ & (2¢) (8¢) blue (on U555)	4.00	3.00	2.75

U563 · U564

SCOTT NO.	DESCRIPTION	FIRST DAY COVER	UNUSED ENTIRE	USED CUT SQ.
U563	8¢ Bowling	1.75	.90	.25
U564	8¢ Conference on Aging	1.75	.75	.25

SCOTT NO.	DESCRIPTION	FIRST DAY COVER	UNUSED ENTIRE	USED CUT SQ.

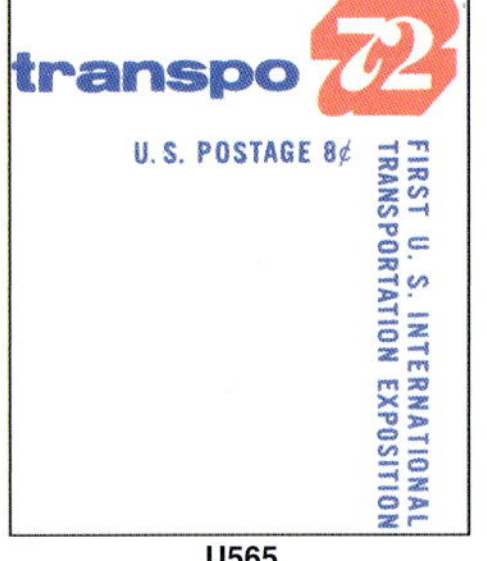

U565

U567

1972

SCOTT NO.	DESCRIPTION	FIRST DAY COVER	UNUSED ENTIRE	USED CUT SQ.
U565	8¢ Transpo '72	1.75	.80	.30

1973

SCOTT NO.	DESCRIPTION	FIRST DAY COVER	UNUSED ENTIRE	USED CUT SQ.
U566	8¢ & 2¢ ultramarine (on U557)	3.00	.65	1.35
U567	10¢ emerald	1.75	.65	.30

U568

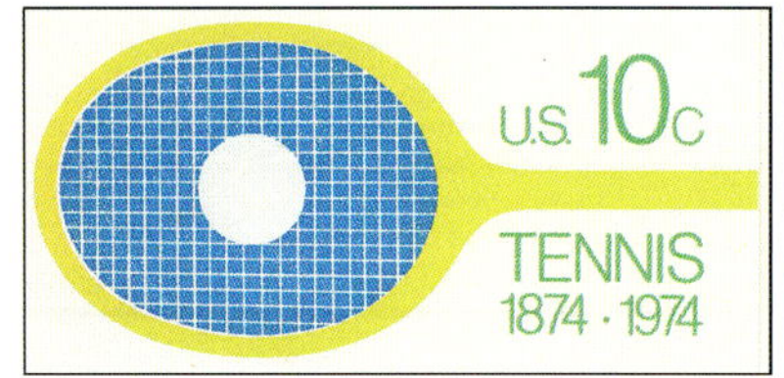

U569

1974

SCOTT NO.	DESCRIPTION	FIRST DAY COVER	UNUSED ENTIRE	USED CUT SQ.
U568	1-8/10¢ blue green	1.75	.85	.30
U569	10¢ Tennis Centenary	2.50	.80	.30

U571

U572

U573

U574

U575

1975-76 BICENTENNIAL ERA

SCOTT NO.	DESCRIPTION	FIRST DAY COVER	UNUSED ENTIRE	USED CUT SQ.
U571	10¢ Seafaring	1.75	.60	.30
U572	13¢ Homemaker (1976)	1.75	.60	.30
U573	13¢ Farmer (1976)	1.75	.60	.30
U574	13¢ Doctor (1976)	1.75	.60	.30
U575	13¢ Craftsman (1976)	1.75	.60	.30

CUT SQUARES: From 1947 to date, Unused Envelope Cut Squares can be supplied at the Unused Entire Price.

U576

1975

SCOTT NO.	DESCRIPTION	FIRST DAY COVER	UNUSED ENTIRE	USED CUT SQ.
U576	13¢ orange brown	1.75	.60	.30

U577

U578

U579

U580

U581

1976-78

SCOTT NO.	DESCRIPTION	FIRST DAY COVER	UNUSED ENTIRE	USED CUT SQ.
U577	2¢ red	1.75	.60	.30
U578	2.1¢ green (1977)	1.75	.70	.30
U579	2.7¢ green (1978)	1.75	.95	.30
U580	(15¢) "A" orange (1978)	1.75	.65	.30
U581	15¢ red & white (1978)	1.75	.65	.30

1976

SCOTT NO.	DESCRIPTION	FIRST DAY COVER	UNUSED ENTIRE	USED CUT SQ.
U582	13¢ Bicentennial (design of U218)	1.75	.55	.30

U583

1977

SCOTT NO.	DESCRIPTION	FIRST DAY COVER	UNUSED ENTIRE	USED CUT SQ.
U583	13¢ Golf	8.00	.80	.35

U584

U585

SCOTT NO.	DESCRIPTION	FIRST DAY COVER	UNUSED ENTIRE	USED CUT SQ.
U584	13¢ Energy Conservation	1.75	.55	.30
U585	13¢ Energy Development	1.75	.55	.30

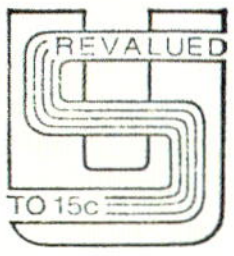

U586, U588

U586

1978

SCOTT NO.	DESCRIPTION	FIRST DAY COVER	UNUSED ENTIRE	USED CUT SQ.
U586	15¢ on 16¢ blue & white	1.75	.55	.25

U587

SCOTT NO.	DESCRIPTION	FIRST DAY COVER	UNUSED ENTIRE	USED CUT SQ.
U587	15¢ Auto Racing	2.00	.95	.45
U588	15¢ on 13¢ white, orange brown (U576)	1.75	.55	.25

U589

U590

1979

SCOTT NO.	DESCRIPTION	FIRST DAY COVER	UNUSED ENTIRE	USED CUT SQ.
U589	3.1¢ ultramarine & white	1.75	.55	.60

1980

SCOTT NO.	DESCRIPTION	FIRST DAY COVER	UNUSED ENTIRE	USED CUT SQ.
U590	3.5¢ purple	1.75	.45	.60

U591

U592

U593

U594

1981-82

SCOTT NO.	DESCRIPTION	FIRST DAY COVER	UNUSED ENTIRE	USED CUT SQ.
U591	5.9¢ brown (1982)	1.85	.45	.60
U592	(18¢) "B" violet & white	1.75	.60	.30
U593	18¢ white & dark blue	1.75	.60	.30
U594	(20¢) "C" brown & white	1.75	60	.30

U595

U596

1979

SCOTT NO.	DESCRIPTION	FIRST DAY COVER	UNUSED ENTIRE	USED CUT SQ.
U595	15¢ Veterinarians	1.75	.85	.30
U596	15¢ Moscow Olympics	1.75	.90	.25

U597

U598

U599

1980

SCOTT NO.	DESCRIPTION	FIRST DAY COVER	UNUSED ENTIRE	USED CUT SQ.
U597	15¢ Bicycle	1.75	.65	.25
U598	15¢ America's Cup	1.75	.65	.25
U599	15¢ Honeybee	1.75	.65	.25

U600

U601

1981

SCOTT NO.	DESCRIPTION	FIRST DAY COVER	UNUSED ENTIRE	USED CUT SQ.
U600	18¢ Blinded Veterans	1.75	.65	.25
U601	20¢ deep magenta & white	1.75	.65	.25

U602

U603

1982

SCOTT NO.	DESCRIPTION	FIRST DAY COVER	UNUSED ENTIRE	USED CUT SQ.
U602	20¢ black, blue & magenta	1.75	.65	.25
U603	20¢ Purple Heart	1.75	.95	.25

U604

U605

U606

1983

SCOTT NO.	DESCRIPTION	FIRST DAY COVER	UNUSED ENTIRE	USED CUT SQ.
U604	5.2¢ orange & white	1.75	.55	1.40
U605	20¢ Paralyzed Veterans	1.75	.65	.25

1984

SCOTT NO.	DESCRIPTION	FIRST DAY COVER	UNUSED ENTIRE	USED CUT SQ.
U606	20¢ Small Business	2.00	.65	.25

U607

U608

U609

1985

SCOTT NO.	DESCRIPTION	FIRST DAY COVER	UNUSED ENTIRE	USED CUT SQ.
U607	22¢ "D"	1.75	.75	.40
U608	22¢ Bison	1.75	.75	.25
U609	6¢ Old Ironsides	1.75	.45	.40

U610

1986

SCOTT NO.	DESCRIPTION	FIRST DAY COVER	UNUSED ENTIRE	USED CUT SQ.
U610	8.5¢ Mayflower	1.75	.65	.80

U611

U612

U613

1988

SCOTT NO.	DESCRIPTION	FIRST DAY COVER	UNUSED ENTIRE	USED CUT SQ.
U611	25¢ Stars	1.75	.85	.25
U612	8.4¢ Constellation	1.75	.65	.90
U613	25¢ Snowflake	1.75	2.60	25.00

U614

U615

U616

U617, U639

1989

SCOTT NO.	DESCRIPTION	FIRST DAY COVER	UNUSED ENTIRE	USED CUT SQ.
U614	25¢ Stamped Return Envelope	1.75	.80	.30
U615	25¢ "USA" and Stars	1.75	.80	.30
U616	25¢ LOVE	1.75	.80	1.00
U617	25¢ Shuttle Docking Hologram	1.75	1.25	.80

U618

U619

1990-91

SCOTT NO.	DESCRIPTION	FIRST DAY COVER	UNUSED ENTIRE	USED CUT SQ.
U618	25¢ Football Hologram	2.75	1.25	.75
U619	29¢ Star	1.75	.95	.35

U620

SCOTT NO.	DESCRIPTION	FIRST DAY COVER	UNUSED ENTIRE	USED CUT SQ.
U620	11.1¢ Birds on Wire	1.75	.65	1.10

U621

U622

SCOTT NO.	DESCRIPTION	FIRST DAY COVER	UNUSED ENTIRE	USED CUT SQ.
U621	29¢ Love	1.75	.95	.70
U622	29¢ Magazine Industry	1.75	.95	1.05

U623

U624

SCOTT NO.	DESCRIPTION	FIRST DAY COVER	UNUSED ENTIRE	USED CUT SQ.
U623	29¢ Star	1.75	.95	.35
U624	26¢ Country Geese	1.75	.95	.70

U625

U626

1992

SCOTT NO.	DESCRIPTION	FIRST DAY COVER	UNUSED ENTIRE	USED CUT SQ.
U625	29¢ Space Station	1.75	1.25	.60
U626	29¢ Saddle & Blanket	1.75	1.05	1.10

U627

U628

SCOTT NO.	DESCRIPTION	FIRST DAY COVER	UNUSED ENTIRE	USED CUT SQ.
U627	29¢ Protect the Environment	1.75	.95	1.10
U628	19.8¢ Star	1.75	.75	.45

U629 U630

SCOTT NO.	DESCRIPTION	FIRST DAY COVER	UNUSED ENTIRE	USED CUT SQ.
U629	29¢ Americans With Disabilities	1.75	1.10	.40
	1993			
U630	29¢ Kitten	1.75	1.35	1.25

U631

U632, U638

1994

SCOTT NO.	DESCRIPTION	FIRST DAY COVER	UNUSED ENTIRE	USED CUT SQ.
U631	29¢ Football	1.75	1.00	1.35

U633, U634

U635

1995

SCOTT NO.	DESCRIPTION	FIRST DAY COVER	UNUSED ENTIRE	USED CUT SQ.
U632	32¢ Liberty Bell	1.95	1.10	.35
U633	(32¢) "G" Old Glory (Design size 49x38mm)	1.95	1.85	2.25
U634	(32¢) "G" Old Glory (Design size 53x44mm)	1.95	2.50	2.25
U635	(5¢) Sheep, Nonprofit	1.95	.60	.55

U636

U637

SCOTT NO.	DESCRIPTION	FIRST DAY COVER	UNUSED ENTIRE	USED CUT SQ.
U636	(10¢) Graphic Eagle, Bulk Rate	1.95	.45	1.60
U637	32¢ Spiral Heart	1.95	1.10	.35
U638	32¢ Liberty Bell, security	1.95	1.10	.35
U639	32¢ Space Station	1.95	1.10	.45

U640

U641

1996

SCOTT NO.	DESCRIPTION	FIRST DAY COVER	UNUSED ENTIRE	USED CUT SQ.
U640	32¢ Save our Environment	1.95	1.10	.45
U641	32¢ Paralympic Games	1.95	1.10	.35

U642, U643

U645

U644

1999-2000

SCOTT NO.	DESCRIPTION	FIRST DAY COVER	UNUSED ENTIRE	USED CUT SQ.
U642	33¢ Flag, yellow, blue & red	1.95	1.35	.35
U642a	same, tagging bars to right of design	1.95	1.35	.35
U643	33¢ Flag, blue & red	1.95	1.35	.35
U644	33¢ Love	1.95	1.10	.35
U645	33¢ Lincoln, blue & black	1.95	1.10	.35

U646

U647

2001-03

SCOTT NO.	DESCRIPTION	FIRST DAY COVER	UNUSED ENTIRE	USED CUT SQ.
U646	34¢ Eagle, blue gray & gray	1.95	1.25	.35
U647	34¢ Lovebirds, rose & dull violet	1.95	1.25	.35

U648

U649

U650

SCOTT NO.	DESCRIPTION	FIRST DAY COVER	UNUSED ENTIRE	USED CUT SQ.
U648	34¢ Community Colleges, dark blue & orange brown	1.95	1.25	.35
U649	37¢ Ribbon Star, red & blue	1.95	1.25	.40
U650	(10¢) Graphic Eagle, Presorted Standard	1.95	1.00	.35

U651

U652

SCOTT NO.	DESCRIPTION	FIRST DAY COVER	UNUSED ENTIRE	USED CUT SQ.
U651	37¢ Nurturing Love	1.95	1.25	.40
U652	$3.85 Jefferson Memorial, pre-paid flat rate	8.75	15.00	8.75

U653

U657

2004

SCOTT NO.	DESCRIPTION	FIRST DAY COVER	UNUSED ENTIRE	USED CUT SQ.
U653	37¢ Goofy, Mickey Mouse, Donald Duck	3.00	3.25	2.50
U654	37¢ Bambi, Thumper	3.00	3.25	2.50
U655	37¢ Mufasa, Simba	3.00	3.25	2.50
U656	37¢ Jiminy Cricket, Pinocchio	3.00	3.25	2.50
	2005			
U657	37¢ Wedding Flowers, letter sheet	1.95	3.25	2.75

U658 U659 U660 U661

SCOTT NO.	DESCRIPTION	FIRST DAY COVER	UNUSED ENTIRE	USED CUT SQ.
	2006			
U658	$4.05 X-Planes, pre-paid flat rate	....	13.00	11.00
U659	39¢ Benjamin Franklin	1.95	1.25	.50
	2007			
U660	$4.60 Air Force One, priority mail, pre-paid flat rate	....	14.00	9.50
U661	$16.25 Marine One, express mail, pre-paid flat rate	....	48.00	30.00

U662 U663

SCOTT NO.	DESCRIPTION	FIRST DAY COVER	UNUSED ENTIRE	USED CUT SQ.
U662	41¢ Horses	2.00	1.35	.50
	2008			
U663	42¢ Elk Mint Entire	3.75	1.35	.50
U663b	42¢ Elk, tagging bar 19mm tall, recycling logo at top right side of statement	....	1.35	....

U664 U667 U668

SCOTT NO.	DESCRIPTION	FIRST DAY COVER	UNUSED ENTIRE	USED CUT SQ.
U664	$4.80 Mount Rushmore	11.00	14.00	9.00
U665	42¢ Sunflower	4.75	3.50	3.50
	2009			
U666	$4.95 Redwood Forest	12.00	14.00	9.50
U667	(44¢) Forever Stamped Envelope	4.75	1.60	.95
U667a	(44¢) Forever Liberty Bell Envelope	2.75	1.60	.95
U668	44¢ Seabiscuit Stamped Envelope	4.75	1.60	.50
U668a	44¢ Seabiscuit Stamped Envelope, typographed	4.75	1.60	.50

U672 U674

SCOTT NO.	DESCRIPTION	FIRST DAY COVER	UNUSED ENTIRE	USED CUT SQ.
U669-73	Gulf Coast Lighthouses	32.50	25.00	....

U675 U676 U677, U678

SCOTT NO.	DESCRIPTION	FIRST DAY COVER	UNUSED ENTIRE	USED CUT SQ.
	2010			
U674	$4.90 Mackinac Bridge	11.00	13.00	9.50
	2011			
U675	$4.95 New River Bridge	11.00	13.00	10.00
	2012			
U676	$5.15 Sunshine Skyway Bridge	12.00	12.50	9.50
U677	(45¢) Purple Martin (design size 33x48 mm)	1.50	1.25	0.65
U678	(45¢) Purple Martin (design size 35x50)	1.50	1.25	0.85
U679	$5.60 Arlington Green Bridge	12.00	12.00	8.50
U680	(46¢) Bank Swallowtail (design size 38x35mm)	2.75	1.50	0.75
U681	(46¢) Bank Swallowtail (design size 41x38mm)	2.75	1.50	0.75
U682	(46¢) Eagle, Shield & Flags	2.75	1.75	0.75
U683	$5.60 Verrazano-Narrows Bridge	12.00		12.00

U680, U681 U684 U685 U686 U687

SCOTT NO.	DESCRIPTION	FIRST DAY COVER	UNUSED ENTIRE	USED CUT SQ.
	2014			
U684	(49¢) Poinsettia	2.50	2.25	1.75
U685	(49¢) Snowflake	2.50	2.25	1.75
U686	(49¢) Snowflake	2.50	2.25	1.75
U687	(49¢) Cardinal	2.50	2.25	1.75
U688	(49¢) Child Making Snowman	2.50	2.25	1.75

U688 U689 U690 U691 U692 U693

SCOTT NO.	DESCRIPTION	FIRST DAY COVER	UNUSED ENTIRE	USED CUT SQ.
	2015			
U689	$5.75 Glade Creek Grist Mill	....	12.50	10.00
U690	(49¢) Pink Water Lily	3.50	2.25	2.25
U691	(49¢) White Water Lily	3.50	2.25	2.25
U692	(49¢) Forget Me Not Missing Children	3.50	2.25	2.25

U694 U695 U696 U700

SCOTT NO.	DESCRIPTION	FIRST DAY COVER	UNUSED ENTIRE	USED CUT SQ.
	2016-2020			
U693	$6.45 La Cueva del Indio Priority Envelope	15.00	15.50	....
U694	(47¢) Northern Cardinal	3.50	2.25	......
U695	$6.65 Liliuokalani Gardens Priority Envelope	15.00	15.50	......
U696	(49¢) Barn Swallow	3.50	2.25	......
U697	$6.70 Byodo-In Temple, Priority Envelope	15.00	15.50	......
U698	$7.35 Joshua Tree, Priority Envelope	16.00	16.00	......
U699	$7.75 Big Bend, Priority Envelope	16.50	16.50	......
U700	(55¢) Flag and Stars	3.50	2.25	......

U701 U702

SCOTT NO.	DESCRIPTION	FIRST DAY COVER	UNUSED ENTIRE	USED CUT SQ.
	2021-2023			
U701	$7.95 Castillo de San Marcos, Priority Envelope	16.50	16.50	.....
U702	(66¢) Northern Cardinal	4.00	2.50	.....

SCOTT NO.	DESCRIPTION	UNUSED ENTIRE	UNUSED CUT SQ.	USED CUT SQ.

UC1

UC2-UC7

Airplane in Circle

Die 1. Vertical rudder not semi-circular, but slopes to the left. Tail projects into "G".
Die 2. Vertical rudder is semi-circular. Tail only touches "G" Die 2a. "6" is 6-1/2mm. wide.
Die 2b. "6" is 6mm. wide.
Die 2c. "6" is 5-1/2mm. wide.
Die 3. Vertical rudder leans forward. "S" closer to "O" than to "T" of "POSTAGE" and "E" has short center bar.

1929-44

SCOTT NO.	DESCRIPTION	UNUSED ENTIRE	UNUSED CUT SQ.	USED CUT SQ.
UC1	5¢ blue, die 1	6.00	4.00	4.00
UC2	5¢ blue, die 2	16.00	12.00	10.00
UC3	6¢ orange, die 2a	2.50	1.75	1.00
UC3n	6¢, die 2a, no border	3.00	1.50	1.00
UC4	6¢, die 2b, with border	72.00	53.00	2.50
UC4n	6¢, die 2b, no border	6.00	4.00	2.50
UC5	6¢, die 2c, no border	1.55	1.00	.50
UC6	6¢ orange on white, die 3	2.25	1.25	.45
UC6n	6¢, die 3, no border	3.00	1.50	.50
UC7	8¢ olive green	21.00	14.50	4.00

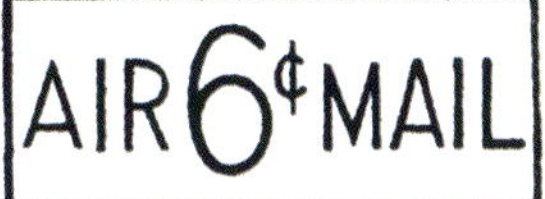

REVALUED
5¢
P.O. DEPT.

Envelopes of 1916-32 surcharged

1945

SCOTT NO.	DESCRIPTION	UNUSED ENTIRE	UNUSED CUT SQ.	USED CUT SQ.
UC8	6¢ on 2¢ carmine on white (U429)	1.75	1.55	1.15
UC9	6¢ on 2¢ carmine on white (U525)	120.00	90.00	72.50

1946

SCOTT NO.	DESCRIPTION	UNUSED ENTIRE	UNUSED CUT SQ.	USED CUT SQ.
UC10	5¢ on 6¢, die 2a (UC3n)	6.00	4.50	2.60
UC11	5¢ on 6¢, die 2b (UC4n)	12.00	11.75	8.50
UC12	5¢ on 6¢, die 2c (UC5)	1.50	1.15	.80
UC13	5¢ on 6¢, die 3 (UC6n)	1.15	1.15	.75

UC14: Die 1. Small projection below rudder is rounded.
UC15: Die 2. Small projection below rudder is sharp pointed.

UC14, UC15, UC18, UC26
DC-4 Skymaster

SCOTT NO.	DESCRIPTION	FIRST DAY COVER	UNUSED ENTIRE	USED CUT SQ.
UC14	5¢ carmine, die 1	2.50	1.25	.75
UC15	5¢ carmine, die 2	......	1.25	.75

UC16
DC-4 Skymaster

UC17
Washington and Franklin, Mail-carrying Vehicles

1947

SCOTT NO.	DESCRIPTION	FIRST DAY COVER	UNUSED ENTIRE	USED CUT SQ.
UC16	10¢ red on blue, Entire "Air Letter" on face, 2-line inscription on back	6.00	9.00	10.50
UC16a	Entire, "Air Letter" on face, 4-line inscription on back	......	18.00	15.00
UC16c	Entire "Air Letter" and "Aerogramme" on face, 4-line inscription on back	......	55.00	13.50
UC16d	Entire "Air Letter" and "Aerogramme" on face, 3-line inscription on back	......	9.50	9.00

1947 CIPEX COMMEMORATIVE

SCOTT NO.	DESCRIPTION	FIRST DAY COVER	UNUSED ENTIRE	USED CUT SQ.
UC17	5¢ carmine	3.00	.65	.60

1950 Design of 1946

SCOTT NO.	DESCRIPTION	FIRST DAY COVER	UNUSED ENTIRE	USED CUT SQ.
UC18	6¢ carmine	1.75	.60	.35

1951 (Shaded Numeral)

SCOTT NO.	DESCRIPTION	FIRST DAY COVER	UNUSED ENTIRE	USED CUT SQ.
UC19	6¢ on 5¢, die 1 (UC14)	......	2.40	1.60
UC20	6¢ on 5¢, die 2 (UC15)	......	1.25	1.60

1952 (Solid Numeral)

SCOTT NO.	DESCRIPTION	FIRST DAY COVER	UNUSED ENTIRE	USED CUT SQ.
UC21	6¢ on 5¢, die 1 (UC14)	......	35.00	19.00
UC22	6¢ on 5¢, die 2 (UC15)	......	9.00	2.75
UC23	6¢ on 5¢ (UC17)	......	2100.00	......

SCOTT NO.	DESCRIPTION	FIRST DAY COVER	UNUSED ENTIRE	USED CUT SQ.

ENVELOPE of 1946 Surcharged

ENVELOPE of 1946-47 Surcharged

1956 FIPEX COMMEMORATIVE

SCOTT NO.	DESCRIPTION	FIRST DAY COVER	UNUSED ENTIRE	USED CUT SQ.
UC25	6¢ red	1.75	1.10	.60

1958 Design of 1946

SCOTT NO.	DESCRIPTION	FIRST DAY COVER	UNUSED ENTIRE	USED CUT SQ.
UC26	7¢ blue	1.75	1.10	.60

UC36

UC27-UC31

Surcharge on Envelopes of 1934 to 1956

UC25

1958

SCOTT NO.	DESCRIPTION	FIRST DAY COVER	UNUSED ENTIRE	USED CUT SQ.
UC27	6¢ & 1¢ (7¢) orange, die 2a (UC3n)	......	420.00	......
UC28	6¢ & 1¢ (7¢), die 2b (UC4n)	......	125.00	82.50
UC29	6¢ & 1¢ (7¢) orange, die 2c (UC5)	......	60.00	52.50
UC30	6¢ & 1¢ (7¢) carmine (UC18)	......	1.35	.60
UC31	6¢ & 1¢ (7¢) red (UC25)	......	1.40	.60

UC32

UC33, UC34

UC35

1958-59

SCOTT NO.	DESCRIPTION	FIRST DAY COVER	UNUSED ENTIRE	USED CUT SQ.
UC32	10¢ blue & red Entire letter sheet, 2-line inscription on back (1959)	......	7.00	5.25
UC32a	Entire letter sheet, 3 line inscription on back	2.25	12.00	5.25

1958

SCOTT NO.	DESCRIPTION	FIRST DAY COVER	UNUSED ENTIRE	USED CUT SQ.
UC33	7¢ blue	1.75	.80	.30

1960

SCOTT NO.	DESCRIPTION	FIRST DAY COVER	UNUSED ENTIRE	USED CUT SQ.
UC34	7¢ carmine	1.75	.85	.30

1961

SCOTT NO.	DESCRIPTION	FIRST DAY COVER	UNUSED ENTIRE	USED CUT SQ.
UC35	11¢ red & blue	3.25	3.00	3.75

1962

SCOTT NO.	DESCRIPTION	FIRST DAY COVER	UNUSED ENTIRE	USED CUT SQ.
UC36	8¢ red	1.75	.85	.25

1965

SCOTT NO.	DESCRIPTION	FIRST DAY COVER	UNUSED ENTIRE	USED CUT SQ.
UC37	8¢ red	1.75	.70	.25
UC38	11¢ J.F. Kennedy	1.75	4.00	4.50

UC37

UC38, UC39

UC40

UC41 (surcharge on UC37)

UC42

1967

SCOTT NO.	DESCRIPTION	FIRST DAY COVER	UNUSED ENTIRE	USED CUT SQ.
UC39	13¢ J.F. Kennedy	1.75	3.50	4.50

1968

SCOTT NO.	DESCRIPTION	FIRST DAY COVER	UNUSED ENTIRE	USED CUT SQ.
UC40	10¢ red	1.75	.85	.25
UC41	8¢ & 2¢ (10¢) red	12.00	.95	.25
UC42	13¢ Human Rights Year	1.75	11.00	8.00

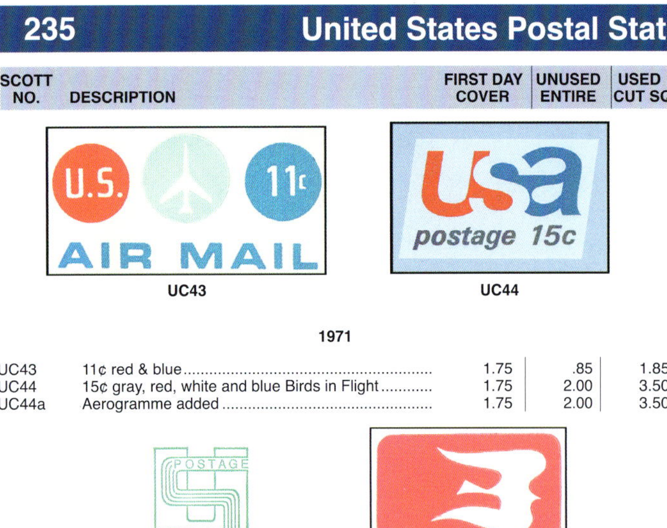

UC43 UC44

1971

SCOTT NO.	DESCRIPTION	FIRST DAY COVER	UNUSED ENTIRE	USED CUT SQ.
UC43	11¢ red & blue	1.75	.85	1.85
UC44	15¢ gray, red, white and blue Birds in Flight	1.75	2.00	3.50
UC44a	Aerogramme added	1.75	2.00	3.50

UC45 (surcharge on UC40)

UC47

1971 Revalued

SCOTT NO.	DESCRIPTION	FIRST DAY COVER	UNUSED ENTIRE	USED CUT SQ.
UC45	10 & (1¢) (11¢) red	6.00	2.50	.25

1973

SCOTT NO.	DESCRIPTION	FIRST DAY COVER	UNUSED ENTIRE	USED CUT SQ.
UC46	15¢ Ballooning	1.75	1.25	1.50
UC47	13¢ rose red	1.75	.75	.25

UC48

UC49

1974

SCOTT NO.	DESCRIPTION	FIRST DAY COVER	UNUSED ENTIRE	USED CUT SQ.
UC48	18¢ red & blue	1.75	1.50	2.25
UC49	18¢ NATO 25th Anniversary	1.75	1.25	2.25

UC50

UC51

1976

SCOTT NO.	DESCRIPTION	FIRST DAY COVER	UNUSED ENTIRE	USED CUT SQ.
UC50	22¢ red, white & blue	1.75	1.55	2.25

1978

SCOTT NO.	DESCRIPTION	FIRST DAY COVER	UNUSED ENTIRE	USED CUT SQ.
UC51	22¢ blue	1.75	1.55	2.25

UC52

UC53, UC54

UC55

1979

SCOTT NO.	DESCRIPTION	FIRST DAY COVER	UNUSED ENTIRE	USED CUT SQ.
UC52	22¢ Moscow Olympics	1.75	2.25	2.25

1980-81

SCOTT NO.	DESCRIPTION	FIRST DAY COVER	UNUSED ENTIRE	USED CUT SQ.
UC53	30¢ red, blue & brown	1.75	1.25	1.75
UC54	30¢ yellow, magenta, blue & black (1981)	1.75	1.25	1.25

1982

SCOTT NO.	DESCRIPTION	FIRST DAY COVER	UNUSED ENTIRE	USED CUT SQ.
UC55	30¢ Made in U.S.A.	1.75	1.45	3.00

UC56

UC57

1983

SCOTT NO.	DESCRIPTION	FIRST DAY COVER	UNUSED ENTIRE	USED CUT SQ.
UC56	30¢ Communications	1.75	1.25	5.50
UC57	30¢ Olympics	1.75	1.25	5.50

UC58

UC59

1985

SCOTT NO.	DESCRIPTION	FIRST DAY COVER	UNUSED ENTIRE	USED CUT SQ.
UC58	36¢ Landsat Satellite	1.75	1.50	5.50
UC59	36¢ Travel	1.75	1.55	3.50
UC60	36¢ Mark Twain, Halley's Comet	1.75	1.75	6.50

UC60

UC61

1986

SCOTT NO.	DESCRIPTION	FIRST DAY COVER	UNUSED ENTIRE	USED CUT SQ.
UC61	39¢ Letters	1.75	2.00	6.50

1989

SCOTT NO.	DESCRIPTION	FIRST DAY COVER	UNUSED ENTIRE	USED CUT SQ.
UC62	39¢ Blair & Lincoln	1.75	1.75	26.00

UC62

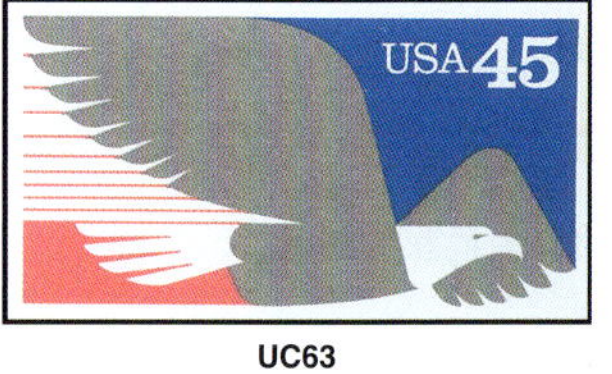

UC63

1991

SCOTT NO.	DESCRIPTION	FIRST DAY COVER	UNUSED ENTIRE	USED CUT SQ.
UC63	45¢ Eagle	1.75	1.75	2.50

1995

SCOTT NO.	DESCRIPTION	FIRST DAY COVER	UNUSED ENTIRE	USED CUT SQ.
UC64	50¢ Thaddeus Lowe	1.95	1.75	5.50

UC64

UC65

1999

SCOTT NO.	DESCRIPTION	FIRST DAY COVER	UNUSED ENTIRE	USED CUT SQ.
UC65	60¢ Voyagers National Park, Minnesota	1.95	2.50	7.75

SCOTT NO.	DESCRIPTION	UNUSED ENTIRE	UNUSED CUT SQ.	USED CUT SQ.

UO1-UO13

UO14-UO17

UO18-UO69
Washington

OFFICIAL ENVELOPES

NOTE: For details on similar appearing varieties please refer to the Scott Specialized Catalogue

POST OFFICE DEPARTMENT

1873 SMALL NUMERALS

SCOTT NO.	DESCRIPTION	UNUSED ENTIRE	UNUSED CUT SQ.	USED CUT SQ.
UO1	2¢ black on lemon	40.00	28.00	11.00
UO2	3¢ black on lemon	38.00	21.00	7.00
UO4	6¢ black on lemon	46.00	31.00	17.00

1874-79 LARGE NUMERALS

SCOTT NO.	DESCRIPTION	UNUSED ENTIRE	UNUSED CUT SQ.	USED CUT SQ.
UO5	2¢ black on lemon	19.00	13.00	5.00
UO6	2¢ black on white	255.00	150.00	40.00
UO7	3¢ black on lemon	5.00	4.00	1.00
UO8	3¢ black on white	5800.00	3250.00	2400.00
UO9	3¢ black on amber	180.00	155.00	42.00
UO12	6¢ black on lemon	31.00	18.00	7.00
UO13	6¢ black on white	5800.00	3250.00	......

1877 POSTAL SERVICE

SCOTT NO.	DESCRIPTION	UNUSED ENTIRE	UNUSED CUT SQ.	USED CUT SQ.
UO14	black on white	12.00	8.00	5.00
UO15	black on amber	955.00	250.00	45.00
UO16	blue on amber	955.00	225.00	38.00
UO17	blue on blue	16.00	10.00	7.00

Portraits for the various denominations are the same as on the regular issue of 1870-73

WAR DEPARTMENT

1873 REAY ISSUE

SCOTT NO.	DESCRIPTION	UNUSED ENTIRE	UNUSED CUT SQ.	USED CUT SQ.
UO18	1¢ dark red on white	1150.00	750.00	325.00
UO19	2¢ dark red on white	3250.00	2500.00	475.00
UO20	3¢ dark red on white	110.00	75.00	48.00
UO22	3¢ dark red on cream	1150.00	1050.00	315.00
UO23	6¢ dark red on white	480.00	350.00	95.00
UO24	6¢ dark red on cream	......	8500.00	440.00
UO25	10¢ dark red on white	......	......	2500.00
UO26	12¢ dark red on white	250.00	190.00	65.00
UO27	15¢ dark red on white	225.00	175.00	65.00
UO28	24¢ dark red on white	250.00	200.00	55.00
UO29	30¢ dark red on white	785.00	600.00	165.00
UO30	1¢ vermillion on white	455.00	225.00	......
WO31	1¢ vermillion on manila	42.00	23.00	15.00
UO32	2¢ vermillion on white	......	550.00	......
WO33	2¢ vermillion on manila	750.00	300.00	......
UO34	3¢ vermillion on white	225.00	110.00	45.00
UO35	3¢ vermillion on amber	400.00	140.00	......
UO36	3¢ vermillion on cream	45.00	20.00	14.00
UO37	6¢ vermillion on white	200.00	110.00	......
UO38	6¢ vermillion on cream	......	600.00	......
UO39	10¢ vermillion on white	655.00	375.00	......
UO40	12¢ vermillion on white	260.00	185.00	......
UO41	15¢ vermillion on white	3250.00	275.00	......
UO42	24¢ vermillion on white	690.00	475.00	......
UO43	30¢ vermillion on white	680.00	550.00	......

1875 PLIMPTON ISSUE

SCOTT NO.	DESCRIPTION	UNUSED ENTIRE	UNUSED CUT SQ.	USED CUT SQ.
UO44	1¢ red on white	275.00	210.00	95.00
UO45	1¢ red on amber	......	1200.00	......
WO46	1¢ red on manila	10.00	5.25	3.00
UO47	2¢ red on white	225.00	170.00	......
UO48	2¢ red on amber	60.00	40.00	18.00
UO49	2¢ red on orange	85.00	72.00	18.00
WO50	2¢ red on manila	250.00	130.00	60.00
UO51	3¢ red on white	25.00	18.00	11.00
UO52	3¢ red on amber	32.00	26.00	11.00
UO53	3¢ red on cream	10.00	8.00	4.00
UO54	3¢ red on blue	7.00	4.50	3.00
UO55	3¢ red on fawn	12.00	7.00	3.00
UO56	6¢ red on white	125.00	75.00	35.00
UO57	6¢ red on amber	150.00	100.00	50.00
UO58	6¢ red on cream	560.00	250.00	95.00
UO59	10¢ red on white	325.00	275.00	90.00
UO60	10¢ red on amber	1600.00	1320.00	......
UO61	12¢ red on white	200.00	75.00	42.00
UO62	12¢ red on amber	1000.00	850.00	......
UO63	12¢ red on cream	1000.00	800.00	......
UO64	15¢ red on white	325.00	275.00	150.00
UO65	15¢ red on amber	1150.00	1000.00	......
UO66	15¢ red on cream	1000.00	850.00	......
UO67	30¢ red on white	250.00	200.00	150.00
UO68	30¢ red on amber	2500.00	1150.00	......
UO69	30¢ red on cream	1400.00	1100.00	......

UO70-UO72

1911 POSTAL SAVINGS

SCOTT NO.	DESCRIPTION	UNUSED ENTIRE	UNUSED CUT SQ.	USED CUT SQ.
UO70	1¢ green on white	120.00	88.00	27.00
UO71	1¢ green on oriental buff	280.00	255.00	77.00
UO72	2¢ carmine on white	29.00	15.00	4.50

UO73

UO74

UO75

1983

SCOTT NO.	DESCRIPTION	FIRST DAY COVER	UNUSED ENTIRE	USED CUT SQ.
UO73	20¢ blue and white	2.50	1.40	40.00

1985

SCOTT NO.	DESCRIPTION	FIRST DAY COVER	UNUSED ENTIRE	USED CUT SQ.
UO74	22¢ blue and white	2.00	1.00	35.00

1987 Design Similar to UO74

SCOTT NO.	DESCRIPTION	FIRST DAY COVER	UNUSED ENTIRE	USED CUT SQ.
UO75	22¢ Savings Bond	3.25	2.50	35.00

UO76 UO77 UO78

UO81

UO83

UO84

1989

SCOTT NO.	DESCRIPTION	FIRST DAY COVER	UNUSED ENTIRE	USED CUT SQ.
UO76	(25¢) "E" black and blue Savings Bonds	2.00	1.65	35.00
UO77	25¢ black and blue	2.00	1.00	25.00
UO78	25¢ black and blue Savings Bonds	2.00	1.45	35.00

1990

SCOTT NO.	DESCRIPTION	FIRST DAY COVER	UNUSED ENTIRE	USED CUT SQ.
UO79	45¢ black & blue seal	2.25	1.55	......
UO80	65¢ black & blue seal	3.00	1.95	......
UO81	45¢ Self-sealing Envelope	2.25	1.55	......
UO82	65¢ Self-sealing Envelope	3.00	1.95	......

UO85

UO86, UO87

UO88, UO89, UO90, UO91, UO92, UO93

1991-92

SCOTT NO.	DESCRIPTION	FIRST DAY COVER	UNUSED ENTIRE	USED CUT SQ.
UO83	(29¢) "F" black and blue Savings Bond	2.00	1.50	36.00
UO84	29¢ black and blue	2.00	1.00	25.00
UO85	29¢ black and blue Savings Bond	2.00	1.00	25.00
UO86	52¢ Consular Service	2.50	6.00	......
UO87	75¢ Consular Service	3.00	12.50	......

1995

SCOTT NO.	DESCRIPTION	FIRST DAY COVER	UNUSED ENTIRE	USED CUT SQ.
UO88	32¢ Great Seal, red and blue	2.00	1.00	25.00

1999

SCOTT NO.	DESCRIPTION	FIRST DAY COVER	UNUSED ENTIRE	USED CUT SQ.
UO89	33¢ Great Seal, red and blue	2.00	1.25	25.00

2001-07

SCOTT NO.	DESCRIPTION	FIRST DAY COVER	UNUSED ENTIRE	USED CUT SQ.
UO90	34¢ Great Seal, red and blue	2.00	1.25	25.00
UO91	37¢ Great Seal, red and blue	2.00	1.25	....
UO92	39¢ Great Seal, red and blue	2.00	1.25	....
UO93	41¢ Great Seal, red and blue	2.00	1.25	....
UO94	42¢ Great Seal, official stamped envelope	2.50	1.25	....

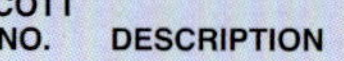

POSTAL CARDS

Prices Are For Entire Cards

MINT: As Issued, no printing or writing added.
UNUSED: Uncancelled, with printing or writing added.

UX1, UX3, U65

UX4, UX5, UX7
Liberty

UX6, UX13, UX16

SCOTT NO.	DESCRIPTION	MINT	UNUSED	USED
	1873			
UX1	1¢ brown, large watermark	425.00	95.00	27.00
UX3	1¢ brown, small watermark	90.00	26.00	4.00
	1875 Inscribed "Write the Address", etc.			
UX4	1¢ black, watermarked	4100.00	800.00	450.00
UX5	1¢ black, unwatermarked	92.00	9.75	.75
	1879			
UX6	2¢ blue on buff	42.00	15.00	38.50
	1881 Inscribed "Nothing but the Address", etc.			
UX7	1¢ black on buff	85.00	9.00	.50

UX8

UX9

Jefferson

UX10, UX11
Grant

SCOTT NO.	DESCRIPTION	MINT	UNUSED	USED
	1885			
UX8	1¢ brown on buff	60.00	15.00	1.50
	1886			
UX9	1¢ black on buff	31.00	3.00	.65
	1891			
UX10	1¢ black on buff	52.00	11.00	1.75
UX11	1¢ blue on grayish white	26.00	6.00	3.00

UX12

UX14

Jefferson

UX15
John Adams

SCOTT NO.	DESCRIPTION	MINT	UNUSED	USED
	1894			
UX12	1¢ black on buff Small Wreath	57.00	3.50	.75
	1897			
UX13	2¢ blue on cream	250.00	95.00	95.00
UX14	1¢ black on buff Large Wreath	50.00	4.00	.75
	1898			
UX15	1¢ black on buff	58.00	15.00	16.00
UX16	2¢ black on buff	18.00	7.00	20.00

UX18

UX19, UX20
McKinley

UX21

SCOTT NO.	DESCRIPTION	MINT	UNUSED	USED
	1902 Profile Background			
UX18	1¢ black on buff	23.00	3.00	.40
	1907			
UX19	1¢ black on buff	65.00	4.00	.60
	1908 Correspondence Space at Left			
UX20	1¢ black on buff	72.00	12.00	4.50
	1910 Background Shaded			
UX21	1¢ blue on bluish	120.00	25.00	14.00

UX22, UX24
Mckiny

UX23, UX26
Lincoln

UX25
Grant

SCOTT NO.	DESCRIPTION	MINT	UNUSED	USED
	White Portrait Background			
UX22	1¢ blue on bluish	29.00	3.25	.85
	1911			
UX23	1¢ red on cream	12.00	4.00	6.00
UX24	1¢ red on cream	14.00	1.50	.40
UX25	2¢ red on cream	1.75	1.25	22.00
	1913			
UX26	1¢ green on cream	15.00	3.00	9.00

UX27
Jefferson

UX28, UX43
Lincoln

UX29, UX30
Jefferson

1
CENT

UX32, UX33 surcharge

SCOTT NO.	DESCRIPTION	MINT	UNUSED	USED
	1914			
UX27	1¢ green on buff	.45	.35	.40
	1917-18			
UX28	1¢ green on cream	1.00	.40	.40
UX29	2¢ red on buff, die 1	52.00	11.00	4.00
UX30	2¢ red on cream, die 2 (1918)	35.00	7.00	1.80

NOTE: On UX29 end of queue slopes sharply down to right while on UX30 it extends nearly horizontally.

SCOTT NO.	DESCRIPTION	MINT	UNUSED	USED
	1920 UX29 & UX30 Revalued			
UX32	1¢ on 2¢ red, die 1	68.00	22.00	15.00
UX33	1¢ on 2¢ red, die 2	18.00	4.00	3.00

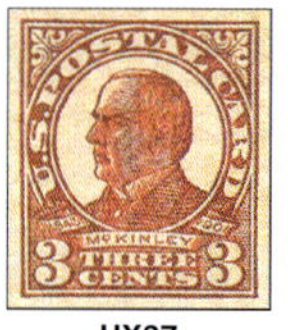

UX37
McKinley

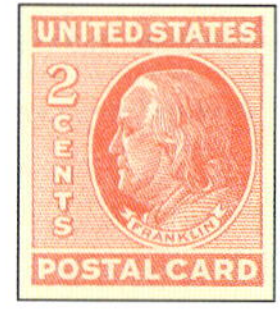

UX38
Franklin

UX39-42 surcharge

SCOTT NO.	DESCRIPTION	MINT	UNUSED	USED
	1926			
UX37	3¢ red on buff	5.50	2.50	17.50

SCOTT NO.	DESCRIPTION	FIRST DAY COVER	MINT	USED
	1951			
UX38	2¢ carmine rose	1.75	.40	.55
	1952 UX27 & UX28 Surcharged by cancelling machine, light green			
UX39	2¢ on 1¢ green	......	.60	.65
UX40	2¢ on 1¢ green	......	.70	.75
	UX27 & UX28 Surcharge Typographed, dark green			
UX41	2¢ on 1¢ green	......	5.75	5.50
UX42	2¢ on 1¢ green	......	6.25	6.00
	1952 Design of 1917			
UX43	2¢ carmine	1.75	.45	1.00

UX44 **UX45, UY16** **UX46, UY17**

SCOTT NO.	DESCRIPTION	FIRST DAY COVER	MINT	USED
	1956 FIPEX COMMEMORATIVE			
UX44	2¢ deep carmine & dark violet	1.75	.45	1.00
	1956 INTERNATIONAL CARD			
UX45	4¢ deep red & ultramarine	1.75	1.95	100.00
	1958			
UX46	3¢ purple	1.75	.65	.25
	As above, but with printed precancel lines			
UX46d	3¢ purple	......	5.00	3.00

ONE CENT
ADDITIONAL
PAID

UX47 surcharge

UX48, UY18
Lincoln

UX49, UX54, UX59, UY19, UY20

SCOTT NO.	DESCRIPTION	FIRST DAY COVER	MINT	USED
	1958 UX38 Surcharged			
UX47	2¢ & 1¢ carmine rose	......	280.00	685.00
	Mint *UX47 has advertising			
	1962-66			
UX48	4¢ red violet	1.75	.60	.25
UX48a	4¢ luminescent (1966)	3.00	.75	.25
	1963			
UX49	7¢ Tourism	1.75	5.50	75.00

UX50

UX51

SCOTT NO.	DESCRIPTION	FIRST DAY COVER	MINT	USED
	1964			
UX50	4¢ Customs Service	1.75	.60	1.00
UX51	4¢ Social Security	1.75	.60	1.00

UX52

UX53

SCOTT NO.	DESCRIPTION	FIRST DAY COVER	MINT	USED
	1965			
UX52	4¢ Coast Guard	1.75	.45	1.00
UX53	4¢ Census Bureau	1.75	.45	1.00
	1967 Design of UX49			
UX54	8¢ Tourism	1.75	5.75	75.00

UX55, UY21
Lincoln

UX56

SCOTT NO.	DESCRIPTION	FIRST DAY COVER	MINT	USED
	1968			
UX55	5¢ emerald	1.75	.40	.75
UX56	5¢ Women Marines	1.75	.45	1.00

UX57

SCOTT NO.	DESCRIPTION	FIRST DAY COVER	MINT	USED
	1970			
UX57	5¢ Weather Bureau	1.75	.45	1.00

UX58, UY22

SCOTT NO.	DESCRIPTION	FIRST DAY COVER	MINT	USED
	1971			
UX58	6¢ Paul Revere	1.75	.40	1.00
	Design of UX49			
UX59	10¢ Tourism	1.75	5.75	65.00

UX60

SCOTT NO.	DESCRIPTION	FIRST DAY COVER	MINT	USED
	1971			
UX60	6¢ New York Hospital	1.75	.40	1.00

UX61

UX62

UX63

UX64, UY23

SCOTT NO.	DESCRIPTION	FIRST DAY COVER	MINT	USED
	1972			
UX61	6¢ U.S.F. Constellation	1.75	1.00	12.00
UX62	6¢ Monument Valley	1.75	.65	12.00
UX63	6¢ Gloucester, Massachusetts	1.75	.65	7.00
UX64	6¢ John Hanson	1.75	.60	1.00

UX66, UY24

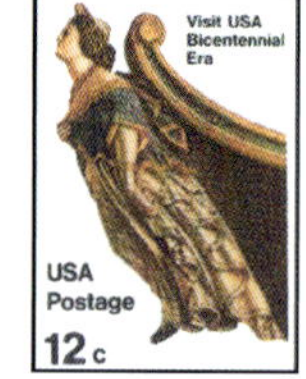

UX67

1973

SCOTT NO.	DESCRIPTION	FIRST DAY COVER	MINT	USED
UX65	6¢ Liberty, magenta, Design of 1873	1.75	.45	1.00
UX66	8¢ Samuel Adams	1.75	.65	1.00

1974

SCOTT NO.	DESCRIPTION	FIRST DAY COVER	MINT	USED
UX67	12¢ Visit USA	1.75	.45	50.00

UX68, UY25

UX69, UY26

UX70, UY27

1975-76

SCOTT NO.	DESCRIPTION	FIRST DAY COVER	MINT	USED
UX68	7¢ Charles Thomson	1.75	.45	12.00
UX69	9¢ J. Witherspoon	1.75	.45	1.00
UX70	9¢ Caesar Rodney	1.75	.45	1.00

UX71

UX72, UY28

1977

SCOTT NO.	DESCRIPTION	FIRST DAY COVER	MINT	USED
UX71	9¢ Federal Court House	1.75	.50	1.00
UX72	9¢ Nathan Hale	1.75	.55	1.00

UX73

UX74, UX75, UY29, UY30

UX76

UX77

1978

SCOTT NO.	DESCRIPTION	FIRST DAY COVER	MINT	USED
UX73	10¢ Music Hall	1.75	.50	1.00
UX74	10¢ John Hancock	1.75	.45	1.00
UX75	10¢ John Hancock	1.75	.50	1.00
UX76	14¢ "Eagle"	1.75	.50	35.00
UX77	10¢ multicolored	1.75	.50	2.00

UX78

UX79

UX80

1979

SCOTT NO.	DESCRIPTION	FIRST DAY COVER	MINT	USED
UX78	10¢ Fort Sackville	1.75	.50	2.00
UX79	10¢ Casimir Pulaski	1.75	.50	2.00
UX80	10¢ Moscow Olympics	1.75	.75	2.00
UX81	10¢ Iolani Palace	1.75	.50	2.00

UX81

UX82

UX83

UX84

UX85

UX86

1980

SCOTT NO.	DESCRIPTION	FIRST DAY COVER	MINT	USED
UX82	14¢ Winter Olympics	1.75	.85	22.00
UX83	10¢ Salt Lake Temple	1.75	.50	2.00
UX84	10¢ Count Rochambeau	1.75	.50	2.00
UX85	10¢ Kings Mountain	1.75	.50	2.00
UX86	19¢ Sir Francis Drake	1.75	1.00	40.00

UX87

UX88, UY31

UX89, UY32

1981

SCOTT NO.	DESCRIPTION	FIRST DAY COVER	MINT	USED
UX87	10¢ Cowpens	1.75	.50	18.50
UX88	"B" 12¢ violet & white	1.75	.45	.75
UX89	12¢ Isaiah Thomas	1.75	.45	.75

UX90

UX91

UX92, UY33

UX93, UY34

SCOTT NO.	DESCRIPTION	FIRST DAY COVER	MINT	USED
UX90	12¢ Eutaw Springs	1.75	.55	17.50
UX91	12¢ Lewis & Clark	1.75	.55	28.00
UX92	13¢ Robert Morris	1.75	.45	.75
UX93	13¢ Robert Morris	1.75	.45	.75

UX94

UX95

UX96

UX97

1982

SCOTT NO.	DESCRIPTION	FIRST DAY COVER	MINT	USED
UX94	13¢ Francis Marion	1.75	.55	1.25
UX95	13¢ La Salle	1.75	.55	1.25
UX96	13¢ Academy of Music	1.75	.55	1.25
UX97	13¢ St. Louis Post Office	1.75	.55	1.25

UX98

UX99

UX100

1983

SCOTT NO.	DESCRIPTION	FIRST DAY COVER	MINT	USED
UX98	13¢ General Oglethorpe	1.75	.55	1.25
UX99	13¢ Washington Post Office	1.75	.55	1.25
UX100	13¢ Olympics	1.75	.55	1.25

UX101

UX102

UX103

Dominguez Adobe Rancho San Pedro The California Ranchos 1784-1984 Historic Preservation USA 13

UX104

1984

SCOTT NO.	DESCRIPTION	FIRST DAY COVER	MINT	USED
UX101	13¢ "Ark" & "Dove"	1.75	.55	1.25
UX102	13¢ Olympics	1.75	.55	1.50
UX103	13¢ Frederic Baraga	1.75	.55	1.25
UX104	13¢ Historic Preservation	1.75	.55	1.25

UX105, UX106, UY35, UY36

UX107

George Wythe Patriot USA 14

UX108

1985

SCOTT NO.	DESCRIPTION	FIRST DAY COVER	MINT	USED
UX105	14¢ Charles Carroll	1.75	.50	.75
UX106	14¢ Charles Carroll	1.75	.50	.60
UX107	25¢ Flying Cloud	1.75	.95	25.00
UX108	14¢ George Wythe	1.75	.50	.90

UX109

UX110

Francis Vigo, Vincennes, 1779 USA 14

UX111

UX112

1986

SCOTT NO.	DESCRIPTION	FIRST DAY COVER	MINT	USED
UX109	14¢ Connecticut	1.75	.55	2.00
UX110	14¢ Stamp Collecting	1.75	.55	1.50
UX111	14¢ Francis Vigo	1.75	.55	1.50
UX112	14¢ Rhode Island	1.75	.55	2.00

UX113

UX114

SCOTT NO.	DESCRIPTION	FIRST DAY COVER	MINT	USED
UX113	14¢ Wisconsin	1.75	.55	1.25
UX114	14¢ National Guard	1.75	.55	1.50

UX115

UX116

USA 14

UX117

1987

SCOTT NO.	DESCRIPTION	FIRST DAY COVER	MINT	USED
UX115	14¢ Steel Plow	1.75	.55	1.50
UX116	14¢ Constitution	1.75	.55	1.00
UX117	14¢ Flag	1.75	.55	.75

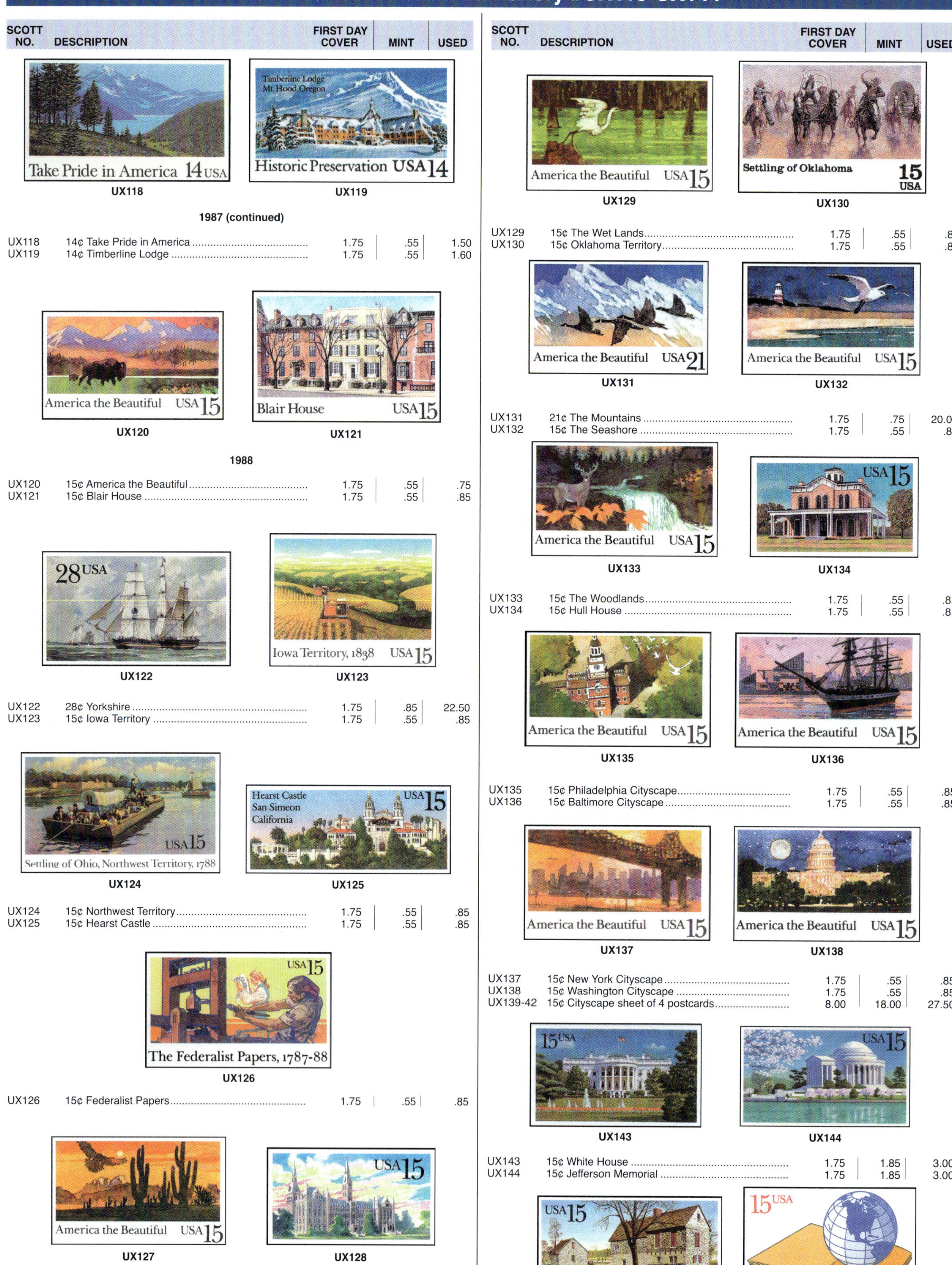

SCOTT NO.	DESCRIPTION	FIRST DAY COVER	MINT	USED
	1987 (continued)			
UX118	14¢ Take Pride in America	1.75	.55	1.50
UX119	14¢ Timberline Lodge	1.75	.55	1.60
	1988			
UX120	15¢ America the Beautiful	1.75	.55	.75
UX121	15¢ Blair House	1.75	.55	.85
UX122	28¢ Yorkshire	1.75	.85	22.50
UX123	15¢ Iowa Territory	1.75	.55	.85
UX124	15¢ Northwest Territory	1.75	.55	.85
UX125	15¢ Hearst Castle	1.75	.55	.85
UX126	15¢ Federalist Papers	1.75	.55	.85
	1989			
UX127	15¢ The Desert	1.75	.55	.85
UX128	15¢ Healy Hall	1.75	.55	.85
UX129	15¢ The Wet Lands	1.75	.55	.85
UX130	15¢ Oklahoma Territory	1.75	.55	.85
UX131	21¢ The Mountains	1.75	.75	20.00
UX132	15¢ The Seashore	1.75	.55	.85
UX133	15¢ The Woodlands	1.75	.55	.85
UX134	15¢ Hull House	1.75	.55	.85
UX135	15¢ Philadelphia Cityscape	1.75	.55	.85
UX136	15¢ Baltimore Cityscape	1.75	.55	.85
UX137	15¢ New York Cityscape	1.75	.55	.85
UX138	15¢ Washington Cityscape	1.75	.55	.85
UX139-42	15¢ Cityscape sheet of 4 postcards	8.00	18.00	27.50
UX143	15¢ White House	1.75	1.85	3.00
UX144	15¢ Jefferson Memorial	1.75	1.85	3.00

SCOTT NO.	DESCRIPTION	FIRST DAY COVER	MINT	USED

UX147

UX148

UX150

UX151

UX152

1990

SCOTT NO.	DESCRIPTION	FIRST DAY COVER	MINT	USED
UX145	15¢ Papermaking	1.75	.55	.50
UX146	15¢ Literacy	1.75	.55	.85
UX147	15¢ Bingham	1.75	1.75	3.00
UX148	15¢ Isaac Royall House	1.75	.55	.85
UX150	15¢ Stanford University	1.75	.55	.85
UX151	15¢ DAR Memorial Hall	1.75	1.60	2.50
UX152	15¢ Chicago Orchestra Hall	1.75	.55	.85

UX153

UX154

UX155

1991

SCOTT NO.	DESCRIPTION	FIRST DAY COVER	MINT	USED
UX153	19¢ Flag	1.75	.65	.85
UX154	19¢ Carnegie Hall	1.75	.65	.85
UX155	19¢ Old Red Administration Building	1.75	.65	.50

UX156

UX157

SCOTT NO.	DESCRIPTION	FIRST DAY COVER	MINT	USED
UX156	19¢ Bill of Rights	1.75	.65	.85
UX157	19¢ University of Notre Dame, Administration Building	1.75	.65	.85

UX158

UX159

SCOTT NO.	DESCRIPTION	FIRST DAY COVER	MINT	USED
UX158	30¢ Niagara Falls	1.75	.90	10.00
UX159	19¢ Old Mill University of Vermont	1.75	.65	1.00

UX160

UX161

UX162

UX163

UX164

UX165

1992

SCOTT NO.	DESCRIPTION	FIRST DAY COVER	MINT	USED
UX160	19¢ Wadsworth Atheneum	1.75	.65	.85
UX161	19¢ Cobb Hall University of Chicago	1.75	.65	.85
UX162	19¢ Waller Hall	1.75	.65	.85
UX163	19¢ America's Cup	1.75	1.95	4.00
UX164	19¢ Columbia River Gorge	1.75	.65	.85
UX165	19¢ Great Hall, Ellis Island	1.75	.65	.85

UX166

UX167

1993

SCOTT NO.	DESCRIPTION	FIRST DAY COVER	MINT	USED
UX166	19¢ National Cathedral	1.75	.65	.85
UX167	19¢ Wren Building	1.75	.65	.85

UX168

UX169

SCOTT NO.	DESCRIPTION	FIRST DAY COVER	MINT	USED
UX168	19¢ Holocaust Memorial	2.00	1.85	4.00
UX169	19¢ Fort Recovery	1.75	.65	.85

UX170

UX171

SCOTT NO.	DESCRIPTION	FIRST DAY COVER	MINT	USED
UX170	19¢ Playmakers Theatre	1.75	.65	.85
UX171	19¢ O'Kane Hall	1.75	.65	.85

UX172

UX173

1993 (continued)

SCOTT NO.	DESCRIPTION	FIRST DAY COVER	MINT	USED
UX172	19¢ Beecher Hall	1.75	.65	.85
UX173	19¢ Massachusetts Hall	1.75	.65	.85

UX174

UX175

UX176

UX177

1994

SCOTT NO.	DESCRIPTION	FIRST DAY COVER	MINT	USED
UX174	19¢ Abraham Lincoln Home	1.75	.65	.85
UX175	19¢ Myers Hall	1.75	.65	.85
UX176	19¢ Canyon de Chelly	1.75	.65	.85
UX177	19¢ St. Louis Union Station	1.75	.65	.85

UX178

Legends of the West

UX178	*Home on the Range*	**UX188**	*Nellie Cashman*
UX179	*Buffalo Bill*	**UX189**	*Charles Goodnight*
UX180	*Jim Bridger*	**UX190**	*Geronimo*
UX181	*Annie Oakley*	**UX191**	*Kit Carson*
UX182	*Native American Culture*	**UX192**	*Wild Bill Hickok*
UX183	*Chief Joseph*	**UX193**	*Western Wildlife*
UX184	*Bill Pickett*	**UX194**	*Jim Beckwourth*
UX185	*Bat Masterson*	**UX195**	*Bill Tilghman*
UX186	*John Fremont*	**UX196**	*Sacagawea*
UX187	*Wyatt Earp*	**UX197**	*Overland Mail*

SCOTT NO.	DESCRIPTION	FIRST DAY COVER	MINT	USED
UX178-97	19¢ Legends of the West, set of 20	35.00	35.00	65.00

UX198

UX199

UX198

1995

SCOTT NO.	DESCRIPTION	FIRST DAY COVER	MINT	USED
UX198	20¢ Red Barn	1.75	.65	.75
UX199	20¢ "G" Old Glory	1.75	4.25	3.00

UX201

Civil War

UX200	*Monitor-Virginia*	**UX210**	*Tubman*
UX201	*Lee*	**UX211**	*Watie*
UX202	*Barton*	**UX212**	*Johnston*
UX203	*Grant*	**UX213**	*Hancock*
UX204	*Shiloh*	**UX214**	*Chestnut*
UX205	*Davis*	**UX215**	*Chancellorsville*
UX206	*Farragut*	**UX216**	*Sherman*
UX207	*Douglass*	**UX217**	*Pember*
UX208	*Semmes*	**UX218**	*Jackson*
UX209	*Lincoln*	**UX219**	*Gettysburg*

SCOTT NO.	DESCRIPTION	FIRST DAY COVER	MINT	USED
UX200-19	20¢ Civil War, set of 20	35.00	60.00	65.00
UX219a	50¢ Eagle	1.75	1.75	10.00

UX220

UX241

SCOTT NO.	DESCRIPTION	FIRST DAY COVER	MINT	USED
UX220	20¢ American Clipper Ships	1.75	.65	.85

UX221

American Comic Strips

UX221	*Yellow Kid*	**UX231**	*Popeye*
UX222	*Katzenjammer Kids*	**UX232**	*Blondie*
UX223	*Little Nemo*	**UX233**	*Dick Tracy*
UX224	*Bring Up Father*	**UX234**	*Alley Oop*
UX225	*Krazy Kat*	**UX235**	*Nancy*
UX226	*Rube Goldberg*	**UX236**	*Flash Gordon*
UX227	*Toonerville Folks*	**UX237**	*Li'l Abner*
UX228	*Gasoline Alley*	**UX238**	*Terry/Pirates*
UX229	*Barney Google*	**UX239**	*Prince Valiant*
UX230	*Little Orphan Annie*	**UX240**	*Brenda Starr*

SCOTT NO.	DESCRIPTION	FIRST DAY COVER	MINT	USED
UX221-40	20¢ American Comic Strips, set of 20	35.00	68.00	80.00

1996

SCOTT NO.	DESCRIPTION	FIRST DAY COVER	MINT	USED
UX241	20¢ Winter Farm Scene	1.75	.65	.50

UX242

Centennial Olympic Games

UX242	*Men's cycling*	**UX252**	*Women's softball*
UX243	*Women's diving*	**UX253**	*Women's swimming*
UX244	*Women's running*	**UX254**	*Men's sprints*
UX245	*Men's canoeing*	**UX255**	*Men's rowing*
UX246	*Decathlon*	**UX256**	*Beach volleyball*
UX247	*Women's soccer*	**UX257**	*Men's basketball*
UX248	*Men's shot put*	**UX258**	*Equestrian*
UX249	*Women's sailboarding*	**UX259**	*Men's gymnastics*
UX250	*Women's gymnastics*	**UX260**	*Men's swimming*
UX251	*Freestyle wrestling*	**UX261**	*Men's hurdles*

SCOTT NO.	DESCRIPTION	FIRST DAY COVER	MINT	USED
UX242-61	20¢ Centennial Olympic Games, set of 20	35.00	77.00	75.00

UX262

UX263

SCOTT NO.	DESCRIPTION	FIRST DAY COVER	MINT	USED
UX262	20¢ McDowell Hall	1.75	.65	.85
UX263	20¢ Alexander Hall	1.75	.65	.85

UX264

Engandered Species

UX264	*Florida panther*
UX265	*Black-footed ferret*
UX266	*American crocodile*
UX267	*Piping plover*
UX268	*Gila trout*
UX269	*Florida manatee*
UX270	*Schaus swallowtail butterfly*
UX271	*Woodland caribou*
UX272	*Thick-billed parrot*
UX273	*San Francisco garter snake*
UX274	*Ocelot*
UX275	*Wyoming toad*
UX276	*California condor*
UX277	*Hawaiian monk seal*
UX278	*Brown pelican*

SCOTT NO.	DESCRIPTION	FIRST DAY COVER	MINT	USED
UX264-78	20¢ Endangered Species, set of 15	26.50	77.00	70.00

UX279

UX280

1997

SCOTT NO.	DESCRIPTION	FIRST DAY COVER	MINT	USED
UX279	20¢ Swans	2.50	6.00	2.00
UX279a	20¢ Swans, set of 12	20.00(8)	60.00	......
UX280	20¢ Shepard Hall	1.75	.65	1.00

UX281

UX282

SCOTT NO.	DESCRIPTION	FIRST DAY COVER	MINT	USED
UX281	20¢ Bugs Bunny	1.75	1.85	2.50
UX282	20¢ Golden Gate Bridge 1.75	.45	1.00	1.00

UX283

UX284

SCOTT NO.	DESCRIPTION	FIRST DAY COVER	MINT	USED
UX283	50¢ Golden Gate Bridge at Sunset	1.95	1.60	3.00
UX284	20¢ Fort McHenry	1.75	.75	.85

UX285

Classic Movie Monsters

UX285 *Lon Chaney as The Phantom of the Opera*
UX286 *Bela Lugosi as Dracula*
UX287 *Boris Karloff as Frankenstein's Monster*
UX288 *Boris Karloff as The Mummy*
UX289 *Lon Chaney Jr. as The Wolfman*

UX291

SCOTT NO.	DESCRIPTION	FIRST DAY COVER	MINT	USED
UX285	20¢ Classic Movie Monsters, set of 5	8.75	12.00	12.00
UX289a	same, bklt of 20 (4 of each)	....	44.00	....

UX290

UX292

1998

SCOTT NO.	DESCRIPTION	FIRST DAY COVER	MINT	USED
UX290	20¢ University of Mississippi	1.75	.65	.85
UX291	20¢ Sylvester & Tweety	1.75	1.75	3.00
UX291a	same, bklt of 10	....	18.00	....
UX292	20¢ Girard College, Philadelphia, PA	1.75	.65	.85

UX293

UX297

UX298

SCOTT NO.	DESCRIPTION	FIRST DAY COVER	MINT	USED
UX293-96	20¢ Tropical Birds, set of 4	7.00	6.50	7.50
UX296a	same, bklt of 20 (5 of each)	....	32.00	....
UX297	20¢ Ballet	1.75	1.75	1.50
UX297a	same, bklt of 10	....	17.00	....
UX298	20¢ Kerr Hall, Northeastern University	1.75	.65	.85

UX299

UX300

UX301

SCOTT NO.	DESCRIPTION	FIRST DAY COVER	MINT	USED
UX299	20¢ Usen Castle, Brandeis University	1.75	.65	.85

1999

SCOTT NO.	DESCRIPTION	FIRST DAY COVER	MINT	USED
UX300	20¢ Love, Victorian	1.75	1.75	2.50
UX301	20¢ University of Wisc.-Madison-Bascom Hill	1.75	.65	.75

UX302

UX303

SCOTT NO.	DESCRIPTION	FIRST DAY COVER	MINT	USED
UX302	20¢ Washington and Lee University	1.75	.65	.60
UX303	20¢ Redwood Library & Anthenaum, Newport, RI...	1.75	.65	.60

UX304

UX305

SCOTT NO.	DESCRIPTION	FIRST DAY COVER	MINT	USED
UX304	20¢ Daffy Duck	1.75	1.75	1.50
UX304a	same, bklt of 10	....	17.00	....
UX305	20¢ Mount Vernon	1.75	.85	.85

UX306

UX307

Famous Trains

UX307 *Super Chief*
UX308 *Hiawatha*
UX309 *Daylight*
UX310 *Congressional*
UX311 *20th Century Limited*

1999

SCOTT NO.	DESCRIPTION	FIRST DAY COVER	MINT	USED
UX306	20¢ Block Island Lighthouse	1.75	.65	.50
UX307-11	20¢ Famous Trains, set of 5	8.75	9.00	6.00
UX311a	same, bklt of 20 (4 of each)	....	33.00	....

UX312

UX313

UX315

UX316

2000

SCOTT NO.	DESCRIPTION	FIRST DAY COVER	MINT	USED
UX312	20¢ University of Utah	1.75	.65	.70
UX313	20¢ Ryman Auditorium, Nashville, Tennessee	1.75	.65	.70
UX314	20¢ Road Runner & Wile E. Coyote	1.75	1.85	1.50
UX314a	same, bklt of 10	....	18.00	....
UX315	20¢ Adoption	1.75	1.85	1.75
UX315a	same, bklt of 10	....	18.00	....
UX316	20¢ Old Stone Row, Middlebury College, Vermont..	1.75	.65	.60

SCOTT NO.	DESCRIPTION	FIRST DAY COVER	MINT	USED

UX336

The Stars and Stripes

- **UX317** *Sons of Liberty Flag, 1775*
- **UX318** *New England Flag, 1775*
- **UX319** *Forster Flag, 1775*
- **UX320** *Continental Colors, 1776*
- **UX321** *Francis Hopkinson Flag, 1777*
- **UX322** *Brandywine Flag, 1777*
- **UX323** *John Paul Jones Flag, 1779*
- **UX324** *Pierre L'Enfant Flag, 1783*
- **UX325** *Indian Peace Flag, 1803*
- **UX326** *Easton Flag, 1814*
- **UX327** *Star-Spangled Banner, 1814*
- **UX328** *Bennington Flag, c. 1820*
- **UX329** *Great Star Flag, 1837*
- **UX330** *29-Star Flag, 1847*
- **UX331** *Fort Sumter Flag, 1861*
- **UX332** *Centennial Flag, 1876*
- **UX333** *38-Star Flag*
- **UX334** *Peace Flag, 1891*
- **UX335** *48-Star Flag, 1912*
- **UX336** *50-Star Flag, 1960*

UX317-36	The Stars and Stripes, set of 20	35.00	85.00	58.00

UX337

Legends of Baseball

- **UX337** *Jackie Robinson*
- **UX338** *Eddie Collins*
- **UX339** *Christy Mathewson*
- **UX340** *Ty Cobb*
- **UX341** *George Sisler*
- **UX342** *Rogers Hornsby*
- **UX343** *Mickey Cochrane*
- **UX344** *Babe Ruth*
- **UX345** *Walter Johnson*
- **UX346** *Roberto Clemente*
- **UX347** *Lefty Grove*
- **UX348** *Tris Speaker*
- **UX349** *Cy Young*
- **UX350** *Jimmie Foxx*
- **UX351** *Pie Traynor*
- **UX352** *Satchel Paige*
- **UX353** *Honus Wagner*
- **UX354** *Josh Gibson*
- **UX355** *Dizzy Dean*
- **UX356** *Lou Gehrig*

UX337-56	20¢ Legends of Baseball, set of 20	35.00	42.00	40.00

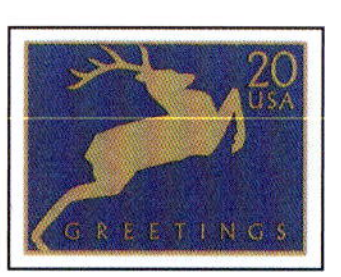

UX357-60

UX361

UX357-60	20¢ Christmas Deer, set of 4	7.00	6.50	5.50

2001

UX361	20¢ Connecticut Hall, Yale University	1.75	.65	.75

UX362

UX363

UX364

UX362	20¢ University of South Carolina	1.75	.65	.85
UX363	20¢ Northwestern University Sesquicentennial 1851-2001	1.75	.65	.85
UX364	20¢ Waldschmidt Hall, The University of Portland	1.75	.65	.75

Legendary Playing Fields

- **UX365** *Ebbets Field*
- **UX366** *Tiger Stadium*
- **UX367** *Crosley Field*
- **UX368** *Yankee Stadium*
- **UX369** *Polo Grounds*
- **UX370** *Forbes Field*
- **UX371** *Fenway Park*
- **UX372** *Comiskey Park*
- **UX373** *Shibe Park*
- **UX374** *Wrigley Field*

2001

UX365-74	21¢ Legendary Playing Fields, set of 10	35.00	55.00	58.00
UX374a	same, bklt of 10	....	55.00	....

UX375

UX376

UX377

UX375	21¢ White Barn	1.75	.70	.70
UX376	21¢ That's All Folks	2.00	2.00	1.75
UX376a	same, bklt of 10	....	18.00	....
UX377-80	21¢ Santas, set of 4	7.50	8.00	7.00
UX380a	same, complete bklt of 20	......	37.00	......

SCOTT NO.	DESCRIPTION	FIRST DAY COVER	MINT	USED

UX381

UX382

UX386

2002

UX381	23¢ Carlsbad Caverns	1.75	.75	.75
UX382-85	23¢ Teddy Bears, set of 4	7.50	6.00	6.00
UX385a	same, complete bklt of 20	......	29.00	......
UX386-89	23¢ Christmas Snowmen, set of 4	7.50	6.00	6.00
UX389a	same, complete bklt of 20	......	29.00	......

UX390

UX395

UX400

2003

UX390-94	23¢ Old Glory, set of 5	8.75	9.75	9.25
UX394a	same, complete booklet of 20 cards	....	36.00	....
UX395-99	23¢ Southern Lighthouses, set of 5	8.75	7.75	7.75
UX399a	same, complete booklet of 20	....	34.00	....
UX400	23¢ Ohio University, 200th Anniversary	1.75	.75	.75
UX401-04	23¢ Christmas Music Makers, set of 4	7.50	7.00	7.00
UX404a	same, complete bklt of 20	......	34.00	......

UX401

UX405

2004

UX405	23¢ Columbia University, 250th Anniversary	1.75	.75	.75

UX406

UX407

UX406	23¢ Harriton House, 300th Anniversary	1.75	.75	.70
UX407-10	23¢ Art of Disney, set of 4	7.00	7.50	8.50
UX410a	same, complete booklet of 20	....	38.00	....

UX411

UX421

UX411-20	23¢ Art of the American Indian, set of 10	17.50	19.00	19.00
UX420a	same, complete booklet of 20	....	33.00	....
UX421-35	23¢ Cloudscapes, set of 15	26.25	28.00	28.00
UX435a	same, complete booklet of 20	....	35.00	....

UX440

UX449

2005

SCOTT NO.	DESCRIPTION	FIRST DAY COVER	MINT	USED
UX436-39	Disney Characters, set of 4	7.00	7.50	7.50
UX439a	same, complete booklet of 20	....	36.00	....
UX440-44	23¢ Sporty Cars, set of 4	7.00	8.00	8.00
UX444a	same, complete booklet of 20	....	30.00	....
UX445-48	23¢ Let's Dance, set of 4	7.00	65.00	6.50
UX448a	same, complete booklet of 20	....	31.00	....

2006

SCOTT NO.	DESCRIPTION	FIRST DAY COVER	MINT	USED
UX449	24¢ Zebulon Pike Expedition, Bicentennial	1.75	.80	.75

UX450

UX454

SCOTT NO.	DESCRIPTION	FIRST DAY COVER	MINT	USED
UX450-53	24¢ Disney Characters, set of 4	7.00	6.50	6.50
UX453a	same, complete booklet of 20	....	30.00	....
UX454-57	24¢ Baseball Sluggers, set of 4	7.00	6.75	6.75
UX457a	same, complete booklet of 20	....	32.00	....

UX458

D.C. Comics Super Heroes

UX458	*Superman Cover*	**UX468**	*The Flash Cover*
UX459	*Superman*	**UX469**	*The Flash*
UX460	*Batman Cover*	**UX470**	*Plastic Man Cover*
UX461	*Batman*	**UX471**	*Plastic Man*
UX462	*Wonder Woman Cover*	**UX472**	*Aquaman Cover*
UX463	*Wonder Woman*	**UX473**	*Aquaman*
UX464	*Green Lantern Cover*	**UX474**	*Supergirl Cover*
UX465	*Green Lantern*	**UX475**	*Supergirl*
UX466	*Green Arrow Cover*	**UX476**	*Hawkman Cover*
UX467	*Green Arrow*	**UX477**	*Hawkman*

SCOTT NO.	DESCRIPTION	FIRST DAY COVER	MINT	USED
UX458-77	24¢ D.C. Comics Super Heroes, set of 20	40.00	38.00	38.00

Southern Florida Wetlands

UX478	*Snail Kite*	**UX483**	*White Ibis*
UX479	*Cape Sable Seaside Sparrow*	**UX484**	*American Crocodile*
UX480	*Wood Storks*	**UX485**	*Everglades Mink*
UX481	*Florida Panthers*	**UX486**	*Roseate Spoonbills*
UX482	*Bald Eagle*	**UX487**	*American Alligators*

UX483

SCOTT NO.	DESCRIPTION	FIRST DAY COVER	MINT	USED
UX478-87	39¢ Southern Florida Wetlands, set of 10	....	53.00	....

UX488

2007

SCOTT NO.	DESCRIPTION	FIRST DAY COVER	MINT	USED
UX488	26¢ Pineapple	1.95	.95	.95

UX501

Star Wars

UX489	*Darth Vader*	**UX496**	*Obi-Wan Kenobi*
UX490	*Luke Skywalker*	**UX497**	*Boba Fett*
UX491	*C-3PO*	**UX498**	*Darth Maul*
UX492	*Queen Padme Amidala*	**UX499**	*Yoda*
UX493	*Millennium Falcon*	**UX500**	*Princess Leia and R2-D2*
UX494	*Emperor Palpatine*	**UX501**	*Chewbacca and Han Solo*
UX495	*Anakin Skywalker and Obi-Wan Kenobi*	**UX502**	*X-wing Starfighter*
		UX503	*Stormtroopers*

SCOTT NO.	DESCRIPTION	FIRST DAY COVER	MINT	USED
UX489-503	26¢ Star Wars, set of 15	27.50	33.00	33.00

UX505

UX509-28

UX529-32

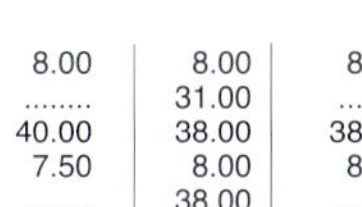

SCOTT NO.	DESCRIPTION	FIRST DAY COVER	MINT	USED
UX504-08	26¢ Pacific Coast Lighthouses, set of 5	8.00	8.00	8.00
UX508a	same, complete booklet of 20	....	31.00	....
UX509-28	26¢ Marvel Comic Book Heroes, set of 20	40.00	38.00	38.00
UX529-32	26¢ Disney Characters, set of 4	7.50	8.00	8.00
	same, complete booklet of 20	....	38.00	....

UX533

UX534

2008

SCOTT NO.	DESCRIPTION	FIRST DAY COVER	MINT	USED
UX533	27¢ Mount St. Mary's University postal card	2.75	.85	.85
UX534	27¢ Corinthian Column postal card	2.75	.85	.85

UX535

SCOTT NO.	DESCRIPTION	FIRST DAY COVER	MINT	USED
UX535-38	27¢ Art of Disney: Imagination, set of 4	7.00	7.75	7.75
UX538a	same, complete booklet of 20	....	38.00	....

UX539

Great Lakes Dunes

UX539	Vesper Sparrow
UX540	Piping Plover
UX541	Easter Hognose Snake
UX542	Common Meransers
UX543	Piping Plover Nestlings
UX544	Red Fox
UX545	Tiger Beetle
UX546	White Footed Mouse
UX547	Spotted Sandpiper
UX548	Red Admiral Butterfly

SCOTT NO.	DESCRIPTION	FIRST DAY COVER	MINT	USED
UX539-48	42¢ Great Lakes Dunes postal cards	....	35.00	....

SCOTT NO.	DESCRIPTION	FIRST DAY COVER	MINT	USED

UX549

Automobiles of the 1950's

UX549 1957 Lincoln Premiere
UX550 1957 Chrysler 300C
UX551 1959 Cadillac Eldorado
UX552 1957 Studebaker Golden Hawk
UX553 1957 Pontiac Safari

UX549-53	27¢ Automobiles of the 1950's, set of 5	9.75	9.50	9.50

UX554

UX556

2009

UX554	27¢ Miami University	2.75	.85	.85
UX555	28¢ Koi Fish Postal Card (white fish, orange & white fish)	1.75	.85	.85
UX556	28¢ Koi Fish Postal Card (black fish, red & white fish)	1.75	.85	.85

Simpsons

UX557 Homer
UX558 Marge
UX559 Bart
UX560 Lisa
UX561 Maggie

UX559

UX562

Gulf Coast Lighthouses

UX562 Matagorda Island
UX563 Sabine Pass
UX564 Biloxi
UX565 Sand Island
UX566 Fort Jefferson

UX557-61	28¢ Simpsons Postal Card, set of 5	9.75	9.75	9.75
UX562-66	28¢ Gulf Coast Lighthouses	19.95	9.95	9.95

UX575

Early TV Memories

UX567 Alfred Hitchcock
UX568 Burns & Allen
UX569 Dinah Shore Show
UX570 Dragnet
UX571 Ed Sullivan Show
UX572 The Honeymooners
UX573 Hopalong Cassidy
UX574 Howdy Doody
UX575 I Love Lucy
UX576 Kukla, Fran & Ollie
UX577 Lassie
UX578 The Lone Ranger
UX579 Ozzie & Harriet
UX580 Perry Mason
UX581 Phil Silvers Show
UX582 Red Skelton Show
UX583 Texaco Star Theatre
UX584 The Tonight Show
UX585 The Twilight Zone
UX586 You Bet Your Life

UX567-86	28¢ Early TV Memories, set of 20	60.00	39.00	39.00

UX587

Kelp Forest

UX587 Western Gull
UX588 Lion's Mane Nudibranch
UX589 Northern Kelp Crab
UX590 Vermillion Rockfish
UX591 Yellowtail Rockfish
UX592 Pacific Rock Crab
UX593 Harbor Seal
UX594 Brown Pelican
UX595 Treefish, Monterey Truban Snail
UX596 Copper Rockfish

UX587-96	44¢ Kelp Forest, set of 10 postal cards	32.50	25.00	....

2010

UX597

Cowboys of the Silver Screen

UX597 Roy Rogers
UX598 Tom Mix
UX599 William S. Hart
UX600 Gene Autrey

UX597-600	28¢ Cowboys of the Silver Screen Postal Cards	9.75	8.50	....

SCOTT NO.	DESCRIPTION	FIRST DAY COVER	MINT	USED

UX606

Scenic American Landscapes

UX601 Acadia
UX602 Badlands
UX603 Bryce Canyon
UX604 Grand Canyon
UX605 Great Smokey Mountains
UX606 Mount McKinley
UX607 Mount Rainier
UX608 St. John, U.S. Virgin Islands
UX609 Yosemite
UX610 Zion

UX601-10	28¢ Scenic American Landscapes	29.00	25.00	....

2011

UX614

Hawaiian Rain Forest

UX611 Hawaii 'amakihi, Hawaii 'elepaio
UX612 'Akepa, 'ope'ape'a
UX613 'I'iwi, haha
UX614 'Oma'o, kanawao, 'ohelo kau lau nui
UX615 'Oha
UX616 Pulehua, kelea lau nui, 'ilihia
UX617 Koele Mountain damselfly, 'akala
UX618 Apapane, Hawaiian Mint
UX619 Jewel Orchid
UX620 Happyface spider, 'ala'ala wai nui

UX611-20	44¢ Hawaiian Rain Forest Postal Cards, set of 10	29.00	25.00	....

UX621

UX625

Pixar: Send a Hello

UX622 Lightening McQueen & Mater
UX623 Remy the Rat & Linquini
UX624 Buzz Lightyear & Two Aliens
UX625 Carl Frederickson & Dug
UX626 Wall-E

UX621	29¢ Common Terns	2.75	.75	.75
UX622-26	29¢ Pixar: Send a Hello Postal Cards	15.00	10.00	....

2012

UX627, UX633

UX630

Pixar: Mail a Smile

UX628 Flik and Dot
UX629 Bob & Dashiell Parr
UX630 Nemo & Squirt
UX631 Jessie, Woody and Bullseye
UX632 Boo, Mike Wazowskie & Sulley

UX627	32¢ Sailboat Postal Card	2.25	.75	.75
UX628-32	45¢ Pixar: Mail a Smile Postal Cards	15.00	9.50	....
UX633	32¢ Sailboat	2.25	.95	....
	same, sheet of 4	....	4.75	....

UX639

Scenic American Landscapes

UX634 13-Mile Woods
UX635 Glacier National Park
UX636 Grand Teton National Park
UX637 Hagatna Bay
UX638 Lancaster County, PA
UX639 Niagra Falls
UX640 Nine-Mile Prarie
UX641 Okefenokee Swamp
UX642 Rio Grande
UX643 Voyageurs National Park

UX634-43	32¢ Scenic American Landscapes	....	17.50	....

2013

UX644

UX644	33¢ Deer	2.25	.95	.95

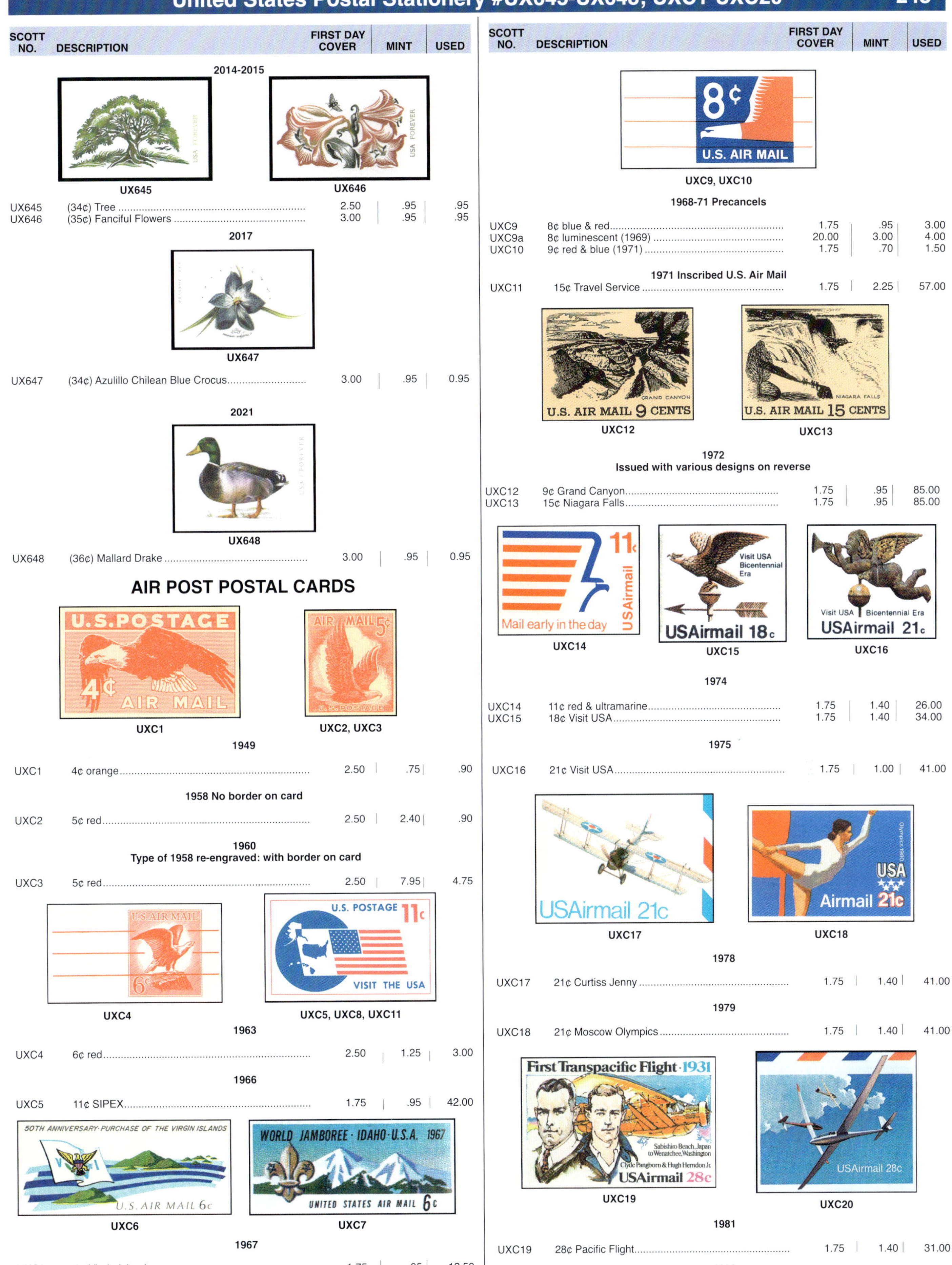

2014-2015

UX645 UX646

SCOTT NO.	DESCRIPTION	FIRST DAY COVER	MINT	USED
UX645	(34¢) Tree	2.50	.95	.95
UX646	(35¢) Fanciful Flowers	3.00	.95	.95

2017

UX647

SCOTT NO.	DESCRIPTION	FIRST DAY COVER	MINT	USED
UX647	(34¢) Azulillo Chilean Blue Crocus	3.00	.95	0.95

2021

UX648

SCOTT NO.	DESCRIPTION	FIRST DAY COVER	MINT	USED
UX648	(36¢) Mallard Drake	3.00	.95	0.95

AIR POST POSTAL CARDS

UXC1 UXC2, UXC3

1949

SCOTT NO.	DESCRIPTION	FIRST DAY COVER	MINT	USED
UXC1	4¢ orange	2.50	.75	.90
	1958 No border on card			
UXC2	5¢ red	2.50	2.40	.90
	1960 Type of 1958 re-engraved: with border on card			
UXC3	5¢ red	2.50	7.95	4.75

UXC4 UXC5, UXC8, UXC11

1963

SCOTT NO.	DESCRIPTION	FIRST DAY COVER	MINT	USED
UXC4	6¢ red	2.50	1.25	3.00
	1966			
UXC5	11¢ SIPEX	1.75	.95	42.00

UXC6 UXC7

1967

SCOTT NO.	DESCRIPTION	FIRST DAY COVER	MINT	USED
UXC6	6¢ Virgin Islands	1.75	.95	12.50
UXC7	6¢ Boy Scout Jamboree	2.50	.95	18.00
UXC8	13¢ AAM Convention	1.75	1.75	46.00

UXC9, UXC10

1968-71 Precancels

SCOTT NO.	DESCRIPTION	FIRST DAY COVER	MINT	USED
UXC9	8¢ blue & red	1.75	.95	3.00
UXC9a	8¢ luminescent (1969)	20.00	3.00	4.00
UXC10	9¢ red & blue (1971)	1.75	.70	1.50
	1971 Inscribed U.S. Air Mail			
UXC11	15¢ Travel Service	1.75	2.25	57.00

UXC12 UXC13

1972
Issued with various designs on reverse

SCOTT NO.	DESCRIPTION	FIRST DAY COVER	MINT	USED
UXC12	9¢ Grand Canyon	1.75	.95	85.00
UXC13	15¢ Niagara Falls	1.75	.95	85.00

UXC14 UXC15 UXC16

1974

SCOTT NO.	DESCRIPTION	FIRST DAY COVER	MINT	USED
UXC14	11¢ red & ultramarine	1.75	1.40	26.00
UXC15	18¢ Visit USA	1.75	1.40	34.00
	1975			
UXC16	21¢ Visit USA	1.75	1.00	41.00

UXC17 UXC18

1978

SCOTT NO.	DESCRIPTION	FIRST DAY COVER	MINT	USED
UXC17	21¢ Curtiss Jenny	1.75	1.40	41.00
	1979			
UXC18	21¢ Moscow Olympics	1.75	1.40	41.00

UXC19 UXC20

1981

SCOTT NO.	DESCRIPTION	FIRST DAY COVER	MINT	USED
UXC19	28¢ Pacific Flight	1.75	1.40	31.00
	1982			
UXC20	28¢ Gliders	1.75	1.40	36.00

UXC21

UXC22

SCOTT NO.	DESCRIPTION	FIRST DAY COVER	MINT	USED
	1983			
UXC21	28¢ Olympics	1.75	1.80	32.00
	1985			
UXC22	33¢ China Clipper	1.75	1.80	32.00

UXC23

UXC24

SCOTT NO.	DESCRIPTION	FIRST DAY COVER	MINT	USED
	1986			
UXC23	33¢ Ameripex '86	1.75	1.35	32.00
	1988			
UXC24	36¢ DC-3	1.75	1.25	32.00

UXC25

SCOTT NO.	DESCRIPTION	FIRST DAY COVER	MINT	USED
	1991			
UXC25	40¢ Yankee Clipper	1.75	1.35	32.00

UXC26

SCOTT NO.	DESCRIPTION	FIRST DAY COVER	MINT	USED
	1995			
UXC26	50¢ Soaring Eagle	1.75	1.25	22.50

UXC27

UXC28

SCOTT NO.	DESCRIPTION	FIRST DAY COVER	MINT	USED
	1999			
UXC27	55¢ Mount Rainier, Washington	1.75	1.75	32.00
	2001			
UXC28	70¢ Badlands National Park, South Dakota	2.25	2.25	22.50

PAID REPLY POSTAL CARDS

UY1m, UY3m

UY2m, UY11m

UY4m

UY1r, UY3r

UY2r, UY11r

UY4r

PAID REPLY CARDS: Consist of two halves—one for your message and one for the other party to use to reply.

SCOTT NO.	DESCRIPTION	MINT	UNUSED	USED
	1892 Card Framed			
UY1	1¢ & 1¢ unsevered	70.00	19.00	9.00
UY1m	1¢ black (Message)	8.00	4.00	2.00
UY1r	1¢ black (Reply)	8.00	4.00	2.00
	1893			
UY2	2¢ & 2¢ unsevered	32.00	18.00	22.00
UY2m	2¢ blue (Message)	7.00	5.00	6.50
UY2r	2¢ blue (Reply)	7.00	5.00	6.50
	1898 Designs of 1892 Card Unframed			
UY3	1¢ & 1¢ unsevered	115.00	18.00	15.00
UY3m	1¢ black (Message)	15.50	7.00	3.00
UY3r	1¢ black (Reply)	15.50	7.00	3.00
	1904			
UY4	1¢ & 1¢ unsevered	75.00	15.00	7.00
UY4m	1¢ black (Message)	12.00	6.00	1.20
UY4r	1¢ black (Reply)	12.00	6.00	1.20

UY5m, UY6m, UY7m, UY13m

UY8m

UY12m

UY5r, UY6r, UY7r, UY13r

UY8r

UY12r

SCOTT NO.	DESCRIPTION	MINT	UNUSED	USED
	1910			
UY5	1¢ & 1¢ unsevered	275.00	55.00	26.00
UY5m	1¢ blue (Message)	16.00	10.00	4.00
UY5r	1¢ blue (Reply)	16.00	10.00	4.00
	1911 Double Line Around Instructions			
UY6	1¢ & 1¢ unsevered	270.00	90.00	25.00
UY6m	1¢ green (Message)	32.00	14.00	7.00
UY6r	1¢ green (Reply)	32.00	14.00	7.00
	1915 Single Frame Line Around Instruction			
UY7	1¢ & 1¢ unsevered	1.85	.95	.60
UY7m	1¢ green (Message)	.40	.30	.25
UY7r	1¢ green (Reply)	.40	.30	.25
	1918			
UY8	2¢ & 2¢ unsevered	155.00	42.00	45.00
UY8m	2¢ red (Message)	36.00	12.00	9.00
UY8r	2¢ red (Reply)	36.00	12.00	9.00

SCOTT NO.	DESCRIPTION	MINT	UNUSED	USED
	1920 UY8 Surcharged			
UY9	1¢/2¢ & 1¢/2¢ unsevered	34.00	14.00	12.00
UY9m	1¢ on 2¢ red (Message)	8.00	3.00	4.00
UY9r	1¢ on 2¢ red (Reply)	8.00	3.00	4.00
	1924 Designs of 1893			
UY11	2¢ & 2¢ unsevered	3.25	1.75	37.00
UY11m	2¢ red (Message)	1.00	.65	15.00
UY11r	2¢ red (Reply)	1.00	.65	15.00
	1926			
UY12	3¢ & 3¢ unsevered	16.50	8.00	30.00
UY12m	3¢ red (Message)	4.00	1.75	7.00
UY12r	3¢ red (Reply)	4.00	1.75	7.00

SCOTT NO.	DESCRIPTION	FIRST DAY COVER	MINT	USED
	1951 Design of 1910 Single Line Frame			
UY13	2¢ & 2¢ unsevered	2.50	2.50	2.25
UY13m	2¢ carmine (Message)	....	.70	1.00
UY13r	2¢ carmine (Reply)	....	.70	1.00
	1952 UY7 Surcharged by cancelling machine, light green			
UY14	2¢/1¢ & 2¢/1¢ unsevered	....	2.50	2.75
UY14m	2¢ on 1¢ green (Message)	....	.50	1.00
UY14r	2¢ on 1¢ green (Reply)	....	.50	1.00
	1952 UY7 Surcharge Typographed, dark green			
UY15	2¢/1¢ & 2¢/1¢ unsevered	....	164.00	50.00
UY15m	2¢ on 1¢ green (Message)	....	20.00	12.00
UY15r	2¢ on 1¢ green (Reply)	....	20.00	12.00
	1956 Design of UX45			
UY16	4¢ & 4¢ unsevered	1.75	1.60	80.00
UY16m	4¢ carmine (Message)	....	.55	40.00
UY16r	4¢ carmine (Reply)	....	.55	40.00
	1958 Design of UX46			
UY17	3¢ & 3¢ purple, unsevered	1.75	6.00	2.50
	1962 Design of UX48			
UY18	4¢ & 4¢ red violet, unsevered	1.75	7.00	2.75
	1963 Design of UX49			
UY19	7¢ & 7¢ unsevered	1.75	5.50	65.00
UY19m	7¢ blue & red (Message)	....	1.75	40.00
UY19r	7¢ blue & red (Reply)	....	1.75	40.00
	1967 Design of UX54			
UY20	8¢ & 8¢ unsevered	1.75	4.50	60.00
UY20m	8¢ blue & red (Message)	....	1.75	40.00
UY20r	8¢ blue & red (Reply)	....	1.75	40.00
	1968 Design of UX55			
UY21	5¢ & 5¢ emerald	1.75	2.50	2.00
	1971 Design of UX58			
UY22	6¢ & 6¢ brown	1.75	1.50	2.00
	1972 Design of UX64			
UY23	6¢ & 6¢ blue	1.75	1.60	2.00
	1973 Design of UX66			
UY24	8¢ & 8¢ orange	1.75	1.35	2.00
	1975			
UY25	7¢ & 7¢ design of UX68	1.75	1.35	9.00
UY26	9¢ & 9¢ design of UX69	1.75	1.35	2.00
	1976			
UY27	9¢ & 9¢ design of UX70	1.75	1.35	2.00
	1977			
UY28	9¢ & 9¢ design of UX72	1.75	1.75	2.00
	1978			
UY29	(10¢ & 10¢) design of UX74	3.00	9.00	10.00
UY30	10¢ & 10¢ design of UX75	1.75	1.75	.40
UY31	(12¢ & 12¢) "B" Eagle, design of UX88	1.75	1.75	2.05
UY32	12¢ & 12¢ light blue, design of UX89	1.75	5.75	2.05
UY33	(13¢ & 13¢) buff, design of UX92	1.75	3.75	2.05
UY34	13¢ & 13¢ buff, design of UX93	1.75	2.00	.25
	1985			
UY35	(14¢ & 14¢) Carroll, design of UX105	1.75	4.75	2.05
UY36	14¢ & 14¢ Carroll, design of UX106	1.75	1.85	2.05
UY37	14¢ & 14¢ Wythe, design of UX108	1.75	1.50	2.05
	1987 -1988			
UY38	14¢ & 14¢ Flag, design of UX117	1.75	1.65	2.25
UY39	15¢ & 15¢ America the Beautiful, design of UX120	1.75	1.50	1.60
	1991			
UY40	19¢ & 19¢ Flag, design of UX153	1.75	1.65	1.50
	1995			
UY41	20¢ & 20¢ Red Barn, design of UX198	1.75	1.65	1.25
	1999			
UY42	20¢ & 20¢ Block Island Lighthouse, design of UX306	1.75	1.65	1.25
	2001-09			
UY43	21¢ & 21¢ White Barn, design of UX375	1.75	1.85	1.50
UY44	23¢ & 23¢ Carlsbad Caverns, design of UX381	1.75	1.85	1.50
UY45	24¢ & 24¢ Zebulon Pike Expedition, design of UX449	1.75	1.85	1.50
UY46	26¢ & 26¢ Pineapple, design of UX488	1.75	1.85	1.50
UY47	27¢ Corinthian Column double-reply postal card	3.75	1.75	1.50
UY48	28¢ Koi Fish reply card	3.50	1.75	1.40
	2011-2012			
UY49	29¢+29¢ Common Terns Postal Reply Card	4.50	1.75	1.75
UY50	32¢+32¢ Sailboat Postal & Reply Card	4.75	1.60	1.75
	2013-2014			
UY51	33¢+33¢ Deer Postal Reply Card	4.75	1.75	1.75
UY52	34¢ + 34¢ tree	4.75	1.75	2.50
	2015			
UY53	35¢ Fanciful Flowers Reply Card	4.75	1.95	2.00
	2017			
UY54	(34¢)+(34¢) Azulillo Chilean Blue Crocus	4.75	1.95	2.00
	2021			
UY55	(36¢)+(36¢) Mallard Drake	4.75	1.95	2.00

OFFICIAL POSTAL CARDS

UZ1

UZ2

UZ3

SCOTT NO.	DESCRIPTION	FIRST DAY COVER	MINT	USED
	1913			
UZ1	1¢ black (Printed Address)	......	755.00	495.00
	1983			
UZ2	13¢ Great Seal	1.75	.95	100.00
	1985			
UZ3	14¢ Great Seal	1.75	.95	90.00

UZ4

UZ5

UZ6

SCOTT NO.	DESCRIPTION	FIRST DAY COVER	MINT	USED
	1988			
UZ4	15¢ Great Seal	1.75	.95	100.00
	1991			
UZ5	19¢ Great Seal	1.75	1.10	100.00
	1995			
UZ6	20¢ Great Seal	1.75	1.10	100.00

1862-71 First Issue

When ordering from this issue be sure to indicate whether the "a", "b" or "c" variety is wanted. Example: R27c. Prices are for used singles.

R1-R4

R5-R15

R16-R42

SCOTT NO.	DESCRIPTION	IMPERFORATE (a) F	AVG	PART PERF. (b) F	AVG	PERFORATED (c) F	AVG
R1	1¢ Express	75.00	58.00	48.00	35.00	1.50	1.15
R2	1¢ Playing Cards	2200.00	1700.00	1600.00	1100.00	195.00	120.00
R3	1¢ Proprietary	1100.00	900.00	275.00	200.00	.60	.40
R4	1¢ Telegraph	600.00	425.00	....	....	18.00	14.00
R5	2¢ Bank Check, blue	1.50	1.15	5.00	2.50	.60	.40
R6	2¢ Bank Check, orange	....	....	60.00	41.25	.30	.20
R7	2¢ Certificate, blue	15.00	11.00	....	....	31.00	22.00
R8	2¢ Certificate, orange	....	....	....	....	43.00	25.00
R9	2¢ Express, blue	15.00	11.00	30.00	28.00	.50	.35
R10	2¢ Express, orange	....	....	1800.00	1200.00	13.00	10.00
R11	2¢ Playing Cards, blue	1500.00	....	270.00	175.00	5.00	3.00
R12	2¢ Playing Cards, orange	....	....	....	....	50.00	38.00
R13	2¢ Proprietary, blue	975.00	610.00	315.00	185.00	.50	.40
R14	2¢ Proprietary, orange	....	....	....	....	60.00	40.00
R15	2¢ U.S. Internal Revenue	....	....	....	....	.40	.35
R16	3¢ Foreign Exchange	....	....	800.00	550.00	5.00	3.25
R17	3¢ Playing Cards	40,000	....	....	....	165.00	115.00
R18	3¢ Proprietary	....	....	800.00	500.00	8.00	6.50
R19	3¢ Telegraph	85.00	63.00	28.00	19.50	3.00	2.10
R20	4¢ Inland Exchange	....	....	....	....	2.25	1.45
R21	4¢ Playing Cards	....	....	....	....	705.00	430.00
R22	4¢ Proprietary	....	....	525.00	325.00	8.00	6.75
R23	5¢ Agreement	....	....	....	....	.50	.40
R24	5¢ Certificate	3.50	2.25	14.00	9.00	.50	.40
R25	5¢ Express	6.50	3.75	7.00	5.50	.50	.40
R26	5¢ Foreign Exchange	....	....	....	....	.50	.40
R27	5¢ Inland Exchange	8.50	6.50	6.50	4.50	.60	.40
R28	5¢ Playing Cards	....	....	....	....	36.00	26.00
R29	5¢ Proprietary	....	....	....	....	24.00	16.00
R30	6¢ Inland Exchange	....	....	....	....	2.00	1.35
R32	10¢ Bill of Lading	50.00	38.00	400.00	325.00	1.75	1.25
R33	10¢ Certificate	300.00	210.00	815.00	540.00	.35	.25
R34	10¢ Contract, blue	....	....	495.00	295.00	.60	.40
R35	10¢ Foreign Exchange	....	....	....	....	12.00	9.00
R36	10¢ Inland Exchange	395.00	250.00	5.00	3.25	.40	.25
R37	10¢ Power of Attorney	895.00	560.00	28.00	19.00	1.00	.65
R38	10¢ Proprietary	....	....	....	....	18.00	12.00
R39	15¢ Foreign Exchange	....	....	....	....	15.00	12.00
R40	15¢ Inland Exchange	38.00	27.00	13.00	9.00	2.00	1.50
R41	20¢ Foreign Exchange	80.00	55.00	....	....	65.00	48.00
R42	20¢ Inland Exchange	16.00	10.00	21.00	15.00	.50	.35

R43-R53

R54-R65

R66-R76

SCOTT NO.	DESCRIPTION	IMPERFORATE (a) F	AVG	PART PERF. (b) F	AVG	PERFORATED (c) F	AVG
R43	25¢ Bond	245.00	185.00	7.00	5.00	3.75	2.85
R44	25¢ Certificate	11.00	8.00	7.00	5.00	.60	.40
R45	25¢ Entry of Goods	21.00	12.50	235.00	150.00	1.40	1.10
R46	25¢ Insurance	12.00	9.00	15.00	12.00	.35	.25
R47	25¢ Life Insurance	47.00	35.00	800.00	600.00	10.00	7.00
R48	25¢ Power of Attorney	8.00	5.50	35.00	25.00	1.25	.75
R49	25¢ Protest	35.00	25.00	860.00	625.00	8.00	6.00
R50	25¢ Warehouse Receipt	50.00	35.00	850.00	670.00	45.00	35.00
R51	30¢ Foreign Exchange	175.00	95.00	8200.00	5000.00	55.00	39.00
R52	30¢ Inland Exchange	65.00	52.00	75.00	50.00	9.00	7.75
R53	40¢ Inland Exchange	2300.00	1500.00	9.00	6.50	8.00	4.75
R54	50¢ Conveyance, blue	18.00	12.00	3.50	2.75	.40	.30
R55	50¢ Entry of Goods	....	....	15.00	10.00	.50	.35
R56	50¢ Foreign Exchange	60.00	40.00	110.00	80.00	7.00	5.00
R57	50¢ Lease	30.00	21.00	170.00	110.00	10.00	7.00
R58	50¢ Life Insurance	45.00	30.00	155.00	95.00	2.00	1.40
R59	50¢ Mortgage	22.00	16.00	5.00	4.00	.70	.50
R60	50¢ Original Process	6.00	4.00	600.00	400.00	1.10	.90
R61	50¢ Passage Ticket	110.00	85.00	400.00	255.00	2.25	1.55
R62	50¢ Probate of Will	52.00	42.00	200.00	135.00	20.00	13.00
R63	50¢ Surety Bond, blue	275.00	185.00	3.00	2.10	.40	.25
R64	60¢ Inland Exchange	110.00	75.00	95.00	55.00	9.00	7.25
R65	70¢ Foreign Exchange	575.00	450.00	165.00	125.00	13.00	9.00

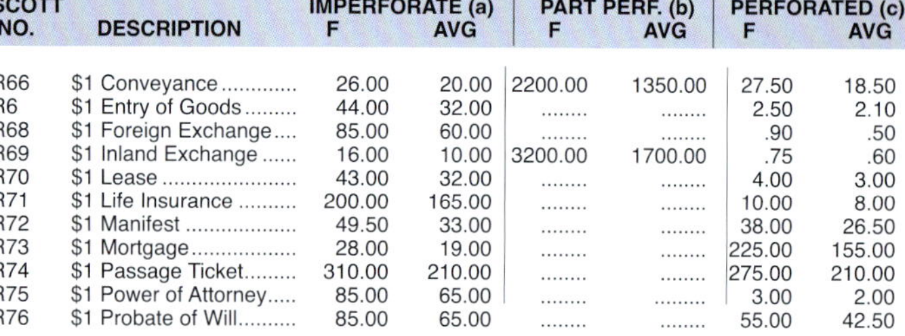

SCOTT NO.	DESCRIPTION	IMPERFORATE (a) F	AVG	PART PERF. (b) F	AVG	PERFORATED (c) F	AVG
R66	$1 Conveyance	26.00	20.00	2200.00	1350.00	27.50	18.50
R6	$1 Entry of Goods	44.00	32.00	....	....	2.50	2.10
R68	$1 Foreign Exchange	85.00	60.00	....	....	.90	.50
R69	$1 Inland Exchange	16.00	10.00	3200.00	1700.00	.75	.60
R70	$1 Lease	43.00	32.00	....	....	4.00	3.00
R71	$1 Life Insurance	200.00	165.00	....	....	10.00	8.00
R72	$1 Manifest	49.50	33.00	....	....	38.00	26.50
R73	$1 Mortgage	28.00	19.00	....	....	225.00	155.00
R74	$1 Passage Ticket	310.00	210.00	....	....	275.00	210.00
R75	$1 Power of Attorney	85.00	65.00	....	....	3.00	2.00
R76	$1 Probate of Will	85.00	65.00	....	....	55.00	42.50

R77-R80

R81-R87

SCOTT NO.	DESCRIPTION	IMPERFORATE (a) F	AVG	PART PERF. (b) F	AVG	PERFORATED (c) F	AVG
R77	$1.30 Foreign Exchange	8000.00	....	....	....	82.00	59.00
R78	$1.50 Inland Exchange	30.00	21.00	....	....	6.50	5.00
R79	$1.60 Foreign Exchange	1250.00	950.00	....	....	120.00	85.00
R80	$1.90 Foreign Exchange	10000.00	....	....	....	115.00	86.00
R81	$2 Conveyance	195.00	135.00	2100.00	1500.00	4.00	3.00
R82	$2 Mortgage	135.00	95.00	....	....	7.00	5.00
R83	$2 Probate of Will	6000.00	4800.00	....	....	75.00	64.00
R84	$2.50 Inland Exchange	8000.00	6500.00	....	....	22.00	18.00
R85	$3 Charter Party	185.00	125.00	....	....	11.00	9.00
R86	$2 Manifest	165.00	105.00	....	....	52.00	38.00
R87	$3.50 Inland Exchange	7000.00	....	....	....	70.00	53.00

R88-R96

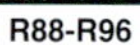
R97-R101

SCOTT NO.	DESCRIPTION	IMPERFORATE (a) F	AVG	PART PERF. (b) F	AVG	PERFORATED (c) F	AVG
R88	$5 Charter Party	300.00	225.00	....	....	10.00	8.00
R89	$5 Conveyance	42.00	35.00	....	....	11.00	8.00
R90	$5 Manifest	185.00	125.00	....	....	90.00	65.00
R91	$5 Mortgage	160.00	135.00	....	....	25.00	17.50
R92	$5 Probate of Will	675.00	550.00	....	....	25.00	17.50
R93	$10 Charter Party	750.00	550.00	....	....	35.00	25.00
R94	$10 Conveyance	125.00	95.00	....	....	75.00	50.00
R95	$10 Mortgage	750.00	550.00	....	....	35.00	25.00
R96	$10 Probate of Will	2100.00	1600.00	....	....	42.00	32.00
R97	$15 Mortgage, blue	2300.00	2100.00	....	....	255.00	180.00
R98	$20 Conveyance	150.00	100.00	....	....	115.00	85.00
R99	$20 Probate of Will	2100.00	1500.00	....	....	2100.00	1500.00
R100	$25 Mortgage	1825.00	1250.00	....	....	185.00	125.00
R101	$50 U.S. Internal Revenue	275.00	195.00	....	....	175.00	150.00

R102

SCOTT NO.	DESCRIPTION	IMPERFORATE (a) F	AVG	PART PERF. (b) F	AVG	PERFORATED (c) F	AVG
R102	$200 U.S. Internal Revenue	2350.00	1850.00	....	....	1000.00	800.00

R103, R104, R134, R135, R151

R105-R111, R136-R139

R112-R114

R115-R117, R142-R143

1871 SECOND ISSUE

NOTE: The individual denominations vary in design from the illustrations shown which are more typical of their relative size.

SCOTT NO.	DESCRIPTION	USED F	USED AVG
R103	1¢ blue and black	82.00	72.00
R104	2¢ blue and black	2.50	2.25
R105	3¢ blue and black	52.00	37.00
R106	4¢ blue and black	140.00	90.00
R107	5¢ blue and black	1.75	1.00
R108	6¢ blue and black	205.00	130.00
R109	10¢ blue and black	1.60	1.20
R110	15¢ blue and black	90.00	55.00
R111	20¢ blue and black	10.00	8.00
R112	25¢ blue and black	1.50	.85
R113	30¢ blue and black	130.00	75.00
R114	40¢ blue and black	110.00	70.00
R115	50¢ blue and black	1.35	.85
R116	60¢ blue and black	200.00	155.00
R117	70¢ blue and black	90.00	75.00

R118-R122, R144

R123-R126, R145-R147

SCOTT NO.	DESCRIPTION	USED F	USED AVG
R118	$1 blue and black	9.25	7.00
R119	$1.30 blue and black	625.00	525.00
R120	$1.50 blue and black	20.00	14.00
R121	$1.60 blue and black	650.00	525.00
R122	$1.90 blue and black	410.00	300.00
R123	$2.00 blue and black	21.00	15.00
R124	$2.50 blue and black	50.00	30.00
R125	$3.00 blue and black	65.00	40.00
R126	$3.50 blue and black	440.00	325.00

R127, R128, R148, R149

R129-R131, R150

SCOTT NO.	DESCRIPTION	USED F	USED AVG
R127	$5 blue and black	32.50	20.00
R128	$10 blue and black	225.00	155.00
R129	$20 blue and black	875.00	525.00
R130	$25 blue and black	925.00	650.00
R131	$50 blue and black	1050.00	660.00

1871-72 THIRD ISSUE

SCOTT NO.	DESCRIPTION	USED F	USED AVG
R134	1¢ claret and black	58.00	40.00
R135	2¢ orange and black	.40	.25
R135b	2¢ orange and black (center inverted)	500.00	450.00
R136	4¢ brown and black	77.00	57.00
R137	5¢ orange and black	.40	.25
R138	6¢ orange and black	85.00	64.00
R139	15¢ brown and black	22.00	17.00
R140	30¢ orange and black	32.00	26.00
R141	40¢ brown and black	80.00	65.00
R142	60¢ orange and black	110.00	85.00
R143	70¢ green and black	85.00	60.00
R144	$1 green and black	3.75	2.50
R145	$2 vermillion and black	40.00	30.00
R146	$2.50 claret and black	100.00	70.00
R147	$3 green and black	80.00	65.00
R148	$5 vermillion and black	40.00	30.00
R149	$10 green and black	310.00	185.00
R150	$20 orange and black	800.00	635.00

1874 on greenish paper

SCOTT NO.	DESCRIPTION	USED F	USED AVG
R151	2¢ orange and black	.40	.25
R151a	2¢ orange and black (center inverted)	650.00	600.00

R152 *Liberty*

I. R.

R153 surcharge

I.R.

R154, R155 surcharge

1875-78

SCOTT NO.	DESCRIPTION	UNUSED F	UNUSED AVG	USED F	USED AVG
R152a	2¢ blue on blue silk paper	....	....	.50	.40
R152b	2¢ watermarked ("USIR") paper	....	....	.40	.30
R152c	2¢ watermarked, rouletted	....	....	35.00	24.00

1898 Postage Stamps 279 & 267 Surcharged

SCOTT NO.	DESCRIPTION	UNUSED F	UNUSED AVG	USED F	USED AVG
R153	1¢ green, small I.R.	5.00	3.50	3.00	2.10
R154	1¢ green, large I.R.	.40	.30	.40	.30
R155	2¢ carmine, large I.R.	.40	.30	.40	.30

DOCUMENTARY STAMPS

Newspaper Stamp PR121 Surcharged

INT. REV.
$5.
DOCUMENTARY.

SCOTT NO.	DESCRIPTION	UNUSED F	UNUSED AVG	USED F	USED AVG
R159	$5 dark blue, red surcharge reading down	475.00	350.00	210.00	175.00
R160	$5 dark blue, red surcharge reading up	150.00	110.00	115.00	95.00

R161-R172

R173-R178, R182, R183

1898 Battleships Inscribed "Documentary"

SCOTT NO.	DESCRIPTION	UNUSED F	UNUSED AVG	USED F	USED AVG
R161	1/2¢ orange	4.00	3.00	20.00	15.00
R162	1/2¢ dark gray	.40	.30	.35	.30
R163	1¢ pale blue	.40	.30	.35	.30
R164	2¢ carmine	.40	.30	.45	.35
R165	3¢ dark blue	3.95	2.10	.45	.35
R166	4¢ pale rose	2.00	1.40	.45	.35
R167	5¢ lilac	.65	.45	.40	.45
R168	10¢ dark brown	2.00	1.40	.35	.30
R169	25¢ purple brown	4.35	4.00	.50	.40
R170	40¢ blue lilac (cut cancel .40)	125.00	90.00	1.50	1.00
R171	50¢ slate violet	36.00	18.00	.35	.30
R172	80¢ bistre (cut cancel .25)	110.00	80.00	.40	.30
R173	$1 dark green	22.00	16.00	.30	.25
R174	$3 dark brown (cut cancel .25)	40.00	28.00	1.00	.70
R175	$5 orange red (cut cancel .25)	66.00	48.00	2.00	1.40
R176	$10 black (cut cancel .70)	145.00	90.00	4.00	2.75
R177	$30 red (cut cancel 50.00)	460.00	350.00	160.00	110.00
R178	$50 gray brown (cut cancel 2.50)	260.00	210.00	6.00	3.95

R179, R225, R246, R248

R180, R226, R249

R181, R224, R227, R247, R250

1899 Various Portraits Inscribed "Series of 1898"

SCOTT NO.	DESCRIPTION	UNUSED F	UNUSED AVG	USED F	USED AVG
R179	$100 yellow brown & black ..... (cut cancel 25.00)	260.00	200.00	39.00	28.50
R180	$500 carmine lake & black.... (cut cancel 325.00)	1400.00	1100.00	850.00	550.00
R181	$1000 green & black .... (cut cancel 150.00)	1300.00	675.00	385.00	300.00

1900

SCOTT NO.	DESCRIPTION	UNUSED F	UNUSED AVG	USED F	USED AVG
R182	$1 carmine .... (cut cancel .40)	38.00	29.00	.75	.50
R183	$3 lake .... (cut cancel 9.00)	300.00	225.00	55.00	42.00

R184-R189 R190-R194

Designs of R173-78 surcharged

SCOTT NO.	DESCRIPTION	UNUSED F	UNUSED AVG	USED F	USED AVG
R184	$1 gray.. (cut cancel .25)	31.00	21.00	.40	.25
R185	$2 gray.. (cut cancel .25)	31.00	21.00	.40	.25
R186	$3 gray...................................... (cut cancel 5.00)	130.00	85.00	16.00	12.00
R187	$5 gray...................................... (cut cancel 1.50)	75.00	55.00	10.00	7.50
R188	$10 gray.................................... (cut cancel 4.00)	200.00	120.00	22.00	15.00
R189	$50 gray.................................. (cut cancel 130.00)	1875.00	1400.00	550.00	375.00

1902

SCOTT NO.	DESCRIPTION	UNUSED F	UNUSED AVG	USED F	USED AVG
R190	$1 green...................................... (cut cancel .35)	44.00	33.00	4.00	3.00
R191	$2 green...................................... (cut cancel .35)	44.00	33.00	2.00	1.25
R191a	$2 surcharged as R185	125.00	85.00	85.00	60.00
R192	$5 green.................................... (cut cancel 5.00)	200.00	140.00	38.00	29.00
R192a	$5 surcharge omitted	250.00	170.00	....	....
R193	$10 green................................ (cut cancel 50.00)	450.00	300.00	145.00	95.00
R194	$50 green.............................. (cut cancel 275.00)	2500.00	1900.00	1100.00	795.00

R195-R216 R217-R223

1914 Inscribed "Series of 1914" Single Line Watermark "USPS"

SCOTT NO.	DESCRIPTION	UNUSED F	UNUSED AVG	USED F	USED AVG
R195	1/2¢ rose	14.00	10.00	5.00	3.50
R196	1¢ rose	2.50	1.75	.40	.25
R197	2¢ rose	4.00	3.00	.40	.25
R198	3¢ rose	77.00	55.00	35.00	25.00
R199	4¢ rose	23.00	17.00	2.25	1.50
R200	5¢ rose	10.00	7.00	.50	.35
R201	10¢ rose	8.00	6.00	.35	.25
R202	25¢ rose	48.00	34.00	.70	.45
R203	40¢ rose	32.00	24.00	3.00	2.00
R204	50¢ rose	13.00	10.00	.35	.25
R205	80¢ rose	210.00	160.00	15.50	12.00

1914 Double Line Watermark "USIR"

SCOTT NO.	DESCRIPTION	UNUSED F	UNUSED AVG	USED F	USED AVG
R206	1/2¢ rose	2.00	1.40	.65	.45
R207	1¢ rose	.35	.25	.30	.20
R208	2¢ rose	.40	.25	.30	.25
R209	3¢ rose	2.00	1.40	.35	.25
R210	4¢ rose	4.50	3.00	.60	.40
R211	5¢ rose	2.00	1.40	.40	.25
R212	10¢ rose	.90	.60	.30	.25
R213	25¢ rose	8.00	6.00	1.75	1.20
R214	40¢ rose .... (cut cancel .60)	120.00	85.00	15.00	10.00
R215	50¢ rose	26.00	18.00	.35	.25
R216	80¢ rose .... (cut cancel 1.25)	175.00	115.00	28.00	21.00
R217	$1 green...................................... (cut cancel .30)	62.00	48.00	.55	.40
R218	$2 carmine .... (cut cancel .25)	82.00	58.00	.85	.60
R219	$3 purple.................................... (cut cancel .60)	110.00	80.00	4.00	2.75
R220	$5 blue .... (cut cancel .60)	95.00	70.00	4.00	2.75
R221	$10 orange.................................. (cut cancel 1.00)	210.00	155.00	6.00	4.00
R222	$30 vermillion............................ (cut cancel 5.50)	675.00	500.00	20.00	14.00
R223	$50 violet .... (cut cancel 375.00)	1700.00	1275.00	1100.00	800.00

1914-15 Various Portraits Inscribed "Series of 1914" or "Series of 1915"

SCOTT NO.	DESCRIPTION	UNUSED F	UNUSED AVG	USED F	USED AVG
R224	$60 brown .... (cut cancel 70.00)	200.00	140.00	150.00	100.00
R225	$100 green............................ (cut cancel 17.00)	68.00	50.00	45.00	30.00
R226	$500 blue .... (cut cancel 275.00)	....	....	650.00	450.00
R227	$1000 orange........................ (cut cancel 300.00)	....	....	700.00	400.00

R228-239, R251-256, R260-263

1917 Perf. 11

SCOTT NO.	DESCRIPTION	UNUSED F	UNUSED AVG	USED F	USED AVG
R228	1¢ carmine rose	.40	.30	.25	.20
R229	2¢ carmine rose	.30	.25	.25	.20
R230	3¢ carmine rose	1.85	1.35	.50	.35
R231	4¢ carmine rose	.85	.70	.30	.25
R232	5¢ carmine rose	.40	.35	.25	.20
R233	8¢ carmine rose	2.75	2.00	.40	.25
R234	10¢ carmine rose	2.00	1.60	.40	.30
R235	20¢ carmine rose	.80	.55	.30	.25
R236	25¢ carmine rose	1.50	1.00	.30	.25
R237	40¢ carmine rose	2.50	1.50	.50	.35
R238	50¢ carmine rose	2.75	1.75	.25	.20
R239	80¢ carmine rose	8.00	6.00	.30	.25

R240-245, R257-259

Same design as issue of 1914-15 Without dates.

SCOTT NO.	DESCRIPTION	UNUSED F	UNUSED AVG	USED F	USED AVG
R240	$1 yellow green...	8.50	6.50	.30	.25
R241	$2 rose..	14.00	10.00	.25	.20
R242	$3 violet .... (cut cancel .30)	55.00	43.00	1.25	.85
R243	$4 yellow brown .... (cut cancel .30)	38.00	28.00	2.00	1.40
R244	$5 dark blue .... (cut cancel .30)	23.00	17.00	.50	.35
R245	$10 orange.................................. (cut cancel .30)	48.00	38.00	1.50	1.00

Types of 1899 Various Portraits Perf. 12

SCOTT NO.	DESCRIPTION	UNUSED F	UNUSED AVG	USED F	USED AVG
R246	$30 deep orange, Grant............ (cut cancel 2.50)	50.00	35.00	15.00	10.00
R247	$60 brown, Lincoln................... (cut cancel 1.00)	60.00	40.00	8.00	5.50
R248	$100 green, Washington............ (cut cancel .45)	40.00	27.00	1.25	.80
R249	$500 blue, Hamilton .... (cut cancel 15.00)	325.00	225.00	40.00	28.00
R249a	$500 Numerals in orange	400.00	275.00	60.00	40.00
R250	$1000 orange, Madison (Perf. In. 3.00) .... (cut cancel 3.50)	160.00	100.00	13.00	8.00

1928-29 Perf. 10

SCOTT NO.	DESCRIPTION	UNUSED F	UNUSED AVG	USED F	USED AVG
R251	1¢ carmine rose	2.25	1.50	1.80	1.20
R252	2¢ carmine rose	.75	.55	.40	.30
R253	4¢ carmine rose	8.00	5.00	5.00	3.50
R254	5¢ carmine rose	1.80	1.20	.75	.50
R255	10¢ carmine rose	2.75	1.85	1.50	1.00
R256	20¢ carmine rose	7.00	5.00	6.00	4.00
R257	$1 green................................... (cut cancel 2.00)	175.00	120.00	40.00	27.00
R258	$2 rose	75.00	50.00	3.00	2.00
R259	$10 orange............................... (cut cancel 7.00)	250.00	175.00	50.00	35.00

1929-30 Perf. 11 x 10

SCOTT NO.	DESCRIPTION	UNUSED F	UNUSED AVG	USED F	USED AVG
R260	2¢ carmine rose	4.00	2.75	3.00	2.00
R261	5¢ carmine rose	3.00	2.00	2.25	1.60
R262	10¢ carmine rose	10.50	7.00	8.00	5.00
R263	20¢ carmine rose	17.00	11.00	9.00	6.00

SCOTT NO.	DESCRIPTION	PLATE BLOCK F/NH	UNUSED F/NH	USED F

R733, R734

1962 CENTENNIAL INTERNAL REVENUE. Inscribed "Established 1862"

SCOTT NO.	DESCRIPTION	PLATE BLOCK F/NH	UNUSED F/NH	USED F
R733	10¢ violet blue & green.	19.50	1.35	.50

1964 Without Inscription Date

SCOTT NO.	DESCRIPTION	PLATE BLOCK F/NH	UNUSED F/NH	USED F
R734	10¢ violet blue & green.	34.00	5.00	.75

PROPRIETARY STAMPS

RB1-2

RB3-7

1871-74 Perforated 12

SCOTT NO.	DESCRIPTION	VIOLET PAPER (a) F	AVG	GREEN PAPER (b) F	AVG
RB1	1¢ green & black	7.00	5.00	13.00	8.00
RB2	2¢ green & black	8.00	6.00	28.00	20.00
RB3	3¢ green & black	25.00	17.00	65.00	40.00
RB4	4¢ green & black	15.00	10.00	24.00	16.00
RB5	5¢ green & black	160.00	110.00	195.00	120.00
RB6	6¢ green & black	60.00	40.00	125.00	85.00
RB7	10¢ green & black	240.00	165.00	65.00	45.00
RB8	50¢ green & black (large)	900.00	600.00	750.00	550.00

RB11-12

RB13-19

SCOTT NO.	DESCRIPTION	SILK PAPER (a) F	AVG	WMKD PERF. (b) F	AVG	ROULETTE (c) F	AVG
RB11	1¢ green	2.50	1.90	.50	.35	135.00	100.00
RB12	2¢ brown	2.75	1.85	1.70	1.00	155.00	95.00
RB13	3¢ orange	14.00	10.00	4.50	3.50	130.00	95.00
RB14	4¢ red brown	11.00	8.00	10.00	6.00	....	....
RB15	4¢ red	....	....	7.00	4.00	260.00	200.00
RB16	5¢ black	180.00	140.00	130.00	90.00	....	1800.00
RB17	6¢ violet blue	38.00	29.00	26.00	19.00	495.00	275.00
RB18	6¢ violet	....	....	37.00	28.00	500.00	350.00
RB19	10¢ blue	....	....	350.00	250.00	....	....

RB20-31

RB32-64

RB65-73

1898 Battleship Inscribed "Proprietary"

SCOTT NO.	DESCRIPTION	UNUSED F	AVG	USED F	AVG
RB20	1/8¢ yellow green	.35	.25	.35	.25
RB21	1/4¢ brown	.35	.25	.25	.20
RB22	3/8¢ deep orange	.30	.25	.50	.40
RB23	5/8¢ deep ultramarine	.30	.25	.30	.25
RB24	1¢ dark green	2.25	1.50	.30	.25
RB25	1-1/4¢ violet	.30	.25	.30	.25
RB26	1-7/8¢ dull blue	16.00	12.00	2.25	1.80
RB27	2¢ violet brown	1.50	1.00	.40	.30
RB28	2-1/2¢ lake	4.50	3.15	.30	.25
RB29	3-3/4¢ olive gray	45.00	30.00	16.00	12.00
RB30	4¢ purple	17.00	12.00	1.60	1.10
RB31	5¢ brown orange	17.00	12.00	1.60	1.10

1914 Watermarked "USPS"

SCOTT NO.	DESCRIPTION	UNUSED F	AVG	USED F	AVG
RB32	1/8¢ black	.30	.25	.30	.25
RB33	1/4¢ black	3.30	2.55	1.60	1.00
RB34	3/8¢ black	.40	.30	.30	.25
RB35	5/8¢ black	6.50	5.00	3.00	2.75
RB36	1-1/4¢ black	5.00	3.50	2.00	1.25
RB37	1-7/8¢ black	60.00	48.00	21.00	15.00
RB38	2-1/2¢ black	14.00	10.00	4.00	2.75
RB39	3-1/8¢ black	130.00	90.00	65.00	45.00
RB40	3-3/4¢ black	62.00	35.00	26.00	19.00
RB41	4¢ black	77.00	55.00	42.00	32.00
RB43	5¢ black	155.00	115.00	105.00	85.00

1914 Watermarked "USIR"

SCOTT NO.	DESCRIPTION	UNUSED F	AVG	USED F	AVG
RB44	1/8¢ black	.40	.30	.30	.25
RB45	1/4¢ black	.30	.25	.30	.25
RB46	3/8¢ black	.80	.60	.50	.40
RB47	1/2¢ black	4.00	2.75	3.50	2.50
RB48	5/8¢ black	.30	.25	.30	.25
RB49	1¢ black	6.00	9.50	6.00	4.50
RB50	1-1/4¢ black	.75	.60	.45	.35
RB51	1-1/2¢ black	4.50	3.50	3.00	2.00
RB52	1-7/8¢ black	1.40	1.00	1.00	.80
RB53	2¢ black	7.00	5.50	6.00	4.00
RB54	2-1/2¢ black	1.80	1.30	2.00	1.40
RB55	3¢ black	5.50	4.00	4.00	3.00
RB56	3-1/8¢ black	7.00	5.00	5.00	4.00
RB57	3-3/4¢ black	17.00	11.00	11.00	8.00
RB58	4¢ black	.60	.50	.30	.25
RB59	4-3/8¢ black	19.00	13.00	11.00	8.00
RB60	5¢ black	4.50	3.50	4.00	3.00
RB61	6¢ black	72.00	60.00	48.00	35.00
RB62	8¢ black	26.00	16.00	15.00	11.00
RB63	10¢ black	17.00	13.00	10.00	7.00
RB64	20¢ black	33.00	23.00	22.00	16.00

1919 Offset Printing

SCOTT NO.	DESCRIPTION	UNUSED F	AVG	USED F	AVG
RB65	1¢ dark blue	.35	.25	.25	.20
RB66	2¢ dark blue	.40	.30	.30	.25
RB67	3¢ dark blue	1.60	1.20	.85	.65
RB68	4¢ dark blue	2.50	2.00	.80	.60
RB69	5¢ dark blue	3.25	2.00	1.40	1.00
RB70	8¢ dark blue	22.00	16.00	14.00	11.00
RB71	10¢ dark blue	10.00	8.00	4.00	2.75
RB72	20¢ dark blue	15.00	12.00	6.00	4.00
RB73	40¢ dark blue	58.00	45.00	15.00	11.00

FUTURE DELIVERY
Type I

FUTURE DELIVERY
Type II

FUTURE DELIVERY STAMPS

Documentary Stamps of 1917 Overprinted

1918-34 Perforated 11, Type I Overprint Lines 8mm. Apart

SCOTT NO.	DESCRIPTION	UNUSED F	AVG	USED F	AVG
RC1	2¢ carmine rose	8.00	5.00	.30	.25
RC2	3¢ carmine rose (cut cancel 13.50)	42.00	32.00	35.00	29.00
RC3	4¢ carmine rose	13.00	9.00	.30	.25
RC3A	5¢ carmine rose	95.00	60.00	4.00	2.75
RC4	10¢ carmine rose	22.00	15.00	.30	.25
RC5	20¢ carmine rose	35.00	25.00	.30	.25
RC6	25¢ carmine rose (cut cancel .25)	65.00	45.00	.75	.55
RC7	40¢ carmine rose (cut cancel .25)	75.00	50.00	.75	.55
RC8	50¢ carmine rose	16.00	11.00	.30	.25
RC9	80¢ carmine rose (cut cancel 1.00)	145.00	95.00	10.00	7.00
RC10	$1 green (cut cancel .25)	60.00	45.00	.30	.25
RC11	$2 rose (cut cancel .25)	65.00	45.00	.30	.25
RC12	$3 violet (cut cancel .30)	185.00	145.00	4.00	3.25
RC13	$5 dark blue (cut cancel .25)	110.00	90.00	.75	.50
RC14	$10 orange (cut cancel .35)	135.00	95.00	1.50	1.00
RC15	$20 olive bistre (cut cancel .75)	350.00	220.00	8.00	6.00

Perforated 12

SCOTT NO.	DESCRIPTION	UNUSED F	AVG	USED F	AVG
RC16	$30 vermillon (cut cancel 2.00)	110.00	85.00	7.00	5.00
RC17	$50 olive green (cut cancel 2.00)	90.00	75.00	6.00	5.00
RC18	$60 brown (cut cancel 1.25)	120.00	90.00	9.00	7.00
RC19	$100 yellow green (cut cancel 8.00)	200.00	180.00	40.00	30.00
RC20	$500 blue (cut cancel6.00)	225.00	130.00	16.00	12.00
RC21	$1000 orange (cut cancel 1.75)	185.00	150.00	8.00	6.00
RC22	1¢ carmine rose (lines 2mm apart)	1.20	.75	.30	.25
RC23	80¢ carmine rose (lines 2mm apart) (cut cancel .40)	190.00	150.00	3.50	2.00

1925-34 Perforated 11 Type II Overprint

SCOTT NO.	DESCRIPTION	UNUSED F	AVG	USED F	AVG
RC25	$1 green (cut cancel .10)	82.00	60.00	2.00	1.00
RC26	$10 orange (cut cancel 5.75)	220.00	170.00	26.00	22.00

STOCK TRANSFER
Type I

STOCK TRANSFER
Type II

STOCK TRANSFER STAMPS

Documentary Stamps Overprinted

1918-22 Perforated 11 Type I Overprint

SCOTT NO.	DESCRIPTION	UNUSED F	AVG	USED F	AVG
RD1	1¢ carmine rose	1.00	.70	.30	.25
RD2	2¢ carmine rose	.30	.25	.30	.25
RD3	4¢ carmine rose	.30	.25	.30	.25
RD4	5¢ carmine rose	.35	.30	.30	.25
RD5	10¢ carmine rose	.35	.30	.30	.25
RD6	20¢ carmine rose	.65	.45	.30	.25
RD7	25¢ carmine rose (cut cancel .25)	2.25	1.75	.30	.25
RD8	40¢ carmine rose	2.25	1.15	.30	.25
RD9	50¢ carmine rose	.80	.50	.30	.25
RD10	80¢ carmine rose (cut cancel .25)	9.00	7.00	.50	.35
RD11	$1 green (red ovverprint) (cut cancel 4.00)	150.00	120.00	28.00	23.00
RD12	$1 green (black overprint)	3.00	2.00	.40	.25
RD13	$2 rose	3.00	2.00	.30	.25
RD14	$3 violet (cut cancel .25)	26.00	19.00	7.00	5.00
RD15	$4 yellow brown (cut cancel .25)	12.00	8.00	.30	.25
RD16	$5 dark blue (cut cancel .25)	8.00	5.00	.30	.25
RD17	$10 orange (cut cancel .25)	27.00	20.00	.50	.45
RD18	$20 olive bistre (cut cancel 3.50)	120.00	95.00	20.00	14.00

Perforated 12

SCOTT NO.	DESCRIPTION	UNUSED F	AVG	USED F	AVG
RD19	$30 vermillion (cut cancel 1.20)	39.00	33.00	6.00	4.00
RD20	$50 olive green (cut cancel 26.00)	130.00	110.00	65.00	55.00
RD21	$60 brown (cut cancel 10.00)	300.00	230.00	28.00	22.00
RD22	$100 green (cut cancel 3.50)	45.00	35.00	7.00	5.00
RD23	$500 blue (cut cancel 80.00)	500.00	450.00	160.00	120.00
RD24	$1000 orange (cut cancel 33.00)	400.00	350.00	100.00	85.00

SCOTT NO.	DESCRIPTION	UNUSED F	UNUSED AVG	USED F	USED AVG
	1928 Perforated 10 Type I Overprint				
RD25	2¢ carmine rose	5.00	4.00	.40	.35
RD26	4¢ carmine rose	5.00	4.00	.40	.35
RD27	10¢ carmine rose	5.00	4.00	.40	.35
RD28	20¢ carmine rose	6.00	5.00	.40	.35
RD29	50¢ carmine rose	10.00	8.00	.60	.45
RD30	$1 green	40.00	28.00	.40	.30
RD31	$2 carmine rose	40.00	28.00	.35	.30
RD32	$10 orange (cut cancel .25)	40.00	28.00	.50	.35
RD33	2¢ carmine rose	11.00	6.00	1.00	.70
RD34	10¢ carmine rose	3.00	2.00	.40	.35
RD35	20¢ carmine rose	6.00	4.00	.30	.25
RD36	50¢ carmine rose	5.00	4.00	.30	.25
RD37	$1 green (cut cancel .30)	70.00	50.00	13.00	9.00
RD38	$2 rose (cut cancel .30)	90.00	70.00	13.00	9.00
	1920-28 Perforated 10 Type II overprint				
RD39	2¢ carmine rose	11.00	9.00	1.00	.70
RD40	10¢ carmine rose	4.00	2.00	.60	.40
RD41	20¢ carmine rose	6.00	4.00	.30	.25

SILVER TAX STAMPS

Documentary Stamps of 1917 Overprinted

1934-36

SCOTT NO.	DESCRIPTION	UNUSED F	UNUSED AVG	USED F	USED AVG
RG1	1¢ carmine rose	1.70	1.25	1.00	.70
RG2	2¢ carmine rose	2.25	1.50	.75	.50
RG3	3¢ carmine rose	2.40	1.25	.90	.60
RG4	4¢ carmine rose	2.40	1.40	1.75	1.25
RG5	5¢ carmine rose	3.60	2.50	1.50	1.00
RG6	8¢ carmine rose	4.85	3.00	3.50	2.50
RG7	10¢ carmine rose	5.25	3.50	4.00	2.50
RG8	20¢ carmine rose	7.75	5.00	4.00	2.50
RG9	25¢ carmine rose	7.75	5.00	5.00	3.50
RG10	40¢ carmine rose	8.50	6.00	6.50	4.50
RG11	50¢ carmine rose	10.00	7.00	8.00	5.00
RG12	80¢ carmine rose	18.00	12.00	11.00	7.00
RG13	$1 green	42.00	35.00	18.00	13.00
RG14	$2 rose	50.00	45.00	27.00	18.00
RG15	$3 violet	82.00	65.00	40.00	28.00
RG16	$4 yellow brown	80.00	50.00	35.00	17.00
RG17	$5 dark blue	82.00	60.00	33.00	20.00
RG18	$10 orange	115.00	90.00	25.00	17.00
RG19	$30 vermillion (cut cancel 20.00)	245.00	140.00	60.00	40.00
RG20	$60 brown (cut cancel 30.00)	280.00	150.00	85.00	60.00
RG21	$100 green	275.00	185.00	35.00	22.50
RG22	$500 blue (cut cancel 110.00)	600.00	400.00	235.00	160.00
RG23	$1000 orange (cut cancel 70.00)	......	......	120.00	77.50
RG26	$100 green, 11mm spacing	600.00	400.00	85.00	55.00
RG27	$1000 orange, 11mm spacing	......	......	1700.00	1450.00

TOBACCO SALE TAX STAMPS

Documentary Stamps of 1917 Overprinted

1934

SCOTT NO.	DESCRIPTION	UNUSED F	UNUSED AVG	USED F	USED AVG
RJ1	1¢ carmine rose	.40	.35	.25	.20
RJ2	2¢ carmine rose	.45	.30	.25	.20
RJ3	5¢ carmine rose	1.40	.90	.45	.30
RJ4	10¢ carmine rose	1.75	1.15	.45	.30
RJ5	25¢ carmine rose	4.75	3.00	1.85	1.20
RJ6	50¢ carmine rose	4.75	3.00	1.85	1.20
RJ7	$1 green	12.00	8.00	1.85	1.20
RJ8	$2 rose	20.00	14.00	2.15	1.40
RJ9	$5 dark blue	25.00	17.00	4.75	3.00
RJ10	$10 orange	40.00	27.00	12.00	7.75
RJ11	$20 olive bistre	100.00	70.00	15.00	9.75

HUNTING PERMIT

RW1

RW2

RW3

RW4

RW5

1934-1938 Inscribed: DEPARTMENT OF AGRICULTURE (NH + 75%)

SCOTT NO.	DESCRIPTION	UNUSED VF	UNUSED F	UNUSED AVG	USED VF	USED F	USED AVG
RW1	1934 $1 Mallards........	650.00	475.00	400.00	160.00	125.00	110.00
RW2	1935 $1 Canvasbacks	575.00	425.00	375.00	185.00	150.00	125.00
RW3	1936 $1 Canada Geese	350.00	250.00	200.00	85.00	70.00	60.00
RW4	1937 $1 Scaup Ducks	290.00	225.00	160.00	65.00	55.00	40.00
RW5	1938 $1 Pintail Drake .	450.00	300.00	225.00	65.00	55.00	40.00

RW6

RW7

RW9

RW8

RW10

RW11

SCOTT NO.	DESCRIPTION	UNUSED VF	UNUSED F	UNUSED AVG	USED VF	USED F	USED AVG
RW6	1939 $1 Green-Winged Teal	200.00	165.00	135.00	55.00	45.00	38.00
RW7	1940 $1 Black Mallards.	200.00	165.00	135.00	55.00	45.00	38.00
RW8	1941 $1 Ruddy Ducks...	200.00	165.00	135.00	55.00	45.00	38.00
RW9	1942 $1 Baldpates	210.00	175.00	140.00	55.00	45.00	35.00
RW10	1943 $1 Wood Ducks....	115.00	85.00	77.00	55.00	42.00	30.00
RW11	1944 $1 White Fronted Geese	130.00	90.00	82.00	47.00	37.00	27.00

RW12

RW13

SCOTT NO.	DESCRIPTION	UNUSED VF	UNUSED F	UNUSED AVG	USED VF	USED F	USED AVG
RW12	1945 $1 Shoveller Ducks	95.00	72.00	62.00	36.00	28.00	22.00
RW13	1946 $1 Redhead Ducks	50.00	35.00	25.00	20.00	15.00	10.00

Note: NH premiums RW6-9 (75%) RW10-16 (50%) RW17-25 (40%)
1939-1958 Inscribed: DEPARTMENT OF INTERIOR

RW14

RW15

SCOTT NO.	DESCRIPTION	UNUSED VF	UNUSED F	UNUSED AVG	USED VF	USED F	USED AVG
RW14	1947 $1 Snow Geese....	50.00	35.00	25.00	20.00	15.00	10.00
RW15	1948 $1 Buffleheads	50.00	35.00	25.00	20.00	15.00	10.00

RW16

RW17

RW18

RW19

RW20

RW21

SCOTT NO.	DESCRIPTION	UNUSED VF	UNUSED F	UNUSED AVG	USED VF	USED F	USED AVG
RW16	1949 $2 Goldeneye Ducks	60.00	40.00	35.00	18.00	15.00	10.00
RW17	1950 $2 Trumpeter Swans	75.00	55.00	45.00	15.00	12.00	9.00
RW18	1951 $2 Gadwall Ducks	75.00	55.00	45.00	15.00	12.00	9.00
RW19	1952 $2 Harlequin Ducks	75.00	55.00	45.00	15.00	12.00	9.00
RW20	1953 $2 Blue-Winged Teal	80.00	60.00	50.00	15.00	12.00	9.00
RW21	1954 $2 Ring-Neck Ducks	85.00	60.00	50.00	13.00	10.00	7.50

RW22

RW23

RW24

RW25

SCOTT NO.	DESCRIPTION	UNUSED VF	UNUSED F	UNUSED AVG	USED VF	USED F	USED AVG
RW22	1955 $2 Blue Geese......	85.00	60.00	50.00	12.00	9.00	7.50
RW23	1956 $2 American Merganser	85.00	60.00	50.00	12.00	9.00	7.50
RW24	1957 $2 Ameriacn Eider	85.00	60.00	50.00	12.00	9.00	7.50
RW25	1958 $2 Canada Geese	85.00	60.00	50.00	12.00	9.00	7.50

PLATE BLOCKS OF 6 RW1-RW25

SCOTT NO.	UNUSED NH F	UNUSED NH AVG	UNUSED OG F	UNUSED OG AVG	SCOTT NO.	UNUSED NH F	UNUSED NH AVG	UNUSED OG F	UNUSED OG AVG
RW1	16000.00	12000.00	13500.00	9500.00	RW14	475.00	375.00	350.00	325.00
RW2	12000.00	9000.00	9500.00	7500.00	RW15	500.00	425.00	425.00	375.00
RW3	5200.00	4300.00	4500.00	3200.00	RW16	575.00	450.00	450.00	400.00
RW4	4600.00	3500.00	4200.00	3300.00	RW17	795.00	650.00	650.00	550.00
RW5	5100.00	4200.00	4400.00	3300.00	RW18	795.00	650.00	650.00	550.00
RW6	4700.00	3800.00	3600.00	2900.00	RW19	795.00	650.00	650.00	550.00
RW7	4700.00	3800.00	3700.00	3100.00	RW20	825.00	675.00	675.00	575.00
RW8	4800.00	3800.00	3700.00	3100.00	RW21	795.00	675.00	675.00	600.00
RW9	4300.00	3600.00	3500.00	2900.00	RW22	795.00	675.00	675.00	600.00
RW10	1075.00	850.00	925.00	775.00	RW23	840.00	725.00	725.00	640.00
RW11	1200.00	875.00	925.00	775.00	RW24	795.00	675.00	650.00	575.00
RW12	900.00	650.00	675.00	550.00	RW25	795.00	675.00	650.00	575.00
RW13	500.00	400.00	350.00	325.00					

Notes on Hunting Permit Stamps

1. Unused stamps without gum (uncancelled) are priced at one-half gummed price.
2. The date printed on the stamp is one year later than the date of issue listed above.
3. #RW1-RW25 and RW31 are plate blocks of 6.

RW26 RW27

RW28 RW29

RW30 RW31

1959-1971 (NH + 40%)

SCOTT NO.	DESCRIPTION	UNUSED VF	UNUSED F	USED VF	USED F
RW26	1959 $3 Dog & Mallard	185.00	135.00	12.00	9.00
RW27	1960 $3 Redhead Ducks	135.00	110.00	12.00	9.00
RW28	1961 $3 Mallard Hen & Ducklings	135.00	110.00	12.00	9.00
RW29	1962 $3 Pintail Drakes	150.00	115.00	12.00	9.00
RW30	1963 $3 Brant Ducks Landing	150.00	115.00	12.00	9.00
RW31	1964 $3 Hawaiian Nene Goose	145.00	115.00	12.00	9.00

RW32 RW33

RW34

RW35

SCOTT NO.	DESCRIPTION	UNUSED VF	UNUSED F	USED VF	USED F
RW32	1965 $3 Canvasback Drakes	145.00	115.00	12.00	9.00
RW33	1966 $3 Whistling Swans	145.00	115.00	12.00	9.00
RW34	1967 $3 Old Squaw Ducks	170.00	125.00	12.00	9.00
RW35	1968 $3 Hooded Mergansers	100.00	72.00	12.00	9.00

RW36

RW37

RW38

RW39

Notes on Hunting Permit Stamps

1. Unused stamps without gum (uncancelled) are priced at one-half gummed price.
2. The date printed on the stamp is one year later than the date of issue listed above.
3. #RW1-RW25 and RW31 are plate blocks of 6.

SCOTT NO.	DESCRIPTION	UNUSED VF	UNUSED F	USED VF	USED F
RW36	1969 $3 White-Winged Scoters	98.00	72.00	12.00	9.00
RW37	1970 $3 Ross's Geese	98.00	72.00	12.00	9.00
RW38	1971 $3 Three Cinnamon Teal	68.00	48.00	12.00	9.00
RW39	1972 $5 Emperor Geese	42.00	32.00	9.00	7.50

RW40 RW41

RW42

RW43

RW44

RW45

1973-1978

SCOTT NO.	DESCRIPTION	UNUSED VF	UNUSED F	USED VF	USED F
RW40	1973 $5 Steller's Eider	32.00	24.00	9.00	7.50
RW41	1974 $5 Wood Ducks	32.00	24.00	9.00	7.50
RW42	1975 $5 Canvasbacks	29.00	22.00	9.00	7.50
RW43	1976 $5 Canada Geese	29.00	22.00	9.00	7.50
RW44	1977 $5 Pair of Ross's Geese	29.00	23.00	9.00	7.50
RW45	1978 $5 Hooded Merganser Drake	29.00	23.00	9.00	7.50

RW46

RW47

RW48

RW49

1979-1986

SCOTT NO.	DESCRIPTION	UNUSED VF	UNUSED F	USED VF	USED F
RW46	1979 $7.50 Green-Winged Teal	29.00	23.00	10.00	9.00
RW47	1980 $7.50 Mallards	29.00	23.00	10.00	9.00
RW48	1981 $7.50 Ruddy Ducks	29.00	23.00	10.00	9.00
RW49	1982 $7.50 Canvasbacks	29.00	23.00	10.00	9.00

RW50 RW51

SCOTT NO.	DESCRIPTION	UNUSED VF	UNUSED F	USED VF	USED F
RW50	1983 $7.50 Pintails	29.00	23.00	10.00	9.00
RW51	1984 $7.50 Widgeon	29.00	23.00	10.00	9.00

PLATE BLOCKS RW26-RW38					
SCOTT NO.	UNUSED NH F	UNUSED OG F	SCOTT NO.	UNUSED NH F	UNUSED OG F
RW26	740.00	550.00	RW33	750.00	573.00
RW27	700.00	525.00	RW34	750.00	573.00
RW28	700.00	550.00	RW35	395.00	300.00
RW29	750.00	550.00	RW36	395.00	300.00
RW30	725.00	485.00	RW37	270.00	300.00
RW31	2800.00	2400.00	RW38	155.00	220.00
RW32	750.00	573.00			

RW52

RW53

SCOTT NO.	DESCRIPTION	UNUSED NH VF	UNUSED NH F	USED VF	USED F
RW52	1985 $7.50 Cinnamon Teal	29.00	23.00	10.00	9.00
RW53	1986 $7.50 Fulvous Whistling	29.00	23.00	10.00	9.00

RW54

RW55

RW56

RW57

1987-1993

SCOTT NO.	DESCRIPTION	UNUSED NH VF	UNUSED NH F	USED VF	USED F
RW54	1987 $10.00 Redhead Ducks	35.00	25.00	13.00	11.00
RW55	1988 $10.00 Snow Goose	35.00	27.00	13.00	11.00
RW56	1989 $12.50 Lesser Scaup	35.00	27.00	13.00	11.00
RW57	1990 $12.50 Black Bellied Whistling Duck	35.00	27.00	13.00	11.00

RW58

RW59

RW60

RW61

SCOTT NO.	DESCRIPTION	UNUSED NH VF	UNUSED NH F	USED VF	USED F
RW58	1991 $15.00 King Eiders	55.00	40.00	18.00	15.00
RW59	1992 $15.00 Spectacled Eider	50.00	35.00	17.00	14.00
RW60	1993 $15.00 Canvasbacks	50.00	35.00	17.00	14.00
RW61	1994 $15.00 Red-Breasted Merganser	50.00	38.00	17.50	12.50

RW62

RW63

RW64

RW65

RW66

RW67

1992-2000

SCOTT NO.	DESCRIPTION	UNUSED NH VF	UNUSED NH F	USED VF	USED F
RW62	1995 $15.00 Mallards	50.00	38.00	17.50	12.50
RW63	1996 $15.00 Surf Scoters	50.00	38.00	17.50	12.50
RW64	1997 $15.00 Canada Goose	50.00	38.00	17.50	12.50
RW65	1998 $15.00 Barrow's Goldeneye	75.00	57.00	32.00	24.00
RW65a	1998 $15.00 Barrow's Goldeneye, self-adhesive, pane of 1	42.00	39.00	18.00	....
RW66	1999 $15.00 Greater Scaup	58.00	47.00	31.00	....
RW66a	1999 $15.00 Greater Scaup, self-adhesive, pane of 1	40.00	34.00	18.00	....
RW67	2000 $15.00 Mottled Duck	40.00	33.00	28.00	....
RW67a	2000 $15.00 Mottled Duck, self-adhesive, pane of 1	37.00	31.00	18.00	....

RW68

RW69

2001-2003

SCOTT NO.	DESCRIPTION	UNUSED NH VF	UNUSED NH F	USED VF	USED F
RW68	2001 $15.00 Northern Pintail	38.00	31.00	26.00	....
RW68a	2001 $15.00 Northern Pintail, self-adhesive, pane of 1	37.00	32.00	18.00	....
RW69	2002 $15.00 Black Scoters	38.00	34.00	26.00	....
RW69a	2002 $15.00 Black Scoters, self-adhesive, pane of 1	37.00	....	18.00	....

RW70

RW71

RW72

RW73

2004-2006

SCOTT NO.	DESCRIPTION	UNUSED NH VF	UNUSED NH F	USED VF	USED F
RW70	2003 $15.00 Snow Geese	40.00	32.00	26.00	....
RW70a	2003 $15.00 Snow Geese, self-adhesive, pane of 1	37.00	....	18.00	....
RW71	2004 $15.00 Redheads	38.00	32.00	23.00	....
RW71a	2004 $15.00 Redheads, self-adhesive, pane of 1	37.00	....	18.00	....
RW72	2005 $15.00 Hooded Mergansers	38.00	32.00	23.00	....
RW72a	2005 $15.00 Hooded Mergansers, self-adhesive, pane of 1	37.00	....	20.00	....
RW73	2006 $15.00 Ross's Goose	38.00	32.00	23.00	....
RW73a	2006 $15.00 Ross's Goose, self-adhesive, pane of 1	37.00	....	20.00	....

RW74

RW75

RW76

RW77

2007-2010

SCOTT NO.	DESCRIPTION	UNUSED NH VF	UNUSED NH F	USED VF	USED F
RW74	2007 $15.00 Ringed-Necked Ducks	38.00	32.00	23.00	....
RW74a	2007 $15.00 Ringed-Necked Ducks, self-adhesive, pane of 1	37.00	....	22.00	....
RW75	2008 $15 Northern Pintail Ducks	38.00	32.00	26.00	....
RW75a	2008 $15 Pintail Ducks, self-adhesive	37.00	....	22.00	....
RW76	2009 $15 Long-Tailed Duck	38.00	32.00	26.00	....
RW76a	2009 $15 Long-Tailed Duck, self-adhesive	37.00	....	22.00	....
RW77	2010 $15 American Widgeon	38.00	32.00	26.00	....
RW77a	2010 $15 American Widgeon, self-adhesive	37.00	....	19.00	....

RW78

RW79

RW80

RW81

2011-2014

SCOTT NO.	DESCRIPTION	UNUSED NH VF	UNUSED NH F	USED VF	USED F
RW78	2011 $15 White-Fronted Geese	38.00	32.00	26.00	....
RW78a	2011 $15 White-Fronted Geese, self-adhesive	35.00	....	19.00	....
RW79	2012 $15 Wood Duck	40.00	....	30.00	....
RW79a	2012 $15 Wood Duck, self-adhesive	45.00	....	20.00	....
RW80	2013 $15 Common Goldeneye	30.00	....	30.00	....
RW80a	2013 $15 Common Goldeneye, self-adhesive	45.00	....	20.00	....
RW81	2014 $15 Canvasbacks	40.00	....	30.00	....
RW81a	2014 $15 Canvasbacks, self-adhesive	45.00	....	20.00	....

RW82

RW83

RW84

RW85

RW86

RW87

2015-2020

SCOTT NO.	DESCRIPTION	UNUSED NH VF	UNUSED NH F	USED VF	USED F
RW82	2015 $25 Ruddy Ducks	95.00	....	40.00	....
RW82a	2015 $25 Ruddy Ducks, self-adhesive	90.00	....	30.00	....
RW83	2016 $25 Trumpeter Swans	95.00	....	40.00	....
RW83a	2016 $25 Trumpeter Swans, self-adhesive	90.00	....	30.00	....
RW84	2017 $25 Canada Geese	50.00	....	40.00	....
RW84a	2017 $25 Canada Geese, self-adhesive	50.00	....	40.00	....
RW85	2018 $25 Mallards	60.00	....	40.00	....
RW85a	2018 $25 Mallards, self-adhesive	60.00	....	40.00	....
RW86	2019 $25 Wood Duck and Decoy	50.00	....	40.00	....
RW86a	2019 $25 Wood Duck and Decoy, self-adhesive	50.00	....	40.00	....
RW87	2020 $25 Black-bellied Whistling Ducks	50.00	....	40.00	....
RW87a	2020 $25 Black-bellied Whistling Ducks, self adhesive	50.00	....	40.00	....

RW88

RW89

2021

SCOTT NO.	DESCRIPTION	UNUSED NH VF	UNUSED NH F	USED VF	USED F
RW88	$25 Lesser Scaup Drake	50.00	....	40.00	....
RW88a	$25 Lesser Scaup Drake	50.00	....	40.00	....

2022

SCOTT NO.	DESCRIPTION	UNUSED NH VF	UNUSED NH F	USED VF	USED F
RW89	$25 Redheads	50.00	....	30.00	....
RW89a	$25 Redheads	50.00	....	30.00	....

RW90

2023

SCOTT NO.	DESCRIPTION	UNUSED NH VF	UNUSED NH F	USED VF	USED F
RW90	$25 Tundra Swans	50.00	....	30.00	....
RW90A	$25 Tundra Swans	50.00	....	30.00	....

RW91

2024

SCOTT NO.	DESCRIPTION	UNUSED NH VF	UNUSED NH F	USED VF	USED F
RW91	$25 Northern Pintail	50.00	....	30.00	....
RW91A	$25 Northern Pintail	50.00	....	30.00	....

PLATE BLOCKS RW39-RW91

SCOTT NO.	UNUSED NH F	SCOTT NO.	UNUSED NH F	SCOTT NO.	UNUSED NH F
RW39	125.00	RW58	150.00	RW77	150.00
RW40	115.00	RW59	150.00	RW78	150.00
RW41	100.00	RW60	150.00	RW79	200.00
RW42	90.00	RW61	150.00	RW80	200.00
RW43	90.00	RW62	150.00	RW81	170.00
RW44	90.00	RW63	150.00	RW82	300.00
RW45	90.00	RW64	150.00	RW83	425.00
RW46	90.00	RW65	225.00	RW84	230.00
RW47	90.00	RW66	150.00	RW85	250.00
RW48	90.00	RW67	150.00	RW86	230.00
RW49	90.00	RW68	150.00	RW87	230.00
RW50	90.00	RW69	150.00	RW88	230.00
RW51	90.00	RW70	150.00	RW89	230.00
RW52	90.00	RW71	150.00	RW90	230.00
RW53	90.00	RW72	150.00	RW91	250.00
RW54	110.00	RW73	150.00		
RW55	110.00	RW74	150.00		
RW56	120.00	RW75	150.00		
RW57	120.00	RW76	150.00		

STATE HUNTING PERMIT

AL7

ALABAMA

NO.	DESCRIPTION	F-VF NH
AL1	'79 $5 Wood Ducks	16.00
AL2	'80 $5 Mallards	14.00
AL3	'81 $5 Canada Geese	14.00
AL4	'82 $5 Green-Winged Teal	14.00
AL5	'83 $5 Widgeons	14.00
AL6	'84 $5 Buffleheads	24.00
AL7	'85 $5 Wood Ducks	17.00
AL8	'86 $5 Canada Geese	17.00
AL9	'87 $5 Pintails	18.00
AL10	'88 $5 Canvasbacks	12.50
AL11	'89 $5 Hooded Mergansers	12.50
AL12	'90 $5 Wood Ducks	12.50
AL13	'91 $5 Redheads	12.50
AL14	'92 $5 Cinnamon Teal	12.50
AL15	'93 $5 Green-Winged Teal	12.50
AL16	'94 $5 Canvasbacks	13.00
AL17	'95 $5 Canada Geese	13.00
AL18	'96 $5 Wood Ducks	13.00
AL19	'97 $5 Snow Geese	13.00
AL20	'98 $5 Barrows Goldeneye	13.00
AL21	'99 $5 Redheads	13.00
AL22	'00 $5 Buffleheads	13.00
AL23	'01 $5 Ruddy Duck	13.00
AL24	'02 $5 Pintail	13.00
AL25	'03 $5 Wood Duck	13.00
AL26	'04 $5 Ring-Necked Duck	13.00
AL27	'05 $5 Canada Geese	13.00
AL28	'06 $5 Canvasback	13.00
AL29	'07 $5 Blue-Winged Teal	13.00
AL30	'08 $5 Hooded Mergansers	13.00
AL31	'09 $5 Wood Duck	13.00
AL32	'10 $5 Pintail	13.00
AL33	'11 $5 Wigeon	11.00
AL34	'12 $6 Ring-necked Duck	11.00
AL35	'13 $5 Canvasbacks	11.00
AL36	'14 $5 Pintails	11.00
AL37	'15 $5 Mallards	11.00
AL38	'16 $10 Wigeons	18.00
AL39	'17 $10 Canada Geese	18.00
AL40	'18 $10 Blue-winged Teal	18.00
AL41	'19 $10 Wood Duck	18.00
AL42	'20 $10 Pintails	18.00

AK1

ALASKA

NO.	DESCRIPTION	F-VF NH
AK1	'85 $5 Emperor Geese	14.00
AK2	'86 $5 Steller's Eiders	13.00
AK3	'87 $5 Spectacled Eiders	15.00
AK4	'88 $5 Trumpeter Swans	11.00
AK5	'89 $5 Barrow's Goldeneyes	11.00
AK6	'90 $5 Old Squaws	12.00
AK7	'91 $5 Snow Geese	14.00
AK8	'92 $5 Canvasbacks	14.00
AK9	'93 $5 Tule White Front Geese	14.00
AK10	'94 $5 Harlequin Ducks	25.00
AK11	'95 $5 Pacific Brant	28.00
AK12	'96 $5 Aleutian Canada Geese	30.00
AK13	'97 $5 King Eiders	22.00
AK14	'98 $5 Barrows Goldeneye	18.00
AK15	'99 $5 Pintail	18.00
AK16	'00 $5 Common Eiders	18.00
AK17	'01 $5 Buffleheads	15.00
AK18	'02 $5 Black Scoter	14.00
AK19	'03 $5 Canada Geese	14.00
AK20	'04 $5 Lesser Scaup	14.00
AK21	'05 $5 Hooded Merganser	14.00
AK22	'06 $5 Pintails, Mallard, green-winged teal	14.00
AK23	'07 Northern Shoveler	14.00
AK24	'08 $5 Pintail	14.00
AK25	'09 $5 Mallards	14.00
AK26	'10 $5 Pintails	14.00
AK27	'11 $5 Canada Goose	13.00
AK28	'12 $5 Harlequin Ducks	11.00
AK29	'13 $5 White-fronted geese	10.00
AK30	'14 $5 White-winged Scoter	10.00
AK31	'15 $5 Northern Pintail	10.00
AK32	'16 $5 Pacific Brant	10.00
AK33	'17 $10 American Wigeon	18.00
AK34	'18 $10 Bufflehead	18.00
AK35	'19 $10 Emperor Goose	18.00
AK36	'20 $10 Gadwall	18.00
AK37	'21 $10 Ring-necked Duck	18.00

AZ1

ARIZONA

NO.	DESCRIPTION	F-VF NH
AZ1	'87 $5.50 Pintails	13.00
AZ2	'88 $5.50 Green-Winged Teal	13.00
AZ3	'89 $5.50 Cinnamon Teal	13.00
AZ4	'90 $5.50 Canada Geese	15.00
AZ5	'91 $5.50 Blue-Winged Teal	13.00
AZ6	'92 $5.50 Buffleheads	13.00
AZ7	'93 $5.50 Mexican Ducks	15.00
AZ8	'94 $5.50 Mallards	15.00
AZ9	'95 $5.50 Widgeon	15.00
AZ10	'96 $5.50 Canvasback	15.00
AZ11	'97 $5.50 Gadwall	15.00
AZ12	'98 $5.50 Wood Duck	15.00
AZ13	'99 $5.50 Snow Geese	15.00
AZ14	'00 $7.50 Ruddy Ducks	22.00
AZ15	'01 $7.50 Redheads	18.00
AZ16	'02 $7.50 Ring-necked ducks	18.00
AZ17	'03 $7.50 Northern Shoveler	18.00
AZ18	'04 $7.50 Lesser Scaup	18.00
AZ19	'05 $7.50 Pintails	18.00
AZ20	'06 $7.50 Canada Geese	18.00
AZ21	'07 $8.75 Wood Duck	18.00
AZ22	'08 $8.75 Canvasback	18.00
AZ23	'09 $8.75 Hooded Mergansers	18.00
AZ24	'10 $8.75 Green-winged teal	18.00
AZ25	'11 $8.75 Bufflehead	18.00
AZ26	'12 $8.75 American Widgeon	18.00
AZ27	'13 $8.75 Pintail	18.00

AR5

ARKANSAS

NO.	DESCRIPTION	F-VF NH
AR1	'81 $5.50 Mallards	50.00
AR2	'82 $5.50 Wood Ducks	40.00
AR3	'83 $5.50 Green-Winged Teal	55.00
AR4	'84 $5.50 Pintails	20.00
AR5	'85 $5.50 Mallards	12.00
AR6	'86 $5.50 Black Swamp Mallards	12.00
AR7	'87 $7 Wood Ducks	12.00
AR8	'88 $7 Pintails	12.00
AR9	'89 $7 Mallards	12.00
AR10	'90 $7 Black Ducks & Mallards	12.00
AR11	'91 $7 Sulphur River Widgeons	12.00
AR12	'92 $7 Shirey Bay Shovelers	12.00
AR13	'93 $7 Grand Prairie Mallards	15.00
AR14	'94 $7 Canada Goose	19.00
AR15	'95 $7 White River Mallards	19.00
AR16	'96 $7 Black Lab	22.00
AR17	'97 $7 Chocolate Lab	18.00
AR18	'98 $7 Labrador retriever, mallards	18.00
AR19	'99 $7.00 Wood Duck	18.00
AR20	'00 $7 Mallards and Golden Retriever	21.00
AR21	'01 $7 Canvasback	18.00
AR22	'02 $7 Mallards	18.00
AR23	'03 $7 Mallards & Chesapeake Bay Retriever	18.00
AR24	'04 $7 Mallards	15.00
AR24a	'04 $20 Mallards	35.00
AR25	'05 $7 Mallards and Labrador Retriever	16.00
AR25a	'05 $20 Mallards and Labrador Retriever	35.00
AR26	'06 $7 Mallards	16.00
AR26a	'06 $20 Mallards	35.00
AR27	'07 $7 Mallards, Labrador Retriever	16.00
AR27a	'07 $20 Mallards, Labrador Retriever	35.00
AR28	'08 $7 Mallards, Labrador Retriever	16.00
AR28a	'08 $20 Mallards, Labrador Retriever	35.00
AR29	'09 $7 Hooded Merganwers	16.00
AR29a	'09 $20 Hooded Merganwers	35.00
AR30	'10 $7 Mallards and Black Labrador Retriever	16.00
AR30a	'10 $20 Mallards and Black Labrador Retriever	40.00
AR31	'11 $7 Mallards	16.00
AR31a	'11 $20 Mallards	35.00
AR32	'12 $7 Green Winged Teal	16.00
AR32a	'12 $20 Green Winged Teal	35.00
AR32b	'$35.00 Green-winged Teal	60.00
AR33	'13 $7 Mallards	16.00
AR33a	'13 $35 Mallards	55.00
AR34	'14 $7 Mallards	16.00
AR34a	'14 $35 Mallards	55.00
AR35	'15 $7 Snow Geese	16.00
AR35a	'15 $35 Snow Geese	55.00
AR36	'16 $7 Mallards	16.00
AR36a	'16 $35 Mallards	55.00
AR37	'17 $7 Mallards	16.00
AR37a	'17 $35 Mallards	55.00
AR38	'18 $7 Ring-necked Ducks	16.00
AR38a	'18 $35 Ring-necked Ducks	55.00
AR39	'19 $7 Mallards	16.00
AR39a	'19 $35 Mallards	55.00
AR40	'20 $7 Green-winged Teal	16.00
AR40a	'20 $7 Green-winged Teal	55.00
AR41	'21 $7 Mallard & Black Lab	16.00
AR41a	'21 $35 Mallard & Black Lab	55.00

CA16

CALIFORNIA

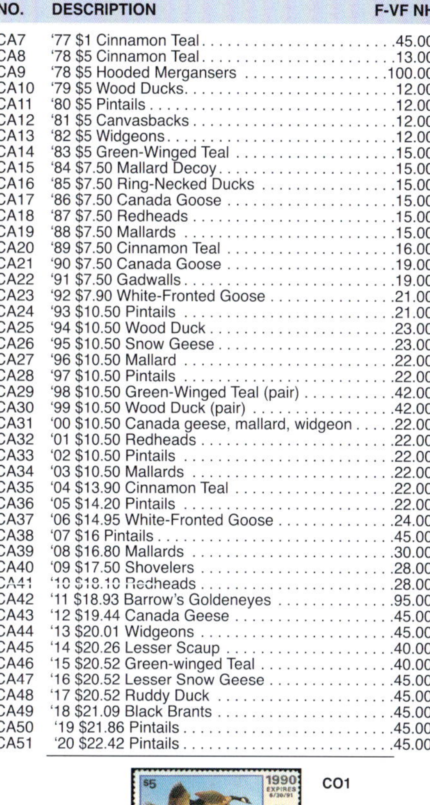

NO.	DESCRIPTION	F-VF NH
CA1	'71 $1 Pintails	500.00
CA2	'72 $1 Canvasbacks	1400.00
CA3	'73 $1 Mallards	15.00
CA4	'74 $1 White-Fronted Geese	4.50
CA5	'75 $1 Green-Winged Teal	150.00
CA6	'76 $1 Widgeons	30.00
CA7	'77 $1 Cinnamon Teal	45.00
CA8	'78 $5 Cinnamon Teal	13.00
CA9	'78 $5 Hooded Mergansers	100.00
CA10	'79 $5 Wood Ducks	12.00
CA11	'80 $5 Pintails	12.00
CA12	'81 $5 Canvasbacks	12.00
CA13	'82 $5 Widgeons	12.00
CA14	'83 $5 Green-Winged Teal	15.00
CA15	'84 $7.50 Mallard Decoy	15.00
CA16	'85 $7.50 Ring-Necked Ducks	15.00
CA17	'86 $7.50 Canada Goose	15.00
CA18	'87 $7.50 Redheads	15.00
CA19	'88 $7.50 Mallards	15.00
CA20	'89 $7.50 Cinnamon Teal	16.00
CA21	'90 $7.50 Canada Goose	19.00
CA22	'91 $7.50 Gadwalls	19.00
CA23	'92 $7.90 White-Fronted Goose	21.00
CA24	'93 $10.50 Pintails	21.00
CA25	'94 $10.50 Wood Duck	23.00
CA26	'95 $10.50 Snow Geese	23.00
CA27	'96 $10.50 Mallard	22.00
CA28	'97 $10.50 Pintails	22.00
CA29	'98 $10.50 Green-Winged Teal (pair)	42.00
CA30	'99 $10.50 Wood Duck (pair)	42.00
CA31	'00 $10.50 Canada geese, mallard, widgeon	22.00
CA32	'01 $10.50 Redheads	22.00
CA33	'02 $10.50 Pintails	22.00
CA34	'03 $10.50 Mallards	22.00
CA35	'04 $13.90 Cinnamon Teal	22.00
CA36	'05 $14.20 Pintails	22.00
CA37	'06 $14.95 White-Fronted Goose	24.00
CA38	'07 $16 Pintails	45.00
CA39	'08 $16.80 Mallards	30.00
CA40	'09 $17.50 Shovelers	28.00
CA41	'10 $18.10 Redheads	28.00
CA42	'11 $18.93 Barrow's Goldeneyes	95.00
CA43	'12 $19.44 Canada Geese	45.00
CA44	'13 $20.01 Widgeons	45.00
CA45	'14 $20.26 Lesser Scaup	40.00
CA46	'15 $20.52 Green-winged Teal	40.00
CA47	'16 $20.52 Lesser Snow Geese	45.00
CA48	'17 $20.52 Ruddy Duck	45.00
CA49	'18 $21.09 Black Brants	45.00
CA50	'19 $21.86 Pintails	45.00
CA51	'20 $22.42 Pintails	45.00

CO1

COLORADO

NO.	DESCRIPTION	F-VF NH
CO1	'90 $5 Canada Geese	17.00
CO2	'91 $5 Mallards	23.00
CO3	'92 $5 Pintails	13.00
CO4	'93 $5 Green-Winged Teal	13.00
CO5	'94 $5 Wood Ducks	13.00
CO6	'95 $5 Buffleheads	13.00
CO7	'96 $5 Cinnamon Teal	13.00
CO8	'97 $5 Widgeon	13.00
CO9	'98 $5 Redhead	13.00
CO10	'99 $5 Blue-winged Teal	13.00
CO11	'00 $5 Gadwalls	13.00
CO12	'01 $5 Ruddy Duck	13.00
CO13	'02 $5 Common Goldeneyes	13.00
CO14	'03 $5 Canvasbacks	13.00
CO15	'04 $5 Snow Geese	13.00
CO16	'05 $5 Shovelers	13.00
CO17	'06 $5 Ring-Necked Ducks	13.00
CO18	'07 $5 Hooded Mergansers	13.00
CO19	'08 $5 Lesser Scaup	13.00
CO20	'09 $5 Barrows's Goldeneye	13.00
CO21	'10 $5 Pintails	13.00
CO22	'11 $5 Green Winged Teal	13.00
CO23	'12 $5 Ross's geese	10.00
CO24	'13 $5 Greater Scaups	10.00
CO25	'14 $5 Canada Geese	10.00
CO26	'15 $7.50 Wood Ducks	13.00
CO27	'16 $10 Marsh Mallards	18.00
CO28	'17 $10 Redheads	18.00
CO29	'18 $10 Ring-necked Ducks	15.00
CO30	'19 $10 Northern Pintails	15.00
CO31	'20 $10 Canvasbacks	15.00
CO32	'21 $10 Canvasbacks	15.00

CT7

CONNECTICUT

NO.	DESCRIPTION	F-VF NH
CT1	'93 $5 Black Ducks	15.00
CT2	'94 $5 Canvasbacks	18.00
CT3	'95 $5 Mallards	18.00
CT4	'96 $5 Old Squaw	23.00
CT5	'97 $5 Green Winged Teal	15.00
CT6	'98 $5 Mallards	15.00
CT7	'99 $5 Canada Geese	28.00
CT8	'00 $5 Wood Duck	15.00
CT9	'01 Bufflehead	15.00
CT10	'02 Greater Scaups	18.00
CT11	'03 $5 Black Duck	15.00
CT12	'04 $5 Wood Duck	15.00
CT13	'05 $10 Mallards	21.00
CT14	'06 $10 Buffleheads	21.00

NO.	DESCRIPTION	F-VF NH
CT15	'07 $10 Black Duck Decoy	21.00
CT16	'08 $10 Common Goldeneyes	21.00
CT17	'09 $10 Black Duck	21.00
CT18	'10 $13 Common Goldeneyes	23.00
CT19	'12 $13 Pintail	25.00
CT20	'13 $13 Wood ducks	25.00
CT21	'14 $13 Hooded Mergansers	25.00
CT22	'15 $13 Canvasbacks	25.00
CT23	'16 $13 Atlantic Brant	25.00
CT24	'17 $17 Canvasbacks and Lighthouse	28.00
CT25	'18 $17 Black Scoter and Lighthouse	28.00
CT26	'19 $17 Buffleheads	28.00
CT27	'20 $17 Wood Ducks	28.00
CT28	'21 $17 Canada Goose	28.00

DE1

DELAWARE

NO.	DESCRIPTION	F-VF NH
DE1	'80 $5 Black Ducks	70.00
DE2	'81 $5 Snow Geese	55.00
DE3	'82 $5 Canada Geese	55.00
DE4	'83 $5 Canvasbacks	40.00
DE5	'84 $5 Mallards	15.00
DE6	'85 $5 Pintail	12.00
DE7	'86 $5 Widgeons	12.00
DE8	'87 $5 Redheads	12.00
DE9	'88 $5 Wood Ducks	10.00
DE10	'89 $5 Buffleheads	10.00
DE11	'90 $5 Green-Winged Teal	10.00
DE12	'91 $5 Hooded Merganser	10.00
DE13	'92 $5 Blue-Winged Teal	10.00
DE14	'93 $5 Goldeneye	10 .00
DE15	'94 $5 Blue Goose	14.00
DE16	'95 $5 Scaup	14.00
DE17	'96 $6 Gadwall	15.00
DE18	'97 $6 White Winged Scoter	15.00
DE19	'98 $6 Blue Winged Teal	14.00
DE20	'99 $6 Tundra Swan	14.00
DE21	'00 $6 American brant	14.00
DE22	'01 $6 Old Squaw	15.00
DE23	'02 $6 Ruddy Ducks	15.00
DE24	'03 $9 Ring Necked Duck	18.00
DE25	'04 $9 Black Scoter	20.00
DE26	'05 $9 Common Merganser and Lighthouse	18.00
DE27	'06 $9 Red-Breasted Mergansers	18.00
DE28	'07 $9 Surf Scooters, Lighthouse	18.00
DE29	'08 $9 Greater Scaup, Lighthouse	18.00
DE30	'09 $9 Black Ducks	18.00
DE31	'10 $9 Canvasback	18.00
DE32	'11 $9 Hooded Mergansers	18.00
DE33	'12 $9 Lesser Scaup	14.00
DE34	'13 $9 Wigeon	14.00
DE35	'14 $9 Blue-winged teal	14.00
DE36	'15 $9 Black Duck	14.00
DE37	'16 $9 Green-winged Teal	14.00
DE38	'17 $15 Canvasbacks and Retriever	25.00
DE39	'18 $15 Pintails and Golden Retriver	25.00
DE40	'19 $15 Long-tailed Duck and Retriever	25.00
DE41	'20 $15 Wigeons & Labrador	28.00
DE42	'21 $15 Mallard	28.00

FL8

FLORIDA

NO.	DESCRIPTION	F-VF NH
FL1	'79 $3.25 Green-Winged Teal	160.00
FL2	'80 $3.25 Pintails	18.00
FL3	'81 $3.25 Widgeon	18.00
FL4	'82 $3.25 Ring-Necked Ducks	18.00
FL5	'83 $3.25 Buffleheads	55.00
FL6	'84 $3.25 Hooded Merganser	20.00
FL7	'85 $3.25 Wood Ducks	18.00
FL8	'86 $3 Canvasbacks	14.00
FL9	'87 $3.50 Mallards	13.00
FL10	'88 $3.50 Redheads	12.00
FL11	'89 $3.50 Blue-Winged Teal	12.00
FL12	'90 $3.50 Wood Ducks	13.00
FL13	'91 $3.50 Northern Pintails	12.00
FL14	'92 $3.50 Ruddy Duck	12.00
FL15	'93 $3.50 American Widgeon	12.00
FL16	'94 $3.50 Mottled Duck	12.00
FL17	'95 $3.50 Fulvous Whistling Duck	13.00
FL18	'96 $3.50 Goldeneyes	23.00
FL19	'97 $3.50 Hooded Mergansers	19.00
FL20	'98 $3.50 Shoveler	36.00
FL21	'99 $3 Pintail	18.00
FL22	'00 $3.50 Rin-necked duck	18.00
FL23	'01 $3.50 Canvasback	18.00
FL24	'02 $3.50 Mottled Duck	66.00
FL25	'03 $3.50 Green-Winged Teal	135.00

GA1

GEORGIA

NO.	DESCRIPTION	F-VF NH
GA1	'85 $5.50 Wood Ducks	19.00
GA2	'86 $5.50 Mallards	12.00
GA3	'87 $5.50 Canada Geese	12.00
GA4	'88 $5.50 Ring-Necked Ducks	12.00
GA5	'89 $5.50 Duckling & Golden Retriever Puppy	22.00
GA6	'90 $5.50 Wood Ducks	12.00
GA7	'91 $5.50 Green-Winged Teal	12.00
GA8	'92 $5.50 Buffleheads	18.00
GA9	'93 $5.50 Mallards	18.00
GA10	'94 $5.50 Ring-Necked Ducks	18.00
GA11	'95 $5.50 Widgeons, Labrador Retriever	42.00
GA12	'96 $5.50 Black Ducks	35.00
GA13	'97 $5.50 Lesser Scaup	58.00
GA14	'98 $5.50 Black Lab with Ringnecks	37.00
GA15	'99 $5.50 Pintails	35.00

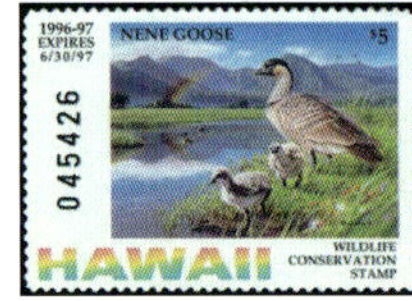

HI1

HAWAII

NO.	DESCRIPTION	F-VF NH
HI1	'96 $5 Nene Geese	13.00
HI2	'97 $5 Hawaiian Duck	13.00
HI3	'98 $5 Wild Turkey	15.00
HI4	'99 $5 Ring-necked Pheasant	18.00
HI5	'00 $5 Erckesls Francolin	15.00
HI6	'01 $5 Japanese Green Pheasant	15.00
HI7	'02 $10 Chukar Partridge	19.00
HI8	'03 $10 Nene Geese	19.00
HI9	'04 $10 Nene Geese	19.00
HI10	'05 $10 California Quail	19.00
HI11	'06 $10 Black Francolin	19.00
HI12	'07 $10 Gray Francolin	19.00
HI13	'08 $10 Chukar Partridge	19.00
HI14	'09 $10 California Quail	19.00
HI15	'11 $10 Green Pheasant	17.50
HI16	'11 $10 Wild Turkey	17.50
HI17	'12 $10 Mouflon Sheep	17.50
HI18	'15 $10 Mouflon Sheep	17.50
HI19	'16 $10 Axis Deer	17.50
HI20	'17 $10 Pheasant and Wild Sheep	17.50
HI21	'18 $10 Boar	17.50
HI22	'19 $10 Mouflon Sheep	17.50
HI23	'20 $10 Black-Tailed Deer	17.50
HI24	'21 $10 Hybrid Sheep	17.50

ID1

IDAHO

NO.	DESCRIPTION	F-VF NH
ID1	'87 $5.50 Cinnamon Teal	20.00
ID2	'88 $5.50 Green-Winged Teal	16.00
ID3	'89 $6 Blue-Winged Teal	14.00
ID4	'90 $6 Trumpeter Swans	28.00
ID6	'91 $6 Widgeons	12.00
ID7	'92 $6 Canada Geese	18.00
ID8	'93 $6 Common Goldeneye	17.00
ID9	'94 $6 Harlequin Ducks	19.00
ID10	'95 $6 Wood Ducks	20.00
ID11	'96 $6 Mallard	28.00
ID12	'97 $6.50 Shovelers	20.00
ID13	'98 $6.50 Canada Geese	20.00

IL11

ILLINOIS

NO.	DESCRIPTION	F-VF NH
IL1	'75 $5 Mallard	400.00
IL2	'76 $5 Wood Ducks	175.00
IL3	'77 $5 Canada Goose	125.00
IL4	'78 $5 Canvasbacks	125.00
IL5	'79 $5 Pintail	85.00
IL6	'80 $5 Green-Winged Teal	85.00
IL7	'81 $5 Widgeons	85.00
IL8	'82 $5 Black Ducks	60.00
IL9	'83 $5 Lesser Scaup	75.00
IL10	'84 $5 Blue-Winged Teal	60.00
IL11	'85 $5 Redheads	21.00
IL12	'86 $5 Gadwalls	21.00
IL13	'87 $5 Buffleheads	18.00
IL14	'88 $5 Common Goldeneyes	16.00
IL15	'89 $5 Ring-Necked Ducks	16.00
IL16	'90 $10 Lesser Snow Geese	21.00
IL17	'91 $10 Labrador Retriever & Canada Goose	21.00
IL18	'92 $10 Retriever & Mallards	35.00
IL19	'93 $10 Pintail Decoys & Puppy	43.00
IL20	'94 $10 Canvasbacks & Retrievers	43.00
IL21	'95 $10 Retriever, Green-Winged Teal, Decoys	43.00
IL22	'96 $10 Wood Ducks	26.00
IL23	'97 $10 Canvasbacks	25.00
IL24	'98 $10 Canada Geese	25.00
IL25	'99 $10 Canada Geese, black labrador retriever	35.00
IL27	'01 $10 Canvasback, yellow labrador	35.00
IL28	'02 $10 Canvasbacks, Chesapeake Retriever	35.00
IL29	'03 $10 Chocolate Lab, Green-winged Teal	32.00
IL30	'04 $10 Wood Ducks	24.00
IL31	'05 $10 Green-winged Teal	24.00
IL32	'06 $10 Northern Pintails	24.00
IL33	'07 $10 Bufflehead	25.00
IL34	'08 $10 Greater Scaup	45.00
IL35	'09 $10 Common Goldeneye	85.00
IL36	'10 $15 Blue Winged Teal	45.00

IN10

INDIANA

NO.	DESCRIPTION	F-VF NH
IN1	'76 $5 Green-Winged Teal	13.00
IN2	'77 $5 Pintail	13.00
IN3	'78 $5 Canada Geese	13.00
IN4	'79 $5 Canvasbacks	13.00
IN5	'80 $5 Mallard Ducklings	13.00
IN6	'81 $5 Hooded Mergansers	13.00
IN7	'82 $5 Blue-Winged Teal	13.00
IN8	'83 $5 Snow Geese	13.00
IN9	'84 $5 Redheads	13.00
IN10	'85 $5 Pintail	13.00
IN11	'86 $5 Wood Duck	13.00
IN12	'87 $5 Canvasbacks	13.00
IN13	'88 $6.75 Redheads	13.00
IN14	'89 $6.75 Canada Goose	13.00
IN15	'90 $6.75 Blue-Winged Teal	13.00
IN16	'91 $6.75 Mallards	13.00
IN17	'92 $6.75 Green-Winged Teal	13.00
IN18	'93 $6.75 Wood Ducks	13.00
IN19	'94 $6.75 Pintail	13.00
IN20	'95 $6.75 Goldeneyes	13.00
IN21	'96 $6.75 Black Ducks	13.00
IN22	'97 $6.75 Canada Geese	13.00
IN23	'98 $6.75 Widgeon	13.00
IN24	'99 $6.75 Bluebills	13.00
IN25	'00 $6.75 Ring-necked Duck	13.00
IN26	'01 $6.75 Green-winged Teal	13.00
IN27	'02 $6.75 Green-winged Teal	13.00
IN28	'03 $6.75 Shoveler	13.00
IN29	'04 $6.75 Hooded Mergansers	13.00
IN30	'05 $6.75 Buffleheads	13.00
IN31	'06 $6.75 Gadwalls	13.00
IN32	'07 $6.75 Pintails	13.00
IN33	'08 $6.75 Shovelers	13.00
IN34	'09 $6.75 Snow Geese	13.00
IN35	'10 $6.75 Black Duck	20.00
IN36	'11 $6.75 Wigeon	13.00
IN37	'12 $6.75 Canada geese	20.00
IN38	'13 $6.75 Wood ducks	11.25
IN39	'14 $6.75 Blue-winged teal	11.25

IA14

IOWA

NO.	DESCRIPTION	F-VF NH
IA1	'72 $1 Mallards	125.00
IA2	'73 $1 Pintails	40.50
IA3	'74 $1 Gadwalls	95.00
IA4	'75 $1 Canada Geese	100.00
IA5	'76 $1 Canvasbacks	31.00
IA6	'77 $1 Lesser Scaup	28.00
IA7	'78 $1 Wood Ducks	55.00
IA8	'79 $5 Buffleheads	275.00
IA9	'80 $5 Redheads	30.00
IA10	'81 $5 Green-Winged Teal	30.00
IA11	'82 $5 Snow Geese	22.00
IA12	'83 $5 Widgeons	22.00
IA13	'84 $5 Wood Ducks	40.00
IA14	'85 $5 Mallard & Mallard Decoy	22.00
IA15	'86 $5 Blue-Winged Teal	14.00
IA16	'87 $5 Canada Goose	14.00
IA17	'88 $5 Pintails	14.00
IA18	'89 $5 Blue-Winged Teal	14.00
IA19	'90 $5 Canvasbacks	14.00
IA20	'91 $5 Mallards	14.00
IA21	'92 $5 Labrador Retriever & Ducks	14.00
IA22	'93 $5 Mallards	14.00
IA23	'94 $5 Green-Winged Teal	14.00
IA24	'95 $5 Canada Geese	14.00

NO.	DESCRIPTION	F-VF NH
IA25	'96 $5 Canvasbacks	14.00
IA26	'97 $5 Canada Geese	14.00
IA27	'98 $5 Pintails	14.00
IA28	'99 $5 Trumpeter Swan	19.00
IA29	'00 $5.50 Hooded Merganser	16.00
IA30	'01 $6 Snow Geese	15.00
IA31	'02 $8.50 Northern Shoveler	27.00
IA32	'03 $8.50 Ruddy Duck	20.00
IA33	'04 $8.50 Wood Ducks	18.00
IA34	'05 $8.50 Green-winged Teals	18.00
IA35	'06 Ring-Necked Duck	18.00
IA36	'07 $8.50 Widgeon	18.00
IA37	'08 $8.50 Wood Duck	18.00
IA38	'09 $10.00 Pintail	23.00
IA39	'10 $8.50 Green-winged teal	31.00
IA40	'11 Hooded Merganser	22.00
IA41	'12 Blue-winged teal	17.50
IA42	'13 Wood ducks	22.50
IA43	'14 Redhead	17.50
IA44	'15 Canada Geese	25.00

KS1

KANSAS

NO.	DESCRIPTION	F-VF NH
KS1	'87 $3 Green-Winged Teal	15.00
KS2	'88 $3 Canada Geese	11.00
KS3	'89 $3 Mallards	11.00
KS4	'90 $3 Wood Ducks	11.00
KS5	'91 $3 Pintail	10.00
KS6	'92 $3 Canvasbacks	10.00
KS7	'93 $3 Mallards	12.00
KS8	'94 $3 Blue-Winged Teal	12.00
KS9	'95 $3 Barrow's Goldeneye	12.00
KS10	'96 $3 Widgeon	13.00
KS11	'97 $3 Mallard (blue)	13.00
KS12	'98 $3 Mallard (green)	13.00
KS13	'99 $3 Mallard (red)	13.00
KS14	'00 $3 Mallard (purple)	13.00
KS15	'01 $3 Mallard (orange)	13.00
KS16	'02 $5 Pintail (blue)	13.00
KS17	'03 $5 Pintail (green)	16.00
KS18	'04 $5 Pintail (red)	16.00

KS1

KENTUCKY

NO.	DESCRIPTION	F-VF NH
KY1	'85 $5.25 Mallards	19.00
KY2	'86 $5.25 Wood Ducks	13.00
KY3	'87 $5.25 Black Ducks	14.00
KY4	'88 $5.25 Canada Geese	14.00
KY5	'89 $5.25 Retriever & Canvasbacks	19.00
KY6	'90 $5.25 Widgeons	12.00
KY7	'91 $5.25 Pintails	13.00
KY8	'92 $5.25 Green-Winged Teal	18.00
KY9	'93 $5.25 Canvasbacks & Decoy	25.00
KY10	'94 $5.25 Canada Goose	21.00
KY11	'95 $7.50 Retriever, Decoy, Ringnecks	29.00
KY12	'96 $7.50 Blue-Winged Teal	18.00
KY13	'97 $7.50 Shovelers	18.00
KY14	'98 $7.50 Gadwalls	19.00
KY15	'99 $7.50 Common Goldeneyes	19.00
KY16	'00 $7.50 Hooded Merganser	26.00
KY17	'01 $7.50 Mallard	18.00
KY18	'02 $7.50 Pintails	18.00
KY19	'03 $7.50 Snow Goose	18.00
KY20	'04 $7.50 Black Ducks	19.00
KY21	'05 $7.50 Canada Geese	18.00
KY22	'06 $7.50 Mallards	18.00
KY23	'07 $7.50 Green-Winged Teal	18.00
KY24	'08 $7.50 Pintails	18.00
KY25	'09 $7.50 Snow Geese	18.00

LA1

LOUISIANA

NO.	DESCRIPTION	F-VF NH
LA1	'89 $5 Blue-Winged Teal	15.00
LA1a	'89 $7.50 Blue-Winged Teal	20.00
LA2	'90 $5 Green-Winged Teal	12.00
LA2a	'90 $7.50 Green-Winged Teal	15.00
LA3	'91 $5 Wood Ducks	12.00
LA3a	'91 $7.50 Wood Ducks	18.00
LA4	'92 $5 Pintails	15.00
LA4a	'92 $7.50 Pintails	18.00
LA5	'93 $5 American Widgeon	15.00
LA5a	'93 $7.50 American Widgeon	18.00
LA6	'94 $5 Mottled Duck	16.00
LA6a	'94 $7.50 Mottled Duck	18.00
LA7	'95 $5 Speckle Bellied Goose	16.00
LA7a	'95 $7.50 Speckle Bellied Goose	18.00
LA8	'96 $5 Gadwall	15.00
LA8a	'96 $7.50 Gadwell	18.00
LA9	'97 $5.00 Ring Necked Duck	16.00
LA9a	'97 $13.50 Ring Necked Duck	30.00
LA10	'98 $5.50 Mallards	15.00
LA10a	'98 $13.50 Mallards	30.00
LA11	'99 $5.50 Snow Geese	15.00
LA11a	'99 $13.50 Snow Geese	30.00
LA12	'00 $5.50 Lesser Scaup	15.00
LA12a	'00 $13.50 Lesser Scaup	45.00
LA13	'01 $5.50 Northern Shoveler	15.00
LA13a	'01 $13.50 Northern Shoveler	45.00
LA14	'02 $5.50 Canvasbacks	15.00
LA14a	'02 $25 Canvasbacks	45.00
LA15	'03 $5.50 Redhead	15.00
LA15a	'03 $25.00 Redhead	45.00
LA16	'04 $5.50 Hooded Merganser	15.00
LA16a	'04 $25 Hooded Merganser	45.00
LA17	'05 $5.50 Pintails and Labrador Retriever	15.00
LA17a	'05 $25 Pintails and Labrador Retriever	45.00
LA18	'06 $5.50 Mallards, Labrador Retriever	15.00
LA18a	'06 $25 Mallards, Labrador Retriever	45.00
LA19	'07 $5.50 Mallards, Labrador Retriever	15.00
LA19a	'07 $25 Mallards, Labrador Retriever	40.00
LA20	'08 $5.50 Wood Ducks, Golden Retriever	15.00
LA20a	'08 $25 Wood Ducks, Golden Retriever	62.50
LA21	'09 $5.50 Ducks, Chesapeake Bay Retriever	15.00
LA21a	'09 $25 Ducks, Chesapeake Bay Retriever	40.00
LA22	'10 $5.50 Pintails	15.00
LA22a	'10 $25 Pintails	40.00
LA23	'11 $5.50 Wood Ducks	20.00
LA23a	'11 $25 Wood Ducks	41.00
LA24	'12 $5.50 Wigeons	20.00
LA24a	'12 $25 Wigeons	35.00
LA25	'13 $5.50 Mallards	20.00
LA25a	'13 $25 Mallards	35.00
LA26	'14 $5.50 White-fronted Geese	15.00
LA26a	'14 $25 White-fronted Geese	35.00
LA27	'15 5.50 Blue-winged Teal	15.00
LA27a	'15 $25 Blue-winged Teal	50.00
LA28	'16 $5.50 Gadwalls	35.00
LA28a	'16 $25 Gadwalls	80.00
LA29	'17 $5.50 Green-winged Teal	40.00
LA29a	'17 $25 Green-tailed Teal	80.00
LA30	'18 $5.50 Canvasbacks	40.00
LA30a	'18 $25 Canvasbacks	80.00
LA31	'19 $5.50 Shovelers	40.00
LA31a	'19 $25 Shovelers	80.00
LA32	'20 $5.50 Ring-necked Ducks	40.00
LA32a	'20 $25 Ring-necked Ducks	80.00
LA33	'21 $5.50 Mottled Duck	40.00
LA33a	'21 $25 Mottled Duck	80.00

ME2

MAINE

NO.	DESCRIPTION	F-VF NH
ME1	'84 $2.50 Black Ducks	25.00
ME2	'85 $2.50 Common Eiders	45.00
ME3	'86 $2.50 Wood Ducks	13.00
ME4	'87 $2.50 Buffleheads	11.00
ME5	'88 $2.50 Green-Winged Teal	11.00
ME6	'89 $2.50 Common Goldeneyes	10.00
ME7	'90 $2.50 Canada Geese	10.00
ME8	'91 $2.50 Ring-Necked Duck	10.00
ME9	'92 $2.50 Old Squaw	10.00
ME10	'93 $2.50 Hooded Merganser	10.00
ME11	'94 $2.50 Mallards	13.00
ME12	'95 $2.50 White-Winged Scoters	15.00
ME13	'96 $2.50 Blue-Winged Teal	15.00
ME14	'97 $2.50 Greater Scaup	15.00
ME15	'98 $2.50 Surf Scoters	15.00
ME16	'99 $2.50 Black Duck	12.00
ME17	'00 $2.50 Common Eider	10.00
ME18	'01 $2.50 Wood Duck	10.00
ME19	'02 $2.50 Bufflehead	10.00
ME20	'03 $5.50 Green-winged Teal	18.00
ME21	'04 $5.50 Barrows Goldeneyes	18.00
ME22	'05 $8.50 Canada Goose	18.00
ME23	'06 $7.50 Ring-Necked Ducks	18.00
ME24	'07 $7.50 Long-Tailed Ducks	18.00
ME25	'08 Hooded Mergansers	18.00
ME26	'09 $7.50 Mallards	18.00
ME27	'10 $7.50 Harlequin Ducks	18.00
ME28	'11 $7.50 Wood Ducks	15.00
ME29	'12 $7.50 Ringed-necked ducks	15.00
ME30	'13 $7.50 Greater Scaup	15.00
ME31	'14 $7.50 Wigeon	15.00
ME32	'15 $7.50 Canvasbacks	15.00
ME33	'16 $7.50 Blue-winged Teal	15.00
ME34	'17 $7.50 Common Eiders	15.00
ME35	'18 $7.50 Northern Pintails	15.00
ME36	'19 $7.50 Canada Goose	15.00
ME37	'20 $7.50 Red-breasted Mergansers	18.00
ME38	'21 $7.50 Long Tailed Ducks	18.00

MD1

MARYLAND

NO.	DESCRIPTION	F-VF NH
MD1	'74 $1.10 Mallards	15.00
MD2	'75 $1.10 Canada Geese	15.00
MD3	'76 $1.10 Canvasbacks	15.00
MD4	'77 $1.10 Greater Scaup	15.00
MD5	'78 $1.10 Redheads	15.00
MD6	'79 $1.10 Wood Ducks	15.00
MD7	'80 $1.10 Pintail Decoy	15.00
MD8	'81 $3 Widgeon	12.00
MD9	'82 $3 Canvasback	12.00
MD10	'83 $3 Wood Duck	17.00
MD11	'84 $6 Black Ducks	18.00
MD12	'85 $6 Canada Geese	18.00
MD13	'86 $6 Hooded Mergansers	18.00
MD14	'87 $6 Redheads	18.00
MD15	'88 $6 Ruddy Ducks	18.00
MD16	'89 $6 Blue-Winged Teal	18.00
MD17	'90 $6 Lesser Scaup	18.00
MD18	'91 $6 Shovelers	18.00
MD19	'92 $6 Bufflehead	18.00
MD20	'93 $6 Canvasbacks	18.00
MD21	'94 $6 Redheads	18.00
MD22	'95 $6 Mallards	40.00
MD23	'96 $6 Canada Geese	50.00
MD24	'97 $6 Canvasbacks	18.00
MD25	'98 $6 Pintails	18.00
MD26	'99 $5 Wood Ducks	18.00
MD27	'00 $6 Oldsquaws	24.00
MD28	'01 $6 American Widgeon	18.00
MD29	'02 $9 Black Scoters	24.00
MD30	'03 $9 Lesser Scaup	24.00
MD31	'04 $9 Pintails	24.00
MD32	'05 $9 Ruddy Duck	24.00
MD33	'06 $9 Canada Geese	24.00
MD34	'07 $9 Wood Ducks	24.00
MD35	'08 $9 Canvasbacks	18.00
MD36	'09 $9 Blue-Winged Teal	18.00
MD37	'10 $9 Hooded Merganser	18.00
MD38	'11 $9 Canada Geese	18.00
MD39	'12 $9 Wigeons	18.00
MD40	'13 $9 Lesser Scaup	18.00
MD41	'14 $9 Ring-necked duck	18.00
MD42	'15 $9 Canvasback	18.00
MD43	'16 $9 Shovelers	18.00
MD44	'17 $9 Black Ducks	18.00
MD45	'18 $9 Green-winged Teal	18.00
MD46	'19 $9 Green Ducks	18.00
MD47	'20 $9 Blue-winged Teal	18.00
MD48	'21 $9 Redheads	18.00

MA12

MASSACHUSETTS

NO.	DESCRIPTION	F-VF NH
MA1	'74 $1.25 Wood Duck Decoy	19.00
MA2	'75 $1.25 Pintail Decoy	16.00
MA3	'76 $1.25 Canada Goose Decoy	16.00
MA4	'77 $1.25 Goldeneye Decoy	16.00
MA5	'78 $1.25 Black Duck Decoy	18.00
MA6	'79 $1.25 Ruddy Turnstone Duck Decoy	24.00
MA7	'80 $1.25 Old Squaw Decoy	19.00
MA8	'81 $1.25 Red-Breasted Merganser Decoy	19.00
MA9	'82 $1.25 Greater Yellowlegs Decoy	19.00
MA10	'83 $1.25 Redhead Decoy	19.00
MA11	'84 $1.25 White-Winged Scoter Decoy	19.00
MA12	'85 $1.25 Ruddy Duck Decoy	19.00
MA13	'86 $1.25 Preening Bluebill Decoy	18.00
MA14	'87 $1.25 American Widgeon Decoy	18.00
MA15	'88 $1.25 Mallard Decoy	18.00
MA16	'89 $1.25 Brant Decoy	18.00
MA17	'90 $1.25 Whistler Hen Decoy	18.00
MA18	'91 $5 Canvasback Decoy	15.00
MA19	'92 $5 Black-Bellied Plover Decoy	15.00
MA20	'93 $5 Red-Breasted Merganser Decoy	15.00
MA21	'94 $5 White-Winged Scoter Decoy	15.00
MA22	'95 $5 Female Hooded Merganser Decoy	15.00
MA23	'96 $5 Eider Decoy	15.00
MA24	'97 $5 Curlew Shorebird	15.00
MA25	'98 $5 Canada Goose	15.00
MA26	'99 $5 Oldsquaw Decoy	15.00
MA27	'00 $5 Merganser Hen decoy	15.00
MA28	'01 $5 Black Duck decoy	15.00
MA29	'02 $5 Bufflehead decoy	15.00
MA30	'03 $5 Green-winged Teal decoy	14.00
MA31	'04 $5 Wood Duck Decoy	14.00
MA32	'05 $5 Oldsquaw Drake Decoy	14.00
MA33	'06 $5 Long-Bellied Curlew Decoy	14.00
MA34	'07 $5 Goldeneye Decoy	14.00
MA35	'08 Black Duck Decoy	14.00
MA36	'09 $5 White-Winged Scoter Decoy	14.00

NO.	DESCRIPTION	F-VF NH
MA37	'10 $5 Canada Goose Decoy	14.00
MA38	'11 $5 Brant Decoy	14.00

MI10

MICHIGAN

NO.	DESCRIPTION	F-VF NH
MI1	'76 $2.10 Wood Duck	7.00
MI2	'77 $2.10 Canvasbacks	355.00
MI3	'78 $2.10 Mallards	32.00
MI4	'79 $2.10 Canada Geese	77.00
MI5	'80 $3.75 Lesser Scaup	25.00
MI6	'81 $3.75 Buffleheads	31.00
MI7	'82 $3.75 Redheads	31.00
MI8	'83 $3.75 Wood Ducks	31.00
MI9	'84 $3.75 Pintails	31.00
MI10	'85 $3.75 Ring-Necked Ducks	31.00
MI11	'86 $3.75 Common Goldeneyes	28.00
MI12	'87 $3.85 Green-Winged Teal	15.00
MI13	'88 $3.85 Canada Geese	12.00
MI14	'89 $3.85 Widgeons	13.00
MI15	'90 $3.85 Wood Ducks	13.00
MI16	'91 $3.85 Blue-Winged Teal	13.00
MI17	'92 $3.85 Red-Breasted Merganser	11.00
MI18	'93 $3.85 Hooded Merganser	11.00
MI19	'94 $3.85 Black Duck	11.00
MI20	'95 $4.35 Blue Winged Teal	11.00
MI21	'96 $4.35 Canada Geese	11.00
MI22	'97 $5 Canvasbacks	30.00
MI23	'98 $5 Pintail	11.00
MI24	'99 $5 Shoveler	13.00
MI25	'00 $5 Mallards	48.00
MI26	'01 $5 Ruddy Duck	12.00
MI27	'02 $5 Wigeons	12.00
MI28	'03 $5 Redhead	12.00
MI29	'04 $5 Wood Duck	12.00
MI30	'05 $5 Blue-winged Teals	12.00
MI31	'06 $5 Widgeon	12.00
MI32	'07 $5 Pintails	12.00
MI33	'08 $5 Wood Ducks	12.00
MI34	'09 $5 Canvasbacks	12.00
MI35	'10 $5 Buffleheads	12.00
MI36	'11 $5 Mallard	10.00
MI37	'12 $5 Ring-necked ducks	10.00
MI38	'13 $5 Black duck	10.00
MI39	'14 $5 Long-tailed ducks	10.00
MI40	'15 $6 Common Goldeneyes	10.00
MI41	'16 $6 Green-winged Teal	10.00
MI42	'17 $6 Shovelers	10.00
MI43	'18 $6 Wingeons and Black Labrador	10.00
MI44	'19 $6 Pintails	10.00
MI45	'20 $6 Canada Geese	15.00
MI46	'21 $6 Wood Duck	15.00

MN2

MINNESOTA

NO.	DESCRIPTION	F-VF NH
MN1	'77 $3 Mallards	18.00
MN2	'78 $3 Lesser Scaup	15.00
MN3	'79 $3 Pintails	15.00
MN4	'80 $3 Canvasbacks	18.00
MN5	'81 $3 Canada Geese	18.00
MN6	'82 $3 Redheads	18.00
MN7	'83 $3 Blue Geese & Snow Goose	18.00
MN8	'84 $3 Wood Ducks	18.00
MN9	'85 $3 White-Fronted Geese	12.00
MN10	'86 $5 Lesser Scaup	12.00
MN11	'87 $5 Common Goldeneyes	15.00
MN12	'88 $5 Buffleheads	12.00
MN13	'89 $5 Widgeons	12.00
MN14	'90 $5 Hooded Mergansers	25.00
MN15	'91 $5 Ross's Geese	12.00
MN16	'92 $5 Barrow's Goldeneyes	12.00
MN17	'93 $5 Blue-Winged Teal	12.00
MN18	'94 $5 Ringneck Duck	12.00
MN19	'95 $5 Gadwall	12.00
MN20	'96 $5 Greater Scaup	14.00
MN21	'97 $5 Shoveler with Decoy	14.00
MN22	'98 $5 Harlequin Ducks	14.00
MN23	'99 $5 Green-winged Teal	14.00
MN24	'00 $5 Red-Breasted Merganser	25.00
MN25	'01 $5 Black Duck	30.00
MN26	'02 $5 Ruddy Duck	18.00
MN27	'03 $5 Long Tailed Duck	18.00
MN28	'04 $7.50 Common Merganser	18.00
MN29	'05 $7.50 White-winged Scoters and Lighthouse	18.00
MN30	'06 $7.50 Mallard	18.00
MN31	'07 $7.50 Lesser Scaups	18.00
MN32	'08 $7.50 Ross's Geese	18.00
MN33	'09 $7.50 Common Goldeneye	18.00
MN34	'10 $7.50 Wood Duck	18.00
MN35	'11 $7.50 Red-Breasted Merganser	18.00
MN36	'12 $7.50 Ruddy Duck	18.00
MN37	'13 $7.50 Pintail	20.00
MN38	'14 $7.50 Canada Geese	25.00
MN39	'15 $7.50 Harlequin Duck	25.00
MN40	'16 $7.50 Wigeon	20.00
MN41	'17 $7.50 Redheads	20.00
MN42	'18 $7.50 White-winged Scoter	20.00
MN43	'19 $7.50 Gadwall	20.00
MN44	'20 $7.50 Snow Geese	20.00
MN45	'21 $7.50 Greater Scaup	20.00

MS10

MISSISSIPPI

NO.	DESCRIPTION	F-VF NH
MS1	'76 $2 Wood Duck	27.00
MS2	'77 $2 Mallards	13.00
MS3	'78 $2 Green-Winged Teal	13.00
MS4	'79 $2 Canvasbacks	12.00
MS5	'80 $2 Pintails	12.00
MS6	'81 $2 Redheads	12.00
MS7	'82 $2 Canada Geese	19.00
MS8	'83 $2 Lesser Scaup	12.00
MS9	'84 $2 Black Ducks	12.00
MS10	'85 $2 Mallards	20.00
MS11	'86 $2 Widgeons	12.00
MS12	'87 $2 Ring-Necked Ducks	12.00
MS13	'88 $2 Snow Geese	12.00
MS14	'89 $2 Wood Ducks	9.00
MS15	'90 $2 Snow Geese	17.00
MS16	'91 $2 Labrador Retriever & Canvasbacks	11.00
MS17	'92 $2 Green-Winged Teal	10.00
MS18	'93 $2 Mallards	11.00
MS19	'94 $2 Canvasbacks	15.00
MS20	'95 $5 Blue-Winged Teal	17.00
MS21	'96 $5 Hooded Merganser	23.00
MS22	'97 $5Wood Duck	30.00
MS23	'98 $5 Pintails	15.00
MS24	'99 $5 Ring-necked Duck	15.00
MS24a	'99 $5 Ring-necked Duck, S/A, die-cut	15.00
MS25	'00 $5 Mallards	15.00
MS25a	'00 $5 Mallards, S/A, die cut	450.00
MS26	'01 $10 Gadwall	15.00
MS26a	'01 $10 Gadwall, S/A, die cut	15.00
MS27	'02 $10 Wood Duck	15.00
MS27a	'02 $10 Wood Duck, S/A, die cut	15.00
MS28	'03 $10 Pintail	15.00
MS28a	'03 $10 Pintail, S/A, die cut	15.00
MS29	'04 $10 Wood Ducks	15.00
MS29a	'04 $10 Wood Ducks, S/A, die cut	15.00
MS30	'05 $10 Blue-Winged Teal	15.00
MS30a	'05 $10 Blue-Winged Teal, S/A, die cut	15.00
MS30b	'05 $15 Blue-Winged Teal, non-resident	24.00
MS31	'06 $10 Labrador Retriever	15.00
MS31a	'06 $10 Labrador Retriever, S/A, die-cut	15.00
MS31b	'06 $15 Labrador Retriever, non-resident	24.00
MS32	'07 $10 Wood Ducks	15.00
MS32a	'07 $15 Wood Duck, S/A, die-cut	15.00
MS32b	'07 $10 Wood Ducks, non-resident	24.00
MS33	'08 $10 Green-winged Teal	15.00
MS33a	'08 $10 Green-winged Teal, S/A, die-cut	15.00
MS33b	'08 $15 Green-winged Teal, non-resident	24.00
MS34	'09 $10 Blue-winged Teal	15.00
MS34a	'09 $10 Blue-winged Teal, S/A, die-cut	15.00
MS34b	'09 $15 Blue-winged Teal, non-resident	24.00
MS35	'10 $10 Mallards	15.00
MS35a	'10 $10 Mallards, S/A, die-cut	15.00
MS35b	'10 $15 Mallards, non-resident	24.00
MS36	'11 $10 Wood Duck	15.00
MS36a	'11 $10 Wood Duck S/A, die-cut	15.00
MS36b	'11 $15 Wood Duck, non-resident	24.00
MS37	'12 $10 Green-winged teal	15.00
MS37a	'12 $10 Green-winged teal, S/A, die-cut	15.00
MS37b	'12 $15 Green-winged teal, non-resident	24.00
MS38	'13 $10 Mallard	15.00
MS38a	'13 $10 Mallard, S/A, die-cut	15.00
MS38b	'13 $15 Mallard, non-resident	24.00
MS39	'14 $10 Wood Ducks	17.00
MS39a	'14 $10 Wood Ducks, S/A, die-cut	17.00
MS39b	'14 $15 Wood Ducks, non-resident	24.00
MS40	'15 $10 Pintail	17.00
MS40a	'15 $10 Pintail, S/A, die-cut	17.00
MS40b	'15 $10 Pintail, non-resident	24.00
MS41	'16 $10 Pintail	20.00
MS41a	'16 $10 Pintail, S/A, die-cut	20.00
MS41b	'16 $10 Pintail, non-resident	30.00
MS42	'17 $10 Gadwall	20.00
MS42a	'17 $10 Gadwall, S/A, die-cut	20.00
MS42b	'17 $15 Gadwall, non-resident	30.00
MS43	'18 $10 Canvasback	20.00
MS43a	'18 $10 Canvasback, S/A, die-cut	20.00
MS43b	'18 $15 Canvasback, non-resident	30.00
MS44	'19 $10 Redheads	20.00
MS44a	'19 $10 Redheads, S/A, die-cut	20.00
MS44b	'19 $15 Redheads, non-resident	30.00
MS45	'20 $10 Black-bellied Whistling Duck	20.00
MS45a	'20 $10 Black-bellied Whistling Duck, die-cut	20.00
MS45b	'20 $15 Black-bellied Whistling Duck, non-resident	30.00
MS46	'21 $10 Black Duck	20.00
MS46a	'21 $10 Black Duck, die-cut	20.00
MS46b	'21 $15 Black Duck, non-resident	30.00

MO9

MISSOURI

NO.	DESCRIPTION	F-VF NH
MO1	'79 $3.40 Canada Geese	400.00
MO2	'80 $3.40 Wood Ducks	90.00
MO3	'81 $3 Lesser Scaup	55.00
MO4	'82 $3 Buffleheads	55.00
MO5	'83 $3 Blue-Winged Teal	57.00
MO6	'84 $3 Mallards	55.00
MO7	'85 $3 American Widgeons	28.00
MO8	'86 $3 Hooded Mergansers	18.00
MO9	'87 $3 Pintails	15.00
MO10	'88 $3 Canvasback	14.00
MO11	'89 $3 Ring-Necked Ducks	11.00
MO12	'90 $5 Redheads	10.00
MO13	'91 $5 Snow Geese	10.00
MO14	'92 $5 Gadwalls	10.00
MO15	'93 $5 Grccn Winged Teal	10.00
MO16	'94 $5 White-Fronted Goose	10.00
MO17	'95 $5 Goldeneyes	12.00
MO18	'96 $5 Black Duck	16.00

MT34

MONTANA

NO.	DESCRIPTION	F-VF NH
MT34	'86 $5 Canada Geese	15.00
MT35	'87 $5 Redheads	18.00
MT36	'88 $5 Mallards	15.00
MT37	'89 $5 Black Labrador Retriever & Pintail	15.00
MT38	'90 $5 Blue-Winged & CinnamonTeal	10.00
MT39	'91 $5 Snow Geese	10.00
MT40	'92 $5 Wood Ducks	10.00
MT41	'93 $5 Harlequin Ducks	10.00
MT42	'94 $5 Widgeons	10.00
MT43	'95 $5 Tundra Swans	10.00
MT44	'96 $5 Canvasbacks	10.00
MT45	'97 $5 Golden Retriever	10.00
MT46	'98 $5 Gadwalls	10.00
MT47	'99 $5 Barrow's Goldeneye	10.00
MT48	'00 $5 Mallard decoy, Chesapeake retriever	10.00
MT49	'01 $5 Canada Geese, Steamboat	10.00
MT50	'02 ($5) Sandhill crane	10.00
MT51	'03 $5 Mallards	80.00

NE1

NEBRASKA

NO.	DESCRIPTION	F-VF NH
NE1	'91 $6 Canada Geese	12.00
NE2	'92 $6 Pintails	12.00
NE3	'93 $6 Canvasbacks	12.00
NE4	'94 $6 Mallards	12.00
NE5	'95 $6 Wood Ducks	12.00
NE6	'06 $5 Wood Ducks	12.00
NE7	'07 $5 Canvasbacks	12.00
NE8	'08 $5 Swans	12.00
NE9	'09 $5 Northern Pintail	12.00

NV7

NEVADA

NO.	DESCRIPTION	F-VF NH
NV1	'79 $2 Canvasbacks & Decoy	50.00
NV2	'80 $2 Cinnamon Teal	10.00
NV3	'81 $2 Whistling Swans	12.00
NV4	'82 $2 Shovelers	12.00
NV5	'83 $2 Gadwalls	12.00
NV6	'84 $2 Pintails	12.00
NV7	'85 $2 Canada Geese	26.00
NV8	'86 $2 Redheads	26.00
NV9	'87 $2 Buffleheads	23.00
NV10	'88 $2 Canvasbacks	15.00
NV11	'89 $2 Ross's Geese	21.00
NV12	'90 $5 Green-Winged Teal	21.00
NV13	'91 $5 White-Faced Ibis	15.00
NV14	'92 $5 American Widgeon	14.00
NV15	'93 $5 Common Goldeneye	14.00
NV16	'94 $5 Mallards	14.00
NV17	'95 $5 Wood Duck	14.00
NV18	'96 $5 Ring Necked Duck	24.00
NV19	'97 $5 Ruddy Duck	14.00

NO.	DESCRIPTION	F-VF NH
NV20	'98 $5 Hooded Merganser	19.00
NV21	'99 $5 Canvasback Decoy	19.00
NV22	'00 $5 Canvasbacks	19.00
NV23	'01 $5 Lesser Scaup	19.00
NV24	'02 $5 Cinnamon teal	15.00
NV25	'03 $5 Green-winged Teal	15.00
NV26	'04 $10 Redhead	19.00
NV27	'05 $10 Gadwalls	19.00
NV28	'06 $10 Tundra Swans	19.00
NV29	'07 $10 Wood Ducks	19.00
NV30	'08 $10 Pintail	19.00
NV31	'09 $10 Canada Goose	19.00
NV32	'10 $10 Shovelers	19.00
NV33	'11 $10 Green Winged Teal	19.00
NV34	'12 $10 Wigeon	18.00
NV35	'13 $10 Snow Goose	18.00
NV36	'14 $10 American Coots	18.00
NV37	'15 $10 White-footed Goose	18.00
NV38	'16 $10 Buffleheads	18.00
NV39	'17 $10 Ruddy Duck	18.00

NH2

NEW HAMPSHIRE

NO.	DESCRIPTION	F-VF NH
NH1	'83 $4 Wood Ducks	130.00
NH2	'84 $4 Mallards	100.00
NH3	'85 $4 Blue-Winged Teal	130.00
NH4	'86 $4 Hooded Mergansers	25.00
NH5	'87 $4 Canada Geese	12.00
NH6	'88 $4 Buffleheads	12.00
NH7	'89 $4 Black Ducks	12.00
NH8	'90 $4 Green-Winged Teal	12.00
NH9	'91 $4 Golden Retriever & Mallards	16.00
NH10	'92 $4 Ring-Necked Ducks	12.00
NH11	'93 $4 Hooded Mergansers	12.00
NH12	'94 $4 Common Goldeneyes	12.00
NH13	'95 $4 Northern Pintails	12.00
NH14	'96 $4 Surf Scoters	16.00
NH15	'97 $4 Old Squaws	12.00
NH16	'98 $4 Canada Goose	12.00
NH17	'99 $4 Mallards	12.00
NH18	'00 $4 Black Ducks	12.00
NH19	'01 $4 Blue-winged Teal	12.00
NH20	'02 $4 Pintails	12.00
NH21	'03 $4 Wood Ducks	12.00
NH22	'04 $4 Wood Ducks	12.00
NH23	'05 $4 Oldsquaw and Lighthouse	12.00
NH24	'06 $4 Common Elders	12.00
NH25	'07 $4 Black Ducks	12.00

NJ1

NEW JERSEY

NO.	DESCRIPTION	F-VF NH
NJ1	'84 $2.50 Canvasbacks	45.00
NJ1a	'84 $5 Canvasbacks	65.00
NJ2	'85 $2.50 Mallards	20.00
NJ2a	'85 $5 Mallards	24.00
NJ3	'86 $2.50 Pintails	23.00
NJ3a	'86 $5 Pintails	16.00
NJ4	'87 $2.50 Canada Geese	24.00
NJ4a	'87 $5 Canada Geese	22.00
NJ5	'88 $2.50 Green-Winged Teal	17.00
NJ5a	'88 $5 Green-Winged Teal	14.00
NJ6	'89 $2.50 Snow Geese	16.00
NJ6a	'89 $5 Snow Geese	16.00
NJ7	'90 $2.50 Wood Ducks	18.00
NJ7a	'90 $5 Wood Ducks	12.00
NJ8	'91 $2.50 Atlantic Brant	18.00
NJ8a	'91 $5 Atlantic Brant	16.00
NJ9	'92 $2.50 Bluebills	16.00
NJ9a	'92 $5 Bluebills	14.00
NJ10	'93 $2.50 Buffleheads	14.00
NJ10a	'93 $5 Buffleheads	14.00
NJ11	'94 $2.50 Black Ducks	16.00
NJ11a	'94 $5 Black Ducks	16.00
NJ12	'95 $2.50 Widgeon, Lighthouse	16.00
NJ12a	'95 $5 Widgeon, Lighthouse	16.00
NJ13	'96 $2.50 Goldeneyes	15.00
NJ13a	'96 $5 Goldeneyes	18.00
NJ14	'97 $5 Oldsquaws	16.00
NJ14a	'97 $10 Oldsquaws	22.00
NJ15	'98 $5 Mallards	17.00
NJ15a	'98 $10.00 Mallards	20.00
NJ16	'99 $5 Redheads	17.00
NJ16a	'99 $10 Redheads	20.00
NJ17	'00 $5 Canvasbacks	18.00
NJ17a	'00 $10 Canvasbacks	20.00
NJ18	'01 $5 Tundra Swans	16.00
NJ18a	'01 $10 Tundra Swans	20.00
NJ19	'02 $5 Wood Ducks	16.00
NJ19a	'02 $10 Wood Ducks	20.00
NJ20	'03 $5 Pintails & Black Lab	15.00
NJ20a	'03 $10 Pintails & Black Lab	20.00

NO.	DESCRIPTION	F-VF NH
NJ21	'04 $5 Merganser/Puppy	13.00
NJ21a	'04 $10 Merganser/Puppy	20.00
NJ22	'05 $5 Canvasback Decoys and Retriever	15.00
NJ22a	'05 $10 Canvasback Decoys and Retriever	20.00
NJ23	'06 $5 Wood Duck Decoy, Golden Retriever	15.00
NJ23a	'06 $10 Wood Duck Decoy, Golden Retriever	20.00
NJ24	'07 $5 Green-Winged Teal, Labrador Retriever	12.00
NJ24a	'07 $10 Green-Winged Teal, Labrador Retriever	18.00
NJ25	'08 $5 Canvasbacks	12.00
NJ25a	'08 $10 Canvasbacks	18.00

NM1

NEW MEXICO

NO.	DESCRIPTION	F-VF NH
NM1	'91 $7.50 Pintails	18.00
NM2	'92 $7.50 American Widgeon	18.00
NM3	'93 $7.50 Mallard	18.00
NM4	'94 $7.50 Green-Winged Teal	25.00

NY3

NEW YORK

NO.	DESCRIPTION	F-VF NH
NY1	'85 $5.50 Canada Geese	14.00
NY2	'86 $5.50 Mallards	10.00
NY3	'87 $5.50 Wood Ducks	10.00
NY4	'88 $5.50 Pintails	10.00
NY5	'89 $5.50 Greater Scaup	10.00
NY6	'90 $5.50 Canvasbacks	10.00
NY7	'91 $5.50 Redheads	12.00
NY8	'92 $5.50 Wood Ducks	12.00
NY9	'93 $5.50 Blue-Winged Teal	12.00
NY10	'94 $5.50 Canada Geese	12.00
NY11	'95 $5.50 Common Goldeneye	12.00
NY12	'96 $5.50 Common Loon	12.00
NY13	'97 $5.50 Hooded Merganser	12.00
NY14	'98 $5.50 Osprey	12.00
NY15	'99 $5.50 Buffleheads	15.00
NY16	'00 $5.50 Wood Ducks	20.00
NY17	'01 $5.50 Pintails	12.00
NY18	'02 $5.50 Canvasbacks	12.00

NC1

NORTH CAROLINA

NO.	DESCRIPTION	F-VF NH
NC1	'83 $5.50 Mallards	60.00
NC2	'84 $5.50 Wood Ducks	45.00
NC3	'85 $5.50 Canvasbacks	25.00
NC4	'86 $5.50 Canada Geese	25.00
NC5	'87 $5.50 Pintails	18.00
NC6	'88 $5 Green-Winged Teal	12.00
NC7	'89 $5 Snow Geese	18.00
NC8	'90 $5 Redheads	18.00
NC9	'91 $5 Blue-Winged Teal	18.00
NC10	'92 $5 American Widgeon	18.00
NC11	'93 $5 Tundra Swans	18.00
NC12	'94 $5 Buffleheads	18.00
NC13	'95 $5 Brant, Lighthouse	18.00
NC14	'96 $5 Pintails	18.00
NC15	'97 $5 Wood Ducks	18.00
NC15a	'97 $5 Wood Ducks, self-adhesive	45.00
NC16	'98 $5 Canada Geese	15.00
NC16a	'98 $5 Canada Geese, self-adhesive	36.00
NC17	'99 $5 Green-winged Teal	22.00
NC17a	'99 $5 Green-winged Teal, self-adhesive	25.00
NC18	'00 $10 Green-winged Teal	24.00
NC18a	'00 $10 Green-winged Teal, self-adhesive	36.00
NC19	'01 $10 Black Duck, lighthouse	23.00
NC19a	'01 $10 Black Duck, lighthouse, self-adhesive	25.00
NC20	'02 $10 Pintails, Hunters, Dog	23.00
NC20a	'02 $10 Pintails, Hunters, Dog, self-adhesive	35.00
NC21	'03 $10 Ringneck & Brittney Spaniel	20.00
NC21a	'03 $10 Ringneck & Brittney Spaniel, self-adhesive	30.00
NC22	'04 $10 Mallard	20.00
NC22a	'04 $10 Mallard, self-adhesive	25.00
NC23	'05 $10 Green-winged Teals	24.00
NC23a	'05 $10 Green-winged Teals, self-adhesive	25.00
NC24	'06 $10 Lesser Scaups, perf.	23.00
NC24a	'06 $10 Lesser Scaups, self-adhesive, die-cut	25.00
NC25	'07 $10 Wood Ducks	23.00
NC25a	'07 $10 Wood Ducks, self-adhesive, die cut	25.00
NC26	'08 $10 Surf Scooters	20.00
NC26a	'08 $10 Surf Scooters, self-adhesive, die cut	25.00
NC27	'09 $10 Wigeons, perf.	18.00
NC27a	'09 $10 Wigeons, self-adhesive	24.00
NC28	'10 $10 Snow Geese	19.00
NC28a	'10 $10 Snow Geese, self-adhesive, die cut	24.00
NC29	'11 $10 Canada Geese	18.00
NC29a	'11 $10 Canada Geese S/A	19.00
NC30	'12 $10 Redheads	17.00
NC30a	'12 $10 Redheads, S/A	18.00
NC31	'13 $10 Shovelers	17.00
NC31a	'13 $10 Shovelers, self-adhesive	18.00
NC32	'14 $10 Hooded Mergansers, W/A	17.00
NC32a	'14 $10 Hooded Mergansers, S/A	18.00
NC33	'15 $10 Black Ducks	17.00
NC33a	'15 $10 Black Ducks, S/A, die-cut	20.00
NC34	'16 $13 Atlantic Brant and Lighthouse	24.00
NC34a	'16 $13 Atlantic Brant and Lighthouse, S/A	24.00
NC35	'17 $13 Gadwalls	24.00
NC35a	'17 $13 Gadwalls, S/A	24.00
NC36	'18 $13 Canvasbacks	24.00
NC36a	'18 $13 Canvasbacks, S/A	24.00
NC37	'19 $13 Ring-necked Ducks	24.00
NC37a	'19 $13 Ring-necked Ducks, S/A	24.00
NC38	'20 $14 Tundra Swans	24.00
NC38a	'20 $14 Tundra Swans, S/A	24.00
NC39	'21 $14 Blue-winged Teals	24.00
NC39a	'21 $14 Blue-winged Teals, S/A	24.00

ND35

NORTH DAKOTA

NO.	DESCRIPTION	F-VF NH
ND32	'82 $9 Canada Geese	120.00
ND35	'83 $9 Mallards	70.00
ND38	'84 $9 Canvasbacks	50.00
ND41	'85 $9 Greater Scaup	25.00
ND44	'86 $9 Pintails	25.00
ND47	'87 $9 Snow Geese	18.00
ND50	'88 $9 White-Winged Scoters	16.00
ND53	'89 $6 Redheads	12.00
ND56	'90 $6 Labrador Retriever & Mallard	12.00
ND59	'91 $6 Green-Winged Teal	12.00
ND62	'92 $6 Blue-Winged Teal	12.00
ND65	'93 $6 Wood Ducks	12.00
ND67	'94 $6 Canada Geese	12.00
ND69	'95 $6 Widgeon	12.00
ND71	'96 $6 Mallards	12.00
ND73	'97 $6 White Fronted Geese	12.00
ND75	'98 $6 Blue Winged Teal	12.00
ND77	'99 $6 Gadwalls	12.00
ND79	'00 $6 Pintails	12.00
ND81	'01 $6 Canada Geese	12.00
ND83	'02 $6 Text, black on green	18.00
ND84	'03 $6 Text, black on green	18.00
ND85	'04 $6 Text, black on green	18.00
ND86	'05 $6 Text, black on green	15.00
ND87	'06 $6 black, green	13.00
ND88	'07 $6 Text, black on green	13.00
ND89	'08 $6 Text, black on green	13.00
ND90	'09 $6 Text, black on green	13.00
ND91	'10 $6 black, green	13.00
ND92	'11 $6 Black	10.00
ND93	'12 $6 Black, green	10.00
ND94	'13 $6 Black, green	10.00
ND95	'14 $10 Black, green	14.00
ND96	'15 $10 Black, green	14.00

OH4

OHIO

NO.	DESCRIPTION	F-VF NH
OH1	'82 $5.75 Wood Ducks	60.00
OH2	'83 $5.75 Mallards	40.00
OH3	'84 $5.75 Green-Winged Teal	40.00
OH4	'85 $5.75 Redheads	35.00
OH5	'86 $5.75 Canvasback	35.00
OH6	'87 $6 Blue-Winged Teal	15.00
OH7	'88 $6 Common Goldeneyes	12.00
OH8	'89 $6 Canada Geese	12.00
OH9	'90 $9 Black Ducks	18.00
OH10	'91 $9 Lesser Scaup	18.00
OH11	'92 $9 Wood Duck	18.00
OH12	'93 $9 Buffleheads	18.00
OH13	'94 $11 Mallards	22.00
OH14	'95 $11 Pintails	25.00
OH15	'96 $11 Hooded Mergansers	25.00
OH16	'97 $11 Widgeons	22.00
OH17	'98 $11 Gadwall	22.00
OH18	'99 $11 Mallard	20.00
OH19	'00 $11 Buffleheads	20.00
OH20	'01 $11 Canvasback	20.00
OH21	'02 $11 Ring Neck	20.00
OH22	'03 $11 Hooded Merganser	20.00
OH23	'04 $15 Tundra Swans	20.00
OH24	'05 $15 Wood Duck	20.00
OH25	'06 $15 Pintail	24.00
OH26	'07 $15 Canada Goose	45.00
OH27	'08 $15 Green-Winged Teal	24.00
OH28	'09 $15 Common Goldeneye	24.00
OH29	'10 $10 Ruddy Ducks	24.00

NO.	DESCRIPTION	F-VF NH
OH30	'11 $15 Red-Breasted Merganser	40.00
OH31	'12 $15 Mallards	24.00
OH32	'13 $15 Blue-winged teal	24.00
OH33	'14 $15 Pintail	30.00
OH34	'15 $15 Shoveler	30.00
OH35	'16 $15 Wood Ducks	30.00
OH36	'17 $15 Wigeons	30.00
OH37	'18 $15 Ring-necked Ducks	30.00
OH38	'19 $15 Black Duck	30.00
OH39	'20 $15 Black Duck	30.00
OH40	'21 $15 Mallard	30.00

OK4

OKLAHOMA

NO.	DESCRIPTION	F-VF NH
OK1	'80 $4 Pintails	50.00
OK2	'81 $4 Canada Goose	20.00
OK3	'82 $4 Green-Winged Teal	12.00
OK4	'83 $4 Wood Ducks	12.00
OK5	'84 $4 Ring-Necked Ducks	12.00
OK6	'85 $4 Mallards	12.00
OK7	'86 $4 Snow Geese	12.00
OK8	'87 $4 Canvasbacks	11.00
OK9	'88 $4 Widgeons	10.00
OK10	'89 $4 Redheads	10.00
OK11	'90 $4 Hooded Merganser	10.00
OK12	'91 $4 Gadwalls	10.00
OK13	'92 $4 Lesser Scaup	10.00
OK14	'93 $4 White-Fronted Geese	10.00
OK15	'94 $4 Blue-Winged Teal	10.00
OK16	'95 $4 Ruddy Ducks	10.00
OK17	'96 $4 Buffleheads	10.00
OK18	'97 $4 Goldeneyes	10.00
OK19	'98 $4 Shoveler	10.00
OK20	'99 $4 Canvasbacks	10.00
OK21	'00 $4 Pintails	12.00
OK22	'01 $4 Canada Goose	12.00
OK23	'02 $4 Green-winged Teal	12.00
OK24	'03 $10 Wood Duck	18.00
OK25	'04 $10 Mallard	18.00
OK26	'05 $10 Snow Geese	18.00
OK27	'06 $10 Widgeons	18.00
OK28	'07 $10 Redheads	18.00
OK29	'08 $10 Mallards, Labrador Retriever	18.00
OK30	'09 $10 Gadwells	18.00
OK31	'10 $10 Ringed-neck Duck	18.00
OK32	'11 $10 Blue Winged Teal	18.00
OK33	'12 $10 White-Fronted Goose	18.00
OK34	'13 $10 Common Goldeneye	18.00
OK35	'14 $10 Canvasback	18.00
OK36	'15 $10 Pintails	18.00
OK37	'16 $10 Mallard	18.00
OK38	'17 $10 Green-winged Teal	18.00
OK39	'18 $10 Shovelers	17.00
OK40	'19 $10 Wood Duck	17.00
OK41	'20 $10 Canada Geese	17.00
OK42	'21 $10 Wigeons	17.00

OR1

OREGON

NO.	DESCRIPTION	F-VF NH
OR1	'84 $5 Canada Geese	25.00
OR2	'85 $5 Lesser Snow Goose	35.00
OR3	'86 $5 Pacific Brant	18.00
OR4	'87 $5 White-Fronted Geese	16.00
OR5	'88 $5 Great Basin Canada Geese	16.00
OR7	'89 $5 Black Labrador Retriever & Pintails	16.00
OR8	'90 $5 Mallards & Golden Retriever	16.00
OR9	'91 $5 Buffleheads & Chesapeake Bay Retriever	16.00
OR10	'92 $5 Green-Winged Teal	16.00
OR11	'93 $5 Mallards	16.00
OR12	'94 $5 Pintails	16.00
OR14	'95 $5 Wood Ducks	16.00
OR16	'96 $5 Mallard/Widgeon/Pintail	16.00
OR18	'97 $5 Canvasbacks	16.00
OR20	'98 $5 Pintail	16.00
OR22	'99 $5 Canada Geese	16.00
OR24	'00 $7.50 Canada Geese, Mallard, Widgeon	16.00
OR25	'01 $7.50 Canvasbacks	16.00
OR26	'02 $7.50 American Wigeon	16.00
OR27	'03 $7.50 Wood Duck	16.00
OR28	'04 $7.50 Ross' Goose	16.00
OR29	'05 $7.50 Hooded Merganser	16.00
OR30	'06 $7.50 Pintail, Mallard	16.00
OR31	'07 $7.50 Wood Ducks	16.00
OR32	'08 $7.50 Pintails	16.00
OR33	'09 $7.50 Mallards	16.00
OR34	'10 $9.50 Wood Duck	18.00
OR35	'11 $9.50 Canvasback	18.00

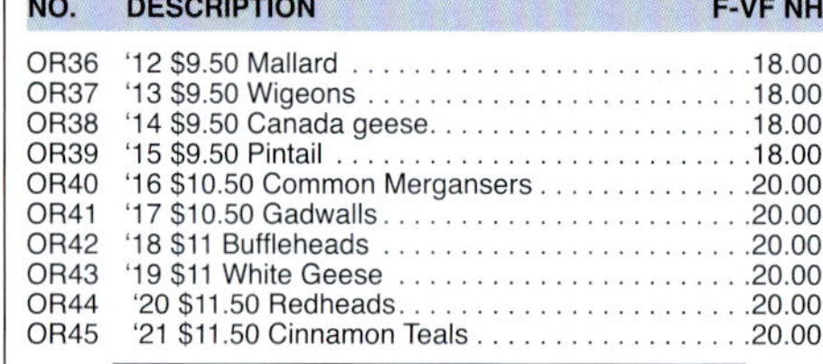

NO.	DESCRIPTION	F-VF NH
OR36	'12 $9.50 Mallard	18.00
OR37	'13 $9.50 Wigeons	18.00
OR38	'14 $9.50 Canada geese	18.00
OR39	'15 $9.50 Pintail	18.00
OR40	'16 $10.50 Common Mergansers	20.00
OR41	'17 $10.50 Gadwalls	20.00
OR42	'18 $11 Buffleheads	20.00
OR43	'19 $11 White Geese	20.00
OR44	'20 $11.50 Redheads	20.00
OR45	'21 $11.50 Cinnamon Teals	20.00

PA1

PENNSYLVANIA

NO.	DESCRIPTION	F-VF NH
PA1	'83 $5.50 Wood Ducks	14.00
PA2	'84 $5.50 Canada Geese	10.00
PA3	'85 $5.50 Mallards	12.00
PA4	'86 $5.50 Blue-Winged Teal	12.00
PA5	'87 $5.50 Pintails	12.00
PA6	'88 $5.50 Wood Ducks	12.00
PA7	'89 $5.50 Hooded Mergansers	10.00
PA8	'90 $5.50 Canvasbacks	10.00
PA9	'91 $5.50 Widgeons	10.00
PA10	'92 $5.50 Canada Geese	10.00
PA11	'93 $5.50 Northern Shovelers	10.00
PA12	'94 $5.50 Pintails	10.00
PA13	'95 $5.50 Buffleheads	10.00
PA14	'96 $5.50 Black Ducks	10.00
PA15	'97 $5.50 Hooded Merganser	10.00
PA16	'98 $5.50 Wood Duck	10.00
PA17	'99 $5.50 Ring-necked Ducks	10.00
PA18	'00 $5.50 Green-Winged Teal	10.00
PA19	'01 $5.50 Pintails	10.00
PA20	'02 $5.50 Snow Geese	10.00
PA21	'03 $5.50 Canvasbacks	10.00
PA22	'04 $5.50 Hooded Mergansers	10.00
PA23	'05 $5.50 Red-breasted Mergansers	10.00
PA24	'06 $5.50 Pintails	10.00
PA25	'07 $5.50 Wood Ducks	10.00
PA26	'08 $5.50 Redheads	10.00
PA27	'09 $5.50 Hooded Merganser	10.00
PA28	'10 $5.50 Canvasbacks	10.50
PA29	'11 $5.50 Wigeons	10.50
PA30	'12 $5.50 Ruddy Ducks	10.00
PA31	'13 $5.50 Black Ducks	10.00
PA32	'14 $5.50 Shoveler	10.00
PA33	'15 $5.50 Green-winged Teal	10.00
PA34	'16 $5.50 Pintail	10.00
PA35	'17 $5.50 Bufflehead	9.50
PA36	'18 $5.50 Mallards	9.50
PA37	'19 $5.50 Long-tailed Duck	9.50
PA38	'20 $5.50 Snow Geese	9.50
PA39	'21 $5.50 Wood Ducks	9.50

RI1

RHODE ISLAND

NO.	DESCRIPTION	F-VF NH
RI1	'89 $7.50 Canvasbacks	15.00
RI2	'90 $7.50 Canada Geese	15.00
RI3	'91 $7.50 Wood Ducks & Labrador Retriever	25.00
RI4	'92 $7.50 Blue-Winged Teal	18.00
RI5	'93 $7.50 Pintails	18.00
RI6	'94 $7.50 Wood Ducks	22.00
RI7	'95 $7.50 Hooded Mergansers	18.00
RI8	'96 $7.50 Harlequin	24.00
RI9	'97 $7.50 Black Ducks	18.00
RI10	'98 $7.50 Black Ducks	18.00
RI11	'99 $7.50 Common Eiders	18.00
RI12	'00 $7.50 Canvasbacks	18.00
RI13	'01 $7.50 Canvasbacks, Mallard, Lighthouse	18.00
RI14	'02 $7.50 White-winged Scoter	17.00
RI15	'03 $7.50 Oldsquaw	15.00
RI16	'04 $7.50 Canvasbacks	15.00
RI17	'05 $7.50 Black Ducks and Lighthouse	15.00
RI18	'06 $7.50 Canvasbacks, Lighthouse	15.00
RI19	'07 $7.50 Harlequin Decoy	15.00
RI20	'08 $7.50 Mallard Decoys	15.00
RI21	'09 $7.50 Hooded Merganser	15.00
RI22	'10 $7.50 Red-breasted Merganser	15.00
RI23	'11 $7.50 Barrow's Goldeneye	15.00
RI24	'12 $7.50 Mallard	15.50
RI25	'13 $7.50 Canvasbacks	15.00
RI26	'14 $7.50 Canvasbacks	18.00
RI27	'15 $7.50 Mallard	18.00
RI28	'16 $7.50 Wood Duck	18.00
RI29	'17 $7.50 Lesser Scaup	18.00
RI30	'18 $7.50 Harlequin, S/A	18.50
RI31	'19 $7.50 Long-tailed Duck	20.00
RI32	'20 $7.50 Canada Geese	20.00
RI33	'21 $7.50 Mallard	20.00

SC5

SOUTH CAROLINA

NO.	DESCRIPTION	F-VF NH
SC1	'81 $5.50 Wood Ducks	65.00
SC2	'82 $5.50 Mallards	100.00
SC3	'83 $5.50 Pintails	100.00
SC4	'84 $5.50 Canada Geese	65.00
SC5	'85 $5.50 Green-Winged Teal	60.00
SC6	'86 $5.50 Canvasbacks	25.00
SC7	'87 $5.50 Black Ducks	20.00
SC8	'88 $5.50 Widgeon & Spaniel	18.00
SC9	'89 $5.50 Blue-Winged Teal	12.00
SC10	'90 $5.50 Wood Ducks	12.00
SC11	'91 $5.50 Labrador Retriever, Pintails & Decoy	12.00
SC12	'92 $5.50 Buffleheads	17.00
SC13	'93 $5.50 Lesser Scaup	17.00
SC14	'94 $5.50 Canvasbacks	17.00
SC15	'95 $5.50 Shovelers, Lighthouse	17.00
SC16	'96 $5.50 Redheads, Lighthouse	18.00
SC17	'97 $5.50 Old Squaws	18.00
SC18	'98 $5.50 Ruddy Ducks	18.00
SC19	'99 $5.50 Barrow's goldeneye	18.00
SC20	'00 $5.50 Wood Ducks, boykin spaniel	18.00
SC21	'01 $5.50 Mallard, yellow labrador,decoy	16.00
SC22	'02 $5.50 Widgeon, Chocolate Labrador	16.00
SC23	'03 $5.50 Green-winged Teal	16.00
SC24	'04 $5.50 Black Labrador	16.00
SC25	'05 $5.50 Canvasbacks	16.00
SC26	'06 $5.50 Black Ducks	16.00
SC27	'07 $5.50 Redheads, Golden Retriever	16.00
SC28	'08 $5.50 Blue-Winged Teal, Labrador Retriever	20.00
SC29	'09 $5.50 Ring-Necked Duck, Labrador Retriever	20.00
SC30	'10 $Wood Duck and Boykin	20.00
SC31	'11 $5.50 Blue Winged Teal & Chocolate Labrador Retriever	20.00
SC32	'12 $5.50 Green-Winged Teal and Golden Retriever	20.00
SC33	'13 $5.50 Black Duck and Boykin Spaniel	20.00
SC34	'14 $5.50 Wood Ducks	20.00
SC35	'15 $5.50 Hooded Mergansers	20.00
SC36	'16 $5.50 Mottled Ducks	20.00
SC37	'17 $5.50 Wigeons	20.00
SC38	'18 $5.50 Pintail	20.00
SC39	'19 $5.50 Canvasbacks and Spaniel	20.00
SC40	'20 $5.50 Wood Duck & Labrador	20.00

SD6

SOUTH DAKOTA

NO.	DESCRIPTION	F-VF NH
SD3	'76 $1 Mallards	30.00
SD4	'77 $1 Pintails	75.00
SD5	'78 $1 Canvasbacks	30.00
SD6	'86 $2 Canada Geese	15.00
SD7	'87 $2 Blue Geese	10.00
SD8	'88 $2 White-Fronted Geese	10.00
SD9	'89 $2 Mallards	8.00
SD10	'90 $2 Blue-Winged Teal	8.00
SD11	'91 $2 Pintails	8.00
SD12	'92 $2 Canvasbacks	8.00
SD13	'93 $2 Lesser Scaup	8.00
SD14	'94 $2 Redheads	8.00
SD15	'95 $2 Wood Ducks	8.00
SD16	'96 $2 Canada Goose	8.00
SD17	'97 $2 Widgeons	8.00
SD18	'98 $2 Green Winged Teal	8.00
SD19	'99 $2 Tundra Swam	10.00
SD20	'00 $3 Buffleheads	10.00
SD21	'01 $3 Mallards	10.00
SD22	'02 $3 Canvasbacks	10.00
SD23	'03 $3 Pintail	10.00
SD24	'04 $3 Text, purple	10.00
SD25	'05 $5 Text, magenta	10.00
SD26	'06 $5 Brown, Orange	10.00
SD27	'07 $5 Text (Brown)	10.00

TN9

TENNESSEE

NO.	DESCRIPTION	F-VF NH
TN1	'79 $2 Mallards	95.00
TN2	'79 $5 Mallards, Non-Resident	550.00
TN3	'80 $2 Canvasbacks	55.00
TN4	'80 $5 Canvasbacks, Non-Resident	185.00
TN5	'81 $2 Wood Ducks	50.00

NO.	DESCRIPTION	F-VF NH
TN6	'82 $6 Canada Geese	60.00
TN7	'83 $6 Pintails	60.00
TN8	'84 $6 Black Ducks	60.00
TN9	'85 $6 Blue-Winged Teal	25.00
TN10	'86 $6 Mallard	15.00
TN11	'87 $6 Canada Geese	15.00
TN12	'88 $6 Canvasbacks	15.00
TN13	'89 $6 Green-Winged Teal	15.00
TN14	'90 $13 Redheads	15.00
TN15	'91 $13 Mergansers	20.00
TN16	'92 $14 Wood Ducks	20.00
TN17	'93 $14 Pintails & Decoy	25.00
TN18	'94 $16 Mallard	30.00
TN19	'95 $16 Ring-Necked Duck	35.00
TN20	'96 $18 Black Ducks	45.00
TN21	'99 $10 Mallard	18.00
TN22	'00 $10 Bufflehead	18.00
TN23	'01 $10 Wood Ducks	18.00
TN24	'02 $10 Green-winged Teal	18.00
TN25	'03 $10 Canada Geese	18.00
TN26	'04 $10 Wood Ducks	18.00
TN27	'05 $10 Mallards	18.00
TN28	'06 $10 Canada Goose	18.00
TN29	'07 $10 Harlequin	18.00
TN30	'08 $10 Wood Ducks	18.00
TN31	'09 $10 Mallards	18.00
TN32	'10 $10 Wood Ducks	18.00
TN33	'11 $10 Wood Ducks	18.00
TN34	'12 $10 Cinnamon Teal	18.00
TN35	'13 $10 King Elders	18.00
TN36	'14 $10 Wood Ducks	18.00
TN37	'15 $10 Green-winged Teal	18.00
TN38	'16 $10 Northern Shoveler	18.00
TN39	'17 $10 Cinnamon Teal	18.00
TN40	'18 $10 Pintails	19.00
TN41	'19 $10 Shovelers	19.00
TN42	'20 $10 Redheads	19.00
TN43	'21 $10 Hooded Merganser	19.00

TX5

TEXAS

NO.	DESCRIPTION	F-VF NH
TX1	'81 $5 Mallards	35.00
TX2	'82 $5 Pintails	25.00
TX3	'83 $5 Widgeons	100.00
TX4	'84 $5 Wood Ducks	30.00
TX5	'85 $5 Snow Geese	11.00
TX6	'86 $5 Green-Winged Teal	11.00
TX7	'87 $5 White-Fronted Geese	11.00
TX8	'88 $5 Pintails	11.00
TX9	'89 $5 Mallards	11.00
TX10	'90 $5 American Widgeons	14.00
TX11	'91 $7 Wood Duck	14.00
TX12	'92 $7 Canada Geese	14.00
TX13	'93 $7 Blue-Winged Teal	14.00
TX14	'94 $7 Shovelers	14.00
TX15	'95 $7 Buffleheads	14.00
TX16	'96 $3 Gadwalls	75.00
TX17	'97 $3 Cinnamon Teal	65.00
TX18	'98 $3 Pintail, Labrador Retriever	65.00
TX19	'99 $3 Canvasbacks	42.00
TX20	'00 $3 Hooded Merganser	35.00
TX21	'01 $3 Snow Goose	25.00
TX22	'02 $3 Redheads	25.00
TX23	'03 $3 Mottled Duck	25.00
TX24	'04 $3 American Goldeneye	18.00
TX25	'05 $7 Mallards	18.00
TX26	'06 $7 Green-Winged Teals	24.00
TX27	'07 $7 Wood Duck	14.00
TX28	'08 $7 Pintails	14.00
TX29	'09 $7 Blue-Winged Teal	14.00
TX30	'10 $7 Wigeons	14.00
TX31	'11 $7 White-Fronted Geese	14.00
TX32	'12 $7 Canada Geese	22.00
TX33	'13 $7 Wood Ducks	14.00
TX34	'14 $7 Cinnamon Teal	14.00
TX35	'15 $7 Ring-necked Duck	14.00

UT1

UTAH

NO.	DESCRIPTION	F-VF NH
UT1	'86 $3.30 Whistling Swans	12.00
UT2	'87 $3.30 Pintails	10.00
UT3	'88 $3.30 Mallards	10.00
UT4	'89 $3.30 Canada Geese	10.00
UT5	'90 $3.30 Canvasbacks	10.00
UT6	'91 $3.30 Tundra Swans	13.00
UT7	'92 $3.30 Pintails	13.00
UT8	'93 $3.30 Canvasbacks	13.00
UT9	'94 $3.30 Chesapeake Retriever & Ducks	100.00
UT10	'95 $3.30 Green-Winged Teal	13.00
UT11	'96 $7.50 White-Fronted Goose	18.00
UT12	'97 $7.50 Redheads, pair	95.00

VT1

VERMONT

NO.	DESCRIPTION	F-VF NH
VT1	'86 $5 Wood Ducks	14.00
VT2	'87 $5 Common Goldeneyes	14.00
VT3	'88 $5 Black Ducks	14.00
VT4	'89 $5 Canada Geese	14.00
VT5	'90 $5 Green-Winged Teal	14.00
VT6	'91 $5 Hooded Mergansers	14.00
VT7	'92 $5 Snow Geese	14.00
VT8	'93 $5 Mallards	14.00
VT9	'94 $5 Ring-Necked Duck	14.00
VT10	'95 $5 Bufflehead	14.00
VT11	'96 $5 Bluebills	14.00
VT12	'97 $5 Pintail	14.00
VT13	'98 $5 Blue-Winged Teal	14.00
VT14	'99 $5 Canvasbacks	14.00
VT15	'00 $5 Widgeons	12.00
VT16	'01 $5 Old Squaw	12.00
VT17	'02 $5 Greater Scaups	12.00
VT18	'03 $5 Mallard	12.00
VT19	'04 $5 Pintails	12.00
VT20	'05 $5 Canvasbacks	12.00
VT21	'06 $5 Canada Goose	12.00
VT22	'07 $5 Ring-Necked Duck	12.00
VT23	'08 $7.50 Harlequin	12.00
VT24	'09 $7.50 Harlequin	12.00
VT25	'10 $7.50 Wood Duck	12.00
VT26	'11 $7.50 Black and Numbered Sticker	12.00
VT27	'12 $7.50 Black and Numbered Sticker	12.00
VT28	'13 $7.50 Black	12.00

VA1

VIRGINIA

NO.	DESCRIPTION	F-VF NH
VA1	'88 $5 Mallards	15.00
VA2	'89 $5 Canada Geese	14.00
VA3	'90 $5 Wood Ducks	10.00
VA4	'91 $5 Canvasbacks	10.00
VA5	'92 $5 Buffleheads	10.00
VA6	'93 $5 Black Ducks	10.00
VA7	'94 $5 Lesser Scaup	10.00
VA8	'95 $5 Snow Geese	10.00
VA9	'96 $5 Hooded Mergansers	10.00
VA10	'97 $5 Pintail, Labrador Retriever	10.00
VA11	'98 $5 Mallards	14.00
VA12	'99 $5 Green-winged Teal	14.00
VA13	'00 $5 Mallards	14.00
VA14	'01 $5 Blue-winged Teal	12.00
VA15	'02 $5 Canvasbacks	12.00
VA16	'03 $5 Mallard	12.00
VA17	'04 $5 Goldeneyes	12.00
VA18	'05 $9.75 Wood Ducks, perforated	18.00
VA18a	'05 $9.75 Wood Ducks, rouletted	18.00
VA18b	'05 $9.75 Wood Ducks, S/A, die cut	18.00
VA19	'06 $9.75 Black Ducks, perforated	18.00
VA19a	'06 $9.75 Wood Ducks, S/A, die cut	18.00
VA20	'07 $10 Canada Geese	18.00
VA20a	'07 $10 Canada Geese, S/A, die cut	18.00
VA21	'08 $10 Widgeons	18.00
VA21a	'08 $10 Widgeons, S/A, die cut	18.00
VA22	'09 $10 Ringed-Neck Duck, perf	18.00
VA22a	'09 $10 Ring-Neck Duck, S/A	18.00
VA23	'10 $10 Green-winged Teal	18.00
VA23a	'10 $10 Green-winged Teal, S/A, die cut	18.00
VA24	'11 $10 Redheads	18.00
VA24a	'11 $10 Redheads S/A	18.00
VA25	'12 $10 Buffleheads	18.00
VA25a	'12 $10 Buffleheads, S/A	18.00
VA26	'13 $10 Hooded Mergansers	18.00
VA26a	'13 $10 Hooded Mergansers, S/A	18.00
VA27	'14 $10 Canvasbacks, W/A	18.00
VA27a	'14 $10 Canvasbacks, S/A	18.00
VA28	'15 $10 Tundra Swans	30.00
VA28a	'15 $10 Tundra Swans, S/A, die-cut	25.00
VA29	'16 $10 Pintails	30.00
VA29a	'16 Pintails, S/A, die-cut	25.00
VA30	'17 $10 Ring-necked Ducks	30.00
VA30a	'17 $10 Ring-necked Ducks, S/A, die-cut	25.00
VA31	'18 $10 Canada Goose	30.00
VA31a	'18 $10 Canada Goose, S/A, die-cut	25.00
VA32	'19 $10 Shoveler	30.00
VA32a	'19 $10 Shoveler, S/A, die-cut	25.00
VA33	'20 $10 Canvasbacks	30.00
VA33a	'20 $10 Canvasbacks, S/A, die-cut	25.00
VA34	'21 $10 Common Goldeneye	30.00
VA34a	'21 $10 Common Goldeneye, S/A, die-cut	25.00

WA1

WASHINGTON

NO.	DESCRIPTION	F-VF NH
WA1	'86 $5 Mallards	10.00
WA2	'87 $5 Canvasbacks	14.00
WA3	'88 $5 Harlequin	11.00
WA4	'89 $5 American Widgeons	11.00
WA5	'90 $5 Pintails & Sour Duck	11.00
WA6	'91 $5 Wood Duck	13.00
WA8	'92 $6 Labrador Puppy & Canada Geese	13.00
WA9	'93 $6 Snow Geese	13.00
WA10	'94 $6 Black Brant	15.00
WA11	'95 $6 Mallards	14.00
WA12	'96 $6 Redheads	24.00
WA13	'97 $6 Canada Geese	14.00
WA14	'98 $6 Goldeneye	18.00
WA15	'99 $6 Bufflehead	18.00
WA16	'00 $6 Canada Geese, Mallard, Widgeon	30.00
WA17	'01 $6 Mallards	22.00
WA18	'02 $10 Green-winged Teal	22.00
WA19	'03 $10 Pintail	22.00
WA20	'04 $10 Canada Goose	18.00
WA21	'05 $10 Barrow's Goldeneyes	18.00
WA22	'06 $10 Widgeons, Mallard	18.00
WA23	'07 $10 Ross's Goose	18.00
WA24	'08 $10 Wood Ducks	18.00
WA25	'09 $11 Canada Goose	18.00
WA26	'10 $10 Pintail	40.00
WA27	'11 $10 Ruddy Duck	30.00
WA28	'12 $15 Brant	30.00
WA29	'13 $15 Shovelers	30.50
WA30	'14 $15 Redheads	30.00
WA31	'15 $15 Canvasbacks	30.00
WA32	'16 $15 Wooded Merganser	30.00
WA33	'17 $15 Cinnamon Teal and Labrador	30.00
WA34	'18 $15 Wood Ducks	30.00
WA35	'19 $15 Ring-necked Duck and Labrador	30.00
WA36	'20 $17 Canada Geese	30.00
WA37	'21 $17 Mallards & Black Labrador	30.00

WV1

WEST VIRGINIA

NO.	DESCRIPTION	F-VF NH
WV1	'87 $5 Canada Geese	18.00
WV2	'87 $5 Canada Geese, Non-Resident	18.00
WV3	'88 $5 Wood Ducks	12.00
WV4	'88 $5 Wood Ducks, Non-Resident	14.00
WV5	'89 $5 Decoys	14.00
WV6	'89 $5 Decoys, Non-Resident	20.00
WV7	'90 $5 Labrador Retriever & Decoy	22.00
WV8	'90 $5 Labrador Retriever & Decoy, Non-Resident	24.00
WV9	'91 $5 Mallards	14.00
WV10	'91 $5 Mallards, Non-Resident	14.00
WV11	'92 $5 Canada Geese	14.00
WV12	'92 $5 Canada Geese, Non-Resident	14.00
WV13	'93 $5 Pintails	14.00
WV14	'93 $5 Pintails, Non-Resident	14.00
WV15	'94 $5 Green-Winged Teal	14.00
WV16	'94 $5 Green-Winged Teal, Non-Resident	14.00
WV17	'95 $5 Mallards	14.00
WV18	'95 $5 Mallards, Non-Resident	14.00
WV19	'96 $5 American Widgeons	14.00
WV20	'96 $5 Widgeon, Non-Resident	14.00

WI3

WISCONSIN

NO.	DESCRIPTION	F-VF NH
WI1	'78 $3.25 Wood Ducks	80.00
WI2	'79 $3.25 Buffleheads	25.00
WI3	'80 $3.25 Widgeons	12.00
WI4	'81 $3.25 Lesser Scaup	12.00
WI5	'82 $3.25 Pintails	11.00
WI6	'83 $3.25 Blue-Winged Teal	11.00
WI7	'84 $3.25 Hooded Merganser	12.00
WI8	'85 $3.25 Lesser Scaup	14.00
WI9	'86 $3.25 Canvasbacks	16.00
WI10	'87 $3.25 Canada Geese	11.00
WI11	'88 $3.25 Hooded Merganser	11.00
WI12	'89 $3.25 Common Goldeneye	11.00

NO.	DESCRIPTION	F-VF NH
WI13	'90 $3.25 Redheads	11.00
WI14	'91 $5.25 Green-Winged Teal	12.00
WI15	'92 $5.25 Tundra Swans	12.00
WI16	'93 $5.25 Wood Ducks	12.00
WI17	'94 $5.25 Pintails	12.00
WI18	'95 $5.25 Mallards	12.00
WI19	'96 $5.25 Green-Winged Teal	12.00
WI20	'97 $7 Canada Geese	18.00
WI21	'98 $7 Snow Geese	18.00
WI22	'99 $7 Greater Scaups	14.00
WI23	'00 $7 Canvasbacks	14.00
WI24	'01 $7 Common Goldeneye	16.00
WI25	'02 $7 Shovelers	12.00
WI26	'03 $7 Canvasbacks	12.00
WI27	'04 $7 Pintail	12.00
WI28	'05 $7 Wood Ducks	14.00
WI29	'06 $7 Green-Winged Teals	14.00
WI30	'07 $7 Redheads	14.00
WI31	'08 $7 Canvasbacks	14.00
WI32	'09 $7 Wigeons	14.00
WI33	'10 $7 Wood Ducks	14.00
WI34	'11 $7 Shovelers	14.00
WI35	'12 $7 Redhead	14.00
WI36	'13 $7 Long-Tailed Ducks	14.00
WI37	'14 $7 Wood Duck	12.00
WI38	'15 $7 Blue-winged Teal	14.00
WI39	'16 $7 Ring-necked Duck	14.00
WI40	'17 $7 Canvasbacks and Lighthouse	14.00
WI41	'18 $7 Canada Geese	13.00
WI42	'19 $7 Redheads	13.00
WI43	'20 $7 Wood Ducks	14.00
WI44	'21 $7 Pintails	22.00

WY10

WYOMING

NO.	DESCRIPTION	F-VF NH
WY1	'84 $5 Meadowlark	72.00
WY2	'85 $5 Canada Geese	64.00
WY3	'86 $5 Antelope	115.00
WY4	'87 $5 Grouse	115.00
WY5	'88 $5 Fish	120.00
WY6	'89 $5 Deer	185.00
WY7	'90 $5 Bear	55.00
WY8	'91 $5 Rams	50.00
WY9	'92 $5 Bald Eagle	40.00
WY10	'93 $5 Elk	25.00
WY11	'94 $5 Bobcat	25.00
WY12	'95 $5 Moose	25.00
WY13	'96 $5 Turkey	25.00
WY14	'97 $5 Rocky Mountain Goats	25.00
WY15	'98 $5 Thunder Swans	25.00
WY16	'99 $5 Brown Trout	25.00
WY17	'00 $5 Buffalo	25.00
WY18	'01 $10 Whitetailed Deer	25.00
WY19	'02 $10 River Otters	25.00
WY20	'03 $10 Mountain Bluebird	25.00
WY21	'04 $10 Cougar	25.00
WY22	'05 $10 Burrowing Owls	25.00
WY23	'06 $10.50 Cut-Throat Trout	25.00
WY24	'07 $10.50 Blue Grouses	25.00
WY25	'08 $12.50 Black-footed Ferret	25.00
WY26	'09 $12.50 Great Gray Owl	25.00
WY27	'10 $12.50 Cinnamon Teal	25.00
WY28	'11 $12.50 Wolverine	20.00
WY29	'12 $12.50 Black Bear	20.00
WY30	'13 $12.50 Greater Short-Horned Lizard	20.00
WY31	'14 $12.50 Ruffled Grouse	22.00
WY32	'15 $12.50 Sauger	22.00
WY33	'16 $12.50 Swift Fox	22.00
WY34	'17 $12.50 Mallard	22.00
WY35	'18 $12.50 Badger	22.00
WY36	'19 $12.50 Mule Deer	24.00
WY37	'20 $20 Cutthroat Trout	35.00
WY38	'21 $20 Osprey	35.00

CANAL ZONE

CANAL ZONE

PANAMA

1904
U.S. Stamp 300, 319, 304, 306-07 overprinted

SCOTT NO.	DESCRIPTION	UNUSED NH F	AVG	UNUSED OG F	AVG	USED F	AVG
4	1¢ blue green	115.00	72.00	50.00	35.00	25.00	20.00
5	2¢ carmine.................	95.00	65.00	43.00	25.00	25.00	20.00
6	5¢ blue.......................	325.00	200.00	150.00	100.00	65.00	50.00
7	8¢ violet black............	575.00	350.00	270.00	175.00	95.00	75.00
8	10¢ pale red brown.....	500.00	350.00	270.00	175.00	100.00	80.00

CANAL

ZONE

1924-25
U.S. Stamps 551-54, 557, 562, 564-66, 569-71 overprinted

Type 1 Flat Tops on Letters "A". Perf. 11

SCOTT NO.	DESCRIPTION	UNUSED NH F	AVG	UNUSED OG F	AVG	USED F	AVG
70	1/2¢ olive brown	3.50	2.50	1.75	1.40	.75	.65
71	1¢ deep green	3.50	2.50	1.75	1.25	1.10	.70
71e	same, bklt pane of 6...	300.00	200.00	170.00	125.00	....	....
72	1-1/2¢ yellow brown ...	5.00	3.50	2.50	1.85	1.60	1.35
73	2¢ carmine.................	20.00	15.00	10.00	7.00	1.75	1.25
73a	same, bklt pane of 6...	400.00	315.00	250.00	185.00	....	....
74	5¢ dark blue...............	50.00	40.00	25.00	20.00	9.00	6.50
75	10¢ orange	110.00	80.00	55.00	40.00	24.00	17.00
76	12¢ brown violet	100.00	75.00	50.00	40.00	27.00	19.50
77	14¢ dark blue.............	75.00	55.00	40.00	30.00	20.00	16.00
78	15¢ gray	125.00	80.00	65.00	45.00	35.00	30.00
79	30¢ olive brown	100.00	65.00	48.00	35.00	25.00	20.00
80	50¢ lilac	210.00	135.00	100.00	70.00	42.00	35.00
81	$1 violet brown	575.00	395.00	300.00	200.00	100.00	85.00

CANAL

ZONE

1925-28
U.S. Stamps 554-55, 557, 564-66, 623, 567, 569-71, overprinted

Type II Pointed Tops on Letters "A"

SCOTT NO.	DESCRIPTION	UNUSED NH F	AVG	UNUSED OG F	AVG	USED F	AVG
84	2¢ carmine.................	80.00	60.00	40.00	30.00	10.00	6.25
84d	same, bklt pane of 6...	450.00	350.00	300.00	260.00	....	....
85	3¢ violet......................	10.00	8.50	5.00	3.75	2.75	1.75
86	5¢ dark blue...............	10.00	8.50	5.00	3.75	2.75	1.75
87	10¢ orange	92.00	70.00	47.00	35.00	10.00	9.00
88	12¢ brown violet	60.00	50.00	30.00	24.00	14.00	10.00
89	14¢ dark blue.............	67.00	50.00	36.00	25.00	16.00	13.00
90	15¢ gray	22.00	16.00	11.00	8.00	4.00	2.50
91	17¢ black....................	11.00	8.00	6.00	4.00	3.00	2.25
92	20¢ carmine rose........	20.00	15.00	11.00	8.00	4.00	3.00
93	30¢ olive brown	15.00	12.00	9.00	6.00	4.00	3.00
94	50¢ lilac	635.00	475.00	310.00	250.00	150.00	135.00
95	$1 violet brown	310.00	250.00	180.00	140.00	50.00	45.00

1926
Type II overprint on U.S. Stamp 627

SCOTT NO.	DESCRIPTION	UNUSED NH F	AVG	UNUSED OG F	AVG	USED F	AVG
96	2¢ carmine rose..........	10.00	7.00	6.00	4.00	3.75	2.50

1927
Type II overprint on U.S. Stamp 583-84, 591
Rotary Press Printing, Perf. 10

SCOTT NO.	DESCRIPTION	UNUSED NH F	AVG	UNUSED OG F	AVG	USED F	AVG
97	2¢ carmine..................	150.00	110.00	80.00	70.00	10.50	8.50
98	3¢ violet......................	25.00	20.00	12.00	10.00	5.00	4.00
99	10¢ orange	50.00	35.00	30.00	20.00	6.75	5.50

SCOTT NO.	DESCRIPTION	PLATE BLOCK F/NH	F	AVG	UNUSED F/NH	F	AVG	USED F	AVG
100	1¢ green	35.00	25.00	22.00	4.25	2.75	2.00	1.30	1.00
101	2¢ carmine..........	45.00	30.00	26.00	4.75	3.00	2.00	.90	.80
101a	same, bklt pane of 6	....	....	....	275.00	175.00	150.00	....	....
102	3¢ violet (1931)....	125.00	90.00	80.00	6.50	4.50	3.00	3.50	2.50
103	5¢ dark blue.........	280.00	200.00	190.00	60.00	40.00	35.00	11.00	9.00
104	10¢ orange (1930)	260.00	180.00	160.00	30.00	23.00	18.00	12.00	10.00

VERY FINE QUALITY: To determine the Very Fine price, add the difference between the Fine and Average prices to the Fine quality price. For example: if the Fine price is $10.00 and the Average price is $6.00, the Very Fine price would be $14.00. From 1935 to date, add 20% to the Fine price to arrive at the Very Fine price.

105,160 106 107

108, 161 109 110 111

112 113 114

1928-40 Builders Issue

SCOTT NO.	DESCRIPTION	PLATE BLOCK F/NH	F	AVG	UNUSED F/NH	F	AVG	USED F	AVG
105-14	**1¢-50¢ complete, 10 varieties.........**	....	....	....	**10.40**	**8.05**	**4.95**	**5.70**	**3.45**
105	1¢ Gorgas...........	3.75	3.00	2.50	.55	.40	.30	.30	.25
106	2¢ Goethals.........	4.50(6)	3.25	2.50	.35	.30	.25	.30	.25
106a	same, bklt pane of 6	....	....	....	22.00	20.00	16.00	....	....
107	5¢ Gaillard Cut (1929).................	24.00(6)	18.00	16.00	1.65	1.40	1.20	.55	.45
108	10¢ Hodges (1932)	8.00(6)	6.00	4.50	.40	.30	.25	.30	.25
109	12¢ Gaillard (1929)	18.00(6)	15.00	12.00	1.50	1.00	.80	.85	.50
110	14¢ Sibert (1937)	25.00(6)	16.00	14.00	1.40	1.25	.95	1.10	.75
111	15¢ Smith (1932).	15.00(6)	12.00	8.00	.80	.65	.45	.50	.40
112	20¢ Rousseau (1932).................	15.00(6)	12.00	8.00	1.25	.75	.65	.30	.25
113	30¢ Williamson (1940).................	19.00(6)	15.00	12.00	1.25	1.15	.85	.95	.75
114	50¢ Blackburn (1929).................	28.00(6)	17.00	13.50	2.75	1.90	1.50	.85	.70

1933
Type II overprint on U.S. Stamps 720 & 695
Rotary Press Printing, Perf. 11 x 10-1/2

SCOTT NO.	DESCRIPTION	PLATE BLOCK F/NH	F	AVG	UNUSED F/NH	F	AVG	USED F	AVG
115	3¢ Washington	56.00	40.00	35.00	4.00	3.50	2.50	.40	.35
116	14¢ Indian...........	90.00	70.00	46.00	8.00	6.00	4.00	3.35	2.75

117, 153

1934

SCOTT NO.	DESCRIPTION	PLATE BLOCK F/NH	F	AVG	UNUSED F/NH	F	AVG	USED F	AVG
117	3¢ Goethals.........	1.75(6)	1.25	1.00	.40	.35	.25	.25	.25
117a	same, bklt pane of 6	....	....	....	100.00	60.00	50.00	....	....

SCOTT NO.	DESCRIPTION	PLATE BLOCK F/NH	F/OG	UNUSED F/NH	F/OG	USED F
	1939 U.S. Stamps 803, 805 overprint					
118	1/2¢ red orange...........	3.75	3.00	.35	.25	.25
119	1-1/2¢ bistre brown	3.25	2.75	.35	.25	.25

FOR YOUR CONVENIENCE, COMPLETE SETS ARE LISTED BEFORE SINGLE STAMP LISTINGS!

120
Balboa—Before

121
Balboa—After

122	*Gaillard Cut—Before*	**123**	*After*
124	*Bas Obispo—Before*	**125**	*After*
126	*Gatun Locks—Before*	**127**	*After*
128	*Canal Channel—Before*	**129**	*After*
130	*Gamboa—Before*	**131**	*After*
132	*Pedro Miguel Locks—Before*	**133**	*After*
134	*Gatun Spillway—Before*	**135**	*After*

1939 25th ANNIVERSARY ISSUE

SCOTT NO.	DESCRIPTION	PLATE BLOCK F/NH	PLATE BLOCK F/OG	UNUSED F/NH	UNUSED F/OG	USED F
120-35	**1¢-50¢ complete, 16 varieties ....**	**........**	**........**	**155.00**	**135.00**	**89.50**
120	1¢ yellow green...........	20.00(6)	16.00	1.25	.95	.45
121	2¢ rose carmine	20.00(6)	16.00	1.25	.85	.50
122	3¢ purple	20.00(6)	16.00	1.25	.85	.25
123	5¢ dark blue	32.00(6)	28.00	2.75	2.00	1.30
124	6¢ red orange..............	80.00(6)	67.00	5.50	3.75	3.25
125	7¢ black........................	80.00(6)	67.00	6.00	4.00	3.25
126	8¢ green.......................	88.00(6)	74.00	7.75	5.50	3.50
127	10¢ ultramarine...........	88.00(6)	74.00	7.00	5.00	5.00
128	11¢ blue hreen	180.00(6)	160.00	12.00	9.00	8.00
129	12¢ brown carmine	160.00(6)	135.00	12.00	9.00	7.00
130	14¢ dark violet.............	180.00(6)	160.00	12.00	9.00	7.00
131	15¢ olive green	210.00(6)	165.00	16.00	12.00	6.00
132	18¢ rose pink	200.00(6)	160.00	17.00	13.00	8.00
133	20¢ brown	240.00(6)	200.00	18.00	14.00	8.00
134	25¢ orange...................	425.00(6)	350.00	27.00	22.00	18.00
135	50¢ violet brown..........	475.00(6)	360.00	35.00	27.00	6.00

136

137

138

139

140

1945-49

SCOTT NO.	DESCRIPTION	PLATE BLOCK F/NH	PLATE BLOCK F/OG	UNUSED F/NH	UNUSED F/OG	USED F
136-40	**1/2¢-25¢ complete 5 varieties ....**	**........**	**........**	**3.50**	**2.50**	**1.75**
136	1/2¢ Major General Davis (1948)................	3.50(6)	2.75	.55	.45	.25
137	1-1/2¢ Gov. Magoon (1948)	3.50(6)	2.75	.55	.45	.25
138	2¢ T. Roosevelt (1948).	2.00(6)	1.50	.35	.25	.25
139	5¢ Stevens..................	3.75(6)	3.00	.50	.40	.25
140	25¢ J.F. Wallace (1948)	12.50(6)	11.00	1.60	1.25	.85

141

1948 CANAL ZONE BIOLOGICAL AREA

SCOTT NO.	DESCRIPTION	PLATE BLOCK F/NH	PLATE BLOCK F/OG	UNUSED F/NH	UNUSED F/OG	USED F
141	10¢ Map & Coat-mundi	11.00(6)	8.50	1.95	1.50	1.20

142

143

144

145

1949 CALIFORNIA GOLD RUSH

SCOTT NO.	DESCRIPTION	PLATE BLOCK F/NH	PLATE BLOCK F/OG	UNUSED F/NH	UNUSED F/OG	USED F
142-45	**3¢-18¢ complete 4 varieties ....**	**........**	**........**	**5.15**	**4.25**	**3.35**
142	3¢ "Forty Niners"..........	7.00(6)	5.00	.70	.55	.35
143	6¢ Journey–Las Cruces	8.25(6)	6.00	.80	.65	.40
144	12¢ Las Cruces–Panama Trail	23.00(6)	19.00	1.75	1.40	1.10
145	18¢ Departure–San Francisco	28.00(6)	23.00	2.60	2.25	2.75

146

147

148

149

150

1951-58

SCOTT NO.	DESCRIPTION	PLATE BLOCK F/NH	PLATE BLOCK F/OG	UNUSED F/NH	UNUSED F/OG	USED F
146	10¢ West Indian Labor.	28.00(6)	23.00	3.25	2.75	2.25
147	3¢ Panama R.R.(1955)	8.00(6)	7.00	1.10	.80	.80
148	3¢ Gorgas Hospital (1957)	6.00	5.00	.60	.50	.45
149	4¢ S.S. Ancon (1958)...	5.00	4.00	.55	.50	.40
150	4¢ T. Roosevelt (1958).	5.00	4.00	.60	.55	.45

151

152, 154

1960-62

SCOTT NO.	DESCRIPTION	PLATE BLOCK F/NH	PLATE BLOCK F/OG	UNUSED F/NH	UNUSED F/OG	USED F
151	4¢ Boy Scout Badge	7.00	5.00	.60	.50	.45
152	4¢ Adminstration Building	1.75	1.35	.35	.25	.25

LINE PAIR

SCOTT NO.	DESCRIPTION	LINE PAIR F/NH	LINE PAIR F/OG	UNUSED F/NH	UNUSED F/OG	USED F
153	3¢ G.W. Goethals, coil .	1.40	1.25	.30	.25	.25
154	4¢ Adminstration Building, coil	1.40	1.25	.30	.25	.25
155	5¢ J.F. Stevens, coil (1962)	1.55	1.25	.40	.30	.25

156

157

PLATE BLOCK

SCOTT NO.	DESCRIPTION	PLATE BLOCK F/NH	PLATE BLOCK F/OG	UNUSED F/NH	UNUSED F/OG	USED F
156	4¢ Girl Scout Badge (1962)	4.75	3.50	.45	.40	.35
157	4¢ Thatcher Ferry Bridge (1962)...........................	5.00	4.00	.40	.35	.30
157a	same, silver omitted (bridge)	....	....	8500.00	....	....

158

159

SCOTT NO.	DESCRIPTION	PLATE BLOCK F/NH	PLATE BLOCK F/OG	UNUSED F/NH	UNUSED F/OG	USED F
	1968-78					
158	6¢ Goethals Memorial..	3.50	....	.40	....	.25
159	8¢ Fort San Lorenzo (1971)	3.00	....	.50	....	.25
	LINE PAIR					
160	1¢ W.C. Gorgas, coil (1975)	1.50	....	.35	....	.25
161	10¢ H.F. Hodges, coil (1975)	6.00	....	.90	....	.55
162	25¢ J.F. Wallace, coil (1975)	26.00	....	3.25	....	3.00

163

165

SCOTT NO.	DESCRIPTION	PLATE BLOCK F/NH	PLATE BLOCK F/OG	UNUSED F/NH	UNUSED F/OG	USED F
	PLATE BLOCK					
163	13¢ Cascades Dredge (1976)	2.50	....	.50	....	.30
163a	same, bklt pane of 4.....	....	....	3.50	....	....
164	5¢ J.F. Stevens (#139) Rotary Press (1977).....	7.00	....	.90	....	1.00
165	15¢ Locomotive (1978)	2.50	....	.60	....	.40

AIR POST

AIR MAIL

105 & 106 Surcharged

25 CENTS 25

SCOTT NO.	DESCRIPTION	PLATE BLOCK F/NH	PLATE BLOCK F	PLATE BLOCK AVG	UNUSED F/NH	UNUSED F	UNUSED AVG	USED F	USED AVG
	1929-31								
C1	15¢ on 1¢ green, Type I..................	225.00(6)	150.00	110.00	15.50	12.00	10.00	6.25	4.50
C2	15¢ on 1¢ yellow green, Type II (1931)......	....	....	....	120.00	110.00	85.00	75.00	68.00
C3	25¢ on 2¢ carmine	200.00	150.00	140.00	7.00	5.00	4.00	2.50	1.85

AIR MAIL

114 & 106 Surcharged

≡10c

SCOTT NO.	DESCRIPTION	PLATE BLOCK F/NH	PLATE BLOCK F	PLATE BLOCK AVG	UNUSED F/NH	UNUSED F	UNUSED AVG	USED F	USED AVG
	1929								
C4	10¢ on 50¢ lilac...	220.00(6)	170.00	150.00	14.00	13.00	8.00	7.00	6.00
C5	20¢ on 2¢ carmine	175.00(6)	135.00	125.00	8.00	7.00	5.00	2.00	1.50

C6-C14

SCOTT NO.	DESCRIPTION	PLATE BLOCK F/NH	PLATE BLOCK F	PLATE BLOCK AVG	UNUSED F/NH	UNUSED F	UNUSED AVG	USED F	USED AVG
	1931-49								
C6-14	**4¢-$1 complete, 9 varieties..........**	....	....	....	**28.00**	**21.00**	**16.00**	**7.60**	**5.00**
C6	4¢ Gaillard Cut, red violet (1949).........	11.00(6)	8.00	6.00	1.25	1.00	.75	1.00	.85
C7	5¢ yellow green...	5.50(6)	4.50	2.75	.75	.55	.40	.45	.35
C8	6¢ yellow brown (1946)..................	9.00(6)	8.00	5.00	1.00	.85	.65	.40	.30
C9	10¢ orange..........	12.50(6)	9.50	6.00	1.30	1.00	.85	.40	.30
C10	15¢ blue..............	13.50(6)	10.50	7.00	1.60	1.35	1.00	.40	.30
C11	20¢ red violet.......	22.00(6)	17.00	13.00	2.85	2.20	1.85	.40	.30
C12	30¢ rose lake (1941)..................	40.00(6)	36.00	28.00	4.50	3.25	2.75	1.30	.80
C13	40¢ yellow...........	40.00(6)	30.00	24.00	4.50	3.50	3.00	1.30	.100
C14	$1 black..............	105.00(6)	82.50	70.00	12.00	9.00	8.00	2.75	2.25

C15

C16

C17

C18

C19

C20

SCOTT NO.	DESCRIPTION	PLATE BLOCK F/NH	PLATE BLOCK F/OG	UNUSED F/NH	UNUSED F/OG	USED F
	1939 25th ANNIVERSARY ISSUE					
C15-20	**5¢-$1 complete 6 varieties ....**	....	....	**95.00**	**75.00**	**52.00**
C15	5¢ Plane over Sosa Hill	50.00(6)	40.00	5.00	4.00	2.75
C16	10¢ Map of Central America........................	65.00(6)	50.00	5.00	4.00	3.50
C17	15¢ Scene near Fort Amador	70.00(6)	60.00	7.50	6.00	1.50
C18	25¢ Clippper at Cristobal Harbor.........................	325.00(6)	250.00	22.00	18.00	9.00
C19	39¢ Clipper over Gaillard Cut	170.00(6)	110.00	21.00	17.00	8.00
C20	$1 Clipper Alighhting....	600.00(6)	450.00	50.00	42.00	29.00

C21-31, C34

SCOTT NO.	DESCRIPTION	PLATE BLOCK F/NH	PLATE BLOCK F/OG	UNUSED F/NH	UNUSED F/OG	USED F
	1951					
C21-26	**4¢-80¢ complete 6 varieties ....**	....	....	**29.25**	**25.50**	**13.00**
C21	4¢ Globe & Wing, red violet	9.00(6)	7.00	1.00	.85	.50
C22	6¢ light brown..............	8.00(6)	6.00	.85	.60	.40
C23	10¢ light red orange.....	11.00(6)	8.50	1.25	1.10	.50
C24	21¢ light blue...............	100.00(6)	85.00	12.00	10.00	5.00
C25	31¢ cerise	100.00(6)	85.00	13.00	11.00	5.00
C26	80¢ Light gray black.....	65.00(6)	48.00	7.75	6.50	2.00
	1958					
C27-31	**5¢-35¢ complete 5 varieties ....**	....	....	**30.75**	**25.00**	**9.70**
C27	5¢ Globe & Wing, yellow green	8.00	6.00	1.20	1.00	.65
C28	7¢ olive........................	8.00	6.00	1.20	1.00	.60
C29	15¢ brown violet..........	47.00	39.00	5.50	4.75	3.25
C30	25¢ orange yellow........	120.00	90.00	14.00	12.00	3.25
C31	35¢ dark blue	70.00	65.00	12.00	10.00	3.25

C32

C33

C35

SCOTT NO.	DESCRIPTION	PLATE BLOCK F/NH	PLATE BLOCK F/OG	UNUSED F/NH	UNUSED F/OG	USED F
	1961-63					
C32	15¢ Emblem Caribbean School	16.00	13.00	1.50	1.40	1.00
C33	7¢ Anti-Malaria (1962)..	3.50	3.00	.60	.40	.50
C34	8¢ Globe & Wing carmine (1968)	8.00	6.00	.85	.60	.40
C35	15¢ Alliance for Progress (1963)	16.00	13.00	1.60	1.35	1.35

C36 C37

C38 C39

C40 C41

1964 50th ANNIVERSARY ISSUE

SCOTT NO.	DESCRIPTION	PLATE BLOCK F/NH	PLATE BLOCK F/OG	UNUSED F/NH	UNUSED F/OG	USED F
C36-41	**6¢-80¢ complete 6 varieties ....**	**........**	**........**	**12.75**	**10.00**	**9.90**
C36	6¢ Cristobal..................	3.85	3.25	.65	.55	.60
C37	8¢ Gatun Locks............	4.25	3.50	.65	.55	.55
C38	15¢ Madden Dam	9.50	8.00	1.25	1.60	1.60
C39	20¢ Gaillard Cut...........	12.50	10.00	2.00	1.60	1.20
C40	30¢ Miraflores Locks....	20.00	16.00	3.50	2.50	3.00
C41	80¢ Balboa..................	28.00	26.00	6.00	5.50	4.50

C42-C53

1965

SCOTT NO.	DESCRIPTION	PLATE BLOCK F/NH	PLATE BLOCK F/OG	UNUSED F/NH	UNUSED F/OG	USED F
C42-47	**6¢-80¢ complete 6 varieties ....**	**........**	**........**	**6.40**	**........**	**2.55**
C42	6¢ Gov. Seal, green & black	3.50	....	.65	....	.40
C43	8¢ rose red & black......	3.50	....	.65	....	.30
C44	15¢ blue & black	7.25	....	.85	....	.35
C45	20¢ lilac & black...........	5.00	....	.85	....	.40
C46	30¢ reddish brown & black	5.25	....	1.25	....	.40
C47	80¢ bistre & balck	19.00	....	2.85	....	1.00

1968-76

SCOTT NO.	DESCRIPTION	PLATE BLOCK F/NH	PLATE BLOCK F/OG	UNUSED F/NH	UNUSED F/OG	USED F
C48-53	**10¢-35¢ complete 6 varieties ....**	**........**	**........**	**4.60**	**........**	**5.50**
C48	10¢ Gov. Seal, dull orange& black	3.75	....	.40	....	.25
C48a	same, bklt pane of 4.....	....	....	4.50	....	....
C49	11¢ Seal, olive & black (1971)	3.75	....	.40	....	.30
C49a	same, bklt pane of 4.....	....	....	3.50	....	....
C50	13¢ Seal, emerald & black (1974)	5.50	....	1.00	....	.35
C50a	same, bklt pane of 4.....	....	....	7.00	....	....
C51	22¢ Seal, violet & black (1976)	6.50	....	1.00	....	2.50
C52	25¢ Seal, pale yellow green & black	6.00	....	.90	....	.75
C53	35¢ Seal, salmon & black (1976)	11.00	....	1.35	....	2.20

AIR MAIL OFFICIAL STAMPS

C7-14 Overprinted
1941-42 Overprint 19 to 20-1/2 mm. long

OFFICIAL
PANAMA CANAL

SCOTT NO.	DESCRIPTION	PLATE BLOCK F/NH	PLATE BLOCK F/OG	UNUSED F/NH	UNUSED F/OG	USED F
CO1-7	**5¢-$1 complete 7 varieties ....**	**........**	**........**	**132.00**	**93.00**	**40.00**
CO1	5¢ Gaillard Cut, yellow green (C7)....................	....	....	7.50	5.75	2.50
CO2	10¢ orange (C9)...........	....	....	12.00	9.00	3.00
CO3	15¢ blue (C10)	....	....	15.00	12.00	3.00
CO4	20¢ red violet (C11)......	....	....	23.00	15.00	5.00
CO5	30¢ rose lake (1942) (C12)	....	....	24.00	20.00	7.00
CO6	40¢ yellow (C13)..........	....	....	24.00	20.00	10.00
CO7	$1 black (C14)..............	....	....	28.00	21.00	14.00

1947 Overprint 19 to 20-1/2mm. long

SCOTT NO.	DESCRIPTION	PLATE BLOCK F/NH	PLATE BLOCK F/OG	UNUSED F/NH	UNUSED F/OG	USED F
CO14	6¢ yellow brown (C8) ...	....	....	25.00	15.00	6.25

POSTAGE DUE STAMPS

1914
U.S. Postage Due Stamps
J45-46, 49 overprint

CANAL ZONE

SCOTT NO.	DESCRIPTION	UNUSED NH F	UNUSED NH AVG	UNUSED OG F	UNUSED OG AVG	USED F	USED AVG
J1	1¢ rose carmine..........	155.00	125.00	85.00	70.00	18.00	14.00
J2	2¢ rose carmine..........	425.00	350.00	225.00	200.00	55.00	45.00
J3	10¢ rose carmine........	1700.00	1400.00	925.00	850.00	55.00	45.00

1924
Type I overprint on U.S. Postage Due Stamps J61-62, 65

SCOTT NO.	DESCRIPTION	UNUSED NH F	UNUSED NH AVG	UNUSED OG F	UNUSED OG AVG	USED F	USED AVG
J12	1¢ carmine rose..........	185.00	145.00	95.00	85.00	30.00	23.00
J13	2¢ deep claret............	125.00	85.00	60.00	55.00	15.00	12.50
J14	10¢ deep claret...........	425.00	350.00	220.00	185.00	55.00	48.00

1925
Canal Zone Stamps
71, 73, 75 overprinted

POSTAGE DUE

SCOTT NO.	DESCRIPTION	UNUSED NH F	UNUSED NH AVG	UNUSED OG F	UNUSED OG AVG	USED F	USED AVG
J15	1¢ deep green	150.00	140.00	85.00	75.00	17.00	14.00
J16	2¢ carmine.................	45.00	35.00	25.00	20.00	7.50	5.50
J17	10¢ orange	85.00	70.00	50.00	40.00	12.50	10.00

1925
Type II overprint on U.S. Postage Due Stamps J61-62, 65

SCOTT NO.	DESCRIPTION	UNUSED NH F	UNUSED NH AVG	UNUSED OG F	UNUSED OG AVG	USED F	USED AVG
J18	1¢ carmine rose..........	18.00	16.00	8.00	6.50	3.00	2.25
J19	2¢ carmine rose..........	32.00	27.00	15.00	13.00	5.00	4.00
J20	10¢ carmine rose........	350.00	300.00	155.00	140.00	20.00	17.00

1929-39
107 Surcharged

POSTAGE DUE
-1-

SCOTT NO.	DESCRIPTION	UNUSED NH F	UNUSED NH AVG	UNUSED OG F	UNUSED OG AVG	USED F	USED AVG
J21	1¢ on 5¢ blue.............	10.00	8.00	5.50	4.50	2.20	1.85
J22	2¢ on 5¢ blue.............	17.00	14.00	9.75	8.00	3.50	2.50
J23	5¢ on 5¢ blue.............	17.00	14.00	9.75	8.00	4.00	3.00
J24	10¢ on 5¢ blue...........	17.00	14.00	9.75	8.00	4.00	3.00

J25

1932-41

SCOTT NO.	DESCRIPTION	UNUSED NH F	UNUSED NH AVG	UNUSED OG F	UNUSED OG AVG	USED F	USED AVG
J25-29	**1¢-15¢ complete, 5 varieties.................**	**5.40**	**4.50**	**4.20**	**3.00**	**3.60**	**2.55**
J25	1¢ claret......................	.50	.40	.40	.30	.30	.25
J26	2¢ claret......................	.50	.40	.40	.30	.30	.25
J27	5¢ claret......................	.90	.70	.70	.50	.30	.40
J28	10¢ claret....................	2.50	1.75	1.75	1.40	1.75	1.40
J29	15¢ claret (1941)	1.95	1.50	1.50	1.00	1.30	.90

OFFICIAL STAMPS

1941
105, 107, 108, 111, 112, 114, 117, 139 overprinted

OFFICIAL
PANAMA
CANAL

OFFICIAL
PANAMA CANAL

"PANAMA" 10mm. Long

SCOTT NO.	DESCRIPTION	UNUSED F/NH	UNUSED F	USED F
O1/9	**1¢-50¢ (O1-2, O4-7, O9) 7 varieties . . . .**	**132.50**	**96.75**	**21.25**
O1	1¢ yellow green (105)	3.50	2.75	.60
O2	3¢ deep violet (117)	7.50	5.50	1.00
O3	5¢ blue (107).	......	......	40.00
O4	10¢ orange (108)	12.00	10.00	2.25
O5	15¢ gray black (111)	20.00	16.00	3.00
O6	20¢ olive brown (112)	25.00	18.00	3.50
O7	50¢ lilac (114)	60.00	50.00	7.50

1947

SCOTT NO.	DESCRIPTION	UNUSED F/NH	UNUSED F	USED F
O9	5¢ deep blue (139)	15.00	13.00	4.50

CANAL ZONE MINT POSTAL STATIONERY ENTIRES

U16

ENVELOPES

SCOTT NO.	DESCRIPTION	MINT ENTIRES
U16	1934, 3¢ purple	1.50
U17	1958, 4¢ blue	1.65
U18	1969, 4¢ + 1¢ blue	1.65
U19	1969, 4¢ + 2¢ blue	3.25
U20	1971, 8¢ Gaillard Cut	1.00
U21	1974, 8¢ + 2¢ Gaillard Cut	1.35
U22	1976, 13¢ Gaillard Cut	1.00
U23	1978, 13¢ + 2¢ Gaillard Cut	1.00

UC5

AIR MAIL ENVELOPES

SCOTT NO.	DESCRIPTION	MINT ENTIRES
UC3	1949, 6¢ DC-4 Skymaster	4.75
UC4	1958, 7¢ DC-4 Skymaster	5.25
UC5	1963, 3¢ + 5¢ purple	7.25
UC6	1964, 8¢ Tail Assembly	3.00
UC7	1965, 4¢ + 4¢ blue	5.25
UC8	1966, 8¢ Tail Assembly	5.75
UC9	1968, 8¢ + 2¢ Tail Assembly	3.50
UC10	1968, 4¢ + 4¢ + 2¢ Tail Assembly	2.75
UC11	1969, 10¢ Tail Assembly	4.75
UC12	1971, 4¢ + 5¢ + 2¢ blue	4.75
UC13	1971, 10¢ + 1¢ Tail Assembly	4.75
UC14	1971, 11¢ Tail Assembly	1.50
UC15	1974, 11¢ + 2¢ Tail Assembly	2.00
UC16	1975, 8¢ + 2¢ + 3¢ emerald	1.75

UX10

POSTAL CARDS

SCOTT NO.	DESCRIPTION	MINT ENTIRES
UX10	1935, 1¢ overprint on U.S. #UX27	2.25
UX11	1952, 2¢ overprint on U.S. #UX38	2.75
UX12	1958, 3¢ Ship in Lock	2.50
UX13	1963, 3¢ + 1¢ Ship in Lock	4.75
UX14	1964, 4¢ Ship in Canal	4.25
UX15	1965, 4¢ Ship in Lock	1.50
UX16	1968, 4¢ + 1¢ Ship in Lock	1.50
UX17	1969, 5¢ Ship in Lock	1.50
UX18	1971, 5¢ + 1¢ Ship in Lock	1.00
UX19	1974, 8¢ Ship in Lock	1.25
UX20	1976, 8¢ + 1¢ Ship in Lock	1.00
UX21	1978, 8¢ + 2¢ Ship in Lock	1.25

AIR MAIL POSTAL CARDS

SCOTT NO.	DESCRIPTION	MINT ENTIRES
UXC1	1958, 5¢ Plane, Flag & Map	4.25
UXC2	1963, 5¢ + 1¢ Plane, Flag & Map	11.00
UXC3	1965, 4¢ + 2¢ Ship in Lock	4.75
UXC4	1968, 4¢ + 4¢ Ship in Lock	3.50
UXC5	1971, 5¢ + 4¢ Ship in Lock	1.50

CONFEDERATE STATES

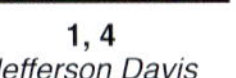

1, 4
Jefferson Davis

2, 5
Thomas Jefferson

(Confederate States 1-14 + 40% for VF Centering)

1861

SCOTT NO.	DESCRIPTION	UNUSED OG F	UNUSED OG AVG	UNUSED F	UNUSED AVG	USED F	USED AVG
1	5¢ green	325.00	190.00	200.00	140.00	175.00	125.00
2	10¢ blue	325.00	225.00	225.00	150.00	200.00	140.00

3
Andrew Jackson

6, 7
Jefferson Davis
6: Fine Print
7: Coarse Print

1862

SCOTT NO.	DESCRIPTION	UNUSED OG F	UNUSED OG AVG	UNUSED F	UNUSED AVG	USED F	USED AVG
3	2¢ green	1150.00	900.00	750.00	550.00	900.00	750.00
4	5¢ blue	275.00	225.00	200.00	125.00	125.00	80.00
5	10¢ rose	1800.00	1200.00	1500.00	1000.00	500.00	450.00
6	5¢ light blue, London Print	45.00	35.00	22.00	18.00	30.00	21.00
7	5¢ blue, Local Print	35.00	25.00	25.00	18.00	21.00	18.00

8
Andrew Jackson

1863

SCOTT NO.	DESCRIPTION	UNUSED OG F	UNUSED OG AVG	UNUSED F	UNUSED AVG	USED F	USED AVG
8	2¢ red brown	90.00	70.00	70.00	60.00	400.00	295.00

9

10, 11 (Die A)
Jefferson Davis

12 (Die B)

SCOTT NO.	DESCRIPTION	UNUSED OG F	UNUSED OG AVG	UNUSED F	UNUSED AVG	USED F	USED AVG
9	10¢ blue (TEN)	1200.00	700.00	650.00	500.00	650.00	550.00
10	10¢ blue (with frame line)	....	....	6000.00	4500.00	2500.00	2250.00
11	10¢ blue (no frame)	22.00	15.00	15.00	10.00	25.00	21.00
12	10¢ blue, filled corner	28.00	20.00	20.00	15.00	23.00	19.00

13
George Washington

14
John C. Calhoun

SCOTT NO.	DESCRIPTION	UNUSED OG F	UNUSED OG AVG	UNUSED F	UNUSED AVG	USED F	USED AVG
13	20¢ green	75.00	60.00	60.00	55.00	400.00	350.00

1862

SCOTT NO.	DESCRIPTION	UNUSED OG F	UNUSED OG AVG	UNUSED F	UNUSED AVG	USED F	USED AVG
14	1¢ orange	160.00	120.00	110.00	80.00	....	....

CUBA

U.S. Administration

1899
U.S. Stamps of 267, 279, 279B, 268, 281, 282C surcharged

CUBA
1 c.
de PESO.

SCOTT NO.	DESCRIPTION	UNUSED NH F	UNUSED NH AVG	UNUSED OG F	UNUSED OG AVG	USED F	USED AVG
221	1¢ on 1¢ yellow green	10.00	8.50	5.50	5.00	.65	.55
222	2¢ on 2¢ carmine	19.00	15.00	10.00	8.00	.85	.70
223	2-1/2¢ on 2¢ carmine	12.00	10.00	5.50	5.00	1.00	.75
224	3¢ on 3¢ purple	27.00	19.00	15.00	13.00	2.00	1.50
225	5¢ on 5¢ blue	27.00	19.00	15.00	13.00	2.50	2.00
226	10¢ on 10¢ brown	65.00	55.00	28.00	23.00	8.00	7.00

227

228

229

230

231

Republic under U.S. Military Rule Watermarked US-C

SCOTT NO.	DESCRIPTION	UNUSED NH F	UNUSED NH AVG	UNUSED OG F	UNUSED OG AVG	USED F	USED AVG
227	1¢ Columbus	7.50	5.50	4.00	3.00	.35	.25
228	2¢ Coconut Palms	7.50	5.50	4.00	3.00	.35	.25
229	3¢ Allegory "Cuba"	7.50	5.50	4.00	3.00	.35	.25
230	5¢ Ocean Liner	9.50	8.00	6.00	4.75	.35	.25
231	10¢ Cane Field	25.00	17.00	15.00	12.00	.75	.55

SPECIAL DELIVERY
1899
Surcharged of 1899 on U.S. E5

SCOTT NO.	DESCRIPTION	UNUSED NH F	UNUSED NH AVG	UNUSED OG F	UNUSED OG AVG	USED F	USED AVG
E1	10¢ on 10¢ blue	270.00	200.00	140.00	95.00	110.00	90.00

E2
Special Delivery Messenger

Republic under U.S. Military Rule
Watermarked US-C Inscribed "Immediate"

SCOTT NO.	DESCRIPTION	UNUSED NH F	UNUSED NH AVG	UNUSED OG F	UNUSED OG AVG	USED F	USED AVG
E2	10¢ orange	115.00	85.00	45.00	30.00	18.00	14.00

POSTAGE DUE STAMPS
1899
Surcharge of 1899 on U.S. J38-39, J41-42

SCOTT NO.	DESCRIPTION	UNUSED NH F	UNUSED NH AVG	UNUSED OG F	UNUSED OG AVG	USED F	USED AVG
J1	1¢ on 1¢ deep claret	90.00	80.00	45.00	40.00	7.00	5.00
J2	2¢ on 2¢ deep claret	90.00	80.00	45.00	40.00	7.00	5.00
J3	5¢ on 5¢ deep claret	95.00	75.00	45.00	40.00	7.00	5.00
J4	10¢ on 10¢ deep claret	60.00	50.00	25.00	20.00	3.00	2.00

GUAM

1899
U.S. Stamps of 279, 267, 268, 272, 280-82C, 284, 275, 276 overprinted

GUAM

SCOTT NO.	DESCRIPTION	UNUSED NH F	UNUSED NH AVG	UNUSED OG F	UNUSED OG AVG	USED F	USED AVG
1	1¢ deep green	40.00	30.00	20.00	13.00	30.00	22.00
2	2¢ red	38.00	30.00	19.00	13.00	29.00	22.00
3	3¢ purple	250.00	200.00	130.00	90.00	160.00	120.00
4	4¢ lilac brown	220.00	190.00	130.00	90.00	160.00	120.00
5	5¢ blue	60.00	40.00	30.00	20.00	50.00	35.00
6	6¢ lake	220.00	170.00	120.00	90.00	180.00	130.00
7	8¢ violet brown	220.00	170.00	120.00	90.00	180.00	130.00
8	10¢ brown (Type I)	80.00	60.00	40.00	20.00	50.00	30.00
10	15¢ olive green	250.00	170.00	140.00	100.00	130.00	100.00
11	50¢ orange	650.00	500.00	300.00	200.00	310.00	220.00
12	$1 black (Type I)	650.00	500.00	300.00	200.00	370.00	200.00

SPECIAL DELIVERY
U.S. Stamp E5 overprint

GUAM

SCOTT NO.	DESCRIPTION	UNUSED NH F	UNUSED NH AVG	UNUSED OG F	UNUSED OG AVG	USED F	USED AVG
E1	10¢ blue	275.00	200.00	140.00	100.00	200.00	150.00

HAWAII

23, 24

25, 26

1864 Laid Paper

SCOTT NO.	DESCRIPTION	UNUSED OG F	UNUSED OG AVG	UNUSED F	UNUSED AVG	USED F	USED AVG
23	1¢ black	300.00	200.00	230.00	150.00	2000.00	1400.00
24	2¢ black	350.00	220.00	240.00	160.00	920.00	620.00

1865 Wove Paper

SCOTT NO.	DESCRIPTION	UNUSED OG F	UNUSED OG AVG	UNUSED F	UNUSED AVG	USED F	USED AVG
25	1¢ dark blue	375.00	220.00	250.00	170.00	....	....
26	2¢ dark blue	375.00	220.00	250.00	170.00	....	....

27-29, 50-51
King Kamehameha IV

1861-63

SCOTT NO.	DESCRIPTION	UNUSED OG F	UNUSED OG AVG	UNUSED F	UNUSED AVG	USED F	USED AVG
27	2¢ pale rose, horizontal laid paper	400.00	275.00	275.00	185.00	275.00	185.00
28	2¢ pale rose, vertical laid paper	400.00	275.00	275.00	185.00	275.00	185.00

1869 Engraved

SCOTT NO.	DESCRIPTION	UNUSED OG F	UNUSED OG AVG	UNUSED F	UNUSED AVG	USED F	USED AVG
29	2¢ red, thin wove paper	50.00	35.00	40.00	35.00	....	....

30
Princess Kamamalu

31
King Kamehameha IV

32, 39, 52C
King Kamehameha V

33

34
Mataia Kekuanaoa

1864-71 Wove Paper

SCOTT NO.	DESCRIPTION	UNUSED OG F	UNUSED OG AVG	UNUSED F	UNUSED AVG	USED F	USED AVG
30	1¢ purple	12.00	9.00	9.00	7.00	8.50	6.00
31	2¢ rose vermillion	70.00	55.00	52.00	43.00	10.00	7.00
32	5¢ blue	200.00	140.00	150.00	95.00	35.00	25.00
33	6 yellow green	45.00	30.00	30.00	20.00	10.00	7.00
34	18¢ dull rose	105.00	70.00	80.00	50.00	40.00	28.00

35, 38, 43
King David Kalakaua

36, 46
Prince William Pitt Leleichoku

1875

SCOTT NO.	DESCRIPTION	UNUSED OG F	UNUSED OG AVG	UNUSED F	UNUSED AVG	USED F	USED AVG
35	2¢ brown	15.00	9.00	6.00	4.00	3.25	2.10
36	12¢ black	110.00	85.00	60.00	38.00	42.00	28.00

37, 42
Princess Likelike

40, 44, 45
King David Kalakaua

41
Queen Kapiolani

47
Statue of King Kamehameha I

48
King William Lunalilo

49
Queen Emma Kaleleonalani

1882

SCOTT NO.	DESCRIPTION	UNUSED OG F	AVG	UNUSED F	AVG	USED F	AVG
37	1¢ blue	22.00	11.00	8.00	6.50	7.00	5.00
38	2¢ lilac rose	280.00	110.00	95.00	75.00	45.00	40.00
39	5¢ ultramarine	30.00	14.00	14.00	10.00	4.00	2.75
40	10¢ black	80.00	60.00	40.00	25.00	22.00	18.00
41	15¢ red brown	110.00	75.00	45.00	32.00	26.00	20.00

1883-86

SCOTT NO.	DESCRIPTION	UNUSED OG F	AVG	UNUSED F	AVG	USED F	AVG
42	1¢ green	6.00	4.00	3.00	2.00	2.10	1.50
43	2¢ rose	10.00	6.00	3.50	2.50	1.25	.85
44	10¢ red brown	70.00	50.00	25.00	20.00	11.00	7.00
45	10¢ vermillion	75.00	55.00	27.00	22.00	15.00	10.00
46	12¢ red lilac	160.00	85.00	58.00	50.00	35.00	30.00
47	25¢ dark violet	290.00	180.00	120.00	100.00	70.00	55.00
48	50¢ red	300.00	210.00	125.00	100.00	90.00	75.00
49	$1 rose red	500.00	200.00	185.00	155.00	250.00	200.00
50	2¢ Orange Vermillion	150.00	95.00	120.00	90.00	....	....
51	2¢ Carmine	30.00	20.00	25.00	20.00	....	....

52
Queen Liliuokalani

1890-91

SCOTT NO.	DESCRIPTION	UNUSED OG F	AVG	UNUSED F	AVG	USED F	AVG
52	2¢ dull violet	12.00	8.00	5.00	3.25	2.00	1.40
52C	5¢ deep indigo	220.00	110.00	77.00	50.00	150.00	100.00

Provisional
GOVT.
1893

1893 Provisional Government
Red Overprint

SCOTT NO.	DESCRIPTION	UNUSED OG F	AVG	UNUSED F	AVG	USED F	AVG
53	1¢ purple	14.00	10.00	6.00	4.25	15.00	11.00
54	1¢ blue	14.00	10.00	6.00	4.25	15.00	11.00
55	1¢ green	3.00	2.00	1.50	1.00	4.00	2.75
56	2¢ brown	20.00	14.00	9.00	6.00	25.00	20.00
57	2¢ dull violet	3.00	2.00	1.50	1.00	1.50	1.00
58	5¢ deep indigo	22.00	15.00	11.00	7.00	30.00	22.00
59	5¢ ultramarine	10.00	8.00	6.00	4.00	3.25	1.95
60	6¢ green	26.00	16.00	13.00	9.00	30.00	20.00
61	10¢ black	20.00	17.00	11.00	8.00	17.00	14.00
62	12¢ black	20.00	17.00	9.00	7.00	18.00	14.00
63	12¢ red lilac	300.00	225.00	130.00	95.00	225.00	170.00
64	25¢ dark violet	55.00	35.00	20.00	15.00	50.00	40.00

Black Overprint

SCOTT NO.	DESCRIPTION	UNUSED OG F	AVG	UNUSED F	AVG	USED F	AVG
65	2¢ rose vermillion	140.00	80.00	40.00	30.00	85.00	60.00
66	2¢ rose	2.00	1.50	1.20	.80	3.00	2.00
67	10¢ vermillion	38.00	25.00	16.00	10.00	35.00	28.00
68	10¢ red brown	14.00	11.00	7.00	5.00	15.00	10.00
69	12¢ red lilac	510.00	425.00	250.00	175.00	600.00	425.00
70	15¢ red brown	35.00	25.00	17.00	13.00	35.00	25.00
71	18¢ dull rose	55.00	40.00	28.00	22.00	40.00	28.00
72	50¢ red	125.00	90.00	55.00	40.00	100.00	70.00
73	$1 rose red	210.00	170.00	105.00	80.00	190.00	130.00

74, 80
Coat of Arms

75, 81
View of Honolulu

76
Statue of King Kamehameha I

1894

SCOTT NO.	DESCRIPTION	UNUSED OG F	AVG	UNUSED F	AVG	USED F	AVG
74	1¢ yellow	4.50	3.25	2.25	1.55	1.40	1.00
75	2¢ brown	4.50	3.25	2.25	1.55	.80	.55
76	5¢ rose lake	10.00	8.50	4.00	2.75	2.00	1.40

77
Star and Palm

78
S.S."Arawa"

79
Pres. S.B. Dole

SCOTT NO.	DESCRIPTION	UNUSED OG F	AVG	UNUSED F	AVG	USED F	AVG
77	10¢ yellow green	12.00	9.00	7.00	5.00	6.00	4.00
78	12¢ blue	28.00	23.00	12.00	8.00	18.00	12.00
79	25¢ deep blue	35.00	29.00	15.00	10.00	16.00	11.00

82
Statue of King Kamehameha I

1899

SCOTT NO.	DESCRIPTION	UNUSED OG F	AVG	UNUSED F	AVG	USED F	AVG
80	1¢ dark green	3.50	2.00	1.50	1.00	1.50	1.00
81	2¢ rose	3.50	2.00	1.50	1.00	1.50	1.00
82	5¢ blue	13.00	10.00	6.00	4.00	4.00	2.80

O1
Lorrin A. Thurston

1896 OFFICIAL STAMPS

SCOTT NO.	DESCRIPTION	UNUSED OG F	AVG	UNUSED F	AVG	USED F	AVG
O1	2¢ green	72.00	50.00	40.00	28.00	20.00	14.00
O2	5¢ black brown	72.00	50.00	40.00	28.00	20.00	14.00
O3	6¢ deep ultramarine	90.00	80.00	40.00	28.00	20.00	14.00
O4	10¢ bright rose	75.00	55.00	40.00	28.00	20.00	14.00
O5	12¢ orange	120.00	90.00	40.00	28.00	20.00	14.00
O6	25¢ gray violet	155.00	110.00	50.00	33.00	20.00	14.00

MARSHALL ISLANDS

The Marshall Islands are a part of the U.S. administered Trust Territories of the Pacific formed in 1947. They were granted postal autonomy in 1984 on their way to independence.

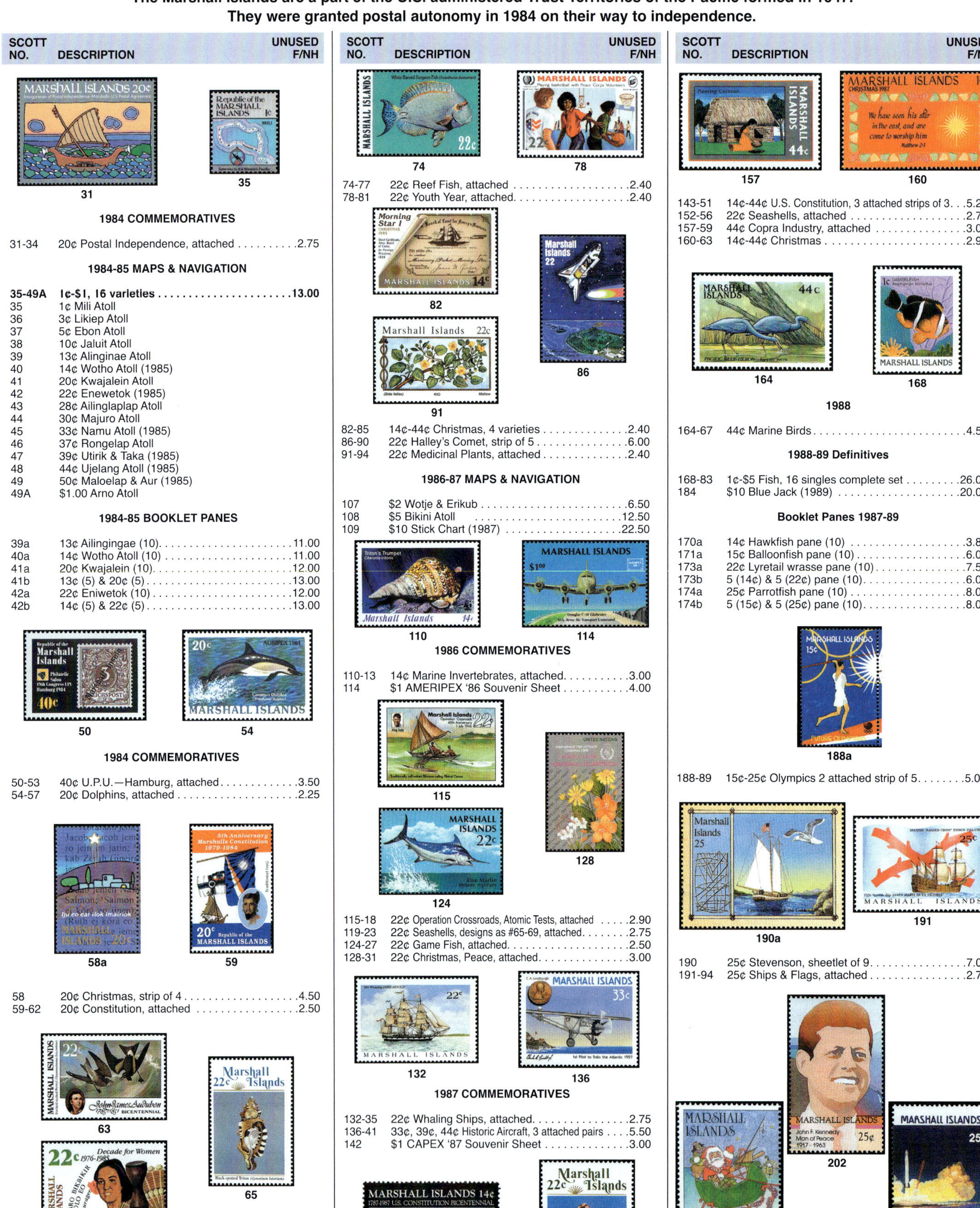

SCOTT NO.	DESCRIPTION	UNUSED F/NH

31 35

1984 COMMEMORATIVES

31-34	20¢ Postal Independence, attached	2.75

1984-85 MAPS & NAVIGATION

35-49A	**1¢-$1, 16 varieties**	**13.00**
35	1¢ Mili Atoll	
36	3¢ Likiep Atoll	
37	5¢ Ebon Atoll	
38	10¢ Jaluit Atoll	
39	13¢ Alinginae Atoll	
40	14¢ Wotho Atoll (1985)	
41	20¢ Kwajalein Atoll	
42	22¢ Enewetok (1985)	
43	28¢ Ailinglaplap Atoll	
44	30¢ Majuro Atoll	
45	33¢ Namu Atoll (1985)	
46	37¢ Rongelap Atoll	
47	39¢ Utirik & Taka (1985)	
48	44¢ Ujelang Atoll (1985)	
49	50¢ Maloelap & Aur (1985)	
49A	$1.00 Arno Atoll	

1984-85 BOOKLET PANES

39a	13¢ Ailingingae (10)	11.00
40a	14¢ Wotho Atoll (10)	11.00
41a	20¢ Kwajalein (10)	12.00
41b	13¢ (5) & 20¢ (5)	13.00
42a	22¢ Eniwetok (10)	12.00
42b	14¢ (5) & 22¢ (5)	13.00

50 54

1984 COMMEMORATIVES

50-53	40¢ U.P.U.—Hamburg, attached	3.50
54-57	20¢ Dolphins, attached	2.25

58a 59

58	20¢ Christmas, strip of 4	4.50
59-62	20¢ Constitution, attached	2.50

63 65 70

1985 COMMEMORATIVES

63-64	22¢ Audubon Birds, attached	1.65
65-69	22¢ Seashells, attached	2.75
70-73	22¢ Decade for Women, attached	2.45

74 78

74-77	22¢ Reef Fish, attached	2.40
78-81	22¢ Youth Year, attached	2.40

82 86 91

82-85	14¢-44¢ Christmas, 4 varieties	2.40
86-90	22¢ Halley's Comet, strip of 5	6.00
91-94	22¢ Medicinal Plants, attached	2.40

1986-87 MAPS & NAVIGATION

107	$2 Wotje & Erikub	6.50
108	$5 Bikini Atoll	12.50
109	$10 Stick Chart (1987)	22.50

110 114

1986 COMMEMORATIVES

110-13	14¢ Marine Invertebrates, attached	3.00
114	$1 AMERIPEX '86 Souvenir Sheet	4.00

115 128 124

115-18	22¢ Operation Crossroads, Atomic Tests, attached	2.90
119-23	22¢ Seashells, designs as #65-69, attached	2.75
124-27	22¢ Game Fish, attached	2.50
128-31	22¢ Christmas, Peace, attached	3.00

132 136

1987 COMMEMORATIVES

132-35	22¢ Whaling Ships, attached	2.75
136-41	33¢, 39¢, 44¢ Historic Aircraft, 3 attached pairs	5.50
142	$1 CAPEX '87 Souvenir Sheet	3.00

143 152

157 160

143-51	14¢-44¢ U.S. Constitution, 3 attached strips of 3	5.25
152-56	22¢ Seashells, attached	2.75
157-59	44¢ Copra Industry, attached	3.00
160-63	14¢-44¢ Christmas	2.90

164 168

1988

164-67	44¢ Marine Birds	4.50

1988-89 Definitives

168-83	1¢-$5 Fish, 16 singles complete set	26.00
184	$10 Blue Jack (1989)	20.00

Booklet Panes 1987-89

170a	14¢ Hawkfish pane (10)	3.80
171a	15¢ Balloonfish pane (10)	6.00
173a	22¢ Lyretail wrasse pane (10)	7.50
173b	5 (14¢) & 5 (22¢) pane (10)	6.00
174a	25¢ Parrotfish pane (10)	8.00
174b	5 (15¢) & 5 (25¢) pane (10)	8.00

188a

188-89	15¢-25¢ Olympics 2 attached strip of 5	5.00

190a 191

190	25¢ Stevenson, sheetlet of 9	7.00
191-94	25¢ Ships & Flags, attached	2.75

202 195 205

195-99	25¢ Christmas, strip of 5	3.00
200-04	25¢ J.F.K. Tribute, strip of 5	3.50
205-08	25¢ Space Shuttle, strip of 4	3.00

SCOTT NO.	DESCRIPTION	UNUSED F/NH

209

1989 COMMEMORATIVES

SCOTT NO.	DESCRIPTION	UNUSED F/NH
209-12	45¢ Links to Japan, attached	4.00

213 216

SCOTT NO.	DESCRIPTION	UNUSED F/NH
213-15	45¢ Alaska Anniv., strip of 3	3.75
216-20	25¢ Seashells, strip of 5	3.00
221	$1 Japanese Art Souvenir Sheet	2.60

222 226

230a 232

SCOTT NO.	DESCRIPTION	UNUSED F/NH
222-25	45¢ Migrant Birds, attached	4.90
226-29	45¢ Postal Service, attached	4.80
230	$1.50 PHILEX-FRANCE Souv. Sheet	12.00
231	$1.00 Postal Service Centenary Souvenir Sheet	12.00
232-38	25¢-$1 20th Anniversary First Moon Landing	20.00
238a	booklet pane of 232-38	20.00

239 248

1989 WWII Anniversary Issues

SCOTT NO.	DESCRIPTION	UNUSED F/NH
239	25¢ Invasion of Poland	1.00
240	45¢ Sinking of HMS Royal Oak	1.65
241	45¢ Invasion of Finland	1.65
242-45	45¢ Battle of River Plate, 4 attached	5.00

1990 WWII Anniversary Issues

SCOTT NO.	DESCRIPTION	UNUSED F/NH
246-47	25¢ Invasion of Denmark and Norway	1.75
248	25¢ Katyn Forest Massacre	1.00
249-50	25¢ Bombing of Rotterdam/25¢ Invasion of Belgium	1.75
251	45¢ Winston Churchill	1.65
252-53	45¢ Evacuation at Dunkirk, 2 attached	3.50
254	45¢ Occupation of Paris	1.65
255	25¢ Battle of Mers-el-Kebir	1.00
256	25¢ Battles for Burma Road	1.00
257-60	45¢ U.S. Destroyers, 4 attached	6.00
261-64	45¢ Battle for Britain, 4 attached	6.00
265	45¢ Tripartite Pact 1940	1.65
266	25¢ Roosevelt Reelected	.90
267-70	25¢ Battle of Taranto, 4 attached	4.00

1991 WWII Anniversary Issues

SCOTT NO.	DESCRIPTION	UNUSED F/NH
271-74	30¢ Roosevelt's Four Freedoms of Speech, 4 attached	4.00
275	30¢ Battle of Beda Fomm	0.95
276-77	29¢ Invasion of Greece and Yugoslavia, 2 attached	1.80
278-81	50¢ Sinking of the Bismarck, 4 attached	7.00
282	30¢ Germany Invades Russia	1.00
283-84	29¢ Atlantic Charter, 2 attached	1.80
285	29¢ Siege of Moscow	1.00

SCOTT NO.	DESCRIPTION	UNUSED F/NH
286-87	30¢ Sinking of the USS Reuben James, 2 attached	1.80
288-91	50¢ Japanese Attack Pearl Harbor, 4 attached	7.00
288-91b	same, 2nd printing (1 title corrected)	30.00
292	29¢ Japanese Capture Guam	1.00
293	29¢ Fall of Singapore	1.00
294-95	50¢ Flying Tigers, 2 attached	3.50
296	29¢ Fall of Wake Island	1.00

1992 WWII Anniversary Issues

SCOTT NO.	DESCRIPTION	UNUSED F/NH
297	29¢ Arcadia Conference	1.00
298	50¢ Fall of Manila	1.50
299	29¢ Japanese take Rabaul	1.00
300	29¢ Battle of Java Sea	1.00
301	50¢ Fall of Rangoon	1.50
302	29¢ Japanese on New Guinea	1.00
303	29¢ MacArthur evacuated from Corregidor	1.00
304	29¢ Raid on Saint-Nazaire	1.00
305	29¢ Bataan/Death March	1.00
306	50¢ Doolittle Raid on Tokyo	1.50
307	29¢ Fall of Corregidor	1.00
308-11	50¢ Battle of the Coral Sea, 4 attached	7.25
308-11b	same, 2nd printing (4 titles corrected)	27.00
312-15	50¢ Battle of Midway, 4 attached	7.25
316	29¢ Village of Lidice destroyed	1.00
317	29¢ Fall of Sevastopol	1.00
318-19	29¢ Convoy PQ 17 Destroyed, 2 attached	2.55
320	29¢ Marines on Guadalcanal	1.00
321	29¢ Battle of Savo Island	1.00
322	29¢ Dieppe Raid	1.00
323	50¢ Battle of Stalingrad	1.90
324	29¢ Battle of Eastern Solomons	1.00
325	50¢ Battle of Cape Esperance	1.90
326	29¢ Battle of El Alamein	1.00
327-28	29¢ Battle of Barents Sea, 2 attached	2.70

1993 WWII Anniversary Issues

SCOTT NO.	DESCRIPTION	UNUSED F/NH
329	29¢ Casablanca Conference	1.00
330	29¢ Liberation of Kharkov	1.00
331-34	50¢ Battle of Bismarck Sea, 4 attached	7.25
335	50¢ Interception of Admiral Yamamoto	1.50
336-37	29¢ Battle of Kursk, 2 attached	2.70

341 346

345a

1989

SCOTT NO.	DESCRIPTION	UNUSED F/NH
341-44	25¢ Christmas 1989, 4 attached	4.70
345	45¢ Milestones in space (25)	35.00

1990

SCOTT NO.	DESCRIPTION	UNUSED F/NH
346-65A	1¢/$2 Birds (21)	35.00
361a	Essen '90 Germany, miniature sheet of 4 (347, 350, 353, 361)	5.70

366 370

377

SCOTT NO.	DESCRIPTION	UNUSED F/NH
366-69	25¢ Children's Games, 4 attached	5.00
370-76	25¢, $1 Penny Black, singles	18.00
376a	booklet pane of 370-76	18.50
377-80	25¢ Endangered Wildlife, 4 attached	6.00

381 382

383 387

SCOTT NO.	DESCRIPTION	UNUSED F/NH
381	25¢ Joint Issue (US & Micronesia)	1.25
382	45¢ German Reunification	1.45
383-86	25¢ Christmas 1990, 4 attached	4.50
387-90	25¢ Breadfruit, 4 attached	4.00

395

1991

SCOTT NO.	DESCRIPTION	UNUSED F/NH
391-94	50¢ 10th Anniversaary of Space Shuttle, 4 attached	5.00
395-98	52¢ Flowers, 4 attached	6.25
398a	52¢ Phila Nippon, sheet of 4	6.25

399 400

SCOTT NO.	DESCRIPTION	UNUSED F/NH
399	29¢ Operation Desert Storm	1.25
400-06	29¢, $1 Birds, set of 7 singles	25.00
406a	same, booklet pane of 7	25.00

407 411

SCOTT NO.	DESCRIPTION	UNUSED F/NH
407-10	12¢-50¢ Air Marshall Islands Aircraft, set of 4	5.00
411	29¢ Admission to the United Nations	1.00

412 413

SCOTT NO.	DESCRIPTION	UNUSED F/NH
412	30¢ Christmas 1991, Dove	1.20
413	29¢ Peace Corps	1.20

414 418

425

1992

SCOTT NO.	DESCRIPTION	UNUSED F/NH
414-17	29¢ Ships, strip of 4	5.00
418-24	50¢, $1 Columbus, set of 7 singles	19.00
424a	same, booklet pane of 7	19.00
425-28	29¢ Handicrafts, 4 attached	3.25

SCOTT NO.	DESCRIPTION	UNUSED F/NH

429

430

429 29¢ Christmas, 1992 . . . . .1.00
430-33 9-45¢ Birds, set of 4 . . . . .4.50

466A

441

478

1993

434-40 50¢, $1 Reef Life, set of 7 singles 24.00
440a same, booklet pane of 7 . . . . .24.50

1993-95

441-66B 10¢-$10 Ships & Sailing Vessels, 28 varieties .79.75
466C "Hong Kong '94" miniature sheet of 4 (#464d-64g) .5.00

1993 WWII Anniversary Issues (continued)

467-70 52¢ Invasion of Sicily, 4 attached 8.00
471 50¢ Bombing of Schweinfurt 1.75
472 29¢ Liberation of Smolensk 1.00
473 29¢ Landings at Bougainville 1.00
474 50¢ Invasion of Tarawa .1.75
475 52¢ Teheran Conference, 1943 . . . . .1.75
476-77 29¢ Battle of North Cape, 2 attached 2.50

1994 WWII Anniversary Issues

478 29¢ Gen. Dwight D. Eisenhower 1.00
479 50¢ Invasion of Anzio 1.75
480 52¢ Siege of Leningrad lifted 1.75
481 29¢ US Liberates Marshall Islands 1.00
482 29¢ Japanese Defeated at Truk 1.00
483 52¢ US Bombs Germany 1.75
484 50¢ Lt. Gen. Mark Clark, Rome Falls to the Allies .1.75
485-88 75¢ D-Day—Allied Landings at Normandy, 4 attached . 11.00
485-88b same, 2nd printing (3 titles corrected) 29.00
489 50¢ V-1 Bombardment of England Begins 1.75
490 29¢ US Marines Land on Saipan 1.00
491 50¢ 1st Battle of Philippine Sea 1.75
492 29¢ US Liberates Guam 1.00
493 50¢ Warsaw Uprising 1.75
494 50¢ Liberation of Paris .1.75
495 29¢ US Marines land on Peliliu 1.75
496 52¢ MacArthur returns to the Philippines 1.75
497 52¢ Battle of Leyte Gulf .1.75
498-99 50¢ Battleship Tirpitz Sunk, 2 attached 4.70
500-03 50¢ Battle of the Bulge, 4 attached 11.00

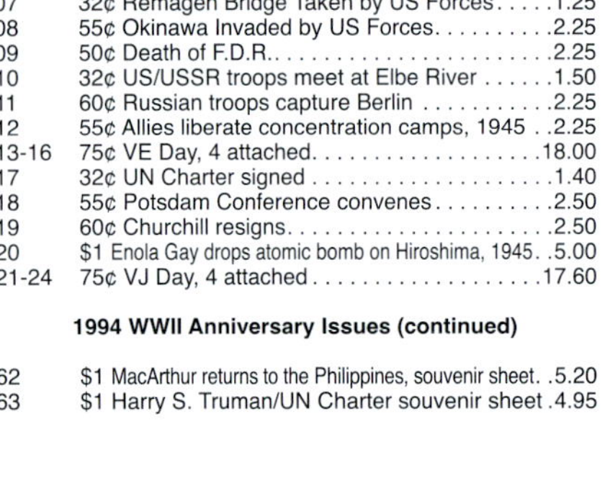

1995 WWII Anniversary Issues

504 32¢ Yalta Conference Begins 1.25
505 55¢ Bombing of Dresden 3.80
506 $1 Iwo Jima Invaded by US Marines 4.50
507 32¢ Remagen Bridge Taken by US Forces 1.25
508 55¢ Okinawa Invaded by US Forces 2.25
509 50¢ Death of F.D.R. 2.25
510 32¢ US/USSR troops meet at Elbe River 1.50
511 60¢ Russian troops capture Berlin 2.25
512 55¢ Allies liberate concentration camps, 1945 . .2.25
513-16 75¢ VE Day, 4 attached 18.00
517 32¢ UN Charter signed .1.40
518 55¢ Potsdam Conference convenes 2.50
519 60¢ Churchill resigns 2.50
520 $1 Enola Gay drops atomic bomb on Hiroshima, 1945 . .5.00
521-24 75¢ VJ Day, 4 attached 17.60

1994 WWII Anniversary Issues (continued)

562 $1 MacArthur returns to the Philippines, souvenir sheet . .5.20
563 $1 Harry S. Truman/UN Charter souvenir sheet .4.95

SCOTT NO.	DESCRIPTION	UNUSED F/NH

567

1993 (continued)

567-70 29¢ New Capitol 2.50

572

576

571 50¢ Super Tanker "Eagle" souvenir sheet 1.35
572-75 29¢ Life in the 1800s, 4 attached 3.00
576 29¢ Christmas 1993 . . . . .1.00

1994

577 $2.90 15th Anniversary Constitution souvenir sheet .6.80
578 29¢ 10th Anniversary Postal Service souvenir sheet . 1.00

579

583

582a

579-80 50¢ World Cup Soccer, 2 attached 5.80
582 50¢ Solar System, Planets, sheetlet of 12 . . . .20.00
583-86 75¢ 25th Anniversary of First Moon Landing, 4 attached . .7.00
586b $3 25th Anniversary of First Moon Landing, souvenir sheet .7.00

587a

588

587 "PHILAKOREA '94" souvenir sheet of 3 . . . . . . .5.50
588 29¢ Christmas 1994 . . . . .1.00

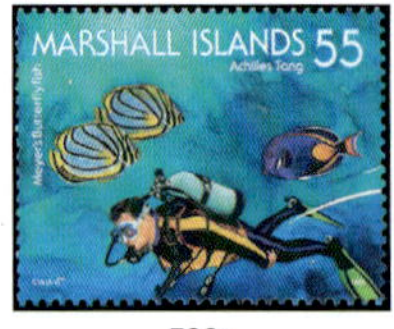
590a

591a

592a

1995

589 50¢ New Year 1995 (Year of the Boar) 1.80
590 55¢ Marine Life, 4 attached 8.80
591 55¢ John F. Kennedy, strip of 6 . . . . .8.00
592 75¢ Marilyn Monroe, 4 attached 8.00

SCOTT NO.	DESCRIPTION	UNUSED F/NH

593a

594a

595a

593 32¢ Cats, 4 attached 3.80
594 75¢ Space Shuttle, 4 attached 6.80
595 60¢ Pacific Game Fish, 8 attached 17.00

596a

597a

596 32¢ Island Legends, 4 attached, plus 4 labels . .3.80
597 32¢ Orchids (Singapore'95), minature sheet of 4 . .3.50
598 50¢ Suzhou Gardens souvenir sheet 1.10

599

600a

601

599 32¢ Christmas 1995 . . . . .1.00
600 32¢ Jet Fighter Planes, sheetlet of 25 . . . . .19.00
601 32¢ Yitzhak Rabin 1.00

603a

604a

1996

602 50¢ New Year 1996 (Year of the Rat) 1.25
603 32¢ Native Birds, 4 attached 7.80
604 55¢ Wild Cats, 4 attached 6.50

SCOTT NO.	DESCRIPTION	UNUSED F/NH

605a  606a  607a  608

605	32¢ Sailing Ships, sheetlet of 25	18.00
606	60¢ Olympic Games Centenary, 4 attached	6.50
607	55¢ History of the Marshall Islands, sheetlet of 12	16.00
608	32¢ Elvis Presley First #1 Hit 40th Anniversary	2.00
609	50¢ The Palance Museum, Shenyang souvenir sheet	1.50

610  611a 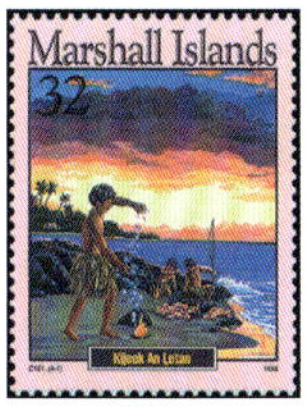 612a

610	32¢ James Dean	1.85
611	60¢ Automobiles, sheet of 8	13.00
612	32¢ Island Legends 1996, 4 attached	3.20

613a  614a  615

613	55¢ Steam Locomotives, sheet of 12	16.00
614	32¢ Marine Life (Taipei '96), miniature sheet of 4	3.20
615	$3 Stick Chart, Canoe & Flag of the Republic	7.35

616  617a  618a

616	32¢ Christmas 1996	1.00
617	32¢ World's Legendary Biplanes, sheet of 25	18.00
618	32¢ Native Crafts, 4 attached	3.20

620 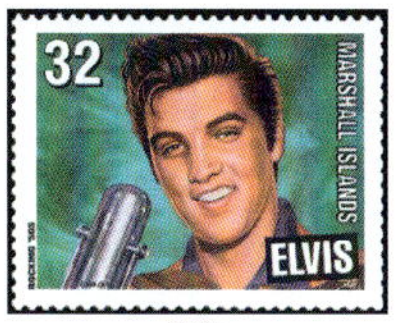 622a  623

1997

619	60¢ New Year 1997 (Year of the Ox)	1.45
620-21	32¢-60¢ Amata Kabua, President of Marshall Islands, set of 2	2.50
622	32¢ Elvis Presley, strip of 3	2.80
623-24	32¢ Hong Kong '97, 2 sheets of 2	2.80

627a 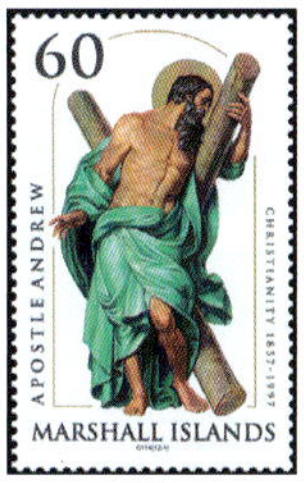 625a  628

625	60¢ The Twelve Apostles, sheet of 12	17.75
626	$3 Rubens "The Last Supper", souvenir sheet	7.50
627	60¢ First Decade of the 20th Century, sheet of 15	22.50
628	60¢ Deng Xiaoping (1904-97), Chinese Leader	1.55
629	32¢ Native Crafts (1996), 4 attached, self-adhesive, Die-Cut	4.65
630	32¢ Native Crafts (1996), 4 attached, self-adhesive, perf.	5.25
631-37	50¢-$1 Anniv. 1st US & Marshall Islands Stamps, booklet of 7	11.40

638  640a  641a

638	16¢ Bristle-Thighed Curlew, strip of 4	3.80
639	50¢ Bank of China, Hong Kong, souvenir sheet	1.80
640	32¢ Canoes, strip of 4	3.80
641	32¢ Legendary Aircraft, sheet of 25	20.00

642a 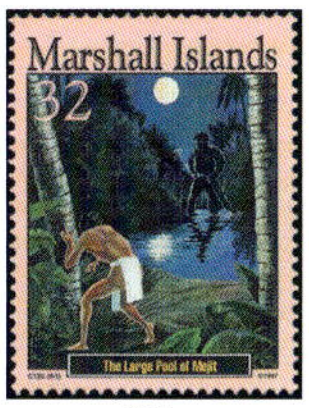 643a

642	32¢ "Old Ironsides" Bicentennial	.95
643	32¢ Island Legends, 4 attached	3.50
644	60¢ Marine Life, 4 attached	6.00
645	60¢ Princess Diana, strip of 3	5.00

646a  649a  647-48

646	60¢ Events of the 20th Century, 1910-19, sheetlet of 15	22.00
647-48	32¢ Christmas, Angel, pair	1.85
649	20¢ US State-Named Warships, sheet of 50	30.00
650	50¢ Treasure Ship, Shanghai '97, souvenir sheet	1.45

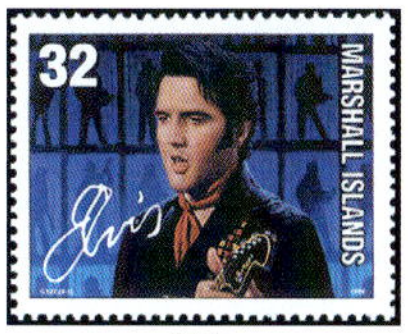

652a  654a  653a  655a

1998

651	60¢ Year of the Tiger, souvenir sheet	1.80
652	32¢ Elvis Presley's 1968 Television Special, strip of 3	2.90
653	32¢ Sea Shells, strip of 4	3.00
654	60¢ Events of the 20th Century, 1920-29, sheetlet of 15	22.00
655	32¢ Canoes of the Pacific, sheetlet of 8	7.00

665  670  667a

656	60¢ Berlin Airlift, 4 attached	6.00
657	60¢ Events of the 20th Century, 1930-39, sheetlet of 15	24.00
658-64	60¢-$3 Tsar Nicholas II, bklt of 7 (60¢ x 6, $3 x 1)	17.00
665	32¢ Babe Ruth	.95
666	32¢ Legendary Aircraft of the US Navy, sheetlet of 25	19.00
667	60¢ Chevrolet Automobiles, sheetlet of 8	12.00
668	33¢ Marshalese Language and Alphabet, sheetlet of 24	18.00
669	33¢ New Buildings in Marshall Islands, strip of 3	2.80
670	32¢ Midnight Angel	.95
671-77	60¢-$3 John Glenn's Return to Space, bklt of 7 (60¢ x 6, $3 x 1)	17.00
678	$3.20 Airplane delivering supplies, souvenir sheet	7.80
679	60¢ Events of the 20th Century, 1940-49, sheetlet of 15	23.00
680	33¢ Warships, sheetlet of 25	20.00

SCOTT NO.	DESCRIPTION	UNUSED F/NH

682

699a

701a

1999

681	60¢ Year of the Rabbit, souvenir sheet	2.50
682-89	1¢-¢10 Birds (8)	28.80
690	33¢ Canoes of the Pacific, sheetlet of 8	7.00
691-98	same, self-adhesive, block of 10 (691-97 x 1, 698 x 3)	8.00
699	60¢ Great American Indian Chiefs, sheetlet of 12	18.00
700	33¢ Marshall Islands National Flag	.95
701	33¢ Flowers of the Pacific, 6 attached	5.50
702	60¢ Events of the 20th Century, 1950-59, sheetlet of 15	23.00
703	$1.20 HMAS Australia, souvenir sheet	3.00
704	33¢ Elvis Presley	1.00
705	60¢ IBRA '99 Exhibition, sheetlet of 4	6.00

706

706	33¢ Marshall Islands Constitution, 20th Anniversary	.95

707a

714

713a

707	33¢ Marshall Islands Postal Service, 15th Anniversary, 4 attached	4.50
708	33¢ Legendary Aircraft, sheetlet of 25	20.00
709	$1 PHILEXFRANCE '99, souvenir sheet	2.80
710	60¢ Tanker Alrehab, souvenir sheet	1.75
711	60¢ Events of the 20th Century, 1960-69, sheetlet of 15	22.00
712	33¢ 1st Manned Moonlanding, 30th Anniversary, sheetlet of 3	2.80
713	33¢ Ships, 4 attached	3.75
714-21	5¢-$5 Birds, set of 8	30.00

722

728a

722	33¢ Christmas	.95
723	60¢ Events of the 20th Century, 1970-79, sheetlet of 15	22.00
724-25	33¢ Millenium, 2 attached	1.85

729a

2000

726	60¢ Events of the 20th Century, 1980-89, sheetlet of 15	22.00
727	60¢ New Year 2000 (Year of the Dragon), souvenir sheet	1.75
728	33¢ Legendary Aircraft, sheetlet of 25	20.00
729	33¢ Roses, 6 attached	5.80
730	60¢ Events of the 20th Century, 1990-99, sheetlet of 15	22.50

731a

739a

731	33¢ Pandas, 6 attached	5.80
732-38	1¢-42¢ American Presidents, 7 sheetlets of 6	20.00
739	33¢ First Zeppelin Flight, 4 attached	3.50

740

740-46	60¢-$1 Sir Winston Churchill, bklt of 7 (60¢ x 6, $1 x 1)	14.00

747a

747	33¢ US Military 225th Anniversary, 3 attached	2.80

748a

748	33¢ National Government, 4 attached	3.50
749	60¢ Ships, 6 attached	9.00

750a

752a

750	60¢ Queen Mother's 100th birthday, 4 attached	7.00
751	33¢ Reef Life, sheetlet of 8	6.95
752	60¢ Butterflies, sheetlet of 12	18.00
753	33¢ Reunification of Germany, 10th Anniversary	.95

754a

754	33¢ Submarines, 4 attached	3.80
755	33¢ Christmas	.85
756	60¢-$1 Sun Yat-sen, bklt of 7 (60¢ x 6, $1 x 1)	12.00

758

2001

757	80¢ Year of the Snake, souvenir sheet	2.80
758	34¢ Carnations, stamp + label	1.00
759	34¢ Violets, stamp + label	1.00
760	34¢ Jonquil, stamp + label	1.00
761	34¢ Sweet Pea, stamp + label	1.00
762	34¢ Lily of the Valley, stamp + label	1.00
763	34¢ Rose, stamp + label	1.00
764	34¢ Larkspur, stamp + label	1.00
765	34¢ Poppy, stamp + label	1.00
766	34¢ Aster, stamp + label	1.00
767	34¢ Marigold, stamp + label	1.00
768	34¢ Chrysanthemum, stamp + label	1.00
769	34¢ Poinsettia, stamp + label	1.00

770

772

770-71	$5-$10 Sailing Canoes	39.00
772-75	34¢-$1 Famous People, set of 4	8.00
776	80¢ Butterflies, sheetlet of 12	24.00

777a

778a

777	34¢ Fairy Tales, 7 varieties attached	7.00
778	34¢ Watercraft Racing, 4 attached	3.80
779	80¢ Manned Spacecraft 40th Anniv, 4 attached	8.50

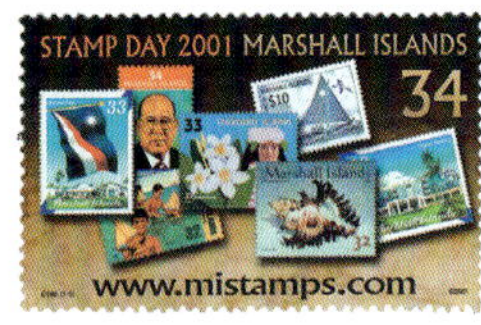
780a

783a

780	34¢ Stamp Day	1.00
781	80¢ American Achievements in Space, 4 attached	8.80
782	34¢ Marine Life, 4 attached	3.75
783	34¢ Sports, 4 attached	5.75
784	57¢ Atlan Anien	1.20

785a

788a

785	34¢ Zodiac Signs, sheetlet of 12	12.00
786	80¢ Phila Nippon 2001, sheetlet of 12	24.00
787	80¢ US Naval Heroes in WWII Pacific Theater, sheetlet of 9	18.50
788	34¢ Classic Cars, 8 attached	8.00
789	34¢-¢1 Remembrance ... of Sept. 11, bklt of 7 (34¢ x 6, $1 x 1)	9.00
790	34¢ Christmas, 4 attached	3.75
791	80¢ Airplanes, 10 attached	20.00

798a

2002

SCOTT NO.	DESCRIPTION	UNUSED F/NH
792	80¢ Year of the Horse, souvenir sheet	2.00
793	34¢ Shells, 6 attached	5.50
794	80¢ Reign of Queen Elizabeth, 50th Anniv., souvenir sheet	2.00
795	34¢ United We Stand	1.00
796	34¢ Classic Cars, 8 attached	7.50
797	34¢ Corals, 4 attached	4.00
798	80¢ Butterflies, sheet of 12	24.00

802a  804

SCOTT NO.	DESCRIPTION	UNUSED F/NH
799	34¢ Horses in Art, sheet of 12	10.00
800	80¢ Horses in Art, souvenir sheet	1.80
801	37¢ Russian Fairy Tale The Frog Princess, sheet of 12	12.80
802	80¢ Carousel Figures, 4 attached	8.00
803	37¢ Birds, sheet of 16	15.80
804	80¢ Benjamin Franklin, 2 attached	4.00
805	37¢ Sea Turtles, 4 attached	4.00
806	80¢ Intl. Federation of Stamp Dealers, 50 Anniv., 6 attached	12.50
807	37¢ U.S. Navy Ships, 6 attached	5.80

808a  812a

SCOTT NO.	DESCRIPTION	UNUSED F/NH
808	23¢ Insects and Spiders, sheet of 20	12.00
809	80¢ Classic Cars, 8 attached	16.00
810	80¢ Queen Mother, redrawn, 4 attached	8.50
811	80¢ Regal Princess Cruise Ship, souvenir sheet	1.80
812	80¢ World War I Heroes, 8 attached	16.00
813	37¢ Snowman cookies, 2 attached	1.80

815  817

2003

SCOTT NO.	DESCRIPTION	UNUSED F/NH
814	80¢ Year of the Ram, souvenir sheet	2.25
815	60¢ UN Membership, 12th Anniv.	1.75
816	50¢ Folktales, block of 4	5.50
817-19	37¢-$13.65 Famous People	40.00
820	37¢ Marshallese Culture, block of 8	7.00

821a

SCOTT NO.	DESCRIPTION	UNUSED F/NH
821	80¢ Butterflies, sheetlet of 12	30.00
822	37¢ Powered Flight Centenary, blk of 10	14.00
823	37¢ Classic Cars, 8 attached	7.50
824	37¢ Marshallese Culture, part 2, 8 attached	7.50
825	37¢ Christmas Ornaments, 4 attached	3.80

827a  833a

2004

SCOTT NO.	DESCRIPTION	UNUSED F/NH
826	$1 Year of the Monkey, souvenir sheet	2.80
827	37¢ Ships, type of 2002, strip of 3	2.80
828	37¢ Classic Cars, type of 2001, 8 attached	7.50
829	37¢ Greetings, sheet of 8	7.50
830-32	37¢ Marshall Islands Postal Service 20th Anniv., set of 3	8.00
833	37¢ Lewis & Clark Expedition, strip of 3	3.75

834a  837a

SCOTT NO.	DESCRIPTION	UNUSED F/NH
834	37¢ D-Day, 60th Anniversary, 4 attached	4.35
835	37¢ Marine Life, 2 attached	2.00
836	60¢ President Ronald Reagan	2.00
837	37¢ First Manned Moon Landing, 35th Anniv., 4 attached	3.80
838	37¢ Festival of the Arts, sheet of 12	11.80
839	23¢ Aircraft, sheet of 50	29.50
840	37¢ Lewis & Clark Expedition, type of 2004, strip of 3	4.75

841  842a  844a

SCOTT NO.	DESCRIPTION	UNUSED F/NH
841	37¢ John Wayne	1.75
842	$1 23rd UPU Congress, Bucharest, Romania, sheet of 4	10.00
843	37¢ Marine Life, sheet of 10	10.00
844	37¢ Christmas, sheet of 9	8.00
845	37¢ Lewis & Clark Expedition, type of 2004, strip of 3	3.75
846	37¢ Battle of the Bulge, 60th Anniv., block of 4	5.75

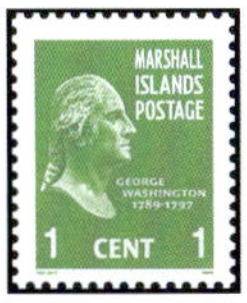

847a 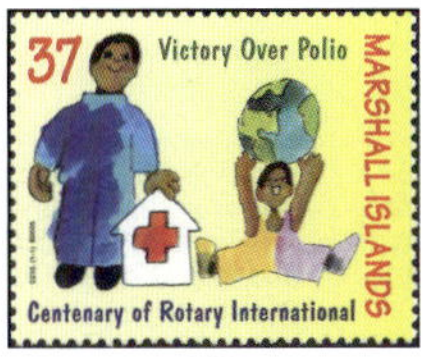 849

2005

SCOTT NO.	DESCRIPTION	UNUSED F/NH
847	1¢-$1 United States Presidents, sheet of 45	39.00
848	$1 Year of the Rooster, souvenir sheet	3.82
849	37¢ Rotary International, Centennial	1.80
850-53	37¢-$1 Hibiscus Varieties, set of 4	8.25

854a  856

SCOTT NO.	DESCRIPTION	UNUSED F/NH
854	$1.56 Turtles souvenir sheet of 2	7.25
855	Lewis & Clark Expedition, type of 2004, strip of 3	3.85
856	37¢ American First Day Cover Society, 50th Anniversary, 4 attached	4.75

857a  860  858a

SCOTT NO.	DESCRIPTION	UNUSED F/NH
857	37¢ VE Day, 60th Anniversary, 4 attached	5.00
858	37¢ Pope John Paul II, 5 attached	5.75
859	37¢-80¢ United Nations, 60th Anniversary, 2 attached	3.80
860-63	1¢-$4 Hibiscus Varieties, set of 4	14.00

864a  865a

SCOTT NO.	DESCRIPTION	UNUSED F/NH
864	37¢ Space Shuttles, 5 attached	5.75
865	37¢ Classic Cars Type of 2001, 8 attached	9.00

866a  867a

SCOTT NO.	DESCRIPTION	UNUSED F/NH
866	37¢ VJ Day, 60th Anniv., 4 attached	6.00
867	37¢ Lewis & Clark Expedition, type of 2004, strip of 3	4.00
868	37¢ Battle of Trafalgar, Bicentennial, sheet of 25	34.00
869	37¢ Battle of Trafalgar, souvenir sheet	2.00

870a  872a  871a  873a

SCOTT NO.	DESCRIPTION	UNUSED F/NH
870	37¢ Christmas, 4 attached	5.00
871	37¢ Lewis & Clark Expedition, type of 2004, strip of 3	3.75
872	37¢ Marshallese Culture, 5 attached	5.50
873	48¢ Benjamin Franklin, sheet of 9	13.50

875 877

2006

SCOTT NO.	DESCRIPTION	UNUSED F/NH
874	$1 Year of the Dog, souvenir sheet	3.95
875	39¢ Love	1.50
876	84¢ Butterflies, sheet of 12	25.50
877	39¢ First Spaceflight by Yuri Gagarin	1.75

880 883a

SCOTT NO.	DESCRIPTION	UNUSED F/NH
878-81	10¢-$4.05 Hibiscus Varieties, set of 4	17.00
882	1/2¢-50¢ Washington 2006 World Philatelic Exhibition, souvenir sheet of 20	9.00
883	39¢ Sharks, 4 attached	5.80
884	39¢ Operations Crossroads, sheet of 6 stamps + 6 labels	7.50
885	39¢ Lewis and Clark, 2 attached	3.00
886	39¢ Marshallese Culture, 5 attached	7.00
887	39¢ Ships, sheet of 10	10.00
888	39¢ Christmas	1.10

2007

SCOTT NO.	DESCRIPTION	UNUSED F/NH
889	39¢ Greetings, 4 attached	5.00
890	$1 Year of the Pig, souvenir sheet	4.00
891	39¢ Railway Passenger Trains, 6 attached	7.00
892	39¢ Dolphins, block of 4	5.50
893-96	26¢-61¢ Fish	4.75
897	41¢ Space Age miniature sheet of 10	14.00
898	41¢ Scouting block of 4	5.25
899	41¢ Purple Heart	1.75
900	41¢ United States Air Force, sheet of 25	31.00
901	41¢ Marshallese Culture strip of 5	6.25

902c 903a

906a 919

SCOTT NO.	DESCRIPTION	UNUSED F/NH
902	41¢ Yacht Registry, sheet of 10	11.50
903	41¢ Santa Claus block of 4	5.25

2008

SCOTT NO.	DESCRIPTION	UNUSED F/NH
904	41¢ Bouquets, sheet of 25	25.00
905	26¢ Chinese New Year, sheet of 12	7.50
906	41¢ U.S. Lighthouses, block of 6	16.50
907	41¢ Wild Cats, sheet of 12	13.00
908	41¢ Ships, sheet of 12	13.00
909	41¢ Constellations, sheet of 20	20.00
910	42¢ U.S. Marine Corps, sheet of 10	10.00
911-23	1¢-$16.50 Tropical Fish, set of 13	75.00
	911 1¢ Banded Butterflyfish	
	912 3¢ Damselfish	
	913 5¢ Pink Skunk Clownfish	
	914 27¢ Copperband Butterflyfish	
	915 42¢ Threadfin Butterflyfish	
	916 60¢ Beau Gregory Damselfish	
	917 61¢ Porkfish	
	918 63¢ Goatfish	
	919 94¢ Common Longnose Butterflyfish	
	920 $1 Royal Gramma	
	921 $4.80 Longfin Bannerfish	
	922 $5 Blue-Striped Blenny	
	923 $16.50 Emperor Butterflyfish	
924	42¢ Birds, sheet of 25	24.00
925	42¢ Dinosaurs, sheet of 12	13.00
926	42¢ Fishing Flies, sheet of 5	5.15
927	42¢ Wild West Portraits, sheet of 16	20.00

928d 932a

SCOTT NO.	DESCRIPTION	UNUSED F/NH
928	42¢ Endangered Species, block of 6	6.75
929	42¢ Marshallese Culture Horiz., strip of 5	5.00
930	42¢ Spacecraft and the Solar System, sheet of 10	11.00
931	42¢ Christmas, sheet of 8	8.00
932	42¢ Owls, block of 6	6.25
933	$1 First U.S. Airmail Stamp Souvenir Sheet	2.50

934b 937L 938g

2009

SCOTT NO.	DESCRIPTION	UNUSED F/NH
934	42¢ Flower Bouquets, sheet of 25	26.00
935	$ Abraham Lincoln, block of 4	9.50
936	42¢ Arctic Explorers, block of 4	4.50
937	44¢ Famous American Indians, sheet of 12	13.00
938	44¢ US Military Air Heroes, sheet of 16	18.00

939 945e

949c

SCOTT NO.	DESCRIPTION	UNUSED F/NH
939	44¢ Marshall Islands Postal Service, souvenir sheet	1.25
940-44	28¢-$1.22 Marine Life	10.00
945	44¢ Constellations, sheet of 20	23.00
946	44¢ Rose Varieties, strip of 5	5.75
947	44¢ Hot Air Balloons, strip of 5	5.75
948	44¢ 2009 Solar Eclipse, strip of 3	3.75
949	44¢ Steam Locomotives, block of 6	7.00
950	44¢ Marshallese Culture, horiz. strip of 5	5.75
951	44¢ Birds of Prey, block of 8	11.00
952	44¢ Dogs, strip of 5	6.00
953	98¢ Dogs, sheet of 4	11.00
954	44¢ Christmas Wreaths, horiz. strip of 5	6.00
955	44¢ Endangered Species, sheet of 8	16.00
956	44¢ Prehistoric Animals, strip of 5	6.00
957	44¢ Shells, block of 4	5.80

965 969b

2010

SCOTT NO.	DESCRIPTION	UNUSED F/NH
958	44¢ Signs of the Zodiac, sheet of 12	16.00
959	44¢ Waterfowl, sheet of 8	10.00
960	44¢ Famous American Indiana, sheet of 12	16.00
961	44¢ Boy Scouts of America, block of 4	5.00
962	98¢ Shells, block of 4	10.00
963	44¢ Astronomers, strip of 5	5.25
964	44¢ Constellations, sheet of 20	25.00
965	28¢ Mandarin Goby	1.80
966	44¢ Marshallese Alphabet, sheet of 24	27.00
967	44¢ Statue of Liberty, sheet of 9	8.00
968	44¢ Classic Cars, sheet of 5	5.50
969	44¢ Carousel Horses, block of 6	6.50
970	44¢ US Warships of WWII, sheet of 15	14.00
971-972	28¢ -98¢ Shells	2.80
973	44¢ Marshallese Culture Strip of 5	4.00
974	44¢ Santa Claus, strip of 4	3.80
975	44¢ President John F. Kennedy, sheet of 6	6.50
976	44¢ Orchids, sheet of 9	8.50
977	44¢ Butterflies, sheet of 12	12.00

986a 1010l

2011

SCOTT NO.	DESCRIPTION	UNUSED F/NH
978	44¢ Tulips, block of 6	6.50
979	98¢ Year of the Rabbit, sheet of 4	9.50
980	44¢ Ronald Reagan, strip of 5	5.50
981	44¢ Firsts in Flight, strip of 5	5.50
982-85	1¢-$10 Turtles	25.00
986	29¢ Corals and Fish, Horizontal Strip of 5	3.75
987	44¢ Famous American Indians, sheet of 12	13.00
988	44¢ Firsts in Flight, strip of 5	5.50
989	$1 First Man in Space, strip of 3	7.50
990	44¢ Wedding of Prince William, sheet of 15	16.00
991	44¢ Apostles of Jesus, sheet of 12	13.00
992	44¢ Garden Life, sheet of 12	13.00
993	98¢ Antartic Treaty, sheet of 9	22.00
994	44¢ Firsts in Flights, strip of 5	5.50
995	$4.95 Outrigger Canoes	12.00
996	$10.95 Plumeria Flowers	26.00
997	$13.95 Marshall Island Flag	34.00
998	$14.95 Coconut Palm Trees and Coconuts	36.00
999	$18.30 Micronesian Pigeons	44.00
1000	$29.95 Triton's Trumpet	73.00
1001	44¢ End of Space Shuttle Missions, sheet of 7	8.00
1002	44¢ Marshallese Culture, strip of 5	5.50
1003	44¢ Fish, sheet of 12	13.00
1004	44¢ Firsts in Flight, horizontal strip of 5	5.50
1005-08	64¢ National Buildings & Symbols, set of 4	6.50
1009	$4.95 Anniversary UN Admission S/S	12.00
1010	Christmas, sheet of 12	19.00
1011	98¢ Compact of Free Association, sheet of 3	7.50

1013a 1018a

1026a 1041a

2012

SCOTT NO.	DESCRIPTION	UNUSED F/NH
1012	44¢ Firsts in Flight, horizontal strip of 5	5.50
1013	44¢ Hanukkah, block of 8	8.75
1014	44¢ American Entry into WWII, sheet of 10 + labels	11.00
1015	44¢ Stained Glass Windows, sheet of 9	9.75
1016	45¢ Rhododendrens, sheet of 9	10.00
1017	45¢ Marine Life	1.25
1018	$1.05 Year of the Dragon, sheet of 4	10.00
1019	32¢ Whales, strip of 4	3.25
1020-25	Priority & Express Mail Stamps	240.00
1020	$5.15 Chuuk War Canoe	12.00
1021	$11.35 Cymbidium Orchid	26.00
1022	$15.45 Arrival of Early Inhabitants	36.00
1023	$16.95 Mandarinfish	39.00
1024	$18.95 Hibiscus Rosa-sinensis	45.00
1025	$38 Seahorses	89.00
1026	$1.05 Queen Elizabeth II, sheet of 6	16.00
1027-28	85¢ - $1.05 Birds	4.75
1029	45¢ Chinese Terra Cotta Warriors, block of 6	6.50
1030	45¢ Inuits, block of 6	6.50
1031	45¢ Creation of Tobolar Coconut Twine and Rope, strip of 4	4.50
1032	45¢ Scientists, sheet of 20	22.00
1033	45¢ Clouds, sheet of 15	16.50
1034	45¢ Birds, block of 10	11.50
1035	45¢ WWII, sheet of 10	11.50
1036	45¢ Introduction of Euro Currency, sheet of 10	13.50
1037	45¢ Civil War, sheet of 5	6.75
1038	45¢ American Indian Dances, block of 6	6.75
1039	$4.95 USSS Constitution and HMS Guerrire S/S	13.50
1040	45¢ Twelve Days of Christmas, sheet of 12	12.00
1041	45¢ Locamotives, sheet of 50	56.00
1042	$5.15 Chuuk War Canoe	13.00

1056c

1043h

1055g

2013

SCOTT NO.	DESCRIPTION	UNUSED F/NH
1043	45¢ Birds of the World, sheet of 10	10.00
1044	46¢ Australia 225th Anniversary, sheet of 10	11.00
1045-53	33¢-$44.95 Marine Life	265.00
1054	$1.10 Year of the Snake sheet of 4	10.00
1055	46¢ Camellias block of 8	8.00
1056	46¢ Birds, sheet of 10	10.00
1057	46¢ Birds, sheet of 10	10.00
1058	46¢ Birds, sheet of 10	10.00

1059a

1060a

SCOTT NO.	DESCRIPTION	UNUSED F/NH
1059	33¢ Cats strip of 6	4.50
1060	46¢ Presidential Medals sheet of 45	45.00
1061	$2 "Ich Bin Ein Berliner" speech by Pres. Kennedy	4.50
1062	46¢ British Steam Locomotives sheet of 10	10.00

1063a

1070a

SCOTT NO.	DESCRIPTION	UNUSED F/NH
1063	46¢ Indian Headressses strip of 5	5.50
1064	46¢ American Civil Rights Movement sheet of 10	10.00
1065	46¢ World War II sheet of 10	10.00
1066	46¢ Traditional Marshallese Children's Games	4.50
1067	46¢ Restarting Space Shuttle Program sheet of 6	6.50
1068	46¢ WWII Aircraft sheet of 25	25.00
1069	46¢ Christmas Block of 6	6.50
1070	46¢ Gettysburg Address sheet of 5	5.50
1071	$2 Thanksgiving S/S	4.75

1074

2014

SCOTT NO.	DESCRIPTION	UNUSED F/NH
1072	46¢ Military Aircraft Diagrams sheet of 15	15.00
1073	$5.60 Marshall Islands Postal Service Authority S/S	12.50
1074-76	34¢-$1.15 Shells set of 3	5.00
1077	$1.15 Year of the Horse Sheet of 4	11.00
1078	49¢ Garden Insects Block of 10	11.00
1079	$1.15 Castles in Great Britain, Strip of 4	10.50
1080	49¢ Historic Flags of US, Sheet of 15 with Labels	16.00
1081	49¢ Traditional Eurpoean Costumes, Sheet of 20	22.00
1082	49¢ Military Aircraft Diagrams, Sheet of 15	16.00
1083	4¢ Hawkwinged Conch	0.50
1084	$19.99 Filled Dogwinkle	42.00
1085	49¢ Trees, Block of 6	7.00
1086	$5.50 Opening of Panama Canal, S/S	12.50
1087	49¢ Amphibians and Reptiles, Sheet of 12	13.00

1088

1100c

SCOTT NO.	DESCRIPTION	UNUSED F/NH
1088	$5.60 Writing of the Star-Spangled Banner, S/S	12.50
1089	49¢ World War II, Sheet of 10 plus 10 Labels	11.00
1090-94	Shells, Set of 5 Singles	105.00
1090	$5.75 Shell	12.50
1091	$5.95 Shell	13.00
1092	$6.10 Shell	14.00
1093	$12.65 Shell	27.50
1094	$17.90 Shell	38.00
1095	49¢ Move Monster, Block of 10	11.00
1096	49¢ Christmas, Block of 6	7.00
1097	49¢ Seahorses, Strip of 4	5.00
1098	49¢ Military Aircraft Diagrams, Sheet of 15	16.00
1099	49¢ Space Adventure for Children, Strip of 4	5.00
1100	49¢ Flowers, Block of 10	11.00

2015

SCOTT NO.	DESCRIPTION	UNUSED F/NH
1101	49¢ Greetings, Block of 6	7.00
1102	34¢ Dinosaurs, Strip of 4	3.25
1103	$1-$2.50 Reef Life, Miniature Sheet of 7	18.00
1104	49¢ Berries, Strip of 5	6.00
1105	$1.15 Year of the Ram, Sheet of 4	10.50
1106-09	49¢ Rays, Set of 4 Singles	4.00
1110	49¢ Seashells, Strip of 4	4.25
1111	49¢ Canoes, Strip of 4	4.25
1112	49¢ Early European Navigators, Strip of 4	4.25
1113	49¢ Sea Wonders, Sheet of 15	15.00
1114	$5.60 Penny Black, Souvenir Sheet	12.00
1115	$5.60 End of the Civil War, Souvenir Sheet	12.00
1116	49¢ Postal Relics, Sheet of 12	12.75
1117	49¢ Winged Wonders, Sheet of 15	15.25
1118a	$3 Apollo & Soyuz Joint Mission, Souvenir Sheet	6.75
1119-22	$1.20 National Icons, Set of 4	10.25

1123a

1124f

SCOTT NO.	DESCRIPTION	UNUSED F/NH
1123	49¢ WWII 70th Anniversary, 1945, Sheet of 10	10.50
1124	$1.00 Best of Marshall Islands, Souvenir Pane of 7	14.75

1127a

SCOTT NO.	DESCRIPTION	UNUSED F/NH
1125	$5.60 25th Anniversary of German Reunification, souvenir Sheet	12.00
1126	49¢ Land Wonders, Sheet of 15	16.00
1127	49¢ Christmas Snowflakes, Sheet of 10	10.50
1128	$1.20 Christmas Snowflakes, Sheet of 4	10.25
1129	49¢ Marshall Islands Legends, Sheet of 16	15.25

1130a

1133b

2016

SCOTT NO.	DESCRIPTION	UNUSED F/NH
1130	49¢ The Art of Haiku, Sheet of 20	21.25
1131	$4 First Concorde Commercial Flight, Souvenir Sheet	8.75
1132	$1.20 Year of the Monkey, Souvenir Sheet	10.25
1133	49¢ Wildlife, Sheet of 10	10.50
1134	49¢ Great Seals of the U.S. I, sheet of 10	10.50
1135	49¢ Great Seals of the U.S. II, sheet of 10	10.50
1136	49¢ Great Seals of the U.S. III, sheet of 10	10.50
1137	49¢ Great Seals of the U.S. IV, sheet of 10	10.50

1138b

1142d

1148f

SCOTT NO.	DESCRIPTION	UNUSED F/NH
1138	49¢ Great Seals of the U.S. V, sheet of 10	10.50
1139	90¢ Queen Elizabeth II 90th Birthday, sheet of 6	11.25
1140	49¢ Semaphore Signals, sheet of 30	30.00
1141	49¢ Art of Howard Koslow, sheet of 20	21.25
1142	49¢ Peace Doves, block of 6	6.00
1143	98¢ Marshall Islands Constitution Commemorative, souvenir sheet	2.00
1144	$3 Marshall Islands Sovereignty 30th Anniversary, souvenir sheet	6.25
1145	49¢ Christmas Ornaments, sheet of 10	10.50
1146	$1.20 Christmas Ornaments, sheet of 4	10.00
1147	$5.75 Pearl Harbor, 75th Anniversary, souvenir sheet	12.00
1148	49¢ U.S. National Parks, sheet of 10	10.00

1149a

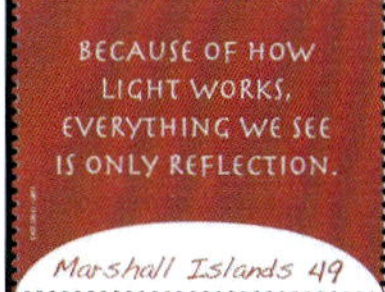

1151a

2017

SCOTT NO.	DESCRIPTION	UNUSED F/NH
1149	$1.20 Year of the Rooster, souvenir sheet of 4	10.00
1150	49¢ Celebration Photography, sheet of 10	10.25
1151	49¢ The Art of Haiku II, sheet of 20	21.25

1152a

1166a

SCOTT NO.	DESCRIPTION	UNUSED F/NH
1152	49¢ Flora, sheet of 10	10.00
1153	49¢ China Clipper, sheet of 6	6.00
1154	49¢ Natural Majesties, sheet of 10	10.25
1155	49¢ Jazz and Blues Instruments, sheet of 10	10.25
1156	49¢ U.S. National Parks II, sheet of 10	10.00
1157	$1 100th Anniversary of John F. Kennedy's birth, souvenir sheet	2.10
1158	$1.50 150th Anniversary of Frank Lloyd Wright's birth, souvenir sheet	3.10
1159	49¢ World Youth, sheet of 20	21.25
1160	49¢ Atolls of Marshall Islands, sheet of 10	10.25
1161	49¢ Honoring the Art of Paul Calle, sheet of 20	21.25
1162	49¢ Steamships, sheet of 10	10.25
1163	49¢ Fire Dancers, sheet of 6	6.00
1164	$5 Launch of QE2, souvenir sheet	10.50
1165	49¢ Eyes of Nature, sheet of 10	10.25
1166	49¢ Christmas Nativity, sheet of 6	6.00
1167	$1.20 Christmas International, sheet of 4	10.25
1168	49¢ U.S. National Parks II, sheet of 10	10.00
1169	49¢ Recovered Birds, sheet of 10	10.00

1172

1175a

2018

SCOTT NO.	DESCRIPTION	UNUSED F/NH
1170-72	1¢-$10 Marine Life, set of 3	21.25
1173	$18.90 Shortin Mako Shark	38.00
1174	$7 The Royal Engagement, souvenir sheet 2	26.00
1175	50¢-$3.50 Year of the Dog, sheet of 4	16.50

1179c

1191

SCOTT NO.	DESCRIPTION	UNUSED F/NH
1176	$2 Winter Olympics, South Korea, sheet of 6 . .	25.00
1177	50¢-$1.75 Shark Sanctuary, sheet of 6.	19.50
1178	$1-$3 Queen Elizabeth II Sapphire Jubilee, sheet of 4 .	16.50
1179	$1.35 Grand Canyon Centennial, sheet of 6 . . .	16.50
1180	$4 Grand Canyon, souvenir sheet.	8.00
1181	$2 Cats, sheet of 4	16.50
1182	$4 Cats, souvenir sheet.	8.00
1183	$1-$2 Visit to Israel President Trump, sheet of 6 .	18.50
1184	$2 Elvis Presley, sheet of 3	12.50
1185	$2 Elvis Presley, sheet of 4	16.50
1186-89	$4 Elvis Presley, set of 4 souvenir sheets	34.00
1190-95	50¢-$24.90 Butterflies, set of 6	135.00

1199d

1202f

1206a

SCOTT NO.	DESCRIPTION	UNUSED F/NH
1196	$1-$4 The Louve Museum, sheet of 4.	21.25
1197	50¢-$2 Seabirds of the Pacific, sheet of 4.	15.00
1198	$2 Birth of Prince Louis, sheet of 4	16.50
1199	$2 Whales, sheet of 4	16.50
1200	$4 Whales, souvenir sheet	8.00
1201	$1.60 First Ladies of the U.S., Barbara Bush, sheet of 5 .	16.50
1202	$1.40 Transcontinental Railroad, sheet of 6 . . .	18.00
1203	$4 Transcontinental Railroad, souvenir sheet . . .	8.00
1204	$1-$3 Royal Wedding Prince Harry & Meghan Markle, sheet of 4	16.50
1205	$5 Royal Wedding, souvenir sheet	10.50
1206	$2 Celestial Wonders-Comets, sheet of 3.	12.50
1207	$2 Peace Summit of President Trump & Kim Jong Un, sheet of 3	12.50
1208-09	50¢-$2 Star Trek Cats, set of 2 sheets of 6. . . .	30.00
1210	$2 Praga 2018 World Stamp Expo, sheet of 4 .	16.50

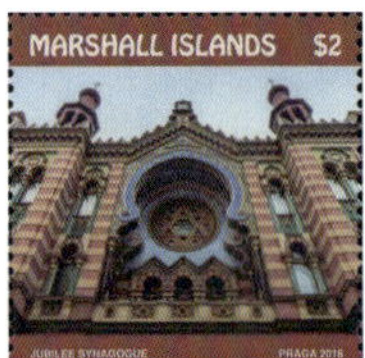

1211d

1212a

1219d

SCOTT NO.	DESCRIPTION	UNUSED F/NH
1211	$2 Praga 2018 World Stamp Expo, Synagogues, sheet of 4 .	16.50
1212	10¢-$1.20 Happy Lunar New Year, sheet of 12 .	16.50
1213	$2 Year of the Boar, souvenir sheet	4.00
1214	$5 20 Years of Diplomatic Relations, sheet of 4 .	41.00
1215-16	$10 Diplomatic Relations, set of 2 souvenir sheets of 2 .	82.00
1217-18B	50¢-$18.90 Christmas Toys, set of 4.	43.00
1219	50¢-$1.75 Owls of the World, sheet of 6.	14.50
1220-21	$1-$2 WWI Razzle Dazzle Ships, set of 2 sheets of 3 .	33.00
1222	$2 Gandhi, 150th Birthday Anniv., sheet of 4 . .	16.50

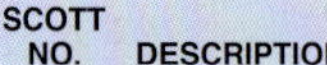

1225d

1233

2019

SCOTT NO.	DESCRIPTION	UNUSED F/NH
1223	$2 Leonardo Da Vinci., sheet of 4.	16.50
1224	$4 Leonardo Da Vinci., souvenir sheet	8.00
1225	$1.50 Birds of Marshall Islands, sheets of 6 . . .	18.50
1226	$5 Birds of Marshall Islands, souvenir sheet. . .	10.50
1227-28	$1.20-$1.50 Colorful Fish, set of 2 sheets of 6 .	35.00
1229-33	5¢-$1.05 Marine Life, set of 5	4.50

1234a

1239

SCOTT NO.	DESCRIPTION	UNUSED F/NH
1234	$1.20 Star Trek Key Comics, sheets of 6	15.00
1235	$1.10 Apollo 11, sheet of 5	12.00
1236	$4 Apollo 11, souvenir sheet	8.00
1237	$2 Jellyfish, sheet of 3.	12.50
1238	$5 Jellyfish, souvenir sheet	10.50
1239	$2 Sacred Kingfisher, sheet of 4	16.50
1240	$5 Sacred Kingfisher, souvenir sheet	10.50
1241	$2 Queen Victoria, 200th, sheet of 4.	16.50
1242	$5 Queen Victoria, 200th, souvenir sheet	10.50

1249

1258a

1254d

SCOTT NO.	DESCRIPTION	UNUSED F/NH
1243	$2 D-Day, 75th Anniversary, sheet of 4	16.50
1244	$7.50 D-Day, 75th Anniversary, souvenir sheet.	16.00
1245	$2 Abdication of Japanese Emperor, sheet of 4 .	16.50
1246	$2 Birth of Archie Mountbatten-Windsor, sheet of 4 .	16.50
1247	$1-$2 Sites & Scenes of Singapore, sheet of 4 .	13.00
1248	$5 Sites & Scenes of Singapore, souvenir sheet .	10.50
1249	$1.50 Dorje Chang Buddha II, single from sheet of 4. .	3.50
1250	$2 Plumeria, sheet of 4	16.50
1251	$5 Plumeria, souvenir sheet	10.50
1252	$2 Morning Glory, sheet of 4	16.50
1253	$5 Morning Glory, souvenir sheet	10.50
1254	$2 Clownfish, sheet of 4	16.50
1255	$7 Clownfish, souvenir sheet	15.00
1256	$2 Pres. Donald Trump Visits Japan, sheet of 4 .	16.50
1257	$5 Pres. Donald Trump Visits Japan, souvenir sheet .	10.50
1258	$10-$25 Beautiful Beaches Crypto MI10, sheet of 6 .	225.00

1259

1275c

2020

SCOTT NO.	DESCRIPTION	UNUSED F/NH
1259-63	6¢-$26.35 Birds, set of 5	105.00
1264-67	55¢-$21.10 Marine Life, set of 4	70.00
1268	$5 Tsakos Group Oil Tanker, souvenir sheet. . .	10.50
1269	$2 COVID-19 Pandemic, sheet of 4	16.50
1270-71	$2 Viet Nam War - 65th Anniversary, set of 2 sheets of 4 .	34.00
1272	$8 Viet Nam War - 65th Anniversary, souvenir sheet .	17.00
1273	$1.60 Victory in Europe - 75th Anniversary, souvenir sheet .	21.00
1274	$1.50 Geese, sheet of 5	16.50
1275	$5 Geese, souvenir sheet	10.50

1283a

SCOTT NO.	DESCRIPTION	UNUSED F/NH
1276	$2 Hibiscus, sheet of 4	16.50
1277	$5 Hisbiscus, souvenir sheet.	10.50
1278-80	$2 Race to the White House, set of 3 sheets of 4 .	51.00
1281	$1.50 Butterflies, sheet of 6.	18.50
1282	$8 Butterflies, souvenir sheet	17.00
1283	$1.50 Antarctic Wildlife, sheet of 6	18.50
1284	$8 Antarctic Wildlife, souvenir sheet	17.00

1291c

1293b

SCOTT NO.	DESCRIPTION	UNUSED F/NH
1285	$4.50 Donald Trump, souvenir sheet	10.00
1286	$4.50 Donald Trump, small souvenir sheet. . . .	10.00
1287	$4.60 Joseph Biden, souvenir sheet.	10.00
1288	$4.60 Joseph Biden, small souvenir sheet	10.00
1289	$2 Rabbits, sheet of 4	16.50
1290	$5 Rabbits, souvenir sheet	10.50
1291	$2 Farm Animals, sheet of 4	16.50
1292	$5 Farm Animals, horse, souvenir sheet.	10.50
1293	$2 Star Fish of the World, sheet of 4.	16.50
1294	$5 Star Fish of the World, souvenir sheet.	10.50
1295	$2 Tea Turles, sheet of 4.	16.50
1296	$3 Turtles of the Sea, souvenir sheet of 2.	10.50
1297	$2 Reptiles of the World, sheet of 4	16.50
1298	$5 Reptiles of the World, box turtle, souvenir sheet .	10.50
1299-1302	$8 Elvis Presley, set of 4 souvenir sheets	67.00
1303	$1 Year of the Ox, sheet of 5.	10.50

1312c

1316

1310b

2021

SCOTT NO.	DESCRIPTION	UNUSED F/NH
1304	$2 Mayflower Pilgrims 400th anniversary, sheet of 4 .	16.50
1305	$5 Mayflower Pilgrims, souvenir sheet	10.50
1306	$1.60 Joseph R. Biden 46th U.S. President, sheet of 5 .	16.50
1307	$4.60 Joseph R. Biden, souvenir sheet.	10.00
1308	$1.90 Empire State Building, sheet of 5	20.00
1309	$4.90 Empire State Building, souvenir sheet . .	10.25
1310	$2 Remembering 9/11, sheet of 4	16.50
1311	$5 Remembering 9/11, souvenir sheet	10.50
1312	$1.95 Queen Elizabeth II 95th Birthday, sheet of 5 .	21.00
1313	$5 Queen Elizabeth II 95th Birthday, souvenir sheet .	10.50
1314	$2 Range Rover 50th anniversary, sheet of 4 . .	16.50
1315	$5 Range Rover, souvenir sheet.	10.50
1316	$1.20 Dorje Chang Buddha III, single from sheet .	2.50
1317	75¢ Birds of Marshall Islands, sheet of 10	16.50
1318	$3 Birds of Marshall Islands, souvenir sheet of 2 .	12.50
1319	$1.35 Crabs of the World, sheet of 6.	17.00
1320	$3 Crabs of the World, souvenir sheet of 2. . . .	12.00
1321	$1.35 Mantis Shrimp of the World, sheet of 6 . .	16.50
1322	$3 Mantis Shrimp of the World, souvenir sheet of 2 .	12.50
1323	$2 Elvis, The King of Rock & Roll, sheet of 4 . .	16.50
1324	$2 Tokyo Summer Olympics, sheet of 4	16.50
1325-37	$3 Queen Elizabeth II / U.S. Presidents, set of 13 souvenir sheets of 2	165.00

SCOTT NO.	DESCRIPTION	UNUSED F/NH

1338c

1338 $2 Owls, sheet of 4 . . . . .16.50
1339 $5 Owls, souvenir sheet 10.50
1340 $1.35 Crocodile, sheet of 6 . . . . .17.00
1341 $5 Crocodile, souvenir sheet. 10.50
1342 $1.50 Space Shuttle Discovery, sheet of 6 . . . .20.00
1343 $1.80 Hubble Space Telescope, sheet of 4. . . .15.00
1344 $3.50 Hubble Space Telescope, souvenir sheet .7.00

1347c

1345 $3.50 Hubble Space Telescope/Earth, souvenir sheet .7.00
1346 $3.50 Space Shuttle Discovery Launch, souvenir sheet .7.00
1347 $2 Metropolitan Museum of Art, sheet of 4 . . . .16.50
1348 $1.60 Prince William & Catherine Middleton, sheet of 5 .16.50
1349 $5 Prince William & Catherine Middleton, souvenir sheet .10.50
1350 $1.60 Prince Harry & Meghan Markel, sheet of 5 . 16.50
1351 $5 Prince Harry & Meghan Markle, souvenir sheet .10.50
1352 $2 Prince Philip, sheet of 4 . . . . .16.50
1353 $5 Prince Philip, souvenir sheet 10.50

1354f

2022

1354 $2 Ducks of Marshall Islands, sheet of 6. . . . . .25.00
1355 $5 Ducks of Marshall Islands, souvenir sheet. . 10.50
1356 $2 Butterflies, sheet of 5 . . . . .21.00
1357 $5 Butterflies, souvenir sheet 10.50
1358 $1 United Arab Emirates, sheet of 4 . . . . .8.00
1359 $20 International Cryptocurrency, souvenir sheet . 40.00
1360 $1 Year of the Tiger, sheet of 6 . . . . .12.00

1361b

1361 $1.70 Queen Elizabeth II-Platinum Jubliee, sheet of 4 .15.00
1362 $4.70 Queen Elizabeth II-Platinum Jubliee, souvenir sheet.10.00
1363 $2 2022 Winter Olympics-Gold Medalists, sheet of 4 . 16.50

1364

1364-73 9¢-$26.95 Fish, set of 10. . . . . .190.00
1374 $5 Peace for Ukraine, souvenir sheet 10.50
1375 $2 Parrots, sheet of 4 .16.50
1376 $5 Parrots, souvenir sheet 10.50
1377 $2 Sharks, sheet of 4 .16.50
1378 $5 Sharks, souvenir sheet. 10.50

1379b

1381a

1379 $2 The World's Jellyfish, sheet of 4. . . . . .16.50
1380 $5 The World's Jellyfish, souvenir sheet 10.50
1381 $1.60 Corals, sheet of 5 . . . . .16.50
1382 $3 Corals, souvenir sheet of 2. . . . . .12.00
1383 $1.60 Bromeliads, sheet of 5. . . . . .16.50
1384 $3 Bromeliads, souvenir sheet of 2 . . . . .12.00
1385 $2 Muhammad Ali, sheet of 4 . . . . .16.50
1386 $5 Muhammad Ali, souvenir sheet 10.50
1387 $1.50 Neil Armstrong, sheet of 5. . . . . .16.00
1388 $5 Neil Armstrong, souvenir sheet 10.00

1390

1391d

1389 $2 King Charles III, sheet of 4 . . . . .16.50
1390 $5 King Charles III, souvenir sheet 10.00
1391 $1.35 Compact of Free Assoc., 35th Anniv, sheet of 4 . . . . .11.50
1392 $1.35 Compact of Free Assoc., 35th Anniv, souvenir sheet of 3 . . . . .9.00

1395b

1393 $1.35 Elvis Presley, sheet of 6 . . . . .17.00
1394 $5 Elvis Presley, souvenir sheet 10.00
1395 $2 Pres. Biden Visits Italy, sheet of 4 . . . . .16.50
1396 $5 Pres. Biden Visits Italy, souvenir sheet 10.00

1400

1395 $2 Pres. Biden Visits Italy, sheet of 4 . . . . .16.50
1396 $5 Pres. Biden Visits Italy, souvenir sheet 10.00
1397 $1.60 Insects, sheet of 5. . . . . .16.50
1398 $3 Insects, souvenir sheet of 2 . . . . .12.00
1399 $1 Mikhail Gorbachev, sheet of 9 . . . . .19.00
1400 $1.96 Queen Elizabeth II, sheet of 6. . . . . .25.00

*Scott numbers and prices are subject to change in the next edition

SEMI-POSTAL

1996

B1 32¢+8¢ 50th Anniv. of Nuclear Testing, sheet of 6 . . . . .7.00

AIR POST

1985

C1-2 44¢ Audubon Birds, attached 3.00

C9 C13

C1-2 44¢ Audubon Birds, attached 3.00

1986-89

C3-6 44¢ AMERIPEX '86, attached 4.75
C7 44¢ Operation Crossroads, souvenir sheet. 6.00
C8 44 Statue of Liberty, Peace 1.40
C9-12 44¢ Girl Scouts, attached 4.65
C13-16 44¢ Marine Birds, attached 4.65

C17

C22

C17-20 44¢ CAPEX '87, attached 4.80
C21 45¢ Space Shuttle. 1.25
C22-25 12¢-45¢ Aircraft 4.50

Booklet Panes

C22a 12¢ Dornier DO288, pane (10) 5.00
C23a 36¢ Boeing 737, pane (10) 12.00
C24a 39¢ Hawker 748, pane (10). 13.00
C25a 45¢ Boeing 727, pane (10) 14.00
C25b 5 (36¢) & 5 (45¢), pane (10) 13.00

UX1

POSTAL STATIONERY

UX1 20¢ Elvis Presley, postal card (1996) 4.95
UX2-5 20¢ Canoes, set of 4. . . . . .6.00
UX6 20¢ Heavenly Angels, Christmas (1996). 2.00
UX7 32¢ Turtle (1997). 2.00

FEDERATED STATES OF MICRONESIA

Micronesia, formed from the major portion of the Caroline Islands, became postally autonomous in 1984. It forms part of the U.S. administered Trust Territories of the Pacific.

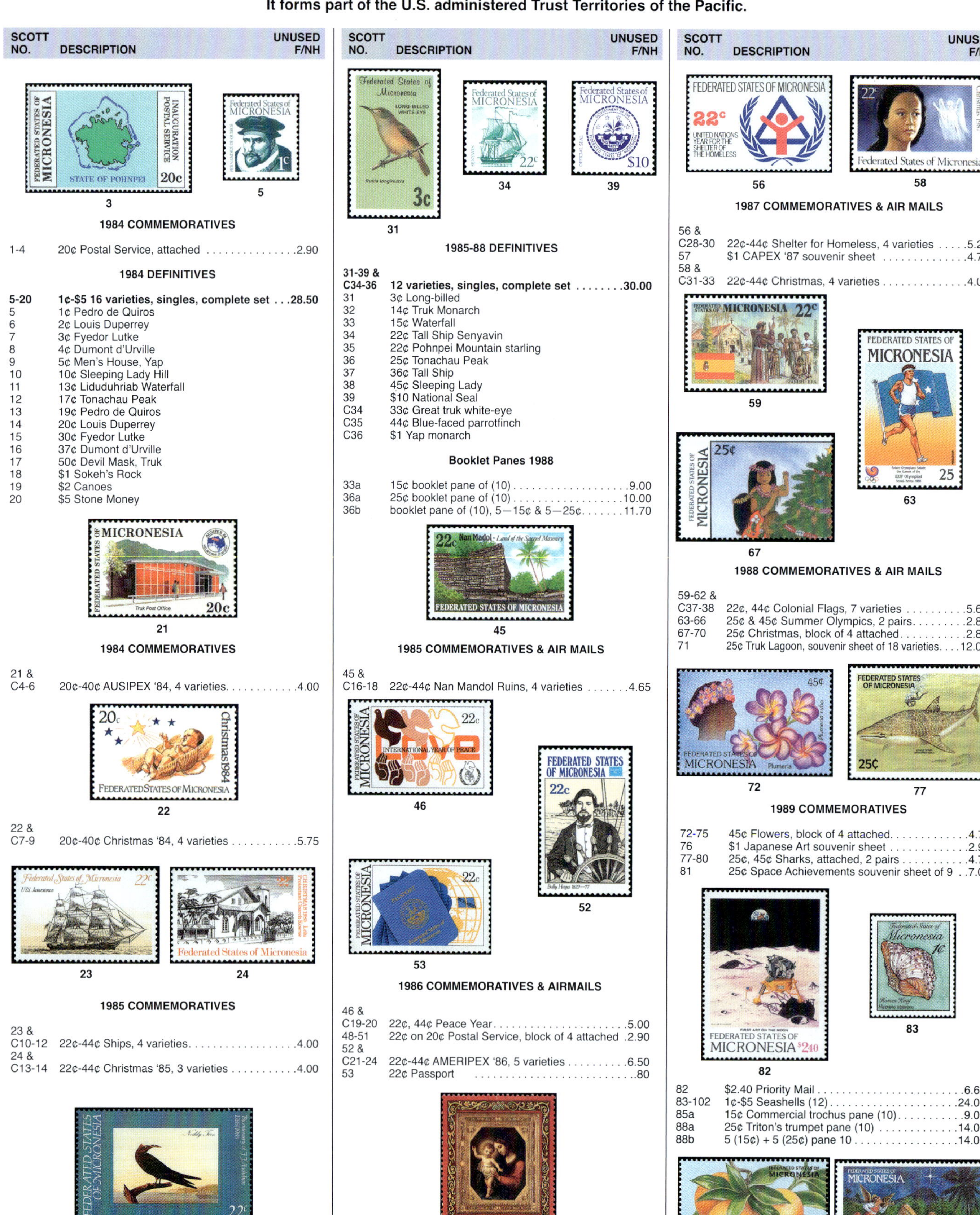

3 5

1984 COMMEMORATIVES

SCOTT NO.	DESCRIPTION	UNUSED F/NH
1-4	20¢ Postal Service, attached	2.90

1984 DEFINITIVES

SCOTT NO.	DESCRIPTION	UNUSED F/NH
5-20	**1¢-$5 16 varieties, singles, complete set**	**28.50**
5	1¢ Pedro de Quiros	
6	2¢ Louis Duperrey	
7	3¢ Fyedor Lutke	
8	4¢ Dumont d'Urville	
9	5¢ Men's House, Yap	
10	10¢ Sleeping Lady Hill	
11	13¢ Liduduhriab Waterfall	
12	17¢ Tonachau Peak	
13	19¢ Pedro de Quiros	
14	20¢ Louis Duperrey	
15	30¢ Fyedor Lutke	
16	37¢ Dumont d'Urville	
17	50¢ Devil Mask, Truk	
18	$1 Sokeh's Rock	
19	$2 Canoes	
20	$5 Stone Money	

21

1984 COMMEMORATIVES

SCOTT NO.	DESCRIPTION	UNUSED F/NH
21 & C4-6	20¢-40¢ AUSIPEX '84, 4 varieties	4.00

22

SCOTT NO.	DESCRIPTION	UNUSED F/NH
22 & C7-9	20¢-40¢ Christmas '84, 4 varieties	5.75

23 24

1985 COMMEMORATIVES

SCOTT NO.	DESCRIPTION	UNUSED F/NH
23 & C10-12	22¢-44¢ Ships, 4 varieties	4.00
24 & C13-14	22¢-44¢ Christmas '85, 3 varieties	4.00

25

SCOTT NO.	DESCRIPTION	UNUSED F/NH
25-28 & C15	22¢ Audubon, booklet of 4 attached, & 44¢ airmail	4.50

31 34 39

1985-88 DEFINITIVES

SCOTT NO.	DESCRIPTION	UNUSED F/NH
31-39 & C34-36	**12 varieties, singles, complete set**	**30.00**
31	3¢ Long-billed	
32	14¢ Truk Monarch	
33	15¢ Waterfall	
34	22¢ Tall Ship Senyavin	
35	22¢ Pohnpei Mountain starling	
36	25¢ Tonachau Peak	
37	36¢ Tall Ship	
38	45¢ Sleeping Lady	
39	$10 National Seal	
C34	33¢ Great truk white-eye	
C35	44¢ Blue-faced parrotfinch	
C36	$1 Yap monarch	

Booklet Panes 1988

SCOTT NO.	DESCRIPTION	UNUSED F/NH
33a	15¢ booklet pane of (10)	9.00
36a	25¢ booklet pane of (10)	10.00
36b	booklet pane of (10), 5—15¢ & 5—25¢	11.70

45

1985 COMMEMORATIVES & AIR MAILS

SCOTT NO.	DESCRIPTION	UNUSED F/NH
45 & C16-18	22¢-44¢ Nan Mandol Ruins, 4 varieties	4.65

46 52 53

1986 COMMEMORATIVES & AIRMAILS

SCOTT NO.	DESCRIPTION	UNUSED F/NH
46 & C19-20	22¢, 44¢ Peace Year	5.00
48-51	22¢ on 20¢ Postal Service, block of 4 attached	2.90
52 & C21-24	22¢-44¢ AMERIPEX '86, 5 varieties	6.50
53	22¢ Passport	.80

54

SCOTT NO.	DESCRIPTION	UNUSED F/NH
54-55 & C26-27	5¢-44¢ Christmas, 4 varieties	4.75

56 58

1987 COMMEMORATIVES & AIR MAILS

SCOTT NO.	DESCRIPTION	UNUSED F/NH
56 & C28-30	22¢-44¢ Shelter for Homeless, 4 varieties	5.20
57	$1 CAPEX '87 souvenir sheet	4.75
58 & C31-33	22¢-44¢ Christmas, 4 varieties	4.00

59 63 67

1988 COMMEMORATIVES & AIR MAILS

SCOTT NO.	DESCRIPTION	UNUSED F/NH
59-62 & C37-38	22¢, 44¢ Colonial Flags, 7 varieties	5.65
63-66	25¢ & 45¢ Summer Olympics, 2 pairs	2.80
67-70	25¢ Christmas, block of 4 attached	2.80
71	25¢ Truk Lagoon, souvenir sheet of 18 varieties	12.00

72 77

1989 COMMEMORATIVES

SCOTT NO.	DESCRIPTION	UNUSED F/NH
72-75	45¢ Flowers, block of 4 attached	4.75
76	$1 Japanese Art souvenir sheet	2.90
77-80	25¢, 45¢ Sharks, attached, 2 pairs	4.75
81	25¢ Space Achievements souvenir sheet of 9	7.00

82 83

SCOTT NO.	DESCRIPTION	UNUSED F/NH
82	$2.40 Priority Mail	6.65
83-102	1¢-$5 Seashells (12)	24.00
85a	15¢ Commercial trochus pane (10)	9.00
88a	25¢ Triton's trumpet pane (10)	14.00
88b	5 (15¢) + 5 (25¢) pane 10	14.00

103a 104

SCOTT NO.	DESCRIPTION	UNUSED F/NH
103	25¢ Fruits & Flowers, sheet of 18	12.00
104-05	Christmas	2.50

SCOTT NO.	DESCRIPTION	UNUSED F/NH

106  110

1990 COMMEMORATIVES

106-09	World Wildlife Fund (4 varieties)	7.50
110-13	45¢ Whaling Ships & Artifacts, 4 attached	4.75
114	$1 Whaling Souvenir Sheet	2.90
115	$1 Penny Black Anniversary Souvenir Sheet	2.90

116  122

116-20	25¢ P.A.T.S. strip of 5	3.75
121	$1 Expo '90 Souvenir Sheet	2.90
122-23	25¢ & 45¢ Loading Mail	2.50

124  127

124-26	25¢ Joint Issue, 3 attached	3.00
127-30	45¢ Moths, 4 attached	4.75

131a

131	25¢ Christmas, sheetlet of 9	7.00

134  138

1991

132	25¢+45¢ Government bldgs., Souvenir Sheet of 2	1.80
133	$1 New Capitol Souvenir Sheet	2.90
134-37	29¢+50¢ Turtles, 2 pairs	7.50
138-41	29¢ Operation Desert Storm, 4 attached	3.00
142	$2.90 Operation Desert Storm Priority Mail	7.20
142a	$2.90 Operation Desert Storm Souvenir Sheet	7.00

143a

143	29¢ Phila Nippon Souvenir Sheet of 3	2.60
144	50¢ Phila Nippon Souvenir Sheet of 3	4.35
145	$1 Phila Nippon Souvenir Sheet	2.75

146  149a

146-48	29¢ Christmas 1991 set of 3	3.50
149	29¢ Pohnpei Rain Forest, sheetlet of 18	17.20

150a  151a

1992

150	29¢ Peace Corps/Kennedy, strip of 5	4.05
151	29¢ Columbus, strip of 3	6.00

152  154

152-53	29¢, 50¢ UN Membership Anniversary	5.20
153a	same, Souvenir Sheet of 2	6.00
154	29¢ Christmas, 1992	2.95

155a  156

1993

155	29¢ Pioneers of Flight I, 8 attached	6.00

1993-94

156-67	10¢-$2.90, Fish, 16 varieties	25.00

168a  172

173  177a

1993

168	29¢ Sailing Ships, sheetlet of 12	18.00
172	29¢ Thomas Jefferson	1.00
173-76	29¢ Canoes, 4 attached	3.80
177	29¢ Local Leaders I, strip of 4	3.00
178	50¢ Pioneers of Flight II, 8 attached	10.00

179  182

179-80	29¢, 50¢ Tourist Attractions, Pohnpei	2.80
181	$1 Tourist Attractions, Souvenir Sheet	2.80
182-83	29¢, 50¢ Butterflies, 2 pairs	4.50

184  186a

184-85	29¢-50¢ Christmas 1993	2.60
186	29¢ Micronesia Culture, sheetlet of 18	15.00

192a  193a  194

1994

187-89	29¢-50¢ Tourist Attractions, Kosrae	3.00
190	"Hong Kong '94" miniature sheet of 4 (#182a, 182b, 183a, 183b)	5.80
191	29¢ Pioneers of Flight III, 8 attached	7.80
192	29¢ 1994 Micronesian Games, 4 attached	3.70
193	29¢ Native Costumes, 4 attached	3.70
194	29¢ Constitution, 15th Anniversary	2.00

195a  196

198a

195	29¢ Flowers, strip of 4	3.80
196-97	50¢ World Cup Soccer, pair	5.75
198	29¢ 10th Anniv. Inauguration Postal Service, 4 attached	5.85

199a  201a

199	"PHILAKOREA '94" Dinosaur, miniature sheet of 3	6.50
200	50¢ Pioneers of Flight IV, 8 attached	10.00
201	29¢ Migratory Birds, 4 attached	6.20

SCOTT NO.	DESCRIPTION	UNUSED F/NH

202

202-03	29¢, 50¢ Christmas 1994	4.90
204-07	32¢ Local Leaders II, set of 4	6.50

208

1995

208	50¢ New Year 1995 (Year of the Boar)	1.75

209a

211a

228a

209	32¢ Chuuk Lagoon, 4 attached	8.00
210	32¢ Pioneers of Flight V, 8 attached	7.20
211	32¢ Dogs, 4 attached	4.00
213-26	32¢-$5.00 Fish, set of 7	30.00
227	32¢ Fish, sheetlet of 25 (1996)	25.00
228	32¢ Flowers II, strip of 4	3.50
229	$1 UN 50th Anniversary Souvenir Sheet	2.80

230a

231a

230	32¢ Orchids (Singapore '95), min. sheet of 4	3.75
231	60¢ US Warships, 4 attached	6.65
232	50¢ Temple of Heaven Souvenir Sheet	1.45
233	60¢ Pioneers of Flight VI, 8 attached	12.50

234

236

234-35	32¢-60¢ Christmas Poinsettias	2.55
236	32¢ Yitzhak Rabin	1.10

238a

239a

240a

241a

1996

237	50¢ New Year 1996 (Year of the Rat)	1.75
238	32¢ Pioneers of Flight VII, 8 attached	8.25
239	32¢ Tourism in Yap, 4 attached	4.00
240	55¢ Sea Stars, 4 attached	6.25
241	60¢ Olympic Games Centenary, 4 attached	7.80
242	50¢ The Tarrying Garden, Suzhou Souvenir Sheet	2.00

243

245a

243-44	32¢ Marine Vessels, 2 attached	3.50
245	55¢ Automobile, sheet of 8	12.00

247

248a

249a

247	32¢ Police Drug Enforcement Dog	1.50
248	32¢ Citrus Fruit, strip of 4	7.25
249	60¢ Pioneers of Flight VIII, 8 attached	16.00

250a

251

253

250	32¢ Fish (Taipei '96), miniature sheet of 4	4.25
251-52	32¢-60¢ Christmas 1996, set of 2	2.55
253	$3 Canoe & Flag of Micronesia	8.00

257, 258

1997

254	60¢ Deng Xiaoping, sheet of 4	7.50
255	$3 Deng Xiaoping, souvenir sheet	8.50
256	$2 Bridge to the Future, salute to Hong Kong, souvenir sheet	6.50
257	32¢ Year of the Ox	1.25
258	$2 Year of the Ox, souvenir sheet	5.00

259

259	60¢ Return of Hong Kong to China, sheet of 6	10.50
260	$3 Return of Hong Kong to China, souvenir sheet	8.75
261	32¢ Sea Goddesses of the Pacific, sheet of 6	4.50
262-64	20¢-60¢ Hiroshige, 3 sheetlets of 3	11.00
265-66	$2 Hiroshige, souvenir sheets(2)	12.00

267a

268a

269a

267	32¢ 2nd Federated States of Micronesia Games, 4 attached	3.50
268	50¢ Elvis Presley, sheetlets of 6	10.00
269	32¢ Undersea Exploration, sheetlet of 9	8.50
270-72	$2 Undersea Exploration, souvenir sheets (3)	16.00

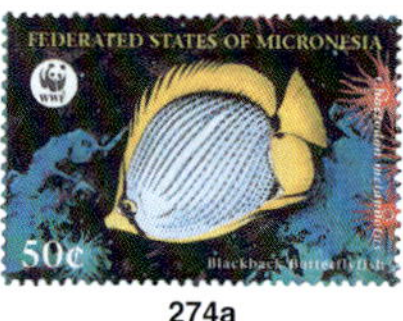
274a

273a

273	60¢ Princess Diana	1.50
274	50¢ World Wildlife Fund, Butterly Fish, 4 attached	7.50

275-76

275-76	32¢ Christmas Paintings, Fra Angelico, pair	1.80
277-78	60¢ Christmas Paintings, Simon Marmion, pair	3.00

SCOTT NO.	DESCRIPTION	UNUSED F/NH

1998

SCOTT NO.	DESCRIPTION	UNUSED F/NH
279-80	50¢ Year of the Tiger, souvenir sheets (2)	3.00
281	$1 Micronesia's Admission to the UN, souvenir sheet	2.75
282	32¢ Disney's Winnie the Pooh, sheetlet of 8	11.00
283-84	$1 Disney's Winnie the Pooh, souvenir sheets (2)	12.50

285a

SCOTT NO.	DESCRIPTION	UNUSED F/NH
285	32¢ 1998 World Cup Soccer Championships, sheetlet of 8	7.00
286-87	$2 1998 World Cup, souvenir sheets (2)	11.00
288	$3 Olympics, souvenir sheet	9.50
289-91	32¢-60¢ Old Testament Bible Stories, 3 sheetlets of 3	9.50
292-94	$2 Old Testament Bible Stories, souvenir sheets (3)	15.50

295a

299a

SCOTT NO.	DESCRIPTION	UNUSED F/NH
295	32¢ International Year of the Ocean, sheetlet of 9	7.00
296-98	$2 International Year of the Ocean, souvenir sheets (3)	15.00
299	50¢ Native Birds, 4 attached	5.00
300	$3 Native Birds, souvenir sheet	7.50

319a

320a

SCOTT NO.	DESCRIPTION	UNUSED F/NH
301-19A	1¢-$10.75 Fish, 20 varieties	59.00
320	32¢ Fala, FDR's Dog, sheetlet of 6	4.80
321-22	32¢-60¢ Christmas, 20th Century Art, 2 sheetlets of 3	7.00
323	$2 Christmas, 20th Century Art, souvenir sheet	5.00
324-25	60¢ John Glenn's Return to Space 2 sheets of 6	24.00
326-27	$2 John Glenn's Return to Space 2 souvenir sheets	10.00

328

334a

342a

1999

SCOTT NO.	DESCRIPTION	UNUSED F/NH
328-33	33¢-$11.75 Fish, 6 varieties	40.00
334	33¢ Russian Space Exploration, sheetlet of 20	17.00
335-36	$2 Russsian Space Exploration 2 souvenir sheets	10.00
337-38	33¢-50¢ "Romance of the 3 Kingdoms" by Lo Kuan-chung, 2 sheetlets of 5	15.00
339	$2 "Romance of the 3 Kingdoms", souvenir sheet	10.00
340-41	55¢ IBRA '99 Exhibition, set of 2	3.00
342	$2 IBRA '99 Exhibition, souvenir sheet	5.50
343	33¢ Voyages of the Pacific, sheetlet of 20	16.00

344a

347a

SCOTT NO.	DESCRIPTION	UNUSED F/NH
344	33¢ Space Achievements, sheetlet of 20	17.00
345-46	$2 Space Achievemnets, 2 souvenir sheets	10.50
347	33¢ Earth Day-Endangered Species sheetlet of 20	17.00
348-49	$2 Earth Day-Endangered Species, 2 souvenir sheets	11.00

356a

358

362a

SCOTT NO.	DESCRIPTION	UNUSED F/NH
350-51	33¢ Hokusai Paintings, 2 sheetlets of 6	10.00
352-53	$2 Hokusai Paintings, 2 souvenir sheets	10.00
354	50¢ Flowers, photomosaic of Princess Diana, sheetlet of 8	10.00
355	20¢ Highlights of the 12th Century, sheetlet of 17	9.50
356	33¢ Science & Technology of Ancient China, sheetlet of 17	16.00
357	33¢ Costumes, sheetlet of 20	17.00
358-60	33¢-$2 Christmas-Van Dyck Paintings	7.50
361	$2 Christmas-Van Dyck Paintings, souvenir sheet	5.50
362	33¢ Millenium-Airplanes, sheetlet of 15	15.00
363-64	$2 Millenium-Airplanes, 2 souvenir sheets	11.00

365a

372a

2000

SCOTT NO.	DESCRIPTION	UNUSED F/NH
365-67	33¢ Orchids, 3 sheetlets of 6	15.00
368-69	$1 Orchids, 2 souvenir sheets	10.00
370	33¢ Leaders of the 20th Century, sheetlet of 12	9.25
371	$2 New Year 2000 (Year of the Dragon), souvenir sheet	6.00
372-73	20¢-55¢ Butterflies, 2 sheetlets of 6	12.00
374-76	$2 Butterflies, 3 souvenir sheets	17.00
377	20¢ Highlights of the 1920's, sheetlet of 17	9.00

378

385a

SCOTT NO.	DESCRIPTION	UNUSED F/NH
378	33¢ Millennium 2000	1.10
379	33¢ Peacemakers, sheetlet of 24	18.00
380	33¢ Philantropists, sheetlet of 16	14.00
381-82	33¢ Mushrooms, 2 sheetlets of 6	10.00
383-34	$2 Mushrooms, 2 souvenir sheets	10.00
385	33¢ Flowers of the Pacific, sheetlet of 6	5.00
386	33¢ Wildflowers, sheetlet of 6	5.00
387	$2 Flowers of the Pacific, souvenir sheet	5.00
388	$2 Wildflowers, souvenir sheet	5.00

389a

390a

SCOTT NO.	DESCRIPTION	UNUSED F/NH
389	33¢ 2000 Summer Olympics, Sydney, souvenir sheet of 4	3.00
390	33¢ Zeppelins & Airships, sheetlet of 6	5.00
391-92	$2 Zeppelins & Airships, 2 souvenir sheets	10.25
393	33¢ Queen Mother Flower Photomosaic, sheet of 8	6.00
394	33¢-$1 2000 Summer Olympics, Sydney, souvenir sheet of 3	4.50

395

SCOTT NO.	DESCRIPTION	UNUSED F/NH
395-98	33¢ Fish, set of 4	3.00
399-400	33¢ Fish, 2 sheetlets of 9	15.00
401-02	$2 Fish, 2 souvenir sheets	10.00
403	50¢ Pope John Paul II Photomosaic, sheet of 8	11.00

404

408a

SCOTT NO.	DESCRIPTION	UNUSED F/NH
404-07	20¢-$3.20 2000 Christmas, set of 4	11.50
408-09	33¢ Dogs & Cats, 2 sheetlets of 6	10.00
410-11	$2 Dogs & Cats, 2 souvenir sheets	10.00

414a

416a

2001

SCOTT NO.	DESCRIPTION	UNUSED F/NH
412-13	60¢ Year of the Snake, 2 souvenir sheets	3.00
414	50¢ Pokemon, sheet of 6	7.50
415	$2 Farfetch'd, souvenir sheet	5.50
416-17	50¢-60¢ Whales, 2 sheetlets of 6	16.00
418-19	$2 Whales, 2 souvenir sheets	10.00

420a

424

SCOTT NO.	DESCRIPTION	UNUSED F/NH
420	34¢ Ecology, sheetlet of 6	5.00
421	60¢ Ecology, sheetlet of 4	6.00
422-23	$2 Ecology, 2 souvenir sheets	11.00
424-28	11¢-$3.50 Fish, set of 5	14.40
429	$12.25 Blue-spotted boxfish	29.00
430-35	34¢ Japanese Art, set of 6	5.00
436	34¢ Japanese Art, sheetlet of 6	5.00
437-38	$2 Japanese Art, 2 imperf sheets	10.00
439	60¢ Toulouse-Lautrec Paintings, sheetlets of 3	4.50
440	$2 Toulouse-Lautrec Paintings, souvenir sheet	5.00
441	60¢ Queen Victoria, sheetlet of 6	9.00
442	$2 Queen Victoria, souvenir sheet	5.00
443	60¢ Queen Elizabeth II, 75th Birthday, sheet of 6	9.00
444	$2 Queen Elizabeth II, 75th Birthday, souvenir sheet	5.00

SCOTT NO.	DESCRIPTION	UNUSED F/NH

445 457a

SCOTT NO.	DESCRIPTION	UNUSED F/NH
445-46	60¢ Marine Life, 2 sheetlets of 6	18.00
447-48	$2 Marine Life, 2 souvenir sheets	10.00
449-52	60¢ Prehistoric Animals, set of 4	6.00
453-54	60¢ Prehistoric Animals, 2 sheetlets of 6	18.00
455-56	$2 Prehistoric Animals, 2 souvenir sheets	10.50
457-58	50¢ Shells, 2 sheetlets of 6	15.00
459-60	$2 Shells, 2 souvenir sheets	10.50

461

469a

473

SCOTT NO.	DESCRIPTION	UNUSED F/NH
461-64	5¢-$2.10 Birds, set of 4	6.50
465-66	60¢ Birds, 2 sheetlets of 6	18.00
467-68	$2 Birds, 2 souvenir sheets	10.50
469-70	60¢ Nobel Prizes Cent., 2 sheetlets of 6	18.00
471-72	$2 Nobel Prizes Cent., 2 souvenir sheets	10.50
473-76	22¢-$1 Christmas, set of 4	5.00
477	$2 Christmas, souvenir sheet	5.00
478-79	60¢ Attack on Pearl Harbor, 60th Anniv., 2 sheetlets of 6	18.00
480-81	$2 Attack on Pearl Harbor, 60th Anniv., 2 souvenir sheets	10.50

485

492a

494a

2002

SCOTT NO.	DESCRIPTION	UNUSED F/NH
482	60¢ Year of the Horse, sheetlet of 5	7.75
483	80¢ Reign of Queen Elizabeth II, 50th Anniv., sheetlet of 4	8.00
484	$2 Reign of Queen Elizabeth II, 50th Anniv., souvenir sheet	5.00
485	$1 United We Stand	2.25
486-87	$1 2002 Winter Olympics, set of 2	5.00
488-89	60¢ Japanese Art, 2 sheetlets of 6	18.00
490-91	$2 Japanese Art, 2 souvenir sheets	10.50
492	80¢ Intl. Year of Mountains, sheet of 4	8.00
493	$2 Intl. Year of Mountains, souvenir sheet	5.00
494	60¢ President John F. Kennedy, sheet of 4	6.50
495	$2 President John F. Kennedy, souvenir sheet	5.00
496	60¢ Princess Diana, sheetlet of 6	9.00
497	$2 Princess Diana, souvenir sheet	5.00

498a

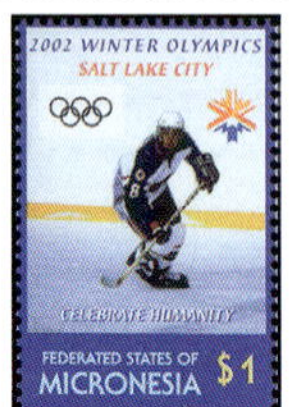

502

SCOTT NO.	DESCRIPTION	UNUSED F/NH
498	80¢ International Year of Eco-Tourism, sheet of 6	12.75
499	$2 International Year of Eco-Tourism, souvenir sheet	5.00
500	$1 20th World Boy Scout Jamboree, Thailand, sheet of 3	8.00
501	$2 20th World Boy Scout Jamboree, Thailand, souvenir sheet	5.00
502-03	$1 2002 Winter Olympics, redrawn smaller rings, set of 2	5.00
503a	$2 2002 Winter Olympics, redrawn smaller rings, souvenir sheet	5.00

504

SCOTT NO.	DESCRIPTION	UNUSED F/NH
504	37¢ Xavier High School, 50th Anniversary	1.00
505	80¢ Queen Elizabeth Memorial, souvenir sheet of 4	8.00
506	$2 Queen Elizabeth Memorial, souvenir sheet	5.00

507a

509

525

SCOTT NO.	DESCRIPTION	UNUSED F/NH
507	80¢ Teddy Bear Centennial, sheet of 4	10.00
508	37¢ Elvis Presley (1935-77), sheetlet of 6	5.25
509-13	15¢-$1 Christmas, set of 5	10.25
514	$2 Christmas, souvenir sheet	5.00
515-19	37¢-80¢ Flora, Fauna & Mushrooms, set of 5 sheets of 6	48.00
520-24	$2 Flora, Fauna & Mushrooms, set of 5 souvenir sheets	25.00
525-37	3¢-$13.65 Bird Definitives, set of 13	70.00

539a

543a

538a

2003

SCOTT NO.	DESCRIPTION	UNUSED F/NH
538	60¢ 1st Non-Stop Solo Transatlantic Flight 75th Anniversary, sheet of 6	9.00
539	37¢ Year of the Ram, sheet of 6	6.00
540	37¢ Astronauts Killed in Shuttle Columbia, In Memorium, sheet of 7	6.50
541	$1 Coronation of Queen Elizabeth II, 50th Anniversary, sheet of 3	7.75
542	$2 Coronation of Queen Elizabeth II, 50th Anniversary, souvenir sheet	5.00
543	$1 Prince Williams, 21st Birthday, sheet of 3	7.75
544	$2 Prince Wllliams, 21st Birthday, souvenir sheet	5.00

545a

551a

SCOTT NO.	DESCRIPTION	UNUSED F/NH
545-46	37¢ Operation Iraqi Freedom, set of 2 sheets of 6	11.50
547	60¢ Tour de France Bicycle Race, Centenary, sheet of 4	6.50
548	$2 Tour de France Bicycle Race, Centenary, souvenir sheet	5.00
549	$1 International Year of Freshwater, sheet of 3	7.75
550	$2 International Year of Freshwater, souvenir sheet	5.00
551	55¢ Powered Flight Centenary, sheet of 6	8.00
552	$2 Powered Flight Centenary, souvenir sheet	5.00
553-54	80¢ Circus Performers, set of 2 sheets of 4	16.00
555	80¢ Paintings of Boy Scouts by Norman Rockwell, sheet of 4	8.00
556	$2 Paintings of Boy Scouts by Norman Rockwell, souvenir sheet, imperf.	5.00

557a

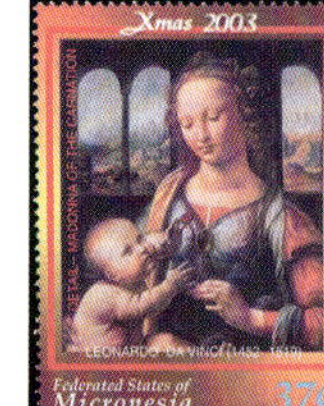

565

SCOTT NO.	DESCRIPTION	UNUSED F/NH
557	80¢ Paintings by Paul Gauguin, sheet of 4	8.00
558	$2 Paintings by Paul Gauguin, souvenir sheet, imperf.	5.00
559-62	37¢-80¢ Paintings by James McNeill Whistler, set of 4	6.00
563	$1 Paintings by James McNeill Whistler, sheet of 3	7.75
564	$2 Paintings by James McNeill Whistler, souvenir sheet, imperf.	5.00
565-68	37¢-80¢ Christmas, set of 4	6.50
569	$2 Christmas, souvenir sheet	5.00
570-73	80¢ Cats, Dogs, Birds & Amphibians, set of 4 sheets of 4	30.00
574-77	$2 Cats, Dogs, Birds & Amphibians, set of 4 souvenir sheets	20.00

578

581

586

2004

SCOTT NO.	DESCRIPTION	UNUSED F/NH
578	37¢ President Bailey Olter	1.00
579	80¢ Paintings by Pablo Picasso, sheet of 4	8.00
580	$2 Painting by Pablo Picasso, souvenir sheet, imperf	5.00
581-84	22¢-$1 Paintings in the Hermitage Museum, set of 4	6.00
585	$2 Painting in the Hermitage Museum, souvenir sheet, imperf.	5.00
586	50¢ Year of the Monkey	1.75
587	$1 Year of the Monkey, souvenir sheet	2.50

588a

591a

SCOTT NO.	DESCRIPTION	UNUSED F/NH
588	80¢ Election of Pope John Paul II, 25th Anniv., sheet of 4	8.00
589	80¢ 2004 European Soccer Championships, sheet of 4	8.00
590	$2 2004 European Soccer Championships, souvenir sheet	5.00
591	50¢ D-Day, 60th Anniversary, sheet of 6	7.50
592	$2 D-Day, 60th Anniversary, souvenir sheet	5.00
593	$2 Deng Xiaoping, souvenir seet	5.00

594a

607a

SCOTT NO.	DESCRIPTION	UNUSED F/NH
594-96	80¢ Locomotives, 3 sheets of 4	25.00
597-99	$2 Locomotives, 3 souvenir sheets	16.00

SCOTT NO.	DESCRIPTION	UNUSED F/NH
600-01	2¢-10¢ Birds, Type of 2002, set of 2	.65
602	80¢ International Year of Peace, sheet of 3	6.65
603-06	37¢-$1 2004 Summer Olympics, Athens, set of 4	7.50
607-08	80¢ Elvis Presley's First Recording, 50th Anniv., 2 sheets of 4	16.00
609	55¢ Flowers, sheet of 6	9.20
610	$2 Flowers, souvenir sheet	5.50
611	80¢ FIFA, Centennial, sheet of 4	8.95
612	$2 FIFA, Centennial, souvenir sheet	5.50
613-14	20¢ National Basketball Assoc. Players, set of 2	2.00

615a

625a

623a

SCOTT NO.	DESCRIPTION	UNUSED F/NH
615-17	80¢ Prehistoric Animals, 3 sheets of 4	26.00
618-20	$2 Preshistoric Animals, 3 souvenir sheets	16.50
621	55¢ Fish and Coral, sheet of 6	9.20
622	$2 Fish and Coral, Great barracuda, souvenir sheet	5.50
623	55¢ Reptiles and Amphibians, sheet of 6	9.20
624	$2 Reptiles and Amphibians, Loggerhead turtle, souvenir sheet	5.50
625	55¢Birds of the Pacific, sheet of 6	9.20
626	2¢ Birds of the Pacific, Golden whistler, souvenir sheet	5.50
627-30	37¢-$1 Christmas, set of 4	8.95
631	$2 Chirstmas, souvenir sheet	5.50

632

634a

2005

SCOTT NO.	DESCRIPTION	UNUSED F/NH
632	50¢ Year of the Rooster	4.00
633	20¢ National Basketball Assoc. Player, Luke Walton	.85
634	55¢ Pres. Ronald Reagan, 2 attached	3.50

635a

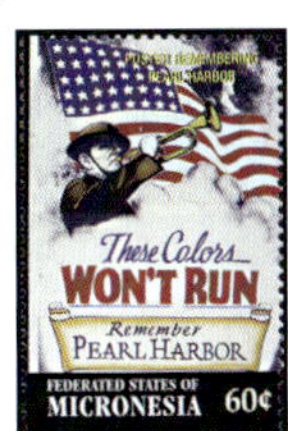

638a

SCOTT NO.	DESCRIPTION	UNUSED F/NH
635-36	60¢ Elvis Presley, 2 sheets of 6	19.00
637-38	60¢ End of World War II, 60th Anniv., 2 sheets of 5	16.00

639a

643

SCOTT NO.	DESCRIPTION	UNUSED F/NH
639	$1 Friedrich von Schiller, sheet of 3	7.75
640	$2 Friedrich von Schiller, souvenir sheet	5.25
641-44	37¢-$1 Battle of Trafalgar, Bicent., set of 4	8.00
645	$2 Battle of Trafalgar, Bicent., souvenir sheet	5.25

646

647a

649a

SCOTT NO.	DESCRIPTION	UNUSED F/NH
646	$1 Pope John Paul II	2.60
647	$1 Rotary International, Cent., sheet of 3	7.75
648	$2 Rotary International, Cent., souvenir sheet	5.25
649	$1 Jules Verne, sheet of 3	7.75
650	$2 Jules Verne, souvenir sheet	5.25

651a

652a

SCOTT NO.	DESCRIPTION	UNUSED F/NH
651	80¢ Nature's Wisdom, Expo 2005, Aichi, Japan, sheet of 4	8.50
652	37¢-$1 Boats, sheet of 4	7.00
653	$2 Boats, sovenir sheet	5.25

654

658

SCOTT NO.	DESCRIPTION	UNUSED F/NH
654-57	4¢-37¢ Kosrae Government Building Complex, set of 4	1.95
658	37¢ Vatican City No. 67	1.35

659e

661

SCOTT NO.	DESCRIPTION	UNUSED F/NH
659	50¢ Worldwide Fund for Nature, 4 attached	5.50
659e	Souvenir Sheet, Worldwide Fund for Nature	11.00
660	$1 Albert Einstein, sheet of 4	10.50
661-64	4¢-37¢ Bananas, set of 4	2.00

665a

668

SCOTT NO.	DESCRIPTION	UNUSED F/NH
665	80¢ Hans Christian Anderson, sheet of 3	6.75
666	$2 Hans Christian Anderson, souvenir shet	5.25
667	80¢ Pope Benedict XVI	2.75
668-71	37¢-$1 Christmas, set of 4	7.25
672	$2 Christmas, souvenir sheet	5.25
673-78	4¢-$1 Flowers, set of 6	6.35
679	80¢ Flowers, sheet of 4	7.75
680-81	$2 Flowers, set of 2 souvenir sheets	10.50

682

2006

SCOTT NO.	DESCRIPTION	UNUSED F/NH
682	50¢ Year of the Dog	1.40
683	$1 Year of the Dog, souvenir sheet	3.75
684-90	24¢-$4.05 Birds, set of 7	18.00
691	39¢ vice President Petrus Tun	1.05
692	$1 Rembrandt, sheet of 4	10.25
693	$2 Rembrandt, souvenir sheet	5.25
694	84¢ Queen Elizabeth II, sheet of 4	8.75
695	$2 Queen Elizabeth II, souvenir sheet	5.25
696	75¢ Space Achievements, sheet of 6	11.00
697-98	$1 Space Achievements, 2 sheets of 4	21.00
699-701	$2 Space Achievements, 3 souvenir sheets	16.00
702-15	1¢-$10 Butterflies	58.00
716-20	22¢-84¢ Christmas, set of 5	6.50
721-22	75¢ Concorde, set of 2 pairs	7.75

730

731

2007

SCOTT NO.	DESCRIPTION	UNUSED F/NH
723	75¢ Year of the Pig	2.00
724	$2 Mozart souvenir sheet	5.50
725	$1 Ludwig Durr souvenir sheet	7.75
726	Marilyn Monroe sheet of 4	11.00
727	$1 Scouting Centenary	8.00
728	$2 Scouting souvenir sheet	5.25
729	50¢ Pope Benedict	1.25
730	60¢ Wedding of Queen Elizabeth II 60th Anniversary sheet of 6	9.50
731	90¢ Princess Diana sheet of 4	9.50
732	$2 Princess Diana souvenir sheet	5.25
733-40	22¢-$4.60 Bananas, set of 8	23.00
741	75¢ Elvis sheet of 6	11.50
742	90¢ Fish sheet of 4	9.25
743	$2 Fish souvenir sheet	5.25
744	90¢ Flowers sheet of 4	9.25
745	$2 Flowers souvenir sheet	5.25
746	90¢ Peace Corp sheet of 4	9.25
747	$1 Gerald Ford miniature sheet of 6	16.00
748	75¢ Penguins sheet of 6	11.50
749	$3.50 Penguins souvenir sheet	9.00
750	90¢ Red Cross sheet of 4	9.50
751-54	22¢-90¢ Cats set of 4	5.75
755	$2 Cats souvenir sheet	5.25
756-59	22¢-90¢ Christmas, churches set of 4	5.00
760	26¢-$2 America's Cup strip of 4	10.00
761	$1 sheet of 4 Helicopters	14.00
762	$2.50 Helicopters souvenir sheet	9.00
763	Princess Diana Sheet	24.00

771

2008

SCOTT NO.	DESCRIPTION	UNUSED F/NH
764	90¢ John F. Kennedy sheet of 4	12.00
765	90¢ Year of the Rat	4.75
766	50¢ 2008 Olympic Games, Beijing, sheet of 4	5.25
767	$2 Breast Cancer Awareness, souvenir sheet	5.25
768	90¢ Hummer, sheet of 4	9.50
769	$2 Hummer, souvenir sheet	5.00
770	$3 World Stamp Championship, Israel	8.00
771	75¢ Elvis Presley, sheet of 6	12.00

SCOTT NO.	DESCRIPTION	UNUSED F/NH

772e

773a

772	42¢ Phoenix Suns, sheet of 9	9.00
773	90¢ Royal Air Force, sheet of 4	9.00
774	94¢ Pope Benedict, sheet of 4	9.50
775	75¢ Muhammad Ali, sheet of 6	10.50
776	94¢ Muhammad Ali, sheet of 4	10.00

777

777	75¢ Star Trek, sheet of 6	11.00
778	94¢ Star Trek, sheet of 4	10.50

779

779-82	22¢-94¢ Christmas, set of 4	5.00
783	94¢ Famous Men, attached pair	5.25

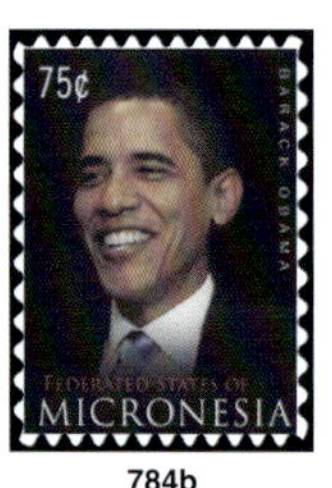

784b

785c

2009

784	Inauguration of Barak Obama, sheet of 6	8.75
785	94¢ Marilyn Monroe, sheet of 4	9.50

800a

801

786-99	Ocean Waves & Surfers	66.00
800	94¢ Year of the Ox, sheet of 4	9.50
801	42¢ Peonies	1.15
802	59¢ Olympic Sports, sheet of 4	5.75

SCOTT NO.	DESCRIPTION	UNUSED F/NH

803b

806

803	59¢ Tang Dynasty Art, sheet of 4	5.75
804	$2.50 Elvis with Stethescope S/S	6.50
805	$2.50 Elvis with Guitar S/S	6.50
806	$2.50 Elvis, strip of film S/S	6.50
807	$2.50 Elvis "Hope" S/S	6.50
808	Michael Jackson, horizontal S/S	5.00
809	Michael Jackson, vertical S/S	5.00
810	75¢ Apollo 11, sheet of 6	9.95
811	98¢ Apollo 11, sheet of 4	9.50

813

830

812-15	Butterflies, set of 4	7.00
816	Butterflies, sheet of 6	11.00
817-22	Fish, set of 6	13.00
823	Fish, sheet of 4	9.50
824-27	Dolphins, set of 4	12.00
828	75¢ Dolphins, sheet of 6	11.00
829-32	Sea Shells, set of 4	10.00

847b

842

833	75¢ Sea Shells, sheet of 6	11.00
834-37	Corals, set of 4	6.50
838	98¢ Corals, sheet of 4	10.00
839	98¢ Corals, sheet of 2	4.75
840	98¢ Abraham Lincoln, sheet of 4	10.00
841	75¢ Chinese Aviation, sheet of 4	7.75
842	$2 Chinese Aviation, souvenir sheet	5.25
843-46	Christmas, set of 4	16.00
847	98¢ Visit of Pope Benedict, sheet of 4	10.00
848	Mandarin Fish, block or strip of 4	5.25

858

849

849-52	Turtles, set of 4	12.50
853	98¢ Turtles, sheet of 4	11.00
854	$1.56 Turtles S/S of 2	8.00
855-58	Birds, set of 4	7.00
859	98¢ Birds, sheet of 4	10.00
860	$1.56 Birds, souvenir sheet of 2	8.00
860c-h	44¢ Diplomatic Relations Between Micronesia and PRC	....
860I	'09 44¢ Diplomatic Relations Between Micronesia and PRC	....
860J	'09 44¢ Diplomatic Relations Between Micronesia and PRC	....
860k	'09 44¢ Diplomatic Relations Between Micronesia and PRC	......
860l	'09 44¢ Diplomatic Relations Between Micronesia and PRC	....

SCOTT NO.	DESCRIPTION	UNUSED F/NH

862a

870

2010

861	22¢ Chinese Zodiac Animals, sheet of 12	7.25
862	$2 Year of the Tiger, souvenir sheet	10.00
863	75¢ Darwin, sheet of 6	11.00
864	75¢ Pope John Paul, sheet of 4	7.75
865-68	Mushrooms, set of 4	6.00
869	75¢ Mushrooms, sheet of 6	11.00
870	80¢ Pre/Nakayama, sheet of 4	8.00
871	$2 Pres/Nakayama, souvenir sheet	5.00
872	94¢ Girl Guides, sheet of 4	9.25

873

873	$2.50 Girl Guides, souvenir sheet	6.25
874-89	1¢-$4.80 Flowers and Fruits	40.00
890	75¢ British Monarchs, sheet of 6	11.00
891	75¢ Botticelli, sheet of 6	11.00
892	94¢ Henri Durant, Red Cross Founder, sheet of 4	11.00
893	$2.50 Henri Durant, souvenir sheet	7.00
894	75¢ Princess Diana, sheet of 4	7.50
895	$2 Issuance of the Penny Black, sheet of 2	10.00
896-900	22¢-$4.95 Christmas, set of 5	15.50
901	75¢ Pope John Paul II	2.00
902	75¢ Pope Benedict XVI, sheet of 4	7.75
903	75¢ Abraham Lincoln, sheet of 4	7.75
904-05	'10 World Cup Soccer Championship, 2 sheets of 6	18.00

2011

906	'11 Year of the Rabbit S/S of 2	7.50
907	75¢ John F. Kennedy, sheet of 4	7.50
908	75¢ Elvis, sheet of 4	7.50
909	95¢ Mohandas K. Gandi	2.50
910	$2.50 Gandhi Souvenir Sheet	6.25
911	75¢ Three Gorges Dam, sheet of 4	7.50
912	$2 Terra Cotta Warriors Souvenir Sheet	5.00
913	94¢ Royal Wedding, sheet of 4	9.75
914	94¢ Royal Wedding, sheet of 4	9.75
915-16	$1.50 Royal Wedding, set of 2 souvenir sheets	19.00
917	75¢ President Obama, sheet of 4	7.25
918	75¢ President Obama, sheet of 4	7.25
919	75¢ President Obama, sheet of 4	7.25
920	98¢ South Pole, sheet of 4	9.75
921-22	98¢ Civil War, 2 sheets of 4	20.00
923	75¢ Abraham Lincoln	1.95
924	$2.50 Abraham Lincoln souvenir sheet	6.75
925	75¢ Pope John Paul II, sheet of 4	7.25
926	$2.50 Pope John Paul II souvenir sheet	6.00
927	75¢ Elvis, sheet of 6	11.00
928	75¢ Elvis, sheet of 6	11.00
929	$2.50 Elvis souvenir sheet	6.50
930	$2.50 Elvis Souvenir Sheet	6.50
931	$2.50 Elvis Souvenir Sheet	6.50
932	$2.50 Elvis Souvenir Sheet	6.50
933-34	98¢ Royal Wedding, 2 sheets of 4	19.75
935	$2.50 Royal Wedding Souvenir Sheet	6.25
936	98¢ Princess Diana, sheet of 4	10.00
937	98¢ Princess Diana, sheet of 4	10.00
938	50¢ Reptiles of Micronesia, sheet of 5	6.25
939	$2.50 Reptiles of Micronesia Souvenir Sheet of 2	6.25
940	98¢ 9/11 sheet of 4	10.00
941	$2.50 World Trade Center Souvenir Sheet	6.25
942	50¢ Women's World Cup, sheet of 8	10.00
943	98¢ Women's World Cup, sheet of 4	10.00
944	$1 Whales, sheet of 3	7.50

945

945	$2.50 Whales souvenir sheet	6.25
946	63¢ Sun Yat-Sen, attached pair	3.25
947	63¢ Sun Yat-Sen, attached pair	3.25
947c	$2 Sr. Sun Yat-Sen Souvenir Sheet of 2	9.00
948	75¢ Sharks, sheet of 4	7.50
949	$2.50 Sharks Souvenir Sheet	6.25

SCOTT NO.	DESCRIPTION	UNUSED F/NH

950

950	$1 Game Fish, sheet of 3	7.25
951-52	$2.50 Game Fish, set of 2 souvenir sheets	12.50
953-56	22¢ - $4.95 Christmas, set of 4	16.00
957	$1.25 Chinese Pottery, sheet of 4	12.50
958	$3.50 Chinese Pottery souvenir sheet	8.75
959	$8 Year of the Dragon	19.75
960	44¢ Peace Corps, sheet of 4	7.50
961	44¢ Erhart Aten, Governor	1.25

2012

962	25¢ 25th Anniversary of Independence	.65
963	$1.25 Pope Benedict Horizontal Pair	5.75
964	$3.50 Pope Benedict S/S	7.75
965	$1.25 President Ronald Reagan	2.75
966	$3.50 Ronald Reagan, Souvenir Sheet	7.75
967	$1.25 Queen Elizabeth II sheet of 4	12.50
968	$3.50 Queen Elizabeth II souvenir sheet	8.75
969	$1.25 Sinking of the Titanic, sheet of 3	9.25
970	$3.50 Sinking of the Titanic, S/S	8.75
971	$1.50 Hindenburg Disaster, sheet of 3	11.00
972	$3.50 Hindenburg Disaster S/S	8.75
973	$1.25 Hybrid Dogs, sheet of 4	12.50
974	$3.50 Hybrid Dogs Souvenir Sheet	8.75
975	$1.25 Mother Teresa	3.25
976	$3.50 Mother Teresa Souvenir Sheet	8.75
977	$1 Three Stooges, sheet of 5	12.50
978	$3.50 Three Stooges Souvenir Sheet	8.75
979	80¢ Summer Olympics sheet of 4	8.00
980	$1.25 Turtles sheet of 4	13.00
981	$1.25 Turtles S/S of 2	6.50
982-86	$3.50 Elvis set of 5 S/S	43.00
987-88	$1.25 Pope Benedict set of 2 Sheets of 4	24.00

990

989

989-90	$1.25 JFK Space Flight Speech set of 2 sheets of 4	24.00
991-92	$1.25 Ranger Moon Program set of 2 sheets of 4	24.00

993

996

993	$1.25 Carnivorous Plants sheet of 4	12.75
994	$1.25 Carnivorous Plants S/S of 2	6.25
995-98	25¢-45¢ Christmas set of 4	3.25
999	$1 Octopus sheet of 5	12.75

1000

1002

1000	$1 Raphael Paintings sheet of 4	10.00
1001	$3.50 Raphael Paintings S/S	9.00
1002	18¢ Year of the Snake sheet of 20	9.00

1003

1005

2013

1003	$1.25 Michelangelo sheet of 4	13.00
1004	$1.25 Michelangelo Sheet of 3	10.00
1005	$1.25 World Radio Day sheet of 4	11.00
1006	$3.50 World Radio Day S/S	8.00

1012

1007

1007-08	$1.20 Vincent van Gohn set of 2 sheets of 4	19.00
1009	$3.50 Vincent van Gohn S.S	8.00
1010	$1.20 Sarah Bernhardt sheet of 4	11.00
1011	$3.50 Sarah Bernhardt S/S	8.00
1012	$1.20 John F. Kennedy sheet of 4	11.00
1013	$3.50 John F. Kennedy S/S	8.00

1014

1017

1014	$1.20 Louis Comfort Tiffany Sheet of 4	11.00
1015	$3.50 Louis Comfort Tiffany S/S	8.00
1016-17	$1.50 Art History set of 2 sheets 3	20.00
1018-19	$3.50 Art History set of 2 S/S	16.00

1028

1021

1020-21	$1.20 Pope Benedict set of 2 Sheets of 4	21.00
1022-23	$3.50 Pope Benedict set of 2 S/S	16.00
1024-25	$1.20 Dolphins set of 2 sheets of 4	22.00
1026-27	$3.50 Dolphins set of 2 S/S	16.00
1028-29	$1.20 Fish of Oceania set of 2 sheets of 4	22.00
1030-31	$3.50 Fish of Oceania set of 2 S/S	16.00
1032	$1.20 Dr. Lois Engelberger	2.75
1033	$3.50 Dr. Lois Engelberger S/S	7.75

1035

1038

1034-35	$1.25 Mushroom set of 2 sheets of 4	22.00
1036-37	$3.50 Mushrooms set of 2 S/S	16.00
1038	46¢ John De Avila	1.25

1041

1039

1045

1039	$1 Sheels sheet of 6	13.00
1040	$3.50 Shells S/S	8.00
1041	75¢ Wildlife of Thailand sheet of 8	13.00
1042	$1.75 Wildlife of Thailand sheet of 2	8.00
1043	$1.50 Internet 30th Anniversary sheet of 3	10.00
1044	$3.50 Internet S/S	7.75
1045	$10 Elvis Presley Foil S/S	22.00

1046a

2014

1046	$1.20 Dogs, Sheet of 4	10.50
1047	$3.50 Dogs, S/S	8.00
1048	$1 Parrots, Sheet of 6	13.00
1049	$3.50 Parrots, S/S	8.00
1050-51	$1.20 World War I, 2 Sheets of 4	21.00
1052-53	$2 World War I, Set of 2 S/S	17.00
1054-55	$1.50 Paintings, 2 Sheets of 3	19.00
1056-57	$4 Paintings, Set of 2 S/S	17.00
1058	$1.75 Pope Francis, Horizontal Pair	7.50
1059	$1.75 Pope Wearing Zucchetto	4.00
1059a	Horizontal Pair,	
1060	$3.50 Pope Francis, Sheet of 2	15.00
1061	$3.50 Pope Francis, Sheet of 2	15.00
1062-63	49¢ College of Micronesia, Set of 2	3.00

1065

1064	$1.20 Birth of Prince George, Sheet of 4	10.50
1065	$4 Birth of Prince George Souvenir Sheet	9.00

1067

1073

1066-73	1¢ - $1 Birds, Set of 8	5.25
1074-75	$1.20 Canonization of Pope John Paul II, 2 Sheets of 4	21.00
1076-77	$2 Canonization of Pope John Paul II, 2 S/S of 2	17.00
1078	$1.75 Nelson Mandela, Sheet of 4	15.00
1079	$1.75 Nelson Mandela, Sheet of 4	15.00
1080-81	$7 Nelson Mandela, Set of 2 Souvenir Sheets	29.00
1082-84	$1 Keitani Graham, Wrestler, Set of 3	6.75
1085	$1.20 South Korean Tourist Attractions, Sheet of 4	10.50
1086	$2 South Korean Tourist Attractions, S/S of 2	9.00
1087	$1.20 Caroline Kennedy, Sheet of 4	10.50
1088	$1.20 Caroline Kennedy, Sheet of 4	10.50
1089	$2 Caroline Kennedy, Souvenir Sheet of 2	9.00
1090	$2 Caroline Kennedy, Souvenir Sheet of 2	9.00
1091	75¢ Fruit, Sheet of 9	14.50
1092	75¢ Polar Bears, Sheet of 4	7.00
1093	$2.50 Polar Bears, S/S	6.00
1094-95	75¢ Tropical Fish, 2 Sheets of 4	13.00

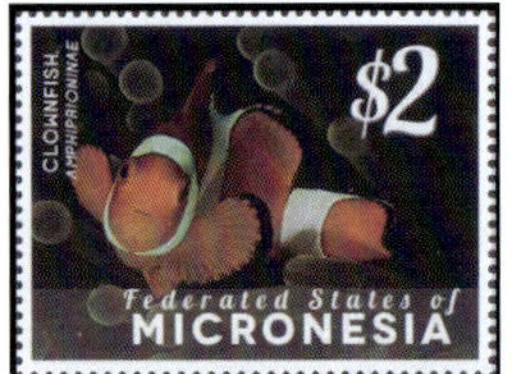

1096

1113

SCOTT NO.	DESCRIPTION	UNUSED F/NH
1096-97	$2 Tropical Fish, 2 S/S of 2	17.00
1098	$2 Bodyboarding	4.50
1099	75¢ Seaglass, Sheet of 4	7.00
1100	75¢ Seaglass, Sheet of 6	10.00
1101-02	$4 Seaglass, 2 Souvenir Sheets	17.00
1103	$1.20 Paintings by Oi Baishi, Sheet of 4	10.50
1104	$1.20 Paintings by Oi Baishi, Sheet of 4	10.50
1105-06	$4 Paintings by Oi Baishi, set of 2 Souvenir Sheets	17.00
1107-08	$1 Alphonse Mucha 75th Anniversary, set of 2 sheets	18.50
1109-10	$1 Sharks, set of 2 sheets	18.50
1113-14	$1 Butterflies, set of 2 sheets	28.75
1115-16	$3.50 Butterflies, set of 2 souvenir sheets	16.75
1117-20	$4 Elvis Presley, set of 4 souvenir sheets	39.00
1121	40¢ Orbicular Batfish, strip of 4	3.25
1122	90¢ Orbicular Batfish, strip of 4	7.50

1126

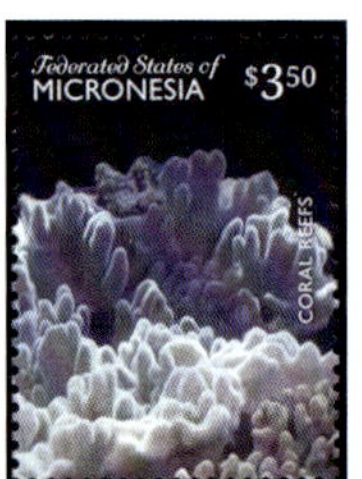

1134

SCOTT NO.	DESCRIPTION	UNUSED F/NH
1123-26	49¢-$2 Christmas, set of 4	8.50
1127	90¢ Year of the Ram, sheet of 4	8.50
1128	$8 Year of the Ram, gold souvenir sheet	18.00
1129	$1 Trans-Siberian Railway, sheet of 4	9.25
1130	$3.50 Trans-Siberian Railway, souvenir sheet	8.25
1131-32	$1 Coral Reefs, set of 2 sheets	18.50
1133-34	$3.50 Coral Reefs, set of 2 souvenir sheets	16.75

1158

2015

SCOTT NO.	DESCRIPTION	UNUSED F/NH
1135-38	29¢ - $3 Sharks, set of 4	11.00
1139	75¢ Pope John Paul II, sheet of 4	6.25
1140	$1 Duke of Cambridge and President Obama, sheet of 4	8.50
1141	$1.75 Duke of Cambridge, souvenir sheet	7.75
1142	$1 WWI Airships, sheet of 6	12.50
1143	$3.50 WWI Airships, souvenir sheet	8.00
1144	$1 Extreme Sports, BMX, sheet of 6	12.50
1145	$3.50 Extreme Sports, BMX, souvenir sheet	8.00
1146-50	1¢ - 10¢ Marine Life, set of 5	.65
1151-54	20¢ - 27¢ Hibiscus Flowers, set of 4	2.75
1155	50¢ Hibiscus Flowers, strip of 5	5.75
1156	$1 Hibiscus Flowers, strip of 5	10.50
1157	$1 London Stamp Expo, British Warbler, sheet of 6	12.50
1158	$3.50 London Stamp Expo, souvenir sheet	8.00

1159

SCOTT NO.	DESCRIPTION	UNUSED F/NH
1159	$1 Queen Elizabeth II and World Leaders, sheet of 6	12.50

1160

SCOTT NO.	DESCRIPTION	UNUSED F/NH
1160	$3.50 Queen Elizabeth II and President Obama	8.00
1161	$1 Mask Artifacts, sheet of 6	12.50
1162	$3.50 Mask Artifacts, souvenir sheet	8.00
1163-64	$1 Submarines, set of 2 sheets	18.50
1165	$1 Sir Winston Churchill, sheet of 6	12.50
1166	$1.75 Sir Winston Churchill, souvenir sheet	7.50
1167	$1 Birth of Princess Charlotte, sheet of 4	9.00

1168

SCOTT NO.	DESCRIPTION	UNUSED F/NH
1168	$3.50 Birth of Princess Charlotte, souvenir sheet	8.00

1170

SCOTT NO.	DESCRIPTION	UNUSED F/NH
1169	$1 Birds of Micronesia, sheet of 6	12.50
1170	$3.50 Birds of Micronesia, souvenir sheet	8.00

1179b

SCOTT NO.	DESCRIPTION	UNUSED F/NH
1171-78	$1 First stamps of U.N. Member States, 8 sheets of 6	......
1178g	$3.50 First stamps of U.N. Members, U.S., souvenir sheet	......
1179	$1 Pope Benedict, sheet of 5	10.75
1180	$3.50 Pope Benedict, souvenir sheet	8.00

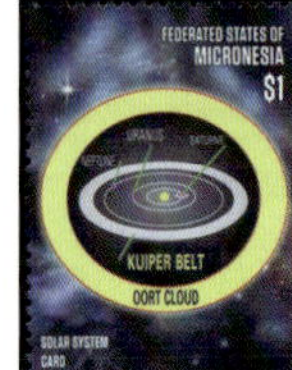

1181a

SCOTT NO.	DESCRIPTION	UNUSED F/NH
1181	$1 Space Anniversary, sheet of 4	9.00
1182	$3.50 Space Anniversary, souvenir sheet	8.00
1183	$1 Vincent van Gogh, sheet of 6	13.50

1185b

SCOTT NO.	DESCRIPTION	UNUSED F/NH
1184	$3.50 Vincent van Gogh, souvenir sheet	8.00
1185	$1 Orchids, sheet of 4	9.00
1186	$3.50 Orchids, souvenir sheet	8.00
1187	$1 Plants and Flowers, sheet of 6	13.50
1188	$3.50 Plants and Flowers, souvenir sheet	8.00
1189	$1 Marine Mammels, sheet of 6	13.50
1190	$3.50 Marine Mammals, souvenir sheet	8.00

1191a

SCOTT NO.	DESCRIPTION	UNUSED F/NH
1191	$1 Battle of Waterloo, sheet of 6	13.50
1192	$3.50 Battle of Waterloo, souvenir sheet	8.00

1193

SCOTT NO.	DESCRIPTION	UNUSED F/NH
1193-96	34¢-$2 Christmas Paintings, set of 4	9.00

C1

1984-94 AIR MAIL

SCOTT NO.	DESCRIPTION	UNUSED F/NH
C1-3	28¢-40¢ Aircraft, set of 3	2.75
C25	$1 Ameripex '86 Souvenir Sheet	4.90

C39

SCOTT NO.	DESCRIPTION	UNUSED F/NH
C39-42	45¢ State Flags, block of 4 attached	4.90
C43-46	22¢-45¢ Aircraft Serving Micronesia (4 varieties)	7.50
C47-48	40¢, 50¢ Aircraft and Ships	5.75
C49	$2.90 25th Anniv. First Moon Landing, souvenir sheet	7.50

Postal Stationery

SCOTT NO.	DESCRIPTION	UNUSED F/NH
U1	20¢ National Flag	17.00
U2	22¢ Tail Ship Senyavin	12.00
U3	29¢ on 30¢ New Capitol	5.00

Postal Cards

SCOTT NO.	DESCRIPTION	UNUSED F/NH
UX1-4	20¢ Scenes, set of 4	7.50

REPUBLIC OF PALAU

Palau is a Strategic Trust of the United States; a designation granted by the United Nations after World War II. It is the first Trust Territory to be granted postal independence, which became effective November 1, 1982. The first stamps were issued March 10, 1983.

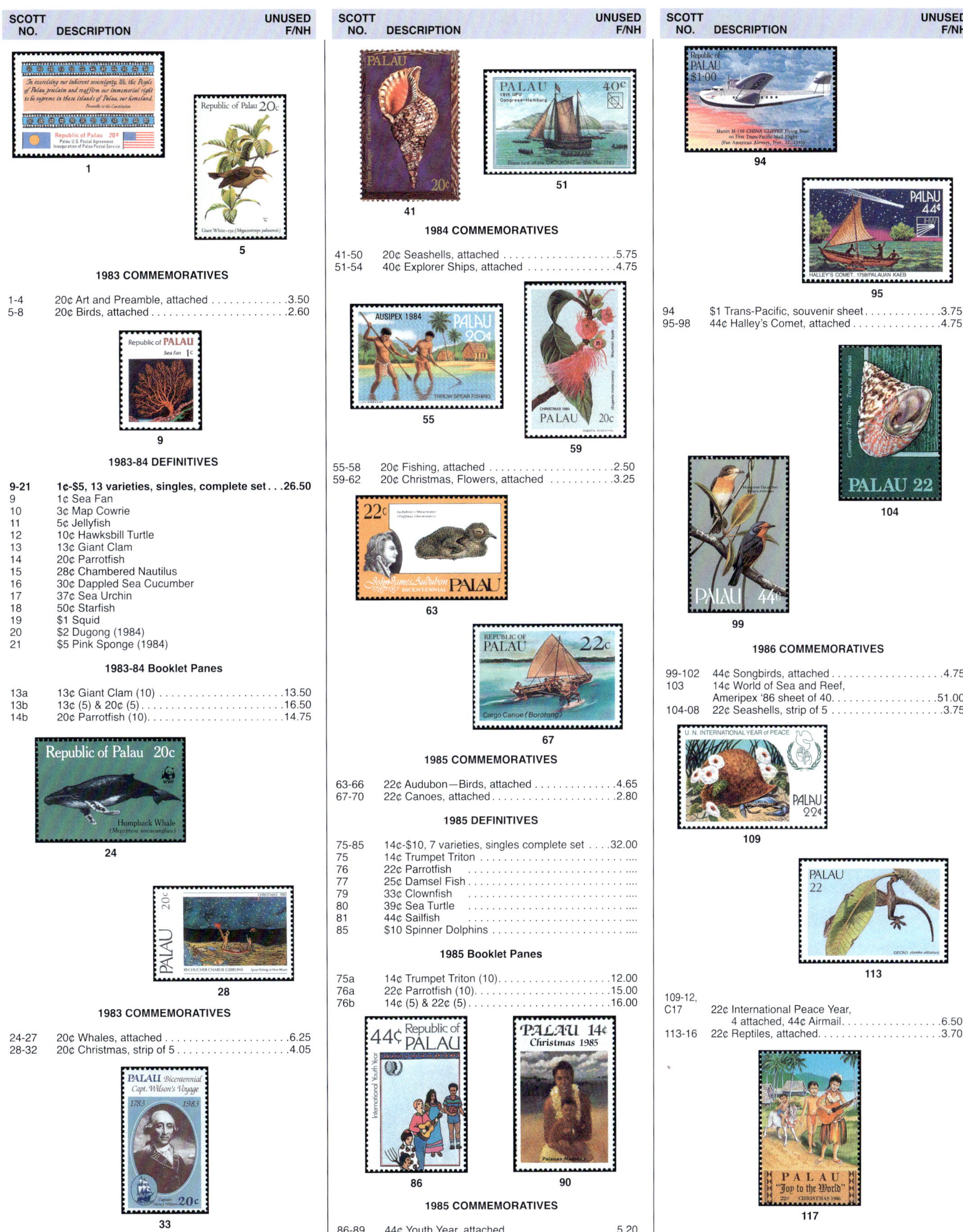

SCOTT NO.	DESCRIPTION	UNUSED F/NH

1 5

1983 COMMEMORATIVES

1-4	20¢ Art and Preamble, attached	3.50
5-8	20¢ Birds, attached	2.60

9

1983-84 DEFINITIVES

9-21	**1¢-$5, 13 varieties, singles, complete set**	**26.50**
9	1¢ Sea Fan	
10	3¢ Map Cowrie	
11	5¢ Jellyfish	
12	10¢ Hawksbill Turtle	
13	13¢ Giant Clam	
14	20¢ Parrotfish	
15	28¢ Chambered Nautilus	
16	30¢ Dappled Sea Cucumber	
17	37¢ Sea Urchin	
18	50¢ Starfish	
19	$1 Squid	
20	$2 Dugong (1984)	
21	$5 Pink Sponge (1984)	

1983-84 Booklet Panes

13a	13¢ Giant Clam (10)	13.50
13b	13¢ (5) & 20¢ (5)	16.50
14b	20¢ Parrotfish (10)	14.75

24

28

1983 COMMEMORATIVES

24-27	20¢ Whales, attached	6.25
28-32	20¢ Christmas, strip of 5	4.05

33

33-40	20¢ When Different Worlds Meet, attached	5.50

41 51

1984 COMMEMORATIVES

41-50	20¢ Seashells, attached	5.75
51-54	40¢ Explorer Ships, attached	4.75

55 59

55-58	20¢ Fishing, attached	2.50
59-62	20¢ Christmas, Flowers, attached	3.25

63

67

1985 COMMEMORATIVES

63-66	22¢ Audubon—Birds, attached	4.65
67-70	22¢ Canoes, attached	2.80

1985 DEFINITIVES

75-85	14¢-$10, 7 varieties, singles complete set	32.00
75	14¢ Trumpet Triton	....
76	22¢ Parrotfish	....
77	25¢ Damsel Fish	....
79	33¢ Clownfish	....
80	39¢ Sea Turtle	....
81	44¢ Sailfish	....
85	$10 Spinner Dolphins	....

1985 Booklet Panes

75a	14¢ Trumpet Triton (10)	12.00
76a	22¢ Parrotfish (10)	15.00
76b	14¢ (5) & 22¢ (5)	16.00

86 90

1985 COMMEMORATIVES

86-89	44¢ Youth Year, attached	5.20
90-93	14¢-44¢ Christmas, 4 varieties	4.05

94

95

94	$1 Trans-Pacific, souvenir sheet	3.75
95-98	44¢ Halley's Comet, attached	4.75

104

99

1986 COMMEMORATIVES

99-102	44¢ Songbirds, attached	4.75
103	14¢ World of Sea and Reef, Ameripex '86 sheet of 40	51.00
104-08	22¢ Seashells, strip of 5	3.75

109

113

109-12, C17	22¢ International Peace Year, 4 attached, 44¢ Airmail	6.50
113-16	22¢ Reptiles, attached	3.70

117

117-21	22¢ Christmas, attached	3.50

121B 122

142

1987 COMMEMORATIVES

SCOTT NO.	DESCRIPTION	UNUSED F/NH
121B-E	44¢ Butterflies, attached	5.50
122-25	44¢ Fruit Bats, attached	5.50

1987-88 FLOWER DEFINITIVES

SCOTT NO.	DESCRIPTION	UNUSED F/NH
126-42	1¢-$5, 17 varieties, single complete set	52.00
126	1¢ Kerdeu	......
127	3¢ Ngemoel	......
128	5¢ Uror	......
129	10¢ Woody Vine	......
130	14¢ Rur	......
131	15¢ Jaml (1988)	......
132	22¢ Denges	......
133	25¢ Ksid (1988)	......
134	36¢ Meldii (1988)	......
135	39¢ Emeridesh	......
136	44¢ Eskeam	......
137	45¢ Shrub (1988)	......
137	45¢ Shrub (1988)	......
138	50¢ Rriu	......
139	$1 Koranges	......
140	$2 Meliin	......
141	$5 Orchid	......
142	$10 Flower Bouquet (1988)	......

1987 Booklet Panes

SCOTT NO.	DESCRIPTION	UNUSED F/NH
130a	14¢ Bikkia Palauensis (10)	5.80
132a	22¢ Bruguiera Gymnorhiza (10)	9.50
132b	14¢ (5) and 22¢ (5)	9.50

1988 Booklet Panes

SCOTT NO.	DESCRIPTION	UNUSED F/NH
131a	15¢ Limnophila (10)	7.00
133a	25¢ Ksid (10)	7.50
133b	15¢ (5) 25¢ (5)	7.20

146 155

SCOTT NO.	DESCRIPTION	UNUSED F/NH
146-49	22¢ Capex '87, attached	2.80
150-54	22¢ Seashells, strip of 5	3.75
155-63	14¢-44¢ U.S. Bicentennial 3 attached, strips of 3	6.50
164-67	12¢-44¢ Japan Links	3.20
168	$1 Japan souvenir sheet	3.20

173

178

SCOTT NO.	DESCRIPTION	UNUSED F/NH
173-77	22¢ Christmas, attached	3.50
178-82	22¢ Marine Species, attached	4.75

187

1988 COMMEMORATIVES

SCOTT NO.	DESCRIPTION	UNUSED F/NH
183-86	44¢ Butterflies, attached	4.55
187-90	44¢ Birds, attached	4.55

196a

SCOTT NO.	DESCRIPTION	UNUSED F/NH
191-95	25¢ Seashells, strip of 5	3.75
196	25¢ Finlandia sheetlet of 6	4.25
197	45¢ PRAGA '88, sheetlet of 6	7.00

198

SCOTT NO.	DESCRIPTION	UNUSED F/NH
198-202	25¢ Christmas, strip of 5	3.75
203	25¢ Chambered Nautilus, sheetlet of 5	4.40

204

208

1989 COMMEMORATIVES

SCOTT NO.	DESCRIPTION	UNUSED F/NH
204-07	45¢ Endangered Birds, attached	5.20
208-11	45¢ Mushrooms, attached	5.20
212-16	25¢ Seashells, strip of 5	3.95
217	$1 Japanese Art souvenir sheet	3.30
218	25¢ Apollo 11 mission, sheetlet of 25	16.00

219

SCOTT NO.	DESCRIPTION	UNUSED F/NH
219	$2.40 Priority Mail	6.25

220a

222

SCOTT NO.	DESCRIPTION	UNUSED F/NH
220	25¢ Literacy (block of 10)	6.50
221	25¢ Stilt Mangrove Fauna, sheetlet of 20	16.00
222-26	25¢ Christmas (strip of 5)	4.00

227

231

1990 COMMEMORATIVES

SCOTT NO.	DESCRIPTION	UNUSED F/NH
227-30	25¢ Soft Coral (4 attached)	3.20
231-34	45¢ Forest Birds (4 attached)	5.20

235a

237

SCOTT NO.	DESCRIPTION	UNUSED F/NH
235	Prince Boo Visit (sheet of 9)	6.50
236	$1 Penny Black Ann	2.90
237-41	45¢ Tropical Orchids (strip of 5)	6.50

242

SCOTT NO.	DESCRIPTION	UNUSED F/NH
242-45	45¢ Butterflies II (4 attached)	5.00
246	25¢ Lagoon Life, sheet of 25	17.00
247-48	45¢ Pacifica, pair	4.50

254

249

SCOTT NO.	DESCRIPTION	UNUSED F/NH
249-53	25¢ Christmas, strip of 5	3.75
254-57	45¢ U.S. Forces in Palau, attached	6.00
258	$1 U.S. Peleliu, souvenir sheet	3.75

SCOTT NO.	DESCRIPTION	UNUSED F/NH

259

263a

1991

259-62 30¢ Hard Corals, attached 4.00
263 30¢ Angaur—The Phosphate Island sheet of 16 . .14.00

267

1991-92

266-83 1¢-$10 Birds, 18 varieties 56.00

1991 Booklet Panes

269b 19¢ Palau fantail booklet pane (10). 5.25
272a Booklet pane of 10, 19¢ (5) + 29¢ (5) 7.00
272b 29¢ Palau fruit dove booklet pane (10) 6.00

288a

289a

288 29¢ Christianity in Palau, sheetlet of 6 . . . . .4.90
289 29¢ Marine Life, sheetlet of 20 . . . . .16.50

294a

290a

290 20¢ Operation Desert Storm, sheetlet of 9 . . . . .5.50
291 $2.90 Operation Desert Storm Priority Mail. 8.00
292 $2.90 Operation Desert Storm Souvenir Sheet. .8.00
293 29¢ 10th Anniversary of Independence, sheetlet of 8 . . . . .6.75
294 50¢ Giant Clams, Souvenir Sheet of 5 . . . . .7.00

295a

295 29¢ Japanese Heritage in Palau, sheet of 6 . . . .5.00

297a

299a

296 $1.00 Phila Nippon, Souvenir Sheet 4.00
297 29¢ Peace Corps, sheetlet of 6. . . . . .5.00
298 29¢ Christmas, 1991, strip of 5 . . . . .5.00
299 29¢ Pearl Harbor/WWII, sheetlet of 10 . . . . . . .11.50

300a

301a

1992

300 50¢ Butterflies, attached 5.50
301 29¢ Shells, strip of 5 . . . . .4.00

302a

302 29¢ Columbus & Age of Discovery, sheetlet of 20. . .16.00
303 29¢ World Environment, sheetlet of 24 . . . . . . .18.00
304-09 50¢ Olympians, set of 6 Souvenir Sheets 8.00

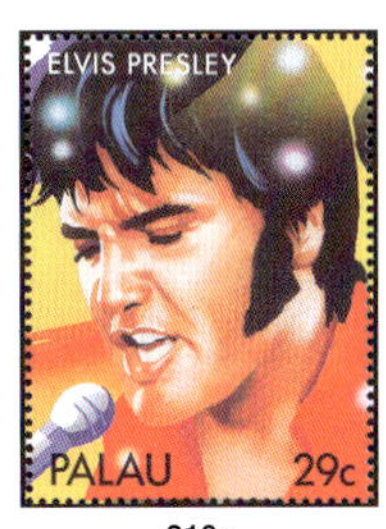

310e

312a

310 29¢ Elvis Presley, sheetlet of 9 . . . . .9.50
311 50¢ WWII Aircraft, sheet of 10. . . . . .12.00
312 29¢ Christmas, strip of 5 . . . . .4.75

313a

314a

1993

313 50¢ Fauna, 4 attached .5.75
314 29¢ Seafood, 4 attached 3.50

315a

316a

315 50¢ Sharks, 4 attached .5.75
316 29¢ WWII in the Pacific, sheetlet of 10 . . . . . . .11.00
317 29¢ Christmas 1993, strip of 5 . . . . .4.50
318 29¢ Prehistoric Sea Creatures, sheet of 25 . . .19.50
319 29¢ International Year of Indigeneous People, sheet of 2 . . . . .3.25
320 $2.90 Quarrying of Stone Money, souvenir sheet. 8.50
321 29¢ Jonah and the Whale, sheet of 25 . . . . . . .19.50

322a

323a

1994

322 40¢ Rays "Hong Kong '94", 4 attached 4.55
323 20¢ Estuarine Crocodile, 4 attached 4.75

324a

327

324 50¢ Large Seabirds, 4 attached 5.80
325 29¢ Action in the Pacific, 1944, sheet of 10 . . .11.00
326 50¢ D-Day, sheet of 10 . . . . .15.00
327 29¢ Pierre de Coubertin 1.05
328-33 50¢-$2 Winter Olympic medalists, souvenir sheet of 1 (6). 15.50

334a

338a

334 29¢ PHILAKOREA '94 (Fish), sheetlet of 8. . . . .8.35
335 40¢ PHILAKOREA '94 (Mammals), sheetlet of 8 . . . . .11.85
336 50¢ PHILAKOREA '94 (Birds), sheetlet of 8 . . .13.85
337 29¢ 25th Anniversary First Manned Moon Landing, sheet of 20 . . . . .16.00
338 29¢ Independence Day, strip of 5 . . . . .4.25
339 $1 50th Anniv. of Invasion of Peleliu, souvenir sheet 3.75

340a

340 29¢ Disney Characters Visit Palau, sheetlet of 9 . . . . .8.50
341-42 $1 Mickey, Donald visiting Palau, souvenir sheet of 1 (2) 6.95
343 $2.90 Pluto, Mickey in Boat, souvenir sheet 8.65

SCOTT NO.	DESCRIPTION	UNUSED F/NH

344a  345a

344	20¢ Int. Year of the Family, sheetlet of 12	6.50
345	29¢ Christmas, strip of 5	4.35
346-48	29¢-50¢ World Cup '94, 3 sheetlets of 12	35.00

351

1995

350	32¢ Elvis Presley, sheetlet of 9	9.25
351-65	1¢-$10 Palau Fishes, set of 15	55.00

1995 Booklet Panes

366a	20¢ Magenta dottyback (10)	5.50
367a	32¢ Reef Lizardfish (10)	8.95
367b	same, 20¢ (5) & 32¢ (5)	7.25

368a

369a

368	32¢ WWII Japanese Sunken Ships, sheetlet of 18	16.00
369	32¢ Flying Dinosaurs, sheetlet of 18	16.00

372a

370a

370	50¢ Experimental Aircraft (Jets), sheetlet of 12	16.00
371	$2 Experimental Aircraft (Concorde) souvenir sheet	5.20
372	32¢ Underwater Submersibles, sheetlet of 18	17.00

373a

374a

373	32¢ Marine Life (Singapore '95), 4 attached	3.75
374	60¢ UN, FAO, 50th Anniversary, 4 attached	6.95
375-76	$2 UN Emblem souvenir sheet (2)	11.00
377-78	20¢-32¢ Independence Anniversary, min. sheet of 4 & single	5.00
379-80	32¢-60¢ 50th End of WWII, sheetlets of 12 & 5	19.50

SCOTT NO.	DESCRIPTION	UNUSED F/NH

381

382a

381	$3 B-29 Nose souvenir sheet	8.95
382	32¢ Christmas 1995, strip of 5	4.95
383	32¢ Life Cycle of the Sea Turtle, sheetlet of 12	11.50

384

384	32¢ John Lennon	1.65

385a

1996

385	10¢ New Year 1996 (Year of the Rat), strip of 4	2.45
386	60¢ New Year 1996 (Year of the Rat), min. sheet of 2	3.95

388a

389a

387	32¢ UNICEF, 50th Anniversary, 4 attached	3.75
388	32¢ Marine Life, strip of 5	4.50
389-90	32¢-60¢ The Circumnavigators, 2 sheetlets of 9	23.65
391-92	$3 The Circumnavigators, 2 souvenir sheets	17.30
392A-F	1¢-6¢ Disney Sweethearts, set of 6	1.45

396a

393a

393	60¢ Disney Sweethearts, sheetlet of 9	16.50
394-95	$2 Disney Sweethearts, 2 souvenir sheets	12.00
396	20¢ Jerusalem Bible Studies, sheetlet of 30	15.75

SCOTT NO.	DESCRIPTION	UNUSED F/NH

397-98

397-98	40¢ 1996 Summer Olympics, pair	2.65

399-400

399-400	60¢ 1996 Summer Olympics, pair	4.00

401a

403a

401	32¢ 1996 Summer Olympics, sheet of 20	17.00
402	50¢ Birds over the Palau Lagoon, sheet of 20	27.00
403	40¢ Military Spy Aircraft, sheet of 12	14.00
404	60¢ Weird & Wonderful Aircraft, sheet of 12	19.00
405	$3 Stealth Bomber, souvenir sheet	8.75
406	$3 Martin Marietta X-24B, souvenir sheet	8.75

407-08

407-08	20¢ Independence, 2nd Anniversary, pair	1.15
409	32¢ Christmas 1996, strip of 5	6.25
410	32¢ Voyage to Mars, sheet of 12	11.25
411-12	$3 Mars rover & Water probe, 2 souvenir sheets	17.00

415

1997

412A	$2 Year of the Ox, souvenir sheet	6.35
413	$1 50th Anniv. of South Pacific Commission, souvenir sheet	2.90
414-19	1¢-$3 Flowers (Hong Kong '97), set of 6	9.50

SCOTT NO.	DESCRIPTION	UNUSED F/NH

420a

422a

420	32¢ Shoreline Plants (Hong Kong '97), 4 attached	3.75
421	50¢ Shoreline Plants (Hong Kong '97), 4 attached	5.80
422-23	32¢-60¢ Bicentennial of the Parachute, sheet of 8	19.75
424-25	$2 Bicentennial of the Parachute, 2 souvenir sheets	12.00
426	20¢ Native Birds & Trees, sheet of 12	8.75

427a

431a

428a

427-28	32¢-60¢ 50th Anniv. of UNESCO, sheet of 8 & 5	15.50
429-30	$2 50th Anniv. of UNESCO, 2 souvenir sheets	12.50
431	32¢ Prints of Hiroshige, sheet of 5	5.75
432-33	$2 Prints of Hiroshige, 2 souvenir sheets	12.00

434a

435

434	32¢ Volcano Goddesses, sheet of 6	6.00
435	32¢ 3rd Anniversary of Independence	.95

436a

440a

436	32¢ Oceanographic Research, sheetlet of 9	8.65
437-39	$2 Oceanographic Research, souvenir sheets (3)	17.00
440	60¢ Princess Diana	2.05

450a

441-46	1¢-10¢ Disney "Let's Read"	1.45
447	32¢ Disney Characters "Reading", sheetlet of 9	8.10
448	$2 Daisy "The library is for everyone" souvenir sheet	6.95
449	$3 Mickey "Books are magical" souvenir sheet	9.25
450	32¢ Children singing Christmas carol, strip of 5	4.90

453a

1998

451-52	50¢ Year of the Tiger. souvenir sheets (2)	3.20
453	32¢ Hubble Space Telescope, sheetlet of 6	5.75
454-56	$2 Hubble Space Telescope, souvenir sheets (3)	16.00

457a

458a

457	60¢ Mother Teresa, sheetlet of 4	7.50
458	32¢ Deep Sea Robots, sheetlet of 18	16.00
459-60	$2 Deep Sea Robots, souvenir sheets (2)	13.00

461a

463a

461	20¢ Israel Stamp Expo ovpt. on Sc. #396, sheetlet of 30	17.00
462	40¢ Legend of Orachel, sheetlet of 12	13.50
463	50¢ 1998 World Cup Soccer, sheetlet of 8	11.00
464	$3 1998 World Cup Soccer, souvenir sheet	8.65
465	32¢ 4th Micronesian Games, sheetlet of 9	8.35

466a

466	32¢ Christmas, Rudolph the Red Nosed Reindeer, strip of 5	4.55
467-70	20¢-60¢ Disney's "A Bug's Life" 4 sheets of 4	17.50
471-74	$2 Disney's "A Bug's Life" 4 souvenir sheets	22.00
475-76	60¢ John Glenn's Return to Space, 2 sheets of 8	26.00
477-78	$2 John Glenn's Return to Space, 2 souvenir sheets	12.00

480a

495a

1999

479	33¢ Environmentalists, sheetlet of 16	13.50
480	33¢ MIR Space Station, sheetlet of 6	5.50
481-84	$2 MIR Space Station, 4 souvenir sheets	22.50
485-94	1¢-$3.20 US & Palau Personalities, set of 10	15.50
495	33¢ Australia '99 World Stamp Expo, sheetlet of 12	10.50

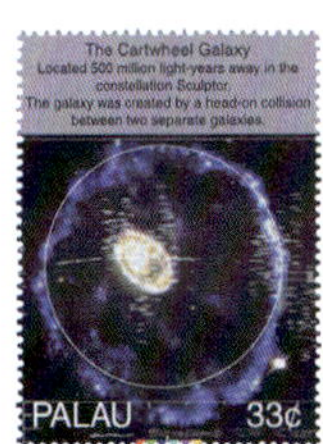
507a

512a

496-97	$2 Australia '99, 2 souvenir sheets	11.25
498-99	55¢ IBRA '99 Exhibition, Caroline Islands Stamps, set of 2	3.10
500	$2 IBRA '99 Exhibition, Caroline Islands Stamps, miniature sheet	5.70
501	33¢ Exploration of Mars, sheetlet of 6	5.70
502-05	$2 Exploration of Mars, 4 souvenir sheets	21.00
506	33¢ Pacific Insects, Earth Day, sheetlet of 20	18.50
507	33¢ International Space Station, sheetlet of 6	5.50
508-11	$2 International Space Station, 4 souvenir sheets	21.50
512	33¢ 20th Century Visionaries, sheetlet of 25	22.50
513-14	33¢ Hokusai Paintings, 2 sheetlets of 6	10.95
515-16	$2 Hokusai Paintings, 2 souvenir sheets	10.50

517a

524a

517	33¢ Apollo 11, 30th Anniversary, sheetlet of 6	5.75
518-21	$2 Apollo 11, 30th Anniversary, 4 souvenir sheets	21.00
522	60¢ Queen Mother (b.1900), sheetlet of 4	6.65
523	$2 Queen Mother (b.1900), souvenir sheet	6.05
524	33¢ Hubble Space Telescope Images, sheetlet of 6	6.05
525-28	$2 Hubble Space Telescope Images, 4 souvenir sheets	22.50
529	20¢ Christmas, Birds and Animals, strip of 5	2.90
530	33¢ Love for Dogs, sheetlet of 10	9.80
531-32	$2 Love for Dogs, 2 souvenir sheets	11.55

SCOTT NO.	DESCRIPTION	UNUSED F/NH
	2000	
533	55¢ Futuristic Space probes, sheetlet of 6	7.75
534-37	$2 Fururistic Space Probes, 4 souvenir sheets	22.50
538-39	20¢ Highlights of 1800-50 and Highlights of 1980-89, 2 Millenium sheetlets of 17	19.00
540	$2 New Year 2000 (Year of the Dragon)	5.75
541-45	$1-$11.75 US Presidents	53.00
546	20¢ 20th Century Discoveries about Prehistoric Life, sheetlet of 20	11.25
547	33¢ 2000 Summer Olympics, Sydney, sheetlet of 4	4.00
548	33¢ Future of Space Exploration, sheetlet of 6	6.00
549-52	$2 Future of Space Exploration, 4 souvenir sheets	22.00

553a

SCOTT NO.	DESCRIPTION	UNUSED F/NH
553-54	20¢-33¢ Birds, 2 sheetlets of 6	8.95

557a

564a

SCOTT NO.	DESCRIPTION	UNUSED F/NH
555-56	$2 Birds, 2 souvenir sheets	10.95
557	33¢ Visionaries of the 20th Century, sheetlet of 20	17.50
558-61	33¢ 20th Century Science and Medicine Advances, 4 sheetlets of 5	17.75
562-63	$2 20th Century Science and Medicine Advances, 2 souvenir sheets	10.00
564-65	33¢ Marine Life, 2 sheetlets of 6	10.00
566-67	$2 Marine Life, 2 souvenir sheets	10.00

568a

SCOTT NO.	DESCRIPTION	UNUSED F/NH
568	20¢ Millennium, sheetlet of 6	3.20
569	55¢ Millennium, sheetlet of 6	9.50

574a

570a

SCOTT NO.	DESCRIPTION	UNUSED F/NH
570-71	33¢ New and Recovering Species, 2 sheetlets of 6	10.00
572-73	$2 New and Recovering Species, 2 souvenir sheets	10.00
574	20¢ Dinosaurs, sheetlet of 6	3.20
575	33¢ Dinosaurs, sheetlet of 6	5.80
576-77	$2 Dinosaurs, 2 souvenir sheets	10.00
578-79	55¢ Queen Mother's 100th birthday, 2 sheetlets of 4	11.50
580	$2 Queen Mother's 100th birthday, souvenir sheet	5.50

581a

584a

SCOTT NO.	DESCRIPTION	UNUSED F/NH
581	55¢ First Zeppelin Flight, sheetlet of 6	8.50
582-83	$2 First Zeppelin Flight, 2 souvenir sheets	10.00
584	33¢ Millennium, sheetlet of 17	17.95
585	50¢ Pope John Paul II, sheetlet of 8	11.00
586-87	60¢ Year of the Snake, 2 souvenir sheets	3.40

589a

SCOTT NO.	DESCRIPTION	UNUSED F/NH
588	55¢ Pacific Ocean Marine Life, sheetlet of 6	8.75
589	20¢ Atlantic Ocean Fish, sheetlet of 6	3.40
590-91	$2 Atlantic Ocean Fish, 2 souvenir sheets	10.00

592a

SCOTT NO.	DESCRIPTION	UNUSED F/NH
592	33¢ Pacific Arts Festival, sheetlet of 9	8.25
593	33¢ National Museum, 45th anniv., sheetlet of 12	10.00

602a

594

SCOTT NO.	DESCRIPTION	UNUSED F/NH
594-97	33¢ Butterflies, set of 4 singles	4.00
598-99	33¢ Butterflies, 2 sheetlets of 6	10.00
600-01	$2 Butterflies, 2 souvenir sheets	10.00
602-03	33¢ Flora and Fauna, 2 sheetlets of 6	10.00
604-05	$2 Flora and Fauna, 2 souvenir sheets	10.00

607

616

SCOTT NO.	DESCRIPTION	UNUSED F/NH
	2001	
606-09	11¢-$12.25 Personalities, set of 3	34.50
610-11	60¢ Phila Nippon, Japan, 2 sheetlets of 5	17.00
612	60¢ Phila Nippon, Japan, sheetlet of 6	10.00
613-15	$2 Phila Nippon, Japan, 3 souvenir sheets	16.00
616-19	20¢-$1 Moths, set of 4	6.00
620-21	34¢-70¢ Moths, 2 sheetlets of 6	16.50
622-23	$2 Moths, 2 souvenir sheets	10.00
624-26	34¢-80¢ Nobel Prizes Cent., 3 sheetlets of 6	27.50
627-29	$2 Nobel Prizes Cent., 3 souvenir sheets	15.75

630a

SCOTT NO.	DESCRIPTION	UNUSED F/NH
630-31	34¢-80¢ 2002 World Cup Soccer, 2 sheetlets of 6	18.00
632-33	$2 2002 World Cup Soccer, 2 souvenir sheets	10.00

634

SCOTT NO.	DESCRIPTION	UNUSED F/NH
634-35	20¢-34¢ Christmas, set of 2	1.65
636	60¢ Queen Mother redrawn, sheet of 4 + label	6.95
637	$2 Queen Mother redrawn, souvenir sheet	5.50

639

638a

SCOTT NO.	DESCRIPTION	UNUSED F/NH
638	60¢ Year of the Horse	2.75
639-40	55¢-60¢ Birds, 2 sheetlets of 6	18.50
641-42	$2 Birds of Palau, 2 souvenir sheets	10.95

645

648

SCOTT NO.	DESCRIPTION	UNUSED F/NH
	2002	
643-44	20¢-30¢ Palau-Japan Friendship Bridge, 2 sheets of 30	43.00
645	$1 United We Stand	3.75
646	80¢ Reign of Queen Elizabeth II, 50th Anniv., sheet of 4	9.20
647	$2 Reign of Queen Elizabeth II, 50th Anniv., souvenir sheet	5.50
648-669	1¢-$10 Birds, set of 22	75.00

SCOTT NO.	DESCRIPTION	UNUSED F/NH

670

678

SCOTT NO.	DESCRIPTION	UNUSED F/NH
670-73	20¢-80¢ Flowers, set of 4	5.50
674-75	60¢ Flowers, 2 sheetlets of 6	19.00
676-77	$2 Flowers, 2 souvenir sheets	10.00
678-79	$1 2002 Winter Olympics, set of 2	5.50

688

680a

SCOTT NO.	DESCRIPTION	UNUSED F/NH
679a	$1 2002 Winter Olympics, souvenir sheet of 2	5.50
680-81	50¢ Cats & Dogs, 2 sheetlets of 6	17.30
682-83	$2 Cats & Dogs, 2 souvenir sheets	10.95
684	80¢ Intl. Year of Mountains, sheet of 4	8.95
685	$2 Intl. Year of Mountains, souvenir sheet	5.50
686	37¢ Flags of Palau and its States, sheet of 17	16.00
687-88	$1 2002 Winter Olympics, redrawn, set of 2	5.50
688a	$1 2002 Winter Olympics, redrawn, souvenir sheet	5.50

696a

705a

SCOTT NO.	DESCRIPTION	UNUSED F/NH
689	60¢ Intl. Year of Ecotourism, sheet of 6	10.00
690	$2 Intl. Year of Ecotourism, souvenir sheet	5.50
691	60¢ Japanese Art, sheet of 6	10.00
692-93	80¢ Japanese Art, 2 sheets of 4	17.00
694-95	$2 Japanese Art, 2 souvenir sheets	10.95
696	60¢ Popeye, sheet of 6	10.00
697	$2 Popeye, souvenir sheet	7.00
698	37¢ Elvis Presley, sheet of 6	6.35
699-703	23¢-$1 Christmas, set of 5	8.10
704	$2 Christmas, souvenir sheet	5.50
705	60¢ Teddy Bears, 100th Birthday, sheet of 4	9.75
706	80¢ Queen Mother, sheet of 4	8.95
707	$2 Queen Mother, souvenir sheet	5.50

708a

2003

SCOTT NO.	DESCRIPTION	UNUSED F/NH
708	60¢ 20th World Scout Jamboree, Thailand, sheet of 6	9.50
709	$2 20th World Scout Jamboree, Thailand, souvenir sheet	5.50

710a

712a

SCOTT NO.	DESCRIPTION	UNUSED F/NH
710	60¢ Shells, sheet of 6	9.50
711	$2 Shells, souvenir sheet	5.50
712	37¢ Year of the Ram, vert. strip of 3	6.05
713	80¢ President John F. Kennedy, sheet of 4	8.95

714

SCOTT NO.	DESCRIPTION	UNUSED F/NH
714-15	26¢-37¢ Birds, unserifed numerals	1.95
716	37¢ Astronauts, Space Shuttle Columbia, sheet of 7	7.20

717a

SCOTT NO.	DESCRIPTION	UNUSED F/NH
717	60¢ Orchids, sheet of 6	9.80
718	$2 Orchids, souvenir sheet	5.50

723a

741

SCOTT NO.	DESCRIPTION	UNUSED F/NH
719	60¢ Insects, sheet of 6	9.80
720	$2 Insects, souvenir sheet	5.50
721	60¢ 1st Non-Stop Solo Transatlantic Flight, 75th Anniversary, sheet of 6	9.80
722	80¢ President Ronald Reagan, sheet of 4	8.95
723	80¢ Princess Diana (1961-97), sheet of 4	8.95
724	$1 Coronation of Queen Elizabeth II, 50th Anniversary, sheet of 3	8.40
725	$2 Coronation of Queen Elizabeth II, 50th Anniversary, souvenir sheet	5.50
726	37¢ Operation Iraqi Freedom, sheet of 6	8.50
727	$1 Prince William, 21st Birthday, sheet of 3	8.40
728	$2 Prince William, 21st Birthday, souvenir sheet	5.50
729	60¢ Tour de France Bicycle Race Centenary, sheet of 4	6.65
730	$2 Tour de France Bicycle Race Centenary, souvenir sheet	5.50
731	55¢ Powered Flight, sheet of 6	9.20
732	$2 Powered Flight, souvenir sheet	5.50
733-36	37¢-$1 Paintings by James McNeil Whistler, set of 4	6.95
737	80¢ Paintings by James McNeil Whistler, sheet of 4	8.95
738	$2 Paintings by James McNeil Whistler, souvenir sheet	5.50
739-40	80¢ Circus Performers, set of 2 sheets of 4	19.50
741-44	37¢-$1 Christmas, set of 4	7.50
745	$2 Christmas, souvenir sheet	5.50

748a

757a

2004

SCOTT NO.	DESCRIPTION	UNUSED F/NH
746	60¢ Sea Turtles, sheet of 6	9.80
747	$2 Sea Turtles, souvenir sheet	5.50
748	80¢ Paintings of Norman Rockwell, sheet of 4	8.95
749	$2 Paintings of Norman Rockwell, souvenir sheet	5.50
750	80¢ Paintings by Pablo Picasso, sheet of 4	8.95
751	$2 Painting by Pablo Picasso, souvenir sheet, imperf.	5.50
752-55	37¢-$1 Paintings in the Hermitage Museum, set of 4	7.20
756	$2 Painting in the Hermitage Museum, souvenir sheet, imperf.	5.50
757	55¢ Marine Life, sheet of 6	9.20
758	$2 Marine Life, souvenir sheet	5.50
759	55¢ Minerals, sheet of 6	9.20
760	$2 Minerals, souvenir sheet	5.50
761	50¢ Year of the Monkey	2.50
762	$1 Year of the Monkey, souvenir sheet	4.25

SCOTT NO.	DESCRIPTION	UNUSED F/NH

763

763-64	26¢-37¢ Ninth Festival of Pacific Arts, 2 sheets of 10	15.50

769a

765a

765-66	26¢-37¢ Marine Life, 2 sheets of 6	10.00
767-68	$2 Marine Life, 2 souvenir sheets	10.0
769	$3 International Year of Peace, sheet of 3	22.00
770	$2 International Year of Peace, souvenir sheet	5.50

771

777a

771-74	37¢-$1 2004 Summer Olympics, set of 4	7.20
775	80¢ Election of Pope John Paul II, 25th Anniv., Sheet of 4	11.00
776	$2 Deng Xiaoping, Chinese Leader, souvenir sheet	5.50
777	50¢ D-Day, 60th Anniversary, sheet of 6	8.35
778	$2 D-Day, 60th Anniversary, souvenir sheet	5.50

779a

781

779	80¢ European Soccer Championships, sheet of 4	8.95
780	$2 European Soccer Championships, souvenir sheet	5.50
781-82	37¢ Babe Ruth, set of 2	3.00

783a

783-84	26¢-37¢ Trains, Bicentennial, 2 sheets of 4	8.35
785-86	$2 Trains, Bicentennial, 2 souvenir sheets	10.50

787a

787-89	80¢ Butterflies, Reptiles, Amphibians, and Birds, 3 sheets of 4	26.80
790-92	$2 Butterflies, Reptiles, Amphibians, and Birds, 3 souvenir sheets	16.45
793-95	26¢-80¢ Dinosaurs, 3 sheets of 4	20.00
796-98	$2 Dinosaurs, 3 souvenir sheets	16.00

799a

799	80¢ FIFA, Centennial, sheet of 4	8.95
800	$2 FIFA, souvenir sheet	5.50

801

804

801-03	26¢ National Basketball Assoc. Players, set of 3	3.25
804-07	$1 Christmas, set of 4	7.80
808	$2 Christmas, souvenir sheet	5.50

809a

809	80¢ Palau-Rep. of China Diplomatic Relations, 5th Anniv., sheet of 4	10.00

811

812a

2005

810	50¢ Year of the Rooster, sheet of 4	5.50
811	80¢ Rotary International, Centennial,sheet of 4	8.50
812	$1 Friedrich von Schiller, sheet of 3	7.75
813	$2 Friedrich von Schiller, souvenir sheet	5.25

814a

816

814	$1 Hans Christian Anderson, sheet of 3	7.75
815	$2 Hans Christian Anderson, souvenir sheet	5.25
816-19	37¢-$1 Battle of Trafalgar, Bicent., set of 4	7.50
820	$2 Battle of Trafalgar, Bicent., souvenir sheet	5.25

821a

821-22	80¢ End of World War II, 60th Anniv., 2 sheets of 4	17.50
823-24	$2 End of World War II, 60th Anniv., 2 souvenir sheets	11.50

825a

825	$1 Jules Verne, sheet of 3	7.75
826	$2 Jules Verne, souvenir sheet	5.25

827

830a

827	$1 Pope John Paul II	2.75
828	80¢ Elvis Presley	3.75
829	80¢ Elvis Presley, sheet of 4	9.50
830	80¢ Trains, sheet of 4	8.00
831	$2 Trains, souvenir sheet	5.25

832a

834a

832	80¢ VJ Day, 60th Anniv., sheet of 4	8.50
833	$2 VJ Day, 60th Anniv., souvenir sheet	5.25
834	80¢ Expo 2005, Aichi, Japan, sheet of 4	8.50

835a

837a

835	80¢ Sailing, sheet of 4	8.50
836	$2 Sailing, souvenir sheet	5.25
837-38	$1 World cup Soccer Championships, 75th Anniv., 2 sheets of 3	15.50
839	$1 Sepp Herberger, souvenir sheet	5.75
840	$1 Franz Beckenbauer, souvenir sheet	5.00
841	37¢ Vatican City No. 61	1.00

842a

843a

842	80¢ Taipei 2005 Intl. Stamp Exhibition, sheet of 4	8.00
843	37¢ Items from the National Museum, sheet of 10	9.50

SCOTT NO.	DESCRIPTION	UNUSED F/NH

844

845

844	80¢ Pope Benedict XVI	2.10
845-48	37¢-$1 Christmas, set of 4	7.25
849	$2 Christmas, souvenir sheet	5.25

850

851

2006

850	50¢ Year of the Dog	1.75
851-52	24¢-39¢ Birds, set of 2	1.85

854a

853a

856a

853	63¢ WWF, 4 attached	6.35
853e	63¢ WWF, souvenir sheet	13.50
854	18¢ World of Sea and Reef, sheet of 40	19.00
855	$2 Mozart, souvenir sheet	5.25
856	84¢ Queen Elizabeth II, sheet of 4	8.75
857	$2 Queen Elizabeth II, souvenir sheet	5.50
858	$1 Rembrandt, sheet of 4	10.50
859	$2 Rembrandt, souvenir sheet	5.50

860a

858a

861a

860	$1 International Space Station, sheet of 4	10.50
861-62	75¢ Space Achievements, 2 sheets of 6	24.00
863-65	$2 Space Achievements, 3 souvenir sheets	16.00
866	$7 Elvis Presley Gold	24.00
867	75¢ Peace Corps, souvenir sheet of 4	11.00
868-69	75¢ Concorde, set of 2 pairs	6.00
870	84¢ Christmas, sheet of 4	9.00

SCOTT NO.	DESCRIPTION	UNUSED F/NH

872c

879

2007

871	75¢ Year of the Pig	1.95
872	84¢ Marilyn Monroe, sheet of 4	8.75
873	39¢ Elvis, sheet of 9	11.00
874	75¢ Elvis, sheet of 6	12.00
875	$1 Scouting sheet of 3	7.75
876	$2 Scouting souvenir sheet	5.25
877	$1 Mushrooms sheet of 4	10.00
878	$2 Mushrooms souvenir sheet	5.25
879-885	10¢-$1 Helicopters, set of 7	9.00
886	$2 Helicopters souvenir sheet	5.25
887	$2 Triton Horn Shell souvenir sheet	5.25

888

890a

888-889	50¢ Birds sheets of 6, set of 2	16.00
890	60¢ Wedding Anniversary of Queen Elizabeth II attached pair	3.25

891a

892a

891	$1 Crabs, souvenir sheet of 4	10.00
892	$1 Flowers sheet of 4	10.00
893	$2 Flowers souvenir sheet	5.25

894

895b

896

894	41¢ Pope Benedict	1.25
895	90¢ Princess Diana, sheet of 4	9.00
896	$2 Princess Diana souvenir sheet	5.25

897

920a

897-916	2¢-$1 Butterflies definitives, set of 20	69.00
917	50¢ Udoud Money Beads, sheet of 6	7.75
918	50¢ Cowries, sheet of 6	7.75
919	75¢ Children & Wildlife, sheet of 4	7.75
920	80¢ Birds of Southeast Asia, sheet of 4	8.00
921	$2 Birds souvenir sheet	5.25

SCOTT NO.	DESCRIPTION	UNUSED F/NH

922d

922	80¢ Tropical Fish, sheet of 4	8.25
923	$2 Tropical Fish souvenir sheet	5.25
924	50¢ Holocaust Rememberance, sheet of 8	10.75
925-28	22¢-90¢ Christmas, set of 4	4.75
929	25¢-$2 America's Cup, strip of 4	10.50

931d

2008

930	50¢ Year of the Rat	1.75
931	90¢ Kennedy, sheet of 4	9.50
932	50¢ 2008 Summer Olympics, sheet of 4	5.50

933d

934

933	50¢ Taiwan Tourist Attractions, sheet of 4	5.50
934	$2 Illuminated Temple Souvenir Sheet	5.50

937

939c

935	$3 2008 World Stamp Championships Sheet	7.50
936	90¢ Sir Edmund Hillary, sheet of 4	9.25
937	75¢ Elvis, sheet of 6	12.00
938	90¢ Pope Benedict, sheet of 4	8.75
939	75¢ Muhammad Ali, sheet of 6	12.00
940	94¢ Muhammad Ali, sheet of 4	10.00

942f

949

941-42	75¢ Space, set of 2 sheets of 6	23.00
943-44	94¢ Space, set of 2 sheets of 4	20.00
945	75¢ Star Trek The Next Generation, sheet of 6	10.75
946	94¢ Star Trek The Next Generation, sheet of 4	10.00
947-50	22¢-94¢ Christmas Angels	4.75

957f

970

2009

SCOTT NO.	DESCRIPTION	UNUSED F/NH
951	94¢ Inauguration of Barak Obama, sheet of 4	9.50
952	$2 President Obama, souvenir sheet	5.25
953	94¢ Year of the Ox, horizontal pair	5.00
954	94¢ Teenage Mutant Ninja Turtles, sheet of 4	9.50
955	44¢ Michael Jackson, sheet of 4	4.50
956	28¢-75¢ Michael Jackson sheet of 4	5.00
957	26¢ Palau Pacific Resort, sheet of 6	4.00
958-61	28¢-$1.05 Dolphins, set of 4	7.00
962	75¢ Dolphins, sheet of 6	12.00
963-66	28¢-$1.05 Shells, set of 6	7.00
967	75¢ Shells, sheet of 6	12.00
968	75¢ Cats, sheet of 6	11.00
969	94¢ Cats, sheet of 4	11.50
970-71	$2 Cats, souvenir sheets (set of 2)	11.00

978

973

SCOTT NO.	DESCRIPTION	UNUSED F/NH
972	75¢ Fish, sheet of 6	12.00
973	44¢ Abraham Lincoln, sheet of 4	4.75
974	98¢-$2 Pope Benedict, sheet of 3	10.00
975	$2.50 Elvis, Steve Grayson	7.00
976	$2.50 Elvis, with Guitar	7.00
977	$2.50 Elvis, Smooth Fast & In Gear	7.00
978	$2.50 Elvis, Speedway Film Clips	7.00
979-991	1¢-$10 Fish	63.00
992	53¢ Worldwide Fund for Nature, block of 4	5.50
992a	53¢ Worldwide Fund for Nature, sheet of 8	10.00
993	98¢ First Man on the Moon, sheet of 4	10.00
994-97	26¢-$2 Christmas, set of 4	9.00

1010a, 1010b

2010

SCOTT NO.	DESCRIPTION	UNUSED F/NH
998	75¢ Charles Darwin, sheet of 6	11.00
999-1002	26¢-$1.05 Reptiles and Amphibians, set of 4	7.50
1003	75¢ Reptiles and Amphibians, sheet of 6	11.00
1004	75¢ Pope John Paul II	2.00
1005	75¢ Abraham Lincoln, sheet of 4	8.00
1006	75¢ Elvis, sheet of 4	8.00
1007	94¢ Girl Guides, sheet of 4	9.75
1008	$2.50 Girl Guides, souvenir sheet	6.50
1009	$1 Palau Governmental Buildings, sheet of 3	7.50
1010	75¢ Princess Diana, pair	3.75
1011	94¢ Mother Theresa, sheet of 4	10.00
1012	94¢ Henri Dunant, sheet of 4	10.00
1013	$2.50 Henri Dunant, souvenir sheet	6.00
1014	94¢ Botticelli Paintings, sheet of 4	9.00
1015	$2.50 Botticelli Paintings, souvenir sheet	6.00
1016	$2 Issuance of the Penny Black, sheet of 2	10.00
1017-20	26¢-$2 Christmas, set of 4	9.50
1021-22	World Cup Soccer, set of 2 sheets of 6	17.50
1023	94¢ Michelangelo, sheet of 4	9.50
1024	$2.50 Michlangelo, souvenir sheet	6.00
1025	75¢ Pope Benedict XVI	2.00
1026	98¢ Napoleon Wrasses, sheet of 3	7.75
1027	98¢ Sharks, sheet of 3	7.75

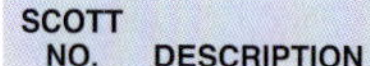

1028b

1028c

SCOTT NO.	DESCRIPTION	UNUSED F/NH
1028	98¢ Sea Turtles, sheet of 3	7.75
1029	98¢ Dugongs, sheet of 3	7.75

2011

SCOTT NO.	DESCRIPTION	UNUSED F/NH
1030	75¢ Lincoln, sheet of 4	7.50
1031	75¢ John Kennedy, sheet of 4	7.50
1032	75¢ President Barack Obama, sheet of 4	7.75
1033	50¢ Indipex 2011, sheet of 6	7.75
1034	$2.50 Indipex Gandhi Souvenir Sheet	6.50
1035	75¢ Whales, sheet of 6	11.00
1036	$2.50 Whales Souvenir Sheet	6.50
1037	94¢ Pope Benedict XVI visit to Spain	9.50
1038	$2.50 Pope Benedict Souvenir Sheet	6.50
1039	98¢ Ronald Reagan, sheet of 4	9.75
1040	75¢ Elvis, sheet of 4	7.50
1041	75¢ Elvis, sheet of 4	7.50
1042-45	$2.50 Elvis, set of 4 Souvenir Sheets	24.00

1048

1055

SCOTT NO.	DESCRIPTION	UNUSED F/NH
1046	75¢ Pope John Paul II, sheet of 4	7.50
1047	$2.50 Pope John Paul II, Souvenir Sheet	6.25
1048	98¢ Royal Wedding	2.50
1049-50	$2 Royal Wedding S/S set of 2	9.75
1051-52	75¢ Princess Diana, set of 2 sheets of 4	14.75
1053	29¢ Taro plant & Inscription, sheet of 30	19.00
1054	$2 President Remeliik Souvenir Sheet	5.00
1055-56	98¢ Birds of Palau, set of 2 sheets of 4	19.00
1057-58	$2 Birds of Palau, set of 2 souvenir sheets	9.75
1059	60¢ Abraham Lincoln, sheet of 5	7.50
1060	$2.50 Abraham Lincoln Souvenir Sheet	6.50
1061	50¢ Peace Corps, sheet of 4	5.00
1062	75¢ Tenth Anniversary of 9/11, sheet of 4	7.50
1063	$2.50 World Trade Center Souvenir Sheet	6.50
1064-65	98¢ World Cup Soccer, 2 sheets of 4	19.00
1066	98¢ Barack Obama 50th Birthday, sheet of 4	10.00
1067	$2.50 President Obama Souvenir Sheet	6.50
1068-69	$1.25 Crustaceans, set of 2 sheets of 4	24.00
1070-71	$3 Crustacians, set of 2 Souvenir Sheets	14.75
1072	75¢ Dangerous Creatures & Coral Reefs, sheet of 5	9.00
1073	$1 Dangerous Creatures & Coral Reefs, sheet of 3	7.50
1074	$2.50 Jolly Fish Souvenir Sheet	6.50
1075	$2.50 Barra Cuda Souvenir Sheet	6.50

1087a

1103a

2012

SCOTT NO.	DESCRIPTION	UNUSED F/NH
1076-79	26¢ - $4.25 Christmas	15.00
1080-81	98¢ Lizards, 2 sheets of 4	20.00
1082-83	$2.50 Lizards, 2 Souvenir Sheets	12.50
1084	50¢ Japan/Palau Friendship Bridge, sheet of 4	5.00
1085	$1.25 Michelangelo, sheet of 3	9.25
1086	$3.50 Michelangelo, Souvenir Sheet	9.00
1087	$1 Titanic, sheet of 4	10.00
1088	$3 Titanic, Souvenir Sheet	7.50
1089	$1.25 Amelia Earhart, sheet of 4	13.00
1090	$1.25 Amelia Earhart, Souvenir Sheet of 2	6.50
1091	80¢ Summer Olympics, sheet of 4	8.00
1092	$1 Blossoms of Flowering Trees, sheet of 6	15.00
1093	$3.50 National Cherry Blossom Festival S/S	9.00
1094	98¢ Elvis, sheet of 4	10.00
1095	98¢ Elvis, sheet of 4	10.00
1096	$1.25 Stingrays, sheet of 4	13.00
1097	$3.50 Stingrays, Souvenir Sheet	9.00
1098-02	$3.50 Elvis Presley, set of 5	44.00
1103	$1.25 Peter Pan, sheet of 4	13.00
1104	$1.25 Televised Tour of the White House, sheet of 4	13.00
1105	$1.25 Pope Benedict, Horizontal Pair	6.50

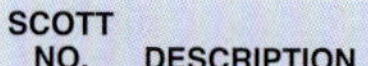

1110a

1111

SCOTT NO.	DESCRIPTION	UNUSED F/NH
1106-07	$1.25 Apollo Moon Missions, set of 2 sheets of 4	24.00
1108	$1 Raphael, sheet of 4	10.00
1109	$3 Raphael, Souvenir Sheet	7.50
1110	$1.25 Dog Breeds, sheet of 4	12.50
1111	$3.50 Dog Breeds, Souvenir Sheet	9.00
1112-15	$3.50 Famous Speeches, set of 4	33.00
1116	$1.25 Carnivorous Plants, sheet of 4	12.00
1117	$3.50 Carnivorous Plants, Souvenir Sheets	9.00
1118-23	29¢-$1.05 Christmas, set of 6	9.00
1124	$3.50 Christmas, Souvenir Sheet	9.00

1125

SCOTT NO.	DESCRIPTION	UNUSED F/NH
1125	$1.20 Hindenburg	12.00
1126	$3.50 Hindenburg, Souvenir Sheet	9.00

1127

2013

SCOTT NO.	DESCRIPTION	UNUSED F/NH
1127	$1.20 World Radio Day Sheet of 4	11.00
1128	$3.50 World Radio Day Souvenir Sheet	8.00
1129	$1.50 Paintings by Paul Signac sheet of 3	10.00
1130	$3.50 Women at the Well Souvenir Sheet	7.75
1131	$1.20 Queen Elizabeth II sheet of 4	10.50
1132	$3.50 Queen Elizabeth II Souvenir Sheet	7.75

1133

1136

SCOTT NO.	DESCRIPTION	UNUSED F/NH
1133	$1.20 Seashells sheet of 4	10.50
1134	$3.50 Seashells Souvenir Sheet	7.75
1135-36	$1.20 Cats set of 2 sheets of 4	21.00

1145

1149

SCOTT NO.	DESCRIPTION	UNUSED F/NH
1137-38	$3.50 Cats set of 2 souvenir sheets	16.00
1139-40	$1.50 History of Art set of 2 sheets of 3	20.00
1141-42	$3.50 History of Art set of 2 souvenir sheets	16.00
1143	$1 Grand Central Terminal sheet of 6	13.50
1144	$3.50 Grand Central Terminal Souvenir sheet	7.75
1145-46	$1.20 John F. Kennedy set of 2 sheets of 4	22.00
1147-48	$3.50 John F. Kennedy set of 2 souvenir sheets	16.00
1149	$1.20 Pope Francis sheet of 4	11.00
1150	$3.50 Pope Francis souvenir sheet	7.75
1151	$1.25 Margaret Thatcher sheet of 4	11.00
1152	$3.50 Margaret Thatcher souvenir sheet	7.75
1153	$1.20 Henry Ford sheet of 4	10.50
1154	$3.50 Henry Ford Souvenir sheet	7.75

SCOTT NO.	DESCRIPTION	UNUSED F/NH

1155

1155-56	$1.20 Tropical Fish set of 2 sheets of 4	21.00
1157-58	$3.50 Tropical Fish set of 2 souvenir sheets	15.00

1161

1163

1159	$1.20 2013 World Stamp Exhibition sheet of 4	10.50
1160	$3.50 2013 World Stamp Exhibition souvenir sheet	7.75
1161	$1.20 Butterflies sheet of 4	10.50
1162	$3.50 Butterflies souvenir sheet	7.75
1163	$2 Pearls sheet of 4	17.50

1174

1164	$4 Pearls souvenir sheet	9.00
1165	$1.20 Birth of Prince George sheet of 4	10.50
1166	$3.50 Birth of Prince George souvenir sheet	7.75
1167-73	$1.10 Sea Life Photos by Kevin Davidson, set of 7 sheets of 6	99.50
1167	$1.10 Sea Life Photos by Kevin Davidson, Sheet of 6, a-f	15.00
1168	$1.10 Sea Life Photos by Kevin Davidson, Sheet of 6, a-f	15.00
1169	$1.10 Sea Life Photos by Kevin Davidson, Sheet of 6, a-e, 1168f	15.00
1170	$1.10 Sea Life Photos by Kevin Davidson, Sheet of 6, a-f	15.00
1171	$1.10 Sea Life Photos by Kevin Davidson, Sheet of 6, a-f	15.00
1172	$1.10 Sea Life Photos by Kevin Davidson, Sheet of 6, a-e, 1171d	15.00
1173	$1.10 Sea Life Photos by Kevin Davidson, Sheet of 6, a-f	15.00
1174	$10 Elvis Presley foil souvenir sheet	22.50

1175

1175	$1.20 Queen Elizabeth II sheet of 4	10.50

1184

1176	$3.50 Queen Elizabeth II souvenir sheet	7.75
1177	$1.20 World Water Day	2.75
1178	$3.50 World Water Day souvenir sheet	7.75
1179-82	29C-$3.50 Christmas set of 4	12.00
1183	$1.20 Nelson Mandella vertical strip of 3	7.75
	same, mint sheet of 6	16.50
1184	$1.20 Nelson Mandella sheet of 6	16.00
1185-86	$3.50 Nelson Mandella souvenir sheets	15.00
1187	$1 Orchids sheet of 6	13.00
1188	$3.50 Orchids Souvenir sheet	7.75
1189	$1.20 Chess in Art sheet of 4	10.50
1190	$3.50 Chess in art souvenir sheet	7.75

1197

2014

1191-92	$1.50 Modern Art, Set of 2 Sheets of 3	19.50
1193-94	$3.50 Modern Art, Set of 2 S/S	15.00
1195-96	$1.75 Seashells, Set of 2 Sheets of 4	29.50
1197-98	$3.50 Set of 2 Souvenir Sheets of 2	29.50

1218

1228

1199	$1.50 Caroline Kennedy, Sheet of 4	13.00
1200	$4 Caroline Kennedy, S/S	9.00
1201	$1.20 Winter Sports, Sheet of 4	10.50
1202	$1.20 Winter Sports, Sheet of 6	15.50
1203-04	$1.20 Pope Francis, Set of 2 Sheets of 4	22.00
1205-06	$2 Pope Francis, Set of 2 Souvenir Sheets of 2	18.00
1207-08	$2.50 World War I, Set of 2 Sheets of 4	42.00
1209-10	$2 World War I, Set of 2 Souvenir Sheets of 2	18.00
1211	$1 South Koreans Stamp Sheet of 8	18.00
1212-13	$3.50 Reptiles, Set of 2 Sheets of 4	58.00
1214-15	$3.50 Set of 2 Souvenir Sheets	16.00
1216-17	$1 Seagulls, Set of 2 Sheets of 6	26.00
1218	75¢ Prince George, Horizontal Strip of 3	5.00
1219	$1 Prince George Attached Pair	4.50
1220-21	Prince George Set of 2 Souvenir Sheets	18.00
1222	45¢ Fish, Sheet of 6	6.00
1223-24	$1.75 Alice in Wonderland, Set of 2 Sheets of 4	30.00
1225-26	$2.50 Alice in Wonderland, 2 Souvenir Sheets of 2	22.00
1227	$1.50 Tourist Attractions in Russia, 2 Sheets of 4	9.75
1228	$2 Tourist Attractions in Russia, Souvenir Sheet of 2	8.75
1229	$1 Owls, Sheet of 4	8.75
1230	$3 Owls Souvenir Sheet	6.50
1231	$4 Owls Souvenir Sheet	8.75

1237

1238

1232-39	2¢ - $1 Marine Life, Set of 8	6.00
1240	$1.20 Trains, Sheet of 4	10.75
1241	$3.50 Trains, Souvenir Sheet	7.50
1242-43	$1.50 Paintings, Set of 2 Sheets of 3	19.00
1244-45	$4 Paintings, Set of 2 Souvenir Sheets	17.00

1249

1263

1246-47	$1.20 Frogs and Toads, 2 Sheet of 4	22.00
1248-49	$4 Frogs and Toads, Set of 2 Souvenir Sheets	18.00
1252-55	34¢ - $3.50 Raphael Christmas Paintings, Set of 4	13.00
1250-51	$1.20 Characters *Downtown Abbey*, set of 2 S/S	26.00
1256	40¢ Lagoon Jellyfish, strip of 4	4.00
1257	90¢ Lagoon Jellyfish, strip of 4	9.00
1258	$1.20 Pope Benedict XVI, sheet of 4	11.00
1259	$4.00 Pope Benedict XVI, souvenir sheet	8.50
1260-61	$1.20 Dinosaurs, set of 2 souvenir sheets	24.00
1262-63	$4.00 Dinosaurs, set of 2 souvenir sheets	20.00

1267

2015

1264	$1.20 Taipei 2015, Bubble Tea, sheet of 6	16.00
1265	$4.00 Taipei 2015, Bubble Tea, souvenir sheet	8.50
1266	75¢ Pope John Paul II	1.60
1267	$1.20 Camouflage of WWI, sheet of 5	12.50

1274

1287d

1268	$4.00 Camouflage of WWI, souvenir sheet	8.50
1269	$1.20 World Heritage Sites, South Pacific, sheet of 5	12.50
1270	$4.00 World Heritage Sites, South Pacific, S/S	9.00
1271-72	45¢ 1940 Evacuation of Dunkirk, set of 2 sheets	30.50
1273	$1.20 Queen Elizabeth II, sheet of 6	15.25
1274	$4.00 Queen Elizabeth II, souvenir sheet	8.50
1275	65¢ Battle of Britain, sheet of 6	8.25
1276	$4.00 Battle of Britain, souvenir sheet	8.50
1277	$1.00 Pope Benedict XVI, sheet of 4	8.25
1278	$3.50 Pope Benedict XVI, souvenir sheet	7.50
1279	65¢ Birds of the South Pacific, sheet of 6	8.25
1280	$4.00 Birds of the South Pacific, souvenir sheet	8.50
1281	$1.20 Birth of Princess Charlotte, sheet of 4	10.00
1282	$4.00 Birth of Princess Charlotte, souvenir sheet	8.50
1283	65¢ Visit of Pope Francis, sheet of 6	8.25
1284	$4.00 Visit of Pope Francis, souvenir sheet	8.50
1285	65¢ President Dwight D. Eisenhower, sheet of 6	8.25
1286	$4.00 President Dwight D. Eisenhower, S/S	8.50
1287	$1.20 Sir Winston Churchill, sheet of 4	10.00
1288	$4.00 Sir Winston Churchill, souvenir sheet	8.50
1289	65¢ William Shakespeare, sheet of 6	8.25
1290	$4.00 William Shakespeare, souvenir sheet	8.50

1295a

1291-94	34¢-$2 Christmas Paintings, set of 4	9.50
1295	$1.20 German Reunification, sheet of 4	10.00
1296	$4.00 German Reunification, souvenir sheet	8.50

1297b

1297	65¢ Star Trek Spacecraft, sheet of 6	9.00
1298	$4.00 Star Trek Spacecraft, souvenir sheet	9.00
1299	$1.20 Marine Mollusks, sheet of 4	10.00
1300	$4.00 Marine Mollusks, souvenir sheets	8.50
1301	65¢ Coral Reef Snakes, sheet of 6	8.50
1302	$4.00 Coral Reef Snakes, souvenir sheets	8.50
1303	65¢ WWII Submarines, sheet of 6	8.25
1304	$4.00 WWI Submarines, souvenir sheet	8.50

1313

2016

SCOTT NO.	DESCRIPTION	UNUSED F/NH
1305	65¢ Flowers and Plants of Palau, sheet of 6	9.00
1306	$4.00 Flowers and Plants of Palau, souvenir sheet	8.50
1307	$1.20 The 2016 Olympic Champions, sheet of 4	10.50
1308	$4 Olympic Champions, Yoshiyuki Tsuruta, souvenir sheet	8.50
1309	65¢ Vincent van Gogh Paintings, sheet of 6	8.25
1310	$4 Vincent van Gogh Paintings, souvenir sheet	8.50
1311-12	65¢ Jimi Hendrix, set of 2 sheets	16.50
1313	$4 Jimi Hendrix, souvenir sheet	8.50
1314-17	$4 Elvis Presley, set of 4 souvenir sheets	34.00
1318	$1.50 Queen Elizabeth II, 90th Birthday, sheet of 3	9.00
1319	$5 Queen Elizabeth II, 90th Birthday, souvenir sheet	10.25
1320	$1.25 New York City, sites and scenes, sheet of 4	10.50
1321	$3 New York City, skyline, souvenir sheet	6.25

1322b

SCOTT NO.	DESCRIPTION	UNUSED F/NH
1322	$1 Nancy Reagan, sheet of 6	12.50
1323	$1.20 Nancy Reagan, sheet of 4	10.50
1324	$2.50 Nancy Reagan, souvenir sheet of 2	10.50
1325	$5 Nancy Reagan, souvenir sheet	10.50

1327a

SCOTT NO.	DESCRIPTION	UNUSED F/NH
1326	47¢ Palau World of Sea and Reef, sheet of 40	39.00
1327	$1 Star Trek, sheet of 6	12.50
1328	$3 Star Trek, souvenir sheet	6.25
1329	$1.50 Rare Birds of Palau, sheet of 4	12.50
1330	$5 Rare Birds of Palau, souvenir sheet	10.50

1339f

1340a

SCOTT NO.	DESCRIPTION	UNUSED F/NH
1331	$1.50 Ngardmau Waterfall, sheet of 4	12.50
1332	$5 Ngardmau Waterfall, souvenir sheet	10.50
1333	$1 Obama Visits UK, sheet of 6	12.50
1334	$2 Obama Visits UK, sheet of 3	12.50
1335	$2.50 Obama Visits U.N., souvenir sheet of 2	10.50
1336	$1 William Shakespeare, sheet of 6	12.50
1337	$1.50 William Shakespeare, sheet of 4	12.00
1338	$5 William Shakespeare, souvenir sheet	10.50
1339	$1.20 Jellyfish Lake, sheet of 6	15.00
1340	$1.20 Giant Clams, sheet of 6	15.00
1341	$1.25 ABAI Mens Meeting Place, sheet of 4	10.75
1342	$1.50 The Rock Islands, sheet of 4	12.50
1343	$1.75 Manta Ray and Devil Ray, sheet of 4	15.00
1344	$1.75 Remembering World War II, sheet of 4	15.00
1345	$1.50 Protected Species, sheet of 3	9.25

1346b

SCOTT NO.	DESCRIPTION	UNUSED F/NH
1346	$1.75 Crabs, sheet of 3	11.75
1347	$1.35 Pearl Harbor, 75th Anniversary, Vintage Posters, sheet of 6	19.00
1348	$3 Pearl Harbor, 75th Anniversary, souvenir sheet	12.50
1349	$1 Palauan Fish, sheet of 6	12.50

1350a

SCOTT NO.	DESCRIPTION	UNUSED F/NH
1350	$2.50 Palauan Fish, souvenir sheet of 2	10.50
1351	75¢-$1 Summer Olympics, sheet of 7	11.75
1352	75¢-$1 Festival of Pacific Arts, sheet of 11	15.00

1353

2017

SCOTT NO.	DESCRIPTION	UNUSED F/NH
1353	$1 Legends of the Wild West, sheet of 6	12.50
1354	$5 Legends of the Wild West, Buffalo Bill, souvenir sheet	10.50
1355	$1-$1.50 Princess Diana's World Travels, sheet of 7	15.00
1356	$1.80 Princess Diana, 20 Years in Memoriam	15.00
1357	$1.35 John F. Kennedy, 100th Birthday, sheet of 6	15.75
1358	$1.60 John F. Kennedy, 100th Birthday, sheet of 4	16.50

1359

SCOTT NO.	DESCRIPTION	UNUSED F/NH
1359	$1.25 Seals of the World, sheet of 6	15.75
1360	$4.50 Seals of the World, souvenir sheet	9.50
1361	$2.00 National Geographic Animals, sheet of 4	17.00
1362	$4.00 National Geographic Animals, souvenir sheet	8.50
1363	$1.60 Gustav Klimt Paintings, sheet of 4	13.50
1364	$4.00 Gustav Klimt Paintings, souvenir sheet	8.50

1365

SCOTT NO.	DESCRIPTION	UNUSED F/NH
1365-68	$4.00 Elvis Presley, set of 4 souvenir sheet	34.00
1369	50¢ PCAA, 50th Anniversary, sheet of 15	16.00

1372b

1379a

2018

SCOTT NO.	DESCRIPTION	UNUSED F/NH
1370	50¢-$2.50 Colorful Birds, sheet of 6	17.00
1371	$1.25-$3.25 Colorful Birds, sheet of 3	13.50
1372	50¢-$3.25 Jellyfish, sheet of 4	15.00
1373	$3.00 Jellyfish, sheet of 2	12.50
1374	50¢-$2.50 Underwater Landscapes, sheet of 4	15.00
1375	$3.00 Underwater Landscapes, sheet of 2	12.50
1376	$1.60 President Donald Trump to Japan, sheet of 4	13.50
1377	$4.00 President Donald Trump to Japan, souvenir sheet	8.50
1378	$3.00 Engagement of Prince Harry, sheet of 2	12.50
1379	50¢-$1.75 Seahorses, sheet of 6	13.50

1383d

1386b

SCOTT NO.	DESCRIPTION	UNUSED F/NH
1380	$2 Elvis Presley, sheet of 4	17.00
1381	$1.50 Marine Life Preservation, sheet of 2	6.00
1382	$2 Fruit Dove	4.00
1383	$2 Palau Nautilus, sheet of 4	17.00
1384	$3 Palau Nautilus, souvenir sheet of 2	12.50
1385	$2 Birth of Prince Louis, sheet of 4	17.00
1386	$1-$4 Royal Wedding Prince Henry and Meghan Markle, sheet of 4	17.00
1387	$4 Royal Wedding, souvenir sheet	8.00
1388	$1 Summit Meeting Pres. Trump and Chairman Kim, sheet of 6	12.50
1389	50¢-$1.75 First Moon Landing, 50th Anniv., sheet of 6	14.00
1390	$4 First Moon Landing, 50th Anniv., souvenir sheet	8.00
1391	$1-$4 Pres. Trump visits Finland, sheet of 4	21.00

1392e

SCOTT NO.	DESCRIPTION	UNUSED F/NH
1392	50¢-$1.75 Sea Turtles, sheet of 6	14.00
1393	$1-$2.50 Giant Clams, sheet of 4	14.50
1394	$4 Giant Clams, souvenir sheet	8.00
1395	$Frangipani Flowers, sheet of 4	17.00
1396	75¢-$2 Whales, sheet of 6	17.50

1397a

1400d

SCOTT NO.	DESCRIPTION	UNUSED F/NH
1397	$3 Whales, souvenir sheet of 2	12.50
1398	25¢-$2.50 Seabirds, sheet of 6	16.00
1399	$1-$3 Seabirds, souvenir sheet of 3	12.50
1400	$1-$4 Dolphins, sheet of 4	21.00
1401	$4 Dolphins, souvenir sheet	8.00
1402	$1-$2.50 Nicobar Pigeons, sheet of 4	15.00
1403	$3 Nicobar Pigeons, souvenir sheet of 2	13.00
1404	50¢-$3 Beautiful Birds, sheet of 4	14.00
1405	25¢-$2 Beautiful Birds, sheet of 6	12.50
1406	$4 Beautiful Birds, souvenir sheet	8.00

SCOTT NO.	DESCRIPTION	UNUSED F/NH

1407d

1414a

1407 $1 Space Shuttle Columbia, sheet of 9 . . . . . . .19.50
1408 50¢-$2 Sharks, sheet of 6 . . . . .16.00
1409 $4 Sharks, souvenir sheet. 8.00
1412-13 50¢-$1.75 Pacific Waterfowl, set of 2, sheets of 6 .29.00
1414 $1-$4 Leonardo da Vinci, sheet of 4 . . . . .22.00
1415 $5 Leonardo da Vinci, souvenir sheet. 11.00
1416-19 $5 Elvis Presley, set of 4 souvenir sheet. 45.00

1421a

2019

1420 $1.95 Protanqila Palau, pair 8.00
..... $1.95 Protanqila Palau, sheet of 4 . . . . .16.50
1421 $1.50 Groupers, sheet of 6 . . . . .18.00
1423-24 $1.20 Sharks, set of 2, sheets of 4 . . . . .20.00
1425 $4 Manta Ray, souvenir sheet. 8.00
1426 $4 Golden Jellyfish, souvenir sheet. 8.00
1427 $1-$4 Strawberry Hermit Crab, sheet of 4. . . . .16.50
1428 $5 Strawberry Hermit Crab, souvenir sheet . . .11.00
1429-30 $1-$3 Mimic Octopus, set of 2, sheets of 3. . . .26.00

1431

1431 $5 Mimic Octopus, souvenir sheet 11.00
1432 $2 Clearfin Lionfish, sheet of 4 . . . . .17.00
1433 $5 Clearfin Lionfish, souvenir sheet 11.00
1434 55¢-$1.20 Palau Conservation Society, sheet of 8 . . . . .13.00
1435 $1.50 U.S. Trans-Continental Railroad, sheet of 4 . . . . .13.00
1436 $1-$3 Honoring Emperor Akihito, sheet of 4 . . .17.00
1437 $2 The Royal Baby, Archie Mountbatten-Windsor, sheet of 4 . . . . .17.00

1438d

1442c

1438 $1-$2 Long-Tailed Macaque, sheet of 4 . . . . . .13.00
1439 $5 Long-Tailed Macaque, souvenir sheet 11.00
1440 50¢-$3.50 Mahatman Gandhi, sheet of 4 . . . . .16.50
1441 $1 H.H. Dorje Chang Buddha III, single from sheet 2.00
1442 $1-$3 Maroon Clownfish, sheet of 3 . . . . .13.00
1443 $3-$4 Maroon Clownfish, souvenir sheet of 2. .14.50

1444a

1444 $1-$2.50 Jellyfish, sheet of 4. . . . . .15.00
1445 $5 Jellyfish, souvenir sheet. 10.00

SCOTT NO.	DESCRIPTION	UNUSED F/NH

1446f

1446 $1 Palau & Japan Diplomatic Relations Anniv, sheet of 6 . . . . .13.00

1447a

1447 $1-$2.50 Butterflies, sheet of 4 . . . . .16.00
1448 $1-$5 Butterflies, sheet of 4 . . . . .20.00
1449 $2 Fruit & Veggie Medley, sheet of 4. . . . . .16.00

1450b

1452a

1450 $3 Fruit & Veggie Medley, souvenir sheet. 13.00
1451 $2 Covid-19, sheet of 4 . . . . .16.00
1452 $1.60 Raphael, sheet of 4 . . . . .14.00
1453 $4 Raphael, souvenir sheet. 8.00
1454-57 $8 Elvis Presley, set of 4 souvenir sheets. 68.00

1458d

1458 $1.50 Westward Expansion, Santa Fe Trail, sheet of 6 . . . . .18.00
1459 $8 Westward Expansion, Santa Fe Trail, souvenir sheet 16.00
1460 25¢ Mahatma Gandhi, single from sheet 0.60

1461b

1461 $1.60 V-E Day, sheet of 6 . . . . .20.00
1462 $2 Rabbits, sheet of 4 .16.00
1463 $3 Rabbits, souvenir sheet of 2. . . . . .13.00

1464a

1464 $2 Sea Turtles, sheet of 4 . . . . .16.00
1465 $3 Sea Turtles, souvenir sheets of 2. . . . . .13.00
1466-67 $2 President Donald Trump-Kim-Jong-un, 2 sheets of 4 . . . . .36.00

SCOTT NO.	DESCRIPTION	UNUSED F/NH

B1

1988 SEMI POSTAL

B1-B4 (25¢ + 5¢) + (45¢ + 5¢) Olympics, 2 pairs. 5.25

C1

AIR MAILS

1984 AIR MAILS

C1-4 40¢ Seabirds, attached .4.55

1985 AIR MAILS

C5 44¢ Audubon Birds 1.65
C6-9 44¢ German Links, attached. 5.50
C10-13 44¢ Transpacific, attached 5.20

C14

C17

1986 AIR MAILS

C14-16 44¢ Remeliik, strip of 3 . . . . .5.50
C17 44¢ Statue of Liberty. 1.30

1989 AIR MAILS

C18-20 36¢-45¢ Aircraft, complete set of 3 . . . . .3.75

C23a

1991 AIR MAILS

C21 50¢ 10th Anniv. Airmail, self-adhesive. 2.45

1989 BOOKLET PANES

C18a 36¢ Aircraft pane (10) .10.10
C19a 39¢ Aircraft pane (10) .10.95
C20a 45¢ Aircraft pane (10). 12.10
C20b 5 (36¢) + 5 (45¢) Aircraft pane (10) 11.55

1995

C22 50¢ World War II, Aircraft, sheetlet of 10. . . . . .15.85
C23 50¢ Birds (Swallows), 4 attached 5.80

1985 ENVELOPE ENTIRES

U1 22¢ Marine Life 5.00
U2 22¢ Spear Fishing. 8.00
U3 25¢ Chambered Nautilus. 2.00
UC1 36¢ Bird, air letter sheet 7.00

1985 POSTAL CARDS

UX1 14¢ Marine Life 3.50

PHILIPPINES

U.S. Stamps of various issues overprinted

PHILIPPINES

1899
On 260. Unwatermarked

SCOTT NO.	DESCRIPTION	UNUSED NH F	UNUSED NH AVG	UNUSED OG F	UNUSED OG AVG	USED F	USED AVG
212	50¢ orange	975.00	775.00	450.00	325.00	250.00	210.00
	On 279, 279d, 267-68, 281, 282C, 283, 284, 275 Double Line Watermarked						
213	1¢ yellow green	10.50	7.00	14.00	3.00	1.00	.85
214	2¢ orange red	4.00	2.95	1.80	1.25	.85	.60
215	3¢ purple	19.95	14.00	9.75	6.75	1.75	1.30
216	5¢ blue	19.90	14.00	10.00	7.00	1.75	1.25
217	10¢ brown (Type I)	78.00	65.00	35.00	28.00	5.00	3.50
217A	10¢ orange brown (Type II)	350.00	250.00	150.00	125.00	35.00	30.00
218	15¢ olive green	85.00	65.00	45.00	35.00	10.00	8.00
219	50¢ orange	295.00	225.00	150.00	110.00	45.00	39.00
	1901 On 280, 282, 272, 276-78						
220	4¢ orange brown	65.00	48.00	35.00	25.00	6.00	5.00
221	6¢ lake	90.00	70.00	48.00	40.00	7.50	6.00
222	8¢ violet brown	90.00	70.00	48.00	40.00	8.00	6.00
223	$1 black (Type I)	975.00	725.00	550.00	450.00	300.00	255.00
223A	$1 black (Type II)	4800.00	3600.00	3600.00	1800.00	900.00	775.00
224	$2 dark blue	1250.00	900.00	550.00	400.00	400.00	330.00
225	$5 dark green	1600.00	1100.00	950.00	795.00	1000.00	875.00
	1903-04 On 300-313						
226	1¢ blue green	15.00	11.00	8.00	6.50	.50	.40
227	2¢ carmine	18.00	14.00	11.00	8.00	1.35	.95
228	3¢ bright violet	140.00	100.00	85.00	60.00	17.50	11.50
229	4¢ brown	150.00	130.00	100.00	80.00	27.00	18.00
230	5¢ blue	34.00	20.00	19.00	16.00	1.50	.95
231	6¢ brownish lake	175.00	125.00	110.00	75.00	24.50	15.95
232	8¢ violet black	125.00	75.00	70.00	55.00	15.00	11.00
233	10¢ pale red brown	70.00	55.00	35.00	27.00	3.75	2.25
234	13¢ purple black	75.00	50.00	45.00	30.00	20.00	16.00
235	25¢ olive green	135.00	105.00	80.00	65.00	20.00	16.00
236	50¢ orange	250.00	195.00	135.00	105.00	42.50	30.00
237	$1 black	900.00	715.00	550.00	400.00	300.00	250.00
238	$2 dark blue	1800.00	1400.00	1000.00	800.00	900.00	800.00
239	$5 dark green	2100.00	1600.00	1300.00	1050.00	6000.00	5500.00
	On 319						
240	2¢ carmine	15.00	10.00	8.00	6.00	2.75	1.85

SPECIAL DELIVERY STAMPS

PHILIPPINES

1901
U.S. E5 Surcharged

SCOTT NO.	DESCRIPTION	UNUSED NH F	UNUSED NH AVG	UNUSED OG F	UNUSED OG AVG	USED F	USED AVG
E1	10¢ dark blue	250.00	185.00	135.00	95.00	100.00	85.00

POSTAGE DUE STAMPS

PHILIPPINES

1899
U.S. J38-44 overprinted

SCOTT NO.	DESCRIPTION	UNUSED NH F	UNUSED NH AVG	UNUSED OG F	UNUSED OG AVG	USED F	USED AVG
J1	1¢ deep claret	13.00	9.00	8.50	6.00	3.00	2.00
J2	2¢ deep claret	13.00	9.00	8.50	6.00	3.00	2.00
J3	5¢ deep claret	26.00	18.00	17.00	12.00	3.00	2.00
J4	10¢ deep claret	40.00	30.00	25.00	18.00	7.00	5.00
J5	50¢ deep claret	375.00	260.00	230.00	160.00	125.00	85.00
	1901						
J6	3¢ deep claret	30.00	20.00	19.00	13.00	9.00	6.50
J7	30¢ deep claret	475.00	325.00	300.00	200.00	130.00	90.00

PUERTO RICO

PORTO RICO

1899
U.S. Stamps 279-79B, 281, 272, 282C overprinted

SCOTT NO.	DESCRIPTION	UNUSED NH F	UNUSED NH AVG	UNUSED OG F	UNUSED OG AVG	USED F	USED AVG
210	1¢ yellow green	13.00	9.50	7.50	6.00	1.75	1.15
211	2¢ carmine	10.00	8.00	6.50	4.00	1.65	1.05
212	5¢ blue	26.00	16.00	14.00	10.00	3.00	2.00
213	8¢ violet brown	85.00	60.00	40.00	28.00	26.00	20.00
214	10¢ brown (I)	50.00	38.00	35.00	25.00	7.00	5.00
	1900 U.S. 279, 279B overprinted (PUERTO RICO)						
215	1¢ yellow green	17.00	12.00	9.00	5.50	1.75	1.50
216	2¢ carmine	13.00	9.00	7.00	5.00	3.00	2.00

POSTAGE DUE STAMPS

PORTO RICO

1899
U.S. Postage Due Stamps J38-39, J41 overprinted

SCOTT NO.	DESCRIPTION	UNUSED NH F	UNUSED NH AVG	UNUSED OG F	UNUSED OG AVG	USED F	USED AVG
J1	1¢ deep claret	47.00	36.00	25.00	18.00	8.00	6.60
J2	2¢ deep claret	42.00	34.00	25.00	18.00	7.00	6.00
J3	10¢ deep claret	375.00	300.00	240.00	165.00	75.00	65.00

The Ryukyu Islands were under U.S. administration from April 1, 1945 until May 15, 1972. Prior to the General Issues of 1948, several Provisional Stamps were used.

RYUKYU ISLANDS

1, 1a, 3, 3a   2, 2a, 5, 5a   4, 4a, 6, 6a   7, 7a

1949 Second Printing

White gum & paper, sharp colors; clean perfs.

SCOTT NO.	DESCRIPTION	UNUSED F/NH	UNUSED F
1-7	**5s to 1y 7 varieties, complete**	**28.75**	**20.50**
1	5s Cycad	3.00	2.75
2	10s Lily	7.00	6.00
3	20s Cycad	4.50	3.75
4	30s Sailing Ship	2.00	1.50
5	40s Lily	2.00	1.50
6	50s Sailing Ship	5.00	4.25
7	1y Farmer	6.75	5.75

1948 First Printing

Thick yellow gum; gray paper; dull colors; rough perfs.

SCOTT NO.	DESCRIPTION	UNUSED F/NH	UNUSED F
1a-7a	**5s to 1y, 7 varieties, complete**	**560.00**	**450.00**
1a	5s Cycad	3.75	3.75
2a	10s Lily	2.25	2.25
3a	20s Cycad	2.25	2.25
4a	30s Sailing Ship	4.50	3.75
5a	40s Lily	70.00	65.00
6a	50s Sailing Ship	5.00	4.25
7a	1y Farmer	500.00	450.00

8

9

10

11

12

13

1950

SCOTT NO.	DESCRIPTION	UNUSED F/NH	UNUSED F
8-13	**50s to 5y, 6 varieties, complete**	**81.50**	**57.65**
8	50s Tile Roof	.30	.25
9	1y Ryukyu Girl	5.00	3.50
10	2y Shun Castle	16.00	11.00
11	3y Dragon Head	35.00	25.00
12	4y Women at Beach	20.00	14.00
13	5y Seashells	9.50	7.00

NOTE: **The 1950 printing of #8 is on toned paper and has yellowish gum. A 1958 printing exhibits white paper and colorless gum.**

14

15

1951

SCOTT NO.	DESCRIPTION	UNUSED F/NH	UNUSED F
14	3y Ryukyu University	65.00	45.00
15	3y Pine Tree	62.00	40.00
16	10y on 50s (no. 8) Type II	14.00	12.00
16a	same, Type I	45.00	45.00
16b	same, Type III	55.00	45.00

18

19

20

21

SCOTT NO.	DESCRIPTION	UNUSED F/NH	UNUSED F
17	100y on 2y (no. 10)	2350.00	1750.00
18	3y Govt. of Ryukyu	135.00	95.00

Type I—Bars are narrow spaced; "10" normal
Type II—Bars are wide spaced; "10" normal
Type III—Bars are wide spaced; "10" wide spaced

1952-53

SCOTT NO.	DESCRIPTION	UNUSED F/NH	UNUSED F
19-26	**1y to 100y, 8 varieties, complete**		**73.85**
19	1y Mandanbashi Bridge		.35
20	2y Main Hall of Shun Castle		.40
21	3y Shurei Gate		.50
22	6y Stone Gate, Sogenji Temple		4.00
23	10y Benzaiten-do Temple		4.50
24	30y Altar at Shuri Castle		18.00
25	50y Tamaudun Shuri		23.00
26	100y Stone Bridge, Hosho Pond		30.00

28

31

29

30

1953

SCOTT NO.	DESCRIPTION	UNUSED F/NH	UNUSED F
27	3y Reception at Shuri Castle		16.00
28	6y Perry and Fleet		1.85
29	4y Chofu Ota and Pencil		13.00

1954

SCOTT NO.	DESCRIPTION	UNUSED F/NH	UNUSED F
30	4y Shigo Toma & Pen		15.00

1954-55

SCOTT NO.	DESCRIPTION	UNUSED F/NH	UNUSED F
31	4y Pottery		1.25
32	15y Lacquerware (1955)		6.00
33	20y Textile Design (1955)		4.00

SCOTT NO.	DESCRIPTION	UNUSED F/NH

34 35 36 37

38 39 40

1955

34	4y Noguni Shrine & Sweet Potato Plant	15.00

1956

35	4y Stylized Trees	13.50
36	5y Willow Dance	1.25
37	8y Straw Hat Dance	3.00
38	14y Group Dance	5.00
39	4y Dial Telephone	15.00
40	2y Garland, Bamboo & Plum	2.50

41 42

1957

41	4y Map & Pencil Rocket	1.25
42	2y Phoenix	.35

43

44-53

1958

43	4y Ryukyu Stamps	1.00
44-53	**1/2¢ to $1.00, 10 varieties, complete, ungummed**	**89.50**
44	1/2¢ Yen, Symbol & Denom., orange	1.00
45	1¢ same, yellow green	1.60
46	2¢ same, dark blue	2.50
47	3¢ same, deep carmine	1.95
48	4¢ same, bright green	2.75
49	same, orange	5.00
50	10¢ same, aquamarine	7.00
51	25¢ same, bright violet blue	9.00
51a	25¢ same, bright violet blue (with gum)	16.00
52	50¢ same, gray	19.00
52a	50¢ same, gray (with gum)	16.50
53	$1 same, rose lilac	14.00

SCOTT NO.	DESCRIPTION	UNUSED F/NH

54 55 56

57 61, 79 63

54	3¢ Gate of Courtesy	1.50
55	1-1/2¢ Lion Dance	.45

1959

56	3¢ Mountains & Trees	.85
57	3¢ Yonaguni Moth	1.35
58-62	**1/2¢ to 17¢, 5 varieties, complete**	**44.00**
58	1/2¢ Hibiscus	.40
59	3¢ Moorish Idol	1.00
60	8¢ Seashell	16.00
61	13¢ Dead Leaf Butterfly	3.25
62	17¢ Jellyfish	28.00
63	1-1/2¢ Toy (Yakaji)	.80

64 65, 81 72

73 74 75

1960

64	3¢ University Badge	1.10

DANCES II

65-68	**1¢-10¢, 4 varieties, complete**	**6.75**
65	1¢ Munsunu	2.25
66	2-1/2¢ Nutwabushi	3.50
67	5¢ Hatomabushi	1.20
68	10¢ Hanafubushi	1.25
72	3¢ Torch & Nago Bay	7.50
73	8¢ Runners	1.25
74	3¢ Egret & Sun	6.00
75	1-1/2¢ Bull Fight	2.00

1960-61 REDRAWN INSCRIPTION

76-80	**1/2¢ to 17¢, 5 varieties, complete**	**21.00**
76	1/2¢ Hibiscus	.85
77	3¢ Moorish Idol	1.50
78	8¢ Seashell	1.75
79	13¢ Dead Leaf Butterfly	2.00
80	17¢ Jellyfish	17.00

SCOTT NO.	DESCRIPTION	UNUSED F/NH

WITH "RYUKYUS" ADDED
1961-64

81-87	**1¢ to $1.00, 8 varieties, Dancers, complete**	**16.00**
81	1¢ Munsuru	.30
82	2-1/2¢ Nutwabushi (1962)	.30
83	5¢ Hatomabushi (1962)	.45
84	10¢ Hanafubushi (1962)	.65
84A	20¢ Shundun (1964)	4.00
85	25¢ Hanagasabushi (1962)	1.50
86	50¢ Nubui Kuduchi	3.00
87	$1 Kutubushi	7.00

88 89 90 91 92

1961

88	3¢ Pine Tree	1.95
89	3¢ Naha, Steamer & Sailboat	2.50
90	3¢ White Silver Temple	3.00
91	3¢ Books & Bird	1.60
92	1-1/2¢ Eagles & Rising Sun	2.75

93 95 98 105 97 103 104

1962

93	1-1/2¢ Steps, Trees & Building	.75
94	3¢ GRI Building	1.00
95	3¢ Malaria Eradication	.70
96	8¢ Eradication Emblem	1.10
97	3¢ Children's Day	1.50
98-102	**1/2¢ to 17¢ varieties, Flowers, complete**	**3.05**
98	1/2¢ Sea Hibiscus	.50
99	3¢ Indian Coral Tree	.45
100	8¢ Iju	.70
101	13¢ Touch-Me-Not	.90
102	17¢ Shell Flower	1.60
103	3¢ Earthenware	4.00
104	3¢ Japanese Fencing	5.25
105	1-1/2¢ Bingata Cloth	1.25

106

107

108

SCOTT NO.	DESCRIPTION	UNUSED F/NH

110 109 111

1963

106	3¢ Stone Relief	1.20
107	1-1/2¢ Gooseneck Cactus	.35
108	3¢ Trees & Hills	1.20
109	3¢ Map of Okinawa	1.50
110	3¢ Hawks & Islands	1.25
111	3¢ Shioya Bridge	1.25

112 113 114 115 116 117

112	3¢ Lacquerware Bowl	3.25
113	3¢ Map of Far East	1.00
114	15¢ Mamaomoto	2.25
115	3¢ Nakagusuku Castle Site	.95
116	3¢ Human Rights	1.00
117	1-1/2¢ Dragon	.75

118 119 120, 120a 121 122, 122a 123 124

1964

118	3¢ Mothers' Day	.50
119	3¢ Agricultural Census	.50
120	3¢ Minsah Obi, rose pink	.65
120a	same, deep carmine	.90
121	3¢ Girl Scout & Emblem	.50
122	3¢ Shuri Relay Station	.90
122a	3¢ same, inverted "1"	40.00
123	8¢ Antenna & map	1.50
124	3¢ Olympic Torch & Emblem	.40

125 126 127

1964-65

125	3¢ Karate, "Naihanchi"	.70
126	3¢ Karate, "Makiwara" (1965)	.60
127	3¢ Karate, "Kumite" (1965)	.60

128 129

1964

SCOTT NO.	DESCRIPTION	UNUSED F/NH
128	3¢ Miyara Dunchi	.40
129	1-1/2¢ Snake & Iris	.40

130 131 132 133 134 135 136 139

1965

SCOTT NO.	DESCRIPTION	UNUSED F/NH
130	3¢ Boy Scouts	.60
131	3¢ Onoyama Stadium	.35
132	3¢ Samisen of King Shoko	.60
133	3¢ Kin Power Plant	.35
134	3¢ ICY and United Nations	.30
135	3¢ Naha City Hall	.30

1965-66

SCOTT NO.	DESCRIPTION	UNUSED F/NH
136	3¢ Chinese Box Turtle	.40
137	3¢ Hawksbill Turtle (1966)	.40
138	3¢ Asian Terrapin (1966)	.40

1965

SCOTT NO.	DESCRIPTION	UNUSED F/NH
139	1-1/2¢ Horse	.30

140 141 143 146 144 145

1966

SCOTT NO.	DESCRIPTION	UNUSED F/NH
140	3¢ Woodpecker	.30
141	3¢ Sika Deer	.35
142	3¢ Dugong	.35
143	3¢ Swallow	.30
144	3¢ Memorial Day	.30
145	3¢ University of Ryukyus	.30
146	3¢ Lacquerware	.30

147 148 149 150

SCOTT NO.	DESCRIPTION	UNUSED F/NH
147	3¢ UNESCO	.30
148	3¢ Government Museum	.30
149	3¢ Nakasone T. Genga's Tomb	.30
150	1-1/2¢ Ram in Iris Wreath	.30

151 156

1966-67

SCOTT NO.	DESCRIPTION	UNUSED F/NH
151-55	**5 varieties, Fish, complete**	**1.70**
151	3¢ Clown Fish	.30
152	3¢ Young Boxfish (1967)	.35
153	3¢ Forceps Fish (1967)	.45
154	3¢ Spotted Triggerfish (1967)	.40
155	3¢ Saddleback Butterflyfish (1967)	.40

1966

SCOTT NO.	DESCRIPTION	UNUSED F/NH
156	3¢ Tsuboya Urn	.30

157 162 163 164 165 166 167 168

1967-68

SCOTT NO.	DESCRIPTION	UNUSED F/NH
157-61	**5 varieties, Seashells, complete**	**1.95**
157	3¢ Episcopal Miter	.30
158	3¢ Venus Comb Murex	.30
159	3¢ Chiragra Spider	.35
160	3¢ Green Turban	.35
161	3¢ Euprotomus Bulla	.75
162	3¢ Roofs & ITY Emblem	.30
163	3¢ Mobile TB Clinic	.30
164	3¢ Hojo Bridge, Enkaku Temple	.30
165	1-1/2¢ Monkey	.30
166	3¢ TV Tower & Map	.35

169 170 171 172 173

1968

SCOTT NO.	DESCRIPTION	UNUSED F/NH
167	3¢ Dr. Nakachi & Helper	.35
168	3¢ Pill Box	.50
169	3¢ Man, Library, Book & Map	.45
170	3¢ Mailmen's Uniforms & 1948 Stamp	.40
171	3¢ Main Gate, Enkaku Temple	.40
172	3¢ Old Man's Dance	.40

SCOTT NO.	DESCRIPTION	UNUSED F/NH

1968-69

173-77	**5 varieties, Crabs, complete**	**2.35**
173	3¢ Mictyris Longicarpus	.40
174	3¢ Uca Dubia Stimpson (1969)	.45
175	3¢ Baptozius Vinosus (1969)	.45
176	3¢ Cardisoma Carnifex (1969)	.60
177	3¢ Ocypode (1969)	.60

178  179  180

1968

178	3¢ Saraswati Pavilion	.40
179	3¢ Tennis Player	.40
180	1-1/2¢ Cock & Iris	.30

181  182  183  184

1969

181	3¢ Boxer	.40
182	3¢ Ink Slab Screen	.60
183	3¢ Antennas & Map	.35
184	3¢ Gate of Courtesy & Emblems	.35

185 187 186 188  189

1969-70

185-89	**5 varieties, Folklore, complete**	**2.70**
185	3¢ Tug of War Festival	.45
186	3¢ Hari Boat Race	.45
187	3¢ Izaiho Ceremony	.45
188	3¢ Mortardrum Dance (1970)	.75
189	3¢ Sea God Dance	.75

SCOTT NO.	DESCRIPTION	UNUSED F/NH

193  191  192  194

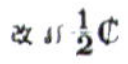

改訂 ½¢
(surcharge)
190

1969

190	1/2¢ on 3¢ (no. 99) Indian Coral Tree	1.25
191	3¢ Nakamura-Ke Farm House	.35
192	3¢ Statue & Maps	.60
193	1-1/2¢ Dog & Flowers	.30
194	3¢ Sake Flask	.35

195  196  197  198  199  200

195-99	**5 varieties, Classic Opera, complete**	**2.85**
195	3¢ "The Bell"	.75
196	3¢ Child & Kidnapper	.75
197	3¢ Robe of Feathers	.75
198	3¢ Vengeance of Two Sons	.75
199	3¢ Virgin & the Dragon	.75
195-99a	**5 varieties, complete, sheets of 4**	**26.00**
195a	3¢ sheet of 4	5.75
196a	3¢ sheet of 4	5.75
197a	3¢ sheet of 4	5.75
198a	3¢ sheet of 4	5.75
199a	3¢ sheet of 4	5.75
200	3¢ Underwater Observatory	.40

201  204  205  206  207

1970-71 Portraits

201	3¢ Noboru Jahana	.60
202	3¢ Saion Gushichan Bunjaku	1.00
203	3¢ Choho Giwan (1971)	.65

1970

204	3¢ Map & People	.35
205	3¢ Great Cycad of Une	.35
206	3¢ Flag, Diet & Map	1.10
207	1-1/2¢ Boar & Cherry Blossoms	.30

SCOTT NO.	DESCRIPTION	UNUSED F/NH

208 210 212

213 214 215

1971

SCOTT NO.	DESCRIPTION	UNUSED F/NH
208-12	**5 varieties, Workers, complete**	**2.10**
208	3¢ Low Hand Loom	.40
209	3¢ Filature	.40
210	3¢ Farmer with Raincoat & Hat	.45
211	3¢ Rice Huller	.55
212	3¢ Fisherman's Box & Scoop	.45
213	3¢ Water Carrier	.45
214	3¢ Old & New Naha	.30
215	2¢ Caesalpinia Pulcherrima	.30
216	3¢ Madder	.30

217 218 220

221 222 223

1971-72 Government Parks

SCOTT NO.	DESCRIPTION	UNUSED F/NH
217	3¢ View from Mabuni Hill	.30
218	3¢ Mt. Arashi from Haneji Sea	.30
219	4¢ Yabuchi Is. from Yakena Port	.35

1971

SCOTT NO.	DESCRIPTION	UNUSED F/NH
220	4¢ Dancer	.30
221	4¢ Deva King	.30
222	2¢ Rat & Chrysanthemums	.30
223	4¢ Student Nurse	.30

224 225

226 227 228

1972

SCOTT NO.	DESCRIPTION	UNUSED F/NH
224	5¢ Birds & Seashore	.55
225	5¢ Coral Reef	.55
226	5¢ Sun Over Islands	.55
227	5¢ Dove & Flags	.95
228	5¢ Antique Sake Pot	.70

C1-3 C4-8

AIR MAIL STAMPS

1950

SCOTT NO.	DESCRIPTION	UNUSED F/NH
C1	8y Dove & Map, bright blue	160.00
C2	12y same, green	40.00
C3	16y same, rose carmine	20.00

1951-54

SCOTT NO.	DESCRIPTION	UNUSED F/NH
C4-8	**13y to 50y, 5 varieties, complete**	**32.25**
C4	13y Heavenly Maiden, blue	3.50
C5	18y same, green	4.50
C6	30y same, cerise	7.00
C7	40y same, red violet (1954)	9.00
C8	50y same, yellow orange (1954)	10.00

C9-13 C14-18 (surcharge) C19-23

C24 C29 C30

1957

SCOTT NO.	DESCRIPTION	UNUSED F/NH
C9-13	**15y to 60y, 5 varieties, complete**	**88.25**
C9	15y Maiden Playing Flute, blue green	10.00
C10	20y same, rose carmine	17.00
C11	35y same, yellow green	19.00
C12	45y same, reddish brown	22.00
C13	60y same, gray	26.00

1959

SCOTT NO.	DESCRIPTION	UNUSED F/NH
C14-18	**9¢ to 35¢, 5 varieties, complete**	**51.50**
C14	9¢ on 15y (no. C9)	3.50
C15	14¢ on 20y (no. C10)	5.00
C16	19¢ on 35y (no. C11)	9.00
C17	27¢ on 45y (no. C12)	18.00
C18	35¢ on 60y (no. C13)	20.00

1960

SCOTT NO.	DESCRIPTION	UNUSED F/NH
C19-23	**9¢ to 35¢, 5 varieties, complete**	**31.00**
C19	9¢ on 4y (no. 31)	4.75
C20	14¢ on 5y (no. 36)	5.50
C21	19¢ on 15y (no. 32)	4.00
C22	27¢ on 14y (no. 38)	11.00
C23	35¢ on 20y (no. 33)	8.00

1961

SCOTT NO.	DESCRIPTION	UNUSED F/NH
C24-28	**9¢ to 35¢, 5 varieties, complete**	**8.75**
C24	9¢ Heavenly Maiden	.45
C25	14¢ Maiden Playing Flute	.95
C26	19¢ Wind God	1.25
C27	27¢ Wind God	4.00
C28	35¢ Maiden Over Tree Tops	3.00

1963

SCOTT NO.	DESCRIPTION	UNUSED F/NH
C29	5-1/2¢ Jet & Gate of Courtesy	.35
C30	7¢ Jet Plane	.40

E1

SPECIAL DELIVERY

1950

SCOTT NO.	DESCRIPTION	UNUSED F/NH
E1	5y Dragon & Map	40.00

UNITED NATIONS (NEW YORK)

1, 6 — 2, 10, UX1-2 — 3, 11 — 4, 7, 9

5 — 8 — 12 — 13-14

1951

SCOTT NO.	DESCRIPTION	FIRST DAY COVERS SING	FIRST DAY COVERS INSC. BLK	INSRIP BLK-4	UNUSED F/NH	USED F
1-11	1¢ to $1 Definitives	85.00	150.00	70.00	15.50	10.00

1952-1953

SCOTT NO.	DESCRIPTION	FIRST DAY COVERS SING	FIRST DAY COVERS INSC. BLK	INSRIP BLK-4	UNUSED F/NH	USED F
12-22	**1952-53 Issues, complete (11)**	......	......	......	**15.50**	......

1952

SCOTT NO.	DESCRIPTION	FIRST DAY COVERS SING	FIRST DAY COVERS INSC. BLK	INSRIP BLK-4	UNUSED F/NH	USED F
12	5¢ United Nations Day	1.75	3.50	3.75	.85	.35
13-14	3¢ & 5¢ Human Rights Day	2.50	7.00	7.75	1.75	.75

15-16 — 17-18 — 19-20

23-24 — 25-26 — 27-28 — 21-22

1953

SCOTT NO.	DESCRIPTION	FIRST DAY COVERS SING	FIRST DAY COVERS INSC. BLK	INSRIP BLK-4	UNUSED F/NH	USED F
15-16	3¢ & 5¢ Refugee Issue	1.80	4.50	6.00	1.50	.95
17-18	3¢ & 5¢ U.P.U. Issue	3.00	7.50	13.00	3.00	1.85
19-20	3¢ & 5¢ Technical Assistance	1.75	4.40	6.00	1.75	1.00
21-22	3¢ & 5¢ Human Rights Day	7.75	18.50	9.50	2.15	1.85

1954

SCOTT NO.	DESCRIPTION	FIRST DAY COVERS SING	FIRST DAY COVERS INSC. BLK	INSRIP BLK-4	UNUSED F/NH	USED F
23-30	**1954 Issues, complete (8)**	......	......		**24.00**	......
23-24	3¢ & 8¢ Food & Agriculture	2.05	5.15	6.00	1.50	1.00
25-26	3¢ & 8¢ International Labor	2.75	6.85	12.00	3.00	2.50
27-28	3¢ & 8¢ Geneva	4.00	10.00	11.00	3.00	2.00
29-30	3¢ & 8¢ Human Rights Day	7.75	18.50	85.00	19.00	5.60

1955

SCOTT NO.	DESCRIPTION	FIRST DAY COVERS SING	FIRST DAY COVERS INSC. BLK	INSRIP BLK-4	UNUSED F/NH	USED F
31/40	**1955 Issues, (9) (No #38)**	......	......	......	**8.00**	......
31-32	3¢ & 8¢ Int. Civil Aviation Org.	3.95	10.00	13.00	3.00	2.50
33-34	3¢ & 8¢ UNESCO	2.00	5.00	5.00	1.25	1.00
35-37	3¢ to 8¢ United Nations	3.25	17.50	14.00	3.50	2.50
38	same, souvenir sheet	85.00	......	......	175.00	60.00
38 var	Second print, retouched	......	......	......	180.00	65.00
39-40	3¢ & 8¢ Human Rights Day	2.00	5.00	6.25	1.40	.90

1956

SCOTT NO.	DESCRIPTION	FIRST DAY COVERS SING	FIRST DAY COVERS INSC. BLK	INSRIP BLK-4	UNUSED F/NH	USED F
41-48	**1956 Issues, complete (8)**	......	......	......	**3.40**	......
41-42	3¢ & 8¢ International Telecommunications	2.00	5.00	5.00	1.30	.90
43-44	3¢ & 8¢ World Health Org.	2.00	5.00	5.00	1.30	.90
45-46	3¢ & 8¢ United Nations Day	1.25	3.15	2.25	.55	.30
47-48	3¢ & 8¢ Human Rights Day	1.25	3.15	2.10	.50	.30

SETS ONLY: Prices listed are for complete sets as indicated. We regrettably cannot supply individual stamps from sets.

57-58 — 59-60 — 61-62

63-64 — 65-66 — 67-68

1957

SCOTT NO.	DESCRIPTION	FIRST DAY COVERS SING	FIRST DAY COVERS INSC. BLK	INSRIP BLK-4	UNUSED F/NH	USED F
49-58	**1957 Issues, complete (10)**	......	......	......	**2.40**	......
49-50	3¢ & 8¢ Meteorological Org.	1.25	3.15	1.35	.35	.30
51-52	3¢ & 8¢ Emergency Force	1.25	3.15	1.35	.35	.30
53-54	same, re-engraved	......	......	6.00	1.40	.45
55-56	3¢ & 8¢ Security Council	1.25	3.15	1.35	.35	.30
57-58	3¢ & 8¢ Human Rights Day	1.25	3.15	1.35	.35	.30

1958

SCOTT NO.	DESCRIPTION	FIRST DAY COVERS SING	FIRST DAY COVERS INSC. BLK	INSRIP BLK-4	UNUSED F/NH	USED F
59-68	**1958 Issues, complete (10**	......	......	......	**1.65**	......
59-60	3¢ & 8¢ Atomic Energy Agency	1.25	3.15	1.35	.35	.30
61-62	3¢ & 8¢ Central Hall	1.25	3.15	1.35	.35	.30
63-64	4¢ & 8¢ U.N. Seal	1.25	3.15	1.35	.35	.30
65-66	4¢ & 8¢ Economic & Social Council	1.25	3.15	1.35	.35	.30
67-68	4¢ & 8¢ Human Rights Day	1.21	3.15	1.35	.35	.30

69-70 — 71-72 — 73-74 — 75-76

1959

SCOTT NO.	DESCRIPTION	FIRST DAY COVERS SING	FIRST DAY COVERS INSC. BLK	INSRIP BLK-4	UNUSED F/NH	USED F
69-76	**1959 Issues, complete (8)**	......	......	......	**1.35**	......
69-70	4¢ & 8¢ Flushing Meadows	1.25	3.15	1.40	.35	.30
71-72	4¢ & 8¢ Economic Commission Europe	1.25	3.15	1.60	.35	.50
73-74	4¢ & 8¢ Trusteeship Council	1.25	3.15	1.90	.40	.30
75-76	4¢ & 8¢ World Refugee Year	1.25	3.15	1.40	.35	.30

77-78 — 79-80 — 81-82 — 83-85 — 86-87

1960

SCOTT NO.	DESCRIPTION	FIRST DAY COVERS SING	FIRST DAY COVERS INSC. BLK	INSRIP BLK-4	UNUSED F/NH	USED F
77/87	**1960 Issues, (10) (No #85)**	......	......	......	**1.65**	...
77-78	4¢ & 8¢ Palais de Chaillot	1.25	3.15	1.40	.35	.30
79-80	4¢ & 8¢ Economic Commission Asia	1.25	3.15	1.40	.35	.30
81-82	4¢ & 8¢ 5th World Forestry Congress	1.25	3.15	1.40	.35	.30
83-84	4¢ & 8¢ 15th Anniversary	1.25	3.15	1.40	.35	.30
85	same, souvenir sheet	4.25	......	......	2.10	1.80
85 var	Broken "V" Variety	135.00	......	......	72.50	67.50
86-87	4¢ & 8¢ International Bank	1.25	3.15	1.40	.35	.30

FIRST DAY COVERS: Prices for United Nations First Day Covers are for cacheted, unaddressed covers with each variety in a set mounted on a separate cover. Complete sets mounted on one cover do exist and sell for a slightly lower price.

UNITED NATIONS (NEW YORK)

1961

SCOTT NO.	DESCRIPTION	FIRST DAY COVERS SING	INSC. BLK	INSRIP BLK-4	UNUSED F/NH	USED F
88-99	**1961 Issues, complete (12)**	.....	.....	.....	2.65	.....
88-89	4¢ & 8¢ International Court of Justice	1.25	3.15	1.35	.35	1.25
90-91	4¢ & 7¢ Int. Monetary Fund	1.25	3.15	1.35	.35	1.25
92	30¢ Abstract Flags	1.25	3.15	3.00	.75	.60
93-94	4¢ & 11¢ Economic Commission Latin America	1.25	3.15	2.70	.60	.50
95-96	4¢ & 11¢ Economic Commission Africa	1.25	3.15	1.25	.35	.35
97-99	3¢, 4¢ & 13¢ Children's Fund	1.25	3.50	2.55	.55	.50

1962

SCOTT NO.	DESCRIPTION	FIRST DAY COVERS SING	INSC. BLK	INSRIP BLK-4	UNUSED F/NH	USED F
100-13	**1962 Issues, complete (14)**	.....	.....	.....	3.05	.....
100-01	4¢ & 7¢ Housing & Community Development	1.25	3.15	1.40	.35	.30
102-03	4¢ & 11¢ Malaria Eradication	1.25	3.15	2.35	.50	.35
104-07	1¢ to 11¢ Definitives	2.00	4.00	3.30	.75	.65
108-09	5¢ & 15¢ Memorial Issue	1.25	3.15	3.40	.75	.55
110-11	4¢ & 11¢ Operation in the Congo	1.25	3.15	3.30	.75	.55
112-13	4¢ & 11¢ Peaceful Uses of Outer Space	1.25	3.15	2.40	.55	.30

1963

SCOTT NO.	DESCRIPTION	FIRST DAY COVERS SING	INSC. BLK	INSRIP BLK-4	UNUSED F/NH	USED F
114-22	**1963 Issues, complete (9)**	.....	.....	.....	2.10	.....
114-15	5¢ & 11¢ Science & Technology	1.25	3.15	1.85	.40	.35
116-17	5¢ & 11¢ Freedom From Hunger	1.25	3.15	1.85	.40	.35
118	25¢ UNTEA	1.10	3.00	3.00	.70	.60
119-20	5¢ & 11¢ General Assem. Bldg.	1.25	3.15	1.85	.40	.35
121-22	5¢ & 11¢ Human Rights	1.25	3.15	1.85	.40	.35

1964

SCOTT NO.	DESCRIPTION	FIRST DAY COVERS SING	INSC. BLK	INSRIP BLK-4	UNUSED F/NH	USED F
123-36	**1964 Issues, complete (14)**	.....	.....	.....	3.30	.....
123-24	5¢ & 11¢ Maritime Organization (IMCO)	1.25	3.15	1.85	.40	.35
125-28	2¢ to 50¢ Definitives	3.25	7.75	7.00	1.60	1.50
129-30	5¢ & 11¢ Trade & Development	1.25	3.15	1.85	.40	.35
131-32	5¢ & 11¢ Narcotics Control	1.25	3.45	1.85	.40	.35
133	5¢ Cessation of Nuclear Testing	.60	1.30	.65	.25	.25
134-36	4¢ to 11¢ Education for Progress	1.30	3.25	2.90	.70	.50

1965

SCOTT NO.	DESCRIPTION	FIRST DAY COVERS SING	INSC. BLK	INSRIP BLK-4	UNUSED F/NH	USED F
137/53	**1965 Issues, (15) (No #145 or 150)**	.....	.....	.....	2.90	.....
137-38	5¢ & 11¢ United Nations Special Fund	1.25	3.15	1.65	.35	.30
139-40	5¢ & 11¢ United Nations Forces in Cyprus	1.25	3.15	1.65	.35	.30
141-42	5¢ & 11¢ I.T.U. Centenary	1.25	3.15	1.65	.35	.30
143-44	5¢ & 15¢ Int'l Cooperation Year	1.25	3.15	1.85	.40	.35
145	same, souvenir sheet	1.75		.....	.60	.50
146-49	1¢ to 25¢ Definitive	3.50	8.75	7.65	1.20	.95

1966

SCOTT NO.	DESCRIPTION	FIRST DAY COVERS SING	INSC. BLK	INSRIP BLK-4	UNUSED F/NH	USED F
150	$1 Definitive	3.10	7.75	9.50	2.50	2.00

1965

SCOTT NO.	DESCRIPTION	FIRST DAY COVERS SING	INSC. BLK	INSRIP BLK-4	UNUSED F/NH	USED F
151-53	4¢ to 11¢ Population Trends	1.60	3.75	2.40	.55	.50

1966

SCOTT NO.	DESCRIPTION	FIRST DAY COVERS SING	INSC. BLK	INSRIP BLK-4	UNUSED F/NH	USED F
154-63	**1966 Issues, complete (10)**	.....	.....	.....	1.90	.....
154-55	5¢ & 15¢ World Federation (WFUNA)	1.25	3.15	2.00	.50	.30
156-57	5¢ & 11¢ World Health Organization	1.25	3.15	1.85	.45	.30
158-59	5¢ & 11¢ Coffee Agreement	1.25	3.15	1.85	.45	.30
160	15¢ Peace Keeping Observers	.60	1.50	1.85	.40	.40
161-63	4¢ to 11¢ UNICEF	1.60	3.75	2.25	.50	.45

1967

SCOTT NO.	DESCRIPTION	FIRST DAY COVERS SING	INSC. BLK	INSRIP BLK-4	UNUSED F/NH	USED F
164/80	**1967 Issues, (16) (No #179)**		.....	.....	3.20	.....
164-65	5¢ & 11¢ Development	1.25	3.15	1.80	.35	.30
166-67	1-1/2 ¢ & 5¢ Definitives	1.25	3.15	1.35	.35	.30
168-69	5¢ & 11¢ Independence	1.25	3.15	1.75	.40	.30
170-74	4¢ to 15¢ Expo '67 Canada	3.00	7.50	4.20	.95	.85

UNITED NATIONS (NEW YORK)

SCOTT NO.	DESCRIPTION	FIRST DAY COVERS SING	FIRST DAY COVERS INSC. BLK	INSRIP BLK-4	UNUSED F/NH	USED F
175-76	5¢ & 15¢ International Tourist Year	1.25	3.15	1.90	.40	.35
177-78	6¢ & 13¢ Towards Disarmament	1.25	3.15	1.90	.40	.35
179	36¢ Chagall Window souvenir sheet	1.25	......	......	.80	.75
180	6¢ Kiss of Peace	.60	......	.90	.25	.25
	1968					
181-91	**1968 Issues, complete (11)**	......	......	......	**4.00**	......
181-82	6¢ & 13 ¢ Secretariat	1.25	3.15	1.90	.40	.35
183-84	6¢ & 75¢ H. Starcke	6.25	15.00	8.00	1.85	1.65
185-86	6¢ & 13¢ Industrial Development	1.25	3.15	1.90	.45	.25
187	6¢ Definitive	.60	1.50	.90	.25	.25
188-89	6¢ & 20¢ Weather Watch	1.25	3.15	2.70	.60	.40
190-91	6¢ & 13¢ International Year—Human Rights	1.25	3.15	2.30	.50	.40
	1969					
192-202	**1969 Issues (11)**	......	......	......	**2.45**	......
192-93	6¢ & 13¢ Institute Training Research	1.25	3.15	2.00	.45	.35
194-95	6¢ & 15¢ U.N. Building—Chile	1.25	3.15	2.15	.45	.40
196	13¢ Definitive	.60	1.50	1.55	.35	.25
197-98	6¢ & 13¢ Peace Through International Law	1.25	3.15	1.95	.40	.35
199-200	6¢ & 20¢ Labor & Development	1.25	3.15	2.55	.60	.45
201-02	6¢ & 13¢ Tunisian Mosaics	1.25	3.15	2.25	.50	.35
	1970					
203/14	**1970 Issues, (11) (No #212)**	......	......	......	**3.25**	......
203-04	6¢ & 25¢ Japanese Peace Bell	1.25	3.15	3.00	.70	.50
205-06	6¢ & 13¢ L. Mekong Delta Devel.	1.25	3.15	2.10	.50	.35
207-08	6¢ & 13¢ Fight Cancer	1.25	3.15	2.10	.50	.35
209-11	6¢ to 25¢ Peace & Progress	1.70	4.25	4.10	.95	.80
212	same, souvenir sheet	1.40	......	......	.95	.85
213-14	6¢ & 13¢ Peace, Justice & Prog.	1.25	3.15	2.25	.50	.35
	1971					
215-25	**1971 Issues (11)**	......	......	......	**3.25**	......
215	6¢ Peaceful Uses Sea-Bed	.60	1.50	.90	.25	.25
216-17	6¢ & 13¢ Support Refugees	1.25	3.15	2.10	.50	.30
218	13¢ World Food Programme	.60	1.50	1.40	.35	.30
219	20¢ Universal Postal Union Building	.70	1.75	1.90	.45	.35
220-21	8¢ & 13¢ Anti-Discrimination	1.25	3.15	2.25	.45	.35
222-23	8¢ & 60¢ Definitives	2.50	6.25	6.75	1.50	1.10
224-25	8¢ & 21¢ International School	1.25	3.15	3.00	.70	.55

SETS ONLY: Prices listed are for complete sets as indicated. We regrettably cannot supply individual stamps from sets.

INSCRIPTION BLOCKS: Each corner of United Nations complete sheets contains the U.N. Emblem plus the name of the issue in the selvage. These are offered as Inscription Blocks of Four.

UNITED NATIONS (NEW YORK)

SCOTT NO.	DESCRIPTION	FIRST DAY COVERS SING	FIRST DAY COVERS INSC. BLK	INSRIP BLK-4	UNUSED F/NH	USED F
	1972					
226-33	**1972 Issues, complete (8)**	......	......	......	**3.85**	......
226	95¢ Definitive	2.75	6.85	9.25	2.00	1.90
227	8¢ Non-Proliferation	.60	1.50	1.00	.25	.25
228	15¢ World Health Org	.60	1.50	1.75	.40	.25
229-30	8¢ & 15¢ Environment	1.25	3.15	2.35	.55	.40
231	21¢ Economic Commission Europe	.75	1.85	2.10	.45	.40
232-33	8¢ & 15¢ Art—Sert Ceiling	1.25	3.15	2.25	.50	.40
	1973					
234-43	**1973 Issues, complete (10)**	......	......	......	**2.60**	......
234-35	8¢ & 15¢ Disarmament Decade	1.25	3.15	2.25	.55	.50
236-37	8¢ & 15¢ Drug Abuse	1.25	3.15	2.50	.55	.50
238-39	8¢ & 21¢ Volunteers Programme	1.25	3.15	2.85	.60	.55
240-41	8¢ & 15¢ Namibia	1.25	3.15	2.75	.55	.50
242-43	8¢ & 21¢ Human Rights	1.25	3.15	3.00	.60	.55
	1974					
244-55	**1974 Issues, complete (12)**	......	......	......	**3.25**	......
244-45	10¢ & 21¢ ILO Headquarters	1.30	3.25	3.25	.70	.65
246	10¢ Universal Postal Union	.60	1.50	.95	.25	.25
247-48	10¢ & 18¢ Brazil Peace Mural	1.25	3.15	2.85	.65	.60
249-51	2¢ to 18¢ Definitives	1.65	4.15	3.00	.65	.60
252-53	10¢ & 18¢ World Population Year	1.35	3.35	3.25	.70	.75
254-55	10¢ & 26¢ Law of the Sea	1.35	3.35	3.50	1.50	.80

231 232-33 234-35 236-37

238-39 240-41 242-43

244-45 246

SCOTT NO.	DESCRIPTION	FIRST DAY COVERS SING	FIRST DAY COVERS INSC. BLK	INSRIP BLK-4	UNUSED F/NH	USED F
	1975					
256/66	**1975 Issues, (10) (No #262)**	......	......	......	**4.10**	......
256-57	10¢ & 26¢ Peaceful Uses of Space	1.35	3.35	3.45	.75	.70
258-59	10¢ & 18¢ Int'l. Women's Year	1.25	3.15	3.25	.65	.65
260-61	10¢ & 26¢ Anniversary	1.30	3.35	3.25	.80	.75
262	same, souvenir sheet	1.55	......	......	1.00	.80
263-64	10¢ & 18¢ Namibia	1.25	3.15	3.10	.65	.65
265-66	13¢ & 26¢ Peacekeeping	1.35	3.35	3.85	.85	.85
	1976					
267-80	**1976 Issues, complete (14)**	......	......	......	**7.90**	......
267-71	3¢ to 50¢ Definitives	3.10	7.75	9.50	2.10	1.85

247-48 249 250, U6 251 252-53

254-55 256-57 258-59 260-62 263-64

265-66 267 268 269 270

271 272-73 274-75 276-77 280

278-79 281-82 283-84 289-90

285-86 287-88

SCOTT NO.	DESCRIPTION	FIRST DAY COVERS SING	FIRST DAY COVERS INSC. BLK	INSRIP BLK-4	UNUSED F/NH	USED F
272-73	13¢ & 26¢ World Federation	1.50	3.75	3.75	.85	.65
274-75	13¢ & 31¢ Conf. on Trade & Dev.	1.45	3.65	4.70	.95	.75
276-77	13¢ & 25¢ Conference on Human Settlements	1.25	3.15	4.00	.85	.75
278-79	13¢ & 31¢ Postal Admin.	9.50	23.50	13.00	4.00	2.25
280	13¢ World Food Council	.60	1.50	1.50	.30	.30
	1977					
281-90	**Issues, complete (10)**	......	......	......	**3.85**	......
281-82	13¢ & 31¢ WIPO	1.40	3.50	4.20	.90	.80
283-84	13¢ & 25¢ Water Conference	1.35	3.40	3.95	.85	.75
285-86	13¢ & 31¢ Security Council	1.50	3.75	4.25	.95	.70
287-88	13¢ & 25¢ Combat Racism	1.35	3.40	3.85	.95	.70
289-90	13¢ & 18¢ Atomic Energy	1.25	3.15	3.00	.65	.70
	1978					
291-303	**1978 Issues, complete (13)**	......	......	......	**6.25**	......
291-93	1¢, 25¢ & $1 Definitives	4.00	10.00	11.00	2.50	2.00
294-95	13¢ & 31¢ Smallpox Eradication	1.40	3.50	4.40	.95	.85
296-97	13¢ & 18¢ Namibia	1.25	3.15	3.00	.70	.60
298-99	13¢ & 25¢ ICAO	1.30	3.25	3.75	.85	.70
300-01	13¢ & 18¢ General Assembly	1.25	3.15	3.25	.70	.65
302-03	13¢ & 31¢ TCDC	1.50	3.75	4.00	.95	.90

291 292 293 294-95

296-97 298-99 300-01 302-03

304 305 306 307

UNITED NATIONS (NEW YORK)

1979

SCOTT NO.	DESCRIPTION	FIRST DAY COVERS SING	INSC. BLK	INSRIP BLK-4	UNUSED F/NH	USED F
304-15	**1979 Issues, complete (12)**	......	......	......	**4.25**	......
304-07	5¢, 14¢, 15¢ & 20¢ Definitives	2.00	5.00	5.25	1.10	1.10
308-09	15¢ & 20¢ UNDRO	1.35	3.40	3.50	.75	.65
310-11	15¢ & 31¢ I.Y.C.	3.75	9.40	4.95	1.10	.95
312-13	15¢ & 31¢ Namibia	1.55	3.85	4.40	1.00	.85
314-15	15¢ & 20¢ Court of Justice	1.40	3.50	3.75	.85	.75

1980 World Flags

326 *Luxembourg*
327 *Fiji*
328 *Viet Nam*
329 *Guinea*
330 *Surinam*
331 *Bangladesh*
332 *Mali*
333 *Yugoslavia*
334 *France*
335 *Venezuela*
336 *El Salvador*
337 *Madagascar*
338 *Cameroon*
339 *Rwanda*
340 *Hungary*

325 308-09 310-11

312-13 314-15 316 317

1980

SCOTT NO.	DESCRIPTION	FIRST DAY COVERS SING	INSC. BLK	INSRIP BLK-4	UNUSED F/NH	USED F
316/42	**1980 Issues, (26) (No #324)**	......	......	......	**7.95**	......
316-17	15¢ & 31¢ Economics	1.65	4.15	4.25	.95	.95
318-19	15¢ & 20¢ Decade for Women	1.35	3.40	3.50	.75	.70
320-21	15¢ & 31¢ Peacekeeping	1.60	4.00	4.25	.90	.90
322-23	15¢ & 31¢ Anniversary	1.55	3.90	4.25	.90	.75
324	same, souvenir sheet	1.45	......	......	.95	.90
325-40	15¢ 1980 World Flags, 16 varieties	10.00	......	22.00	5.00	3.75
341-42	15¢ & 20¢ Economic & Social Council	1.30	3.25	4.00	.85	.75

318-19 320 321 322

323 341 342 343

344 345 346-47 348

349 366 367

1981 World Flags

350 *Djibouti*
351 *Sri Lanka*
352 *Bolivia*
353 *Equatorial Guinea*
354 *Malta*
355 *Czechoslovakia*
356 *Thailand*
357 *Trinidad*
358 *Ukraine*
359 *Kuwait*
360 *Sudan*
361 *Egypt*
362 *United States*
363 *Singapore*
364 *Panama*
365 *Costa Rica*

368 369

370 371 372 373 390-91

1981

SCOTT NO.	DESCRIPTION	FIRST DAY COVERS SING	INSC. BLK	INSRIP BLK-4	UNUSED F/NH	USED F
343-67	**1981 Issues, complete (25)**	......	......	......	**11.00**	......
343	15¢ Palestinian People	.75	1.85	1.60	.35	.30
344-45	20¢ & 35¢ Disabled Persons	1.70	4.25	5.50	1.25	1.00
346-47	20¢ & 31¢ Fresco	1.60	4.00	5.50	1.25	1.00
348-49	20¢ & 40¢ Sources of Energy	1.90	4.75	5.75	1.20	1.00
350-65	20¢ 1981 World Flags, 16 varieties	13.50	......	28.00	7.00	5.50
366-67	18¢ & 28¢ Volunteers Program	1.55	3.85	5.50	1.20	.95

1982

SCOTT NO.	DESCRIPTION	FIRST DAY COVERS SING	INSC. BLK	INSRIP BLK-4	UNUSED F/NH	USED F
368-91	**1982 Issues, complete (24)**	......	......	......	**11.50**	......
368-70	17¢, 28¢ & 49¢ Definitives	2.50	6.25	9.25	2.00	1.80
371-72	20¢ & 40¢ Human Environment	1.95	4.85	7.00	1.40	1.25
373	20¢ Space Exploration	.90	2.25	3.25	.70	.60
374-89	20¢ World Flags, 16 varieties	13.00	......	29.00	7.00	5.50
390-91	20¢ & 28¢ Nature Conservation	1.75	4.35	5.75	1.20	1.00

1982 World Flags

374 *Austria*
375 *Malaysia*
376 *Seychelles*
377 *Ireland*
378 *Mozambique*
379 *Albania*
380 *Dominica*
381 *Solomon Islands*
382 *Philippines*
383 *Swaziland*
384 *Nicaragua*
385 *Burma*
386 *Cape Verde*
387 *Guyana*
388 *Belgium*
389 *Nigeria*

392 393

394 395 396 397 398

1983 World Flags

399 *United Kingdom*
400 *Barbados*
401 *Nepal*
402 *Israel*
403 *Malawi*
404 *Byelorussian SSR*
405 *Jamaica*
406 *Kenya*
407 *China*
408 *Peru*
409 *Bulgaria*
410 *Canada*
411 *Somalia*
412 *Senegal*
413 *Brazil*
414 *Sweden*

415 416 417-18

1983

SCOTT NO.	DESCRIPTION	FIRST DAY COVERS SING	INSC. BLK	INSRIP BLK-4	UNUSED F/NH	USED F
392-416	**1983 Issues, complete (25)**	......	......	......	**12.50**	......
392-93	20¢ & 40¢ World Communications Year	2.05	5.15	6.00	1.40	1.25
394-95	20¢ & 37¢ Safety at Sea	1.95	4.75	6.00	1.40	1.25
396	20¢ World Food Program	.85	2.10	3.95	.85	.50
397-98	20¢ & 28¢ Trade & Development	1.60	4.00	7.25	1.60	1.25
399-414	20¢ World Flags, 16 varieties	13.00	......	29.00	6.50	7.00
415-16	20¢ & 40¢ Human Rights	2.50	6.25	7.00	2.00	1.50

419 420 421 423

1984 World Flags

425 *Burundi*
426 *Pakistan*
427 *Benin*
428 *Italy*
429 *Tanzania*
430 *United Arab Emirates*
431 *Ecuador*
432 *Bahamas*
433 *Poland*
434 *Papua New Guinea*
435 *Uruguay*
436 *Chile*
437 *Paraguay*
438 *Bhutan*
439 *Central African Republic*
440 *Australia*

422 424

UNITED NATIONS (NEW YORK)

SCOTT NO.	DESCRIPTION	FIRST DAY COVERS SING	FIRST DAY COVERS INSC. BLK	INSRIP BLK-4	UNUSED F/NH	USED F
417-42	**1984 Issues, complete (25)**	......	......	......	20.40	......
417-18	20¢ & 40¢ Population	2.10	5.25	6.50	1.75	1.25
419-20	20¢ & 40¢ Food Day	2.10	5.25	6.50	2.00	1.25
421-22	20¢ & 50¢ Heritage	2.25	5.50	8.00	2.25	1.50
423-24	20¢ & 50¢ Future for Refugees	2.25	5.50	8.00	2.00	1.35
425-40	20¢ 1984 World Flags, 16 varieties	13.00	......	39.00	11.50	10.00
441-42	20¢ & 35¢ Youth Year	2.10	5.25	9.00	2.00	1.70

1985 World Flags

450 *Grenada*
451 *Germany-West*
452 *Saudi Arabia*
453 *Mexico*
454 *Uganda*
455 *Sao Tome & Principie*
456 *U.S.S.R.*
457 *India*
458 *Liberia*
459 *Mauritius*
460 *Chad*
461 *Dominican Republic*
462 *Oman*
463 *Ghana*
464 *Sierra Leone*
465 *Finland*

443

444

445

1985

SCOTT NO.	DESCRIPTION	FIRST DAY COVERS SING	FIRST DAY COVERS INSC. BLK	INSRIP BLK-4	UNUSED F/NH	USED F
443/67	**1985 Issues, (24) (No #449)**	......	......	......	25.00	......
443	23¢ ILO—Turin Centre	1.00	2.50	3.50	.85	.60
444	50¢ United Nations University in Japan	1.65	4.15	6.75	1.65	1.25
445-46	22¢ & $3 Definitives	8.00	20.00	29.00	6.50	5.25
447-48	22¢ & 45¢ 40th Anniversary	2.30	5.75	7.75	1.75	1.50
449	same, souvenir sheet	2.50	......	......	2.50	1.50
450-65	22¢ 1985 World Flags, 16 varieties	14.00	......	44.00	12.50	10.00
466-67	22¢ & 33¢ Child Survival	2.25	5.65	6.75	1.50	1.20

1986 World Flags

477 *New Zealand*
478 *Lao PDR*
479 *Burkina Faso*
480 *Gambia*
481 *Maldives*
482 *Ethiopia*
483 *Jordan*
484 *Zambia*
485 *Iceland*
486 *Antigua & Barbuda*
487 *Angola*
488 *Botswana*
489 *Romania*
490 *Togo*
491 *Mauritania*
492 *Colombia*

446

447

448

466

441

468

469

473

475

476

1986

SCOTT NO.	DESCRIPTION	FIRST DAY COVERS SING	FIRST DAY COVERS INSC. BLK	INSRIP BLK-4	UNUSED F/NH	USED F
468-92	**1986 Issues (25)**	......	......	......	24.50	......
468	22¢ African Crisis	1.05	2.60	3.25	.70	.60
469-72	22¢ Development, 4 varieties, attached	2.50	3.25	7.00	6.00	5.00
473-74	22¢ & 44¢ Philately	2.30	5.75	7.50	1.75	1.00
475-76	22¢ & 33¢ Peace Year	2.25	5.65	10.50	2.25	1.00
477-92	22¢ 1986 World Flags, 16 varieties	14.00	......	44.00	12.50	10.00

493a

494

495

497

1987 World Flags

499 *Comoros*
500 *Democratic Yemen*
501 *Mongolia*
502 *Vanuatu*
503 *Japan*
504 *Gabon*
505 *Zimbabwe*
506 *Iraq*
507 *Argentina*
508 *Congo*
509 *Niger*
510 *St. Lucia*
511 *Bahrain*
512 *Haiti*
513 *Afghanistan*
514 *Greece*

515

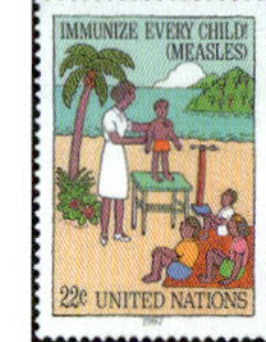

517

1986

SCOTT NO.	DESCRIPTION	FIRST DAY COVERS SING	FIRST DAY COVERS INSC. BLK	INSRIP BLK-4	UNUSED F/NH	USED F
493	22¢ to 44¢ World Federation of United Nations Associations Souvenir sheet of 4	4.00	......	......	5.50	4.00

1987

SCOTT NO.	DESCRIPTION	FIRST DAY COVERS SING	FIRST DAY COVERS INSC. BLK	INSRIP BLK-4	UNUSED F/NH	USED F
494-518	**1987 Issues (25)**	......	......	......	19.00	......
494	22¢ Trygve Lie	1.05	2.60	5.00	1.00	.75
495-96	22¢ & 44¢ Shelter Homeless	2.25	5.65	8.50	1.85	1.75
497-98	22¢ & 33¢ Anti-Drug Campaign	2.25	5.65	8.25	1.85	1.75
499-514	22¢ 1987 World Flags, 16 varieties	14.00	......	44.00	12.50	10.00
515-16	22¢ & 39¢ United Nations Day	2.30	5.75	7.50	1.50	1.30
517-18	22¢ & 44¢ Child Immunization	2.35	5.70	14.00	3.25	3.00

519

521

524

1988 World Flags

528 *Spain*
529 *St. Vincent & Grenadines*
530 *Ivory Coast*
531 *Lebanon*
532 *Yemen*
533 *Cuba*
534 *Denmark*
535 *Libya*
536 *Qatar*
537 *Zaire*
538 *Norway*
539 *German Democratic Republic*
540 *Iran*
541 *Tunisia*
542 *Samoa*
543 *Belize*

526

544-45

546

548

549

550

1988

SCOTT NO.	DESCRIPTION	FIRST DAY COVERS SING	FIRST DAY COVERS INSC. BLK	INSRIP BLK-4	UNUSED F/NH	USED F
519/44	**1988 Issues (24) (No #522-23)**	......	......	......	19.25	......
519-20	22¢ & 33¢ World without Hunger	2.25	5.65	8.50	2.35	1.75
521	3¢ For a Better World	.90	2.25	.90	.25	.25
				Sheetlets		
522-23	25¢ & 44¢ Forest Conservation (set of 6, includes Geneva and Vienna)	15.00	40.00	130.00	27.50	25.00
524-25	25¢ & 50¢ Volunteer Day	2.60	6.50	10.50	2.25	2.00
526-27	25¢ & 38¢ Health in Sports	2.30	5.75	12.00	2.75	2.00
528-43	25¢ 1988 World Flags, 16 varieties	14.50	......	44.00	12.50	10.00
544	25¢ Human Rights	1.75	4.25	4.00	.75	.75
545	$1 Human Rights souvenir sheet	2.75	......	......	2.50	2.00

552

553

570-71

1989 World Flags

554 *Indonesia*
555 *Lesotho*
556 *Guatamala*
557 *Netherlands*
558 *South Africa*
559 *Portugal*
560 *Morocco*
561 *Syrian Arab Republic*
562 *Honduras*
563 *Kampuchea*
564 *Guinea-Bissau*
565 *Cyprus*
566 *Algeria*
567 *Brunei*
568 *St. Kitts & Nevis*
569 *United Nations*

572

573-74

1989

SCOTT NO.	DESCRIPTION	FIRST DAY COVERS SING	FIRST DAY COVERS INSC. BLK	INSRIP BLK-4	UNUSED F/NH	USED F
546-71	**1989 Issues (26)**	......	......	......	30.00	......
546-47	25¢ & 45¢ World Bank	2.60	6.50	12.00	2.75	2.00
548	25¢ Nobel Peace Prize	1.10	1.65	3.75	1.10	.95
549	45¢ United Nations Definitive	1.40	2.10	5.75	1.10	.95
550-51	25¢ & 36¢ Weather Watch	2.30	5.75	12.00	3.50	2.50
552-53	25¢ & 90¢ U.N. Offices in Vienna	3.75	9.25	24.00	6.25	5.50
554-69	25¢ 1989 World Flags, 16 varieties	14.50	......	50.00	13.50	11.00
				Sheetlets (12)		
570-71	25¢ & 45¢ Human Rights 40th Ann. (strips of 3 with tabs)	2.60	6.50	21.00	5.00	....

UNITED NATIONS (NEW YORK)

SCOTT NO.	DESCRIPTION	FIRST DAY COVERS SING	FIRST DAY COVERS INSC. BLK	INSRIP BLK-4	UNUSED F/NH	USED F
	1990					
572/83	**1990 Issues (11) (No #579)**	......	......	......	**25.50**	......
572	25¢ International Trade Center	1.75	2.95	8.00	2.10	1.80
573-74	25¢ & 40¢ AIDS	2.60	6.50	11.00	2.75	2.25
575-76	25¢ & 90¢ Medicinal Plants	3.75	9.25	12.00	3.50	2.50
577-78	25¢ & 45¢ United Nations 45th Anniversary	2.60	6.50	16.50	4.00	3.50
579	25¢ & 45¢ United Nations 45th Anniversary Souvenir Sheet	2.10	......	......	8.00	8.00
580-81	25¢ & 36¢ Crime Prevention	2.30	5.75	15.00	4.00	3.00
				Sheetlets (12)		
582-83	25¢ & 45¢ Human Rights (strips of 3 with tabs)	2.60	6.50	23.00	5.00	....

575-76

577-78

580-81

584

588

590

591

592

593

595

597

603 605 609

SCOTT NO.	DESCRIPTION	FIRST DAY COVERS SING	FIRST DAY COVERS INSC. BLK	INSRIP BLK-4	UNUSED F/NH	USED F
	1991					
584-600	**1991 Issues (17)**	......	......	......	**29.00**	......
584-87	30¢ Econ. Comm. for Europe, 4 varieties, attached	4.50	7.50	7.00	5.75	5.50
588-89	30¢ & 50¢ Namibia—A New Nation	3.50	8.75	12.00	2.75	2.75
590-91	30¢ & 50¢ Definitives	4.00	10.00	10.50	2.35	2.25
592	$2 Definitive	5.50	13.50	21.00	4.75	4.00
593-94	30¢ & 70¢ Children's Rights	4.00	10.00	17.00	4.00	4.00
595-96	30¢ & 90¢ Banning of Chemical	4.25	10.50	21.00	5.00	5.00
597-98	30¢ & 40¢ 40th Anniversary of UNPA	3.50	8.75	12.00	2.50	2.50
				Sheetlets (12)		
599-600	30¢ & 50¢ Human Rights (strips of 3 with tabs)	3.00	7.50	31.50	7.00	....

611

613

614

618

620

624

626

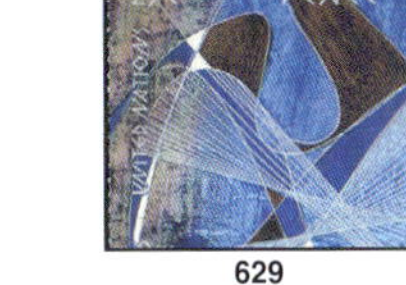
629

633

SCOTT NO.	DESCRIPTION	FIRST DAY COVERS SING	FIRST DAY COVERS INSC. BLK	INSRIP BLK-4	UNUSED F/NH	USED F
	1992					
601-17	**1992 Issues (17)**	......	......	......	**23.00**	......
601-02	29¢-50¢ World Heritage—UNESCO	3.60	9.00	10.00	2.50	2.00
603-04	29¢ Clean Oceans, 2 varieties, attached	2.50	4.95	4.95	1.70	1.50
605-08	29¢ Earth Summit, 4 varieties, attached	3.50	4.25	6.00	5.00	4.50
609-10	29¢ Mission to Planet Earth, 2 varieties, attd	2.50	4.95	15.00	6.75	6.50
611-12	29¢-50¢ Science and Technology	3.60	9.00	8.75	1.95	1.75
613-15	4¢-40¢ Definitives	3.40	8.50	9.75	2.00	1.95
				Sheetlets (12)		
616-17	20¢-50¢ Human Rights (strips of 3 with tabs)	3.00	9.50	25.00	7.50	....
	1993					
618-36	**1993 Issues (19)**	......	......	......	**22.75**	......
618-19	29¢-52¢ Aging	3.00	9.50	11.00	3.00	3.00
620-23	29¢ Endangered Species, 4 attached	3.50	4.25	3.50	3.00	3.00
624-25	29¢-50¢ Health Environment	3.60	9.00	10.00	2.50	2.35
626	5¢ Definitive	2.00	4.00	1.00	.25	.25
	Sheetlets (12)					
627-28	29¢-35¢ Human Rights (strips of 3 with tabs)	3.00	9.50	20.00	6.75	....
629-32	29¢ Peace, 4 attached	3.50	8.00	12.00	11.00	10.00
633-36	29¢ Environment—Climate, strip of 4	3.50	7.00	12.00(8)	5.00	4.75

637

643

644

645

646

647

651

653

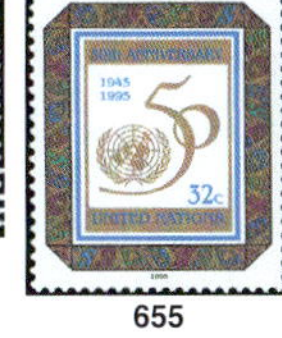
655

SCOTT NO.	DESCRIPTION	FIRST DAY COVERS SING	FIRST DAY COVERS INSC. BLK	INSRIP BLK-4	UNUSED F/NH	USED F
	1994					
637-54	**1994 Issues (18)**	......	......	......	**21.50**	......
637-38	29¢-45¢ International Year of the Family	2.25	8.50	13.00	3.00	3.00
639-42	29¢ Endangered Species, 4 attached	3.00	4.25	3.50	3.00	2.50
643	50¢ Refugees	1.75	5.75	8.00	1.50	1.50
644-46	10¢-$1 Definitives (3)	3.50	12.50	13.00	3.25	3.00
647-50	29¢ International Decade for Natural Disaster Reduction, 4 attached	3.00	4.25	12.50	10.50	10.00
651-52	29¢-52¢ Population and Development	2.25	9.00	11.00	2.50	2.25
653-54	29¢-50¢ Development through Partnership	2.25	9.00	8.75	1.75	1.50

656

661

663

SCOTT NO.	DESCRIPTION	FIRST DAY COVERS SING	FIRST DAY COVERS INSC. BLK	INSRIP BLK-4	UNUSED F/NH	USED F
	1995					
655/69	**1995 Issues (14) (No #665)**	......	......	......	**34.00**	......
655	32¢ 50th Anniversary of the UN	1.75	4.00	6.75	2.00	1.50
656	50¢ Social Summit	1.75	5.75	6.50	1.40	1.25
657-60	29¢ Endangered Species, 4 attached	3.00	4.25	3.50	3.00	3.00
661-62	32¢-55¢ Youth: Our Future	2.50	11.00	12.00	3.00	3.00
663-64	32¢-50¢ 50th Anniversary of the UN	2.50	11.00	12.00	3.50	3.00

UNITED NATIONS (NEW YORK)

SCOTT NO.	DESCRIPTION	FIRST DAY COVERS SING	FIRST DAY COVERS INSC. BLK	INSRIP BLK-4	UNUSED F/NH	USED F

666

668

SCOTT NO.	DESCRIPTION	FDC SING	FDC INSC. BLK	INSRIP BLK-4	UNUSED F/NH	USED F
665	82¢ 50th Anniversary of the UN, Souvenir Sheet	2.50	....	....	4.50	4.25
666-67	32¢-40¢ 4th World Conference on Women	2.50	9.00	10.50	2.40	2.25
668	20¢ UN Headquarters	1.75	....	2.25	.45	.45

669a

SCOTT NO.	DESCRIPTION	FDC SING	FDC INSC. BLK	INSRIP BLK-4	UNUSED F/NH	USED F
669	32¢ 50th Anniversary, Miniature Sheet of 12	....	....	....	18.00	....
669a-l	32¢ 50th Anniversary of the UN, booklet single	1.75	....	....	.75	.25
670	same, souvenir booklet of 4 panes of 3...	....	....	....	22.00	....

671

672

1996

SCOTT NO.	DESCRIPTION	FDC SING	FDC INSC. BLK	INSRIP BLK-4	UNUSED F/NH	USED F
671/89	**1996 Issues (18) (No 685)**	....	....	....	**19.00**	....
671	32¢ WFUNA 50th Anniversary	1.75	4.00	3.75	.85	.75
672-73	32¢-60¢ Definitives	2.50	9.00	9.00	2.25	2.10
674-77	32¢ Endangered Species, 4 attached	3.00	4.25	4.50	3.50	3.00
678-82	32¢ City Summit (Habitat II), strip of 5	3.75	5.00	17.00	8.00	7.00
683-84	32¢-50¢ Sport & the Environment	2.50	9.00	15.00	3.50	3.00
685	82¢ Sport & the Environment souvenir sheet	2.50	....	....	3.50	3.50

686

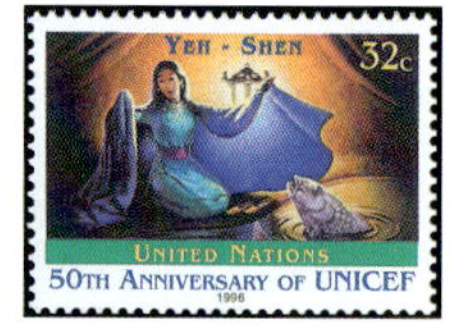

688

SCOTT NO.	DESCRIPTION	FDC SING	FDC INSC. BLK	INSRIP BLK-4	UNUSED F/NH	USED F
686-87	32¢-60¢ A Plea for Peace	2.50	9.00	9.75	2.25	2.00
688-89	32¢-60¢ UNICEF 50th Anniversary	2.50	9.00	24.00	2.40	2.25

1997 World Flags

690 *Tadjikistan*
691 *Georgia*
692 *Armenia*
693 *Namibia*
694 *Liechtenstein*
695 *South Korea*
696 *Kazakhstan*
697 *Latvia*

698

1997

SCOTT NO.	DESCRIPTION	FDC SING	FDC INSC. BLK	INSRIP BLK-4	UNUSED F/NH	USED F
690/717	**1997 Issues (27) (No. #708, 708A)**	....	....	....	**26.00**	....
690-97	1997 World Flags, 8 varieties	12.50	....	41.00	11.00	10.00
698-99	8¢-55¢ Flowers, UN headquarters	2.25	8.00	8.00	1.85	1.50

700-03

704-07

SCOTT NO.	DESCRIPTION	FDC SING	FDC INSC. BLK	INSRIP BLK-4	UNUSED F/NH	USED F
700-03	32¢ Endangered Species, 4 attached	3.00	4.25	4.00	3.30	3.10
704-07	32¢ Earth Summit +5, 4 attached	3.00	4.25	6.50	5.25	5.00
708	$1 Earth Summit +5, souvenir sheet	2.50	....	....	4.75	4.50
708a	$1 1997 Pacific '97 overprint on #708	15.00	....	....	23.00	23.00

709-13

SCOTT NO.	DESCRIPTION	FDC SING	FDC INSC. BLK	INSRIP BLK-4	UNUSED F/NH	USED F
709-13	32¢ Transporation, strip of 5	3.75	5.00	11.00(10)	5.00	5.00

714

716

SCOTT NO.	DESCRIPTION	FDC SING	FDC INSC. BLK	INSRIP BLK-4	UNUSED F/NH	USED F
714-15	32¢-50¢ Tribute to Philately	2.50	9.00	18.00	4.50	4.25
716-17	32¢-60¢ Terracota Warriors	2.50	9.00	11.50	2.75	2.50
718	same, Souvenir bklt of 6 panes of 4	....	....	....	13.00	....

1998 World Flags

719 *Micronesia*
720 *Slovakia*
721 *Dem. People's Rep. of Korea*
722 *Azerbaijan*
723 *Uzbekistan*
724 *Monaco*
725 *Czeh Republic*
726 *Estonia*

730-33

1998

SCOTT NO.	DESCRIPTION	FDC SING	FDC INSC. BLK	INSRIP BLK-4	UNUSED F/NH	USED F
719-26	1998 World Flags, 8 varieties	12.50	....	33.00	8.75	8.00
727-29	1¢-21¢ Definitives	4.50	10.00	4.50	1.00	.95
730-33	32¢ Endangered Species, 4 attached	3.00	4.25	4.50	3.75	3.00

734a

SCOTT NO.	DESCRIPTION	FDC SING	FDC INSC. BLK	INSRIP BLK-4	UNUSED F/NH	USED F
734	32¢ Intl. Year of the Ocean, sheetlet of 12	15.00	....	....	15.00	....
735	32¢Rain Forest, Jaguar	1.75	4.25	4.00	.85	.75
736	$2 Rain Forest, Jaguar, souvenir sheet	7.00	....	....	5.00	4.75
737-38	32¢-40¢ 50 Year of Peacekeeping	3.75	9.00	8.50	1.85	1.75
739-40	32¢-50¢ 50th of the Dec. of Human Rights	4.00	9.50	9.00	2.25	2.00
741-42	32¢-60¢ Schonbrunn Castle	4.25	10.00	11.00	2.40	2.25
743	same, souvenir bklt of 6 panes	....	....	....	23.00	....

UNITED NATIONS (NEW YORK)

1999 World Flags

744 *Lithuania*
745 *San Marino*
746 *Turkmenistan*
747 *Marshall Islands*
748 *Moldova*
749 *Kyrgyzstan*
750 *Bosnia & Herzegovia*
751 *Eritrea*

754

1999

SCOTT NO.	DESCRIPTION	FIRST DAY COVERS SING	FIRST DAY COVERS INSC. BLK	INSRIP BLK-4	UNUSED F/NH	USED F
744-51	1999 World Flags, 8 varieties	12.50	....	36.00	9.50	9.00
752-53	33¢-$5 Definitives	12.00	30.00	58.00	13.00	12.00
754-55	33¢-60¢ World Heritage Sites, Australia .	4.25	10.00	12.00	2.50	2.40
756	same, souvenir bklt of 6 panes	....	....	....	18.00	....

757-60

SCOTT NO.	DESCRIPTION	FIRST DAY COVERS SING	FIRST DAY COVERS INSC. BLK	INSRIP BLK-4	UNUSED F/NH	USED F
757-60	33¢ Endangered Species, 4 attached	3.00	4.25	4.00	3.50	3.25

761-62

764-67

SCOTT NO.	DESCRIPTION	FIRST DAY COVERS SING	FIRST DAY COVERS INSC. BLK	INSRIP BLK-4	UNUSED F/NH	USED F
761-62	33¢ Unispace III Conference	1.75	4.25	6.50	2.40	2.25
763	$2 Unispace III Conference, souvenir sheet	7.00	....	....	5.50	5.00
764-67	33¢ Universal Postal Union	1.75	4.25	4.75	3.75	3.50

770-71

SCOTT NO.	DESCRIPTION	FIRST DAY COVERS SING	FIRST DAY COVERS INSC. BLK	INSRIP BLK-4	UNUSED F/NH	USED F
768	33¢ In Memorium	1.75	4.25	7.50	1.65	1.50
769	$1 In Memorium, souvenir sheet	3.25	....	....	2.75	2.75
770-71	33¢-60¢ Education-Keystone to the 21st Century	4.25	10.00	11.00	2.40	2.40

772

773-76

2000

SCOTT NO.	DESCRIPTION	FIRST DAY COVERS SING	FIRST DAY COVERS INSC. BLK	INSRIP BLK-4	UNUSED F/NH	USED F
772	33¢ International Year of Thanksgiving	1.75	4.25	4.25	1.00	.85
773-76	33¢ Endangered Species, 4 attached	3.00	4.25	4.25	3.50	3.00

777

787

782

SCOTT NO.	DESCRIPTION	FIRST DAY COVERS SING	FIRST DAY COVERS INSC. BLK	INSRIP BLK-4	UNUSED F/NH	USED F
777-78	33¢-60¢ Our World 2000	4.25	10.00	11.00	2.50	2.25
779-80	33¢-55¢ 55th Anniversary of the UN	4.25	10.00	11.00	2.25	2.00
781	same, 33¢-55¢ souvenir sheet	....	....	....	3.75	3.50
782	33¢ International Flag of Peace	1.75	4.25	4.00	.90	.90
783	33¢ United Nations in the 21st Century, sheet of 6	5.00	4.25	11.00	11.00	11.00
784-85	33¢-60¢ World Heritage Sites, Spain	4.25	10.00	14.00	3.00	3.00
786	same, souvenir bklt of 6 panes of 4	....	....	....	13.00	....
787	33¢ Respect for Refuges	1.75	4.25	4.50	.95	.95
788	$1 Respect for Refuges, souvenir sheet	3.25	....	....	3.50	3.50

793

789-92

2001

SCOTT NO.	DESCRIPTION	FIRST DAY COVERS SING	FIRST DAY COVERS INSC. BLK	INSRIP BLK-4	UNUSED F/NH	USED F
789-92	34¢ Endangered Species, 4 attached	3.00	4.25	4.00	3.50	3.00
793-94	34¢-80¢ Intl. Volunteers Year	4.50	10.00	12.00	2.75	2.50
795-802	2001 World Flags, 8 varieties	12.50	....	40.00	11.00	9.00
803-04	7¢-34¢ Definitives	3.50	8.50	5.00	1.00	1.00
805-06	34¢-70¢ World Heritage Sites, Japan	4.50	10.00	11.00	2.50	2.40
807	same, souvenir bklt of 6 panes of 4	....	....	....	16.00	....

808

816

809

SCOTT NO.	DESCRIPTION	FIRST DAY COVERS SING	FIRST DAY COVERS INSC. BLK	INSRIP BLK-4	UNUSED F/NH	USED F
808	80¢ Dag Hammarskjold	2.50	4.00	9.25	1.95	1.85
809-10	34¢-80¢ 50th Anniv. of the UNPA	4.50	10.00	14.00	3.00	3.00
811	same, $2.40 souvenir sheet	6.50	....	....	8.00	8.00
812-15	34¢ Climate Change, strip of 4	3.00	4.25	11.00	5.00	5.00
816	34¢ Nobel Peace Prize	1.75	4.25	4.75	1.40	1.00

817

822

2002

SCOTT NO.	DESCRIPTION	FIRST DAY COVERS SING	FIRST DAY COVERS INSC. BLK	INSRIP BLK-4	UNUSED F/NH	USED F
817	80¢ Children and Stamps	2.50	4.00	8.50	1.95	1.75
818-21	34¢ Endangered Species, 4 attached	3.00	4.25	4.00	3.50	3.50
822-23	34¢-57¢ Independence of East Timor	4.00	9.00	10.50	2.25	2.25
824-27	34¢-80¢ Intl. Year of Mountains, 2 pairs	5.00	11.00	7.00	9.00	8.50
828-31	37¢-60¢ Johannesburg Summit, 2 pairs	4.50	10.00	....	9.00	9.00

UNITED NATIONS (NEW YORK)

832

837

SCOTT NO.	DESCRIPTION	FIRST DAY COVERS SING	FIRST DAY COVERS INSC. BLK	INSRIP BLK-4	UNUSED F/NH	USED F
832-33	34¢-80¢ World Heritage Sites, Italy	4.50	10.00	14.50	3.75	3.50
834	same, souvenir bklt of 6 panes of 4	....	....	....	15.00	....
835	70¢ UNAIDS Awareness, semi postal	2.25	3.75	8.00	1.75	1.65
	2003					
836	37¢ Indigenous Art, sheet of 6	7.00	....	....	8.00	8.00
837-39	23¢-70¢ Definitives	3.50	4.50	14.00	3.50	3.50
840-41	23¢-70¢ Centenary of First Flight, 2 attach.	3.00	4.00	6.00	3.25	3.00

842-45

SCOTT NO.	DESCRIPTION	FIRST DAY COVERS SING	FIRST DAY COVERS INSC. BLK	INSRIP BLK-4	UNUSED F/NH	USED F
842-45	37¢ Endangered Species, 4 attached	3.50	4.50	4.50	3.75	3.50
846-47	23¢-37¢ Intl. Year of Freshwater, 2 attach.	2.25	3.75	6.00	2.25	2.25
848	37¢ Ralph Bunche	1.75	4.50	4.50	1.00	1.00
849	60¢ In Memoriam, UN Complex Bombing in Iraq	2.25	4.50	7.50	2.00	1.40
850-51	37¢-80¢ World Heritage Sites, United States	4.25	9.50	14.00	3.00	2.75
852	same, souvenir bklt of 6 panes of 4	....	....	....	12.00	....
853-57	37¢ UN Headquarters + labels, vert strip of 5	....	....	....	26.00	....
....	same, sheet of 4 (853-57)	....	....	....	100.00	....

863

865

866

SCOTT NO.	DESCRIPTION	FIRST DAY COVERS SING	FIRST DAY COVERS INSC. BLK	INSRIP BLK-4	UNUSED F/NH	USED F
	2004					
859-61	37¢ Endangered Species, 4 attached	4.00	6.00	4.75	4.00	3.75
862	37¢ Indigenous Art, sheet of 6	7.50	....	....	7.00	7.00
863-64	37¢-70¢ Road Safety	4.50	10.00	11.00	2.75	2.50
865	80¢ Japanese Peace Bell, 50th Anniv.	2.50	5.00	9.00	2.00	1.85
866-67	37¢-60¢ World Heritage Sites, Greece	4.25	9.50	11.00	2.50	2.25
868	same, souvenir bklt. of 6 panes of 4	....	....	....	19.00	....
869-70	37¢-80¢ My Dream for Peace	4.50	10.00	13.00	3.75	2.85
871-72	37¢-70¢ Human Rights	4.50	10.00	19.50(8)	2.75	2.50
873	37¢ Disarmament	1.75	4.50	4.25	.95	.95

874

876-79

SCOTT NO.	DESCRIPTION	FIRST DAY COVERS SING	FIRST DAY COVERS INSC. BLK	INSRIP BLK-4	UNUSED F/NH	USED F
	2005					
874	80¢ U.N. 60th Anniversary	2.50	5.00	9.00	2.00	2.00
875	$1 U.N. 60th Anniv., souvenir sheet	3.25	....	....	22.50	18.00
876-79	37¢ Orchids, 4 attached	4.00	6.00	4.75	3.75	3.75
880-84	80¢ Sculptures-personalized stamps, 5 attached	25.00	50.00	275.00	135.00	135.00
885-86	37¢ Nature's Wisdom	4.50	10.00	14.00	3.00	2.50
887-88	37¢-70¢ International Year of Sports	4.50	10.00	13.00	2.75	2.75
889-90	37¢-80¢ World Heritage Sites, Egypt	4.50	10.00	14.00	3.00	2.90
891	same, souvenir bklt. of 6 panes of 4	....	....	....	19.00	....
892-93	37¢-80¢ My Dream for Peace type of 2004	4.50	10.00	14.00	3.00	2.75
894-95	37¢-80¢ Food for Life	4.50	10.00	14.00	3.50	2.75

896

898

SCOTT NO.	DESCRIPTION	FIRST DAY COVERS SING	FIRST DAY COVERS INSC. BLK	INSRIP BLK-4	UNUSED F/NH	USED F
	2006					
896	25¢ Stylized Flags in Heart and Hands	1.75	4.25	3.00	.70	.65
897	37¢ Indigenous Art, sheet of 6	7.50	....	....	7.00	7.00
898-902	39¢ UN Headquarters + labels, strip of 5	7.00	....	....	11.00	....
....	same, sheet of 4	....	....	....	47.00	....

903

908-11

SCOTT NO.	DESCRIPTION	FIRST DAY COVERS SING	FIRST DAY COVERS INSC. BLK	INSRIP BLK-4	UNUSED F/NH	USED F
903-07	84¢ Sculptures + label, strip of 5	11.00	....	....	22.00	22.00
....	same, sheet of 2	....	....	....	35.00	....
908-11	39¢ Endangered Species, 4 attached	5.00	10.00	4.75	4.25	4.25

913

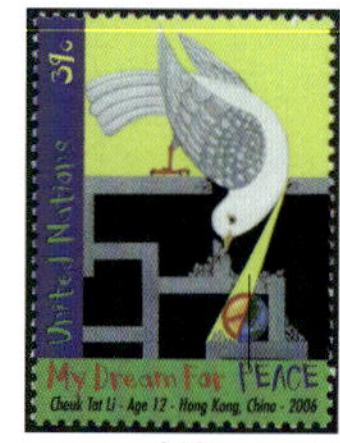
918

SCOTT NO.	DESCRIPTION	FIRST DAY COVERS SING	FIRST DAY COVERS INSC. BLK	INSRIP BLK-4	UNUSED F/NH	USED F
912	75¢ Peace personalized stamp	2.25	....	18.00	3.50	3.50
913-914	39¢-84¢ Day of Families	4.50	10.00	15.00	3.25	3.00
915-16	39¢-84¢ World Heritage Sites, France	4.50	10.00	15.00	3.25	3.00
917	same, bklt of 6 panes of 4	....	....	....	19.00	....
918-19	39¢-84¢ My Dream of Peace One Day	4.50	10.00	15.00	3.00	3.00
920	39¢ Flags and Coins, sheet of 8	10.00	....	....	9.00	9.00

925-28

SCOTT NO.	DESCRIPTION	FIRST DAY COVERS SING	FIRST DAY COVERS INSC. BLK	INSRIP BLK-4	UNUSED F/NH	USED F
	2007					
921-24	39¢ Flags, 4 varieties	5.00	10.00	19.00	5.00	5.00
925-28	39¢ Endangered Species, 4 attached	5.00	10.00	5.50	4.50	4.50
929	84¢ UN Emblem + label	....	....	105.00	27.00	22.00
....	same, sheet of 10 + 10 labels	....	....	....	160.00	....
930	39¢ Flags and Coins, sheet of 8	10.00	....	....	8.50	8.50
931	84¢ UN Emblem + label	....	....	19.00	3.50	3.00
....	same, sheet of 10 + 10 labels	....	....	....	60.00	....
932-33	39¢-84¢ Peaceful Vision	4.50	10.00	13.00	3.25	3.25
934-38	UN symbols personalized stamps, strip of 5 attached	....	....	....	11.00	....
	same sheet of 4	....	....	....	42.00	....
939	90¢ UN Flag & Label	....	....	25.00	5.50	....
	same sheet of 10	....	....	....	48.00	....
940	90¢ UN Peacekeeping Helmet	3.00	4.50	10.00	2.50	3.50
941-42	41¢-90¢ World Heritage Sites, South America	5.50	11.00	14.00	3.75	3.00
943	same, bklt panes of 6 panes of 4	....	....	....	23.00	....
944	90¢ Universal Postal Union, joint issue with Swiss Post Humanitarian Mail	3.00	4.50	18.50	3.50	2.50
945-46	41¢-90¢ Space for Humanity	5.50	11.00	19.00	4.00	3.00
947	$1 Space for Humanity souvenir sheet	3.25	....	....	3.50	3.50

UNITED NATIONS (NEW YORK)

948

949

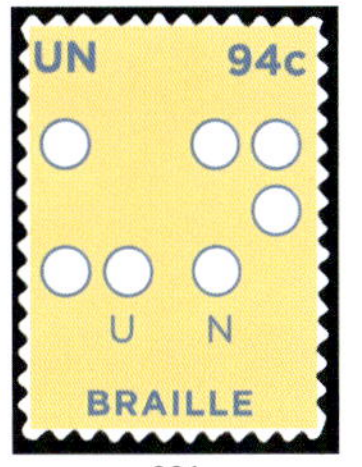
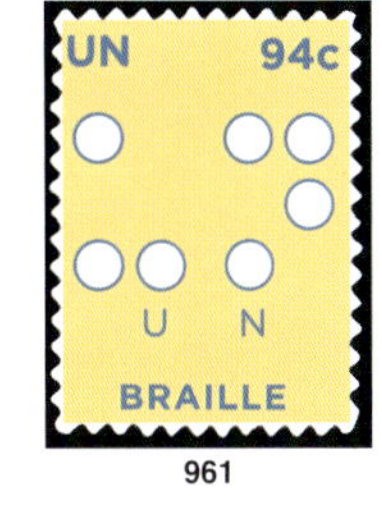

961

2008

SCOTT NO.	DESCRIPTION	FIRST DAY COVERS SING	FIRST DAY COVERS INSC. BLK	INSRIP BLK-4	UNUSED F/NH	USED F
948	41¢ Holocaust Remeberance Day	2.00	…….	4.50	1.00	1.00
	same, sheet of 9	…….	…….	…….	9.00	…….
949-52	41¢ Endangered Species	4.75	…….	5.00	4.25	4.00
	same, sheet of 16	…….	…….	…….	18.00	…….
953	41¢ Flags and Coins, sheet of 8	10.00	…….	…….	9.00	9.00
954-58	42¢ UN Personalized, strip of 5 w/labels	…….	…….	…….	9.50	9.50
	same, sheet of 20	…….	…….	…….	38.00	75.00
959	94¢ UN Emblem + Label	3.50	…….	…….	4.00	4.00
960	42¢ Wheelchair Accessibility	3.50	…….	4.00	1.25	1.25
961	94¢ "UN" In Braille	7.75	…….	11.00	2.25	2.25

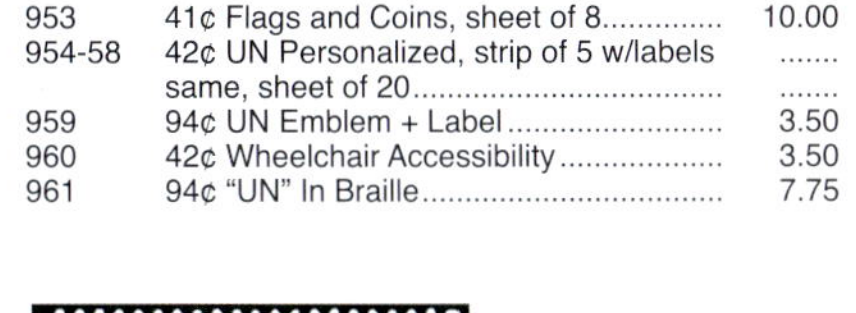

963

965

967

SCOTT NO.	DESCRIPTION	FIRST DAY COVERS SING	FIRST DAY COVERS INSC. BLK	INSRIP BLK-4	UNUSED F/NH	USED F
962	42¢ Sprinter	3.50	…….	5.00	1.25	1.25
963	94¢ Hurdler	5.00	…….	11.00	2.25	2.25
964	$1.25 Sprinter, souvenir sheet	5.75	…….	…….	3.25	3.25
965	94¢ Sport for Peace with label	7.75	…….	…….	4.00	4.00
966	42¢ Children's Art, "We Can End Poverty"	3.00	…….	5.00	1.25	1.25
967	94¢ Children's Art, "We Can End Poverty"	3.75	…….	10.00	2.25	2.25
968	42¢ Climate Change, sheet of 4	4.75	…….	…….	5.00	5.00
968a	42¢ Climate Change, bklt pane of 4	4.75	…….	…….	5.00	5.00
969	94¢ Climate Change, sheet of 4	10.00	…….	…….	10.00	10.00
970	Climate Change, souvenir booklet	…….	…….	…….	21.00	…….

2009

SCOTT NO.	DESCRIPTION	FIRST DAY COVERS SING	FIRST DAY COVERS INSC. BLK	INSRIP BLK-4	UNUSED F/NH	USED F
971-73	1¢-10¢ Flowers, set of 3	3.50	…….	3.50	.75	.75
974	94¢ U Thant	3.50	…….	11.00	3.00	3.00
975-78	42¢ Endangered Species, block of 4	7.75	…….	5.00	4.50	4.50

985

990

SCOTT NO.	DESCRIPTION	FIRST DAY COVERS SING	FIRST DAY COVERS INSC. BLK	INSRIP BLK-4	UNUSED F/NH	USED F
979-80	44¢-98¢ World Heritage Sites, Germany	5.50	…….	16.00	3.75	3.75
981	World Heritage Sites, souvenir booklet	…….	…….	…….	22.00	…….
982-86	44¢ Personalized Stamps, vert. strip of 5 with labels	…….	…….	…….	8.50	8.50
	same, full sheet	…….	…….	…….	35.00	…….
987-91	98¢ Personalized Stamps, vert. strip of 5 with labels	…….	…….	…….	22.00	22.00
	same, full sheet	…….	…….	…….	43.00	…….
992-93	44¢-98¢ Economic & Social Council	4.75	…….	16.00	4.00	4.00

994

995d

SCOTT NO.	DESCRIPTION	FIRST DAY COVERS SING	FIRST DAY COVERS INSC. BLK	INSRIP BLK-4	UNUSED F/NH	USED F
994	98¢ UN Emblem with label	…….	…….	…….	4.50	…….
	same, sheet	…….	…….	…….	48.00	…….
995	44¢ Millennium Development Goals, sheet of 8	10.00	…….	…….	9.00	9.00
996	$1 Mohandas K. Gandhi	3.95	…….	12.00	2.50	2.50
997	44¢ Indigenous People, sheet of 6	…….	…….	…….	7.00	7.00

2010

SCOTT NO.	DESCRIPTION	FIRST DAY COVERS SING	FIRST DAY COVERS INSC. BLK	INSRIP BLK-4	UNUSED F/NH	USED F
998	44¢ Flags & Coins, sheet of 8	10.00	…….	…….	9.00	9.00

998a *Bahamas* **998d** *Kuwait* **998g** *St. Lucia*
998b *Jamaica* **998e** *Panama* **998h** *Yemen*
998c *Honduras* **998f** *Guatemala*

SCOTT NO.	DESCRIPTION	FIRST DAY COVERS SING	FIRST DAY COVERS INSC. BLK	INSRIP BLK-4	UNUSED F/NH	USED F
999-1002	44¢ Endangered Species	5.00	10.00	5.50	4.50	4.50

1004b

1008

SCOTT NO.	DESCRIPTION	FIRST DAY COVERS SING	FIRST DAY COVERS INSC. BLK	INSRIP BLK-4	UNUSED F/NH	USED F
1003	44¢ One Planet, One Ocean, sheet of 4	…….	…….	…….	4.25	4.25
1004	98¢ One Planet, One Ocean, sheet of 4	…….	…….	…….	8.75	8.75
1005	One Planet, One Ocean, souvenir booklet		…….	…….	21.00	…….
1006-07	3¢-4¢ People of Different Cultures	3.75	…….	2.00	.75	.50
1008-09	98¢ Expo 2010 Shanghi	6.50	…….	…….	7.25	7.25
1009a	Pane of 5, Expo 2010 Shanhi	…….	…….	42.00	…….	…….
1010	98¢ UN 65th Anniversary	3.75	…….	11.00	2.50	2.50
1011	UN 65th Anniversary S/S	6.25	…….	…….	5.00	5.00

1012-16

1019e

SCOTT NO.	DESCRIPTION	FIRST DAY COVERS SING	FIRST DAY COVERS INSC. BLK	INSRIP BLK-4	UNUSED F/NH	USED F
1012-16	44¢ UN Transport	3.25	…….	12.00	5.50	5.50
1017-18	15¢ - $1.50 Int. Year of Biodiversity	7.75	…….	19.00	4.00	4.00
1019	44¢ Indigenous People, sheet of 6	8.75	…….	…….	7.00	7.00
1020-21	11¢-$5 UN Headquarters	14.00	…….	49.00	12.00	11.00
1022	44¢ Flags & Coins, sheet of 8	10.00	…….	…….	9.00	9.00
1023	98¢ UN Emblem Plus Label	…….	…….	…….	3.50	…….
	Same, sheet of 10 + labels	…….	…….	…….	32.50	…….
1024	44¢ 50th Anniversary of Human Space Flight, sheet of 16	19.00	…….	…….	15.50	…….
1025	Human Space Flight S/S sheet of 2	4.75	…….	…….	3.75	…….
1026-27	44¢-98¢ World Heritage Sites in Nordic Countries	6.00	…….	13.50	4.00	…….
	same, 2 panes of 20	…….	…….	…….	62.00	…….
1028	44¢ AIDS ribbon	3.75	…….	…….	1.20	…….
	same, pane of 4	…….	…….	…….	3.75	…….
1029-30	44¢-98¢ Economic & Social Council	5.95	…….	12.50	3.25	…….

1027

1031

SCOTT NO.	DESCRIPTION	FIRST DAY COVERS SING	FIRST DAY COVERS INSC. BLK	INSRIP BLK-4	UNUSED F/NH	USED F
1031-34	44¢ Endangered Species	5.95	…….	4.75	4.00	4.00
1035-36	44¢-98¢ International Year of Forests	4.50	…….	8.00	3.25	3.25
1037	$1.05 UN Emblem and Label	…….	…….	…….	3.50	3.50
1038	Personalized sheet of 10 with labels	…….	…….	…….	34.00	…….
1039	45¢ Flags & Coins, sheet of 8	12.50	…….	…….	8.00	…….
1040-41	$1.05 Autism Awareness	5.95	…….	11.00	5.00	5.00

2012

SCOTT NO.	DESCRIPTION	FIRST DAY COVERS SING	FIRST DAY COVERS INSC. BLK	INSRIP BLK-4	UNUSED F/NH	USED F
1042-45	45¢ Endangered Species	5.75	…….	5.00	4.00	3.75
1046-47	$1.05 Conservation with labels, vertical pair	…….	…….	…….	6.75	6.75
	same, sheet of 10 with labels	…….	…….	…….	32.50	…….
1048	$1.05 Conference on Stable Development	4.50	…….	8.75	2.50	2.50
1049-50	45¢-$1.05 Sport for Peace	…….	…….	13.50	3.25	3.25
1050a	Sport for Peace, Souvenir Sheet	…….	…….	…….	2.50	2.50
1051-52	42¢-$1.05 UNESCO World Heritage sites in Africa	4.75	…….	13.00	3.25	3.25
1053	45¢ Indigenous People, sheet of 6	9.00	…….	…….	6.25	6.25

2013

SCOTT NO.	DESCRIPTION	FIRST DAY COVERS SING	FIRST DAY COVERS INSC. BLK	INSRIP BLK-4	UNUSED F/NH	USED F
1054	$1.10 UN Emblem and Label	…….	…….	…….	3.00	3.00
1055	$1.10 Sheet of 10	…….	…….	…….	32.50	…….
1056-57	46¢-$1.10 World Radio Day	5.75	…….	14.00	3.50	3.50
1058-59	$1.10-$3.00 Circle of People and United Nations Headquarters	12.00	…….	35.00	9.00	9.00

UNITED NATIONS (NEW YORK)

1058

1061

SCOTT NO.	DESCRIPTION	FIRST DAY COVERS SING	FIRST DAY COVERS INSC. BLK	INSRIP BLK-4	UNUSED F/NH	USED F
1060-61	46c-$1.10 World Heritage Sites, China...	5.00	....	13.50	3.50	....
1062	World Heritage Sites, China, Souvenir Booklet		....	....	22.00	....
1063-66	$1.10 Flags, pane of 16	36.00		10.00	9.50	9.50

1067a

1068-1069

SCOTT NO.	DESCRIPTION	FIRST DAY COVERS SING	FIRST DAY COVERS INSC. BLK	INSRIP BLK-4	UNUSED F/NH	USED F
1067	46c World Ocean's Day sheet of 12	15.00	....	....	15.00	....
1068-69	$1.10 Nebulae	6.75	....	9.75	5.00	4.75
1070	46c Nebulae Souvenir sheet of 1	2.75	....	....	1.25	1.25
1071	$1.10 World Humanitarian Day sheet of 10	....	....	....	32.00	32.00
1072-73	46c-$1.10 Works of Disable Artists	4.75	....	13.50	3.50	3.50
1074-77	$1.10 endangered Species	12.00	....	11.00	9.50	9.50
1078	46c Flags & Coins sheet of 8	12.00	....	....	8.50	8.50

2014

SCOTT NO.	DESCRIPTION	FIRST DAY COVERS SING	FIRST DAY COVERS INSC. BLK	INSRIP BLK-4	UNUSED F/NH	USED F
1079	$1.15 UN emblem & label	3.75		....	3.75	3.75
1080	$1.15 Personalized sheet of 10 with labels	....		....	33.00	33.00

1082

1083

SCOTT NO.	DESCRIPTION	FIRST DAY COVERS SING	FIRST DAY COVERS INSC. BLK	INSRIP BLK-4	UNUSED F/NH	USED F
1081-82	47¢-$1.15 Int. Day of Happiness	4.50	....	15.00	4.25	4.25
1083-86	$1.15 Flags set of 4	12.00	....	....	11.50	11.50
1087	49¢ International Year of Jazz, Sheet of 12	16.00	....	....	13.50	15.00
1088-89	33¢ - $2 Definitives	7.00	....	20.00	5.50	5.50
1090-91	49¢ - $1.15 Taj Majal	5.75	....	15.00	4.25	4.25
1092	Taj Majah Souvenir Booklet	....	....	22.50	....	....
1093-94	49¢ - $1.15 International Year of Family Farming, Set of 2	4.50	....	15.00	4.25	4.25

1093

1097

SCOTT NO.	DESCRIPTION	FIRST DAY COVERS SING	FIRST DAY COVERS INSC. BLK	INSRIP BLK-4	UNUSED F/NH	USED F
1095	$1.15 Global Education First Initiative	4.25	....	10.50	2.75	2.75
1096	$1.50 Global Education First Initiative Souvenir Sheet	6.00	....	....	3.75	3.75
1097-1100	$1.15 Endangered Species, Block of 4...	12.00	....	10.50	10.50	10.50
1101	$1.15 ASDA 100th Anniversary Personalized Sheet of 10	....	....	....	32.00	....

1107

1114

1123

2015

SCOTT NO.	DESCRIPTION	FIRST DAY COVERS SING	FIRST DAY COVERS INSC. BLK	INSRIP BLK-4	UNUSED F/NH	USED F
1102	$1.15 UN emblem & label	....	....	30.00 (10)	3.50	3.50
1103	49¢ Flags & Coins, sheet of 8	12.00	....	....	8.50	....
1104-05	49¢ and $1.20 World Poetry Day, 2 sheets of 8	27.00	....	....	22.00	....
1106-09	$1.20 Endangered Species, set of 4	16.00	....	10.50	10.25	....
1110-11	35¢ - 40¢ Definitives	4.50	....	7.00	1.75	....
1112	$1.20 Greetings from New York, sheet of 10	....	....	....	30.00	....
1113-14	49¢ - $1.20 World Heritage Sites, Southeast Asia	5.75	....	14.00	3.75	....
1115	$1.20 World Heritage Sites, souvenir booklet	....	....	....	22.00	....
1116-17	49¢ - $1.20 End Violence Against Children	6.00	....	14.00	3.75	....
1118	$1.20 UN Emblem and Label	....	....	32.00(10)	3.25	....
1119-22	49¢ - $1.20 UN Building	9.75	....	14.00	7.50	....
1123	$1.20 U.N. 70th Anniversary, souvenir sheet.	....	....	....	2.50	....
1124	$1.20 UNESCO Emblem	....	....	32.00(10)	3.25	....
1125	$1.20 UN Climate Change Conference	4.50	....	10.00	2.75	....

1127

1134

2016

SCOTT NO.	DESCRIPTION	FIRST DAY COVERS SING	FIRST DAY COVERS INSC. BLK	INSRIP BLK-4	UNUSED F/NH	USED F
1126	$1.20 Year of the Monkey, sheet of 10	....	....	32.00	3.50	....
1127-28	49¢-$1.20 LGBT Equality	6.00	....	14.50	3.75	....
1129-30	49¢-$1.20 U.N. Woman-HeforShe	6.00	....	14.50	3.75	....

1131b

1145c

SCOTT NO.	DESCRIPTION	FIRST DAY COVERS SING	FIRST DAY COVERS INSC. BLK	INSRIP BLK-4	UNUSED F/NH	USED F
1131	$1.15 Angry Birds, sheet of 10	....	....	32.00	3.50	....
1132-33	47¢-$1.15 International Dance Day, 2 sheets of 6	....	....	25.00(2)	....	....
1134-35	47¢-$1.15 U.N. Peacekeepers	6.00	....	14.50	3.75	....
1136	$1.15 UNPA 65th Anniversary, sheet of 10	....	....	32.00	....	....
1137-40	47¢-$1.15 Sport for Peace & Development, 2 pairs	8.50	....	....	7.50	....
1141	$1.15, 2fr, 170e, 32nd Asian International Stamp Expo	....	....	15.50	....	....
1142-43	47¢-$1.15 World Heritage Sites, Czech Republic	6.00	....	15.50	3.75	....
1144	$9.72 World Heritage Sites, souvenir bklt	....	....	....	22.00	....
1145	$1.15 Eye on Africa, sheet of 4	....	....	....	10.00	....
1146	$1.15 World Post Day, sheet of 10	....	....	30.00	30.00	....
1147	47¢ Sustainable Development Goals, sheet of 17	....	....	19.50	19.50	....
1148	$1.15, 2fr, 1.70e Monkey King, souvenir sheet	....	....	15.50	....	....

1167

1173

2017

SCOTT NO.	DESCRIPTION	FIRST DAY COVERS SING	FIRST DAY COVERS INSC. BLK	INSRIP BLK-4	UNUSED F/NH	USED F
1149	$1.15 Year of the Rooster, sheet of 10	.....	.....	32.00	3.50	.....
1150-57	$1.15 World Flag Series set of 8	25.00(8)	.....	85.00	22.00	.....
1158	$1.15 Smurfs International Day of Happiness, sheet of 10	......	.....	32.00	3.75	.....
1159-60	49¢-$1.15 International Dance Day, 2 sheets of 6	......	.....	25.00(2)	.....	.....
1161	$1.15, 2fr, 1.70e Asian International Stamp Expo, sheet of 3	......	.....	15.50	.....	......
1162-65	$1.15 Endangered Species, block of 4	12.00	.....	12.50	12.50	.....
1166-67	49¢-$1.15 World Environment Day	6.00	.....	15.50	3.75	.....
1168	$1.15 International Day of Yoga, sheet of 10	.....	.....	32.00	.....	.....
1169-70	49¢-$1.15 World Heritage Sites, Along the Silk Road	6.00	.....	15.50	3.75	.....
1171	$9.96 World Heritage Sites, souvenir bklt ..	.....	.....	.....	22.00	.....
1172-73	49¢-$1.15 International Day of Peace	6.00	.....	15.50	3.75	.....
1174	$1.15 Inter. Day of Peace, souvenir sheet .	.....	.....	.....	2.75	.....
1175-76	49¢-$1.15 World Food Day	6.00	.....	15.50	3.75	.....
1177	$1.15, 2fr, 1.70e Universal Declaration of Human Rights, sheet of 3	.....	.....	15.50	.....	......
1178	$1.15, 2fr, 1.70e Autumn Philatelic Fair in Paris, sheet of 3	.....	.....	15.50	.....	......

UNITED NATIONS (NEW YORK)

1179 1205 1192

2018

SCOTT NO.	DESCRIPTION	FIRST DAY COVERS SING	FIRST DAY COVERS INSC. BLK	INSRIP BLK-4	UNUSED F/NH	USED F
1179-86	$1.15 World Flag Series, set of 8	25.00(8)		85.00	22.00	
1187	$1.15 Year of the Dog (2018 date), sheet of 10			32.00	3.50	
1188-91	$1.15 Endangered Species, block of 4	12.00		12.50	12.50	
1192-93	50¢-$1.15 World Health Day	6.00		15.50	3.75	
1194	$2.50 Declaration of Human Rights			24.75	5.75	
1195	65¢ What are You Doing for Peace?			6.75	1.50	
1196-97	50¢-$1.15 UNISPACE, 50th Anniv. Global Conference in Outer Space			15.50	3.75	
1198	$1.15 UNISPACE souvenir sheet				2.75	
1199-1200	50¢-$1.15 World Heritage Sites, UK	6.00		15.50	3.75	
1201	$10.20 World Heritage Sites, UK, prestige booklet				23.50	
1202	$1.15 Thomas and Friends, sheet of 10			32.00		
1203	$1.15, 2fr, 1.70e Asian Inter. Stamp Expo, Macau, sheet of 3			15.50		
1204	c Music Day 2018, sheet of 12			13.50		
1205	1¢ Non-Violence Gun, Regular Issue	3.00		1.00	0.25	
1206-07	$1.15 Diwali Festival, sheet of 10			32.00		
1208	$1.15, 2fr, 1.70e Veronafil, souvenir sheet of 3			15.50		

1212

1224

2019

SCOTT NO.	DESCRIPTION	FIRST DAY COVERS SING	FIRST DAY COVERS INSC. BLK	INSRIP BLK-4	UNUSED F/NH	USED F
1209	$1.15 Year of the Pig, sheet of 10			32.00	3.50	
1210	65¢ World Languages, sheet of 6				8.50	
1211	85¢ Stop Sexual Exploitation & Abuse	3.00		8.00	1.95	
1212-15	$1.15 Endangered Species, block of 4	12.00		12.50	12.50	
1216	$3 World Bee Day, souvenir sheet				7.00	
1217	$1.30 Kofi Annan, single	4.50		14.00	3.50	
1218	$1.15, 2fr, 1.80e Pandas, China 2019 Expo, souvenir sheet of 3				14.00	
1218d	$1.15, 2fr, 1.80e Pandas, SINGPEX 2019, souvenir sheet of 3				14.00	
1219-23	55¢ Inter. Labour Organization, strip of 5	18.00		15.50	7.00	
1224-25	55¢-$1.15 Climate Change	6.00		17.00	4.25	

1227

SCOTT NO.	DESCRIPTION	FIRST DAY COVERS SING	FIRST DAY COVERS INSC. BLK	INSRIP BLK-4	UNUSED F/NH	USED F
1226	$1.15 Climate Change, souvenir sheet				2.75	
1227	$2.75 Mahatma Gandi, single	5.50		30.00	7.00	
1228-29	55¢-$1.15 World Heritage Sites, Cuba	6.50		17.00	4.25	
1230	$10.80 World Heritage Sites, Cuba, prestige booklet				25.00	

1234

1258

1238

2020

SCOTT NO.	DESCRIPTION	FIRST DAY COVERS SING	FIRST DAY COVERS INSC. BLK	INSRIP BLK-4	UNUSED F/NH	USED F
1231	$1.20 Year of the Rat, sheet of 10			32.00	3.50	
1232-35	$1.20 Endangered Species, block of 4	12.00		12.50	12.50	

SCOTT NO.	DESCRIPTION	FIRST DAY COVERS SING	FIRST DAY COVERS INSC. BLK	INSRIP BLK-4	UNUSED F/NH	USED F
1231	$1.20 Year of the Rat, sheet of 10			32.00	3.50	
1232-35	$1.20 Endangered Species, block of 4	12.00		12.50	12.50	

SCOTT NO.	DESCRIPTION	FIRST DAY COVERS SING	FIRST DAY COVERS INSC. BLK	INSRIP BLK-4	UNUSED F/NH	USED F
1236	$1.20 Hello Kitty, set of 2, souvenir sheets of 1 with labels				8.00	
......	same, folded booklets, ($1.20, 2fr, e1.80)			30.00		
1237	$1.20 Act Now Climate Change, sheet of 10			35.00		
1238-39	55¢-$1.20 Each Day 2020	6.00		16.00	3.50	
1240-44	$1.20 International Day of U.N. Women Peacekeepers, 5 varieties			32.00	17.00	
1245-52	$1.20 World Flag Series, set of 8	25.00(8)		85.00(32)	23.00(8)	
1253-54	55¢-$1.20 World Heritage Site, Russia	6.50		17.00	4.25	
1255	$10.80 World Heritage Sites, Russia, prestige booklet				25.00	
1256	$1.20 U.N. 75th Anniv., souvenir sheet of 2				6.00	
1257	$7.75 U.N. Crypto Stamp, souvenir sheet				18.00	
1258-62	$1.20 World Soil Day, 5 varieties			32.00	17.00	

1264

1265

1270-72

2021

SCOTT NO.	DESCRIPTION	FIRST DAY COVERS SING	FIRST DAY COVERS INSC. BLK	INSRIP BLK-4	UNUSED F/NH	USED F
1263	$1.20 Year of the Ox, sheet of 10			32.00	3.50	
1264	$1.20 United Against Racism & Discrimination			14.00	3.50	
1265-68	$1.20 Endangered Species, block of 4	12.00		38.00	12.50	
1269	$1.20 UNPA, 50th Anniv., sheet of 10			35.00		
1270-75	55¢-$1.20 Sports for Peace, horiz strips of 4				18.00(2)	
1276	$1.20 Sports for Peace, souvenir sheet				3.50	
1277	$1.80 Mother Teresa			22.00	4.25	
1278-79	55¢-$1.20 World Heritage, Waterways, Railways, & Bridges	6.50		17.00	4.25	
1280	$10.80 World Heritage, prestige booklet			25.00		
1281	$1.30, 2fr, 180e Dubai UAE Expo, souvenir sheet of 3				14.00	
1282	$1.30, 2fr, 180e U.N. Biodiversity, souvenir sheet of 3				14.00	
1283	$1.30 U.N. Celebrations, sheet of 10			35.00		
1284	58¢ World Toilet Day			6.00	1.50	
1285	$1.30 UNICEF, 75th Anniv., sheet of 10			35.00		

1290-91

1299

1304

2022

SCOTT NO.	DESCRIPTION	FIRST DAY COVERS SING	FIRST DAY COVERS INSC. BLK	INSRIP BLK-4	UNUSED F/NH	USED F
1286-89	58¢-$1.30 Sports for Peace, pairs			25.00(2)	9.00(2)	
1290-91	$1.30 Year of the Tiger, pair, sheet of 10			35.00	7.00	
1292-96	$1.30 Troll Food Heroes, strip of 5, sheet of 10			35.00	17.50	
1297-1300	$1.30 Endangered Species, block of 4	12.00		12.50	12.50	
1301-02	58¢-$1.30 Exploration of Mars	7.00		42.00(2)	4.50	
1303	$1.30 Exploration of Mars, souvenir sheet	6.00			3.50	
1304-05	60¢-$1.40 World Heritage, European Spa Towns	7.00		24.00(2)	6.00	
1306	$11.76 World Heritage, prestige booklet			30.00		
1307	$1.40 Guided Tours of U.N., 70th Anniv., sheet of 10			35.00		
1308	$4.50 Crypto, souvenir sheet			10.00		

UNITED NATIONS (NEW YORK)

1313

1326

SCOTT NO.	DESCRIPTION	FIRST DAY COVERS SING	FIRST DAY COVERS INSC. BLK	INSRIP BLK-4	UNUSED F/NH	USED F
	2023					
1309-10	$1.40 Year of the Rabbit, pair, sheet of 10	.....	.....	35.00	7.50	.....
1311-14	$1.45 Endangered Species, block of 4....	12.00	.....	12.50	12.50	.....
1315	$1.45, 2.30fr, e1.90 5th U.N. Conference LDC5 DOHA, souvenir sheet	.....	.....	16.00	.....	
1316	$1.45, 1.10fr U.N. Emblem, WHO, generic or personalized	.....	.....	35.00	7.50	
1316c	same, Commemorating 60th Anniv. UNITAR, sheet of 10		.....	38.00	8.00	.....
1317-18	63c-$1.45 World Art Day	10.00	.....	50.00(2)	4.50	.....
1319	63c World Oceans Day, sheet of 9	20.00	.....	17.00	.....	.....
1320	$1.45 "Don't Choose Extinction", souvenir sheet	7.00	.....	3.50	.....	.....
1321	66c Tajiquan, Body, Mind & Soul	5.00	.....	6.00	1.50	.....
1322	$1.50 Tajiquan, Body, Mind & Soul, souvenir sheet	7.00	.....	3.50	.....	.....
1323-24	66c-$1.50 World Heritage, Turkey	7.00	.....	24.00(2)	6.00	.....
1325	$14.04 World Heritage, Turkey, prestige booklet	.....	.....	.....	35.00	.....
1326	$1.50 World Mental Health Day	7.00	.....	12.00	3.50	.....
1327	$1.50, 1.10fr U.N. Climate Change Conference, sheet of 10	.....	.....	38.00	7.50	.....

*Scott numbers and prices are subject to change in the next edition.

SEMI-POSTAL

SCOTT NO.	DESCRIPTION	SING	INSC. BLK	BLK-4	F/NH	F
	2002					
B1	37¢ + 6¢ UN AIDS Awareness, souv. sheet	2.00	....	....	3.00	3.00
	2020					
B2	55¢ + 50¢, $1.20 + 50¢, Geneva 1fr + 50fr, 1.50fr + 50fr, Vienna e0.85 + e0.50, e1.00 + e0.05	.....	.....	30.00	.....	
	2021					
B3	$1.30 + 50¢ John Lennon	.....	.....	17.00	4.25	.....
B4	$2.60 + $1 John Lennon, souvenir sheet	.....	.....	.....	10.00	.....
	2022					
B5	$1.40 + 50¢ World Humanitarian Day	.....	.....	17.00	4.25	.....

AIR POST ISSUE

C1-2, UC5

C3-C4, UC1-2

SCOTT NO.	DESCRIPTION	SING	INSC. BLK	BLK-4	F/NH	F
	1951-77					
C1-C23	**AIR MAILS, complete (23)**	......	......	**39.50**	**8.50**	......

C5-6, UXC1, UXC3

C7, UC4

SCOTT NO.	DESCRIPTION	SING	INSC. BLK	BLK-4	F/NH	F
	1951-59					
C1-4	6¢, 10¢, 15¢ & 20¢	24.50	60.00	9.00	2.00	2.00
C5-7	4¢, 5¢ & 7¢ (1957-59)	1.65	4.15	2.25	.55	.45

C8, UXC4

C10

C9, UC6, UC8

C11

C12

SCOTT NO.	DESCRIPTION	SING	INSC. BLK	BLK-4	F/NH	F
	1963-77					
C8-12	6¢, 8¢, 13¢, 15¢, & 25¢ (1963-64)	3.25	8.00	8.50	1.85	1.85

C13

C14

SCOTT NO.	DESCRIPTION	SING	INSC. BLK	BLK-4	F/NH	F
C13-14	10¢ & 20¢ (1968-69)	2.00	4.95	3.65	.75	.75

C15, UXC8

C17, UXC10

C16, UC10

C18

SCOTT NO.	DESCRIPTION	SING	INSC. BLK	BLK-4	F/NH	F
C15-18	9¢, 11¢, 17¢, & 21¢ (1972)	2.40	6.00	6.00	1.85	1.15

C19, UC11

C20, UXC11

C21

SCOTT NO.	DESCRIPTION	SING	INSC. BLK	BLK-4	F/NH	F
C19-21	13¢, 18¢, & 26¢ (1974)	2.75	6.95	6.00	1.50	1.25

C22

C23

SCOTT NO.	DESCRIPTION	SING	INSC. BLK	BLK-4	F/NH	F
C22-23	25¢ & 31¢ (1977)	2.50	6.25	6.00	1.50	1.25

ENVELOPES AND AIR LETTER SHEETS (New York)

U1-U2 · U8, U49 · UC3 · U3 · U7 · (Surcharge) U12, U13 · (Surcharge) U9 · U10, U11, U12, U13

UC6 · UC14, UC15 · UC16, UC17 · UC7 · UC13 · UC9, UC22 · (surcharge) UC19, UC24 · (surcharge) UC15, UC17 · UC20, UC21 · UC23, UC24 · UC18, UC19 · (surcharge) UC21

SCOTT NO.	DESCRIPTION	FIRST DAY COVER	UNUSED ENTIRE
	1953		
U1	3¢ blue	4.50	1.00
	1958		
U2	4¢ ultramarine	.95	.75
	1963		
U3	5¢ multicolored (design #128)	1.00	.45
	1969		
U4	6¢ multicolored (design #128)	.95	.55
	1973		
U5	8¢ multicolored (design #187)	.95	1.00
	1975		
U6	10¢ multicolored (design #250)	.95	.70
	1985		
U7	22¢ Strip Bouquet	11.00	11.00
	1989		
U8	25¢ U.N. Headquarters	4.50	4.50
U9	25¢+4¢ surcharge (U8)	4.75	4.75
U9a	25¢+7¢ surcharge (U8)	7.50	4.00
	1997		
U10	32¢ Cripticandina (79x38mm)	3.50	3.50
U11	32¢ Cripticandina (89x44mm)	4.25	4.00
	1999		
U12	32¢+1¢ surcharge (U10)	3.75	4.00
U13	32¢+1¢ surcharge (U11)	3.75	4.00
	2001		
U14	34¢ NY Headquarters (34x34mm)	3.50	3.75
U15	34¢ NY Headquarters (36x36mm)	3.50	3.75
	2002		
U16	34¢+3¢ surcharge (U14)	2.75	3.00
U17	34¢+3¢ surcharge (U15)	2.75	3.00
	2003		
U18	37¢ U.N. Headquarters (37X47mm)	1.50	1.95
U19	37¢ U.N. Headquarters (40X52mm)	1.50	1.95
	2006		
U20	37¢+2¢ surcharge on #U18	1.50	1.95
U21	37¢+2¢ surcharge on #U19	1.50	1.95
	2007		
U22	37¢+4¢ U18 surcharged	2.25	2.25
U23	37¢+4¢ U19 sucharged	2.25	2.25
U24	41¢ UN Emblem #6 3/4	2.25	2.00
U25	41¢ UN Emblem #10	2.25	2.00
	2008		
U26	41¢+1¢ U24 surcharged	1.60	2.00
U27	41¢+1¢ U25 surcharged	1.60	2.00
	2009		
U28	41¢+3¢ U24 surcharged	1.25	1.75
U29	41¢+3¢ U25 surcharged	1.25	1.85
	2010		
U30	44¢ UN Headquarters & Cherry Blossoms, #6 3/4	2.75	1.50
U31	44¢ UN Headquarters & Cherry Blossoms, #10	2.75	1.50
	2012		
U32	44¢+1¢ U30 Surcharged	2.5	1.25
U33	44¢+1¢ U31 Surcharged	2.5	1.25
	2013		
U34	46¢ Orange Circle and Dots, #6 3/4 entire	1.50	1.25
U35	46¢ Orange Circle and Dots, #10 entire	1.50	1.25
	2014		
U36	46¢+3¢ #U34 Surcharged	1.75	1.75
U37	46¢+3¢ #U35 Surcharged	1.75	1.75
	2017		
U38	49¢ U.N. Headquarters, #6 3/4 entire	2.00	1.95
U39	49¢ U.N. Headquarters, #10 entire	2.00	1.95
	2018		
U40	39¢+1¢ U.N. Sculpture, #6 3/4 entire	......	1.85
U41	39¢+1¢ U.N. Sculpture, #10 entire	......	1.85

AIRMAILS

SCOTT NO.	DESCRIPTION	FIRST DAY COVER	UNUSED ENTIRE
	1952		
UC1	10¢ blue, air letter (design #C3)	8.00	30.00
	1954		
UC2	10¢ royal blue, white borders aerogramme (design of #C3)	......	9.75
	1958		
UC2a	10¢ royal blue, no border (design #C3)	......	8.00
	1959		
UC3	7¢ blue	1.00	2.00
	1960		
UC4	10¢ ultramarine on bluish, letter sheet (design of #C7)	.95	.75
	1961		
UC5	11¢ ultramarine on bluish, letter sheet (design of #C1)	1.25	1.55
	1965		
UC5a	11¢ dark blue on green, letter sheet (design of #C1)	......	2.75
	1963		
UC6	8¢ multicolored (design #C9)	1.00	.75
	1958		
UC7	13¢ shades-blue, letter sheet	.95	.90
	1969		
UC8	10¢ multicolored (design #C9)	.95	.85
	1972-73		
UC9	15¢ shades-blue, letter sheet	.95	.90
UC10	11¢ multicolored (design #C16)	.95	1.00
	1975		
UC11	13¢ multicolored (design #C19)	1.00	.95
UC12	18¢ multicolored, aerogramme (design of #222)	1.00	.80
	1977		
UC13	22¢ multicolored, aerogramme	1.25	.90
	1982		
UC14	30¢ black, aerogramme	3.00	2.50
	1988-89		
UC15	30¢+6¢ Surcharge on #UC14	11.50	63.00
UC16	39¢ U.N. Headquarters aerogramme	2.25	5.00
UC17	39¢+6¢ Surcharge on #UC16	2.25	19.75
	1982		
UC18	45¢ Winged Hand	1.95	4.00
	1995		
UC19	45¢+5¢ Surcharge on #UC18	5.00	7.00
	1997/1999		
UC20	50¢ Cherry Blossoms	1.65	3.50
UC21	50¢+10¢ surcharge on #UC20	1.75	3.25
	2001-2008		
UC22	50¢+20¢ on UC9	1.75	4.25
UC23	70¢ Cherry Blossoms	1.75	3.25
UC24	70¢+5¢ surcharge on #UC23	1.75	2.50
UC25	70¢+20¢ Multicolored Airletter	3.25	3.00
UC26	90¢ UN Emblem & Airplane	3.25	2.95
UC27	90¢+4¢ UC26 Surcharged	2.25	2.95
	2009		
UC28	90¢+8¢ UC24 Surcharged	2.75	2.95
	2010		
UC29	98¢ IM Emblem and Airplane	3.25	2.95
	2012		
UC30	98¢+7¢ UC29 Surcharged	2.75	2.75
	2013		
UC31	$1.10 Orange Circles and Dots	2.75	2.75
	2014		
UC32	$1.10+5¢ #UC24 Surcharged	3.00	3.00

POSTAL CARDS (New York)

SCOTT NO.	DESCRIPTION	FIRST DAY COVER	UNUSED ENTIRE
	1952		
UX1	2¢ blue on buff (design of #2)	1.65	.35
	1958		
UX2	3¢ gray olive on buff (design of #2)	.90	.35

UX3

SCOTT NO.	DESCRIPTION	FIRST DAY COVER	UNUSED ENTIRE
	1963		
UX3	4¢ multicolored (design of #125)	.90	.35

UX4

SCOTT NO.	DESCRIPTION	FIRST DAY COVER	UNUSED ENTIRE
	1969		
UX4	5¢ blue & black	.95	.35

UX5-6

SCOTT NO.	DESCRIPTION	FIRST DAY COVER	UNUSED ENTIRE
	1973		
UX5	6¢ multicolored	.90	.35
	1975		
UX6	8¢ multicolored	1.00	.75

UX7  UX8

SCOTT NO.	DESCRIPTION	FIRST DAY COVER	UNUSED ENTIRE
	1977		
UX7	9¢ multicolored	1.00	.90
	1982		
UX8	13¢ multicolored	1.10	.60

UX9

SCOTT NO.	DESCRIPTION	FIRST DAY COVER	UNUSED ENTIRE
	1989		
UX9	15¢ UN Complex	1.10	2.00
UX10	15¢ UN Complex with trees	1.10	2.00
UX11	15¢ Flags	1.10	2.00
UX12	15¢ General Assembly	1.10	2.00
UX13	15¢ UN Complex from East River	1.10	2.00
UX14	36¢ UN Complex and Flags	1.50	2.75
UX15	36¢ Flags	1.50	2.75
UX16	36¢ UN Complex at Dusk	1.50	2.75
UX17	36¢ Security Council	1.50	2.75
UX18	36¢ UN Complex and Sculpture	1.50	2.75
UX19	40¢ UN Headquarters	1.60	6.25
	1998		
UX20	21¢ Secretariat Bldg., Roses	1.75	1.40
UX21	50¢ UN Complex	1.75	2.00
	2001		
UX22	70¢ NY Headquarters	1.75	3.00
UX23	70¢ Cherry Blossoms	1.75	2.50
	2003		
UX24	23¢ Equestrian Statue	1.75	1.40
UX25	23¢ Lobby	1.75	1.40
UX26	23¢ U.N. Headquarters	1.75	1.40
UX27	23¢ Meeting Room	1.75	1.40
UX28	23¢ Post Office	1.75	1.40
UX29	70¢ Meeting Room	1.75	2.00
UX30	70¢ Peace Bell	1.75	2.00
UX31	70¢ Statue	1.75	2.00
UX32	70¢ U.N. Headquarters	1.75	2.00
UX33	70¢ General Assembly	1.75	2.00

AIR MAILS

SCOTT NO.	DESCRIPTION	FIRST DAY COVER	UNUSED ENTIRE
	1957		
UXC1	4¢ maroon on buff (design of #C5)	.60	.35

(surcharge)
UXC2

SCOTT NO.	DESCRIPTION	FIRST DAY COVER	UNUSED ENTIRE
	1959		
UXC2	4¢ & 1¢ (on UXC1)	......	.75
UXC3	5¢ crimson on buff (design of #C6)	.70	1.00

UXC4  UXC5-6

SCOTT NO.	DESCRIPTION	FIRST DAY COVER	UNUSED ENTIRE
UXC4	6¢ black & blue (design of #C8)	.85	.95
	1965		
UXC5	11¢ multicolored	1.00	.50
	1968		
UXC6	13¢ yellow & green	.95	.65

UXC7, UXC9

SCOTT NO.	DESCRIPTION	FIRST DAY COVER	UNUSED ENTIRE
	1969		
UXC7	8¢ multicolored	.90	.80
	1972		
UXC8	9¢ multicolored (design of #C15)	1.00	.65
UXC9	15¢ multicolored	1.00	.70
	1975		
UXC10	11¢ shades—blue (design of #C17)	1.00	.65
UXC11	18¢ multicolored (design of #C20)	1.20	.65

UXC12

SCOTT NO.	DESCRIPTION	FIRST DAY COVER	UNUSED ENTIRE
	1982		
UXC12	28¢ multicolored	1.40	.80

UNITED NATIONS;
OFFICES IN GENEVA, SWITZERLAND
Denominations in Swiss Currency

NOTE: Unless illustrated, designs can be assumed to be similar to the equivalent New York or Vienna issues

4 22 61 65 67 69 71 73 74 77 79 82

SCOTT NO.	DESCRIPTION	FIRST DAY COVERS SING	FIRST DAY COVERS INSC. BLK	INSRIP BLK-4	UNUSED F/NH	USED F
	1969-70					
1-14	5¢ to 10fr Definitives	45.00	110.00	85.00	18.00	12.00
	1971					
15-21	**1971 Issues, complete (7)**	......	......	......	**4.25**	......
15	30¢ Peaceful Uses Sea Bed	.95	2.40	1.40	.30	.30
16	50¢ Support for Refugees	1.10	2.75	2.40	.55	.40
17	50¢ World Food Programme	1.40	3.50	2.65	.55	.45
18	75¢ U.P.U. Building	2.75	6.85	4.25	.90	.80
19-20	30¢ & 50¢ Anti-Discrimination	2.25	5.65	4.25	.90	.60
21	1.10fr International School	3.65	9.00	6.25	1.35	1.15
	1972					
22-29	**1972 Issues, complete (8)**	......	......	......	**5.95**	......
22	40¢ Definitive	1.10	2.75	1.90	.40	.35
23	40¢ Non Proliferation	2.15	5.40	3.50	.75	.75
24	80¢ World Health Day	2.15	5.40	3.75	.85	.85
25-26	40¢ & 80¢ Environment	3.75	9.50	7.00	1.75	1.40
27	1.10fr Economic Committee Europe	3.25	8.15	7.00	1.60	1.35
28-29	40¢ & 80¢ Art—Sert Ceiling	3.50	8.75	7.00	1.70	1.00
	1973					
30-36	**1973 Issues, complete (6)**	......	......	......	**5.50**	......
30-31	60¢ & 1.10fr Disarmament Decade	3.50	8.75	8.00	2.00	1.50
32	60¢ Drug Abuse	2.00	5.00	3.25	.70	.65
33	80¢ Volunteer	2.50	6.25	4.00	.95	.75
34	60¢ Namibia	2.05	5.15	3.00	.75	.75
35-36	40¢ & 80¢ Human Rights	2.65	6.65	6.50	1.40	1.00
	1974					
37-45	**1974 Issues, complete (9)**	......	......	......	**7.15**	......
37-38	60¢ & 80¢ ILO Headquarters	2.75	6.85	7.50	1.50	1.25
39-40	30¢ & 60¢ U.P.U. Centenary	2.25	5.65	6.00	1.25	1.00
41-42	60¢ & 1fr Brazil Peace Mural	3.00	7.50	8.50	1.75	1.45
43-44	60¢ & 80¢ World Population Year	2.50	6.25	8.00	1.70	1.85
45	1.30fr Law of the Sea	2.25	5.65	7.00	1.50	1.15
	1975					
46/56	**1975 Issues, (10) (No #52)**	......	......	......	**9.25**	......
46-47	60¢ & 90¢ Peaceful Use of Space	2.40	6.00	8.75	1.90	1.40
48-49	60¢ & 90¢ International Women's Year	2.75	6.85	8.00	1.75	1.40
50-51	60¢ & 90¢ 30th Anniversary	2.25	5.65	8.00	1.75	1.25
52	same, souvenir sheet	2.50	......	......	1.75	1.40
53-54	50¢ & 1.30fr Namibia	2.50	6.25	8.00	2.00	1.40
55-56	60¢ & 70¢ Peacekeeping	2.10	5.25	7.00	1.50	1.25
	1976					
57-63	**1976 Issues, (7)**	......	......	......	**8.95**	......
57	90¢ World Federation	1.80	4.50	5.75	1.25	1.20
58	1.10fr Conference T.& D.	2.10	5.25	6.00	1.25	1.20
59-60	40¢ & 1.50fr Human Settlement	3.00	7.50	9.00	2.00	1.50
61-62	80¢ & 1.10fr Postal Administration	12.00	29.50	14.00	5.00	4.50
63	70¢ World Food Council	1.40	3.50	4.00	.85	.65

SCOTT NO.	DESCRIPTION	FIRST DAY COVERS SING	FIRST DAY COVERS INSC. BLK	INSRIP BLK-4	UNUSED F/NH	USED F
	1977					
64-72	**1977 Issues, complete (9)**	......	......	......	**7.50**	......
64	80¢ WIPO	1.40	3.50	4.00	.90	.70
65-66	80¢ & 1.10fr Water Conference	3.00	7.50	9.00	2.00	1.45
67-68	80¢ & 1.10fr Security Council	3.00	7.50	9.00	2.00	1.45
69-70	40¢ & 1.10fr Combat Racism	2.50	6.25	7.00	1.75	1.40
71-72	80¢ & 1.10fr Atomic Energy	3.00	7.50	9.00	2.00	1.45
	1978					
73-81	**1978 Issues, complete (9)**	......	......	**30.95**	**7.20**	......
73	35¢ Definitive	.95	2.40	2.20	.45	.40
74-75	80¢ & 1.10fr Smallpox Eradication	2.95	7.50	10.75	2.00	1.70
76	80¢ Namibia	1.50	3.75	5.00	1.25	1.00
77-78	70¢ & 80¢ ICAO	2.25	5.65	8.00	1.65	1.25
79-80	70¢ & 1.10fr General Assembly	3.00	7.50	9.00	2.00	1.65
81	80¢ TCDC	1.40	3.50	4.25	.95	.90
	1979					
82-88	**1979 Issues, complete (7)**	......	......	......	**7.50**	......
82-83	80¢ & 1.50fr UNDRO	3.10	7.75	10.00	2.75	1.95
84-85	80¢ & 1.10fr I.Y.C.	4.75	11.85	7.00	2.00	1.40
86	1.10fr Namibia	1.90	4.75	5.00	1.25	.95
87-88	80¢ & 1.10fr Court of Justice	3.00	7.50	8.00	2.00	1.55
	1980					
89/97	**1980 Issues, (8) (No #95)**	......	......	......	**5.40**	......
89	80¢ Economics	1.50	4.75	5.25	1.15	1.15
90-91	40¢ & 70¢ Decade for Women	1.95	6.00	5.50	1.25	1.10
92	1.10fr Peacekeeping	1.85	6.00	5.25	1.25	1.00
93-94	40¢ & 70¢ 35th Anniversary	2.00	6.00	5.50	1.25	1.15
95	Same, Souvenir Sheet	2.75	......	......	1.40	1.25
96-97	40¢ & 70¢ Economic & Social Council	1.85	6.00	6.00	1.25	1.25
	1981					
98-104	**1981 Issues, complete (7)**	......	......	......	**6.00**	......
98	80¢ Palestinian People	1.70	4.25	4.00	1.00	.70
99-100	40¢ & 1.50fr Disabled People	2.75	6.85	9.00	2.00	1.70
101	80¢ Fresco	1.50	3.75	4.50	1.00	1.00
102	1.10fr Sources of Energy	1.50	3.75	5.00	1.25	1.00
103-04	40¢ & 70¢ Conservation	1.75	4.50	8.00	1.70	1.70
	1982					
105-12	**1982 Issues, complete (8)**	......	......	......	**7.00**	......
105-06	30¢ & 1fr Definitives	2.10	5.25	7.50	1.50	1.40
107-08	40¢ & 1.20fr Human Environment	2.40	6.00	9.00	1.85	1.70
109-10	80¢ & 1fr Space Exploration	2.65	6.65	9.50	2.00	1.70
111-12	40¢ & 1.50fr Conservation	2.75	6.95	10.00	2.25	1.75

84 87 90 93 97 104 105 106 110 107 115 118 119

SCOTT NO.	DESCRIPTION	FIRST DAY COVERS SING	FIRST DAY COVERS INSC. BLK	INSRIP BLK-4	UNUSED F/NH	USED F
	1983					
113-20	**1983 Issues, complete (8)**	......	......	......	**8.35**	......
113	1.20fr World Communications	1.75	4.40	7.25	1.55	1.35
114-15	40¢ & 80¢ Safety at Sea	1.75	4.40	7.25	1.55	1.45
116	1.50fr World Food Program	2.25	5.65	8.50	1.70	1.45
117-18	80¢ & 1.10fr Trade & Development	2.75	6.95	9.75	1.95	1.70
119-20	40¢ & 1.20fr Human Rights	3.50	8.75	9.00	2.05	1.80
	1984					
121-28	**1984 Issues, complete (8)**	......	......	......	**9.20**	......
121	1. 20fr Population	1.75	4.50	7.00	1.50	1.25
122-23	50¢ & 80¢ Food Day	1.75	4.50	7.00	1.75	1.25
124-25	50¢ & 70¢ Heritage	1.75	4.50	8.00	2.25	1.25
126-27	35¢ & 1.50fr Future for Refugees	2.75	6.95	9.00	2.25	1.75
128	1.20fr Youth Year	1.75	4.50	8.00	1.95	1.25
	1985					
129/39	**1985 Issues, (10) (No #137)**	......	......	......	**11.50**	
129-30	80¢-1.20fr Turin Centre	2.75	6.95	9.00	2.25	1.75
131-32	50¢-80¢ U.N. University	2.00	5.00	8.00	1.95	1.50
133-34	20¢-1.20fr Definitives	2.25	5.65	9.00	2.00	1.60
135-36	50¢-70¢ 40th Anniversary	2.00	5.80	8.00	1.95	1.60
137	same, souvenir sheet	2.75	......	......	2.50	2.50
138-39	50¢-1.20fr Child Survival	5.75	14.50	10.00	2.00	2.50
	1986					
140-49	**1986 Issues (10)**	......	......	......	**17.25**	......
140	1.40fr Africa in Crisis	2.00	5.00	8.00	2.50	1.40
141-44	35¢ Development, 4 varieties, attached	2.00	2.75	12.00	10.50	9.00
145	5¢ Definitive	1.10	2.75	1.00	.25	.25
146-47	50¢ & 80¢ Philately	1.85	4.65	9.50	2.00	1.80
148-49	45¢ & 1.40fr Peace Year	2.75	6.95	12.50	3.00	2.25
150	35¢-70¢ WFUNA, souvenir sheet	2.75	......	......	5.50	4.00
	1987					
151-61	**1987 Issues (11)**	......	......	......	**13.00**	......
151	1.40fr Trygve Lie	2.00	5.00	8.00	2.00	1.75
152-53	90¢-1.40fr Definitive	3.50	8.75	11.00	2.50	2.00
154-55	50¢-90¢ Shelter Homeless	2.00	5.00	9.50	1.95	1.75
156-57	80¢-1.20fr Anti-Drug Campaign	2.75	6.95	11.00	2.50	1.75
158-59	35¢-50¢ United Nations Day	3.50	8.75	8.50	1.50	1.45
160-61	90¢-1.70fr Child Immunization	1.85	4.65	20.00	4.25	4.00

120 122 123 124

125 126 127 128 145

130 133 134 148

149 152 153 164 178

183 184 185 179

201 202 203 204 213

205 206 255 256

SCOTT NO.	DESCRIPTION	FIRST DAY COVERS SING	FIRST DAY COVERS INSC. BLK	INSRIP BLK-4	UNUSED F/NH	USED F
	1988					
162/172	**1988 Issues, (8) (No #165-66, 172)**	......	......	......	**9.00**	......
162-63	35¢-1.40fr World without Hunger	2.50	6.25	11.00	2.75	2.00
164	50¢ For a Better World	1.25	3.15	4.00	.85	.85
					Sheetlets (12)	
165-66	50¢-1.10fr Forest Conservation	15.00	40.00	14.00	8.00	7.50
	(set of 6, includes NY and Vienna)			130.00	27.50	25.00
167-68	80¢-90¢ Volunteer Day	2.50	6.25	10.00	2.40	2.25
169-70	50¢-1.40fr Health in Sports	2.75	6.95	11.00	2.25	2.00
171	90¢ Human Rights 40th Anniversary	2.00	5.00	6.00	1.25	1.00
172	2fr Human Rights 40th Anniversary souvenir sheet	2.75	....	....	3.25	3.00
	1989					
173-81	**1989 Issues (9)**	......	......	....	**19.50**	....
173-74	80¢ & 1.40fr. World Bank	2.75	6.95	17.00	4.00	3.25
175	90¢ Nobel Peace Prize	1.50	3.75	8.00	1.40	1.10
176-77	90¢ & 1.10fr World Weather Watch	2.75	6.95	19.25	4.25	4.25
178-79	50¢ & 2fr UN Offices in Vienna	4.00	10.00	24.50	5.25	5.25
					Sheetlets (12)	
180-81	35¢ & 80¢ Human Rights 40th Ann. (strips of 3 w/tabs)	1.85	4.65	24.00	7.00	....
	1990					
182/94	**1990 Issues, No #190 (12)**	......	......	....	**33.50**	......
182	1.50fr International Trade	2.15	5.40	14.00	3.00	2.75
183	5fr Definitive	7.75	19.50	25.00	6.00	5.25
184-85	50¢ & 80¢ SIDA (AIDS)	2.15	5.50	15.50	3.25	3.25
186-87	90¢ & 1.40fr Medicinal Plants	3.60	9.00	17.00	3.50	3.50
188-89	90¢ & 1.10fr Anniversary of U.N.	3.00	7.50	19.00	4.00	4.00
190	same, souvenir sheet	3.00		......	7.00	7.00
191-92	50¢ & 2fr Crime Prevention	4.15	10.50	22.00	4.50	4.50
193-94	35¢ & 90¢ Human Rights (strips of 3 w/tabs)	1.95	4.95	30.00	7.50	....
	1991					
195-210	**1991 Issues (17)**	......	......	.....	**31.00**	......
195-98	90¢ Econ. Comm. for Europe, 4 varieties, attached	5.75	6.75	7.75	6.75	6.75
199-200	70¢ & 90¢ Namibia—A New Nation	3.85	9.60	19.50	4.25	4.25
201-02	80¢ & 1.50fr Definitives	5.00	12.50	19.50	4.25	4.25
203-04	80¢ & 1.10fr Children's Rights	4.50	11.25	19.50	4.25	4.25
205-06	80¢ & 1.40fr Banning of Chemical Weapons	5.00	12.50	29.00	7.00	7.00
207-08	50¢ & 1.60fr 40th Anniv. of the UNPA	4.75	11.95	19.50	4.25	4.25
					Sheetlets (12)	
209-10	50¢ & 90¢ Human Rights (strips of 3 w/tabs)	2.75	7.50	38.00	9.50	....
	1992					
211-25	**1992 Issues (15)**	......	......	......	**38.00**	......
211-12	50¢-1.10fr. World Heritage—UNESCO	3.60	9.00	19.00	4.25	4.25
213	3fr Definitive	6.00	15.00	19.00	4.75	4.75
214-15	80¢ Clean Oceans, 2 varieties, attached	2.75	5.35	7.50	2.50	2.50
216-19	75¢ Earth Summit, 4 varieties, attached	4.00	4.95	9.00	7.00	7.00
220-21	1.10fr Mission to Planet Earth, 2 varieties, attached	4.00	6.95	13.00	5.75	5.75
222-23	90¢-1.60fr Science and Technology	4.75	11.75	25.00	6.00	6.00
224-25	50¢-90¢ Human Rights (strips of 3 w/tabs)	2.75	6.50	38.00	9.50	......
	1993					
226-43	**1993 Issues (18)**	......	......	......	**36.00**	......
226-27	50¢-1.60fr Aging	3.60	9.00	19.00	4.00	3.75
228-31	80¢ Endangered Species, 4 attached	4.00	5.00	6.50	5.25	5.25
232-33	60¢-1fr Healthy Environment	3.00	8.00	19.00	4.25	4.25
234-35	50¢-90¢ Human Rights (strips of 3 w/tabs)	3.00	7.00	38.00	9.50	....
236-39	60¢ Peace, 4 attached	3.50	4.50	11.00	9.50	7.50
240-43	1.10fr Environment—Climate, strip of 4	3.50	8.00	20.00(8)	9.75	9.75

277 279 294 280-83

284-88

SCOTT NO.	DESCRIPTION	FIRST DAY COVERS SING	INSC. BLK	INSRIP BLK-4	UNUSED F/NH	USED F
	1994					
244-61	**1994 Issues (18)**	....	....	....	**33.50**	....
244-45	80¢-1fr Intl. Year of the Family	3.50	12.50	17.50	3.75	3.75
246-49	80¢ Endangered Species, 4 attached	4.50	5.00	7.00	5.75	5.75
250	1.20fr Refugees	2.50	9.25	16.00	3.50	4.85
251-54	60¢ Intl. Decade for Natural Disaster Reduction, 4 attached	3.50	4.25	10.00	9.00	8.00
255-57	60¢-1.80fr Definitives (3)	5.00	17.50	26.00	5.50	5.50
258-59	60¢-80¢ Population and Development	4.00	10.00	16.00	4.00	3.50
260-61	80¢-1fr Development through Partnership	3.50	12.50	18.00	3.75	3.75
	1995					
262/75	**1995 Issues (13) (No #272)**	....	....	....	**40.00**	....
262	80¢ 50th Anniversary of the UN	1.75	6.50	7.00	1.75	1.75
263	1fr Social Summit	2.25	7.50	9.00	2.00	2.00
264-67	80¢ Endangered Species, 4 attached	4.50	5.00	7.50	6.50	6.50
268-69	80¢-1fr Youth: Our Future	3.50	12.50	24.00	5.25	5.25
270-71	60¢-1.80fr 50th Anniversary of the UN	4.75	15.50	24.00	5.25	5.25
272	2.40fr 50th Anniversary of the UN, souvenir sheet	4.50	....	....	6.00	6.00
273-74	60¢-1fr 4th Conference on Women	3.00	10.00	23.00	5.25	5.25
275	30¢ 50th Anniversary, min. sheet of 12	....	....	....	21.00	....
276	same, souvenir booklet of 4 panes of 3	....	....	....	23.00	....

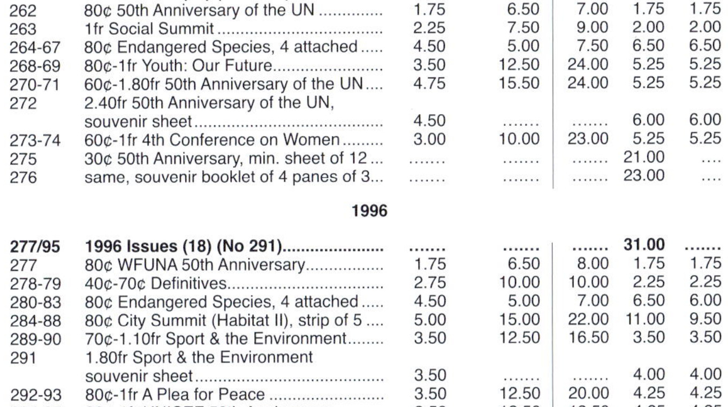

SCOTT NO.	DESCRIPTION	FIRST DAY COVERS SING	INSC. BLK	INSRIP BLK-4	UNUSED F/NH	USED F
	1996					
277/95	**1996 Issues (18) (No 291)**	....	....	....	**31.00**	....
277	80¢ WFUNA 50th Anniversary	1.75	6.50	8.00	1.75	1.75
278-79	40¢-70¢ Definitives	2.75	10.00	10.00	2.25	2.25
280-83	80¢ Endangered Species, 4 attached	4.50	5.00	7.00	6.50	6.00
284-88	80¢ City Summit (Habitat II), strip of 5	5.00	15.00	22.00	11.00	9.50
289-90	70¢-1.10fr Sport & the Environment	3.50	12.50	16.50	3.50	3.50
291	1.80fr Sport & the Environment souvenir sheet	3.50	....	....	4.00	4.00
292-93	80¢-1fr A Plea for Peace	3.50	12.50	20.00	4.25	4.25
294-95	80¢-1fr UNICEF 50th Anniversary	3.50	12.50	13.50	4.25	4.25

302-05

312

296

314

SCOTT NO.	DESCRIPTION	FIRST DAY COVERS SING	INSC. BLK	INSRIP BLK-4	UNUSED F/NH	USED F
	1997					
296/315	**1997 Issues (19) (No.# 306)**	....	....	....	**26.50**	....
296-97	10¢-$1 10fr. Definitives	2.75	10.00	11.75	2.75	2.00
298-301	80¢ Endangered Species, 4 attached	4.50	5.00	7.00	5.50	5.00
302-05	45¢ Earth Summit +5, 4 attached	2.50	2.75	6.50	5.50	5.00
306	1.10Fr Earth Summit, souvenir sheet	2.40	....	....	4.25	3.75
307-11	70¢ Transporation, strip of 5	5.50	13.50	16.00(10)	7.00	6.75
312-13	70¢-1.10Fr Tribute to Philately	3.50	12.50	18.50	4.00	3.50
314-15	45¢-70¢ Terracota Warriors	2.75	10.00	18.50	4.00	3.50
316	same, Souvenir bklt of 6 pane of 4	....	....	....	15.00	....

317 322a 318-21

SCOTT NO.	DESCRIPTION	FIRST DAY COVERS SING	INSC. BLK	INSRIP BLK-4	UNUSED F/NH	USED F
	1998					
	1998 Issues (12) (No #322, 321, 331)	....	....	....	**24.50**	....
317	2fr Definitive	4.00	9.00	15.50	3.25	3.25
318-21	80¢ Endangered Species, 4 attached	4.50	5.00	6.50	5.75	5.75
322	45¢ Intl. Year of the Ocean, sheetlet of 12	15.00	....	....	15.00	....
323	70¢ Rain Forests, Orangutans	2.00	4.50	6.00	1.50	1.50
324	3fr Rain Forests, Orangutans, souvenir sheet	7.00	....	....	6.00	6.00
325-26	70¢-90¢ 50 Years of Peacekeeping	4.00	9.00	14.00	3.25	3.25
327-28	90¢-1.80fr 50th of the Dec. of Human Rights	6.75	15.00	18.00	5.50	5.00
329-30	70¢-1.10fr Schonbrunn Castle	4.50	10.00	14.50	3.65	3.25
331	same, souvenir bklt of 6 panes	....	....	....	18.00	....

332 333

SCOTT NO.	DESCRIPTION	FIRST DAY COVERS SING	INSC. BLK	INSRIP BLK-4	UNUSED F/NH	USED F
	1999					
	1999 Issues (16) (No #355, 342, 348)	....	....	....	**25.50**	....
332	1.70fr Denfinitive	4.00	9.00	13.00	3.25	2.75
333-34	90¢-1.10fr World Heritage Sites, Australia	4.50	10.00	15.00	3.85	3.25
335	same, souvenir bklt of 6 panes	....	....	....	13.00	....

336-39

347

SCOTT NO.	DESCRIPTION	FIRST DAY COVERS SING	INSC. BLK	INSRIP BLK-4	UNUSED F/NH	USED F
336-39	90¢ Endangered Species, 4 attached	4.50	5.00	7.50	6.50	6.00
340-41	45¢ Unispace III Conference	1.95	4.00	6.00	2.50	2.50
342	2fr Unispace III Conference, souvenir sheet	6.00	....	....	5.50	5.50
343-46	70¢ Universal Postal Union	2.00	4.50	6.00	5.25	4.75
347	1.10fr In Memorium	2.40	5.00	8.50	2.00	2.00
348	2fr In Memoriam, souvenir sheet	3.75	....	....	3.75	3.75

349

351

SCOTT NO.	DESCRIPTION	FIRST DAY COVERS SING	INSC. BLK	INSRIP BLK-4	UNUSED F/NH	USED F
349-50	70¢-1.80fr Education-Keystone to the 21st Century	6.50	14.00	21.00	5.00	4.50
	2000					
351	90¢ International Year of Thanksgiving	1.95	4.00	7.25	1.65	1.65
352-55	90¢ Endangered Species, 4 attached	4.50	5.00	8.75	7.50	7.50
356-57	90¢-1.10fr Our World 2000	4.50	10.00	16.00	3.85	3.50
358-59	90¢-1.40fr 55th Anniversary of the UN	4.75	11.00	19.00	4.00	4.00
360	same, 90¢-1.40fr souvenir sheet	....	....	....	5.00	4.50
361	50¢ United Nations in the 21st Century	7.50	7.50	....	10.00	10.00
362-63	1fr-1.20fr World Heritage Sites, Spain	5.25	11.50	19.00	4.50	4.50
364	same, souvenir bklt of 6 panes	....	....	....	13.00	....
365	80¢ Respect for Regugees	1.75	6.50	7.00	1.50	1.50
366	1.80fr Respect for Refugees, souvenir sheet	3.50	....	....	3.25	3.25

371

384

2001

SCOTT NO.	DESCRIPTION	FIRST DAY COVERS SING	FIRST DAY COVERS INSC. BLK	INSRIP BLK-4	UNUSED F/NH	USED F
367-70	90¢ Endangered Species, 4 attached	4.50	5.00	7.25	6.25	6.25
371-72	90¢-1.10fr Intl. Volunteers Year	4.50	10.00	17.00	3.85	3.85
373-74	1.20fr-1.80fr World Hertiage Sites, Japan	6.00	12.50	22.00	5.50	5.00
375	same, souvenir bklt of 6 panes	....	....	....	14.00	....
376	2fr Dag Hammarskjold	3.50	7.50	15.50	3.50	3.50
377-78	90¢-1.30fr 50th Anniv. of UNPA	4.50	10.00	20.00	5.00	5.00
379	same, 3.50fr souvenir sheet	4.50	....	....	8.00	8.00
380-83	90¢ Climate Change, strip of 4	4.50	5.00	14.00	6.25	6.25
384	90¢ Nobel Peace Prize	1.95	4.00	7.00	1.65	1.65

385

400

2002

SCOTT NO.	DESCRIPTION	FIRST DAY COVERS SING	FIRST DAY COVERS INSC. BLK	INSRIP BLK-4	UNUSED F/NH	USED F
385	1.30fr Palais des Nations	2.75	6.00	10.00	2.50	2.35
386-89	90¢ Endangered Species, 4 attached	4.50	5.00	7.00	6.00	5.95
390-91	90¢-1.30fr Independence of East Timor	4.50	7.50	17.50	5.75	3.75
392-95	70¢-1.20fr Intl. Year of Mountains, 2 pairs	4.50	5.00	11.00	7.00	7.00
396-99	90¢-1.80fr Johannesburg Summit, 2 pairs	6.00	7.00	32.00	13.00	12.00
400-01	90¢-1.30fr World Heritage Sites, Italy	4.50	7.50	17.00	3.50	3.50
402	same, souvenir bklt of 6 panes of 4	....	....	....	32.00	....
403	1.30fr UNAIDS Awareness, semi postal	2.75	6.00	10.00	2.50	2.50
404	3fr Entry of Switzerland into United Nations	7.00	15.00	25.00	5.50	5.50
B1	90¢+30¢ UNAIDS Awareness, souvenir sheet	2.40	....	....	5.00	5.00

406

413

2003

SCOTT NO.	DESCRIPTION	FIRST DAY COVERS SING	FIRST DAY COVERS INSC. BLK	INSRIP BLK-4	UNUSED F/NH	USED F
405	90¢ Indigenous Art, sheet of 6	11.00	....	....	12.00	12.00
406	90¢ Interparliamentary Union	1.95	4.00	8.25	2.00	1.75
407-10	90¢ Endangered Species, 4 attached	4.50	5.00	9.00	7.50	7.00
411-12	70¢-1.30fr Intl. Year of Freshwater, 2 attached	4.25	9.50	14.00	4.00	4.00
413	1.80fr Ralph Bunche	3.75	9.50	16.00	3.50	3.50
414	85¢ In Memorium of Victims	4.50	5.00	9.00	1.75	1.75
415-16	90¢-1.30fr World Heritage Sites, United States	4.50	7.50	19.00	4.40	4.40
417	same, souvenir bklt of 6 panes of 4	....	....	....	13.00	....

429

433

2004

SCOTT NO.	DESCRIPTION	FIRST DAY COVERS SING	FIRST DAY COVERS INSC. BLK	INSRIP BLK-4	UNUSED F/NH	USED F
418-21	1fr Endangered Species, 4 attached	8.00	10.00	9.00	8.25	8.25
422	1fr Indigenous Art, sheet of 6	12.00	....	....	13.00	....
423-24	85¢-1fr Road Safety	4.25	8.00	18.00	4.00	3.80
425	1.30fr Japanese Peace Bell, 50th Anniv.	3.00	7.75	12.00	2.75	2.50
426-27	1fr-1.30fr World Heritage Sites, Greece	4.50	7.50	22.00	5.00	4.50
428	same, souvenir bklt of 6 panes of 4	....	....	....	18.50	....
429-30	85¢-1.20fr My Dream for Peace	4.25	8.00	19.00	4.00	3.75
431-32	85¢-1.30fr Human Rights	5.00	9.00	35.00(8)	4.50	4.50
433	180¢ Sports	4.50	8.50	16.00	4.00	4.00

434

440

2005

SCOTT NO.	DESCRIPTION	FIRST DAY COVERS SING	FIRST DAY COVERS INSC. BLK	INSRIP BLK-4	UNUSED F/NH	USED F
434	1.30fr U.N. 60th Anniv.	3.00	7.75	12.00	3.00	3.00
435	3fr U.N. 60th Anniv., souvenir sheet	7.00	....	....	8.00	8.00
436-39	1fr Orchids, 4 attached	8.00	10.00	9.50	8.00	8.00
440-41	1fr-1.30fr Nature's Wisdom	4.50	7.50	22.00	5.00	4.50
442-43	1fr-1.30fr International Year of Sports	4.50	7.50	22.00	5.00	4.50

444

449

SCOTT NO.	DESCRIPTION	FIRST DAY COVERS SING	FIRST DAY COVERS INSC. BLK	INSRIP BLK-4	UNUSED F/NH	USED F
444-45	1fr-1.30fr World Heritage Sites, Egypt	4.50	7.50	24.00	5.50	5.00
446	same, souvenir bklt of 6 panes	....	....	....	18.50	....
447-48	1fr-1.30fr My Dream for Peace type of 2004	4.50	7.50	22.00	5.00	4.50
449-50	1fr-1.30fr Food for life	4.50	7.50	22.00	5.00	4.50

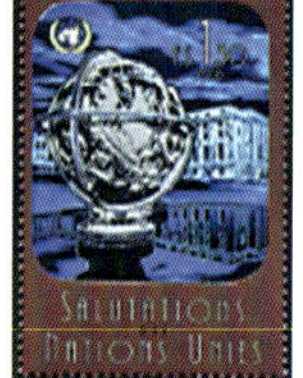

451

453

457

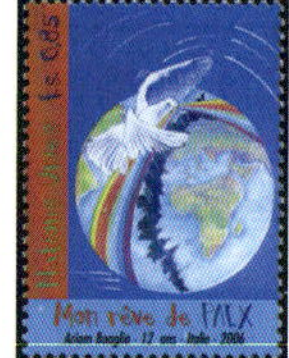

462

2006

SCOTT NO.	DESCRIPTION	FIRST DAY COVERS SING	FIRST DAY COVERS INSC. BLK	INSRIP BLK-4	UNUSED F/NH	USED F
451	1.30fr Armillary Sphere, Palais des Nations	3.50	6.50	12.00	2.75	2.60
452	1.20fr Indigenous Art, sheet of 6	15.00	....	....	15.00	15.00
453-56	1fr Endangered Species, 4 attached	8.00	10.00	9.75	8.50	8.00
457-58	1fr-1.30fr Day of Families	4.50	7.50	22.00	5.00	4.50
459-60	1fr-1.30fr World Heritage Sites, France	4.50	7.50	22.00	5.00	4.00
461	same, 20¢-50¢ souvenir bklt of 6 panes	....	....	....	18.50	....
462-63	85¢-1.20fr My Dream of Peace One Day	4.25	8.00	20.00	4.50	4.50
464	85¢ Flags and Coins, sheet of 8	15.00	....	....	18.50	18.50

465-68

2007

SCOTT NO.	DESCRIPTION	FIRST DAY COVERS SING	FIRST DAY COVERS INSC. BLK	INSRIP BLK-4	UNUSED F/NH	USED F
465-68	1fr Endangered Species, 4 attached	8.00	10.00	10.00	8.50	8.00
469	85¢ Flags and Coins, sheet of 8	15.00	....	....	16.00	16.00
470-71	1.20fr-1.80fr Peaceful Visions	6.00	8.00	31.00	8.00	8.00
472-73	1fr-1.80fr World Heritage Series, South America	6.00	8.00	24.00	5.50	5.50
474	same, 20¢-50¢ souvenir bklt of 6 panes	....	....	....	22.50	....
475	1.80fr Universal Postal Union, joint issue with Swiss Post Humanitarian Mail	4.00	7.00	11.00	4.00	4.00
476-77	1.00fr-1.80fr Space for Humanity	5.00	8.00	15.00	6.00	6.00
478	3fr Space for Humanity souvenir sheet	6.50	....	....	7.00	....

479

480-83

2008

SCOTT NO.	DESCRIPTION	FIRST DAY COVERS SING	FIRST DAY COVERS INSC. BLK	INSRIP BLK-4	UNUSED F/NH	USED F
479	85¢ Holocaust Remembrance Day	2.75	....	10.00	2.50	2.50
	same, sheet of 9	....	....	....	19.00	....
480-83	1fr Endangered Species block of 4	9.00	....	10.00	9.50	9.00
	same, pane of 16	....	....	....	35.00	....

485

487

491

SCOTT NO.	DESCRIPTION	FIRST DAY COVERS SING	FIRST DAY COVERS INSC. BLK	INSRIP BLK-4	UNUSED F/NH	USED F
484	85¢ Flags and Coins, sheet of 8	18.00			16.50	16.50
485	1 fr Handshake	3.50		11.00	2.50	2.50
486	1.80 fr Sign Language	6.00		18.00	4.50	4.50
487	1 fr Gymnast	3.50		11.00	3.00	3.00
488	1.80 fr Tennis Player	6.00		18.00	4.50	4.50
489	3 fr Gymnast, souvenir sheet	7.75			8.00	8.00
490	1 fr Childrens' Art "We Can End Poverty"	3.50		11.00	2.75	2.75
491	1.80 fr Childrens' Art "We Can End Poverty"	7.75		18.00	4.25	4.25
492	1.20 fr Climate Change, sheet of 4	12.00			12.00	12.00
493	1.80 fr Climate Change, sheet of 4	17.00			17.00	17.00
494	Climate Change, souvenir booklet				24.00	

503a

505e

2009

SCOTT NO.	DESCRIPTION	FIRST DAY COVERS SING	FIRST DAY COVERS INSC. BLK	INSRIP BLK-4	UNUSED F/NH	USED F
495	1.30 fr U Thant			14.00	3.50	3.50
496-99	1 fr Endangered Species, block of 4	3.75		10.00	9.00	
8.50						
500-01	1 fr-1.30fr World Heritage, Germany	6.75		27.00	6.00	6.00
502	World Heritage Sites, souvenir booklet				23.00	
	1 fr-180 fr Economic Social Council	5.75		24.00	8.00	7.00
503-04	85¢-1.80 fr Economic and Social Council	7.50		29.00	7.00	6.75
505	1.30 fr UN Millennium Goals, sheet of 8	21.00			23.00	
506-10	1 fr 40th Anniversary UNPA in Geneva, strip of 5 with labels				35.00	35.00
	same, sheet of two strips				68.00	
511	1.30 fr Indigenous People, sheet of 6				19.00	

2010

SCOTT NO.	DESCRIPTION	FIRST DAY COVERS SING	FIRST DAY COVERS INSC. BLK	INSRIP BLK-4	UNUSED F/NH	USED F
512	85¢ Flags & Coins, sheet of 8				16.00	16.00

512a *Equatorial Guinea* **512e** *Argentina*
512b *Loas* **512f** *Morocco*
512c *Seychelles* **512g** *Sudan*
512d *Mauritania* **512h** *Brunei*

SCOTT NO.	DESCRIPTION	FIRST DAY COVERS SING	FIRST DAY COVERS INSC. BLK	INSRIP BLK-4	UNUSED F/NH	USED F
513-16	1fr Endangered Species	8.00	11.00	12.00	9.00	9.00
517	1.60fr Arachnid	4.75	15.00	16.00	4.25	1.25
518	1.90fr Starfish	5.75	17.00	18.00	4.75	4.75

520a

524

SCOTT NO.	DESCRIPTION	FIRST DAY COVERS SING	FIRST DAY COVERS INSC. BLK	INSRIP BLK-4	UNUSED F/NH	USED F
519	85¢ One Planet, One Ocean, Sheet of 4				10.00	10.00
520	1 fr One Planet, One Ocean, sheet of 4				11.00	11.00
521	One Planet, One Ocean, souvenier bklt				23.00	
522	1.90fr UN 65th Anniversary				4.50	4.50
522a	UN 65th Anniversary S/S				10.00	10.00
523-27	1fr UN Transport	12.75		22.00	12.00	12.00
528	1.90 fr Campaign Against Child Labor, sheet of 10				36.00	36.00
529	1.30 fr Indigenous People, sheet of 6				20.00	20.00

2011

SCOTT NO.	DESCRIPTION	FIRST DAY COVERS SING	FIRST DAY COVERS INSC. BLK	INSRIP BLK-4	UNUSED F/NH	USED F
530-31	10¢-50¢ UN Headquarters	5.75		6.75	1.65	1.65
532	85¢ Flag & Coins, sheet of 8	17.50			16.00	16.00

533

SCOTT NO.	DESCRIPTION	FIRST DAY COVERS SING	FIRST DAY COVERS INSC. BLK	INSRIP BLK-4	UNUSED F/NH	USED F
533	Anniversary of Human Space Flight, sheet of 16	22.50			20.00	
534	Anniversary of Human Space Flight, S/S of 2	5.75			4.75	
535-536	85¢-1fr World Heritage Sites in Nordic Countries			22.00	5.00	5.00
	same, sheet of 20				88.00	
537	1.30fr Aids Ribbon	6.75			3.75	
	same, pane of 4				14.50	
538-39	1fr-1.30fr Economic & Social Counsil	7.50		26.00	6.50	
540-43	1fr Endangered Species	12.50		11.50	10.75	
544-45	85¢-1.40fr Intl. Year of Forests	7.25		12.00	6.75	6.00

2012

SCOTT NO.	DESCRIPTION	FIRST DAY COVERS SING	FIRST DAY COVERS INSC. BLK	INSRIP BLK-4	UNUSED F/NH	USED F
546	85¢ Flags & Coins, sheet of 8	19.50			18.00	
547-548	1.40fr Autism Awareness	8.00		16.00	7.50	7.00
549-552	1 fr Endangered Species	10.75				
553	1.40fr Conference on Sustainable Development	5.50		15.00	4.50	4.50
554-555	1fr-1.40fr Sport for Peace				6.75	6.75
555a	Sport for Peace, Souvenir Sheet				4.50	4.50
556-557	85¢-1fr UNESCO World Heritage sites in Africa	5.75		19.00	4.95	4.95
558	85¢ Indigenous People, sheet of 6	9.00			12.75	

561

562

564

2013

SCOTT NO.	DESCRIPTION	FIRST DAY COVERS SING	FIRST DAY COVERS INSC. BLK	INSRIP BLK-4	UNUSED F/NH	USED F
559-560	1.40fr-1.90fr World Radio Day	9.75		34.00	9.00	9.00
561-562	1fr-1.40fr People and Dove	8.95		25.50	6.75	6.75
563-64	1.40fr-1.90fr World Heritage Sites, China			33.00	8.50	8.50
565	World HeritageSites, China, Souvenir Booklet				25.00	

566k-566l

567

568

SCOTT NO.	DESCRIPTION	FIRST DAY COVERS SING	FIRST DAY COVERS INSC. BLK	INSRIP BLK-4	UNUSED F/NH	USED F
566	World Oceans' Day sheet of 12	27.00			26.00	26.00
566	World Oceans' Day sheet of 12	27.00			26.00	26.00
567-68	1.40fr Nebulae	8.00		15.00	7.50	7.50
569	1fr Nebulae Souvenir sheet of 1	3.75			2.75	2.75
570-71	1.40fr-1.90fr Works of disable artists	11.00		34.00	8.50	8.50
572-75	1.40fr Endangered Species	14.50		14.00	13.50	13.50
576	1.40fr Flags & Coins sheet of 8	29.00			27.00	27.00

577

583

585

2014

SCOTT NO.	DESCRIPTION	FIRST DAY COVERS SING	FIRST DAY COVERS INSC. BLK	INSRIP BLK-4	UNUSED F/NH	USED F
577-78	1fr-1.40fr International Day of Happiness	7.00		25.00	6.50	6.50
579	1fr International Year of Jazz, Sheet of 12	35.00			31.00	
580-81	2.20fr-2.60fr Definitives	14.00		50.00	13.00	13.00
582-83	1.40fr-1.90fr Taj Majal, Set of 2	9.75		35.00	9.50	9.50
584	Taj Mahal Souvenir Booklet				26.00	
585-86	1.30fr - 1.60fr International Year of Family Farming	8.75		31.00	8.50	8.50
587	1.30fr Personalized Sheet of 10 with Labels				39.00	
588	1.90fr Global Education First Initiative	6.75		20.00	5.50	5.50
589	1.90fr Global Education First Initiative Souvenir Sheet	6.75			5.50	5.50
590-93	1.40fr Endangered Species	16.00		15.00	14.50	

598

601

2015

SCOTT NO.	DESCRIPTION	FIRST DAY COVERS SING	FIRST DAY COVERS INSC. BLK	INSRIP BLK-4	UNUSED F/NH	USED F
594	90¢ Flags and Coins, sheet of 8	19.00	....	....	17.00	....
595-96	1fr - 1.40fr World Poetry Day, 2 sheets of 6	39.00	....	....	35.00	....
597-600	1.40fr Endangered Species	15.00	....	14.50	14.00	....
601-02	1.40fr - 1.90fr World Heritage Sites, Southeast Asia	10.50	....	32.00	8.25	....
603	World Heritage Souvenir Booklet	....	....	....	24.50	....

604

605

SCOTT NO.	DESCRIPTION	FIRST DAY COVERS SING	FIRST DAY COVERS INSC. BLK	INSRIP BLK-4	UNUSED F/NH	USED F
604-05	1fr - 1.40fr End Violence Against Children	8.75	....	24.00	5.95	....
606	Greetings from the United Nations, sheet of 10 plus Labels	....	....	....	39.00	....

611

613

SCOTT NO.	DESCRIPTION	FIRST DAY COVERS SING	FIRST DAY COVERS INSC. BLK	INSRIP BLK-4	UNUSED F/NH	USED F
607-10	1fr - 1.90fr UN Building	16.00	....	29.00	15.50	....
611	1.40fr Souvenir Sheet	4.75	....	....	3.75	....
612	1.40fr UN Climate Change Conference	4.75	....	14.00	3.75	....
613-14	1fr-1.50fr LGBT Equality	....	....	24.00	6.00	....

619

628b

635

2016

SCOTT NO.	DESCRIPTION	FIRST DAY COVERS SING	FIRST DAY COVERS INSC. BLK	INSRIP BLK-4	UNUSED F/NH	USED F
615-16	1fr-2fr U.N. Women-HeforShe	....	....	29.00	6.50	.....
617-18	1r-1.50fr International Dance Day, 2 sheets of 6	....	....	38.00(2)	.....	.....
619-20	1fr-1.50fr U.N Peacekeepers	....	....	24.00	6.00	.....
621-24	1fr-2fr Sports for Peace & Development, 2 pairs	....	....	28.00	15.00	.....
625-26	1fr-1.50fr World Heritage Sites, Czech Republic	....	....	24.00	6.00	.....
627	9.60fr World Heritage Sites, souvenir booklet	....	....	....	27.00	.....
628	2fr Eye on Africa, sheet of 4	....	....	....	17.00	.....
629	1fr Sustainable Development Goals, sheet of 17	....	....	40.00	40.00	.....
630-31	1fr-1.50fr International Dance Day, 2 sheets of 6	.....	.....	38.00(2)	.....	.....
632-35	1.50fr Endangered Species, block of 4	.....	.....	15.00	13.00	.....

637

644

2017

SCOTT NO.	DESCRIPTION	FIRST DAY COVERS SING	FIRST DAY COVERS INSC. BLK	INSRIP BLK-4	UNUSED F/NH	USED F
636-37	1fr-2fr World Environment Day	.....	.....	24.00	6.00	.....
638-39	1fr-1.50fr World Heritage Sites, Along the Silk Road	.....	.....	24.00	6.00	.....
640	9.60fr World Heritage Sites, souvenir booklet	.....	.....	.....	27.00	.....
641-42	1fr-2fr International Day of Peace	.....	.....	24.00	6.00	.....
643	2fr International Day of Peace	.....	.....	.....	6.00	.....
644-45	1fr-1.50fr World Food Day	.....	.....	24.00	6.00	.....

650

656

2018

SCOTT NO.	DESCRIPTION	FIRST DAY COVERS SING	FIRST DAY COVERS INSC. BLK	INSRIP BLK-4	UNUSED F/NH	USED F
646-49	1.50fr Endangered Species, block of 4	.....	.....	15.00	13.00	
650-51	1fr-2fr World Health Day	.....	.....	30.00	7.00	.....
652	1.50fr NABA Lugano 2018, sheet 10	.....	.....	38.00	.....	.....
653-54	1fr-1.50fr UNISPACE, 50th Anniv.	.....	.....	27.00	7.00	.....
655	2fr UNISPACE, souvenir sheet	.....	.....	.....	5.00	.....
656	2fr Nelson Mandela	.....	.....	.....	5.00	.....
657-58	1fr-1.50fr World Heritage Sites, United Kingdom	.....	.....	24.00	6.00	.....
659	9.60fr World Heritage Sites, prestige booklet		.....	.....	27.00	.....
660	1fr Music Day 2018, sheet of 12	.....	.....	.....	26.00	.....

663

673

2019

SCOTT NO.	DESCRIPTION	FIRST DAY COVERS SING	FIRST DAY COVERS INSC. BLK	INSRIP BLK-4	UNUSED F/NH	USED F
661	1fr International Languages, sheet of 6	.....	.....	.....	13.00	
662	1.50fr Sexual Equality, single	.....	.....	.....	4.25	.....
663-66	1.50fr Endangered Species, block of 4	.....	.....	15.00	13.00	.....
667	2.60fr World Bee Day, souvenir sheet	.....	.....	.....	6.00	.....
668-72	1fr International Labour Organization, strip of 5	.....	.....	25.00	12.00	.....
673-74	1fr-1.50fr Climate Change	.....	.....	25.00	6.00	.....
675	2fr Climate Change, souvenir sheet	.....	.....	.....	5.00	.....
676	1.50fr UNPA 50th Anniv., personalized sheet of 10	.....	.....	.....	36.00	.....
677-78	1fr-1.50fr World Heritage Sites, Cuba	.....	.....	25.00	6.00	.....
679	9.60fr World Heritage Sites, Cuba, prestige booklet	.....	.....	.....	27.00	.....

681

686

2020

SCOTT NO.	DESCRIPTION	FIRST DAY COVERS SING	FIRST DAY COVERS INSC. BLK	INSRIP BLK-4	UNUSED F/NH	USED F
680-83	1.50fr Endangered Species, block of 4	.....	.....	15.00	13.00	.....
684	2fr Hello Kitty, set of 2, souvenir sheet of 1 with labels	.....	.....	.....	10.00	.....
	same, folded booklets, ($1.20, 2fr, e1.80)	.....	.....	30.00	.....	.....
685-86	1fr-1.50fr Earth Day 2020	.....	.....	28.00	7.00	.....
687	1.70fr Eradication of Smallpx, single	.....	.....	17.00	4.50	.....
688-89	1fr-1.50fr World Heritage Sites, Russia	.....	.....	28.00	7.00	.....
690	9.60fr World Heritage Sites, Russia, prestige booklet	.....	.....	.....	27.00	.....
691	2fr U.N. 75th Anniv., souvenir sheet of 2	.....	.....	.....	10.00	.....
692	8fr U.N. Crypto Stamp, souvenir sheet	.....	.....	.....	20.00	.....

698-700

SCOTT NO.	DESCRIPTION	FIRST DAY COVERS SING	FIRST DAY COVERS INSC. BLK	INSRIP BLK-4	UNUSED F/NH	USED F
	2021					
693	2fr United Against Racism & Discrimination	.....	.....	22.00	5.75	
694-97	1.50fr Endangered Species, block of 4 ...	.....	.....	18.00	16.00	.....
698-703	1fr-1.50fr Sports for Peace, horiz strips of 4	.....	.....	70.00(2)	55.00(2)	......
704	2fr Sports for Peace, souvenir sheet.......	.....	.....	.....	10.00	......
705-06	1fr-1.50fr World Heritage, Waterways, Railways, & Bridges	.....	.....	28.00	7.00	.....
707	9.60fr World Heritage, prestige booklet...	.....	.....	.....	27.00	.....
708	1.20fr U.N. Celebrations, sheet of 10......	.....	.....	60.00	.....	.....
709	1fr World Toilet Day	.....	.....	12.00	2.75	......

710-11

SCOTT NO.	DESCRIPTION	FIRST DAY COVERS SING	FIRST DAY COVERS INSC. BLK	INSRIP BLK-4	UNUSED F/NH	USED F
	2022					
710-13	1.10fr-2fr Sports for Peace, pairs	.....	.....	47.00(2)	16.00(2)	.....
714-17	1.50fr Endangered Species, block of 4 ...	.....	.....	18.00	16.00	.....
718-19	1.10fr-1.50fr Exploration of Mars............	10.00	.....	65.00(2)	7.00	.....
720	2fr Exploration of Mars, souvenir sheet...	6.00	.....	.....	6.00	......
721	1.50fr World Bicycle Days, sheet of 10 ...	.....	.....	45.00	.....	.....
722-23	1.10fr-1.50fr World Heritage, European Spa Towns	.....	.....	28.00(2)	7.00	.....
724	9.60fr World Heritage, prestige booklet...	.....	.....	.....	27.00	.....
725	3.80fr Crypto, souvenir sheet	.....	.....	10.00	.....	.....

727

741

SCOTT NO.	DESCRIPTION	FIRST DAY COVERS SING	FIRST DAY COVERS INSC. BLK	INSRIP BLK-4	UNUSED F/NH	USED F
	2023					
726-29	1.80fr Endangered Species, block of 4 ...	.....	.....	19.00	17.00	.....
730-31	1.10fr-2.30fr World Art Day.....................	15.00	.....	35.00(2)	7.50	.....
732	1.10fr International Tea Day, sheet of 10.	.....	.....	36.00	.....	.....
733	1.10fr World Oceans Day, sheet of 9	30.00	.....	25.00	.....	.....
734	2.30fr "Don't Choose Extinction", souvenir sheet...	10.00	.....	6.00	.....	.....
735	1.10fr Calligraphy, Body, Mind & Soul	5.00	.....	13.50	3.00	.....
736	2.30fr Calligraphy, Body, Mind & Soul, souvenir sheet...	8.00	.....	6.00	.....	.....
737-38	1.10fr-1.80fr World Heritage, Turkey......	.....	.....	30.00(2)	7.00	.....
739	9.60fr World Heritage, Turkey, prestige booklet...	.....	.....	.....	28.00	.....
740	1.80fr World Mental Health Day	7.00	.....	18.00	5.00	.....
741	2.30fr Marie Curie, Physicist and Chemist	9.00	.....	25.00	6.50	.....

*Scott numbers and prices are subject to change in the next edition.

SEMI-POSTAL

SCOTT NO.	DESCRIPTION	FIRST DAY COVERS SING	FIRST DAY COVERS INSC. BLK	INSRIP BLK-4	UNUSED F/NH	USED F
	2002					
B1	90¢ + 30¢ AIDS Awareness, souv. sheet	.....	....	....	5.75	.....
	2021					
B2	1.30fr + 50¢ John Lennon	.....	.....	22.00	5.75	.....
B3	$2.60 + $1 John Lennon, souvenir sheet	.....	.....	.....	10.50	.....
	2022					
B4	2fr + 50¢ World Humanitarian Day........	.....	60.00	6.00	.....	

AIR LETTER SHEETS & POSTAL CARDS

SCOTT NO.	DESCRIPTION	UNUSED F/NH	USED F
	1969		
UC1	65¢ ultramarine & light blue	4.50	1.90
	1969		
UX1	20¢ olive green & black...	1.65	.50
UX2	30¢ violet blue, blue, light & dark green......................	1.65	.70

UX3

UX4

SCOTT NO.	DESCRIPTION	UNUSED F/NH	USED F
	1977		
UX3	40¢ multicolored...	1.25	.75
UX4	70¢ multicolored...	1.65	1.35

UX5

UX6

SCOTT NO.	DESCRIPTION	UNUSED F/NH	USED F
	1985		
UX5	50¢ Six languages	1.25	6.00
UX6	70¢ Birds & Rainbow	1.65	5.25

UX7

UX10

SCOTT NO.	DESCRIPTION	UNUSED F/NH	USED F
	1986		
UX7	70¢+10¢ Surcharge on UX6	8.00	3.65
	1992-93		
UX8	90¢ U.N. Buildings	1.75	3.00
UX9	50¢ + 10¢ Surcharge on UX5	1.75	3.00
UX10	80¢ Postal Card	1.75	3.50

UX11

UX12

SCOTT NO.	DESCRIPTION	UNUSED F/NH	USED F
	1997		
UX11	50¢+20¢ Surcharge on UX5	1.75	3.75
UX12	80¢+30¢ Surcharge on UX10	2.00	3.75

UX13

UX14

SCOTT NO.	DESCRIPTION	UNUSED F/NH	USED F
	1998		
UX13	70¢ Assembly Hall	2.00	3.25
UX14	1.10fr Palais des Nations	2.50	3.50
	2001		
UX15	1.30fr Palais des Nations	2.75	3.50
UX16	70¢+15¢ Surcharge on UX13	2.10	2.25
UX17	90¢+10¢ Surcharge on UX8	2.50	2.50
UX18	1.10fr+10¢ Surcharge on UX14	2.75	3.75
UX19	85¢ Ceiling Sculpture..	2.95	2.50
UX20	1 fr Broken Chair Memorial..	2.95	3.00
UX21	1.80 fr League of Nations Building................................	3.95	5.00

UNITED NATIONS: OFFICES IN VIENNA, AUSTRIA

Denominations in Austrian Currency

NOTE: Unless illustrated, designs can be assumed to be similar to the equivalent New York or Geneva issue

3  5  9  19  24  37  38  40  41  42  43

SCOTT NO.	DESCRIPTION	FIRST DAY COVERS SING	FIRST DAY COVERS INSC. BLK	INSRIP BLK-4	UNUSED F/NH	USED F
	1979					
1-6	50g to 10s Definitives	6.75	16.95	10.00	2.25	2.50
	1980					
7/16	**1980 Issues, (9) (No #14)**	......	......	......	**6.50**	.....
7	4s International Economic Order	3.75	9.50	11.50	1.25	1.20
8	2.50s International Economic Definitive	1.85	2.15	(B)8.75	.80	.70
9-10	4s & 6s Decade for Women	3.10	7.75	6.50	1.50	1.40
11	6s Peacekeeping	1.95	4.85	5.25	1.15	1.05
12-13	4s & 6s 35th Anniversary	3.15	7.85	6.50	1.25	1.40
14	same, souvenir sheet	3.85	......	......	1.40	1.40
15-16	4s & 6s Economic and Social Council	2.35	5.85	6.50	1.40	1.20
	1981					
17-23	**1981 Issues, complete (7)**	......	......	......	**5.65**	......
17	4s Palestinian People	1.55	3.85	3.75	.85	.75
18-19	4s & 6s Disabled Persons	2.40	6.00	5.50	1.50	1.50
20	6s Fresco	1.45	3.65	4.40	1.00	1.50
21	7.50s Sources of Energy	1.95	4.85	3.95	1.00	1.00
22-23	5s & 7s Volunteers Program	2.75	6.85	7.75	1.75	1.75
	1982					
24-29	**1982 Issues, complete (6)**	......	......	......	**4.85**	......
24	3s Definitive	.85	2.15	3.00	.65	.45
25-26	5s & 7s Human Environment	2.50	6.25	9.00	1.95	1.75
27	5s Space Exploration	1.25	3.15	3.95	.85	.85
28-29	5s & 7s Nature Conservation	2.50	6.25	7.75	1.75	1.75
	1983					
30-38	**1983 Issues, complete (9)**	......	......	......	**7.00**	......
30	4s World Communications	.85	2.15	3.95	.85	.55
31-32	4s & 6s Safety at Sea	2.15	5.35	6.15	1.40	1.40
33-34	5s & 7s World Food Program	2.60	6.50	7.00	1.75	1.65
35-36	4s & 8.50s Trade & Develop.	2.75	6.95	8.95	1.95	1.85
37-38	5s & 7s Human Rights	3.15	7.85	8.95	1.95	1.85
	1984					
39-47	**1984 Issues, complete (9)**	....	....	......	**8.55**	....
39	7s Population	1.40	3.50	4.50	1.00	.95
40-41	4.50s & 6s Food Day	1.85	4.65	7.25	1.50	1.50
42-43	3.50s & 15s Heritage	3.50	8.75	10.50	2.50	2.25
44-45	4.50s & 8.50s Future for Refugees	2.25	5.65	10.50	2.25	1.75
46-47	3.50s & 6.50s Youth Year	1.80	4.50	9.00	2.00	1.65
	1985					
48/56	**1985 Issues, (8) (No #54)**	......	......	......	**10.90**	......
48	7.50s I.L.O. Turin Centre	1.25	3.15	5.50	1.40	1.00
49	8.50s U.N. University	1.35	3.40	5.50	1.50	1.10
50-51	4.50s & 15s Definitives	3.15	7.95	13.75	3.25	2.35
52-53	6.50s & 8.50s 40th Anniversary	2.50	6.25	12.00	3.00	3.50
54	Same, Souvenir Sheet	3.25	......	......	3.00	2.90
55-56	4s-6s Child Survival	2.15	5.40	13.00	3.00	2.85

SCOTT NO.	DESCRIPTION	FIRST DAY COVERS SING	FIRST DAY COVERS INSC. BLK	INSRIP BLK-4	UNUSED F/NH	USED F
	1986					
57-65	**1986 Issues (9)**	......	......	......	**17.00**	......
57	8s Africa in Crisis	1.35	3.40	6.00	1.50	.90
58-61	4.50s Development, 4 varieties, attached	3.05	7.65	13.00	12.00	2.25
62-63	3.50s & 6.50s Philately	1.95	4.95	9.75	2.00	1.15
64-65	5s & 6s Peace Year	2.25	5.65	12.00	2.50	1.95
66	4s to 7s WFUNA, souvenir sheet	3.05	......	......	5.50	5.00
	1987					
67-77	**1987 Issues (11)**	......	......	......	**13.40**	....
67	8s Trygve Lie	1.35	3.40	6.00	1.10	1.00
68-69	4s & 9.50s Shelter Homeless	2.35	5.95	10.00	2.25	2.00
70-71	5s & 8s Anti-Drug Campaign	2.25	5.65	8.00	2.25	2.00
72-73	2s & 17s Definitives	3.45	8.65	11.00	2.75	2.25
74-75	5s & 6s United Nations Day	2.25	5.65	10.00	2.75	2.50
76-77	4s & 9.50s Child Immunization	2.35	5.95	14.00	3.00	3.00
	1988					
78/86	**1988 Issues, (7) (No #80-81, 87)**	....	....	....	**13.00**	....
78-79	4s & 6s World Without Hunger	2.25	5.65	8.00	2.00	1.50
				Sheetlets		
80-81	4s & 5s Forest Conservation	22.50	65.00	18.00	8.00	8.00
	(set of 6, includes NY and Geneva)			130.00	35.00	25.00
82-83	6s & 7.50s Volunteer Day	2.35	5.95	12.00	2.75	2.00
84-85	6s & 8s Health in Sports	2.50	6.25	14.50	3.25	2.00
86	5s Human Rights 40th Anniversary ...	1.00	2.50	4.00	1.50	1.50
87	11s Human Rights 40th Anniversary souvenir sheet	1.75	....	....	3.00	2.25
	1989					
88-96	**1989 Issues (9)**	....	....	....	**18.75**	....
88-89	5.50s & 8s World Bank	2.35	5.95	16.50	3.50	3.00
90	6s Nobel Peace Prize	1.25	3.15	6.75	1.35	1.00
91-92	4s & 9.50s World Weather Watch	2.35	5.95	19.50	4.00	3.50
93-94	5s & 7.50s UN Office in Vienna	2.25	5.65	24.00	5.50	5.00
				Sheetlets(12)		
95-96	4s & 6s Human Rights, 40th Ann. (strips of 3 w/tabs)	2.25	5.65	25.00	5.50	....
	1990					
97/109	**1990 Issues, (12) (No #105)**	....	....	....	**27.95**	....
97	12s Int'l. Trade Center	2.15	5.40	8.00	2.00	1.50
98	1.50s Definitive	.85	2.15	1.80	.40	.30
99-100	5s & 11s AIDS	2.75	6.95	18.00	4.25	3.00
101-02	4.50s & 9.50s Medicinal Plants	2.50	6.25	21.00	4.50	3.00
103-04	7s & 9s 45th Anniv. of U.N.	2.75	6.95	21.00	4.50	3.50
105	same, souvenir sheet	2.75	......	......	7.75	6.00
106-07	6s & 8s Crime Prevention	2.50	6.25	18.00	4.00	3.25
				Sheetlets(12)		
108-09	4.50s & 7s Human Rights (strips of 3 w/tabs)	2.35	5.95	30.00	7.00	....

44  45  46  50  51  64  72  73  93  94  98  116  117  137  118  119  120  138

149

167

168

169

193

194

195

196-99

200-04

1991

SCOTT NO.	DESCRIPTION	FIRST DAY COVERS SING	FIRST DAY COVERS INSC. BLK	INSRIP BLK-4	UNUSED F/NH	USED F
110-24	**1991 Issues, (15)**	....	....	....	**29.50**	....
110-13	5s Econ. Comm. for Europe, 4 varieties, attached	5.50	13.75	6.50	5.75	5.50
114-15	6s & 9.50s Namibia—A New Nation	4.50	11.25	23.00	5.00	5.00
116	20s Definitive Issue	4.75	11.85	16.00	3.75	3.00
117-18	7s & 9s Children's Rights	4.50	11.25	18.00	4.00	3.00
119-20	5s & 10s Chemical Weapons	4.75	11.95	22.00	5.00	5.00
121-22	5s & 8s 40th Anniv. of U.N.P.A.	4.15	10.35	15.00	3.50	3.00
				Sheetlets (12)		
123-24	4.50s & 7s Human Rights (strips of 3 w/tabs)	2.50	6.25	39.00	8.50	
....						

1992

SCOTT NO.	DESCRIPTION	FIRST DAY COVERS SING	FIRST DAY COVERS INSC. BLK	INSRIP BLK-4	UNUSED F/NH	USED F
125-40	**1992 Issues, (17)**	....	....	....	**32.00**	....
125-26	5s-9s World Heritage—UNESCO	4.25	10.75	18.00	3.50	3.00
127-28	7s Clean Oceans, 2 varieties, attached	4.25	5.50	7.50	3.00	2.50
129-32	5.50s Earth Summit, 4 varieties, attached		4.25	8.95	8.50	7.00
5.00						
133-34	10s Mission to Planet Earth, 2 varieties, attached	4.25	5.50	16.00	7.00	6.50
135-36	5.50s-7s Science & Technology	4.00	10.25	13.00	2.75	2.25
137-38	5.50s-7s Definitives	4.00	10.25	13.00	2.75	2.50
				Sheetlets (12)		
139-40	6s-10s Human Rights (strips of 3 w/tabs)	2.75	6.95	38.00	10.00	....

1993

SCOTT NO.	DESCRIPTION	FIRST DAY COVERS SING	FIRST DAY COVERS INSC. BLK	INSRIP BLK-4	UNUSED F/NH	USED F
141-59	**1993 Issues, (19)**	....	....	....	**35.00**	....
141-42	5.50s-7s Aging	4.00	10.25	12.00	2.50	2.25
143-46	7s Endangered Species, 4 attached	5.00	6.00	7.50	6.00	5.50
147-48	6s-10s Healthy Environment	4.00	11.50	17.50	4.00	3.00
149	13s Definitive	4.00	10.25	12.50	3.50	3.50
				Sheetlets (12)		
150-51	5s-6s Human Rights	3.00	7.00	40.00	10.00	....
152-55	5.50s Peace, 4 attached (strips of 3 w/tabs)	2.50	6.00	11.00	9.00	9.00
156-59	7s Environment—Climate, strip of 4	4.00	7.00	22.00(8)	9.75	9.75

1994

SCOTT NO.	DESCRIPTION	FIRST DAY COVERS SING	FIRST DAY COVERS INSC. BLK	INSRIP BLK-4	UNUSED F/NH	USED F
160-77	**1994 Issues (18)**	....	....	....	**33.00**	....
160-61	5.50s-8s Intl. Year of the Family	3.00	10.75	16.00	3.50	3.25
162-65	7s Endangered Species, 4 attached	6.25	7.50	7.50	6.50	6.50
166	12s Refugees	3.50	12.00	9.00	2.25	1.75
167-69	50g-30s Definitives (3)	8.50	33.50	32.50	7.00	7.00
170-73	6s Intl. Decade for Natural Disaster Reduction, 4 attached	5.50	6.50	10.00	9.00	8.50
174-75	5.50s-7s Population and Development	3.00	10.25	17.00	4.00	3.50
176-77	6s-7s Development through Partnership	3.50	10.25	16.00	3.50	3.50

1995

SCOTT NO.	DESCRIPTION	FIRST DAY COVERS SING	FIRST DAY COVERS INSC. BLK	INSRIP BLK-4	UNUSED F/NH	USED F
178/91	**1995 Issues (13) (No #188)**	....	....	....	**53.95**	....
178	7s 50th Anniversary of the UN	2.00	7.25	8.00	1.75	1.75
179	14s Social Summit	3.50	12.50	14.00	3.00	3.00
180-83	7s Endangered Species, 4 attached	6.25	7.50	8.00	7.00	6.50
184-85	6s-7s Youth: Our Future	3.50	10.25	18.00	4.00	4.00
186-87	7s-10s 50th Anniversary of the UN	4.00	11.50	19.00	4.00	4.00
188	17s 50th Anniversary of the UN, souvenir sheet	3.50	....	....	6.00	6.00
189-90	5.50s-6s 4th World Conference on Women	3.25	10.50	19.00	4.00	4.00
191	3s 50thAnniversary, min. sheet of 12	....	....	....	23.00	....
192	same, souvenir booklet of 4 panes of 3	....	....	....	28.00	....

1996

SCOTT NO.	DESCRIPTION	FIRST DAY COVERS SING	FIRST DAY COVERS INSC. BLK	INSRIP BLK-4	UNUSED F/NH	USED F
193/211	**1996 Issues (18) (No 207)**	....	....	....	**27.50**	....
193	7s WFUNA 50th Anniversary	2.00	7.25	8.00	1.60	1.35
194-95	1s-10s Definitives	3.25	10.50	10.50	2.50	2.25
196-99	7s Endangered Species, 4 attached	6.25	7.50	8.00	7.00	6.00
200-04	6s City Summit (Habitat II), strip of 5	6.75	16.50	28.00	10.00	10.00
205-06	6s-7s Sport & the Environment	3.50	10.25	16.00	3.00	3.00
207	13s Sport & theEnvrinronment souvenir sheet	3.25	....	....	3.50	3.00
208-09	7s-10s A Plea for Peace	4.00	11.50	18.00	3.50	5.50
210-11	5.5s-8s UNICEF 50th Anniversary	3.50	10.25	11.50	3.00	3.00

207

208

209

210

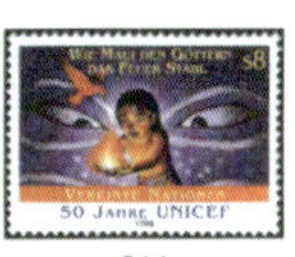
211

218-21

214-17

212

228

230

223-27

1997

SCOTT NO.	DESCRIPTION	FIRST DAY COVERS SING	FIRST DAY COVERS INSC. BLK	INSRIP BLK-4	UNUSED F/NH	USED F
212/31	**1997 Issues (19) (No. #222)**	....	....	....	**27.50**	....
212-13	5s-6s Definitives	3.25	10.50	10.50	2.50	2.25
214-17	7s Endangered Species, 4 attached	6.25	7.50	8.00	7.00	6.00
218-21	3.5s Earth Summit +5, 4 attached	3.25	3.75	7.00	5.50	5.00
222	11s Earth Summit +5, souvenir sheet	2.50	....	....	3.50	3.50
223-27	7s Transportation, strip of 5	6.75	9.50	16.00(10)	7.00	7.00
228-29	6.50s-7s Tribute to Philately	3.50	10.25	15.00	3.50	3.00
230-31	3s-6s Terracota Warriors	2.75	8.25	16.00	3.50	3.50
232	same, Souvenir bklt of 6 panes of 4	....	....	....	14.00	....

233

239a

1998

SCOTT NO.	DESCRIPTION	FIRST DAY COVERS SING	FIRST DAY COVERS INSC. BLK	INSRIP BLK-4	UNUSED F/NH	USED F
233-34	6.50-9s Definitives	3.75	8.00	15.00	3.00	3.00
235-38	7s Endangered Species, 4 attached	6.25	7.50	7.00	6.00	5.50
239	3.50s Intl. Year of the Ocean, sheetlet of 12	15.00	....	16.00	16.00	....
240	6.50s Rain Forest, Ocelot	2.00	4.50	6.75	1.50	1.25
241	22s Rain Forests, Ocelot, souvenir sheet	6.50	....	4.50	4.50	4.00
242-43	4s-7.50s 50 Years of Peacekeeping	3.25	7.00	11.00	2.50	2.25
244-245	4.40s-7s 50th of the Dec. of Human Rights	3.25	7.00	11.00	2.50	2.25
246-47	3.50s-7s Schonbrunn Palace	3.25	7.00	8.25	1.95	1.95
248	33s Schonbrunn Palace booklet	....	....	....	18.00	....

249

253-56

1999

SCOTT NO.	DESCRIPTION	FIRST DAY COVERS SING	FIRST DAY COVERS INSC. BLK	INSRIP BLK-4	UNUSED F/NH	USED F
249	8s Definitives	2.50	6.75	9.50	2.25	2.25
250-51	4.50s-6.50s World Heritage Sites, Australia	3.00	6.50	11.00	2.50	2.35
252	same, souvenir bklt of 6 panes	....	....	....	10.50	....
253-56	7s Endangered Species, 4 attached	6.25	7.50	7.00	6.00	5.50
257-58	3.50s Unispace III Conference	1.95	4.50	5.50	2.00	2.00
259	13s Unispace III Conference, souvenir sheet	3.50	....	....	5.00	5.00
260-63	6.50s Universal Postal Union	2.00	4.50	6.75	5.00	5.00

264

266

SCOTT NO.	DESCRIPTION	FIRST DAY COVERS SING	FIRST DAY COVERS INSC. BLK	INSRIP BLK-4	UNUSED F/NH	USED F
264	3.50s In Memorium	1.95	4.50	5.50	1.25	1.25
265	14s In Memorium	3.50	....	....	3.00	3.00
266-67	7s-13s Education-Keystone to the 21st Century	5.00	11.50	18.00	4.75	4.00

268

273

2000

SCOTT NO.	DESCRIPTION	FIRST DAY COVERS SING	FIRST DAY COVERS INSC. BLK	INSRIP BLK-4	UNUSED F/NH	USED F
268	7s International Year of Thanksgiving	1.95	4.50	7.00	1.50	1.50
269-72	7s Endangered Species, 4 attached	6.25	7.50	7.00	6.00	5.50
273-74	7s-8s Our World 2000	4.50	10.50	15.00	4.00	3.00

275

288

SCOTT NO.	DESCRIPTION	FIRST DAY COVERS SING	FIRST DAY COVERS INSC. BLK	INSRIP BLK-4	UNUSED F/NH	USED F
275-76	7s-9s 55th Anniversary of the UN	4.50	10.50	15.00	4.00	4.00
277	same, 7s-9s souvenir sheet	....	....	....	4.00	4.00
278	3.50s United Nations in the 21st Century	1.75	4.50	....	6.75	6.75
279-80	4.50s-6.50s World Heritage Series, Spain	3.00	6.50	10.00	2.35	2.25
281	same, souvenir bklt of 6 panes	....	....	....	11.00	....
282	7s Respect for Refugees	1.95	4.50	6.50	1.50	1.50
283	25s Respect for Refugees, souvenir sheet	7.00	....	....	5.50	5.50

2001

SCOTT NO.	DESCRIPTION	FIRST DAY COVERS SING	FIRST DAY COVERS INSC. BLK	INSRIP BLK-4	UNUSED F/NH	USED F
284-87	7s Endangered Species, 4 attached	6.25	7.50	7.00	6.00	5.50
288-89	10s-12s Intl. Volunteers Year	5.50	12.50	21.00	5.00	5.00
290-91	7s-15s World Heritage Sites, Japan	5.50	12.50	22.00	5.00	5.00

293

294

SCOTT NO.	DESCRIPTION	FIRST DAY COVERS SING	FIRST DAY COVERS INSC. BLK	INSRIP BLK-4	UNUSED F/NH	USED F
292	36s World Heritage Sites, Japan Prestige Booklet	....	....	....	14.00	....
293	7s Dag Hammarskjold	1.95	4.50	6.50	1.50	1.50
294-95	7s-8s 50th Anniv. of the UNPA	4.50	10.50	12.00	4.00	3.00
296	same, 28s souvenir sheet	7.50	....	....	5.50	5.00
297-300	7s Climate Change, strip of 4	6.25	7.50	12.50	6.00	5.50
301	7s Nobel Peace Prize	1.95	4.50	6.00	1.25	1.25

302

312

2002

SCOTT NO.	DESCRIPTION	FIRST DAY COVERS SING	FIRST DAY COVERS INSC. BLK	INSRIP BLK-4	UNUSED F/NH	USED F
302-07	e0.07-e2.03 Austrian Tourist Attractions	5.50	15.00	52.00	11.00	11.00
308-11	e0.51 Endangered Species, 4 attached	5.00	6.00	7.00	6.00	6.00
312-13	e0.51-1.09 Independence of East Timor	3.50	8.00	19.00	4.00	4.00
314-17	e0.22-0.51 Intl. Year of Mountains, 2 pairs	3.50	4.50	19.00	5.50	5.50
318-21	e0.51-0.58 Johannesburg Summit, 2 pairs	4.50	5.50	8.00	7.00	6.50

322

SCOTT NO.	DESCRIPTION	FIRST DAY COVERS SING	FIRST DAY COVERS INSC. BLK	INSRIP BLK-4	UNUSED F/NH	USED F
322-23	e0.51-0.58 World Heritage Sites, Italy	2.25	7.00	14.00	3.00	3.50
324	same, souvenir bklt of 6 panes of 4	....	....	....	20.00	....
325	e0.51-0.25 UNAIDS Awareness, souvenir sheet	2.25	....	....	5.00	5.00

327

333-34

2003

SCOTT NO.	DESCRIPTION	FIRST DAY COVERS SING	FIRST DAY COVERS INSC. BLK	INSRIP BLK-4	UNUSED F/NH	USED F
326	e0.51 Indigenous Art, sheet of 6	9.50	....	....	10.00	10.00
327-28	e0.25-e1.00 Austrian Tourist Attractions	2.50	7.50	16.00	3.50	3.50
329-32	e0.51 Endangered Species, 4 attached	5.00	6.00	7.00	6.00	6.00
333-34	e0.55-e0.75 Intl. Year of Freshwater, 2 attach	2.50	8.00	12.00	5.50	5.50

335

341

SCOTT NO.	DESCRIPTION	FIRST DAY COVERS SING	FIRST DAY COVERS INSC. BLK	INSRIP BLK-4	UNUSED F/NH	USED F
335	e0.04 Schloss Eggenberg, Graz	1.75	4.50	4.50	1.00	.75
336	e2.10 Ralphe Bunche	3.75	9.50	28.00	6.00	6.00
337	e2.10 In Memoriam , UN Complex Bomding in Iraq	3.75	9.50	28.00	6.00	6.00
338-39	e0.51-e0.75 World Heritage Sites, United States	2.50	17.00	18.00	4.00	4.00
340	same, souvenir bklt of 6 panes of 4	....	....	....	14.00	....

353

355

2004

SCOTT NO.	DESCRIPTION	FIRST DAY COVERS SING	FIRST DAY COVERS INSC. BLK	INSRIP BLK-4	UNUSED F/NH	USED F
341	e0.55 Schloss Schonbrunn, Vienna	2.10	4.00	7.50	1.75	.85
342-45	e0.55 Endangered Species, 4 attached	7.00	9.00	7.00	6.50	6.50
346	e0.55 Indigenous Art, sheet of 6	10.50	....	....	11.00	11.00
347-48	e0.55-e0.75 Road Safety	2.50	8.00	18.00	4.00	4.00
349	e2.10 Japanese Peace Bell, 50th Anniv.	3.75	9.50	29.00	6.75	6.75
350-51	e0.55-e0.75 World Heritage Sites, Greece	2.50	8.00	17.50	4.00	4.00
352	same, souvenir bklt of 6 panes of 4	....	....	....	21.00	....
353-54	e0.55-e1.00 My Dream for Peace	2.75	8.50	22.00	4.50	4.50
355-56	e0.55-e1.25 Human Rights	3.25	....	....	5.75	5.50

357

360

366

2005

SCOTT NO.	DESCRIPTION	FIRST DAY COVERS SING	FIRST DAY COVERS INSC. BLK	INSRIP BLK-4	UNUSED F/NH	USED F
357	e0.55 U.N. 60th Anniv.	2.10	4.00	10.00	2.25	2.25
358	e2.10 U.N. 60th Anniv.	3.75	....	....	6.75	6.75
359	e0.75 Definitive	2.35	5.00	11.00	2.50	2.50
360-63	e0.55 Orchids, 4 attached	7.00	9.00	7.75	7.00	6.50
364-65	e0.55-e0.75 Nature's Wisdom	2.50	8.00	19.00	4.00	4.00
366-67	e0.55-e1.10 International Year of Sports	2.75	8.50	27.00	6.00	6.00

368

371

373

SCOTT NO.	DESCRIPTION	FIRST DAY COVERS SING	FIRST DAY COVERS INSC. BLK	INSRIP BLK-4	UNUSED F/NH	USED F
368-69	e0.55-e0.75 World Heritage Sites, Egypt	2.50	8.00	21.00	4.00	5.00
370	same, souvenir bklt of 6 panes of 4	....	....	....	23.00	....
371-72	e0.55-e1.00 My Dream for Peace, type of 2004	2.75	8.50	22.50	5.00	5.00
373-74	e0.55-e1.25 Food for Life	2.75	8.50	26.50	6.00	6.00

376

380

382

2006

SCOTT NO.	DESCRIPTION	FIRST DAY COVERS SING	FIRST DAY COVERS INSC. BLK	INSRIP BLK-4	UNUSED F/NH	USED F
375	e0.55 Indigenous Art, sheet of 6	11.50	....	....	11.00	11.00
376-79	e0.55 Endangered Species, 4 attached	7.00	9.00	8.50	7.25	6.75
380-81	e0.55-e1.25 Day of Families	2.75	8.50	28.00	6.00	6.00
382-83	e0.55-e0.75 World Heritage Sites, France	2.50	8.00	20.00	4.50	4.00
384	same, souvenir bklt of 6 panes of 4	....	....	....	22.00	....

385

387a

SCOTT NO.	DESCRIPTION	FIRST DAY COVERS SING	FIRST DAY COVERS INSC. BLK	INSRIP BLK-4	UNUSED F/NH	USED F
385-86	e0.55-e1.00 My Dream for Peace One Day	2.75	8.50	24.00	5.75	5.75
387	e0.55 Flags and Coins, sheet of 8	15.00	....	....	18.00	18.00

388-91

2007

SCOTT NO.	DESCRIPTION	FIRST DAY COVERS SING	FIRST DAY COVERS INSC. BLK	INSRIP BLK-4	UNUSED F/NH	USED F
388-91	e0.55 Endangered Species, 4 attached	7.00	9.00	8.00	7.00	6.50
392	e0.55 Flags and Coins, sheet of 8	15.00	....	....	14.00	14.00
393-97	e0.55 UN Headquarters + labels, strip of 5	....	....	....	48.00	....
....	same, sheet of 2 (393-97)	....	....	....	100.00	....
398-99	e0.55-e1.25 Peaceful Visions	5.00	6.25	31.00	8.00	8.00
400-01	e0.55-e0.75 World Heritage Sites, South America	2.50	8.00	22.00	5.00	5.00
....	e0.75 Universal Postal Union, joint issue with					
402	same, booklet of 6 panes of 4	....	....	....	24.00	....
403	e0.75 UPU, joint issue with Swiss Post Humanitarian Mail	2.50	5.00	9.00	2.00	2.00
404-08	Space, vert. strip of 5 + labels	....	....	....	48.00	....
	same, sheet of 10 + labels	....	....	....	100.00	....
409-10	65¢+e1.15 Space for Humanity, set of 2	12.75	....	24.00	8.00	8.00
	same, 2 sheets of 6	....	....	....	38.00	....
411	e2.10 Space for Humanity souvenir sheet	7.25	....	....	7.00	7.00

414

415

412

2008

SCOTT NO.	DESCRIPTION	FIRST DAY COVERS SING	FIRST DAY COVERS INSC. BLK	INSRIP BLK-4	UNUSED F/NH	USED F
412	65¢ International Holocaust Remembrance Day	3.25	....	11.00	2.50	2.50
	same, sheet of 9	....	....	....	22.00	....
413-16	Sculptures	....	....	42.00	9.00	9.00
413	10¢ Johann Strauss Memorial, Vienna	1.25	....	1.50	.60	.60
	same, pane of 20	....	....	....	7.50	....
414	15¢ Pallas Athene Fountain, Vienna	1.25	....	2.50	.95	.95
	same, pane of 20	....	....	....	11.00	....
415	65¢ Pegasus Fountain, Saizburg	3.50	....	9.50	3.00	3.00
	same, pane of 20	....	....	....	46.00	....
416	e1.40 Statue, Beledere Palace Gardens, Vienna	7.50	....	20.00	6.00	6.00
	same, pane of 20	....	....	....	97.00	....

417-20

SCOTT NO.	DESCRIPTION	FIRST DAY COVERS SING	FIRST DAY COVERS INSC. BLK	INSRIP BLK-4	UNUSED F/NH	USED F
417-20	65¢ Endangered Species block of 4	9.00	....	12.00	9.00	9.00
	same, pane of 16	....	....	....	45.00	....

428

429

433

SCOTT NO.	DESCRIPTION	FIRST DAY COVERS SING	FIRST DAY COVERS INSC. BLK	INSRIP BLK-4	UNUSED F/NH	USED F
421	65¢ Flags and Coins, sheet of 8	21.00	....	....	4.00	21.00
422-26	UN Personalized, strip of 5 w/labels	....	....	....	45.00	....
427-428	55¢-1.40e Disabled Persons and Sport for Peace	12.00	....	35.00	8.00	8.50
429-430	65¢-1.30e Man On Rings and Swimmer	12.00	....	31.00	7.50	7.50
431	2.10e Man On Rings, souvenir sheet	9.00	....	....	9.00	9.00
432-433	65¢- 75¢ Childrens' Art "We Can End Poverty"	8.00	....	24.00	6.00	6.00
434	65¢ Climate Change, sheet of 4	10.00	....	....	11.00	11.00
435	1.15e Climate Change, sheet of 4	18.00	....	....	18.00	18.00
436	Climate Change, souvenir booklet	....	....	....	30.00	....

444b

446

2009

SCOTT NO.	DESCRIPTION	FIRST DAY COVERS SING	FIRST DAY COVERS INSC. BLK	INSRIP BLK-4	UNUSED F/NH	USED F
437	1.15e U Thant	....	....	15.00	3.75	3.75
438-41	65¢ Endangered Species, block of 4	4.50	....	10.00	8.50	8.50
442-43	65¢-1.40e World Heritage Sites, Germany	7.95	....	32.00	7.00	7.00
444	World Heritage Sites, souvenir booklet	....	....	....	28.00	....
445-449	65¢ Personalized Stamp, strip of 5 with labels	....	....	....	17.00	17.00
	same, sheet	....	....	....	35.00	....
450-51	55¢-75¢ Economic/Social Council	7.95	....	20.00	4.50	4.50

454

457h

471

SCOTT NO.	DESCRIPTION	FIRST DAY COVERS SING	FIRST DAY COVERS INSC. BLK	INSRIP BLK-4	UNUSED F/NH	USED F
452-56	e1.40 Personalized, strip of 5 with labels	....	....	....	38.00	....
	same, sheet of 10	....	....	....	80.00	....
457	65¢ UN Millennium Goals, sheet of 8	19.50	....	....	17.00	....
458	65¢ Indigenous People, sheet of 6	....	....	....	15.00	....

2010

SCOTT NO.	DESCRIPTION	FIRST DAY COVERS SING	FIRST DAY COVERS INSC. BLK	INSRIP BLK-4	UNUSED F/NH	USED F
459	65¢ Flags & Coins, sheet of 8	....	....	....	19.00	19.00

459a *Romania* **459b** *Slovenia* **459c** *Azerbaijan* **459d** *Bangladesh*
459e *Belarus* **459f** *Malta* **459g** *Swaziland* **459h** *Jordan*

SCOTT NO.	DESCRIPTION	FIRST DAY COVERS SING	FIRST DAY COVERS INSC. BLK	INSRIP BLK-4	UNUSED F/NH	USED F
460-64	65¢ Human Trafficking, vertical strip of 5 with labels	....	....	....	26.00	26.00
	same, sheet of 2 strips	....	....	....	52.00	....
465-68	65¢ Endangered Species	9.75	11.75	10.50	9.75	9.75
469	5¢ Colonial Algae	2.25	3.75	1.00	0.35	0.35
470	20¢ Boxfish	2.75	4.5	3.25	0.85	0.85
471-72	55¢-65¢ One Planet, One Ocean Miniature Sheet of 4 (2)	....	....	....	21.00	21.00
473	7.80 One Planet, One Ocean, One Prestige Booklet	....	....	....	26.00	....
474	75¢ UN 60th Anniversary	....	....	12.50	3.00	3.00
474a	75¢ UN 60th Anniversary S/S of 2	....	....	....	6.00	6.00

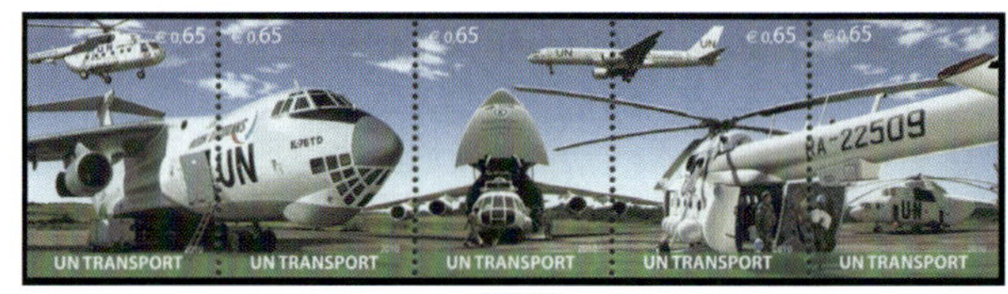

475-79

SCOTT NO.	DESCRIPTION	FIRST DAY COVERS SING	FIRST DAY COVERS INSC. BLK	INSRIP BLK-4	UNUSED F/NH	USED F
475-79	e0.65 UN Transport	11.00	....	19.50	10.00	10.00
480	e0.65 Indigenous People, sheet of 6	14.50	....	....	14.00	14.00

2011

SCOTT NO.	DESCRIPTION	FIRST DAY COVERS SING	FIRST DAY COVERS INSC. BLK	INSRIP BLK-4	UNUSED F/NH	USED F
481-82	e1.25 - e2.85 UN Headquarters	12.50	....	62.00	13.50	13.50
483	e0.65 Flag and Coins, sheet of 8	17.50	....	....	16.00	16.00
484	Anniversary of Human Space Flight, sheet of 16	22.50	....	....	19.50	....
485	Anniversary of Human Space Flight, S/S of 2	6.50	....	....	5.00	....
486-90	62¢ strip of 5, with labels	....	....	....	12.00	....
	same, sheet of 20	....	....	....	48.00	....
491-95	70¢ strip of 5, with labels	....	....	....	17.50	....
	same, sheet of 10, with labels	....	....	....	36.00	....
496	62¢ World Heritage Sites in Nordic Countries	3.75	....	8.50	2.25	2.25
	same, pane of 20	....	....	....	32.00	....
497	70¢ World Heritage Sites in Nordic Countries	5.75	....	9.25	2.75	2.75
	same, pane of 20	....	....	....	45.00	....
498	70¢ Aids Ribbon	3.75	....	....	2.50	2.50
	same, pane of 4	....	....	....	10.75	....
499-500	62¢-70¢ Economic and Social Council	....	....	19.75	4.75	4.75
501-04	$0.70 Endangered Species	10.75	....	11.00	9.75	9.00
505-06	$0.62-$0.70 Int. Year of Forests	5.25	....	9.75	4.75	4.75

513

523

524

2012

SCOTT NO.	DESCRIPTION	FIRST DAY COVERS SING	FIRST DAY COVERS INSC. BLK	INSRIP BLK-4	UNUSED F/NH	USED F
507	$0.70 Flags & Coins, sheet of 8	19.50	....	....	19.00	....
508-509	$0.70 Autism Awareness	5.50	....	11.00	5.00	5.00
510	70¢ UN Seal and Label	....	....	....	3.50	....
	same, sheet of 10 + 10 labels	....	....	....	35.00	....
511-514	70¢ Endangered Species	9.50	....	9.00	8.75	....
515	70¢ Conference on Stable Development	....	....	9.00	3.25	....
516-517	62¢-70¢ Sport for Peace	....	....	17.50	4.50	....
517a	Sport for Peace, Souvenir Sheet	....	....	....	3.00	....
518-519	62¢-70¢ UNESCO World Heritage sites in Africa	5.50	....	16.50	4.25	....
520	45¢ Indigenous People, sheet of 6	14.50	....	....	12.50	....

2013

SCOTT NO.	DESCRIPTION	FIRST DAY COVERS SING	FIRST DAY COVERS INSC. BLK	INSRIP BLK-4	UNUSED F/NH	USED F
521-522	e0.70-e1.70 World Radio Day	9.25	....	30.00	8.00	....
523-524	e0.62-e2.20 People in Handprint and Heart	11.00	....	36.00	9.50	....

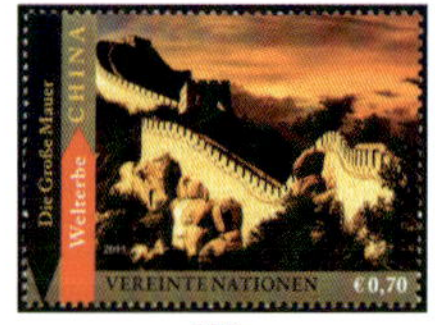

525

526

SCOTT NO.	DESCRIPTION	FIRST DAY COVERS SING	FIRST DAY COVERS INSC. BLK	INSRIP BLK-4	UNUSED F/NH	USED F
525-26	e0.70-e1.70 World Heritage Sites, China	10.00	....	29.00	7.50	7.50
527	World Heritage Sites, China, Souvenir Booklet	....	....	26.00	....	....
528	World Oceans Day sheet of 12	27.00		....	25.00	25.00

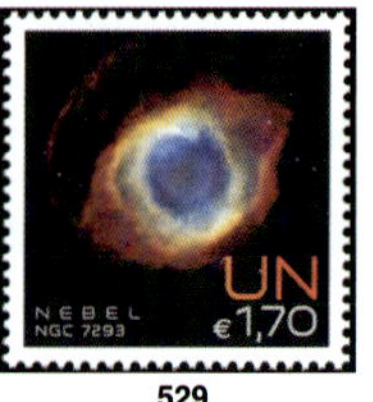

529

530

SCOTT NO.	DESCRIPTION	FIRST DAY COVERS SING	FIRST DAY COVERS INSC. BLK	INSRIP BLK-4	UNUSED F/NH	USED F
529-530	e1.70 Nebulae	12.00		22.00	11.00	11.00
531	e0.62 Nebulae S/S of 1	3.25	....	....	2.25	2.25
532-33	e0.70-e1.70 Works of Disabled Artists	8.75	....	29.00	7.50	7.50
534-37	e0.70 Endangered Species	9.50	....	8.75	8.50	8.50
538	70¢ UN emblem & tab	....	....	3.50	3.50	....
	same, sheet of 10	....	....	32.5	....	....
539	e0.70 Flags & Coins sheet of 8	19.00	....	....	17.00	17.00

546 553 547

2014

SCOTT NO.	DESCRIPTION	FIRST DAY COVERS SING	FIRST DAY COVERS INSC. BLK	INSRIP BLK-4	UNUSED F/NH	USED F
540-41	e0.90-e1.70 International Day of Happiness	9.50	.....	33.00	9.00	9.00
542	70¢ International Year of Jazz, Sheet of 12	29.00	.....	.....	27.00	27.00
543	70¢ Vienna International Center, Sheet of 10		.....	.....	32.00	32.00
544-45	70¢-e1.70 Definitives	8.75	.....	31.00	8.50	8.50
546-47	90¢ - e1.70 Taj Majal	9.75	.....	34.00	9.00	9.00
548	Taj Majal Souvenir Booklet	.....	.....	.....	28.00	.....
549-550	62¢-e1.70 International Year of Family Farming	7.50	.....	22.00	5.75	5.75
551	e1.70 Global Education First Initiative	6.75	.....	22.00	5.75	5.75
552	e2 Global Education First Initiative Souvenir Sheet	6.75	.....	.....	6.75	6.75
553-56	70¢ Endangered Species Block of 4	16.00	.....	15.00	15.00	15.00

564 570 576

2015

SCOTT NO.	DESCRIPTION	FIRST DAY COVERS SING	FIRST DAY COVERS INSC. BLK	INSRIP BLK-4	UNUSED F/NH	USED F
557	e0.80 Greetings from the United Nations, sheet of 10 with labels	.....	.....	.....	32.00	.....
558	e0.80 Flags and Coins, sheet of 8	22.00	.....	.....	19.00	.....
559-60	e0.68-e0.80 World Poetry Day, 2 sheets of 6		.....	.....	26.00	.....
561-64	e0.80 Endangered Species, set of 4	9.75	.....	9.00	8.25	.....
565-66	e0.68-e0.80 Definitives	5.75	.....	16.00	4.25	.....
567-68	e0.80-e1.70 World Heritage Sites, Southeast Asia	8.25		7.00	7.00	.....
569	World Heritage Sites, Southeast Asia, Souvenir booklet	.....	.....	.....	22.50	.....
570-71	e0.68-e0.80 End Violence Against Children	6.25	.....	16.00	4.25	.....
572-75	e0.80-e1.70 World Heritage Sites, Southeast Asia	15.00	.....	27.00	13.50	.....
576	e1.70 Trusteeship Council, Souvenir Sheet	6.25	.....	.....	4.75	.....
577	e0.80 70th Anniversary of the UN + Label	.....	.....	.....	3.00	.....
	same, sheet of 10		.....	.....	30.00	.....
578	e0.80 UN Climate Change Conference	4.00	.....	9.00	2.50	.....

579 586

2016

SCOTT NO.	DESCRIPTION	FIRST DAY COVERS SING	FIRST DAY COVERS INSC. BLK	INSRIP BLK-4	UNUSED F/NH	USED F
579-80	e0.68-e0.80 LGBT Equality	.....	.....	16.00	4.25	.....
581-82	e0.68-e0.80 U.N. Women-HeforShe	.....	.....	16.00	4.25	.....
583-84	e0.68-e0.80 International Dance Day, 2 sheets of 6	.....	.....	20.00(2)	.....	.....
585	e0.80 UNIDO 50th Anniversary, sheet of 10	.....	.....	25.00	.....	.....
586-87	e0.68-e0.80 U.N. Peacekeepers	.....	.....	16.00	4.25	.....
588-91	e0.68-e1.70 Sports for Peace & Development, 2 pairs	.....	.....	25.00	10.50	.....
592-93	e0.30-e0.40 World Heritage Sites, Czech Republic	.....	.....	27.50	6.50	.....
594	e8.40 World Heritage Sites, souvenir booklet	.....	.....	.....	27.00	.....

595b 598H

SCOTT NO.	DESCRIPTION	FIRST DAY COVERS SING	FIRST DAY COVERS INSC. BLK	INSRIP BLK-4	UNUSED F/NH	USED F
595	e0.80 CTBTO, Test Ban Treaty, sheet of 10	.....	.....	25.00	.....	.....
596	e1.70 Eye on Africa, sheet of 4	.....	.....	.....	15.00	.....
597	e0.68 Sustainable Development Goals, sheet of 17	.....	.....	30.00	.....	.....

2017

SCOTT NO.	DESCRIPTION	FIRST DAY COVERS SING	FIRST DAY COVERS INSC. BLK	INSRIP BLK-4	UNUSED F/NH	USED F
598	e0.80 Smurfs International Day of Happiness, sheet of 10	.....	.....	25.00	.....	.....
599-600	e0.68-e0.80 International Dance Day, 2 sheets of 6	.....	.....	22.00(2)	.....	.....

604 611

SCOTT NO.	DESCRIPTION	FIRST DAY COVERS SING	FIRST DAY COVERS INSC. BLK	INSRIP BLK-4	UNUSED F/NH	USED F
601-04	e0.80 Endangered Species, block of 4	.....	.....	9.00	8.25	.....
605-06	e0.68-e1.70 World Environment Day	.....	.....	27.50	6.25	.....
607-08	e0.80-e1.70 World Heritage Sites, Along the Silk Road	.....	.....	28.00	6.25	.....
609	e8.40 World Heritage Sites, Along the Silk Road	.....	.....	28.00		
610	e0.68 UNPA at the Traunsee, sheet of 10	.....	.....	28.00	.....	.....
611-12	e0.68-e1.70 International Day of Peace	.....	.....	27.50	6.25	.....
613	e1.70 International Day of Peace	.....	.....	.....	5.50	.....
614-15	e0.68-e0.80 World Food Day	.....	.....	18.00	4.25	.....

621 630

2018

SCOTT NO.	DESCRIPTION	FIRST DAY COVERS SING	FIRST DAY COVERS INSC. BLK	INSRIP BLK-4	UNUSED F/NH	USED F
616-19	e0.80 Endangered Species, block of 4	.....	.....	9.00	8.25	.....
520-21	e0.68-e0.70 World Health Day	.....	.....	27.50	6.25	.....
622	e0.80 Shorta Rustavel, sheet of 10	.....	.....	27.50	.....	.....
623-24	e0.68-e1.80 UNISPACE, 50th Anniv. in Outer Space	.....	.....	18.00	4.25	.....
625	e1.70 UNISPACE, souvenir sheet	.....	.....	.....	4.50	.....
625v	e8.40 World Day Against Trafficking, sheet of 10	.....	.....	27.50	.....	
626-27	e0.80-e1.70 World Heritage sites, UK	.....	28.00	28.00	6.25	
628	e8.40 World Heritage Sites, UK prestige booklet	.....	.....	27.50	.....	.....
629	e0.68 Music Day 2018, sheet of 12	.....	.....	.....	.....	.....
630-31	e0.90-e1.70 Non-Violence, Regular Issue	.....	.....	30.00	8.25	

633 634 641

2019

SCOTT NO.	DESCRIPTION	FIRST DAY COVERS SING	FIRST DAY COVERS INSC. BLK	INSRIP BLK-4	UNUSED F/NH	USED F
632	e0.80 International Language, sheet of 6	.....	.....	.....	10.00	.....
633	e1.80 Migration, single	.....	.....	22.00	4.50	.....
634-37	e0.90 Endangered Species, block of 4	.....	.....	11.50	10.00	.....
638	e2.70 World Bee Day, souvenir sheet	.....	.....	.....	7.50	.....
639-43	e0.80 Inter. Labour Organization, strip of 5	.....	.....	22.00	10.00	.....
644-48	e0.90 UNPA Vienna Inter. Center, sheet of 20	.....	.....	28.50	.....	
649-50	e0.80-e0.90 Climate Change	.....	.....	20.00	4.50	.....
651	e1.80 Climate Change, souvenir sheet	.....	.....	.....	5.00	.....
652-53	e1.90-e1.80 World Heritage Sites, Cuba	.....	.....	29.00	7.50	.....
654	e8.40 World Heritage Sites, Cuba, prestige booklet	.....	.....	29.00	.....	.....

655 662

2020

SCOTT NO.	DESCRIPTION	FIRST DAY COVERS SING	FIRST DAY COVERS INSC. BLK	INSRIP BLK-4	UNUSED F/NH	USED F
655-58	e0.90 Endangered Species, block of 4	.....	.....	11.50	10.00	.....
659	e1.80 Hello Kitty, set of 2, souvenir sheet of 1 with labels	.....	.....	.....	10.00	.....
.....	same, folded booklets ($1.20, 2fr, e1.80)	.....	.....	30.00	.....	.....
660-61	e0.85-e0.90 Climate Change	.....	.....	25.00	6.00	.....
662	e1.35 Florence Nightingale, single	.....	.....	.....	4.00	.....
663-64	e1-e1.80 World Heritage Sites, Russia	.....	.....	30.00	7.50	.....

2020 continued

SCOTT NO.	DESCRIPTION	FIRST DAY COVERS SING	INSC. BLK	INSRIP BLK-4	UNUSED F/NH	USED F
665	e9.00 World Heritage Sites, Russia, prestige booklet	.....	.....	30.00	.....	.....
666	e1 UNPA at OVEBRIA, sheet of 10	.....	.....	32.00	.....	.....
667	e1.80 U.N. 75th Anniv., souvenir sheet of 2	.....	.....	.....	10.00	.....
668	e7 U.N. Crypto Stamp, souvenir sheet	.....	.....	.....	20.00	.....

674-76

2021

SCOTT NO.	DESCRIPTION	FIRST DAY COVERS SING	INSC. BLK	INSRIP BLK-4	UNUSED F/NH	USED F
669	e1.80 United Against Racism & Discrimination			22.00	5.75	.....
670-73	e0.80 Endangered Species, block of 4	.....	.....	14.00	12.00	.....
674-79	e0.85-e1 Sports for Peace, horiz strips of 4	.....	.....	30.00(2)	24.00(2)	......
680	e1.80 Sports for Peace, souvenir sheet	.....	.....	.....	5.75	......
681-82	1e-1.50e World Heritage, Waterways, Railways, & Bridges	.....	.....	40.00	9.00	.....
683	e9.00 World Heritage, prestige booklet	.....	.....	.....	28.00	.....
684	e1.00 CBTBO-25th Anniv., sheet of 10	.....	.....	48.00	.....	.....
685	e1.00 U.N. Celebrations, sheet of 10	.....	.....	55.00	.....	.....
686	e1.00 World Toilet Day	.....	.....	12.00	2.75	......

687-88

2022

SCOTT NO.	DESCRIPTION	FIRST DAY COVERS SING	INSC. BLK	INSRIP BLK-4	UNUSED F/NH	USED F
687-90	e.85-e1.80 Sports for Peace, pairs	.....	.....	40.00(2)	14.00(2)	.....
691-94	e1 Endangered Species, block of 4	.....	.....	14.00	12.00	.....
695	e.85 Wangari Maathai	.....	.....	12.00	2.75	......
696-97	e.85r-e1.00 Exploration of Mars	10.00	.....	48.00(2)	5.00	.....
698	e1.80 Exploration of Mars, souvenir sheet	7.50	.....	.....	5.00	......
699	e1.00 World Chess Day, sheet of 10	.....	.....	35.00	.....	.....
700-01	e1-e1.80 World Heritage, European Spa Towns	.....	.....	40.00	9.00	.....
702	e9.00 World Heritage, prestige booklet	.....	.....	.....	28.00	.....
703	e3.65 Crypto, souvenir sheet	.....	.....	10.00	.....	.....

704

717

2023

SCOTT NO.	DESCRIPTION	FIRST DAY COVERS SING	INSC. BLK	INSRIP BLK-4	UNUSED F/NH	USED F
704-07	e1.20 Endangered Species, block of 4	.....	.....	13.00	13.00	.....
708-09	e1-e1.90 World Art Day	15.00	.....	30.00(2)	7.50	.....
710	e1 World Oceans Day, sheet of 9	30.00	.....	26.00	.....	.....
711	e1.90 "Don't Choose Extinction", souvenir sheet	9.00	.....	5.00	.....	.....
712	e1 Guqin, Body, Mind & Soul	5.00	.....	13.50	3.00	.....
713	e1.90 Guqin, Body, Mind & Soul, souvenir sheet	8.00	.....	5.00	.....	.....
714-15	e1.20-e2.10 World Heritage, Turkey	.....	40.00	9.00	.....	
716	e9.00 World Heritage,Turkey, prestige booklet	.....	.....	.....	30.00	.....
717	e1.20 World Mental Health Day	6.00	.....	13.50	3.00	.....

*Scott numbers and prices are subject to change in the next edition.

SEMI-POSTAL

2002

SCOTT NO.	DESCRIPTION	FIRST DAY COVERS SING	INSC. BLK	INSRIP BLK-4	UNUSED F/NH	USED F
B1	51¢ + 25¢ AIDS Awareness, souv. sheet	.....	....	....	5.75	.....

2021

SCOTT NO.	DESCRIPTION	FIRST DAY COVERS SING	INSC. BLK	INSRIP BLK-4	UNUSED F/NH	USED F
B2	e1.00 + 50¢ John Lennon	.....	.....	20.00	5.00	.....
B3	e2.85 + e1 John Lennon, souvenir sheet	.....	.....	.....	12.00	.....

2022

SCOTT NO.	DESCRIPTION	FIRST DAY COVERS SING	INSC. BLK	INSRIP BLK-4	UNUSED F/NH	USED F
B4	e1.80r + 50¢ World Humanitarian Day	.....	.....	60.00	6.00	.....

AIR LETTER SHEETS & POSTAL CARDS

U1

1995

SCOTT NO.	DESCRIPTION	UNUSED F/NH	USED F
U1	6s Vienna International Center	1.75	5.25
U2	7s Vienna Landscape	1.75	3.75

1998

SCOTT NO.	DESCRIPTION	UNUSED F/NH	USED F
U3	13s multicolored	4.00	4.60

2002-03

SCOTT NO.	DESCRIPTION	UNUSED F/NH	USED F
U4	e0.51 Vienna International Center	2.50	3.60
U5	e1.09 Vienna International Center	3.75	5.25
U6	e0.51+e0.4 surcharged envelope (U4)	2.50	4.00
U7	e1.09+e0.16 surcharged envelope (U5)	3.75	5.50
U8	e0.55 U.N. Headquarters, Vienna	2.75	2.50
U9	e1.25 U.N. Headquarters, Vienna	4.25	5.75
U10	e0.55+e0.10 surcharged envelope (U8)	4.00	4.00
U11	e1.25+e0.15 surcharged envelope (U9)	6.50	7.00
U12	65¢ Vienna International Center	3.95	4.25
U13	e1.40 Vienna International Center	3.95	7.00
U14	(U12) Surcharged, 65¢+5¢	3.75	4.25
U15	(U13) Surgharged, E1.40+30¢	6.75	6.75
U16	e0.68 Dull Orange, UN Emblem	3.25	......
U17	e0.80 Yellow/Green UN Emblem	3.50	......
U18	e1.70 Lilac UN Emblemt	5.75	......
U19	68¢ Vienna Interternational Center	3.50	.....
U20	90¢ Vienna Internatrional Center	4.00	.....

UC1

UC5

UC3

1962

SCOTT NO.	DESCRIPTION	UNUSED F/NH	USED F
UC1	9s multicolored	4.00	4.50

1967

SCOTT NO.	DESCRIPTION	UNUSED F/NH	USED F
UC2	9s+2s surcharge on UC1	40.00	68.00
UC3	11s Birds in Flight	3.50	5.50
UC4	11s+1s surcharged	9.00	65.00
UC5	12s Vienna Office	4.00	8.75

UX2

UX3

UX7

UX11

1982-85

SCOTT NO.	DESCRIPTION	UNUSED F/NH	USED F
UX1	3s multicolored (1982)	1.25	1.75
UX2	5s multicolored (1982)	1.75	1.50
UX3	4s U.N. Emblem (1985)	1.25	4.95

1992-94

SCOTT NO.	DESCRIPTION	UNUSED F/NH	USED F
UX4	5s+1s surcharged	....	28.00
UX5	6s Reg Schek Painting	1.75	5.00
UX6	5s Postal Card	1.75	19.00
UX7	6s Postal Card	1.75	5.00
UX8	5s + 50g surcharge on UX6	1.75	6.75

1997

SCOTT NO.	DESCRIPTION	UNUSED F/NH	USED F
UX9	6s+50s surcharge on UX5	2.50	3.50
UX10	6s+1s surcharge on UX7	2.50	3.50

1998-2018

SCOTT NO.	DESCRIPTION	UNUSED F/NH	USED F
UX11	6.50s multicolored	2.00	2.00
UX12	7s The Gloriette	2.00	2.50
UX13	7s multicolored, type of 1983	2.00	2.75
UX14	e.0.51 Clock tower Graz, Austria	1.75	3.25
UX15	e.0.51+e0.04 surcharged postal card (UX14)	1.75	3.75
UX16	e0.55 U.N. Headquarters, Vienna	2.75	3.75
UX17	e0.55+e0.10 surcharged postal card (UX16)	4.50	4.50
UX18	65¢ Vienna International Center	3.95	4.50
UX19	62¢ Vienna International Center and Flagpoles	3.75	4.25
UX20	70¢ Fish-eye views of Vienna International Center	4.25	5.00
UX21	e1.70 Vienna International Center at night	7.00	7.00
UX22	e0.68 Dove and Vienna International Center	3.25	....
UX23	e0.80 Vienna International Center	3.50	....
UX24	e1.70 Woman Free, Sculpture by Edwina Sandys	5.75	....
UX25	e0.68+e0.22 Surcharge on UX22	3.50	....
UX26	e1.70+e0.10 Surcharge on UX24	6.00	....

CANADA

1, 4, 12
Beaver

2, 5, 10, 13
Prince Albert

7
Jacques Cartier

8, 11

9

14

Queen Victoria

15
Beaver

SCOTT NO.	DESCRIPTION	UNUSED VF	UNUSED F	UNUSED AVG	USED VF	USED F	USED AVG
	1851 Laid paper, Imperforate (OG + 75%)						
1	3p red	40000.00	32000.00	28000.00	1200.00	900.00	750.00
2	6p grayish purple	41000.00	36000.00	28000.00	1600.00	1100.00	900.00
3	12p black	....	....	....	....	....	....
	1852-55 Wove paper						
4	3p red	1550.00	1350.00	1200.00	200.00	175.00	125.00
4d	3p red (thin paper)	1650.00	1400.00	1000.00	225.00	175.00	125.00
5	6p slate gray	31000.00	24000.00	1100.00	1550.00	1300.00	1100.00
	1855						
7	10p blue	10500.00	8000.00	6000.00	1800.00	1400.00	1000.00
	1857						
8	1/2p rose	1150.00	800.00	650.00	700.00	550.00	475.00
9	7-1/2p green	10500.00	8500.00	6000.00	3600.00	2800.00	2100.00
	Very thick soft wove paper						
10	6p reddish purple	33000.00	25000.00	18000.00	7700.00	5400.00	3500.00
	1858-59 Perf. 12						
11	1/2p rose	3600.00	2800.00	1900.00	2000.00	1600.00	1000.00
12	3p red	18500.00	14000.00	9000.00	1200.00	900.00	600.00
13	6p brown violet	22700.00	16000.00	10000.00	7500.00	5500.00	4500.00
	1859 (OG + 35%)						
14	1¢ rose	430.00	350.00	260.00	95.00	75.00	60.00
15	5¢ vermillion	500.00	400.00	300.00	30.00	22.00	18.00
16	10¢ black brown	20000.00	16000.00	10000.00	6000.00	5300.00	3900.00
17	10¢ red lilac	1600.00	1100.00	800.00	160.00	105.00	80.00
18	12-1/2¢ yellow green	950.00	800.00	600.00	125.00	100.00	85.00
19	17¢ blue	1300.00	1100.00	775.00	225.00	175.00	110.00
	1864						
20	2¢ rose	550.00	400.00	275.00	250.00	180.00	120.00

16, 17
Prince Albert

18
Queen Victoria

19
Jacques Cartier

20
Queen Victoria

21

22, 23, 31

24, 32

25, 33

Original Gum: Prior to 1897, the Unused price is for stamps either without gum or with partial gum. If you require full original gum, use the OG premium. Never hinged quality is scarce on those issues. Please write for specific quotations for NH.

SCOTT NO.	DESCRIPTION	UNUSED VF	UNUSED F	UNUSED AVG	USED VF	USED F	USED AVG
	1868-75 Wove paper, Perf. 12, unwkd. (OG + 35%)						
21	1/2¢ black	125.00	105.00	70.00	77.00	55.00	40.00
22	1¢ brown red	850.00	700.00	500.00	100.00	80.00	50.00
23	1¢ yellow orange	1800.00	1500.00	1100.00	2300.00	160.00	115.00
24	2¢ green	1050.00	950.00	650.00	80.00	50.00	40.00
25	3¢ red	2000.00	1650.00	1200.00	35.00	26.00	16.00
26	5¢ olive gr. (pf. 11-1/2x12)	1800.00	1500.00	1200.00	200.00	155.00	110.00
27	6¢ dark brown	2300.00	1900.00	1400.00	130.00	90.00	70.00
28	12-1/2¢ blue	1200.00	1000.00	775.00	105.00	80.00	45.00
29	15¢ gray violet	125.00	95.00	70.00	55.00	40.00	30.00
29b	15¢ red lilac	1158.00	975.00	675.00	120.00	90.00	65.00
30	15¢ gray	100.00	88.00	65.00	60.00	40.00	28.00

26

27

28

29, 30

SCOTT NO.	DESCRIPTION	UNUSED VF	UNUSED F	UNUSED AVG	USED VF	USED F	USED AVG
	1873-74 Wove paper. Perf. 11-1/2 x 12, unwatermarked						
21a	1/2¢ black	165.00	145.00	100.00	77.00	60.00	45.00
29a	15¢ gray violet	1750.00	1400.00	1100.00	400.00	300.00	200.00
30a	15¢ gray	1400.00	1200.00	850.00	400.00	300.00	200.00
	1868 Wove paper. Perf. 12 watermarked						
22a	1¢ brown red	......	3000.00	1900.00	......	475.00	275.00
24a	2¢ green	......	3100.00	1900.00	......	400.00	300.00
25a	3¢ red	......	4800.00	3500.00	......	475.00	325.00
27b	6¢ dark brown	......	9000.00	6000.00	......	2100.00	1400.00
28a	12-1/2¢ blue	......	4600.00	1900.00	......	400.00	300.00
29c	15¢ gray violet	......	6000.00	4500.00	......	1200.00	450.00
	1868 Laid Paper (OG + 20%)						
31	1¢ brown red	......	23000.00	18000.00	6000.00	4500.00	3000.00
33	3¢ bright red	......	21000.00	15000.00	......	2100.00	1400.00
	1870-89 Perf. 12						
34	1/2¢ black	21.00	14.00	7.00	11.00	9.00	7.00
35	1¢ yellow	48.00	36.00	25.00	1.25	.80	.60
35a	1¢ orange	180.00	140.00	110.00	10.00	7.00	4.25
36	2¢ green	80.00	60.00	45.00	2.75	1.50	1.25
36d	2¢ blue green	105.00	85.00	67.00	4.75	3.00	2.50
37	3¢ dull red	175.00	120.00	75.00	3.00	2.25	1.50
37c	3¢ orange red	130.00	100.00	85.00	3.25	2.50	1.50
37d	3¢ copper red, pf. 12-1/2	12500.00	7725.00	6000.00	1350.00	900.00	650.00
38	5¢ slate green	950.00	800.00	500.00	23.00	15.00	11.00
39	6¢ yellow brown	750.00	600.00	450.00	35.00	28.00	20.00
40	10¢ dull rose lilac	1150.00	800.00	575.00	77.00	65.00	50.00

34

35

36

37, 41

38, 42

39, 43

40, 45

44

SCOTT NO.	DESCRIPTION	UNUSED VF	UNUSED F	UNUSED AVG	USED VF	USED F	USED AVG
	1873-79 Perf. 11-1/2 x 12 (OG + 20%)						
35d	1¢ orange	500.00	400.00	350.00	21.00	17.00	13.00
36e	2¢ green	775.00	600.00	500.00	24.00	16.00	9.50
37e	3¢ red	475.00	400.00	350.00	11.00	7.75	5.00
38a	5¢ slate green	1300.00	1100.00	900.00	52.00	41.00	30.00
39b	6¢ yellow brown	1050.00	800.00	600.00	65.00	55.00	40.00
40c	10¢ pale milky rose lilac	1750.00	1500.00	1375.00	325.00	195.00	130.00

SCOTT NO.	DESCRIPTION	UNUSED VF	UNUSED F	UNUSED AVG	USED VF	USED F	USED AVG
	1888-93 Perf. 12						
41	3¢ bright vermillion	60.00	40.00	25.00	.60	.45	.35
41a	3¢ rose carmine	495.00	300.00	200.00	9.00	6.00	4.00
42	5¢ gray	210.00	150.00	90.00	4.50	3.50	2.25
43	6¢ red brown	210.00	150.00	90.00	12.50	8.50	5.00
43a	6¢ chocolate	400.00	350.00	225.00	30.00	21.00	12.50
44	8¢ gray	250.00	185.00	120.00	5.00	3.75	2.50
45	10¢ brown red	730.00	575.00	400.00	60.00	50.00	35.00
46	20¢ vermillion	495.00	385.00	275.00	120.00	85.00	65.00
47	50¢ deep blue	495.00	385.00	275.00	85.00	65.00	45.00

46, 47

50-65
Queen Victoria in 1837 & 1897

SCOTT NO.	DESCRIPTION	UNUSED OG VF	UNUSED OG F	UNUSED OG AVG	USED VF	USED F	USED AVG
	1897 Jubilee Issue (NH + 150%)						
50	1/2¢ black	160.00	135.00	77.00	95.00	85.00	76.00
51	1¢ orange	35.00	25.00	18.00	10.00	8.50	5.50
52	2¢ green	40.00	30.00	18.00	14.00	11.00	9.00
53	3¢ bright rose	25.00	21.00	12.00	2.50	2.00	1.25
54	5¢ deep blue	80.00	65.00	50.00	48.00	35.00	29.00
55	6¢ yellow brown	275.00	240.00	175.00	135.00	140.00	125.00
56	8¢ dark violet	160.00	105.00	70.00	60.00	48.00	35.00
57	10¢ brown violet	172.00	125.00	85.00	120.00	80.00	60.00
58	15¢ steel blue	350.00	275.00	200.00	175.00	140.00	115.00
59	20¢ vermillion	350.00	300.00	175.00	175.00	140.00	115.00
60	50¢ ultramarine	440.00	325.00	225.00	183.00	140.00	115.00
61	$1 lake	1100.00	900.00	700.00	710.00	620.00	500.00
62	$2 dark purple	1900.00	1500.00	1200.00	550.00	440.00	340.00
63	$3 yellow bistre	1900.00	1500.00	1200.00	1100.00	800.00	650.00
64	$4 purple	1900.00	1500.00	1200.00	1100.00	800.00	650.00
65	$5 olive green	1900.00	1500.00	1200.00	1100.00	800.00	650.00

66-73

74-84

Queen Victoria

85-86
Map Showing British Empire

77: 2¢ Die I. Frame of four thin lines
77a: 2¢ Die II. Frame of thick line between two thin lines

SCOTT NO.	DESCRIPTION	UNUSED OG VF	UNUSED OG F	UNUSED OG AVG	USED VF	USED F	USED AVG
	1897-98 Maple Leaves (NH + 150%)						
66	1/2¢ black	17.00	12.00	9.00	6.75	5.00	3.75
67	1¢ blue green	52.00	37.00	25.00	1.50	1.15	.85
68	2¢ purple	57.00	37.00	25.00	2.25	1.50	.85
69	3¢ carmine (1898)	85.00	65.00	35.00	1.10	.75	.55
70	5¢ dark blue, bluish paper	205.00	165.00	125.00	10.00	6.75	5.50
71	6¢ brown	165.00	135.00	110.00	36.00	29.00	22.00
72	8¢ orange	335.00	260.00	180.00	13.00	10.00	8.00
73	10¢ brown violet (1898)	640.00	450.00	300.00	82.00	72.00	62.00
	1898-1902 Numerals (NH + 150%)						
74	1/2¢ black	16.00	9.50	7.00	2.40	1.80	1.25
75	1¢ gray green	60.00	35.00	25.00	.35	.25	.20
76	2¢ purple (I)	60.00	35.00	25.00	.35	.25	.20
77	2¢ carmine (I) (1899)	65.00	40.00	25.00	.35	.25	.25
77a	2¢ carmine (II)	85.00	55.00	35.00	.60	.45	.35
78	3¢ carmine	85.00	70.00	55.00	1.15	.85	.60
79	5¢ blue, bluish paper	255.00	200.00	150.00	2.25	1.50	1.00
80	6¢ brown	260.00	165.00	120.00	46.00	39.00	32.00
81	7¢ olive yellow (1902)	200.00	153.00	110.00	23.00	19.00	14.00
82	8¢ orange	400.00	275.00	200.00	27.00	18.50	14.00
83	10¢ brown violet	625.00	425.00	300.00	25.00	17.00	14.00
84	20¢ olive green (1900)	795.00	625.00	350.00	100.00	85.00	60.00
	1898 IMPERIAL PENNY POSTAGE COMMEMORATIVE						
85	2¢ black, lavender & carmine	52.00	37.00	25.00	8.50	5.00	3.25
86	2¢ black, blue & carmine	52.00	37.00	25.00	7.25	5.00	3.25
	1899 69 & 78 surcharged						
87	2¢ on 3¢ carmine	26.00	19.00	13.00	7.75	6.00	4.50
88	2¢ on 3¢ carmine	35.00	30.00	20.00	6.50	5.75	4.75

89-95
King Edward VII

SCOTT NO.	DESCRIPTION	UNUSED NH F	UNUSED NH AVG	UNUSED OG F	UNUSED OG AVG	USED F	USED AVG
	1903-08						
89	1¢ green	125.00	70.00	50.00	30.00	.35	.25
90	2¢ carmine	135.00	75.00	55.00	35.00	.35	.25
90a	2¢ carmine, imperf. pair	100.00	75.00	60.00	35.00	.....	.....
91	5¢ blue, blue paper	650.00	425.00	250.00	175.00	5.00	3.50
92	7¢ olive bistre	750.00	400.00	280.00	175.00	5.00	3.50
93	10¢ brown lilac	1200.00	700.00	725.00	300.00	8.00	6.00
94	20¢ olive green	2000.00	1100.00	750.00	500.00	30.00	35.00
95	50¢ purple (1908)	2500.00	1400.00	850.00	600.00	90.00	50.00

96
Princess and Prince of Wales in 1908

97
Jacques Cartier and Samuel Champlain

98
Queen Alexandra and King Edward

99
Champlain's Home in Quebec

100
Generals Montcalm and Wolfe

101
View of Quebec in 1700

102
Champlain's Departure for the West

103
Arrival of Cartier at Quebec

104-34, 136-38, 184
King George V

Never Hinged: From 1897 to 1949, Unused OG is for stamps with original gum that have been hinged. If you desire Never Hinged stamps, order from the NH listings.

SCOTT NO.	DESCRIPTION	UNUSED NH F	UNUSED NH AVG	UNUSED OG F	UNUSED OG AVG	USED F	USED AVG
	1908 QUEBEC TERCENTENARY ISSUE						
96-103	1/2¢-20¢ complete, 8 varieties	2300.00	1600.00	900.00	695.00	495.00	325.00
96	1/2¢ black brown	24.00	12.00	9.00	7.50	4.50	3.00
97	1¢ blue green	80.00	48.00	35.00	18.00	4.50	3.00
98	2¢ carmine	95.00	75.00	40.00	29.00	1.50	.85
99	5¢ dark blue	225.00	140.00	85.00	50.00	50.00	38.00
100	7¢ olive green	375.00	275.00	200.00	160.00	85.00	60.00
101	10¢ dark violet	475.00	325.00	220.00	160.00	125.00	80.00
102	15¢ red orange	550.00	375.00	270.00	175.00	140.00	80.00
103	20¢ yellow brown	600.00	475.00	285.00	220.00	160.00	110.00
	1912-25						
104-22	1¢-$1 complete 18 varieties	3400.00	1975.00	1350.00	800.00	39.00	29.00
104	1¢ green	50.00	35.00	20.00	12.00	.25	.20
104a	same, booklet pane of 6	85.00	50.00	45.00	25.00	.....	.....
105	1¢ yellow (1922)	55.00	34.00	20.00	15.00	.25	.20
105a	same, booklet pane of 4	125.00	80.00	60.00	40.00	.....	.....
105b	same, booklet pane of 6	150.00	85.00	70.00	45.00	.....	.....
106	2¢ carmine	62.00	38.00	25.00	15.00	.25	.20
106a	same, booklet pane of 6	85.00	55.00	40.00	30.00	.....	.....
107	2¢ yellow green (1922)	55.00	35.00	17.00	12.00	.25	.20
107b	same, booklet pane of 4	150.00	100.00	75.00	50.00	.....	.....
107c	same, booklet pane of 6	700.00	425.00	350.00	200.00	.....	.....
108	3¢ brown (1918)	50.00	35.00	20.00	15.00	.25	.20
108a	same, booklet pane of 4	200.00	120.00	100.00	60.00	.....	.....

SCOTT NO.	DESCRIPTION	UNUSED NH F	AVG	UNUSED OG F	AVG	USED F	AVG
109	3¢ carmine (1923)	50.00	38.00	26.00	16.00	.30	.25
109a	same, booklet pane of 4	160.00	100.00	80.00	52.00	.....	.....
110	4¢ olive bistre (1922)	120.00	78.00	55.00	40.00	3.50	2.75
111	5¢ dark blue	395.00	260.00	150.00	110.00	1.00	.75
112	5¢ violet (1922)	100.00	68.00	45.00	30.00	.75	.45
113	7¢ yellow ochre	125.00	100.00	55.00	30.00	3.50	2.00
114	7¢ red brown (1924)	55.00	40.00	30.00	18.00	9.00	8.00
115	8¢ blue (1925)	90.00	60.00	40.00	23.00	10.00	8.00
116	10¢ plum	725.00	450.00	300.00	250.00	3.00	2.00
117	10¢ blue (1922)	145.00	95.00	65.00	38.00	2.25	1.50
118	10¢ bistre brown (1925)	135.00	80.00	45.00	30.00	2.25	1.25
119	20¢ olive green	300.00	200.00	125.00	70.00	2.00	1.00
120	50¢ black brown (1925)	225.00	180.00	85.00	60.00	3.00	2.50
120a	50¢ black	625.00	400.00	200.00	150.00	7.00	6.00
122	$1 orange (1923)	250.00	200.00	110.00	75.00	9.00	8.00

1912 Coil Stamps; Perf. 8 Horizontally

SCOTT NO.	DESCRIPTION	UNUSED NH F	AVG	UNUSED OG F	AVG	USED F	AVG
123	1¢ dark green	300.00	180.00	120.00	80.00	55.00	35.00
124	2¢ carmine	300.00	180.00	120.00	75.00	55.00	35.00

1912-24 Perf. 8 Vertically

SCOTT NO.	DESCRIPTION	UNUSED NH F	AVG	UNUSED OG F	AVG	USED F	AVG
125-30	**1¢-3¢ complete, 6 varieties**	**310.00**	**270.00**	**160.00**	**110.00**	**16.00**	**13.00**
125	1¢ green	65.00	38.00	30.00	20.00	2.00	1,50
126	1¢ yellow (1923)	25.00	17.00	15.00	10.00	7.50	5.00
126a	1¢ block of 4	120.00	75.00	65.00	45.00	.....	.....
127	2¢ carmine	90.00	65.00	50.00	25.00	2.00	1.50
128	2¢ green (1922)	40.00	25.00	15.00	10.00	2.00	1.00
128a	2¢ block of 4	120.00	75.00	75.00	50.00	.....	.....
129	3¢ brown (1918)	70.00	45.00	35.00	25.00	1.50	1.00
130	3¢ carmine (1924)	175.00	130.00	75.00	50.00	8.50	6.50
130a	3¢ block of 4	1600.00	1100.00	1000.00	650.00	.....	.....

1915-24 Perf. 12 Horizontally

SCOTT NO.	DESCRIPTION	UNUSED NH F	AVG	UNUSED OG F	AVG	USED F	AVG
131	1¢ dark green	17.00	10.00	8.50	6.00	8.00	5.00
132	2¢ carmine	70.00	45.00	30.00	20.00	9.00	7.00
133	2¢ yellow green (1924)	170.00	100.00	80.00	50.00	60.00	35.00
134	3¢ brown (1921)	25.00	17.00	12.00	7.00	6.00	3.95

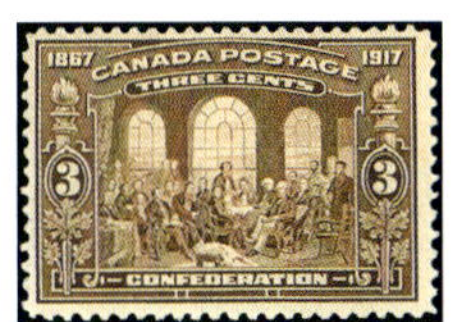

135
Quebec Conference of 1867

1917 CONFEDERATION ISSUE

SCOTT NO.	DESCRIPTION	UNUSED NH F	AVG	UNUSED OG F	AVG	USED F	AVG
135	3¢ brown	140.00	80.00	55.00	35.00	1.50	1.00

1924 Imperforate

SCOTT NO.	DESCRIPTION	UNUSED NH F	AVG	UNUSED OG F	AVG	USED F	AVG
136	1¢ yellow	75.00	55.00	45.00	35.00	35.00	28.00
137	2¢ green	70.00	50.00	40.00	30.00	35.00	28.00
138	3¢ carmine	35.00	25.00	20.00	15.00	16.00	12.00

1926
109 Surcharged

SCOTT NO.	DESCRIPTION	UNUSED NH F	AVG	UNUSED OG F	AVG	USED F	AVG
139	2¢ on 3¢ carmine	110.00	75.00	65.00	40.00	55.00	41.00

109 Surcharged

SCOTT NO.	DESCRIPTION	UNUSED NH F	AVG	UNUSED OG F	AVG	USED F	AVG
140	2¢ on 3¢ carmine	65.00	40.00	30.00	25.00	25.00	20.00

141
Sir John Macdonald

142
The Quebec Conference of 1867

143
The Parliment Building at Ottawa

144
Sir Wilfred Laurier

145
Map of Canada

1927 CONFEDERATION ISSUE

SCOTT NO.	DESCRIPTION	UNUSED NH F	AVG	UNUSED OG F	AVG	USED F	AVG
141-45	**1¢-12¢ complete, 5 varieties**	**36.25**	**24.75**	**21.75**	**15.25**	**13.00**	**9.00**
141	1¢ orange	7.00	4.00	4.00	2.50	1.50	1.00
142	2¢ green	4.00	2.75	2.75	1.45	.25	.20
143	3¢ brown carmine	20.00	13.00	12.00	8.00	6.00	4.00
144	5¢ violet	9.00	6.00	5.00	4.00	3.50	2.25
145	12¢ dark blue	50.00	30.00	30.00	18.00	7.00	5.00

146
Thomas McGee

147
Sir Wilfred Laurier and Sir John Macdonald

148
Robert Baldwin and L.H. Lafontaine

1927 HISTORICAL ISSUE

SCOTT NO.	DESCRIPTION	UNUSED NH F	AVG	UNUSED OG F	AVG	USED F	AVG
146-48	**5¢-20¢ complete, 3 varieties**	**75.00**	**48.00**	**45.00**	**30.00**	**12.00**	**8.75**
146	5¢ violet	8.50	6.00	5.00	2.50	3.00	2.25
147	12¢ green	20.00	15.00	12.00	8.00	6.00	4.00
148	20¢ brown carmine	55.00	38.00	35.00	24.00	7.50	5.00

149-154, 160, 161
King George V

155
Mt. Hurd

156
Quebec Bridge

157
Harvesting Wheat

158
Fishing Schooner "Bluenose"

159
The Parliament Building at Ottawa

1928-29

SCOTT NO.	DESCRIPTION	UNUSED NH F	AVG	UNUSED OG F	AVG	USED F	AVG
149-59	**1¢-$1 complete, 11 varieties**	**1035.00**	**825.00**	**525.00**	**355.00**	**130.00**	**95.00**
149-55	**1¢-10¢, 7 varieties**	**200.00**	**125.00**	**51.50**	**33.00**	**17.15**	**10.15**
149	1¢ orange	10.00	7.50	7.00	5.00	.50	.35
149a	same, booklet pane of 6	45.00	30.00	30.00	20.00	.....	.....
150	2¢ green	3.00	2.25	1.85	1.25	.30	.20
150a	same, booklet pane of 6	45.00	30.00	35.00	18.00	.....	.....
151	3¢ dark carmine	60.00	40.00	38.00	25.00	12.00	8.00
152	4¢ bistre (1929)	50.00	35.00	30.00	20.00	6.00	4.00
153	5¢ deep violet	30.00	18.00	18.00	12.00	3.00	2.00
153a	same, booklet pane of 6	275.00	200.00	200.00	130.00	.....	.....
154	8¢ blue	40.00	30.00	24.00	17.00	7.00	5.00
155	10¢ green	45.00	33.00	30.00	22.00	2.25	1.75
156	12¢ gray (1929)	90.00	60.00	55.00	30.00	7.00	4.50
157	20¢ dark carmine (1929)	125.00	70.00	60.00	40.00	12.00	9.00
158	50¢ dark blue (1929)	475.00	300.00	250.00	175.00	65.00	50.00
159	$1 olive green (1929)	600.00	400.00	325.00	225.00	80.00	60.00

1929 Coil Stamps. Perf. 8 Vertically

SCOTT NO.	DESCRIPTION	UNUSED NH F	AVG	UNUSED OG F	AVG	USED F	AVG
160	1¢ orange	75.00	55.00	40.00	30.00	23.00	16.50
161	2¢ green	75.00	55.00	35.00	22.50	3.50	2.25

2¢ Die I. Above "POSTAGE" faint crescent in ball of ornament. Top letter "P" has tiny dot of color.

162-172, 178-183
King George V

173
Parliament Library at Ottawa

2¢ Die II. Stronger and clearer crescent, spot of color in "P" is larger.

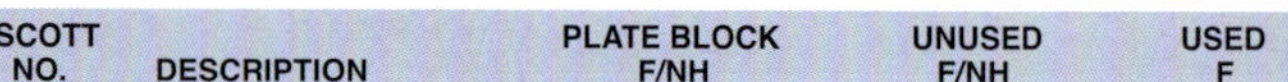

174
The Old Citadel at Quebec

175
Harvesting Wheat on the Prairies

176
The Museum at Grand Pre and Monument to Evangeline

177
Mt. Edith Cavell

VERY FINE QUALITY: To determine the Very Fine price, add the difference between the Fine and Average prices to the Fine quality price. For example: if the Fine price is $10.00 and the Average price is $6.00, the Very Fine price would be $14.00. From 1935 to date, add 20% to the Fine price to arrive at the Very Fine price.

1930-31

SCOTT NO.	DESCRIPTION	PLATE BLOCK F/NH		UNUSED F/NH		USED F	
162-77	1¢-$1 complete, 16 varieties	695.00	575.00	400.00	188.25	60.00	45.00
162-72	1¢-8¢, 11 varieties	105.00	85.00	45.00	30.00	19.00	16.00
162	1¢ orange	2.75	1.50	1.35	.95	.60	.40
163	1¢ deep green	4.50	2.75	2.25	1.50	.30	.25
163a	same, booklet pane of 4	175.00	120.00	120.00	85.00	.....	.....
163c	same, booklet pane of 6	35.00	25.00	20.00	15.00	.....	.....
164	2¢ dull green	3.75	2.25	1.75	1.00	.30	.25
164a	same, booklet pane of 6	55.00	35.00	35.00	25.00	.....	.....
165	2¢ deep red, die II	3.50	2.50	1.75	1.00	.30	.25
165a	2¢ deep red, die I	3.25	2.50	3.00	1.50	.30	.25
165b	same, booklet pane of 6	40.00	28.00	28.00	20.00	.....	.....
166	2¢ dark brown, die II (1931)	4.75	3.00	.90	.70	.35	.30
166a	same, booklet pane of 4	195.00	130.00	125.00	85.00	.....	.....
166b	2¢ dark brown, die I (1931)	7.50	5.00	4.00	2.75	4.00	2.75
166c	same, booklet pane of 6	90.00	60.00	60.00	40.00	.....	.....
167	3¢ deep red (1931)	7.50	6.00	1.55	.95	.25	.20
167a	same, booklet pane of 4	65.00	50.00	45.00	30.00	.....	.....
168	4¢ yellow bistre	27.00	18.00	13.00	9.00	7.00	5.00
169	5¢ dull violet	18.00	12.00	9.00	6.00	4.50	3.00
170	5¢ dull blue	13.00	10.00	9.00	6.00	.35	.25
171	8¢ dark blue	52.00	40.00	30.00	22.00	12.50	9.00
172	8¢ red orange	13.00	8.00	6.50	4.50	5.25	3.50
173	10¢ olive green	26.00	19.00	13.00	9.00	1.25	.80
174	12¢ gray black	55.00	42.00	26.00	16.00	5.50	3.50
175	20¢ brown red	85.00	70.00	50.00	37.00	1.25	.85
176	50¢ dull blue	400.00	300.00	200.00	150.00	13.00	8.00
177	$1 dark olive green	400.00	300.00	200.00	150.00	26.00	16.00

Note: **Coil Pairs for Canada can be supplied at double the single price**

1930-31 Coil Stamps. Perf. 8-1/2 Vertically

SCOTT NO.	DESCRIPTION	PLATE BLOCK F/NH		UNUSED F/NH		USED F	
178-83	1¢-3¢ complete, 6 varieties	97.00	70.00	60.00	45.00	15.50	11.00
178	1¢ orange	26.00	18.00	13.00	9.00	9.00	6.50
179	1¢ deep green	17.00	9.00	8.50	5.00	5.50	3.50
180	2¢ dull green	11.00	8.00	5.50	3.75	3.00	2.00
181	2¢ deep red	47.00	30.00	24.00	16.00	3.00	1.75
182	2¢ dark brown (1931)	21.00	12.00	11.00	8.00	.75	.50
183	3¢ deep red (1931)	38.00	23.00	16.50	12.00	.75	.50

1931 Design of 1912-25. Perf. 12x8

SCOTT NO.	DESCRIPTION	PLATE BLOCK F/NH		UNUSED F/NH		USED F	
184	3¢ carmine	20.00	17.00	8.00	5.00	4.25	2.75

1931

SCOTT NO.	DESCRIPTION	PLATE BLOCK F/NH		UNUSED F/NH		USED F	
190	10¢ dark green	32.00	20.00	13.00	10.00	.30	.25

1932
165 & 165a surcharged

SCOTT NO.	DESCRIPTION	PLATE BLOCK F/NH		UNUSED F/NH		USED F	
191	3¢ on 2¢ deep red, die II	2.25	1.50	1.35	.85	.30	.25
191a	3¢ on 2¢ deep red, die I	4.25	2.50	2.75	1.50	1.65	1.00

190
Sir George Etienne Cartier

192
King George V

193
Prince of Wales

194
Allegorical Figure of Britannia Surveying the Britsh Empire

1932 OTTAWA CONFERENCE ISSUE

SCOTT NO.	DESCRIPTION	PLATE BLOCK F/NH		UNUSED F/NH		USED F	
192-94	3¢-13¢ complete, 3 varieties	34.00	19.50	16.00	10.00	6.50	5.00
192	3¢ deep red	2.50	1.85	1.25	.85	.25	.20
193	5¢ dull blue	14.00	8.50	7.00	5.00	2.25	1.75
194	13¢ deep green	20.00	12.00	10.00	7.00	5.50	3.50

195-200, 205-207
King George V

201
The Old Citadel at Quebec

1932

SCOTT NO.	DESCRIPTION	PLATE BLOCK F/NH		UNUSED F/NH		USED F	
195-201	1¢-31¢ complete, 7 varieties	290.00	205.00	154.00	115.00	13.00	7.50
195	1¢ dark green	2.50	1.75	1.25	.85	.25	.20
195a	same, booklet pane of 4	130.00	90.00	80.00	60.00	.....	.....
195b	same, booklet pane of 6	130.00	90.00	80.00	60.00	.....	.....
196	2¢ black brown	2.50	1.75	1.50	1.00	.25	.20
196a	same, booklet pane of 4	175.00	120.00	120.00	80.00	.....	.....
196b	same, booklet pane of 6	125.00	85.00	80.00	55.00	.....	.....
197	3¢ deep red	2.50	2.00	1.50	1.00	.25	.20
197a	same, booklet pane of 4	80.00	60.00	50.00	30.00	.....	.....
198	4¢ ochre	95.00	70.00	60.00	40.00	6.50	4.00
199	5¢ dark blue	25.00	16.00	13.00	8.00	.25	.20
200	8¢ red orange	85.00	60.00	45.00	35.00	3.50	2.50
201	13¢ dull violet	85.00	60.00	45.00	35.00	3.50	2.50

202
Parliament Buildings at Ottawa

203

204
S.S. Royal William

208

209

210

1933-34 COMMEMORATIVES

SCOTT NO.	DESCRIPTION	PLATE BLOCK F/NH		UNUSED F/NH		USED F	
202/10	(202-04, 208-10), 6 varieties	238.00	183.00	135.00	117.00	33.00	25.50

1933

SCOTT NO.	DESCRIPTION	PLATE BLOCK F/NH		UNUSED F/NH		USED F	
202	5¢ Postal Union	20.00	15.00	9.50	8.50	3.25	3.25
203	20¢ Grain Exhibition	80.00	60.00	45.00	35.00	13.00	10.00
204	5¢ Trans-Atlantic Crossing	19.00	14.00	11.00	9.00	5.25	4.50

1933 Coil Stamps Perf. 8-1/2 Vertically

SCOTT NO.	DESCRIPTION	PLATE BLOCK F/NH		UNUSED F/NH		USED F	
205	1¢ dark green	28.00	21.00	17.00	14.00	2.75	2.25
206	2¢ black brown	34.00	26.00	22.00	16.00	1.25	1.00
207	3¢ deep red	28.00	19.00	16.00	12.00	.45	.35

1934

SCOTT NO.	DESCRIPTION	PLATE BLOCK F/NH		UNUSED F/NH		USED F	
208	3¢ Jacques Cartier	8.50	6.75	4.50	3.50	1.50	1.00
209	10¢ Loyalists Monument	50.00	44.00	27.00	23.00	7.00	6.00
210	2¢ New Brunswick	6.75	5.00	4.25	3.00	2.25	1.50

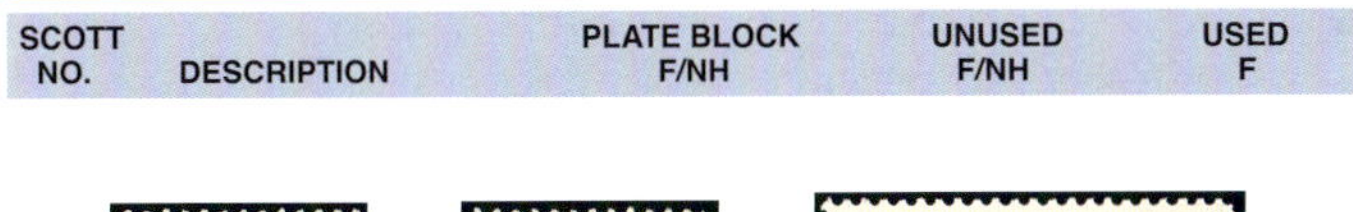

211

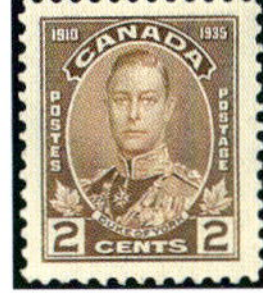
212

213

214

215

216

1935 SILVER JUBILEE ISSUE

SCOTT NO.	DESCRIPTION	PLATE BLOCK F/NH		UNUSED F/NH		USED F
211-16	1¢-13¢ complete, 6 varieties	.....	.....	45.00	34.00	11.00
211	1¢ Princess Elizabeth	11.00	9.00	1.00	.75	.35
212	2¢ Duke of York	13.00	10.00	1.75	1.25	.25
213	3¢ George & Mary	26.00	20.00	3.50	1.75	.25
214	5¢ Prince of Wales	75.00	65.00	9.00	7.00	2.75
215	10¢ Windsor Castle	105.00	90.00	13.00	10.00	3.50
216	13¢ Royal Yacht	115.00	90.00	15.00	11.00	5.50

217-22, 228-30
King George V

223

224

225

226

227

1935

SCOTT NO.	DESCRIPTION	PLATE BLOCK F/NH		UNUSED F/NH		USED F
217-27	1¢-$1 complete, 11 varieties	.....	.....	220.00	146.00	17.00
217	1¢ green	7.25	5.00	.50	.35	.25
217a	same, booklet pane of 4	.....	.....	95.00	65.00	.....
217b	same, booklet pane of 4	.....	.....	72.00	48.00	.....
218	2¢ brown	6.00	4.00	1.00	.75	.25
218a	same, booklet pane of 4		.....	95.00	65.00	.....
219	3¢ dark carmine	13.00	8.00	1.00	.75	.25
219a	same, booklet pane of 4		.....	48.00	33.00	.....
220	4¢ yellow	60.00	45.00	4.00	2.75	.60
221	5¢ blue	60.00	45.00	5.50	3.50	.25
222	8¢ deep orange	60.00	45.00	5.00	3.50	2.25
223	10¢ Mounted Policeman	125.00	95.00	11.00	7.50	2.25
224	13¢ Conference of 1864	125.00	95.00	13.00	9.00	.75
225	20¢ Niagara Falls	250.00	200.00	33.00	22.00	.75
226	50¢ Parliament Building	325.00	275.00	48.00	33.00	6.00
227	$1 Champlain Monument	650.00	450.00	110.00	70.00	10.00

1935 Coil Stamps Perf. 8 Vertically

SCOTT NO.	DESCRIPTION	PLATE BLOCK F/NH		UNUSED F/NH		USED F
228-30	1¢-3¢ coils, complete, 3 varieties	.....	.....	59.00	46.00	4.00
228	1¢ green	.....	.....	20.00	15.00	2.75
229	2¢ brown	.....	.....	24.00	16.00	.85
230	3¢ dark carmine	.....	.....	20.00	15.00	.60

231-236, 238-240
King George VI

237

241

242

243

244

245

246

247

248

1937

SCOTT NO.	DESCRIPTION	PLATE BLOCK F/NH		UNUSED F/NH		USED F
231-36	1¢-8¢ complete, 6 varieties	.....	.....	22.75	10.75	1.60
231	1¢ green	3.25	2.40	.50	.40	.25
231a	same, booklet pane of 4	.....	.....	22.00	16.00	.....
231b	same, booklet pane of 6	.....	.....	9.00	7.00	.....
232	2¢ brown	5.25	3.40	1.00	.75	.25
232a	same, booklet pane of 4	.....	.....	24.00	16.00	.....
232b	same, booklet pane of 6	.....	.....	15.00	10.00	.....
233	3¢ carmine	6.00	4.25	1.00	.75	.25
233a	same, booklet pane of 4	.....	.....	9.50	6.75	.....
234	4¢ yellow	29.00	21.00	4.00	3.00	.25
235	5¢ blue	29.00	22.00	5.00	3.25	.25
236	8¢ orange	29.00	22.00	4.00	2.75	.50
237	3¢ Coronation	3.35	2.60	.40	.30	.25

Coil Stamps Perf. 8 Vertically

SCOTT NO.	DESCRIPTION	PLATE BLOCK F/NH		UNUSED F/NH		USED F
238-40	1¢-3¢ coils, complete, 3 varieties	.....	.....	17.75	11.50	1.75
238	1¢ green	.....	.....	3.65	2.75	1.25
239	2¢ brown	.....	.....	7.25	5.25	.40
240	3¢ carmine	.....	.....	11.50	8.50	.25

1938

SCOTT NO.	DESCRIPTION	PLATE BLOCK F/NH		UNUSED F/NH		USED F
241-45	10¢-$1 complete, 5 varieties	.....	.....	235.00	152.00	12.50
241	10¢ Memorial Hall	66.00	48.00	14.00	10.00	.25
242	13¢ Halifax Harbor	95.00	77.00	19.00	13.00	.50
243	20¢ Fort Garry Gate	145.00	98.00	25.00	18.00	.45
244	50¢ Vancouver Harbor	270.00	195.00	65.00	42.00	5.50
245	$1 Chateau de Ramezay	530.00	380.00	125.00	77.00	6.75

1939 Royal Visit

SCOTT NO.	DESCRIPTION	PLATE BLOCK F/NH		UNUSED F/NH		USED F
246-48	1¢-3¢ complete, 3 varieties	4.25	3.25	1.05	.85	.60
246	1¢ Princess Elizabeth & Margaret	2.50	2.05	.55	.35	.25
247	2¢ War Memorial	2.90	2.05	.55	.35	.25
248	3¢ King George VI & Queen Elizabeth	2.90	2.05	.55	.35	.25

249, 255, 263, 278

250, 254, 264, 267, 279, 281
King George VI

253

256

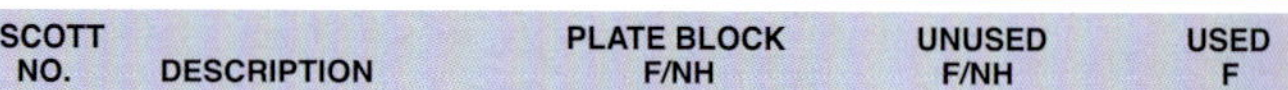

257

258, 259

260

261

262

1942-43 WAR ISSUE

SCOTT NO.	DESCRIPTION	PLATE BLOCK F/NH		UNUSED F/NH		USED F
249-62	**1¢-$1 complete, 14 varieties**	.....	.....	**195.00**	**138.00**	**15.00**
249	1¢ green	3.65	2.75	.55	.40	.25
249a	same, booklet pane of 4	.....	.....	5.00	3.50	.....
249b	same, booklet pane of 6	.....	.....	6.50	4.50	.....
249c	same, booklet pane of 3	.....	.....	3.50	2.25	.....
250	2¢ brown	4.25	2.85	.65	.45	.25
250a	same, booklet pane of 4	.....	.....	9.50	6.50	.....
250b	same, booklet pane of 6	.....	.....	12.50	8.50	.....
251	3¢ dark carmine	5.00	3.75	1.00	.70	.25
251a	same, booklet pane of 4	.....	.....	5.50	3.75	.....
252	3¢ rose violet (1943)	4.50	3.00	.80	.60	.25
252a	same, booklet pane of 4	.....	.....	4.75	3.25	.....
252b	same, booklet pane of 3	.....	.....	4.25	3.00	.....
252c	same, booklet pane of 6	.....	.....	4.75	3.25	.....
253	4¢ Grain Elevators	14.50	10.50	2.50	1.35	.65
254	4¢ dark carmine (1943)	5.00	3.25	1.00	.70	.25
254a	same, booklet pane of 6	.....	.....	7.00	4.75	.....
254b	same, booklet pane of 3	.....	.....	4.50	3.00	.....
255	5¢ deep blue	13.00	9.25	2.00	1.30	.25
256	8¢ Farm Scene	19.00	14.00	2.50	1.75	.60
257	10¢ Parliament Buildings	48.00	34.00	7.75	5.50	.25
258	13¢ "Ram" Tank	58.00	35.00	7.75	5.25	3.75
259	14¢ "Ram" Tank (1943)	67.00	47.00	12.00	8.50	.40
260	20¢ Corvette	72.00	53.00	14.00	9.50	.25
261	50¢ Munitions Factory	255.00	180.00	55.00	38.00	1.95
262	$1 Destroyer	590.00	475.00	110.00	68.00	7.75

Coil Stamps Perf. 8 Vertically

SCOTT NO.	DESCRIPTION	PLATE BLOCK F/NH		UNUSED F/NH		USED F
263-67	**1¢-4¢ complete, 5 varieties**	.....	.....	**18.75**	**13.00**	**3.30**
263	1¢ green	.....	.....	1.95	1.35	.55
264	2¢ brown	.....	.....	3.00	2.00	1.10
265	3¢ dark carmine	.....	.....	3.00	2.00	1.10
266	3¢ rose violet (1943)	.....	.....	5.25	3.75	.40
267	4¢ dark carmine (1943)	.....	.....	7.50	5.00	.30

268

269

270

271

272

273

1946 PEACE ISSUE

SCOTT NO.	DESCRIPTION	PLATE BLOCK F/NH		UNUSED F/NH		USED F
268-73	**8¢-$1 complete, 6 varieties**	......	......	**86.50**	**71.00**	**5.50**
268	8¢ Farm Scene	13.00	9.00	2.60	1.85	5.50
269	10¢ Great Bear Lake	30.00	14.00	4.00	3.00	.25
270	14¢ Hydro-Electric Power Station	25.00	18.00	4.75	3.50	.25
271	20¢ Reaper & Harvester	32.00	23.00	6.25	4.50	.25
272	50¢ Lumber Industry	112.00	77.00	25.00	20.00	1.85
273	$1 New Train Ferry	268.00	188.00	48.00	40.00	3.25

274

275

276

277

282

283

1947-49 COMMEMORATIVES

SCOTT NO.	DESCRIPTION	PLATE BLOCK F/NH		UNUSED F/NH		USED F
274/83	**274-77, 282-83, complete, 6 varieties**	**4.00**	**3.40**	**1.25**	**.85**	**.95**
274	4¢ Alexander G. Bell	1.70	1.10	.35	.30	.25
275	4¢ Canadian Citizen	1.70	1.10	.35	.30	.25
	1948					
276	4¢ Princess Elizabeth	1.70	1.10	.35	.30	.25
277	4¢ Parliament Building	1.70	1.10	.35	.30	.25

Designs of 1942-43 Coil Stamps Perf. 9-1/2 Vertically

SCOTT NO.	DESCRIPTION	PLATE BLOCK F/NH		UNUSED F/NH		USED F
278-81	**1¢-4¢ complete, 4 varieties**	.....	......	**43.00**	**36.50**	**13.75**
278	1¢ green			6.25	4.50	2.00
279	2¢ brown			18.00	15.00	8.50
280	3¢ rose violet			12.00	9.00	2.25
281	4¢ dark carmine			16.00	12.50	2.50
	1949					
282	4¢ Cabot's "Matthew"	1.25	.75	.30	.25	.25
283	4¢ Founding of Halifax	1.25	.75	.30	.25	.25

COMMEMORATIVES: Commemorative stamps are special issues released to honor or recognize persons, organizations, historical events or landmarks. They are usually issued in the current first class denomination to supplement regular issues.

284, 289, 295, 297 — 285, 290, 298, 305, 309 — 286, 291, 296, 299 — 287, 292, 300, 306, 310 — 288, 293

King George VI

1949 (with "Postes-Postage")

SCOTT NO.	DESCRIPTION	PLATE BLOCK F/NH	UNUSED F/NH	USED F
284-88	**1¢-5¢ complete, 5 varieties**	**10.70**	**2.70**	**1.00**
284	1¢ green	1.25	.30	.25
284a	same, booklet pane of 3	......	1.25	......
285	2¢ sepia	1.60	.35	.25
286	3¢ rose violet	2.00	.45	.25
286a	same, booklet pane of 3	......	2.80	......
286b	same, booklet pane of 4	......	3.50	......
287	4 dark carmine	3.00	.65	.25
287a	same, booklet pane of 3	......	13.50	......
287b	same, booklet pane of 6	......	19.00	......
288	5¢ deep blue	7.25	1.40	.25

1950 Type of 1949
(without "Postes-Postage")

SCOTT NO.	DESCRIPTION	PLATE BLOCK F/NH	UNUSED F/NH	USED F
289-93	**1¢-5¢ complete, 5 varieties**	**9.50**	**2.90**	**1.95**
289	1¢ green	1.30	.30	.25
290	2¢ sepia	3.00	.45	.25
291	3¢ rose violet	2.00	.45	.25
292	4¢ dark carmine	2.00	.45	.25
293	5¢ deep blue	7.75	1.55	1.25
294	50¢ Oil Wells, Alberta	60.50	12.65	1.65

Coil Stamps Perf. 9-1/2 Vertically

SCOTT NO.	DESCRIPTION	PLATE BLOCK F/NH	UNUSED F/NH	USED F
295-300	**1¢-4¢ complete, 6 vars.**	......	**25.50**	**3.75**
	(without "Postes-Postage")			
295	1¢ green	......	.70	.35
296	3¢ rose violet	......	1.25	.65
	(with "Postes-Postage")			
297	1¢ green	......	.45	.25
298	2¢ sepia	......	3.60	1.80
299	3¢ rose violet	......	2.40	.25
300	4¢ dark carmine	......	19.00	.95
301	10¢ Fur Resources	6.00	1.15	.25
302	$1 Fishing	275.00	65.00	14.00

294 — 301 — 302 — 303

304 — 311 — 314 — 315

1951

1951-52 COMMEMORATIVES

SCOTT NO.	DESCRIPTION	PLATE BLOCK F/NH	UNUSED F/NH	USED F
303/19	**(303-04, 311-15, 317-19) complete, 10 vars.**	**26.40**	**9.25**	**3.70**
303	3¢ Sir Robert L. Borden	1.85	.30	.25
304	4¢ William L.M. King	1.85	.35	.25
	(with "Postes-Postage")			
305	2¢ olive green	1.35	.25	.25
306	4¢ orange vermillion	1.85	.40	.25
306a	same, booklet pane of 3	......	6.00	......
306b	same, booklet pane of 6	......	5.50	......
	Coil Stamps Perf. 9-1/2 Vertically			
309	2¢ olive green	......	1.55	.80
310	4¢ orange vermillion	......	3.25	.95
	1951 "CAPEX" Exhibition			
311	4¢ Trains of 1851 & 1951	3.50	.70	.25
312	5¢ Steamships	11.00	2.25	1.80
313	7¢ Stagecoach & Plane	6.50	1.35	.45
314	15¢ "Three Pence Beaver"	7.00	1.50	.30
315	4¢ Royal Visit	1.30	.35	.25

317 — 318 — 1952 — 319 — 316

SCOTT NO.	DESCRIPTION	PLATE BLOCK F/NH	UNUSED F/NH	USED F
316	20¢ Paper Production	10.00	1.85	.25
317	4¢ Red Cross	1.50	.36	.25
318	3¢ J.J.C. Abbott	1.35	.30	.25
319	4¢ A. Mackenzie	1.55	.35	.25

1952-53

SCOTT NO.	DESCRIPTION	PLATE BLOCK F/NH	UNUSED F/NH	USED F
320	7¢ Canada Goose	2.40	.50	.25
321	$1 Indian House & Totem Pole (1953)	55.00	12.00	1.15

1953-54 COMMEMORATIVES

SCOTT NO.	DESCRIPTION	PLATE BLOCK F/NH	UNUSED F/NH	USED F
322/50	**(322-24, 330, 335-36, 349-50) complete, 8 varieties**	**8.95**	**1.90**	**1.60**
322	2¢ Polar Bear	1.35	.30	.25
323	3¢ Moose	1.40	.30	.25
324	4¢ Bighorn Sheep	1.75	.30	.25

320 — 321 — 322 — 323 — 324

1953

SCOTT NO.	DESCRIPTION	PLATE BLOCK F/NH	UNUSED F/NH	USED F
325-29	**1¢-5¢ complete, 5 vars.**	**4.50**	**1.25**	**.95**
325	1¢ violet brown	1.35	.25	.25
325a	same, booklet pane of 3	......	1.50	
326	2¢ green	1.35	.25	.25
327	3¢ carmine rose	1.40	.25	.25
327a	same, booklet pane of 3	1.85	......	
327b	same, booklet pane of 4	2.50	......	
328	4¢ violet	1.40	.25	.25
328a	same, bklt. pane of 3	......	2.50	......
328b	same, bklt. pane of 6	......	2.25	......
329	5¢ ultramarine	3.00	.40	.25
330	4¢ Queen Elizabeth II	1.35	.40	.25

Coil Stamps Perf. 9-1/2 Vertically

SCOTT NO.	DESCRIPTION	PLATE BLOCK F/NH	UNUSED F/NH	USED F
331-33	**2¢-4¢ complete, 3 vars.**	......	**8.00**	**3.60**
331	2¢ green	......	1.60	1.25
332	3¢ carmine rose	......	1.60	1.25
333	4¢ violet	......	3.30	1.90
334	50¢ Textile Industry	23.00	4.70	.25

325-29, 331-33 — 330 — 334 — 335

336 — 337-342, 345-348 — 343

1954

SCOTT NO.	DESCRIPTION	PLATE BLOCK F/NH	UNUSED F/NH	USED F
335	4¢ Walrus	1.85	.30	.25
336	5¢ Beaver	2.25	.35	.25
336a	same, booklet pane of 5	......	1.95	......
337-43	**1¢-15¢ cpl., 7 vars.**	**11.75**	**2.75**	**1.50**
337	1¢ violet brown	1.40	.25	.25
337a	same, booklet pane of 5	......	1.40	......
338	2¢ green	1.40	.25	.25
338a	mini pane of 25	......	4.40	......
338a	sealed pack of 2	......	9.50	......
339	3¢ carmine rose	1.40	.25	.25
340	4¢ violet	1.40	.25	.25
340a	same, booklet pane of 5	......	1.65	......
340b	same, booklet pane of 6	......	5.50	......
341	5¢ bright blue	1.75	.25	.25
341a	same, booklet pane of 5	......	1.65	......
341b	mini sheet of 20	......	8.25	......
342	6¢ orange	2.75	.55	.25
343	15¢ Gannet	7.75	1.60	.25

SCOTT NO.	DESCRIPTION	PLATE BLOCK F/NH	UNUSED F/NH	USED F

349 350 351 352 353

Coil Stamps Perf. 9-1/2 Vertically

SCOTT NO.	DESCRIPTION	PLATE BLOCK F/NH	UNUSED F/NH	USED F
345-48	**2¢-4¢ complete, 3 vars**	......	**4.50**	**.75**
345	2¢ green	......	.65	.25
347	4¢ violet	......	1.60	.25
348	5¢ bright blue	......	2.50	.25
349	4¢ J.S.D. Thompson	1.85	.35	.25
350	5¢ M. Bowell	1.85	.35	.25

1955

SCOTT NO.	DESCRIPTION	PLATE BLOCK F/NH	UNUSED F/NH	USED F
351	10¢ Eskimo in Kayak	2.25	.40	.20

1955-56 COMMEMORATIVES

SCOTT NO.	DESCRIPTION	PLATE BLOCK F/NH	UNUSED F/NH	USED F
352/64	**(352-61, 364 (complete, 11 varieties**	**26.00**	**3.75**	**2.10**
352	4¢ Musk Ox	1.85	.40	.25
353	5¢ Whooping Cranes	2.00	.45	.25

1955

SCOTT NO.	DESCRIPTION	PLATE BLOCK F/NH	UNUSED F/NH	USED F
354	5¢ Intl. Civil Aviation Org.	2.40	.50	.25
355	5¢ Alberta-Saskatchewan	2.40	.50	.25
356	5¢ Boy Scout Jamboree	2.40	.50	.25
357	4¢ R.B. Bennett	2.40	.50	.25
358	5¢ C. Tupper	2.40	.50	.25

1956

SCOTT NO.	DESCRIPTION	PLATE BLOCK F/NH	UNUSED F/NH	USED F
359	5¢ Hockey Players	2.25	.50	.25
360	4¢ Caribou	2.40	.50	.25
361	5¢ Mountain Goat	2.40	.50	.25
362	20¢ Paper Industry	9.50	1.55	.25
363	25¢ Chemical Industry	10.75	1.85	.25
364	5¢ Fire Prevention	1.85	.40	.25

354  355  356  357

358  359  360  361

362  363  364  365

1957 COMMEMORATIVES

SCOTT NO.	DESCRIPTION	PLATE BLOCK F/NH	UNUSED F/NH	USED F
365-74	**complete, 10 varieties**	**20.50(7)**	**6.20**	**4.50**
365-68	Recreation, attached	2.95	2.10	1.60
365	5¢ Fishing	......	.40	.25
366	5¢ Swimming	......	.40	.25
367	5¢ Hunting	......	.40	.25
368	5¢ Skiing	......	.40	.25
369	5¢ Loon	1.75	.40	.25
370	5¢ D. Thompson, Explorer	1.75	.40	.25
371	5¢ Parliament Building	1.75	.40	.25
372	15¢ Posthorn & Globe	12.50	2.50	2.25
373	5¢ Coal Miner	1.75	.35	.25
374	5¢ Royal Visit	1.75	.35	.25

1958 COMMEMORATIVES

SCOTT NO.	DESCRIPTION	PLATE BLOCK F/NH	UNUSED F/NH	USED F
375-82	**complete, 8 varieties**	**13.75(6)**	**2.75**	**1.80**
375	5¢ Newspaper	......	.35	.25
376	5¢ Int'l. Geophysical Year	......	.35	.25
377	5¢ Miner Panning Gold	3.25	.35	.25
378	5¢ La Verendrye, Explorer	2.50	.35	.25
379	5¢ S. deChamplain	5.25	.35	.25
380	5¢ National Health	2.30	.35	.25
381	5¢ Petroleum Industry	2.30	.35	.25
382	5¢ Speaker's Chair & Mace	2.30	.35	.25

369  370  371  372

373  374  375  376

377  378  379

380  381  382

1959 COMMEMORATIVES

SCOTT NO.	DESCRIPTION	PLATE BLOCK F/NH	UNUSED F/NH	USED F
383-88	**complete, 6 varieties**	**14.65**	**2.00**	**1.25**
383	5¢ Old & Modern Planes	2.40	.35	.25
384	5¢ NATO Anniversary	2.40	.35	.25
385	5¢ Woman Tending Tree	2.40	.35	.25
386	5¢ Royal Tour	2.40	.35	.25
387	5¢ St. Lawrence Seaway	5.25	.35	.25
387a	same, center inverted	...	9800.00	8000.00
388	5¢ Plains of Abraham	2.40	.35	.25

1960-62 COMMEMORATIVES

SCOTT NO.	DESCRIPTION	PLATE BLOCK F/NH	UNUSED F/NH	USED F
389-400	**complete, 12 varieties**	**17.50**	**4.00**	**2.25**
389	5¢ Girl Guides Emblem	1.85	.45	.25
390	5¢ Battle of Long Sault	1.85	.45	.25

1961

SCOTT NO.	DESCRIPTION	PLATE BLOCK F/NH	UNUSED F/NH	USED F
391	5¢ Earth Mover	1.85	.45	.25
392	5¢ E.P. Johnson	1.85	.45	.25

383 384 385

386  387  388  389

390  391  392

SCOTT NO.	DESCRIPTION	PLATE BLOCK F/NH	UNUSED F/NH	USED F
393	5¢ A. Meighen	1.85	.40	.25
394	5¢ Colombo Plan	1.85	.40	.25
395	5¢ Natural Resources	1.85	.40	.25
	1962			
396	5¢ Education	1.85	.40	.25
397	5¢ Red River Settlement	1.85	.40	.25
398	5¢ Jean Talon	1.85	.40	.25
399	5¢ Victoria, B.C.	1.85	.40	.25
400	5¢ Trans-Canada	1.85	.40	.25

393 395 396 394 397 398 399 400 401-09

1962-63

SCOTT NO.	DESCRIPTION	PLATE BLOCK F/NH	UNUSED F/NH	USED F
401-05	**1¢-5¢ complete, 5 varieties**	**7.00**	**1.00**	**.85**
401	1¢ deep brown (1963)	1.10	.30	.25
401a	same, booklet pane of 5	......	3.30	......
402	2¢ green (1963)	3.60	.30	.25
402a	mini pane of 25	......	8.00	......
402a	same, sealed pack of 2	......	18.50	......
403	3¢ purple (1963)	1.25	.30	.25
404	4¢ carmine (1963)	1.25	.30	.25
404a	same, booklet pane of 5	......	3.70	......
404b	mini pane of 25	......	13.00	......
405	5¢ violet blue	1.50	.30	.25
405a	same, booklet pane of 5	......	5.00	......
405b	mini pane of 20	......	15.00	......

1963-64 Coil Stamps, Perf. 9-1/2 Horiz.

SCOTT NO.	DESCRIPTION	PLATE BLOCK F/NH	UNUSED F/NH	USED F
406-09	**2¢-5¢ complete, 4 varieties**	......	**15.50**	**6.00**
406	2¢ green	......	4.65	2.25
407	3¢ purple (1964)	......	3.00	1.75
408	4¢ carmine	......	4.65	2.15
409	5¢ violet blue	......	4.65	.85

1963-64 COMMEMORATIVES

SCOTT NO.	DESCRIPTION	PLATE BLOCK F/NH	UNUSED F/NH	USED F
410/35	**(410, 412-13, 416-17, 431-35) 10 varieties**	**10.20**	**2.50**	**1.60**
410	5¢ Sir Casimir S. Gzowski	1.60	.35	.25
411	$1 Export Trade	74.25	15.00	2.50
412	5¢ Sir M. Frobisher, Explorer	1.60	.35	.25
413	5¢ First Mail Routes	1.60	.35	.25
	1963-64			
414	7¢ Jet Takeoff (1964)	2.75	.60	.55
415	15¢ Canada Geese	11.00	2.20	.25
	1964			
416	5¢ World Peace	1.50	.35	.25
417	5¢ Canadian Unity	1.50	.35	.25

410 411 412 413 414, 430, 436 415 416 417

COATS OF ARMS & FLORAL EMBLEMS

419 *Quebec & White Garden Lily*
420 *Nova Scotia & Mayflower*
421 *New Brunswick & Purple Violet (1965)*
422 *Manitoba & Prairie Crocus (1965)*
423 *British Columbia & Dogwood (1965)*
424 *Prince Edward Island & Lady's Slipper (1965)*
425 *Saskatchewan & Prairie Lily (1966)*
426 *Alberta & Wild Rose (1966)*
427 *Newfoundland & Pitcher Plant (1966)*
428 *Yukon & Fireweed (1966)*
429 *Northwest Territories & Mountain Avens (1966)*

418
Ontario & White Trillium

429A
Canada & Maple Leaf

1964-66

SCOTT NO.	DESCRIPTION	PLATE BLOCK F/NH	UNUSED F/NH	USED F
418-29A	**complete, 13 varieties**	**15.00**	**3.55**	**2.75**
418	5¢ red brown, buff & green	1.60	.35	.25
419	5¢ green, yellow & orange	1.60	.35	.25
420	5¢ blue, pink & green	1.60	.35	.25
421	5¢ carmine, green & violet	1.60	.35	.25
422	5¢ red brown, lilac & green	2.75	.35	.25
423	5¢ lilac, green & bistre	1.60	.35	.25
424	5¢ violet, green & deep rose	1.60	.35	.25
425	5¢ sepia, orange & green	1.60	.35	.25
426	5¢ green, yellow & carmine	1.60	.35	.25
427	5¢ black, green & carmine	1.60	.35	.25
428	5¢ dark blue, rose & green	2.75	.35	.25
429	5¢ olive, yellow & green	1.60	.35	.25
429A	5¢ dark blue & red (1966)	1.60	.35	.25
	1964 Surcharged on 414			
430	8¢ on 7¢ Jet Takeoff	......	.50	.40
431	5¢ Charlottetown Conference	1.60	.35	.25
432	5¢ Quebec Conference	1.60	.35	.25
433	5¢ Queen Elizabeth's Visit	1.60	.35	.25
434	3¢ Christmas	1.60	.35	.25
434a	mini sheet of 25	......	8.25	......
434a	same, sealed pack of 2	......	17.50	......
435	5¢ Christmas	1.60	.35	.25
	Jet Type of 1964			
436	8¢ Jet Takeoff	2.30	.50	.25

1965 COMMEMORATIVES

SCOTT NO.	DESCRIPTION	PLATE BLOCK F/NH	UNUSED F/NH	USED F
437-44	**8 varieties**	**9.00**	**2.50**	**1.65**
437	5¢ I.C.Y.	1.65	.35	.25

431 432 433 434, 435 437 438 439 440 441 442 443-44

SCOTT NO.	DESCRIPTION	PLATE BLOCK F/NH	UNUSED F/NH	USED F
438	5¢ Sir Wilfred Grenfell	1.60	.35	.25
439	5¢ National Flag	1.60	.35	.25
440	5¢ Winston Churchill	1.60	.35	.25
441	5¢ Inter-Parliamentary	1.60	.35	.25
442	5¢ Ottawa, National Capital	1.60	.35	.25
443	3¢ Christmas	1.60	.35	.25
443a	mini pane of 25	......	7.00	......
443a	same, sealed pack of 2	......	15.00	......
444	5¢ Christmas	1.60	.35	.25

1966 COMMEMORATIVES

SCOTT NO.	DESCRIPTION	PLATE BLOCK F/NH	UNUSED F/NH	USED F
445-52	**8 varieties**	**11.50**	**2.35**	**1.70**
445	5¢ Alouette II Satellite	1.60	.35	.25
446	5¢ La Salle Arrival	1.60	.35	.25
447	5¢ Highway Safety	1.60	.35	.25
448	5¢ London Conference	1.60	.35	.25
449	5¢ Atomic Reactor	1.60	.35	.25
450	5¢ Parliamentary Library	1.60	.35	.25
451	3¢ Christmas	1.60	.35	.25
451a	mini pane of 25	......	5.25	......
451a	same, sealed pack of 2	......	11.00	......
452	5¢ Christmas	1.60	.35	.25

445 446 447 448

449 451, 452 450 453

1967 COMMEMORATIVES

SCOTT NO.	DESCRIPTION	PLATE BLOCK F/NH	UNUSED F/NH	USED F
453/77	**(453, 469-77) complete, 10 varieties**	**10.00**	**2.70**	**2.10**
453	5¢ National Centennial	1.60	.35	.25

454 455 456, 466 457, 467

458, 468 459-460F, 468A-B, 543-49 461 465B

Regional Views & Art Designs 1967-72 Perf.12 except as noted

SCOTT NO.	DESCRIPTION	PLATE BLOCK F/NH	UNUSED F/NH	USED F
454-65B	**1¢-$1 complete, 14 varieties**	**95.50**	**18.25**	**3.60**
454-64	**1¢-20¢, 11 varieties**	**21.00**	**3.35**	**1.85**
454	1¢ brown	1.35	.30	.25
454a	same, booklet pane of 5	......	1.35	......
454b	booklet pane, 1¢(1), 6¢(4)	......	3.30	......
454c	booklet pane, 1¢(5), 3¢(5)	......	3.85	......

NOTE: **#454d, 454e, 456a, 457d, 458d, 460g, and 460h are Booklet Singles**

SCOTT NO.	DESCRIPTION	PLATE BLOCK F/NH	UNUSED F/NH	USED F
454d	1¢ perf. 10 (1968)	......	.35	.25
454e	1¢ 12-1/2 x 12 (1969)	......	.45	.25
455	2¢ green	1.40	.30	.25
455a	booklet pane 2¢(4), 3¢(4)	......	1.80	......
456	3¢ dull purple	2.10	.30	.25
456a	3¢ 12-1/2 x 12 (1971)	......	2.20	1.20
457	4¢ carmine rose	2.10	.30	.25
457a	same, booklet pane 5	......	1.50	......
457b	miniature pane of 25	......	26.00	......
457c	same, booklet pane of 25	......	9.00	......
457d	4¢ perf.10 (1968)	......	.70	.30
458	5¢ blue	1.55	.30	.25
458a	same, booklet pane of 5	......	6.50	......
458b	miniature pane of 20	......	34.00	......
458c	booklet pane of 20, perf.10	......	8.50	......
458d	5¢ perf. 10 (1968)	......	.70	.30
459	6¢ orange, perf. 10 (1968)	3.85	.35	.25
459a	same, booklet pane of 25	......	10.00	......
459b	6¢ orange 12-1/2x12 (1969)	3.30	.35	.25
460	6¢ black, 12-1/2x12 (1970)	2.30	.30	.25
460a	booklet pane of 25, perf.10	......	15.85	......
460b	booklet pane of 25, 12-1/2x12	......	18.50	......
460c	6¢ black, 12-1/2x12 (1970)	2.20	.35	.25
460d	booklet pane of 4, 12-1/2x12	......	5.50	......
460e	booklet pane of 4, perf.10	......	12.00	......
460f	6¢ black, perf. 12 (1972)	2.50	.50	.35
460g	6¢ black, perf. 10 (I)	......	1.75	.40
460h	6¢ black, perf. 10 (II)	......	4.00	1.25

460, 460a, b,& g: Original Die. Weak shading lines around 6.
460 c, d, e, & h: Reworked plate lines strengthened, darker.
460f: Original Die. Strong shading lines, similar to 468B, but Perf 12x12 .

SCOTT NO.	DESCRIPTION	PLATE BLOCK F/NH	UNUSED F/NH	USED F
461	8¢ "Alaska Highway"	3.00	.35	.25
462	10¢ "The Jack Pine"	1.80	.35	.25
463	15¢ "Bylot Island"	3.55	.55	.25
464	20¢ "The Ferry, Quebec"	3.55	.70	.25
465	25¢ "The Solemn Land"	7.60	1.50	.25
465A	50¢ "Summer Stores"	22.00	4.40	.25
465B	$1 "Imp. Wildcat No. 3"	49.50	9.90	.80

1967-70 Coil Stamps

SCOTT NO.	DESCRIPTION	PLATE BLOCK F/NH	UNUSED F/NH	USED F
466-68B	3¢-6¢ complete, 5 varieties	......	7.40	3.35

Perf. 9-1/2 Horizontally

SCOTT NO.	DESCRIPTION	PLATE BLOCK F/NH	UNUSED F/NH	USED F
466	3¢ dull purple	......	4.00	1.10
467	4¢ carmine rose	......	1.25	.65
468	5¢ blue	......	2.75	.85

Perf. 10 Horizontally

SCOTT NO.	DESCRIPTION	PLATE BLOCK F/NH	UNUSED F/NH	USED F
468A	6¢ orange (1969)	......	.50	.25
468B	6¢ black (1970)	......	.45	.25

NOTE: **See #543-50 for similar issues**

469 470 471

472 473 474

1967

SCOTT NO.	DESCRIPTION	PLATE BLOCK F/NH	UNUSED F/NH	USED F
469	5¢ Expo '67	1.60	.35	.25
470	5¢ Women's Franchise	1.60	.35	.25
471	5¢ Royal Visit	1.60	.35	.25
472	5¢ Pan-American Games	1.60	.35	.25
473	5¢ Canadian Press	1.60	.35	.25
474	5¢ George P. Vanier	1.60	.35	.25
475	5¢ View of Toronto	1.60	.35	.25
476	3¢ Christmas	1.30	.35	.25
476a	miniature pane of 25	......	4.25	......
476a	same, sealed pack of 2	......	8.50	......
477	5¢ Christmas	1.30	.20	.25

475 476, 477 478 479

480 481 482

483 484 485 486

1968 COMMEMORATIVES

SCOTT NO.	DESCRIPTION	PLATE BLOCK F/NH	UNUSED F/NH	USED F
478-89	**complete, 12 varieties**	**22.00**	**5.25**	**3.75**
478	5¢ Gray Jays	4.40	.55	.25
479	5¢ Weather Map & Inst .	1.55	.35	.25
480	5¢ Narwhal	1.55	.35	.25
481	5¢ Int'l Hydro. Decade	1.55	.35	.25
482	5¢ Voyage of "Nonsuch"	1.55	.35	.25
483	5¢ Lacrosse Players	1.55	.35	.25
484	5¢ G. Brown, Politician	1.55	.35	.25
485	5¢ H. Bourassa, Journalist	1.55	.35	.25
486	15¢ W.W.I Armistice	11.00	2.25	1.70

NOTE: **Beginning with #478, some issues show a printer's inscription with no actual plate number.**

487 488 490 491 492 493

SCOTT NO.	DESCRIPTION	PLATE BLOCK F/NH	UNUSED F/NH	USED F
487	5¢ J. McCrae	1.60	.35	.25
488	5¢ Eskimo Family	1.20	.25	.25
488a	same, booklet pane of 10	.....	3.15	.....
489	6¢ Mother & Child	1.20	.25	.25

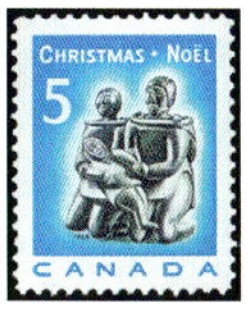

1969 COMMEMORATIVES

SCOTT NO.	DESCRIPTION	PLATE BLOCK F/NH	UNUSED F/NH	USED F
490-504	**complete, 15 varieties**	**48.25**	**12.50**	**9.00**
490	6¢ Game of Curling	1.55	.35	.25
491	6¢ V. Massey	1.55	.35	.25
492	50¢ A. deSuzor-Cote, Artist	20.00	3.85	3.30
493	6¢ I.L.O.	1.55	.35	.25
494	15¢ Vickers Vimy Over Atlantic	9.50	2.85	1.80
495	6¢ Sir W. Osler	1.55	.35	.25
496	6¢ White Throated Sparrows	2.00	.45	.25
497	10¢ Ipswich Sparrow	3.85	.75	.50
498	25¢ Hermit Thrush	9.60	2.10	2.00
499	6¢ Map of Prince Edward Island	1.55	.30	.25
500	6¢ Canada Games	1.55	.30	.25
501	6¢ Sir Isaac Brock	1.55	.30	.25
502	5¢ Children of Various Races	1.55	.30	.25
502a	booklet pane of 10	......	4.00	......
503	6¢ Children Various Races	1.35	.35	.25
504	6¢ Stephen Leacock	1.55	.35	.25

1970 COMMEMORATIVES

SCOTT NO.	DESCRIPTION	PLATE BLOCK F/NH	UNUSED F/NH	USED F
505/31	**(505-18, 531) 15 varieties**	**26.00**	**13.75**	**12.00**
505	6¢ Manitoba Cent.	1.55	.35	.25
506	6¢ N.W. Territory Centenary	1.55	.35	.25
507	6¢ International Biological	1.55	.35	.25
508-11	Expo '70 attached	12.00	9.75	9.75
508	25¢ Emblems	......	2.50	2.50
509	25¢ Dogwood	......	2.50	2.50
510	25¢ Lily	......	2.50	2.50
511	25¢ Trilium	......	2.50	2.50

494  495  496  500  501  499 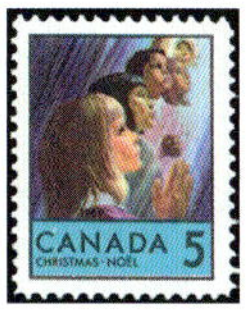 502, 503  504  505  506  507  508  509  512  513-514

515 516 517 518 519 524 529 530

SCOTT NO.	DESCRIPTION	PLATE BLOCK F/NH	UNUSED F/NH	USED F
512	6¢ H. Kelsey—Explorer	1.55	.35	.25
513	10¢ 25th U.N. Anniversary	3.85	.80	.65
514	15¢ 25th U.N. Anniversary	6.25	1.25	1.10
515	6¢ L. Riel—Metis Leader	1.55	.35	.25
516	6¢ Sir A. Mackenzie-Explorer	1.55	.35	.25
517	6¢ Sir O. Mowat Confederation Father	1.55	.35	.25
518	6¢ Isle of Spruce	1.55	.35	.25
519-30	**5¢-15¢ complete, 12 varieties**	**18.00**	**5.50**	**3.50**
519-23	5¢ Christmas, attached	7.95(10)	3.10	2.80
519	5¢ Santa Claus	......	.45	.25
520	5¢ Sleigh	......	.45	.25
521	5¢ Nativity	......	.45	.25
522	5¢ Skiing	......	.45	.25
523	5¢ Snowman & Tree	......	.45	.25
524-28	6¢ Christmas, attached	10.00(10)	3.55	3.25
524	6¢ Christ Child	......	.55	.25
525	6¢ Tree & Children	......	.55	.25
526	6¢ Toy Store	......	.55	.25
527	6¢ Santa Claus	......	.55	.25
528	6¢ Church	......	.55	.25

NOTE: We cannot supply blocks or pairs of the 5¢ & 6¢ Christmas designs in varying combinations of designs.

SCOTT NO.	DESCRIPTION	PLATE BLOCK F/NH	UNUSED F/NH	USED F
529	10¢ Christ Child	2.20	.60	.40
530	15¢ Snowmobile & Trees	4.80	1.25	1.00
531	6¢ Sir Donald A. Smith	1.55	.35	.25

1971 COMMEMORATIVES

SCOTT NO.	DESCRIPTION	PLATE BLOCK F/NH	UNUSED F/NH	USED F
532/58	**(532-42, 552-58) complete, 18 varieties**	**31.00**	**8.50**	**7.95**
532	6¢ E. Carr—Painter & Writer	1.55	.35	.25
533	6¢ Discovery of Insulin	1.55	.35	.25
534	6¢ Sir E. Rutherford—Physicist	1.55	.35	.25
535-38	6¢-7¢ Maple Leaves	6.75	1.20	.80
535	6¢ Maple Seeds	1.75	.35	.25
536	6¢ Summer Leaf	1.75	.35	.25
537	Autumn Leaf	1.75	.35	.25
538	7¢ Winter Leaf	1.75	.35	.25
539	6¢ L. Papineau—Polit. Reform	1.55	.35	.25
540	6¢ Copper Mine Expedition	1.55	.35	.25
541	15¢ Radio Canada Int'l	9.95	2.00	1.50
542	6¢ Census Centennial	1.55	.35	.25

531  532  533  534  535  539  540  541 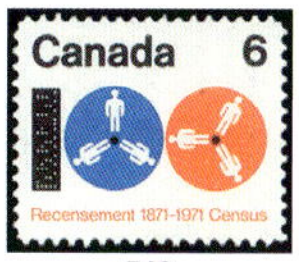 542  543, 549  544, 550

552

553

554-55

556-57

558

559

560

561

1971

SCOTT NO.	DESCRIPTION	PLATE BLOCK F/NH	UNUSED F/NH	USED F
543	7¢ Trans. & Communication	3.70	.40	.20
543a	bklt. pane, 7¢(3), 3¢(1), 1¢(1)	......	4.50	......
543b	bklt. pane 7¢(12), 3¢(4), 1¢(4)	......	8.50	......
544	8¢ Parliamentary Library	2.95	.50	.20
544a	bklt. pane 8¢(2), 6¢(1), 1¢(3)		2.55	......
544b	bklt. pane 8¢(11), 6¢(1), 1¢(6)	......	6.95	......
544c	bklt. pane 8¢(5), 6¢(1), 1¢(4)	......	3.85	......

1971 Coil Stamps Perf.10 Horizontally

SCOTT NO.	DESCRIPTION	PLATE BLOCK F/NH	UNUSED F/NH	USED F
549	7¢ Trans. & Communication	......	.40	.25
550	8¢ Parliamentary Library	......	.35	.25
552	7¢ B.C. Centennial	1.55	.35	.25
553	7¢ Paul Kane	3.20	.50	.25
554-57	6¢-15¢ Christmas	8.00	1.65	1.50
554	6¢ Snowflake, dark blue	1.25	.35	.25
555	7¢ same, bright green	1.25	.35	.25
556	10¢ same, deep carmine & silver	2.20	.45	.40
557	15¢ same, light ultramarine, deep carmine & silver	4.00	.85	.85
558	7¢ P. Laporte	2.70	.35	.25

1972 COMMEMORATIVES

SCOTT NO.	DESCRIPTION	PLATE BLOCK F/NH	UNUSED F/NH	USED F
559/610	**(559-61, 582-85, 606-10) 12 varieties**	**47.85(9)**	**10.40**	**8.60**
559	8¢ Figure Skating	1.55	.35	.25
560	8¢ W.H.O. Heart Disease	1.80	.40	.25
561	8¢ Frontenac & Ft. St. Louis	1.55	.35	.25

VERY FINE QUALITY: From 1935 to date, add 20% to the Fine price. Minimum of 3¢ per stamp.

1972-76 INDIAN PEOPLES OF CANADA

SCOTT NO.	DESCRIPTION	PLATE BLOCK F/NH	UNUSED F/NH	USED F
562-81	**complete, 20 varieties**	**17.25**	**7.35**	**4.40**
562-63	Plains, attached	2.15	.90	.60
562	8¢ Buffalo Chase	......	.45	.30
563	8¢ Indian Artifacts	......	.45	.30
564-65	Plains, attached	2.15	.90	.60
564	8¢ Thunderbird Symbolism	......	.45	.30
565	8¢ Sun Dance Costume	......	.45	.30
566-67	Algonkians, attached (1973)	2.15	.90	.60
566	8¢ Algonkian Artifacts	......	.45	.30
567	8¢ Micmac Indians	......	.45	.30
568-69	Algonkians, attached (1973)	2.00	.80	.75
568	8¢ Thunderbird Symbolism	......	.45	.30
569	8¢ Costume	......	.45	.30
570-71	Pacific, attached (1974)	2.00	.80	.60
570	8¢ Nootka Sound House	......	.45	.30
571	8¢ Artifacts	......	.45	.30
572-73	Pacific, attached (1974)	2.00	.80	1.00
572	8¢ Chief in Chilkat Blanket	......	.45	.30
573	8¢ Thunderbird—Kwakiutl	......	.45	.30
574-75	Subarctic, attached (1975)	1.70	.70	.60
574	8¢ Canoe & Artifacts	......	.35	.25
575	8¢ Dance—Kutcha-Kutchin	......	.35	.25
576-77	Subarctic, attached (1975)	1.70	.70	.65
576	8¢ Kutchin Costume	......	.35	.25
577	8¢ Ojibwa Thunderbird	......	.35	.25
578-79	Iroquois, attached (1976)	1.70	.70	.60
578	10¢ Masks	......	.35	.25
579	10¢ Camp	......	.35	.25
580-81	Iroquois, attached (1976)	1.70	.70	.60
580	10¢ Iroquois Thunderbird	......	.35	.25
581	10¢ Man & Woman	......	.35	.25

562

564

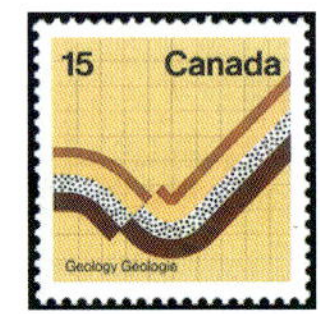
582

1972 EARTH SCIENCES

SCOTT NO.	DESCRIPTION	PLATE BLOCK F/NH	UNUSED F/NH	USED F
582-85	Sciences, attached	38.50(16)	8.25	8.00
582	15¢ Geology	......	2.00	1.75
583	15¢ Geography	......	2.00	1.75
584	15¢ Photogrammetry	......	2.00	1.75
585	15¢ Cartography	......	2.00	1.75

NOTE: **Plate Block Price is for a miniature pane of 16 Stamps.**

1973-76 DEFINITIVE ISSUE PERF. 12 x 12-1/2

SCOTT NO.	DESCRIPTION	PLATE BLOCK F/NH	UNUSED F/NH	USED F
586-93A	**1¢-10¢, 9 varieties**	**8.85**	**1.85**	**1.60**
586	1¢ Sir J. Macdonald	1.30	.25	.25
586a	bklt. pane 1¢(3), 6¢(1), 8¢(2)	......	1.25	......
586b	bklt. pane 1¢(6), 6¢(1), 8¢(11)	......	3.00	......
586c	bklt. pane 1¢(2), 2¢(4), 8¢(4)	......	1.70	......
587	2¢ Sir W. Laurier	1.30	.30	.25
588	3¢ Sir R.L. Borden	1.30	.30	.25
589	4¢ W.L. Mackenzie King	1.30	.30	.25
590	5¢ R.B. Bennett	1.30	.30	.25
591	6¢ L.B. Pearson	1.30	.30	.25
592	7¢ L. St. Laurent (1974)	1.30	.30	.25
593	8¢ Queen Elizabeth	1.30	.30	.25
593b	same (pf. 13x13-1/2) (1976)	4.95	1.00	.50
593A	10¢ Queen Elizabeth (perf 13x13-1/2) (1976)	1.55	.35	.50
593c	10¢ same, perf 12x12-1/2 booklet single	......	.50	.50

586

593, 593b, 593A, 604-605

594, 594a, 594B

599, 599a, 600

1972-73 Photogravure & Engraved Perf. 12-1/2x12

SCOTT NO.	DESCRIPTION	PLATE BLOCK F/NH	UNUSED F/NH	USED F
594-99	**10¢-$1, 6 varieties**	**26.00**	**5.10**	**6.45**
594	10¢ Forests	1.80	.40	.25
595	15¢ Mountain Sheep	1.90	.45	.25
596	20¢ Prairie Mosaic	3.30	.60	.25
597	25¢ Polar Bears	3.30	.65	.25
598	50¢ Seashore	5.95	1.25	.25
599	$1 Vancouver Skyline(1973)	13.75	2.80	.75

NOTE: **#594-97 exist with 2 types of phosphor tagging. Prices are for Ottawa tagged.**

1976-77 Perf. 13

SCOTT NO.	DESCRIPTION	PLATE BLOCK F/NH	UNUSED F/NH	USED F
594a	10¢ Forests	1.80	.40	.25
595a	15¢ Mountain Sheep	13.00	.65	.25
596a	20¢ Prairie Mosaic	3.25	.65	.25
597a	25¢ Polar Bears	3.60	.75	.25
598a	50¢ Seashore	9.50	1.90	.25
599a	$1 Vancouver Skyline(1977)	13.75	2.80	.45

1972 Lithographed & Engraved Perf. 11

SCOTT NO.	DESCRIPTION	PLATE BLOCK F/NH	UNUSED F/NH	USED F
600	$1 Vancouver Skyline	29.00	6.00	2.30
601	$2 Quebec Buildings	25.00	5.00	3.25

1974-76 Coil Stamps

SCOTT NO.	DESCRIPTION	PLATE BLOCK F/NH	UNUSED F/NH	USED F
604	8¢ Queen Elizabeth	......	.30	.25
605	10¢ Queen Elizabeth (1976)	......	.40	.25

1972

SCOTT NO.	DESCRIPTION	PLATE BLOCK F/NH	UNUSED F/NH	USED F
606-09	6¢-15¢ Christmas	8.40	1.70	1.45
606	6¢ Five candles	1.30	.40	.25
607	8¢ same	1.55	.40	.25
608	10¢ Six candles	2.30	.45	.25
609	15¢ same	3.50	.80	.80
610	8¢ C.Krieghoff—Painter	2.60	.40	.25

606, 607

608, 609

610

611

1973 COMMEMORATIVES

SCOTT NO.	DESCRIPTION	PLATE BLOCK F/NH	UNUSED F/NH	USED F
611-28	**18 varieties, complete**	**28.40**	**6.70**	**5.40**
611	8¢ Monseignor De Laval	1.55	.25	.25
612	8¢ G.A. French & Map	1.55	.30	.25
613	10¢ Spectrograph	2.00	.45	.35
614	15¢ "Musical Ride"	3.95	.75	.70
615	8¢ J. Mance—Nurse	1.55	.35	.25
616	8¢ J. Howe	1.55	.35	.25
617	15¢ "Mist Fantasy" Painting	3.30	.70	.65
618	8¢ P.E.I. Confederation	1.55	.35	.25
619	8¢ Scottish Settlers	1.55	.35	.25
620	8¢ Royal Visit	1.55	.35	.25
621	15¢ same	3.25	.70	.60
622	8¢ Nellie McClung	1.55	.35	.25
623	8¢ 21st Olympic Games	1.55	.35	.25
624	15¢ same	3.30	.70	.60
625-28	6¢ to 15¢ Christmas	5.75	1.30	1.25
625	6¢ Skate	1.30	.25	.25
626	8¢ Bird Ornament	1.30	.25	.25
627	10¢ Santa Claus	1.55	.30	.30
628	15¢ Shepherd	3.30	.65	.65

612 615 616 617 618 619 620, 621 622 623, 624 627 625 629 633 634

1974 COMMEMORATIVES

SCOTT NO.	DESCRIPTION	PLATE BLOCK F/NH	UNUSED F/NH	USED F
629-55	**complete, 27 varieties**	**22.40(16)**	**11.25**	**7.50**
629-32	Summer Olympics, attached	2.00	1.65	1.35
629	8¢ Children Diving	......	.45	.25
630	8¢ Jogging	......	.45	.25
631	8¢ Bicycling	......	.45	.25
632	8¢ Hiking	......	.45	.25
633	8¢ Winnipeg Centenary	1.55	.25	.25
634-39	Postal Carriers, attached	4.60(6)	3.85	3.85
634	8¢ Postal Clerk & Client	......	.75	.50
635	8¢ Mail Pick-up	......	.75	.50
636	8¢ Mail Handler	......	.75	.50
637	8¢ Sorting Mail	......	.75	.50
638	8¢ Letter Carrier	......	.75	.50
639	8¢ Rural Delivery	......	.75	.35
640	8¢ Agriculture Symbol	1.55	.35	.25
641	8¢ Antique to Modern Phones	1.55	.35	.25
642	8¢ World Cycling Championship	1.55	.35	.25
643	8¢ Mennonite Settlers	1.55	.35	.25
644-47	Winter Olympics, attached	2.00	1.75	1.40
644	8¢ Snowshoeing	......	.40	.25
645	8¢ Skiing	.....	.40	.25
646	8¢ Skating	.....	.40	.25
647	8¢ Curling	.....	.40	.25
648	8¢ U.P.U. Cent.	1.55	.35	.25
649	15¢ same	4.80	1.00	.70
650-53	6¢ to 15¢ Christmas	8.00	1.55	1.40
650	6¢ Nativity	1.30	.25	.25
651	8¢ Skaters in Hull	1.30	.25	.25
652	10¢ The Ice Cone	2.00	.45	.35
653	15¢ Laurentian Village	3.60	.60	.50
654	8¢ G. Marconi—Radio Inventor	1.55	.35	.25
655	8¢ W.H. Merritt & Welland Canal	1.55	.35	.25

640 641 642 643 644 648, 649 650 651 654 655 656 657

1975 COMMEMORATIVES

SCOTT NO.	DESCRIPTION	PLATE BLOCK F/NH	UNUSED F/NH	USED F
656-80	**complete, 25 varieties**	**67.50(18)**	**16.60**	**15.00**
656	$1 "The Sprinter"	11.75	2.85	2.75
657	$2 "The Plunger"	25.35	5.75	5.50
658-59	Writers, attached	1.55	.90	.50
658	8¢ L.M. Montgomery—Author	......	.35	.25
659	8¢ L. Hemon—Author	......	.35	.25
660	8¢ M. Bourgeoys—Educator	1.55	.35	.25
661	8¢ A. Desjardins—Credit Union	1.55	.35	.25
662-63	Religious, attached	1.55	.70	.70
662	8¢ S Chown & Church	......	.30	.25
663	8¢ J. Cook & Church	......	.30	.25
664	20¢ Pole Vaulter	3.30	.75	.50
665	25¢ Marathon Runner	3.85	.85	.55
666	50¢ Hurdler	7.75	1.50	1.40
667	8¢ Calgary Centenary	1.55	.35	.25
668	8¢ Int'l. Women's Year	1.55	.35	.25
669	8¢ "Justice"	1.55	.35	.25
670-73	Ships, attached	2.75	2.20	1.85
670	8¢ W.D. Lawrence	......	.55	.35
671	8¢ Beaver	......	.55	.35
672	8¢ Neptune	......	.55	.35
673	8¢ Quadra	......	.55	.35
674-79	6¢ to 15¢ Christmas	5.60(4)	1.75	1.50
674-75	Christmas, attached	1.35	.60	.35
674	6¢ Santa Claus	......	.30	.25
675	6¢ Skater	......	.30	.25
676-77	Christmas, attached	1.50	.55	.45
676	8¢ Child	......	.30	.25
677	8¢ Family & Tree	......	.30	.25
678	10¢ Gift	1.55	.35	.25
679	15¢ Trees	2.40	.55	.55
680	8¢ Horn & Crest	1.55	.35	.25

658 659 660 661 662-63 664 666 667 668 669 670

674 676

679

680

681

687

689 690 684

691

1976 COMMEMORATIVES

SCOTT NO.	DESCRIPTION	PLATE BLOCK F/NH	UNUSED F/NH	USED F
681-703	complete, 23 varieties	75.00(18)	21.25	16.90
681	8¢ Olympic Flame	1.50	.35	.25
682	20¢ Opening Ceremony	3.70	.85	.70
683	25¢ Receiving Medals	4.95	1.10	.85
684	20¢ Communication Arts	6.95	1.35	.70
685	25¢ Handicraft Tools	8.25	1.65	.75
686	50¢ Performing Arts	12.50	2.50	1.65
687	$1 Notre Dame & Tower	17.00	3.50	2.75
688	$2 Olympic Stadium	28.00	5.80	5.35
689	20¢ Olympic Winter Games	5.00	1.00	.85
690	20¢ "Habitat"	2.95	.65	.65
691	10¢ Benjamin Franklin	1.85	.40	.25
692-93	Military College, attached	1.55	.70	.50
692	8¢ Color Parade	......	.30	.25
693	8¢ Wing Parade	......	.30	.25
694	20¢ Olympiad—Phys. Disabled	3.25	.65	.60
695-96	Authors, attached	1.55	.60	.50
695	8¢ R.W. Service—Author	......	.30	.25
696	8¢ G. Guevremont—Author	......	.30	.25
697	8¢ Nativity Window	1.30	.30	.25
698	10¢ same	1.55	.30	.25
699	20¢ same	2.80	.65	.65
700-03	Inland Vessels, attached	2.30	1.85	1.75
700	10¢ Northcote	......	.45	.40
701	10¢ Passport	......	.45	.40
702	10¢ Chicora	......	.45	.40
703	10¢ Athabasca	......	.45	.40

692-93

694

695

696

697

700

704

1977 COMMEMORATIVES

SCOTT NO.	DESCRIPTION	PLATE BLOCK F/NH	UNUSED F/NH	USED F
704/51	(704, 732-51) complete, 21 varieties	20.85(14)	7.25	5.50
704	25¢ Silver Jubilee	3.85	.80	.70

705, 781, 781a

713, 713a, 716, 716a , 789, 789a, 791, 792

714, 715, 729, 730, 790, 797, 800, 806

1977-79 Definitives Perf. 12x12-1/2

SCOTT NO.	DESCRIPTION	PLATE BLOCK F/NH	UNUSED F/NH	USED F
705-27	1¢ to $2 complete, 22 varieties	66.50	19.50	6.40
705	1¢ Bottle Gentian	1.10	.25	.25
707	2¢ Western Columbine	1.10	.25	.25
708	3¢ Canada Lily	1.10	.25	.25
709	4¢ Hepatica	1.10	.25	.25
710	5¢ Shooting Star	1.10	.25	.25
711	10¢ Lady's Slipper	1.10	.25	.25
711a	same, perf.13 (1978)	1.35	.25	.25
712	12¢ Jewelweed, perf 13x13-1/2 (1978)	3.80	.30	.25
713	12¢ Queen Elizabeth II, perf.13x13-1/2	1.55	.35	.25
713a	same, perf.12x12-1/2	......	.35	.25
714	12¢ Parliament, perf.13	1.55	.25	.25
715	14¢ same, perf.13 (1978)	1.80	.30	.25
716	14¢ Queen Elizabeth II perf. 13x13-1/2	1.80	.30	.25
716a	14¢ same, perf 12x12-1/2	......	.30	.25
716b	same, booklet pane of 25	......	6.25	......

NOTE: **713a and 716a are from booklet panes. 713a will have one or more straight edges, 716a may or may not have straight edges.**

717

723, 723A

726

Perforated 13-1/2

SCOTT NO.	DESCRIPTION	PLATE BLOCK F/NH	UNUSED F/NH	USED F
717	15¢ Trembling Aspen	2.50	.50	.25
718	20¢ Douglas Fir	2.65	.55	.25
719	25¢ Sugar Maple	3.30	.70	.25
720	30¢ Oak Leaf	3.70	.80	.25
721	35¢ White Pine (1979)	4.20	.90	.35
723	50¢ Main Street (1978)	6.85	1.40	.30
723A	50¢ same, 1978 Lic. Plate	6.50	1.25	.45
723C	60¢ Ontario House	7.75	1.55	.45
724	75¢ Row Houses (1978)	9.00	1.90	.70
725	80¢ Maritime (1978)	9.75	1.95	.90
726	$1 Fundy Park (1979)	12.00	2.50	.70
727	$2 Kluane Park (1979)	26.00	5.25	1.60

1977-78 Coil Stamps Perf. 10 Vert.

SCOTT NO.	DESCRIPTION	PLATE BLOCK F/NH	UNUSED F/NH	USED F
729	12¢ Parliament	......	.30	.25
730	14¢ same (1978)	......	.40	.25

732

733

735

736

737

1977 COMMEMORATIVES

SCOTT NO.	DESCRIPTION	PLATE BLOCK F/NH	UNUSED F/NH	USED F
732	12¢ Cougar	1.55	.35	.25
733-34	Thomson, attached	1.55	.70	.45
733	12¢ Algonquin Park	......	.35	.25
734	12¢ Autumn Birches	......	.35	.25
735	12¢ Crown & Lion	1.55	.35	.25
736	12¢ Badge & Ribbon	1.55	.35	.25
737	12¢ Peace Bridge	1.55	.35	.25

738-39

740

741

SCOTT NO.	DESCRIPTION	PLATE BLOCK F/NH	UNUSED F/NH	USED F
738-39	Pioneers, attached	1.60	.70	.45
738	12¢ Bernier & CGS Arctic	......	.30	.25
739	12¢ Fleming & RR Bridge	......	.30	.25
740	25¢ Peace Tower	3.85	.75	.75
741	10¢ Braves & Star	1.20	.25	.20
742	12¢ Angelic Choir	1.55	.25	.20
743	25¢ Christ Child	3.55	.80	.60
744-47	Sailing Ships	1.55	1.35	1.15
744	12¢ Pinky	......	.35	.25
745	12¢ Tern	......	.35	.25
746	12¢ Five Masted	......	.35	.25
747	12¢ Mackinaw	......	.35	.25
748-49	Inuit, attached	1.55	.60	.50
748	12¢ Hunting Seal	......	.35	.25
749	12¢ Fishing	......	.35	.25
750-51	Inuit, attached	1.55	.60	.50
750	12¢ Disguised Archer	......	.35	.25
751	12¢ Hunters of Old	......	.35	.25

1978 COMMEMORATIVES

SCOTT NO.	DESCRIPTION	PLATE BLOCK F/NH	UNUSED F/NH	USED F
752/79	**(No #756a)28 varieties**	**33.00(19)**	**13.45**	**8.65**
752	12¢ Peregrine Falcon	1.55	.35	.25
753	12¢ CAPEX Victoria	1.55	.35	.25
754	14¢ CAPEX Cartier	1.80	.35	.25
755	30¢ CAPEX Victoria	3.75	.70	.55
756	$1.25 CAPEX Albert	15.50	3.25	1.40
756a	$1.69 CAPEX sheet of 3	.....	4.50	4.50
757	14¢ Games Symbol	1.80	.40	.25
758	30¢ Badminton Players	3.70	.80	.50
759-60	Comm. Games, attached	1.80	.80	.55
759	14¢ Stadium	......	.40	.25
760	14¢ Runners	......	.40	.25
761-62	Comm. Games, attached	3.70	1.65	1.35
761	30¢ Edmonton	......	.85	.60
762	30¢ Bowls	......	.85	.60
763-64	Captain Cook, attached	1.80	.80	.45
763	14¢ Captain Cook	......	.35	.25
764	14¢ Nootka Sound	......	.35	.25
765-66	Resources, attached	1.80	.80	.45
765	14¢ Miners	......	.35	.25
766	14¢ Tar Sands	......	.35	.25
767	14¢ CNE 100th Anniversary	1.80	.35	.25
768	14¢ Mere d'Youville	1.80	.35	.25
769-70	Inuit, attached	1.80	.85	.45
769	14¢ Woman Walking	......	.35	.25
770	14¢ Migration	......	.35	.25
771-72	Inuit, attached	1.80	.85	.45
771	14¢ Plane over Village	......	.35	.25
772	14¢ Dog Team & Sled	......	.35	.25

744

748-49

763

752

753

757

764

759

765-66

767

768

769-70

773

780

813

815

SCOTT NO.	DESCRIPTION	PLATE BLOCK F/NH	UNUSED F/NH	USED F
773	12¢ Mary & Child w/pea	1.60	.35	.25
774	14¢ Mary & Child w/apple	1.80	.40	.25
775	30¢ Mary & Child w/goldfinch	3.85	.80	.35
776-79	Ice Vessels, attached	1.80	1.60	1.40
776	14¢ Robinson	......	.40	.25
777	14¢ St. Roch	......	.40	.25
778	14¢ Northern Light	......	.40	.25
779	14¢ Labrador	......	.40	.25

1979 COMMEMORATIVES

SCOTT NO.	DESCRIPTION	PLATE BLOCK F/NH	UNUSED F/NH	USED F
780/846	**(780, 813-20, 833-46) complete, 23 varieties**	**36.00(16)**	**9.75**	**4.55**
780	14¢ Quebec Winter Carnival	1.75	.40	.25

1977-83 Definitives Perf 13x131/2

SCOTT NO.	DESCRIPTION	PLATE BLOCK F/NH	UNUSED F/NH	USED F
781-92	**1¢-32¢ complete, 11 varieties**	**16.00**	**4.15**	**2.00**
781	1¢ Gentian (1979)	1.00	.25	.25
781a	1¢ same, perf 12x12-1/2	......	.25	.25
781b	booklet pane, 1¢ (2—781a), 12¢ (4—713a)	......	1.75	......
782	2¢ Western Columbine (1979)	1.00	.25	.25
782a	booklet pane, 2¢ (4—782b), 12¢ (3—716a)	......	1.75	......
782b	2¢ same, perf 12x121/2 (1978)	.....	.25	.25
783	3¢ Canada Lily (1979)	1.00	.25	.25
784	4¢ Hepatica (1979)	1.00	.25	.25
785	5¢ Shooting Star (1979)	1.00	.25	.25
786	10¢ Lady's-Slipper (1979)	1.25	.30	.25
787	15¢ Violet (1979)	2.00	.40	.25
789	17¢ Queen Elizabeth II (1979)	2.00	.75	.65
789a	17¢ same, 12x12-1/2 (1979)	.....	.40	.25
789b	booklet pane of 25	.....	11.00	.....
790	17¢ Parliament Bldg. (1979)	2.00	.45	.25
791	30¢ Queen Elizabeth II (1982)	3.25	.75	.25
792	32¢ Queen Elizabeth II (1983)	3.60	.80	.25

NOTE: **781a, 782b, 797 & 800 are from booklet panes and will have one or more straight edges. 789a may or may not have straight edges.**

1979 Perf 12x12-1/2

SCOTT NO.	DESCRIPTION	PLATE BLOCK F/NH	UNUSED F/NH	USED F
797	1¢ Parliament Building	.....	.75	.30
797a	booklet pane 1¢ (1—797), 5¢ (3—800), 17¢ (2—789a)	.....	2.60	.....
800	5¢ Parliament Building	.....	.35	.25

1979 Coil Stamps Perf 10 Vertical

SCOTT NO.	DESCRIPTION	PLATE BLOCK F/NH	UNUSED F/NH	USED F
806	17¢ Parliament Building, slate green	.....	.50	.25

1979

SCOTT NO.	DESCRIPTION	PLATE BLOCK F/NH	UNUSED F/NH	USED F
813	17¢ Turtle	2.00	.45	.25
814	35¢ Whale	4.60	.95	.35
815-16	Postal Code, attached	2.00	.90	.45
815	17¢ Woman's Finger	......	.50	.25
816	17¢ Man's Finger	......	.50	.25
817-18	Writers, attached	2.00	.90	.60
817	17¢ "Fruits of the Earth"	......	.50	.25
818	17¢ "The Golden Vessel"	......	.50	.25
819-20	Colonels, attached	2.00	.90	.60
819	17¢ Charles de Salaberry	......	.50	.25
820	17¢ John By	......	.50	.25

817-18

819-20

821 *Ontario*

PROVINCIAL FLAGS

821 *Ontario* · **822** *Quebec* · **823** *Nova Scotia*
824 *New Brunswick* · **825** *Manitoba* · **826** *British Columbia*
827 *Prince Edward Island* · **828** *Saskatchewan* · **829** *Alberta*
830 *Newfoundland* · **831** *Northern Teritories* · **832** *Yukon Territory*

SCOTT NO.	DESCRIPTION	PLATE BLOCK F/NH	UNUSED F/NH	USED F
832a	17¢ Sheet of 12 varieties, attached	......	5.00	......
821-32	set of singles	......	4.90	3.30
Any	17¢ single	......	.45	.25
833	17¢ Canoe—kayak	2.00	.45	.25
834	17¢ Field Hockey	2.00	.45	.25
835-36	Inuit, attached	2.00	.90	.60
835	17¢ Summer Tent	......	.40	.25
836	17¢ Igloo	......	.40	.25
837-38	Inuit, attached	2.00	.90	.60
837	17¢ The Dance	......	.40	.25
838	17¢ Soapstone Figures	......	.40	.25
839	15¢ Wooden Train	1.75	.40	.25
840	17¢ Horse Pull Toy	2.00	.55	.25
841	35¢ Knitted Doll	4.50	.90	.55
842	17¢ I.Y.C.	2.00	.45	.25
843-44	Flying Boats, attached	2.00	.90	.60
843	17¢ Curtiss, HS2L	......	.45	.25
844	17¢ Canadair CL215	......	.45	.25
845-46	Flying Boats, attached	4.50	1.85	1.75
845	35¢ Vichers Vedette	......	.85	.60
846	35¢ Consolidated Canso	......	.85	.60

833 · 834 · 839 · 835-36 · 842 · 843 · 847 · 848

1980 COMMEMORATIVES

SCOTT NO.	DESCRIPTION	PLATE BLOCK F/NH	UNUSED F/NH	USED F
847-77	**complete, 31 varieties**	**5250(23)**	**15.95**	**10.25**
847	17¢ Arctic Islands Map	2.00	.45	.25
848	35¢ Olympic Skiing	4.40	.90	.60
849-50	Artists, attached	2.00	.90	.55
849	17¢ School Trustees	......	.40	.25
850	17¢ Inspiration	......	.40	.25
851-52	Artists, attached	4.40	1.85	1.50
851	35¢ Parliament Bldgs	......	.90	.70
852	35¢ Sunrise on the Saguenay	......	.90	.70
853	17¢ Atlantic Whitefish	2.25	.40	.25
854	17¢ Greater Prairie Chicken	2.25	.40	.25

849

853

855

856

857-58

859 · 870 · 860 · 862 · 863 · 865 · 873 · 866-67 · 878 · 877

SCOTT NO.	DESCRIPTION	PLATE BLOCK F/NH	UNUSED F/NH	USED F
855	17¢ Gardening	2.00	.45	.25
856	17¢ Rehabilitation	2.00	.45	.25
857-58	"O Canada", attached	2.00	.90	.55
857	17¢ Bars of Music	......	.45	.25
858	17¢ Three Musicians	......	.45	.25
859	17¢ John Diefenbaker	2.00	.45	.25
860-61	Musicians, attached	2.00	.90	.55
860	17¢ Emma Albani	......	.45	.25
861	17¢ Healy Willan	......	.45	.25
862	17¢ Ned Hanlan	2.00	.45	.25
863	17¢ Saskatchewan	2.00	.45	.25
864	17¢ Alberta	2.00	.45	.25
865	35¢ Uranium Resources	4.40	.90	.35
866-67	Inuit, attached	2.00	.90	.50
866	17¢ Sedna	......	.45	.20
867	17¢ Sun	......	.45	.20
868-69	Inuit, attached	4.40	1.85	1.50
868	35¢ Bird Spirit	......	.90	.45
869	35¢ Shaman	......	.90	.45
870	15¢ Christmas	1.75	.35	.25
871	17¢ Christmas	2.00	.40	.25
872	35¢ Christmas	4.40	.90	.45
873-74	Aircraft	2.00	.90	.65
873	17¢ Avro Canada CF-100	......	.45	.20
874	17¢ Avro Lancaster	......	.45	.20
875-76	Aircraft, attached	4.40	1.85	1.65
875	35¢ Curtiss JN-4	......	.85	.65
876	35¢ Hawker Hurricane	......	.85	.65
877	17¢ Dr. Lachapelle	2.00	.45	.25

1981 COMMEMORATIVES

SCOTT NO.	DESCRIPTION	PLATE BLOCK F/NH	UNUSED F/NH	USED F
878-906	**complete, 29 varieties**	**37.00(19)**	**13.50**	**8.75**
878	17¢ Antique Instrument	2.00	.45	.25
879-82	Feminists, attached	2.25	1.90	1.70
879	17¢ Emily Stowe	......	.50	.30
880	17¢ Louise McKinney	......	.50	.30
881	17¢ Idola Saint-Jean	......	.50	.30
882	17¢ Henrietta Edwards	......	.50	.30
883	17¢ Marmot	2.00	.45	.25
884	35¢ Bison	4.40	.90	.80
885-86	Women, attached	2.00	.85	.70
885	17¢ Kateri Tekakwitha	......	.45	.25
886	17¢ Marie de L'Incarnation	......	.45	.25
887	17¢ "At Baie Saint-Paul"	2.00	.45	.25
888	17¢ Self-Portrait	2.00	.45	.25
889	35¢ Untitled No. 6	4.40	.90	.80

879 · 883

885

887

890 894 896 897

898 899 900 903

SCOTT NO.	DESCRIPTION	PLATE BLOCK F/NH	UNUSED F/NH	USED F
890-93	Canada Day, attached	3.85(8)	1.85	1.80
890	17¢ Canada in 1867	......	.55	.50
891	17¢ Canada in 1873	......	.55	.50
892	17¢ Canada in 1905	......	.55	.50
893	17¢ Canada in 1949	......	.55	.50
894-95	Botanists, attached	2.00	.75	.60
894	17¢ Frere Marie Victorin	......	.45	.25
895	17¢ John Macoun	......	.45	.25
896	17¢ Montreal Rose	2.00	.45	.25
897	17¢ Niagara-on-the-Lake	2.00	.45	.25
898	17¢ Acadians	2.00	.45	.25
899	17¢ Aaron Mosher	2.00	.45	.25
900	15¢ Christmas Tree in 1781	2.00	.45	.25
901	15¢ Christmas Tree in 1881	2.00	.45	.25
902	15¢ Christmas Tree in 1981	2.00	.45	.25
903-04	Aircraft, attached	2.00	.90	.50
903	17¢ Canadair CL-41 Tutor	......	.45	.25
904	17¢ de Havilland Tiger Moth	......	.45	.25
905-06	Aircraft, attached	4.40	1.85	1.55
905	35¢ Avro Canada C-102	......	.85	.70
906	35¢ de Havilland Canada Dash-7	......	.85	.70
907	(30¢) "A" Maple Leaf	7.75	1.75	.25
908	(30¢) "A" Maple Leaf, Coil	......	1.90	.25

907, 908

909

914

915

1982 COMMEMORATIVES

SCOTT NO.	DESCRIPTION	PLATE BLOCK F/NH	UNUSED F/NH	USED F
909/75	**(909-16, 954, 967-75) 18 varieties, complete**	**51.25(16)**	**15.25**	**8.00**
909	30¢ 1851 Beaver	3.30	.75	.25
910	30¢ 1908 Champlain	3.30	.75	.25
911	35¢ 1935 Mountie	4.15	.90	.75
912	35¢ 1928 Mt. Hurd	4.15	.90	.75
913	60¢ 1929 Bluenose	6.90	1.50	1.25
913a	$1.90 Phil. Exhib. sheet of 5	......	4.85	......
914	30¢ Jules Leger	3.30	.75	.25
915	30¢ Terry Fox	3.30	.75	.25
916	30¢ Constitution	3.30	.75	.25

916

917

925/952, 1194, 1194A

938

939

926

1982-87 DEFINITIVES

SCOTT NO.	DESCRIPTION	PLATE BLOCK F/NH	UNUSED F/NH	USED F
917-37	**1¢-$5 complete, 23 varieties**	**135.00**	**36.00**	**11.00**
917a-21a	**1¢-10¢, 5 varieties**	**4.10**	**1.00**	**.70**
917	1¢ Decoy	1.00	.25	.25
917a	1¢ perf.13x13-1/2 (1985)	1.25	.25	.25
918	2¢ Fishing Spear	1.00	.25	.25
918a	2¢ perf.13x13-1/2 (1985)	1.00	.25	.25
919	3¢ Stable Lantern	1.00	.25	.25

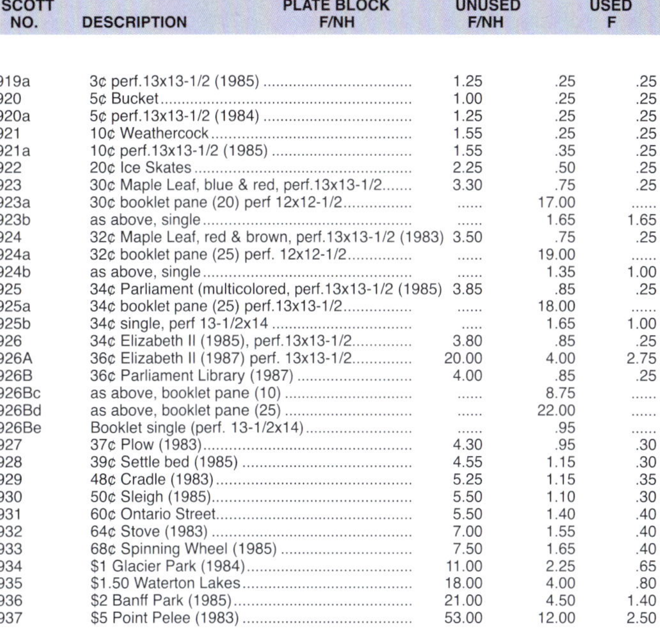

SCOTT NO.	DESCRIPTION	PLATE BLOCK F/NH	UNUSED F/NH	USED F
919a	3¢ perf.13x13-1/2 (1985)	1.25	.25	.25
920	5¢ Bucket	1.00	.25	.25
920a	5¢ perf.13x13-1/2 (1984)	1.25	.25	.25
921	10¢ Weathercock	1.55	.25	.25
921a	10¢ perf.13x13-1/2 (1985)	1.55	.35	.25
922	20¢ Ice Skates	2.25	.50	.25
923	30¢ Maple Leaf, blue & red, perf.13x13-1/2	3.30	.75	.25
923a	30¢ booklet pane (20) perf 12x12-1/2	......	17.00	......
923b	as above, single	......	1.65	1.65
924	32¢ Maple Leaf, red & brown, perf.13x13-1/2 (1983)	3.50	.75	.25
924a	32¢ booklet pane (25) perf. 12x12-1/2	......	19.00	......
924b	as above, single	......	1.35	1.00
925	34¢ Parliament (multicolored, perf.13x13-1/2 (1985)	3.85	.85	.25
925a	34¢ booklet pane (25) perf.13x13-1/2	......	18.00	......
925b	34¢ single, perf 13-1/2x14	......	1.65	1.00
926	34¢ Elizabeth II (1985), perf.13x13-1/2	3.80	.85	.25
926A	36¢ Elizabeth II (1987) perf. 13x13-1/2	20.00	4.00	2.75
926B	36¢ Parliament Library (1987)	4.00	.85	.25
926Bc	as above, booklet pane (10)	......	8.75	......
926Bd	as above, booklet pane (25)	......	22.00	......
926Be	Booklet single (perf. 13-1/2x14)	......	.95	......
927	37¢ Plow (1983)	4.30	.95	.30
928	39¢ Settle bed (1985)	4.55	1.15	.30
929	48¢ Cradle (1983)	5.25	1.15	.35
930	50¢ Sleigh (1985)	5.50	1.10	.30
931	60¢ Ontario Street	5.50	1.40	.40
932	64¢ Stove (1983)	7.00	1.55	.40
933	68¢ Spinning Wheel (1985)	7.50	1.65	.40
934	$1 Glacier Park (1984)	11.00	2.25	.65
935	$1.50 Waterton Lakes	18.00	4.00	.80
936	$2 Banff Park (1985)	21.00	4.50	1.40
937	$5 Point Pelee (1983)	53.00	12.00	2.50

1982-87 BOOKLET SINGLES

SCOTT NO.	DESCRIPTION	PLATE BLOCK F/NH	UNUSED F/NH	USED F
938-948	**1¢-36¢ complete, 11 varieties**	**......**	**6.45**	**4.95**
938	1¢ East Block (1987)	......	.35	.30
939	2¢ West Block (1985)	......	.35	.30
940	5¢ Maple Leaf (1982)	......	.35	.30
941	5¢ East Block (1985)	......	.30	.25
942	6¢ West Block (1987)	......	.30	.25
943	8¢ Maple Leaf (1983)	......	.60	.60
944	10¢ Maple Leaf (1982)	......	.45	.45
945	30¢ Maple Leaf, red perf. 12x12-1/2 (1982)	......	.75	.80
945a	booklet pane 2# 940, 1 #944, 1 #945	......	1.65	......
946	32¢ Maple Leaf, brown on white, perf.12x12-1/2 (1983)		......	.75
.65				
946b	booklet pane 2 #941, 1 #943, 1 #946	......	1.65	......
947	34¢ Library, slate blue, perf.12x12-1/2 (1985)	......	1.40	.95
947a	booklet pane, 3 #939, 2 #941, 1 #947	......	2.80	......
948	36¢ Parliament Library (1987)	......	1.50	.95
948a	booklet pane, 2 #938, 2 #942, #948	......	2.40	......

1982-1987 COILS

SCOTT NO.	DESCRIPTION	PLATE BLOCK F/NH	UNUSED F/NH	USED F
950-53	30¢-36¢ complete, 4 varieties	......	3.50	.85
950	30¢ Maple Leaf (1982)	......	.95	.25
951	32¢ Maple Leaf (1983)	......	.85	.25
952	34¢ Parliament (1985)	......	.90	.25
953	36¢ Parliament (1987)	......	.95	.25

954

955 *Yukon Territories*

Paintings

956 *Quebec* **957** *Newfoundland* **958** *Northwest Territories*
959 *Prince Edward Island* **960** *Nova Scotia* **961** *Saskatchewan*
962 *Ontario* **963** *New Brunswick* **964** *Alberta*
965 *British Columbia* **966** *Manitoba*

1982 COMMEMORATIVES

SCOTT NO.	DESCRIPTION	PLATE BLOCK F/NH	UNUSED F/NH	USED F
954	30¢ Salvation Army	3.30	.75	.25
955-66	set of singles	......	9.75	8.50
......	same, any 30¢ single	......	.95	.50
966a	sheet of 12 varieties, attached	......	10.00	......
967	30¢ Regina	3.30	.75	.25
968	30¢ Henley Regatta	3.30	.75	.25
969-70	30¢ Aircraft, attached	4.30	1.80	1.25
969	30¢ Fairchild FC-2W1	......	.70	.30

967

968

969

SCOTT NO.	DESCRIPTION	PLATE BLOCK F/NH	UNUSED F/NH	USED F
970	30¢ De Havilland Canada Beaver	....	.85	.25
971-72	Aircraft, attached	6.75	3.00	2.40
971	60¢ Noorduyn Norseman	....	1.50	.95
972	60¢ Fokker Super Universal	....	1.50	.95
973	30¢ Joseph, Mary & Infant	3.50	.70	.25
974	35¢ Shepherds	4.25	.90	.60
975	60¢ Wise Men	7.00	1.45	1.00

973

976

978

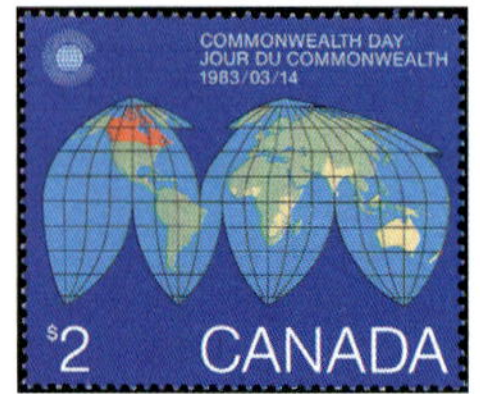

977

1983 COMMEMORATIVES

SCOTT NO.	DESCRIPTION	PLATE BLOCK F/NH	UNUSED F/NH	USED F
976/1008	**(976-82, 993-1008) complete, 23 varieties**	**80.25(20)**	**26.75**	**12.40**
976	32¢ World Comm. Year	3.60	.80	.25
977	$2 Commonwealth Day	46.00	10.00	4.75
978-79	Poet/Author, attached	3.60	1.75	1.10
978	32¢ Laure Conan	......	.80	.25
979	32¢ E.J. Pratt	......	.80	.25
980	32¢ St.John Ambulance	3.50	.75	.25
981	32¢ University Games	3.50	.75	.25
982	64¢ University Games	7.25	1.50	1.00

Forts

984 *Ft. William*
985 *Ft. Rodd Hill*
986 *Ft. Wellington*
987 *Fort Prince of Wales*
988 *Halifax Citadel*
989 *Ft. Chambly*
990 *Ft. No. 1 Pt. Levis*
991 *Ft. at Coteau-du-Lac*
992 *Fort Beausejour*

SCOTT NO.	DESCRIPTION	PLATE BLOCK F/NH	UNUSED F/NH	USED F
992a	32¢ Forts, pane of 10	......	9.50	9.00
983-92	set of singles	......	8.40	8.00
......	Any 32¢ single Fort	......	.75	.60
993	32¢ Boy Scouts	3.55	.80	.60
994	32¢ Council of Churches	3.55	.80	.60
995	32¢ Humphrey Gilbert	3.55	.80	.60
996	32¢ Nickel	3.55	.80	.60
997	32¢ Josiah Henson	3.55	.80	.60
998	32¢ Fr. Antoine Labelle	3.55	.80	.60

980

981

983 *Ft. Henry*

993

994

995

996

997

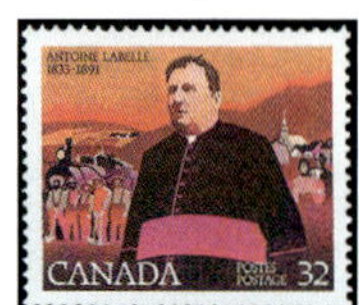

998

999

1003

1004

1007

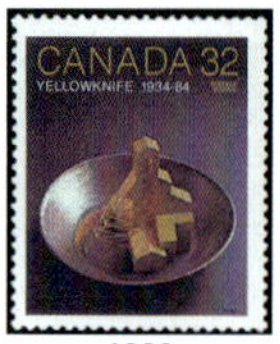

1009

1010

1011

1012

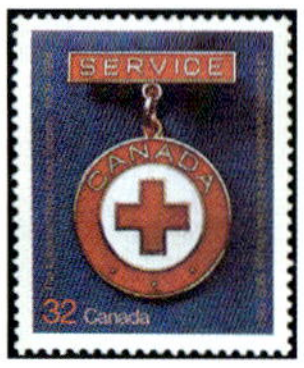

1013

1014

1015

SCOTT NO.	DESCRIPTION	PLATE BLOCK F/NH	UNUSED F/NH	USED F
999-1000	Steam Trains, attached	14.00	3.85	2.50
999	32¢ Toronto 4-4-0	......	.85	.65
1000	32¢ Dorchester 0-4-0	......	.85	.65
1001	37¢ Samson 0-6-0	4.40	.95	.75
1002	64¢ Adam Brown 4-4-0	7.25	1.60	1.25
1003	32¢ Law School	3.55	.80	.25
1004	32¢ City Church	3.55	.80	.25
1005	37¢ Family	4.40	.95	.65
1006	64¢ County Chapel	6.45	1.55	1.50
1007-08	Army Regiment, attached	3.55	1.60	1.50
1007	32¢ Canada & Br.Reg.	.....	.75	.30
1008	32¢ Winn. & Dragoons	.....	.75	.30

1984 COMMEMORATIVES

SCOTT NO.	DESCRIPTION	PLATE BLOCK F/NH	UNUSED F/NH	USED F
1009/44	**(1009-15, 1028-39, 1040-44) complete, 24 varieties**	**8.50**	**60.15(20)**	**19.75**
1009	32¢ Yellowknife	3.60	.80	.25
1010	32¢ Year of the Arts	3.60	.80	.25
1011	32¢ Cartier	3.60	.80	.25
1012	32¢ Tall Ships	3.60	.80	.25
1013	32¢ Canadian Red Cross	3.60	.80	.25
1014	32¢ New Brunswick	3.60	.80	.25
1015	32¢ St. Lawrence Seaway	3.60	.80	.25

PROVINCIAL LANDSCAPES BY JEAN PAUL LEMIEUX

1016 *New Brunswick*
1017 *British Columbia*
1018 *Yukon Territory*
1019 *Quebec*
1020 *Manitoba*
1021 *Alberta*
1022 *Prince Edward Island*
1023 *Saskatchewan*
1024 *Nova Scotia*
1025 *Northwest Territories*
1026 *Newfoundland*
1027 *Ontario*

1016

SCOTT NO.	DESCRIPTION	PLATE BLOCK F/NH	UNUSED F/NH	USED F
1027a	sheet of 12 varieties attached	......	11.00	9.00
1016-27	set of singles	......	9.55	5.75
.....	Any 32¢ single Provinces		.85	.50
1028	32¢ Loyalists	3.60	.70	.25
1029	32¢ Catholicism	3.60	.70	.25
1030	32¢ Papal Visit	3.60	.70	.25
1031	64¢ Papal Visit	7.25	1.45	.90

1028

1029

1030

1032

1036

1040

1043

1044

1045

1046

SCOTT NO.	DESCRIPTION	PLATE BLOCK F/NH	UNUSED F/NH	USED F
1032-35	Lighthouses, attached	3.80	3.50	1.75
1032	32¢ Louisbourg	......	.75	.25
1033	32¢ Fisgard	......	.75	.25
1034	32¢ Ile Verte	......	.75	.25
1035	32¢ Gilbraltar Point	......	.75	.25
1036-37	Locomotives, attached	3.60	1.65	1.20
1036	32¢ Scotia 0-6-0	......	.75	.30
1037	32¢ Countess of Dufferin 4-4-0	......	.75	.30
1038	37¢ Grand Trunk 2-6-0	4.70	.95	.80
1039	64¢ Canadian Pacific 4-6-0	7.25	1.65	1.15
1039a	32¢-64¢ Locomotive S/S	......	4.25	4.25
1040	32¢ Christmas	3.60	.80	.25
1041	37¢ Christmas	4.40	.95	.75
1042	64¢ Christmas	7.25	1.55	1.00
1043	32¢ Royal Air Force	3.60	.75	.25
1044	32¢ Newspaper	3.60	.75	.25

1985 COMMEMORATIVES

SCOTT NO.	DESCRIPTION	PLATE BLOCK F/NH	UNUSED F/NH	USED F
1045/76	**(1045-49, 1060-66, 1067-76) complete, 21 varieties**	**49.40(16)**	**19.00**	**8.25**
1045	32¢ Youth Year	3.60	.80	.30
1046	32¢ Canadian Astronaut	3.60	.80	.30
1047-48	Women, attached	3.60	1.65	1.25
1047	32¢ T. Casgrain	......	.80	.25
1048	32¢ E. Murphy	......	.80	.25
1049	32¢ G. Dumont	3.60	.80	.25
1059a	34¢ Forts pane of 10	......	16.00	15.00
1050-59	set of singles	......	11.00	9.00
......	any Fort single	......	.95	.65
1060	34¢ Louis Hebert	3.80	.85	.25
1061	34¢ Inter-Parliamentary	3.80	.85	.25
1062	34¢ Girl Guides	3.80	.85	.25
1063-66	Lighthouses, attached	3.80	3.75	2.95
1063	34¢ Sisters Islets	......	.90	.30
1064	34¢ Pelee Passage	......	.90	.30
1065	34¢ Haut-fond Prince	......	.90	.30
1066	34¢ Rose Blanche	......	.90	.30
1066b	Lighthouse Souvenir Sheet	......	5.00	5.00
1067	34¢ Christmas	3.75	.85	.25
1068	39¢ Christmas	4.25	.95	.70
1069	68¢ Christmas	7.50	1.65	1.15
1070	32¢ Christmas, booklet single	......	1.25	.50
1070a	same, booklet pane of 10	......	13.00	......
1071-72	Locomotives, attached	4.75	1.90	1.25
1071	34¢ GT Class K2	......	.95	.65
1072	34¢ CP Class P2a	......	.95	.65
1073	39¢ CMoR Class 010a	4.50	.85	.85
1074	68¢ CGR Class H4D	7.75	1.60	1.35
1075	34¢ Royal Navy	3.85	.85	.25
1076	34¢ Montreal Museum	3.85	.85	.25

1047-48

1049

1050

1060

1061

1062

FORTS

1050 *Lower Ft. Garry* · **1051** *Fort Anne* · **1052** *Fort York*
1053 *Castle Hill* · **1054** *Fort Whoop Up* · **1055** *Fort Erie*
1056 *Fort Walsh* · **1057** *Fort Lennox* · **1058** *York Redoubt*
1059 *Fort Frederick*

1063

1067

1075

1076

1077

1078

1986 COMMEMORATIVES

SCOTT NO.	DESCRIPTION	PLATE BLOCK F/NH	UNUSED F/NH	USED F
1077/1121	**(1077-79, 1090-1107,1108-16, 1117-21) complete, 35 varieties**	**70.50**	**29.50**	**15.00**
1077	34¢ Computer Map	3.80	.85	.25
1078	34¢ Expo '86	3.80	.85	.25
1079	39¢ Expo '86	4.40	.95	.60

1987 HERITAGE ARTIFACTS

SCOTT NO.	DESCRIPTION	PLATE BLOCK F/NH	UNUSED F/NH	USED F
1080	25¢ Butter Stamp	3.30	.75	.30
1081	42¢ Linen Chest	5.25	1.10	.35
1082	55¢ Iron Kettle	7.25	1.55	.45
1083	72¢ Hand-drawn Cart	8.75	1.85	.60

1986-87 Definitive

SCOTT NO.	DESCRIPTION	PLATE BLOCK F/NH	UNUSED F/NH	USED F
1084	$5 La Mauricie	58.00	12.50	3.50

1090

1091

1092

1094

1103

1104

1095

1099

1986 COMMEMORATIVES

SCOTT NO.	DESCRIPTION	PLATE BLOCK F/NH	UNUSED F/NH	USED F
1090	34¢ Philippe Aubert de Gaspe	3.85	.85	.25
1091	34¢ Molly Brant	3.85	.85	.25
1092	34¢ Expo '86	3.85	.85	.25
1093	68¢ Expo '86	7.75	1.65	.75
1094	34¢ Canadian Forces Postal Service	3.80	.75	.20
1095-98	Birds, attached	4.75	3.80	3.25
1095	34¢ Great Blue Heron	......	1.10	.45
1096	34¢ Snow Goose	......	1.10	.45
1097	34¢ Great Horned Owl	......	1.10	.45
1098	34¢ Spruce Grouse	......	1.10	.45
1099-1102	Science & Technology, attached	4.85	4.25	3.25
1099	34¢ Rotary Snowplow	......	.85	.30
1100	34¢ Canadarm	......	.85	.30
1101	34¢ Anti-gravity Flight Suit	......	.85	.30
1102	34¢ Variable-pitch Propeller	......	.85	.30
1103	34¢ CBC	3.70	.85	.20
1104-07	Exploration, attached	4.65	3.75	3.00
1104	34¢ Continent	......	.85	.30
1105	34¢ Vikings	......	.85	.30
1106	34¢ John Cabot	......	.85	.30
1107	34¢ Hudson Bay	......	.85	.30
1107b	CAPEX souvenir sheet	......	3.75	3.50

SCOTT NO.	DESCRIPTION	PLATE BLOCK F/NH	UNUSED F/NH	USED F
1108-09	Frontier Peacemakers, attached	3.85	1.75	1.25
1108	34¢ Crowfoot	......	.85	.30
1109	34¢ J.F. Macleod	......	.85	.30
1110	34¢ Peace Year	3.85	.85	.25
1111-12	Calgary, attached	3.85	1.75	1.25
1111	34¢ Ice Hockey	......	.85	.25
1112	34¢ Biathlon	......	.85	.25
1113	34¢ Christmas Angels	3.85	.85	.25
1114	39¢ Christmas Angels	4.30	.95	.55
1115	68¢ Christmas Angels	7.65	1.65	1.15
1116	29¢ Christmas Angels, booklet singles	......	1.65	1.45
1116a	same, booklet pane of 10	......	15.00	......

1108 1110 1111 1113 1117 1122

SCOTT NO.	DESCRIPTION	PLATE BLOCK F/NH	UNUSED F/NH	USED F
1117	34¢ John Molson	4.00	.85	.25
1118-19	Locomotive, attached	4.50	1.95	1.40
1118	34¢ CN V1a	......	.95	.30
1119	34¢ CP T1a	......	.95	.30
1120	39¢ CN U2a	4.75	.95	.90
1121	68¢ CP H1c	7.75	1.65	1.40

1987 COMMEMORATIVES

SCOTT NO.	DESCRIPTION	PLATE BLOCK F/NH	UNUSED F/NH	USED F
1122/54	(1122-25, 1126-54) complete, 33 varieties	68.75	28.50	13.25
1122	34¢ Toronto P.O.	3.70	.75	.25

1987 CAPEX EXHIBITION

SCOTT NO.	DESCRIPTION	PLATE BLOCK F/NH	UNUSED F/NH	USED F
1123	36¢ Nelson-Miramichi: Post Office	3.95	.90	.30
1124	42¢ Saint Ours P.O.	4.95	1.05	.40
1125	72¢ Battleford P.O.	8.25	1.75	1.40
1125A	CAPEX Souvenir Sheet	......	4.50	4.25
1126-29	Exploration, attached	4.00	3.50	3.25
1126	34¢ Brule	......	.95	.45
1127	34¢ Radisson	......	.95	.45
1128	34¢ Jolliet	......	.95	.45
1129	34¢ Wilderness	......	.95	.45
1130	36¢ Calgary Olympics	3.95	.90	.30
1131	42¢ Calgary Olympics	4.95	1.00	.75
1132	36¢ Volunteers	4.00	.90	.30
1133	36¢ Charter of Freedom	4.00	.90	.30
1134	36¢ Engineering	4.00	.90	.30

1987 COMMEMORATIVES

SCOTT NO.	DESCRIPTION	PLATE BLOCK F/NH	UNUSED F/NH	USED F
1135-38	Science & Tech., attached	4.40	3.80	2.80
1135	36¢ Reginald A. Fessenden	......	.90	.40
1136	36¢ Charles Fenerty	......	.90	.40
1137	36¢ Desbarats & Leggo	......	.90	.40
1138	36¢ Frederick N. Gisborne	......	.90	.40
1139-40	Steamships, attached	4.25	1.75	1.25
1139	36¢ Segwun	......	.90	.35
1140	36¢ Princess Marguerite	......	.90	.35
1141-44	Historic Shipwrecks, att'd	4.40	3.80	3.25
1141	36¢ Hamilton & Scourge	......	.90	.35
1142	36¢ San Juan	......	.90	.35
1143	36¢ Breadalbane	......	.90	.35
1144	36¢ Ericsson	......	.90	.35
1145	36¢ Air Canada	3.95	.90	.30

1132 1133 1134 1135 1139 1141 1145

1146 1147 1148 1154 1155 1162 1163 1165 1166 1169

SCOTT NO.	DESCRIPTION	PLATE BLOCK F/NH	UNUSED F/NH	USED F
1146	36¢ Quebec Summit	3.95	.90	.30
1147	36¢ Commonwealth Mtg.	3.95	.90	.30
1148	36¢ Christmas	3.95	.90	.30
1149	42¢ Christmas	3.95	.90	.40
1150	72¢ Christmas	8.00	1.75	1.25
1151	31¢ Christmas booklet single	......	.85	.50
1151a	same, booklet pane of 10	......	7.75	......
1152-53	Calgary Olympics, attached	3.95	1.85	1.10
1152	36¢ Cross-Country Skiing	......	.90	.30
1153	36¢ Ski Jumping	......	.90	.30
1154	36¢ Grey Cup	3.95	.90	.30

1987-91 DEFINITIVE ISSUES

SCOTT NO.	DESCRIPTION	PLATE BLOCK F/NH	UNUSED F/NH	USED F
1155	1¢ Flying Squirrel	1.00	.25	.25
1156	2¢ Porcupine	1.00	.25	.25
1157	3¢ Muskrat	1.00	.25	.25
1158	5¢ Hare	1.00	.25	.25
1159	6¢ Red Fox	1.00	.25	.25
1160	10¢ Skunk	1.25	.25	.25
1160a	same, perf. 13x12-1/2	......	9.00	.60
1161	25¢ Beaver	2.80	.65	.20
1162	37¢ Elizabeth II	4.40	.95	.30
1163	37¢ Parliament	4.40	.95	.30
1163a	same, bklt. pane of 10 (1988)	......	9.00	7.50
1163b	same, bklt. pane of 25 (1988)	......	23.00	16.00
1163c	37¢, perf. 13-1/2x14 (1988)	......	1.20	......
1164	38¢ Elizabeth II (1988)	4.40	.95	.30
1164a	38¢, perf. 13x13-1/2	......	1.65	.75
1164b	same, booklet pane of 10	......	11.00	8.00
1165	38¢ Clock Tower (1988)	4.40	1.00	.25
1165a	same, booklet pane of 10	......	10.00	6.00
1165b	same, booklet pane of 25	......	24.00	22.00
1166	39¢ Flag & Clouds	4.60	1.00	.20
1166a	same, booklet pane of 10	......	9.50	7.50
1166b	same, booklet pane of 25	......	28.00	22.50
1166c	same, perf. 12-1/2x13	......	27.00	1.00
1167	39¢ Elizabeth II	4.40	1.00	.25
1167a	same, booklet pane of 10	......	9.50	9.00
1167b	39¢, perf. 13 (1990)	94.00	19.00	.90
1168	40¢ Elizabeth II (1990)	4.40	1.00	.25
1168a	same, booklet pane of 10	......	9.00	8.00
1169	40¢ Flag and Mountains (1990)	4.40	1.00	.25
1169a	same, booklet pane of 25	......	33.00	28.00
1169b	same, booklet pane of 10	......	10.00	9.00
1170	43¢ Lynx	6.00	1.25	.45
1171	44¢ Walrus (1989)	8.25	1.75	.25
1171a	44¢, perf. 12-1/2x13	......	3.00	1.75
1171b	same, booklet pane of 5	....	15.00	....
1171c	perf., 13-1/2x13	....	560.00	65.00
1172	45¢ Pronghorn (1990)	4.95	1.15	.30
1172b	same, booklet pane of 5	......	15.00	12.00
1172d	45¢, perf. 13	135.00	26.00	1.40
1172f	Perf. 12-1/2x13	....	2.75	.50
1172A	46¢, Wolverine (1990)	5.25	1.15	.35
1172Ac	46¢, perf. 12-1/2x13	......	1.50	.60
1172Ae	same, booklet pane of 5	......	7.50	5.25
1172Ag	same, perf. 14-1/2x14	31.00	6.75	.50
1173	57¢ Killer Whale	6.50	1.40	.45
1174	59¢ Musk-ox (1989)	7.00	1.55	.45
1174a	same, perf. 13	60.00	14.00	8.00
1175	61¢ Timber Wolf (1990)	7.00	1.50	.50
1175a	61¢, perf. 13	450.00	90.00	8.50
1176	63¢ Harbor Porpoise	17.00	3.50	.50
1176a	63¢, perf. 13	60.00	14.00	5.75
1177	74¢ Wapiti (1988)	10.00	2.00	.95
1178	76¢ Grizzly Bear (1989)	10.00	2.25	.75
1178a	76¢, perf. 12-1/2x13	......	3.50	2.80
1178b	same, booklet pane of 5	....	17.00	....
1178c	same, perf. 13	210.00	45.00	20.00
1179	78¢ Beluga (1990)	12.00	2.50	.95
1179a	same, booklet pane of 5	......	17.00	......
1179b	78¢, perf. 13	195.00	40.00	8.50
1179c	same, perf. 12-1/2x13	......	3.30	2.75
1180	80¢ Peary caribou (1990)	9.75	2.00	.95
1180a	80¢, perf. 12-1/2x13	......	3.50	1.25
1180b	same, booklet pane of 5	....	17.50	....
1180c	80¢, perf. 14-1/2x14	33.00	6.50	3.00

1181 · 1184 · 1191, 1192, 1193 · 1203

SCOTT NO.	DESCRIPTION	PLATE BLOCK F/NH	UNUSED F/NH	USED F
1181	$1 Runnymede Library	11.00	2.40	.80
1182	$2 McAdam Train Station	23.00	4.80	1.50
1183	$5 Bonsecours Market	62.00	13.00	4.00

BOOKLET STAMPS

SCOTT NO.	DESCRIPTION	PLATE BLOCK F/NH	UNUSED F/NH	USED F
1184	1¢ Flag, booklet single (1990)	......	.30	.25
1184a	same, perf. 12-1/2 x 13	......	15.00	15.00
1185	5¢ Flag, booklet single (1990)	......	.30	.25
1185a	same, perf. 12-1/2x13	......	10.00	10.00
1186	6¢ Parliament East (1989)	......	.75	.30
1187	37¢ Parliament booklet single	......	1.10	.75
1187a	booklet pane (4), 1 #938, 2 #942, 1 #1187	......	1.90	......
1188	38¢ Parliament Library booklet single (1989)	......	1.10	.45
1188a	booklet pane (5), 3 #939a, 1 #1186, 1 #1188	......	2.25	......
1189	39¢ Flag booklet single (1990)	......	1.15	.45
1189b	perf. 12-1/2x13	......	20.00	20.00
1189c	booklet pane (4) #11896	......	62.00	......
1189a	booklet pane (4), 1 #1184, 2 #1185, 1 #1189	......	2.00	......
1190	40¢ Flag booklet single (1990)	......	1.75	.65
1190a	booklet pane (4) 2 #1184, 1 #1185, 1 #1190	......	2.50	......

1204 · 1206 · 1210 · 1216 · 1214 · 1215 · 1217-20 · 1221

SELF-ADHESIVE BOOKLET STAMPS

SCOTT NO.	DESCRIPTION	PLATE BLOCK F/NH	UNUSED F/NH	USED F
1191	38¢ Flag, forest (1989)	......	1.75	.95
1191a	same, booklet pane of 12	......	19.00	......
1192	39¢ Flag field (1990)	......	1.55	.95
1192a	same, booklet pane of 12	......	17.00	......
1193	40¢ Flag, seacoast (1991)	......	1.70	.95
1193a	same, booklet pane of 12	......	18.00	......

COIL STAMPS

SCOTT NO.	DESCRIPTION	PLATE BLOCK F/NH	UNUSED F/NH	USED F
1194	37¢ Parliament Library (1988)	......	.95	.25
1194A	38¢ Parliament Library (1989)	......	1.25	.25
1194B	39¢ Flag (1990)	......	1.00	.25
1194C	40¢ Flag (1990)	......	1.00	.25

1988 COMMEMORATIVES

SCOTT NO.	DESCRIPTION	PLATE BLOCK F/NH	UNUSED F/NH	USED F
1195/1236	**(1195-1225, 1226-36) complete, 39 varieties**	**74.75**	**38.25**	**15.75**
1195-96	Calgary Olympics, att'd.	4.50	2.00	1.15
1195	37¢ Alpine Skiing	......	.95	.35
1196	37¢ Curling	......	.95	.35
1197	43¢ Figure Skating	5.00	1.10	.85
1198	74¢ Luge	8.35	1.85	1.10
1199-1202	Explorers, attached	4.60	3.85	3.10
1199	37¢ Anthony Henday	......	.90	.45
1200	37¢ George Vancouver	......	.90	.45
1201	37¢ Simon Fraser	......	.90	.45
1202	37¢ John Palliser	......	.90	.45
1203	50¢ Canadian Art	5.75	1.25	1.15
1204-05	Wildlife Conservation, att'd.	4.40	1.95	1.15
1204	37¢ Ducks Unlimited	......	.95	.35
1205	37¢ Moose	......	.95	.35
1206-09	Science & Technology, att'd.	4.40	3.85	3.40
1206	37¢ Kerosene	......	.95	.40
1207	37¢ Marquis Wheat	......	.95	.40
1208	37¢ Electron Microscope	......	.95	.40
1209	37¢ Cancer Therapy	......	.95	.40
1210-13	Butterflies, attached	4.40	3.80	3.40
1210	37¢ Short-tailed Swallowtail	......	.90	.45
1211	37¢ Northern Blue	......	.90	.45
1212	37¢ Macoun's Arctic	......	.90	.45
1213	37¢ Tiger Swallowtail	......	.90	.45
1214	37¢ Harbor Entrance	4.40	.95	.25
1215	37¢ 4-H Club Anniv.	4.40	.95	.25
1216	37¢ Les Forges Du St. Maurice	4.40	.95	.25
1217-20	Dogs, attached	5.25	4.50	4.25

1222 · 1226 · 1227 · 1228 · 1229-32

SCOTT NO.	DESCRIPTION	PLATE BLOCK F/NH	UNUSED F/NH	USED F
1217	37¢ Tahltan Bear Dog	......	1.20	.45
1218	37¢ Nova Scotia Retriever	......	1.20	.45
1219	37¢ Canadian Eskimo Dog	......	1.20	.45
1220	37¢ Newfoundland Dog	......	1.20	.45
1221	37¢ Baseball	4.25	.95	.25
1222	37¢ Christmas Nativity	4.40	.95	.25
1223	43¢ Virgin & Child	4.80	1.10	.75
1224	74¢ Virgin & Child	8.30	1.85	1.15
1225	32¢ Christmas Icons booklet single	......	1.15	.95
1225a	same, booklet pane of 10	......	10.00	9.50
1226	37¢ Charles Inglis	4.40	.95	.30
1227	37¢ Ann Hopkins	4.40	.95	.30
1228	37¢ Angus Walters	4.40	.95	.30
1229-32	Small Craft Series, attached	4.40	3.85	3.25
1229	37¢ Chipewyan Canoe	......	.95	.45
1230	37¢ Haida Canoe	......	.95	.45
1231	37¢ Inuit Kayak	......	.95	.45
1232	37¢ Micmac Canoe	......	.95	.45
1233-36	Explorers, attached	4.40	3.85	3.75
1233	38¢ Matonabbee	......	.95	.45
1234	38¢ Sir John Franklin	......	.95	.45
1235	38¢ J.B.Tyrrell	......	.95	.45
1236	38¢ V. Stefansson	......	.95	.45

1237 · 1243 · 1245 · 1249 · 1251 · 1256, 1256a · 1259, 1259a · 1260 · 1252

1989 COMMEMORATIVES

SCOTT NO.	DESCRIPTION	PLATE BLOCK F/NH	UNUSED F/NH	USED F
1237/63	**(1237-56, 1257, 1258, 1259, 1260-63) complete, 26 varieties**	......	**25.00**	**12.00**
1237-40	Canadian Photography, att'd.	4.40	3.80	3.50
1237	38¢ W. Notman	......	.95	.45
1238	38¢ W.H. Boorne	......	.95	.45
1239	38¢ A. Henderson	......	.95	.45
1240	38¢ J.E. Livernois	......	.95	.45
1241	50¢ Canadian Art	6.00	1.35	.95
1243-44	19th Century Poets, att'd.	4.40	1.95	1.50
1243	38¢ L.H.Frechette	......	.95	.45
1244	38¢ A. Lampman	......	.95	.45
1245-48	Mushrooms, attached	4.40	3.85	3.40
1245	38¢ Cinnabar Chanterelle	......	.95	.45
1246	38¢ Common Morel	......	.95	.45
1247	38¢ Spindell Coral	......	.95	.45
1248	38¢ Admirable Boletus	......	.95	.45
1249-50	Canadian Infantry, attached	225.00	1.95	1.70
1249	38¢ Light Infantry	......	.95	.45
1250	38¢ Royal 22nd Regiment	......	.95	.45
1251	38¢ International Trade	4.40	.95	.30
1252-55	Performing Arts, attached	4.40	3.95	3.40
1252	38¢ Dance	......	.95	.45
1253	38¢ Music	......	.95	.45
1254	38¢ Film	......	.95	.45
1255	38¢ Theatre	......	.95	.45
1256	38¢ Christmas 1989	4.40	.95	.45
1256a	same, booklet single	....	4.95	......
1256b	same, booklet pane of 10 perf., 13x12-1/2	....	53.00	......
1257	44¢ Christmas 1989	4.95	1.10	.75
1257a	same, booklet single	....	4.50	.75
1257a	same, booklet pane of 5	....	22.50	......
1258	76¢ Christmas 1989	8.75	1.85	1.40
1258a	same, booklet single	....	7.25	7.25
1258a	same, booklet pane of 5	....	34.00	......
1259	33¢ Christmas, booklet single	......	1.15	1.65
1259a	same, booklet pane of 10	......	15.00	....
1260-63	WWII 50th Anniversary, att'd.	4.95	4.10	4.00
1260	38¢ Declaration of War	......	.95	.65
1261	38¢ Army Mobilization	......	.95	.65
1262	38¢ Navy Convoy System	......	.95	.65
1263	38¢ Commonwealth Training	......	.95	.65

1264

1270

1272-73

1274

1990 COMMEMORATIVES

SCOTT NO.	DESCRIPTION	PLATE BLOCK F/NH	UNUSED F/NH	USED F
1264/1301	**(1264-73, 1274-94, 1295, 1296, 1297, 1298-1301) complete, 38 vars.**	**62.25**	**35.50**	**17.50**
1264-65	Norman Bethune, attached	7.75	2.50	1.85
1264	39¢ Bethune in Canada	.....	1.25	.50
1265	39¢ Bethune in China	.....	1.25	.50
1266-69	Small Craft Series, att'd.	4.70	3.95	3.50
1266	39¢ Dory	.....	1.00	.45
1267	39¢ Pointer	.....	1.00	.45
1268	39¢ York Boat	.....	1.00	.45
1269	39¢ North Canoe	.....	1.00	.45
1270	39¢ Multiculturalism	4.40	1.00	.25
1271	50¢ Canadian Art,"The West Wind"	5.95	1.30	1.15
1272-73	Canada Postal System 39¢ booklet pair	.....	2.40	2.40
1273a	same, booklet pane of 8	.....	8.25	.....
1273b	same, booklet pane of 9	.....	13.00	.....
1274-77	Dolls of Canada, attached	4.70	4.00	3.60
1274	39¢ Native Dolls	.....	.95	.40
1275	39¢ Settlers' Dolls	.....	.95	.40
1276	39¢ Four Commercial Dolls	.....	.95	.40
1277	39¢ Five Commercial Dolls	.....	.95	.40

1278

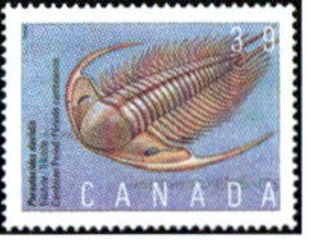
1279

1283

1287

1288

1289

1293

1294

1297

SCOTT NO.	DESCRIPTION	PLATE BLOCK F/NH	UNUSED F/NH	USED F
1278	39¢ Canada/Flag Day	4.50	.90	.25
1279-82	Prehistoric Life, attached	4.70	3.95	3.50
1279	39¢ Trilobite	......	.95	.40
1280	39¢ Sea Scorpion	......	.95	.40
1281	39¢ Fossil Algae	......	.95	.40
1282	39¢ Soft Invertebrate	......	.95	.40
1283-86	Canadian Forests, attached	4.70	3.95	3.50
1283	39¢ Acadian	......	.95	.40
1284	39¢ Great Lakes—St.Lawrence	......	.95	.40
1285	39¢ Coast	......	.95	.40
1286	39¢ Boreal	......	.95	.40
1287	39¢ Climate Observations	4.50	.95	.40
1288	39¢ Int'l. Literacy Year	4.50	.95	.40
1289-92	Can. Lore & Legend, attached	5.25	4.40	3.85
1289	39¢ Sasquatch	......	1.00	.75
1290	39¢ Kraken	......	1.00	.75
1291	39¢ Werewolf	......	1.00	.75
1292	39¢ Ogopogo	......	1.00	.75
1293	39¢ Agnes Macphail	4.40	.95	.25
1294	39¢ Native Mary & Child	4.40	.95	.25
1294a	same, booklet pane of 10	......	10.00	......
1295	45¢ Inuit, Mother & Child	5.40	1.25	.85
1295a	same, booklet pane of 5	......	9.70	......
1296	78¢ Raven Children	9.60	2.00	1.40
1296a	same, booklet pane of 5	......	15.00	......
1297	34¢ Christmas, booklet sgl	......	1.25	.50
1297a	same, booklet pane of 10	......	9.60	......
1298-1301	World War II—1940, att'd	5.00	4.25	4.00
1298	39¢ Home Front	......	1.10	.95
1299	39¢ Communal War Efforts	......	1.10	.95
1300	39¢ Food Production	......	1.10	.95
1301	39¢ Science and War	......	1.10	.95

1302

1311

1316

1321

1991 COMMEMORATIVES

SCOTT NO.	DESCRIPTION	PLATE BLOCK F/NH	UNUSED F/NH	USED F
1302-43, 1345-48, 46 varieties		**41.75**	**45.00**	**21.00**
1302-05	Canadian Doctors, att'd.	4.75	4.00	3.25
1302	40¢ Jennie Trout	......	1.00	.45
1303	40¢ Wilder Penfield	......	1.00	.45
1304	40¢ Sir Frederick Banting	......	1.00	.45
1305	40¢ Harold Griffith	......	1.00	.45
1306-09	Prehistoric Life, attached	4.75	4.25	3.25
1306	40¢ Microfossils	......	1.00	.45
1307	40¢ Early tree	......	1.00	.45
1308	40¢ Early fish	......	1.00	.45
1309	40¢ Land reptile	......	1.00	.45
1310	50¢ Canadian Art, "Forest, British Columbia"	6.25	1.35	1.15
1311	40¢ The Butchart Gardens, attached booklet single	......	1.10	.45
1312	40¢ International Peace Garden, booklet single	......	1.10	.45
1313	40¢ Royal Botanical Garden, booklet single	......	1.10	.45
1314	40¢ Montreal Botanical Garden, booklet single	......	1.10	.45
1315	40¢ Halifax Public Gardens, booklet single	......	1.10	.45
1315a	Public Gardens, strip of 5	......	4.75	3.00
1315b	Public Gardens, attached booklet pane of 10	......	9.75	....
1316	40¢ Canada Day	4.60	.95	.45
1317-20	Small Craft Series, attached	4.60	4.10	3.30
1317	40¢ Verchere Rowboat	......	.95	.45
1318	40¢ Touring Kayak	......	.95	.45
1319	40¢ Sailing Dinghy	......	.95	.45
1320	40¢ Cedar Strip Canoe	......	.95	.45
1321	40¢ South Nahanni River	......	.95	.45
1322	40¢ Athabasca River	......	.95	.45
1323	40¢ Voyageur Waterway	......	.95	.45
1324	40¢ Jacques Cartier River	......	.95	.45
1325	40¢ Main River	......	.95	.45
1325a	Canadian Rivers, strip of 5	......	4.75	4.00
1325b	Canadian Rivers, attached booklet pane of 10	......	9.75	......
1326-29	Arrival of the Ukrainians, attached	4.75	4.10	3.25
1326	40¢ Leaving	....	.95	.45
1327	40¢ Winter in Canada	....	.95	.45
1328	40¢ Clearing Land	....	.95	.45
1329	40¢ Growing Wheat	....	.95	.45
1330-33	Dangerous Public Service Occupations, attached	6.60	5.60	4.75
1330	40¢ Ski Patrol	....	1.25	.45
1331	40¢ Police	....	1.25	.45
1332	40¢ Firefighters	....	1.25	.45
1333	40¢ Search & Rescue	....	1.25	.45
1334-37	Folktales, attached	4.75	4.20	3.25
1334	40¢ Witched Canoe	....	.95	.45
1335	40¢ Orphan Boy	....	.95	.45
1336	40¢ Chinook Wind	....	.95	.45
1337	40¢ Buried Treasure	....	.95	.45
1338	40¢ Queen's University, booklet, single	....	.95	.75
1338a	Same booklet pane of 10	....	9.50	....
1339	40¢ Santa at Fireplace	4.75	1.00	.25
1339a	Same, booklet pane of 10	....	9.50	....
1340	46¢ Santa with White horse, tree	5.25	1.15	.80
1340a	Same, booklet pane of 5	....	5.50	....
1341	80¢ Sinterklaas, girl	8.60	1.95	1.25
1341a	Same, booklet pane of 5	....	9.55	....
1342	35¢ Santa with Punchbowl, booklet, single	....	.95	.25
1342a	Same, booklet pane of 10	....	9.00	....
1343	40¢ Basketball Centennial	4.40	.95	.35
1344	40¢-80¢ Basketball Souvenir Sheet of 3	....	6.00	....
1345-48	World War II—1941, att'd.	5.00	4.00	3.75
1345	40¢ Women's Armed Forces	....	1.10	.95
1346	40¢ War Industry	....	1.10	.95
1347	40¢ Cadets and Veterans	....	1.10	.95
1348	40¢ Defense of Hong Kong	....	1.10	.95

1326

1330

1334

1338

1343

1349

1339

1342

1991-96 Regular Issue

SCOTT NO.	DESCRIPTION	PLATE BLOCK F/NH	UNUSED F/NH	USED F
1349	1¢ Blueberry (1992)	.95	.25	.25
1350	2¢ Wild Strawberry (1992)	.95	.25	.25
1351	3¢ Black Crowberry (1992)	.95	.25	.25
1352	5¢ Rose Hip (1992)	.95	.25	.25
1353	6¢ Black Raspberry (1992)	.95	.25	.25
1354	10¢ Kinnikinnick (1992)	1.25	.30	.25
1355	25¢ Saskatoon berry (1992)	2.90	.65	.25
1356	42¢ Flag + Rolling Hills	4.75	1.00	.25
1356a	Same, booklet pane of 10	....	11.00	8.00
1356b	Same, booklet pane of 50	....	112.00	....
1356c	Same, booklet pane of 25	....	23.00	....
1357	42¢ Queen Elizabeth II (Karsh)	4.75	1.05	.25
1357a	Same, booklet pane of 10	....	10.00	9.50
1358	43¢ Queen Elizabeth II (Karsh) (1992)	5.50	1.25	.25
1358a	Same, booklet pane of 10	....	12.00	8.50
1359	43¢ Flag + Prairie (1992)	5.50	1.10	.25
1359a	Same, booklet pane of 10	....	11.00	8.50
1359b	Same, booklet pane of 25	....	33.00	....
1360	45¢ Queen Elizabeth II (Karsh) (1995)	6.65	1.30	.25
1360a	Same, booklet pane of 10	....	13.00	9.50
1361	45¢ Flag & Building (1995)	5.95	1.10	.25
1361a	Same, booklet pane of 10	....	12.00	11.50
1361b	Same, booklet pane of 25	....	33.00	....
1362	45¢ Flag & Building, perf. 13¹/2 x 13	5.25	1.25	.25
1362a	Same, booklet pane of 10	....	11.00	9.00
1362b	Same, booklet pane of 30	....	33.00	....
1363	48¢ McIntosh Apple Tree, perf. 13	5.50	1.20	.25
1363a	Same, perf. 14¹/2 x 14	....	1.75	.40
1363b	Same, booklet pane of 5	....	8.75	....
1364	49¢ Delicious Apple perf.13 (1992)	5.60	1.25	.25
1364a	Same, perf. 14¹/2 x 14	....	3.00	.40
1364b	Same, booklet pane of 5	....	16.00	....
1365	50¢ Snow Apple (1994)	5.75	1.25	.45
1365a	Same, booklet pane of 5	....	7.75	....
1365b	Same, perf. 14¹/2 x 14	....	3.00	.50
1365c	Same, booklet pane of 5	....	15.00	....
1366	52¢ Gravenstein apple (1995)	7.50	1.70	.45
1366a	Same, booklet pane of 5	....	9.00	6.00
1366b	52¢ Gravenstein apple, perf. 14¹/2 x 14	12.00	2.50	.55
1366c	Same, booklet pane of 5	....	12.00	....
1367	65¢ Black Walnut Tree	7.60	1.65	.45
1368	67¢ Beaked Hazelnut (1992)	7.60	1.65	.45
1369	69¢ Shagbark Hickory (1994)	8.00	1.65	.45
1370	71¢ American Chestnut (1995)	8.25	1.65	.45
1371	84¢ Stanley Plum Tree, perf. 13	9.75	2.25	.45
1371a	Same, perf. 14¹/2 x 14	....	2.75	.50
1371b	Same, booklet pane of 5	....	13.50	....
1372	86¢ Bartlett Pear, perf. 13 (1992)	12.00	2.65	.75
1372a	Same, perf. 14¹/2 x 14	13.15	3.50	1.65
1372b	Same, booklet pane of 5 (perf. 14-1/2x14)	....	16.00	....
1372c	Same, booklet pane of 5	....	19.00	....
1373	88¢ Westcot Apricot (1994)	10.00	2.15	.60
1373b	Same, perf. 14¹/2 x 14	....	4.75	2.35
1363c	Same, booklet pane of 5	....	24.50	....
1374	90¢ Elberta Peach (1995)	11.00	2.40	.65
1374a	Same, booklet pane of 5	....	12.00	....
1374b	perf. 14¹/2 x 14	....	4.25	1.75
1374c	Same, booklet pane of 5	....	22.00	....
1375	$1 Yorkton Court House (1994)	11.50	2.50	.65
1375b	perf. 13-1/2x13	12.00	2.50	.65
1376	$2 Provincial Normal School, Nova Scotia (1994)	23.00	5.00	1.25
1378	$5 Carnegie Public Library, Victoria	58.00	12.00	2.75
1388	42¢ Flag and Mountains, quick-stick (1992)	....	1.65	.85
1388a	Same, booklet pane of 12	....	19.00	....
1389	43¢ Flag, estuary shore (1993)	....	1.65	.85
1394	42¢ Canadian Flag + Rolling Hills, coil	....	1.00	.30
1395	43¢ Canadian Flag, coil (1992)	....	1.00	.30
1396	45¢ Canadian Flag, coil (1995)	....	1.15	.30

1363 1399 1404

1992 COMMEMORATIVES

SCOTT NO.	DESCRIPTION	PLATE BLOCK F/NH	UNUSED F/NH	USED F
1399-1455, 57 varieties		**44.15**	**56.10**	**22.25**
1399	42¢ Ski Jumping	....	1.10	.45
1400	42¢ Figure Skating	....	1.10	.45
1401	42¢ Hockey	....	1.10	.45
1402	42¢ Bobsledding	....	1.10	.45
1403	42¢ Alpine Skiing	....	1.10	.45
1403a	Olympic Winter Games, Strips of 5	....	5.50	4.75
1403b	Olympic Winter Games, booklet pane of 10	....	11.00	10.00
1404-05	350th Anniversary of Montreal, attached	4.75	2.25	1.00
1404	42¢ Modern Montreal	....	1.00	.40
1405	42¢ Early Montreal	....	1.00	.40
1406	48¢ Jaques Cartier	5.50	1.20	.85
1407	84¢ Columbus	9.50	2.10	1.10
1407a	42¢-84¢ Canada '92, Souvenir Sheet of 4	....	5.75	5.75
1408	42¢ The Margaree River	....	1.00	.40
1409	42¢ Eliot or West River	....	1.00	.40
1410	42¢ Ottowa River	....	1.00	.40
1411	42¢ Niagara River	....	1.00	.40
1412	42¢ South Saskatchewan River	....	1.00	.40
1412a	Canadian Rivers II, Strip of 5	....	5.25	4.00
1412b	Canadian Rivers II, booklet pane of 10	....	10.00	....

1413 1420

SCOTT NO.	DESCRIPTION	PLATE BLOCK F/NH	UNUSED F/NH	USED F
1413	42¢ 50th Anniversary of the Alaska Highway	4.80	1.00	.35
1414	42¢ Gymnastics	....	1.00	.35
1415	42¢ Track and Field	....	1.00	.35
1416	42¢ Diving	....	1.00	.35
1417	42¢ Cycling	....	1.00	.35
1418	42¢ Swimming	....	1.00	.35
1418a	Olympic Summer Games, Strip of 5, attached	....	5.50	8.50
1418b	Olympic Summer Games, booklet pane of 10	....	11.00	10.00
1419	50¢ Canadian Art "Red Nasturtiums"	5.95	1.20	1.50
1420	Nova Scotia	....	2.10	1.50
1421	Ontario	....	2.10	1.50
1422	Prince Edward Island	....	2.10	1.50
1423	New Brunswick	....	2.10	1.50
1424	Quebec	....	2.10	1.50
1425	Saskatchewan	....	2.10	1.50
1426	Manitoba	....	2.10	1.50
1427	Northwest Territories	....	2.10	1.50
1428	Alberta	....	2.10	1.50
1429	British Columbia	....	2.10	1.50
1430	Yukon	....	2.10	1.50
1431	Newfoundland	....	2.10	1.50
1431a	42¢ 125th Anniversary of Canada, 12 various attached	....	24.00	22.00

1432 1436

SCOTT NO.	DESCRIPTION	PLATE BLOCK F/NH	UNUSED F/NH	USED F
1432-35	Canadian Folk Heroes, attached	4.95	4.25	3.50
1432	42¢ Jerry Potts	....	1.00	.35
1433	42¢ Capt. William Jackman	....	1.00	.35
1434	42¢ Laura Secord	....	1.00	.35
1435	42¢ Joseph Montferrand	....	1.00	.35
1436	42¢ Copper	....	1.00	.45
1437	42¢ Sodalite	....	1.15	.45
1438	42¢ Gold	....	1.15	.45
1439	42¢ Galena	....	1.15	.45
1440	42¢ Grossular	....	1.15	.45
1440a	Minerals, Strip of 5	....	5.50	4.25
1440b	Minerals, booklet pane of 10	....	11.50	9.50

1441

1443a

SCOTT NO.	DESCRIPTION	PLATE BLOCK F/NH	UNUSED F/NH	USED F
1441-42	Canadian Space Exploration, attached	4.95	2.25	2.25
1441	42¢ Anik E2 Satellite	....	1.00	.75
1442	42¢ Earth, Space Shuttle	....	1.10	1.00
1443-45	National Hockey League, booklet singles	....	3.25	.95
1443a	Skates, Stick, booklet pane of 8	....	8.00	....
1444a	Team Emblems, booklet pane of 8	....	8.00	....
1445a	Goalie's Mask, booklet pane of 9	....	10.00	....

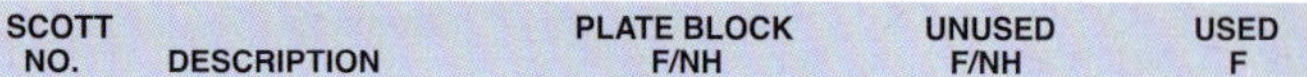

SCOTT NO.	DESCRIPTION	PLATE BLOCK F/NH	UNUSED F/NH	USED F

1446-47

1452

SCOTT NO.	DESCRIPTION	PLATE BLOCK F/NH	UNUSED F/NH	USED F
1446-47	Order of Canada + D. Michener, attached	5.25	2.25	1.50
1446	42¢ Order of Canada	....	1.10	.35
1447	42¢ Daniel Roland Michener	....	1.10	.35
1448-51	World War II—1942, att'd	4.95	4.25	3.30
1448	42¢ War Reporting	....	1.10	.50
1449	42¢ Newfoundland Air Bases	....	1.10	.50
1450	42¢ Raid on Dieppe	....	1.10	.50
1451	42¢ U-boats offshore	....	1.10	.50
1452	42¢ Jouluvana—Christmas	4.50	1.00	.25
1452a	Same, perf. 13-1/2	....	1.15	.25
1452b	Same, booklet pane of 10	....	11.00	....
1453	48¢ La Befana—Christmas	6.00	1.35	.75
1453a	Same, booklet pane of 5	....	6.75	....
1454	84¢ Weihnachtsmann	9.25	2.00	.85
1454a	Same, booklet pane of 5	....	11.00	....
1455	37¢ Santa Claus	....	1.00	.95
1455a	Same, booklet pane of 10	....	9.75	....

1455

1456

1460

1993 COMMEMORATIVES

SCOTT NO.	DESCRIPTION	PLATE BLOCK F/NH	UNUSED F/NH	USED F
1456-89, 1491-1506, 50 varieties		**41.00**	**42.50**	**19.50**
1456-59	Canadian Women, attached	5.50	4.80	3.50
1456	43¢ Adelaide Sophia Hoodless	....	1.10	.35
1457	43¢ Marie-Josephine Gerin-Lajoie	...	1.10	.35
1458	43¢ Pitseolak Ashoona	...	1.10	.35
1459	43¢ Helen Kinnear	....	1.10	.35
1460	43¢ Stanley Cup Centennial	5.25	1.10	.35

1461

1467

SCOTT NO.	DESCRIPTION	PLATE BLOCK F/NH	UNUSED F/NH	USED F
1461	43¢ Coverlet "Bed Rugg", New Brunswick	....	1.10	.35
1462	43¢ Pieced Quilt, Ontario	....	1.10	.35
1463	43¢ Doukhobor Bedcover, Saskatchewan	....	1.10	.35
1464	43¢ Kwakwaka'wakw ceremonial robe, British Columbia	....	1.10	.35
1465	43¢ Boutonne coverlet, Quebec	....	1.10	.35
1465a	Handcrafted Textiles, Strip of 5	....	5.75	3.00
1465b	Handcrafted Textiles, booklet pane of 10	....	11.50	7.00
1461-65	Same, set of 5 singles	....	5.00	....
1466	86¢ Canadian Art—"Drawing for the Owl"	9.75	2.25	1.25
1467	43¢ Empress Hotel, Victoria, B.C.	....	1.15	.35
1468	43¢ Banff Springs Hotel, Banff, Alberta	....	1.15	.35
1469	43¢ Royal York Hotel, Toronto, Ontario	....	1.15	.35
1470	43¢ Chateau Frontenac, Quebec City, Quebec	....	1.15	.35
1471	43¢ Algonquin Hotel, St. Andrews, N.B.	....	1.15	.35
1471a	Canadian Pacific Hotels, strip of 5	....	6.25	4.00
1471b	Canadian Pacific Hotels, booklet pane of 10	....	12.50	....

1472

1484

1490a

SCOTT NO.	DESCRIPTION	PLATE BLOCK F/NH	UNUSED F/NH	USED F
1472	43¢ Algonquin Park, Ontario	....	1.25	1.10
1473	43¢ De la Gaspesie Park, Quebec	....	1.25	1.10
1474	43¢ Cedar Dunes Park, P.E.I.	....	1.25	1.10
1475	43¢ Cape St. Mary's Reserve, Newfoundland	....	1.25	1.10
1476	43¢ Mount Robson Park, B.C.	....	1.25	1.10
1477	43¢ Writing-On-Stone Park, Alberta	....	1.25	1.10
1478	43¢ Spruce Woods Park, Manitoba	....	1.25	1.10
1479	43¢ Herschel Island Park, Yukon	....	1.25	1.10
1480	43¢ Cypress Hills Park, Saskatchewan	....	1.25	1.10
1481	43¢ The Rocks Park, New Brunswick	....	1.25	1.10
1482	43¢ Blomidon Park, Nova Scotia	....	1.25	1.10
1483	43¢ Katannilik Park, Northwest Territories	....	1.25	1.10
1483a	100th Anniversary of Territorial Parks, 12 varieties attached	...	18.00	18.00
1484	43¢ Toronto Bicentennial	5.25	1.10	.40
1485	43¢ Fraser River	...	1.10	.40
1486	43¢ Yukon River	...	1.10	.40
1487	43¢ Red River	...	1.10	.40
1488	43¢ St. Lawrence River	...	1.10	.40
1489	43¢ St. John River	...	1.10	.40
1489a	Canadian Rivers III, strip of 5	...	6.00	4.25
1489b	Canadian Rivers III, booklet pane of 10	...	11.00	8.50

1491

1495

1499

SCOTT NO.	DESCRIPTION	PLATE BLOCK F/NH	UNUSED F/NH	USED F
1490	43¢-86¢ Canadian Motor Vehicles souvenir sheet of 6	...	9.50	9.00
1491-94	Canadian Folklore—Folk Songs, attached	5.50	4.50	3.50
1491	43¢ The Alberta Homesteader	...	1.10	.35
1492	43¢ Les Raftmans	...	1.10	.35
1493	43¢ I'se the B'y that Builds the Boat	...	1.10	.35
1494	43¢ Bear Song	...	1.10	.35

1502

1507

SCOTT NO.	DESCRIPTION	PLATE BLOCK F/NH	UNUSED F/NH	USED F
1495-98	Dinosaurs, attached	5.50	4.75	3.50
1495	43¢ Massospondylus (Jurassic period)	...	1.20	.35
1496	43¢ Styracosaurus (Cretaceous period)	...	1.20	.35
1497	43¢ Albertosaurus (Cretaceous period)	...	1.20	.35
1498	43¢ Platecarpus (Cretaceous period)	...	1.20	.35
1499	43¢ Santa Claus—Poland	4.85	1.10	.25
1499a	same, booklet pane of 10	...	11.00	...
1500	49¢ Santa Claus—Russia	6.00	1.25	.55
1500a	same, booklet pane of 5	...	6.75	...
1501	86¢ Father Christmas, Australia	10.00	2.40	.65
1501a	same, booklet pane of 5	...	11.00	...
1502	38¢ Santa Claus	...	1.00	.65
1502a	same, booklet pane of 10	...	9.00	...
1503-06	World War II—1943	5.30	4.50	4.00
1503	43¢ Aid to Allies	...	1.15	.65
1504	43¢ Canada's Bomber Force	...	1.15	.65
1505	43¢ Battle of the Atlantic	...	1.15	.65
1506	43¢ Invasion of Italy	...	1.15	.65

1994

SCOTT NO.	DESCRIPTION	PLATE BLOCK F/NH	UNUSED F/NH	USED F
1507-08	43¢ Greeting booklet (10 stamps w/35 stickers)	...	11.00	...

1509

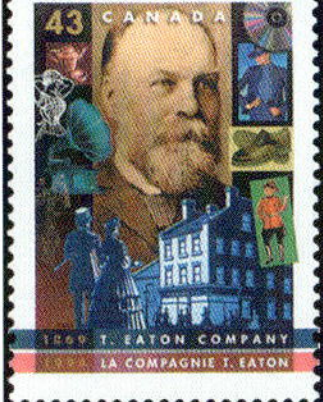
1510

1517

1994 COMMEMORATIVES

SCOTT NO.	DESCRIPTION	PLATE BLOCK F/NH	UNUSED F/NH	USED F
	1509-22, 1524-26, 1528-40, 41 varieties	...	**34.00**	**13.75**
1509	43¢ Jeanne Sauve	5.50	1.10	.40
1510	43¢ T. Eaton Prestige	...	1.10	.40
1510a	43¢ T. Eaton Prestige, booklet of 10	...	11.00	...
1511	43¢ Saguenay River	...	1.25	.35
1512	43¢ French River	...	1.25	.35
1513	43¢ Mackenzie River	...	1.25	.35
1514	43¢ Churchill River	...	1.25	.35
1515	43¢ Columbia River	...	1.25	.35
1515a	Canadian Rivers IV, strip of 5	...	5.75	5.00
1515b	Canadian Rivers IV, booklet pane of 10	...	12.00	...
1516	88¢ Canadian Art "Vera"	10.50	2.25	1.25

1523a

1524a

1525

SCOTT NO.	DESCRIPTION	PLATE BLOCK F/NH	UNUSED F/NH	USED F
1517-18	Commonwealth Games, attached	5.25	2.25	1.50
1517	43¢ Lawn Bowls	...	1.10	.35
1518	43¢ Lacrosse	...	1.10	.35
1519-20	Commonwealth Games, attached	5.25	2.25	1.50
1519	43¢ Wheelchair Marathon	...	1.10	.35
1520	43¢ High Jump	...	1.10	.35
1521	50¢ Commonwealth Games (Diving)	5.60	1.25	.80
1522	88¢ Commonwealth Games (Cycling)	9.75	2.25	1.15
1523	43¢ Intl. Year of the Family, souvenir sheet of 5	...	6.00	5.50
1524	Canada Day—Maple Trees, 12 varieties, attached	...	14.00	13.00
1525-26	Famous Canadians, attached	5.25	2.25	1.15
1525	43¢ Billy Bishop, Fighter Ace	...	1.10	.35
1526	43¢ Mary Travers, Folk Singer	...	1.10	.35
1527	43¢-88¢ Historic Motor Vehicles, souvenir sheet of 6	...	8.75	8.50

1528

1533

1536

SCOTT NO.	DESCRIPTION	PLATE BLOCK F/NH	UNUSED F/NH	USED F
1528	43¢ 50th Anniversary of ICAO	6.00	1.35	.35
1529-32	Dinosaurs, attached	5.35	4.75	3.75
1529	43¢ Coryphodon	...	1.20	.35
1530	43¢ Megacerops	...	1.20	.35
1531	43¢ Short-Faced Bear	...	1.20	.35
1532	43¢ Woolly Mammoth	...	1.20	.35
1533	43¢ Family Singing Carols	5.25	1.10	.25
1533a	same, booklet pane of 10	...	11.00	...
1534	50¢ Choir	5.75	1.25	.65
1534a	same, booklet pane of 5	...	6.75	...
1535	88¢ Caroling	9.75	2.25	1.15
1535a	same, booklet pane of 5	...	11.00	...
1536	38¢ Caroling Soloist, booklet single	...	1.00	.65
1536a	same, booklet pane of 10	...	9.75	...
1537-40	World War II—1944, attached	5.60	4.75	3.75
1537	43¢ D-Day Beachhead	...	1.15	.45
1538	43¢ Artillery—Normandy	...	1.15	.45
1539	43¢ Tactical Air Forces	...	1.15	.45
1540	43¢ Walcheren and Scheldt	...	1.15	.45

1995 COMMEMORATIVES

SCOTT NO.	DESCRIPTION	PLATE BLOCK F/NH	UNUSED F/NH	USED F
	1541-51, 1553-58, 1562-67, 1570-90, 47 varieties	......	**48.75**	**17.75**
1541-44	World War II—1945, attached	5.35	4.75	3.75
1541	43¢ Veterans Return Home	......	1.10	.45
1542	43¢ Freeing the POW	......	1.10	.45
1543	43¢ Libertation of Civilians	......	1.10	.45
1544	43¢ Crossing the Rhine	......	1.10	.45
1545	88¢ Canadian Art "Floraison"	9.50	2.25	1.25
1546	(43¢) Canada Flag over Lake	5.25	1.15	.35
1547	(43¢) Louisbourg Harbor, ships near Dauphin Gate	......	1.15	.35
1548	(43¢) Walls, streets & buildings of Louisbourg	......	1.15	.35
1549	(43¢) Museum behind King's Bastion	......	1.15	.35
1550	(43¢) Drawing of King's Garden, Convent, Hospital & barracks	......	1.15	.35
1551	(43¢) Partially eroded fortifications	......	1.15	.35
1551a	(43¢) Fortress of Louisbourg, strip of 5	......	6.00	4.75
1551b	(43¢) Fortress of Louisbourg, booklet pane of 10	......	11.00	9.00
1552	43¢-88¢ Historic Land Vehicles/Farm and Frontier souvenir sheet of 6	......	9.00	9.00
1553	43¢ Banff Springs Golf Club	......	1.20	.35
1554	43¢ Riverside Country Club	......	1.20	.35
1555	43¢ Glen Abbey Golf Club	......	1.20	.35
1556	43¢ Victoria Golf Club	......	1.20	.35
1557	43¢ Royal Montreal Golf Club	......	1.20	.35
1557a	43¢ Royal Canadian Golf Assoc., strip of 5	......	6.50	5.00
1557b	43¢ Royal Canadian Golf Assoc., booklet pane of 10	......	12.50	11.00
1558	43¢ Lunenberg Academy Centennial	5.00	1.20	.35
1559-61	43¢ Group of Seven 75th Anniv. 3 souv. sheets (2 w/3 stamps and 1 w/4 stamps)	......	11.75	11.50
1562	43¢ Winnipeg, Manitoba 125th Anniversary	5.00	1.10	.35
1563-66	Migratory Wildlife, attached	5.50	4.75	3.00
1563, 65-67	Migratory Wildlife, attached (revised inscription)	6.00	5.25	5.25
1563	45¢ Monarch Butterfly	......	1.10	.40
1564	45¢ Belted Kingfisher	......	1.10	.40
1565	45¢ Northern Pintail	......	1.10	.40
1566	45¢ Hoary Bat	......	1.10	.40
1568-69	45¢ Canadian Memorial College, Toronto, Greetings Booklet (10 stamps w/15 stickers)	......	12.75	......
1570-73	45¢ Canadian Bridges, attached	5.50	4.75	3.75
1570	45¢ Quebec Bridge, Quebec	......	1.15	.40
1571	45¢ Highway 403-401-410 interchange, Ontario	......	1.15	.40
1572	45¢ Hartland Covered Wooden Bridge, New Brunswick	......	1.15	.40
1573	45¢ Alex Fraser Bridger, British Columbia	......	1.15	.40

1546

1547

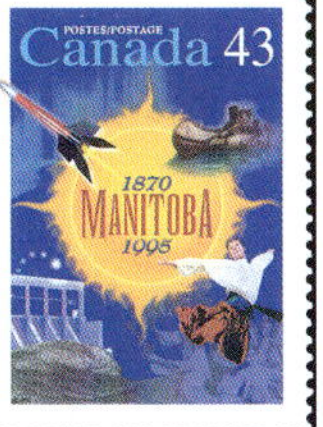
1553

1558

1559a

1562

1563

1570

1574

SCOTT NO.	DESCRIPTION	PLATE BLOCK F/NH	UNUSED F/NH	USED F
1574	45¢ Polar bear, caribou	....	1.15	.40
1575	45¢ Arctic poppy, cargo canoe	....	1.15	.40
1576	45¢ Inuk man, igloo, sled dogs	....	1.15	.40
1577	45¢ Dog-sled team, ski plane	....	1.15	.40
1578	45¢ Children	....	1.15	.40
1578a	45¢ Canadian Arctic, strip of 5	....	6.00	5.50
1578b	45¢ Canadian Arctic, booklet pane of 10	....	11.00	11.00
1579	45¢ Superman	....	1.45	.40
1580	45¢ Johnny Canuck	....	1.45	.40
1581	45¢ Nelvana	....	1.45	.40
1582	45¢ Captain Canuck	....	1.45	.40
1583	45¢ Fleur de Lys	....	1.45	.40
1583a	45¢ Comic Book Characters, strip of 5	....	7.00	3.00
1583b	45¢ Comic Book Characters, booklet pane of 10	....	13.50	12.00
1584	45¢ United Nations, 50th Anniversary	6.50	1.40	.40
1585	45¢ The Nativity	5.00	1.15	.40
1585a	same, booklet pane of 10	....	11.00	....
1586	52¢ The Annunciation	6.25	1.35	.65
1586a	same, booklet pane of 5	....	6.75	....
1587	90¢ Flight to Egypt	9.75	2.25	.70
1587a	same, booklet pane of 5	....	11.00	....
1588	40¢ Holly, booklet single	....	1.00	.70
1588a	same, booklet pane of 10	....	9.75	....
1589	45¢ La Francophonie's Agency, 25th Anniversary	5.10	1.15	.35
1590	45¢ End of the Holocaust, 50th Anniversary	5.10	1.15	.35

1579

1585

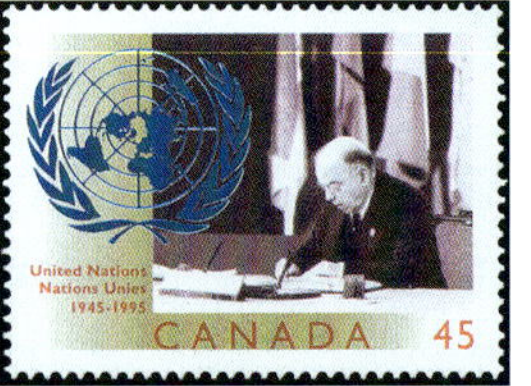

1584

1588

1589

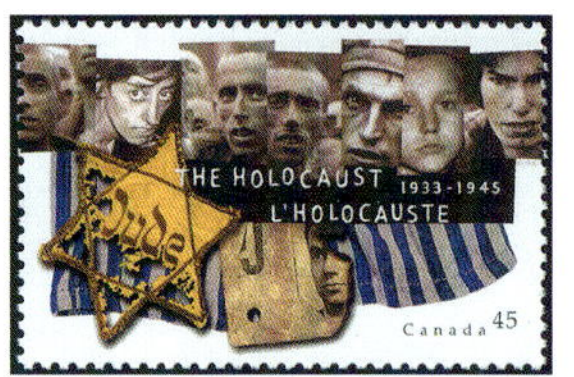

1590

1591

1595

1600

1602

1996 COMMEMORATIVES

SCOTT NO.	DESCRIPTION	PLATE BLOCK F/NH	UNUSED F/NH	USED F
1591-98, 1602-03, 1606-14, 1617-21, 1622-29, 36 varieties		**........**	**44.50**	**16.75**
1591-94	Birds, attached	....	5.00	4.25
1591	45¢ American Kestrel	....	1.15	.35
1592	45¢ Atlantic Puffin	....	1.15	.35
1593	45¢ Pileated Woodpecker	....	1.15	.35
1594	45¢ Ruby-throated Hummingbird	....	1.15	.35
1595-98	High Technology Industries, attached	....	5.25	4.25
1595	45¢ Ocean technology	....	1.25	.45
1596	45¢ Aerospace technology	....	1.25	.45
1597	45¢ Information technology	....	1.25	.45
1598	45¢ Biotechnology	....	1.25	.45
1598b	Booklet pane of 12	....	14.50	....
1600-01	45¢ Special Occasions, Greetings Booklet (10 stamps w/35 stickers)	....	18.00	....
1602	90¢ Canadian Art—"The Spirit of Haida Gwaii"	10.00	2.25	1.25
1603	45¢ AIDS Awareness	5.25	1.15	.25
1604	45¢-90¢ Historic Canadian Industrial & Commercial Vehicles souvenir sheet of 6	....	10.00	9.50
1605	5¢-45¢ CAPEX '96 souvenir pane of 25 vehicle stamps	....	10.00	9.50
1606	45¢ Yukon Gold Rush centennial, strip of 5	....	6.75	6.00
1606a	45¢ Jim Mason's discovery on Rabbit Creek, 1896	....	1.25	.65
1606b	45¢ Miners trekking to gold fields, boats on Lake Laberge	....	1.25	.65
1606c	45¢ Supr. Sam Steele, North West Mounted Police	....	1.25	.65
1606d	45¢ Dawson, boom town, city of entertainment	....	1.25	.65
1606e	45¢ Klondike gold fields	....	1.25	.65
1607	45¢ Canada Day (Maple Leaf), self-adhesive	....	1.15	.35
1607a	same, pane of 12	....	13.00	....
1608	45¢ Ethel Catherwood, high jump, 1928	....	1.30	.90
1609	45¢ Etienne Desmarteau, 56 lb. weight throw, 1904	....	1.30	.90
1610	45¢ Fanny Rosenfeld, 100m, 400m relay, 1928	....	1.30	.90
1611	45¢ Gerald Ouellette, smallbore, fifle, prone, 1956	....	1.30	.90
1612	45¢ Percy Williams, 100m, 200m, 1928	....	1.30	.90
1612a	45¢ Canadian Gold Medalists, strip of 5	....	6.50	4.75
1612b	45¢ Canadian Gold Medalists, booklet pane of 10	....	13.00	....
1613	45¢ 125th Anniv. of British Columbia's Entry into Confederation	5.25	1.15	.35
1614	45¢ Canadian Heraldy	5.25	1.15	.35
1615	45¢ Motion Pictures Centennial, self-adhesive, sheet of 5	....	6.00	5.50
1615a	45¢ L'arrivee d'un train en gate, Lumiere cinematography, 1896	....	1.25	1.10
1615b	45¢ Back to God's Country, Nell & Ernest Shipman, 1919	....	1.25	1.10
1615c	45¢ Hen Hop, Norman McLaren, 1942	....	1.25	1.10
1615d	45¢ Pour la suite du monde, Pierre Perrault, Michel Brault, 1963	....	1.25	1.10
1615e	45¢ Goin' Down the Road, Don Shebib, 1970	....	1.25	1.10

1603

1604a

1607

1606a

1608

1613

1614

1615a

1617

1618 1622 1627 1645 1647 1650 1630 1631 1635 1636 1637 1638 1639 1640 1641 1659 1661 1665

SCOTT NO.	DESCRIPTION	PLATE BLOCK F/NH	UNUSED F/NH	USED F
1616	45¢ Motion Pictures Centennial, self-adhesive, sheet of 5	....	6.00	5.50
1616a	45¢ Mon oncle Antoine, Claude Jutra, 1971	....	1.25	1.10
1616b	45¢ The Apprenticeship of Duddy Kravitz, Ted Kotcheff, 1974	....	1.25	1.10
1616c	45¢ Les Ordres, Michel Brault, 1974	....	1.25	1.10
1616d	45¢ Les Bons Debarras, Francis Mankiewicz, 1980	....	1.25	1.10
1616e	45¢ The Grey Fox, Phillip Borsos, 1982	....	1.25	1.10
1617	45¢ Edouard Montpetit, Educator	2.25	1.15	.50
1618-21	Winnie the Pooh, attached	....	5.25	5.25
1618	45¢ Winnie, Lt. Colebourne, 1914		1.25	.80
1619	45¢ Winnie, Christopher Robin, 1925	....	1.25	.80
1620	45¢ Milne and Shepard's Winnie the Pooh, 1926	....	1.25	.80
1621	45¢ Winnie the Pooh at Walt Disney World, 1996	....	1.25	.80
1621b	same, souvenir sheet of 4 (#1618-21)	....	9.25	9.25
1621c	same, booklet pane of 16	....	20.00	....
	same, 2 booklet panes plus souvenir book	....	24.00	....
1622	45¢ Margaret Laurence (1926-1987)	....	1.25	.45
1623	45¢ Donald G. Creighton (1902-1979)	....	1.25	.45
1624	45¢ Gabrielle Roy (1909-1983)	....	1.25	.45
1625	45¢ Felix-Antoine Savard (1896-1982)	....	1.25	.45
1626	45¢ Thomas C. Halliburton (1796-1865)	....	1.25	.45
1626a	45¢ Canadian Authors, strip of 5	....	7.25	6.75
1626b	45¢ Canadian Authors, booklet pane of 10	....	14.00	14.00
1627	45¢ Children on snowshoes, sled	5.25	1.15	.25
1627a	same, booklet pane of 10	....	11.00	....
1628	52¢ Santa Claus skiing	6.00	1.30	.40
1628a	same, booklet pane of 5	....	7.00	....
1629	90¢ Children skating	9.50	2.25	.65
1629a	same, booklet pane of 5	....	12.00	....

1997 COMMEMORATIVES

SCOTT NO.	DESCRIPTION	PLATE BLOCK F/NH	UNUSED F/NH	USED F
1630, 1631-48, 1649-72, 43 varieties		**.......**	**39.00**	**18.00**
1630	45¢ New Year 1997 (Year of the Ox)	5.50	1.25	.60
1630a	same, souvenir sheet of 2	....	3.25	3.25
	same, souvenir sheet of 2, with Hong Kong '97 overprint	....	10.00	....
1631-34	Birds of Canada, attached	5.50	4.75	3.75
1631	45¢ Mountain bluebird	....	1.20	.35
1632	45¢ Western grebe	....	1.20	.35
1633	45¢ Northern gannet	....	1.20	.35
1634	45¢ Scarlet tanager	....	1.20	.35
1635	90¢ Canadian Art "York Boat on Lake Winnipeg"	10.00	2.30	1.25
1636	45¢ Canadian Tire, 75th Anniv.	5.00	1.15	.35
1637	45¢ Father Charles-Emile Gadbois (1906-1981)	5.00	1.15	.35
1638	45¢ Blue poppy	....	1.15	.35
1638a	same, booklet pane of 12	....	13.00	....
1639	45¢ Victorian Order of Nurses	5.00	1.15	.35
1640	45¢ Law Society of Upper Canada	5.00	1.15	.35
1641-44	45¢ Ocean Fish, attached	5.25	4.75	3.25
1641	45¢ Great White Shark		1.15	.35
1642	45¢ Pacific Halibut		1.15	.35
1643	45¢ Atlantic Sturgeon		1.15	.35
1644	45¢ Bluefin Tuna		1.15	.35
1645-46	45¢ Confederation Bridge, attached	5.35	2.75	1.50
1645	45¢ Lighthouse and Bridge	....	1.15	.35
1646	45¢ Bridge and Bird	....	1.15	.35
1647	45¢ Gilles Villeneuve, Formula 1 driver	5.15	1.15	.35
1648	90¢ Gilles Villeneuve, Formula 1 d iver	10.00	2.25	1.15
1648b	45¢-90¢ Gilles Villeneuve, souvenir sheet of 8	....	14.00	....
1649	45¢ John Cabot	5.10	1.15	.35
1650-53	45¢ Canada's scenic highways (Canada Day), attached	5.35	4.75	3.75
1650	45¢ Sea to Sky Highway, British Columbia	....	1.20	.75
1651	45¢ The Cabot Trail, Nova Scotia	....	1.20	.75
1652	45¢ The Wine Route, starting in Ontario	....	1.20	.75
1653	45¢ The Big Muddy, Saskatchewan	....	1.20	.75
1654	45¢ Industrial Design	5.10	1.20	.75
1654v	same, sheet of 24 w/12 different Labels	....	30.00	....
1655	45¢ Highland Games	5.10	1.20	.35
1656	45¢ Knights of Columbus in Canada	5.10	1.20	.35
1657	45¢ World Congress of the PTT	5.10	1.20	.35
1658	45¢ Canada's Year of Asia Pacific	5.10	1.20	.35
1659-60	45¢ Ice Hockey "Series of the Century", bklt singles	....	2.25	1.30
1660a	same, bklt pane of 10 (5 of each)	....	11.00	....
1661-64	Famous Politicians, attached	5.25	4.75	3.75
1661	45¢ Martha Black	....	1.15	.75
1662	45¢ Lionel Chevrier	....	1.15	.75
1663	45¢ Judy LaMarsh	....	1.15	.75
1664	45¢ Real Caouette	....	1.15	.75
1665-68	Supernatural, 4 attached	5.25	4.75	3.75
1665	45¢ Vampire	....	1.15	.35
1666	45¢ Werewolf	....	1.15	.35
1667	45¢ Ghost	....	1.15	.35
1668	45¢ Goblin	....	1.15	.35
1669	45¢ Christmas, Stained Glass Window	5.25	1.15	.30
1669a	same, bklt pane of 10	....	11.00	....
1670	52¢ Christmas, Stained Glass Window	6.25	1.25	.50
1670a	same, bklt pane of 5	....	7.00	....
1671	90¢ Christmas, Stained Glass Window	9.75	2.25	.75
1671a	same, bklt pane of 5	....	11.00	....
1672	45¢ 75th Royal Agriculture Winter Fair, Toronto	5.25	1.15	.35

1997-2000 Regular Issues

SCOTT NO.	DESCRIPTION	PLATE BLOCK F/NH	UNUSED F/NH	USED F
1673	1¢ Bookbinding	.95	.25	.25
1674	2¢ Ironwork	.95	.25	.25
1675	3¢ Glass blowing	.95	.25	.25
1676	4¢ Oyster farmer	.95	.25	.25
1677	5¢ Weaving	.95	.25	.25
1678	9¢ Quilting	1.25	.30	.25
1679	10¢ Artistic woodworking	1.25	.30	.25
1680	25¢ Leatherworking	2.85	.65	.25
1681	46¢ Queen Elizabeth II	5.00	1.15	.25
1682	46¢ Flags Over Icebergs	5.25	1.15	.25
1682a	same, booklet pane of 10		11.50	....
1684	55¢ Maple Leaf	6.25	1.35	.40
1684a	same, booklet pane of 5 + label	....	6.30	....
1685	73¢ Maple Leaf	8.50	1.85	.60
1686	95¢ Maple Leaf	11.00	2.40	.95
1686a	same, booklet pane of 5 + label	....	12.00	....
1687	$1 Loon	11.00	2.40	.70
1688-89	$1 Atlantic Walrus & White Tailed Deer	11.00	4.75	3.00
1688	$1 White-Tailed Deer	....	2.50	1.25
1689	$1 Atlantic Walrus	....	2.50	1.25
1689b	Souvenir Sheet Deer and Walrus	....	10.00	10.00
1690	$2 Polar Bear	22.00	5.00	2.25
1691-92	$2 Peregrine Falcons & Sable Island Horses	22.00	10.00	5.50
1691	$2 Peregrine Falcons	....	4.75	2.25
1692	$2 Sable Island Horses	....	4.75	2.25
1692b	Souvenir Sheet, 2 each 1691-92	....	20.00	20.00
1693	$5 Moose	....	13.00	2.25
1694	$8 Grizzly Bear	....	18.50	5.50
1695	46¢ Flag, coil	....	1.15	.35
1696	45¢ Maple Leaf	....	1.65	1.50
1696b	same, booklet pane of 18	....	38.00	....
1697	45¢ Maple Leaf	....	1.40	.75
1698	46¢ Flags Over Icebergs	....	1.40	.75
1698a	same, booklet pane of 30	....	35.00	....
1699	46¢ Maple Leaf	....	3.00	2.85
1699a	same, booklet pane of 18	....	58.00	....
1700	47¢ Flag and Inukshuk	....	1.20	.25
1700a	same, booklet pane of 10	....	11.00	....
1700b	same, booklet pane of 30	....	32.00	....

1708

1709a

1710

1696

1715

1721

1722

1723

1725

1735

1736

1750

1756

1761

1764

1998 COMMEMORATIVES

SCOTT NO.	DESCRIPTION	PLATE BLOCK F/NH	UNUSED F/NH	USED F
1708,1710-13,1715-20,1721-24,1735-37,1738-42, 1750-54,1760-61,1761-66 set of 40 1998 commemoratives		....	**43.00**	**19.00**
1708	45¢ Year of the Tiger	5.25	1.15	.35
1708a	same, souvenir sheet of 2	....	2.40	2.00
1709	45¢ Provincial Leaders. sheetlet of 10	....	14.00	12.00
1710-13	Birds, attached	5.20	4.75	3.75
1710	45¢ Hairy Woodpecker	....	43.00	19.00
1711	45¢ Great Crested Flycatcher	....	1.25	.45
1712	45¢ Eastern Screech Owl	....	1.25	.45
1713	45¢ Gray Crowned Rosy-Finch	....	1.25	.45
1715-20	Fly Fishing, strip of 6, from bklt pane	....	7.75	5.75
1715	45¢ Coquihalla orange, steelhead trout	....	1.15	.55
1716	45¢ Steelhead bee, steelhead trout	....	1.15	.55
1717	45¢ Dark Montreal, brook trout	....	1.15	.55
1718	45¢ Lady Amherst, Atlantic salmon	....	1.15	.55
1719	45¢ Coho blue, coho salmon	....	1.15	.55
1720	45¢ Cosseboom special, Atlantic salmon	....	1.15	.55
1720a	same, bklt pane of 12	....	13.75	....
1721	45¢ Canadian Inst. of Mining Centennial	5.25	1.25	.35
1722	45¢ Imperial Penny Post Centennial	5.25	1.25	.35
1723-24	Sumo Wrestling Tournament, attached	5.25	2.50	2.50
1723	45¢ Rising sun, Mapleleaf and two wrestlers	....	1.15	.35
1724	45¢ Rising sun, Mapleleaf and Sumo champion	....	1.15	.35
1724b	45¢ Sumo Wrestling Tournament, souvenir sheet of 2	....	4.25	4.25
1725	45¢ St. Peters Canal, Nova Scotia	....	1.50	.75
1726	45¢ St. Ours Canal, Quebec	....	1.50	.75
1727	45¢ Port Carling Lock, Ontario	....	1.50	.75
1728	45¢ Locks, Rideau Canal, Onrtario	....	1.50	.75
1729	45¢ Peterborough lift lock, Trent-Severn Waterway, Ontario		1.50	.75
1730	45¢ Chambly Canal, Quebec	....	1.50	.75
1731	45¢ Lachine Canal, Quebec	....	1.50	.75
1732	45¢ Ice skating on Rideau Canal, Ottawa	....	1.50	.75
1733	45¢ Boat on Big Chute Marine Railway, Trent-Severn Waterway	....	1.50	.75
1734	45¢ Sault Ste. Marie Canal, Ontario	....	1.50	.75
1734a	45¢ Canals of Canada, bklt pane of 10 plus labels	....	16.00	....
1735	45¢ Health Professionals	5.25	1.15	.35
1736-37	Royal Canadian Mounted Police 125th Anniv. attd.	5.40	2.50	1.50
1736	45¢ Male mountie, native horse	....	1.15	.35
1737	45¢ Female mountie, helicopter, cityscape	....	1.15	.3
1737b	same, souvenir sheet of 2	....	3.00	2.75
1737c	same, souvenir sheet of 2 with signature	....	4.00	3.50
1737d	same, souvvenir sheet of 2 with Portugal '98 emblem	....	4.50	3.50
1737e	same, souvenir sheet of 2 with Italia '98 emblem	....	4.50	3.50
1738	45¢ William Roue, designer of Bluenose	5.25	1.15	.35

1739

SCOTT NO.	DESCRIPTION	PLATE BLOCK F/NH	UNUSED F/NH	USED F
1739-42	Scenic Highways, 4 attached	5.75	4.75	3.75
1739	45¢ Dempster Highway, Yukon	....	1.15	.45
1740	45¢ Dinosaur Trail, Alberta	....	1.15	.45
1741	45¢ River Valley, Scenic Drive, New Burnswick	....	1.15	.45
1742	45¢ Blue Heron Route, Prince Edward Isalnd ...	....	1.15	.45
1743	45¢ "Peinture", Jean-Paul Riopelle, self-adhesive	....	1.25	.45
1744	45¢ "La demiere campagne de Napolean", Fernand Leduc, self-adhesive	....	1.25	.65
1745	45¢ "Jet fuligineux sur noir torture", Jean -Paul Monusseau, self-adhesive	....	1.25	.65
1746	45¢ "Le fond du garde-robe", Pierre Gauvreau, self-adhesive	....	1.25	.65
1747	45¢ "Jean lacustre", Paul-Emile Borduas, self-adhesive	....	1.25	.65
1748	45¢ "Syndicat des gens de met", Marcelle Ferron, self-adhesive	....	1.25	.65
1749	45¢ "Le tumulte a la machoire crispee", Marcel Barbeau, self-adhesive	....	1.25	.65
1749a	45¢ The Automatists, 50th Anniversary, self-adhesive, bklt pane of 7	....	10.00	9.50
1750-53	Canadian Legendary Heroes, 4 attached	5.75	4.75	3.50
1750	45¢ Napoleon-Alexandre Comeau (1848-1923) outdoorsman	....	1.15	.45
1751	45¢ Phyllis Munday (1894-1990), mountaineer	....	1.15	.45
1752	45¢ Bill Mason (1929-1988), film maker	....	1.15	.45
1753	45¢ Harry "Red" Foster (1905-1985), sports enthusiast	....	1.15	.45
1754	90¢ Canadian Art "The Farmer's Family"	10.00	2.25	1.10
1755	45¢ Housing in Canada, sheetlet of 9	....	14.00	14.00
1756	45¢ University of Ottawa, 150th Anniversary	5.25	1.15	.30
1757	45¢ Elephant, bear performing tricks	....	1.15	.30
1758	45¢ Women standing on horse, aerial act	....	1.15	.30
1759	45¢ Lion tamer	....	1.15	.30
1760	45¢ Contortionists, acrobats	....	1.15	.30
1760a	45¢ The Circus, bklt pane of 12	....	14.00	....
1760b	same, souvenir sheet of 4	....	5.65	5.00
1761	45¢ John Peters Humphrey, Human Rights author	5.25	1.15	.35
1762-63	Canadian Naval Reserve, 75th Anniversary, attached	5.25	2.50	1.75
1762	45¢ HMCS Sackville	....	1.15	.35
1763	45¢ HMCS Shawinigan	....	1.15	.35
1764	45¢ Christmas, Sculpted wooden angels	5.25	1.15	.30
1764a	same, bklt pane of 10	....	43.00	....
1765	52¢ Christmas, Sculpted wooden angels	5.75	1.35	.55
1765a	same, bklt pane of 5	....	20.00	....
1766	90¢ Christmas, Sculpted wooden angels	10.00	2.20	.85
1766a	same, bklt pane of 5	....	43.00	....

1767

1770

1999 COMMEMORATIVES

SCOTT NO.	DESCRIPTION	PLATE BLOCK F/NH	UNUSED F/NH	USED F
1767	46¢ New Year 1999, Year of the Rabbit	5.25	1.15	.40
1768	same, souvenir sheet of 2	....	2.75	2.50
1769	46¢ Le Theatre du Rideau Vert, 50th Anniversary	5.25	1.15	.40
1770-73	Birds, 4 attached	5.95	4.75	2.50
1770	46¢ Northern goshawk	....	1.15	.45
1771	46¢ Red-winged blackbird	....	1.15	.45
1772	46¢ American goldfinch	....	1.15	.45
1773	46¢ Sandhill crane	....	1.15	.45
1774	46¢ Northern goshawk, self-adhesive	....	1.20	.55
1775	46¢ Red-winged blackbird, self-adhesive	....	1.20	.55
1776	46¢ American goldfinch, self-adhesive	....	1.20	.55
1777	46¢ Sandhill crane, self-adhesive	....	1.20	.55
1777a	same, bklt pane of 6 (1774 x 2, 1775 x 2, 1776 x 2, 1777x 1), self-adhesive	....	7.50	....
1777b	same, bklt pane of 6 (1774 x 1, 1775 x 1, 1776 x 2, 1777 x 2), self-adhesive	....	7.50	....

1778

1779

1999 COMMEMORATIVES (continued)

SCOTT NO.	DESCRIPTION	PLATE BLOCK F/NH	UNUSED F/NH	USED F
1778	46¢ Univ. of British Columbia Museum of Anthropology. 50th Anniversary	5.26	1.15	.35
1779	46¢ Sailing Ship Marco Polo	5.26	1.15	.35
1779a	same, souvenir sheet of 2 (1779 x 1, Australia 1631 x 1)	....	3.50	3.50
1780-83	Canada's Scenic Highways, 4 attached	5.95	4.75	3.75
1780	46¢ Gaspe Peninsula, Highway 132, Quebec	....	1.25	.45
1781	46¢ Yellowghead Highway (PTH 16), Manitoba	....	1.25	.45
1782	46¢ Dempster Highway 8, Northwest Territories	....	1.25	.45
1783	46¢ Discovery Trail, Route 230N, Newfoundland	....	1.25	.45
1784	46¢ Creation of the Nunavnt Territory	5.25	1.15	.35
1785	46¢ International Year of Older Persons	5.25	1.15	.35
1786	46¢ Baisakhi, Religious Holiday of Sikh Canadians, 300 th Anniversary	9.25	2.25	.35
1787	46¢ Canadian orchid, Arethusa bulbosa, self-adhesive	....	1.25	.45
1788	46¢ Canadian orchid, Amerorchis rotundifolia, self-adhesive	....	1.25	.45
1789	46¢ Canadian orchid, Platanthera psycodes, self-adhesive	....	1.25	.45
1790	46¢ Canadian orchid, Cypripedium pubescens, self-adhesive	....	1.25	.45
1790a	same, bklt pane of 12 (1787-90 x 3)	....	15.00	....
1790b	same, souvenir sheet of 4 w/ China '99 emblem	....	4.95	4.95

1791

1799

SCOTT NO.	DESCRIPTION	PLATE BLOCK F/NH	UNUSED F/NH	USED F
1791-94	Horses, 4 attached	5.95	4.95	4.25
1791	46¢ Northern Dancer, thorough-bred race horse	....	1.25	.45
1792	46¢ Kingsway Skoal, bucking horse	....	1.25	.45
1793	46¢ Big Ben, show horse	....	1.25	.45
1794	46¢ Ambro Flight, harness race horse	....	1.25	.45
1795	46¢ Northern Dancer, thorough-bred race horse, self-adhesive	....	1.25	.45
1796	46¢ Kingsway Skoal, bucking horse, self-adhesive	....	1.25	.45
1797	46¢ Big Ben, show horse, self-adhesive	....	1.25	.45
1798	46¢ Ambro Flight, harness race horse, self-adhesive	....	1.25	.45
1798a	same, bklt pane of 12 (1795-98 x 3)	....	15.75	....
1799	46¢ Quebec Bar Association, 150th Anniversary	5.25	1.15	.35

1800

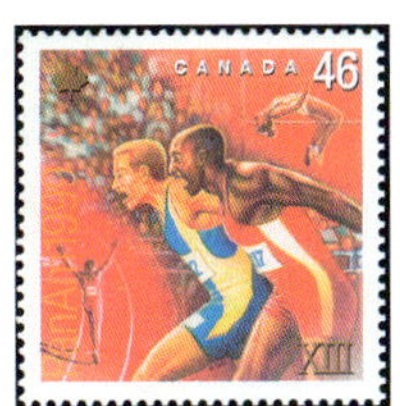

1801

SCOTT NO.	DESCRIPTION	PLATE BLOCK F/NH	UNUSED F/NH	USED F
1800	95¢ Canadian Art "Unicorn Rooster"	10.50	2.40	1.35
1801-04	46¢ Pan-American Games XIII, 4 attached	5.95	4.75	3.50
1801	46¢ Track & Field	....	1.25	.50
1802	46¢ Cycling, weight lifting, gymnastics	....	1.25	.50
1803	46¢ Swimming, sailboarding, kayaking	....	1.25	.50
1804	46¢ Soccer, tennis, medals winners	....	1.25	.50

1805

1806

SCOTT NO.	DESCRIPTION	PLATE BLOCK F/NH	UNUSED F/NH	USED F
1805	46¢ World Rowing Championships	5.25	1.15	.35
1806	46¢ Universal Postal Union	5.25	1.15	.35

1807a

1808a

SCOTT NO.	DESCRIPTION	PLATE BLOCK F/NH	UNUSED F/NH	USED F
1807	46¢ Canadian Int. Air Show, 50th Anniv., sheetlet of 4		6.50	6.50
1807a	46¢ Fokker DR-1, CT-114 Tutors	....	1.50	1.25
1807b	46¢ Tutors, H101 Salto sailplane	....	1.50	1.25
1807c	46¢ De Havilland DH100 Vampire MKIII	....	1.50	1.25
1807d	46¢ Stearman A-75	....	1.50	1.25
1808	46¢ Royal Canadian Air Force, 75th Anniv, sheetlet of 16	....	24.00	24.00
1808a	46¢ De Havilland Mosquito FVBI	....	1.25	1.25
1808b	46¢ Sopwith F1 Camel	....	1.25	1.25
1808c	46¢ De Havilland Canada DHC-3 Otter	....	1.25	1.25
1808d	46¢ De Havilland Canada CC-108 Caribou	....	1.25	1.25
1808e	46¢ Canadair DL-28 Argus MK 2	....	1.25	1.25
1808f	46¢ North American F86 Sabre 6	....	1.25	1.25
1808g	46¢ McDonnell Douglas CF-18 Hornet	....	1.25	1.25
1808h	46¢ Sopwith SF-1 Dolphin	....	1.25	1.25
1808i	46¢ Armstrong Whitworth Siskin IIIA	....	1.25	1.25
1808j	46¢ Canadian Vickers (Northrop) Delta II	....	1.25	1.25
1808k	46¢ Sikorsky CH-124A Sea King Helicopter	....	1.25	1.25
1808l	46¢ Vickers-Armstrong Wellington MKII	....	1.25	1.25
1808m	46¢ Avro Anson MKI	....	1.25	1.25
1808n	46¢ Canadair (Lockheed) CF-104G Starfighter	....	1.25	1.25
1808o	46¢ Burgess-Dunne seaplane	....	1.25	1.25
1808p	46¢ Avro 504K	....	1.25	1.25

1809

1810

SCOTT NO.	DESCRIPTION	PLATE BLOCK F/NH	UNUSED F/NH	USED F
1809	46¢ NATO, 50th Anniversary	5.25	1.15	.35
1810	46¢ Frontier College, 100th Anniversary	5.25	1.15	.35

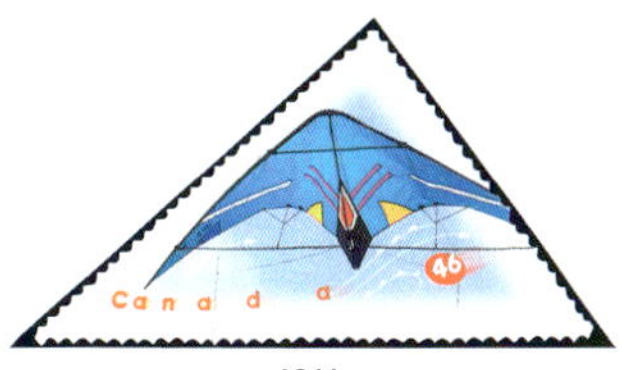

1811a

1813

SCOTT NO.	DESCRIPTION	PLATE BLOCK F/NH	UNUSED F/NH	USED F
1811	33¢ Kites, bklt pane of 8	....	10.50	....
1811a	33¢ Master Control, sport kite by Lam Hoac (triangular)		2.50	.50
1811b	33¢ Indian Garden Flying Carpet, edo kite by Skye Morrison (trapezoidal)	....	2.50	.50
1811c	33¢ Gibson Girl, Manufactured box kite (rectangular)		2.50	.50
1811d	33¢ Dragon centipede kite by Zhang tian Wei (oval)	....	2.50	.50
1812	Holographic Dove & 2000	....	1.25	.50
....	same, pane of 4	....	6.50	6.50
1813	55¢ Girl & Dove	....	1.50	.95
....	same, pane of 4	....	6.50	6.50

1814

1815

SCOTT NO.	DESCRIPTION	PLATE BLOCK F/NH	UNUSED F/NH	USED F
1814	95¢ Millenium Dove	....	2.50	1.95
....	same, pane of 4	....	8.00	....
1815	46¢ Christmas, Angel, drum	5.25	1.15	.35
1815a	same, bklt pane of 10	....	11.00	....
1816	55¢ Christmas, Angel, toys	6.25	1.40	.50
1816a	same, bklt pane of	....	6.75	....
1817	95¢ Christmas, Angel, candle	10.50	2.50	1.25
1817a	same, bklt pane of 5	....	12.00	....

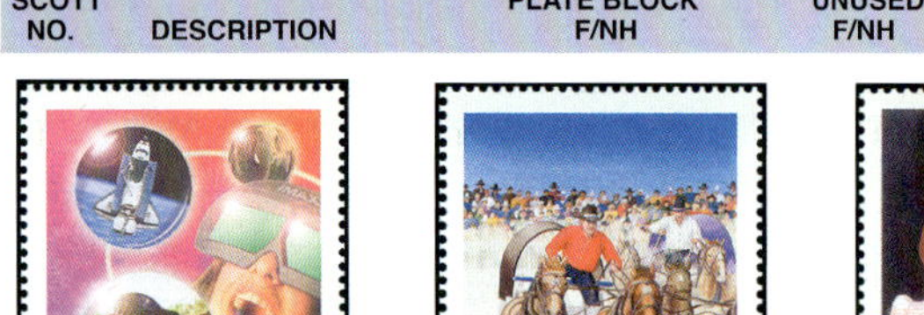

1818a

1819a

1820a

SCOTT NO.	DESCRIPTION	PLATE BLOCK F/NH	UNUSED F/NH	USED F
1818	46¢ Millenium Collection-Media Tech. sheet of 4	....	....	9.50
1818a	46¢ IMAX Movies	....	2.50	2.00
1818b	46¢ Softimage animation software	....	2.50	2.00
1818c	46¢ Ted Rogers Sr. (1900-39) and radio tube	....	2.50	2.00
1818d	46¢ Invention of radio facsimile device by Sir William Stephenson (1896-1989)	....	2.50	2.00
1819	46¢ Millenium Collection-Canadian Entertainment, sheet of 4	....	9.50	....
1819a	46¢ Calgary Stampede	....	2.50	2.00
1819b	46¢ Performers from Cirque du Soleil	....	2.50	2.00
1819c	46¢ Hockey Night in Canada	....	2.50	2.00
1819d	46¢ La Soiree du Hockey	....	2.50	2.00
1820	46¢ Millenium Collection-Entertainers, sheet of 4	....	....	9.50
1820a	46¢ Portia White (1911-68), singer	....	2.50	2.00
1820b	46¢ Glenn Gould (1932-82), pianist	....	2.50	2.00
1820c	46¢ Guy Lombardo (1902-77), band leader	....	2.50	2.00
1820d	46¢ Felix Leclerc (1914-88), singer, guitarist	....	2.50	2.00

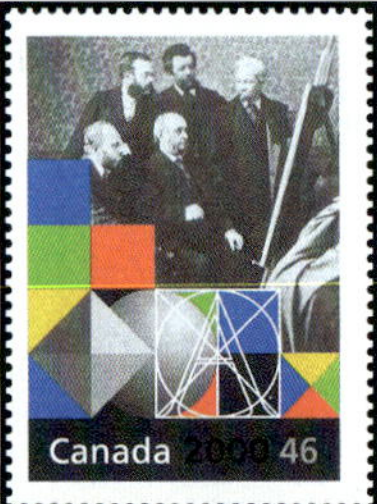

1821a

1822a

1823a

SCOTT NO.	DESCRIPTION	PLATE BLOCK F/NH	UNUSED F/NH	USED F
1821	46¢ Millenium Collection-Fostering Canadian Talent, sheet of 4	....	9.50	....
1821a	46¢ Royal Canadian Academy of Arts (men viewing painting)	....	2.50	2.00
1821b	46¢ Canada Council (sky, musical staff, "A")	....	2.50	2.00
1821c	46¢ National Film Board of Canada	....	2.50	2.00
1821d	46¢ Canadian Broadcasting Corp.	....	2.50	2.00
1822	46¢ Millenium Collection-Medical Innovators, sheet of 4	....	9.50	....
1822a	46¢ Sir Frederic Banting (1891-1941), co-discoverer of insulin, syringe and dog	....	2.50	2.00
1822b	46¢ Dr. Armand Frappier (1904-91), microbiologist, holding flask	....	2.50	2.00
1822c	46¢ Dr. Hans Selye (1907-82), endocrinologist and molecular diagram	....	2.50	2.00
1822d	46¢ Maude Abbott (1869-1940), pathologist, and roses	....	2.50	2.00
1823	46¢ Millenium Collection-Social Progress, sheet of 4	....	9.50	....
1823a	46¢ Nun, doctor, hospital	....	2.50	2.00
1823b	46¢ Statue of women holding decree	....	2.50	2.00
1823c	46¢ Alphonse Desjardins (1854-1920) and wife, credit union founders	....	2.50	2.00
1823d	46¢ Father Moses Coady (1882-1959), educator of adults	....	2.50	2.00

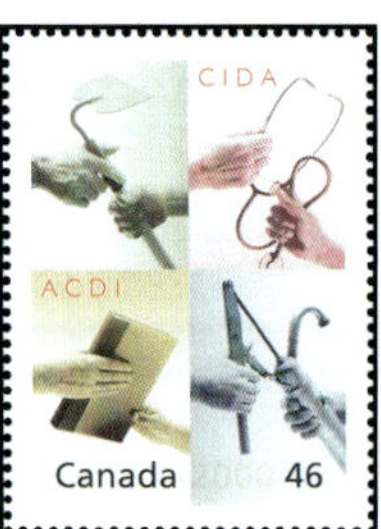

1824a

1825a

SCOTT NO.	DESCRIPTION	PLATE BLOCK F/NH	UNUSED F/NH	USED F
1824	46¢ Millenium Collection-Charity, sheet of 4	....	9.50	....
1824a	46¢ Canadian Inter. Development Agency (hand and tools)	....	2.50	2.00
1824b	46¢ Dr. Lucille Teasdale (1929-96), hospital administrator in Uganda	....	2.50	2.00
1824c	46¢ Marathon of Hope inspired by Terry Fox (1958-81)	....	2.50	2.00
1824d	46¢ Meals on Wheels program	....	2.50	2.00
1825	46¢ Millenium Collection-Humanitarians and Peacekeepers, sheet of 4	....	9.50	....
1825a	46¢ Raoul Dandurand (1861-1942)	....	2.50	2.00
1825b	46¢ Pauline Vanier (1898-1991), Elizabeth Smellie (1884-1968) nurses	....	2.50	2.00
1825c	46¢ Lester B. Pearson (1897-1972), prime minister and Nobel Peace Prize winner	....	2.50	2.00
1825d	46¢ Amputee and shadow (Ottawa Convention on Land Mines)	....	2.50	2.00

1826a

1827a

1828a

2000 COMMEMORATIVES

SCOTT NO.	DESCRIPTION	PLATE BLOCK F/NH	UNUSED F/NH	USED F
1826	46¢ Millenium Collection-Canada's First People, sheet of 4	....	9.50	....
1826a	46¢ Chief Pontiac (c.1720-69)	....	2.50	2.00
1826b	46¢ Tom Longboat (1887-1949), marathon runner	....	2.50	2.00
1826c	46¢ Inuit sculpture of shaman	....	2.50	2.00
1826d	46¢ Medicine man	....	2.50	2.00
1827	46¢ Millenium Collection-Canada's Cultural Fabric, sheet of 4	....	9.50	....
1827a	46¢ Norse boat, L'Anse aux Meadows	....	2.50	2.00
1827b	46¢ Immigrants on Halifax Pier 21	....	2.50	2.00
1827c	46¢ Neptune Theater, Halifax (head of Neptune)	....	2.50	2.00
1827d	46¢ Stratford Festival (actor and theater)	....	2.50	2.00
1828	46¢ Millenium Collection-Literary Legends, sheet of 4	....	9.50	....
1828a	46¢ W.O. Mitchell (1914-98), novelist, and prairie scene	....	2.50	2.00
1828b	46¢ Gratien Gelinas (1909-99), actor and playwright, and stars	....	2.50	2.00
1828c	46¢ Le Cercle du Livre de France book club	....	2.50	2.00
1828d	46¢ Harlequin paperback books	....	2.50	2.00

1829a

1830a

1831a

SCOTT NO.	DESCRIPTION	PLATE BLOCK F/NH	UNUSED F/NH	USED F
1829	46¢ Millenium Collection-Great Thinkers, sheet of 4	....	9.50	....
1829a	46¢ Marshall McLuhan (1911-80), philosopher, and television set	....	2.50	2.00
1829b	46¢ Northrop Frye (1912-91), literary critic, and word "code"	....	2.50	2.00
1829c	46¢ Roger Lemelin (1919-92), novelist, and cast of "The Plouffe Family" TV series	....	2.50	2.00
1829d	46¢ Hilda Marion Neatby (1904-75), historian, and farm scene	....	2.50	2.00
1830	46¢ Millenium Collection-A Tradition of Generosity, sheet of 4	....	9.50	....
1830a	46¢ Hart Massey (1823-96), Hart House, University of Toronto	....	2.50	2.00
1830b	46¢ Dorothy (1899-1965) & Izaak Killam (1885-1955), philantropists	....	2.50	2.00
1830c	46¢ Eric Lafferty Harvive (1892-1975), philantropist, and mountain scene	....	2.50	2.00
1830d	46¢ Macdonald Stewart Foundation	....	2.50	2.00
1831	46¢ Millenium Collection-Engineering and Tech. Marvels, sheet of 4	....	9.50	....
1831a	46¢ Map of Roger Pass, locomotive and tunnel diggers	....	2.50	2.00
1831b	46¢ Manic Dams	....	2.50	2.00
1831c	46¢ Canadian satellites, Remote Manipulator Arm	....	2.50	2.00
1831d	46¢ CN Tower	....	2.50	2.00

1832a

1833a

1834a

SCOTT NO.	DESCRIPTION	PLATE BLOCK F/NH	UNUSED F/NH	USED F
1832	46¢ Millenium Collection-Fathers of Invention, sheet of 4	....	9.50	....
1832a	46¢ George Klein (1904-92), gearwheels	....	2.50	2.00
1832b	46¢ Abraham Gesner (1797-1864), beaker of kerosene and lamp	....	2.50	2.00
1832c	46¢ Alexander Graham Bell (1847-1922), passenger-carrying kite, hydrofoil	....	2.50	2.00
1832d	46¢ Joseph-Armand Bombardier (1907-64), snowmobile	....	2.50	2.00
1833	46¢ Millenium Collection-Food, sheet of 4	....	9.50	....
1833a	46¢ Sir Charles Saunders (1867-1937), Marquis wheat	....	2.50	2.00
1833b	46¢ Pablum	....	2.50	2.00
1833c	46¢ Dr. Archibald Gowanlock Huntsman (1883-1973), marketer of frozen fish	....	2.50	2.00
1833d	46¢ Products of McCain Foods, Ltd., tractor	....	2.50	2.00
1834	46¢ Millenium Collection-Enterprising Giants, sheet of 4	....	9.50	....
1834a	46¢ Hudson's Bay Company (Colonist, Indian, canoe)	....	2.50	2.00
1834b	46¢ Bell Canada Enterprises (earth ,satellite, string of binary digits)	....	2.50	2.00
1834c	Vachon Co., snack cakes	....	2.50	2.00
1834d	46¢ George Weston Limited (Baked Goods, eggs)	....	2.50	2.00

1837a

1838a

SCOTT NO.	DESCRIPTION	PLATE BLOCK F/NH	UNUSED F/NH	USED F
1835	46¢ Millenium-2000	5.25	1.15	.35
1836	46¢ New Year 2000, Year of the Dragon	5.25	1.15	.35
1837	95¢ New Year 2000, Year of the Dragon, souvenir sheet of 1	....	2.50	2.50
1838	46¢ 50th National Hockey League All-Star, sheet 6	....	7.50	6.75
1838a	46¢ Wayne Gretsky (Oilers jersey No. 99)	....	1.75	1.00
1838b	46¢ Gordie Howe (Red Wings jersey No. 9)	....	1.75	1.00
1838c	46¢ Maurice Richard (red, white and blue Canadian jersey No. 9)	....	1.75	1.00
1838d	46¢ Doug Harvey (Canadians jersey No. 2)	....	1.75	1.00
1838e	46¢ Bobby Orr (Bruins jersey No. 4)	....	1.75	1.00
1838f	46¢ Jacques Plante (Canadians jersey No. 1)	....	1.75	1.00

1839

1847

SCOTT NO.	DESCRIPTION	PLATE BLOCK F/NH	UNUSED F/NH	USED F
1839-42	46¢ Birds, 4 attached	5.95	4.95	3.95
1839	46¢ Canada warbler	....	1.25	.45
1840	46¢ Osprey	....	1.25	.45
1841	46¢ Pacific Loon	....	1.25	.45
1842	46¢ Blue Jay	....	1.25	.45
1843	46¢ Canada warbler, self-adhesive	....	1.50	.45
1844	46¢ Osprey, self-adhesive	....	1.50	.45
1845	46¢ Pacific Loon, self-adhesive	....	1.50	.45
1846	46¢ Blue Jay, self-adhesive	....	1.50	.45
1846a	same, bklt pane of 6 (1843x2, 1844x2, 1845x1, 1846x1)		7.00	....
1846b	same, bklt pane of 6 (1843x1, 1844x1, 1845x2, 1846x2)		7.00	....
1847	46¢ Supreme Court, 125th Anniversary	5.25	1.15	.35

1850

1854a

SCOTT NO.	DESCRIPTION	PLATE BLOCK F/NH	UNUSED F/NH	USED F
1848	46¢ Ritual of the Calling of an Engineer, 75 Anniv.	5.25	1.15	.30
1848a	same, tete-beche pair	....	2.35	1.55
1849	46¢ Decorated Rural Mailboxes, Ship, fish, house designs		1.25	.45
1850	same, Flower, cow and church designs	....	1.25	.45
1851	same, Tractor design	....	1.25	.45
1852	same, Goose head, house designs	....	1.25	.45
1852a	same, bklt pane of 12 (1849-52x3)	....	16.00	....
1853	46¢ Picture Frame, self-adhesive	....	1.25	.45
1853a	same, bklt pane of 5 plus 5 labels	....	6.00	....
1853b	same, pane of 25	....	85.00	....
1854	55¢ Fresh Waters, bklt pane of 5, self-adhesive	....	11.00	....
1855	95¢ Fresh Waters, bklt pane of 5, self-adhesive	....	14.00	....

1856

1858

SCOTT NO.	DESCRIPTION	PLATE BLOCK F/NH	UNUSED F/NH	USED F
1856	95¢ Queen Mother's 100th Birthday	4.50	2.40	1.15
1857	46¢ Boys' and Girls' clubs, Centennial	5.25	1.20	.35
1858	46¢ Seventh Day Adventists	6.00	1.35	.35

1859

1866

SCOTT NO.	DESCRIPTION	PLATE BLOCK F/NH	UNUSED F/NH	USED F
1859-62	46¢ Stampin' the Future, 4 attached	5.50	4.50	3.50
1859	46¢ Rainbow, Spacevechile, astronauts, flag	....	1.15	.35
1860	46¢ Children in space vechile, children on ground	....	1.15	.35
1861	46¢ Children and map of Canada	....	1.15	.35
1862	46¢ Two astronauts in space vechile, planets	....	1.15	.35
1862b	Souvenir Sheet	....	4.75	4.00
1863	95¢ Canadian Artists, The Artist at Niagara	10.50	2.25	1.15
1864-65	46¢ Tall Ships in Halifax Harbor, 2 attached	....	2.25	.95
1865a	same, bklt of 10 (1864-65 x 5)	....	11.00	....
1866	46¢ Department of Labor	5.25	1.15	.35
1867	46¢ Petro-Canada, 25th anniversary	....	1.15	.35
1867a	same, bklt pane of 12	....	15.00	....
1867b	same, die cut inverted (2 points at TL)	....	4.50	3.75

1868

1873

1876

1877

SCOTT NO.	DESCRIPTION	PLATE BLOCK F/NH	UNUSED F/NH	USED F
1868-71	46¢ Centaceans, 4 attached	4.50	4.50	3.50
1868	46¢ Monodon monoceros	....	1.25	.45
1869	46¢ Balaenoptera musculus	....	1.25	.45
1870	46¢ Balaena mysticetus	....	1.25	.45
1871	46¢ Delphinapterus leucas	....	1.25	.45
1872	46¢ Christmas frame	....	1.40	.90
1872a	same, bklt pane of 5 + 5 labels	....	6.00	....
1873	46¢ Adoration of the shepherds	5.00	1.15	.35
1873a	same, bklt pane of 10	....	11.00	....
1874	55¢ Creche	6.00	1.40	.45
1874a	same, bklt pane of 6	....	8.50	....
1875	95¢ Flight into Egypt	10.50	2.50	.85
1875a	same, bklt pane of 6	....	13.50	....
1876-77	46¢ Regiments, 2 attached	5.50	2.40	.95
1876	46¢ Lord Stratchcona's Horse Regiment	....	1.25	.45
1877	46¢ Les Voltigeurs de Quebec	....	1.25	.45

1879 1880 1881

SCOTT NO.	DESCRIPTION	PLATE BLOCK F/NH	UNUSED F/NH	USED F
1878	47¢ Maple leaves, coil	....	1.25	.30
1879	60¢ Red fox, coil	....	1.50	.50
1879a	same, bklt pane of 6	....	12.50	....
1880	75¢ Gray wolf, coil	....	1.85	.65
1881	$1.05 White-tailed deer, coil	....	2.75	.95
1881a	same, bklt pane of 6	....	16.00	....
1882	47¢ Picture Frames, booklet pane of 5	....	6.75	....
1882a-e	47¢ Picture Frames, set of singles	....	6.55	6.00

1883

1885a

SCOTT NO.	DESCRIPTION	PLATE BLOCK F/NH	UNUSED F/NH	USED F
1883	47¢ Year of the Snake	5.50	1.25	.40
1884	$1.05 Year of the Snake, souvenir sheet	....	3.00	3.00

1886, 1890

1900

2001 COMMEMORATIVES

SCOTT NO.	DESCRIPTION	PLATE BLOCK F/NH	UNUSED F/NH	USED F
1885	47¢ National Hockey League, sheet of 6 + 3 labels	....	8.50	8.25
1885a	47¢ Jean Beliveau (Canadiens jersey No. 4)....	....	1.50	....
1885b	47¢ Terry Sawchuk (goalie in Red Wings uniform)	....	1.50	....
1885c	47¢ Eddie Shore (Bruins jersey No.2)	....	1.50	....
1885d	47¢ Denis Potvin (Islanders jersey No. 5)	....	1.50	....
1885e	47¢ Bobby Bull (Black Hawks jersey No.9)	....	1.50	....
1885f	47¢ Syl Apps, Sr. (Toronto Maple leafs jersey)	....	1.50	....
1886-89	47¢ Birds, 4 attached	7.00	5.50	3.50
1886	47¢ Golden Eagle	....	1.25	.45
1887	47¢ Arctic tern	....	1.25	.45
1888	47¢ Rock ptarmigan	....	1.25	.45
1889	47¢ Lapland longspur	....	1.25	.50
1890	47¢ Golden Eagle, self-adhesive	....	1.50	.50
1891	47¢ Artic tern, self-adhesive	....	1.50	.50
1892	47¢ Rock ptarmigan, self-adhesive	....	1.50	.50
1893	47¢ Lapland longspur, self-adhesive	....	1.50	.50
1893a	same, bklt pane of 6 (1890 x 2, 1891 x 2, 1892 x 1, 1893 x 1)	....	8.00	....
1893b	same, bklt pane of 6 (1892 x 2, 1893 x 2, 1890 x 1, 1891 x 1)	....	8.00	....

1901

1903a

SCOTT NO.	DESCRIPTION	PLATE BLOCK F/NH	UNUSED F/NH	USED F
1894-95	47¢ Games of La Francophonie, 2 attached	5.95	2.50	1.50
1894	47¢ High jumper	....	1.25	.45
1895	47¢ Dancer	....	1.25	.45
1896-99	47¢ World Figure Skating, 4 attached	5.95	5.00	4.00
1896	47¢ Pairs	....	1.25	.50
1897	47¢ Ice dancing	....	1.25	.50
1898	47¢ Men's singles	....	1.25	.50
1899	47¢ Women's singles	....	1.25	.50
1900	47¢ First Canadian postage stamp	5.75	1.25	.40
1901	47¢ Toronto Blue Jays Baseball Team, 25th anniv.	....	1.25	.40
1901a	same, bklt pane of 8	....	12.00	....
1902	47¢ Summit of the Americans, Quebec	5.75	1.25	.40
1903	60¢ Tourist Attractions, bklt pane of 5, self-adhesive	....	7.75	....
1904	$1.05 Tourist Attraction, bklt pane of 5, self-adhesive	....	15.00	....

1905

1906

SCOTT NO.	DESCRIPTION	PLATE BLOCK F/NH	UNUSED F/NH	USED F
1905	47¢ Armenian Apostolic Church	5.75	1.25	.40
1906	47¢ Royal Military College	5.75	1.25	.40

1909

1911

SCOTT NO.	DESCRIPTION	PLATE BLOCK F/NH	UNUSED F/NH	USED F
1907-08	47¢ Intl. Amateur Athletic Federation World Championship, 2 attached	5.95	2.50	1.65
1907	47¢ Pole Vault	....	1.25	.45
1908	47¢ Runner	....	1.25	.45
1909	47¢ Pierre Elliot Trudeau	5.75	1.25	.40
1909a	same, souvenir sheet of 4	....	5.00	....
1910	47¢ Canadian Roses, souvenir sheet of 4	....	5.75	5.75
1911	47¢ Morden Centennial Rose	....	1.25	.70
1912	47¢ Agnes Rose	....	1.25	.70
1913	47¢ Champion Rose	....	1.25	.70
1914	47¢ Canadian White Star Rose	....	1.25	.70
1914a	same, bklt pane of 4 (1911-14)	....	5.25	....
....	same, complete booklet (1914a x 3)	....	14.00	....

1915

1917

1919-20

SCOTT NO.	DESCRIPTION	PLATE BLOCK F/NH	UNUSED F/NH	USED F
1915	47¢ Great Peace of Montreal	5.75	1.25	.40
1916	$1.05 Canadian Artists, "The Space Between Columns"	12.00	2.75	1.35
1917	47¢ Shriners	5.75	1.25	.40
1918	47¢ Picture Frame, bklt pane of 5 + 5 labels	....	7.00	....
1919-20	47¢ Theater Anniversaries, 2 attached	5.95	2.50	1.25
1919	47¢ Theatre du Nouveau Monde	....	1.20	.45
1920	47¢ Grand Theater	....	1.20	.45

1921a

1922

SCOTT NO.	DESCRIPTION	PLATE BLOCK F/NH	UNUSED F/NH	USED F
1921	47¢ Hot Air Balloons, self-adhesive, bklt of 8	....	10.00	....
1922	47¢ Horse-drawn sleigh	5.75	1.25	.35
1922a	same, bklt pane of 10	....	12.00	....
1923	60¢ Skaters	6.75	1.50	.50
1923a	same, bklt pane of 6	....	9.00	....
1924	$1.05 Children making snowman	12.00	2.75	1.00
1924a	same, bklt pane of 6	....	16.00	....

1927 1931

1928 1929 1930

2002 COMMEMORATIVES

SCOTT NO.	DESCRIPTION	PLATE BLOCK F/NH	UNUSED F/NH	USED F
1925	47¢ YMCA in Canada	5.75	1.25	.35
1926	47¢ Royal Canadian Legion	5.75	1.25	.35
1927	48¢ Maple Leaves, self-adhesive coil	....	1.25	.35
1928	65¢ Jewelry making, coil	....	1.70	.60
1928a	same, bklt pane of 6	....	11.00	....
1929	77¢ Basket weaving, coil	....	2.50	.75
1930	$1.25 Sculpture, coil	....	3.25	.95
1930a	same, bklt pane of 6	....	19.00	....
1931	48¢ Flag & Canada Post Headquarters	....	1.25	.30
1931a	same, bklt pane of 10	....	13.00	....
1931b	same, bklt pane of 30	....	40.00	....

1932 1933 1935a

SCOTT NO.	DESCRIPTION	PLATE BLOCK F/NH	UNUSED F/NH	USED F
1932	48¢ Regin of Queen Elizabeth, 50th Anniv.	5.75	1.25	.40
1933	48¢ Year of the Horse	5.75	1.25	.40
1934	$1.25 Year of the Horse, souvenir sheet	....	3.50	3.50
1935	48¢ National Hockey League Stars, sheet of 6 + 3 labels	....	7.50	7.50
1935a	48¢ Tim Horton	....	1.25	.75
1935b	48¢ Guy Lafleur	....	1.25	.75
1935c	48¢ Howie Morenz	....	1.25	.75
1935d	48¢ Glenn Hall	....	1.25	.75
1935e	48¢ Red Kelly	....	1.25	.75
1935f	48¢ Phil Esposito	....	1.25	.75

1936 1940

SCOTT NO.	DESCRIPTION	PLATE BLOCK F/NH	UNUSED F/NH	USED F
1936-39	48¢ 2002 Winter Olympics, 4 attached	6.00	4.95	3.50
1936	48¢ Short track speed skating	....	1.25	.50
1937	48¢ Curling	....	1.25	.50
1938	48¢ Freestyle aerial skiing	....	1.25	.50
1939	48¢ Women's hockey	....	1.25	.50
1940	48¢ Appoint. of First Canadian Governor General	5.75	1.25	.40

1941

1942

SCOTT NO.	DESCRIPTION	PLATE BLOCK F/NH	UNUSED F/NH	USED F
1941	48¢ University of Manitoba	....	1.25	.40
1941a	same, bklt pane of 8	....	9.25	....
1942	48¢ Laval University	....	1.25	.40
1942a	same, bklt pane of 8	....	9.25	....
1943	48¢ University of Trinity College	....	1.25	.40
1943a	same, bklt pane of 8	....	9.25	....
1944	48¢ Saint Mary's University, Halifax	....	1.25	.40
1944a	same, bklt pane of 8	....	9.25	....

1945 1946a

SCOTT NO.	DESCRIPTION	PLATE BLOCK F/NH	UNUSED F/NH	USED F
1945	$1.25 Canadian Art, Church and Horse	14.00	3.25	1.40
1946	48¢ Canadian Tulips, bklt pane of 4, self-adhesive	....	4.75	3.25
1946a	48¢ City of Vancouver tulip	....	1.35	.95
1946b	48¢ Monte Carlo tulip	....	1.35	.95
1946c	48¢ Ottawa tulip	....	1.35	.95
1946d	48¢ The Bishop tulip	....	1.35	.95
1947	48¢ Canadian Tulips, souvenir sheet of 4, perforted	....	5.25	5.25

1948

SCOTT NO.	DESCRIPTION	PLATE BLOCK F/NH	UNUSED F/NH	USED F
1948-51	48¢ Corals, 4 attached	5.75	4.75	3.95
1948	48¢ Dendronepthea Giagantea & Dendronepthea Corals	....	1.25	.50
1949	48¢ Tubastrea & Echinogorgia Corals	....	1.25	.50
1950	48¢ North Atlantic Pink Tree, Pacific Orange Cup & North Pacific Horn Corals	....	1.25	.50
1951	48¢ North Atlantic Giant Orange Tree & Black Coral	....	1.25	.50
1951b	same, souvenir sheet of 4	....	7.25	7.25

1954-55

SCOTT NO.	DESCRIPTION	PLATE BLOCK F/NH	UNUSED F/NH	USED F
1952	65¢ Tourists Attractions, bklt pane of 5, self-adhesive	....	8.50	8.50
1952a	65¢ Yukon Quest, Yukon Territory	....	1.75	.95
1952b	65¢ Icefields Parkway, Alberta	....	1.75	.95
1952c	65¢ Agawa Canyon, Ontario	....	1.75	.95
1952d	65¢ Old Port of Montreal, Quebec	....	1.75	.95
1952e	65¢ Kings Landing, New Burnswick	....	1.75	.95
1953	$1.25 Tourists Attractions, bklt pane of 5, self-adhesive	....	17.00	17.00
1953a	$1.25 Northern Lights, Northwest Territories	....	3.25	1.50
1953b	$1.25 Stanley Park, Vancouver, British Columbia	....	3.25	1.50
1953c	$1.25 Head-Smashed-In Buffalo Jump, Alberta.	....	3.25	1.50
1953d	$1.25 Saguenay Fjord, Quebec	....	3.25	1.50
1953e	$1.25 Peggy's Cove, Nova Scotia	....	3.25	1.50
1954-55	48¢ Sculpture, Lumberjacks & Embacle, 2 attached	5.95	2.50	1.25
1954	48¢ Sculpture "Embacle" by Charles Daudelin	....	1.25	.45
1955	48¢ Sculpture "Lumberjacks" by Leo Mol	....	1.25	.45

1956

1957

SCOTT NO.	DESCRIPTION	PLATE BLOCK F/NH	UNUSED F/NH	USED F
1956	48¢ Canadian Postmasters & Assistants Assoc.	5.75	1.25	.40
1957	48¢ World Youth Day, self-adhesive	....	1.25	.40
1957a	48¢ World Youth Day, bklt pane of 8, self-adhesive	....	9.25	....

SCOTT NO.	DESCRIPTION	PLATE BLOCK F/NH	UNUSED F/NH	USED F

1958

1959

SCOTT NO.	DESCRIPTION	PLATE BLOCK F/NH	UNUSED F/NH	USED F
1958	48¢ Public Services International World Congress	5.75	1.25	.40
1959	48¢ Public Pensions, 75th Anniv.	5.75	1.25	.40
1960	48¢ Mountains, 8 attached	....	10.00	10.00
1960a	48¢ Mt. Logan ,Canada	....	1.25	1.25
1960b	48¢ Mt. Elbrus, Russia	....	1.25	1.25
1960c	48¢ Puncak Java, Indonesia	....	1.25	1.25
1960d	48¢ Mt. Everest, Nepal & China	....	1.25	1.25
1960e	48¢ Mt. Kilimanjaro, Tanzania	....	1.25	1.25
1960f	48¢ Vinson Massif, Antarctica		1.25	1.25
1960g	48¢ Mt. Aconcagua, Argentina	....	1.25	1.25
1960h	48¢ Mt. Mckinley, Alaska	....	1.25	1.25

1961

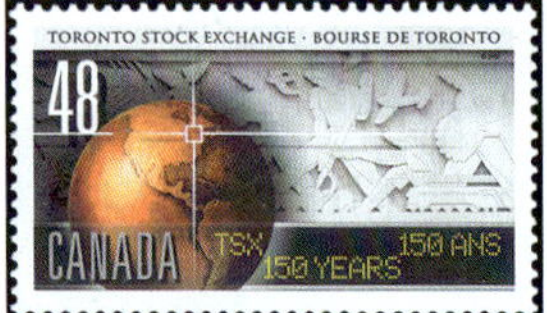

1962

SCOTT NO.	DESCRIPTION	PLATE BLOCK F/NH	UNUSED F/NH	USED F
1961	48¢ World Teacher's Day	5.75	1.25	.40
1962	48¢ Toronto Stock Exchange	5.75	1.25	.40

1963-64

SCOTT NO.	DESCRIPTION	PLATE BLOCK F/NH	UNUSED F/NH	USED F
1963-64	48¢ Communication Technology Centenaries, 2 attach	5.75	2.50	1.50
1963	48¢ Sir Sandford Fleming 91827-1915, cable-laying ship	....	1.25	.45
1964	48¢ Guglielmo Marconi 1874-19370, radio and transmission towers	....	1.25	.45

1965

1968

SCOTT NO.	DESCRIPTION	PLATE BLOCK F/NH	UNUSED F/NH	USED F
1965	48¢ "Genesis" by Daphne Odjig	5.75	1.25	.35
1965a	same, bklt pane of 10	....	12.00	....
1966	65¢ "Winter Travel" by Cecil Youngfox	7.25	1.65	.50
1966a	same, bklt pane of 6	....	8.50	....
1967	$1.25 "Mary and Child" sculpture by Irene Katak Angutitaq	14.00	3.25	1.00
1967a	same, bklt pane of 6	....	18.00	....
1968	48¢ Quebec Symphony Orchestra Centenary	5.75	1.25	.40

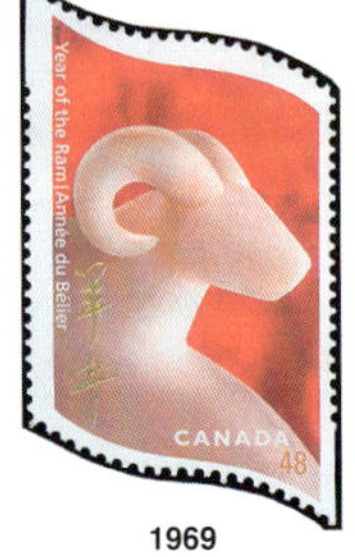

1969

1971a, 1972a

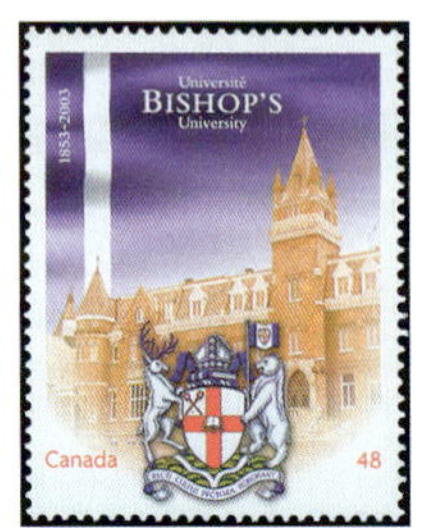

1973

2003 COMMEMORATIVES

SCOTT NO.	DESCRIPTION	PLATE BLOCK F/NH	UNUSED F/NH	USED F
1969	48¢ Year of the Ram	5.25	1.25	.45
1970	$1.25 Year of the Ram, souvenir sheet	....	3.50	3.50
1971	48¢ National Hockey League All-Star Game, sheet of 6	....	23.00	20.00
1971a	48¢ Frank Mahovlich	....	3.25	2.50
1971b	48¢ Raymond Bourque	....	3.25	2.50
1971c	48¢ Serge Savard	....	3.25	2.50
1971d	48¢ Stan Mikita	....	3.25	2.50
1971e	48¢ Mike Bossy	....	3.25	2.50
1971f	48¢ Bill Durnan	....	3.25	2.50
1972	48¢ National Hockey League All-Star Game, sheet of 6, self-adhesive	....	86.00	23.00
1972a	48¢ Frank Mahovlich, self-adhesive	....	12.00	3.00
1972b	48¢ Raymond Bourque, self-adhesive	....	12.00	3.00
1972c	48¢ Serge Savard, self-adhesive	....	12.00	3.00
1972d	48¢ Stan Mikita, self-adhesive	....	12.00	3.00
1972e	48¢ Mike Bossy, self-adhesive	....	12.00	3.00
1972f	48¢ Bill Durnan, self-adhesive	....	12.00	3.00
1973	48¢ Bishop's University, Quebec, 150th Anniv.	....	1.25	.50
1973a	same, bklt pane of 8	....	9.25	....
1974	48¢ University of Western Ontario, 125th Anniv.	....	1.25	.40
1974a	same, bklt pano of 8	....	9.25	....
1975	48¢ St. Francis Xavier University, Antigonis, 150th Anniv.	....	1.25	.40
1975a	same, bklt pane of 8	....	9.25	....
1976	48¢ Macdonald Institute, Guelph, Ont., Centennial	....	1.25	.40
1976a	same, bklt pane of 8	....	9.25	....
1977	48¢ University of Montreal, 125th Anniversary	....	1.25	.40
1977a	same, bklt pane of 8	....	9.25	....

1979

1984

SCOTT NO.	DESCRIPTION	PLATE BLOCK F/NH	UNUSED F/NH	USED F
1979-82	Bird paintings by John James Audubon, 4 attached	5.95	4.95	3.50
1979	48¢ Leach's Storm Petrel	....	1.25	.40
1980	48¢ Brant	....	1.25	.40
1981	48¢ Great Cormorant	....	1.25	.40
1982	48¢ Common Murre	....	1.25	.40
1983	65¢ Gyfalcon, self-adhesive	....	1.25	.60
1983a	same, bklt pane of 6	....	9.75	....
1984	48¢ Canadian Rangers	5.75	1.25	.40
1985	48¢ American Hellenic Educational Progressive Assoc. in Canada, 75th Anniversary	5.75	1.25	.40
1986	48¢ Volunteer Firefighters	5.75	1.25	.40
1987	48¢ Coronation of Queen Elizabeth II, 50th Anniv.	5.75	1.25	.40
1988	48¢ Pedro da Silva, First Courier in New France	5.75	1.25	.40

1992

1991

1993

SCOTT NO.	DESCRIPTION	PLATE BLOCK F/NH	UNUSED F/NH	USED F
1989	65¢ Tourist Attractions, bklt pane of 5, self-adhesive	....	9.25	....
1989a	65¢ Wilbeforce Falls, Nunavult	....	1.85	1.25
1989b	65¢ Inside Passage, B.C.	....	1.85	1.25
1989c	65¢ Royal Canadian Mounted Police Depot Division	....	1.85	1.25
1989d	65¢ Casa Loma, Toronto	....	1.85	1.25
1989e	65¢ Gatineau Park, Quebec	....	1.85	1.25
1990	$1.25 Tourist Attractions, bklt pane of 5, self-adhesive	....	17.00	16.00
1990a	$1.25 Dragon boat races, Vancouver, B.C.	....	3.50	1.25
1990b	$1.25 Polar bear watching, Manitoba	....	3.50	1.25
1990c	$1.25 Nigara Falls, Ontario	....	3.50	1.25
1990d	$1.25 Magdalen Islands, Quebec	....	3.50	1.25
1990e	$1.25 Charlottestown, P.E.I.	....	3.50	1.25
1991	48¢ "Vancouver 2010" overprint	....	2.00	1.25
1991a	same, bklt pane of 10	....	48.00	....
1991b	same, bklt pane of 30	....	145.00	....
1991C-Da	($1.25) Canada-Alaska Cruise Scenes, self-adhesive, 2 attached	....	28.00	....
1991C	($1.25) Totem Pole	....	14.00	14.00
1991D	($1.25) Whale's Tail	....	14.00	14.00
1992	48¢ Lutheran World Federation 10th Assem	5.75	1.25	.40
1993	48¢ Korean War Armistice, 50th Anniv.	5.75	1.25	.40

1994

1998

SCOTT NO.	DESCRIPTION	PLATE BLOCK F/NH	UNUSED F/NH	USED F
1994-97	48¢ National Library, 50th Anniv. 4 attached	....	4.95	3.50
1994	48¢ Anne Hebert (1916-2000)	....	1.25	.50
1995	48¢ Hector de Saint-Denys Garneau (1912-43)	....	1.25	.50
1996	48¢ Morley Callaghan (1903-90)	....	1.25	.50
1997	48¢ Susanna Moodie (1803-85), Catharine Parr Trail (1802-99)	....	1.25	.50
1997b	same, bklt pane of 8 (1994-97 x 2)	....	9.50	....
1998	48¢ World Road Cycling Championships, Hamilton, Ont.	....	1.25	.60
1998a	same, bklt pane of 8	....	9.50	....
1999	48¢ Canadian Astronauts, self-adhesive, sheet of 8	....	12.00	....
1999a	48¢ Marc Garneau, self-adhesive	....	1.50	1.10
1999b	48¢ Roberta Bondar, self-adhesive	....	1.50	1.10
1999c	48¢ Steve MacLean, self-adhesive	....	1.50	1.10
1999d	48¢ Chris Hadfield, self-adhesive	....	1.50	1.10
1999e	48¢ Robert Thrisk, self-adhesive	....	1.50	1.10
1999f	48¢ Bjarni Tryggvason, self-adhesive	....	1.50	1.10
1999g	48¢ Dave Williams, self-adhesive	....	1.50	1.10
1999h	48¢ Julie Payette, self-adhesive	....	1.50	1.10

2000-01

2002a

SCOTT NO.	DESCRIPTION	PLATE BLOCK F/NH	UNUSED F/NH	USED F
2000-01	48¢ Trees of Canada and Thailand, 2 attached	5.75	2.75	1.75
2000	48¢ Acer Saccharum leaves (Canada)	....	1.25	.45
2001	48¢ Cassia fistula (Thailand)	....	1.25	.45
2001b	48¢ Trees of Canada and Thailand, souvenir sheet of 2	....	9.50	9.50
2002	48¢ L'Hommage a Rosa Luxemburg by Jean-Paul Riopelle, sheet of 6	....	9.00	9.00
2002a	48¢ Red & Blue dots between birds at LR	....	1.50	1.15
2002b	48¢ Bird with yellow beak at center	....	1.50	1.15
2002c	48¢ Three birds in circle at R	....	1.50	1.15
2002d	48¢ Sun at UR	....	1.50	1.15
2002e	48¢ Birds with purple outlines ar L	....	1.50	1.15
2002f	48¢ Birds with red outline in circle at R	....	1.50	1.15
2003	$1.25 Pink bird in red circle at R, souvenir sheet	....	3.75	3.75

2004

SCOTT NO.	DESCRIPTION	PLATE BLOCK F/NH	UNUSED F/NH	USED F
2004	48¢ Gift boxes and Ice skates	....	1.25	.35
2004a	same, bklt pane of 6	....	7.00	....
2005	65¢ Gift boxes and Teddy bear	....	1.75	.75
2005a	same, bklt pane of 6	....	10.00	....
2006	$1.25 Gift boxes and Toy duck	....	3.25	1.25
2006a	same, bklt pane of 6	....	18.00	....
2008	49¢ Maple Leaf and Samara, self-adhesive, coil	....	1.25	.40
2009	80¢ Maple Leaf on Twig, self-adhesive, coil	....	1.95	.75
2010	$1.40 Maple Leaf on Twig, self-adhesive, coil	....	3.40	1.25
2011	49¢ Flag over Edmonton, Alberta, self-adhesive	....	1.25	.40
2011a	same, bklt pane of 10	....	12.00	....
2012	49¢ Queen Elizabeth II, self-adhesive	....	1.25	.40
2012a	same, bklt pane of 10	....	12.00	....
2013	80¢ Maple Leaf on Twig, self-adhesive	....	2.00	.75
2013a	same, bklt pane of 6	....	12.00	....
2014	$1.40 Maple Leaf Twig, self-adhesive	....	3.50	1.25
2014a	same, bklt pane of 6	....	19.50	....

2015

2024

2026

2004 COMMEMORATIVES

SCOTT NO.	DESCRIPTION	PLATE BLOCK F/NH	UNUSED F/NH	USED F
2015	49¢ Year of the Monkey	5.75	1.25	.40
2016	$1.40 Year of the Monkey souvenir sheet	....	3.75	3.75
2016a	same, with 2004 Hong Kong overprint	....	7.75	7.75
2017	49¢ National Hockey League Stars, sheet of 6	....	10.00	10.00
2017a	49¢ Larry Robinson	....	2.00	.95
2017b	49¢ Marcel Dionne	....	2.00	.95
2017c	49¢ Ted Lindsay	....	2.00	.95
2017d	49¢ Johnny Bower	....	2.00	.95
2017e	49¢ Brad Park	....	2.00	.95
2017f	49¢ Milt Schmidt	....	2.00	.95
2018	49¢ National Hockey League Stars, sheet of 6, self-adhesive	....	18.00	....
2018a	49¢ Larry Robinson, self-adhesive	....	3.00	1.10
2018b	49¢ Marcel Dionne, self-adhesive	....	3.00	1.10
2018c	49¢ Ted Lindsay, self-adhesive	....	3.00	1.10
2018d	49¢ Johnny Bower, self-adhesive	....	3.00	1.10
2018e	49¢ Brad Park, self-adhesive	....	3.00	1.10
2018f	49¢ Milt Schmidt, self-adhesive	....	3.00	1.10
2019	49¢ Quebec Winter Carnival, self-adhesive	....	1.25	.50
2019a	same, bklt pane of 6	....	7.50	....
2020	49¢ St. Joseph's Oratory, Montreal, self-adhesive	....	1.25	.50
2020a	same, bklt pane of 6	....	7.50	....
2021	49¢ International Jazz Festival	....	1.25	.50
2021a	same, booklet pane of 6	....	7.50	....
2022	49¢ Traversee Internationale Swimming Marathon	....	1.25	.50
2022a	same, booklet pane of 6	....	7.50	....
2023	49¢ Canadian National Exhibition	....	1.25	.50
2023a	same, booklet pane of 6	....	7.50	....
2024	49¢ Governor General Ramon John Hnatyshyn	5.75	1.25	.40
2025	49¢ Royal Canadian Army Cadets, 125th Anniv, self-adhesive	....	1.25	.40
2025a	same, bklt pane of 4	....	5.00	....
2026	49¢ The Farm, Ship of Otto Sverdrup, Arctic Explorer	5.75	1.25	.40
2027	$1.40 The Farm, Ship of Otto Sverdrup, Arctic Explorer, souvenir sheet	....	5.75	5.75
2028-31	49¢ Urban Transit & Light Rail Systems, 4 attached	11.00	4.95	4.00
2028	49¢ Toronto Transit Commission	....	1.25	.45
2029	49¢ Translink Skytrain, Vancouver	....	1.25	.45
2030	49¢ Societe de Transport de Montreal	....	1.25	.45
2031	49¢ Calgary Transit Light Rail	....	1.25	.45

2035

2043

SCOTT NO.	DESCRIPTION	PLATE BLOCK F/NH	UNUSED F/NH	USED F
2032	49¢ Home Hardware, 40th Anniv., self-adhesive	....	1.25	.40
2032a	same, bklt pane of 10	....	12.00	....
2033	49¢ University of Sherbrooke, 50th Anniv.	....	1.25	.40
2033a	same, bklt pane of 8	....	9.75	....
2034	49¢ University of Prince Edwards Island, Bicenn	....	1.25	.40
2034a	same, bklt pane of 8	....	9.75	....
2035	49¢ Montreal Children's Hospital Centenary, self-adhesive	....	1.25	.40
2035a	same, bklt pane of 4	....	5.00	....
2036-39	49¢ Bird Paintings by John James Audubon, 4 attached	5.75	4.95	4.25
2036	49¢ Ruby-crowned Kinglet	....	1.25	.45
2037	49¢ White-winged Crossbill	....	1.25	.45
2038	49¢ Bohemian Waxwing	....	1.25	.45
2039	49¢ Borcal Chickadee	....	1.25	.45
2040	80¢ Lincoln's Sparrow by J.J. Audubon, self-adhesive	....	1.95	.95
2040a	same, bklt pane of 6	....	11.50	....
2041-42	49¢ Pioneers of Trans Mail Service, 2 attached	5.75	2.50	1.75
2041	49¢ Sir Samuel Cunard	....	1.25	.40
2042	49¢ Sir Hugh Allan	....	1.25	.40
2043	49¢ D-Day 60th Anniversary	5.75	1.25	.40
2044	49¢ Pierre Dugua de Mons, Leader of First French Settlement in Acadia	5.75	1.25	.40
2045	(49¢) Butterfly and Flower, self-adhesive	....	15.00	15.00
2045a	same, bklt pane of 2	....	30.00	....
....	complete bklt, 2045a + phonecard in greeting card	....	60.00	....
2046	(49¢) Children on Beach, self-adhesive	....	15.00	15.00
2046a	same, bklt pane of 2	....	50.00	....
....	complete bklt, 2046a + phonecard in greeting card	....	60.00	....
2047	(49¢) Rose, self-adhesive	....	15.00	15.00
2047a	same, bklt pane of 2	....	30.00	....
....	complete bklt, 2047a + phonecard in greeting card	....	60.00	....
2048	(49¢) Dog, self-adhesive	....	15.00	15.00
2048a	same bklt pane of 2	....	30.00	....
....	complete bklt, 2048a + phonecard in greeting card	....	60.00	....

2049-50

SCOTT NO.	DESCRIPTION	PLATE BLOCK F/NH	UNUSED F/NH	USED F
2049-50	49¢ 2004 Summer Olympics , Athens, 2 attached	5.75	2.50	1.50
2049	49¢ Spyros Louis 1896 Marathon Gold Medalist	....	1.25	.45
2050	49¢ Soccer net inscribed “Canada” girls soccer	....	1.25	.45

2051

2056

SCOTT NO.	DESCRIPTION	PLATE BLOCK F/NH	UNUSED F/NH	USED F
2051-52	49¢ Canadian Open Golf Championship, self-adhesive, set of 2	....	2.50	.85
2051	49¢ Canadian Open Golf Championship, ‘finishing swing”	....	1.25	.45
2052	49¢ Canadian Open Golf Championship, “ready to putt”	....	1.25	.45
2053	49¢ Maple Leaf and Samara, self-adhesive, coil	....	1.25	.40
2054	80¢ Maple Leaf on Twig, self-adhesive, die-cut 8.25, coil	....	2.50	.75
2055	$1.40 Maple Leaf on Twig, self-adhesive, die-cut 8.25, coil	....	6.00	1.40
2056	49¢ Montreal Heart Institute, 50th Anniversary..	....	1.35	.40
2056a	same, booklet pane of 4	....	5.25	....
2057	49¢ Pets – Fish	....	1.25	.45
2058	49¢ Pets – Cats	....	1.25	.45
2059	49¢ Pets – Rabbit	....	1.25	.45
2060	49¢ Pets – Dog	....	1.25	.45
2060a	same, booklet pane of 4	....	5.25	....

2061

2065

SCOTT NO.	DESCRIPTION	PLATE BLOCK F/NH	UNUSED F/NH	USED F
2061-62	49¢ Nobel Laureates in chemistry, 2 attached...	5.75	2.50	1.50
2061	49¢ Gerhard Herzberg, 1971 laureate & molecular structures	....	1.25	.50
2062	49¢ Michael Smith, 1993 laureate & DNA double helix	....	1.25	.50
2063-64	(49¢) Ribbon Frame & Picture Album Frame, self-adhesive, 2 attached	....	2.50	1.60
2063	(49¢) Ribbon Frame, self-adhesive	....	1.50	.50
2064	(49¢) Picture Album Frame, self-adhesive	....	1.50	.50
2065-66	49¢ Victoria Cross 150th Anniv., 2 attached	4.00	2.50	1.50
2065	49¢ Victoria Cross	....	1.25	.50
2066	49¢ Design for Victoria Cross approved w/ QEII’s signature	....	1.25	.50

2068

2069

SCOTT NO.	DESCRIPTION	PLATE BLOCK F/NH	UNUSED F/NH	USED F
2067	47¢ “Self-Portrait” by Jean Paul Lemieux, perf 13 x 13.24	4.00	1.25	.40
2067a	Same, perf. 13 .....4.00	....	2.75	2.75
2068	47¢ – $1.40 Paintings of Jean Paul Lemieux, souvenir sheet of 3	....	9.50	....
2069	49¢ Santa Claus and Sleigh, self-adhesive	....	1.25	.40
2069a	same, booklet pane of 6	....	7.75	....
2070	80¢ Santa Claus and Automobile, self-adhesive	....	1.95	.75
2070a	same, booklet pane of 6	....	12.00	....
2071	$1.40 Santa Claus and Train, self-adhesive	....	3.40	1.25
2071a	same, booklet pane of 6	....	19.50	....

2072

2075

2080

SCOTT NO.	DESCRIPTION	PLATE BLOCK F/NH	UNUSED F/NH	USED F
2072	50¢ Red Calla Lilies, self-adhesive, coil	....	1.25	.40
2072a	same, serpentine die cut 6.75	....	1.25	.40
2072b	same, serpentine die cut 7.25	....	7.50	.40
2073	85¢ Yellow Calla Lilies, self-adhesive, coil	....	2.25	.75
2073a	same, serpentine die cut 6.75	....	6.50	.75
2074	$1.45 Iris, self-adhesive, coil	....	3.75	1.25
2074a	same, serpentine die cut 6.75	....	7.75	3.75
2075	50¢ Queen Elizabeth II, self-adhesive	....	1.25	.40
2075a	same, booklet pane of 10	....	12.00	....
2076	50¢ Flag and Saskatoon, Saskatchewan, self-adhesive	....	1.55	.40
2077	50¢ Flag and Durrell, Newfoundland, self-adhesive	....	1.55	.40
2078	50¢ Flag and Shannon Falls, British Columbia, self-adhesive	....	1.55	.40
2079	50¢ Flag and Mont-Saint-Hillaire, Quebec, self-adhesive	....	1.55	.40
2080	50¢ Flag and Toronto, self-adhesive	....	1.25	.40
2080a	same, booklet pane of 10 (#2076-80 x 2)	....	12.00	....
2081	85¢ Yellow Calla Lilies, self-adhesive	....	2.25	.50
2081a	same, booklet pane of 6	....	14.00	....
2082	$1.45 Iris, self-adhesive	....	3.75	1.25
2082a	same, booklet pane of 6	....	22.00	....

2083

2086a

2005 COMMEMORATIVES

SCOTT NO.	DESCRIPTION	PLATE BLOCK F/NH	UNUSED F/NH	USED F
2083	50¢ Year of the Rooseter	5.75	1.25	.40
2084	$1.45 Year of the Rooster, souvenir sheet	....	4.25	4.25
2084a	same, with dates, Canadian and Chinese flags in sheet margin	....	7.00	7.00
2085	50¢ National Hockey League Stars, sheet of 6..	....	10.00	....
2085a	50¢ Henri Richard	....	1.75	1.00
2085b	50¢ Grant Fuhr	....	1.75	1.00
2085c	50¢ Allan Stanley	....	1.75	1.00
2085d	50¢ Pierre Pilote	....	1.75	1.00
2085e	50¢ Bryan Trottier	....	1.75	1.00
2085f	50¢ John Bucyk	....	1.75	1.00
2086	50¢ National Hockey League Stars, self-adhesive, pane of 6		10.00	....
2086a	50¢ Henri Richard, self-adhesive	....	1.75	.80
2086b	50¢ Grant Fuhr, self-adhesive	....	1.75	.80
2086c	50¢ Allen Stanley, self-adhesive	....	1.75	.80
2086d	50¢ Pierre Pilote, self-adhesive	....	1.75	.80
2086e	50¢ Bryan Trottier, self-adhesive	....	1.75	.80
2086f	50¢ John Bucyk, self-adhesive	....	1.75	.80

2087a, 2088a

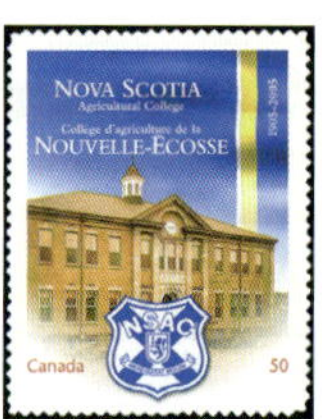

2089

SCOTT NO.	DESCRIPTION	PLATE BLOCK F/NH	UNUSED F/NH	USED F
2087	50¢ Fishing Flies, sheet of 4	....	9.00	9.00
2087a	50¢ Alevin	....	2.25	1.75
2087b	50¢ Jock Scott	....	2.25	1.75
2087c	50¢ P.E.I. Fly	....	2.25	1.75
2087d	50¢ Mickey Finn	....	2.25	1.75
2088	50¢ Fishing Flies, self-adhesive, bklt pane of 4.	....	5.25	5.25
2088a	50¢ Alevin, self-adhesive	....	1.40	.45
2088b	50¢ Jock Scott. self-adhesive	....	1.40	.45
2088c	50¢ P.E.I. Fly, self-adhesive	....	1.40	.45
2088d	50¢ Mickey Finn, self-adhesive	....	1.40	.45
2089	50¢ Nova Scotia Agricultural College, self-adhesive	....	1.40	.45
2089a	same, booklet pane of 4	....	5.00	....

2090

2092

SCOTT NO.	DESCRIPTION	PLATE BLOCK F/NH	UNUSED F/NH	USED F
2090	50¢ EXPO 2005, Aichi, Japan	5.75	1.25	.40
2091	50¢ Daffodils, souvenir sheet of 2	......	3.50	3.50
2092	50¢ Yellow Daffodils, self-adhesive	....	1.50	1.00
2093	50¢ White Daffodils, self-adhesive	....	1.50	1.00
2093a	50¢ Daffodils, self-adhesive, bklt pane of 10	....	12.00	....

2094

2099

SCOTT NO.	DESCRIPTION	PLATE BLOCK F/NH	UNUSED F/NH	USED F
2094	50¢ TD Bank Financial Group, 150th Anniv., self-adhesive	....	1.25	.45
2094a	same, booklet pane of 10	....	12.50	....
2095-98	50¢ Bird Paintings by John James Audubon, 4 attached	5.75	5.00	3.75
2095	50¢ Horned lark	....	1.25	.45
2096	50¢ Piping plover	....	1.25	.45
2097	50¢ Stilt sandpiper	....	1.25	.45
2098	50¢ Willow ptarmigan	....	1.25	.45
2099	85¢ Double-crested Cormorant by John James Audubon, self-adhesive	....	2.25	.75
2099a	same, booklet pane of 6	....	12.50	....

2100

2104

SCOTT NO.	DESCRIPTION	PLATE BLOCK F/NH	UNUSED F/NH	USED F
2100-03	50¢ Bridges, self-adhesive, 4 attached	5.75	5.00	3.50
2100	50¢ Jacques Cartier Bridge, Quebec	....	1.25	.45
2101	50¢ Souris Swinging Bridge, Manitoba	....	1.25	.45
2102	50¢ Angus L. MacDonald Bridge, Nova Scotia	....	1.25	.45
2103	50¢ Canso Causeway, Nova Scotia	....	1.25	.45
2104	50¢ Maclean's Magazine	5.75	1.25	.45

2105-06

SCOTT NO.	DESCRIPTION	PLATE BLOCK F/NH	UNUSED F/NH	USED F
2105-06	50¢ Biosphere Reserves of Canada and Ireland, 2 attached	5.75	2.50	1.75
2105	50¢ Saskatoon Berries, Waterton Lakes National Park	....	1.25	.40
2106	50¢ Deer, Killarney National Park	....	1.25	.40
2106b	Souvenir Sheet	....	2.95	2.95

2107

2108

SCOTT NO.	DESCRIPTION	PLATE BLOCK F/NH	UNUSED F/NH	USED F
2107	50¢ Battle of the Atlantic, World War II	5.75	1.25	.40
2108	50¢ Opening of Canadian War Museum, Ottawa, self-adhesive	....	1.25	.40
2108a	same, booklet pane of 4	....	5.00	....

2109

2112

SCOTT NO.	DESCRIPTION	PLATE BLOCK F/NH	UNUSED F/NH	USED F
2109	50¢ Paintings by Homer Watson	5.75	1.30	.40
2109a	perf. 13-1/2x13	....	3.50	1.25
2110	$1.35 Paintings by Homer Watson, souvenir sheet of 2	....	6.50	6.50
2111	50¢ Search and Rescue, sheet of 8	....	12.00	12.00
2112	50¢ Ellen Fairclough	5.75	1.25	.40
2113-14	50¢ 9th FINA World Championships, Montreal, 2 attached	....	2.50	1.00
2113	50¢ Diver	....	1.25	.40
2114	50¢ Swimmer	....	1.25	.40

2115

2117

SCOTT NO.	DESCRIPTION	PLATE BLOCK F/NH	UNUSED F/NH	USED F
2115	50¢ Founding of Port Royal, Nova Scotia, 400th Anniv.	5.75	1.25	.40
2116	50¢ Province of Alberta, Centennial, self-adhesive	5.75	1.25	.40
2117	50¢ Province of Saskatchewan, Centennial	5.75	1.25	.40

2118

2120

SCOTT NO.	DESCRIPTION	PLATE BLOCK F/NH	UNUSED F/NH	USED F
2118	50¢ Oscar Peterson, Pianist, 80th Birthday	5.75	1.25	.40
2118a	same, souvenir sheet of 4	....	4.75	....
2119	50¢ Acadiaan Deportation, 250th Anniversary	5.75	1.25	.40
2120	50¢ Mass Polio Vaccinations in Canada, 50th Anniv.	5.75	1.25	.40
2121	50¢ Youth Sports, self-adhesive, complete booklet of 8 (2121a-d X2)	....	9.95	....
2121a	50¢ Wall Climbing, self-adhesive	....	1.25	.50
2121b	50¢ Skateboarding, self-adhesive	....	1.25	.50
2121c	50¢ Mountain biking, self-adhesive	....	1.25	.50
2121d	50¢ Snowboarding, self-adhesive	....	1.25	.50

2122-23

SCOTT NO.	DESCRIPTION	PLATE BLOCK F/NH	UNUSED F/NH	USED F
2122-23	50¢ Wildcats, 2 attached	5.75	2.50	1.65
2122	50¢ Puma concolor	....	1.25	.50
2123	50¢ Panthera pardus orientalis	....	1.25	.50
2123b	Souvenir Sheet	....	2.60	2.60

2124

2125

SCOTT NO.	DESCRIPTION	PLATE BLOCK F/NH	UNUSED F/NH	USED F
2124	50¢ Snowmen, self-adhesive	....	1.25	.40
2124a	same, booklet pane of 6	....	7.25	....

SCOTT NO.	DESCRIPTION	PLATE BLOCK F/NH	UNUSED F/NH	USED F
2125	50¢ Creche Figures, St. Joseph Oratory, Montreal, self-adhesive	....	1.25	.40
2125a	same, booklet pane of 6	....	7.25	....
2126	85¢ Creche Figures, St. Joseph Oratory, Montreal, self-adhesive	....	2.25	.75
2126a	same, booklet pane of 6	....	14.00	....
2127	$1.45 Creche Figures, St. Joseph Oratory, Montreal, self-adhesive	....	3.75	....
2127a	same, booklet pane of 6	....	21.00	....

2128

2131, 2134

2135

SCOTT NO.	DESCRIPTION	PLATE BLOCK F/NH	UNUSED F/NH	USED F
2128	51¢ Red bergamot flower, self-adhesive, coil	....	1.35	.40
2129	89¢ Yellow lady's slipper, self-adhesive, coil	....	2.25	.90
2130	$1.05 Pink fairy slipper, self-adhesive, coil	....	2.60	1.00
2131	$1.49 Himalayan blue poppy, self-adhesive, coil	....	3.75	1.35
2132	89¢ Yellow lady's slipper, self-adhesive	....	2.40	.90
2132a	same, booklet pane of 6	....	13.50	....
2133	$1.05 Pink fairy slipper, self-adhesive	....	2.75	1.00
2133a	same, booklet pane of 6	....	15.50	....
2134	$1.49 Himalayan blue poppy, self-adhesive	....	3.75	1.35
2134a	same, booklet pane of 6	....	21.00	....
2135	51¢ Flag and Houses, New Glasgow, Prince Edward Island, self-adhesive	....	1.25	.40
2136	51¢ Flag and Bridge, Bouctouche, New Brunswick, self-adhesive	....	1.25	.40
2137	51¢ Flag and Windmills, Pincher Creek, Alberta self-adhesive	....	1.25	.40
2138	51¢ Flag and Lower Fort Garry, Manitoba, self-adhesive		1.25	.40
2139	51¢ Flag and Dogsled, Yukon Territory, self-adhesive	....	1.25	.40
2139a	Flags, booklet pane of 10 (2135-39 x 2)	....	12.00	....

2140

2142

2006 COMMEMORATIVES

SCOTT NO.	DESCRIPTION	PLATE BLOCK F/NH	UNUSED F/NH	USED F
2140	51¢ Year of the Dog	6.00	1.35	.40
2141	$1.49 Year of the Dog, Dog and pup, souvenir sheet	....	5.00	5.00
2142	51¢ Queen Elizabeth II, 80th Birthday, self-adhesive	....	1.35	.40
....	same, bookelt pane of 10	....	12.50	....

2143

2146

SCOTT NO.	DESCRIPTION	PLATE BLOCK F/NH	UNUSED F/NH	USED F
2143-44	51¢ 2006 Winter Olympics, Turin, Italy, 2 attached	6.00	2.75	1.35
2143	51¢ Team pursuit speed skating	....	1.25	.45
2144	51¢ Skeleton	....	1.25	.45
2145	51¢ Gardens, complete booklet of 8	....	10.50	....
2145a	51¢ Shade garden	....	1.25	.50
2145b	51¢ Flower garden	....	1.25	.50
2145c	51¢ Water garden	....	1.25	.50
2145d	51¢ Rock garden	....	1.25	.50
2146	51¢ Party Balloons, self-adhesive	....	1.40	.50
2146a	same, booklet pane of 6	....	7.50	....

2147

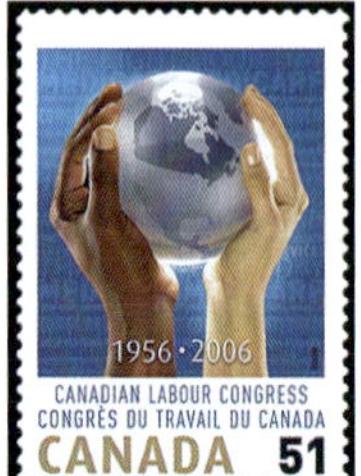

2149

SCOTT NO.	DESCRIPTION	PLATE BLOCK F/NH	UNUSED F/NH	USED F
2147	51¢ Paintings by Dorothy Knowles	6.00	1.40	.45
2147a	same, single from souvenir sheet, perf. 12.75 X 12.5	....	2.25	2.25
2148	51¢-89¢ Paintings by Dorothy Knowles, souvenir sheet	....	5.25	5.25
2148a	89¢ single from souvenir sheet	....	3.25	3.25
2149	51¢ Canadian Labor Congress, 50th Anniversary	6.00	1.40	.45
2150	$1.49 Queen Elizabeth 80th Birthday, souvenir sheet of 2	....	7.75	....
2150a	single from souvenir sheet	....	4.00	4.00

2151

2152

2154c

2155, 2156a

SCOTT NO.	DESCRIPTION	PLATE BLOCK F/NH	UNUSED F/NH	USED F
2151	51¢ McClelland & Stewart Publishing, self-adhesive	....	1.40	.45
....	same, booklet pane of 8	....	10.00	....
2152	89¢ Canadian Museum of Civilization, self adhesive	....	2.25	1.00
....	same, booklet pane of 8	....	17.00	....
2153	51¢ Canadians in Hollywood, souvenir sheet of 4	....	6.75	....
2154	same, booklet pane of 4	....	6.00	....
2154a	51¢ John Candy, self-adhesive	....	1.50	1.00
2154b	51¢ Mary Pickford, self-adhesive	....	1.50	1.00
2154c	51¢ Fay Wray, self adhesive	....	1.50	1.00
2154d	51¢ Lorne Greene, self-adhesive	....	1.50	1.00
2154e	same, booklet of 8, Wray on cover	....	9.95	....
2154f	same, booklet of 8, Pickford on cover	....	9.95	....
2154g	same, booklet of 8, Greene on cover	....	9.95	....
2154h	same, booklet of 8, Candy on cover	....	9.95	....
2155	51¢ Champlain Surveys the East Coast	....	1.40	.50
2156	2-39¢ and 2-51¢ Champlain, souvenir sheet sheet of 4, joint issue with the U.S.	....	8.95	....
2156a	51¢ single from souvenir sheet	....	1.95	1.95

2157

2160

SCOTT NO.	DESCRIPTION	PLATE BLOCK F/NH	UNUSED F/NH	USED F
2157	51¢ Vancouver Aquarium, 50th Anniv., self-adhesive	....	1.40	.50
2157a	same, booklet pane of 10	....	12.00	....
2158-59	51¢ Canadian Forces Snowbirds, 2 attached	6.00	2.75	1.75
2158	51¢ view from cockpit	....	1.40	.75
2159	51¢ three C-114 Tutor jets	....	1.40	.75
2159b	same, souvenir sheet of 2	....	3.50	....
2160	51¢ Atlas of Canada	....	1.35	.50

2161

2162

SCOTT NO.	DESCRIPTION	PLATE BLOCK F/NH	UNUSED F/NH	USED F
2161	51¢ 2006 World Lacrosse Championship, self-adhesive	....	1.35	.45
2161a	same, booklet pane of 8	....	10.00	....
2162	51¢ Mountaineering, self-adhesive	....	1.35	.45
2162a	same, booklet pane of 8	....	10.00	....

2163-66

2167

2168

SCOTT NO.	DESCRIPTION	PLATE BLOCK F/NH	UNUSED F/NH	USED F
2163-2166	51¢ Duck decoys	6.00	5.25	....
2163	51¢ Barrow's Golden Eye decoy	....	1.25	.60
2164	51¢ Mallard decoy	....	1.25	.60
2165	51¢ Red Breasted Merganser decoy	....	1.25	.60
2166	51¢ Black Duck decoy	....	1.25	.60
2166b	same, souvenir sheet of 4	....	5.95	....

SCOTT NO.	DESCRIPTION	PLATE BLOCK F/NH	UNUSED F/NH	USED F
2167	51¢ Society of Graphic Designers	6.00	1.40	.50
2168	51¢ Three glasses of wine, self-adhesive	....	1.25	.50
2169	51¢ Wine taster, self-adhesive	....	1.25	.50
2170	51¢ Various cheeses, self-adhesive	....	1.25	.50
2171	51¢ Woman with tray of cheeses, self-adhesive	....	1.25	.50
2171a	same, booklet of 8, 2 each 2168-2171	....	9.95	....

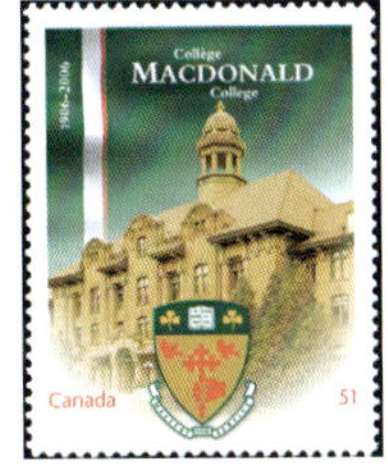

2172

2174

SCOTT NO.	DESCRIPTION	PLATE BLOCK F/NH	UNUSED F/NH	USED F
2172	51¢ MacDonald College, self-adhesive	....	1.35	.50
2172a	same, booklet pane of 4	....	5.00	....
2173	51¢ Endangered Species, souvenir sheet of 4 + 4 labels	....	7.00	....
2174	51¢ Newfoundland Marten	....	1.25	.60
2175	51¢ Blotched Tiger Salamander	....	1.25	.60
2176	51¢ Blue Racer	....	1.25	.60
2177	51¢ Swift Fox	....	1.25	.60
2177b	same, booklet of 8 (2174-2177 x 2)	....	10.00	....

2178

2183

SCOTT NO.	DESCRIPTION	PLATE BLOCK F/NH	UNUSED F/NH	USED F
2178-82	51¢ Opera singers, strip of 5	....	6.50	5.00
2178	51¢ Maureen Forrester	....	1.25	.50
2179	51¢ Raorel Jobin	....	1.25	.50
2180	51¢ Simoneau and Alarie	....	1.25	.50
2181	51¢ Jon Vickers	....	1.25	.50
2182	51¢ Edward Johnson	....	1.25	.50
2183	51¢ Madonna and Child, self-adhesive	....	1.35	.50
2183	same, booklet of pane of 12	....	14.75	....
2184	51¢ Snowman, self-adhesive	....	1.35	.40
2184a	same, booklet pane of 12	....	14.75	....
2185	89¢ Winter Joys, self-adhesive	....	2.25	.90
2185a	same, booklet pane of 6	....	12.75	....
2186	$1.49 Contemplation, self-adhesive	....	3.75	1.50
2186a	same, booklet pane of 6	....	21.00	....

2187

2188

2192

SCOTT NO.	DESCRIPTION	PLATE BLOCK F/NH	UNUSED F/NH	USED F
2187	"P" Spotted coalroot flower, self-adhesive, coil	....	1.35	.50
2188	Nondenominated "P" Queen Elizabeth II, self-adhesive	....	1.35	.50
2188a	same, booklet pane of 10	....	12.75	....
2189	"P" Flag and Sirmilik National Park Nunaunt, self-adhesive	....	1.50	.50
2190	"P" Flag and Cliff near Chemainus, British Columbia self-adhesive	....	1.50	.50
2191	"P" Flag and Polar bears near Churchill, Manitoba self-adhesive	....	1.50	.50
2192	"P" Flag and Bras d'Or Lake, Nova Scotia, self-adhesive		1.50	.50
2193	"P" Flag and Tuktut Nogait National Park, Northwest Territories, self-adhesive	....	1.50	.50
2193a	same, booklet pane of 10 (2189-2193 x 2)	....	13.00	....
2193b	same, booklet of 30 (2189-2193 x 6)	....	38.00	....

2195

2196

2197

SCOTT NO.	DESCRIPTION	PLATE BLOCK F/NH	UNUSED F/NH	USED F
2194	Flowers souvenir sheet of 4	....	10.50	....
2195	93¢ Flat-leaved Bladderwort, self-adhesive, coil	....	2.40	.85
2196	$1.10 March Skullcap, self-adhesive, coil	....	2.75	1.00
2197	$1.55 Little Larkspur, self-adhesive, coil	....	4.00	1.50
2198	93¢ Flat-leaved Bladderwort, self-adhesive	....	2.40	.85
2198a	same, booklet pane of 6	....	13.50	....
2199	$1.10 March Skullcap, self-adhesive	....	3.00	1.00
2199a	same, booklet pane of 6	....	16.00	....
2200	$1.55 Little Larkspur, self-adhesive	....	4.00	1.50
2200a	same, booklet pane of 6	....	22.00	....

2201

2203

2007 COMMEMORATIVES

SCOTT NO.	DESCRIPTION	PLATE BLOCK F/NH	UNUSED F/NH	USED F
2201	52¢ Year of the Pig	6.00	1.35	.50
2202	$1.55 Year of the Pig, souvenir sheet	....	5.25	5.25
2203	52¢ Celebration	....	1.35	.50
2203a	same, booklet pane of 6	....	7.50	....

2204-05

SCOTT NO.	DESCRIPTION	PLATE BLOCK F/NH	UNUSED F/NH	USED F
2204-05	52¢ International Polar Year, 2 attached	....	2.75	1.75
2204	52¢ Somateria spectabilis	....	1.35	.50
2205	52¢ Crossota millsaeare	....	1.35	.50
2205b	52¢ International Polar Year, souvenir sheet of 2	....	3.25	3.25
2206	52¢ Lilacs, souvenir sheet of 2	....	3.25	3.25
2207	52¢ White lilacs, self-adhesive	....	1.40	.60
2208	52¢ Purple lilacs, self-adhesive	....	1.40	.60
2208a	same, booklet pane of 10 (2207-08 x 2)	....	13.00	....

2209

2211

SCOTT NO.	DESCRIPTION	PLATE BLOCK F/NH	UNUSED F/NH	USED F
2209	52¢ HEC Montreal College, self-adhesvie	....	1.40	.50
2209a	same, booklet pane of 4	....	4.95	....
2210	52¢ University of Saskatchewan, self-adhesive	....	1.40	.50
2210a	same, booklet pane of 4	....	5.25	....
2211	52¢ Jelly Shelf by Mary Pratt	6.00	1.40	.50
2212	52¢-$1.55 Art by Mary Pratt, souvenir sheet	....	6.50	....
2212a	$1.55 Iceberg in North Atlantic by Mary Pratt	....	5.50	5.00

2214

2215

SCOTT NO.	DESCRIPTION	PLATE BLOCK F/NH	UNUSED F/NH	USED F
2213	52¢-$1.55 Ottawa 150th Anniversary souvenir sheet of 2	....	5.50	....
2213a	52¢ Ottawa 150th Anniversary	....	2.00	1.50
2213b	$1.55 Ottawa 150th Anniversary	....	3.50	3.00
2214	52¢ Ottawa 150th Anniversary, self-adhesive	....	1.35	.45
2214a	same, booklet pane of 4	....	5.25	....
2215-18	52¢ Royal Architectural Institute, strip of 4	....	5.25	3.50
2215	52¢ University of Lethbridge	....	1.25	.65
2216	52¢ St. Mary's Church	....	1.25	.65
2217	52¢ Ontario Science Center	....	1.25	.65
2218	52¢ National Gallery of Canada	....	1.25	.65

2219

2220

SCOTT NO.	DESCRIPTION	PLATE BLOCK F/NH	UNUSED F/NH	USED F
2219	$1.55 Captain George Vancouver	17.75	4.00	1.75
2219a	same, souvenir sheet of 1	....	4.00	3.25
2220	52¢ FIFA World Youth Championship	6.00	1.35	.55
2221	52¢ Canadian Recording Artists, souvenir sheet	....	7.75	....
2222	same, booklet of 8	....	14.00	....
	same, booklet of 4	....	7.50	....
2222a	52¢ Gordon Lightfoot, self-adhesive	....	1.75	.60
2222b	52¢ Joni Mitchell, self-adhesive	....	1.75	.60
2222c	52¢ Anne Murray, self-adhesive	....	1.75	.60
2222d	52¢ Paul Anka, self-adhesive	....	1.75	.60

2223

2234

2242

SCOTT NO.	DESCRIPTION	PLATE BLOCK F/NH	UNUSED F/NH	USED F
2223	52¢ Terra Nova National Park, self-adhesive	....	1.40	.55
2223a	same, booklet pane of 5	....	6.00	....
2223BOOK	same, booklet of 10	....	15.00	....
2224	52¢ Jasper National Park, self-adhesive	....	1.40	.55
2224a	same, booklet pane of 5	....	7.75	....
2224BOOK	same, booklet of 10	....	15.00	....
2225	52¢ 100 Years of Scouting, self-adhesive	....	1.40	.55
2225a	same, booklet of 8	....	11.00	....
2226	52¢ Henri Membertou	6.00	1.40	.55
2227	52¢ Law Society of Saskatchewan	....	1.90	.85
2228	52¢ Law Society of Alberta, Canada	6.00	1.40	.55
2229	52¢ Endangered Animals sheet of 4 + 4 lables	....	6.00	6.00
2229a	52¢ North Atlantic Right Whale	....	1.50	.65
2229b	52¢ Northern Cricket Frog	....	1.50	.65
2229c	52¢ White Sturgeon	....	1.50	.65
2229d	52¢ Leatherback Turtle	....	1.50	.65
2230-33	52¢ Endangered Animals block of 4	....	6.00	....
2230	52¢ North Atlantic Right Whale bklt single	....	1.50	.65
2231	52¢ Northern Cricket Frog bklt single	....	1.50	.65
2232	52¢ White Sturgeon bklt single	....	1.50	.65
2233	52¢ Leatherback Turtle bklt single	....	1.50	.65
2233b	bklt pane of 8	....	11.00	....
2234-38	1¢-25¢ Beneficial Insects	7.00	1.50	1.25
2234	1¢ Convergent Lady Beetle	.80	.30	.25
2235	3¢ Golden-Eyed Lacewing	.90	.30	.25
2235b	3¢ Golden-Eyed Lacewing, dated 2012	....	.30	.25
2236	5¢ Northern Bumblebee	1.00	.30	.25
2237	10¢ Canada Darner	1.20	.30	.25
2238	25¢ Cecropia Moth	3.25	.60	.30
2238a	souvenir sheet of 5	....	1.50	1.50
2239	52¢ Reindeer & Snowflakes	....	1.35	.60
2239a	same bklt pane of 6	....	7.50	....
2240	52¢ Holy Family	....	1.40	.60
2240a	same bklt pane of 6	....	7.50	....
2241	93¢ Angel Over Town	....	2.40	1.25
2241	same bklt pane of 6	....	14.50	....
2242	$1.55 Dove	....	4.00	1.85
2242a	same bklt pane of 6	....	23.00	....

2248a

2249

2261

SCOTT NO.	DESCRIPTION	PLATE BLOCK F/NH	UNUSED F/NH	USED F
2243	$1.60 Orchids sheet of 4	....	11.00	11.00
2244-47	$1.60 Orchids coils	....	11.00	8.00
2244	Odontioda Island Red Orchid coil	....	1.35	.60
2244a	Odontioda Island Red Orchid coil, die-cut 9.1	....	2.50	....
2245	95¢ Potinara Janet Elizabeth "Fire Dancer" Orchid coil	....	2.40	1.00
2246	$1.15 Laeliocattieya Memorial Evelyn Light Orchid coil	....	2.95	1.25
2247	$1.60 Masdevallia Kaleidoscope "Conni" Orchid coil	....	4.00	1.75
2248	Queen Elizabeth II	....	1.35	.60
2248a	same bklt pane of 10	....	12.50	....
2249	Flag & Sambro Island Lighthouse, Nova Scotia	....	1.40	.60
2250	Flag & Point Clark Lighthouse, Ontario	....	1.40	.60
2251	Flag & Cap-des-Rosiars	....	1.40	.60
2252	Flag & Warren Landing Lighthouse, Manitoba	....	1.40	.60
2253	Flag & Panchena Point Lighthouse, British Columbia	....	1.40	.60
2253a	bklt pane of 10, 2 each 2249-2253	....	12.50	....
2253b	Flag & Pachena Point Lighthouse, British Columbia	....	1.40	.65
2253c	same bklt pane of 10, 2 ea. 2249-52, 2253b	....	13.00	....
2253d	same bklt pane of 40, 6 ea. 2249-52, 2253b	....	38.00	....
2254	95¢ Potinara Janet Elizabeth "Fire Dancer" Orchid	....	2.45	1.10
2254a	same bklt pane of 6	....	14.00	....
2255	$1.15 Laeliocattieya Memorial Evelyn Light Orchid	....	3.00	1.35
2255a	same bklt pane of 6	....	17.00	....
2256	$1.60 Masdevallia Kaleidoscope "Conni" Orchid	....	4.00	1.75
2256a	same bklt pane of 6	....	23.00	....

2008

SCOTT NO.	DESCRIPTION	PLATE BLOCK F/NH	UNUSED F/NH	USED F
2257	52¢ Year of the Rat	5.75	1.25	.60
2258	$1.60 Year of the Rat souvenir sheet	....	4.00	4.00
2259	Fireworks	....	1.25	.60
2259a	same bklt pane of 6	....	7.50	....
2260	52¢ Peonies sheet of 2	....	3.25	2.50
2261-62	52¢ Peonies bklt singles	....	3.25	1.25
2262b	bklt pane of 10, 5 each of 2261 & 2262	....	12.00	....
2263	52¢ University of Alberta	....	1.25	.60
2263a	same bklt pane of 8	....	9.50	....

2273

2280d

2287

SCOTT NO.	DESCRIPTION	PLATE BLOCK F/NH	UNUSED F/NH	USED F
2264	52¢ University of British Columbia	....	1.25	.60
2264a	same bklt pane of 8	....	9.25	....
2264b	gutter pane, 4 each of 2263-64	....	21.00	....
2265	52¢ Int. Ice Hockey Federation Championships	....	1.25	....
2265a	same bklt pane of 10	....	13.00	....
2266	52¢ Guide Dog	....	1.25	.60
2266a	same bklt pane of 10	....	13.00	....
2267-68	52¢ Canadian Oil & Gas Industries attached pair	....	2.50	2.25
2267	Transcanada Pipeline Completion	....	1.25	.60
2268	First Commercial Oil Well	....	1.25	.60
2268a	52¢ Canadian Industries bklt pane of 10	....	12.00	....
2269	Founding of Quebec City	5.75	1.25	.60
2270	52¢ Yousuf Karsh self-portrait	5.75	1.25	.60
2271	Souvenir sheet of 3, 2270, 2271a, 2271b	....	7.50	7.25
2271a	96¢ Audrey Hepburn	....	2.50	1.00
2271b	$1.60 Winston Churchill	....	3.75	1.75
2272	96¢ Audry Hepburn	....	2.50	1.00
2272a	same bklt pane of 4	....	9.00	....
2273	$1.60 Winston Churchill	....	3.75	1.75
2273a	same bklt pane of 4	....	15.00	....
2274	52¢ Royal Canadian Mint	....	1.25	.65
2275	52¢ Canadian Nurses Association	....	1.25	.65
2275a	same, booklet pane of 10	....	12.00	....
2276	Anne of Green Gables, sheetlet of 2	....	4.50	4.50
2276a	52¢ Anne Holding Buttercups	....	3.75	.95
2276b	52¢ Green Gables House	....	1.75	.95
2277	52¢ Anne Holding Buttercups, booklet single	....	1.50	.65
2278	52¢ Green Gables House, booklet single	....	1.50	.65
2278a	Anne of Green Gables, bklt pane of 10	....	12.00	....
2279	Canadians in Hollywood, souvenir sheet of 4	....	8.00	....
2279a	Norma Shearer	....	2.00	1.25
2279b	Chief Dan George	....	2.00	1.25
2279c	Marie Dressler	....	2.00	1.25
2279d	Raymond Burr	....	2.00	1.25
2280	Canadians in Hollywood, booklet pane of 4	....	6.25	....
	same, complete booklet	....	12.00	....
2280a	Marie Dressler, booklet single	....	1.60	1.25
2280b	Chief Dan George, booklet single	....	1.60	1.25
2280c	Norma Shearer, booklet single	....	1.60	1.25
2280d	Raymond Burr, booklet single	....	1.60	1.25
2281	52¢ Beijing Summer Olympics	....	1.25	.65
2281a	same, booklet pane of 10	....	12.00	....
2282	52¢ Lifesaving Society	....	1.25	.65
2282a	same, booklet pane of 10	....	12.00	....
2283	52¢ British Columbia 150th Anniversary	5.75	1.25	.65
2284	52¢ R. Samuel McLaughlin, Buick Automobile	5.75	1.25	.65
2285	Endangered Animal, sheet of 4 + labels	....	5.25	5.25
2285a	Prothonotary Warbler	....	1.25	.65
2285b	Taylor's Checkerspot Butterfly	....	1.25	.65
2285c	Roseate Tern	....	1.25	.65
2285d	Burrowing Owl	....	1.25	.65
2286	Prothonotary Warbler, booklet single	....	1.25	.65
2287	Taylor's Checkerspot Butterfly, booklet single	....	1.25	.65
2288	Roseate Tern, booklet single	....	1.25	.65
2289	Burrowing Owl, booklet single	....	1.25	.65
2289a	Endangered Animal, bklt pane of 4, #2286-89	....	5.00	....
2289b	Endangered Animal, bklt pane, 2 of #2289a	....	9.75	....
2290	52¢ 12th Francophone Summit	5.45	1.25	.50
2291	Winter Scenes, sheet of 3	....	7.75	....
2291a	Making Snow Angel	....	1.50	1.15
2291b	95¢ Skiing	....	2.50	1.85
2291c	$1.60 Tobogganing	....	3.75	3.00
2292	Christmas	....	1.25	.50
2292a	same, booklet pane of 6	....	7.25	....
	same, complete booklet, #2292a	....	13.95	....
2293	Making Snow Angle, booklet single	....	1.25	.50
2293a	same, booklet pane of 6	....	7.25	....
	same, complete bklt, 2 of #2293a	....	13.95	....
2294	95¢ Skiing, booklet single	....	2.25	.90
2294a	same, booklet pane of 6	....	13.00	....
2295	$1.60 Tobogganing, booklet single	....	3.85	1.50
2295a	same, booklet pane of 6	....	22.00	....
2295b	same, gutter pane, #2294a, 2295a	....	39.00	....

2300

2301

2303

2009 COMMEMORATIVES

SCOTT NO.	DESCRIPTION	PLATE BLOCK F/NH	UNUSED F/NH	USED F
2296	Year of the Ox	5.50	1.25	.50
2297	$1.65 Year of the Ox, souvenir sheet	....	4.25	4.25

SCOTT NO.	DESCRIPTION	PLATE BLOCK F/NH	UNUSED F/NH	USED F
2297a	same, w/China 2009 emblem overprinted in gold	....	4.75	4.75
2298	Queen Elizabeth II	....	1.25	.50
2298a	same, booklet pane of 10	....	12.50	....
2299	Sports of the Winter Olympics, sheet of 5	....	7.00	4.75
2299a	Curling	....	1.50	1.00
2299b	Bobsledding	....	1.50	1.00
2299c	Snowboarding	....	1.50	1.00
2299d	Freestyle Skiing	....	1.50	1.00
2299e	Ice-Sled Hockey	....	1.50	1.00
2299f	#2299, "Vancouver/2010" overprinted in sheet margin in silver	....	11.00	9.75
2300	Freestyle Skiing, booklet single	....	1.25	1.00
2301	Ice-Sled Hockey, booklet single	....	1.25	1.00
2302	Bobsledding, booklet single	....	1.25	1.00
2303	Curling, booklet single	....	1.25	1.00
2304	Snowboarding, booklet single	....	1.25	1.00
2304a	booklet pane of 10, 2 ea. 2300-2304	....	12.00	....
2304b	booklet pane of 30, 6 ea. 2300-2304	....	36.00	....
2305	Olympics, sheet of 5	....	11.00	11.00
2306	"P" 2010 Winter Olympics Emblem, die cut 9 1/4, rounded tips	....	2.25	1.75
2307	"P" 2010 Vancouver Winter Paralympics Emblem, die cut 9 1/4, rounded tips	....	2.25	1.75
2307a	"P" 2010 Winter Olympics Emblem, die cut 9-9 1/4, sawtooth tips	....	2.25	1.75
2307b	"P" 2010 Vancouver Winter Paralympics Emblem, die cut 9-9 1/4, sawtooth tips	....	2.25	1.75
2308	98¢ MIGA, Winter Olympics Mascot, die cut 8 1/4 - 9 1/4, sawtooth tips	....	3.25	1.75
2309	$1.18 SUMI, Paralympics Mascot, die cut 8 1/4 - 9 1/4, sawtooth tips	....	4.50	1.75
2310	$1.65 Quatchi, Winter Olympics Mascot, die cut 8 1/4 - 9 1/4, sawtooth tips	....	4.50	1.75
2311	98¢ MIGA, Winter Olympics Mascot, die cut 9 1/4, rounded tips	....	2.75	1.75
2312	$1.18 SUMI, Paralympics Mascot, die cut 9 1/4, rounded tips	....	3.25	1.75
2313	$1.65 Quatchi, Winter Olympics Mascot, die cut 9 1/4, rounded tips	....	4.25	1.75

2316

2321

2326

SCOTT NO.	DESCRIPTION	PLATE BLOCK F/NH	UNUSED F/NH	USED F
2314	Celebration	....	1.25	.50
2314a	same, booklet pane of 6	....	7.25	5.75
2315	54¢ Rosemary Brown	....	1.25	.90
2316	54¢ Abraham Doras Shadd	....	1.25	.90
2316a	pair, 2315-16	....	2.50	1.00
2317	"P" First Airplane Flight in Canada	....	1.25	.50
2318	54¢ Rhododendrons, sheet of 2	....	3.25	2.50
2319	54¢ White and Pink Rhododendrons	....	1.25	.50
2320	54¢ Pink Rhododendrons	....	1.25	.50
2320a	54¢ Rhododendrons, bklt pane of 10	....	12.50	....
2321	54¢ Jack Bush Painting, striped column, per 13 x 13 1/4	....	1.25	.50
2321a	54¢ Jack Bush Painting, striped column, per 12 1/2 x 13 1/4	....	1.75	1.75
2322	54¢ - $1.65 souvenir sheet, Paintings by Jack Bush	....	5.75	5.75
2323	54¢ Astronomy, souvenir sheet of 2	....	3.25	3.25
2323c	same as 2323, w/buff bkgrnd behind product code	....	5.00	5.00
2324	54¢ Canada-France-Hawaii Telescope	....	1.25	.50
2325	54¢ Horsehead Nebula	....	1.25	.50
2325a	booklet pane of 10, each 2324 & 2325	....	13.00	....
2326	54¢ Polar Bear	....	1.25	.50
2327	54¢ Arctic Tern	....	1.25	.50
2327b	souvenir sheet, 1 ea. 2326-2327	....	3.50	....
2328	2¢ Caterpillar	....	.25	.25
2329	54¢ Canadian Horse	....	1.25	.50
2330	54¢ Newfoundland Pony	....	1.25	.50
2330a	booklet pane of 10, 5 ea. 2329-2330	....	12.50	....
2331	54¢ Boundary Water Treaty	....	1.25	.60
2333	54¢ Popular Singers, sheet of 4	....	6.50	5.75
2333a	54¢ Robert Charlebois	....	1.75	1.25
2333b	54¢ Edith Butler	....	1.75	1.25

2334a

2337

2338a

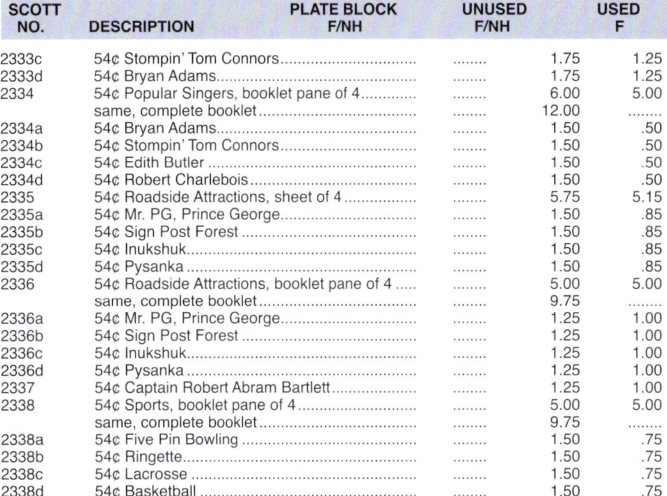

SCOTT NO.	DESCRIPTION	PLATE BLOCK F/NH	UNUSED F/NH	USED F
2333c	54¢ Stompin' Tom Connors	....	1.75	1.25
2333d	54¢ Bryan Adams	....	1.75	1.25
2334	54¢ Popular Singers, booklet pane of 4	....	6.00	5.00
	same, complete booklet	....	12.00	....
2334a	54¢ Bryan Adams	....	1.50	.50
2334b	54¢ Stompin' Tom Connors	....	1.50	.50
2334c	54¢ Edith Butler	....	1.50	.50
2334d	54¢ Robert Charlebois	....	1.50	.50
2335	54¢ Roadside Attractions, sheet of 4	....	5.75	5.15
2335a	54¢ Mr. PG, Prince George	....	1.50	.85
2335b	54¢ Sign Post Forest	....	1.50	.85
2335c	54¢ Inukshuk	....	1.50	.85
2335d	54¢ Pysanka	....	1.50	.85
2336	54¢ Roadside Attractions, booklet pane of 4	....	5.00	5.00
	same, complete booklet	....	9.75	....
2336a	54¢ Mr. PG, Prince George	....	1.25	1.00
2336b	54¢ Sign Post Forest	....	1.25	1.00
2336c	54¢ Inukshuk	....	1.25	1.00
2336d	54¢ Pysanka	....	1.25	1.00
2337	54¢ Captain Robert Abram Bartlett	....	1.25	1.00
2338	54¢ Sports, booklet pane of 4	....	5.00	5.00
	same, complete booklet	....	9.75	....
2338a	54¢ Five Pin Bowling	....	1.50	.75
2338b	54¢ Ringette	....	1.50	.75
2338c	54¢ Lacrosse	....	1.50	.75
2338d	54¢ Basketball	....	1.50	.75

2339

2341

2343b

2359

SCOTT NO.	DESCRIPTION	PLATE BLOCK F/NH	UNUSED F/NH	USED F
2339	P Montreal Canadians Hockey Jersey	....	1.25	.55
2339a	same, booklet pane of 10	....	12.50	....
2340	$3 500 Goal Scorers of the Montreal Canadians	....	25.00	....
2340a	$3 Maurice Richard	....	8.50	6.00
2340b	$3 Jean Beliveau	....	8.50	6.00
2340c	$3 Guy Lafleur	....	8.50	6.00
2341	P National War Memorial	....	2.50	2.25
2341a	P National War Memorial Souvenir Sheet of 2	....	3.25	3.25
2342	P National War Memorial, booklet single	....	1.25	.55
2342a	same, booklet pane of 10	....	12.50	....
2343	Christmas, sheet of 4 + 6 labels	....	9.50	....
2343a	P Christmas	....	1.50	.55
2343b	P Madonna & Child	....	2.00	2.00
2343c	98¢ Magus	....	3.50	3.25
2343d	$1.65 Shepherd & Lamb	....	5.00	4.75
2344	P Christmas Tree	....	1.25	.55
2344a	same, booklet pane of 6	....	7.25	....
	complete booklet	....	14.50	....
2345	P Madonna & child, booklet stamp	....	1.25	.55
2345a	same, booklet pane of 6	....	7.50	....
	complete booklet	....	14.50	....
2346	98¢ Magus booklet stamp	....	2.50	1.10
2346a	same, booklet pane of 6	....	13.50	....
2347	$1.65 Shepherd & Lamb booklet stamp	....	3.75	1.75
2347a	booklet pane of 6	....	22.50	....
2347b	booklet pane of 12, 6 each 2346-2347	....	42.00	....
2348	P Tiger in circle	....	1.25	.65
2349	$1.70 Sculpted Tiger Seal	....	4.50	3.00

2356a

2373a

2010 COMMEMORATIVES

SCOTT NO.	DESCRIPTION	PLATE BLOCK F/NH	UNUSED F/NH	USED F
2350	Souvenir sheet of 5	....	7.50	....
2350a	P Flag over Watson's Mill	....	1.50	1.00
2350b	P Flag over Keremeos Grist Mill	....	1.50	1.00
2350c	P Flag over Old Stone Mill	....	1.50	1.00
2350d	P Flag over Riordon Grist Mill	....	1.50	1.00
2350e	P Flag over Cornell Mill	....	1.50	1.00
2351	P Flag over Watson's Mill S/A booklet single	....	1.50	1.00
2352	P Flag over Keremeos Grist Mill S/A bklt single	....	1.50	1.00
2353	P Flag over Old Stone Mill S/A booklet single	....	1.50	1.00
2354	P Flag over Riordon Grist Mill S/A bklt single	....	1.50	1.00
2355	P Flag over Cornell Mill S/A booklet single	....	1.50	1.00
2355a	Booklet pane of 10, 2 each 2351-55	....	13.50	....
2355b	Booklet pane of 30, 6 each 2351-55	....	42.00	....
2356	Orchids souvenir sheet of 4	....	11.00	....
2356a	P Striped Coralroot Orchid	....	1.50	1.25
2356b	$1 Giant Helleborine Orchid	....	2.50	2.00
2356c	$1.22 Rose Pogonia Orchid	....	3.00	2.50

SCOTT NO.	DESCRIPTION	PLATE BLOCK F/NH	UNUSED F/NH	USED F
2356d	$1.70 Grass Pink Orchid	....	4.00	3.50
2357	P Striped Coralroot Orchid S/A coil (sawtooth tips)	....	1.35	.60
2358	$1 Giant Helleborine Orchid S/A coil (sawtooth tips)	....	2.50	1.10
2359	$1.22 Rose Pogonia Orchid S/A coil (sawtooth tips)	....	3.00	1.35
2360	$1.70 Grass Pink Orchid S/A coil (sawtooth tips)	....	4.00	1.75
2361	P Striped Coralroot Orchid S/A coil (rounded tips)	....	1.75	.60
2362	$1 Giant Helleborine Orchid booklet stamps	....	2.50	1.00
2362a	booklet pane of 6	....	13.50	....
2363	$1.22 Rose Pogonia Orchid booklet stamps	....	3.00	1.00
2363a	booklet pane of 6	....	17.00	....
2364	$1.70 Grass Pink Orchid booklet stamp	....	4.00	1.75
2364a	booklet pane of 6	....	24.00	....
2365	P Queen Elizabeth II	....	1.25	.60
2365a	same, booklet pane of 10	....	13.00	....
2366	57¢ souvenir sheet of 2	....	3.25	2.50
2366a	57¢ Whistler, B.C.	....	1.50	.75
2366b	57¢ Vancouver	....	1.50	.75
2366c	#2366 with "Vancouver/2010" overprinted in sheet margin in gold	....	5.50	5.00
2367	57¢ Whistler, B.C.	....	1.25	.75
2368	57¢ Vancouver	....	1.25	.75
2368a	Booklet pane of 10, 5 each 2367-2368	....	13.00	....
2369	57¢ William Hall	....	1.25	.75
2370	57¢ Romeo LeBlanc	....	1.25	.75
2371	57¢ Gold Medal sheet of 2	....	4.00	4.00
2371a	57¢ Gold Medal single stamp	....	1.25	.75
2372	57¢ Gold Medal S/S booklet stamp	....	1.25	.75
2372a	same, booklet pane of 10	....	13.00	.75
2373	57¢ Winter Olympics souvenir sheet of 2	....	3.50	3.50
2373a	57¢ Woman with painted face at left	....	1.50	.60
2373b	57¢ Woman with painted face at right	....	1.50	.60
2374	57¢ Woman with painted face at left S/A booklet stamp	....	1.25	.60

2377

2378

2383

SCOTT NO.	DESCRIPTION	PLATE BLOCK F/NH	UNUSED F/NH	USED F
2375	57¢ Woman with painted face at right S/A bklt stamp	....	1.25	.60
2375a	Booklet pane of 10, 5 each 2374-2375	....	12.50	....
2376	African Violet Hybrids, souvenir sheet of 2	....	3.50	3.50
2377	P red African violet	....	1.50	.75
2378	P purple african violet	....	1.50	.75
2378a	same, booklet pane of 10	....	12.50	....
2379	$1.70 Canada-Israel Friendship	....	3.75	1.95
2379a	same, booklet pane of 3 + label	....	11.50	....
2380-83	57¢ Indian Kings	....	5.50	5.00
2380	57¢ Tee Yee Neen Ho Ga Row	....	1.40	0.75
2381	57¢ Sa Ga Yeath Qua Pieth Tow	....	1.40	0.75
2382	57¢ Ho Nee Yeath Taw No Row	....	1.40	0.75
2383	57¢ Etow Oh Koam	....	1.40	0.75
2383b	Souvenir sheet of 4	....	6.75	6.75
2383c	Souvenir sheet of 4 with London 2010, emblem on sheet margin	.....	9.00	9.00
2384	57¢ Canadian Navy Cent, sheet of 2	....	3.50	3.50
2384a	57¢ Male Sailor	....	1.50	.85
2384b	57¢ Female Sailor	....	1.50	.85
2385	57¢ Male Sailor	....	1.50	.85
2386	57¢ Female Sailor	....	1.50	.85
2386a	same, bklt pane of 10	....	12.50	....

2387b

2394

2395

SCOTT NO.	DESCRIPTION	PLATE BLOCK F/NH	UNUSED F/NH	USED F
2387	57¢ Mammals, sheet of 2	....	3.60	3.60
2387a	57¢ Hasrbor porpoise	....	1.25	.85
2387b	57¢ Sea Otter	....	1.25	.85
2387c	57¢ Hasrbor porpoise, perf 13x12.75 syncopated	....	1.25	.85
2387d	57¢ Sea Otter, perf 13x12.75 sycopated	....	1.25	.85
2387e	same, booklet pane of 8	....	10.00	....
2388	57¢ Canadian Geographic wildlife photography, sheet of 5	....	7.75	7.75
2388a	57¢ Ardia Herodias	....	1.70	1.30
2388b	57¢ Vulpees Vulpees	....	1.70	1.30
2388c	57¢ Tetigonlidae	....	1.70	1.30
2388d	57¢ Tachycineta bicolor	....	1.70	1.30
2388e	57¢ Selaphorus rufus	....	1.70	1.30
2389-93	57¢ Canadian Geographic wildlife photography, d/c 13.25	....	7.50	7.50
2389	57¢ Ardia Herodias	....	1.50	1.50
2390	57¢ Vulpees Vulpees	....	1.50	1.50
2391	57¢Tetigonlidae, die cut 13.25	....	1.50	1.50
2392	57¢ Tachycineta bicolor, die cut 13.25	....	1.50	1.50
2393	57¢ Selaphorus rufus, die cut 13.25	....	1.50	1.50
2393a	57¢ Canadian Geographic wildlife photography, bklt pane of 10	.....	12.50	....
2394	57¢ Rotary International	....	1.35	.65
2394a	same, bklt pane of 8	....	10.00	....
2395	57¢ Rollande	....	1.30	.65

2410

2397d

2414

SCOTT NO.	DESCRIPTION	PLATE BLOCK F/NH	UNUSED F/NH	USED F
2396	57¢, $1.70 Paintings by Prudence Heward, souvenir sheet of 2	....	6.50	6.50
2396a	$1.70 At the Theatre	....	5.50	4.50
2397	Roadside Attractions, sheet of 4	....	6.50	6.50
2397a	P Coffee Pot	....	1.50	1.00
2397b	P Happy Rock	....	1.50	1.00
2397c	P Wawa Goose	....	1.50	1.00
2397d	P Puffin	....	1.50	1.00
2398	P Coffee Pot, booklet single	....	1.40	1.00
2399	P Happy Rock, booklet single	....	1.40	1.00
2400	P Wawa Goose, booklet single	....	1.40	1.00
2401	P Puffin, booklet single	....	1.40	1.00
2401a	Booklet pane of 4	....	5.50	....
	Complete Booklet	....	11.00	....
2402	P Girl Guides	....	1.35	.65
2402a	same, bklt pane of 10	....	12.50	....
2403	57¢ Founding of Cupids, Newfoundland	....	1.35	.65
2404	57¢ Year of British Home Children	....	1.35	.65
2405	$10 Blue Whale	....	22.00	13.00
2406	4¢ Paper Wasp	....	.25	.25
2406a	4¢ Paper Wasp, added microprinting and small design features	....	.30	.25
2407	6¢ Assassin Bug	....	.25	.25
2408	7¢ Large Milkweed Bug	....	.25	.25
2409	8¢ Margined Leatherwing	....	.25	.25
2409a	8¢ Margined Leathewing, added microprinting and small design features	....	.30	.25
2409b	Souvenir sheet of 3, #2235b, 2406a, 2409a	....	.45	.45
2410	9¢ Dogbane Beetle	....	.25	.25
2410a	Souvenir sheet of 5 Beneficial Insects	....	1.05	.95
2411	Souvenir sheet of 3 Christmas Ornaments	....	8.25	8.25
2411a	P Christmas Ornament	....	1.50	.75
2411b	$1 Christmas Ornament	....	2.25	1.25
2411c	$1.70 Christmas Ornament	....	3.75	2.00
2412	(57¢) P Madonna & Child	....	1.40	.75
2412a	same, booklet pane of 6	....	7.75	....
2413	P Christmas Ornament	....	1.35	.75
2413a	same, booklet pane of 6	....	7.75	....
2414	$1 Christmas Ornament	....	2.25	1.25
2414a	same, booklet pane of 6	....	13.50	....
2415	$1.70 Christmas Ornament	....	3.75	2.00
2415a	same, booklet pane of 6	....	23.50	....
2415b	Gutter pane, #2414a, 2415a	....	40.00	....

2416

2428

2433

2011 COMMEMORATIVES

SCOTT NO.	DESCRIPTION	PLATE BLOCK F/NH	UNUSED F/NH	USED F
2416	P Year of the Rabbit	....	1.50	.75
2417	$1.75 Year of the Rabbit Souvenir Sheet	....	4.50	4.25
2418	P Canadian Flag, sheet of 5	....	7.75	6.75
2418a	P Canadian Flag on Soldier's Uniform	....	1.50	.65
2418b	P Canadian Flag on Hot Air Balloon	....	1.50	.65
2418c	P Canadian Flag of Search & Rescue Team's Uniform	....	1.50	.65
2418d	P Canadian Flag on Canadarm	....	1.50	.65
2418e	P Canadian Flag on Backpack	....	1.50	.65
2419	P Canadian Flag on Soldier's Uniform	....	1.50	.65
2420	P Canadian Flag on Hot Air Balloon	....	1.50	.65
2421	P Canadian Flag of Search & Rescue Team's Uniform	....	1.50	.65
2422	P Canadian Flag on Canadarm	....	1.50	.65
2423	P Canadian Flag on Backpack	....	1.50	.65
2423a	Booklet Pane of 10, 2 each #2419-23	....	13.00	....
2423b	Booklet Pane of 30, 6 each #2419-23	....	39.00	....
2424	Juvenile Wildlife, sheet of 4	....	10.50	10.50
2424a	P Arctic hare leverets	....	1.35	.75
2424b	$1.05 Red Fox Kit in hollow log	....	2.25	1.25
2424c	$1.25 Canada goslings	....	2.75	1.50
2424d	$1.75 Polar Bear Cub	....	3.75	2.00
2425	P Arctic hare leverets coil, D/C 9.25	....	1.90	1.55
2426	P Arctic hare leverets coil, D/C 8.25	....	1.90	.75
2427	$1.03 Red Fox Kit in hollow log coil, D/C 8.25	....	2.50	1.25
2428	$1.25 Canada goslings coil D/C 8.50	....	2.90	1.50
2429	$1.75 Polar Bear Cub coil D/C 8.25	....	3.95	2.00
2430	$1.03 Red Fox Kit in hollow log bklt single	....	2.25	1.25
2430a	same, booklet pane of 6	....	13.50	....
2431	$1.25 Canada goslings bklt single	....	2.75	1.50
2431a	same, booklet pane of 6	....	17.00	....
2432	$1.75 Polar Bear Cub bklt single	....	4.00	2.00
2432a	Same, booklet pane of 6	....	23.50	....

SCOTT NO.	DESCRIPTION	PLATE BLOCK F/NH	UNUSED F/NH	USED F
2433	59¢ Carrie Best, Order of Canada Recipient	....	1.35	.75
2433a	same, bklt pane of 10	....	13.50	....

2434

2436

SCOTT NO.	DESCRIPTION	PLATE BLOCK F/NH	UNUSED F/NH	USED F
2434	59¢ Ferguson Jenkins, order of Canada Recipient	....	1.35	.75
2434a	same, bklt pane of 10	....	13.50	....
2435	P Gift Box	....	1.35	.75
2435a	Same, bklt pane of 6	....	8.00	....
2436	59¢ Pow-wow Dancer	....	1.35	.75
2437	Paintings of Daphne Odjig, sheet of 3	....	8.50	8.25
2437a	$1.03 Pow-wow	....	2.25	1.25
2437b	$1.75 Spiritual Renewal	....	4.00	2.00
2438	$1.03 Pow-wow	....	2.25	1.25
2438a	same, booklet pane of 6	....	13.50	....
2439	$1.75 Spiritual Renewal	....	3.75	2.00
2439a	same, booklet pane of 6	....	24.00	....
2440	P Sunflower, sheet of 2	....	3.00	2.75
2440A	P Prado Red	....	1.40	.75
2440B	P Sunbright	....	1.40	.75

2442

2448b

SCOTT NO.	DESCRIPTION	PLATE BLOCK F/NH	UNUSED F/NH	USED F
2441-42	P Sunflower, coil pair	....	3.00	....
2441	P Prado Red, coil	....	1.35	.75
2442	P Sunbright, coil	....	1.35	.75
2443	P Prado Red, booklet single	....	1.35	.75
2444	P Sunbright, booklet single	....	1.35	.75
2444A	P Sunflower, booklet pane of 10	....	13.50	....
2445	Signs of the Zodiac, sheet of 4	....	6.25	6.00
2446	Signs of the Zodiac, sheet of 4	....	6.25	6.00
2446a	P Leo	....	1.50	.95
2446b	P Virgo	....	1.50	.95
2446c	P Libra	....	1.50	.95
2446d	P Scorpio	....	1.50	.95
2447	Signs of the Zodiac, sheet of 4	....	6.25	5.50
2447a	P Sagittarius	....	1.50	.95
2447b	P Capricorn	....	1.50	.95
2447c	P Aquarius	....	1.50	.95
2447d	P Pisces	....	1.50	.95
2448	Signs of the Zodiac, sheet of 12	....	18.00	18.00
2448a	P Aries	....	1.50	.75
2448b	P Taurus	....	1.50	.75
2448c	P Gemini	....	1.50	.75
2448d	P Cancer	....	1.50	.75
2448e	P Leo	....	1.50	.75
2448f	P Virgo	....	1.50	.75
2448g	P Libra	....	1.50	.75
2448h	P Scorpio	....	1.50	.75
2448i	P Sagittarius	....	1.50	.75
2448j	P Capricorn	....	1.50	.75
2448k	P Aquarius	....	1.50	.75
2448l	P Pisces	....	1.50	.75
2449	P Aries, booklet single	....	1.50	.75
2449a	same, booklet pane of 10	....	13.50	....
2450	P Taurus, booklet single	....	1.50	.75
2450a	same, booklet pane of 10	....	13.50	....
2450b	Gutter pane of 12, 6 each 2449-50	....	17.50	....
2451	P Gemini, booklet single	....	1.50	.75
2451a	same, booklet pane of 10	....	13.50	....
2452	P Cancer, booklet single	....	1.50	.75
2452a	same, booklet pane of 10	....	13.50	....
2452b	gutter pane of 12, 6 each 2451-52	....	17.00	....
2453	P Leo Booklet Single	....	1.50	.75
2453a	same, booklet pane of 10	....	13.50	....
2454	P Virgo Booklet Single	....	1.50	.75
2454a	same, booklet pane of 10	....	13.50	....
2455	P Libra Booklet Single	....	1.50	.75
2455a	same, booklet pane of 10	....	13.50	....
2456	P Scorpio Booklet Single	....	1.50	.75
2456a	same, booklet pane of 10	....	13.50	....
2457	P Sagittarius Booklet Single	....	1.50	.75
2457a	same, booklet pane of 10	....	13.50	....
2458	P Capricorn Booklet Single	....	1.50	.75
2458a	same, booklet pane of 10	....	13.50	....
2459	P Aquarius Booklet Single	....	1.50	.75
2459a	same, booklet pane of 10	....	13.50	....
2460	P Pisces Booklet Single	....	1.50	.75
2460a	same, booklet pane of 10	....	13.50	....
2461	P International Year of the Forest, sheet of 2	....	2.75	2.75
2461a	P Tree	....	1.35	.75
2461b	P Mushroom and Plants on Forest Floor	....	1.35	.75
2462	P Tree, booklet single	....	1.35	.75
2463	P Mushroom & Plants on Forest Floor, bklt single	....	1.35	.75
2463a	Booklet pane of 8, 4 each of 2462 & 2463	....	11.00	....

2462

2463

2464-65

SCOTT NO.	DESCRIPTION	PLATE BLOCK F/NH	UNUSED F/NH	USED F
2464-65	59¢ - $1.75 Royal Wedding, pair	....	5.50	5.00
2464	P Couple with Prince William at right	....	1.35	1.00
2465	$1.75 Couple with Prince William at right	....	4.00	2.00
2465b	same, souvenir sheet of 2	....	5.75	5.75
2465c	same, souvenir sheet of 2 with coat of arms overprint	....	7.00	7.00
2466	59¢ Royal Wedding, booklet single	....	1.25	.75
2466a	Same, booklet pane of 10	....	13.50	10.00
2467	$1.75 Royal Wedding, booklet single	....	3.75	3.25
2467a	Same, booklet pane of 10	....	39.00	....
2467b	Gutter pane, 6 #2466, 4 #2467	....	27.50	....

2468-2469

SCOTT NO.	DESCRIPTION	PLATE BLOCK F/NH	UNUSED F/NH	USED F
2468-69	59¢ Mail Delivery Pair	....	2.75	2.25
2468	59¢ Ponchon	....	1.35	.75
2469	59¢ Dog Sled	....	1.35	.75
2470	59¢ Canada Parks Centennial	....	1.35	.75
2470a	same, booklet pane of 10	....	13.50	....
2471	P Art Deco, sheet of 5	....	7.00	7.00
2471a	P Burrard Bridge	....	1.50	.75
2471b	P Cormier House	....	1.50	.75
2471c	P R.C. Water House Treatment Plant	....	1.50	.75
2471d	P Supreme Court of Canada	....	1.50	.75
2471e	P Dominion Building	....	1.50	.75
2472	P Burrard Bridge, booklet single	....	1.50	.75
2473	P Cormier House, booklet single	....	1.50	.75
2474	P R.C. Water House Treatment Plant, bklt single	....	1.50	.75
2475	P Supreme Court of Canada, booklet single	....	1.50	.75
2476	P Dominion Building, booklet single	....	1.50	.75
2476a	Art Deco Structures, booklet pane of 10	....	13.50	....
2477	Royal Wedding, sheet of 2	....	2.75	2.75
2477b	same, with Royal Tour Emblem, overprinted in sheet margin	....	3.00	3.00
2478	P Royal Wedding, booklet single	....	1.50	.75
2478a	same, booklet pane of 10	....	13.50	....
2479	P Ginette Reno	....	1.50	.75
2479a	P Ginette Reno, perf 12.5x13	....	1.50	.75

2483b

2486a

SCOTT NO.	DESCRIPTION	PLATE BLOCK F/NH	UNUSED F/NH	USED F
2480	P Bruce Cockburn	....	1.50	.75
2480a	P Bruce Cockburn, perf 12.5x13	....	1.50	.75
2481	P Robbie Robertson	....	1.50	.75
2481a	P Robbie Robertson, perf 12.5x13	....	1.50	.75
2482	P Kate and Anna McGarrigle	....	1.50	.75
2482a	P Kate and Anna McGarrigle, perf 12.5x13	....	1.50	.75
2482b	Popular Singers Souvenir Sheet of 4	....	6.00	....
2483	Popular Singers, booklet pane of 4	....	6.00	....
2483a	P Bruce Cockburn, booklet single	....	1.50	.75
2483b	P Kate and Anna McGarrigle, booklet single	....	1.50	.75
2483c	P Ginette Reno, booklet single	....	1.50	.75
2483d	P Robbie Robertson, booklet single	....	1.50	.75
2484	P Roadside Attractions Sheet of 4	....	6.00	2.75
2484a	P World's Largest Lobster	....	1.50	.75
2484b	P Wild Blueberry	....	1.50	.75
2484c	P Big Potato	....	1.50	.75
2484d	P Giant Squid	....	1.50	.75
2485	P Roadside Attractions, booklet pane of 4	....	6.00	....
2485a	P World's Largest Lobster, booklet single	....	1.50	.75
2485b	P Wild Blueberry, booklet single	....	1.50	.75
2485c	P Big Potato, booklet single	....	1.50	.75
2485d	P Giant Squid, booklet single	....	1.50	.75
2486	Miss Supertest S/S of 2	....	5.50	5.25
2486a	P Miss Supertest III	....	1.50	.75
2486b	$1.75 Miss Supertest III	....	3.75	1.95
2487	P Miss Supertest, booklet single	....	1.50	.75
2487a	same, booklet pane of 10	....	13.50	....

2488b 2490c 2495

SCOTT NO.	DESCRIPTION	PLATE BLOCK F/NH	UNUSED F/NH	USED F
2488	Canadian Inventions, booklet pane of 4	....	5.75	....
2488a	59¢ Pacemaker, Dr. John Hopps	....	1.35	.75
2488b	59¢ Blackberry, Research in Motion	....	1.35	.75
2488c	59¢ Electric Oven, Thomas Ahern	....	1.35	.75
2488d	59¢ Electric Wheelchair, George J. Klein	....	1.35	.75
2489	P Dr. John Charles Polanyi	....	1.35	.75
2489a	same, booklet pane of 10	....	13.50	....
2490	Christmas, sheet of 3	....	7.50	7.50
2490a	P Angel	....	1.50	.75
2490b	$1.03 Nativity	....	2.25	1.25
2490c	$1.75 Epiphany	....	3.75	2.25
2491	P Christmas	....	1.35	.65
2491a	same, booklet pane of 6	....	7.75	....
2492	P Angel, booklet single	....	1.50	.75
2492a	same, booklet pane of 6	....	7.75	....
2493	$1.03 Nativity, booklet single	....	2.25	1.25
2493a	$1.75 Epiphany	....	13.50	....
2494	$1.75 Epiphany, booklet single	....	3.75	2.25
2494a	$1.75 Epiphany	....	24.00	....

2498 2505 2508

2012 COMMEMORATIVES

SCOTT NO.	DESCRIPTION	PLATE BLOCK F/NH	UNUSED F/NH	USED F
2495	P Year of the Dragon	....	1.50	.75
2496	$1.80 Year of the Dragon	....	4.00	2.00
2496a	Year of the Dragon souvenir sheet of 2	....	7.50	4.25
2497	$1.80 Year of the Dragon, booklet single	....	4.00	2.00
2497a	same, booklet pane of 6	....	25.00	....
2498	P Flag, souvenir sheet of 5	....	6.75	....
2498a	P Flag on Coast Guard Ship	....	1.35	.65
2498b	P Flag in Van Window	....	1.35	.65
2498c	P Oympic Athlete Carrying Flag	....	1.35	.65
2498d	P Flag on Bobsled	....	1.35	.65
2498e	P Inuit Child waving Flag	....	1.35	.65
2499	P Flag on Coast Guard Ship, booklet single	....	1.35	.65
2499a	P Flag on Coast Guard Ship, "Canada" visible on reverse of stamp	....	1.50	.75
2500	P Flag in Van Window, booklet single	....	1.35	.65
2500a	P Flag in Van window, "Canada" visible on reverse of stamps	....	1.50	.75
2501	P Olympic Athlete Carrying Flag, booklet single	....	1.35	.65
2501a	P Olympic athlete carrying flag, "Canada" visible on reverse of stamps	....	1.50	.75
2502	P Flag on Bobsled, booklet single	....	1.35	.65
2502a	P Flag on Bobsled, microprinting with corrected spelling "Lueders"	....	1.50	.75
2502b	P Flag on Bobsled, microprinting with "Canada" visible on reverse of stamp	....	1.50	.75
2503c	booklet pane of 10, 2 each, 2499-2502, 2502a, 2503	....	13.50	....
2503d	P Inuit child waving flag, "Canada" visible on reverse of stamp	....	1.50	.75
2503e	booklet pane of 10, 2 each, 2499a, 2500a, 2501a, 2502b, 2503d	....	13.50	....
2504	Juvenile Wildlife Souvenir Sheet of 4	....	10.50	10.50
2504a	P Three Raccoon Kits	....	1.40	.70
2504b	$1.05 Two Caribou Calves	....	2.30	1.25
2504c	$1.29 Adult Loon and Two Chicks	....	2.75	1.50
2504d	$1.80 Moose Calves	....	4.25	2.25
2505	P Three Raccoon Kits Coil, D/C 9.25	....	1.40	.70
2506	P Three Raccoon Kits Coil, D/C 8.25	....	1.40	.70
2507	$1.05 Two Caribou Calves Coil, D/C 8.25	....	2.30	1.25
2508	$1.29 Adult Loon and Two Chicks Coil, D/C 8.25	....	2.75	1.50
2509	$1.80 Moose Calves Coil, D/C 8.25	....	4.25	2.25

2520 2527

SCOTT NO.	DESCRIPTION	PLATE BLOCK F/NH	UNUSED F/NH	USED F
2510	$1.05 Two Caribou Calves, booklet single	....	2.25	1.25
2510a	same, booklet pane of 6	....	14.00	....
2511	$1.29 Adult Loon and Two Chicks, booklet single	....	2.75	1.50
2511a	same, booklet pane of 6	....	17.00	....
2512	$1.80 Moose Calves, booklet single	....	3.95	2.00
2512a	same, booklet pane of 6	....	23.00	....
2513	P Crown, Canada #330	....	1.40	.70
2514	P Map of Canada, Canada #471	....	1.40	.70
2515	P Reign of Queen Elizabeth II, 60th Anniversary	....	1.40	.70
2516	P Queen Elizabeth II Flowers, Canada #1168	....	1.40	.70
2517	P Queen Elizabeth II Tiara, Canada #1932	....	1.40	.70
2518	P Queen Elizabeth II	....	1.35	.65
2519	P Queen Elizabeth II Wearing Robe and Tiara	....	1.40	.70
2519A	same, booklet pane of 10	....	14.00	....
2520	P John Ware	....	1.40	.70
2520a	booklet pane of 10	....	14.00	....
2521	P Viola Desmond	....	1.40	.70
2521a	booklet pane of 10	....	14.00	....
2521b	gutter pane of 12, 6 each 2519, 2520	....	16.00	....
2522	P Smoothly She Shifted, by Joe Fafard	....	1.40	.70
2523	Souvenir sheet, Sculptures by Joe Fafard	....	7.50	7.50
2523a	$1.05 Dear Vincent	....	2.25	1.25
2523b	$1.80 Capillery	....	4.25	2.25
2524	$1.05 Dear Vincent, booklet single	....	2.25	1.25
2524a	same, booklet pane of 6	....	13.75	....
2525	$1.80 Capillary, booklet single	....	4.25	2.25
2525a	same, booklet pane of 6	....	23.50	....
2526	Daylilies Souvenir Sheet of 2	....	2.75	2.75
2526a	P Orange Daylily	....	1.50	.65
2526b	P Purple Daylily	....	1.50	.65
2527-28	P Daylilies Coil Pair	....	2.75	....
2527	P Orange Daylily Coil	....	1.50	.65
2528	P Purple Daylily Coil	....	1.50	.65
2529	P Orange Daylily, booklet single	....	1.50	.65
2530	P Purple Daylily, booklet single	....	1.50	.65
2530a	same, booklet pane of 10	....	13.50	....

2536 2537 2539

SCOTT NO.	DESCRIPTION	PLATE BLOCK F/NH	UNUSED F/NH	USED F
2531-34	P Sinking of the Titanic	....	5.50	5.50
2531	P White Star Line Flag & Bow of Titanic, map showing Halifax	....	1.35	.65
2532	P Bow of Titanic & Map showing Southhampton, England	....	1.35	.65
2533	P Propellers of Titanic, three men	....	1.35	.65
2534	P Propellers of Titanic, six men	....	1.35	.65
2535	$1.80 Titanic Souvenir Sheet	....	4.50	4.50
2536	P White Star Line Flag & Titanic map showing Halifax, booklet single	....	1.35	.65
2537	P Bow of Titanic & map showing Southampton, England, bklt single	....	1.35	.65
2537a	P Titanic, booklet pane of 10	....	13.00	....
2538	$1.80 White Star Line Flag & Titanic	....	4.25	2.25
2538a	same, booklet pane of 6	....	23.50	....
2539	P Thomas Douglas, 5th Earl of Selkirk	....	1.35	.70
2540	$2 Reign of Queen Elizabeth II	....	4.50	2.50
2540a	$2 Reign of Queen Elizabeth II, souvenir sheet	....	4.50	4.50

2542 2547 2557

SCOTT NO.	DESCRIPTION	PLATE BLOCK F/NH	UNUSED F/NH	USED F
2541	P Franklin the Turtle, miniature sheet of 4	....	5.50	5.50
2541a	P Franklin, Beaver and Teddy Bear	....	1.40	.70
2541b	P Franklin helping young turtle to read book	....	1.40	.70
2541c	P Franklin and snail	....	1.40	.70
2541d	P Franklin watching bear feed fish in bowl	....	1.40	.70
2542	P Franklin, beaver & teddy bear, booklet single.	....	1.40	.70
2543	P Franklin helping young turtle to read, bklt single	....	1.40	.70
2544	P Franklin and snail, booklet single	....	1.40	.70
2545	P Franklin watching bear feed fish in bowl, bklt single	....	1.40	.70
2545a	P Franklin the turtle booklet pane of 12	....	16.00	....
2546	P Calgary Stampede Centennial Souvenir Sheet of 2	....	4.00	4.00
2546a	P Saddle on Rodeo Horse	....	1.50	.70
2546b	$1.05 Commemorative Belt Buckle	....	2.50	1.25
2547	P Saddle on Rodeo Horse, booklet single	....	1.50	.70
2547a	same, booklet pane of 10	....	13.00	....
2548	$1.05 Commemorative Belt Buckle, bklt single.	....	2.50	1.25
2548a	same, booklet pane of 10	....	24.00	....
2549	P Order of Canada Recipients Miniature sheet of 4	....	5.50	5.50
2549a	P Louise Arbour	....	1.50	.70
2549b	P Rick Hansen	....	1.50	.70
2549c	P Sheila Watt-Cloutier	....	1.50	.70
2549d	P Michael J. Fox	....	1.50	.70
2550	P Louise Arbour booklet single	....	1.50	.70
2550a	same, booklet pane of 10	....	13.50	....

SCOTT NO.	DESCRIPTION	PLATE BLOCK F/NH	UNUSED F/NH	USED F
2551	P Rick Hansen booklet single	....	1.50	.70
2551a	same, booklet pane of 10	....	13.50	....
2552	P Sheila Watt-Cloutier booklet single	....	1.50	.70
2552a	same, booklet pane of 10	....	13.50	....
2553	P Michael J. Fox	....	1.50	.70
2553A	same, booklet pane of 10	....	13.50	....
2554-55	P War of 1812 Bicentennial	....	2.75	2.75
2554	P Sir Isaac Brock	....	1.50	.70
2555	P Tecumseh	....	1.50	.70
2556	P 2012 Summer Olympics	....	1.50	.75
2556a	same, booklet pane of 10	....	13.50	....
2557	P Tommy Douglas	....	1.50	.75

2559

2566

SCOTT NO.	DESCRIPTION	PLATE BLOCK F/NH	UNUSED F/NH	USED F
2558	P Canadian Football League Sheet of 8	....	12.50	....
2558a	P British Columbia Lions	....	1.50	.75
2558b	P Edmonton Eskimos	....	1.50	.75
2558c	P Calgary Stampeders	....	1.50	.75
2558d	P Saskatchewan Roughriders	....	1.50	.75
2558e	P Winnipeg Blue Bombers	....	1.50	.75
2558f	P Hamilton-Tiger-Cats	....	1.50	.75
2558g	P Toronto Argonauts	....	1.50	.75
2558h	P Montreal Alouettes	....	1.50	.75
2559-66	P Canadian Football Leagues Coil	....	12.80	....
2559	P British Columbia Lions Coil Single	....	1.50	.75
2560	P Edmonton Eskimos Coil Single	....	1.50	.75
2561	P Calgary Stampeders Coil Single	....	1.50	.75
2562	P Saskatchewan Roughriders Coil Single	....	1.50	.75
2563	P Winnipeg Blue Bombers Coil Single	....	1.50	.75
2564	P Hamilton-Tiger-Cats Coil Single	....	1.50	.75
2565	P Toronto Argonauts Coil Single	....	1.50	.75
2566	P Montreal Alouettes Coil Single	....	1.50	.75

2568

2578

SCOTT NO.	DESCRIPTION	PLATE BLOCK F/NH	UNUSED F/NH	USED F
2567	P Grey Cup Centennial, sheet of 9	....	12.50	12.50
2567a	P Two football players and cup	....	1.50	.75
2567b	P British Columbia Lions player Geroy Simon	....	1.50	.75
2567c	P Edmonton Eskimos play Tom Wilkinson	....	1.50	.75
2567d	P Calgary Stampeders player "Thumper" Wayne Harris	....	1.50	.75
2567e	P Saskatchewan Roughriders player George Reed	....	1.50	.75
2567f	P Winnipeg Blue Bombers player Ken Pipen	....	1.50	.75
2567g	P Hamilton-Tiger-Cats player Danny McMannus	....	1.50	.75
2567h	P Toronto Argonauts player Michael "Pinball" Cannon	....	1.50	.75
2567i	P Montreal Alouettes player Anthony Calvillo	....	1.50	.75
2568	P Two football players and cup booklet single	....	1.50	.75
2568a	same, booklet pane of 10	....	13.50	....
2569	P British Columbia Lions player Geroy Simon, booklet single	....	1.50	.75
2569a	same, booklet pane of 10	....	13.50	....

2570

2582

SCOTT NO.	DESCRIPTION	PLATE BLOCK F/NH	UNUSED F/NH	USED F
2570	P Edmonton Eskimos player Tom Wilkinson, booklet single	....	1.50	.75
2570a	same, booklet pane of 10	....	13.50	....
2571	P Calgary Stampeders player "Thumper" Wayne Harris	....	1.50	.75
2571a	same, booklet pane of 10	....	13.50	....
2572	P Saskatchewan Roughriders player George Reed, booklet single	....	1.50.	.75
2572a	same, booklet pane of 10	....	13.50	....
2573	P Winnipeg Blue Bombers player Ken Pipen, booklet single	....	1.50	.75
2573a	same, booklet pane of 10	....	13.50	....
2574	P Hamilton-Tiger-Cats player Danny McMannus, booklet single	....	1.50	.75
2574a	same, booklet pane of 10	....	13.50	....
2575	P Toronto Argonauts player Michael "Pinball" Cannon, booklet single	....	1.50	.75
2575a	same, booklet pane of 10	....	13.50	....
2576	P Montreal Alouettes player Anthony Calvillo, booklet single	....	1.50	.75
2576a	same, booklet pane of 10	....	13.50	....
2577	P Military Regiments, souvenir sheet of 3	....	4.25	4.25
2577a	P Black Watch (Royal Highland) Regiment of Canada, perf 13x13.5	....	1.35	.75
2577b	P Royal Hamilton Light Infantry (Wentworth Regiment), perf 13x13.5	....	1.35	.75
2577c	P Royal Regiment of Canada, perf 13x13.5	....	1.35	.75
2578	P Black Watch (Royal Highland) Regiment of Canada, perf 13.25x13	....	1.35	.75
2578a	same, booklet pane of 10	....	13.50	....

2581a, 2583

2581b, 2584

2581c, 2585

SCOTT NO.	DESCRIPTION	PLATE BLOCK F/NH	UNUSED F/NH	USED F
2579	P Royal Hamilton Light Infantry (Wentworth Regiment), perf 13.25x13	....	1.35	.75
2579a	same, booklet pane of 10	....	13.50	....
2580	P Royal Regiment of Canada, perf 13.25x13	....	1.35	.75
2580a	same, booklet pane of 10	....	13.50	....
2581	Gingerbread Cookies Souvenir Sheet of 3	....	7.75	7.75
2581a	P Man and Woman Gingerbread Cookies	....	1.50	.75
2581b	$1.05 Five-Pointed Star Gingerbread Cookie	....	2.25	1.25
2581c	$1.80 Snowfake Gingerbread Cookie	....	4.25	2.25
2582	Stained Glass Window	....	1.50	.75
2582a	same, booklet pane of 12	....	15.50	....
2583	P Man and Woman Gingerbread Cookies, bklt single	....	1.50	.75
2583a	same, booklet pane of 12	....	15.50	....
2584	$1.05 Five-Pointed Star Gingerbread Cookie, bklt single	....	2.25	1.25
2584a	same, booklet pane of 6	....	13.50	....
2585	$1.80 Snowflake Gingerbread Cookie, bklt single	....	4.25	2.25
2585a	same, booklet pane of 6	....	23.00	....
2586	P Gray Dots	....	1.50	1.50
2586a	P Gray Dots, personalized issue	....	....	....
2587	P Gray Frame	....	1.50	1.50
2587a	P Gray Frame, personalized issue	....	....	....
2588	P Gray and Red Hearts	....	1.50	1.50
2588a	P Gray and Red Hearts, personalized issue	....	....	....
2589	P Multicolored Creatures	....	1.50	1.50
2589a	P Multicolored Creatures, personalized issue	....	....	....
2590	P Multicolored Butterflies	....	1.50	1.50
2590a	P Multicolored Butterflies, personalized issue	....	....	....
2591	P Multicolored Maple Leaves	....	1.50	1.50
2591a	P Multicolored Maple Leaves, personalized issue	....	....	....
2592	P Multicolored Flowers	....	1.50	1.50
2592a	P Multicolored Flowers, personalized issue	....	....	....
2593	P Multicolored Snowflakes	....	1.50	1.50
2593a	P Multicolored Snowflakes, personalized issue	....	....	....
2594	P Gray and Black Wedding Bells	....	1.50	1.50
2594a	P Gray and Black Wedding Bells, personalied issue	....	....	....
2595	P Gray Doves and Flowers	....	1.50	1.50
2595a	P Gray Doves and Flowers, personalized issue	....	....	....
2596	P Multicolored Balloons, Stars, Party	....	1.50	1.50
2596a	P Multicolored Balloons, Stars, Party, personalized issue	....	....	....
2597	P Multicolored Holly	....	1.50	1.50
2597a	P Multicolored Holly, personalized issue	....	....	....
2598	P Gray Cup Victory of Toronto Argonauts	....	1.35	.65
2598a	same, booklet pane of 10	....	13.00	....

2599

2602b, 2605, 2608

2013 COMMEMORATIVES

SCOTT NO.	DESCRIPTION	PLATE BLOCK F/NH	UNUSED F/NH	USED F
2599	P Year of the Snake	....	1.50	.75
2600	$1.85 Snake's Head	....	4.25	4.25
2600a	Year of the Snake Souvenir Sheet of 2	....	8.25	8.25
2601	$1.85 Snake's Head Booklet Single	....	4.25	4.25
2601a	same, booklet pane of 6	....	23.50	....
2602	Juvenile Wildlife Souvenir Sheet of 4	....	11.00	11.00
2602a	P Four Woodchuck Pups	....	1.35	.75
2602b	$1.10 Pocupette	....	2.50	1.25
2602c	$1.34 Fawn	....	3.00	1.50
2602d	$1.85 Bear Cub	....	4.25	2.00
2603	P Four Woodchuck Pups coil D/C 9.25 horizontal	....	1.35	.75
2604	P Four Woodchuck Pups coil D/C 8.25 horizontal	....	1.35	.75
2605	$1.10 Pocupette Coil	....	2.50	1.25
2606	$1.34 Fawn coil	....	3.00	1.50
2607	$1.85 Bear Cub Coil	....	4.25	2.00

SCOTT NO.	DESCRIPTION	PLATE BLOCK F/NH	UNUSED F/NH	USED F
2608	$1.10 Porcupette booklet single	....	2.50	1.25
2608a	same, booklet pane of 6	....	14.50	....
2609	$1.34 Fawn booklet single	....	3.00	1.50
2609a	same, booklet pane of 6	....	17.50	....
2610	$1.85 Bear Cub Booklet Single	....	4.25	2.00
2610a	same, booklet pane of 6	....	24.00	....

2612 2613 2614 2615 2616

SCOTT NO.	DESCRIPTION	PLATE BLOCK F/NH	UNUSED F/NH	USED F
2611	P Flags, souvenir sheet of 5	....	6.75	6.75
2611a	P Flag design on chairs	....	1.35	.75
2611b	P Flag on hay roll	....	1.35	.75
2611c	P Flag Design onSpinnaker	....	1.35	.75
2611d	P Flag in flower bed	....	1.35	.75
2611e	P Flag design on hut	....	1.35	.75
2612	P Flag design on chairs booklet single	....	1.35	.75
2612a	P Flag design on chairs booklet single, "Canada" visible on reverse of stamp	....	1.35	.75
2613	P Flag on hay roll booklet single	....	1.35	.75
2613a	P Flag on hay roll booklet single, "Canada" visible on reverse of stamp	....	1.35	.75
2614	P Flag design onSpinnaker booklet single	....	1.35	.75
2614a	P Flag design onSpinnaker booklet single, "Canada" visible on reverse of stamp	....	1.35	.75
2615	P Flag in flower bed booklet single	....	1.35	.75
2615a	P Flag in flower bed booklet single, "Canada" visible on reverse of stamps	....	1.35	.75
2616	P Flag design on Hut, booklet single	....	1.35	.75
2616a	P Flag design on Hut booklet single, "Canada" visible on reverse of stamp	....	1.35	.75
2616b	Booklet pane of 10, 2 each, 2612-2616	....	13.50	....
2616c	Booklet pane of 10, 2 each, 2612a-2616a	....	13.50	....
2616d	Booklet pane of 30, 6 each of 2612-2616	....	38.50	....
2616e	Booklet pane of 30, 6 each of 2612a-2616a	....	38.50	....
2617	P Queen Elizabeth II, booklet single	....	1.35	.75
2617a	same, booklet pane of 10	....	13.50	....
2617b	same, Canada visible on reverse of stamp	....	1.50	.75
2617c	same, booklet pane of 10	....	13.50	....
2618	$1.85 Raoul Wallenberg	....	4.25	2.25
2618a	same, booklet pane of 6	....	23.50	....

2619

2620

2624

SCOTT NO.	DESCRIPTION	PLATE BLOCK F/NH	UNUSED F/NH	USED F
2619	P Oliver Jones booklet single	....	1.35	.75
2619a	same, booklet pane 10	....	13.50	....
2620	P Joe Fortes booklet single	....	1.35	.75
2620a	same, booklet pane of 10	....	13.50	....
2621	Magnolias Souvenir sheet of 2	....	2.75	3.75
2621a	P Yellow Flower	....	1.35	.75
2621b	P White Flower	....	1.35	.75
2622-23	Magnolias Coils	....	2.75	....
2622	P Yellow Flower Coil	....	1.35	.75
2623	P White Flower Coil	....	1.35	.
2624	P Yellow Flower Booklet Single	....	1.35	.75

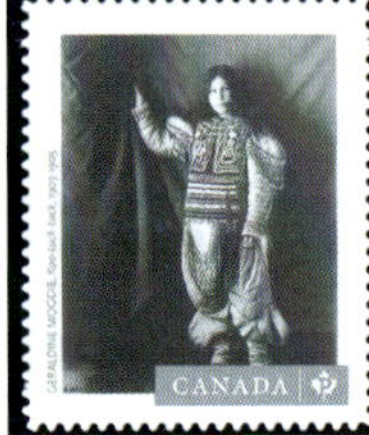

2632

2635

SCOTT NO.	DESCRIPTION	PLATE BLOCK F/NH	UNUSED F/NH	USED F
2625	P White Flower Booklet Single	....	1.35	.75
2625a	same, booklet pane of 10, 2 each 2624-2625	....	13.50	....
2626	P Photography sheet of 3	....	4.00	4.00
2627	P Photography sheet of 4	....	8.75	8.75
2628	P Hot Properties #1, by Jim Bruekelman	....	1.50	.75
2629	P Louis-Joseph Papineau by Thomas Coffin Doane	....	1.50	.75
2630	P The Kitchen Sink, by Margaret Watkins	....	1.50	.75
2631	P Andor Pasztor by Gabor Szilasi	....	1.50	.75
2632	P Koo-tuck-tuck by Geraldine Moodie	....	1.50	.75
2632a	Booklet pane of 10, 2 each #2628-32	....	13.50	....
2633	$1.10 basement Camera Shop circa 1937	....	2.50	1.25
2633a	same, booklet pane of 6	....	14.50	....
2634	$1.85 Yousuf Karsh by Arnaud Maggs	....	4.25	2.25
2634a	same, booklet pane of 6	....	24.00	....
2635	P The Prince of Wales Own Regiment	....	1.50	.75
2635a	same, booklet pane of 10	....	13.50	....

2640

2644

2645

SCOTT NO.	DESCRIPTION	PLATE BLOCK F/NH	UNUSED F/NH	USED F
2636	P Pet Adoption sheet of 5	....	6.50	6.50
2637	P Cat with bird on branch in background	....	1.50	.75
2638	P Parrot on perch	....	1.50	.75
2639	P Dog with squirrel, butterfly, flower and ball in background	....	1.50	.75
2640	P Dog with fireplace, dog bed and bone in background	....	1.50	.75
2641	P Cat with cat toys in background	....	1.50	.75
2641a	same, booklet pane of 10	....	13.50	....
2642	P Chinatown Gares sheet of 8	....	11.00	....
2642a	P Toronto	....	1.50	.75
2642b	P Montreal	....	1.50	.75
2642c	P Winnipeg	....	1.50	.75
2642d	P Edmonton	....	1.50	.75
2642e	P Vancouver	....	1.50	.75
2642f	P Ottawa	....	1.50	.75
2642g	P Mississauga	....	1.50	.75
2642h	P Victoria	....	1.50	.75
2643	P Chinatown Gares booklet pane of 8	....	11.00	....
2643a	P Toronto	....	1.50	.75
2643b	P Montreal	....	1.50	.75
2643c	P Winnipeg	....	1.50	.75
2643d	P Edmonton	....	1.50	.75
2643e	P Vancouver	....	1.50	.75
2643f	P Ottawa	....	1.50	.75
2643g	P Mississauga	....	1.50	.75
2643h	P Victoria	....	1.50	.75
2644	P Coronation of Queen Elizabeth II	....	1.50	.75
2644a	same, booklet pane of 10	....	13.50	....
2645	P Big Brothers, Big Sisters	....	1.50	.75
2645a	same, booklet page of 10	....	13.50	....

2647 - 2648

2650

SCOTT NO.	DESCRIPTION	PLATE BLOCK F/NH	UNUSED F/NH	USED F
2646	Motorcyles sheet of 2	....	3.00	3.00
2646a	P 1908 CCM	....	1.50	.70
2646b	P 1914 Indian	....	1.50	.70
2647	P 1908 CCM bklt single	....	1.50	.70
2648	P 1914 Indian bklt single	....	1.50	.70
2648a	same, booklet pane of 10	....	13.50	....
2649	P Benjamin Franklin and Quebec Harbor	....	1.50	.70
2649a	same, booklet pane of 10	....	13.50	....

2653-2654

SCOTT NO.	DESCRIPTION	PLATE BLOCK F/NH	UNUSED F/NH	USED F
2650	P Lieutenant Colonel Charles de Salaberry	....	1.50	.70
2651	P Laura Secord	....	1.50	.70
2651a	attached pair, 2650-51	....	3.25	3.25
2652	P Children's Literature Souvenir Sheet of 2	....	2.75	2.75
2652a	P Stella hanging by legs from tree	....	1.50	.70
2652b	P Stella, brother Sam, and dog, Fred	....	1.50	.70
2653	P Stella hanging by legs from tree, booklet single	....	1.50	.70
2654	P Stella, brother Sam, and dog, Fred, booklet single	....	1.50	.70
2654a	Same, booklet pane of 10, 5 each of 2653 & 2654	....	13.5	....

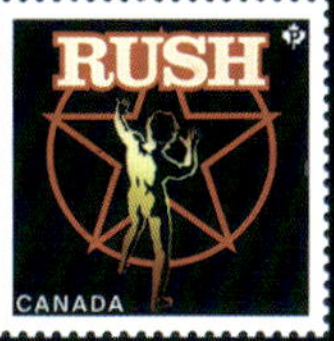

2655

SCOTT NO.	DESCRIPTION	PLATE BLOCK F/NH	UNUSED F/NH	USED F
2655	P Canadian Bands Souvenir Sheet of 4	....	5.50	5.50
2655a	P The Tragically Hip	....	1.50	.70
2655b	P Rush	....	1.50	.70
2655c	P Beau Dommage	....	1.50	.70
2655d	P The Guess Who	....	1.50	.70
2656	P The Tragically Hip, booklet single	....	1.50	.70
2656a	same, booklet pane of 10	....	13.50	....
2657	P Rush, booklet single	....	1.50	.70
2657a	same, booklet pane of 10	....	13.50	....
2658	P Beau Dommage, booklet single	....	1.50	.70
2658a	same, booklet pane of 10	....	13.50	....
2659	P The Guess Who, booklet single	....	1.50	.70
2659a	same, booklet pane of 10	....	13.50	....

2660

2662

2672

SCOTT NO.	DESCRIPTION	PLATE BLOCK F/NH	UNUSED F/NH	USED F
2660	63¢ Robertson Davies	....	1.50	.70
2660a	same, booklet pane of 10	....	13.50	....
2661	63¢ Pucks with Canadian National Hockey League Team Emblems		9.25	9.25
2661a	63¢ Vancouver Canucks	....	1.50	.70
2661b	63¢ Edmonton Oilers	....	1.50	.70
2661c	63¢ Toronto Maple Leafs	....	1.50	.70
2661d	63¢ Montreal Canadians	....	1.50	.70
2661e	63¢ Calgary Flames	....	1.50	.70
2661f	63¢ Winnipeg Jets	....	1.50	.70
2661g	63¢ Ottawa Senators	....	1.50	.70
2662-68	63¢ Pucks with Canadian NHL Team Emblems Coil Stamps		9.75	5.75
2662	63¢ Vancouver Canucks Coil	....	1.50	.70
2663	63¢ Edmonton Oilers coil	....	1.50	.70
2664	63¢ Toronto Maple Leafs coil	....	1.50	.70
2665	63¢ Montreal Canadians coil	....	1.50	.70
2666	63¢ Calgary Flames coil	....	1.50	.70
2667	63¢ Winnipeg Jets coil	....	1.50	.70
2668	63¢ Ottawa Senators coil	....	1.50	.70
2669	63¢ Home and Away Uniforms of Canadian NHL teams Sheet of 7		9.75	9.75
2669a	63¢ Vancouver Canucks Player and Fan	....	1.50	.70
2669b	63¢ Edmonton Oilers Player and Fan	....	1.50	.70
2669c	63¢ Toronto Maple Leafs Player and Fan	....	1.50	.70
2669d	63¢ Montreal Canadians Player and Fan	....	1.50	.70
2669e	63¢ Calgary Flames Player and Fan	....	1.50	.70
2669f	63¢ Winnipeg Jets Player and Fan	....	1.50	.70
2669g	63¢ Ottawa Senators Player and Fan	....	1.50	.70
2670	63¢ Vancouver Canucks Player and Fan booklet single		1.50	.70
2670a	same, booklet pane of 10		13.50	....
2671	63¢ Edmonton Oilers Player and Fan booklet single		1.50	.70
2671a	same, booklet pane of 10		13.50	....
2672	63¢ Toronto Maple Leafs Player and Fan booklet single		1.50	.70
2672a	same, booklet pane of 10		13.50	....
2673	63¢ Montreal Canadians Player and Fan booklet single		1.50	.70
2673a	same, booklet pane of 10		13.50	....
2674	63¢ Calgary Flames Player and Fan booklet single	....	1.50	.70
2674a	same, booklet pane of 10		13.50	....
2675	63¢ Winnipeg Jets Player and Fan booklet single	....	1.50	.70
2675a	same, booklet pane of 10		13.50	....
2676	63¢ Ottawa Senators Player and Fan booklet single		1.50	.70
2676a	same, booklet pane of 10		13.50	....

2677

SCOTT NO.	DESCRIPTION	PLATE BLOCK F/NH	UNUSED F/NH	USED F
2677	P Superman Sheet of 5	....	7.25	7.25
2677a	P Superman leaping tall buildings	....	1.50	.70
2677b	P Superman and lightening bolts	....	1.50	.70
2677c	P Superman breaking chanins	....	1.50	.70
2677d	P Superman over Daily Planet	....	1.50	.70
2677e	P Superman in stormy sky	....	1.50	.70
2678	P Superman Comics 75th Anniversary	....	1.50	.70
2679	P Superman leaping tall buildings booklet single	....	1.50	.70
2680	P Superman and lightening bolts booklet single	....	1.50	.70
2681	P Superman breaking chanins booklet single	....	1.50	.70

2678

2686

SCOTT NO.	DESCRIPTION	PLATE BLOCK F/NH	UNUSED F/NH	USED F
2682	P Superman over Daily Planet booklet single	....	1.50	.70
2683	P Superman in stormy sky booklet single	....	1.50	.70
2683a	Same, booklet pane of 10, 2 each of 2679-83	....	13.50	....
2684	P Hastings and Prince Edward Regiment	....	1.50	.70
2684a	same, bklt pane of 10	....	13.50	....
2685	P Birth of Prince George sheet of 2	....	3.00	3.00
2685a	P Birth of Prince George single from sheet	....	1.50	.70
2686	P Birth of Prince George booklet single	....	1.50	.70
2686a	same, bklt pane of 10	....	13.50	....
2687	Christmas sheet of 3	....	7.75	....
2687a	63¢ Christmas horn single from sheet	....	1.50	.70
2687b	$1.10 Cross-Stitched reindeer	....	2.50	1.50
2687c	$1.85 Cross-stitched Christmas Tree	....	3.75	2.00
2688	63¢ Cross-stitched Horn bklt single, D/C	....	1.50	.70
2688a	Same, bklt pane of 12	....	16.00	....
2689	63¢ Cross-stitched Horn bklt single, D/C 13.25 x 13	....	1.50	.70
2689a	Same, bklt pane of 12	....	16.00	....
2690	$1.10 Cross-Stitched reindeer	....	2.50	1.25
2690a	Same, bklt pane of 6	....	14.00	....
2691	$1.85 Cross-stitched Christmas Tree	....	3.75	2.00
2691a	Same, bklt pane of 6	....	22.00	....
2692	63¢ four woodchuck pups coil D/C	....	1.50	1.50
2692a	63¢ four woodchuck pups coil D/C 8.25 horiz.	....	1.50	1.50
2693	63¢ Flag Design on Chairs, bklt single D/C	....	1.50	1.50
2694	63¢ Flag on Hay Roll, bklt single D/C	....	1.50	1.50
2695	63¢ Flag Design on Spinnaker, bklt single, D/C	....	1.50	1.50
2696	63¢ Flag in Flower Bed, bklt single, D/C	....	1.50	1.50
2697	63¢ Flag Design on Hut, bklt single, D/C	....	1.50	1.50
2697a	same, bklt pane of 10, 2 each 2693-97	....	13.50	....
2698	63¢ Queen Elizabeth II, bklt single D/C	....	1.50	1.50
2698a	same, bklt pane of 10	....	13.50	....

2699

2704c

2705

2014 COMMEMORATIVES

SCOTT NO.	DESCRIPTION	PLATE BLOCK F/NH	UNUSED F/NH	USED F
2699	$1.85 Year of the Horse	....	1.50	1.50
2700	$1.85 Year of the Horse	....	3.75	3.75
2700a	$1.85 Year of the Horse S/S of 2, #2600 & #2700	....	7.50	7.50
2701	$1.85 Year of the Horse bklt single D/C	....	3.95	....
2701a	same, bklt pane of 6	....	25.00	....
2702	63¢ Africville, Halifax, Nova Scotia bklt single D/C	....	1.50	1.50
2702a	same, bklt pane of 10	....	13.50	....
2703	63¢ Hogan's Alley, Vancouver, BC bklt single D/C13.25	....	1.50	1.50
2703a	same, bklt pane of 10	....	13.50	....
2704	63¢ Female Athletes, sheet of 3	....	4.50	4.50
2704a	63¢ Barbara Ann Scott, figure skater	....	1.50	1.50
2704b	63¢ Sandra Schmirler, curler	....	1.50	1.50
2704c	63¢ Sarah Burke, freestyle skier	....	1.50	1.50
2705	63¢ Barbara Ann Scott, figure skater, bklt single D/C 13.25	....	1.50	1.50
2705a	same, bklt pane of 10	....	13.50	....
2706	63¢ Sandra Schmirler, curler, bklt single D/C 13.25	....	1.50	1.50
2706a	same, bklt pane of 10	....	13.50	....

2711

2714

SCOTT NO.	DESCRIPTION	PLATE BLOCK F/NH	UNUSED F/NH	USED F
2707	63¢ Sarah Burke, freestyle skier, bklt single D/C	....	1.50	1.50
2707a	same, bklt pane of 10	....	13.50	....
2708	22¢ Monarch butterfly, perf 13.25 x 13	....	.50	.35
2709	Juvenile Wildlife S/S of 5	....	15.00	15.00
2709a	P Beaver Kits	....	1.75	.90
2709b	$1.00 Burrowing Owl Chicks	....	2.15	1.00

SCOTT NO.	DESCRIPTION	PLATE BLOCK F/NH	UNUSED F/NH	USED F
2709c	$1.20 Mountain Goat Kid	....	2.50	1.25
2709d	$1.80 Puffin chicks	....	3.50	1.75
2709e	$2.50 Newborn wapiti	....	4.75	2.50
2710	$1 Burrowing Owl Chicks coil, D/C 13.50	....	2.15	1.00
2710a	P Beaver Kits	....	1.75	.85
2711	P Beaver Kits coil D/C 8.25	....	1.75	.90
2712	$1.20 Mountain Goat Kid coil D/C 8.25	....	2.50	1.25
2713	$1.80 Puffin chicks coil, D/C 8.25	....	3.50	1.75
2714	$2.50 Newborn wapiti coil, D/C 8.25	....	4.75	2.50
2715	$1.20 Mountain Goat Kid, bklt single D/C 9.25	....	2.50	1.25
2715a	same, bklt pane of 6	....	14.50	....
2716	$1.80 Puffin chicks, bklt single D/C 9.25	....	3.50	1.75
2716a	same, bklt pane of 6	....	21.00	....
2717	$2.50 Newborn wapiti, bklt single, D/C 9.25	....	4.75	2.50
2717a	same, bklt pane of 6	....	28.00	....
2718	P National Parks souvenir sheet of 5	....	9.00	9.00
2718a	P Gros Morne National Park	....	1.75	.95
2718b	P Joggins Fossil Cliffs	....	1.75	.95
2718c	P Canadian Rocky Mountains Park	....	1.75	.95
2718d	P Nahinni National Park	....	1.75	.95
2718e	Miguasha National Park	....	1.75	.95
2719	P Gros Morne Nat. Park bklt single, D/C 13.25	....	1.75	.95
2720	P Nahinni National Park bklt single D/C 13.25	....	1.75	.95
2721	P Joggins Fossil Cliffs bklt single d/c 13.25	....	1.75	.95
2722	Miguasha National Park bklt single D/C 13.25	....	1.75	.95

2725

2727a-b

SCOTT NO.	DESCRIPTION	PLATE BLOCK F/NH	UNUSED F/NH	USED F
2723	P Canadian Rocky Mtns. Park bklt single D/C13.25	....	1.75	.95
2723a	same, bklt pane of 10, 2 each 2719-23	....	18.00	....
2723b	same, Booklet pane of 30	....	49.00	....
2724	P Unesco World Heritage Sites sheet of 2	....	3.75	3.75
2724a	P Shiva Natajara Sculpture, mummified cat & bison		1.75	1.00
2724b	P Hadrasaur skeleton & Luohan Chinese sculpture		1.75	1.00
2725	P Shiva Natajara Sculpture, mummified cat & bison bklt single		1.75	1.00
2726	P Hadrasaur skeleton & Luohan Chinese sculpture bklt single		1.75	1.00
2726a	same, bklt pane of 10, 5 each 2725-26		18.00	....
2727	P Roses, Sheet of 2	....	3.25	3.25
2727a	P Konrad Henkel (Red) Rose	....	1.75	.95
2727b	P Maid of Honor (White) Rose	....	1.75	.95
2728-29	P Roses Coil Pair	....	3.50	....
2728	P Maid of Honor (White)Coil Rose	....	1.75	.95
2729	P Konrad Henkel (Red) Coil Rose	....	1.75	.95
2730	P Konrad Henkel (Red) Rose Booklet Single	....	1.75	.95
2731	P Maid of Honor (White) Rose Booklet Single	....	1.75	.95
2731a	Same, Booklet pane of 10	....	17.50	....
2732	$2.50 Komagata Maru Incident Booklet Single	....	5.00	3.50
2732a	Same, Booklet Pane of 6	....	32.50	....
2733	National Film Board, Sheet of 5 + Label	....	8.50	8.50
2733a	P Flamenco at 5:15	....	1.75	.95
2733b	P The Railrodder	....	1.75	.95
2733c	P Mon Oncle Antoine	....	1.75	.95
2733d	P Log Driver's Waltz	....	1.75	.95
2733e	P Neighbours	....	1.75	.95
2734	P Flamenco at 5:15 Booklet Single	....	1.75	.95
2735	P The Railrodder Booklet Single	....	1.75	.95
2736	P Mon Oncle Antoine Booklet Single	....	1.75	.95
2737	P Log Driver's Waltz Booklet Single	....	1.75	.95
2738	P Neighbours Booklet Single	....	1.75	.95
2738a	National Film Board, Sheet of 6	....	17.50	....
2739	UNESCO World Heritage Sites Miniature Sheet	....	17.50	17.50
2739a	$1.20 Head-Smashed-In Buffalo Jump	....	2.50	1.25
2739b	$1.20 Old Town Lunenburg	....	2.50	1.25
2739c	$1.20 Landscape of Grand Pre	....	2.50	1.25
2739d	$2.50 SGang Gwaay	....	5.00	2.50
2739e	$2.50 Rideau Canal	....	5.00	2.50
2740	$1.20 Old Town Lunenburg Booklet Single	....	2.50	1.25
2741	$1.20 Head-Smashed-In Buffalo Jump Bklt Single	....	2.50	1.25
2742	$1.20 Landescape of Grand Pre Booklet Single	....	2.50	1.25
2742a	Booklet Pane of 6	....	14.50	....
2743	$2.50 SGang Gwaay Booklet Single	....	5.00	2.50
2744	$2.50 Rideau Canal Booklet Single	....	5.00	2.50
2744a	Booklet Pane of 6	....	29.50	....

2746

2748c

SCOTT NO.	DESCRIPTION	PLATE BLOCK F/NH	UNUSED F/NH	USED F
2745	P Empress of Ireland	....	1.75	.95
2746	$2.50 Empress of Ireland Souvenir Sheet	....	5.00	2.50
2747	P Empress of Ireland Booklet Single	....	1.75	.95
2747a	Same, Booklet Pane of 10	....	17.50	....
2748	P Haunted Canada, Sheet of 5	....	8.50	8.50
2748a	P Ghost Bride	....	1.75	.95
2748b	P Ghost Train	....	1.75	.95
2748c	P Apparitions of Fort George	....	1.75	.95
2748d	P Count of Frontenac Hotel	....	1.75	.95
2748e	P Phantom Ship	....	1.75	.95
2749	P Ghost Bride Booklet Single	....	1.75	.95
2750	P Phantom Ship Booklet Single	....	1.75	.95
2751	P Ghost Train Booklet Single	....	1.75	.95
2752	P Count of Frontenac Hotel Booklet Single	....	1.75	.95
2753	P Apparitions of Fort George Booklet Single	....	1.75	.95
2753a	Booklet Pane of 10	....	17.50	....

2758

2765c

2771

SCOTT NO.	DESCRIPTION	PLATE BLOCK F/NH	UNUSED F/NH	USED F
2754	P Russ Jackson in Ottawa Rough Riders Uniform	....	1.75	.95
2755	P Russ Jackson in Ottawa Rough Riders Uniform Booklet Single	....	1.75	.95
2755a	Same, Booklet pane of 10	....	17.50	....
2756	Photography, Sheet of 3	....	5.75	5.75
2756a	P Unidentified Chinese Man	....	1.75	.95
2756b	P St. Joseph's Covenant School	....	1.75	.95
2756c	$1.20 Sitting Bull and Buffalo Bill	....	3.25	1.50
2757	Photography, Sheet of 4	....	10.50	10.50
2757a	P Untitled by Lynne Cohen	....	1.75	.95
2757b	P La Ville de Quebec en Hiver	....	1.75	.95
2757c	P Bogner's Grocery	....	1.75	.95
2757d	$2.50 Rallcuts #1	....	5.50	2.75
2758	P Bogner's Grocery Booklet Single	....	1.75	.95
2759	P St. Joseph's Convenant School Booklet Single	....	1.75	.95
2760	P La Ville de Quebec en Hiver	....	1.75	.95
2761	P Untitled by Lynne Cohen, Booklet Single	....	1.75	.95
2762	P Unidentified Chinese Man	....	1.75	.95
2762a	Booklet pane of 10, 2 each of 2758-62	....	17.50	....
2763	$1.20 Sitting Bull and Buffalo Bill Booklet Single	....	2.50	1.25
2763a	Booklet Pane of 6	....	14.50	....
2764	$2.50 Rallcuts #1 Booklet Single	....	5.25	2.75
2764a	Same, Booklet Pane of 6	....	31.00	....
2765	Country Music Recording Artists, Sheet of 5	....	9.00	9.00
2765a	P Hand Snow	....	1.75	.95
2765b	P Renee Martel	....	1.75	.95
2765c	P Shania Twain	....	1.75	.95
2765d	P Tommy Hunter	....	1.75	.95
2765e	P K. D. Lang	....	1.75	.95
2766	P Hank Snow Booklet Single	....	1.75	.95
2766a	Same, Booklet of 10	....	17.50	....
2767	P Renee Martel Booklet Single	....	1.75	.95
2767a	Same, Booklet Pane of 10	....	17.50	....
2768	P Shania Twain Booklet Single	....	1.75	.95
2768a	Same, Booket Pane of 10	....	17.50	....
2769	P Tommy Hunter Booket Single	....	1.75	.95
2769a	Same, Booklet Pane of 10	....	17.50	....
2770	P K. D. Lang Booklet Single	....	1.75	.95
2770a	Same, Booklet Pane of 10	....	17.50	....
2771	P Canadian Museum for Human Rights	....	1.75	.95
2771a	Same, Booklet Pane of 10	....	17.50	....

2772b

2772e

SCOTT NO.	DESCRIPTION	PLATE BLOCK F/NH	UNUSED F/NH	USED F
2772	P Comedians, Sheet of 5	....	9.00	....
2772a	P Mike Myers	....	1.75	.95
2772b	P Martin Short	....	1.75	.95
2772c	P Catherine O'Hara	....	1.75	.95
2772d	P Olivier Guimond	....	1.75	.95
2772e	P Jim Carrey	....	1.75	.95
2773	P Mike Myers Booklet Single	....	1.75	.95
2773a	Booklet pane of 10, 6 of 2773, 1 each of 2774-77	....	17.50	....
2774	P Martin Short Booklet Single	....	1.75	.95
2774a	Booklet pane of 10, 6 of 2774, 1 each of 2773, 2775-77	....	17.50	....
2775	P Catherine O'Hara Booklet Single	....	1.75	.95
2775a	Booklet pane of 10, 6 of 2775, 1 each of 2773-74, 2776-77	....	17.50	....
2776	P Olivier Guimond Booklet Single	....	1.75	.95
2776a	Booklet pane of 10, 6 of 2776, 1 each of 2773-75, 2777	....	17.50	....
2777	P Jim Carrey Booklet Single	....	1.75	.95
2777a	Booklet pane of 10, 6 of 2777, 1 each of 2773-76	....	17.50	....

2779

2787a

SCOTT NO.	DESCRIPTION	PLATE BLOCK F/NH	UNUSED F/NH	USED F
2778	P Canadian NHL Zambonis Sheet of 7	....	12.00	12.00
2778a	P Winnipeg Jets	....	1.75	.95
2778b	P Ottawa Senators	....	1.75	.95
2778c	P Toronto Maple Leafs	....	1.75	.95
2778d	P Montreal Canadians	....	1.75	.95
2778e	P Vancouver Canucks	....	1.75	.95
2778f	P Calgary Flames	....	1.75	.95
2778g	P Edmonton Oilers	....	1.75	.95
2779-85	P Canadian NHL Zambonis Coil	....	12.00	....
2779	P Winnipeg Jets Coil	....	1.75	.95
2780	P Ottawa Senators Coil	....	1.75	.95
2781	P Toronto Maple Leafs Coil	....	1.75	.95
2782	P Montreal Canadians Coil	....	1.75	.95
2783	P Vancouver Canucks Coil	....	1.75	.95
2784	P Calgary Flames Coil	....	1.75	.95
2785	P Edmonton Oilers Coil	....	1.75	.95
2786	P NHL Hall of Fame Defensemen, Sheet of 6	....	10.50	10.50
2786a	P Tim Horton	....	1.75	.95
2786b	P Doug Harvey	....	1.75	.95
2786c	P Bobby Orr	....	1.75	.95
2786d	P Harry Howell	....	1.75	.95
2786e	P Pierre Pilote	....	1.75	.95
2786f	P Red Kelly	....	1.75	.95
2787	P NHL Hall of Fame Defensemen, Bklt Pane of 6	....	10.50	....
2787a	P Tim Horton Booklet Single	....	1.75	.95
2787b	P Doug Harvey Booklet Single	....	1.75	.95
2787c	P Bobby Orr Booklet Single	....	1.75	.95
2787d	P Harry Howell Booklet Single	....	1.75	.95
2787e	P Pierre Pilote Booklet Single	....	1.75	.95
2787f	P Red Kelly Booklet Single	....	1.75	.95
2788	$2.50 Tim Horton Souvenir Sheet	....	5.00	2.50
2789	$2.50 Doug Harvey Souvenir Sheet	....	5.00	2.50
2790	$2.50 Bobby Orr Souvenir Sheet	....	5.00	2.50
2791	$2.50 Harry Howell Souvenir Sheet	....	5.00	2.50
2792	$2.50 Pierre Pilote Souvenir Sheet	....	5.00	2.50
2793	$2.50 Red Kelly Souvenir Sheet	....	5.00	2.50

2794

2797

2799

2801

2804

SCOTT NO.	DESCRIPTION	PLATE BLOCK F/NH	UNUSED F/NH	USED F
2794	P "Wait for me Daddy"	....	1.75	.95
2795	P "Wait for me Daddy" Booklet Single	....	1.75	.95
2795a	Same, Booklet Pane of 10	....	17.50	....
2796	Santa Claus, Sheet of 3	....	9.00	9.00
2796a	P Santa Writing Letter	....	1.75	.95
2796b	$1.20 Santa Carrying Sack	....	1.75	.95
2796c	$2.50 Santa with Dove	....	1.75	.95
2797	P Virgin & Child with John the Baptist	....	1.75	.95
2797a	Same, Booklet Pane of 12	....	19.00	....
2798	P Santa Writing Letter, Booklet Single	....	1.75	.95
2798a	Same, Booklet Pane of 12	....	19.00	....
2799	$1.20 Santa Carrying Sack, Booklet Single	....	2.50	1.25
2799a	Same, Booklet Pane of 6	....	14.50	....
2800	$2.50 Santa with Dove, Booklet Single	....	5.00	2.50
2800a	Same, Booklet Pane of 6	....	29.50	....

2015 COMMEMORATIVES

SCOTT NO.	DESCRIPTION	PLATE BLOCK F/NH	UNUSED F/NH	USED F
2801	P Year of the Ram	....	1.75	.95
2802	$2.50 Year of the Ram, Souvenir Sheet	....	4.50	4.50
2802a	Year of the Ram, Souvenir Sheet of 2, #2700, 2802	....	7.75	7.75
2803	$2.50 Year of the Ram, Booklet Single	....	4.50	2.50
2803a	Same, Booklet Pane of 6	....	26.50	....
2804	P Sir John A MacDonald, First Prime Minister	....	1.75	.95
2804a	Same, Booklet Pane of 10	....	17.50	....

SCOTT NO.	DESCRIPTION	PLATE BLOCK F/NH	UNUSED F/NH	USED F
2805	$2.50 Nelson Mandela Souvenir Sheet	....	4.50	4.50
2806	P Nelson Mandela	....	1.65	.85
2806a	Same, Booklet Pane of 10	....	16.50	....
2807	P Canadian Flag	....	1.65	.85
2807a	Same, Booklet Pane of 10	....	16.50	....
2808	$5 Canadian Flag, 50th Anniversary Souvenir Sheet	....	9.50	9.50
2809	P Pansies Souvenir Sheet of 2	....	3.00	3.00
2809a	P Delta Premium Pure Light Blue Pansy (blue and yellow flower)	....	1.50	.85
2809b	P Midnight Glow Pansy (purple and yellow flower)	....	1.50	.85

2823c

2831

2833

SCOTT NO.	DESCRIPTION	PLATE BLOCK F/NH	UNUSED F/NH	USED F
2810-11	P Pansies Attached Pair	....	3.00	....
2810	P Delta Premium Pure Light Blue Pansy Coil	....	1.50	.85
2811	P Midnight Glow Pansy Coil	....	1.50	.85
2812	P Delta Premium Pure Light Blue Pansy Booklet Single	....	1.50	.85
2813	P Midnight Glow Pansy Booklet Single	....	1.50	.85
2813a	Same, Booklet Pane of 10, 5 each of 2812-13	....	15.50	....
2814	Photography sheet of 3	....	7.75	7.75
2814a	P Shoeshine Stand	....	1.75	.85
2814b	P Southan Sisters	....	1.75	.85
2814c	$2.50 La Voie Lactee	....	4.50	2.50
2815	Photography sheet of 4	....	7.00	7.00
2815a	P Angels	....	1.75	.85
2815b	P Isaac's First Swim	....	1.75	.85
2815c	P Friends and Family and Trips	....	1.75	.85
2815d	$1.20 Alex Colville	....	2.25	1.25
2816	P Angels booklet single	....	1.75	.85
2817	P Southan Sisters booklet single	....	1.75	.85
2818	P Friends and Family and Trips booklet single	....	1.75	.85
2819	P Isaac's First Swim booklet single	....	1.75	.85
2820	P Shoeshine Stand booklet single	....	1.75	.85
2820a	P Photography, booklet pane of 10	....	16.00	....
2821	$1.20 Photography	....	2.25	1.25
2821a	same, booklet pane of 6	....	13.50	....
2822	$2.50 Photography	....	4.50	2.50
2822a	same, booklet pane of 6	....	27.00	....
2823	P Dinosaurs, sheet of 5	....	8.50	....
2823a	P Euplocephalus Tutus	....	1.75	.85
2823b	P Chasmosaurus Belli	....	1.75	.85
2823c	P Tyrannosaurus Rex	....	1.75	.85
2823d	P Ornithomimus Edmontonicus	....	1.75	.85
2823e	P Tylosaurus Pembinensis	....	1.75	.85
2824	P Tyrannosaurus Rex booklet single	....	1.75	.85
2825	P Tylosaurus Pembinensis booklet single	....	1.75	.85
2826	P Chasmosaurus Belli booklet single	....	1.75	.85
2827	P Euplocephalus Tutus booklet single	....	1.75	.85
2828	P Ornithomimus Edmontonicus booklet single	....	1.75	.85
2828a	same, booklet pane of 10	....	17.50	....
2829	P Love Your Pet, sheet of 5	....	8.50	....
2829a	P Cat in Head Cone Sniffing Flowers	....	1.65	.85
2829b	P Dog Chasing Snowball	....	1.65	.85
2829c	P Veterinarian Examining Cat	....	1.65	.85
2829d	P Dog Drinking Water from Bowl	....	1.65	.85
2829e	P Cat on Leash Weraing ID Tags	....	1.65	.85
2830	P Cat in Head Cone Sniffing Flowers, bklt single	....	1.65	.85
2831	P Dog Chasing Snowball, booklet single	....	1.65	.85
2832	P Veterinarian Examining Cat, booklet single	....	1.65	.85
2833	P Cat on Leash Wearing ID Tags, booklet single	....	1.65	.85
2834	P Dog Drinking Water from Bowl, booklet single	....	1.65	.85
2834a	P Love Your Pet, booklet of 10	....	16.50	....

2838b

2838d

SCOTT NO.	DESCRIPTION	PLATE BLOCK F/NH	UNUSED F/NH	USED F
2835	P In Flander's Field	....	1.65	.85
2836	P In Flander's Field, booklet single	....	1.65	.85
2836a	same, booklet pane of 10	....	16.50	....
2837	P Woman's World Cup Soccer Championships	....	1.65	.85
2837a	same, booklet pane of 10	....	16.50	....
2838	P Weather Phenomena, sheet of 5 plus label	....	7.50	7.50
2838a	P Lightening	....	1.50	.75
2838b	P Double Rainbow	....	1.50	.75
2838c	P Sun Dog Over Iqaluit, Nunavut	....	1.50	.75
2838d	P Fog near Cape Spear Lighthouse	....	1.50	.75
2838e	P Hoar Frost on Tree	....	1.50	.75
2839	P Lightening	....	1.50	.75
2840	P Hoar Frost on Tree	....	1.50	.75
2841	P Fog near Cape Spear Lighthouse	....	1.50	.75
2842	P Sun Dog Over Iqaluit, Nunavut	....	1.50	.75
2843	P Double Rainbow	....	1.50	.75
2843a	same, booklet pane of 10	....	15.00	....

SCOTT NO.	DESCRIPTION	PLATE BLOCK F/NH	UNUSED F/NH	USED F

2844b, 2847

2844e, 2849

SCOTT NO.	DESCRIPTION	PLATE BLOCK F/NH	UNUSED F/NH	USED F
2844	UNESCO World Heritage Sites, sheet of 5	....	....	....
2844a	$1.20 Hoodoos, Alberta	....	....	....
2844b	$1.20 Woods Buffalo National Park	....	....	....
2844c	$1.20 Red Bay Basque Whaling Station	....	....	....
2844d	$2.50 Waterton Glacier International Peace Park	....	....	....
2844e	$2.50 Kluane National Park, Yukon	....	....	....
2845	$1.20 Hoodoos, Alberta	....	....	....
2846	$1.20 Red Bay Basque Whaling Station	....	....	....
2847	$1.20 Woods Buffalo National Park	....	....	....
2847a	$1.20 Canada Sites, booklet pane of 6	....	....	....
2848	$2.50 Waterton Glacier International Peace Park	....	4.50	2.50
2849	$2.50 Kluane National Park, Yukon	....	4.50	2.50
2849a	same, booklet pane of 6	....	26.00	....

2851

2860a

SCOTT NO.	DESCRIPTION	PLATE BLOCK F/NH	UNUSED F/NH	USED F
2850	P Alice Munro, 2013 Nobel Literature Laureate	....	1.50	.75
2850a	same, booklet pane of 10	....	15.00	....
2851-52	P Franklin Expedition, set of 2	....	3.00	1.50
2851	P HMS Erebus Trapped in Ice	....	1.50	.75
2852	P Map of Northern Canadian Islands	....	1.50	.75
2853	$2.50 Franklin Expedition, souvenir sheet	....	4.00	2.00
2854	P HMS Erebus Trapped in Ice	....	1.50	.75
2855	P Map of Northern Canadian Islands	....	1.50	.75
2855a	same, booklet pane of 10, 5 each 2853-54	....	15.00	....
2856	$2.50 Wreckage and Diagram of HMS Erebus	....	4.25	2.25
2856a	same, booklet pane of 6	....	23.50	....
2857	UNESCO World Heritage Sites, sheet of 5, Reissue	....	16.00	....
2846-47, 58	$1.20-$2.50 Reissue singles, set of 3	....	7.75	....
2858a	same, booklet pane of 6	....	12.50	....
2859	P Queen Elizabeth II	....	1.50	.75
2859a	same, booklet pane of 10	....	15.00	....
2860	P Haunted Canada, sheet of 5	....	7.50	7.50
2860a	P Brakeman Ghost, Vancouver, BC	....	1.50	.75
2860b	P Red River Trail Oxcart, Winnepeg	....	1.50	.75
2860c	P Gray Lady of the Citadel, Halifax	....	1.50	.75
2860d	P Ghost of Marie-Josephte Corriveau, Levis	....	1.50	.75
2860e	P Ghost of Caribou Hotel, Carcross, Yukon	....	1.50	.75
2861	P Brakeman Ghost, Vancouver, BC	....	1.50	.75
2862	P Ghost of Marie-Josephte Corriveau, Levis	....	1.50	.75
2863	P Gray Lady of the Citadel, Halifax	....	1.50	.75
2864	P Red River Trail Oxcart, Winnepeg	....	1.50	.75
2865	P Ghost of Caribou Hotel, Carcross, Yukon	....	1.50	.75
2865a	same, booklet pane of 10, 2 each	....	15.00	....

2866a

2879

SCOTT NO.	DESCRIPTION	PLATE BLOCK F/NH	UNUSED F/NH	USED F
2866	P Hockey Goaltenders, sheet of 6	....	7.75	7.75
2866a	P Ken Dryden	....	1.50	.75
2866b	P Tony Esposito	....	1.50	.75
2866c	P Johnny Bower	....	1.50	.75
2866d	P Gump Worsley	....	1.50	.75
2866e	P Bernie Parent	....	1.50	.75
2866f	P Martin Brodeur	....	1.50	.75
2867	P Ken Dryden, booklet single	....	1.50	.75
2868	P Tony Esposito, booklet single	....	1.50	.75
2869	P Johnny Bower, booklet single	....	1.50	.75
2870	P Gump Worsley, booklet single	....	1.50	.75
2871	P Bernie Parent, booklet single	....	1.50	.75
2872	P Martin Brodeur, booklet single	....	1.50	.75
2872a	same, booklet pane of 6	....	9.00	....
2873	P Ken Dryden, souvenir sheet	....	3.25	....
2874	P Tony Esposito, souvenir sheet	....	3.25	....
2875	P Johnny Bower, souvenir sheet	....	3.25	....
2876	P Gump Worsley, souvenir sheet	....	3.25	....
2877	P Bernie Parent, souvenir sheet	....	3.25	....
2878	P Martin Brodeur, souvenir sheet	....	3.25	....
2879	P $1.20-$2.50 Christmas, sheet of 3	....	9.50	....
2879a	P Moose	....	1.50	....
2879b	$1.20 Beaver	....	2.25	....
2879c	$2.50 Polar Bear	....	4.50	....

2880

2884

2888

SCOTT NO.	DESCRIPTION	PLATE BLOCK F/NH	UNUSED F/NH	USED F
2880	P Adoration of the Magi		1.50	....
2880a	same, booklet pane of 12		17.50	....
2881	P Moose, booklet single		1.50	....
2881a	same, booklet pane of 12		17.50	....
2882	$1.20 Beaver, booklet single		2.25	....
2882a	same, booklet pane of 6		12.50	....
2883	$2.50 Polar Bear, booklet single		4.50	....
2883a	same, booklet pane of 6		12.50	....

2897, 2899 2898, 2900

2901

2016 COMMEMORATIVES

SCOTT NO.	DESCRIPTION	PLATE BLOCK F/NH	UNUSED F/NH	USED F
2884	P Year of the Monkey		1.50	....
2885	$2.50 Year of the Monkey, souvenir sheet		4.50	....
2885a	$2.50 souvenir sheet of 2, 2885 and 2802b		7.75	....
2886	P Year of the Monkey, booklet single		1.50	....
2886a	same, booklet pane of 10		13.00	....
2887	$2.50 Year of the Monkey, booklet single		4.50	....
2887a	same, booklet pane of 6		23.50	....
2888	P Queen Elizabeth II		1.50	....
2888a	same, booklet pane of 10		13.00	....
2889	UNESCO World Heritage Sites, sheet of 5		6.50	....
2889a	P Landscape of Grand Pre, Nova Scotia		1.50	....
2889b	P Rideau Canal, Ontario		1.50	....
2889c	P Sgang Gwaay, British Columbia		1.50	....
2889d	P Head-Smashed-in Buffalo Jump, Alberta		1.50	....
2889e	P Old Town Lunenburg, Nova Scotia		1.50	....
2890	P Landscape of Grand Pre, Nova Scotia, bklt single		1.50	....
2891	P Sgang Gwaay, British Columbia, bklt single		1.50	....
2892	P Old Town Lunenburg, Novia Scotia, bklt single		1.50	....
2893	P Rideau Canal, Ontario, booklet single		1.50	....
2894	P Head-Smashed-in Buffalo Jump, Alberta, booklet single		1.50	....
2894a	same, booklet pane of 10		13.00	....
2894b	same, booklet pane of 30		39.00	....
2895	P Organization of No. 2 Construction Battalion		1.50	....
2895a	same, booklet page of 10		13.50	....
2896	P Hydrangeas, sheet of 2, water activated		3.00	....
2896a	P Hydrangea Macrophylia		1.50	....
2896b	P Hydrangea Arborescens		1.50	....
2897-98	P Hydrangea coil pair, self-adhesive		3.00	....
2897	P Hydrangea Macrophylia coil, 8.25 vert		1.50	....
2898	P Hydrangea Arborescens coil, 8.25 vert		1.50	....
2899	P Hydrangea Macrophylia, booklet single		1.50	....
2900	P Hydrangea Arborescens, booklet single		1.50	....
2900a	same, booklet pane of 10, 5 each 2899 and 2900		13.00	....
2901	P Woman's Suffrage Centennial		1.50	....
2901a	same, booklet pane of 10		13.00	....

2910

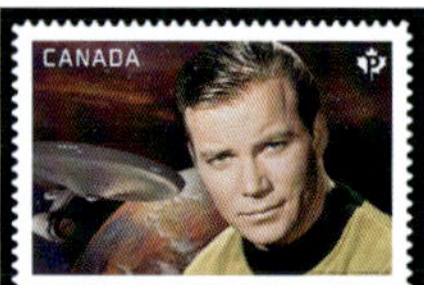

2912a, 2917

2911a, 2913

2911b, 2914

SCOTT NO.	DESCRIPTION	PLATE BLOCK F/NH	UNUSED F/NH	USED F
2902	P Photography, sheet of 4		7.00	....
2903	P-$2.50 Photography, sheet of 3		8.00	....
2904	P Toronto, booklet single		1.50	....
2905	P Window, booklet single		1.50	....
2906	P Freighter's Boat on Banks of Red River, booklet single		1.50	....
2907	P Victoria Bridge, Grand Trunk Railway, booklet single		1.50	....
2908	P Sans Titre 0310/La Chambre Noire, booklet single		1.50	....
2908a	same, booklet pane of 10		14.00	....
2909	$1.20 Climbing Mt. Habel, booklet single		2.25	....
2909a	same, booklet pane of 6		12.50	....
2910	$2.50 Grey Owl, booklet single		4.50	....
2910a	same, booklet pane of 6		26.00	....
2911	P Star Trek Ships, sheet of 2		3.00	....

SCOTT NO.	DESCRIPTION	PLATE BLOCK F/NH	UNUSED F/NH	USED F
2912	P-$2.50 Star Trek, sheet of 5		14.00	....
2912a	P Captain James T. Kirk		1.50	....
2912b	$1 Klingon Commander Kor		2.00	....
2912c	$1.20 Dr. Leonard "Bones" McCoy		2.25	....
2912d	$1.80 Montgomery "Scotty" Scott		3.50	....
2912e	$2.50 Commander Spock		4.50	....
2913-14	P Star Trek Ships, coil pair		3.00	....
2913	P U.S.S. Enterprise, coil single, die cut 8.25		1.50	....
2914	P Klingon Battle Cruiser, coil single, die cut 8.25		1.50	....
2915	P U.S.S. Enterprise, booklet single, die cut 13.75		1.50	....
2916	P Klingon Battle Cruiser, booklet single, die cut 13.75		1.50	....
2916V	P-$2.50 Star Trek Prestige Booklet Complete		35.00	....
2917	P Captain James T. Kirk, booklet single		1.50	....
2918	P Montgomery "Scotty" Scott, booklet single		1.50	....
2919	P Klingon Commander Kor, booklet single		1.50	....
2920	P Commander Spock, booklet single		1.50	....
2921	P Dr. Leonard "Bones" McCoy, booklet single		1.50	....
2921a	same, booklet pane of 10		14.00	....
2922	$5 Star Trek, three-dimensional souvenir sheet of 2		20.00	....

2929b, 2931

2923b, 2926

2935a, 2940

SCOTT NO.	DESCRIPTION	PLATE BLOCK F/NH	UNUSED F/NH	USED F
2923	P Dinosaurs, sheet of 5		8.00	....
2923a	P Troodon Inequalis		1.50	....
2923b	P Dimetrodon Borealis		1.50	....
2923c	P Comox Valley Elasmosaur		1.50	....
2923d	P Cypretherium Coarctatum		1.50	....
2923e	P Acrotholus Audeti		1.50	....
2924	P Troodon Inequalis, booklet single		1.50	....
2925	P Cypretherium Coarctatum		1.50	....
2926	P Dimetrodon Borealis		1.50	....
2927	P Acrotholus Audeti		1.50	....
2928	P Comox Valley Elasmosaur		1.50	....
2928a	same, booklet of 10		14.00	....
2929	P Birds of Canada, sheet of 5		8.00	....
2929a	P Rock Ptarmigan (Lagopus Muta)		1.50	....
2929b	P Great Horned Owl (Bubo Virginianus)		1.50	....
2929c	P Common Raven (Corvus Corax)		1.50	....
2929d	P Atlantic Puffin (Fratercula Arctica)		1.50	....
2929e	P Sharp-tailed Grouse (Tympanuchus Phasianellus)		1.50	....
2930	P Sharp-tailed Grouse (Tympanuchus Phasianellus)		1.50	....
2931	P Great Horned Owl (Bubo Virginianus)		1.50	....
2932	P Atlantic Puffin (Fratercula Arctica)		1.50	....
2933	P Common Raven (Corvus Corax)		1.50	....
2934	P Rock Ptarmigan (Lagopus Muta)		1.50	....
2934a	same, booklet pane of 10		14.00	....
2935	P Haunted Canada, sheet of 5		8.00	....
2935a	P Bell Island Hag		1.50	....
2935b	P Dungarvon Whooper		1.50	....
2935c	P Winter Garden Theatre Ghost		1.50	....
2935d	P Lady in White		1.50	....
2935e	P Phantom Bell Ringers		1.50	....
2936	P Bell Island Hag, booklet single		1.50	....
2937	P Dungarvon Whooper, booklet single		1.50	....
2938	P Lady in White, booklet single		1.50	....
2939	P Winter Garden Theatre Ghost, booklet single		1.50	....
2940	P Phantom Bell Ringers, booklet single		1.50	....
2940a	same, booklet pane of 10		14.00	....

2941e, 2946

2955

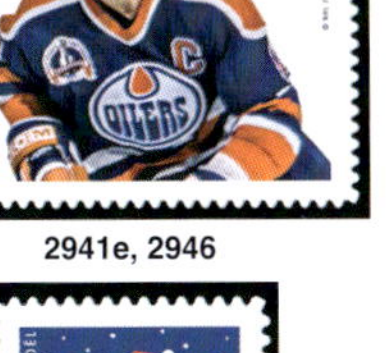

2957

2958

SCOTT NO.	DESCRIPTION	PLATE BLOCK F/NH	UNUSED F/NH	USED F
2941	P National Hockey League Forwards, sheet of 6		9.25	....
2941a	P Sidney Crosby		1.50	....
2941b	P Phil Esposito		1.50	....
2941c	P Guy Lafleur		1.50	....
2941d	P Steve Yzerman		1.50	....
2941e	P Mark Messier		1.50	....
2941f	P Darryl Sittler		1.50	....
2942	P Sidney Crosby, booklet single		1.50	....
2943	P Phil Esposito, booklet single		1.50	....
2944	P Guy Lafleur, booklet single		1.50	....
2945	P Steve Yzerman, booklet single		1.50	....
2946	P Mark Messier, booklet single		1.50	....
2947	P Darryl Sittler, booklet single		1.50	....
2947a	same, booklet pane of 6		9.25	....
2948	$1.80 Sidney Crosby, souvenir sheet		3.50	....
2949	$1.80 Phil Esposito, souvenir sheet		3.50	....
2950	$1.80 Guy Lafleur, souvenir sheet		3.50	....
2951	$1.80 Steve Yzerman, souvenir sheet		3.50	....
2952	$1.80 Mark Messier, souvenir sheet		3.50	....
2953	$1.80 Darryl Sittler, souvenir sheet		3.50	....
2954	P-$2.50 Christmas Trees, sheet of 3		8.00	....
2955	P Virgin and Child, booklet single		1.50	....
2955a	same, booklet pane of 12		18.00	....
2956	P Santa & Christmas Tree, booklet single		1.50	....
2956a	same, booklet pane of 12		18.00	....
2957	$1.20 Christmas Tree in Hat, booklet single		2.25	....
2957a	same, booklet pane of 6		12.25	....
2958	$2.50 Dove & Christmas Tree, booklet single		4.50	....
2958a	same, booklet pane of 6		26.00	....

2959, 2959a, 2961

2963a, 2966

2017 COMMEMORATIVES

SCOTT NO.	DESCRIPTION	PLATE BLOCK F/NH	UNUSED F/NH	USED F
2959	P Year of the Rooster, perf. 12.5 x 13.25		1.50	....
2959a	same, perf. 13.25 x 12.5		1.50	....
2960	$2.50 Year of the Rooster, souvenir sheet		4.50	....
2960a	$2.50 Souvenir Sheet of 2, 2885a, 2960		11.00	....
2961	P Year of the Rooster, booklet single		1.50	....
2961a	same, booklet pane of 10		14.00	....
2962	$2.50 Year of the Rooster, booklet single		4.50	....
2962a	same, booklet pane of 6		27.00	....
2963	P UNESCO World Heritage Sites, sheet of 5		8.00	....
2963a	P Dinosaur Provincial Park		1.50	....
2963b	P Mistaken Point		1.50	....
2963c	P Historic District of Old Quebec		1.50	....
2963d	P L'Anse aux Meadows		1.50	....
2963e	P Red Bay Basque Whaling Station		1.50	....
2964	P Dinosaur Provincial Park, booklet single		1.50	....
2965	P Historic District of Old Quebec, booklet single		1.50	....
2966	P Red Bay Basque Whaling Station, booklet single		1.50	....
2967	P Mistaken Point, booklet single		1.50	....
2968	P L'Anse aux Meadows, booklet single		1.50	....
2968a	same, booklet pane of 10		14.00	....
2968b	same, booklet pane of 30		44.00	....

2969

2970c, 2973

SCOTT NO.	DESCRIPTION	PLATE BLOCK F/NH	UNUSED F/NH	USED F
2969	P Matieu Da Costa, booklet single		1.50	....
2969a	same, booklet pane of 10		14.00	....
2970	P Canadian Opera, sheet of 5		8.00	....
2970a	P *Filumena*		1.50	....
2970b	P Gerald Finley		1.50	....
2970c	P Adrianne Pieczonka		1.50	....
2970d	P Irving Guttman		1.50	....
2970e	P *Louis Riel*		1.50	....
2971	P *Filumena*, booklet single		1.50	....
2972	P Gerald Finley, booklet single		1.50	....
2973	P Adrianne Pieczonka, booklet single		1.50	....
2974	P Irving Guttman, booklet single		1.50	....
2975	P *Louis Riel*, booklet single		1.50	....
2975a	same, booklet pane of 10		14.00	....

2979

2982

2980

SCOTT NO.	DESCRIPTION	PLATE BLOCK F/NH	UNUSED F/NH	USED F
2976	P Daisies, sheet of 2		3.25	....
2977-78	P Daisies, coil pair		3.00	....
2977	P Purple Daisy, coil single		1.50	....
2978	P Yellow Daisy, coil single		1.50	....

SCOTT NO.	DESCRIPTION	UNUSED F/NH	USED F
2979-80	P Daisies, booklet pair	3.00	
2979	P Purple Daisy, booklet single	1.50	
2980	P Yellow Daisy, booklet single	1.50	
2980a	same, booklet pane of 10	14.00	
2981	$2.50 Battle of Vimy Ridge, sheet of 2	10.00	
2982	P Battle of Vimy, booklet single	1.50	
2982a	same, booklet pane of 10	14.00	

2983c, 2989

2983e, 2987

SCOTT NO.	DESCRIPTION	UNUSED F/NH	USED F
2983	P-$2.50 Star Trek II, sheet of 5	14.00	
2983a	P Admiral James T. Kirk	1.50	
2983b	$1 Captain Jonathan Archer	2.00	
2983c	$1.20 Captain Kathryn Janeway	2.25	
2983d	$1.80 Captain Benjamin Sisko	3.50	
2983e	$2.50 Captain Jean-Luc Picard	4.50	

2984

12991

SCOTT NO.	DESCRIPTION	UNUSED F/NH	USED F
2984	$5 Borg Cube, booklet single	11.00	
2984V	P-$5 Star Trek II, Prestige Booklet Complete	36.00	
2985	P Galileo Shuttle, coil single, die cut 8	1.50	
2986	P Admiral James T. Kirk	1.50	
2987	P Captain Jean-Luc Picard	1.50	
2988	P Captain Benjamin Sisko	1.50	
2989	P Captain Kathryn Janeway	1.50	
2990	P Captain Jonathan Archer	1.50	
2990a	same, booklet pane of 10	14.00	
2991	P Galileo Shuttle, bklt single, die cut 13.75	2.75	

2992c, 2995

2999c, 3002

SCOTT NO.	DESCRIPTION	UNUSED F/NH	USED F
2992	P Formula 1 Race Car Drivers, sheet of 5	8.00	
2992a	P Sir Jackie Stewart	1.50	
2992b	P Gilles Villeneuve	1.50	
2992c	P Ayrton Senna	1.50	
2992d	P Micheal Schumacher	1.50	
2992e	P Lewis Hamilton	1.50	
2993	P Sir Jackie Stewart, booklet single	1.50	
2994	P Gilles Villeneuve, booklet single	1.50	
2995	P Ayrton Senna, booklet single	1.50	
2996	P Micheal Schumacher, booklet single	1.50	
2997	P Lewis Hamilton, booklet single	1.50	
2997a	same, booklet pane of 10	14.50	
2998	P EID, booklet single	1.50	
2998a	same, booklet pane of 10	14.50	
2999	P Canadian Confederation, 150th Anniv., sheet of 10	14.50	
2999a	P Habitat 67 at Expo'67	1.50	
2999b	P Route Marker Trans-Canada Hwy.	1.50	
2999c	P Summit Series	1.50	
2999d	P Terry Fox Marathon of Hope	1.50	
2999e	P Canadarm in Space	1.50	
2999f	P Canadian Constitution	1.50	
2999g	P Woman of Nunavut	1.50	
2999h	P Rainbow Flag	1.50	
2999i	P Canadian Olympic Athlete	1.50	
2999j	P Paralympic Skiier	1.50	
3000	P Habitat 67 at Expo'67, booklet single	1.50	
3001	P Route Marker Trans-Canada Hwy., booklet single	1.50	
3002	P Summit Series, booklet single	1.50	
3003	P Terry Fox Marathon of Hope, booklet single	1.50	
3004	P Canadarm in Space, booklet single	1.50	
3005	P Canadian Constitution, booklet single	1.50	
3006	P Woman of Nunavut, booklet single	1.50	
3006a	P Woman of Nunavut, booklet pane of 8	11.50	
3007	P Rainbow Flag, booklet single	1.50	
3007a	P Rainbow Flag, booklet pane of 8	11.50	
3008	P Canadian Olympic Athlete, booklet single	1.50	
3009	P Paralympic Skiier, booklet single	1.50	
3009a	same, 3000-09 one each, booklet pane of 10	14.50	

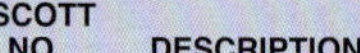

3017c, 3021

3012

SCOTT NO.	DESCRIPTION	UNUSED F/NH	USED F
3010	P Photography, sheet of 2	3.00	
3011	P Photography, sheet of 3	4.50	
3012	P Ti-Noir Lajeunesse, Violinist, booklet single	1.50	
3013	P Enlacees, booklet single	1.50	
3014	P Ontario, Canada, booklet single	1.50	
3015	P Construction of the Parliament Buildings, booklet single	1.50	
3016	P Sir John A. Macdonald, booklet single	1.50	
3016a	same, booklet pane of 10	14.50	
3017	P Birds of Canada, sheet of 5	8.00	
3017a	P Cyanocitta Cristata	1.50	
3017b	P Falco Rusticolus	1.50	
3017c	P Strix Nebulosa	1.50	
3017d	P Pandion Haliaetus	1.50	
3017e	P Gavia Immer	1.50	
3018	P Pandion Haliaetus, booklet single	1.50	
3019	P Falco Rusticolus, booklet single	1.50	
3020	P Cyanocitta Cristata, booklet single	1.50	
3021	P Strix Nebulosa, booklet single	1.50	
3022	P Gavia Immer, booklet single	1.50	
3022a	same, 3018-22 two each, booklet pane of 10	14.50	
3023	$2.50 - $25.00 Diwali - India Joint Issue, sheet of 2	5.25	
3024	P Diwali, floral flame, booklet single	1.50	
3025	P Diwali, single flame, booklet single	1.50	
3025a	P Diwali, 3024-25 five each, booklet of 10	14.50	

3026f, 3032

3044

SCOTT NO.	DESCRIPTION	UNUSED F/NH	USED F
3026	P National Hockey League, Ultimate Six, sheet of 6	9.25	
3026a	P Maurice Richard	1.50	
3026b	P Jean Beliveau	1.50	
3026c	P Gordie Howe	1.50	
3026d	P Bobby Orr	1.50	
3026e	P Mario Lemieux	1.50	
3026f	P Wayne Gretzky	1.50	
3027	P Maurice Richard, booklet single	1.50	
3028	P Jean Beliveau, booklet single	1.50	
3029	P Gordie Howe, booklet single	1.50	
3030	P Bobby Orr, booklet single	1.50	
3031	P Mario Lemieux, booklet single	1.50	
3032	P Wayne Gretzky, booklet single	1.50	
3032a	same, booklet pane of 6	9.25	
3033	$1.80 Maurice Richard, souvenir sheet	3.50	
3034	$1.80 Jean Beliveau, souvenir sheet	3.50	
3035	$1.80 Gordie Howe, souvenir sheet	3.50	
3036	$1.80 Bobby Orr, souvenir sheet	3.50	
3037	$1.80 Mario Lemieux, souvenir sheet	3.50	
3038	$1.80 Wayne Gretzky, souvenir sheet	3.50	
3039	P History of Hockey - U.S. Joint Issue, sheet of 2	3.00	

3047

3048

3049

SCOTT NO.	DESCRIPTION	UNUSED F/NH	USED F
3040	P Hockey Player in Gear, booklet single	1.50	
3041	P Hockey Player in Hat & Scarf, booklet single	1.50	
3041a	same, 3040-41 five each, booklet pane of 10	14.50	
3042	$5 Emblem of Toronto Maple Leafs, souvenir sheet	8.75	
3043	P Emblem of Toronto Maple Leafs, coil single	1.50	
3044	P Maple Leaf and 100, booklet single	1.50	
3044a	same, booklet pane of 10	14.50	
3045	P-$2.50 Christmas Animals, sovenir sheet of 3	8.00	
3046	P Adoration of the Shepherds, booklet single	1.50	
3046a	same, booklet pane of 12	18.00	
3047	P Polar Bear, booklet single	1.50	
3047a	same, booklet pane of 12	18.00	
3048	$1.20 Cardinal, booklet single	2.25	
3048a	same, booklet pane of 6	12.25	
3049	$2.50 Caribou, booklet single	4.50	
3049a	same, booklet pane of 6	26.00	
3050	P Halifax Harbor Cent., booklet single	1.50	
3050a	same, booklet pane of 10	14.50	
3051	P Hanukkah, booklet single	1.50	
3051a	same, booklet pane of 10	14.50	

3057, 3062, 3071

3085

2018 COMMEMORATIVES

SCOTT NO.	DESCRIPTION	UNUSED F/NH	USED F
3052	P Year of the Dog	1.50	.....
3053	$2.50 Year of the Dog, souvenir sheet	4.50	.....
3053a	$2.50 Year of the Dog and Rooster, souvenir sheet	11.50	.....
3054	P Year of the Dog, booklet single	1.50	.....
3054a	same, booklet pane of 10	14.50	.....
3054b	same, booklet pane of 30	44.00	.....
3055	$2.50 Year of the Dog, booklet single	4.50	.....
3055a	same, booklet pane of 6	27.00	.....
3056	P-$2.50 From Far and Wide, souvenir sheet of 9	20.00	.....
3057-61	P From Far and Wide, horiz. coil strip of 5, die-cut 9.25	8.00	.....
3057	P St. John's, coil single, die-cut 9.25	1.50	.....
3058	P Hopewell Rocks, coil single, die-cut 9.25	1.50	.....
3059	P MacMillan Provincial Park, coil single, die-cut 9.25	1.50	.....
3060	P Prince Edwards National Park,coil single, die-cut 9.25	1.50	.....
3061	P Parc National de l'Ile-Bonaventure-et-du-Rocher-Perce, coil single, die-cut 9.25	1.50	.....
3062-66	P From Far and Wide, vert. coil strip of 5, die-cut 8.5	8.00	.....
3062	P St. John's, coil single, die-cut 8.5	1.50	.....
3063	P Hopewell Rocks, coil single, die-cut 8.5	1.50	.....
3064	P MacMillan Provincial Park, coil single, die-cut 8.5	1.50	.....
3065	P Prince Edwards National Park,coil single, die-cut 8.5	1.50	.....
3066	P Parc National de l'Ile-Bonaventure-et-du-Rocher-Perce, coil single, die-cut 8.5	1.50	.....
3067	$1.20 Point Pelle, coil single	2.25	.....
3068	$1.80 Naats'jhch'oh National Park, coil single	3.50	.....
3069	$2.50 Arctic Bay, coil single	4.50	.....
3070	$1 Pisew Falls Park, coil single	2.00	.....
3071	P St. John's, booklet single	1.50	.....
3072	P Hopewell Rocks, booklet single	1.50	.....
3073	P MacMillan Provincial Park, booklet single	1.50	.....
3074	P Prince Edwards National Park, booklet single	1.50	.....
3075	P Parc National de l'Ile-Bonaventure-et-du-Rocher-Perce, booklet single	1.50	.....
3075a	same, booklet pane of 10	14.50	.....
3075b	same, booklet pane of 30	44.00	.....
3076	$1.20 Point Pelle, booklet single	2.25	.....
3076a	same, booklet pane of 6	12.25	.....
3077	$1.80 Naats'jhch'oh National Park, booklet single	3.50	.....
3077a	same, booklet pane of 6	21.00	.....
3078	$2.50 Arctic Bay, booklet single	4.50	.....
3078a	same, booklet pane of 6	27.00	.....
3079	P Canadian Women in Winter Sports, sheet of 5	8.00	.....
3079a	P Nancy Greene	1.50	.....
3079b	P Sharon and Shirley Firth	1.50	.....
3079c	P Danielle Goyette	1.50	.....
3079d	P Clara Hughes	1.50	.....
3079e	P Sonja Gaudet	1.50	.....
3080	P Nancy Greene, booklet single	1.50	.....
3081	P Sharon and Shirley Firth, booklet single	1.50	.....
3082	P Danielle Goyette, booklet single	1.50	.....
3083	P Clara Hughes, booklet single	1.50	.....
3084	P Sonja Gaudet, booklet single	1.50	.....
3084a	same, 3080-84 two each, booklet pane of 10	14.50	.....
3085	P Kay Livingstone, booklet single	1.50	.....
3085a	same, booklet pane of 10	14.50	.....
3086	P Lincoln Alexander, booklet single	1.50	.....
3086a	same, booklet pane of 10	14.50	.....

3088, 3090

3089, 3091

3098

SCOTT NO.	DESCRIPTION	UNUSED F/NH	USED F
3087	P Lotus Flowers, souvenir sheet of 2	3.25	.....
3088-89	P Lotus Flowers, coil pair	3.00	.....
3088	P Pink Lotus, coil single	1.50	.....
3089	P Yellow Lotus, coil single	1.50	.....
3090-91	P Lotus Flowers, booklet pair	3.00	.....
3090	P Pink Lotus, booklet single	1.50	.....
3091	P Yellow Lotus, booklet single	1.50	.....
3091a	same, booklet pane of 10	14.50	.....
3092	P Canadian Illustrators, souvenir sheet of 5	8.00	.....
3092a	P Anita Kunz	1.50	.....
3092b	P Will Davies	1.50	.....
3092c	P Blair Drawson	1.50	.....
3092d	P Gerard Dubois	1.50	.....
3092e	P James Hill	1.50	.....
3093	P Anita Kunz, booklet single	1.50	.....
3094	P Will Davies, booklet single	1.50	.....
3095	P Blair Drawson, booklet single	1.50	.....
3096	P Gerard Dubois, booklet single	1.50	.....
3097	P James Hill, booklet single	1.50	.....
3097a	same, 3093-97 two each, booklet pane of 10	14.50	.....

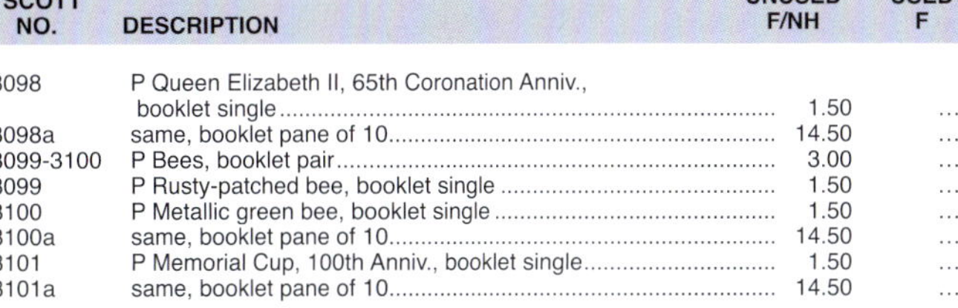

SCOTT NO.	DESCRIPTION	UNUSED F/NH	USED F
3098	P Queen Elizabeth II, 65th Coronation Anniv., booklet single	1.50	.....
3098a	same, booklet pane of 10	14.50	.....
3099-3100	P Bees, booklet pair	3.00	.....
3099	P Rusty-patched bee, booklet single	1.50	.....
3100	P Metallic green bee, booklet single	1.50	.....
3100a	same, booklet pane of 10	14.50	.....
3101	P Memorial Cup, 100th Anniv., booklet single	1.50	.....
3101a	same, booklet pane of 10	14.50	.....

3102b

3105a, 3110

SCOTT NO.	DESCRIPTION	UNUSED F/NH	USED F
3102	P Royal Astronomical Society, souvenir sheet of 2	3.25	.....
3103-04	P Royal Astronomical Society, pair	3.00	.....
3103	P Milky Way, booklet single	1.50	.....
3104	P Northern Lights, booklet single	1.50	.....
3104a	same, booklet pane of 10	14.50	.....
3105	P Sharks, souvenir sheet of 5	8.00	.....
3105a	P Isurus Oxyrinchus	1.50	.....
3105b	P Cetorhimus	1.50	.....
3105c	P Carcharodon	1.50	.....
3105d	P Somniosus	1.50	.....
3105e	P Prionace Glauca	1.50	.....
3106	P Carcharodon, booklet single	1.50	.....
3107	P Cetorhinus, booklet single	1.50	.....
3108	P Somniosus, booklet single	1.50	.....
3109	P Prionace Glauca, booklet single	1.50	.....
3110	P Isurus Oxyrinchus, booklet single	1.50	.....
3110a	same, booklet of 10	14.50	.....

3117a, 3118

3111c, 3115

3117c, 3122

SCOTT NO.	DESCRIPTION	UNUSED F/NH	USED F
3111	P Weather Wonders, souvenir sheet of 5	8.00	.....
3111a	P Steam Fog	1.50	.....
3111b	P Waterspout	1.50	.....
3111c	P Lenticular Clouds	1.50	.....
3111d	P Light Pillars	1.50	.....
3111e	P Moon Halo	1.50	.....
3112	P Steam Fog, booklet single	1.50	.....
3113	P Waterspout, booklet single	1.50	.....
3114	P Lenticular Clouds, booklet single	1.50	.....
3115	P Light Pillars, booklet single	1.50	.....
3116	P Moon Halo, booklet single	1.50	.....
3116a	same, booklet pane of 10	14.50	.....
3117	P Birds of Canada, souvenir sheet of 5	8.00	.....
3117a	P Poecile Atricapillus	1.50	.....
3117b	P Bubo Scandiacus	1.50	.....
3117c	P Cyanocitta Stelleri	1.50	.....
3117d	P Branta Canadensis	1.50	.....
3117e	P Grus Americana	1.50	.....
3117f	P Birds of Canada, Overprint, souvenir sheet of 5	8.00	.....
3118	P Poecile Atricapillus, booklet singles	1.50	.....
3119	P Grus Americana, booklet singles	1.50	.....
3120	P Branta Canadensis, booklet single	1.50	.....
3121	P Bubo Scandiacus, booklet single	1.50	.....
3122	P Cyanocitta Stelleri, booklet single	1.50	.....
3122a	same, booklet pane of 10	14.50	.....

3123d, 3127

3130, 3131

3134

SCOTT NO.	DESCRIPTION	UNUSED F/NH	USED F
3123	P Emergency Responders, souvenir sheet of 5	8.00	.....
3123a	P Canadian Armed Forces and Raft	1.50	.....
3123b	P Paramedics, Ambulances and Helicopter	1.50	.....
3123c	P Firefighters	1.50	.....
3123d	P Police Officers and Skyline	1.50	.....
3123e	P Search and Rescue Crew and Helicopter	1.50	.....
3124	P Canadian Armed Forces and Raft, booklet single	1.50	.....
3125	P Firefighters, booklet single	1.50	.....
3126	P Paramedics, Ambulances and Helicopter, bklt single	1.50	.....
3127	P Police Officers and Skyline, booklet single	1.50	.....
3128	P Search and Rescue Crew and Helicopter, bklt single	1.50	.....
3128a	same, booklet pane of 10	14.50	.....
3129	$4 Rocky Mountain Bighorn Sheep	7.50	.....
3130	P WWI Armistice	1.50	.....
3131	P WWI Armistice, booklet single	1.50	.....
3131a	same, booklet pane of 10	14.50	.....

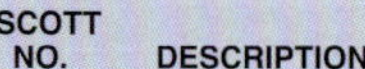

SCOTT NO.	DESCRIPTION	UNUSED F/NH	USED F
3132	P $2.50 Christmas, Warm & Cozy, souvenir sheet 3	8.00	.....
3133	P Nativity Scene, booklet single	1.50	.....
3133a	same, booklet pane of 12	18.00	.....
3134	P Socks, booklet single	1.50	.....
3134a	same, booklet pane of 12	18.00	.....
3135	$1.20 Cap, booklet single	2.25	.....
3135b	same, booklet pane of 6	12.25	.....
3136	$2.50 Mittens, booklet single	4.50	.....
3136a	same, booklet pane of 6	26.00	.....

3137

3152

2019 COMMEMORATIVES

SCOTT NO.	DESCRIPTION	UNUSED F/NH	USED F
3137	P (90c) Queen Elizabeth II	1.60	.....
3137a	same, booklet pane of 10	15.50	.....
3138	P $2.50 From Far and Wide, souvenir sheet of 9	21.00	.....
3139-43	P From Far and Wide, coil strip of 5, die-cut 9	8.50	.....
3139	P Tombstone Terri. Park, coil single, die cut 9	1.60	.....
3140	P Athabasca Falls, coil single, die-cut 9	1.60	.....
3141	P Quttinirpaaq National Park, coil single, die-cut 9	1.60	.....
3142	P Mahone Bay, coil single, die-cut 9	1.60	.....
3143	P Little Limestone Lake Provincial Park, coil single, die-cut 9	1.60	.....
3144-48	P From Far and Wide, vert. coil strip of 5, die-cut 8	8.50	.....
3144	P Tombstone Terri. Park, coil single, die-cut 8	1.60	.....
3145	P Athabasca Falls, coil single, die-cut 8	1.60	.....
3146	P Quttinirpaaq National Park, coil single, die-cut 8	1.60	.....
3147	P Mahone Bay, coil single, die-cut 8	1.60	.....
3148	P Little Limestone Lake Provincial Park, coil single, die-cut 8	1.60	.....
3149	$1.05 Castle Butte, coil single, die-cut 13.25	2.25	.....
3150	$1.27 Algonquin Provi. Park, coil single, die-cut 8.25	2.50	.....
3151	$1.90 Mingan Archipelago, coil single, die-cut 8.25	3.75	.....
3152	$2.65 Iceburg Alley, coil single, die-cut 8.25	4.75	.....
3153	P Tombstone Terri. Park, booklet single	1.60	.....
3154	P Quttinirpaaq National Park, booklet single	1.60	.....
3155	P Little Limestone Lake Provincial Park, booklet single	1.60	.....
3156	P Athabasca Falls, booklet single	1.60	.....
3157	P Mahone Bay, booklet single	1.60	.....
3157a	same, booklet pane of 10	15.50	.....
3158	$1.27 Algonquin Provi. Park, booklet single	2.50	.....
3158a	same, booklet pane of 6	15.00	.....
3159	$1.90 Mingan Archipelago, booklet single	3.75	.....
3159a	same, booklet pane of 6	24.00	.....
3160	$2.65 Iceburg Alley, booklet single	4.75	.....
3160a	same, booklet pane of 6	28.50	.....

3161

3168, 3170 3167, 3169

SCOTT NO.	DESCRIPTION	UNUSED F/NH	USED F
3161	P Year of the Pig 2019	1.50	.....
3162	$2.65 Year of the Pig, souvenir sheet	4.75	.....
3162a	$2.65+$2.50 Year of the Pig & Dog (3053b), sheet of 2	9.00	.....
3163	P Year of the Pig, booklet single	1.60	.....
3163a	same, booklet pane of 10	15.50	.....
3164	$2.65 Year of the Pig, booklet single	4.75	.....
3164a	same, booklet pane of 6	28.50	.....
3165	P Albert Jackson, Black History, booklet single	1.60	.....
3165a	same, booklet pane of 10	15.50	.....
3166	P Gardenia, souvenir sheet of 2	3.50	.....
3166a	P Pink Gardenia	1.60	.....
3166b	P Blue Green Gardenia	1.60	.....
3167-68	P Gardenia, coil pair	3.50	.....
3167	P Pink Gardenia, coil single	1.60	.....
3168	P Blue Green Gardenia, coil single	1.60	.....
3169-70	P Gardenia, booklet pair	3.50	.....
3169	P Pink Gardenia, booklet single	1.60	.....
3170	P Blue Green Gardenia, booklet single	1.60	.....
3170a	same, booklet pane of 10	15.50	.....
3171	P Canadians in Flight, sheet of 5	8.50	.....
3171a	P Elizabeth MacGill	1.60	.....
3171b	P Ultraflight Lazair Aircraft	1.60	.....
3171c	P Avro CF-105	1.60	.....
3171d	P C.H. Dickins	1.60	.....
3171e	P William George Barker	1.60	.....
3172	P Elizabeth MacGill, booklet single	1.60	.....
3173	P William George Barker, booklet single	1.60	.....
3174	P C.H. Dickins, booklet single	1.60	.....
3175	P Avro CF-105, booklet single	1.60	.....
3176	P Ultraflight Lazair Aircraft, booklet single	1.60	.....
3176a	same, booklet pane of 10	15.50	.....

3176

3178

3179a

SCOTT NO.	DESCRIPTION	UNUSED F/NH	USED F
3177	P Canada Sweets, sheet of 5	8.50	.....
3177a	P Sugar Pie	1.60	.....
3177b	P Butter Tart	1.60	.....
3177c	P Saskatoon Berry Pie	1.60	.....
3177d	P Nanaimo Bar	1.60	.....
3177e	P Blue-berry Grunt	1.60	.....
3177f	same, booklet pane of 10	15.50	.....
3178	P 1940 Vancouver Asahi Baseball	1.60	.....
3178a	same, booklet pane of 10	15.50	.....
3179	P Endangered Turtles, souvenir sheet of 2	3.25	.....
3179a	P Clemmys Guttatta	1.60	.....
3179b	P Emydoidea Blandingii	1.60	.....
3179c	same, booklet pane of 10	15.50	.....
3180	P Historic Covered Bridges, sheet of 5	8.50	.....
3180a	P Hartland, New Brunswick	1.60	.....
3180b	P Powerscourt, Quebec	1.60	.....
3180c	P Felix-Gabriel-Marchand, Quebec	1.60	.....
3180d	P West Montrose, Ontario	1.60	.....
3180e	P Ashnola No.1, British Columbia	1.60	.....
3181	P Hartland, New Brunswick, booklet single	1.60	.....
3182	P Powerscourt, Quebec, booklet single	1.60	.....
3183	P Felix-Gabriel-Marchand, Quebec, booklet single	1.60	.....
3184	P West Montrose, Ontario, booklet single	1.60	.....
3185	P Ashnola No.1, British Columbia, booklet single	1.60	.....
3185a	same, booklet pane of 10	15.50	.....
3186	P Command and Service Modules, Earth	1.60	.....
3187	P Lunar Module and Moon	1.60	.....
3186-87	P Apollo 11, 50th Anniv. pair	3.50	.....
3188-89	P Apollo 11, 50th Anniv., booklet pair	3.50	.....
3188	P Command and Service Modules, Earth, booklet single	1.60	.....
3189	P Lunar Module and Moon, booklet single	1.60	.....
3189a	same, booklet pane of 10	15.50	.....

3200

3190a

3204

SCOTT NO.	DESCRIPTION	UNUSED F/NH	USED F
3190	P Bears, sheet of 4	7.50	.....
3190a	P Grizzly Bear	1.60	.....
3190b	P Polar Bear	1.60	.....
3190c	P American Black Bear	1.60	.....
3190d	P Kermode Bear	1.60	.....
3191	P American Black Bear, booklet single	1.60	.....
3192	P Polar Bear, booklet single	1.60	.....
3193	P Kermode Bear, booklet single	1.60	.....
3194	P Grizzly Bear, booklet single	1.60	.....
3194a	same, booklet pane of 8	13.50	.....
3195	P, $1.27, $1.90, $2.65 Leonard Cohen, sheet of 6	15.00	.....
3196	P Leonard Cohen, squatting, booklet single	1.60	.....
3197	P Leonard Cohen, standing, booklet single	1.60	.....
3198	P Leonard Cohen, holding eyeglasses, booklet single	1.60	.....
3198a	same, booklet pane of 8	14.50	.....
3199	P, $1.27, $2.65 Shiney and Bright, sheet of 3	8.50	.....
3200	P Magi, booklet single	1.60	.....
3200a	same, booklet pane of 12	18.50	.....
3201	P Reindeer, booklet single	1.60	.....
3201a	same, booklet pane of 12	18.50	.....
3202	$1.27 Dancers, booklet single	2.25	.....
3202a	same, booklet pane of 6	12.50	.....
3203	$2.65 Patridge and Pears, booklet single	4.50	.....
3203a	same, booklet pane of 6	27.00	.....
3204	P Red River Resistance, booklet single	1.60	.....
3204a	same, booklet pane of 10	15.50	.....
3205	P Hanukkah, booklet single	1.60	.....
3205a	same, booklet pane of 10	15.50	.....

3207, 3212

3209, 3214

3208, 3213

SCOTT NO.	DESCRIPTION	UNUSED F/NH	USED F

3210, 3115

3211, 3216

2020 COMMEMORATIVES

SCOTT NO.	DESCRIPTION	UNUSED F/NH	USED F
3206	P(92c)-$2.71 From Far and Wide, souvenir sheet of 9	21.00	.....
3207-11	P From Far and Wide, coil strip of 5, die-cut 9.25	8.50	.....
3207	P Abraham Lake, coil single, die-cut 9.25	1.60	.....
3208	P Athabaska Sand Dunes, coil single, die-cut 9.25	1.60	.....
3209	P Herschel Island-Qikiqtaruk, coil single, die-cut 9.25	1.60	.....
3210	P French River, coil single, die-cut 9.25	1.60	.....
3211	P Magdalen Islands, coil single, die-cut 9.25	1.60	.....
3212-16	P From Far and Wide, coil strip of 5, die-cut 8.5	8.50	.....
3212	P Abraham Lake, coil single, die cut 8.5	1.60	.....
3213	P Athabaska Sand Dunes, coil single, die-cut 8.5	1.60	.....
3214	P Herschel Island-Qikiqtaruk, coil single, die-cut 8.5	1.60	.....
3215	P French River, coil single, die-cut 8.5	1.60	.....
3216	P Magdalen Islands, coil single, die-cut 8.5	1.60	.....
3217	$1.30 Kootenay National Park, coil single, die-cut 8.25	2.50	.....
3218	$1.94 Swallowtail Lighthouse, coil single, die-cut 8.25	3.75	.....
3219	$2.71 Cabot Trail, coil single, die-cut 8.25	4.75	.....
3220	$1.07 Carcajou Falls, coil single, die-cut 13.25	2.25	.....
3221	P Abraham Lake, booklet single	1.60	.....
3222	P Herschel Island-Qikiqtaruk, booklet single	1.60	.....
3223	P Magdalen Islands, booklet single	1.60	.....
3224	P Athabaska Sand Dunes, booklet single	1.60	.....
3225	P French River, booklet single	1.60	.....
3225a	same, booklet pane of 10	15.50	.....
3226	$1.30 Kootenay National Park, booklet single, die-cut 9.25	2.50	.....
3226a	same, booklet pane of 6	15.00	.....
3227	$1.94 Swallowtail Lighthouse, booklet single, die-cut 9.25	3.75	.....
3227a	same, booklet pane of 6	24.00	.....
3228	$2.71 Cabot Trail, booklet single, die-cut 9.25	4.75	.....
3228a	same, booklet pane of 6	28.50	.....

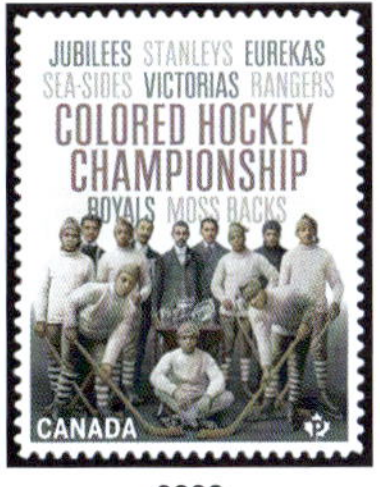

3233

3229

3239

3235,3237 3236,3238

SCOTT NO.	DESCRIPTION	UNUSED F/NH	USED F
3229	P(92c) Year of the Rat, 2020	1.60	.....
3230	$2.71 Year of the Rat, souvenir sheet	4.75	.....
3230a	$2.71 + $2.65 Year of the Rat & Pig (3162a), sheet of 2	9.75	.....
3231	P Year of the Rat, booklet single	1.60	.....
3231a	same, booklet pane of 10	15.75	.....
3232	$2.75 Year of the Rat, booklet single	4.75	.....
3232a	same, booklet pane of 6	28.50	.....
3233	P Colored Hockey Championship, booklet single	1.60	.....
3233a	same, booklet pane of 10	15.75	.....
3234	P Dahlias, souvenir sheet of 2	3.50	.....
3235-36	P Dahlias, coil pair	3.50	.....
3235	P Dahlias, without background, coil single	1.60	.....
3236	P Dahlias, light blue background, coil single	1.60	.....
3237-38	P Dahlias, booklet pair	3.50	.....
3237	P Dahlias without background, booklet single	1.60	.....
3238	P Dahlias, light blue background, booklet single	1.60	.....
3238a	same, booklet pane of 10	15.50	.....
3239	P EID, booklet single	1.60	.....
3239a	same, booklet pane of 10	15.50	.....

3240 3241

SCOTT NO.	DESCRIPTION	UNUSED F/NH	USED F
3240-41	P Victory in Europe, 75th Anniv., booklet pair	3.50	.....
3240	P Leo Major, booklet single	1.60	.....
3241	P Veronica Foster, booklet single	1.60	.....
3241a	same, booklet pane of 10	15.50	.....
3242	P Paintings by Group Seven, sheet of 7	12.50	.....
3243	same, booklet pane of 7	12.50	.....

3244 3245

SCOTT NO.	DESCRIPTION	UNUSED F/NH	USED F
3244-45	P Radio History Canada, booklet pair	3.50	.....
3244	P Microphone, booklet single	1.60	.....
3245	P Radio Receiver, booklet single	1.60	.....
3245a	same, booklet pane of 10	15.50	.....

3246

3252

3255

SCOTT NO.	DESCRIPTION	UNUSED F/NH	USED F
3246	P Dr. James Till & Dr. Ernest McCulloch, booklet single	1.60	.....
3247	P Dr. M. Vera Peters, booklet single	1.60	.....
3248	P Dr. Julio Montaner, booklet single	1.60	.....
3249	P Dr. Balfour Mount, booklet single	1.60	.....
3250	P Dr. Bruce Chown, booklet single	1.60	.....
3250a	P Medical Researchers, booklet pane of 10	15.50	.....
3251	P Diwali, booklet single	1.60	.....
3251a	same, booklet pane of 10	15.50	.....
3252	P Trenches on the Somme Painting, booklet single	1.60	.....
3252a	same, booklet pane of 10	15.50	.....
3253	P-$2.71 Folk Art Paintings by Maud Lewis, sheet of 3	8.50	.....
3254	P Holy Family, booklet single	1.60	.....
3254a	same, booklet pane of 12	18.50	.....
3255	P Winter Slight Ride, booklet single	1.60	.....
3255a	same, booklet pane of 12	18.50	.....
3256	$1.30 Team of Oxen, booklet single	2.25	.....
3256a	same, booklet pane of 6	12.50	.....
3257	$2.71 Family and Sled, booklet single	4.50	.....
3257a	same, booklet pane of 6	27.00	.....
3258	P Hanukkah, booklet single	1.60	.....
3258a	same, booklet pane of 10	15.50	.....

3273

3278

3282, 3285 3283, 3284

2021 COMMEMORATIVES

SCOTT NO.	DESCRIPTION	UNUSED F/NH	USED F
3259	P Lunar New Year, sheet of 12 varieties	25.00	.....
3260	$2.71 Lunar New Year, sheet of 12 varieties	....	.....
3261	P Year of the Rat, booklet single	1.60	.....
3262	P Year of the Ox, booklet single	1.60	.....
3263	P Year of the Tiger, booklet single	1.60	.....
3264	P Year of the Rabbit, booklet single	1.60	.....
3265	P Year of the Dragon, booklet single	1.60	.....
3266	P Year of the Snake, booklet single	1.60	.....
3267	P Year of the Horse, booklet single	1.60	.....
3268	P Year of the Ram, booklet single	1.60	.....
3269	P Year of the Monkey, booklet single	1.60	.....
3270	P Year of the Rooster, booklet single	1.60	.....
3271	P Year of the Dog, booklet single	1.60	.....
3272	P Year of the Pig, booklet single	1.60	.....
3272a	P Lunar New Year, booklet pane of 12	18.50	.....
3273	P Amber Valley Settlers, booklet single	1.60	.....
3274	P Willow Grove Settlers, booklet single	1.60	.....
3274a	P Black History, booklet pane of 10	15.50	.....
3275	P Snow Mammals, sheet of 5	8.50	.....
3276	P Ermine, booklet single	1.60	.....
3277	P Snowshoe Hare, booklet single	1.60	.....
3278	P Peary Caribou, booklet single	1.60	.....
3279	P Arctic Fox, booklet single	1.60	.....
3280	P Northern Collared Lemming, booklet single	1.60	.....
3280a	P Snow Mammals, booklet pane of 10	15.50	.....

SCOTT NO.	DESCRIPTION	UNUSED F/NH
3281	P Crabapple Blossoms, souvenir sheet of 2	3.50
3282-83	P Crabapple Blossoms, coil pair	3.50
3282	P Malus "Maybride", coil single	1.60
3283	P Malus "Rosseau", coil single	1.60

3287

3291

SCOTT NO.	DESCRIPTION	UNUSED F/NH
3284-85	P Crabapple Blossoms, booklet pair	3.50
3284	P Malus "Rosseau", booklet single	1.60
3285	P Malus "Maybride", booket single	1.60
3285a	same, booklet pane of 10	15.50
3286	P Juno Awards, booklet single	1.60
3286a	same, booklet pane of 5	8.50
3287	P Insulin Cenntennial, booklet single	1.60
3287a	same, booklet pane of 10	15.50
3288	P EID, booklet single	1.60
3288a	same, booklet pane of 10	15.50
3289	P Legends of Ballet Dancers, souvenir sheet of 2	3.50
3290	P Fernans Nault, booklet single	1.60
3290a	same, booklet pane of 6	9.50
3290	P Fernans Nault, booklet single	1.60
3290a	same, booklet pane of 6	9.50
3291	P Karen Kain, booklet single	1.60
3291a	same, booklet pane of 6	9.50
3292	P John Turner, booklet single	1.60
3292a	same, booklet pane of 10	15.50
3293	P Schooner Bluenose, souvenir sheet of 2	3.50
3293c	P Schooner Bluenose, souvenir sheet of 2, CAPEX 22 Ovpt.	3.50

3294 3295

SCOTT NO.	DESCRIPTION	UNUSED F/NH
3294-95	P Schooner Blue nose, booklet pair	3.50
3294	P Bluenose & fisherman in boat, booklet single	1.60
3295	P Bluenose racing, booklet single	1.60
3295a	same booklet pane of 10	15.50
3296	P Stan Rogers, booklet single	1.60
3296a	same, booklet pane of 10	15.50
3297	P Editorial Cartoon by Brian Gable, booklet single	1.60
3298	P Editorial Cartoon by Terry Mosher, booklet single	1.60
3299	P Editorial Cartoon by Duncan Macpherson, booklet single	1.60
3300	P Editorial Cartoon by Serge Chapleau, booklet single	1.60
3301	P Editorial Cartoon by Bruce MacKinnon, booklet single	1.60
3301a	same, booklet pane of 10	15.50
3302	P Christopher Plummer, sheet of 6	9.75
3303	P Christopher Plummer, booklet single	1.60
3303a	P Christopher Plummer, booklet pane of 10	15.50
3304	P Diwali, booklet single	1.60
3304a	P Diwali, booklet pane of 10	15.50
3305	P Valour Road, sheet of 5	8.00

3308a, 3310

3315

SCOTT NO.	DESCRIPTION	UNUSED F/NH
3306	P Valour Road, booklet single	1.60
3306a	P Valour Road, booklet pane of 10	15.50
3307	P Remembrance Poppy, booklet single	1.60
3307a	P Remembrance Poppy, booklet pane of 10	15.50
3308	P-$2.71 Holiday Portraits, sheet of 3	8.50
3309	P Christmas Angel, booklet single	1.60
3309a	P Christmas Angel, booklet pane of 12	18.50
3310	P Santa Portrait, booklet single	1.60
3310a	P Santa Portrait, booklet pane of 12	18.50
3311	$1.30 Reindeer Portrait, booklet single	2.25
3311a	$1.30 Reindeer Portrait, booklet pane of 6	12.50
3312	$2.71 Elf Portrait, booklet single	4.50
3312a	$2.71 Elf Portrait, booklet pane of 6	27.00
3313	P Hanukkah, booklet single	1.60
3313a	P Hanukkah, booklet pane of 10	15.50
3314	P Buffy Sainte-Marie, booklet single	1.60
3314a	P Buffy Sainte-Marie, booklet pane of 10	15.50
3315	P Margaret Atwood, booklet single	1.60
3315a	P Margaret Atwood, booklet pane of 10	15.50

3317, 3318

3324

3327a, 3329

2022 COMMEMORATIVES

SCOTT NO.	DESCRIPTION	UNUSED F/NH
3316	P Eleanor Collins, booklet single	1.60
3316a	P Eleanor Collins, booklet pane of 6	9.75
3317	P Queen Elizabeth II, Platinum Jubilee, single	1.60
3318	P Queen Elizabeth II, Platinum Jubilee, booklet single	1.60
3318a	P Queen Elizabeth II, Platinum Jubilee, booklet pane of 10	15.50
3319	P Calla Lilies, souvenir sheet of 2	3.50
3319c	P Calla Lilies, souvenir sheet of 2, CAPEX 22 Ovpt.	3.50
3320-21	P Calla Lilies, coil pair	3.50
3320	P Calla Lilies, pink background, coil single	1.60
3321	P Calla Lilies, white background, coil single	1.60
3322-23	P Calla Lilies, booklet pair	3.50
3322	P Calla Lilies, white background, booklet single	1.60
3323	P Calla Lilies, pink background, booklet single	1.60
3323a	same, booklet pane of 10	15.50
3324	P Organ & Tissue Donation, booklet single	1.60
3324a	P Organ & Tissue Donation, booklet pane of 10	15.50
3325	P EID Lantern, booklet single	1.60
3325a	P EID Lantern, booklet pane of 6	9.75
3326	P Salome Bey, booklet single	1.60
3326a	P Salome Bey, booklet pane of 6	9.75
3327	P Endangered Whales, sheet of 5	8.00
3327a	P Orcinus Orca	1.60
3327b	P Delphinapterus Leucas	1.60
3327c	P Balaenoptera Musculus	1.60
3327d	P Hyperoodon Ampullatus	1.60
3327e	P Eubalaena Glacialis	1.60
3328	P Delphinapterus Leucas, booklet single	1.60
3329	P Orcinus Orca, booklet single	1.60
3330	P Eubalaena Glacialis, booklet single	1.60
3331	P Balaenoptera Musculus, booklet single	1.60
3332	P Hyperoodon Ampullatus, booklet single	1.60
3332a	same, booklet pane of 10	15.50

3333a, 3334

3339b, 3341

3343a, 3344

SCOTT NO.	DESCRIPTION	UNUSED F/NH
3333	P Vintage Travel Posters, sheet of 5	8.00
3333f	P Vintage Travel Posters, sheet of 5, CAPEX 22 Ovpt.	8.00
3334	P Mont Tremblant, booklet single	1.60
3335	P The Royal York Hotel, booklet single	1.60
3336	P Travel the Canadian, booklet single	1.60
3337	P Cruise the Great Lakes, booklet single	1.60
3338	P Canada's Picturesque East Coast, booklet single	1.60
3338a	same, booklet pane of 10	15.50
3339	P Indigenous Leaders, sheet of 3	5.00
3340	P Marie-Anne Day Walker-Pelletier, booklet single	1.60
3340a	P Marie-Anne Day Walker-Pelletier, booklet pane of 6	9.75
3341	P Jose Kusugak, booklet single	1.60
3341a	P Jose Kusugak, booklet pane of 6	9.75
3342	P Harry Daniels, booklet single	1.60
3342a	P Harry Daniels, booklet pane of 6	9.75
3343	P Carousel Animals, sheet of 5	8.00
3343a	P Horse, Rosneath	1.60
3343b	P Horse, La Ronde	1.60
3343c	P Lion, Lakeside Park	1.60
3343d	P Horse, Heritage Park	1.60
3343e	P Horse, Burnaby Village	1.60
3344-48	P Carousel Animals, pane of 5	8.00
3344	P Horse, Rosneath, booklet single	1.60
3345	P Horse, La Ronde, booklet single	1.60
3346	P Lion, Lakeside Park, booklet single	1.60
3347	P Horse, Heritage Park, booklet single	1.60
3348	P Horse, Burnaby Village, booklet single	1.60
3348a	same, booklet pane of 10	15.50
3349	P The Summit Series, booklet single	1.60
3349a	same, booklet pane of 10	15.50
3350-53	P Truth and Reconciliation, pane of 4	6.25
3350	P Bunchberry and Faces, booklet single	1.60
3351	P Woman Lighting Inuit Stone Lamp, booklet single	1.60
3352	P Hands and Tears, booklet single	1.60
3353	P Beadede Flowers Over Map, booklet single	1.60
3353a	same, booklet pane of 8	12.50
3354	P Diwali, booklet single	1.60
3354a	same, booklet pane of 6	9.50
3355	P Canadians in Flight, sheet of 5	8.00
3355a	P Violet Milstead	1.60
3355b	P De Havilland	1.60
3355c	P CAE Flight Simulator	1.60
3355d	P Dr. Wilbur R. Franks	1.60
3355e	P W. Rupert Turnbull	1.60

SCOTT NO.	DESCRIPTION	UNUSED F/NH
3356	P Violet Milstead, booklet single	1.60
3357	P Dr. Wilbur R. Franks, booklet single	1.60
3358	P W. Rupert Turnbull, booklet single	1.60
3359	P De Havilland, booklet single	1.60
3360	P CAE Flight Simulator, booklet single	1.60
3360a	same, booklet pane of 10	15.50

3361, 3362

3363b, 3366

SCOTT NO.	DESCRIPTION	UNUSED F/NH
3361	P Tommy Price	1.60
3362	P Tommy Price, booklet single	1.60
3362a	same, booklet pane of 10	15.50
3363	P-$2.71 Holiday Birds, souvenir sheet of 3	8.50
3364	P Christmas Star, booklet single	1.60
3364a	same, booklet pane of 12	18.50
3365	P Cardinal, booklet single	1.60
3365a	same, booklet pane of 12	18.50
3366	$1.30 Blue Jay, booklet single	2.25
3366a	same, booklet pane of 6	12.50
3367	$2.71 Grosbeck, booklet single	4.50
3367a	same, booklet pane of 6	27.00
3368	P Hanukkah, booklet single	1.60
3368a	same, booklet pane of 6	9.50

3369, 3370

SCOTT NO.	DESCRIPTION	UNUSED F/NH
3369	P Monique Mercure	1.60
3370	P Monique Mercure, booklet single	1.60
3370a	same, booklet pane of 6	9.50

3371

3373, 3375 3374, 3376

2023 COMMEMORATIVES

SCOTT NO.	DESCRIPTION	UNUSED F/NH
3371	P Chloe Cooley, booklet single	1.60
3371a	same, booklet pane of 6	9.50
3372	P Ranunculus Flowers, souvenir sheet of 2	3.50
3373-74	P Ranunculus Flowers, coil pair	3.50
3373	P Ranunculus, nine flowers, coil single	1.60
3374	P Ranunculus, one flower, coil single	1.60
3375-76	P Ranunculus Flowers, booklet pair	3.50
3375	P Ranunculus, nine flowers, booklet single	1.60
3376	P Ranunculus, one flower, booklet single	1.60
3376b	P Ranunculus, booklet pane of 10	15.50

3377

3381

3386

SCOTT NO.	DESCRIPTION	UNUSED F/NH
3377	P Eid, booklet single	1.60
3377a	same, booklet pane of 6	9.50
3378	P Animals and Their Young, souvenir sheet of 2	3.50
3379-80	P Animals and Their Young, booklet pair	3.50
3379	P Enhydra Lutris, booklet single	1.60
3380	P Podiceps Grisegena, booklet single	1.60
3380a	same, booklet pane of 6	9.50
3381	P King Charles III, booklet single	1.60
3381a	same, booklet pane of 10	15.50
3382	P Royal Canadian Mounted Police	1.60
3382a	same, booklet pane of 6	9.50
3383	P Indigenous Leaders, sheet of 3	5.00
3384	P Thelma Chalifoux, booklet single	1.60
3384a	same, booklet pane of 6	9.50
3385	P Nellie Cournoyea, booklet single	1.60
3385a	same, booklet pane of 6	9.50
3386	P George Manuel, booklet single	1.60
3386a	same, booklet pane of 6	9.50

3389

3401

3402

SCOTT NO.	DESCRIPTION	UNUSED F/NH
3387	P Denys Arcand, booklet single	1.60
3387a	same, booklet pane of 6	9.50
3388	P Ferries, sheet of 5	8.00
3388a	P Spirit of British Columbia	1.60
3388b	P Chi-Cheemaun	1.60
3388c	P Trillium	1.60
3388d	P Alphonse-Desjardins	1.60
3388e	P Grand Manan V	1.60
3389	P Spirit of British Columbia	1.60
3390	P Chi-Cheemaun	1.60
3391	P Trillium	1.60
3392	P Alphonse-Desjardins	1.60
3393	P Grand Manan V	1.60
3393a	P Ferries, booklet pane of 10	15.50
3394	P Simonne Monet-Chartrand, booklet single	1.60
3395	P Madeleine Parent, booklet single	1.60
3396	P Lea Roback, booklet single	1.60
3396a	P Quedec Feminists, booklet pane of 6	9.50
3397	P Kamloops Redidential School, booklet single	1.60
3398	P Ile-a-la-Crosse Residential School, booklet single	1.60
3399	P Sept-Iles Residential School, booklet single	1.60
3400	P Grollier Hall, booklet single	1.60
3400a	P National Day of Truth and Reconciliation, booklet of 8	12.50
3401	P Donald Sutherland, booklet single	1.60
3401a	same, booklet pane of 10	15.50

3404

3405

3408

SCOTT NO.	DESCRIPTION	UNUSED F/NH
3402	P Willie O'Ree, booklet single	1.60
3402a	same, booklet pane of 6	9.50
3403	P, $1.20, $2.71, Holiday Winter Scenes, souvenir sheet of 3	8.50
3404	P Madonna & Child, booklet single	1.60
3404a	same, booklet pane of 12	18.50
3505	P Mountain Village in Winter, booklet single	1.60
3505a	same, booklet pane of 12	18.50
3506	$1.30 Skaters on Frozen Pond, booklet single	2.25
3506a	same, booklet pane of 6	12.50
3407	$2.71 Seacoast in Winter, booklet single	4.50
3407a	same, booklet pane of 6	27.00
3408	P Mona Parsons	1.60
3409	P Mona Parsons, booklet single	1.60
3409a	same, booklet pane of 10	15.50
3410	P Diwali, booklet single	1.60
3410a	same, booklet pane of 6	9.50
3411	P Hanukkah, booklet single	1.60
3411a	same, booklet pane of 6	9.50

3412

3414-15

3418

2024 COMMEMORATIVES

SCOTT NO.	DESCRIPTION	UNUSED F/NH
3412	P Mary Ann Shadd, booklet single	1.60
3412a	same, booklet pane of 6	9.50
3413	P Wildflowers, souvenir sheet of 2	3.50
3414-15	P Wildflowers, coil pair	3.50
3414	P Asclepias Tuberosa, coil single	1.60
3415	P Monarda Punctata, coil single	1.60
3416-17	P Wildflowers, booklet pair	3.50
3416	P Asclepias Tuberosa, booklet single	1.60
3417	P Monarda Punctata, booklet single	1.60
3417a	P Wildflowers, booklet pane of 10	15.50
3418	P Total Solar Eclipse, booklet single	1.60
3418a	same, booklet pane of 10	15.50
3419	P Eid, booklet single	1.60
3419a	same, booklet pane of 6	9.50

CANADA PHOSPHOR TAGGED ISSUES

Overprinted with barely visible phosphorescent ink

TYPES OF TAGGING

I = Wide Side Bars
II = Wide Bar in Middle
III = Bar at Right or Left
IV = Narrow Bar in Middle
V = Narrow Side Bars

SCOTT NO.	DESCRIPTION			UNUSED F/NH
	1962-63 Queen Elizabeth II			
337-41p	1¢-5¢ Elizabeth	(5)	52.50	10.60
401-5p	1¢-5¢ Elizabeth	(5)	10.75	1.75
404pIV	4¢ Carmine—IV		6.00	1.25
404pII	4¢ Carmine—II		17.50	4.00
405q	5¢ Elizabeth, mini. pane of 25		......	41.25
	1964-67			
434-35p	3¢-5¢ 1964 Christmas	(2)	13.00	2.25
434q	3¢ mini. pane of 25		......	12.10
434q	same, sealed pack of 2		......	25.00
443-44p	3¢-5¢ 1965 Christmas	(2)	3.50	.65
443q	3¢ mini. pane of 25		......	7.70
443q	same, sealed pack of 2		......	15.75
451-52p	3¢-5¢ 1966 Christmas	(2)	3.50	.80
451q	3¢ mini. pane of 25		......	5.15
451q	same, sealed pack of 2		......	10.50
453p	5¢ Centennial		2.25	.45
	1967-72 Queen Elizabeth II			
454-58pI	1¢-5¢—I	(4)	12.50	1.75
454-58pII	1¢-5¢—II	(4)	12.50	1.65
454-57pV	1¢-5¢—V	(4)	7.75	.95
454ep	1¢ booklet single—V		......	.25
457p	4¢ carmine—III		2.75	.35
458q	5¢ mini. pane of 20		......	65.00
459p	6¢ orange, perf.10—I		4.50	.65
459bp	6¢ orange, perf.12-1/2x12—I		4.50	.65
460p	6¢ black, perf 12-1/2x12—I		5.50	.40
460cp	6¢ black, perf 12-1/2x12—II		4.25	.50
460gp	6¢ black, booklet single, perf.10—V		......	.75
460pII	6¢ black, perf. 12—II		4.00	.55
460pV	6¢ black, perf. 12—V		4.00	.50
	1967 Views			
462-65pI	10¢-25¢—I	(4)	45.00	9.00
462-63pV	10¢-15¢—V	(2)	12.50	2.00
	1967-69			
476-77p	3¢-5¢ 1967 Christmas	(2)	3.50	.65
476q	3¢ mini. pane of 25		......	3.30
476q	same, sealed pack of 2		......	7.00
488-89p	5¢-6¢ 1968 Christmas	(2)	3.75	.70
488q	5¢ booklet pane of 10		......	4.15
502-3p	5¢-6¢ 1969 Christmas	(2)	3.50	.60
502q	5¢ booklet pane of 10		......	3.85
	1970-71			
505p	6¢ Manitoba		1.75	.35
508-11p	25¢ Expo '70	(4)	12.50	11.00
513-14p	10¢-15¢ U.N.	(2)	20.00	3.15
519-30p	5¢-15¢ Christmas	(12)	23.50	6.05
541p	15¢ Radio Canada		17.25	3.05
	1971 Queen Elizabeth II			
543-44p	7¢-8¢—I	(2)	9.25	1.05
544q	booklet pane, 8¢(2), 6¢(1), 1¢(3)		......	2.20
544r	booklet pane, 8¢(11), 6¢(1), 1¢(6)		......	6.05
544s	booklet pane, 8¢(5), 6¢(1), 1¢(4)		......	2.75
544pV	8¢ slate—V		4.25	.60
550p	8¢ slate, coil		......	.30
	1971-72			
554-57p	6¢-15¢ Christmas	(4)	11.00	2.50
560p	8¢ World Health Day		3.25	.65
561p	8¢ Frontenac		5.75	.95
562-63p	8¢ Indians	(2)	3.75	1.20
564-65p	8¢ Indians	(2)	3.75	1.20
582-85p	15¢ Sciences	(4)	16.00	13.20
	1972 Pictorials			
594-97	10¢-25¢—V	(4)	10.50	2.25
594-97p I	10¢-25¢—I	(4)	35.00	7.50
	1972			
606-09p	6¢-15¢ Christmas—V	(4)	12.75	2.65
606-09pI	6¢-15¢ Christmas—I	(4)	15.00	3.50
610p	8¢ Krieghoff		3.50	.40

B20

B24

B22

SEMI-POSTAL STAMPS

SCOTT NO.	DESCRIPTION	PLATE BLOCK F/NH	UNUSED F/NH	USED F
	1974-76			
B1-12	**Olympics, 12 varieties**	**28.50**	**6.25**	**6.25**
	1974 -1976			
B1-3	Emblems, 3 varieties	7.50	1.95	1.95
B1	8¢ + 2¢ Olympic Emblem	1.95	.55	.55
B2	10¢ + 5¢ same	2.65	.65	.65
B3	15¢ + 5¢ same	3.85	.95	.95
B4-6	Water Sports, 3 varieties	7.25	1.95	1.95
B4	8¢ + 2¢ Swimming	1.85	.45	.50
B5	10¢ + 5¢ Rowing	2.75	.65	.65
B6	15¢ + 5¢ Sailing	3.85	.85	.85
B7-9	Combat Sports, 3 varieties	7.25	1.75	1.50
B7	8¢ + 2¢ Fencing	1.75	.45	.45
B8	10¢ + 5¢ Boxing	2.75	.65	.65
B9	15¢ + 5¢ Judo	3.85	.95	.95
B10-12	Team Sports, 3 varieties	8.75	2.00	2.00
B10	8¢ + 2¢ Basketball	1.85	.45	.45
B11	10¢ + 5¢ Gymnastics	2.75	.65	.65
B12	20¢ + 5¢ Soccer	4.75	1.15	1.15
	1997-2015			
B13	45¢ + 5¢ Literacy	....	1.40	.75
B13a	same, booklet pane of 10	....	13.50	....
B14	Mental Health	....	1.40	1.40
B14a	same, booklet pane of 10	....	13.50	....
B15	P + 10¢ Mental Health semi-postal	....	1.40	1.40
B15a	same, booklet pane of 10	....	14.50	....
B16	P + 10¢ Mental Health semi-postal	....	1.60	1.60
B16a	same, booklet pane of 10	....	15.50	....
B17	Mental Health Souvenir Sheet of 2	....	2.95	2.95
B17a	P + 10¢ Mental Health Semi-postal	....	1.50	1.50
B18	P + 10¢ Mental Health Semi-postal S/A booklet single	....	1.50	1.50
B18a	same, booklet pane of 10	....	16.00	....
B19	P+10¢, Hands and Heart	....	1.65	1.65
B19a	same, booklet pane of 10	....	16.50	....
B20	63¢ +10¢ Children's Art by Ezra Peters	....	1.75	1.75
B20a	same, booklet pane of 10	....	1.75	....
B21	P +10¢ Children in Paper Boat, single	....	1.75	....
B21a	same, booklet pane of 10	....	16.50	....
B22	P +10¢ Children Reading Story Under Tented Bedsheet	....	1.75	....
B22a	same, booklet pane of 10	....	16.50	....
B23-24	P+10¢ Stylized Bird, pair	....	3.00	17.00
B24a	same, booklet pane of 10	....	17.00	....
	2017-2021			
B25-26	P+10c Stylized Cats, pair	8.75	2.50	2.00
B26a	same, B25-B26 five each, booklet pane of 10	1.85	17.50	.45
B27	P+10c Child on Hill	2.75	1.75	....
B27a	same, booklet pane of 10	2.75	17.50	....
B28-29	P+10c Ice Cream Cone & Ice Pop	....	1.75	....
B29a	same, booklet pane of 10	....	17.50	....
B30	P+10c Animals in Tree, booklet single	....	1.75	.....
B30a	same, booklet pane of 10	....	17.50	.....
B31	P+10c Fireflies, booklet single	....	1.75	.....
B31a	same, booklet pane of 10	....	17.50	.....
	2022			
B32	P+10c Sunflowers, booklet single	....	1.75	....
B32a	same, booklet pane of 10	....	17.50	....
B33	P+10c Treehouses, booklet single	....	1.75	....
B33a	same, booklet pane of 10	....	17.50	....
	2023			
B34	P+10c Animals Reading Book, booklet single	....	1.75	....
B34a	same, booklet pane of 10	....	17.50	....

AIR POST STAMPS

C2

C5

SCOTT NO.	DESCRIPTION	UNUSED NH VF	F	AVG	UNUSED OG VF	F	AVG	USED VF	F	AVG
	1928									
C1	5¢ brown olive	33.00	22.00	17.00	18.00	14.00	12.00	4.50	3.50	2.75
	1930									
C2	5¢ olive brown	165.00	125.00	100.00	92.00	70.00	55.00	28.00	21.00	16.00

SCOTT NO.	DESCRIPTION	UNUSED NH VF	F	AVG	UNUSED OG VF	F	AVG	USED VF	F	AVG
	1932									
C3	6¢ on 5¢ brown olive	23.00	17.00	12.00	14.00	11.00	7.50	3.50	2.60	1.50
C4	6¢ on 5¢ olive brown	82.00	60.00	50.00	48.00	38.00	32.00	11.50	8.75	5.50

C6

C7

C9

SCOTT NO.	DESCRIPTION	PLATE BLOCK F/NH	F/OG	UNUSED F/NH	F/OG	USED F
	1935					
C5	6¢ red brown	40.00	25.00	5.50	4.00	1.25
	1938					
C6	6¢ blue	25.00	16.00	4.50	3.25	.45
	1942-43					
C7	6¢ deep blue	33.00	23.00	7.50	5.00	1.00
C8	7¢ deep blue (1943)	6.50	4.50	1.50	1.00	.25
	1946					
C9	7¢ deep blue	6.00	4.00	1.25	.90	.25
C9a	same, booklet pane of 4	...	....	4.00	...	...

AIR POST SPECIAL DELIVERY

CE1

CE3

SCOTT NO.	DESCRIPTION	PLATE BLOCK F/NH	F/OG	UNUSED F/NH	F/OG	USED F
	1942-43					
CE1	16¢ bright ultramarine	14.00	10.00	3.50	2.50	1.85
CE2	17¢ bright ultramarine (1943)	19.00	14.00	4.50	3.00	2.75
	1946					
CE3	17¢ bright ultramarine (circumflex "E")	31.00	22.00	6.00	4.25	4.00
	1947					
CE4	17¢ bright ultramarine (grave "E")	31.00	22.00	6.00	4.75	4.00

SPECIAL DELIVERY STAMPS

E1

E2

E3

SCOTT NO.	DESCRIPTION	UNUSED NH VF	F	AVG	UNUSED O.G VF	F	AVG	USED VF	F	AVG
	1898									
E1	10¢ blue green	415.00	250.00	190.00	150.00	75.00	48.00	11.00	7.50	5.00
	1922									
E2	20¢ carmine	330.00	210.00	150.00	140.00	90.00	60.00	9.00	7.00	4.50
	1927									
E3	20¢ orange	110.00	70.00	48.00	49.00	30.00	18.00	12.50	9.00	6.75
	1930									
E4	20¢ henna brown	138.00	95.00	75.00	82.00	60.00	45.00	16.50	12.50	8.75
	1933									
E5	20¢ henna brown	140.00	90.00	75.00	85.00	60.00	44.00	19.00	14.00	10.00

E4

E6

E7

E10

SCOTT NO.	DESCRIPTION	PLATE BLOCK F/NH	F/OG	UNUSED F/NH	F/OG	USED F
	1935					
E6	20¢ dark carmine	105.00	75.00	19.00	14.00	7.00
	1938-39					
E7	10¢ dark green(1939)	50.00	38.00	11.00	8.00	3.75
E8	20¢ dark carmine	265.00	178.25	45.00	30.00	27.00
E9	10¢ on 20¢ dark carmine (#E8) (1939)	50.00	35.00	10.00	7.00	5.50
	1942					
E10	10¢ green	22.50	16.00	5.00	3.75	2.00
	1946					
E11	10¢ green	22.00	15.00	4.00	3.00	1.25

WAR TAX STAMPS

MR1

MR3

2¢ + 1¢ Die I. Below large letter "T" there is a clear horizontal line of color. Die II. Right side of line is replaced by two short lines and five dots.

SCOTT NO.	DESCRIPTION	UNUSED NH F	AVG	UNUSED F	AVG	USED F	AVG
	1915						
MR1	1¢ green	52.00	42.00	33.00	16.50	.30	.25
MR2	2¢ carmine	55.00	42.00	33.00	16.50	.30	.25
	1916 Perf 12						
MR3	2¢ + 1¢ carmine (I)	75.00	65.00	48.00	31.00	.30	.25
MR3a	2¢ + 1¢ carmine(II)	375.00	275.00	160.00	95.00	5.00	3.60
MR4	2¢ + 1¢ brown (II)	42.00	34.00	18.00	10.00	.35	.30
MR4a	2¢ + 1¢ brown(I)	950.00	750.00	550.00	350.00	10.00	8.00
	Perf 12 x 8						
MR5	2¢ + 1¢ carmine	125.00	85.00	75.00	48.00	28.00	20.00
	Coil Stamps Perf. 8 Vertically						
MR6	2¢ + 1¢ carmine (I)	275.00	200.00	190.00	115.00	8.50	6.50
MR7	2¢ + 1¢ brown (II)	85.00	60.00	58.00	35.00	1.25	.90
MR7a	2¢ + 1¢ brown (I)	350.00	280.00	230.00	140.00	8.00	6.00

REGISTRATION STAMPS

F2

1875-88 Perf. 12 (NH+50%)

SCOTT NO.	DESCRIPTION	UNUSED O.G. VF	F	AVG	UNUSED VF	F	AVG	USED VF	F	AVG
F1	2¢ orange	95.00	75.00	55.00	70.00	46.75	28.50	4.00	3.50	2.75
F1a	2¢ vermillion	130.00	80.00	50.00	82.50	55.00	33.00	9.50	6.35	3.40
F1b	2¢ rose carmine	285.00	210.00	150.00	165.00	110.00	66.00	110.00	72.50	40.00
F1d	2¢ orange, perf 12x11-1/2	365.00	308.00	220.00	305.00	203.50	132.50	88.00	58.85	32.50
F2	5¢ dark green	100.00	85.00	60.00	82.50	55.00	34.50	4.50	3.25	1.95
F2d	5¢ dark green, perf 12x11-1/2	1140.00	960.00	500.00	950.00	800.00	450.00	185.00	125.00	90.00
F3	8¢ blue	550.00	365.00	245.00	455.00	305.00	205.00	410.00	275.00	148.50

POSTAGE DUE STAMPS

J1

J11

J6

J15

J21

SCOTT NO.	DESCRIPTION	UNUSED NH F	AVG	UNUSED F	AVG	USED F	AVG
	1906-28						
J1	1¢ violet	35.00	20.00	14.50	9.25	4.50	2.75
J2	2¢ violet	35.00	20.00	14.50	9.25	.90	.65
J3	4¢ violet (1928)	105.00	80.00	62.00	48.00	22.00	16.00
J4	5¢ violet	35.00	17.50	14.50	9.25	1.75	1.25
J5	10¢ violet (1928)	135.00	110.00	75.00	55.00	13.00	9.50
	1930-32						
J6	1¢ dark violet	22.00	18.00	12.00	8.50	4.00	3.00
J7	2¢ dark violet	12.00	9.00	7.00	5.50	1.00	.70
J8	4¢ dark violet	35.00	28.00	20.00	15.00	5.75	4.50
J9	5¢ dark violet	42.00	34.00	23.00	18.00	6.75	5.25
J10	10¢ dark violet (1932)	175.00	140.00	100.00	75.00	10.00	7.75
	1933-34						
J11	1¢ dark violet (1934)	23.00	18.00	15.00	11.00	6.75	5.25
J12	2¢ dark violet	15.00	11.00	14.00	8.00	1.25	.75
J13	4¢ dark violet	24.00	17.00	14.00	11.00	7.25	5.75
J14	10¢ dark violet	45.00	32.50	40.00	28.00	5.75	4.50

SCOTT NO.	DESCRIPTION	UNUSED NH F	AVG	UNUSED F	AVG	USED F
	1935-65					
J15-20	**1¢-10¢ complete, 7 varieties**	**6.50**	**5.25**	**5.50**	**4.95**	**3.35**
J15	1¢ dark violet	.80	.55	.35	.25	.25
J16	2¢ dark violet	.80	.55	.35	.25	.25
J16B	3¢ dark violet (1965)	2.25	1.75	1.95	1.35	1.00
J17	4¢ dark violet	.50	.40	.35	.25	.25
J18	5¢ dark violet (1948)	.50	.40	.40	.30	.40
J19	6¢ dark violet (1957)	2.25	1.70	1.95	1.35	1.50
J20	10¢ dark violet	.50	.40	.35	.25	.25

POSTAGE DUES

SCOTT NO.	DESCRIPTION	PLATE BLOCK F/NH	UNUSED F/NH	USED F
	1967 Perf. 12 Regular Size Design 20mm X 17mm			
J21-27	**1¢-10¢ cpl., 7 vars.**	**22.00**	**3.50**	**3.40**
J21	1¢ carmine rose	8.25	.25	.25
J22	2¢ carmine rose	1.40	.25	.25
J23	3¢ carmine rose	1.40	.25	.25
J24	4¢ carmine rose	2.75	.45	.25
J25	5¢ carmine rose	10.00	1.65	1.35
J26	6¢ carmine rose	3.00	.40	.25
J27	10¢ carmine rose	3.00	.45	.25
	1969-78 Perf. 12 (White or Yellow Gum) Modular Size Design 20mm x 15-3/4 mm			
J28/37 (J28-31, J33-37) 9 vars.		**14.00**	**2.95**	**1.90**
J28	1¢ carmine rose (1970)	3.00	.55	.45
J29	2¢ carmine rose (1972)	2.25	.45	.35
J30	3¢ carmine rose (1974)	1.70	.30	.25
J31	4¢ carmine rose (1969)	1.75	.35	.25
J32a	5¢ carmine rose (1977)	125.00	24.75	24.75
J33	6¢ carmine rose (1972)	1.50	.30	.25
J34	8¢ carmine rose	1.50	.30	.25
J35	10¢ carmine rose (1969)	1.50	.65	.25
J36	12¢ carmine rose (1969)	5.00	.85	.65
J37	16¢ carmine rose (1974)	2.00	.40	.35
	1977-78 Perf. 12-1/2 X 12			
J28a-40	**1¢-50¢ cpl., 9 vars.**	**22.00**	**5.05**	**4.75**
J28a	1¢ carmine rose	.95	.25	.25
J31a	4¢ carmine rose	.95	.25	.25
J32	5¢ carmine rose	.95	.25	.25
J34a	8¢ carmine rose (1978)	2.50	.40	.25
J35a	10¢ carmine rose	1.35	.30	.25
J36a	12¢ carmine rose	11.00	2.25	1.40
J38	20¢ carmine rose	2.60	.55	.45
J39	24¢ carmine rose	3.25	.65	.45
J40	50¢ carmine rose	4.60	1.25	1.00

OFFICIAL STAMPS

1949-50
#249, 250, 252, 254, 269-73 overprinted O.H.M.S.

SCOTT NO.	DESCRIPTION	PLATE BLOCK F/NH	UNUSED F/NH	USED F
O1-10	**1¢-$1 complete, 9 vars.**	......	**315.00**	**165.00**
O1-8	**1¢-20¢, 7 varieties**	......	**47.50**	**18.50**
O1	1¢ green	12.00	2.50	1.85
O2	2¢ brown	110.00	15.40	8.00
O3	3¢ rose violet	12.00	2.50	1.35
O4	4¢ dark carmine	17.50	3.30	.70
O6	10¢ olive	22.00	5.55	.65
O7	14¢ black brown	32.00	7.50	2.25
O8	20¢ slate black	85.00	18.50	3.00
O9	50¢ dark blue green	1100.00	203.50	100.00
O10	$1 red violet	450.00	73.00	40.00
	1950 #294 overprinted O.H.M.S.			
O11	50¢ dull green	300.00	39.00	26.50
	1950 #284-88 overprinted O.H.M.S.			
O12-15A	**1¢-5¢ cpl., 5 vars.**	**26.75**	**6.95**	**3.25**
O12	1¢ green	3.50	.75	.40
O13	2¢ sepia	5.00	1.50	.75
O14	3¢ rose violet	5.25	1.50	.60
O15	4¢ dark carmine	5.25	1.50	.20
O15A	5¢ deep blue	11.00	2.40	1.60
	1950 #284-88, 269-71, 294, 273 overprinted G			
O16-25	**1¢-$1 complete, 10 vars.**	......	**148.00**	**85.00**
O16-24	**1¢-50¢, 9 varieties**	......	**37.00**	**8.00**
O16	1¢ green	4.25	.90	.25
O17	2¢ sepia	7.00	1.75	.85
O18	3¢ rose violet	7.00	1.75	.25
O19	4¢ dark carmine	7.00	1.75	.25
O20	5¢ deep blue	14.00	2.75	.95
O21	10¢ olive	17.00	3.75	.50
O22	14¢ black brown	38.00	7.15	2.25
O23	20¢ slate black	90.00	16.50	1.05
O24	50¢ dull green	60.00	11.00	5.75
O25	$1 red violet	475.50	112.00	82.00
	1950-51 #301, 302 overprinted G			
O26	10¢ black brown	8.00	1.30	.30
O27	$1 bright ultramarine	450.00	100.00	85.00

SCOTT NO.	DESCRIPTION	PLATE BLOCK F/NH	UNUSED F/NH	USED F
	1951-53 #305-06, 316, 320-21 overprinted G			
O28	2¢ olive green	3.50	.70	.25
O29	4¢ orange vermillion ('52)	4.95	.95	.25
O30	20¢ gray (1952)	17.00	3.75	.25
O31	7¢ blue (1952)	19.75	4.10	1.25
O32	$1 gray (1953)	90.00	16.25	10.25
	1953 #325-29, 334 overprinted G			
O33-37	**1¢-5¢ complete, 5vars**	**8.40**	**2.40**	**1.15**
O33	1¢ violet brown	2.00	.40	.25
O34	2¢ green	2.00	.40	.25
O35	3¢ carmine	2.00	.40	.25
O36	4¢ violet	3.00	.50	.25
O37	5¢ ultramarine	3.00	.50	.25
O38	50¢ lightgreen	27.00	5.25	1.00
	1955 #351 overprinted G			
O39	10¢ violet brown	6.50	1.40	.25

SCOTT NO.	DESCRIPTION	PLATE BLOCK F/NH	UNUSED F/NH	USED F
	1955-56 #337, 338, 340, 341, 362 overprinted G			
O40-45	**1¢-20¢ cpl., 5vars.**	**17.00**	**6.50**	**1.35**
O40	1¢ violet brown(1956)	3.00	.85	.45
O41	2¢ green (1956)	3.00	.85	.25
O43	4¢ violet(1956)	7.00	1.85	.25
O44	5¢ bright blue	3.00	.85	.25
O45	20¢ green(1956)	9.95	2.25	.25
	1963 #401, 402, 404, 405 overprinted G			
O46-49	**1¢-5¢ cpl., 4 vars.**	**14.60**	**4.30**	**2.95**
O46	1¢ deep brown	4.00	1.20	.85
O47	2¢ green	4.00	1.20	.85
O48	4¢ carmine	8.00	1.40	.85
O49	5¢ violet blue	2.75	.85	.55
	1949-50 AIR POST OFFICIAL STAMPS			
CO1	7¢ deep blue, O.H.M.S.(C9)	45.00	10.00	4.50
CO2	7¢ deep blue, G (C9)	90.00	18.15	13.75
	1950 SPECIAL DELIVERY OFFICIAL STAMPS			
EO1	10¢ green, O.H.M.S.(E11)	99.00	16.00	12.25
EO2	10¢ green, G (E11)	185.00	25.00	25.00

British Columbia & Vancouver Island #1-18

1

2
Queen Victoria

4

7
Seal

SCOTT NO.	DESCRIPTION	UNUSED O.G. VF	UNUSED O.G. F	UNUSED O.G. AVG	UNUSED VF	UNUSED F	UNUSED AVG	USED VF	USED F	USED AVG
	1860 Imperforate									
1	2-1/2p dull rose	...	...	...	...	21,000.00	15000.00	...	...	...
	1860 Perforated 14									
2	2-1/2p dull rose	950.00	650.00	425.00	475.00	375.00	240.00	300.00	225.00	150.00
	VANCOUVER ISLAND									
	1865 Imperforate									
3	5¢ rose	....	....	....	....	....	....	....	....	....
4	10¢ blue	4500.00	2450.00	1650.00	3000.00	1975.00	1200.00	1350.00	725.00	450.00
	Perforated 14									
5	5¢ rose	1050.00	700.00	450.00	700.00	530.00	340.00	525.00	430.00	270.00
6	10¢ blue	1050.00	700.00	450.00	700.00	530.00	340.00	525.00	430.00	270.00
	BRITISH COLUMBIA									
	1865									
7	3p blue	350.00	220.00	110.00	170.00	110.00	70.00	300.00	160.00	95.00
	New Values surcharged on 1865 design									
	1867-69 Perforated 14									
8	2¢ brown	400.00	225.00	150.00	250.00	165.00	95.00	240.00	160.00	95.00
9	5¢ bright red	625.00	375.00	225.00	400.00	272.00	160.00	400.00	320.00	185.00
10	10¢ lilac rose	4500.00	2450.00	1300.00	2450.00	1300.00	700.00	...	...	...
11	25¢ orange	800.00	550.00	325.00	450.00	325.00	190.00	410.00	320.00	185.00
12	50¢ violet	2400.00	1225.00	850.00	1500.00	975.00	575.00	1450.00	995.00	570.00
13	$1 green	3800.00	2250.00	1500.00	2400.00	1600.00	980.00	...	...	...
	1869 Perforated 12-1/2									
14	5¢ bright red	5200.00	2800.00	1675.00	3600.00	2250.00	1350.00	2550.00	1950.00	990.00
15	10¢ lilac rose	3000.00	1900.00	1050.00	1700.00	1250.00	795.00	1650.00	1295.00	770.00
16	25¢ orange	1950.00	1400.00	800.00	1250.00	810.00	500.00	900.00	825.00	500.00
17	50¢ violet	3150.00	1550.00	950.00	1400.00	795.00	775.00	1450.00	825.00	650.00
18	$1 green	4750.00	2800.00	1550.00	2400.00	1155.00	1150.00	2875.00	1950.00	1175.00

1, 15A, 16

2, 11, 17

3, 11A

4, 12, 18

6, 13, 20

7, 21

8, 22

9, 15, 23

24, 38
Codfish

25, 26, 40
Seal

SCOTT NO.	DESCRIPTION	UNUSED O.G. VF	UNUSED O.G. F	UNUSED O.G. AVG	UNUSED VF	UNUSED F	UNUSED AVG	USED VF	USED F	USED AVG
	1857 Imperforate, Thick Paper									
1	1p brown violet	125.00	100.00	75.00	72.50	55.00	38.50	200.00	165.00	135.00
2	2p scarlet vermillion	17500.00	14000.00	12000.00	13000.00	11000.00	9000.00	5800.00	4800.00	3500.00
3	3p green	540.00	410.00	260.00	360.00	275.00	175.00	485.00	375.00	300.00
4	4p scarlet vermillion	12000.00	8600.00	7000.00	9000.00	7500.00	6500.00	3800.00	2800.00	2300.00
5	5p brown violet	300.00	225.00	195.00	250.00	200.00	165.00	380.00	300.00	265.00
6	6p scarlet vermillion	23000.00	17000.00	12000.00	19000.00	16000.00	13500.00	4800.00	4100.00	3000.00
7	6-1/2p scarlet vermillion	4500.00	3800.00	3000.00	3900.00	3000.00	2500.00	3800.00	3100.00	2600.00
8	8p scarlet vermillion	475.00	400.00	325.00	425.00	350.00	300.00	480.00	400.00	350.00
9	1sh scarlet vermillion	46000.00	40000.00	35000.00	42000.00	37000.00	31000.00	10000.00	8100.00	6300.00
	1860 Thin Paper									
11	2p orange	400.00	325.00	290.00	350.00	300.00	265.00	450.00	375.00	300.00
11A	3p green	80.00	62.00	39.50	53.50	41.25	26.40	110.00	85.00	60.00
12	4p orange	3300.00	2800.00	23000.00	2900.00	2400.00	1900.00	1100.00	850.00	600.00
12A	5p violet brown	127.50	100.00	49.50	85.00	66.00	33.00	180.00	138.00	95.00
13	6p orange	5600.00	4600.00	3800.00	4100.00	3500.00	3100.00	1000.00	750.00	600.00
	1861-62 Thin Paper									
15	1sh orange	30000.00	23000.00	16000.00	25000.00	19000.00	16000.00	10000.00	8200.00	6000.00
15A	1p violet brown	195.00	150.00	100.00	130.00	100.00	66.00	225.00	200.00	165.00
16	1p reddish brown	8500.00	6000.00	4500.00	5500.00	3400.00	2800.00	...	...	...
17	2p rose	195.00	150.00	100.00	130.00	100.00	66.00	175.00	138.00	95.00
18	4p rose	58.75	45.00	25.50	39.25	30.25	17.00	75.00	60.00	40.00
19	5p reddish brown	64.50	44.50	33.00	43.00	33.00	22.00	78.00	63.00	44.00
20	6p rose	32.25	24.75	13.20	21.50	16.50	8.80	69.00	53.00	35.75
21	6-1/2p rose	96.75	74.25	39.60	64.50	49.50	26.40	320.00	240.00	190.00
22	8p rose	82.50	63.50	33.00	55.00	42.35	22.00	320.00	240.00	190.00
23	1sh rose	48.50	37.00	19.75	32.00	24.75	13.20	260.00	170.00	90.00

27
Prince Albert

28, 29
Queen Victoria

30
Fishing Ship

31
Queen Victoria

32, 32A, 37
Prince of Wales

35, 36
Queen Victoria

1865-94 Perforate 12 Yellow Paper

SCOTT NO.	DESCRIPTION	UNUSED O.G. VF	UNUSED O.G. F	UNUSED O.G. AVG	UNUSED VF	UNUSED F	UNUSED AVG	USED VF	USED F	USED AVG
24	2¢ green	88.00	72.00	55.00	72.00	60.00	50.00	32.00	25.00	16.00
24a	2¢ green (white paper)	115.00	95.00	85.00	100.00	85.00	70.00	46.00	40.00	36.00
25	5¢ brown	560.00	430.00	300.00	430.00	360.00	230.00	375.00	310.00	255.00
26	5¢ black (1868)	450.00	350.00	240.00	350.00	290.00	190.00	155.00	130.00	100.00
27	10¢ black	440.00	330.00	250.00	370.00	260.00	170.00	71.50	55.00	43.00
27a	10¢ black (thin yellowish paper)	425.00	360.00	300.00	375.00	280.00	170.00	120.00	100.00	80.00
28	12¢ pale red brown	70.00	60.00	50.00	65.00	55.00	49.00	48.00	40.00	34.00
28a	12¢ pale red brown (thin yellowish paper)	510.00	460.00	390.00	485.00	435.00	320.00	195.00	160.00	120.00
29	12¢ brown (1894)	58.00	48.00	35.00	55.00	48.00	36.00	46.00	36.00	29.00
30	13¢ orange	230.00	195.00	180.00	185.00	160.00	130.00	120.00	95.00	82.00
31	24¢ blue	53.00	45.00	38.00	49.00	42.00	39.00	31.00	24.00	19.00

1868-94

SCOTT NO.	DESCRIPTION	UNUSED O.G. VF	UNUSED O.G. F	UNUSED O.G. AVG	UNUSED VF	UNUSED F	UNUSED AVG	USED VF	USED F	USED AVG
32	1¢ violet	185.00	125.00	80.00	150.00	105.00	70.00	61.00	45.00	30.00
32A	1¢ brown lilac, re-engraved (1871)	165.00	135.00	105.00	202.00	150.00	45.00	65.00	52.00	32.00
33	3¢ vermillion (1870)	525.00	450.00	325.00	320.00	260.00	200.00	175.00	135.00	85.00
34	3¢ blue (1873)	525.00	450.00	315.00	300.00	250.00	220.00	78.00	55.00	35.00
35	6¢ dull rose (1870)	23.00	20.00	16.00	20.00	17.00	14.00	15.00	11.00	7.50
36	6¢ carmine lake (1894)	38.00	33.00	26.00	34.00	26.00	15.00	23.00	12.00	8.00

1876-79 Rouletted

SCOTT NO.	DESCRIPTION	UNUSED O.G. VF	UNUSED O.G. F	UNUSED O.G. AVG	UNUSED VF	UNUSED F	UNUSED AVG	USED VF	USED F	USED AVG
37	1¢ brown lilac (1877)	165.00	120.00	75.00	159.00	120.00	65.00	50.00	38.00	23.00
38	2¢ green (1879)	200.00	175.00	110.00	175.00	150.00	100.00	50.00	38.00	23.00
39	3¢ blue (1877)	430.00	330.00	200.00	350.00	300.00	180.00	15.00	11.50	8.00
40	5¢ blue	280.00	225.00	180.00	230.00	200.00	160.00	15.00	11.50	8.00

41-45
Prince of Wales

46-48
Codfish

53-55
Seal

56-58
Newfoundland Dog

1880-96 Perforate 12

SCOTT NO.	DESCRIPTION	UNUSED O.G. VF	UNUSED O.G. F	UNUSED O.G. AVG	UNUSED VF	UNUSED F	UNUSED AVG	USED VF	USED F	USED AVG
41	1¢ violet brown	53.00	41.00	33.00	50.00	38.00	32.00	11.00	9.00	7.00
42	1¢ gray brown	53.00	41.00	33.00	50.00	38.00	32.00	11.00	9.00	7.00
43	1¢ brown (Reissue) (1896)	110.00	80.00	65.00	85.00	60.00	40.00	60.00	45.00	35.00
44	1¢ deep green (1887)	20.00	15.00	10.00	15.00	11.00	8.50	4.00	2.75	2.00
45	1¢ green (Reissue) (1897)	20.00	15.00	10.00	18.00	13.00	10.00	6.50	4.95	2.75
46	2¢ yellow green	47.00	35.00	25.00	36.00	24.00	16.00	15.00	12.00	7.50
47	2¢ green (Reissue) (1896)	88.00	68.00	54.00	78.00	60.00	49.00	28.00	22.00	17.00
48	2¢ red orange (1887)	32.00	24.00	20.00	26.00	22.00	18.00	10.00	8.00	6.00
49	3¢ blue	56.00	47.00	33.00	46.00	38.00	34.00	7.00	5.00	3.50
51	3¢ umber brown (1887)	43.00	35.00	31.00	35.00	29.00	22.00	5.00	3.50	2.50
52	3¢ violet brown (Reissue) (1896)	120.00	100.00	60.00	95.00	70.00	55.00	90.00	80.00	73.00
53	5¢ pale blue	380.00	300.00	50.00	300.00	225.00	165.00	11.25	8.80	5.00
54	5¢ dark blue (1887)	170.00	130.00	100.00	140.00	85.00	50.00	8.50	6.60	4.00
55	5¢ bright blue (1894)	55.00	44.00	37.00	44.00	37.00	31.00	6.50	4.95	3.00

59
Schooner

60
Queen Victoria

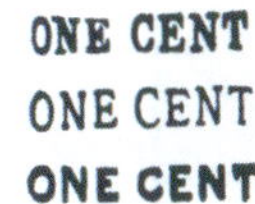

1897
60a surcharged in black

61
Queen Victoria

62
John Cabot

63
Cape Bonavista

1887-96

SCOTT NO.	DESCRIPTION	UNUSED O.G. VF	UNUSED O.G. F	UNUSED O.G. AVG	UNUSED VF	UNUSED F	UNUSED AVG	USED VF	USED F	USED AVG
56	1/2¢ rose red	10.00	8.50	6.50	9.00	7.75	6.00	7.50	6.25	5.00
57	1/2¢ orange red (1896)	80.00	65.00	45.00	30.00	50.00	40.00	48.00	36.00	28.00
58	1/2¢ black (1894)	16.00	6.50	4.25	7.50	5.50	4.00	7.50	6.00	4.00
59	10¢ black	125.00	100.00	75.00	85.00	70.00	50.00	67.00	48.00	36.00

1890

SCOTT NO.	DESCRIPTION	UNUSED O.G. VF	UNUSED O.G. F	UNUSED O.G. AVG	UNUSED VF	UNUSED F	UNUSED AVG	USED VF	USED F	USED AVG
60	3¢ slate	30.00	25.00	20.00	27.00	23.00	18.00	1.60	1.30	.90

64
Caribou Hunting

65
Mining

66
Logging

67
Fishing

68
Cabot's Ship

69
Ptarmigan

70
Seals

71
Salmon Fishing

72
Seal of Colony

73
Coast Scene

74
King Henry VII

1897 CABOT ISSUE

SCOTT NO.	DESCRIPTION	UNUSED O.G. VF	UNUSED O.G. F	UNUSED O.G. AVG	UNUSED VF	UNUSED F	UNUSED AVG	USED VF	USED F	USED AVG
61-74	**1¢-60¢ complete, 14 varieties ....**	**360.00**	**275.00**	**170.00**	**250.00**	**225.00**	**130.50**	**185.00**	**150.00**	**95.00**
61	1¢ deep green	4.50	2.85	1.95	2.25	1.75	1.25	1.75	1.40	.95
62	2¢ carmine lake	5.00	3.85	2.75	2.50	1.85	1.35	1.55	1.20	.75
63	3¢ ultramarine	8.50	5.75	3.85	4.25	3.25	2.55	1.45	1.10	.60
64	4¢ olive green	13.00	8.75	6.50	6.50	4.25	3.75	3.55	2.75	1.65
65	5¢ violet	20.00	13.75	10.00	10.00	7.00	5.00	3.55	2.75	1.65
66	6¢ red brown	14.00	9.00	7.00	7.00	4.50	3.00	4.30	3.30	2.00
67	8¢ red orange	45.00	31.00	22.00	22.00	16.00	9.00	14.00	12.00	9.00
68	10¢ black brown	45.00	31.00	22.00	22.00	16.00	9.00	14.00	12.00	9.00
69	12¢ dark blue	55.00	38.00	25.00	27.00	18.00	10.00	17.00	14.00	11.00
70	15¢ scarlet	55.00	38.00	25.00	27.00	18.00	10.00	17.00	14.00	11.00
71	24¢ gray violet	70.00	48.00	38.00	38.00	26.00	19.00	22.00	18.00	15.00
72	30¢ slate	130.00	95.00	60.00	65.00	45.00	35.00	55.00	48.00	29.00
73	35¢ red	290.00	200.00	150.00	140.00	90.00	65.00	64.75	49.50	25.00
74	60¢ black	45.00	30.00	24.00	25.00	16.00	10.00	12.00	9.00	7.00

1897

SCOTT NO.	DESCRIPTION	UNUSED O.G. VF	UNUSED O.G. F	UNUSED O.G. AVG	UNUSED VF	UNUSED F	UNUSED AVG	USED VF	USED F	USED AVG
75	1¢ on 3¢ gray lilac, Type a	200.00	120.00	95.00	90.00	48.00	36.00	30.00	26.00	23.00
76	1¢ on 3¢ gray lilac, Type b	600.00	325.00	250.00	260.00	185.00	150.00	195.00	170.00	120.00
77	1¢ on 3¢ gray lilac, Type c	1500.00	1000.00	750.00	825.00	525.00	395.00	700.00	610.00	550.00

78
Edward, Prince of Wales

79, 80
Queen Victoria

81, 82
King Edward VII

83
Queen Alexandria

84
Queen Mary

85
King George V

1897-1901 ROYAL FAMILY ISSUE

SCOTT NO.	DESCRIPTION	UNUSED O.G. VF	UNUSED O.G. F	UNUSED O.G. AVG	UNUSED VF	UNUSED F	UNUSED AVG	USED VF	USED F	USED AVG
78-85	**1/2¢-5¢ complete, 8 varieties ....**	**110.00**	**95.50**	**70.50**	**74.00**	**61.25**	**42.00**	**18.75**	**14.50**	**8.10**
78	1/2¢ olive green	8.00	5.00	3.75	4.25	2.75	2.00	2.65	2.05	1.10
79	1¢ carmine rose	10.00	6.75	3.50	5.75	3.75	8.25	4.95	3.75	2.75
80	1¢ yellow green (1898)	9.75	6.00	5.00	5.00	3.50	2.50	.30	.25	.20
81	2¢ orange	12.00	8.00	7.00	6.50	4.25	2.50	4.30	3.30	2.00
82	2¢ vermillion (1898)	25.00	15.00	8.00	12.50	8.00	5.50	.75	.55	.35
83	3¢ orange (1898)	60.00	38.00	27.00	30.00	20.00	14.00	.75	.55	.35
84	4¢ violet (1901)	85.00	58.00	30.00	42.00	28.00	16.00	4.30	3.30	1.85
85	5¢ blue (1899)	105.00	63.00	40.00	52.00	35.00	24.00	3.00	2.50	1.75

86
Map of Newfoundland

87
King James I

88
Arms of the London & Bristol Company

89
John Guy

90
Guy's Ship the "Endeavour"

91
View of the Town of Cupids

92, 92A, 98
Lord Bacon

93, 99
View of Mosquito Bay

94, 100
Logging Camp

95, 101
Paper Mills

96, 102
King Edward VII

SCOTT NO.	DESCRIPTION	UNUSED O.G. VF	F	AVG	UNUSED VF	F	AVG	USED VF	F	AVG
					1908					
86	2¢ rose carmine	140.00	78.00	65.00	70.00	41.00	25.00	2.00	1.60	1.25

1910 JOHN GUY ISSUE—Lithographed Perf.12

SCOTT NO.	DESCRIPTION	UNUSED O.G. VF	F	AVG	UNUSED VF	F	AVG	USED VF	F	AVG
87/97	**(87-92, 92A, 93-97) 12 varieties**	**845.00**	**675.00**	**470.00**	**653.00**	**521.75**	**382.00**	**637.50**	**440.75**	**272.25**
87	1¢ deep green, perf. 12x11	4.25	3.00	1.85	2.25	1.50	1.00	1.10	.85	.50
87a	1¢ deep green	9.00	6.50	4.50	6.80	3.85	2.25	2.15	1.65	1.00
87b	1¢ deep green, perf. 12x14	8.00	5.50	4.00	4.50	3.00	2.00	2.25	1.85	1.40
88	2¢ carmine	21.00	15.00	11.00	11.50	7.50	4.00	1.20	.95	.70
88a	2¢ carmine, perf. 12x14	15.00	10.00	7.00	8.00	5.00	3.00	.85	.65	.40
88c	2¢ carmine, perf. 12x11-1/2	600.00	425.00	300.00	500.00	340.00	270.00	350.00	275.00	175.00
89	3¢ brown olive	40.00	27.00	20.00	19.00	14.00	9.00	15.00	13.00	10.00
90	4¢ dull violet	40.00	27.00	20.00	19.00	14.00	9.00	12.00	9.50	7.50
91	5¢ ultramarine, perf. 14x12	40.00	27.00	20.00	19.00	14.00	8.00	4.25	3.50	2.25
91a	5¢ ultramarine	52.00	35.00	25.00	25.00	18.00	12.00	7.50	6.00	4.75
92	6¢ claret (I)	185.00	126.00	85.00	90.00	65.00	45.00	65.00	54.00	38.00
92A	6¢ claret (II)	85.00	110.00	40.00	44.00	32.00	26.00	38.00	33.00	26.00
93	8¢ pale brown	175.00	110.00	70.00	85.00	55.00	30.00	55.00	45.00	26.00
94	9¢ olive green	175.00	110.00	70.00	85.00	55.00	30.00	55.00	45.00	26.00
95	10¢ violet black	175.00	110.00	70.00	85.00	55.00	30.00	55.00	45.00	26.00
96	12¢ lilac brown	175.00	110.00	70.00	85.00	55.00	30.00	55.00	45.00	26.00
97	15¢ gray black	185.00	120.00	75.00	90.00	60.00	35.00	65.00	54.00	40.00

#92 Type I. "Z" of "COLONIZATION" is reversed. #92A Type II. "Z" is normal

97, 103
King George V

104
Queen Mary

105
King George

106

107

108
Princess Mary

109
Prince Henry

1911 Engraved. Perf. 14

SCOTT NO.	DESCRIPTION	UNUSED O.G. VF	F	AVG	UNUSED VF	F	AVG	USED VF	F	AVG
98-103	**6¢-15¢ complete, 6 varieties**	**650.00**	**450.00**	**380.00**	**390.00**	**240.00**	**150.00**	**340.00**	**240.00**	**175.00**
98	6¢ brown violet	65.00	45.00	32.00	35.00	25.00	19.00	23.00	20.00	15.00
99	8¢ bistre brown	180.00	115.00	90.00	85.00	65.00	40.00	68.00	50.00	48.00
100	9¢ olive green	140.00	96.00	75.00	75.00	50.00	35.00	58.00	43.00	34.00
101	10¢ violet black	210.00	133.00	160.00	100.00	70.00	50.00	95.00	83.00	64.00
102	12¢ red brown	185.00	115.00	90.00	95.00	65.00	40.00	75.00	71.00	56.00
103	15¢ slate brown	185.00	115.00	90.00	95.00	65.00	40.00	75.00	71.00	56.00

110
Prince George

111
Prince John

112
Queen Alexandria

113
Duke of Connaught

114
Seal of Colony

1911 ROYAL FAMILY ISSUE

SCOTT NO.	DESCRIPTION	UNUSED O.G. VF	UNUSED O.G. F	UNUSED O.G. AVG	UNUSED VF	UNUSED F	UNUSED AVG	USED VF	USED F	USED AVG
104-14	**1¢-15¢ complete, 11 varieties..........**	**750.00**	**475.00**	**370.00**	**425.00**	**240.00**	**91.25**	**210.00**	**175.00**	**130.00**
104	1¢ yellow green.................................	7.00	5.00	3.50	5.00	3.00	2.00	.30	.25	.20
105	2¢ carmine...	7.25	5.00	3.75	5.00	3.00	2.00	.85	.70	.60
106	3¢ red brown......................................	54.00	40.00	30.00	35.00	27.00	18.00	19.00	15.00	13.00
107	4¢ violet..	42.00	33.00	28.00	29.00	19.00	15.00	13.50	11.00	9.00
108	5¢ ultramarine....................................	24.00	18.00	13.00	19.00	13.00	9.00	1.80	1.40	.75
109	6¢ black...	52.00	37.00	26.00	30.00	24.00	17.00	23.00	20.00	17.00
110	8¢ blue (paper colored).......................	185.00	115.00	90.00	96.00	65.00	50.00	65.00	53.00	39.00
110a	8¢ peacock blue (white paper)...........	195.00	125.00	95.00	108.00	70.00	55.00	70.00	60.00	45.00
111	9¢ blue violet......................................	52.00	34.00	25.00	35.00	24.00	15.00	21.00	18.00	13.00
112	10¢ dark green..................................	95.00	67.00	45.00	55.00	36.00	29.00	38.00	33.00	27.00
113	12¢ plum..	90.00	58.00	40.00	48.00	34.00	26.00	38.00	33.00	27.00
114	50¢ magenta......................................	75.00	49.00	38.00	38.00	26.00	18.00	38.00	33.00	27.00

115

116

72
surcharged

70 & 73
surcharged

131

132

133

134

135

136

137

138

139

140

1919 TRAIL OF THE CARIBOU ISSUE

SCOTT NO.	DESCRIPTION	UNUSED O.G. VF	UNUSED O.G. F	UNUSED O.G. AVG	UNUSED VF	UNUSED F	UNUSED AVG	USED VF	USED F	USED AVG
115-26	**1¢ -36¢ complete, 12 varieties ....**	**300.00**	**220.00**	**140.00**	**220.00**	**175.00**	**105.00**	**170.00**	**140.00**	**95.00**
115	1¢ green...	5.50	3.50	2.25	3.25	2.10	1.40	.40	.30	.20
116	2¢ scarlet..	5.65	3.75	2.50	3.40	2.25	1.50	.55	.40	.25
117	3¢ red brown.....................................	7.00	4.75	3.50	4.25	3.00	2.60	.35	.25	.15
118	4¢ violet..	10.00	6.50	5.00	5.75	4.00	2.25	1.45	1.10	.65
119	5¢ ultramarine...................................	18.00	13.00	10.00	11.00	7.00	3.50	1.45	1.10	.65
120	6¢ gray..	40.00	29.00	19.00	26.00	17.00	11.00	22.00	18.75	14.50
121	8¢ magenta.......................................	40.00	29.00	19.00	26.00	17.00	11.00	18.00	16.50	13.50
122	10¢ dark green..................................	28.00	19.00	12.00	18.00	10.00	7.00	12.00	11.00	10.00
123	12¢ orange..	140.00	90.00	65.00	82.00	55.00	40.00	62.00	56.00	48.00
124	15¢ dark blue....................................	90.00	60.00	40.00	55.00	36.00	20.00	42.00	38.00	32.00
125	24¢ bistre..	90.00	60.00	40.00	55.00	36.00	20.00	42.00	37.00	30.00
126	36¢ olive green..................................	75.00	50.00	35.00	45.00	32.00	18.00	40.00	36.00	29.00

SCOTT NO.	DESCRIPTION	UNUSED O.G. F	UNUSED O.G. AVG	UNUSED F	UNUSED AVG	USED F	USED AVG
	1920						
127	2¢ on 30¢ slate	9.00	6.75	8.25	5.75	5.50	4.00
	Bars 10-1/2mm apart						
128	3¢ on 15¢ scarlet	325.00	265.00	280.00	195.00	225.00	170.00
	Bars 13-1/2mm apart						
129	3¢ on 15¢ scarlet	26.00	20.00	23.00	16.00	11.00	8.55
130	3¢ on 35¢ red	17.00	13.00	15.00	11.00	9.50	7.50

141

142

143

144

145, 163, 172
Map of Newfoundland

146, 164, 173
S.S. Caribou

1923-24 PICTORIAL ISSUE

SCOTT NO.	DESCRIPTION	UNUSED O.G. F	UNUSED O.G. AVG	UNUSED F	UNUSED AVG	USED F	USED AVG
131-44	**1¢-24¢ complete, 14 varieties**	**210.00**	**135.00**	**140.00**	**80.00**	**85.00**	**62.00**
131	1¢ gray green	3.50	2.35	2.25	1.60	.25	.20
132	2¢ carmine	3.50	2.35	2.25	1.55	.25	.20
133	3¢ brown	4.75	3.00	2.85	1.95	.25	.20
134	4¢ brown violet	5.50	3.50	3.25	2.25	1.85	1.25
135	5¢ ultramarine	10.00	8.00	6.00	3.75	2.25	1.70
136	6¢ gray black	9.00	7.50	6.00	4.00	5.30	3.95
137	8¢ dull violet	7.25	6.00	6.00	4.00	4.25	3.25
138	9¢ slate green	52.00	45.00	48.00	35.00	28.00	20.00
139	10¢ dark violet	6.25	5.00	6.00	4.50	2.50	1.90
140	11¢ olive green	10.50	8.00	9.75	7.00	7.00	4.75
141	12¢ lake	10.50	8.00	9.75	7.00	7.75	5.75
142	15¢ deep blue	13.00	9.00	12.00	8.00	8.00	5.75
143	20¢ red brown (1924)	19.00	16.00	17.50	12.00	7.50	6.00
144	24¢ black brown (1924)	82.00	60.00	77.00	48.00	45.00	38.00

147, 165, 174
Queen Mary and King George

148, 166, 175
Prince of Wales

149, 167, 176
Express Train

150, 168, 177
Newfoundland Hotel, St. John's

151, 178
Town of Heart's Content

152
Cabot Tower, St. John's

153, 169, 179
War Memorial, St. John's

154, 158
Post Office, St. John's

156, 170, 180
First Airplane to Cross Atlantic Non-Stop

157, 171, 181
House of Parliament, St. John's

159, 182
Grand Falls, Labrador

1928 Tourist Publicity Issue
Unwatermarked. Thin paper, dull colors

SCOTT NO.	DESCRIPTION	UNUSED O.G. F	UNUSED O.G. AVG	UNUSED F	UNUSED AVG	USED F	USED AVG
145-59	**1¢-30¢ complete, 15 varieties**	**140.00**	**90.00**	**99.00**	**70.00**	**68.00**	**44.00**
145	1¢ deep green	2.10	1.55	1.25	.95	.75	.60
146	2¢ deep carmine	4.25	3.25	2.50	1.85	.65	.50
147	3¢ brown	4.25	3.25	4.00	2.00	.50	.32
148	4¢ lilac rose	5.25	5.00	5.00	3.50	1.85	1.20
149	5¢ slate green	12.25	11.75	9.50	7.50	4.50	2.80
150	6¢ ultramarine	8.25	7.75	7.75	5.00	5.00	4.00
151	8¢ light red brown	10.25	8.50	8.75	6.50	4.50	3.50
152	9¢ myrtle green	10.25	8.50	10.00	7.00	7.00	5.00
153	10¢ dark violet	12.50	11.00	12.00	7.50	4.50	3.25
154	12¢ brown carmine	8.50	7.00	7.75	6.00	5.00	5.00
155	14¢ red brown	17.00	13.00	16.00	12.00	7.00	6.00
156	15¢ dark blue	12.00	11.00	12.00	7.50	7.00	6.00
157	20¢ gray black	17.00	15.00	16.00	12.00	6.75	4.00
158	28¢ gray green	40.00	36.00	38.00	28.00	24.00	18.00
159	30¢ olive brown	21.00	17.50	19.00	15.00	7.75	5.75

1929

SCOTT NO.	DESCRIPTION	UNUSED O.G. F	UNUSED O.G. AVG	UNUSED F	UNUSED AVG	USED F	USED AVG
160	3¢ on 6¢ gray black	5.50	4.00	5.00	3.25	3.35	2.85

1929-31 Tourist Publicity Issue
Types of 1928 re-engraved
Unwatermarked. Thicker paper, brighter colors

SCOTT NO.	DESCRIPTION	UNUSED O.G. F	UNUSED O.G. AVG	UNUSED F	UNUSED AVG	USED F	USED AVG
163-71	**1¢-20¢ complete, 9 varieties**	**155.00**	**115.00**	**135.00**	**90.00**	**64.90**	**50.00**
163	1¢ green	3.00	2.50	2.75	2.00	.65	.50
164	2¢ deep carmine	3.00	2.50	2.75	2.00	.35	.25
165	3¢ deep red brown	3.00	2.50	2.75	2.00	.35	.25
166	4¢ magenta	5.25	4.00	5.00	3.50	1.50	.75
167	5¢ slate green	11.00	9.00	10.00	8.00	1.50	.75
168	6¢ ultramarine	15.00	13.00	12.00	7.00	9.00	7.00
169	10¢ dark violet	12.50	9.00	12.00	8.00	2.50	1.75
170	15¢ deep blue (1930)	72.00	60.00	65.00	45.00	38.00	33.00
171	20¢ gray black (1931)	110.00	90.00	97.00	65.00	28.00	22.00

1931 Tourist Publicity Issue
Types of 1928 re-engraved, watermarked, coat of arms
Thicker paper, brighter colors

SCOTT NO.	DESCRIPTION	UNUSED O.G. F	UNUSED O.G. AVG	UNUSED F	UNUSED AVG	USED F	USED AVG
172-82	**1¢-30¢ complete, 11 varieties**	**250.00**	**180.00**	**225.00**	**140.00**	**105.00**	**75.00**
172	1¢ green	4.25	3.00	3.95	2.00	1.25	.85
173	2¢ red	11.00	8.00	10.00	7.50	1.30	.90
174	3¢ red brown	5.25	4.00	5.00	3.00	1.30	.85
175	4¢ rose	6.25	5.00	5.75	4.00	2.75	1.85
176	5¢ greenish gray	19.00	14.00	15.00	12.00	7.00	6.00
177	6¢ ultramarine	30.00	25.00	29.00	18.00	16.00	13.00
178	8¢ light red brown	30.00	25.00	29.00	18.00	16.00	13.00
179	10¢ dark violet	21.00	16.00	19.00	16.00	9.00	7.50
180	15¢ deep blue	59.00	50.00	56.00	40.00	28.00	21.00
181	20¢ gray black	75.00	60.00	65.00	45.00	18.00	14.00
182	30¢ olive brown	60.00	48.00	56.00	39.00	26.00	21.00

THREE CENTS

160
136 surcharged in red

183, 253
Codfish

185, 186
King George

187
Queen Mary

188, 189
Prince of Wales

190, 191, 257
Caribou

192
Princess Elizabeth

193, 260
Salmon

194, 261
Newfoundland Dog

195, 262
Northern Seal

196, 263
Trans-Atlantic Beacon

1932-37 RESOURCES ISSUE Perf. 13-1/2

SCOTT NO.	DESCRIPTION	UNUSED O.G. F	UNUSED O.G. AVG	UNUSED F	UNUSED AVG	USED F	USED AVG
183-99	**1¢-48¢ complete, 17 varieties**	**97.25**	**70.50**	**85.00**	**60.00**	**48.50**	**36.50**
183	1¢ green	3.85	2.50	3.50	2.75	.55	.40
184	1¢ gray black	1.35	.90	.90	.70	.25	.20
185	2¢ rose	3.75	3.50	2.75	2.00	.35	.30
186	2¢ green	2.00	1.50	1.50	.85	.25	.20
187	3¢ orange brown	2.00	.95	1.50	.70	.35	.30
188	4¢ deep violet	8.50	7.00	8.00	6.00	1.40	.90
189	4¢ rose lake	1.00	.80	.90	.50	.30	.30
190	5¢ violet brown (I)	14.00	11.00	13.00	10.00	1.40	.30
191	5¢ deep violet (II)	2.00	1.50	1.75	1.00	.25	.20
191a	5¢ deep violet (I)	14.00	11.00	13.00	10.00	1.00	.60
192	6¢ dull blue	14.00	11.00	13.00	10.00	11.00	8.00
193	10¢ olive black	1.90	1.40	1.75	1.25	.85	.60
194	14¢ black	4.75	3.50	4.90	3.00	2.50	2.00
195	15¢ magenta	3.95	2.75	5.50	2.50	2.00	1.75
196	20¢ gray green	4.00	3.00	3.60	2.50	1.00	.70
197	25¢ gray	3.95	3.00	3.60	2.50	2.25	1.75
198	30¢ ultramarine	36.00	30.00	33.00	28.00	24.00	19.00
199	48¢ red brown (1937)	14.85	10.00	13.00	8.00	5.00	3.75

197, 265
Sealing Fleet

198, 266
Fishing Fleet

208
The Duchess of York

209, 259
Corner Brook Paper Mills

210, 264
Loading Iron Ore, Bell Island

1932 Perf. 13-1/2

SCOTT NO.	DESCRIPTION	UNUSED O.G. F	UNUSED O.G. AVG	UNUSED F	UNUSED AVG	USED F	USED AVG
208-10	7¢-24¢ complete, 3 varieties	7.25	5.50	6.00	4.50	5.00	3.95
208	7¢ red brown	1.90	1.35	1.75	1.15	1.25	1.00
209	8¢ orange red	1.90	1.35	1.75	1.15	1.25	1.00
210	24¢ light blue	3.85	2.50	3.60	2.25	3.25	2.25

1933 LAND & SEA OVERPRINT

SCOTT NO.	DESCRIPTION	UNUSED O.G. F	UNUSED O.G. AVG	UNUSED F	UNUSED AVG	USED F	USED AVG
211	15¢ brown	15.50	13.00	14.00	12.00	9.50	7.55

L. & S. Post.

211
No. C9 with Overprint and Bars

212
Sir Humphrey Gilbert

213
Compton Castle, Devon

214
The Gilbert Arms

216
Token to Gilbert from Queen Elizabeth

215
Eton College

217
Gilbert Commissioned by Queen Elizabeth

218
Gilbert's Fleet Leaving Plymouth

219
The Fleet Arriving at St. John's

220
Annexation of Newfoundland

221
Coat of Arms of England

1933 SIR HUMPHREY GILBERT ISSUE

SCOTT NO.	DESCRIPTION	UNUSED O.G. F	UNUSED O.G. AVG	UNUSED F	UNUSED AVG	USED F	USED AVG
212-25	**1¢-32¢ complete, 14 varieties**	185.00	155.00	150.00	138.00	104.00	96.00
212	1¢ gray black	1.65	1.40	1.25	1.00	.75	.70
213	2¢ green	1.75	1.40	1.25	1.00	.75	.70
214	3¢ yellow brown	3.25	2.50	2.60	2.00	.95	.70
215	4¢ carmine	2.75	2.25	2.25	2.00	.75	.70
216	5¢ dull violet	4.25	3.50	3.50	3.00	1.00	.75
217	7¢ blue	26.00	21.00	22.00	19.00	12.65	12.00
218	8¢ orange red	11.00	9.00	10.00	9.00	6.50	6.00
219	9¢ ultramarine	12.00	9.50	10.00	9.00	7.00	5.75
220	10¢ red brown	12.00	9.50	10.00	9.00	7.00	5.50
221	14¢ black	23.00	16.00	20.00	17.00	15.00	14.00
222	15¢ claret	21.00	16.00	20.00	17.00	15.00	14.00
223	20¢ deep green	19.00	14.00	15.00	14.00	11.00	9.00
224	24¢ violet brown	35.00	26.00	28.00	20.00	23.00	20.00
225	32¢ gray	35.00	26.00	28.00	20.00	23.00	20.00

222
Gilbert on the "Squirrel"

223
1624 Map of Newfoundland

224
Queen Elizabeth I

225
Gilbert Statue at Truro

226
Windsor Castle and King George

1935 SILVER JUBILEE

SCOTT NO.	DESCRIPTION	UNUSED F/NH	UNUSED F	USED F
226-29	**4¢-24¢ complete, 4 varieties**	23.00	19.90	10.00
226	4¢ bright rose	3.00	2.75	.75
227	5¢ violet	3.50	3.00	.90
228	7¢ dark blue	6.50	4.50	3.50
229	24¢ olive green	13.00	10.00	7.50

1937 CORONATION ISSUE

SCOTT NO.	DESCRIPTION	UNUSED F/NH	UNUSED F	USED F
230-32	**2¢-5¢ complete, 3 varieties**	9.75	5.50	2.60
230	2¢ deep green	2.75	1.75	.75
231	4¢ carmine rose	2.75	1.75	.75
232	5¢ dark violet	5.25	3.50	1.50

230
King George VI and Queen Elizabeth

233

234
Die I: Fine Impression
Die II: Coarse Impression

235

236

237

238

239

240

241

242

245, 254
King George VI

243

1937 LONG CORONATION ISSUE

SCOTT NO.	DESCRIPTION	UNUSED F/NH	UNUSED F	USED F
233-43	**1¢-48¢ complete, 11 varieties**	45.00	41.00	25.10
233	1¢ Codfish	.85	.50	.35
234	3¢ Map, die I	3.75	3.25	1.10
234a	3¢ same, die II	2.60	2.75	1.00
235	7¢ Caribou	3.75	3.25	2.60
236	8¢ Paper Mills	3.75	3.25	2.60
237	10¢ Salmon	6.00	5.50	4.25
238	14¢ Newfoundland Dog	6.00	5.50	3.50
239	15¢ Northern Seal	5.25	4.75	3.50
240	20¢ Cape Race	4.00	3.50	2.50
241	24¢ Bell Island	5.25	4.25	3.50
242	25¢ Sealing Fleet	5.25	4.25	3.50
243	48¢ Fishing Fleet	8.00	7.25	3.50

249

2 CENTS

250
249 surcharged

1938 ROYAL FAMILY Perf. 13-1/2

SCOTT NO.	DESCRIPTION	UNUSED F/NH	UNUSED F	USED F
245-48	**2¢-7¢ complete, 4 varieties**	7.25	5.10	2.65
245	2¢ green	2.50	1.75	.25
246	3¢ dark carmine	2.50	1.75	.25
247	4¢ light blue	3.00	2.25	.25
248	7¢ dark ultramarine	2.25	2.00	1.20
249	5¢ violet blue	1.75	1.50	1.15

249 SURCHARGED

SCOTT NO.	DESCRIPTION	UNUSED F/NH	UNUSED F	USED F
250	2¢ on 5¢ violet blue	1.65	1.25	.95
251	4¢ on 5¢ violet blue	1.25	.95	.95

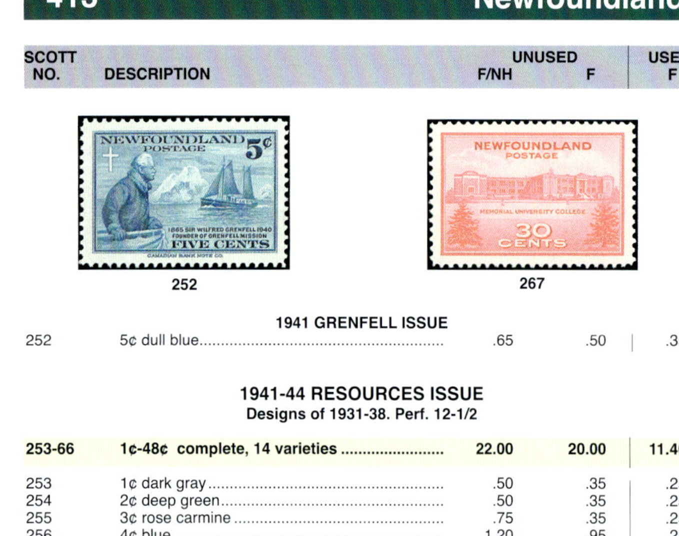

252 267

SCOTT NO.	DESCRIPTION	UNUSED F/NH	UNUSED F	USED F
	1941 GRENFELL ISSUE			
252	5¢ dull blue	.65	.50	.35
	1941-44 RESOURCES ISSUE Designs of 1931-38. Perf. 12-1/2			
253-66	**1¢-48¢ complete, 14 varieties**	**22.00**	**20.00**	**11.40**
253	1¢ dark gray	.50	.35	.25
254	2¢ deep green	.50	.35	.25
255	3¢ rose carmine	.75	.35	.25
256	4¢ blue	1.20	.95	.25
257	5¢ violet	1.20	.95	.25
258	7¢ violet blue (1942)	1.60	1.40	1.00
259	8¢ red	1.85	1.40	.70
260	10¢ brownish black	1.85	1.40	.65
261	14¢ black	2.60	2.40	2.00
262	15¢ pale rose violet	2.60	2.25	1.45
263	20¢ green	2.60	2.25	1.20
264	24¢ deep blue	3.30	2.80	2.00
265	25¢ slate	3.30	2.80	2.00
266	48¢ red brown (1944)	5.00	4.00	1.80

TWO

CENTS

268

269

270

SCOTT NO.	DESCRIPTION	UNUSED F/NH	UNUSED F	USED F
	1943-47			
267	30¢ Memorial University	2.20	1.60	1.10
268	2¢ on 30¢ University (1946)	.45	.35	.30
269	4¢ Princess Elizabeth (1947)	.45	.35	.25
270	5¢ Cabot (1947)	.45	.35	.25

AIR POST STAMPS

Trans-Atlantic
AIR POST,
1919.
ONE DOLLAR.

C2
70 surcharged

AIR MAIL
to Halifax, N.S.
1921

C3

Air Mail
DE PINEDO
1927

C4
74 overprinted

Trans-Atlantic
AIR MAIL
By B. M.
"Columbia"
September
1930
Fifty Cents

C5
126 surcharged

C6, C9
Airplane and Dog Team

SCOTT NO.	DESCRIPTION	UNUSED O.G. VF	UNUSED O.G. F	UNUSED O.G. AVG	UNUSED VF	UNUSED F	UNUSED AVG	USED VF	USED F	USED AVG
	1919									
C2	$1 on 15¢ scarlet	275.00	195.00	165.00	225.00	170.00	135.00	225.00	185.00	165.00
C2a	same without comma after "POST"	310.00	270.00	190.00	250.00	200.00	170.00	260.00	205.00	165.00
	1921									
C3	35¢ red	195.00	165.00	125.00	140.00	105.00	78.75	185.00	150.00	125.00
C3a	same with period after "1921"	225.00	175.00	135.00	175.00	131.25	98.00	205.00	160.00	140.00

C7, C10
First Trans-atlantic Airmail

C8, C11
Routes of Historic Trans-atlantic Flights

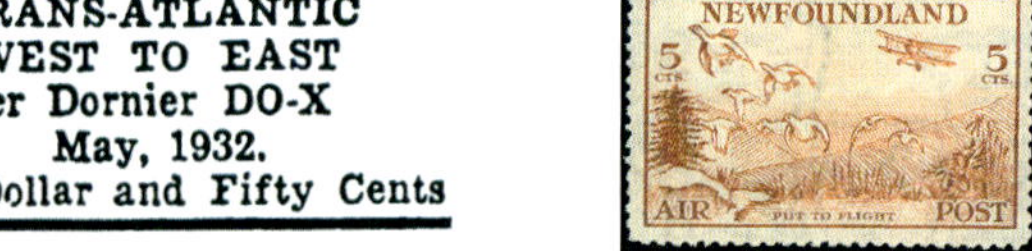

C12
C11 surcharged

C13

SCOTT NO.	DESCRIPTION	UNUSED O.G. VF	UNUSED O.G. F	UNUSED O.G. AVG	UNUSED VF	UNUSED F	UNUSED AVG	USED VF	USED F	USED AVG
	1931 Unwatermarked									
C6	15¢ brown	15.00	13.00	11.00	12.50	10.75	9.00	8.50	6.60	4.40
C7	50¢ green	48.00	34.00	26.00	42.00	31.00	27.00	26.00	20.00	16.00
C8	$1 blue	110.00	85.00	60.00	90.00	78.00	56.00	60.00	46.75	31.35
	Watermarked Coat of Arms									
C9	15¢ brown	16.00	13.00	9.00	13.00	11.00	7.00	7.75	6.00	4.00
C10	50¢ green	90.00	72.00	63.00	85.00	65.00	40.00	36.00	29.00	22.00
C11	$1 blue	155.00	118.00	72.00	120.00	90.00	65.00	92.00	77.00	58.00
	1932 TRANS-ATLANTIC FLIGHT									
C12	$1.50 on $1 blue	470.00	360.00	225.00	375.00	295.00	195.00	360.00	275.00	181.50

C14

C15

SCOTT NO.	DESCRIPTION	UNUSED O.G. VF	UNUSED O.G. F	UNUSED O.G. AVG	UNUSED VF	UNUSED F	UNUSED AVG	USED VF	USED F	USED AVG
	1933 LABRADOR ISSUE									
C13-17	**5¢-75¢ complete, 5 varieties**	**206.00**	**172.50**	**103.50**	**150.00**	**112.50**	**75.00**	**156.00**	**135.50**	**100.00**
C13	5¢ "Put to Flight"	15.85	13.20	7.95	11.00	9.00	7.00	10.50	9.00	7.25
C14	10¢ "Land of Heart's Delight"	23.75	19.80	11.85	16.00	12.00	8.00	18.00	16.00	14.00
C15	30¢ "Spotting the Herd"	39.50	33.00	19.75	30.50	22.00	17.00	31.00	27.00	21.00
C16	60¢ "News from Home"	71.00	59.00	36.00	60.00	40.00	29.00	58.00	52.00	38.00
C17	75¢ "Labrador, The Land of Gold"	71.00	59.00	36.00	60.00	40.00	30.00	58.00	52.00	38.00

C16

C17

1933
GEN. BALBO
FLIGHT.
$4.50

C18
C17 Surcharged

C19

SCOTT NO.	DESCRIPTION	UNUSED O.G. VF	UNUSED O.G. F	UNUSED O.G. AVG	UNUSED VF	UNUSED F	UNUSED AVG	USED VF	USED F	USED AVG
	1933 BALBOA FLIGHT ISSUE									
C18	$4.50 on 75¢ bistre	650.00	545.00	330.00	460.00	385.00	302.50	460.00	385.00	302.50
	1943									
C19	7¢ St. John's	.55	.45	.40	.50	.40	.35	.35	.30	.25

POSTAGE DUE STAMPS

C: J1

SCOTT NO.	DESCRIPTION	UNUSED F/NH	UNUSED F	USED F
	1939 Unwatermarked, Perf. 10-1/2x10			
J1	1¢ yellow green	7.50	4.00	5.25
J2	2¢ vermillion	11.00	7.00	5.25
J3	3¢ ultramarine	11.00	7.50	6.00
J4	4¢ yellow orange	15.00	12.00	10.00
J5	5¢ pale brown	18.00	14.00	5.00
J6	10¢ dark violet	12.00	8.00	5.00

SCOTT NO.	DESCRIPTION	UNUSED F/NH	UNUSED F	USED F
	1946-49 Unwatermarked, Perf. 11			
J1a	1¢ yellow green	9.50	6.00	5.50
	Unwatermarked, Perf. 11x9			
J2a	2¢ vermillion	10.00	7.00	5.50
J3a	3¢ ultramarine	10.00	7.00	7.50
J4a	4¢ yellow orange	17.00	15.00	15.00
	Watermarked, Perf. 11			
J7	10¢ dark violet	18.00	12.00	14.00

New Brunswick #1-11

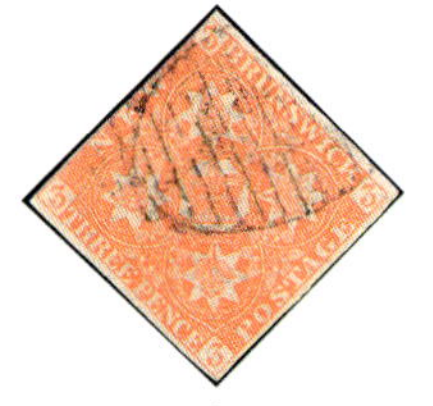

1
Crown of Great Britain surrounded by Heraldic Flowers of the United Kingdom

6

7

8

9

10

11

1851 PENCE ISSUE. Imperforate

SCOTT NO.	DESCRIPTION	UNUSED O.G. VF	UNUSED O.G. F	UNUSED O.G. AVG	UNUSED VF	UNUSED F	UNUSED AVG	USED VF	USED F	USED AVG
1	3p red	5200.00	3900.00	2850.00	2600.00	2100.00	1600.00	450.00	350.00	300.00
2	6p olive yellow	7000.00	5000.00	2900.00	3700.00	3000.00	2200.00	850.00	700.00	600.00
3	1sh bright red violet	30500.00	26000.00	19000.00	16000.00	13000.00	10000.00	6600.00	5000.00	4500.00
4	1sh dull violet	35500.00	30000.00	22000.00	23000.00	18000.00	13500.00	7600.00	6300.00	4600.00

1860-63 CENTS ISSUE
(NH + 50%)

SCOTT NO.	DESCRIPTION	UNUSED O.G. VF	UNUSED O.G. F	UNUSED O.G. AVG	UNUSED VF	UNUSED F	UNUSED AVG	USED VF	USED F	USED AVG
6	1¢ Locomotive	40.00	30.00	22.50	30.00	22.50	17.00	38.00	32.00	28.00
7	2¢ Queen Victoria, orange (1863)	16.00	14.00	12.00	12.50	9.50	7.00	14.00	10.50	7.75
8	5¢ same, yellow green	31.00	25.00	18.00	16.00	13.00	11.00	23.00	16.00	11.00
9	10¢ same, vermillion	60.00	45.00	33.00	42.00	31.50	23.75	48.00	39.00	33.00
10	12-1/2¢ Ships	100.00	75.00	60.00	60.00	45.00	33.75	80.00	64.00	54.00
11	17¢ Prince of Wales	55.00	44.00	32.00	42.00	31.50	23.75	67.00	54.00	47.00

Nova Scotia #1-13

1

2, 3
Royal Crown and Heraldic Flowers of the United Kingdom

1851-53 PENCE ISSUE
Imperf. Blue Paper

SCOTT NO.	DESCRIPTION	UNUSED O.G. VF	UNUSED O.G. F	UNUSED O.G. AVG	UNUSED VF	UNUSED F	UNUSED AVG	USED VF	USED F	USED AVG
1	1p Queen Victoria	3600.00	3100.00	2700.00	3200.00	2300.00	1800.00	675.00	530.00	485.00
2	3p blue	1450.00	1200.00	900.00	1100.00	950.00	800.00	250.00	210.00	185.00
3	3p dark blue	1775.00	1350.00	1000.00	1200.00	1000.00	850.00	315.00	255.00	200.00
4	6p yellow green	5100.00	4000.00	3100.00	3700.00	2900.00	2450.00	695.00	540.00	430.00
5	6p dark green	10000.00	7000.00	5600.00	6600.00	5100.00	4100.00	1800.00	1550.50	1400.00
6	1sh reddish violet	26000.00	21000.00	18000.00	19000.00	15000.00	13000.00	5400.00	4100.00	3400.00
7	1sh dull violet	26000.00	21000.00	18000.00	19000.00	15000.00	13000.00	6600.00	5300.00	4800.00

8

11
Queen Victoria

12

1860-63 CENTS ISSUE
White or Yellowish Paper, Perf. 12
(NH + 50%)

SCOTT NO.	DESCRIPTION	UNUSED O.G. VF	UNUSED O.G. F	UNUSED O.G. AVG	UNUSED VF	UNUSED F	UNUSED AVG	USED VF	USED F	USED AVG
8	1¢ black	13.00	10.00	7.00	8.00	6.50	4.95	8.50	6.50	5.50
9	2¢ lilac	12.50	10.00	7.00	8.00	6.00	4.50	13.00	9.00	7.00
10	5¢ blue	410.00	310.00	250.00	285.00	210.00	165.00	11.50	8.00	6.00
11	8-1/2¢ green	13.00	11.00	9.50	9.00	8.00	7.00	19.75	15.00	11.00
12	10¢ vermillion	13.00	11.00	9.75	9.00	8.00	6.50	12.00	9.00	6.00
13	12-1/2¢ black	38.00	28.00	23.00	28.00	21.00	16.00	38.00	30.00	22.00

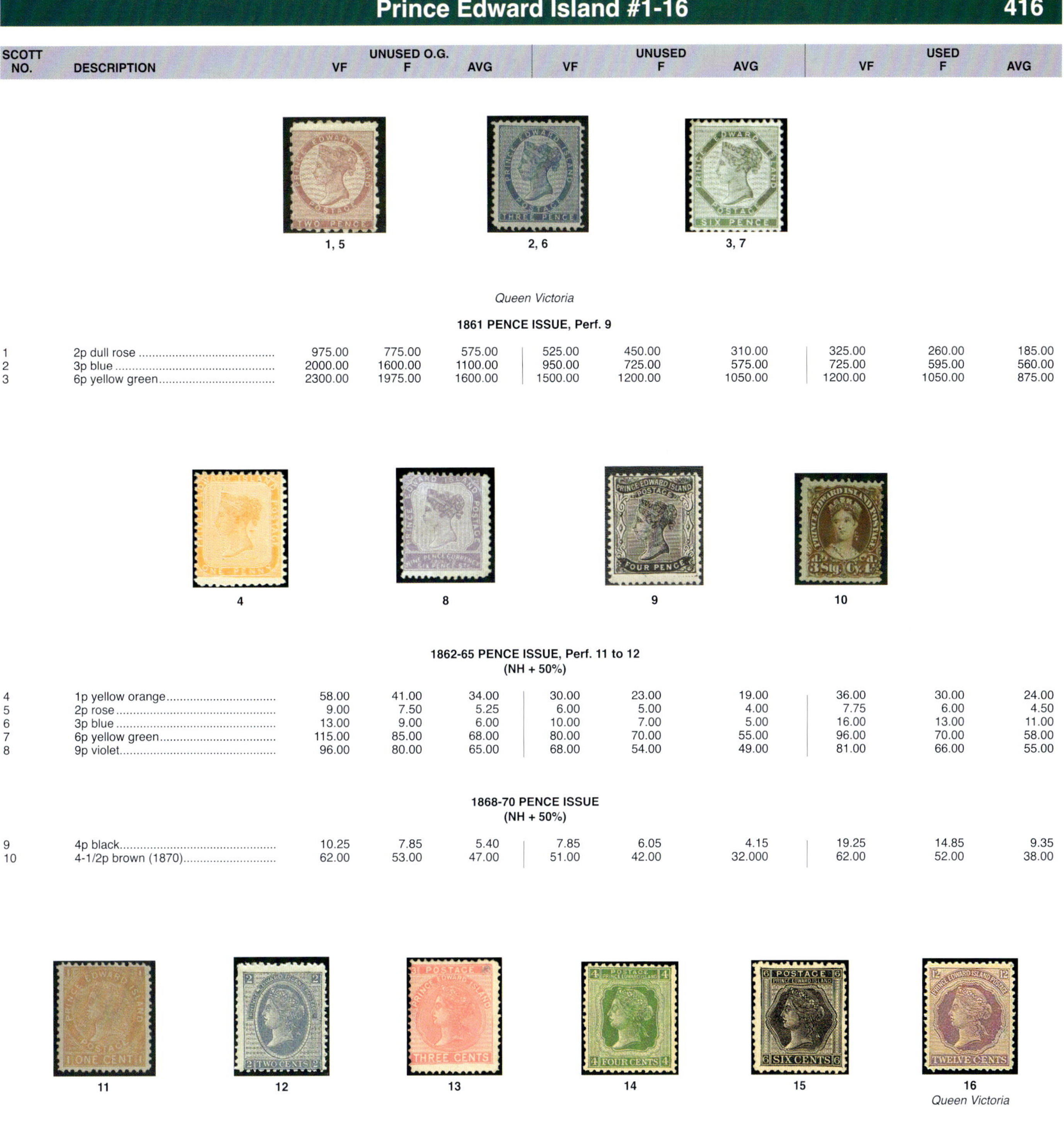

1, 5 2, 6 3, 7

Queen Victoria

4 8 9 10

11 12 13 14 15 16

Queen Victoria

SCOTT NO.	DESCRIPTION	UNUSED O.G. VF	UNUSED O.G. F	UNUSED O.G. AVG	UNUSED VF	UNUSED F	UNUSED AVG	USED VF	USED F	USED AVG
	1861 PENCE ISSUE, Perf. 9									
1	2p dull rose	975.00	775.00	575.00	525.00	450.00	310.00	325.00	260.00	185.00
2	3p blue	2000.00	1600.00	1100.00	950.00	725.00	575.00	725.00	595.00	560.00
3	6p yellow green	2300.00	1975.00	1600.00	1500.00	1200.00	1050.00	1200.00	1050.00	875.00
	1862-65 PENCE ISSUE, Perf. 11 to 12 (NH + 50%)									
4	1p yellow orange	58.00	41.00	34.00	30.00	23.00	19.00	36.00	30.00	24.00
5	2p rose	9.00	7.50	5.25	6.00	5.00	4.00	7.75	6.00	4.50
6	3p blue	13.00	9.00	6.00	10.00	7.00	5.00	16.00	13.00	11.00
7	6p yellow green	115.00	85.00	68.00	80.00	70.00	55.00	96.00	70.00	58.00
8	9p violet	96.00	80.00	65.00	68.00	54.00	49.00	81.00	66.00	55.00
	1868-70 PENCE ISSUE (NH + 50%)									
9	4p black	10.25	7.85	5.40	7.85	6.05	4.15	19.25	14.85	9.35
10	4-1/2p brown (1870)	62.00	53.00	47.00	51.00	42.00	32.000	62.00	52.00	38.00
	1872 CENTS ISSUE (NH + 40%)									
11	1¢ brown orange	6.00	4.60	3.00	5.00	3.85	2.50	9.30	7.15	4.70
12	2¢ ultramarine	25.00	21.00	18.00	22.00	18.00	16.00	31.00	27.00	21.00
13	3¢ rose	25.00	19.00	16.00	17.25	13.20	10.00	23.00	20.00	16.00
14	4¢ green	10.00	7.75	6.00	6.50	5.00	4.50	26.50	20.35	13.75
15	6¢ black	8.00	6.00	4.00	7.00	5.00	3.50	23.50	18.15	12.10
16	12¢ violet	9.00	6.50	4.00	8.00	6.00	3.75	35.75	27.50	20.35

HOW TO WRITE YOUR ORDER

PLEASE USE ORDER FORM

1.) Please use black or blue ink (NO PENCIL) and print all requested information (name, address, etc.)
2.) Indicate quantity, country (U.S., UN, Canada or province), catalog number, item description (single, plate block, etc.)
3.) Specify condition (F, VF, NH, etc.) and check whether it is mint or used
4.) Enter price as listed in this catalog
5.) Total all purchases, adding shipping/handling charge from table below. Alabama residents (only) also add sales tax.
6.) Payment may be made by check, money order, or credit card (VISA, Discover, American Express or Mastercard are accepted). ORDERS FROM OUTSIDE THE UNITED STATES MUST BE PAID WITH A CREDIT CARD and all payments must be made in U.S. funds.

SHIPPING AND HANDLING CHARGES*
Safe delivery is guaranteed. We assume all losses.

If ordering STAMPS ONLY Orders under $150.00 .... add $5.95
If order includes supply items and totals
Orders under $50.00 .... add $6.95
Orders from $50.00 to $149.99 .... add $9.95
Orders from $150.00 to $299.99 .... add $12.95
Orders over $300.. add $15.95

*The following charges may not fully cover the actual postage or freight, insurance and handling cost for foreign orders, and additional charges may be added.

RETURN POLICY

H.E. Harris offers a 30 day money-back guarantee on every item. The customer has 30 days to examine, grade (at customer's expense) and evaluate every stamp to insure customer satisfaction. If the customer is not completely satisfied with their purchase, they can return it for a full refund or exchange:

- Call 1-800-546-2995, for a Return Authorization Number. You will not receive a credit for the product returned unless you have a Return Authorization Number. The Return Authorization Number must be written on the outside of all boxes returned.
- Please keep a list of the products being sent back.

The credit will be processed after we receive your return. Please allow 4 weeks for the return to show on the account. Sorry, we cannot accept C.O.D. freight or refund the original or return shipping costs. If you have questions about returning a Whitman Publishing product, please contact our customer service department at 1-800-546-2995 during normal business hours, 8 a.m. to 5 p.m. Central Standard Time.

H.E. HARRIS PERFORMANCE PLEDGE

• All stamps are genuine, exactly as described, and have been inspected by our staff experts.
• H.E. Harris & Co. upholds the standards set forth by the American Philatelic Society and the American Stamp Dealers Association.
• If you have any problem with your order, please call our customer service department at 1-800-546-2995. We will handle it to your complete satisfaction.

Note: Coupon ONLY valid with order of $50.00 or more from the H.E. Harris 2025 US/BNA Catalog. Copies of coupon will not be accepted. Please include this coupon with order and payment. **If placing order by phone, please mention code US**. Coupon expires December 31, 2025.

Note: Coupon ONLY valid with order of $50.00 or more from the H.E. Harris 2025 US/BNA Catalog. Copies of coupon will not be accepted. Please include this coupon with order and payment. **If placing order by phone, please mention code US**. Coupon expires December 31, 2025.

Note: Coupon ONLY valid with order of $50.00 or more from the H.E. Harris 2025 US/BNA Catalog. Copies of coupon will not be accepted. Please include this coupon with order and payment. **If placing order by phone, please mention code US**. Coupon expires December 31, 2025.

NOTES

4001 Helton Drive, Bldg. A · Florence, AL 35630
www.heharris.com
You may also order by phone 1-800-546-2995 or Fax 1-256-246-1116

See Page 417 for Return Policy.
Sorry, no CODs.

Make payment in U.S. dollars by personal check, money order, Visa, Master Card, Discover or American Express. Please do not send cash.

Orders for shipment outside the U.S. must be paid by credit card and shipping charges will be added.

We Thank You For Your Order!

RUSH SHIPMENT TO:

Name ______________________________

Address ______________________________

City/State/Zip ______________________________

Phone *(in case of question about your order)* ______________________________

FAST CREDIT CARD ORDERING

☐ VISA ☐ mastercard ☐ DISCOVER ☐ AMERICAN EXPRESS

Card # ______________________________

Expiration Date ____________CVV____________

Signature ______________________________

Catalog or Stock No.	Qty.	Description	Mint	Used	Unit Price	Total Price

Shipping & Handling

If ordering STAMPS ONLY Orders under $150.00..................add $5.95
If order includes supply items and totals
Orders under $50.00..add $6.95
Orders from $50.00 to $149.99 ....add $9.95
Orders from $150.00 to $299.99 ....add $12.95
Orders over $300...add $15.95
Foreign orders: S&H will be added separately.
Please apply your tax rate if you live in the following states:
AL, AR, GA, IL, IN, IA, KS, KY, MI, MN, NE, NV, NJ, NC, ND, NY, OH, OK, RI, SD, TN, UT, VT, VA, WA, WV, WI, WY

TOTAL FRONT	
TOTAL REVERSE	
DISCOUNTS–If applicable	
SUBTOTAL	
SHIPPING CHARGE	
SALES TAX IF APPLICABLE	
TOTAL PURCHASE	

For Office Use Only

2025-USBNA

Catalog or Stock No.	Qty.	Description	Mint	Used	Unit Price	Total Price
				TOTAL THIS SIDE		

4001 Helton Drive, Bldg. A • Florence, AL 35630
www.heharris.com
You may also order by phone 1-800-546-2995 or Fax 1-256-246-1116

See Page 417 for Return Policy.

Sorry, no CODs.

Make payment in U.S. dollars by personal check, money order, Visa, Master Card, Discover or American Express. Please do not send cash.

Orders for shipment outside the U.S. must be paid by credit card and shipping charges will be added.

We Thank You For Your Order!

RUSH SHIPMENT TO:

Name ______________________

Address ______________________

City/State/Zip ______________________

Phone *(in case of question about your order)* ______________________

FAST CREDIT CARD ORDERING

☐ VISA ☐ mastercard ☐ DISCOVER ☐ AMERICAN EXPRESS

Card # ______________________

Expiration Date ____________ CVV ____________

Signature ______________________

Catalog or Stock No.	Qty.	Description	Mint	Used	Unit Price	Total Price

Shipping & Handling

If ordering STAMPS ONLY Orders under $150.00..................add $5.95
If order includes supply items and totals
Orders under $50.00....................add $6.95
Orders from $50.00 to $149.99 ....add $9.95
Orders from $150.00 to $299.99 ....add $12.95
Orders over $300.................... add $15.95
Foreign orders: S&H will be added separately.
Please apply your tax rate if you live in the following states:
AL, AR, GA, IL, IN, IA, KS, KY, MI, MN, NE, NV, NJ, NC, ND, NY, OH, OK, RI, SD, TN, UT, VT, VA, WA, WV, WI, WY

TOTAL FRONT	
TOTAL REVERSE	
DISCOUNTS–If applicable	
SUBTOTAL	
SHIPPING CHARGE	
SALES TAX IF APPLICABLE	
TOTAL PURCHASE	

For Office Use Only

2025-USBNA

Catalog or Stock No.	Qty.	Description	Mint	Used	Unit Price	Total Price
					TOTAL THIS SIDE	